THE EXPLORATION OF ECONOMICS

ROBERT L. SEXTON | 5E

Pepperdine University

Australia • Brazil • Japan • Korea • Mexico • Singapore • Spain • United Kingdom • United States

The Exploration of Economics, 5e
Robert L. Sexton

Vice President of Editorial, Business:
  Jack W. Calhoun

Publisher: Joe Sabatino

Acquisitions Editor: Steven Scoble

Developmental Editor: Daniel Noguera

Associate Marketing Manager: Betty Jung

Marketing Coordinator: Suellen Ruttkay

Content Project Manager:
  D. Jean Buttrom

Media Editor: Deepak Kumar

Frontlist Buyer, Manufacturing:
  Sandee Milewski

Production Service: S4Carlisle Publishing Services

Compositor: S4Carlisle Publishing Services

Senior Art Director: Michelle Kunkler

Cover Images:
  © Shutterstock

Photo Credits:
  b/w image: Comstock images
  color image: shutterstock images/ Kheng Guan Toh

Photography Manager: Deanna Ettinger

Photo Researcher: Scott Rosen, Bill Smith Group

Printed in China
by China Translation & Printing Services Limited
1 2 3 4 5 6 7 13 12 11 10

© 2011, 2008 South-Western, Cengage Learning

ALL RIGHTS RESERVED. No part of this work covered by the copyright herein may be reproduced, transmitted, stored, or used in any form or by any means graphic, electronic, or mechanical, including but not limited to photocopying, recording, scanning, digitizing, taping, web distribution, information networks, or information storage and retrieval systems, except as permitted under Section 107 or 108 of the 1976 United States Copyright Act, without the prior written permission of the publisher.

> For product information and technology assistance, contact us at
> **Cengage Learning Customer & Sales Support, 1-800-354-9706**
>
> For permission to use material from this text or product, submit all requests online at **www.cengage.com/permissions**
> Further permissions questions can be emailed to
> **permissionrequest@cengage.com**

Exam*View*® is a registered trademark of eInstruction Corp. Windows is a registered trademark of the Microsoft Corporation used herein under license. Macintosh and Power Macintosh are registered trademarks of Apple Computer, Inc. used herein under license.

© 2008 Cengage Learning. All Rights Reserved.

Library of Congress Control Number: 2009939189

International Student Edition ISBN 13: 978-0-538-75189-6
International Student Edition ISBN 10: 0-5387-5189-4

Cengage Learning International Offices

Asia
cengageasia.com
tel: (65) 6410 1200

Australia/New Zealand
cengage.com.au
tel: (61) 3 9685 4111

Brazil
cengage.com.br
tel: (011) 3665 9900

India
cengage.co.in
tel: (91) 11 30484837/38

Latin America
cengage.com.mx
tel: +52 (55) 1500 6000

UK/Europe/Middle East/Africa
cengage.co.uk
tel: (44) 207 067 2500

Represented in Canada by Nelson Education, Ltd.
nelson.com
tel: (416) 752 9100 / (800) 668 0671

For product information: **www.cengage.com/international**
Visit your local office: **www.cengage.com/global**
Visit our corporate website: **www.cengage.com**

THE EXPLORATION OF ECONOMICS

To
Elizabeth,
Katherine,
and Tommy

Brief Contents

PART 1 INTRODUCTION

Chapter 1
The Role and Method of Economics 2

Chapter 2
The Economic Way of Thinking 36

Chapter 3
Scarcity, Trade-Offs, and Production Possibilities 66

PART 2 SUPPLY AND DEMAND

Chapter 4
Supply and Demand 92

Chapter 5
Bringing Supply and Demand Together 121

Chapter 6
Elasticities 151

PART 3 MARKET EFFICIENCY, MARKET FAILURE, AND THE PUBLIC SYSTEM

Chapter 7
Market Efficiency and Welfare 182

Chapter 8
Market Failure 209

Chapter 9
Public Sector and Public Choice 233

PART 4 HOUSEHOLDS AND MARKET STRUCTURE

Chapter 10
Consumer Choice Theory 258

Chapter 11
The Firm: Production and Costs 289

Chapter 12
Firms in Perfectly Competitive Markets 328

Chapter 13
Monopoly and Antitrust 361

Chapter 14
Monopolistic Competition and Product Differentiation 400

Chapter 15
Oligopoly and Strategic Behavior 421

PART 5 INPUT MARKETS AND MICROECONOMIC POLICY ISSUES

Chapter 16
The Markets for Labor, Capital, and Land 454

Chapter 17
Income and Poverty 482

Chapter 18
The Environment 513

Chapter 19
Health Care 539

PART 6 MACROECONOMIC FOUNDATIONS

Chapter 20
Introduction to Macroeconomics: Unemployment, Inflation, and Economic Fluctuations 562

Chapter 21
Measuring Economic Performance 607

Chapter 22
Economic Growth in the Global Economy 631

Chapter 23
Financial Markets, Saving, and Investment 653

PART 7 THE MACROECONOMIC MODELS

Chapter 24
Aggregate Demand and Aggregate Supply 688

Chapter 25
The Aggregate Expenditure Model 731

PART 8 MACROECONOMIC POLICY

Chapter 26
Fiscal Policy 758

Chapter 27
Monetary Institutions 801

Chapter 28
The Federal Reserve System and Monetary Policy 832

Chapter 29
Issues in Macroeconomic Theory and Policy 877

PART 9 THE GLOBAL ECONOMY

Chapter 30
International Trade 914

Chapter 31
International Finance 949

Table of Contents

PART 1 INTRODUCTION

CHAPTER 1
The Role and Method of Economics 2

1.1 Economics: A Brief Introduction 3
   Economics—A Word with Many Different Meanings 3
   Economics Is All Around Us 3
   Why Study Economics? 4

1.2 Economic Behavior 7
   Self-Interest 7
   What Is Rational Behavior? 7

1.3 Economic Theory 10
   Economic Theories 10
   Abstraction Is Important 10
   Developing a Testable Proposition 11
   Science and Stories 11
   The *Ceteris Paribus* Assumption 12
   Why Are Observation and Prediction Harder in the Social Sciences? 12
   Why Do Economists Predict on a Group Level? 12
   The Two Branches of Economics: Microeconomics and Macroeconomics 13

1.4 Pitfalls to Avoid in Scientific Thinking 14
   Confusing Correlation and Causation 14
   The Fallacy of Composition 14

1.5 Positive Statements and Normative Statements 16
   Positive Statement 16
   Normative Statement 17
   Positive Versus Normative Analysis 17
   Disagreement Is Common in Most Disciplines 17
   Often Economists Do Agree 19

Interactive Chapter Summary 20
   Key Terms and Concepts 21
   Section Check Answers 21
   Study Guide 24
   Appendix: Working with Graphs 28

CHAPTER 2
The Economic Way of Thinking 36

2.1 Scarcity 37
   Scarcity 37
   Scarcity and Resources 37
   What Are Goods and Services? 38
   What Are Bads? 38
   Are Those Who Want More Greedy? 38
   Does Everyone Face Scarcity? 38
   Will Scarcity Ever Be Eradicated? 39

2.2 Choices, Costs, and Trade-Offs 40
   Scarcity Forces Us to Choose 40
   Trade-Offs 40
   To Choose Is to Lose 40
   The Opportunity Cost of Going to College or Having a Child 41
   Is That Really a Free Lunch, a Freeway, or a Free Beach? 41

2.3 Marginal Thinking 42
   Many Choices We Face Involve Marginal Thinking 42

2.4 Incentives Matter 47
   People Respond to Changes in Incentives 47
   Positive and Negative Incentives 47

2.5 Specialization and Trade 49
   Why Do People Specialize? 49
   We All Specialize 49
   The Advantages of Specialization 49
   Specialization and Trade Lead to Greater Wealth and Prosperity 51

2.6 Markets and Improved Efficiency 52
   How Does the Market Work to Allocate Resources? 52
   Market Prices Provide Important Information 52
   What Effect Do Price Controls Have on the Market System? 53
   Market Failure 53

Interactive Chapter Summary 55
   Key Terms and Concepts 56
   Section Check Answers 56
   Study Guide 60

CHAPTER 3
Scarcity, Trade-Offs, and Production Possibilities 66

3.1 The Three Economic Questions Every Society Faces 67
   Scarcity and the Allocation of Resources 67
   What Goods and Services Will Be Produced? 67
   How Will the Goods and Services Be Produced? 68
   Who Will Get the Goods and Services Produced? 68

3.2 The Circular Flow Model 71
Product Markets 71
Factor Markets 71
The Simple Circular Flow Model 71

3.3 The Production Possibilities Curve 73
The Production Possibilities Curve 73
Using Resources Efficiently 75
Inefficiency and Efficiency 76
The Law of Increasing Opportunity Cost 76

3.4 Economic Growth and the Production Possibilities Curve 78
Generating Economic Growth 78
Growth Does Not Eliminate Scarcity 78
The Effects of a Technological Change on the Production Possibilities Curve 79
Summing Up the Production Possibilities Curve 80

Interactive Chapter Summary 81
Key Terms and Concepts 82
Section Check Answers 82
Study Guide 85

PART 2 SUPPLY AND DEMAND

CHAPTER 4
Supply and Demand 92

4.1 Markets 93
Defining a Market 93
Buyers and Sellers 94

4.2 Demand 94
The Law of Demand 94
Individual Demand 95
What Is a Market Demand Curve? 95

4.3 Shifts in the Demand Curve 97
A Change in Demand Versus a Change in Quantity Demanded 97
Shifts in Demand 98
The Prices of Related Goods 98
Income 99
Number of Buyers 101
Consumer's Preferences and Information 101
Expectations 101
Changes in Demand Versus Changes in Quantity Demanded—Revisited 102

4.4 Supply 104
The Law of Supply 104
A Positive Relationship Between Price and Quantity Supplied 105
An Individual Supply Curve 105
The Market Supply Curve 105

4.5 Shifts in the Supply Curve 106
A Change in Quantity Supplied Versus a Change in Supply 106
Shifts in Supply 107
Change in Supply Versus Change in Quantity Supplied—Revisited 109

Interactive Chapter Summary 111
Key Terms and Concepts 111
Section Check Answers 112
Study Guide 114

CHAPTER 5
Bringing Supply and Demand Together 121

5.1 Market Equilibrium Price and Quantity 122
Equilibrium Price and Quantity 122
Shortages and Surpluses 123
Scarcity and Shortages 123

5.2 Changes in Equilibrium Price and Quantity 127
A Change in Demand 127
A Change in Supply 127
Changes in Both Supply and Demand 129
The Combinations of Supply and Demand Shifts 130
Supply, Demand, and the Market Economy 134

5.3 Price Controls 135
Price Controls 135
Price Ceilings: Rent Controls 135
Price Floors: The Minimum Wage 137
Price Ceilings: Price Controls on Gasoline 138
Unintended Consequences 139

Interactive Chapter Summary 141
Key Terms and Concepts 142
Section Check Answers 142
Study Guide 145

CHAPTER 6
Elasticities 151

6.1 Price Elasticity of Demand 152
Is the Demand Curve Elastic or Inelastic? 152
Types of Demand Curves 152
Calculating the Price Elasticity of Demand: The Midpoint Method 154
The Determinants of the Price Elasticity of Demand 155

6.2 Total Revenue and the Price Elasticity of Demand 158
How Does the Price Elasticity of Demand Impact Total Revenue? 158
Price Elasticity Changes Along a Linear Demand Curve 159

6.3 Other Types of Demand Elasticities 163
The Cross-Price Elasticity of Demand 163
Cross-Price Elasticity and Sodas 163
The Income Elasticity of Demand 163

6.4 Price Elasticity of Supply 165
What Is the Price Elasticity of Supply? 165
Elasticities and Taxes: Combining Supply and Demand Elasticities 166

Interactive Chapter Summary 172
  Key Terms and Concepts 172
  Section Check Answers 173
  Study Guide 175

PART 3 MARKET EFFICIENCY, MARKET FAILURE, AND THE PUBLIC SYSTEM

CHAPTER 7
Market Efficiency and Welfare 182

7.1 Consumer Surplus and Producer Surplus 183
  Consumer Surplus 183
  Marginal Willingness to Pay Falls as More Is Consumed 183
  Price Changes and Changes in Consumer Surplus 184
  Producer Surplus 184
  Market Efficiency and Producer and Consumer Surplus 185

7.2 The Welfare Effects of Taxes, Subsidies, and Price Controls 190
  Using Consumer and Producer Surplus to Find the Welfare Effects of a Tax 190
  Elasticity and the Size of the Deadweight Loss 192
  The Welfare Effects of Subsidies 193
  Price Ceilings and Welfare Effects 193
  Applications of Consumer and Producer Surplus 194
  Price Floors 196
  The Welfare Effects of a Price Floor When the Government Buys the Surplus 196
  Deficiency Payment Program 198

Interactive Chapter Summary 200
  Key Terms and Concepts 200
  Section Check Answers 201
  Study Guide 203

CHAPTER 8
Market Failure 209

8.1 Externalities 210
  Negative Externalities in Production 210
  What Can the Government Do to Correct for Negative Externalities? 211
  Positive Externalities in Consumption 213
  What Can the Government Do to Correct for Positive Externalities? 214
  Nongovernmental Solutions to Externalities 214

8.2 Public Goods 216
  Private Goods Versus Public Goods 216
  Public Goods and the Free-Rider Problem 217
  The Government and Benefit-Cost Analysis 217
  Common Resources and the Tragedy of the Commons 218

8.3 Asymmetric Information 219
  What Is Asymmetric Information? 219
  What Is Moral Hazard? 222

Interactive Chapter Summary 226
  Key Terms and Concepts 227
  Section Check Answers 227
  Study Guide 229

CHAPTER 9
Public Sector and Public Choice 233

9.1 Other Functions of Government 234
  Property Rights and the Legal System 234
  Insufficient Competition in Markets 234
  Income Redistribution 234

9.2 Government Spending and Taxation 237
  Growth in Government 237
  Generating Government Revenue 238
  Financing State and Local Government Activities 239
  Should We Have a Flat Tax? 240
  Taxes: Efficiency and Equity 243

9.3 Public Choice 245
  What Is Public Choice Theory? 245
  Scarcity and the Public Sector 245
  The Individual Consumption-Payment Link 246
  Majority Rule and the Median Voters 246
  Voters and Rational Ignorance 247
  Special Interest Groups 248

Interactive Chapter Summary 249
  Key Terms and Concepts 250
  Section Check Answers 251
  Study Guide 253

PART 4 HOUSEHOLDS AND MARKET STRUCTURE

CHAPTER 10
Consumer Choice Theory 258

10.1 Consumer Behavior 259
  Wants Versus Needs 259
  Do We Need More Freeways? 260
  Utility 260
  Utility Is a Personal Matter 260
  Total Utility and Marginal Utility 261
  Diminishing Marginal Utility 263

10.2 The Consumer's Choice 266
  What Is the "Best" Decision for Consumers? 266
  Consumer Equilibrium 266
  The Law of Demand and the Law of Diminishing Marginal Utility 267

Interactive Chapter Summary 272
  Key Terms and Concepts 273
  Section Check Answers 273

Study Guide 275
Appendix: A More Advanced Theory
    of Consumer Choice 279

CHAPTER 11
The Firm: Production and Costs 289

11.1 Firms and Profits: Total Revenues Minus Total Costs 290
Explicit Costs 290
Implicit Costs 290
Profits 290
Are Accounting Profits the Same as Economic Profits? 290
A Zero Economic Profit Is a Normal Profit 292
Sunk Costs 292

11.2 Production in the Short Run 293
The Short Run Versus the Long Run 293
Production in the Short Run 293
Diminishing Marginal Product 294

11.3 Costs in the Short Run 296
Fixed Costs, Variable Costs, and Total Costs 296
Average Total Costs 296
Marginal Costs 297
How Are These Costs Related? 298

11.4 The Shape of the Short-Run Cost Curves 300
The Relationship Between Marginal Costs and Marginal Product 300
The Relationship Between Marginal and Average Amounts 301
Why Is the Average Total Cost Curve U-Shaped? 301
The Relationship Between Marginal Costs and Average Variable and Average Total Costs 302

11.5 Cost Curves: Short-Run Versus Long-Run 304
Why Are Long-Run Cost Curves Different from Short-Run Cost Curves? 304
What Are Economies of Scale? 306
Why Do Economies and Diseconomies of Scale Occur? 306

Interactive Chapter Summary 307
Key Terms and Concepts 308
Section Check Answers 308
Study Guide 311
Appendix: Using Isoquants and Isocosts 320

CHAPTER 12
Firms in Perfectly Competitive Markets 328

12.1 A Perfectly Competitive Market 329
A Perfectly Competitive Market 329

12.2 An Individual Price Taker's Demand Curve 330
An Individual Firm's Demand Curve 330
A Change in Market Price and the Firm's Demand Curve 331

12.3 Profit Maximization 332
Revenues in a Perfectly Competitive Market 332
Total Revenue 333
Average Revenue and Marginal Revenue 333
How Do Firms Maximize Profits? 333
Equating Marginal Revenue and Marginal Cost 333

12.4 Short-Run Profits and Losses 335
The Three-Step Method 335
Evaluating Economic Losses in the Short Run 337
Deriving the Short-Run Market Supply Curve 338

12.5 Long-Run Equilibrium 341
Economic Profits and Losses Disappear in the Long Run 341
The Long-Run Equilibrium for the Competitive Firm 343

12.6 Long-Run Supply 344
A Constant-Cost Industry 344
An Increasing-Cost Industry 344
A Decreasing-Cost Industry 346
Perfect Competition and Economic Efficiency 347

Interactive Chapter Summary 348
Key Terms and Concepts 350
Section Check Answers 350
Study Guide 353

CHAPTER 13
Monopoly and Antitrust 361

13.1 Monopoly: The Price Maker 362
What Is a Monopoly? 362
Pure Monopoly Is a Rarity 362
Barriers to Entry 362

13.2 Demand and Marginal Revenue in Monopoly 363
The Monopolist's Price in the Elastic Portion of the Demand Curve 366

13.3 The Monopolist's Equilibrium 368
How Does the Monopolist Determine the Profit-Maximizing Output? 368
Three-Step Method for the Monopolist 368
Profits for a Monopolist 368
Losses for the Monopolist 369
Patents 370

13.4 Monopoly and Welfare Loss 371
Does Monopoly Promote Inefficiency? 371
Does Monopoly Retard Innovation? 373

13.5 Monopoly Policy 373
Antitrust Policies 374
Antitrust Laws 374
Have Antitrust Policies Been Successful? 375

Government Regulation 375
Difficulties in Average Cost Pricing 377

13.6 Price Discrimination and Peak Load Pricing 378
Price Discrimination 378
Conditions for Price Discrimination 378
Why Does Price Discrimination Exist? 379
Examples of Price Discrimination 379
The Welfare Effects of Price Discrimination 381
Peak Load Pricing 385

Interactive Chapter Summary 387
Key Terms and Concepts 388
Section Check Answers 388
Study Guide 392

CHAPTER 14
Monopolistic Competition and Product Differentiation 400

14.1 Monopolistic Competition 401
What Is Monopolistic Competition? 401
The Three Basic Characteristics of Monopolistic Competition 401

14.2 Price and Output Determination in Monopolistic Competition 403
The Firm's Demand and Marginal Revenue Curve 403
Determining Short-Run Equilibrium 404
Short-Run Profits and Losses in Monopolistic Competition 405
Determining Long-Run Equilibrium 406
Achieving Long-Run Equilibrium 407

14.3 Monopolistic Competition Versus Perfect Competition 408
The Significance of Excess Capacity 408
Failing to Meet Allocative Efficiency, Too 409
What Are the Real Costs of Monopolistic Competition? 410
Are the Differences Between Monopolistic Competition and Perfect Competition Exaggerated? 410

14.4 Advertising 411
Why Do Firms Advertise? 411
Is Advertising "Good" or "Bad" from Society's Perspective? 412

Interactive Chapter Summary 414
Key Terms and Concepts 415
Section Check Answers 415
Study Guide 417

CHAPTER 15
Oligopoly and Strategic Behavior 421

15.1 Oligopoly 422
What Is Oligopoly? 422
Mutual Interdependence 422
Why Do Oligopolies Exist? 422
Measuring Industry Concentration 422
Economies of Scale as a Barrier to Entry 423
Equilibrium Price and Quantity in Oligopoly 423

15.2 Collusion and Cartels 424
Uncertainty and Pricing Decisions 424
Collusion 424
Joint Profit Maximization 424
Why Are Most Collusive Oligopolies Short Lived? 427

15.3 Other Oligopoly Models 427
The Kinked Demand Curve Model—Price Rigidity 427
Price Leadership 428
What Happens in the Long Run If Entry Is Easy? 429
How Do Oligopolists Deter Market Entry? 429
Antitrust and Mergers 430
Antitrust and Pricing Strategies 430

15.4 Game Theory and Strategic Behavior 433
Some Strategies for Noncollusive Oligopolies 433
What Is Game Theory? 433
Cooperative and Noncooperative Games 433
The Prisoners' Dilemma 434
Profits Under Different Pricing Strategies 435
Advertising 436
Repeated Games 438
Network Externalities 439

Interactive Chapter Summary 442
Key Terms and Concepts 443
Section Check Answers 443
Study Guide 446

PART 5   INPUT MARKETS AND MICROECONOMIC POLICY ISSUES

CHAPTER 16
The Markets for Labor, Capital, and Land 454

16.1 Input Markets 455
Determining the Price of a Productive Factor: Derived Demand 455

16.2 Supply and Demand in the Labor Market 456
Will Hiring That Input Add More to Revenue Than Costs? 456
The Demand Curve for Labor Slopes Downward 457
How Many Workers Will an Employer Hire? 458
The Market Labor Supply Curve 459

16.3 Labor Market Equilibrium 461
Determining Equilibrium in the Competitive Labor Market 461
Shifts in the Labor Demand Curve 461
Shifting the Labor Supply Curve 463
Monopsony 464

16.4 Labor Unions 465
　　Labor Unions in the United States 465
　　Why Are There Labor Unions? 466
　　Union Impact on Labor Supply and Wages 466
　　Wage Differences for Similarly Skilled Workers 466
　　Can Unions Lead to Increased Productivity? 467

16.5 The Markets for Land and Capital 468
　　The Supply of and Demand for Land 468
　　Supply and Demand in the Capital Market 468
　　The Interdependence of Input Markets 469
　　Income Distribution and Marginal Productivity 470

Interactive Chapter Summary 470
　　Key Terms and Concepts 471
　　Section Check Answers 472
　　Study Guide 475

CHAPTER 17
Income and Poverty 482

17.1 Income Distribution 483
　　Measuring Income Inequality 483
　　The Lorenz Curve 484
　　Are We Overstating the Disparity in the Distribution of Income? 485
　　Permanent Income Hypothesis 486
　　How Much Movement Happens on the Economic Ladder? 486
　　Why Do Some Earn More Than Others? 487
　　Income Distribution in Other Countries 489

17.2 Income Redistribution 490
　　Equality 491
　　Income Redistribution Can Reduce Incentives to Work, Invest, and Save 491
　　Revisiting Marginal Productivity Theory 492

17.3 The Economics of Discrimination 493
　　Job-Entry Discrimination 493
　　Wage Discrimination 493
　　Discrimination or Differences in Productivity? 493
　　Why Do People Discriminate? 494
　　The Costs of Discrimination 495

17.4 Poverty 496
　　Defining Poverty 496
　　An Alternative Definition of Poverty 496
　　Income Redistribution 498

Interactive Chapter Summary 503
　　Key Terms and Concepts 504
　　Section Check Answers 504
　　Study Guide 507

CHAPTER 18
The Environment 513

18.1 Negative Externalities and Pollution 514
　　What Are Social Costs? 514
　　Negative Externalities and Pollution 514
　　Measuring Externalities 515

18.2 Public Policy and the Environment 517
　　Why Is a Clean Environment Not Free? 517
　　The Costs and Benefits of Pollution Control 517
　　Command and Control Policies: Regulation 519
　　Pollution (Pigovian) Taxes: A Market-Based Policy 520
　　Transferable Pollution Rights 520
　　What Is an Ideal Pollution Control Policy? 521

18.3 Property Rights 525
　　Property Rights and the Environment 525
　　The Coase Theorem 525
　　Transaction Costs and the Coase Theorem 525

Interactive Chapter Summary 528
　　Key Terms and Concepts 528
　　Section Check Answers 529
　　Study Guide 531

CHAPTER 19
Health Care 539

19.1 The Rising Cost of Health Care 540

19.2 The Health Care Market 542
　　Income 542
　　Insurance and Third-Party Payers 543
　　Demographic Changes 544
　　The Supply of Health Care 544
　　Doctors as Gatekeepers 544
　　Technological Progress and Quality of Care 545
　　Imperfect Competition 545
　　Shortages 546
　　The Market for Human Organs 547
　　Health Saving Account (HSA) 547
　　The Debate over Health Care Reform 549

Interactive Chapter Summary 552
　　Key Terms and Concepts 553
　　Section Check Answers 553
　　Study Guide 555

PART 6 MACROECONOMIC FOUNDATIONS

CHAPTER 20
Introduction to Macroeconomics: Unemployment, Inflation, and Economic Fluctuations 562

20.1 Macroeconomic Goals 563
　　Three Major Macroeconomic Goals 563
　　Acknowledging Our Goals: The Employment Act of 1946 563

20.2 Employment and Unemployment 564
　　The Consequences of High Unemployment 564
　　What Is the Unemployment Rate? 564
　　The Worst Case of U.S. Unemployment 565
　　Variations in the Unemployment Rate 565

Are Unemployment Statistics Accurate Reflections of the Labor Market? 565
Who Are the Unemployed? 566
Categories of Unemployed Workers 566
How Much Unemployment? 567
How Long Are People Usually Unemployed? 567
Labor Force Participation Rate 568

20.3 Types of Unemployment 569
Frictional Unemployment 569
Should We Worry About Frictional Unemployment? 569
Structural Unemployment 570
Some Unemployment Is Unavoidable 570
Cyclical Unemployment 570
The Natural Rate of Unemployment 571

20.4 Reasons for Unemployment 573
Why Does Unemployment Exist? 573
Minimum Wages and Unemployment 573
The Impact of Unions on the Unemployment Rate 574
Efficiency Wage 574
Job Search 574
Unemployment Insurance 575
Does New Technology Lead to Greater Unemployment? 575

20.5 Inflation 576
Stable Price Level as a Desirable Goal 576
Measuring Inflation 577
The Consumer Price Index and the GDP Deflator 578
How Is a Price Index Created? 578
Producer Price Index 579
GDP Deflator Versus CPI 579
The Price Level over the Years 579
Who Loses with Inflation? 582
Other Costs of Inflation 583
Inflation and Interest Rates 584
Do Creditors Always Lose During Inflation? 585
Protecting Ourselves from Inflation 585

20.6 Economic Fluctuations 587
Short-Term Fluctuations in Economic Growth 587
The Phases of a Business Cycle 587
How Long Does a Business Cycle Last? 588
Seasonal Fluctuations Affect Economic Activity 589
Forecasting Cyclical Changes 589

Interactive Chapter Summary 590
Key Terms and Concepts 592
Section Check Answers 593
Study Guide 597

CHAPTER 21
Measuring Economic Performance 607

21.1 National Income Accounting: A Standardized Way to Measure Economic Performance 608
What Is Gross Domestic Product? 608
Production, Income, and the Circular Flow Model 608

21.2 Measuring Total Production 610
The Expenditure Approach to Measuring GDP 610
Consumption (C) 610
Investment (I) 611
Government Purchases (G) 612
Exports (X − M) 612

21.3 Other Measures of Total Production and Total Income 613

21.4 Problems in Calculating an Accurate GDP 614
Problems in Calculating an Accurate GDP 614
How Do We Solve This Problem? 614
A Price-Level Index 614
Real GDP 614
Is Real GDP Always Less Than Nominal GDP? 615
Real GDP per Capita 615
Why Is the Measure of per Capita GDP So Important? 616

21.5 Problems with GDP as a Measure of Economic Welfare 617
Nonmarket Transactions 617
The Underground Economy 617
Measuring the Value of Leisure 617
GDP and Externalities 617
Quality of Goods 620
Other Measures of Economic Well-Being 620

Interactive Chapter Summary 621
Key Terms and Concepts 622
Section Check Answers 622
Study Guide 624

CHAPTER 22
Economic Growth in the Global Economy 631

22.1 Economic Growth 632
Defining Economic Growth 632
The Rule of 70 632

22.2 Determinants of Economic Growth 634
Factors That Contribute to Economic Growth 634
New Growth Theory 637

22.3 Public Policy and Economic Growth 638
    The Impact of Economic Growth 638
    Saving Rates, Investment, Capital Stock, and
        Economic Growth 638
    Infrastructure 638
    Research and Development 638
    The Protection of Property Rights Impacts
        Economic Growth 639
    Free Trade and Economic Growth 639
    Education 640

22.4 Population and Economic Growth 642
    Population Growth and Economic Growth 642
    The Malthusian Prediction 643

Interactive Chapter Summary 644
    Key Terms and Concepts 645
    Section Check Answers 645
    Study Guide 647

CHAPTER 23
Financial Markets, Saving, and Investment 653

23.1 Financial Institutions and Intermediaries 654
    Bonds 654
    Stocks 654
    Retained Earnings 655
    The Value of Securities 655
    Reading Stock Tables 656
    Financial Intermediaries 657

23.2 Saving, Investment, and the Financial System 658
    The Macroeconomics of Saving and
        Investment 659
    The Market for Loanable Funds 659
    Analyzing the Market for Loanable Funds 661
    Interest Rates and the Inflow and Outflow
        of Capital 666

23.3 The Financial Crisis of 2008 667
    Low Interest Rates (2002–2004) Led to Aggressive
        Borrowing 668
    Deregulation in the Housing Market and Subprime
        Mortgages 668
    Who Bought These Risky Subprime
        Mortgages? 669
    The Fed Raises Interest Rates and the Housing
        Bust 670

Interactive Chapter Summary 673
    Key Terms and Concepts 674
    Section Check Answers 674
    Study Guide 677
    Appendix: Calculating Present Value 684

PART 7 THE MACROECONOMIC MODELS

CHAPTER 24
Aggregate Demand and Aggregate Supply 688

24.1 The Determinants of Aggregate Demand 689
    What Is Aggregate Demand? 689
    Consumption (C) 689
    Investment (I) 689
    Government Purchases (G) 689
    Net Exports $(X - M)$ 689

24.2 The Aggregate Demand Curve 690
    How Is the Quantity of Real GDP Demanded
        Affected by the Price Level? 690
    Why Is the Aggregate Demand Curve Negatively
        Sloped? 691

24.3 Shifts in the Aggregate Demand Curve 692
    Shifts Versus Movements Along the Aggregate
        Demand Curve 692
    Aggregate Demand Curve Shifters 692

24.4 The Aggregate Supply Curve 694
    What Is the Aggregate Supply Curve? 694
    Why Is the Short-Run Aggregate Supply Curve
        Positively Sloped? 695
    Why Is the Long-Run Aggregate Supply Curve
        Vertical? 695

24.5 Shifts in the Aggregate Supply Curve 697
    Shifting Short-Run and Long-Run
        Supply Curves 697
    What Factors Shift Short-Run Aggregate Supply
        Only? 698

24.6 Macroeconomic Equilibrium 700
    Determining Macroeconomic Equilibrium 700
    Recessionary and Inflationary Gaps 700
    Demand-Pull Inflation 701
    Cost-Push Inflation 701
    What Helped the United States Recover
        in the 1980s? 703
    A Decrease in Aggregate Demand
        and Recessions 703
    Adjusting to a Recessionary Gap 704
    Slow Adjustments to a Recessionary Gap 704
    What Causes Wages and Prices to Be
        Sticky Downward? 704
    Adjusting to an Inflationary Gap 705
    Price Level and RGDP Over Time 706

24.7 The Classical and the Keynesian Macroeconomic Model   707
The Classical School and Say's Law   707
Changes in Aggregate Demand in the Classical Model   708
The Keynesian Short-Run Aggregate Supply Curve—Sticky Prices and Wages   709

Interactive Chapter Summary   711
Key Terms and Concepts   713
Section Check Answers   713
Study Guide   718

CHAPTER 25
The Aggregate Expenditure Model   731

25.1 Simple Aggregate Expenditure Model   732
Why Do We Assume the Price Level Is Fixed?   732
The Simplest Aggregate Expenditure Model: Autonomous Consumption Only   732
What Are the Autonomous Factors That Influence Spending?   733

25.2 Finding Equilibrium in the Aggregate Expenditure Model   734
Revisiting Marginal Propensity to Consume and Save   735
Marginal Propensity to Save   735
Equilibrium in the Aggregate Expenditure Model   736
Disequilibrium in the Aggregate Expenditure Model   737

25.3 Adding Investment, Government Purchases, and Net Exports   739

25.4 Shifts in Aggregate Expenditure and the Multiplier   741

25.5 From Aggregate Expenditures to Aggregate Demand   744
Shifts in Aggregate Demand   745
Limitations of the Aggregate Expenditure Model   746

Interactive Chapter Summary   748
Key Terms and Concepts   749
Section Check Answers   749
Study Guide   752

PART 8   MACROECONOMIC POLICY

CHAPTER 26
Fiscal Policy   758

26.1 Fiscal Policy   759
Fiscal Policy   759
Fiscal Stimulus Affects the Budget   759
The Government and Total Spending   759

26.2 Fiscal Policy and the *AD/AS* Model   761
Fiscal Policy and the *AD/AS* Model   761

26.3 The Multiplier Effect   765
Government Purchases, Taxes, and Aggregate Demand   765
The Multiplier Effect   765
The Multiplier Effect at Work   766
Changes in the MPC Affect the Multiplier Process   767
The Multiplier and the Aggregate Demand Curve   767
Tax Cuts and the Multiplier   767
Taxes and Investment Spending   768
A Reduction in Government Purchases and Tax Increases   768
Time Lags, Saving, and Imports Reduce the Size of the Multiplier   769
The 2008–09 Recession   769

26.4 Supply-Side Effects of Tax Cuts   770
What Is Supply-Side?   770
Impact of Supply-Side Policies   770
Research and Development and the Supply Side of the Economy   770
How Do Supply-Side Policies Affect Long-Run Aggregate Supply?   771
Critics of Supply-Side Economics   771
The Supply-Side and Demand-Side Effects of a Tax Cut   771

26.5 Possible Obstacles to Effective Fiscal Policy   775
The Crowding-Out Effect   775
Time Lags in Fiscal Policy Implementation   776

26.6 Automatic Stabilizers   779
Automatic Stabilizers   779
How Do the Tax System and Transfer Payments Stabilize the Economy?   779

26.7 The National Debt   781
Fiscal Stimulus Affects the Budget   781
How Government Finances the Debt   781
Why Run a Budget Deficit?   781
An Increase in the Budget Deficit: Short-Run and Long-Run Effects   782
The Burden of Public Debt   783

Interactive Chapter Summary   786
Key Terms and Concepts   788
Section Check Answers   788
Study Guide   792

CHAPTER 27
Monetary Institutions   801

27.1 What Is Money?   802
The Functions of Money   802

27.2 Measuring Money   806
Currency   806
Currency as Legal Tender   806

Demand Deposits and Other
  Checkable Deposits 806
The Popularity of Demand Deposits and Other
  Checkable Deposits 807
Credit Cards 807
Savings Accounts 808
Money Market Mutual Funds 808
Stocks and Bonds 808
Liquidity 809
The Money Supply 809
How Was Money "Backed"? 809
What Really Backs Our Money Now? 810

27.3 How Banks Create Money 812
Financial Institutions 812
The Functions of Financial Institutions 812
How Do Banks Create Money? 812
How Do Banks Make Profits? 813
Reserve Requirements 813
Fractional Reserve System 813
A Balance Sheet 814
The Required Reserve Ratio 815
Loaning Excess Reserves 815
Is More Money More Wealth? 817

27.4 The Money Multiplier 818
The Multiple Expansion Effect 818
New Loans and Multiple Expansions 818
The Money Multiplier 819
Why Is It Only "Potential" Money Creation? 819

27.5 The Collapse of America's Banking System, 1920–1933 821
What Happened to the Banking Industry? 821
What Caused the Collapse? 821
Bank Failures Today 822

Interactive Chapter Summary 823
Key Terms and Concepts 824
Section Check Answers 824
Study Guide 827

CHAPTER 28
The Federal Reserve System and Monetary Policy 832

28.1 The Federal Reserve System 833
The Functions of a Central Bank 833
Location of the Federal Reserve System 833
The Fed's Relationship to the Federal
  Government 834
The Fed's Ties to the Executive Branch 834
Fed Operations 835

28.2 How Does the Federal Reserve Change the Money Supply? 836
Open Market Operations 836
The Reserve Requirement 837
The Discount Rate 837
How the Fed Reduces the Money Supply 838
How the Fed Increases the Money Supply 838
Difficulties in Controlling the Money Supply 839

28.3 Money, Interest Rates, and Aggregate Demand 839
The Money Market 839
The Demand for Money and the Nominal Interest
  Rate 840
Why Is the Supply of Money Relatively
  Inelastic? 841
The Money Market 841
How Do Income Changes Affect the Equilibrium
  Position? 842
How Would an Increase in the Money Supply
  Affect Equilibrium Interest Rates and Aggregate
  Demand? 842
Does the Fed Target the Money Supply or Interest
  Rates? 843
Which Interest Rate Does the Fed Target? 844
Does the Fed Influence the Real Interest Rate in the
  Short Run? 845

28.4 Expansionary and Contractionary Monetary Policy 848
Expansionary Monetary Policy in a Recessionary
  Gap 848
Contractionary Monetary Policy in an Inflationary
  Gap 848
Monetary Policy in the Open Economy 850

28.5 Money and Inflation 854
The Inflation Rate and the Growth in the Money
  Supply 854
The Equation of Exchange 855

28.6 Problems in Implementing Monetary and Fiscal Policy 857
Problems in Conducting Monetary Policy 857
How Do Commercial Banks Implement the Fed's
  Monetary Policies? 858
Banks That Are Not Part of the Federal Reserve
  System and Policy Implementation 858
Fiscal and Monetary Coordination
  Problems 858
Alleviating Coordination Problems 858
Imperfect Information 859
Overall Problems with Monetary and
  Fiscal Policy 859

Interactive Chapter Summary 861
Key Terms and Concepts 863
Section Check Answers 864
Study Guide 868

CHAPTER 29
Issues in Macroeconomic Theory and Policy 877

29.1 The Phillips Curve 878
Unemployment and Inflation 878
The Phillips Curve 878
The Slope of the Phillips Curve 878
The Phillips Curve and Aggregate Supply
  and Demand 879

29.2 The Phillips Curve over Time 880
The Phillips Curve—The 1960s 880
The Short-Run Phillips Curve Versus the Long-Run Phillips Curve 881
Supply Shocks 883

29.3 Rational Expectations and Real Business Cycles 885
Can Human Behavior Counteract Government Policy? 885
The Rational Expectations Theory 885
Rational Expectations and the Consequences of Government Macroeconomic Policies 886
Anticipation of an Expansionary Monetary Policy 886
Unanticipated Expansionary Policy 887
When an Anticipated Expansionary Policy Change Is Less Than the Actual Policy Change 888
Critics of Rational Expectations Theory 888
New Keynesians and Rational Expectations 889
What Is the Real Business Cycle Theory? 889

29.4 Controversies in Macroeconomic Policy 891
Are Fiscal and Monetary Policies Effective? 891
Policy Difficulties with Supply Shocks 892
What Should the Central Bank Do? 892
Inflation Targeting 892
Indexing and Reducing the Costs of Inflation 896

Interactive Chapter Summary 898
Key Terms and Concepts 900
Section Check Answers 900
Study Guide 903

PART 9 THE GLOBAL ECONOMY

CHAPTER 30
International Trade 914

30.1 The Growth in World Trade 915
Importance of International Trade 915
Trading Partners 915

30.2 Comparative Advantage and Gains from Trade 917
Economic Growth and Trade 917
The Principle of Comparative Advantage 918
Comparative Advantage, Specialization, and the Production Possibilities Curves 918
Regional Comparative Advantage 923

30.3 Supply and Demand in International Trade 926
The Importance of Trade: Producer and Consumer Surplus 926
Free Trade and Exports—Domestic Producers Gain More Than Domestic Consumers Lose 927
Free Trade and Imports—Domestic Consumers Gain More Than Domestic Producers Lose 928

30.4 Tariffs, Import Quotas, and Subsidies 929
Tariffs 929
The Domestic Economic Impact of Tariffs 929
Arguments for Tariffs 931
Import Quotas 932
The Domestic Economic Impact of an Import Quota 932
The Economic Impact of Subsidies 932

Interactive Chapter Summary 938
Key Terms and Concepts 939
Section Check Answers 939
Study Guide 942

CHAPTER 31
International Finance 949

31.1 The Balance of Payments 950
Balance of Payments 950
The Current Account 950
The Capital Account 953

31.2 Exchange Rates 954
The Need for Foreign Currencies 954
The Exchange Rate 954
Changes in Exchange Rates Affect the Domestic Demand for Foreign Goods 954
The Demand for a Foreign Currency 954
The Supply of a Foreign Currency 955
Determining Exchange Rates 955
The Demand Curve for a Foreign Currency 955
The Supply Curve for Foreign Currency 956
Equilibrium in the Foreign Exchange Market 956

31.3 Equilibrium Changes in the Foreign Exchange Market 957
Determinants in the Foreign Exchange Market 957
Increased Tastes for Foreign Goods 957
Relative Income Increases or Reductions in U.S. Tariffs 957
European Incomes Increase, Reductions in European Tariffs, or Changes in European Tastes 958
How Do Changes in Relative Real Interest Rates Affect Exchange Rates? 959
Changes in the Relative Inflation Rate 959
Expectations and Speculation 960

31.4 Flexible Exchange Rates 962
The Flexible Exchange Rate System 962
Are Exchange Rates Managed at All? 962
When Exchange Rates Change 963
The Advantages of Flexible Rates 963
Fixed Exchange Rates Can Result in Currency Shortages 963
Flexible Rates Solve the Currency Shortage Problem 964
Flexible Rates Affect Macroeconomic Policies 964
The Disadvantages of Flexible Rates 964

Interactive Chapter Summary 969
Key Terms and Concepts 970
Section Check Answers 970
Study Guide 973

Glossary 980

Index 988

Preface

About the Book

The *Exploration of Economics*, **5th Edition,** was written to not only be a student-friendly textbook, but one that was relevant, one that focused on those few principles and applications that demonstrate the enormous breadth of economics to everyday life. This text is lively, motivating, and exciting, and it helps students relate economics to their world.

The Section-by-Section Approach

Many students are not lacking in ability, but rather are lacking a strategy. Information needs to be moved from short-term memory to long-term memory and then retrieved. Learning theory provides several methods for helping students do this.

The Exploration of Economics uses a section-by-section approach in its presentation of economic ideas. Information is presented in small, self-contained sections rather than in large blocks of text. Learning theorists call this *chunking*. That is, more information can be stored in the working memory as a result of learning in smaller blocks of information. Also, by using shorter bite-sized pieces, students are not only more likely to read the material but also more likely to reread it, leading to better comprehension and test results. Learning theorists call this *rehearsal*.

Unlike standard textbook construction, this approach is distinctly more compatible with the modern communication style with which most students are familiar and comfortable: short, intense, and exciting bursts of information. Rather than being distracted and discouraged by the seeming enormity of the task before them, students are more likely to work through a short, self-contained section before getting up from their desks. More importantly, instructors benefit from having a student population that has actually read the textbook and prepared for class!

In executing the section-by-section approach in *The Exploration of Economics,* every effort has been made to take the intimidation out of economics. The idea of sticking to the basics and reinforcing student mastery, concept by concept, has been done with the student in mind. But students aren't the only ones to benefit from this approach. The section-by-section presentation allows instructors greater flexibility in planning their courses.

The Exploration of Economics was created with flexibility in mind in order to accommodate a variety of teaching styles. Many of the chapters are self-contained, allowing instructors to customize their course. For example, in Part 3, the theory of the firm chapters can be presented in any order. The theory of the firm chapters are introduced in the textbook from the most competitive market structure (perfect competition) to the least competitive market structure (monopoly). After all, almost all firms face a downward-sloping demand curve, not just monopolists. However, instructors who prefer can teach monopoly immediately following perfect competition because each chapter is self-contained. And for those who do not have sufficient time to cover the Aggregate expenditure model, the Fiscal Policy chapter has an extensive section on the multiplier.

Each chapter is comprised of approximately six to ten short sections. These sections are self-contained learning units, typically presented in three to six pages that include these helpful learning features:

- **Key Questions.** Each section begins with a list of questions that highlight the primary ideas that students should learn from the material. These questions are intended to serve as a preview and to pique interest in the material to come. They also serve as landmarks: if students can answer these questions after reading the material, they have prepared well.

- **Section Checks.** It is also important that students learn to self-manage: They should ask themselves: How well am I doing? How does this relate to what I already know? The section-by-section approach provides continual self-testing along every step of the way. Each section ends with four to six short sentences emphasizing the important points in each section. It also includes four to six questions designed to test comprehension of the basic points of the section just covered. Answers are provided at the end of each chapter so students can check their responses. If students can answer these Section Check questions correctly, they can feel confident about proceeding to the next topic.

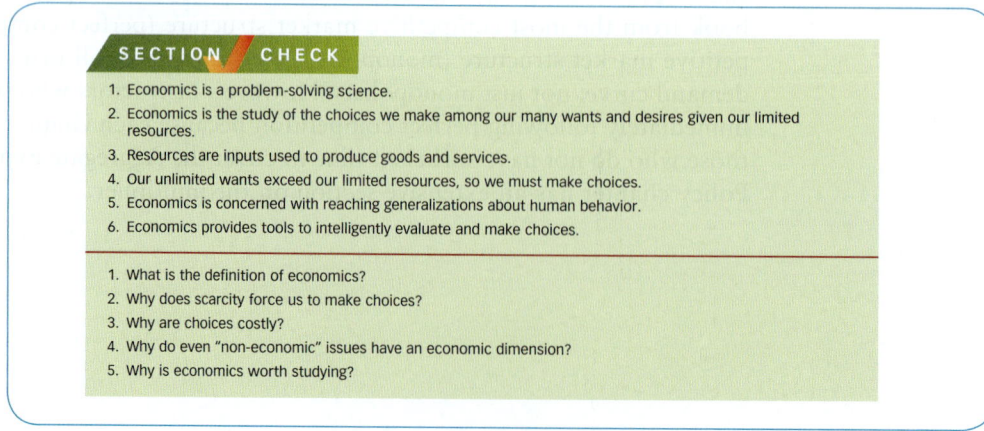

* **Integrated Study Guide pages!** These pages, found at the end of each chapter, guide students through various exercises designed to test their comprehension and mastery, including true-false, multiple-choice, and application-type questions. Organized in chronological order to follow the chapter, students can easily refer back to the chapter content for review and support as they proceed through the exercises.

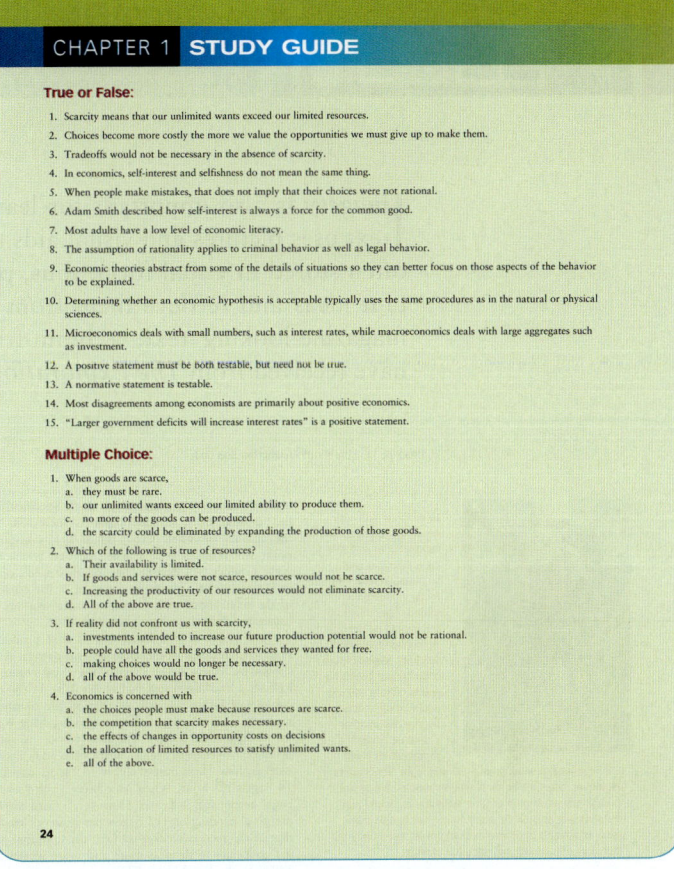

Other End-of-Chapter Material Includes:

* **Interactive Chapter Summary.** Each chapter ends with an interactive summary of the main ideas in the chapter. Students can fill in the blanks and check their answers against those provided at the end of the summary. It is a useful refresher before class or tests and a good starting point for studying.

* **Key Terms and Concepts.** A list of key terms concludes each chapter. If students can define all these terms, they have a good head start on studying.

TAKE OUT

Visual Learning Features

Imagery is also important for learning. Visual stimulus helps the learning process. This text uses pictures and visual aids to reinforce valuable concepts and ideas. Information is often stored in visual form; thus, pictures are important in helping students retain important ideas and retrieve them from their long-term memory. Students want a welcoming, magazine-looking text; a brain-friendly environment. The most consistent remark we have received from *The Exploration of Economics* adopters is that their students are reading their book, and reading the text leads to better test performance.

At every turn this text has been designed with interesting graphics so that visual cues help students learn and remember:

✴ **Photos.** The text contains a number of colorful pictures. They are not, however, mere decoration; rather, these photos are an integral part of the book, for both learning and motivation purposes. The photos are carefully placed where they reinforce important concepts, and they are accompanied with captions designed to encourage students to extend their understanding of particular ideas.

✴ **Exhibits.** Graphs, tables, and charts are important economic tools. These tools are used throughout *The Exploration of Economics* to illustrate, clarify, and reinforce economic principles. Text exhibits are designed to be as clear and simple as possible, and they are carefully coordinated with the text material.

xxii

Applications

There are numerous applications to everyday life situations scattered throughout the text. These applications were chosen specifically with students in mind, and they are designed to help them find the connection between economics and their life. With that, economic principles are applied to everyday problems and issues, such as teen smoking, property rights and song swapping, crime, online betting, the NCAA, gift giving, and many others. There are also five special types of boxed applications scattered throughout each chapter:

✻ **In the News.** These applications focus primarily on current news stories that are relevant and thought-provoking. These articles are placed strategically throughout the text to solidify particular concepts. In an effort to emphasize the breadth and diversity of the situations to which economic principles can be applied, these articles have been chosen from a wide range of sources.

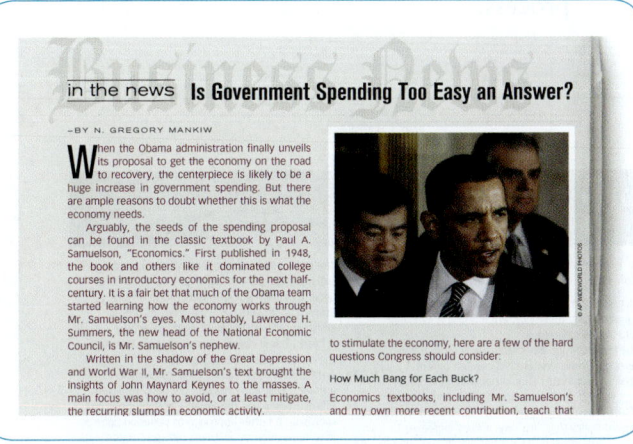

✻ **Global Watch.** Whether we are concerned with understanding yesterday, today, or tomorrow, and whether we are looking at a small, far-away country or a large next door neighbor, economic principles can strengthen our grasp of many global issues. "Global Watch" articles were chosen to help students understand the magnitude and character of the changes occurring around the world today and to introduce them to some of the economic causes and implications of these changes. To gain a greater perspective on a particular economy or the planet as a whole, it is helpful to compare important economic indicators around the world. For this reason, "Global Watch" applications are sometimes also used to present relevant comparative statistics.

xxiii

xxiv Applications

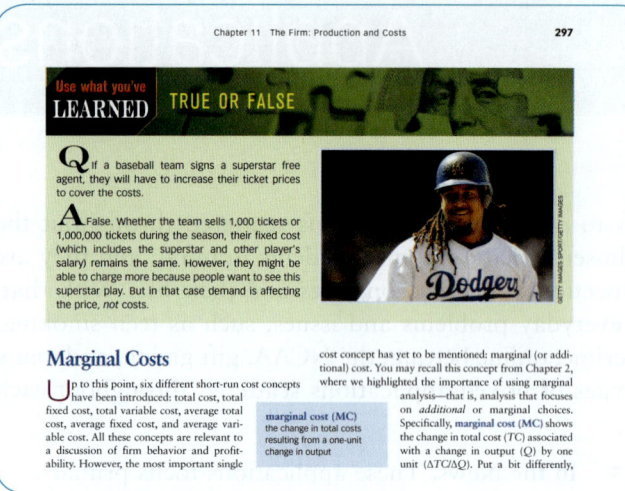

❋ **Using What You've Learned.** Economic principles aren't just definitions to memorize; they are valuable tools that can help students analyze a whole host of issues and problems in the world around them. Part of learning economics is learning when and how to use new tools. These special boxes are scattered throughout the text as a way of reinforcing and checking students' true comprehension of important or more difficult concepts by assessing their ability to apply what they have learned to a real-world situation. Students can check their work against the answer given in the self-contained box, providing them with immediate feedback and encouragement in the learning process.

❋ **Policy Application.** These features focus primarily on news stories that involve a government policy decision based upon economic concepts. These applications are scattered throughout the text as a way of reinforcing important or more difficult concepts.

❋ **Interactive Summary.** Picking up the terminology of economics is not enough; students have to learn when and how to use their new tools. It is this philosophy that serves as the focus for the problem-solving approach in *The Exploration of Economics*, which is designed to serve two key purposes: (1) to facilitate student mastery of concepts both theoretically and in application, and (2) to communicate a sense of relevancy to students.

Instructor's Resources

The 5th Edition offers an array of instructor resources designed to enhance teaching.

Instructor's Manual

Prepared by Gary Galles (Pepperdine University), the Instructor's Manual, available online at www.cengage.com/international, follows the textbook's concept-by-concept approach in two parts: chapter outlines and teaching tips. The Teaching Tips section provides analogies, illustrations, and examples to help instructors reinforce each section of the text. Answers to all of the end-of-chapter text questions can also be found in the Instructor's Manual.

Test Bank

Test bank questions, available online at www.cengage.com/international have been thoroughly updated. The test bank includes approximately 150 test questions per chapter, consisting of multiple-choice, true-false, and short-answer questions.

ExamView® Testing Software

ExamView®—Computerized Testing Software contains all of the questions in the printed test banks. ExamView is an easy-to-use test creation software compatible with Microsoft Windows. Instructors can add or edit questions, instructions, and answers, and select questions by previewing them on the screen, selecting them randomly, or selecting them by number. Instructors can also create and administer quizzes online over the Internet.

Microsoft PowerPoint® Presentation Slides

- **Lecture Presentation in PowerPoint.** This PowerPoint presentation covers all the essential sections presented in each chapter of the book. Graphs, tables, lists, and concepts are animated sequentially to visually engage students. Additional examples and applications are used to reinforce major lessons. The slides are crisp, clear, and colorful. Instructors may adapt or add slides to customize their lectures.
- **Exhibits from the Text in PowerPoint.** Every graph and table within the text has been recreated in PowerPoint. These exhibits are available within the lecture presentation, but we have also made them available as a separate batch of slides for those instructors who don't want the lecture slides.

Both the Lecture and Exhibit PowerPoint presentations are available for downloading at the Sexton Companion Web site: http://www.cengage.com/international

Availability of resources may differ by region. Check with your local Cengage Learning representative for details.

Student Resources

The 5th Edition offers an array of resources to help students test their understanding of chapter concepts and enhance their overall learning. Found at the student Companion Web site, these interactive resources provide exam preparation and help students get the most from their Principles of Economics course.

Interactive Quizzes

Students can test their understanding of the chapter's concepts with the interactive quiz. Each quiz contains multiple-choice questions, like those found on a typical exam. Questions include detailed feedback for each answer, so that students may know instantly whether they have answered correctly or incorrectly. In addition, they may email the results of the quiz to themselves or their instructor, with a listing of correct and incorrect answers. An Internet connection is required to take the quizzes.

Key Term Glossary and Flashcards

As a study aid, students may use the glossary terms as flashcards to test their knowledge. Students can state the definition of a term, then click on the term to check the correctness of their statement.

Internet Review Quizzes

These exercises are designed to spark students' excitement about researching on the Internet by asking them to access economic data and then answer questions related to the content of the chapter. All Internet exercises are on the Sexton Web site with direct links to the addresses so that students will not have the tedious and error-prone task of entering long Web site addresses.

Availability of resources may differ by region. Check with your local Cengage Learning representative for details.

Technology Solutions
with Sexton's 5th Edition

Global Economic Watch

The global economic downturn, the most important economic event in generations, unfolds day-to-day and hour-to hour. Cengage Learning's Global Economic Watch is a powerful online portal for bringing current events into the classroom.

The Watch includes:

- A content-rich blog of breaking news, expert analysis, and commentary
- A real-time database of hundreds of relevant and vetted journal, newspaper, and periodical articles, videos, and podcasts—updated four times daily
- A thorough overview and timeline of events leading up to the global economic crisis
- Discussion and testing content and other teaching/study resources
Visit www.cengage.com/thewatch

EconCentral

Multiple resources for learning and reinforcing principles and concepts are now available in one place!

EconCentral is your one-stop shop for the learning tools and activities to help you succeed. Available for an additional price, EconCentral equips you with a portal to a wealth of resources that help you both study and apply economic concepts. As you read and study the chapters, you can access video tutorials with Ask the Instructor videos. You can also review with Flashcards and the Graphic Workshop, as well as check your understating of the chapter with interactive quizzing.

Ready to apply chapter concepts to the real world? EconCentral gives you ABC News videos, EconNews articles, Economic debates, Links to economic data, and more. All the study and application resources in EconCentral are organized by chapter to help you get the most from *The Exploration of Economics,* 5e, and from your lectures.

Visit www.cengage.com/economics/econcentral to see the study options available!

APLIA™

Created by Paul Romer, one of the nation's leading economists, Aplia enhances teaching and learning by providing online interactive tools and experiments that help economics students become "active learners." This application allows a tight content correlation between Sexton's 5th Edition and Aplia's online tools.

Students Come to Class Prepared

It is a proven fact that students do better in their course work if they come to class prepared. Aplia's activities are engaging and based on discovery learning, requiring students to take an active role in the learning process. When assigned online homework, students are more apt to read the text, come to class better prepared to participate in discussions, and are more able to relate to the economic concepts and theories presented. Learning by doing helps students feel involved, gain confidence in the materials, and see important concepts come to life.

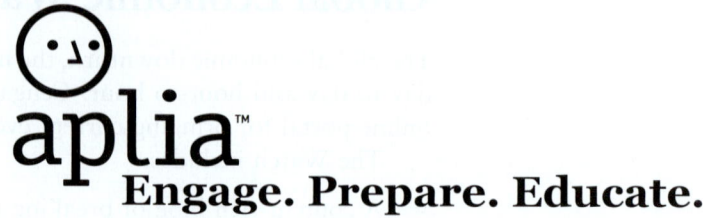

Assign Homework in an Effective and Efficient Way

Now you can assign homework without increasing your workload! Together, Sexton and Aplia provide the best text and technology resources to give you multiple teaching and learning solutions. Through Aplia, you can assign problem sets and online activities that automatically give feedback and are tracked and graded, all without requiring additional effort. Since Aplia's assignments are closely integrated with Sexton's 5th Edition, your students are applying what they have learned from the text to their homework.

Contact your local Cengage South-Western representative to find out how you can incorporate this exciting technology into your course. For more information, please visit: www.aplia.com.

JoinIn™ on TurningPoint®

Made on demand, JoinIn™ on TurningPoint is the only classroom response software tool that gives you true PowerPoint integration. With JoinIn, you are no longer tied to your computer. You can walk about your classroom as you lecture, showing slides while collecting and displaying responses with ease. There is simply no easier or more effective way to turn your lecture hall into a personal, fully interactive experience for your students. If you can use PowerPoint, you can use JoinIn on TurningPoint with Sexton's 5th Edition.

Availability of resources may differ by region. Check with your local Cengage Learning representative for details.

About the Author

Robert L. Sexton is Distinguished Professor of Economics at Pepperdine University. Professor Sexton has also been a Visiting Professor at the University of California at Los Angeles in the Anderson Graduate School of Management and the Department of Economics. He was also an Assistant Coach in the movie *Benchwarmers* (2006).

Professor Sexton's research ranges across many fields of economics: economics education, labor economics, environmental economics, law and economics, and economic history. He has written several books and has published numerous reference articles, many in top economic journals such as *The American Economic Review, Southern Economic Journal, Economics Letters, Journal of Urban Economics,* and *The Journal of Economic Education*. Professor Sexton has also written more than 100 other articles that have appeared in books, magazines, and newspapers.

Professor Sexton received the Pepperdine Professor of the Year Award in 1991 and he was named a Harriet and Charles Luckman Teaching Fellow in 1994.

Professor Sexton resides in Agoura Hills, California, with his wife, Julie, and their three children, Elizabeth, Katherine, and Tommy.

Acknowledgments

I would like to extend special thanks to the following colleagues for their valuable insight during the manuscript phase of this project. I owe a debt of gratitude to Edward Merkel, Troy University; Doug McNiel and Salvador Contreras, McNeese State University; David McClough, Ohio Northern University; Tim Bettner, University of La Verne; Inge O'Connor, Syracuse University; William Coomber, University of Maryland; Michael Marlow, Cal Poly; Nand Arora, Cleary University; Carlos F. Liard, Central Connecticut State University; Howard Cochran, Belmont University; Abdulhamid Sukar, Cameron University; Harry Karim, Los Angeles Community College; Maria DaCosta, University of Wisconsin-Eau Claire; Kelli Mayes-Denker, Carl Sandburg College; Elnora Farmer, Griffin Technical College; Robert Shoffner, Central Piedmont Community College; Mark Strazicich, Appalachian State University; and Jeffrey Phillips, SUNY Morrisville.

I also wish to thank Gary Galles of Pepperdine University for his help preparing the ancillaries that accompany the 5th Edition, and Mike Ryan of Gainesville State College for providing an invaluable verification of the text and updating the Test Bank.

I am truly indebted to the excellent team of professionals at Cengage Learning. My appreciation goes to Steve Scoble, Senior Acquisitions Editor; Daniel Noguera, Developmental Editor; Jean Buttrom, Content Project Manager; and Michelle Kunkler, Art Director. Also thanks to Joe Sabbatino, Publisher; Betty Jung, Associate Marketing Manager, Bill Hendee, VP/Marketing, Jack Calhoun, VP/Editorial Director, and the Cengage Sales Representatives. I sincerely appreciate your hard work and effort.

In addition, my family deserves special gratitude—my wife, Julie; my daughters, Elizabeth and Katherine; and my son, Tommy. They are an inspiration to my work. Also, special thanks to my brother Bill for all of his work that directly and indirectly helped this project come to fruition.

Thanks to all of my colleagues who reviewed this material for the 5th Edition. From very early on in the revision all the way up to publication, your comments were very important to me.

Robert L. Sexton

PART 1 INTRODUCTION

Chapter 1 The Role and Method of Economics *2*

Appendix: Working with Graphs *28*

Chapter 2 The Economic Way of Thinking *36*

Chapter 3 Scarcity, Trade-Offs, and Production Possibilities *66*

1 The Role and Method of Economics

1.1 Economics: A Brief Introduction
1.2 Economic Behavior
1.3 Economic Theory
1.4 Pitfalls to Avoid in Scientific Thinking
1.5 Positive Statements and Normative Statements
APPENDIX: Working with Graphs

As you begin your first course in economics, you may be asking yourself why you're here. What does economics have to do with your life?

Although we can list many good reasons to study economics, perhaps the best reason is that many issues in our lives are at least partly economic in character. A good understanding of economics would allow you to answer such questions as, Why do 10 A.M. classes fill up more quickly than 8 A.M. classes during registration? Why is it so hard to find an apartment in cities such as San Francisco, Berkeley, and New York? Why is teenage unemployment higher than adult unemployment? Why is the price of your prescription drugs so high? How does inflation impact you and your family? Will higher taxes on cigarettes reduce the number of teenagers smoking? If so, by how much? Why do female models make more than male models? Why is it easier for college graduates to find jobs in some years rather than others? Why do U.S. auto producers like tariffs (taxes) on imported cars? Is outsourcing jobs to India a good idea? Is globalization good for the economy? The study of economics improves your understanding of these and many other concerns.

Economics is a unique way of analyzing many areas of human behavior. Indeed, the range of topics to which economic analysis can be applied is broad. Many researchers discover that the economic approach to human behavior sheds light on social problems that have been with us for a long time: discrimination, education, crime, divorce, political favoritism, and more. In fact, your daily newspaper is filled with economics. You can find economics on the domestic page, the international page, the business page, the sports page, the entertainment page, and even the weather page—economics is all around us.

However, before we delve into the details and models of economics, it is important that we present an overview of how economists approach problems—their methodology. How does an economist apply the logic of science to approach a problem? And what are the pitfalls that economists should avoid in economic thinking? We also discuss why economists disagree. ∎

SECTION 1.1

Economics: A Brief Introduction

* What is economics?
* What is scarcity?

Economics—A Word with Many Different Meanings

Some individuals think economics involves the study of the stock market and corporate finance, and it does—in part. Others think that economics is concerned with the wise use of money and other matters of personal finance, and it is—in part. Still others think that economics involves forecasting or predicting what business conditions will be in the future, and again, it does—in part. The word *economics* is, after all, derived from the Greek *Oeconomicus*, which referred to the management of household affairs.

Precisely defined, **economics** is the study of the choices we make among our many wants and desires given our limited resources. What are resources? **Resources** are inputs—land, human effort and skills, and machines and factories, for instance—used to produce goods and services. The problem is that our unlimited wants exceed our limited resources, a fact that we call **scarcity**. Scarcity forces us to decide how best to use our limited resources. This is **the economic problem:** Scarcity forces us to choose, and choices are costly because we must give up other opportunities that we value. Consumers must make choices on what to buy, how much to save, and how much to invest of their limited incomes. Workers must decide what types of jobs they want, when to enter the workforce, where they will work, and number of hours they wish to work. Firms must decide what kinds of products to produce, how much to produce, and how to produce those goods and services at the lowest cost. That is, consumers, workers, and firms all face choices because of scarity.

The economic problem is evident in every aspect of our lives. You may find that the choice between shopping for groceries and browsing at the mall, or between finishing a research paper and going to a movie, is easier to understand when you have a good handle on the "economic way of thinking."

The front pages of our daily newspapers are filled with articles related to economics—either directly or indirectly. News headlines may cover topics such as unemployment, deficits, financial markets, health care, social security, energy issues, war, global warming, and so on.

economics
the study of choices we make among our many wants and desires given our limited resources

resources
inputs used to produce goods and services

scarcity
exists when human wants (material and nonmaterial) exceed available resources

the economic problem
scarcity forces us to choose, and choices are costly because we must give up other opportunities that we value

Economics Is All Around Us

The tools of economics are far reaching. In fact, other social scientists have accused economists of being imperialistic because their tools have been used in so many fields outside the formal area of economics, like crime, education, marriage, divorce, addiction, finance, health, law, politics, and religion.

So while you might think that much of what you desire in life is "non-economic," economics concerns everything an individual might consider worthwhile, including things that you might consider "priceless." For instance, although we may long for love, sexual fulfillment, or spiritual enlightenment, few of us would

in the news: Americans Score Poorly on Economic Literacy

Average American Grade: F

In 1999, the National Council of Economic Education tested 1,010 adults and 1,085 high school students on their knowledge of basic economic principles. On average, adults got a grade of 57 percent on a test on the basics of economics. Among high school students, the average grade was 48 percent.

* Almost two-thirds of those tested did not know that in times of inflation, money does not hold its value.
* Only 58 percent of the students understood that when the demand for a product goes up but the supply doesn't, its price is likely to increase.
* Half of the adults and about two-thirds of the students didn't know that the stock market brings people who want to buy stocks together with those who want to sell them.
* Just over one in three Americans realize that society must make choices about how to use resources.

In 2005, the survey was repeated. As in 1999, virtually all adults (97 percent) and high school students (93 percent) believe it is important for Americans to have a good understanding of economics. Almost all adults (97 percent) believe that economics should be included in high school education. It also showed some good news—students' understanding of economic knowledge increased from a mean score of 51 in 1999 to 62, and the number of students scoring an "A" or "B" nearly doubled.

SOURCE: "What American Teens and Adults Know About Economics," National Council of Economic Education, 1999 and 2005.

---

be able to set a price for them. But even these matters have an economic dimension. Consider spirituality, for example. Concern for spiritual matters has led to the development of institutions such as churches, synagogues, and temples that conduct religious and spiritual services. In economic terms, these services are goods that many people desire. Love and sex likewise have received economists' scrutiny. One product of love, the institution of the family, is an important economic decision-making unit.

Even time has an economic dimension. In fact, in modern culture, time has become perhaps the single most precious resource we have. Everyone has the same limited amount of time per day, and how we divide our time between work and leisure (including study, sleep, exercise, and so on) is a distinctly economic matter. If we choose more work, we must sacrifice leisure. If we choose to study, we must sacrifice time with friends or time spent sleeping or watching TV. Virtually everything we decide to do, then, has an economic dimension.

Living in a world of scarcity involves trade-offs. As you are reading this text, you are giving up other things you value: shopping, spending time on Facebook or My Space, going to the movies, sleeping, or working out. When we know what the trade-offs are, we can make better choices from the options all around us, every day. George Bernard Shaw stated, "Economy is the art of making the most of life."

Why Study Economics?

Among the many good reasons to study economics, perhaps the best reason is that so many of the things of concern in the world around us are at least partly economic in character. A quick look at newspaper headlines reveals the vast range of problems that are related to economics—global warming, health care, education, and Social Security. The study of economics improves your understanding of these concerns. A student of economics becomes aware that, at a basic level, much of economic life involves choosing among alternative possible courses of action—making choices between our conflicting wants and desires in a world of scarcity. Economics provides some clues as to how to intelligently evaluate these options and determine

in the news How Much Is Your Major Worth?

Another reason you might want to study economics is that starting salaries are high compared to many other majors. According to a recent poll (2008), economics majors can expect an average starting salary of $50,100. Compare this with other majors in terms of starting salaries and mid-career median salaries.

Undergraduate Major	Starting Median Salary	Mid-Career Median Salary
Accounting	$46,000.00	$77,100.00
Agriculture	$42,600.00	$71,900.00
Anthropology	$36,800.00	$61,500.00
Architecture	$41,600.00	$76,800.00
Art History	$35,800.00	$64,900.00
Biology	$38,800.00	$64,800.00
Business Management	$43,000.00	$72,100.00
Chemical Engineering	$63,200.00	$107,000.00
Chemistry	$42,600.00	$79,900.00
Civil Engineering	$53,900.00	$90,500.00
Communications	$38,100.00	$70,000.00
Computer Engineering	$61,400.00	$105,000.00
Computer Science	$55,900.00	$95,500.00
Criminal Justice	$35,000.00	$56,300.00
Drama	$35,900.00	$56,900.00
Economics	**$50,100.00**	**$98,600.00**
Education	$34,900.00	$52,000.00
Electrical Engineering	$60,900.00	$103,000.00
English	$38,000.00	$64,700.00
Film	$37,900.00	$68,500.00
Finance	$47,900.00	$88,300.00
Geography	$41,200.00	$65,500.00
Geology	$43,500.00	$79,500.00
History	$39,200.00	$71,000.00
Information Technology (IT)	$49,100.00	$74,800.00
International Relations	$40,900.00	$80,900.00
Journalism	$35,600.00	$66,700.00
Management Information Systems (MIS)	$49,200.00	$82,300.00
Marketing	$40,800.00	$79,600.00
Math	$45,400.00	$92,400.00
Mechanical Engineering	$57,900.00	$93,600.00
Music	$35,900.00	$55,000.00
Nursing	$54,200.00	$67,000.00
Nutrition	$39,900.00	$55,300.00
Philosophy	$39,900.00	$81,200.00
Physics	$50,300.00	$97,300.00
Political Science	$40,800.00	$78,200.00
Psychology	$35,900.00	$60,400.00
Religion	$34,100.00	$52,000.00
Sociology	$36,500.00	$58,200.00
Spanish	$34,000.00	$53,100.00

SOURCE: Pay Scale Inc.

the most appropriate choices in given situations. But economists learn quickly that there are seldom easy, clear-cut solutions to the problems we face—the easy problems were solved long ago!

Many students take introductory college-level economics courses because they are required to as part of a general education curriculum or breadth requirements. But why do the committees that establish these requirements include economics? In part, economics helps develop a disciplined method of thinking about problems. The problem-solving tools you will develop by studying economics will prove valuable to you both in your personal and professional life, regardless of your career choice. In short, the study of economics provides a systematic, disciplined way of thinking.

Will You Ever Really Use This Stuff?

The basic tools of economics are valuable to people in all walks of life and in all career paths. Newspaper reporters benefit from economics, because the problem-solving perspective it teaches trains them to ask intelligent questions whose answers will better inform their readers. Engineers, architects, and contractors usually have alternative ways to build. Architects learn to combine technical expertise and artistry with the limitations imposed by finite resources. That is, they learn how to evaluate their options from an economic perspective. Clothing designers face similar problems, because costs are a constraint in both creating and marketing new apparel. Will the added cost of a more expensive fabric be outweighed by the added sales revenues that are expected to result? Economists cannot answer such questions in a general sense because the answers depend on the circumstances. Economists can, however, pose these questions and provide criteria that clothing designers can use in evaluating the appropriateness of one fabric as compared to another. The point is that the economic way of thinking causes those in many types of fields to ask the right kind of questions. As John Maynard Keynes once remarked:

> The object of our analysis is not to provide a machine or method of blind manipulation, which will furnish an infallible answer, but to provide ourselves with an organized and orderly method of thinking out particular problems; and, after we have reached a provisional conclusion by isolating the complicating factors one by one, we then have to go back on ourselves and allow, as well as we can, for the probable interactions of the factors amongst themselves. This is the nature of economic thinking.[1]

Will an Understanding of Economics Make You a Financial Wizard?

Some people think that economics may be a useful course of study, hoping that it will tell them how to become successful in a financial sense. If becoming wealthy is your goal in studying economics, you may be disappointed. Although most economists make a good living, few have become rich from their knowledge of economics. In fact, if economists had some secret for making money in, for example, the stock market, they would likely be using those secrets to their own financial advantage rather than making less money doing things such as teaching. Moreover, if economists did have some secret for making money, they would not be likely to let non-economists in on it, because economic theory suggests (as will be clear later) that disclosure of the secret would reduce or eliminate the possibility of the economists' earning further income from this knowledge. Still, having some knowledge of the workings of market forces is likely to help individuals make more informed and appropriate decisions, including financial decisions. In short, economics won't necessarily make you richer, but it may keep you from making some decisions that would make you poorer.

SECTION CHECK

1. Economics is a problem-solving science.
2. Economics is the study of the choices we make among our many wants and desires given our limited resources.
3. Resources are inputs used to produce goods and services.
4. Our unlimited wants exceed our limited resources, so we must make choices.
5. Economics is concerned with reaching generalizations about human behavior.
6. Economics provides tools to intelligently evaluate and make choices.

---

1. What is the definition of economics?
2. Why does scarcity force us to make choices?
3. Why are choices costly?
4. Why do even "non-economic" issues have an economic dimension?
5. Why is economics worth studying?

---

[1] See J. M. Keynes, *General Theory of Employment Interest and Money* (New York: Harcourt Brace, 1936), p. 297.

SECTION 1.2 Economic Behavior

* What is self-interest?
* Why is self-interest not the same as selfishness?
* What is rational behavior?

Self-Interest

Economists assume that individuals act *as if* they are motivated by self-interest and respond in predictable ways to changing circumstances. In other words, self-interest is a good predictor of human behavior in most situations. For example, to a worker, self-interest means pursuing a higher-paying job and/or better working conditions. To a consumer, it means gaining a higher level of satisfaction from limited income and time.

We seldom observe employees asking employers to cut their wages and increase their workload to increase a company's profits. Or how often do you think customers walk into a supermarket demanding to pay more for their groceries? In short, a great deal of human behavior can be explained and predicted by assuming people act *as if* they are motivated by their own self-interest.

There is no question that self-interest is a powerful force that motivates people to produce goods and services. But self-interest can include benevolence. Think of the late Mother Teresa, who spent her life caring for others. One could say that her work was in her self-interest, but who would consider her actions selfish? Similarly, workers may be pursuing self-interest when they choose to work harder and longer to increase their charitable giving or saving for their children's education. That is, self-interest to an economist is not a narrow monetary self-interest. The enormous amount of money and time donated to victims of Hurricane Katrina is an example of self-interest too—the self-interest was to help others in need. So don't confuse self-interest with selfishness.

In the United States, people typically give more than $250 billion annually to charities. They also pay more money for environmentally friendly goods. Consumers can derive utility or satisfaction from these choices. It is clearly not selfish—it is in their best interest to care about the environment and those who are less fortunate than themselves.

rational behavior
people do the best they can, based on their values and information, under current and anticipated future circumstances

There was an enormous amount of money and time donated to the victims of Hurricane Katrina. Economists believe that individuals act to promote those items which interest them. Is this self-interested act selfish? Acting in one's own self-interest is only selfish if one's interests are selfish.

What Is Rational Behavior?

Economists assume that people, for the most part, engage in rational behavior. And you might think that could not possibly apply to your brother, sister, or roommates. But the key is in the definition. To an economist, **rational behavior** merely means that people do the best they can, based on their values and information, under current and anticipated future circumstances. It is even rational when people make choices they later regret, because they have limited information. Rational behavior applies to the actions people take to pursue their own goals—whatever those goals may be—and they need not be materialistic or widely shared. Therefore, rational behavior applies to criminals and people who dedicate their lives to caring for others. In

Use what you've LEARNED: THE BENEVOLENCE OF SELF-INTEREST

Q How can economists expect to be taken seriously, non-economists are given to complain, when their model of man is so patently inadequate? Mainstream economics assumes that people are driven by the rational pursuit of self-interest. But, as everybody knows, people are not rational and they often act selflessly. Where in this view of man as desiccated calculating-machine is there recognition of the centrality of love, duty, and self-sacrifice in human conduct? What use is a purported science of social behavior that is blind to the necessary conditions for social behavior?

A These questions would be telling if "rational" and "self-interest" meant what these critics take them to mean. But they do not. In mainstream economics, to say that people are rational is not to assume that they never make mistakes, as critics usually suppose. It is merely to say that they do *not* make systematic mistakes; that is, they do not keep making the same mistake over and over again. And when economists talk of self-interest, they are referring not just to satisfaction of material wants, but to a broader idea of "preferences" that can easily encompass, among other things, the welfare of others.

Even when the terms are properly understood, "rational pursuit of self-interest" is a simplifying assumption. But the right question is whether this simplification is fruitful, or so gross that it hides what needs to be examined. Human behavior is far too complicated to be analyzed—to yield patterns and suggest generalizations—without employing some such simplification. And in nearly every branch of economics, rationality has proved a useful one. . . .

Turning from means to ends, what about self-interest? Here the issues are subtler. If economics supposed, at one extreme, that people seek only to maximize their material consumption, then it would be plain wrong, and that would be that. If, at the other extreme, it assumed that people seek to satisfy their preferences (or some such formula), then it would be true merely by virtue of the meaning of the words—and it would not tell you anything. The assumption built into mainstream economics is much closer to the second of these than the first. . . .

However, the assumption of self-interest is not entirely tautological. Many kinds of apparently selfless behavior may in fact be self-interested in the way economics proposes. . . .

People show consideration for others in the hope or expectation that the favor will be returned. Behavior that establishes a reputation for honesty, or that signals a willingness to enter into commitments, is also, as a rule, self-interested in this sense. That makes it no less conducive to a flourishing society, no less to be praised and encouraged . . . it is self-interest, not love, that holds society together. . . .

When Adam Smith, one of the greatest economic thinkers and author of *The Wealth of Nations* published in 1776, pointed out that if people want dinner, they look not to the benevolence of the butcher, brewer, or baker, but to their regard for their own interest, his aim was not to portray social interaction as mean and narrow. Rather it was to draw attention to the extraordinary and improbable power of self-interest: this stunted, inward-looking trait is transformed, through spontaneous social cooperation, into a force for the common good.

Smith regarded this as almost miraculous. So it is. The main task of economics has been to understand this astonishing process. And by and large, thanks to its simplifying assumptions, it has succeeded. That's not so dismal, is it?

SOURCE: From "The Benevolence of Self-Interest", 'The Economist' (online edition), March 30, 2000. © The Economist Newspaper Limited, London 2000. Reprinted with permission.

GREAT ECONOMIC THINKERS
ADAM SMITH (1723–1790)

Adam Smith was born in a small fishing village just outside of Edinburgh, Scotland, in 1723. At age 4, gypsies (called *tinkers* in Scotland) kidnapped Smith, but he was rescued through the efforts of his uncle. He began studying at Glasgow College when he was just 14 and later continued his studies at Oxford University. He returned to Glasgow at age 28 as a professor of philosophy and logic. (Until the nineteenth century, economics was considered a branch of philosophy, thus Smith never took nor taught a class in economics.) He later resigned that position to become the private tutor to the stepson of Charles Townshend.

Although known for his intelligence, warm hospitality, and charitable spirit, Smith was not without his eccentricities. Notorious for his absent-mindedness, there is a story about Smith taking a trip to a tanning factory and, while engaged in conversation with a friend, walking straight into a large tanning vat. Another tale features Smith walking 15 miles in his sleep, awakening from his sleepwalk to the ringing of church bells, and scurrying back home in his nightgown. Most astonishing and unfortunate, Smith, without explanation, had the majority of his unpublished writings destroyed before his death in 1790.

Adam Smith is considered the founder of economics. He addressed problems of both economic theory and policy in his famous book, *An Inquiry into the Nature and Causes of the Wealth of Nations*, published in 1776. The book was a success from the beginning, with its first edition selling out in just six months, and people have continued to read it for well over two centuries.

Smith believed that the wealth of a nation did not come from the accumulation of gold and silver—the prevailing thought of the day. Smith observed that people tend to pursue their own personal interests and that an "invisible hand" (the market) guides their self-interest, increasing social welfare and general economic well-being. Smith's most powerful and enduring contribution was this idea of an invisible hand of market incentives channeling individuals' efforts and promoting social welfare.

Smith also showed that through division of labor and specialization of tasks, producers could increase their output markedly. While Smith did not invent the market, he demonstrated that free markets, unfettered by monopoly and government regulation, and free trade were at the very foundation of the wealth of a nation. Many of Smith's insights are still central to economics today.

Smith is buried in a small cemetery in Edinburgh, Scotland. The money left on the grave site is usually gone by morning; the homeless prey on the donations to use for food and spirits. Adam Smith is probably smiling somewhere. He had a reputation as a charitable man—"a scale much beyond what might have been expected from his fortunes."

COURTESY OF ROBERT L. SEXTON

addition, rational behavior does not mean that people do not make mistakes, but it does mean that people learn from past mistakes and that their decisions in the future reflect that information. That is, they do not keep making the same mistake.

In short, rational individuals weigh the benefits and costs of their actions and they only pursue actions if they perceive the benefits to be greater than the costs. We will discuss this concept more thoroughly in the next chapter.

SECTION CHECK

1. Economists assume that people act as if they are motivated by self-interest and respond predictably to changing circumstances.
2. Do not confuse self-interest with selfishness.
3. Rational behavior means that people do the best they can based on their values and information, under current and future anticipated consequences.

---

1. What do economists mean by self-interest?
2. What does rational self-interest involve?
3. How are self-interest and selfishness different?
4. What is rational behavior?

SECTION 1.3 Economic Theory

- What are economic theories?
- What can we expect from theories?
- Why do we need to abstract?
- What is a hypothesis?
- What is empirical analysis?
- What is the *ceteris paribus* assumption?
- What are microeconomics and macroeconomics?

Economic Theories

A **theory** is an established explanation that accounts for known facts or phenomena. Specifically, economic theories are statements or propositions about patterns of human behavior that occur expectedly under certain circumstances. These theories help us sort out and understand the complexities of economic behavior and guide our analysis. We expect a good theory to explain and predict well. A good economic theory, then, should help us better understand and, ideally, predict human economic behavior.

theory
statement or proposition used to explain and predict behavior in the real world

Abstraction Is Important

Economic theories cannot realistically include every event that has ever occurred. A theory weeds out the irrelevant facts from the relevant ones. We must abstract. A road map of the United States may not include every creek, ridge, and gully between Los Angeles and Chicago; indeed, such an all-inclusive map would be too large and too detailed to be of value. A road map designating major interstate highways will provide enough information to travel by car from Los Angeles to Chicago. Likewise, an economic

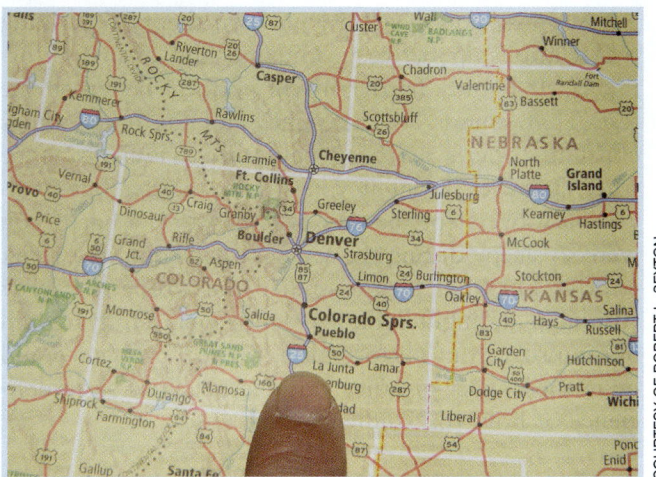

How is economic theory like a map? Because of the complexity of human behavior, economists must abstract to focus on the most important components of a particular problem. It is similar to the way that maps highlight the important information (and assume away many minor details) to help people get from here to there.

theory provides a broad view, not a detailed examination, of human economic behavior.

Without abstraction or simplification, the world is too complex to analyze. For the same reason, economists make a number of simplifying *assumptions* in their models. Sometimes economists make very strong assumptions, such as that all people seek self-betterment or all firms attempt to maximize profits. Of course, this may not hold for every single person or firm. Only when we test our models using these assumptions do we find out if they were too simplified or too limiting.

Developing a Testable Proposition

The beginning of any theory is a **hypothesis**, a testable proposition that makes some type of prediction about behavior in response to certain changes in conditions based on our assumptions. In economic theory, a hypothesis is a testable prediction about how people will behave or react to a change in economic circumstances. For example, if we notice an increase in the price of digital video discs (DVDs), we might hypothesize that sales of DVDs will drop, or if the price of DVDs decreases, our hypothesis might be that

DVDs sales will rise. Once we state our hypothesis, we test it by comparing what it predicts will happen to what actually happens.

Using Empirical Analysis

To determine whether our hypothesis is valid, we must engage in **empirical analysis.** That is, we must examine the data to see whether our hypothesis fits well with the facts. If the hypothesis is consistent with real-world observations, we can accept it; if it does not fit well with the facts, we must "go back to the drawing board."

Determining whether a hypothesis is acceptable is more difficult in economics than it is in the natural or physical sciences. Chemists, for example, can observe chemical reactions under laboratory conditions. They can alter the environment to meet the assumptions of the hypothesis and can readily manipulate the variables (chemicals, temperatures, and so on) crucial to the proposed relationship. Such controlled experimentation is seldom possible in economics. The laboratory of economists is usually the real world. Unlike chemists in their labs, economists cannot easily control all the variables that might influence human behavior.

From Hypothesis to Theory

After gathering their data, economic researchers must evaluate the results to determine whether their hypothesis is supported or refuted. If supported, the hypothesis can be tentatively accepted as an economic theory.

hypothesis
a testable proposition

empirical analysis
the use of data to test a hypothesis

Every economic theory is on lifelong probation; the hypothesis underlying an economic theory is constantly being tested against empirical findings. Do the observed findings support the prediction? When a hypothesis survives a number of tests, it is accepted until it no longer predicts well.

Science and Stories

Much of scientific discovery is expressed in terms of stories, not unlike the stories told by writers of novels. This similarity is not accidental. The novelist tries to persuade us that a story could almost be true; the scientist tries to persuade us that certain events fall into a certain meaningful pattern. The scientist does not (or is not supposed to) invent the underlying "facts" of the story, whereas the novelist is not so constrained. However, a scientist does select *certain* facts from among many facts that could have been chosen, just as the novelist chooses from an infinite number of possible characters and situations to make the story most persuasive. In both cases, the author "invents" the story. Therefore, we should not be surprised to find order in economic theory any more than we are surprised to find order in a good novel. Scientists would not bother to write about "life" if they were not convinced that they had stories worth telling.

What makes a story "worth telling?" When we look for order in nature, we cannot suppose that the "facts" are a sufficient basis for understanding observed events. The basic problem is that the facts of a complex world simply do not organize themselves. Understanding requires that a *conceptual order* be imposed on these "facts" to counteract the confusion that would otherwise result. For example, objects of different weights falling freely in the air do **not** travel at *precisely* the same rate (largely because of the different effects of air resistance). Yet this piece of information is generally much less significant than the fact that falling bodies do travel at *almost* the same rate (which presumably would be identical in a vacuum). By focusing on the most significant fact—the similarity, not the difference—Galileo was able to impose order on the story of gravity.

In the same way, to interpret the impact of rising housing prices on the amount of housing desired, economists must separate out the impact of increasing wealth, population, and other contributing factors. Failing to do so would obscure the central insight that people tend to buy less housing at higher prices. Without a story—a theory of causation—scientists could not sort out and understand the complex reality that surrounds us.

The *Ceteris Paribus* Assumption

Virtually all economic theories share a condition usually expressed by the Latin phrase **ceteris paribus**. A rough translation of the phrase is "letting everything else be equal" or "holding everything else constant." When economists try to assess the effect of one variable on another, they must keep the relationship between the two variables isolated from other events that might also influence the situation that the theory tries to explain or predict. A couple of examples will make this concept clearer.

Suppose you develop your own theory describing the relationship between studying and exam performance: If I study harder, I will perform better on the test. That sounds logical, right? Holding other things constant (*ceteris paribus*), your theory is likely to be true. However, what if you studied harder but inadvertently overslept the day of the exam? What if you were so sleepy during the test that you could not think clearly? Or what if you studied the wrong material? Although it might look like additional studying did not improve your performance, the real problem could lie in the impact of other variables, such as sleep deficiency or how you studied.

Why Are Observation and Prediction Harder in the Social Sciences?

ceteris paribus
holding all other things constant

Working from observations, scientists try to make generalizations that will enable them to predict certain events. However, observation and prediction are more difficult in the social sciences than in physical sciences such as physics, chemistry, and astronomy. Why? The major reason for the difference is that the social scientists, including economists, are concerned with *human* behavior. And human behavior is more variable and often less readily predictable than the behavior of experiments observed in a laboratory. However, by looking at the actions of a large group of people, economists can still make many reliable predictions about human behavior.

Why Do Economists Predict on a Group Level?

Economists' predictions usually refer to the collective behavior of large groups rather than to that of specific individuals. Why is this? Looking at the behaviors of a large group allows economists to discern general patterns of actions. For example, consider what would happen if the price of air travel from the United States to Europe was reduced drastically, say from $1,000 to $400, because of the invention of a more fuel-efficient jet. What type of predictions could we make about the effect of this price reduction on the buying habits of typical consumers?

What Does Individual Behavior Tell Us?

Let's look first at the responses of individuals. As a result of the price drop, some people will greatly increase their intercontinental travel, taking theater weekends in London or week-long trips to France to indulge in French food. Some people, however, are terribly afraid to fly, and the price reduction will not influence their behavior in the slightest. Others might detest Europe and, despite the lowered airfares, prefer to spend a few days in Aspen, Colorado, instead. A few people might respond to the airfare reduction in precisely the opposite way from ours: At the lower fare, they might make fewer trips to Europe, because they might believe (rightly or wrongly) that the price drop would be accompanied by a reduction in the quality of service, greater crowding, or reduced safety. In short, we cannot predict with any level of certainty how a given individual will respond to this airfare reduction.

What Does Group Behavior Tell Us?

Group behavior is often more predictable than individual behavior. When the weather gets colder, more firewood will be sold. Some individuals may not buy firewood, but we can predict with great accuracy that a group of individuals will establish a pattern of buying more firewood. Similarly, while we cannot say what each individual will do, within a group of persons, we can predict with great accuracy that more flights to Europe from Los Angeles will be sold at lower prices than at higher prices, holding other things such as income and preferences constant. We cannot predict exactly how many more airline tickets will be sold at $400 than at $1,000, but we can predict the direction of the impact and approximate the extent of the impact. By observing the relationship between the price of goods and services and the quantities people purchase in different places and during different time periods, it is possible to make some reliable generalizations about how much people will react to changes in the prices of goods and services. Economists use this larger picture of the group for most of their theoretical analysis.

The Two Branches of Economics: Microeconomics and Macroeconomics

Conventionally, we distinguish two main branches of economics, microeconomics and macroeconomics. **Microeconomics,** deals with the smaller units within the economy, attempting to understand the decision-making behavior of firms and households and their interaction in markets for particular goods or services. Microeconomic topics include discussions of health care, agricultural subsidies, the price of everyday items such as running shoes, the distribution of income, and the impact of labor unions on wages. **Macroeconomics,** in contrast, deals with the aggregate, or total economy; it looks at economic problems as they influence the whole of society. Topics covered in macroeconomics include discussions of inflation, unemployment, business cycles, and economic growth. To put it simply, microeconomics looks at the trees while macroeconomics looks at the forest.

microeconomics
the study of household and firm behavior and how they interact in the marketplace

macroeconomics
the study of the whole economy, including the topics of inflation, unemployment, and economic growth

aggregate
the total amount—such as the *aggregate level of output*

SECTION CHECK

1. Economic theories are statements used to explain and predict patterns of human behavior.
2. We must abstract and focus on the most important components of a particular problem.
3. A hypothesis makes a prediction about human behavior and is then tested.
4. We use empirical analysis to examine the data and see whether our hypothesis fits well with the facts.
5. In order to isolate the effects of one variable on another, we use the *ceteris paribus* assumption.
6. It is rational for people to act in their own self-interest and try to improve their situation.
7. Microeconomics focuses on smaller units within the economy—firms and households—and how they interact in the marketplace.
8. Macroeconomics deals with the aggregate, or total, economy.

continued

1. What are economic theories?
2. What is the purpose of a theory?
3. Why must economic theories be abstract?
4. What is a hypothesis? How do we determine whether it is tentatively accepted?
5. Why do economists hold other things constant (*ceteris paribus*)?
6. Why are observation and prediction more difficult in the social sciences?
7. Why do economic predictions refer to the behavior of groups of people rather than individuals?
8. Why is the market for running shoes considered a microeconomic topic?
9. Why is inflation considered a macroeconomic topic?

SECTION 1.4 Pitfalls to Avoid in Scientific Thinking

* If two events usually occur together, does it mean one event caused the other to happen?
* What is the fallacy of composition?

In our discussion of economic theory we have not yet mentioned that there are certain pitfalls to avoid that may hinder scientific and logical thinking: confusing correlation and causation, and the fallacy of composition.

Confusing Correlation and Causation

Without a theory of causation, no scientist could sort out and understand the enormous complexity of the real world. But one must always be careful not to confuse correlation with causation. In other words, the fact that two events usually occur together (**correlation**) does not necessarily mean that one caused the other to occur (**causation**). For example, say a groundhog awakes after a long winter of hibernation, climbs out of his hole, and sees his shadow—then six weeks of bad weather ensue. Did the groundhog cause the bad weather? In Europe, the stork population has fallen and so have birth rates. Does this mean that the one event caused the other to occur? It is highly unlikely.

Perhaps the causality runs in the opposite direction. A rooster may always crow before the sun rises, but it does not cause the sunrise; rather, the early light from the sunrise causes the rooster to crow.

correlation
when two events occur together

causation
when one event brings about another event

fallacy of composition
the incorrect view that what is true for the individual is always true for the group

Why Is The Correlation Between Ice Cream Sales and Property Crime Positive?

Did you know that when ice cream sales rise, so do property crime rates? What do you think causes the two events to occur together? The explanation is that property crime peaks in the summer because of warmer weather, more people on vacations (leaving their homes vacant), teenagers out of school, and so on. It just happens that ice cream sales also peak in those months because of the weather. It is the case of a third variable causing both to occur. Or what if there were a positive correlation between sales of cigarette lighters and the incidence of cancer? The suspect might well turn out to be the omitted variable (the so-called "smoking gun"): the cigarette.

The Fallacy of Composition

Economic thinking requires us to be aware of the problems associated with aggregation (adding up all the parts). One of the biggest problems is the **fallacy of composition**. This fallacy states that even if something is true for an individual, it is not necessarily true for many individuals as a group. For example, say you

in the news: Sex on Television and Teenage Pregnancy

When it comes to television programming, sex sells—maybe too well. According to a Rand Corporation study authored by Anita Chandra, there is a link between teenagers' exposure to sexual content on TV and teen pregnancies. Specifically, the study found that teens exposed to high levels of sexual content on television were twice as likely to be involved in a pregnancy in the following three years as teens with limited exposure. The results were published in the November, 2008, edition of the journal *Pediatrics*.

The study's author is quick to point out that the factors leading to teen pregnancies are varied and complex—but warns it is important for parents, teachers, and pediatricians to understand that TV can be one of them.

consider this:

While sex on television may lead to increases in teen pregnancy, isn't it possible the causality runs in the opposite direction—teenagers that are more susceptible to teen pregnancy watch shows with more sexual content? In addition, there are a host of other variables that could be much more statistically significant such as low self-esteem, single-parent households, household income, years of schooling, heavy drug and alcohol use, GPA, child abuse, peer pressure, and so on.

In fact, more women of all ages, not just teenagers, are having children out of wedlock. Actually, the teen birth rate was much higher in 1957 than it is today. The growing concern is over the rise in unwed teenage mothers. However, births to single teens actually account for a smaller percentage of all non-marital births than 20 years ago—so is television to blame? Heed the–author's warning: "the reasons for the rise in teen pregnancies are varied and complex."

---

are at a football game and you decide to stand up to get a better view of the playing field. This works as long as the people seated around you don't stand up. But what happens if everyone stands up at the same time? Then your standing up does nothing to improve your view. Thus, what is true for an individual does not always hold true in the aggregate. The same can be said of getting to school early to get a better parking place—what if everyone arrived early? Or studying harder to get a better grade in a class that is graded on a curve—what if everyone studied harder? These are all examples of the fallacy of composition.

Normally, people expect more accidents at higher speeds. This expectation seems reasonable; yet, as shown in the picture, slower driving can be correlated with more accidents. Why the positive correlation? It is a third variable—icy roads—that leads to both lower speeds and increased accidents.

> ### SECTION CHECK
>
> 1. The fact that two events are related does not mean that one caused the other to occur.
> 2. What is true for the individual is not necessarily true for the group.
>
> ---
>
> 1. What is the relationship between correlation and causation?
> 2. What types of misinterpretation result from confusing correlation and causation?
> 3. What is the fallacy of composition?
> 4. If you can sometimes get a high grade on an exam without studying, does it mean that additional studying does not lead to higher grades? Explain your answer.

SECTION 1.5 Positive Statements and Normative Statements

* What is a positive statement?
* What is a normative statement?
* Why do economists disagree?

Positive Statement

Most economists view themselves as scientists seeking the truth about the way people behave. They make speculations about economic behavior, and then, ideally, they assess the validity of those predictions based on human experience. Their work emphasizes how people *do* behave, rather than how people *should* behave. In the role of scientist, an economist tries to observe patterns of behavior objectively, without reference to the appropriateness or inappropriateness of that behavior. This objective, value-free approach, based on the scientific method, is called positive analysis. In positive analysis, we want to know the impact of variable *A* on variable *B*. We want to be able to test a hypothesis. For example, the following is a **positive statement**: If rent controls are imposed, vacancy rates will fall. This statement is testable. A positive statement does not have to be a true statement, but it does have to be a testable statement.

Keep in mind, however, that it is doubtful that even the most objective scientist can be totally value free in

positive statement
an objective, testable statement that describes what happens and why it happens

his or her analysis. An economist may well emphasize data or evidence that supports a hypothesis, putting less weight on other evidence that might be contradictory. This tendency, alas, is human nature. But a good economist/scientist strives to be as fair and objective as possible in evaluating evidence and in stating conclusions based on the evidence. In some sense, economists are like engineers; they try to figure out how things work and then describe what would happen if you changed something.

Normative Statement

Economists, like anyone else, have opinions and make value judgments. And when economists, or anyone else for that matter, express opinions about an economic policy or statement, they are indicating in part how they believe things should be, not stating facts about the way things are. In other words, they are performing normative analysis. **Normative statements** involve judgments about what should be or what ought to happen. For example, normative questions might include: Should the government raise the minimum wage? Should the government increase spending in the space program? Should the government give "free" prescription drugs to senior citizens?

> **normative statements**
> a subjective, contestable statement that attempts to describe what should be done

Positive Versus Normative Analysis

The distinction between positive and normative analysis is important. It is one thing to say that everyone should have universal health care, an untestable normative statement, and quite another to say that universal health care would lead to greater worker productivity, a testable positive statement. It is important to distinguish between positive and normative analysis because many controversies in economics revolve around policy considerations that contain both. For example, what impact would a 3 percent reduction in income taxes across the board have on the economy? This question requires positive analysis. Whether we should have a 3 percent reduction in income taxes requires normative analysis as well. When economists are trying to explain the way the world works, they are scientists. When economists start talking about how the economy should work rather than how it does work, they have entered the normative world of the policymaker. In short, positive statements are attempts to *describe* what happens and why it happens, while normative statements are attempts to *prescribe* what should be done.

Disagreement Is Common in Most Disciplines

Although economists do frequently have opposing views on economic policy questions, they probably disagree less than the media would have you believe. Disagreement is common in most disciplines: Seismologists differ over predictions of earthquakes or volcanic eruption; historians can be at odds over the interpretation of historical events; psychologists disagree on proper ways to rear children; and nutritionists debate the merits of large doses of vitamin C.

The majority of disagreements in economics stem from normative issues; differences in values or policy beliefs result in conflict. For example, a policy might increase efficiency at the expense of a sense of fairness or equity, or it might help a current generation at the expense of a future generation. Because policy decisions involve trade-offs, they will always involve the potential for conflict.

Freedom Versus Fairness

Some economists are concerned about individual freedom and liberty, thinking that any encroachment on individual decision making is bad, other things being equal. People with this philosophic bent are inclined to be skeptical of any increased government involvement in the economy.

On the other hand, some economists are concerned with what they consider an unequal, "unfair," or unfortunate distribution of income, wealth, or power, and view governmental intervention as desirable in righting injustices that they believe exist in a market economy. To these persons, the threat to individual liberty alone is not sufficiently great to reject governmental intervention in the face of perceived economic injustice.

The Validity of an Economic Theory

Aside from philosophic differences, a second reason helps explain why economists may differ on any given policy question. Specifically, they may disagree about the validity of a given economic theory for the policy in question—that is, they disagree over the positive analysis. Why would they disagree over positive analysis? For at least two reasons. One, a particular model may yield mixed results: some empirical evidence supporting it and some not. Two, the information available may be insufficient to make a compelling theory.

in the news

A Brighter Day for the Dismal Science— Economics Becomes the Hot Major for Undergrads World-Wide

—BY JESSICA E. VASCELLARO

What's your major? Around the world, college undergraduates' time-honored question is increasingly drawing the same answer: Economics.

U.S. colleges and universities awarded 16,141 degrees to economics majors in the 2003–2004 academic year, up nearly 40 percent from five years earlier. This is according to John. J. Siegfried, an economics professor at Vanderbilt University in Nashville, Tennessee, who tracks 272 colleges and universities around the country for the *Journal of Economic Education*.

Since the mid-1990s, the number of students majoring in economics has been rising, while the number majoring in political science and government has declined and the number majoring in history and sociology has barely grown, according to the U.S. government's National Center for Education Statistics.

"There has been a clear explosion of economics as as major," says Mark Gertler, a professor and chairman of New York University's economics department.

The number of students majoring in economics has been rising even faster at the United States' top colleges. At New York University, for example, the number of economics majors has more than doubled to nearly 800 in the past 10 years. It is now the most popular major.

Economics also is the most popular major at Harvard University, Cambridge, Massachusetts, where 964 students majored in the subject this year. The number of economics majors at Columbia University, New York, has risen 67 percent since 1995. The University of Chicago said that last year 24 percent of its graduating class, or 240 students, departed with economics degrees.

The trend marks a big switch for the so-called dismal science, which experienced large declines in undergraduate enrollments in the early 1990s, as interest in other areas, like sociology, was growing. Behind the turnaround is a clear-eyed reading of supply and demand: In a global economy filled with uncertainty, many students see economics as the best vehicle for landing a job promising good pay and security.

And as its focus broadens, there are even some signs that economics is becoming cool.

In addition to probing the mechanics of inflation and exchange rates, academics now use statistics and an economist's view of how people respond to incentives to study issues such as AIDS research, obesity, and even terrorism. The surprise best seller of the spring, for instance, was *Freakonomics*, co-authored by University of Chicago economist Steven Levitt, that examines issues ranging from corruption among real-estate agents to sumo wrestling.

Pooja Jotwani, a recent graduate of Georgetown University, Washington, says she is certain her economics degree helped her land a job in Lehman Brothers Holdings Inc.'s sales and trading division, where she will earn the industry's standard starting salary of $55,000, or about 45,000 euros, not including bonus. She says the major strengthened her business skills and provided her with something very simple: "financial security."

"People are fascinated with applying the economic mode of reasoning to a wide variety of issues, and these forces are causing them to study economics more and more," says Lawrence Summers, [former] president of Harvard, former U.S. Treasury Secretary, [and head of the Council of Economic Advisors].

Economics and business majors ranked among the five most desirable majors in a 2004 survey of employers by the National Association of Colleges and Employers, along with accounting, electrical engineering, and mechanical engineering. It wasn't just banks and insurance companies that expressed interest in hiring economics majors: Companies in industries such as utilities and retailing did, too . . . .

Roberto Angulo, chief executive of AfterCollege Inc., a San Francisco online recruiting service with

267,000 registered users, says an economics major has practical value on the job. "Students are more employable if they study economics," he says. He graduated from Stanford University in California with an economics degree five years ago.

It isn't just the job calculus that is drawing students to the major: It also is the rapid spread of economic globalization. Many students around the world are wondering what effect global economic trends will have on them.

Foreign students studying in the United States are flocking to the major. Sabrina De Abreu, a student from Argentina about to start her senior year at Harvard, says her country's experiences made her choice easy. "When I grew up in Argentina, my country plunged into a recession," she says. "Understanding economics has become a fundamental part of my life."

Indeed, the rising popularity of the economics major appears to be a global phenomenon. A recent McKinsey Global Institute study found that the share of degrees in economics and business awarded in Poland from 1996 to 2002 more than doubled, to 36 percent from 16 percent; in Russia, the share jumped to 31 percent from 18 percent....

John Sutton, chairman of the economics department at the London School of Economics, says the school's popularity is at an all-time high, in part the result of interest among students from Eastern Europe, where there is a "huge pent-up demand for well-trained professional economists." Dr. Sutton says that as these countries become increasingly open to capitalism, "bright young students are beginning to see economic issues highlighted."

SOURCE: From Jessica E. Vascellaro, "Career Journal: The Hot Major For Undergrads Is Economics", 'The Wall Street Journal', July 5, 2005, p. A7. Reprinted by permission of The Wall Street Journal, copyright © 2005 Dow Jones & Company, Inc. All Rights Reserved Worldwide.

POLICY application: ECONOMISTS DO AGREE

Most economists agree that these statements are correct:

1. A ceiling on rents (rent control) reduces the quantity and quality of rental housing available (93 percent agree).
2. Tariffs and import quotas usually reduce general economic welfare (93 percent agree).
3. The United States should not restrict employers from outsourcing work to foreign countries (90.1 percent agree).
4. Fiscal policy (e.g., tax cuts and/or increases in government expenditure) has significant stimulative impact on an economy that is less than fully employed (90 percent agree).
5. Flexible and floating exchange rates offer an effective international monetary arrangement (90 percent).
6. The gap between Social Security funds and expenditures will become unsustainably large within the next 50 years if the current policies remain unchanged (85 percent agree).
7. The United States should eliminate agricultural subsidies (85 percent agree).
8. Local and state governments in the United States should eliminate subsidies to professional sport franchises (85 percent agree).
9. A large budget deficit has an adverse effect on the economy (83 percent agree).
10. A minimum wage increases unemployment among young and unskilled (79 percent agree).
11. Effluent taxes and marketable pollution permits represent a better approach to pollution control than imposition of pollution ceilings (78 percent agree).
12. Economist favor expanding competition and market forces in education (67.1 percent agree).

SOURCE: From Jessica E. Vascellaro, "Career Journal: The Hot Major For Undergrads Is Economics", 'The Wall Street Journal', July 5, 2005, p. A7. Reprinted by permission of The Wall Street Journal, copyright © 2005 Dow Jones & Company, Inc. All Rights Reserved Worldwide.

Often Economists Do Agree

Although you may not believe it after reading the previous discussion, economists don't always disagree. In fact, according to a survey among members of the American Economic Association, most economists agree on a wide range of issues, including rent control, import tariffs, export restrictions, the use of wage and price controls to curb inflation, and the minimum wage (see Policy Application: Economists Do Agree, in this section).

SECTION CHECK

1. Positive analysis is objective and value-free.
2. Normative analysis involves value judgments and opinions about the desirability of various actions.
3. Disagreement is common in most disciplines.
4. Most disagreement among economists stems from normative issues.

---

1. What is a positive statement? Must positive statements be testable?
2. What is a normative statement? Is a normative statement testable?
3. Why is the positive/normative distinction important?
4. Why do policy disagreements arise among economists?
5. Is the statement "UFOs land in my backyard at least twice a week" a positive statement? Why or why not?

Interactive Chapter Summary

Fill in the blanks:

1. Economics is the study of the choices we make among our many wants and desires given our _____ resources.
2. _____ occurs because our unlimited wants exceed our limited resources.
3. Resources are _____ used to produce goods and services.
4. The economic problem is that _____ forces us to choose, and choices are costly because we must give up other opportunities that we _____.
5. Living in a world of scarcity means _____.
6. Economics provided the tools to intelligently evaluate _____ and make _____.
7. _____ deals with the aggregate (the forest), or total economy, while _____ deals with the smaller units (the trees) within the economy.
8. Economists assume that individuals act as if they are motivated by _____ and respond in _____ ways to changing circumstances.
9. Economists believe that it is _____ for people to anticipate the likely future consequences of their behavior.
10. Actions have _____.
11. Rational self-interest implies that people do not make _____ mistakes.
12. Economic _____ are statements or propositions used to _____ and _____ patterns of human economic behavior.

13. Because of the complexity of human behavior, economists must _____ to focus on the most important components of a particular problem.

14. A(n) _____ in economic theory is a testable prediction about how people will behave or react to a change in economic circumstances.

15. _____ analysis is the use of data to test a hypothesis.

16. In order to isolate the effects of one variable on another, we use the _____ assumption.

17. When two events usually occur together, it is called _____.

18. When one event brings on another event, it is called _____.

19. The _____ is the incorrect view that what is true for an individual is always true for the group.

20. The objective, value-free approach to economics, based on the scientific method, is called _____ analysis.

21. _____ analysis involves judgments about what should be or what ought to happen.

22. _____ analysis is descriptive; normative analysis is _____.

23. "A tax increase will lead to a lower rate of inflation" is a(n) _____ economic statement.

Answers: 1. limited; unlimited 2. Scarcity 3. inputs 4. scarcity; value 5. trade-offs 6. options; choices 7. Macroeconomics; microeconomics 8. self-interest; predictable 9. rational 10. consequences 11. systematic 12. theories; explain; predict 13. abstract 14. hypothesis 15. Empirical 16. *ceteris paribus* 17. correlation 18. causation 19. fallacy of composition 20. positive 21. Normative 22. Positive; prescriptive 23. positive

Key Terms and Concepts

economics 3
resources 3
scarcity 3
the economic problem 3
rational behavior 7
theory 10

hypothesis 11
empirical analysis 11
ceteris paribus 12
microeconomics 13
macroeconomics 13
aggregate 13

correlation 14
causation 14
fallacy of composition 14
positive statement 16
normative statement 17

Section Check Answers

1.1 Economics: A Brief Introduction

1. **What is the definition of economics?**
   Economics is the study of the choices we make among our many wants and desires given our limited resources.

2. **Why does scarcity force us to make choices?**
   Scarcity—the fact that our wants exceed what our resources can produce—means that we are forced to make choices on how best to use these limited resources.

3. **Why are choices costly?**
   In a world of scarcity, whenever we choose one option, we also choose to do without something else that we also desire. The want that we choose not to satisfy is the opportunity cost of that choice.

4. **Why do even "non-economic" issues have an economic dimension?**
   Even apparently non-economic issues have an economic dimension because economics concerns anything worthwhile to some human being (including love, friendship, charity, etc.) and the choices we make among those things we value.

5. **Why is economics worth studying?**
   Perhaps the best reason to study economics is that so many of the things that concern us are at least partly economic in character. Economics helps us to intelligently evaluate our options and determine the most appropriate choices in many given situations. It helps develop a disciplined method of thinking about problems.

1.2 Economic Behavior

1. **What do economists mean by self-interest?**
   By self-interest, economists simply mean that people try to improve their own situation (as they see it, not necessarily as others see it). Self-interest can also include benevolence.

2. **What does rational self-interest involve?**
   Economists consider individuals to be acting in their rational self-interest if they are striving to do their best

to achieve their goals with their limited income, time, and knowledge, and given their expectations of the likely future consequences (both benefits and costs) of their behavior.

3. **How are self-interest and selfishness different?**
Self-interest means people are striving to do their best to achieve their goals, which may or may not be selfish. Parents working more hours to give more to their children or a favorite charity can be self-interested but are not selfish.

4. **What is rational behavior?**
Rational behavior is when people do the best they can based on their values and information, under current and anticipated future consequences. Rational individuals weigh the benefits and costs of their actions and they only pursue actions if they perceive their benefits to be greater than the costs.

1.3 Economic Theory

1. **What are economic theories?**
A theory is an established explanation that accounts for known facts or phenomena. Economic theories are statements or propositions about patterns of human behavior that are expected to take place under certain circumstances.

2. **What is the purpose of a theory?**
The purpose of a theory is primarily to explain and predict well. Theories are necessary because the facts of a complex world do not organize themselves.

3. **Why must economic theories be abstract?**
Economic theories must be abstract because they could not possibly include every possible event, circumstance, or factor that might affect behavior. Like a road map, an economic theory abstracts from some issues to focus more clearly and precisely on the central questions it is designed to understand.

4. **What is a hypothesis? How do we determine whether it is tentatively accepted?**
A hypothesis is a testable proposal that makes some type of prediction about behavior in response to certain changed conditions. An economic hypothesis is a testable proposal about how people will behave or react to a change in economic circumstances. It is tentatively accepted if its predictions are consistent with what actually happens. In economics, testing involves empirical analysis to see whether the hypothesis is supported by the facts.

5. **Why do economists hold other things constant (*ceteris paribus*)?**
The hold other things constant, or *ceteris paribus*, assumption is used in economics because in trying to assess the effect of one variable on another, we must isolate their relationship from other important events or variables that might also influence the situation the theory tries to explain or predict.

6. **Why are observation and prediction more difficult in the social sciences?**
Observation and prediction are more difficult in the social sciences than in physical sciences because social sciences are concerned with human behavior, which is more variable and often less readily predictable than the behavior of experiments observed in a laboratory. Social scientists can seldom run truly "controlled" experiments like those of the biological scientists.

7. **Why do economic predictions refer to the behavior of groups of people rather than individuals?**
Economists' predictions usually refer to the collective behavior of large groups rather than individuals because looking at the behaviors of a large group of individuals allows economists to discern general patterns of actions and therefore make more reliable generalizations.

8. **Why is the market for running shoes considered a microeconomic topic?**
Because a single industry is "small" relative to the economy as a whole, the market for running shoes (or the running-shoe industry) is a microeconomic topic.

9. **Why is inflation considered a macroeconomic topic?**
Inflation—a change in the overall price level—has effects throughout the entire economy, rather than just in certain small areas of the economy, which makes it a macroeconomic topic.

1.4 Pitfalls to Avoid in Scientific Thinking

1. **What is the relationship between correlation and causation?**
Correlation means that two things are related; causation means that one thing caused the other to occur. Even though causation implies correlation, correlation does not necessarily imply causation.

2. **What types of misinterpretation result from confusing correlation and causation?**
Confusing correlation between variables with causation can lead to misinterpretation where a person "sees" causation between two variables or events where none exists or where a third variable or event is responsible for causing both of them.

3. **What is the fallacy of composition?**
The fallacy of composition is the incorrect idea that if something is true for an individual, it must also be true for many individuals as a group.

4. **If you can sometimes get a high grade on an exam without studying, does it mean that additional studying does not lead to higher grades? Explain your answer.**

   In some instances a student can get a high grade on an exam without studying. However, because additional studying increases mastery of the material, additional studying would typically increase test performance and grades. That is, even though added studying would not raise grades in some unusual situations, as a generalization, additional studying does lead to higher grades.

1.5 Positive Statements and Normative Statements

1. **What is a positive statements? Must positive statements be testable?**

   Positive statements focus on how people actually behave, rather than on how people should behave. They deal with how variable *A* impacts variable *B*. Positive statements must be testable to determine whether their predictions are borne out by the evidence.

2. **What is a normative statement? Is a normative statement testable?**

   Normative statements focus on what should be or what ought to happen; They involve opinions about the desirability of various actions or results. Normative statements are not testable, because it is not scientifically possible to establish whether one value judgment is better than another value judgment.

3. **Why is the positive/normative distinction important?**

   It is important to distinguish between positive and normative statements because many controversies in economics revolve around policy considerations that contain both. Deciding whether a policy is good requires both positive analysis (what will happen) and normative analysis (is what happens good or bad).

4. **Why do policy disagreements arise among economists?**

   As with most disciplines, economists do disagree. However, the majority of those disagreements stem from differences in normative analysis, because the evidence cannot establish whether one set of value judgments is better or more appropriate than other sets of value judgments.

5. **Is the statement "UFOs land in my backyard at least twice a week" a positive statement? Why or why not?**

   A positive statement need not be true; it simply needs to be testable to determine whether it is borne out by the evidence.

CHAPTER 1 STUDY GUIDE

True or False:

1. Scarcity means that our unlimited wants exceed our limited resources.
2. Choices become more costly the more we value the opportunities we must give up to make them.
3. Tradeoffs would not be necessary in the absence of scarcity.
4. In economics, self-interest and selfishness do not mean the same thing.
5. When people make mistakes, that does not imply that their choices were not rational.
6. Adam Smith described how self-interest is always a force for the common good.
7. Most adults have a low level of economic literacy.
8. The assumption of rationality applies to criminal behavior as well as legal behavior.
9. Economic theories abstract from some of the details of situations so they can better focus on those aspects of the behavior to be explained.
10. Determining whether an economic hypothesis is acceptable typically uses the same procedures as in the natural or physical sciences.
11. Microeconomics deals with small numbers, such as interest rates, while macroeconomics deals with large aggregates such as investment.
12. A positive statement must be both testable, but need not be true.
13. A normative statement is testable.
14. Most disagreements among economists are primarily about positive economics.
15. "Larger government deficits will increase interest rates" is a positive statement.

Multiple Choice:

1. When goods are scarce,
   a. they must be rare.
   b. our unlimited wants exceed our limited ability to produce them.
   c. no more of the goods can be produced.
   d. the scarcity could be eliminated by expanding the production of those goods.

2. Which of the following is true of resources?
   a. Their availability is limited.
   b. If goods and services were not scarce, resources would not be scarce.
   c. Increasing the productivity of our resources would not eliminate scarcity.
   d. All of the above are true.

3. If reality did not confront us with scarcity,
   a. investments intended to increase our future production potential would not be rational.
   b. people could have all the goods and services they wanted for free.
   c. making choices would no longer be necessary.
   d. all of the above would be true.

4. Economics is concerned with
   a. the choices people must make because resources are scarce.
   b. the competition that scarcity makes necessary.
   c. the effects of changes in opportunity costs on decisions.
   d. the allocation of limited resources to satisfy unlimited wants.
   e. all of the above.

5. Which of the following would not reflect self-interested behavior to an economist?
    a. A worker quitting a higher-paying job with better working conditions for a lower paying job with worse working conditions.
    b. A student attending class less frequently when attendance represents a larger part of the grade, other things equal.
    c. Mother Teresa using her Nobel Prize money to care for the poor.
    d. None of the above reflects self-interested behavior.
    e. Neither a. nor b. reflects self-interested behavior, but c. is consistent with self-interested behavior.
6. When economists assume that people act rationally, it means they
    a. do the best they can based on their values and information about their current and future circumstances.
    b. make decisions based solely on what is best for society.
    c. always make decisions based on complete and accurate information.
    d. commit no errors in judgment.
    e. make decisions they will not regret later.
7. Analyzing a particular industry is studying _____; analyzing inflation is studying _____.
    a. normative economics; positive economics.
    b. positive economics; normative economics.
    c. microeconomics; macroeconomics.
    d. macroeconomics; microeconomics.
8. Which of the following would be a topic of discussion in microeconomics?
    a. An increase in the overall price level in the economy.
    b. An increase in the production of HD televisions by a consumer electronics company.
    c. A sharp increase in the unemployment rate.
    d. The stability of the economy as a whole.
    e. None of the above are microeconomics issues.
9. Economists use theories to
    a. mimic the complexities of the world as completely as possible.
    b. prescribe how people ought to behave.
    c. explain and help predict human behavior.
    d. do all of the above.
10. The *ceteris paribus*, or other things equal, assumption
    a. enables economists to analyze the relationship between two variables apart from the influence of other variables.
    b. enables economists to separate normative economic issues from positive economic ones.
    c. enables economists to generalize from individual behavior to group behavior.
    d. enables economists to do all of the above.
11. When Event 1 and Event 2 are correlated,
    a. Event 1 caused Event 2.
    b. Event 2 caused Event 1.
    c. A third variable must be causing both Event 1 and Event 2.
    d. The observed correlation may be accidental.
12. Billy notices that people who play basketball are taller than average and if, as a result, he decides to play basketball because it will make him taller, Billy is
    a. violating the *ceteris paribus* assumption.
    b. committing the fallacy of composition.
    c. committing the fallacy of decomposition.
    d. mistaking correlation for causation.
13. Which of the following correlations is likely to involve primarily one variable causing the other, rather than a third variable causing them both?
    a. Higher ice cream sales and higher crime rates both tend to increase at the same time.
    b. A lower price of a particular good and a higher quantity purchased tend to occur at the same time.
    c. The amount of time a team's third string plays in the game tends to be greater, the larger the team's margin of victory.
    d. The likelihood of rain tends to be greater after you have washed your car.

14. Which of the following is not a normative statement?
    a. Teenage unemployment should be reduced.
    b. An increase in tax rates will reduce unemployment.
    c. New tax laws are needed to help the poor.
    c. We should increase Social Security payments to the elderly.
    e. All of the above are normative statements.

Problems:

1. If you had to define economics, what would be the main elements in the definition?

2. Would you expect the birth rate to rise or fall as economic opportunities for men increased in relatively underdeveloped countries? What if the economic opportunities for women increased?

3. Answer the following questions:
    a. Why are observation and prediction more difficult in economics than in chemistry?
    b. Why do economists look at group behavior rather than individual behavior?
    c. What is the difference between self-interest and selfishness?
    d. Why does inaction have consequences?

4. Using the map analogy from the chapter, talk about the importance of abstraction. How do you abstract when taking notes in class?

5. Identify which of the following headlines represents a microeconomic topic and which represents a macroeconomic topic.
    A. "U.S. Unemployment Rate Reaches Historic Laws"
    B. "Colorado Rockies Make Outfielder Highest Paid Ballplayer"
    C. "OPEC Action Result in a General Increase in Prices"
    D. "General Motors Closes Auto Plant in St. Louis"
    E. "Lawmakers Worry about the Possibility of a US Recession"
    F. "Companies Cut the Cost of Health Care for Employees"

6. Would the following topics be discussed as part of microeconomics or macroeconomics?
    a. Changes in the inflation rate.
    b. The price of concert tickets.
    c. Changes in the country's economic growth rate.
    d. The effects of an increase in the supply of lumber on the home-building industry.
    e. Changes in the national unemployment rate.

7. You are trying to understand the causes of urban pollution. You develop the following two hypotheses. Hypothesis I: Air pollution will be greater, the higher the average temperature in the urban area. Hypothesis II: Air pollution will be greater, the greater the population of the urban area. Test each hypothesis with the information given below. Which hypothesis fits the facts better? Have you developed a theory?

Metropolitan Statistical Area	Days with Polluted Air*	Average Maximum Temperature	Population (thousands)
Cincinnati, OH	30	64.0	1,979
EI Paso, TX	13	77.1	680
Milwaukee, WI	12	55.9	1,690
Atlanta, GA	24	72.0	4,112
Philadelphia, PA	33	63.2	5,101
Albany, NY	8	57.6	876
San Diego, CA	20	70.8	2,814
Los Angeles, CA	80	70.6	9,519

*Air Quality Index greater than 100 (2002)

8. In the 1940s, Dr. Melvin Page conducted a national campaign to stop adults from drinking milk, which he considered a leading cause of cancer. He pointed to the fact that a larger proportion of people died of cancer in Wisconsin, America's leading milk producing state, than any other state as proof of his claim. How would you evaluate Dr. Page's claim?

9. Do any of the following statements involve fallacies? If so, which ones do they involve?
   a. An increase in the amount of money I have will make me better off, but an increase in the supply of money in the economy will not make Americans as a group better off.
   b. When a basketball team spends more to get better players, it is more successful, which proves that all the teams should spend more to get better players.
   c. Because sitting in the back of classrooms is correlated with getting lower grades in the class, students should always sit closer to the front of the classroom.
   d. Gasoline prices were higher last year than in 1970, yet people purchased more gas, which contradicts the law of demand.
   e. Historically, the stock market rises in years the NFC team wins the Super Bowl and falls when the AFC wins the Super Bowl; I am rooting for the NFC team to win for the sake of my investment portfolio.

10. In the debate about clean air standards we have often heard the statement, "A nation as rich as the United States should have no pollution." Why is this a normative statement? Would it help you make a decision on national air quality standards? Describe two positive statements that might be useful in determining the air quality standards.

11. Are the following statements normative or positive, or do they contain both normative and positive statements?
    a. An increase in the price of corn will decrease the amount of corn purchased. However, it will increase the amount of wheat purchased.
    b. A decrease in the price of butter will increase the amount of butter purchased, but that would be bad because it would increase Americans' cholesterol levels.
    c. The birth rate is reduced as economies urbanize, but it also leads to a decreased average age of developing countries' populations.
    d. A higher income-tax rate would generate increased tax revenues. Those extra revenues should be used to give more government aid to the poor.
    e. The study of physics is more valuable than the study of sociology, but both should be studied by all college students.

APPENDIX
Working with Graphs

Graphs Are an Important Economic Tool

Sometimes the use of visual aids, such as graphs, greatly enhances our understanding of a theory. It is much the same as finding your way to a friend's house with the aid of a map rather than with detailed verbal or written instructions. Graphs are important tools for economists. They allow us to understand better the workings of the economy. To economists, a graph can be worth a thousand words. This textbook will use graphs throughout to enhance the understanding of important economic relationships. This appendix provides a guide on how to read and create your own graphs.

The most useful graph for our purposes is one that merely connects a vertical line (the **Y-axis**) with a horizontal line (the **X-axis**), as seen in Exhibit 1. The intersection of the two lines occurs at the *origin*, which is where the value of both variables is equal to zero. In Exhibit 1, the graph has four quadrants, or boxes. In this textbook, we will be primarily concerned with the shaded box in the upper-right corner. This portion of the graph deals exclusively with positive numbers. Always keep in mind that moving to the right on the horizontal axis and moving up along the vertical axis both lead to higher values.

Y-axis
the vertical axis on a graph

X-axis
the horizontal axis on a graph

Using Graphs and Charts

Exhibit 2 presents four common types of graphs. The **pie chart** in Exhibit 2(a) shows the revenues received from various taxes levied on households and corporations. Each slice in the pie chart represents the percentage of finances that are derived from different sources—for example, personal income taxes account for 43 percent of the federal government's tax revenues. Therefore, pie charts are used to show the relative size of various quantities that add up to 100 percent.

Exhibit 2(b) is a **bar graph** that shows the unemployment rate by age and sex in the United States. The height of the line represents the unemployment rate. Bar graphs are used to show a comparison of quantities.

Exhibit 2(c) is a **time-series graph.** This type of graph shows changes in the value of a variable over time. This visual tool allows us to observe important trends over a certain time period. In Exhibit 2(c) we see a graph that shows trends in the inflation rate over time. The horizontal axis shows us the passage of time, and the vertical axis shows us the inflation rate (annual percent change). From the graph, we can see the trends in the inflation rate from 1961 to 2005.

Exhibit 2(d) is a **scatter diagram.** Each point on this graph represents a point that corresponds to an actual observation along the X-axis and Y-axis. It shows the relationship of one variable to another. A linear curve is usually fitted to the scatter of points—it

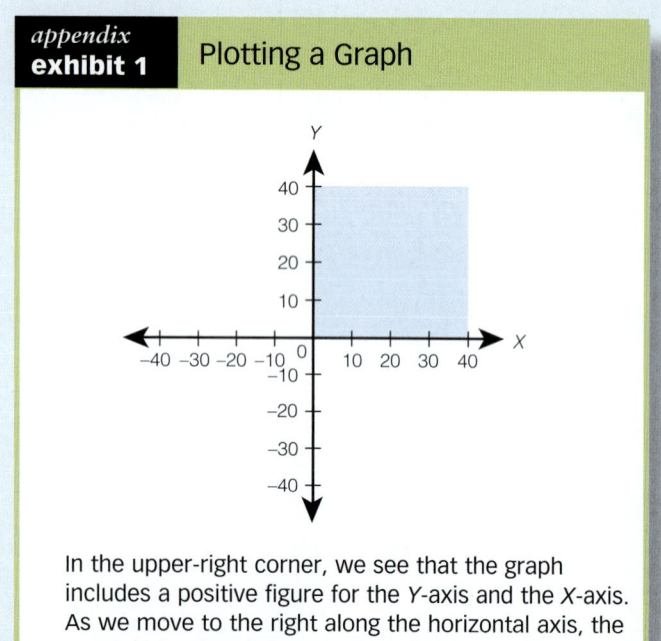

appendix **exhibit 1** Plotting a Graph

In the upper-right corner, we see that the graph includes a positive figure for the Y-axis and the X-axis. As we move to the right along the horizontal axis, the numerical values increase. As we move up along the vertical axis, the numerical values increase.

pie chart
visual display showing the relative size of various quantities that add up to 100 percent

bar graph
visual display showing the comparison of quantities

time-series graph
visual tool to show changes in a variable's value over time

scatter diagram
a graph showing the relationship of one variable to another

APPENDIX Working with Graphs

appendix exhibit 2: Pie Chart, Bar Graph, Time-Series Graph, and Scatter Diagram

a. Pie Chart—Tax Revenues—Federal Government

- Other Taxes 7%
- Personal Income Taxes 44%
- Social Security Tax (Payroll Tax) 38%
- Corporate Income Taxes 11%

SOURCE: Economic Report of the President and Bureau of Economic Analysis, 2009.

b. Bar Graph—U.S. Unemployment, by Sex and Age

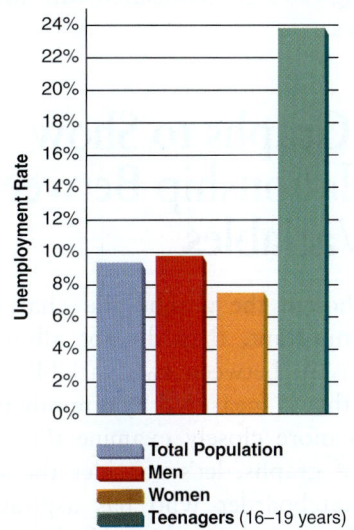

- Total Population
- Men
- Women
- Teenagers (16–19 years)

SOURCE: Bureau of Labor Statistics, August 2009.

c. Time-Series Graph—Inflation Rate

SOURCE: Bureau of Labor Statistics, 2009.

d. Scatter Diagram—Saving Rates and GDP Growth

SOURCE: World Bank, World Development Report, 1996, Oxford University Press, 1996. Republished with permission of the World Bank, from World Bank Development Report 1996; permission conveyed through Copyright Clearance Center, Inc.

represents the best fit for the observations. In this case, the graph shows that rates of economic growth are positively associated with saving rates. Higher saving rates lead to greater economic growth rates, and lower saving rates are associated with lower economic growth rates.

Using Graphs to Show the Relationship Between Two Variables

Even though the graphs and chart in Exhibit 2 are important, they do not allow us to show the relationship between two variables (a **variable** is something that is measured by a number, such as your height). To more closely examine the structures and functions of graphs, let's consider the story of Josh, an avid skateboarder who has aspirations of winning the Z Games next year. He knows that to get there, he'll need to put in many hours of practice. But how many hours? In search of information about the practice habits of other skateboarders, he logs onto the Internet, where he pulls up the results of a study that looked at the score of each Z Games competitor in relation to the amount of practice time per week spent by each skateboarder. As Exhibit 3 shows, the results of the study indicate that skateboarders had to practice 10 hours per week to receive a score of 4, 20 hours per week to receive a score of 6, 30 hours per week to get a score of 8, and 40 hours per week to get a perfect score of 10. How does this information help Josh? By using a graph, he can more clearly understand the relationship between practice time and overall score.

A Positive Relationship

The study on scores and practice times reveals what is called a direct relationship, also called a positive relationship. A **positive relationship** means that the variables change in the same direction. That is, an increase in one variable (practice time) is accompanied by an increase in the other variable (overall score), or a decrease in one variable (practice time) is accompanied by a decrease in the other variable (overall score). In short, the variables change in the same direction.

A Negative Relationship

When two variables change in opposite directions, they have an inverse relationship, also called a **negative**

appendix **exhibit 3** A Positive Relationship

The skateboarders' practice times and scores in the competition are plotted on the graph. Each participant is represented by a point. The graph shows that those skateboarders who practiced the most scored the highest, which indicates a positive, or direct, relationship.

variable something that is measured by a number, such as your height

negative relationship when two variables change in opposite directions

positive relationship when two variables change in the same direction

relationship. That is, when one variable rises, the other variable falls, or when one variable decreases, the other variable increases.

The Graph of a Demand Curve

Let's now examine one of the most important graphs in economics—the demand curve. In Exhibit 4, we see Emily's individual demand curve for DVDs. It shows the price of DVDs on the vertical axis and the quantity of DVDs purchased per month on the horizontal axis. Every point in the space shown represents a price and quantity combination. The downward-sloping line, labeled "Demand curve," shows the different combinations of price and quantity purchased. Note that the higher the price of the DVDs, as shown on the vertical axis, the smaller the quantity purchased, as shown on the horizontal axis, and the lower the price shown on the vertical axis, the greater the quantity purchased shown on the horizontal axis.

appendix exhibit 4 A Negative Relationship

The downward slope of the curve means that price and quantity purchased are inversely, or negatively, related: When one increases, the other decreases. That is, moving down along the demand curve from point A to point E, we see that as the price falls, the quantity purchased increases. Moving up along the demand curve from point E to point A, we see that as the price increases, the quantity purchased falls.

In Exhibit 4, we see that moving up the vertical price axis from the origin, the price of DVDs increases from $5 to $25 in increments of $5. Moving out along the horizontal quantity axis, the quantity purchased increases from zero to five DVDs per month. Point A represents a price of $25 and a quantity of one DVD, point B represents a price of $20 and a quantity of two DVDs, point C a price of $15 and a quantity of three DVDs, and so on. When we connect all the points, we have what economists call a curve. As you can see, curves are sometimes drawn as straight lines for ease of illustration. Moving down along the curve, we see that as the price falls, a greater quantity is demanded; moving up the curve to higher prices, a smaller quantity is demanded. That is, when DVDs become less expensive, Emily buys more DVDs. When DVDs become more expensive, Emily buys fewer DVDs, perhaps choosing to go to the movies or buy a pizza instead.

Using Graphs to Show the Relationship Among Three Variables

Although only two variables are shown on the axes, graphs can be used to show the relationship among three variables. For example, say we add a third variable—income—to our earlier example. Our three variables are now income, price, and quantity purchased. If Emily's income rises—say she gets a raise at work—she is now able and willing to buy more DVDs than before at each possible price. As a result, the whole demand curve shifts outward (to the right) compared with the old curve. That is, the new income gives her more money to use buying more DVDs. This shift is seen in the graph in Exhibit 5(a). On the other hand, if her income falls—say she quits her job to go back to school—she would have less income to buy DVDs. A decrease in this variable causes the whole demand curve to shift inward (to the left) compared with the old curve. This shift is seen in the graph in Exhibit 5(b).

The Difference Between a Movement Along and a Shift in the Curve

It is important to remember the difference between a movement between one point and another along a curve and a shift in the whole curve. A change in one of the variables on the graph, like price or quantity purchased, will cause a movement along the curve, say from point A to point B, as shown in Exhibit 6. A change in one of the variables not shown (held constant in order to show only the relationship between price and quantity), such as income in our example, will cause the whole curve to shift. The change from D_1 to D_2 in Exhibit 6 shows such a shift.

slope
the ratio of rise (change in the Y variable) over run (change in the X variable)

Slope

In economics, we sometimes refer to the steepness of a line or curve on a graph as the slope. A slope can be either positive (upward sloping) or negative (downward sloping). A curve that is downward sloping represents an inverse, or negative, relationship between the two variables and slants downward from left to right, as seen in Exhibit 7(a). A curve that is upward sloping represents a direct, or positive, relationship between the two variables and slants upward from left to right, as seen in Exhibit 7(b). The numeric value of the slope shows the number of units of change of the Y-axis variable for each unit of change in the X-axis variable. Slope provides the direction (positive or negative) as well as the magnitude of the relationship between the two variables.

Measuring the Slope of a Linear Curve

A straight-line curve is called a linear curve. The slope of a linear curve between two points measures the

appendix exhibit 5: Shifting a Curve

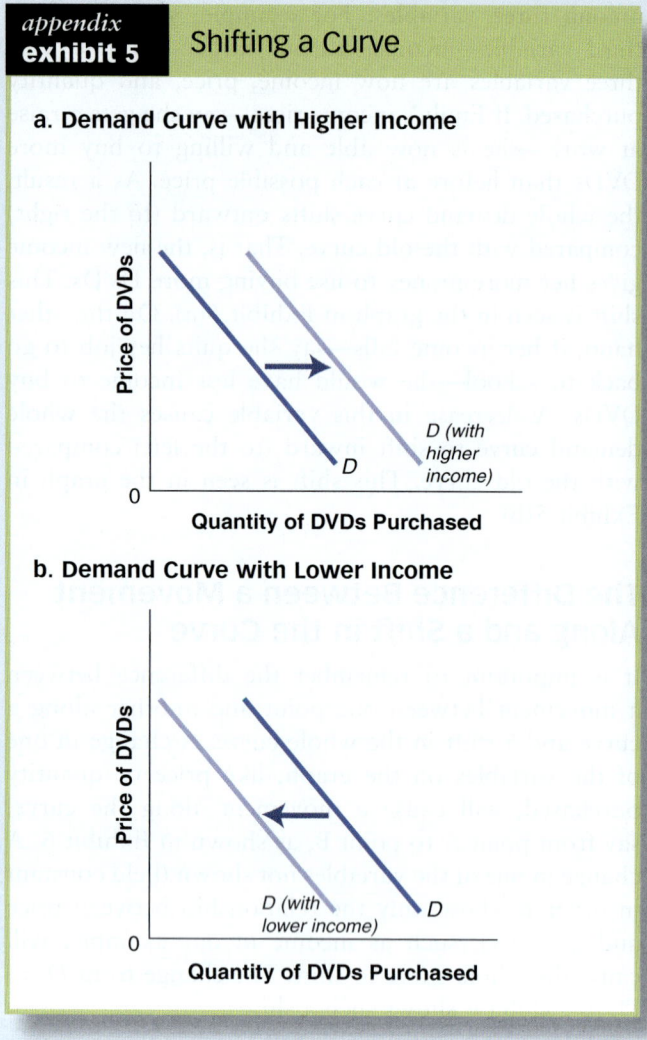

a. Demand Curve with Higher Income

b. Demand Curve with Lower Income

appendix exhibit 7: Downward- and Upward-Sloping Linear Curve

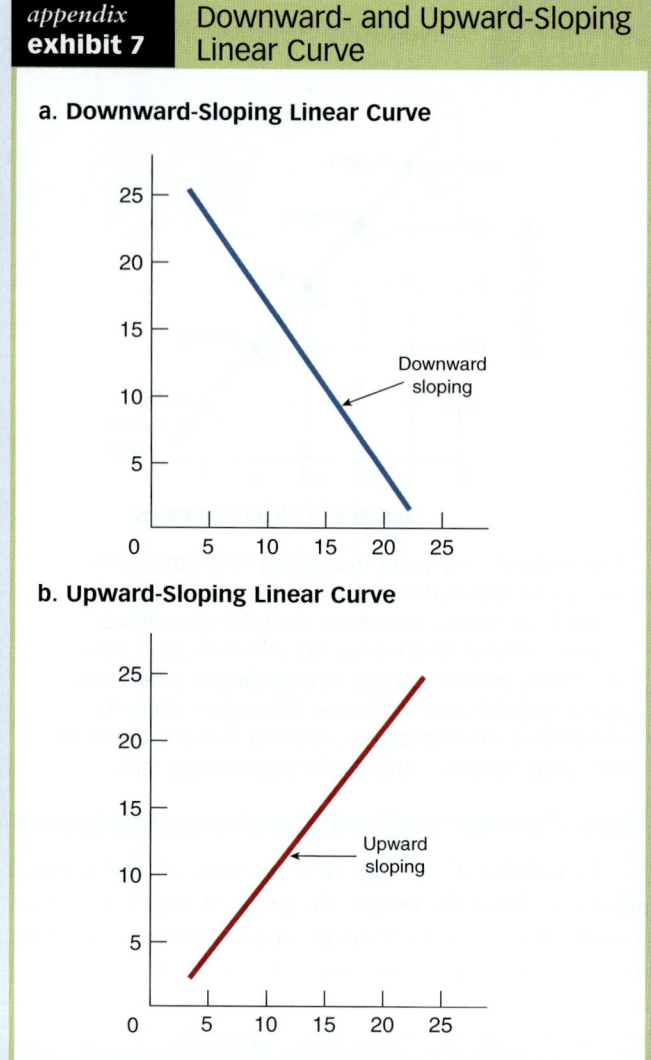

a. Downward-Sloping Linear Curve

b. Upward-Sloping Linear Curve

appendix exhibit 6: Shifts Versus Movements

relative rates of change of two variables. Specifically, the slope of a linear curve can be defined as the ratio of the change in the Y value to the change in the X value. The slope can also be expressed as the ratio of the rise over the run, where the rise is the vertical change and the run is the horizontal change.

Exhibit 8 shows two linear curves, one with a positive slope and one with a negative slope. In Exhibit 8(a), the slope of the positively sloped linear curve from point A to B is 1/2, because the rise is 1 (from 2 to 3) and the run is 2 (from 1 to 3). In Exhibit 8(b), the negatively sloped linear curve has a slope of −4: A rise of −8 (a fall of 8, from 10 to 2) and a run of 2 (from 2 to 4) gives us a slope of −8/2, or −4. Notice the appropriate signs on the slopes: The negatively sloped line carries a minus sign and the positively sloped line, a plus sign.

Finding the Slope of a Nonlinear Curve

In Exhibit 9, we show the slope of a nonlinear curve. A nonlinear curve is a line that actually curves. Here the slope varies from point to point along the curve.

appendix exhibit 8 Slopes of Positive and Negative Curves

a. Positive Slope
b. Negative Slope

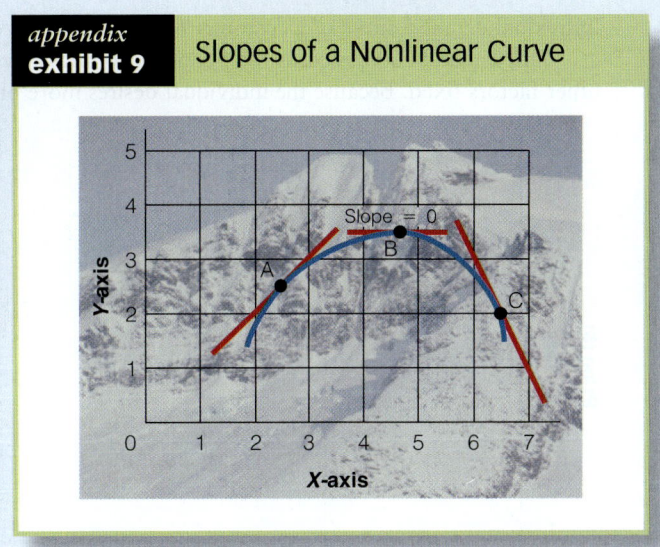

appendix exhibit 9 Slopes of a Nonlinear Curve

However, we can find the slope of this curve at any given point by drawing a straight line tangent to that point on the curve. A tangency is when a straight line just touches the curve without actually crossing it. At point A, we see that the positively sloped line that is tangent to the curve has a slope of 1: the line rises 1 and runs 1. At point B, the line is horizontal, so it has zero slope. At point C, we see a slope of –2, because the negatively sloped line has a rise of –2 (a fall of 2) for every run of 1.

Remember, many students have problems with economics simply because they fail to understand graphs, so make sure that you understand this material before going on to Chapter 2.

Key Terms and Concepts

Y-axis 28
X-axis 28
pie chart 28
bar graph 28

time-series graph 28
scatter diagram 28
variable 30
positive relationship 30

negative relationship 30
slope 31

Problems:

1. The following table gives the prices and quantity demanded of oranges (pounds) for the week of December 10–16.

Price ($/lb.)	Quantity Demanded (lbs.)
$0.80	0
0.70	3
0.60	4
0.50	5
0.40	7
0	

   a. Plot the data from the table into a graph.
   b. Is it a positive or negative relationship? Explain.

   Answer

   We have created a negatively sloped demand curve. That is, the price and quantity demanded of oranges are inversely related:

   $$\uparrow P \Rightarrow \downarrow Q_D \text{ and } \downarrow P \Rightarrow \uparrow Q_D$$

Individual demand curve of a customer for oranges of a certain grade, Week of December 10–16.

The demand curve records the pounds of oranges a consumer desires at various prices in a given week, holding all other factors fixed. Because the individual desires more oranges at lower prices, the demand curve slopes downward.

2. Which of the following will lead to a positive relationship? A negative relationship?
   a. Hours studied and grade in a course
   b. The price of ice cream and the amount of ice cream purchased
   c. The amount of seasonal snowfall and the sale of snow shovels

   Answer
   a. positive
   b. negative
   c. positive

3. Below is Emily's demand curve for iTunes. How do we add income, a third variable, to price and quantity purchased on our graph? Using a graph, explain what would happen if Emily had an increase in income. What would happen if Emily has a decrease in income?

Answer

When income increases, Emily can purchase more at each and every price—a rightward shift from D_1 to D_2. If Emily's income falls, her demand will shift leftward from D_1 to D_3.

4. Use the information in the following table to plot a graph. Is it a positive or negative relationship? What is the slope?

X	Y
1	2
2	4
3	6
4	8
5	10

Answer

5. What is a pie chart? Bar graph? Time-series graph? Scatter diagram?

Answer

Pie charts are used to show the relative size of various quantities that add up to 100 percent. Bar graphs are used to show a comparison of quantities of similar items. Time-series graphs allow us to see important trends over a period of time. Scatter diagrams display points of actual observations. Generally, a curve is fitted to the scatter of points to show a trend.

2 The Economic Way of Thinking

2.1 Scarcity
2.2 Choices, Costs, and Trade-Offs
2.3 Marginal Thinking

2.4 Incentives Matter
2.5 Specialization and Trade
2.6 Markets and Improved Efficiency

Studying economics may teach you how to "think better," because economics helps develop a disciplined method of thinking about problems.

A student of economics becomes aware that, at a basic level, much of economic life involves choosing one course of action rather than another—making choices among our conflicting wants and desires in a world of scarcity. Economics provides insights about how to intelligently evaluate these options and determine the most appropriate choices in given situations. *Most of economics really involves knowing certain principles well and knowing when and how to apply them.*

This chapter presents some important tools that will help you understand the economic way of thinking. The economic way of thinking provides a logical framework for organizing and analyzing your understanding of a broad set of issues, many of which do not even seem directly related to economics as you now know it.

The basic ideas that you learn in this chapter will occur repeatedly throughout the text. If you develop a good understanding of these principles and master the problem-solving skills inherent in them, they will serve you well for the rest of your life. Learning to think like an economist takes time. Like most disciplines, economics has its own specialized vocabulary, including such terms as *elasticity, comparative advantage, supply and demand, deadweight loss,* and *consumer surplus*. Learning economics requires more than picking up this new terminology; however, it also involves using its powerful tools to improve your understanding of a whole host of issues in the world around you. ∎

SECTION 2.1 Scarcity

- What are goods and services?
- What are tangible and intangible goods?
- What are economic goods?

Scarcity

Economics is concerned primarily with **scarcity**—how we satisfy our unlimited wants in a world of limited resources. We may want "essential" items such as food, clothing, schooling, and health care. We may want many other items, such as vacations, cars, computers, and concert tickets. We may want more friendship, love, knowledge, and so on. We also may have many goals—perhaps an A in this class, a college education, and a great job. Unfortunately, people are not able to fulfill all their wants and desires, material and nonmaterial. And as long as human wants exceed available resources, scarcity will exist.

Don't confuse scarcity with rarity. Something may be rare, but if it is not desirable, it is not scarce. You won't find many baseball cards of my son (rare)—about 10—but at the same time, few people outside of the immediate family want one. Therefore, the card is rare but not scarce. However, if he becomes a major league star, those cards could become scarce—rare and desirable.

All the things you see here—grass, trees, rocks, animals—are considered land to economists.

Scarcity and Resources

The scarce resources used in the production of goods and services can be grouped into four categories: labor, land, capital, and entrepreneurship.

Labor is the total of both physical and mental effort expended by people in the production of goods and services. The services of a teacher, nurse, cosmetic surgeon, professional golfer, and an electrician all fall under the general category of labor.

Land includes the "gifts of nature" or the natural resources used in the production of goods and services. Economists consider land to include trees, animals, water, minerals, and so on, along with the physical space we normally think of as land.

scarcity
exists when human wants (material and nonmaterial) exceed available resources

labor
the physical and human effort used in the production of goods and services

land
the natural resources used in the production of goods and services

capital
the equipment and structures used to produce goods and services

human capital
the productive knowledge and skill people receive from education, on-the-job training, health, and other factors that increase productivity

entrepreneurship
the process of combining labor, land, and capital to produce goods and services

Capital is the equipment and structures used to produce goods and services. Office buildings, tools, machines, and factories are all considered capital goods. When we invest in factories, machines, research and development, or education, we increase the potential to create more goods and services in the future. Capital also includes **human capital**—the productive knowledge and skill people receive from education and on-the-job training.

Entrepreneurship is the process of combining labor, land, and capital to produce goods and services. Entrepreneurs make the tough and risky decisions about what and how to produce goods and services. Entrepreneurs are always looking for new ways to improve production techniques or to create new products. They are lured by the chance of making a profit. It is this opportunity to make a profit that leads entrepreneurs to take risks.

However, not every entrepreneur is a Bill Gates (Microsoft) or a Henry Ford (Ford Motor Company). In some sense, we are all entrepreneurs when we try new products or when we find better ways to manage our households or our study time. Rather than money, then, our profits might take the form of greater enjoyment, additional time for recreation, or better grades.

What Are Goods and Services?

Goods are the items that we value or desire. Goods tend to be **tangible**—objects that can be seen, held, heard, tasted, or smelled. But other goods that we cannot reach out and touch are called intangible goods. **Intangible goods** include fairness for all, friendship, leisure, knowledge, security, prestige, respect, and health.

Services are intangible acts for which people are willing to pay, such as legal counsel, medical care, and education. Services are intangible because they are less overtly visible, but they are certainly no less valuable than goods.

All goods and services, whether tangible or intangible, are produced from scarce resources and can be subjected to economic analysis. Scarce goods created from scarce resources are called **economic goods**. These goods are *desirable but limited* in supply. Without enough economic goods for all of us, we are forced to compete. That is, scarcity ultimately leads to competition for the available goods and services, a subject we will return to often in the text.

What Are Bads?

In contrast to goods, **bads** are those items that we do not desire or want. For most people, garbage, pollution, weeds, and crime are bads. People tend to eliminate or minimize bads, so they will often pay to have bads, like garbage, removed. The elimination of the bad—garbage removal, for example—is a good.

Are Those Who Want More Greedy?

We all want more tangible and intangible goods and services. In economics, we assume that more goods lead to greater satisfaction. However, just

goods
items we value or desire

tangible goods
items we value or desire that we can reach out and touch

intangible goods
goods that we cannot reach out and touch, such as friendship and knowledge

services
intangible items of value provided to consumers, such as education

economic goods
scarce goods created from scarce resources—goods that are desirable but limited in supply

bads
items that we do not desire or want, where less is preferred to more, like terrorism, smog, or poison oak.

because economics assumes that we want more goods does not mean that economics also assumes that we are selfish and greedy. That is, scarcity does not result from people just wanting more for themselves. Many people give much of their income and time to charitable or religious organizations. The ways people allocate their income and time reveal their preferences. The fact that people are willing to give up their money and time for causes that they believe to be important reveals quite conclusively that charitable endeavors are a desirable good. Clearly, then, many desires, such as the desire to build new friendships or help charities, can hardly be defined as selfish; yet they are desires that many people share. In other words, *self-interest* is not the same as *selfishness* or *greed*. Indeed, in a world without scarcity, we would have no use for generosity.

Does Everyone Face Scarcity?

We all face scarcity because we cannot have all the goods and services we desire. However, because we all have different wants and desires,

Not even millionaire lottery winners can escape scarcity. The problem is that as we get more affluent, we learn of new luxuries to provide us with satisfaction. Even lottery winners may become less content as the excitement wears off and they begin looking for new satisfactions. A 78-year-old man from Michigan just won his second $1 million scratch-off lottery. He says, "I am now going for three."

scarcity affects everyone differently. For example, a child in a developing country may face a scarcity of food and clean drinking water, while a rich man may face a scarcity of garage space for his growing antique car collection. Likewise, a harried middle-class working mother may find time for exercise particularly scarce, while a pharmaceutical company may be concerned with the scarcity of the natural resources it uses in its production process. Its effects may vary, but no one can escape scarcity.

We often hear it said of rich people that "He has everything" or "She can buy anything she wants." Actually, even the richest person must live with scarcity and must, at some point, choose one want or desire over another. And of course, we all have only 24 hours in a day! The problem is that as we get more affluent, we learn of new luxuries to provide us with satisfaction. Wealth, then, creates a new set of wants to be satisfied. No evidence indicates that people would not find a valuable use for additional income, no matter how rich they became. Even the wealthy individual who decides to donate all her money to charity faces the constraints of scarcity. If she had greater resources, she could do still more for others.

Will Scarcity Ever Be Eradicated?

It is probably clear by now that scarcity never has and never will be eradicated. The same creativity that develops new methods to produce goods and services in greater quantities also reveals new wants. Fashions are always changing. Clothes and shoes that are "in" one year will likely be "out" the next. New wants quickly replace old ones. It is also quite possible that over a period of time, a rising quantity of goods and services will not increase human happiness. Why? Because our wants may grow as fast—if not faster—than our ability to meet those wants.

SECTION CHECK

1. We all have many wants and goals.
2. Scarcity exists when our wants exceed the available resources.
3. Scarce resources can be categorized as: land (all of our natural resources), labor (the physical and mental efforts expended in the production of goods and services), capital (the equipment and structures used to produce goods and services, and the productive knowledge and skill people receive from education and on-the-job training), and entrepreneurship (the process of combining land, labor, and capital into production of goods and services).
4. Goods and services are things that we value.
5. Goods can be tangible (physical) or intangible (love, compassion, and intelligence).
6. Economic goods are goods created from limited resources.
7. We all face scarcity—rich and poor alike.
8. Our wants grow over time, so scarcity will never be eliminated.

---

1. What must be true for something to be an economic good?
2. Does wanting more tangible and intangible goods and services make us selfish?
3. Why does scarcity affect everyone?
4. How and why does scarcity affect each of us differently?
5. Why do you think economists often refer to training that increases the quality of workers' skills as "adding to human capital"?
6. What are some of the ways that students act as entrepreneurs as they seek higher grades?
7. Why might sunshine be scarce in Seattle but not in Tucson?
8. Why can't a country become so technologically advanced that its citizens won't have to choose?

SECTION 2.2 Choices, Costs, and Trade-Offs

* Why do we have to make choices?
* What do we give up when we have to choose?
* Why are "free" lunches not free?

Scarcity Forces Us to Choose

Each of us may want a nice home, two luxury cars, wholesome and good-tasting food, a personal trainer, and a therapist, all enjoyed in a pristine environment with zero pollution. If we had unlimited resources, and thus an ability to produce all the goods and services everyone wants, we would not have to choose among those desires. However, we all face scarcity, and as a consequence, we must make choices. If we did not have to make meaningful economic choices, the study of economics would not be necessary. The essence of economics is to understand fully the implications that scarcity has for wise decision making.

Trade-Offs

In a world of scarcity, we all face trade-offs. If you spend more time at work you might give up an opportunity to go shopping at the mall or watch your favorite TV show. Or when you decide how to spend your income, buying a new car may mean you have to forgo a summer vacation. Businesses have trade-offs too. If a farmer chooses to plant his land in cotton this year, he gives up the opportunity to plant his land in wheat. If a firm decides to produce only cars, it gives up the opportunity to use those resources to produce refrigerators or something else that people value. Society, too, must make trade-offs. For example, the federal government faces trade-offs when it comes to spending tax revenues; additional resources used to enhance the environment may come at the expense of additional resources to provide health, education or national defense.

To Choose Is to Lose

Every choice involves a cost. The highest or best forgone opportunity resulting from a decision is called the **opportunity cost.** Another way to put it is that "to choose is to lose" or "an opportunity cost is an opportunity lost." To get more of anything that is desirable, you must accept less of something else that you also value.

For example, time spent exercising costs time that could be spent doing something else that is valuable—perhaps relaxing with friends or studying for an upcoming exam. One of the reasons drivers talk so much on their cell phones is because they have little else to do with their time while driving—a low opportunity cost. However, drivers using cell phones should pay attention; otherwise, they are giving up safety. Trade-offs are everywhere. The famous poet, Robert Frost, understood that to live is to choose. In his poem, "The Road Not Taken," he writes, "two roads diverged in a yellow wood, and sorry I could not travel both."

Bill Gates, Tiger Woods, and Oprah Winfrey all quit college to pursue their dreams. Tiger Woods dropped out of Stanford (an economics major) to join the PGA golf tour. Bill Gates dropped out of Harvard to start a software company. Oprah Winfrey dropped out of Tennessee State to pursue a career in broadcasting. At the early age of 19, she became the co-anchor of the evening news. Staying in school would have cost each of them millions of dollars. We cannot say it would have been the wrong decision to stay in school; but it would have been costly. Their opportunity cost of staying in school was high.

opportunity cost
the value of the best forgone alternative that was not chosen

Money Prices and Costs

If you go to the store to buy groceries you have to pay for the items you bought. This amount is called the *money price*. It is an opportunity cost, because you could have used that money to purchase other goods or services. However, additional opportunity costs include the nonprice costs incurred to acquire the groceries—time spent getting to the grocery store, finding a parking place, actual shopping, and waiting in the checkout line. The nonprice costs are measured by assessing the sacrifice involved—the value you place on what you would have done with that time if you had not gone shopping. So the cost of grocery shopping is the price paid for the goods, plus the nonprice costs incurred. Or your concert ticket may have only been $50. But what if you had to wait in line for six hours in the freezing cold? Waiting and enduring the cold are costs too. Seldom are costs just dollars and cents. Shopping at a large discount store may save you on the money price, but cost you time waiting in long checkout lines. Also, buying food in bulk quantities may be less expensive per ounce, but cost inventory space in your pantry, or the food may spoil before it is eaten.

Remember that many costs do not involve money but are still costs. Do I major in economics or engineering? Do I go to Billy Madison University or Tech State University? Should I get an MBA now or work and wait a few years to go back to school?

Policy makers are unavoidably faced with opportunity costs too. Consider airline safety. Both money cost and time costs affect airline safety. New airline safety devices cost money (luggage inspection devices, smoke detectors, fuel tank safeguards, new radar equipment, and so on), and time costs are quite evident with the new security checks. Time waiting in line costs time doing something else that is valuable. New airline safety requirements could also actually cost lives. If the new safety equipment costs are passed on in the form of higher airline ticket prices, people may choose to travel by car, which is far more dangerous per mile traveled than by air. Opportunity costs are everywhere!

How often do people consider the full opportunity of raising a child to age 18? The obvious money costs include food, visits to the doctor, clothes, piano lessons, time spent at soccer practices, and so on. According to the Department of Agriculture, a middle-income family with a child born in 2007 can expect to spend about $270,000 for food, shelter, and other necessities to raise that child through age 17. Other substantial opportunity costs are incurred in rearing a child as well. Consider the opportunity cost of one parent choosing to give up his or her job to stay at home. For a parent who makes that choice, the time spent in child rearing is time that could have been used earning money and pursuing a career.

Is That Really a Free Lunch, a Freeway, or a Free Beach?

The expression "there's no such thing as a free lunch" clarifies the relationship between scarcity and opportunity cost. Suppose the school cafeteria is offering "free" lunches today. Although the lunch is free to you, is it really free from society's perspective?

The Opportunity Cost of Going to College or Having a Child

The average person often does not correctly calculate opportunity costs. For example, the (opportunity) cost of going to college includes not just the direct expenses of tuition and books. Of course, those expenses do involve an opportunity cost because the money used for books and tuition could be used to buy other things that you value. But what about the nonmoney costs? That is, going to college also includes the opportunity cost of your time. Specifically, the time spent going to school is time that could have been spent on a job earning, say, $30,000 over the course of an academic year. What about room and board? That aspect is a little tricky because you would presumably have to pay room and board whether you went to college or not. The relevant question may be how much more it costs you to live at school rather than at home (and living at home may have substantial nonmoney costs). Even if you stayed at home, your parents would sacrifice something; they could rent your room out or use the room for some other purpose such as storage, guest room, home office, a sibling's room, and so on.

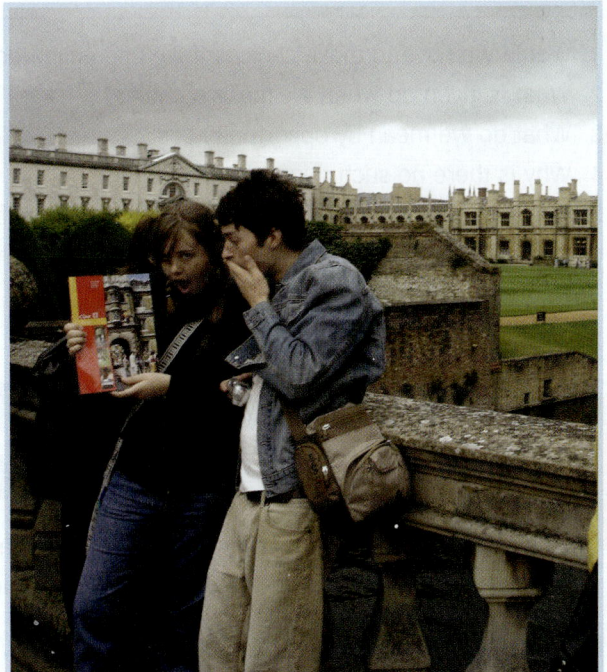

You may think tuition, room and board are expensive! Now add the opportunity cost of your time—perhaps working during those nine months.

Is air free? How about clean air? Clean air is desirable but limited in cities—that is, it is a scarce good. How about air to a scuba diver? Or how about air to a climbing expedition on Mount Everest? What if you want to fill your tires at this gas station but you didn't buy gas? So in many situations, air is not free; it is scarce.

The answer is no, because some of society's scarce resources will have been used in the preparation of the lunch. The issue is whether the resources that went into creating that lunch could have been used to produce something else of value. Clearly, the scarce resources that went into the production of the lunch—the labor and materials (food-service workers, lettuce, meat, plows, tractors, fertilizer, and so forth)—could have been used in other ways. They had an opportunity cost and thus were not free.

Do not confuse free with a zero monetary price. A number of goods—freeways, free beaches, and free libraries, for instance—do not cost consumers money, but they are still scarce. Few things are free in the sense that they use none of society's scarce resources. So what does a free lunch really mean? It is, technically speaking, a "subsidized" lunch—a lunch using society's scarce resources, but one that the person receiving it does not have to pay for personally.

SECTION CHECK

1. Scarcity means we all have to make choices.
2. When we are forced to choose, we give up the next highest-valued alternative.
3. Opportunity cost is what you give up when you make a choice.

---

1. Would we have to make choices if we had unlimited resources?
2. What is given up when we make a choice?
3. What do we mean by opportunity cost?
4. Why is there no such thing as a free lunch?
5. Why was the opportunity cost of staying in college higher for Tiger Woods than for most undergraduates?
6. Why is the opportunity cost of time spent getting an MBA typically lower for a 22-year-old straight out of college than for a 45-year-old experienced manager?

Marginal Thinking

- What do we mean by marginal thinking?
- What is the rule of rational choice?
- Why do we use the word *expected* with marginal benefits and costs?

Many Choices We Face Involve Marginal Thinking

Some decisions are "all or nothing," like whether to start a new business or go to work for someone else, or whether to attend graduate school or take a job. But many choices we face involve how *much* of something to do rather than whether to do something. It is not *whether* you eat but *how much* you eat. Or, how many caffe lattes will I buy this week? Or, how often do I change the oil in my car? Or how much of my check do I spend, and how much do I save? Your instructors hope that the question is not *whether* you study this semester but *how much* you study. You might think to yourself, "If I studied a little more, I might be able to improve my grade," or "If I had a little better concentration when I was studying, I could improve my grade." That is, spending more time has an additional expected benefit (a higher grade) and an additional expected cost (giving up time to do something else that is valuable, such as watching TV or sleeping). These examples reflect what economists call **marginal thinking** because the focus is on the additional, or marginal, choices available to you. Or think of marginal as the edge—marginal decisions are made around the edge of what you are currently doing. Marginal choices involve the effects of adding or subtracting from the current situation. In short, they are the small (or large) incremental changes to a plan of action.

Businesses are constantly engaged in marginal thinking. For example, firms have to decide whether the additional (marginal) revenue received from increasing production is greater than the marginal cost of that production.

Always watch out for the difference between average and marginal costs. Suppose an airline had 10 unoccupied seats on a flight from Los Angeles to New York, and the average cost was $400 per seat (the total cost divided by the number of seats—$100,000/250). If 10 people are waiting on standby, each willing to pay $300, should the airline sell them the tickets? Yes! The unoccupied seats earn nothing for the airline. What are the additional (marginal) costs of a few more passengers? The marginal costs are minimal—slight wear and tear on the airplane, handling some extra baggage, and 10 extra in-flight meals. In this case, thinking at the margin can increase total profits, even if it means selling at less than the average cost of production.

Another good example of marginal thinking is an auction. Prices are bid up marginally as the auctioneer calls out one price after another. When bidders view the new price (the marginal cost) to be greater than the value they place on the good (the marginal benefit), they withdraw from further bidding.

In trying to make themselves better off, people alter their behavior if the expected marginal benefits from doing so outweigh the expected marginal costs, which is the **rule of rational choice.** Economic theory is often called marginal analysis because it assumes that people are always weighing the expected marginal benefits against the expected marginal costs. The term *expected* is used with *marginal benefits* and *marginal costs* because the world is uncertain in many important respects, so the actual result of changing behavior may not always make people better off—but on average it will. However, as a matter of rationality, people are assumed to engage only in behavior that they think ahead of time will make them better off. That is, individuals will only pursue an activity if their expected marginal benefits are greater than their expected marginal costs of pursuing that activity one step further, $E(MB) > E(MC)$.

This fairly unrestrictive and realistic view of individuals seeking self-betterment can be used to analyze a variety of social phenomena.

Suppose that you have to get up for an 8 A.M. class but have been up very late. When the alarm goes off at 7 A.M. you are weighing the marginal benefits and marginal costs of an extra 15 minutes of sleep. If you perceive the marginal benefits of 15 additional minutes of sleep to be greater than the marginal costs of those extra minutes, you may choose to hit the snooze button. Or perhaps you may decide to blow off class completely. But it's unlikely that you will choose that action if it's the day of the final exam—because it is now likely that the **net benefits** (the difference between the expected marginal benefits and the expected marginal costs) of skipping class have changed. When people have opportunities to make themselves better off they usually take them. And they will continue to seek those opportunities as long as they expect a net benefit from doing so.

The rule of rational choice is simply the rule of being sensible, and most economists believe that individuals act *as if* they are sensible and apply the rule of rational choice to their daily lives. It is a rule that can help us understand our decisions to study, walk, shop, exercise, clean house, cook, and perform just about every other action.

It is also a rule that we will continue to use throughout the text. Because whether it is consumers, producers, or policy makers, they all must compare the expected marginal benefits and the expected marginal cost to determine the best level to consume, produce, or provide public programs.

Zero Pollution Would Be Too Costly

Let's use the concept of marginal thinking to evaluate pollution levels. We all know the benefits of a cleaner environment, but what would we have to give up—that is, what marginal costs would we have to incur—to achieve zero pollution? A lot! You could not drive a

---

marginal thinking
focusing on the additional, or marginal, choices; marginal choices involve the effects of adding or subtracting, from the current situation, the small (or large) incremental changes to a plan of action

rule of rational choice
individuals will pursue an activity if the expected marginal benefits are greater than the expected marginal costs

net benefit
the difference between the expected marginal benefits and the expected marginal costs

POLICY application

ECONOMICS AND FOOTBALL: WEIGHING THE BENEFITS AND COSTS OF GOING FOR IT ON FOURTH DOWN

With just over five minutes to play in yesterday's game against the New York Jets, the Washington Redskins found themselves on their own 23-yard line facing a fourth and one. The team, which was ahead by just three points, elected to do what teams normally do in such situations: They played it safe and punted rather than try to keep the drive alive.

The Jets promptly came back to kick a field goal, tying the game and sending it into overtime. While this particular story had a happy ending for Washington, which won, 23-20, it illustrated the value of an analysis by David Romer, an economist at the University of California, who has concluded that football teams are far too conservative in play calling in fourth-down situations.

You don't have to be particularly interested in sports to find Romer's conclusion intriguing: His hunch about human behavior in general was that although people say they have a certain goal and are willing to do everything they can to achieve it, their actual behavior regularly departs from the optimal path to reach that goal.

In his analysis of football teams, Romer specifically looked at a single question -- whether teams should punt or kick the football on fourth down, or take a chance and run or throw the ball. Romer's calculations don't necessarily tell teams what to do in specific situations such as yesterday's game. But on average, teams that take the risk seem to win more often than lose.

Data from a large number of NFL games show that coaches rarely follow what Romer's calculations predict would give them the best chance of victory. While fans often suggest more aggressive play calling, even fans usually don't go as far as the economist does—his calculations show that teams should regularly be going for it on fourth down, even if it is early in the game, even if the score is tied, and even if the ball is on their own side of the field.

Romer's calculations have been backed up by independent analyses. Coaches have not raised a serious challenge to Romer's analysis, but they have simply ignored his finding.

New England Patriots coach Bill Belichick is among those who has said he agrees with Romer, and Belichick happens to be one of the more successful coaches in the league. Two Sundays ago, as the Patriots were piling up an astronomical score against Washington, Belichick took a chance on a fourth-down play and got his team seven points instead of the three he might have gotten had the team tried a field goal.

When asked by reporters why he took the chance, Belichick's response was the response of someone who really means what he says about maximizing points: "What do you want us to do, kick a field goal?"

Owners and fans have been receptive to Romer's ideas. However, in informal conversations Romer has had with the coaching staffs of various teams, the economist said he has been told to mind his own business in the ivory tower.

Indeed, since Romer wrote his paper a couple of years ago, NFL coaches seem to have gotten even more conservative in their play calling, which the economist attributes to their unwillingness to follow the advice of an academic, however useful it might be. . . .

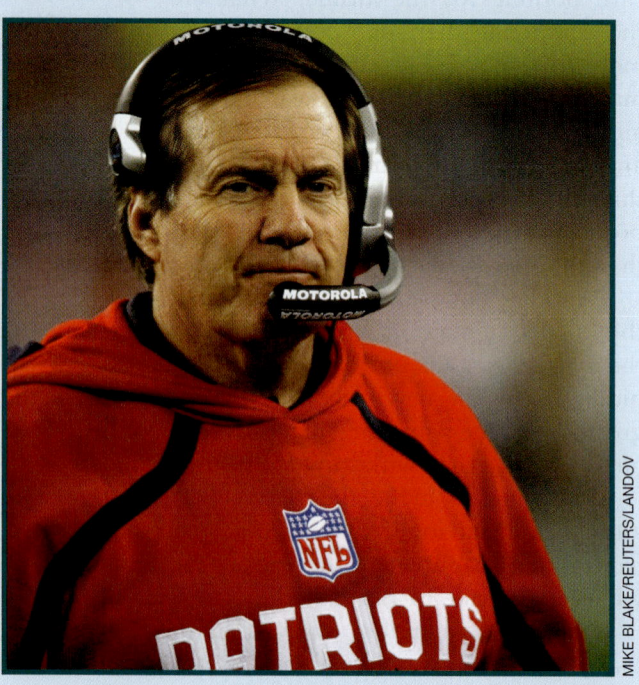

Policy application

"It used to be that going for it on fourth down was the macho thing to do," Romer said. But after his findings were widely publicized in sports circles, he said: "Now going for it on fourth down is the egghead thing to do. Would you rather be macho or an egghead?"

The interesting question raised by Romer's research applies to a range of settings that have nothing to do with sports. Why do coaches persist in doing something that is less than optimal, when they say their only goal is to win? One theory that Romer has heard is that coaches—like generals, stock fund directors and managers in general—actually have different goals than the people they lead and the people they must answer to. Everyone wants to win, but managers are held to different standards than followers when they lose, especially when they lose after trying something that few others are doing.

consider this:

Coaches must weigh the expected marginal benefits and costs of "going for it" on fourth down. So why don't coaches go for it more often if the data suggests that teams should take more risks? Does Coach Belichick take more risks because he was an economics major in college and has figured it out? Or is it because coaches tend to be more risk averse than their fans and owners because coaches are held to different standards when they lose? So coaches often do what other coaches do and play it safe and punt.

SOURCE: From Shankar Vedantam, "Go for It on Fourth Down, Coach? Maybe You Should Ask an Egghead", 'Washington Post', November 5, 2007, p. A3. Copyright © 2007 The Washington Post. All rights reserved. Used by permission and protected by the Copyright Laws of the United States. The printing, copying, redistribution, or retransmission of the material without express writtten permission is prohibited.

Even thrill seekers would likely slow down if fines were higher and/or law enforcement were increased, because such measures would alter the driver's cost-benefit calculation for reckless driving (as would bad brakes, bald tires, and poor visibility). On the other hand, compulsory seat belts and airbags would also alter behavior, because they change the driver's incentives. Seat belts and airbags make accidents less costly, by reducing the chance of serious injury or death; thus they reduce the benefit to safe driving, causing some motorists to drive more recklessly.

car, fly in a plane, or even ride a bicycle, especially if everybody else were riding bikes, too (because congestion is a form of pollution). How would you get to school or work, or go to the movies or the grocery store? Everyone would have to grow their own food because transporting, storing, and producing food uses machinery and equipment that pollute. And even growing your own food would be a problem because many plants emit natural pollutants. We could go on and on. The point is *not* that we shouldn't be concerned about the environment; rather, we have to weigh the expected marginal benefits of a cleaner environment against the expected marginal costs of a cleaner environment. This discussion is not meant to say the environment should not be cleaner, only that zero pollution levels would be far too costly in terms of what we would have to give up.

Optimal (Best) Levels of Safety

Like pollution, crime and safety can have optimal (or best) levels that are greater than zero. Take crime. What would it cost society to have zero crime? It would be prohibitively costly to divert a tremendous amount of our valuable resources toward the complete elimination of crime. In fact, it would be impossible to eliminate crime totally. Even reducing crime significantly would be costly. Because lower crime rates are costly, society must decide how much it is willing to give up. The additional resources for crime prevention can only come from limited resources, which could be used to produce something else the people may value even more.

The same is true for safer products. Nobody wants defective tires on their cars, or cars that are unsafe and roll over at low speeds. However, optimal amounts of safety that are greater than zero are available. The issue is not safe versus unsafe products but rather *how much* safety we want. It is not risk versus no-risk but rather *how much* risk we are willing to take. Additional safety can only come at higher costs. To make all products perfectly safe would be impossible, so we must weigh the benefits and costs of safer products. In fact, according to one study by Sam Peltzman, a University of Chicago economist, additional safety regulations in cars (mandatory safety belts and padded dashboards) in the late 1960s may have had little impact on highway fatalities. Peltzman found that making cars safer led to more reckless driving and more accidents. The safety regulations did result in fewer deaths per automobile accident, but the total number of deaths remained unchanged because more accidents occurred.

Reckless driving has a benefit in the form of getting somewhere more quickly, but it can also have a cost—an accident or even a fatality. Most people will compare the marginal benefits and marginal costs of safer driving and make the choices that they believe will get them to their destination safely.

SECTION CHECK

1. Economists are usually interested in the effects of additional, or marginal, changes in a given situation.
2. People try to make themselves better off.
3. People make decisions based on what they expect to happen.
4. The rule of rational choice states that individuals will pursue an activity if they expect the marginal benefits to be greater than the marginal costs, or $E(MB) > E(MC)$.
5. The optimal (best) levels of pollution, crime, and safety are greater than zero.

1. What are marginal choices? Why does economics focus on them?
2. What is the rule of rational choice?
3. How could the rule of rational choice be expressed in terms of net benefits?
4. Why does rational choice involve expectations?
5. Why do students often stop taking lecture notes when a professor announces that the next few minutes of material will not be on any future test or assignment?
6. If you decide to speed to get to a doctor's appointment and then get in an accident due to speeding, does your decision to speed invalidate the rule of rational choice? Why or why not?
7. If pedestrians felt far safer using crosswalks to cross the street, how could adding crosswalks increase the number of pedestrian accidents?
8. Imagine driving a car with daggers sticking out of the steering wheel—pointing directly at your chest. Would you drive more safely? Why?

SECTION 2.4 Incentives Matter

* Can we predict how people will respond to changes in incentives?
* What are positive incentives?
* What are negative incentives?

People Respond to Changes in Incentives

Because most people are seeking opportunities to make themselves better off, they respond to changes in incentives. That is, they are reacting to changes in expected marginal benefits and expected marginal costs. In fact, much of human behavior can be explained and predicted as a response to incentives.

Positive and Negative Incentives

Almost all of economics can be reduced to incentive [$E(MB)$ versus $E(MC)$] stories, where consumers and producers are driven by incentives that affect expected costs or benefits. Prices, wages, profits, taxes, and subsidies are all examples of economic incentives. Incentives can be classified into two types: positive and negative. **Positive incentives** are those that either increase benefits or reduce costs and thus result in an increased level of the related activity or behavior. **Negative incentives,** on the other hand, either reduce benefits or increase costs, resulting in a decreased level of the related activity or behavior. For example, a tax on cars that emit lots of pollution (an increase in costs) would be a negative incentive that would lead to a reduction in emitted pollution. On the other hand, a subsidy (the opposite of a tax) on hybrid cars—part electric, part internal combustion—would be a positive incentive that would encourage greater production and consumption of hybrid cars. Human behavior is influenced in predictable ways by such changes in economic incentives, and economists use this information to predict what will happen when the benefits and costs of any choice are changed. In short, economists study the incentives and consequences of particular actions.

A subsidy on hybrid electric vehicles would be a positive incentive that would encourage greater production and consumption of these vehicles. A wide variety of incentives are offered at the federal, state, and local levels to encourage the expanded use of alternative-fuel vehicles.

positive incentive
an incentive that either reduces costs or increases benefits, resulting in an increase in an activity or behavior

negative incentive
an incentive that either increases costs or reduces benefits, resulting in a decrease in the activity or behavior

Because most people seek opportunities that make them better off, we can predict what will happen when incentives are changed. If salaries increase for engineers and decrease for MBAs, we would predict fewer people would go to graduate school in business and more would go into engineering. A permanent change to a much higher price of gasoline would lead us to expect fewer gas guzzlers on the highway. People who work on commission tend to work harder. If the price of downtown parking increased, we would predict that commuters would look for alternative methods to get to work that would save money. If households were taxed to conserve water economists would expect people to use less water and substantially less water than if they were simply asked to conserve water. Incentives matter.

in the news: Incentives Matter

Estonia's Total Fertility Rate Increasing in Part Because of Government Program Encouraging Women to Give Birth

Estonia's total fertility rate has increased to an average of 1.5 children per woman from an average of 1.3 children per woman in the late 1990s, which could be the result of a government initiative aimed at sustaining the nation's population by providing women who have children with monthly stipends, the *Wall Street Journal* reports. The initiative, launched in 2004, was pushed after a 2001 world population report by the United Nations showed that Estonia was "one of the fastest-shrinking nations on earth," according to the *Journal*. Under the program, Estonia provides employed women who have children with their monthly salary, up to $1,560 monthly, over a 15-month period and unemployed women with $200 monthly. According to the *Journal*, the average monthly salary in Estonia is $650. The program has helped raise the total fertility rate because many employed women in the country could not afford to take time off from work to have children and because taking time off could have a negative impact on job security, according to the *Journal*. Some other factors that contributed to the lower total fertility rate include advances in birth control and ideas about personal freedom and happiness, the *Journal* reports. Estonia's program could serve as a model for other countries with low total fertility rates, according to the *Journal*. The Estonian government plans to continue formulating strategies—such as expanding preabortion counseling and subsidizing child-care providers and private day care—to help improve the total fertility rate, the *Journal* reports. According to the *Journal*, Estonia needs a total fertility rate of 2.1 children per woman to maintain its current population.

COURTESY OF ROBERT L. SEXTON

consider this:

Estonia is using positive incentives. But what would happen to birth rates if the tax deduction for dependents is removed? Although it would not change everyone's behavior, overall we would expect birth rates to fall if the tax deduction for dependents was eliminated, because it would then be more expensive for couples to raise children. We would also predict that couples would choose to have fewer children if the government imposed a birth tax on couples. Clearly, both of these policy changes would serve as negative incentives to having children, because both increase the costs of having kids. In essence, what either of these policies would do is change the benefit-cost equation, and altering this equation typically leads to predictable results.

SOURCE: Reprinted with permission from http://www.kaisernetwork.org. You can view the entire Kaiser Daily Health Policy Report, search the archives, or sign up for email delivery at http://www.kaisernetwork.org/dailyreports/healthpolicy. The Kaiser Daily Health Policy Report is published for kaisernetwork.org, a free service of The Henry J. Kaiser Family Foundation. © 2005 Advisory Board Company and Kaiser Family Foundation. All rights reserved.

SECTION CHECK

1. People respond to incentives in predictable ways.
2. A positive incentive decreases costs or increases benefits, thus encouraging consumption or production.
3. A negative incentive increases costs or reduces benefits, thus discouraging consumption or production.

---

1. What is the difference between positive incentives and negative incentives?
2. According to the rule of rational choice, would you do more or less of something if its expected marginal benefits increased? Why?
3. According to the rule of rational choice, would you do more or less of something if its expected marginal costs increased? Why?
4. How does the rule of rational choice imply that young children are typically more likely to misbehave at a supermarket checkout counter than at home?
5. Why do many parents refuse to let their children have dessert before they eat the rest of their dinner?

SECTION 2.5 Specialization and Trade

* What is the relationship between opportunity cost and specialization?
* What are the advantages of specialization in production?

Why Do People Specialize?

As you look around, you can see that people specialize in what they produce. They tend to dedicate their resources to one primary activity, whether it be child rearing, driving a cab, or making bagels. Why? The answer, short and simple, is opportunity costs. By concentrating their energies on only one, or a few, activities, individuals are **specializing.** This focus allows them to make the best use of (and thus gain the most benefit from) their limited resources. A person, a region, or a country can gain by specializing in the production of the good in which they have a comparative advantage. That is, if they can produce a good or service at a lower opportunity cost than others, we say that they have a **comparative advantage** in the production of that good or service.

> **specializing**
> concentrating in the production of one, or a few, goods
>
> **comparative advantage**
> occurs when a person or country can produce a good or service at a lower opportunity cost than others

specialization. For example, we may specialize in selling or fixing automobiles. The wages from that work can then be used to buy goods from a farmer who has chosen to specialize in the production of food. Likewise, the farmer can use the money earned from selling his produce to get his tractor fixed by someone who specializes in that activity.

Specialization is evident not only among individuals but among regions and countries as well. In fact, the story of the economic development of the United States and the rest of the world involves specialization. Within the United States, the Midwest with its wheat, the coastal waters of the Northeast with its fishing fleets, and the Northwest with its timber are each examples of regional specialization.

We All Specialize

We all specialize to some extent and rely on others to produce most of the goods and services we want. The work that we choose to do reflects our

The Advantages of Specialization

In a small business, every employee usually performs a wide variety of tasks—from hiring to word processing to marketing. As the size of the company increases, each employee can perform a more specialized job, with a consequent increase in output per worker. The

Use what you've LEARNED

SPECIALIZATION, COMPARATIVE ADVANTAGE, AND BASEBALL

Specialization and comparative advantage are important in sports, as they are in other fields. In baseball and softball, teams have resources that they must place in alternative positions to increase the likelihood of a victory. The resource is labor—human effort used to produce something. We can be even more specific, and talk about the particular characteristics or skills of the labor. That is, we have strength of arms, speed, fielding, power hitting, and contact hitting. Where do we play each of these players in the field or place them in the batting line-up to increase our chances to win? The teams that specialize with their varied talent have a better chance of winning. Quicker players are usually positioned in the middle of the field—shortstop, second base, and center field. Slower (less quick) fielders are usually on the corners—third base, first base, left field, and right field. Strength of arm—pitchers, catchers, and right field (it is a long throw from right field to third base). Hitting—speed and contact in the one and two spots, power in the three, four, and five spots, and the relatively poorer contact hitters at the bottom of the line-up.

It is also easy to see the importance of comparative advantage in this example. Suppose there are two players on your softball team, Jessica and Mariah, and you are not sure where they should play in the field. Jessica is good at infield and good at outfield. Mariah is good at infield and bad at outfield, but not as good at Jessica at either. Where should they play Mariah, since Jessica has an absolute advantage over Mariah in the infield and outfield? It would be best to play Mariah in the infield because she is just a little worse than Jessica in the infield and a lot worse than Jessica in the outfield. Remember, comparative advantage is a relative concept.

Finally, why did hitters put up higher batting averages 100 years ago? Ted Williams was the last player to hit over 400, and that was in 1941. Over 30 hitters exceeded that mark from 1880–1930. Were hitters better back in the old days? Or are pitchers better today? It is probably that pitchers are better today. Part of the reason is training and nutrition for pitchers. But the other reason is specialization. Pitchers rarely throw complete games these days. Often they are only asked to throw five innings of a nine-inning game. It is then up to the middle relievers and the closers to finish up the game. There are also specialty pitchers for different situations—if you need a ground ball you might bring in your sinker ball pitcher. If your computer records suggest that the left-handed batter coming up struggles against left-handed pitching, you might bring in a left-handed reliever. Specialization has changed the game.

primary advantages of specialization are that employees acquire greater skill from repetition, they avoid wasted time in shifting from one task to another, and they do the types of work for which they are best suited—and specialization promotes the use of specialized equipment for specialized tasks.

The advantages of specialization are seen throughout the workplace. For example, in larger firms, specialists conduct personnel relations, and accounting is in the hands of full-time accountants instead of someone with half a dozen other tasks. Owners of small retail stores select the locations for their stores primarily through guesswork, placing them where they believe sales will be high or where empty low-rent buildings are available. In contrast, larger chains have store sites selected by experts who have experience in analyzing the factors that make different locations relatively more desirable, such as traffic patterns, income levels, demographics, and so on.

Use what you've LEARNED: COMPARATIVE ADVANTAGE

Q Should an attorney who types 100 words per minute hire an administrative assistant to type her legal documents, even though he can only type 50 words per minute? If the attorney does the job, she can do it in five hours; if the administrative assistant does the job, it takes him 10 hours. The attorney makes $100 an hour, and the administrative assistant earns $10 an hour. Which one has the comparative advantage (the lowest opportunity cost) in typing documents?

A If the attorney types her own documents, it will cost $500 ($100 per hour x 5 hours). If she has the administrative assistant type her documents, it will cost $100 ($10 per hour x 10 hours). Clearly, then, the lawyer should hire the administrative assistant to type her documents, because the administrative assistant has the comparative advantage (lowest opportunity cost) in this case, despite being half as good in absolute terms.

Specialization and Trade Lead to Greater Wealth and Prosperity

Trade, or voluntary exchange, directly increases wealth by making both parties better off (or they wouldn't trade). It is the prospect of wealth-increasing exchange that leads to productive specialization. That is, trade increases wealth by allowing a person, a region, or a nation to specialize in those products that it produces at a lower opportunity cost and to trade them for products that others produce at a lower opportunity cost. That is, we trade with others because it frees up time and resources to do other things that we do better.

In short, if we divide tasks and produce what we do *relatively* best and trade for the rest, we will be better off than if we were self-sufficient—that is, without trade. Imagine life without trade, where you were completely self-sufficient—growing your own food, making your own clothes, working on your own car, building your own house—do you think you would be better off? For example, say the United States is better at producing wheat than is Brazil, and Brazil is better at producing coffee than is the United States. The United States and Brazil would each benefit if the United States produces wheat and trades some of it to Brazil for coffee. Coffee growers in the United States could grow coffee in expensive greenhouses, but it would result in higher coffee costs and prices, while leaving fewer resources available for employment in more beneficial jobs, such as wheat production.

This concept is true for individuals as well. Imagine Tom had 10 pounds of tea and Katherine had 10 pounds of coffee. However, Tom preferred coffee to tea and Katherine preferred tea to coffee. So if Tom traded his tea to Katherine for her coffee, both parties would be better off. Trade simply reallocates existing goods, and voluntary exchange increases wealth by making both parties better off—otherwise, they would not agree to trade.

In the words of growth theorist, Paul Romer, "There are huge potential gains from trade. Poor countries can supply their natural and human resources. Rich countries can supply their know-how. When these are combined, everyone can be better off. The challenge is for a country to arrange its laws and institutions so that both sides can profitably engage in trade." Standards of living can be increased through trade and exchange. In fact, the economy as a whole can create more wealth when each person specializes in a task that he or she does best. And through specialization and trade, a country can gain a greater variety of goods and services at a lower cost. So while counties may be competitors inn the global market they are also partners.

SECTION CHECK

1. We all specialize.
2. Specialization is important for individuals, businesses, regions, and nations.
3. Specialization and trade increase wealth.
4. The person, region, or country that can produce a good or service at a lower opportunity cost than other producers has a comparative advantage in the production of that good or service.

(continued)

1. Why do people specialize?
2. What do we mean by comparative advantage?
3. Why does the combination of specialization and trade make us better off?
4. If you can mow your lawn in half the time it takes your spouse or housemate to do it, do you have a comparative advantage in mowing the lawn?
5. If you have a current comparative advantage in doing the dishes, and you then become far more productive than before in completing yard chores, could that eliminate your comparative advantage? Why or why not?
6. Could a student who gets a C in one class but a D or worse in everything else have a comparative advantage over someone who gets a B in that class but an A in everything else? Explain this concept using opportunity cost.

SECTION 2.6 Markets and Improved Efficiency

* How does a market economy allocate scarce resources?
* What are the important signals that market prices communicate?
* What are the effects of price controls?
* What is a market failure?

How Does the Market Work to Allocate Resources?

In a world of scarcity, competition is inescapable, and one method of allocating resources among competing uses is the market economy. The market economy provides a way for millions of producers and consumers to allocate scarce resources. For the most part, markets are efficient. To an economist, **efficiency** is achieved when the economy gets the most out of its scarce resources. In short, efficiency makes the economic pie as large as possible.

Competitive markets are powerful—they can make existing products better and/or less expensive, they can improve production processes, and they can create new products, from video games to lifesaving drugs. Buyers and sellers indicate their wants through their action and inaction in the marketplace, and it is this collective "voice" that determines how resources are allocated. But how is this information communicated? Market prices serve as the language of the market system. By understanding what these market prices mean, you can get a better understanding of the vital function that the market economy performs.

Markets may not always lead to your desired tastes and preferences. You may think that markets produce too many pet rocks, chia pets, breast enhancements, and face lifts. Some markets are illegal—the market for cocaine, the market for stolen body parts, the market for child pornography, and the market for indecent radio announcers. Markets do not come with a moral compass; they simply provide what buyers are willing and able to pay for and what sellers are willing and able to produce.

efficiency
when an economy gets the most out of its scarce resources

Market Prices Provide Important Information

Market prices communicate important information to both buyers and sellers. These prices communicate information about the relative availability of products to buyers, and they provide sellers with critical information about the relative value that consumers place on those products. In short, buyers look at the price and decide how much they are willing and able to demand and sellers look at the price and decide how much they are able and willing to supply. The market price reflects the value a buyer places on a good and the cost to society of producing that good. Thus, market prices provide a way for both buyers and sellers to communicate about the relative value of resources. To paraphrase Adam Smith, prices adjust like an "invisible hand" to direct buyers and sellers to an outcome that is socially desirable. We will see how this works beginning in Chapter 4.

The basis of a market economy is voluntary exchange and the price system that guides people's choices and produces solutions to the questions of what goods to produce and how to produce and distribute them.

Take something as simple as the production of a pencil. Where did the wood come from? Perhaps the Northwest or Georgia. The graphite may have come from the mines in Michigan and the rubber may be from Malaysia. The paint, the glue, the metal piece that holds the eraser—who knows? The point is that market forces coordinated this production activity among literally thousands of people, some of whom live in different countries and speak different languages. The market brought these people together to make a pencil that sells for 25 cents at your bookstore. It all happened because the market economy provided the incentive for people to pursue activities that benefit others. This same process produces millions of goods and services around the world, from automobiles and computers to pencils and paper clips.

The same is true of the IPod and IPhone. The entrepreneur of Apple have learned how to combine almost 500 generic parts to make something of much greater value. The whole is greater than the sum of the parts.

> **price controls**
> government-mandated minimum or maximum prices
>
> **market failure**
> when the economy fails to allocate resources efficiently on its own

What Effect Do Price Controls Have on the Market System?

Government policies called **price controls** sometimes force prices above or below what they would be in a market economy. Unfortunately, these controls often impose harm on the same people they are trying to help, in large part by short-circuiting the market's information-transmission function. That is, price controls effectively strip the market price of its meaning for both buyers and sellers (as we will see in Chapter 5). A sales tax also distorts price signals, leading to a misallocation of resources (as we will see in Chapter 6).

Market Failure

The market mechanism is a simple but effective and efficient general means of allocating resources among alternative uses. When the economy fails to allocate resources efficiently on its own, however, it is known as **market failure.** For example, a steel mill might put soot and other forms of "crud" into the air as a by-product of making steel. When it does,

POLICY application: COUNTRIES THAT DO NOT RELY ON A MARKET SYSTEM

Countries that do not rely on the market system have no clear communication between buyers and sellers. The former Soviet Union, where quality was virtually nonexistent, experienced many shortages of quality goods and surpluses of low-quality goods. For example, thousands of tractors had no spare parts and millions of pairs of shoes were left on shelves because the sizes did not match those of the population. Before the breakup of the Soviet Union, one of President Reagan's favorite stories concerned a man who goes to the Soviet bureau of transportation to order an automobile. He is informed that he will have to put down his money now, but there is a 10-year wait. The man fills out all the various forms, has them processed through the various agencies, and finally he gets to the last agency. He pays them his money and they say, "Come back in 10 years and get your car." He asks, "Morning or afternoon?" The man from the agency says, "We're talking 10 years from now. What is the difference?" He replies, "The plumber is coming in the morning."

Even though designating these parking spaces for disabled drivers may not be an efficient use of scarce parking spaces (because they are often not used), many believe it is fair to give these drivers a convenient spot. The debate between efficiency and equity is often heated.

it imposes costs on others not connected with using or producing steel from the steel mill. The soot may require homeowners to paint their homes more often, entailing a cost. And studies show that respiratory diseases are greater in areas with more severe air pollution, imposing costs that may even include life itself. In addition, the steel mill might discharge chemicals into a stream, thus killing wildlife and spoiling recreational activities for the local population. In this case, the steel factory does not bear the costs of its polluting actions, and it continues to emit too much pollution. In other words, by transferring the pollution costs onto society, the firm lowers its costs of production and so produces more than the ideal output—which is inefficient because it is an overallocation of resources.

Markets sometimes produce too little of a good—research, for example. Therefore, the government might decide to subsidize promising scientific research that could benefit many people—such as cancer research. When one party prevents other parties from participating in mutually beneficial exchange, it also causes a market failure. This situation occurs in a monopoly, with its single seller of goods. Because the monopolist can raise its end price above the competitive price, some potential consumers are kept from buying the goods they would have bought at the lower price, and inefficiency occurs. Whether the market economy has produced too little (underallocation) or too much (overallocation), the government can improve society's well-being by intervening. The case of market failure will be taken up in more detail in Chapter 8.

We cannot depend on the market economy to always communicate accurately. Some firms may have market power to distort prices in their favor. For example, the only regional cement company in the area has the ability to charge a higher price and provide lower-quality services than if the company were in a highly competitive market. In this case, the lack of competition can lead to higher prices and reduced product quality. And without adequate information, unscrupulous producers may be able to misrepresent their products to the disadvantage of unwary consumers.

In sum, government *can* help promote efficiency when there is a market failure—making the economic pie larger.

Does the Market Distribute Income Fairly?

Sometimes a painful trade-off exists between how much an economy can produce efficiently and how that output is distributed—the degree of equality. An efficient market rewards those that produce goods and services that others are willing and able to buy. But this does not guarantee a "fair" or equal distribution of income. That is, how the economic pie is divided up. A market economy cannot guarantee everyone adequate amounts of food, shelter, and health care. That is, not only does the market determine what goods are going to be produced and in what quantities, but it also determines the distribution of output among members of society.

As with other aspects of government intervention, the degree-of-equity argument can generate some sharp disagreements. What is "fair" for one person may seem highly "unfair" to someone else. One person may find it terribly unfair for some individuals to earn many times the amount earned by other individuals who work equally hard, and another person may find it highly unfair to ask one group, the relatively rich, to pay a much higher proportion of their income in taxes than another group pays.

Government Is Not Always the Solution

However, just because the government could improve the situation does not mean it will. After all, the political process has its own set of problems, such as special interests, shortsightedness, and imperfect information. For example, government may reduce competition through tariffs and quotas, or it may impose inefficient regulations that restrict entry. That is, there is government failure as well as market failure.

SECTION CHECK

1. Scarcity forces us to allocate our limited resources.
2. Market prices provide important information to buyers and sellers.
3. Price controls distort market signals.
4. A market failure is said to occur when the economy fails to allocate resources efficiently.

---

1. Why must every society choose some manner in which to allocate its scarce resources?
2. How does a market system allocate resources?
3. What do market prices communicate to others in society?
4. How do price controls undermine the market as a communication device?
5. Why can markets sometimes fail to allocate resources efficiently?

Interactive Chapter Summary

Fill in the blanks:

1. As long as human _____ exceed available _____, scarcity will exist.
2. Something may be rare, but if it is not _____ it is not scarce.
3. The scarce resources that are used in the production of goods and services can be grouped into four categories: _____, _____, _____, and _____.
4. Capital includes human capital, the _____ people receive from _____.
5. Entrepreneurs are always looking for new ways to improve _____ or _____. They are lured by the chance of making a _____.
6. _____ goods include fairness, friendship, knowledge, security, and health.
7. _____ are intangible items of value, such as education, provided to consumers.
8. Scarce goods created from scarce resources are called _____ goods.
9. Scarcity ultimately leads to _____ for the available goods and services.
10. Because we all have different _____, scarcity affects everyone differently.
11. Economics is the study of the choices we make among our many _____ and _____.
12. In a world of scarcity, we all face _____.
13. The highest or best forgone alternative resulting from a decision is called the _____.
14. The cost of grocery shopping is the _____ paid for the goods plus the _____ costs incurred.
15. Many choices involve _____ of something to do rather than whether to do something.
16. Economists emphasize _____ thinking because the focus is on additional, or _____, choices, which involve the effects of _____ or _____ the current situation.
17. The rule of rational choice is that in trying to make themselves better off, people alter their behavior if the _____ to them from doing so outweigh the _____ they will bear.
18. In acting rationally, people respond to _____.
19. If the benefits of some activity _____ and/or if the costs _____, economists expect the amount of that activity to rise. Economists call these _____ incentives. Likewise, if the benefits of some activity _____ and/or if the costs _____, economists expect the amount of that activity to fall. Economists call these _____ incentives.
20. Because most people seek opportunities that make them better off, we can _____ what will happen when incentives are _____.
21. People _____ by concentrating their energies on the activity to which they are best suited because

individuals incur _____ opportunity costs as a result.

22. If a person, a region, or a country can produce a good or service at a lower opportunity cost than others can, we say that they have a(n) _____ in the production of that good or service.

23. The primary advantages of specialization are that employees acquire greater _____ from repetition, they avoid _____ time in shifting from one task to another, and they do the types of work for which they are _____ suited.

24. We trade with others because it frees up time and resources to do other things we do _____.

25. Produce what we do _____ best and _____ for the _____.

26. Market prices serve as the _____ of the market system. They communicate information about the _____ to buyers, and they provide sellers with critical information about the _____ that buyers place on those products. This communication results in a shifting of resources from those uses that are _____ valued to those that are _____ valued.

27. The basis of a market economy is _____ exchange and the _____ system that guides people's choices regarding what goods to produce and how to produce those goods and distribute them.

28. _____ can lead the economy to fail to allocate resources efficiently, as in the cases of pollution and scientific research.

29. Sometimes a painful trade-off exists between how much an economy can produce _____ and how that output is _____.

30. In the case of market _____, appropriate government policies could improve on market outcomes.

Answers: 1. wants; resources 2. desirable 3. land; labor; capital; entrepreneurship 4. knowledge and skill; education and on-the-job training 5. production techniques; products; profit 6. Intangible 7. Services 8. economic 9. competition 10. wants and desires 11. wants; desires 12. trade-offs 13. opportunity cost 14. prices; nonprice 15. how much 16. marginal 17. expected marginal benefits; expected marginal costs 18. incentives 19. rise; fall; positive; negative 20. predict; changed 21. specialize; lower value; less; more 27. voluntary; price 28. Market failure 29. efficiently; distributed 30. failure
22. comparative advantage 23. skill; wasted; best 24. better 25. relatively; trade; rest 26. language; relative availability of products; relative

Key Terms and Concepts

scarcity 37
labor 37
land 37
capital 37
human capital 37
entrepreneurship 37
goods 38
tangible goods 38

intangible goods 38
services 38
economic goods 38
bads 38
opportunity cost 40
marginal thinking 43
rule of rational choice 43
net benefit 43

positive incentive 47
negative incentive 47
specializing 49
comparative advantage 49
efficiency 52
price controls 53
market failure 53

Section Check Answers

2.1 Scarcity

1. **What must be true for something to be an economic good?**
   An economic good, tangible or intangible, is any good or service that we value or desire. This definition includes the reduction of things we don't want—bads—as a good.

2. **Does wanting more tangible and intangible goods and services make us selfish?**
   No. Among the goods many of us want more of are helping others (charity), so to say we all want more goods and services does not imply that we are selfish.

3. **Why does scarcity affect everyone?**
   Because no one can have all the goods and services that he or she desires, we all face scarcity as a fact of life.

4. **How and why does scarcity affect each of us differently?**
   Because our desires and the extent of the resources we have available to meet those desires vary, scarcity affects each of us differently.

5. **Why do you think economists often refer to training that increases the quality of workers' skills as "adding to human capital"?**
   Training increases a worker's ability to produce further goods, just as capital goods increase an economy's ability to produce further goods. Because of this similarity in their effects on productive abilities, training is often referred to as adding to workers' human capital.

6. **What are some of the ways that students act as entrepreneurs as they seek higher grades?**
   Students act as entrepreneurs in seeking higher grades in a wide variety of ways. They sometimes form study groups, often assigning different material to different members. They often share notes. They study harder for those questions they believe will be more likely to be tested. Sometimes they try to get hold of old tests or to cheat. All of these activities and more are part of different students' efforts to discover the lowest-cost way for them to get higher grades.

7. **Why might sunshine be scarce in Seattle but not in Tucson?**
   For a good to be scarce means we want more of it than we are able to have. Residents of Tucson typically have all the sunshine they wish, while rain may be something that is scarce relative to residents' desires. For residents of Seattle, where the sun shines much less and it rains much more, the opposite might well be true.

8. **Why can't a country become so technologically advanced that its citizens won't have to choose?**
   No matter how productive a country becomes, citizens' desires will continue to outstrip their ability to satisfy them. As we get more productive, and incomes grow, we discover new wants that we would like to satisfy, so our ability to produce never catches up with our wants.

2.2 Choices, Costs, and Trade-Offs

1. **Would we have to make choices if we had unlimited resources?**
   We would not have to make choices if we had unlimited resources, because we would then be able to produce all the goods and services anyone wanted, and having more of one thing would not require having less of other goods or services.

2. **What is given up when we make a choice?**
   What is given up when we make a choice is the opportunity to pursue other valued alternatives with the same time or resources.

3. **What do we mean by opportunity cost?**
   The opportunity cost of a choice is the highest valued forgone opportunity resulting from a decision. It can usefully be thought of as the value of the opportunity a person would have chosen if his most preferred option was taken away from him.

4. **Why is there no such thing as a free lunch?**
   There is no such thing as a free lunch because the production of any good uses up some of society's resources, which are therefore no longer available to produce other goods we want.

5. **Why was the opportunity cost of staying in college higher for Tiger Woods than for most undergraduates?**
   The forgone alternative to Tiger Woods of staying in school—starting a highly paid professional golf career sooner than he could otherwise—was far more lucrative than the alternatives facing most undergraduates. Because his forgone alternative was more valuable for Tiger Woods, his opportunity cost of staying in school was higher than for most.

6. **Why is the opportunity cost of time spent getting an MBA typically lower for a 22-year-old straight out of college than for a 45-year-old experienced manager?**
   The opportunity cost of time for a 45-year-old experienced manager—the earnings he would have to give up to spend a given period getting an MBA—is higher than that of a 22-year-old straight out of college, whose income earning alternatives are far less.

2.3 Marginal Thinking

1. **What are marginal choices? Why does economics focus on them?**
   Marginal choices are choices of how much of something to do, rather than whether to do something. Economics focuses on marginal choices because those are the sorts of choices we usually face: Should I do a little more of this or a little less of that?

2. **What is the rule of rational choice?**
   The rule of rational choice is that in trying to make themselves better off, people alter their behavior if the expected marginal benefits from doing so outweigh the expected marginal costs they will bear. If the expected marginal benefits of an action exceed the expected marginal costs, a person will do more of that action; if the expected marginal benefits of an action are less than the expected marginal costs, a person will do less of that action.

3. **How could the rule of rational choice be expressed in terms of net benefits?**
   Because net benefits are expected to be positive when expected marginal benefits exceed expected marginal cost to the decision maker, the rule of rational choice

could be restated as: People will make choices for which net benefits are expected to be positive.

4. **Why does rational choice involve expectations?**
Because the world is uncertain in many important respects, we can seldom know for certain whether the marginal benefits of an action will in fact exceed the marginal costs. Therefore, the rule of rational choice deals with expectations decision makers hold at the time they make their decisions, recognizing that mistakes can be made.

5. **Why do students often stop taking lecture notes when a professor announces that the next few minutes of material will not be on any future test or assignment?**
The benefit, in terms of grades, from taking notes in class falls when the material discussed will not be tested or "rewarded," and when the benefits of lecture note taking are smaller in this situation, students do less of it.

6. **If you decide to speed to get to a doctor's appointment and then get in an accident due to speeding, does your decision to speed invalidate the rule of rational choice? Why or why not?**
No. Remember, the rule of rational choice deals with expectations at the time decisions were made. If you thought you would get in an accident due to speeding in this situation, you would not have decided to speed. The fact that you got in an accident doesn't invalidate the rule of rational choice; it only means your expectations at the time you decided to speed were incorrect.

7. **If pedestrians felt far safer using crosswalks to cross the street, how could adding crosswalks increase the number of pedestrian accidents?**
Just like safer cars can lead people to drive less safely, if pedestrians felt safer in crosswalks, they might cross less safely, such as taking less care to look both ways. The result of pedestrians taking less care may well be an increase in the number of pedestrian accidents.

8. **Imagine driving a car with daggers sticking out of the steering wheel—pointing directly at your chest. Would you drive more safely? Why?**
Because the cost to you of an accident would be so much higher in this case, you would drive far more safely as a result.

2.4 Incentives Matter

1. **What is the difference between positive incentives and negative incentives?**
Positive incentives are those that either increase benefits or decrease costs of an action, encouraging the action; negative incentives are those that either decrease benefits or increase costs of an action, discouraging the action.

2. **According to the rule of rational choice, would you do more or less of something if its expected marginal benefits increased? Why?**
You would do more of something if its expected marginal benefits increased, because then the marginal expected benefits would exceed the marginal expected costs for more "units" of the relevant action.

3. **According to the rule of rational choice, would you do more or less of something if its expected marginal costs increased? Why?**
You would do less of something if its expected marginal costs increased, because then the marginal expected benefits would exceed the marginal expected costs for fewer "units" of the relevant action.

4. **How does the rule of rational choice imply that young children are typically more likely to misbehave at a supermarket checkout counter than at home?**
When a young child is at a supermarket checkout counter, the benefit of misbehaving—the potential payoff to pestering Mom or Dad for candy—is greater. Also, because his parents are less likely to punish him, or to punish him as severely, in public as in private when he pesters them, the costs are lower as well. The benefits of misbehavior are higher and the costs are lower at a supermarket checkout counter, so more child misbehavior is to be expected there.

5. **Why do many parents refuse to let their children have dessert before they eat the rest of their dinner?**
Children often find that the costs of eating many foods at dinner exceed the benefits (e.g., "If it's green, it must be disgusting."), but that is seldom so of dessert. If parents let their children eat dessert first, they would often not eat the food that was "good for them." But by adding the benefit of getting dessert to the choice of eating their other food, parents can often get their children to eat the rest of their dinner, too.

2.5 Specialization and Trade

1. **Why do people specialize?**
People specialize because by concentrating their energies on the activities to which they are best suited, individuals incur lower opportunity costs. That is, they specialize in doing those things they can do at lower opportunity costs than others, and let others who can do other things at lower opportunity costs than they can specialize in doing them.

2. **What do we mean by comparative advantage?**
A person, region, or country has a comparative advantage in producing a good or service when it can produce it at a lower opportunity cost than other persons, regions, or countries.

3. **Why does the combination of specialization and trade make us better off?**
   Trade increases wealth by allowing a person, region, or a nation to specialize in those products that it produces relatively better than others and to trade for those products that others produce relatively better than they do. Exploiting our comparative advantages, and then trading, allows us to produce, and therefore consume, more than we could otherwise from our scarce resources.

4. **If you can mow your lawn in half the time it takes your spouse or housemate to do it, do you have a comparative advantage in mowing the lawn?**
   Your faster speed at mowing the lawn does not establish that you have a comparative advantage in mowing. That can only be established relative to other tasks. The person with a comparative advantage in mowing lawns is the one with the lowest opportunity cost, and that could be your spouse or housemate in this case. For instance, if you could earn $12 an hour, mowing the lawn in half an hour implies an opportunity cost of $6 of forgone output elsewhere. If they could only earn $5 per hour (because they were less than half as productive doing other things compared to you), the opportunity cost of them mowing the lawn in an hour is $5. In this case, your spouse or housemate has a comparative advantage in mowing the lawn.

5. **If you have a current comparative advantage in doing the dishes, and you then become far more productive than before in completing yard chores, could that eliminate your comparative advantage? Why or why not?**
   The opportunity cost of you doing the dishes is the value of other chores you must give up to do the dishes. Therefore, an increase in your productivity doing yard chores would increase the opportunity cost of doing the dishes, and could well eliminate your current comparative advantage in doing the dishes compared to other members of your family.

6. **Could a student who gets a C in one class but a D or worse in everything else have a comparative advantage over someone who gets a B in that class but an A in everything else? Explain this concept using opportunity cost.**
   A student who gets a C in a class is less good, in an absolute sense, at that class than a student who gets a B in it. But if the C student gets Ds in other classes, he is relatively, or comparatively, better at the C class, while if the B student gets As in other classes, she is relatively, or comparatively, worse at that class.

2.6 Markets and Improved Efficiency

1. **Why must every society choose some manner in which to allocate its scarce resources?**
   Every society must choose some manner in which to allocate its scarce resources because the collective wants of its members always far outweigh what the scarce resources nature has provided can produce.

2. **How does a market system allocate resources?**
   A market system allows individuals, both as producers and consumers, to indicate their wants and desires through their actions—how much they are willing to buy or sell at various prices. The market then acts to bring about that level of prices that allows buyers and sellers to coordinate their plans.

3. **What do market prices communicate to others in society?**
   The prices charged by suppliers communicate the relative availability of products to consumers; the prices consumers are willing to pay communicate the relative value consumers place on products to producers. That is, market prices provide a way for both consumers and suppliers to communicate about the relative value of resources.

4. **How do price controls undermine the market as a communication device?**
   Price controls—both price floors and price ceilings—prevent the market from communicating relevant information between consumers and suppliers. A price floor set above the market price prevents suppliers from communicating their willingness to sell for less to consumers. A price ceiling set below the market price prevents consumers from indicating their willingness to pay more to suppliers.

5. **Why can markets sometimes fail to allocate resources efficiently?**
   Markets can sometimes fail to allocate resources efficiently. Such situations, called market failures, represent situations such as externalities, where costs can be imposed on some individuals without their consent (e.g., from dumping "crud" in their air or water), where information in the market may not be communicated honestly and accurately, and where firms may have market power to distort prices in their favor (against consumers' interests).

CHAPTER 2 STUDY GUIDE

True or False:

1. In economics, labor as a factor of production does not include mental effort, and land does not include natural resources found under land, such as oil deposits.
2. Entrepreneurship is motivated by the prospect of earning profits.
3. Economic analysis only applies to tangible goods.
4. Everyone except the wealthiest faces scarcity.
5. Increases in production could enable us to reduce poverty but not eliminate scarcity.
6. Even unlimited resources would not eliminate the necessity to choose among our desires.
7. "There's no such thing as a free lunch" is a way of saying that every choice has an opportunity cost.
8. Following the rule of rational choice does not guarantee that their choices will always make people better off.
9. Trying to achieve zero levels of pollution, crime, and risk are sensible applications of the rule of rational choice.
10. While some choices are all or nothing, most choices are marginal choices involving how much of something to do.
11. Treating average costs as if they were marginal costs can lead to mistaken choices.
12. Positive incentives increase benefits or costs, increasing the level of the related activity or behavior; negative incentives reduce benefits or costs, decreasing the level of the related activity or behavior.
13. The economic analysis of safety focuses not on whether a product is safe in an absolute sense, but rather on the tradeoffs between additional safety and additional amounts of other goods and services.
14. Voluntary trade increases wealth because both parties expect to be better off. Fraud, however, can result in a trader being worse off.
15. People gain by specializing in the production of whichever goods in which they have a absolute advantage.
16. When there are greater restrictions on the ability to trade, people would gain less by specializing in those areas where they have a comparative advantage.
17. Government price floors can make goods appear scarcer than they actually are to buyers.
18. When the economy produces too little or too much of something, government intervention will always improve society's well-being.
19. Governments can easily change the distribution of output among members of society without changing what goods will be produced and in what quantities.

Multiple Choice:

1. Which of the following is not part of the economic way of thinking?
    a. When an option becomes less costly, individuals will become more likely to choose it.
    b. Costs are incurred whenever scarce resources are used to produce goods or services.
    c. The value of a good is determined by its cost of production.
    d. In choosing between two goods with the same opportunity cost, individuals choose the good that they expect will give them a greater benefit.
2. Ted has decided to buy a burger and fries at a restaurant but is considering whether to buy a drink as well. If the price of a burger is 3 Euros, fries are 2 Euros, and drinks are 2 Euros, but a meal with all three costs 5.40 Euros, the marginal cost to Ted of the drink is
    a. 5.40 Euros.
    b. 1.40 Euros.
    c. 0.40 Euros.
    d. 2.00 Euros.
    e. impossible to determine from the information given.

3. If a country wants to maximize the value of its output,
   a. each job should be carried out by the person who has the highest opportunity cost of doing it.
   b. each job should be carried out by the person who has an absolute advantage in it.
   c. each job should be carried out by the person who can complete it most rapidly.
   d. each job should be carried out by the person who enjoys that job the most.
   e. None of the above is correct.

4. Who would be most likely to drop out of college before graduation?
   a. A chemistry major who has just been reading about the terrific jobs available for those with chemistry degrees.
   b. A star basketball player who has just received a multimillion-dollar professional contract offer after his junior year.
   c. A math major with a B average.
   d. An economics major who wishes to go to graduate school.

5. "If I hadn't been set up on this blind date tonight, I would have saved $50 and spent the evening watching TV." The opportunity cost of the date is
   a. smaller, the more you enjoy the date.
   b. higher, the more you like that night's TV shows.
   c. $50, plus the cost to you of giving up a night of TV.
   d. $50.
   e. described by both b. and c.

6. Say you had an 8 A.M. accounting class, but you would still come to campus at the same time even if you skipped your accounting class. The cost of choosing to go to the accounting class would not include
   a. the cost of the gasoline it took to get to campus.
   b. the value of the time it took to drive to campus.
   c. the cost of insuring the car for that day.
   d. any of the above.

7. Which of the following would not raise your opportunity cost of attending a big basketball game this Sunday night?
   a. You find out that your personal favorite player, who normally doesn't play much, will start for the first time in that game.
   b. Late Friday afternoon, your physics professor makes a surprise announcement that there will be a major exam on Monday morning.
   c. Your employer offers you double your usual wage to work this Sunday night.
   d. A friend calls you up and offers you free tickets to a concert by one of your favorite bands on Sunday night.
   e. All of the above will raise the opportunity cost of attending the game

8. Which of the following demonstrates marginal thinking?
   a. Deciding to never eat meat
   b. Deciding to spend one more hour studying economics tonight because you think the improvement on your next test will be large enough to make it worthwhile to you
   c. Working out an extra hour per week
   d. Both b. and c. demonstrate marginal thinking.

9. If resources and goods are free to move between countries, and Spanish producers choose to specialize in growing oranges while Portugese producers choose to specialize in growing tangerines, then we could reasonably conclude that
   a. the opportunity cost of growing tangerines is lower in Portugal than in Spain.
   b. the opportunity cost of growing oranges is lower in Spain than in Portugal.
   c. Portugal has a comparative advantage in producing tangerines.
   e. Spain has a comparative advantage in producing oranges.
   e. all of the above are true.

10. If an American driver who had no change and whose cell phone battery was dead got stranded near a pay phone and chose to buy two quarters from a passerby for a dollar bill,
    a. the passerby was made better off and the driver was made worse off by the transaction.
    b. the transaction made the driver worse off by 50 cents.
    c. both a. and b. are true.
    d. both the passerby and the driver were made better off by the transaction.

11. Which of the following is true?
    a. What one trader gains from a trade, the other must lose.
    b. Voluntary exchange is expected to be advantageous to both parties to the exchange.
    c. Voluntary trades involve exchanges of things of equal value.
    d. If one party to a potential voluntary trade decides it does not advance his interests, he can veto the potential trade.
    e. Both b. and d. are true.

12. Which of the following is correct?
    a. Only by eliminating scarcity could a minimal level of income conceivably be provided to all individuals.
    b. Even in the wealthiest of countries, the desire for material goods is greater than productive capabilities.
    c. If not for greed, scarcity would not exist.
    d. Scarcity and poverty are basically the same thing.
    e. Both a. and b. are correct.

13. Which of the following would economists consider a capital resource?
    a. 20,000 Euros in a bank account.
    b. A bond issued by a company selling construction equipment.
    c. An electric generator.
    d. Shares of stock in a computer software company.

14. Which of the following statements is false?
    a. The opportunity cost of a decision can exceed the monetary cost.
    b. The opportunity cost of a decision is the value of the best forgone alternative.
    c. The lowest dollar cost option need not be the lowest opportunity cost option.
    d. The opportunity cost of attending college is the same for all students at the same university but may differ among students at different universities.
    e. All of the above statements are true.

15. The opportunity cost of choosing to attend college is does not include which of the following?
    a. Tuition fees.
    b. The income you forgo in order to attend classes.
    c. The cost of food eaten during the school term.
    d. The cost of required textbooks.
    e. The cost of paper and pencils needed to take notes.

16. The opportunity cost of a passenger taking a particular airplane flight
    a. differs between passengers only to the extent that each traveler pays a different airfare.
    b. can differ between passengers who pay the same airfare.
    c. differs between passengers only to the extent that the foregone value of the travel time differs.
    d. cannot change once she has booked her flight.
    e. Both b. and d. are true.

17. Rene's boss offers him triple his usual wage rate to work tonight instead of taking his girlfriend on a romantic date. This offer will likely
    a. not affect the opportunity cost of going on the date.
    b. increase the opportunity cost of going on the date.
    c. reduce the opportunity cost of going on the date because giving up the additional work dollars will make his girlfriend feel even more appreciated.
    d. not be taken into consideration by Rene when deciding what to do tonight.

18. Which of the following is most consistent with rational behavior?
    a. analyzing the average costs of a decision.
    b. analyzing the total benefits of a decision.
    c. continuing to undertake an activity as long as the total benefits exceed the total costs.
    d. undertaking activities whenever the marginal benefit exceeds the marginal cost.
    e. undertaking activities as long as the marginal benefit exceeds zero.

19. Liters of milk at a local store are priced at one for 2 Euros or two for 3 Euros. The marginal cost of buying a second gallon of milk equals
    a. Zero.
    b. 1 Euro.
    c. 2 Euros.
    d. 3 Euros.
    e. 5 Euros.
20. Which of the following statements is most consistent with the rule of rational choice?
    a. Police forces should be enlarged until virtually all crime is eliminated.
    b. Manufacturers of automobiles should seek to make cars safer, no matter the costs involved.
    c. We should strive to eliminate virtually all air and water pollution.
    d. When evaluating new prescription drugs, one should weigh each drug's potential health benefits against the potential health risks posed by known side effects.
21. Megan is an attorney who is also an excellent typist. She can type 120 words per minute, but she is pressed for time because she has all the legal work she can handle at 150 Euros per hour. Megan's friend Robert works as a waiter and would like some typing work (provided that he can make at least his wage, including tips, as a waiter, which is 50 Euros per hour). Robert can type 60 words per minute. According to the law of comparative advantage,
    a. Megan should do all the typing because she is faster.
    b. Megan should hire Robert to type for her.
    c. If Robert suddenly could only type 50 words per minute, Megan should still hire Robert to type for her.
    d. Both b. and c. are correct.

Problems:

1. The automotive revolution after World War II reduced the time involved for travel and shipping goods. This innovation allowed the economy to produce more goods and services since it freed resources involved in transportation for other uses. The transportation revolution also increased wants. Identify two ways the car and truck revealed new wants.

2. Which of the following goods are scarce?
    a. clothes
    b. garbage
    c. salt water in the ocean
    d. a public library
    e. clean air in a big city
    f. dirty air in a big city

3. Explain why scarcity and poverty are not the same thing.

4. List some things that you need. Then ask yourself if you would still want some of those things if the price were five times higher. Would you still want them if the price were 10 times higher?

5. List the opportunity costs of the following:
    a. going to college.
    b. missing a lecture in a college class.
    c. withdrawing and spending 100 Euros from your savings account, which earns 5 percent interest annually.
    d. going snowboarding on the weekend before final examinations.

6. McDonald's once ran a promotion that whenever St. Louis Cardinal's slugger Mark McGwire hit a home run into the upper deck at Busch Stadium, McDonald's gave anyone with a ticket to that day's game a free Big Mac. If holders of ticket stubs have to stand in line for ten minutes, is the Big Mac really "free?"

7. The price of a one-way Chunnel trip from Great Britain to France is 150 pounds. Sarah, a school teacher, pays the same price in February (during the school year) as in July (during her vacation), so the opportunity cost of the trip to her is the same in February as in July. Do you agree?

8. Explain why following the rule of rational choice can make a person better off.

9. Which of the following activities require marginal thinking. Why?
    a. studying
    b. eating
    c. driving
    d. shopping
    e. getting ready for a night out

10. Should you go to the movies this Friday? List the factors that affect the possible benefits and costs of this decision. Explain where uncertainty affects the benefits and costs.

11. Modern medicine has made organ transplants a common occurrence, yet the number of organs that people want far exceeds the available supply. According to CNN, ten people die each day because of a lack of transplantable organs like kidneys and livers. Some economists have recommended that an organ market be established through which doctors and others could pay people for the right to use their organs when they die. The law currently forbids the sale of organs. What do you think of such a proposal? What kind of incentives would an organ market provide for people to allow others to use their organs? What would happen to the supply of organs if, instead of relying on donated kidneys, livers, and retinas, doctors and hospitals could bid for them? What drawbacks would a free market in organs have? Have you made arrangements to leave your organs to your local organ bank? Would you do so if you could receive 50,000 Euros for them?

12. Which of the following are positive incentives? Negative incentives? Why?
    a. a fine for not cleaning up after your dog defecates in the park.
    b. a trip to Hawaii paid for by your parents or significant other for earning an A in your economics course.
    c. a higher tax on cigarettes and alcohol.
    d. a subsidy for installing solar panels on your house.

13. Throughout history, many countries have chosen the path of self-sufficiency, choosing to not trade with other countries. Explain why this path would make a country poorer.

14. Why is it important that the country or region with the lower opportunity cost produce the good? How would you use the concept of comparative advantage to argue for reducing restrictions on trade between countries?

15. Farmer John can grow soybeans and corn. He can grow 50 bushels of soybeans or 100 bushels of corn on an acre of his land for the same cost. The price of soybeans is $1.50 per bushel and the price of corn is $.60 per bushel. Show the benefits to John of specialization. What should he specialize in?

16. Which region do you think has a comparative advantage in the following goods:
    a. Wheat: Colombia or the United States?
    b. Coffee: Colombia or the United States?
    c. Timber: Iowa or Washington?
    d. Corn: Iowa or Washington?

17. Which of the following would cause the relative value and, hence, price, of potatoes to rise?
    a. The prices of wheat, rice, and other substitutes for potatoes fall dramatically.
    b. A fungus infestation wipes out half the Idaho potato crop.
    c. The price of potato chips rises.
    d. Scientists find that eating potato chips makes you better looking.

18. People communicate with each other in the market through the effect their decisions to buy or sell have on prices. Indicate whether each of the following would increase or decrease the price of the good in question.
    a. What happens to the price of Jack Russell terriers after people who see an energetic and loveable Jack Russell Terrier in a popular TV series want Jack Russell Terriers as pets?
    b. What would happen to the price of housing in Tampa, Florida, if aging retirees begin flocking there to live?
    c. What would happen to the price of coffee if weather-related crop failures in Colombia and Costa Rica reduce coffee supplies?
    d. What would happen to the price of sugar if sugar cane fields in Hawaii and Louisiana are replaced with housing?
    e. What would happen to the wages of American doctors if more and more students graduate from U.S. medical schools?
    f. What would happen to the price of gasoline if Americans begin driving bigger, gas-guzzling cars like SUVs, and driving them more miles?

19. Imagine that you are trying to decide whether to cross a street without using the designated crosswalk at the traffic signal. What are the expected marginal benefits of crossing? The expected marginal costs? How would the following conditions change your benefit–cost equation?
    a. The closest crosswalk was 10 feet away.
    b. The closest crosswalk was a mile away.
    c. A police officer was standing 100 feet away.
    d. You were in a huge hurry.
    e. The street was empty and it was 3 A.M.
    f. The street was busy.

3 Scarcity, Trade-Offs, and Production Possibilities

3.1 The Three Economic Questions Every Society Faces

3.2 The Circular Flow Model

3.3 The Production Possibilities Curve

3.4 Economic Growth and the Production Possibilities Curve

This chapter builds on the foundations of the preceding chapters. We have learned that we have unlimited wants and limited resources—that is, we all face scarcity. And scarcity forces us to choose.

To get one thing we like, we usually have to give up something else we want—that is, people face trade-offs. Recognizing these trade-offs will allow us to make better decisions.

Every economy must transform the resources that nature provides into goods and services. Economics is the study of that process. This chapter begins with a discussion of how every economy must respond to three fundamental questions: What goods and services will be produced? How will the goods and services be produced? Who will get the goods and services?

In this chapter, we introduce our first economic models: the circular flow model and the production possibilities curve. In the circular flow model, we show how decisions made by households and firms interact with each other. Our second model, the production possibilities curve, employs many of the most important concepts in economics: scarcity, trade-offs, increasing opportunity costs, efficiency, investment in capital goods, and economic growth. ■

SECTION 3.1 The Three Economic Questions Every Society Faces

* What goods and services will be produced?
* How will the goods and services be produced?
* Who will get the goods and services?

Scarcity and the Allocation of Resources

Collectively, our wants far exceed what can be produced from nature's scarce resources. So how should we allocate those scarce resources? Some methods of resource allocation might seem bad and counterproductive—for example, the "survival of the fittest" competition that takes place on the floor of the jungle. Physical violence has been used since the beginning of time, as people, regions, and countries attacked one another to gain control over resources. We could argue that government should allocate scarce resources on the basis of equal shares or according to need. However, this approach poses problems because of diverse individual preferences, the difficulty of ascertaining needs, and the negative work and investment incentives involved. In reality, society is made up of many approaches to resource allocation. For now, we will focus on one form of allocating goods and services found in most countries—the market economy.

Because of scarcity, certain economic questions must be answered, regardless of the level of affluence of the society or its political structure. We will consider three fundamental questions that every society inevitably faces: (1) What goods and services will be produced? (2) How will the goods and services be produced? (3) Who will get the goods and services produced? These questions are unavoidable in a world of scarcity.

What Goods and Services Will Be Produced?

How do individuals control production decisions in market-oriented economies? Questions arise such as should society produce more baseball stadiums or more schools? Should Apple produce more iPhones or laptops? The government has a limited budget, too,

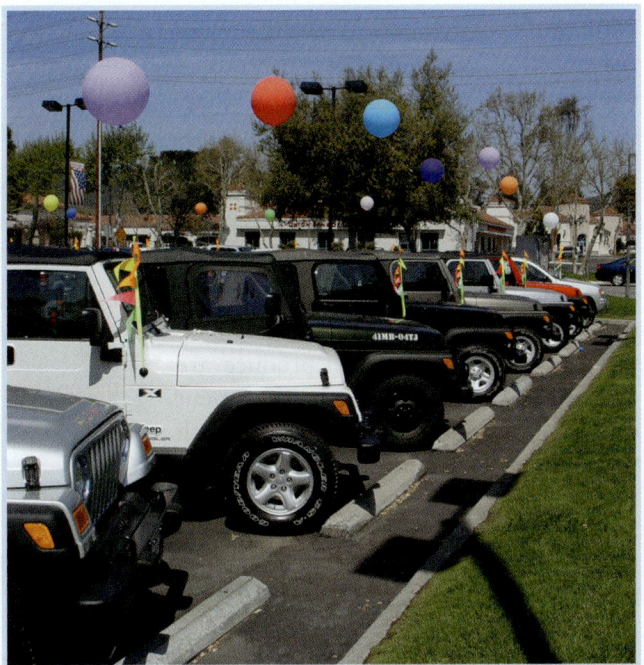

How do we decide which colors and options to include with these cars?

consumer sovereignty consumers vote with their dollars in a market economy; this accounts for what is produced

and must make choices on how much to spend on defense, health care, highways, and education. In short, consumers, firms, and government must all make choices about what goods and services will be produced and each one of those decisions has an opportunity cost—the highest valued alternative forgone. In the marketplace, the answer to these and other similar questions is that people "vote" in economic affairs with their dollars (or pounds or yen). This concept is called **consumer sovereignty**. Consumer sovereignty explains how individual consumers in market economies determine what is to be produced.

Televisions, DVD players, cell phones, ipods, camcorders, and computers, for example, became part of our lives because consumers "voted" hundreds of dollars apiece on these goods. As they bought more color TVs, consumers "voted" fewer dollars on regular color

TVs and more on high definition TVs. Similarly, vinyl record albums gave way to tapes, CDs to downloadable music as consumers voted for these items with their dollars. If consumers vote for more fuel efficient cars and healthier foods, then firms that wish to remain profitable must listen and respond.

How Different Types of Economic Systems Answer the Question "What Goods and Services Will Be Produced?"

Economies are organized in different ways to answer the question of what is to be produced. The dispute over the best way to answer this question has inflamed passions for centuries. Should a central planning board make the decisions, as in North Korea and Cuba? Sometimes this highly centralized economic system is referred to as a **command economy**. Under this type of regime, decisions about how many tractors or automobiles to produce are largely determined by a government official or committee associated with the central planning organization. That same group decides on the number and size of school buildings, refrigerators, shoes, and so on. Other countries, including the United States, much of Europe, and, increasingly, Asia and elsewhere have largely adopted a decentralized decision-making process where literally millions of individual producers and consumers of goods and services determine what goods, and how many of them, will be produced. A country that uses such a decentralized decision-making process is often said to have a **market economy**. Actually, no nation has a pure market economy. The United States, along with most countries, is said to have a **mixed economy**. In such an economy, the government and the private sector together determine the allocation of resources.

> **command economy**
> economy in which the government uses central planning to coordinate most economic activities
>
> **market economy**
> an economy that allocates goods and services through the private decisions of consumers, input suppliers, and firms
>
> **mixed economy**
> an economy where government and the private sector determine the allocation of resources
>
> **labor intensive**
> production that uses a large amount of labor
>
> **capital intensive**
> production that uses a large amount of capital

machines or more workers. For example, a company might decide to move their production to a plant in another country that uses more workers and fewer machines.

A ditch can be dug by many workers using their hands, by a few workers with shovels, or by one person with a backhoe. Someone must decide which method is most appropriate. From this example, you might be tempted to conclude that it is desirable to use the biggest, most elaborate form of capital. But would you really want to plant your spring flowers with huge earthmoving machinery? That is, the most capital-intensive method of production may not always be the best. The best method is the least-cost method.

What Is the Best Form of Production?

The best or "optimal" form of production will usually vary from one economy to the next. For example, earthmoving machinery is used in digging large ditches in the United States and Europe, while in developing countries, shovels are often used. Why do these optimal forms of production vary? Compared with capital, labor is relatively cheap and plentiful in developing countries but relatively scarce and expensive in the United States. In contrast, capital (machines and tools, mainly) is comparatively plentiful and cheap in the United States but scarcer and more costly in developing countries. That is, in developing countries, production tends to be more **labor intensive**, or labor driven. In the United States, production tends to be more **capital intensive**, or capital driven. Each nation tends to use the production processes that conserve its relatively scarce (and thus relatively more expensive) resources and use more of its relatively abundant resources.

How Will the Goods and Services Be Produced?

All economies, regardless of their political structure, must decide how to produce the goods and services that they want—because of scarcity. Goods and services can generally be produced in several ways. Firms may face a trade-off between using more

Who Will Get the Goods and Services Produced?

In every society, some mechanism must exist to determine how goods and services are to be distributed among the population. Who gets what? Why do some people get to consume or use far more goods and services than others? This question of distribution is so important that wars and revolutions have been fought over it. Both the French and Russian revolutions were concerned fundamentally with the distribution of goods and services. Even in societies where political questions are usually settled peacefully, the question of the distribution of income is an issue that always arouses strong emotional responses. As we will see, in a market economy with private ownership and control of the means of production, the amounts of goods and services an individual can obtain depend on her or his income. Income, in turn, will depend on the quantity and quality of the scarce resources the individual controls. Income is also determined by the price others are willing and able to pay for what you have to sell. If you are a medical doctor and make $300,000 a year, that is income you will have available to buy goods and services. If you also own a condominium you rent out in Aspen, Colorado, you will have an even greater amount of income to spend on goods and services. For instance, markets reward education, hard work, and training. Education (years of schooling) and earnings are highly (positively) correlated. For example, Oprah Winfrey makes a lot of money because she has unique and marketable skills as a talk show host. This basis for distribution may or may not be viewed as "fair," an issue we will look at in detail later in this book.

Castaway and Resource Allocation

In the movie *Castaway,* Chuck Noland's (played by Tom Hanks) plane crashes and he finds himself on a

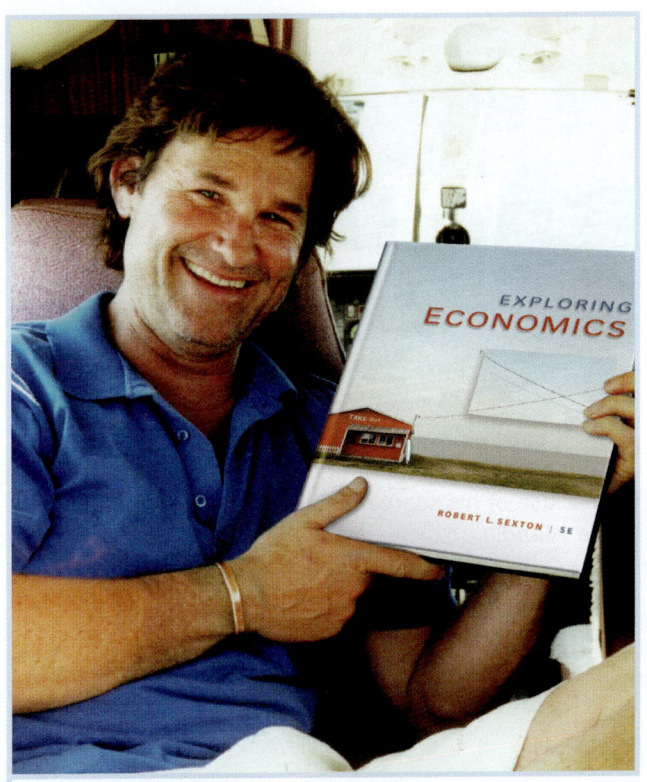

Actor Kurt Russell gets paid a lot of money because he controls scarce resources: his talent and his name recognition. As we will see in Chapter 5, people's talents and other goods and services in limited supply relative to demand will command high prices. He also has good taste in his reading material!

Use what you've LEARNED — MARKET SIGNALS

Q Adam was a college graduate with a major in art. A few years ago, Adam decided that he wanted to pursue a vocation that utilized his talent. In response, he shut himself up in his studio and created a watercolor collection. With high hopes, Adam put his collection on display for buyers. After several years of displaying his art, however, the only one interested in the collection was his 18-year-old sister, who wanted the picture frames for her room. Recognizing that Adam was having trouble pursuing his chosen occupation, Adam's friend Karl told him that the market had failed. In the meantime, Adam turned to house painting (interior and exterior) and business was booming. Adam hired five workers and would often be painting all day and into the evenings and weekends. Do you think the market has failed?

A No. Markets provide important signals, and the signal being sent in this situation is that Adam should look for some other means of support—something that society values. Remember the function of consumer sovereignty in the marketplace. Clearly, consumers were not voting for Adam's art. The market seems to be telling Adam: less painting on canvas and more painting on walls, doors, and trim.

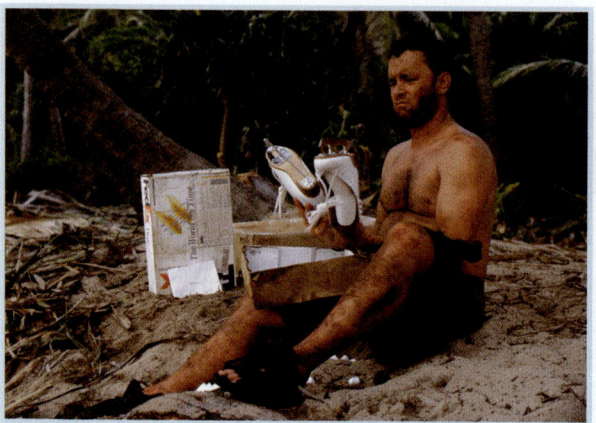

Chuck Noland (Tom Hanks) had to make the best use of his scarce resources to survive on the island.

deserted island, and he has to find a way to survive. On the island, he must find answers to the *what*, *how*, and *for whom* questions. The *for whom* question is pretty easy: He is the only one on the island—he gets what is produced. The *what* question is pretty easy, too: He is trying to survive, so he is looking to produce food, shelter, and clothing. The *how* question is where this scene becomes interesting. Noland salvages several boxes from the plane crash. After a failed attempt to leave the island, he decides to open the boxes to see whether they contain anything useful. He first finds a pair of ice skates. He uses the blades of the ice skates as a knife to open coconuts, to cut a dress to convert into a fishing net, and to sharpen a stick to use as a spear for catching fish. He uses the laces from the skate and the bubble wrap in the package to dress an injury. He uses the raft as a lean-to for his shelter. He builds a fire and even "makes" a friend out of a volleyball. In short, Noland must use his entrepreneurial talents to make the best use of the scarce resources to survive on the island.

SECTION CHECK

1. Every economy has to decide what goods and services to produce.
2. In a decentralized market economy, millions of buyers and sellers determine what and how much to produce.
3. In a mixed economy, the government and the private sector determine the allocation of resources.
4. The best form of production is the one that conserves the relatively scarce (more costly) resources and uses more of the abundant (less costly) resources.
5. When capital is relatively scarce and labor plentiful, production tends to be labor intensive.
6. When capital is relatively abundant and labor relatively scarce, production tends to be capital intensive.
7. In a market economy, the amount of goods and services one is able to obtain depends on one's income.
8. The amount of an individual's income depends on the quantity and quality of the scarce resources that he or she controls.

---

1. Why does scarcity force us to decide what to produce?
2. How is a command economy different from a market economy?
3. How does consumer sovereignty determine production decisions in a market economy?
4. Do you think that what and how much an economy produces depends on who will get the goods and services produced in that economy? Why or why not?
5. Why do consumers have to "vote" for a product with their dollars for it to be a success?
6. Why must we choose among multiple ways of producing the goods and services we want?
7. Why might production be labor intensive in one economy but be capital intensive in another?
8. If a tourist from the United States on an overseas trip notices that other countries don't produce crops "like they do back home," would he be right to conclude that farmers in the other countries produce crops less efficiently than U.S. farmers?
9. In what way does scarcity determine income?
10. What are the most important functions of the market system?

SECTION 3.2 The Circular Flow Model

* What are product markets?
* What are factor markets?
* What is the circular flow model?

How do we explain how the millions of people in an economy interact when it comes to buying, selling, producing, working, hiring, and so on? A continuous flow of goods and services is bought and sold between the producers of goods and services (which we call firms) and the buyers of goods and services (which we call households). A continuous flow of income also moves from firms to households as firms buy inputs to produce the goods and services they sell. In our simple economy, these exchanges take place in product markets and factor markets.

Product Markets

Product markets are the markets for consumer goods and services. In the product market, households are buyers and firms are sellers. Households buy the goods and services that firms produce and sell. The payments from the households to the firms, for the purchases of goods and services, flow to the firms at the same time as goods and services flow to the households.

Factor Markets

Factor or input markets are where households sell the use of their inputs (capital, land, labor, and entrepreneurship) to firms. In the factor market, households are the sellers and firms are the buyers. Households receive money payments from firms as compensation for the labor, land, capital, and entrepreneurship needed to produce goods and services. These payments take the form of wages (salaries), rent, interest payments, and profit.

> **product markets**
> markets where households are buyers and firms are sellers of goods and services
>
> **factor (or input) markets**
> markets where households sell the use of their inputs (capital, land, labor, and entrepreneurship) to firms
>
> **simple circular flow model**
> an illustration of the continuous flow of goods, services, inputs, and payments between firms and households

The Simple Circular Flow Model

The simple circular flow model is illustrated in Exhibit 1. In the top half of the exhibit, the product markets, households purchase goods and services that firms have produced. In the lower half of the exhibit, the factor (or input) markets, households sell the inputs that firms use to produce goods and services. Households receive income (wages, rent, interest, and profit) from firms for the inputs used in production (capital, land, labor, and entrepreneurship).

Let's take a simple example to see how the circular flow model works. Suppose a teacher's supply of labor generates personal income in the form of wages (the factor market), which she can use to buy automobiles, vacations, food, and other goods (the product market). Suppose she buys an automobile (product market); the automobile dealer now has revenue to pay for his inputs (factor market)—wages to workers, purchase of new cars to replenish his inventory, rent for his building, and so on. So we see that in the simple circular flow model, income flows from firms to households (factor markets), and spending flows from households to firms (product markets). The simple circular flow model shows how households and firms interact in product markets and factor markets and how the two markets are interrelated.

section 3.2
exhibit 1 — The Circular Flow Diagram

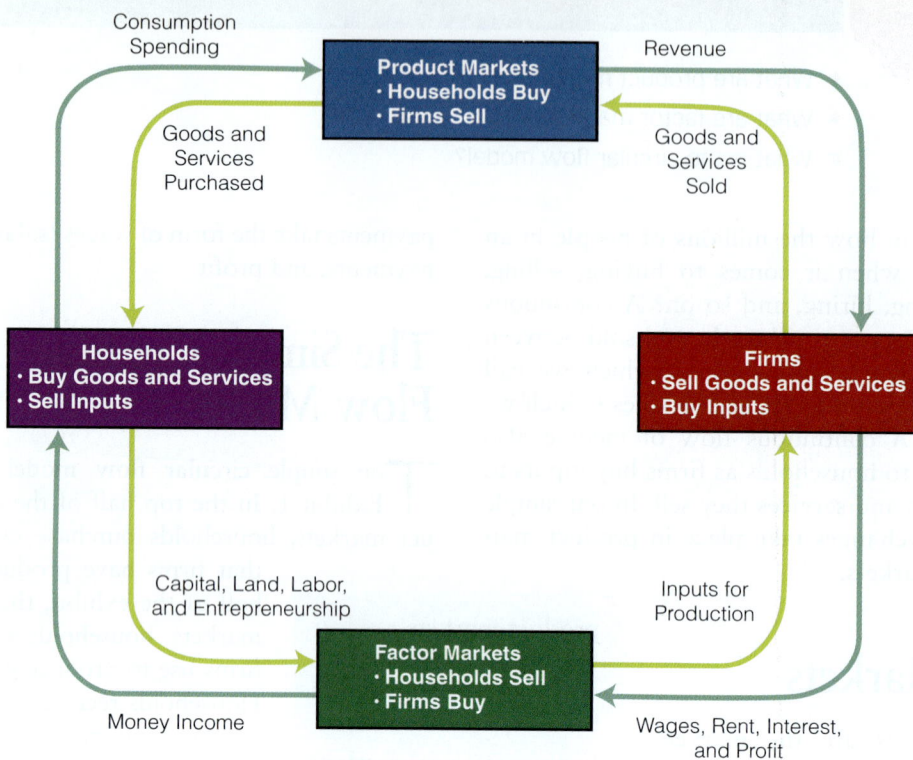

The circular flow diagram is a visual model of the economy. Households and firms interact with each other in product markets (where households buy and firms sell) and factor markets (where households sell and firms buy). For example, households receive income from firms in exchange for working and providing other inputs. Households then recycle that income to firms in exchange for goods and services. Dollars flow clockwise, and goods and services flow counterclockwise.

SECTION CHECK

1. In the product market, households are buyers and firms are sellers.
2. In the factor market, households are sellers and firms are buyers.
3. Wages, rent, interest, and profits are the payments for the labor, land, capital, and entrepreneurship needed to produce goods and services. These transactions are carried out in factor, or input, markets.
4. The circular flow model illustrates the flow of goods, services, and payments among firms and households.

---

1. Why does the circular flow of money move in the opposite direction from the flow of goods and services?
2. What is bought and sold in factor markets?
3. What is bought and sold in product markets?

SECTION 3.3 The Production Possibilities Curve

- What is a production possibilities curve?
- What are unemployed resources?
- What are underemployed resources?
- What is efficiency?
- What is the law of increasing opportunity costs?

The Production Possibilities Curve

production possibilities curve the potential total output combinations of any two goods for an economy

The economic concepts of scarcity, choice, and trade-offs can be illustrated visually by means of a simple graph called a production possibilities curve. The **production possibilities curve** represents the potential total output combinations of any two goods for an economy, given the inputs and technology available to the economy. That is, it illustrates an economy's potential for allocating its limited resources in producing various combinations of goods, in a given time period.

The Production Possibilities Curve for Grades in Economics and History

What would the production possibilities curve look like if you were "producing" grades in two of your classes—say, economics and history? Exhibit 1 shows a hypothetical production possibilities curve for your expected grade in economics (on the vertical axis), and your expected grade in history (on the horizontal axis). Suppose you have a part-time restaurant job, so you choose to study 10 hours a week. You like both courses and are equally adept at studying for both.

We see in Exhibit 1 that the production possibilities curve is a straight line. For example, if you spend the full 10 hours studying economics, your expected grade in economics is 95 percent (an A), and your expected grade in history is 55 percent (an F). Of course, this outcome assumes you can study zero

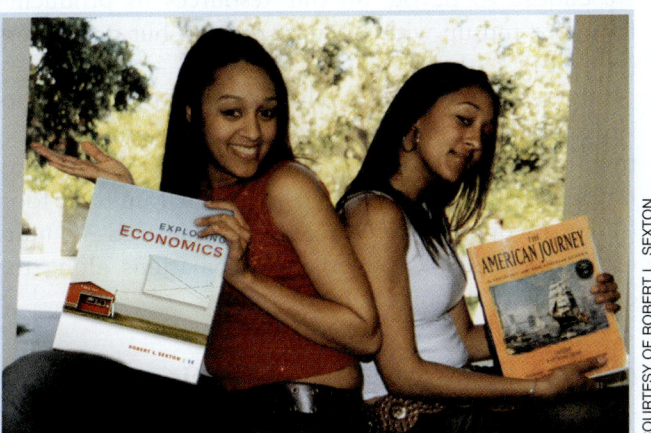

Because Tia and Tamera only have so many hours a week to study, studying more for economics and less for history might hurt their grade in history, *ceteris paribus*. Life is full of trade-offs.

section 3.3 exhibit 1 Production Possibilities Curve: "Producing" Grades in Economics and History

A 95% — 10 Hours Economics, 0 Hours History
B 85% — 7.5 Hours Economics, 2.5 Hours History
C 75% — 5 Hours Economics, 5 Hours History
D 65% — 2.5 Hours Economics, 7.5 Hours History
F 55% — 0 Hours Economics, 10 Hours History

Expected Grade in History: 55% F, 65% D, 75% C, 85% B, 95% A

The production possibilities curve highlights the concept of trade-offs. Assuming you choose to study a total of 10 hours a week, moving down the production possibilities curve shows that if you use your time to study history instead of economics, you can raise your expected grade in history but only at the expense of lowering your expected grade in economics. That is, with a straight-line production possibilities curve, the opportunity costs are constant.

section 3.3 exhibit 2 Production Possibilities Curve: The Trade-Off Between Food and Shelter

Combinations	Shelter (units)	Food (units)
A	10	0
B	9	20
C	7	40
D	4	60
E	0	80

Each point on the production possibilities curve represents the potential amounts of food and shelter that can be produced in a given period, with a given quantity and quality of resources in the economy to use for production. All the points on the production possibilities curve are efficient. Any point in the shaded area, such as point I, is inefficient. Any point outside the production possibilities curve, such as point N, is not presently attainable.

hours a week and still get a 55 percent average or study the full 10 hours a week and get a 95 percent average. Moving down the production possibilities curve, we see that as you spend more of your time studying history and less on economics, you can raise your expected grade in history but only at the expense of lowering your expected grade in economics. Specifically, moving down along the straight-line production possibilities curve, the trade-off is one lower percentage point in economics for one higher percentage point in history. That is, with a straight-line production possibilities curve, the opportunity costs are constant.

Of course, if you were to increase your overall study time, you would expect higher grades in both courses. But that would be on a different production possibilities curve. Along the production possibilities curve shown in Exhibit 1, we assume that technology and the number of study hours are given.

The Production Possibilities Curve for Food and Shelter

To illustrate the production possibilities curve more clearly, imagine living in an economy that produces just two goods, food and shelter. The fact that we have many goods in the real world makes actual decision making more complicated, but it does not alter the basic principles being illustrated. Each point on the production possibilities curve shown in Exhibit 2 represents the potential amounts of food and shelter that we can produce in a given period, with a given quantity and quality of resources in the economy available for production.

Notice in Exhibit 2 that if we devote all our resources to making shelters, we can produce 10 units of shelter but no food (point A). If, on the other hand, we choose to devote all our resources to producing food, we end up with 80 units of food but no shelters (point E).

In reality, nations rarely opt for production possibility A or E, preferring instead to produce a mixture of goods. For example, our fictional economy might produce 9 units of shelter and 20 units of food (point B) or perhaps 7 units of shelter and 40 units of food (point C). Still other combinations along the curve, such as point D, are possible.

Off the Production Possibilities Curve

The economy cannot operate at point N (not attainable) during the given period because not enough resources are currently available to produce that level of output. However, it is possible the economy can operate inside the production possibilities curve, at point I (inefficient). If the economy is operating at point I, or any other point inside the production possibilities curve, it is not at full capacity and is operating inefficiently. In short, the economy is not using all its scarce resources efficiently; as a result, actual output is less than potential output.

Using Resources Efficiently

Most modern economies have resources that are idle, at least some of the time—during periods of high unemployment, for instance. If those resources were not idle, people would have more scarce goods and services available for their use. Unemployed resources create a serious problem. For example, consider an unemployed coal miner who is unable to find work at a "reasonable" wage, or those unemployed in depressed times when factories are already operating below capacity. Clearly, the resources of these individuals are not being used efficiently.

The fact that factories can operate below capacity suggests that it is not just labor resources that should be most effectively used. Rather, all resources entering into production should be used effectively. However,

---

Use what you've LEARNED: THE PRODUCTION POSSIBILITIES CURVE

Q Imagine that you are the overseer on a small island that only produces two goods, cattle and wheat. About a quarter of the land is not fertile enough for growing wheat, so cattle graze on it. What would happen if you tried to produce more and more wheat, extending your planting even to the less fertile soil?

A Under the law of increasing opportunity cost, as you plant more and more of your acreage in wheat, you would move into some of the rocky, less fertile land, and, consequently, wheat yields on the additional acreage would fall. If you try to plant the entire island with wheat, you would find that some of the rocky, less fertile acreage would yield virtually no extra wheat. It would, however, have been great for cattle grazing—a large loss. Thus, the opportunity cost of using that marginal land for wheat rather than cattle grazing would be high. The law of increasing opportunity cost occurs because resources are not homogeneous (identical) and are not equally adaptable for producing cattle and wheat; some acres are more suitable for cattle grazing, while others are more suitable for wheat growing. This relationship is shown in Exhibit 3, where the vertical lines represent the opportunity cost of growing 10 more bushels of wheat in terms of cattle production sacrificed. You can see that as wheat production increases, the opportunity cost in terms of lost cattle production rises.

section 3.3 exhibit 3 — Opportunity Costs for Cattle and Wheat

The opportunity cost of each 10 bushels of wheat in terms of forgone cattle is measured by the vertical distances. Moving from point A to point F, the opportunity cost of wheat in terms of forgone cattle rises.

social concern focuses on labor, for several reasons. A primary reason is that labor costs are the largest share of production costs. Another major reason is that unemployed or underemployed laborers (whose resources are not being used to their full potential) may have mouths to feed at home, while an unemployed machine does not (although the owner of the unemployed machine may).

Inefficiency and Efficiency

Suppose for some reason employment is widespread or resources are not being put to their best uses. The economy would then be operating at a point inside the production possibilities curve, such as I in Exhibit 2, where the economy is operating inefficiently. At point I, 4 units of shelter and 40 units of food are being produced. By putting unemployed resources to work or by putting already employed resources to better uses, we could expand the output of shelter by 3 units (moving to point C) without giving up any units of food. Alternatively, we could boost food output by 20 units (moving to point D) without reducing shelter output. We could even get more of both food and shelter by moving to a point on the curve between C and D.

Increasing or improving the utilization of resources, then, can lead to greater output of all goods. You may recall from Chapter 2, an efficient use of our resources means that more of everything we want can be available for our use. Thus, *efficiency* requires society to use its resources to the fullest extent—getting the most from our scarce resources and wasting none. If resources are being used efficiently—that is, at some point along a production possibilities curve—then more of one good or service requires the sacrifice of another good or service. Efficiency does not tell us which point along the production possibilities curve is *best*, but it does tell us that points inside the curve cannot be best, because some resources are wasted.

The Law of Increasing Opportunity Cost

As in Exhibit 2, the production possibilities curve in Exhibit 4 is not a straight line like that in Exhibit 1. It is concave from below (that is, bowed outward from the origin). Looking at Exhibit 4, you can see that at low food output, an increase in the amount of food produced will lead to only a small reduction in the

| section 3.3 exhibit 4 | Increasing Opportunity Cost and the Production Possibilities Curve |

The production possibilities curve also illustrates the opportunity cost of producing more of a given product. For example, if we are to increase food output from 40 units to 60 units (moving from point C to point D), we must produce 3 fewer units of shelter. The opportunity cost of those 20 additional units of food is the 3 units of shelter we must forgo. We can see that, moving down the curve from A to E, each additional 20 units of food costs society more and more shelter—the law of increasing opportunity cost.

number of units of shelter produced. For example, increasing food output from 0 to 20 (moving from point A to point B on the curve) requires the use of resources capable of producing 1 unit of shelter. In other words, for the first 20 units of food, 1 unit of shelter must be given up. When food output is higher, however, more units of shelter must be given up when switching additional resources from the production of shelter to food. Moving from point D to point E, for example, an increase in food output of 20 (from 60 to 80) reduces the production of shelters from 4 to 0. At this point, then, the cost of those 20 additional units of food is 4 units of shelter, considerably more than the 1 unit of shelter required in the earlier scenario. This difference shows us that opportunity costs do not remain constant but rise because more units of food and fewer units of shelter are produced. It is this **increasing opportunity cost,** then, that is represented by the bowed production possibilities curve.

> **increasing opportunity cost**
> the opportunity cost of producing additional units of a good rises as society produces more of that good

What Is the Reason for the Law of Increasing Opportunity Cost?

The basic reason for the increasing opportunity cost is that some resources and skills cannot be easily adapted from their current uses to alternative uses. And, the more you produce of one good, the more you are forced to employ inputs that are relatively more suitable for producing other goods. For example, at low levels of food output, additional increases in food output can be obtained easily by switching relatively low skilled carpenters from making shelters to producing food. However, to get even more food output, workers who are less well suited or appropriate for producing food (i.e., they are better adapted to making shelters) must be released from shelter making to increase food output. For example, a skilled carpenter may be an expert at making shelters but a very bad farmer because he lacks the training and skills necessary in that occupation. So using the skilled carpenter to farm results in a relatively greater opportunity cost than using the unskilled carpenter to farm. The production of additional units of food becomes increasingly costly as progressively lower-skilled farmers (but good carpenters) convert to farming.

In short, resources tend to be specialized. As a result, we lose some of their productivity when we transfer those resources from producing what they are relatively good at to producing something they are relatively bad at.

SECTION CHECK

1. The production possibilities curve represents the potential total output combinations of two goods available to a society given its resources and existing technology.
2. If the economy is operating within the production possibilities curve, the economy is operating inefficiently; actual output is less than potential output. A point outside the production possibilities curve is currently unattainable.
3. Efficiency requires society to use its resources to the fullest extent—no wasted resources.
4. A bowed production possibilities curve means that the opportunity costs of producing additional units of a good rise as society produces more of that good (the law of increasing opportunity costs).

1. What does a production possibilities curve illustrate?
2. How are opportunity costs shown by the production possibilities curve?
3. Why do the opportunity costs of added production increase with output?
4. How does the production possibilities curve illustrate increasing opportunity costs?
5. Why are we concerned with widespread amounts of unemployed or underemployed resources in a society?
6. What do we mean by *efficiency,* and how is it related to underemployment of resources?
7. How are efficiency and inefficiency illustrated by a production possibilities curve?
8. Will a country that makes being unemployed illegal be more productive than one that does not? Why or why not?
9. If a 68-year-old worker in the United States chooses not to work at all, does that mean that the United States is functioning inside its production possibilities curve? Why or why not?

SECTION 3.4 Economic Growth and the Production Possibilities Curve

* How much should we sacrifice today to get more in the future?
* How do we show economic growth on the production possibilities curve?

Generating Economic Growth

How have some nations been able to rapidly expand their outputs of goods and services over time, while others have been unable to increase their standards of living at all?

The economy can only grow with qualitative or quantitative changes in the factors of production—land, labor, capital, and entrepreneurship. Advancement in technology, improvements in labor productivity, or new sources of natural resources (such as previously undiscovered oil) could lead to outward shifts of the production possibilities curve.

In terms of the production possibilities curve, an outward shift in the possible combinations of goods and services produced leads to economic growth, as seen in Exhibit 1. With growth comes the possibility of having more of both goods than was previously available. Suppose we were producing at point C (7 units of shelter, 40 units of food) on our original production possibilities curve. Additional resources and/or new methods of using them (technological progress) can lead to new production possibilities, creating the potential for more of all goods (or more of some with no less of others). These increases will push the production possibilities curve outward. For example, if we invest in human capital by training the workers making the shelters, it will increase the productivity of those workers. As a result, they will produce more units of shelter. Ultimately, then, we will use fewer resources to make shelters, freeing them to be used for farming, which will result in more units of food. Notice that at point F (future) on the new curve, we can produce 9 units of shelter and 70 units of food, more of both goods than we previously could produce, at point C.

Growth Does Not Eliminate Scarcity

With all of this discussion of growth, it is important to remember that growth, or increases in a society's output, does not make scarcity disappear.

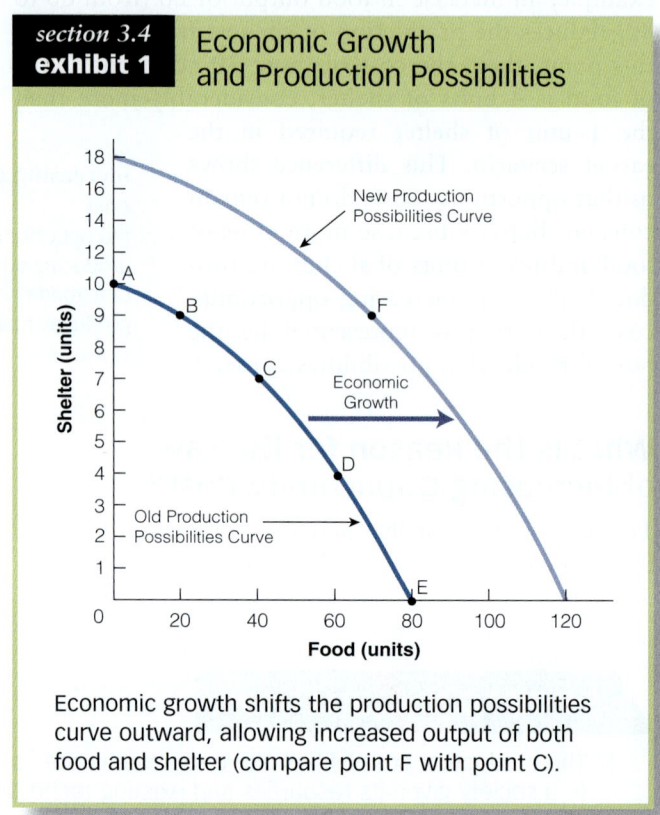

section 3.4 exhibit 1 Economic Growth and Production Possibilities

Economic growth shifts the production possibilities curve outward, allowing increased output of both food and shelter (compare point F with point C).

When output grows more rapidly than population, people are better off. But they still face trade-offs; at any point along the production possibilities curve, to get more of one thing, you must give up something else. There are no free lunches on the production possibilities curve.

Capital Goods Versus Consumption Goods

Economies that choose to invest more of their resources for the future will grow faster than those that don't. To generate economic growth, a society must produce fewer consumer goods—video games, DVD players, cell phones, cars, vacations, and so on—in the present and produce more capital goods—machines, factories, tools, education, and the like. The society that devotes a larger share of its productive capacity to capital

section 3.4 exhibit 2 — Economic Growth and Production Possibilities Curve

Because Economy A invests relatively more in capital goods than does Economy B, Economy A will experience greater economic growth.

goods than to consumer goods will experience greater economic growth. It must sacrifice some present consumption of consumer goods and services to experience growth in the future. Why? Investing in capital goods, such as computers and other new technological equipment, as well as upgrading skills and knowledge, expands the ability to produce in the future. It shifts the economy's production possibilities curve outward, increasing the future production capacity of the economy. That is, the economy that invests more now (consumes less now) will be able to produce, and therefore consume, more in the future. In Exhibit 2, we see that Economy A invests more in capital goods than Economy B. Consequently, Economy A's production possibilities curve shifts outward further than does Economy B's over time.

The Effects of a Technological Change on the Production Possibilities Curve

In Exhibit 3, we see that a technological advance does not have to impact all sectors of the economy equally. There is a technological advance in food production but not in housing production. The technological advance in agriculture causes the production possibilities curve to extend out further on the horizontal axis which measures food production. We can move to any point on the new production possibilities curve. For example, we could move from point A on the original production possibilities curve to point B on the new production possibilities curve. This would lead to 150 more units of food and the same amount of housing—200 units. Or, we could move from point A to point C, which would allow us to produce more units of both food and housing. How do we produce more housing, when the technological

section 3.4 exhibit 3 — The Effects of a Technological Change on the Production Possibilities Curve

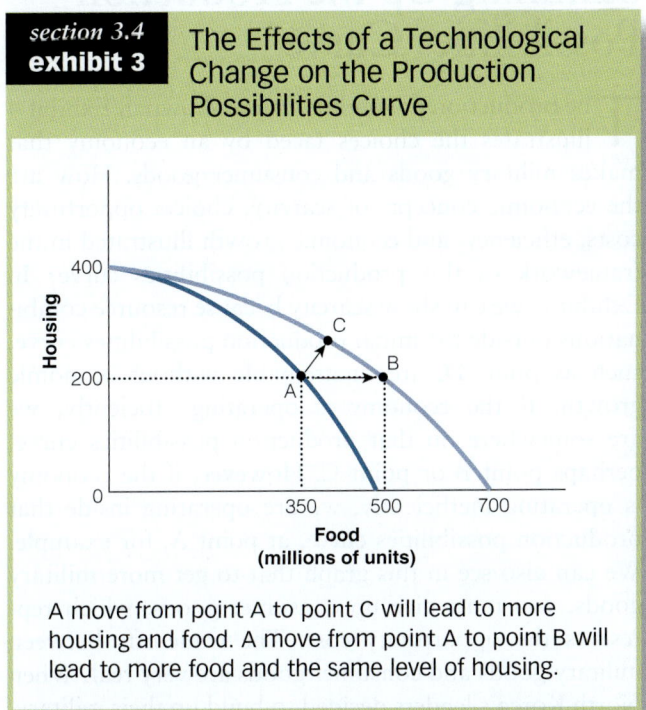

A move from point A to point C will lead to more housing and food. A move from point A to point B will lead to more food and the same level of housing.

Use what you've LEARNED
GUNS AND BUTTER

During most of the 1930s, the United States economy suffered from high rates of unemployment and factories operated far below capacity (point A). As the United States became engaged in the war effort, the economy moved onto its production possibilities curve (point B). The graph shows this scenario, using the production possibilities curve.

advance occurred in agriculture? The answer is that the technological advance in agriculture allows us to produce more from a given quantity of resources. That is, it allows us to shift some of our resources out of agriculture into housing. This is actually an ongoing story in U.S. economic history. In colonial days, about 90 percent of the population made a living in agriculture. Today it is less than 3 percent.

Summing Up the Production Possibilities Curve

The production possibilities curve shown in Exhibit 4 illustrates the choices faced by an economy that makes military goods and consumer goods. How are the economic concepts of scarcity, choice, opportunity costs, efficiency, and economic growth illustrated in the framework of this production possibilities curve? In Exhibit 4, we can show scarcity because resource combinations outside the initial production possibilities curve, such as point D, are unattainable without economic growth. If the economy is operating efficiently, we are somewhere on that production possibilities curve, perhaps point B or point C. However, if the economy is operating inefficiently, we are operating inside that production possibilities curve, at point A, for example. We can also see in this graph that to get more military goods, you must give up consumer goods, which represents the opportunity cost. The trade-offs between military goods and consumer goods are very real. When North Korea's leaders decided to build up their military,

section 3.4 exhibit 4 — Production Possibilities Curve

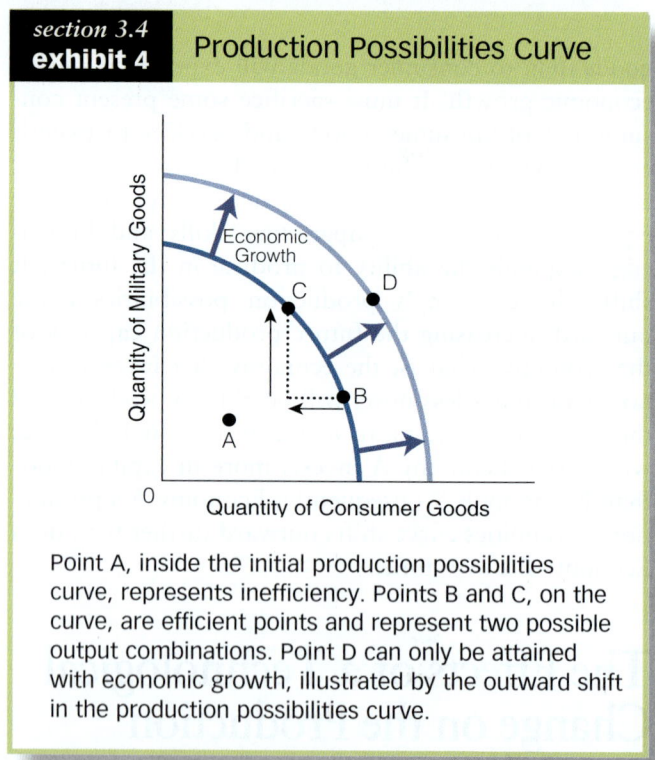

Point A, inside the initial production possibilities curve, represents inefficiency. Points B and C, on the curve, are efficient points and represent two possible output combinations. Point D can only be attained with economic growth, illustrated by the outward shift in the production possibilities curve.

it came at the expense of consumer goods. North Korea experienced a devastating famine in the 1990s and was again on the brink of famine in 2008. The 1990s famine was estimated to have killed roughly 4 percent of their population. Finally, we see that over time, with economic growth, the whole production possibilities curve can shift outward, making point D attainable.

SECTION CHECK

1. Economies must decide how much current consumption they are willing to sacrifice for greater growth in the future.
2. Economic growth is represented by an outward shift of the production possibilities curve.
3. Economic growth increases the possibility of producing more of all goods.
4. Despite economic growth, scarcity inevitably remains a fact of life.

---

1. What is the essential question behind issues of economic growth?
2. What is the connection between sacrifices and economic growth?
3. How is economic growth shown in terms of production possibilities curves?
4. Why doesn't economic growth eliminate scarcity?
5. What would happen to the production possibilities curve in an economy where a new innovation greatly increased its ability to produce shelter but did not change its ability to produce food?
6. If people reduced their saving (thus reducing the funds available for investment), what would that change do to society's production possibilities curve over time?

Interactive Chapter Summary

Fill in the blanks:

1. Because of scarcity, certain economic questions must be answered regardless of the level of affluence of the society or its political structure. Three fundamental questions that inevitably must be faced in a world of scarcity are (1) _____ will be produced? (2) _____ the goods and services be produced? (3) _____ the goods and services produced?

2. Market economies largely rely on a(n) _____ decision-making process, where literally millions of individual producers and consumers of goods and services determine what will be produced.

3. Most countries, including the United States, have _____ economies, in which the government and private sector determine the allocation of resources.

4. The _____-cost method is the most appropriate method for producing a given product.

5. Methods of production used where capital is relatively scarce will be _____, and methods of production used where labor is relatively scarce will be _____.

6. In a market economy, the amount of goods and services one is able to obtain depends on one's _____, which depends on the quality and quantity of the scarce _____ he or she controls.

7. The markets where households are buyers and firms are sellers of goods and services are called _____ markets.

8. The markets where households sell the use of their _____ (capital, land, labor, and entrepreneurship) to _____ are called _____ or _____ markets.

9. The simple _____ model shows the continuous flow of goods, services, inputs, and payments through the _____ and _____ markets among households and _____.

10. A(n) _____ curve represents the potential total output combinations of any two goods for an economy.

11. On a production possibilities curve, we assume that the economy has a given quantity and quality of _____ and _____ available to use for production.

12. On a straight-line production possibilities curve, the _____ are constant.

13. If an economy is operating _____ its production possibilities curve, it is not at full capacity and is operating _____. Such an economy's actual output is less than _____ output.

14. By putting _____ resources to work or by putting already employed resources to _____ uses, we could expand output.

15. _____ requires society to use its resources to the fullest extent—getting the _____ we can out of our scarce resources.

16. If the production possibilities curve is concave from below (that is, bowed outward from the origin), it reflects _____ opportunity costs of producing additional amounts of a good.

17. On a bowed production possibilities curve (concave to the origin), the opportunity costs of producing additional units of a good rises as society produces more of that good. This relationship is called the law of _____.

18. Resources tend to be specialized, so we lose some of their productivity when we transfer those resources from producing what they are relatively _____ at to producing something they are relatively _____ at.

19. To generate economic growth, a society must produce _____ consumer goods and _____ capital goods in the present.

20. Advancements in _____, improvements in _____, or new _____ could all lead to outward shifts of the production possibilities curve.

21. Increases in a society's output do not make _____ disappear. Even when output has grown more rapidly than population so that people are made better off, they still face _____.

22. The production possibilities curve can be used to illustrate the economic concepts of _____ (resource combinations outside the production possibilities curve are unattainable), _____ (selecting among the alternative bundles available along the production possibilities curve), _____ (how much of one good you give up to get another unit of the second good as you move along the production possibilities curve), _____ (being on the production possibilities curve rather than inside it), and _____ (shifting the production possibilities curve outward).

Answers: 1. what goods and services; who will get; how much 2. decentralized 3. mixed 4. least 5. labor intensive; capital intensive 6. income; resources 7. product 8. inputs; firms; factor; input 9. circular flow; product; factor; firms 10. production possibilities 11. resources; technology 12. opportunity costs 13. inside; inefficiently; potential 14. unemployed 15. Efficiency; better 15. increasing 17. increasing opportunity costs 18. good; bad 19. fewer; more 20. technology; labor productivity; natural resource finds 21. scarcity; trade-offs 22. scarcity; choice; opportunity costs; efficiency; economic growth

Key Terms and Concepts

consumer sovereignty 67
command economy 68
market economy 68
mixed economy 68

labor intensive 68
capital intensive 68
product markets 71
factor (or input) markets 71

simple circular flow model 71
production possibilities curve 73
increasing opportunity cost 77

Section Check Answers

3.1 The Three Economic Questions Every Society Faces

1. **Why does scarcity force us to decide what to produce?**
   Because our wants exceed the amount of goods and services that can be produced from our limited resources, it must be decided which wants should have priority over others.

2. **How is a command economy different from a market economy?**
   A command economy makes decisions about what and how much to produce centrally by members of a planning board or organization. A market economy makes those decisions as the result of decentralized decision making by individual producers and consumers, coordinated by their offers to buy and sell on markets.

3. **How does consumer sovereignty determine production decisions in a market economy?**
   Consumer sovereignty determines production decisions in a market economy because producers make what they believe consumers will "vote" for by being willing to pay for them.

4. **Do you think that what and how much an economy produces depends on who will get the goods and services produced in that economy? Why or why not?**
   Who will get the goods produced in an economy affects the incentives of the producers. The less a producer will benefit from increased production, the smaller are incentives to increase production, and the smaller will be total output in an economy.

5. **Why do consumers have to "vote" for a product with their dollars for it to be a success?**
   In the market sector, products can be profitable only if they attract dollar votes from consumers.

6. **Why must we choose among multiple ways of producing the goods and services we want?**
   We must choose among multiple ways of producing the goods and services we want because goods can generally be produced in several ways, using different combinations of resources.

7. **Why might production be labor intensive in one economy but be capital intensive in another?**
   Production will tend to be labor intensive where labor is relatively plentiful, and therefore relatively less expensive; it will tend to be capital intensive where capital is relatively plentiful, and therefore relatively less expensive. When the manner of production is different in different situations because factors of production have different relative prices, each of those methods will be more efficient where they are used.

8. **If a tourist from the United States on an overseas trip notices that other countries don't produce crops "like they do back home," would he be right to conclude that farmers in the other countries produce crops less efficiently than U.S. farmers?**
   No. The different ways of farming in different areas reflect the different relative scarcities of land, labor, and capital they face. Factors of production that are relatively scarce in an economy are also relatively costly there as a result. Producers there economize on the use of those more costly resources by using more of relatively less scarce, and less costly, resources instead. For example, where land is scarce, it is intensively cultivated with relatively cheaper (less scarce) labor and capital, but where capital is scarce, relatively cheaper (less scarce) land and labor are substituted for capital.

9. **In what way does scarcity determine income?**
   Relative scarcity determines the market values of the scarce resources people offer to others in exchange for income.

10. **What are the most important functions of the market system?**
    They transmit information through price signals, they provide incentives, and they distribute income.

3.2 The Circular Flow Model

1. **Why does the circular flow of money move in the opposite direction from the flow of goods and services?**
   The circular flow of money moves in the opposite direction from the flow of goods and services because the money flows are the payments made in exchange for the goods and services.

2. **What is bought and sold in factor markets?**
   The factors of production—capital, land, labor, and entrepreneurship—are sold in factor, or input, markets.

3. **What is bought and sold in product markets?**
   Consumer and investment goods and services are sold in product markets.

3.3 The Production Possibilities Curve

1. **What does a production possibilities curve illustrate?**
   The production possibilities curve illustrates the potential output combinations of two goods in an economy operating at full capacity, given the inputs and technology available to the economy.

2. **How are opportunity costs shown by the production possibilities curve?**
   Opportunity cost—the forgone output of one good necessary to increase output of another good—is illustrated by the slope, or trade-off, between the two goods at a given point on the production possibilities curve.

3. **Why do the opportunity costs of added production increase with output?**
   Opportunity costs of added production increase with output because some resources cannot be easily adapted from their current uses to alternative uses. At first, easily adaptable resources can be switched to producing more of a good. But once those easily adapted resources have been switched, producing further output requires the use of resources less well adapted to expanding that output, raising the opportunity cost of output.

4. **How does the production possibilities curve illustrate increasing opportunity costs?**
   Increasing opportunity costs are illustrated by a bowed (concave from below) production possibilities curve. It shows that initial units of one good can be produced by giving up little of another good, but progressive increases in output will require greater and greater sacrifices of the other good.

5. **Why are we concerned with widespread amounts of unemployed or underemployed resources in a society?**
   We are concerned with widespread amounts of unemployed or underemployed resources in a society because, if we could reduce the extent of unemployed or underemployed resources, people could have more scarce goods and services available for their use.

6. **What do we mean by *efficiency,* and how is it related to underemployment of resources?**
   Efficiency means getting the most we can out of our scarce resources. Underemployment of resources means a society is not getting the most it can out of these resources, either because they are not fully employed or because they are not matched to the uses best suited to them.

7. **How are efficiency and inefficiency illustrated by a production possibilities curve?**
   Efficient combinations of outputs are illustrated by points on the production possibilities curve, along which more of one good can be produced only if less of some other good is also produced. Inefficient combinations of outputs are illustrated by points inside the production possibilities curve, because more of both goods could then be produced with the resources available to the economy.

8. **Will a country that makes being unemployed illegal be more productive than one that does not? Why or why not?**
   A more productive economy is one that makes the best use of those who wish to work. Making unemployment illegal (as was true in the old USSR) does not eliminate underemployment, nor does it guarantee that people and other resources are employed where they are most productive (especially because it is more difficult to search for a better job when you are working than when you are not working).

9. **If a 68-year-old worker in the United States chooses not to work at all, does that mean that the United States is functioning inside its production possibilities curve? Why or why not?**
   Individuals who choose retirement rather than work must consider themselves better off not working, when all the relevant considerations are taken into account. They are therefore as fully employed, given their circumstances, as they would like to be, and so the choice does not imply that the United States would be inside its production possibilities curve as a result. However, if such workers became more willing to work, that would shift the United States' production possibilities curve outward.

3.4 Economic Growth and the Production Possibilities Curve

1. **What is the essential question behind issues of economic growth?**
   The essential question behind issues of economic growth is: How much are we willing to give up today to get more in the future?

2. **What is the connection between sacrifices and economic growth?**
   The more current consumption is sacrificed in an economy, the larger the fraction of its current resources it can devote to producing investment goods, which will increase its rate of economic growth.

3. **How is economic growth shown in terms of production possibilities curves?**
   Economic growth—the expansion of what an economy can produce—is shown as an outward shift in the production possibilities curve, with formerly unattainable output combinations now made possible.

4. **Why doesn't economic growth eliminate scarcity?**
   Economic growth doesn't eliminate scarcity because people's wants still exceed what they are capable of producing, so that trade-offs among scarce goods must still be made.

5. **What would happen to the production possibilities curve in an economy where a new innovation greatly increased its ability to produce shelter but did not change its ability to produce food?**
   This innovation would increase the amount of shelter the economy could produce, shifting out the production possibilities curve's intercept on the shelter axis, but not changing its intercept on the food axis. If shelter is on the vertical axis and food is on the horizontal axis of the production possibilities curve, such a technological change would leave the vertical intercept unchanged, but make it less steep (reflecting the reduced opportunity cost of producing additional food), shifting out the curve's intercept with the horizontal axis.

6. **If people reduced their saving (thus reducing the funds available for investment), what would that change do to society's production possibilities curve over time?**
   The less people save, the slower the capital stock of the economy will grow through new investment (because saving is the source of the funds for investment), and so the slower the production possibilities curve would shift out over time.

CHAPTER 3 STUDY GUIDE

True or False:

1. Consumer sovereignty describes how individual consumers in market economies determine what is to be produced.
2. Command economies rely on central planning, where decisions about what and how many are largely determined by a government official associated with the central planning organization.
3. All economies, regardless of political structure, must decide how, from several possible ways, to produce the goods and services that they want.
4. In any economy, it would always be less efficient to dig ditches by having many workers use their hands than to use workers with shovels or a backhoe.
5. Each nation tends to use the production processes that conserve its relatively scarce (and thus relatively more expensive) resources and use more of its relatively abundant resources.
6. In a market economy, with private ownership and control of the means of production, the amount of output one is able to obtain depends on the quantity and quality of the scarce resources that the individual controls.
7. The market where households sell the use of their inputs to firms is called the product market.
8. The circular flow model illustrates the continuous flow of goods, services, inputs, and payments between firms and households.
9. With a straight-line production possibilities curve, the opportunity cost of producing another unit of a good increases with its output.
10. The economy cannot produce beyond the levels indicated by the production possibilities curve during a given time period, but it is possible to operate inside the production possibilities curve.
11. Underutilized resources or those not being put to their best uses are illustrated by output combinations along the production possibilities curve.
12. We all have an interest in the efficient use of all of society's resources because more of everything we care about can be available for our use as a result.
13. If resources are being used efficiently, at a point along a production possibilities curve, more of one good or service requires the sacrifice of another good or service as a cost.
14. The basic reason for increasing opportunity cost is that some resources and skills cannot be easily adapted from their current uses to alternative uses.
15. Investing in capital goods will increase the future production capacity of an economy, so an economy that invests more now (consumes less now) will be able to produce, and therefore consume, more in the future.
16. An economy can grow despite a lack of qualitative and quantitative improvements in the factors of production.
17. Economic growth means a movement along an economy's production possibilities curve in the direction of producing more consumer goods.
18. From a point inside the production possibilities curve, in order to get more of one thing, an economy must give up something else.

Multiple Choice:

1. Which of the following is not a question that all societies must answer?
    a. How can scarcity be eliminated?
    b. What goods and services will be produced?
    c. Who will get the goods and services?
    d. How will the goods and services be produced?
    e. All of the above are questions that all societies must answer.

2. Economic disputes over the distribution of income are generally associated with which economic question?
   a. Who should produce the goods?
   b. What goods and services will be produced?
   c. Who will get the goods and services?
   d. How will the goods and services be produced?

3. Three economic questions must be determined in all societies. What are they?
   a. How much will be produced? When will it be produced? How much will it cost?
   b. What will the price of each good be? Who will produce each good? Who will consume each good?
   c. What is the opportunity cost of production? Does the society have a comparative advantage in production? Will consumers desire the goods being produced?
   d. What goods and services will be produced? How will the goods and services be produced? Who will get the goods and services?

4. The private ownership of property and the use of the market system to direct and coordinate economic activity are most characteristic of
   a. a command economy.
   b. a mixed economy.
   c. a market economy.
   d. a traditional economy.

5. The degree of government involvement in the economy is greatest in
   a. a command economy.
   b. a mixed economy.
   c. a market economy.
   d. a traditional economy.

6. When a command economy is utilized to resolve economic questions regarding the allocation of resources, then
   a. everyone will receive an equal share of the output produced.
   b. the preferences of individuals are of no importance.
   c. economic efficiency will be assured.
   d. the role of markets will be replaced by political decision making.

7. In a circular flow diagram,
   a. goods and services flow in a clockwise direction.
   b. goods and services flow in a counterclockwise direction.
   c. product markets appear at the top of the diagram.
   d. factor markets appear at the left of the diagram.
   e. both b and c are true.

8. Which of the following is true?
   a. In the product markets, firms are buyers and households are sellers.
   b. In the factor markets, firms are sellers and households are buyers.
   c. Firms receive money payments from households for capital, land, labor, and entrepreneurship.
   d. All of the above are true.
   e. None of the above are true.

9. In the circular flow model,
   a. firms supply both products and resources.
   b. firms demand both products and resources.
   c. firms demand resources and supply products.
   d. firms supply resources and demand products.

10. A point beyond the boundary of an economy's production possibilities curve is
    a. efficient.
    b. inefficient.
    c. attainable.
    d. unattainable.
    e. both attainable and efficient.

Use the diagram to answer questions 11 through 14.

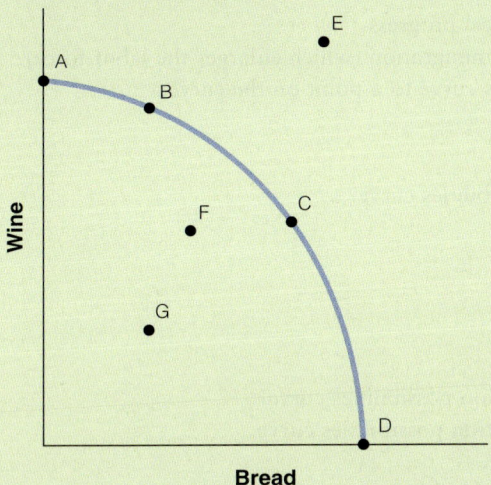

11. Currently, it is not possible to produce at
    a. point A.
    b. point B.
    c. point E.
    d. point G.
    e. either point E or point G.

12. An economy is operating at full employment, and then workers in the bread industry are laid off. This change is portrayed in the movement from
    a. A to B.
    b. B to E.
    c. C to F.
    d. G to F.
    e. None of the above are correct.

13. Along the production possibilities curve, the most efficient point of production depicted is
    a. point B.
    b. point C.
    c. point D.
    d. point G.
    e. All points on the production possibilities curve are equally efficient.

14. The opportunity cost of one more unit of bread is greater at point _____ than at point _____.
    a. G; B
    b. C; A
    c. A; C
    d. None of the above. The opportunity cost of a good is constant everywhere along the production possibilities curve.

15. Which of the following is consistent with the implications of the production possibilities curve?
    a. If the resources in an economy are being used efficiently, scarcity will not be a problem.
    b. If the resources in an economy are being used efficiently, more of one good can be produced only if less of another good is produced.
    c. Producing more of any one good will require smaller and smaller sacrifices of other goods as more of that good is being produced in an economy.
    d. An economy will automatically attain that level of output at which all of its resources are fully employed.
    e. Both b and c are consistent with the implications of the production possibilities curve.

16. Consider a production possibilities curve for an economy producing bicycles and video game players. It is possible to increase the production of bicycles without sacrificing video game players if
    a. the production possibilities curve shifts outward due to technological progress.
    b. the production possibilities curve shifts outward due to increased immigration (which enlarges the labor force).
    c. the economy moves from a point inside the production possibilities curve to a point on the curve.
    d. any of the above occurs.
    e. either a or b, but not c, occurs.

17. What determines the position and shape of a society's production possibilities curve?
    a. the physical resources of that society
    b. the skills of the workforce
    c. the level of technology of the society
    d. the number of factories available to the society
    e. all of the above

18. Which of the following is the most accurate statement about a production possibilities curve?
    a. An economy can produce at any point inside or outside its production possibilities curve.
    b. An economy can produce only on its production possibilities curve.
    c. An economy can produce at any point on or inside its production possibilities curve, but not outside the curve.
    d. An economy can produce at any point inside its production possibilities curve, but not on or outside the curve.

19. Which of the following is most likely to shift the production possibilities curve outward?
    a. an increase in unemployment
    b. a decrease in the stock of physical or human capital
    c. a decrease in the labor force
    d. a technological advance

20. Which of the following is least likely to shift the production possibilities curve outward?
    a. a change in preferences away from one of the goods and toward the other
    b. an invention that reduces the amount of natural resources necessary for producing a good
    c. the discovery of new natural resources
    d. a reduction in people's preferences for leisure

21. Inefficiency is best illustrated by which of the following?
    a. forgoing civilian goods in order to produce more military goods
    b. limiting economic growth by reducing capital spending
    c. having high levels of unemployment of labor and other resources that could be productively employed
    d. producing outside the production possibilities frontier
    e. all of the above

22. Suppose Country A produces few consumption goods and many investment goods while Country B produces few investment goods and many consumption goods. Other things being equal, you would expect
    a. per capita income to grow more rapidly in Country B.
    b. population to grow faster in Country B.
    c. the production possibilities curve for Country A to shift out more rapidly than that of Country B.
    d. that if both countries started with identical production possibilities curves, in 20 years, people in Country B will be able to produce more consumer goods than people in Country A.
    e. that both c and d are true.

23. A virulent disease spreads throughout the population of an economy, causing death and disability. This event can be portrayed as
    a. a movement from a point on the production possibilities curve to a point inside the curve.
    b. a movement from a point on the production possibilities curve to the northeast.
    c. a movement along the production possibilities curve to the southeast.
    d. an outward shift of the production possibilities curve.
    e. an inward shift of the production possibilities curve.

24. Say that a technological change doubles an economy's ability to produce good X and triples the economy's ability to produce good Y. As a result,
    a. the economy will tend to produce less X and more Y than before.
    b. the opportunity cost of producing units of Y in terms of X forgone will tend to fall.

c. the production possibilities curve will shift out further along the X-axis than along the Y-axis.
d. both b and c would be true.

Problems:

1. What are the three basic economic questions? How are decisions made differently in a market economy than in planned economies?

2. Recently the American Film Institute selected *Citizen Kane* as the best movie of all time. *Citizen Kane* is a fictional psychological biography of one of the most powerful newspaper publishers in history, William Randolph Hearst. *Titanic*, an epic romance about the sinking of the *Titanic*, has made the most money of any film in history. Unlike *Titanic*, *Citizen Kane* was not a box office success. Do you think Hollywood will make more movies like *Titanic* or like *Citizen Kane*? Why?

3. As women's wages and employment opportunities have expanded over the past 50 years, Americans have purchased more and more labor-saving home appliances like automatic washers and dryers, dishwashers, and microwave ovens. Do you think these phenomena are related? Could higher wages and better job opportunities lead to a more capital-intensive way of performing household chores? Explain.

4. Identify where the appropriate entries go in the circular flow diagram.

5. Identify whether each of the following transactions takes place in the factor market or the product market.
   a. Billy buys a sofa from Home Time Furniture for his new home.
   b. Home Time Furniture pays its manager her weekly salary.
   c. The manager buys dinner at Billy's Café.
   d. After he pays all of his employees their wages and pays his other bills, the owner of Billy's Café takes his profit.

6. Given the following production possibilities curve:

   a. Does this production possibilities curve show increasing opportunity costs? Explain.
   b. What is the opportunity cost of moving from point I to point D? Explain.

c. What is the opportunity cost of moving from point C to point B?
d. Which of points A–E is the most efficient? Explain.

7. During wartime, countries shift production from civilian goods, like automobiles and clothing, to military goods, like tanks and military uniforms. When the United States entered World War I in April 1917, for example, the federal government created the War Industries Board and charged it with determining production priorities and converting plants to meet war needs. In the following year, automobile production fell 43 percent as output of military vehicles soared. When the war ended, 19 months later, in November 1918, the government cancelled $2.5 billion in military contracts and the nation resumed normal production. Assuming that in 1917 the United States was at point A on the production possibilities curves shown, show what happened between April 1917 and November 1918. Show what happened once the war ended.

8. How would the following events be shown using a production possibilities curve for shelter and food?
    a. The economy is experiencing double-digit unemployment.
    b. Economic growth is increasing at more than 5 percent per year.
    c. Society decides it wants less shelter and more food.
    d. Society decides it wants more shelter and less food.

9. In *A Bend in the River*, Nobel Prize winner V. S. Naipaul describes an underdeveloped country in which the government's constantly changing tax policies and vague laws regarding ownership of property cause entrepreneurs to become demoralized and unresponsive to economic opportunities. Could this be a case of idle or unemployed entrepreneurs? How can tax laws and rules governing property affect entrepreneurs' willingness to start new businesses or improve existing enterprises?

10. Using the following table, answer the questions:

	Combinations				
	A	B	C	D	E
Guns	1	2	3	4	5
Butter	20	18	14	8	0

    a. What are the assumptions for a given production possibilities curve?
    b. What is the opportunity cost of one gun when moving from point B to point C? When moving from point D to point E?
    c. Do these combinations demonstrate constant or increasing opportunity costs?

11. Economy A produces more capital goods and fewer consumer goods than Economy B. Which economy will grow more rapidly? Draw two production possibilities curves, one for Economy A and one for Economy B. Demonstrate graphically how one economy can grow more rapidly than the other.

12. Why one nation experiences economic growth and another doesn't is a question that has intrigued economists since Adam Smith wrote *An Inquiry into the Nature and Causes of the Wealth of Nations* in 1776. Explain why each of the following would limit economic growth.
    a. The politically connected elite secure a large share of a country's output and put the proceeds in Swiss banks.
    b. A country has a very low output per person.
    c. The national philosophy is live for the moment and forget about tomorrow.
    d. The government closes all of the schools so more people will be available for work.
    e. The country fears military invasion and spends half of its income on military goods.

13. How does education add to a nation's capital stock?

14. How does a technological advance that increases the efficiency of shoe production affect the production possibilities curve between shoes and pizza? Is it possible to produce more shoes and pizza or just more shoes? Explain.

15. A politician running for president of the United States promises to build new schools and new space stations during the next four years without sacrificing any other goods and services. Using a production possibilities curve between schools and space stations, explain under what conditions the politician would be able to keep his promise.

PART 2 SUPPLY AND DEMAND

Chapter 4 Supply and Demand *92*

Chapter 5 Bringing Supply and Demand Together *121*

Chapter 6 Elasticities *151*

4 Supply and Demand

4.1 Markets
4.2 Demand
4.3 Shifts in the Demand Curve
4.4 Supply
4.5 Shifts in the Supply Curve

According to Thomas Carlyle, a nineteenth-century philosopher, "Teach a parrot the term 'supply and demand' and you've got an economist." Unfortunately, economics is more complicated than that.

However, if Carlyle was hinting at the importance of supply and demand, he was right on target. Supply and demand is without a doubt the most powerful tool in the economist's toolbox. It can help explain much of what goes on in the world and help predict what will happen tomorrow. In this chapter, we begin with an introduction to markets. Every market has a demand side and a supply side. Buyers represent the demand side of the market and sellers represent the supply side. In this chapter, we will learn about the law of demand and the law of supply and the factors that can change supply and demand. In the following chapter, we will put it together to show markets in motion.

SECTION 4.1 Markets

* What is a market?
* Why is it so difficult to define a market?

Defining a Market

Although we usually think of a market as a place where some sort of exchange occurs, a market is not really a place at all. A **market** is the process of buyers and sellers exchanging goods and services. Supermarkets, the New York Stock Exchange, drug stores, roadside stands, garage sales, Internet stores, and restaurants are all markets.

market
the process of buyers and sellers exchanging goods and services

Every market is different. That is, the conditions under which the exchange between buyers and sellers takes place can vary. These differences make it difficult to precisely define a market. After all, an incredible variety of exchange arrangements exist in the real world—organized securities markets, wholesale auction markets, foreign exchange markets, real estate markets, labor markets, and so forth.

Goods being priced and traded in various ways at various locations by various kinds of buyers and sellers further compound the problem of defining a market.

The stock market involves many buyers and sellers; and profit statements and stock prices are readily available. New information is quickly understood by buyers and sellers and is incorporated into the price of the stock. When people expect a company to do better in the future, the price of the stock rises; when people expect the company to do poorly in the future, the price of the stock falls.

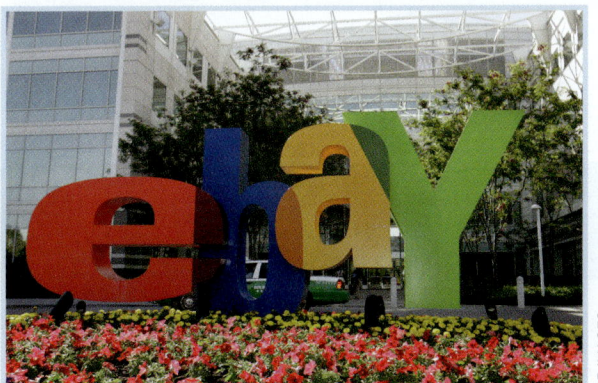

eBay is an Internet auction company that brings together millions of buyers and sellers from all over the world. The gains from these mutually beneficial exchanges are large. Craigslist also uses the power of the internet to connect many buyers and sellers in local markets.

For some goods, such as housing, markets are numerous but limited to a geographic area. Homes in Santa Barbara, California, for example (about 100 miles from downtown Los Angeles), do not compete directly with homes in Los Angeles. Why? Because people who work in Los Angeles will generally look for homes within commuting distance. Even within cities, separate markets for homes are differentiated by amenities such as more living space, newer construction, larger lots, and better schools.

In a similar manner, markets are numerous but geographically limited for a good such as cement. Because transportation costs are so high relative to the selling price, the good is not shipped any substantial distance, and buyers are usually in contact only with local producers. Price and output are thus determined in a number of small markets. In other markets, such as those for gold or automobiles, markets are global. The important point is not what a market looks like, but what it does—it facilitates trade.

Buyers and Sellers

The roles of buyers and sellers in markets are important. Buyers, as a group, determine the demand side of the market. Buyers include the consumers who purchase the goods and services and the firms that buy inputs—labor, capital, and raw materials. Sellers, as a group, determine the supply side of the market. Sellers include the firms that produce and sell goods and services and the resource owners who sell their inputs to firms—workers who "sell" their labor and resource owners who sell raw materials and capital. The interaction of buyers and sellers determines market prices and output—through the forces of supply and demand.

In the next few chapters, we focus on how supply and demand work in a **competitive market**. A competitive market is one in which a number of buyers and sellers are offering similar products, and no single buyer or seller can influence the market price. That is, buyers and sellers have little market power. Because many markets contain a large degree of competitiveness, the lessons of supply and demand can be applied to many different types of problems.

The supply and demand model is particularly useful in markets like agriculture, finance, labor, construction, services, wholesale, and retail.

In short, a model is only as good as it explains and predicts. The model of supply and demand is very good at predicting changes in prices and quantities in many markets large and small.

competitive market
a market where the many buyers and sellers have little market power—each buyer's or seller's effect on market price is negligible

SECTION CHECK

1. Markets consist of buyers and sellers exchanging goods and services with one another.
2. Markets can be regional, national, or global.
3. Buyers determine the demand side of the market and sellers determine the supply side of the market.

---

1. Why is it difficult to define a market precisely?
2. Why do you get your produce at a supermarket rather than directly from farmers?
3. Why do the prices people pay for similar items at garage sales vary more than for similar items in a department store?

SECTION 4.2 Demand

* What is the law of demand?
* What is an individual demand curve?
* What is a market demand curve?

The Law of Demand

Sometimes observed behavior is so pervasive it is called a law—the law of demand, for example. According to the **law of demand**, the quantity of a good or service demanded varies inversely (negatively) with its price, *ceteris paribus*. More directly, the law of demand says that, other things being equal, when the price (P) of a good or service falls, the quantity demanded (Q_D) increases. Conversely, if the price of a good or service rises, the quantity demanded decreases.

law of demand
the quantity of a good or service demanded varies inversely (negatively) with its price, *ceteris paribus*

$$P \uparrow \Rightarrow Q_D \downarrow \quad \text{and} \quad P \downarrow \Rightarrow Q_D \uparrow$$

Individual Demand

An Individual Demand Schedule

The **individual demand schedule** shows the relationship between the price of the good and the quantity demanded. For example, suppose Elizabeth enjoys drinking coffee. How many pounds of coffee would Elizabeth be willing and able to buy at various prices during the year? At a price of $3 a pound, Elizabeth buys 15 pounds of coffee over the course of a year. If the price is higher, at $4 per pound, she might buy only 10 pounds; if it is lower, say $1 per pound, she might buy 25 pounds of coffee during the year. Elizabeth's demand for coffee for the year is summarized in the demand schedule in Exhibit 1. Elizabeth might not be consciously aware of the amounts that she would purchase at prices other than the prevailing one, but that does not alter the fact that she has a schedule in the sense that she would have bought various other amounts had other prices prevailed. It must be emphasized that the schedule is a list of alternative possibilities. At any one time, only one of the prices will prevail, and thus a certain quantity will be purchased.

> **individual demand schedule**
> a schedule that shows the relationship between price and quantity demanded
>
> **individual demand curve**
> a graphical representation that shows the inverse relationship between price and quantity demanded
>
> **market demand curve**
> the horizontal summation of individual demand curves

An Individual Demand Curve

By plotting the different prices and corresponding quantities demanded in Elizabeth's demand schedule in Exhibit 1 and then connecting them, we can create the **individual demand curve** for Elizabeth shown in Exhibit 2. From the curve, we can see that when the price is higher, the quantity demanded is lower, and when the price is lower, the quantity demanded is higher. The demand curve shows how the quantity demanded of the good changes as its price varies.

What Is a Market Demand Curve?

Although we introduced the concept of the demand curve in terms of the individual, economists usually speak of the demand curve in terms of large groups of people—a whole nation, a community, or a trading area. That is, to analyze how the market works, we will need to use market demand. As you know, every individual has his or her demand curve for every product. The horizontal summing of the demand curves of many individuals is called the **market demand curve**.

Suppose the consumer group is composed of Homer, Marge, and the rest of their small community, Springfield, and that the product is still coffee. The effect of price on the quantity of coffee demanded by Marge, Homer, and the rest of Springfield is given in the demand schedule and demand curves shown in Exhibit 3. At $4 per pound, Homer would be willing and able to buy 20 pounds of coffee per year, Marge would be willing and able to buy 10 pounds, and the rest of Springfield would be willing and able to buy 2,970 pounds. At $3 per pound, Homer would be

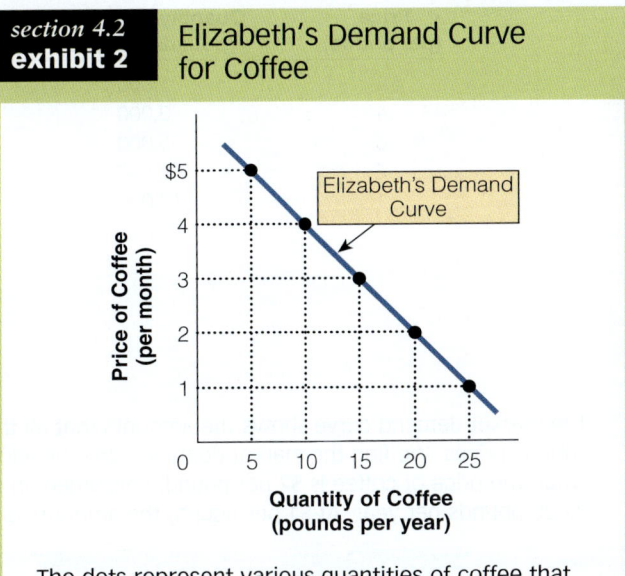

section 4.2 exhibit 2 Elizabeth's Demand Curve for Coffee

The dots represent various quantities of coffee that Elizabeth would be willing and able to buy at different prices in a given period. The demand curve shows how the quantity demanded varies inversely with the price of the good when we hold everything else constant—*ceteris paribus*. Because of this inverse relationship between price and quantity demanded, the demand curve is downward sloping.

section 4.2 exhibit 1 Elizabeth's Demand Schedule for Coffee

Price of Coffee (per pound)	Quantity of Coffee Demanded (pounds per year)
$5	5
4	10
3	15
2	20
1	25

section 4.2 exhibit 3 — Creating a Market Demand Curve

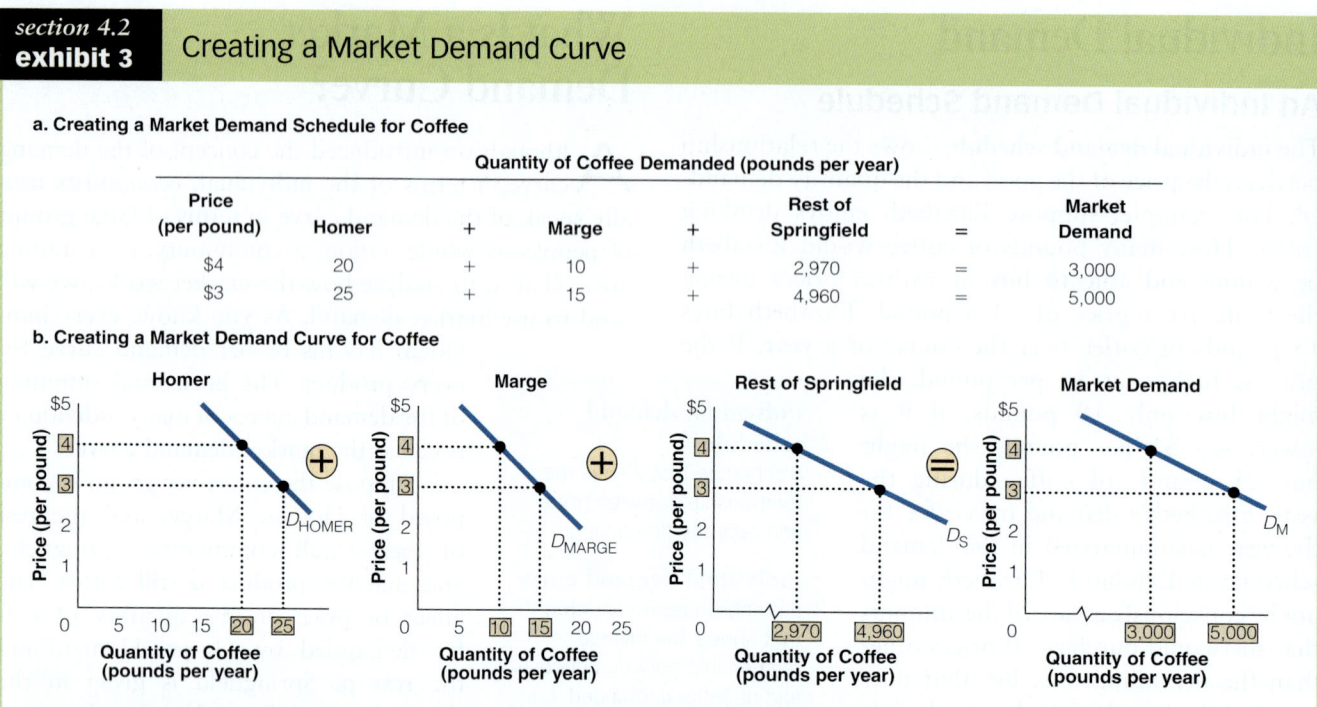

section 4.2 exhibit 4 — A Market Demand Curve

a. Market Demand Schedule for Coffee

Price (per pound)	Quantity Demanded (pounds per year)
$5	1,000
4	3,000
3	5,000
2	8,000
1	12,000

b. Market Demand Curve for Coffee

The market demand curve shows the amounts that all the buyers in the market would be willing and able to buy at various prices. We find the market demand curve by adding horizontally the individual demand curves. For example, when the price of coffee is $2 per pound, consumers in the market collectively would be willing and able to buy 8,000 pounds per year. At $1 per pound, the amount collectively demanded would be 12,000 pounds per year.

willing and able to buy 25 pounds of coffee per year, Marge would be willing and able to buy 15 pounds, and the rest of Springfield would be willing and able to buy 4,960 pounds. The market demand curve is simply the (horizontal) sum of the quantities Homer, Marge, and the rest of Springfield demand at each price. That is, at $4, the quantity demanded in the market would be 3,000 pounds of coffee (20 + 10 + 2,970 = 3,000), and at $3, the quantity demanded in the market would be 5,000 pounds of coffee (25 + 15 + 4,960 = 5,000).

In Exhibit 4, we offer a more complete set of prices and quantities from the market demand for coffee during the year. Remember, the market demand curve shows the amounts that all the buyers in the market would be willing and able to buy at various prices. For example, when the price of coffee is $2 per pound, consumers in the market collectively would be willing and able to buy 8,000 pounds per year. At $1 per pound, the amount collectively demanded would be 12,000 pounds per year. The market demand curve is the negative (inverse) relationship between price and the total quantity demanded, while holding all other factors that affect how much consumers are able and willing to pay constant, *ceteris paribus*. For the most part, we are interested in how the market works, so we will primarily use market demand curves.

SECTION CHECK

1. The law of demand states that when the price of a good falls (rises), the quantity demanded rises (falls), *ceteris paribus*.
2. An individual demand curve is a graphical representation of the relationship between the price and the quantity demanded.
3. The market demand curve shows the amount of a good that all buyers in the market would be willing and able to buy at various prices.

1. What is an inverse relationship?
2. How do lower prices change buyers' incentives?
3. How do higher prices change buyers' incentives?
4. What is an individual demand schedule?
5. What is the difference between an individual demand curve and a market demand curve?
6. Why does the amount of dating on campus tend to decline just before and during final exams?

SECTION 4.3 Shifts in the Demand Curve

* What is the difference between a change in demand and a change in quantity demanded?
* What are the determinants of demand?
* What are substitutes and complements?
* What are normal and inferior goods?
* How does the number of buyers affect the demand curve?
* How do changes in taste affect the demand curve?
* How do changing expectations affect the demand curve?

A Change in Demand Versus a Change in Quantity Demanded

Consumers are influenced by the prices of goods when they make their purchasing decisions. At lower prices, people prefer to buy more of a good than they do at higher prices, holding other factors constant. Why? Primarily, it is because many goods are substitutes for one another. For example, an increase in the price of coffee might tempt some buyers to switch from buying coffee to buying tea or soft drinks.

Understanding this relationship between price and quantity demanded is so important that economists make a clear distinction between it and the various other factors that can influence consumer behavior. A change in a good's own price is said to lead to a **change in quantity demanded**. That is, it "moves you along"

change in quantity demanded
a change in a good's own price leads to a change in quantity demanded, a move along a given demand curve

a given demand curve. The demand curve is drawn under the assumption that all other things are held constant, except the price of the good. However, economists know that price is not the only thing that affects the quantity of a good that people buy. The other factors that influence the demand curve are called *determinants of demand*, and a change in these other factors *shifts the entire demand curve*. These determinants of demand are called demand shifters and they lead to **changes in demand**.

> **change in demand**
> the prices of related goods, income, number of buyers, tastes, and expectations can change the demand for a good; that is, a change in one of these factors shifts the entire demand curve

possible demand shifters are the prices of related goods, income, number of buyers, tastes, and expectations. We will now look more closely at each of these variables.

The Prices of Related Goods

In deciding how much of a good or service to buy, consumers are influenced by the price of that good or service, a relationship summarized in the law of demand. However, sometimes consumers are also influenced by the prices of *related* goods and services—substitutes and complements.

Substitutes

Substitutes are generally goods for which one could be used in place of the other. To many, substitutes would include butter and margarine, domestic and foreign cars, movie tickets and video rentals, jackets and sweaters, Exxon and Shell gasoline, and Nikes and Reeboks.

Suppose you go into a store to buy a couple of six packs of Coca-Cola and you see that Pepsi is on sale for half its usual price. Is it possible that you might decide to buy Pepsi instead of Coca-Cola? Economists argue that many people would. Empirical tests have confirmed that consumers are responsive to both the price of the good in question and the prices of related goods. When goods are substitutes, the more people buy of one good, the less they will buy of the other. Suppose there is a fall in the price of Pepsi; this would cause an increase in the quantity demanded for Pepsi (a movement down along the demand

Shifts in Demand

An increase in demand shifts the demand curve to the right; a decrease in demand shifts the demand curve to the left, as shown in Exhibit 1. Some

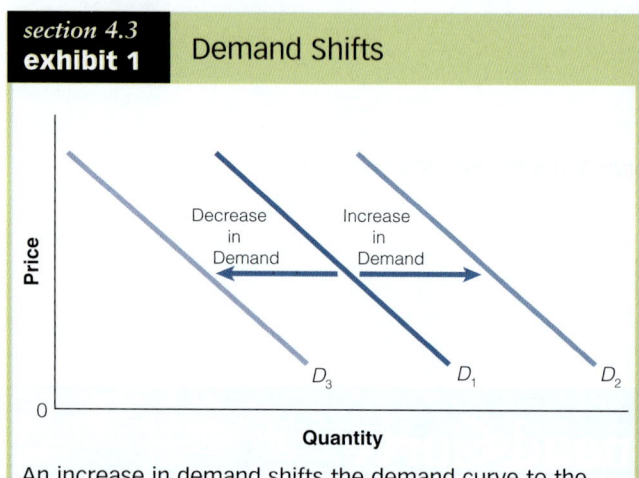

section 4.3 exhibit 1 Demand Shifts

An increase in demand shifts the demand curve to the right. A decrease in demand shifts the demand curve to the left.

Use what you've LEARNED: SUBSTITUTE GOODS

Q Can you describe the change we would expect to see in the demand curve for Sprite if the relative price for 7-Up increased significantly?

A If the price of one good increases and, as a result, an individual buys more of another good, the two related goods are substitutes. That is, buying more of one reduces purchases of the other. In Exhibit 2(a), we see that as the price of 7-Up increases—a movement up along the demand curve for 7-Up, from point A to point B. The price increase for 7-Up causes a reduction in the quantity demanded of 7-Up. If the two goods are substitutes, the higher price for 7-Up will cause an increase in the demand for Sprite (a rightward shift), as seen in Exhibit 2 (b).

section 4.3
exhibit 2

Substititute Goods

curve). Many Coke drinkers may switch to the new relatively lower priced Pepsi—causing a reduction in demand for Coca-Cola; shifting the demand curve for Coca-Cola to the left. Alternatively, if there is an increase in the price of Pepsi, this causes a decrease in the quantity demanded of Pepsi (a movement up along the demand curve). At the new higher price for Pepsi, many Pepsi drinkers will switch to the relatively lower priced Coca-Cola—shifting the demand curve for Coca-Cola to the right. In this example, Pepsi and Coca-Cola are said to be substitutes.

Two goods are **substitutes** if an increase (a decrease) in the price of one good causes the demand curve for another good to shift to the right (left)—a direct (or positive) relationship.

substitutes
an increase (decrease) in the price of one good causes the demand curve for another good to shift to the right (left)

complements
an increase (decrease) in the price of one good shifts the demand curve for another good to the left (right)

rise—a movement down along the demand curve for motorcycles. As more people buy motorcycles, they will demand more motorcycle helmets—the demand curve for motorcycle helmets shifts to the right. In short, when goods are **complements,** the more people buy of one good, the more they will buy of the other. That is, if a decrease in the price of good A leads to an increase in the demand for good B, the two goods are complements. Alternatively, if an increase in the price of good A leads to a decrease in the demand for good B, the two goods are complements.

Complements

$$P_{\text{GOOD A}} \uparrow \Rightarrow \downarrow D_{\text{GOOD B}}$$
$$P_{\text{GOOD A}} \downarrow \Rightarrow \uparrow D_{\text{GOOD B}}$$

Substitutes

$$P_{\text{GOOD A}} \uparrow \Rightarrow \uparrow D_{\text{GOOD B}}$$
$$P_{\text{GOOD A}} \downarrow \Rightarrow \downarrow D_{\text{GOOD B}}$$

Complements

Complements are goods that "go together," often consumed and used simultaneously, such as skis and bindings, peanut butter and jelly, hot dogs and buns, digital music players and downloadable music, and printers and ink cartridges. For example, if the price of motorcycles falls, the quantity of motorcycles demanded will

Income

Economists have observed that generally the consumption of goods and services is positively related to the income available to consumers. Empirical studies support the notion that as individuals receive more income, they tend to increase their purchases of most goods and services. Other things held equal, rising income usually leads to an increase in the demand for goods (a rightward shift of the demand curve), and decreasing income usually leads to a decrease in the demand for goods (a leftward shift of the demand curve).

Use what you've LEARNED
COMPLEMENTARY GOODS

Q If the price of computers fell markedly, what do you think would happen to the demand for printers?

A If computers and printers are complements, the decrease in the price of computers will lead to more computers purchased (a movement down along the demand curve from point A to point B) and an increase in the demand for printers (a rightward shift). Of course, the opposite is true too—an increase in the price of computers will lead to fewer people purchasing computers (a movement up along the demand curve for computers from point B to point A) and a lower demand for printers (a leftward shift).

section 4.3 exhibit 3 Complementary Goods

Normal and Inferior Goods

If demand for a good increases when incomes rise and decreases when incomes fall, the good is called a **normal good**. Most goods are normal goods. Consumers will typically buy more CDs, clothes, pizzas, and trips to the movies as their incomes rise. However, if demand for a good decreases when incomes rise or if demand increases when incomes fall, the good is called an **inferior good**. These goods include inexpensive cuts of meat, second-hand clothing, or retread tires, which customers generally buy only because they cannot afford more expensive substitutes. As incomes rise, buyers shift to preferred substitutes and decrease their demand for the inferior goods. Suppose most individuals prefer hamburger to beans, but low-income families buy beans because they are less expensive. As incomes rise, many consumers may switch from buying beans to buying hamburgers. Hamburgers may be inferior too; as incomes rise still further, consumers may substitute steak or chicken for hamburger. The term *inferior* in this sense does not refer to the quality of the good in question but shows that demand decreases when income increases and demand increases when income decreases. So beans are inferior not because they are low quality, but because you buy less of them as income increases.

Or, if people's incomes rise and they increase their demand for movie tickets, we say that movie tickets are a normal good. But if people's incomes fall and they increase their demand for bus rides, we say bus rides are an inferior good. Whether goods are normal or inferior, the point here is that income influences demand—usually positively, but sometimes negatively.

normal good
if income increases, the demand for a good increases; if income decreases, the demand for a good decreases

inferior good
if income increases, the demand for a good decreases; if income decreases, the demand for a good increases

Normal Good

Income ↑ ⇒ Demand ↑

Income ↓ ⇒ Demand ↓

Inferior Good

Income ↑ ⇒ Demand ↓

Income ↓ ⇒ Demand ↑

Number of Buyers

The demand for a good or service will vary with the size of the potential consumer population. The demand for wheat, for example, rises as population increases, because the added population wants to consume wheat products, such as bread or cereal. Marketing experts, who closely follow the patterns of consumer behavior regarding a particular good or service, are usually vitally concerned with the *demographics* of the product—the vital statistics of the potential consumer population, including size, race, income, and age characteristics. For example, market researchers for baby food companies keep a close watch on the birth rate.

Consumer's Preferences and Information

The demand for a good or service may increase or decrease suddenly with changes in people's tastes or preferences. Changes in taste may be triggered by advertising or promotion, by a news story, by the behavior of some popular public figure, and so on. Changes in taste are particularly noticeable in apparel. Skirt lengths, coat lapels, shoe styles, and tie sizes change frequently.

Changes in preferences naturally lead to changes in demand. A person may grow tired of one type of recreation or food and try another type. People may decide they want more organic food; consequently, we will see more stores and restaurants catering to this change in taste. Changes in occupation, number of dependents, state of health, and age also tend to alter preferences. The birth of a baby might cause a family to spend less on recreation and more on food and clothing. Illness increases the demand for medicine and lessens purchases of other goods. A cold winter increases the demand for heating oil. Changes in customs and traditions also affect preferences, and the development of new products draws consumer preferences away from other goods. Compact discs replaced record albums, just as DVD players replaced VCRs. A change in information can also impact consumers' demand. For example, a breakout of *E. coli* or new information about a defective and/or dangerous product, such as a baby's crib, can reduce demand.

Expectations

Sometimes the demand for a good or service in a given period will dramatically increase or decrease because consumers expect the good to change in price or availability at some future date. If people expect the future price to be higher, they will purchase more of the good now before the price increase. If people expect the future price to be lower, they will purchase less of the good now and wait for the price decrease. For example, if you expect the price of computers to fall soon, you may be less willing to buy one today. Or, if you expect to earn additional income next month, you may be more willing to dip into your current savings to buy something this month.

Body piercing and tattoos have risen in popularity in recent years. The demand for these services has been pushed to the right. According to the Pew Research Center thirty-six percent of 18-25 year olds have at least one tattoo.

Use what you've LEARNED: NORMAL AND INFERIOR GOODS

Q Chester Field owns a high-quality furniture shop. If a boom in the economy occurs (higher average income per person and fewer people unemployed), can Chester expect to sell more high-quality furniture?

A Yes. Furniture is generally considered a normal good, so a rise in income will increase the demand for high-quality furniture, as shown in (a). However, if Chester sells unfinished, used, or low-quality furniture, the demand for his products might fall, as higher incomes allow customers to buy furniture that is finished, new, or of higher quality. Chester's furniture would then be an inferior good, as shown in Exhibit 4(b).

section 4.3 exhibit 4 — Normal and Inferior Goods

a. Rising Income and a Normal Good

b. Rising Income and an Inferior Good

Changes in Demand Versus Changes in Quantity Demanded—Revisited

Economists put particular emphasis on the impact on consumer behavior of a change in the price of a good. We are interested in distinguishing between consumer behavior related to the price of a good itself (movement *along* a demand curve) and behavior related to changes in other factors (shifts of the demand curve).

As indicated earlier, if the price of a good changes, it causes a *change in quantity demanded*. If one of the other factors (determinants) influencing consumer behavior changes, it results in a *change in demand*. The effects of some of the determinants that cause changes in demand (shifters) are reviewed in Exhibit 5. For example, there are two different ways to curb teenage smoking: raise the price of cigarettes (a reduction in the quantity of cigarettes demanded) or decrease the demand for cigarettes (a leftward shift in the demand curve for cigarettes). Both would reduce the amount of smoking. Specifically, to increase the price of cigarettes, the government could impose a higher tax on manufacturers. Most of this would be passed on to consumers in the form of higher prices (more on this in Chapter 6). Or to shift the demand curve leftward, the government could adopt policies to discourage smoking, such as advertising bans and increasing consumer awareness of the harmful side effects of smoking—disease and death.

section 4.3 exhibit 5 — Possible Demand Shifters

Price of complement falls or price of substitute rises

Income increases (normal good)

Income increases (inferior good)

Increase in the number of buyers in the market

Taste change in favor of the good

Future price increase expected

Use what you've LEARNED
CHANGES IN DEMAND VERSUS CHANGES IN QUANTITY DEMANDED

Q How would you use a graph to demonstrate the two following scenarios? (1) Someone buys more DVDs because the price of DVDs has fallen; and (2) a student buys more DVDs because she just got a 20 percent raise at work giving her additional income.

A In Exhibit 6, the movement from A to B is called an increase in quantity demanded; the movement from B to A is called a decrease in quantity demanded. Economists use the phrase "increase or decrease in quantity demanded" to describe movements along a given demand curve. However, the change from A to C is called an increase in demand, and the change from C to A is called a decrease in demand. The phrase "increase or decrease in demand" is reserved for a shift in the whole curve. So if an individual buys more DVDs because the price fell, we call it an increase in quantity demanded. However, if she buys more DVDs even at the current price, say $15, we say it is an increase in demand. In this case, the increase in income was responsible for the increase in demand, because she chose to spend some of her new income on DVDs.

section 4.3 exhibit 6 — Change in Demand Versus Change in Quantity Demanded

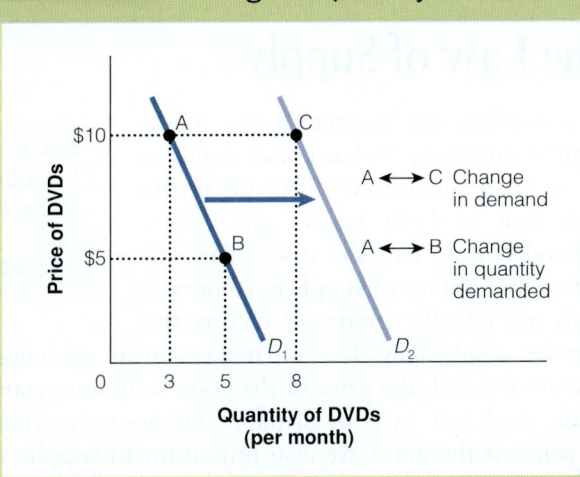

A ↔ C Change in demand
A ↔ B Change in quantity demanded

SECTION CHECK

1. A change in the quantity demanded describes a movement along a given demand curve in response to a change in the price of the good.
2. A change in demand shifts the entire demand curve. An increase in demand shifts the demand curve to the right; a decrease shifts it to the left.
3. A change in the price of a substitute shifts the demand curve for the good in question. The relationship is direct.
4. A change in the price of a complement shifts the demand curve for the good in question. The relationship is inverse.
5. Changes in income cause demand curve shifts. For normal goods the relationship is direct; for inferior goods it is inverse.
6. The position of the demand curve will vary according to the number of consumers in the market.
7. Changes in taste will shift the demand curve.
8. Changes in expected future prices and income can shift the current demand curve.

---

1. What is the difference between a change in demand and a change in quantity demanded?
2. If the price of zucchini increases, causing the demand for yellow squash to rise, what do we call the relationship between zucchini and yellow squash?
3. If incomes rise and, as a result, demand for jet skis increases, how do we describe that good?
4. How do expectations about the future influence the demand curve?
5. Would a change in the price of ice cream cause a change in the demand for ice cream? Why or why not?
6. Would a change in the price of ice cream likely cause a change in the demand for frozen yogurt, a substitute?
7. If plane travel is a normal good and bus travel is an inferior good, what will happen to the demand curves for plane and bus travel if people's incomes increase?

SECTION 4.4 Supply

* What is the law of supply?
* What is an individual supply curve?
* What is a market supply curve?

The Law of Supply

In a market, the answer to the fundamental question, "What do we produce, and in what quantities?" depends on the interaction of both buyers and sellers. Demand is only half the story. The willingness and ability of suppliers to provide goods are equally important factors that must be weighed by decision makers in all societies. As with demand, the price of the good is an important factor. And just as with demand, factors other than the price of the good are also important to suppliers, such as the cost of inputs or advances in technology. While behavior will vary among individual suppliers, economists expect that, other things being equal, the quantity supplied will vary directly with the price of the good, a relationship called the **law of supply.** According to the law of supply, the higher the price of the good (P), the greater the quantity supplied (Q_s), and the lower the price of the good, the smaller the quantity supplied.

law of supply
the higher (lower) the price of the good, the greater (smaller) the quantity supplied

$$P \uparrow \Rightarrow Q_s \uparrow \quad \text{and} \quad P \downarrow \Rightarrow Q_s \downarrow$$

The relationship described by the law of supply is a direct, or positive, relationship, because the variables move in the same direction.

A Positive Relationship Between Price and Quantity Supplied

Firms supplying goods and services want to increase their profits, and the higher the price per unit, the greater the profitability generated by supplying more of that good. For example, if you were a coffee grower, wouldn't you much rather be paid $5 a pound than $1 a pound, *ceteris paribus*?

When the price of coffee is low, the coffee business is less profitable and less coffee will be produced. Some suppliers may even shut down, reducing their quantity supplied to zero.

An Individual Supply Curve

To illustrate the concept of an **individual supply curve,** consider the amount of coffee that an individual supplier, Juan Valdes, is willing and able to supply in one year. The law of supply can be illustrated, like the law of demand, by a table or graph. Juan's supply schedule for coffee is shown in Exhibit 1(a). The combinations of price and quantity supplied were then plotted and joined to create the individual supply curve shown in Exhibit 1(b). Note that the individual supply curve is upward sloping as you move from left to right. At higher prices, it will be more attractive to increase production. Existing firms or growers will produce more at higher prices than at lower prices.

The Market Supply Curve

The **market supply curve** may be thought of as the horizontal summation of the supply curves for individual firms. The market supply curve shows how the total quantity supplied varies positively with the price of a good, while holding constant all other factors that affect how much producers are able and willing to supply. The market supply schedule, which reflects the total quantity supplied at each price by all of the coffee producers, is shown in Exhibit 2(a). Exhibit 2(b) illustrates the resulting market supply curve for this group of coffee producers.

individual supply curve
a graphical representation that shows the positive relationship between the price and quantity supplied

market supply curve
a graphical representation of the amount of goods and services that suppliers are willing and able to supply at various prices

---

section 4.4 exhibit 1   An Individual Supply Curve

a. Juan's Supply Schedule for Coffee

Price (per pound)	Quantity Supplied (pounds per year)
$5	80
4	70
3	50
2	30
1	10

Other things being equal, the quantity supplied will vary directly with the price of the good. As the price rises (falls), the quantity supplied increases (decreases).

b. Juan's Supply Curve for Coffee

section 4.4 exhibit 2: A Market Supply Curve

a. Market Supply Schedule for Coffee

Price (per pound)	Juan	+	Other Producers	=	Market Supply
$5	80	+	7,920	=	8,000
4	70	+	6,930	=	7,000
3	50	+	4,950	=	5,000
2	30	+	2,970	=	3,000
1	10	+	990	=	1,000

b. Market Supply Curve for Coffee

The dots on this graph indicate different quantities of coffee that producers would be willing and able to supply at various prices. The line connecting those combinations is the market supply curve.

SECTION CHECK

1. The law of supply states that the higher (lower) the price of a good, the greater (smaller) the quantity supplied.
2. The relationship between price and quantity supplied is positive because profit opportunities are greater at higher prices and because the higher production costs of increased output mean that suppliers will require higher prices.
3. The market supply curve is a graphical representation of the amount of goods and services that suppliers are willing and able to supply at various prices.

---

1. What are the two reasons why a supply curve is positively sloped?
2. What is the difference between an individual supply curve and a market supply curve?

SECTION 4.5 Shifts in the Supply Curve

* What is the difference between a change in supply and a change in quantity supplied?
* What are the determinants of supply?
* How does the number of suppliers affect the supply curve?
* How does technology affect the supply curve?
* How do taxes affect the supply curve?

A Change in Quantity Supplied Versus a Change in Supply

Changes in the price of a good lead to changes in the quantity supplied by suppliers, just as changes in the price of a good lead to changes in the quantity demanded by buyers. Similarly, a change in supply, whether an increase or a decrease, can occur for reasons other than changes in the price of the product itself, just as changes in demand may be due to factors (determinants) other than the price of the good. In other words, a change in the price of the good in question is shown as a movement along a given supply curve, leading to a change in quantity supplied. A change in any other factor that can affect supplier behavior (input prices, the prices of related products, expectations, number of suppliers, technology, regulation, taxes and subsidies, and weather) results in *a shift in the entire supply curve,* leading to a change in supply.

Shifts in Supply

An increase in supply shifts the supply curve to the right; a decrease in supply shifts the supply curve to the left, as shown in Exhibit 1. Anything that affects the costs of production will influence supply and the position of the supply curve. We will now look at some of the possible determinants of supply—factors that determine the position of the supply curve—in greater depth.

Input Prices

Suppliers are strongly influenced by the costs of inputs used in the production process, such as steel used for automobiles or microchips used in computers. For example, higher labor, materials, energy, or other input costs increase the costs of production, causing the supply curve to shift to the left at each and every price. If input prices fall, the costs of production decrease, causing the supply curve to shift to the right—more will be supplied at each and every price.

Prices of Related Goods

The supply of a good increases if the price of one of its substitutes in production falls; and the supply of a good decreases if the price of one of its substitutes in production rises. Suppose you own your own farm, on which you plant cotton and wheat. One year, the price of wheat falls, and farmers reduce the quantity of wheat supplied, as shown in Exhibit 2(a). What effect does the lower price of wheat have on your cotton production? It increases the supply of cotton. You want to produce relatively less of the crop that has fallen in price (wheat) and relatively more of the now more attractive other crop (cotton). Cotton and wheat are *substitutes in production* because both goods can be produced using the same resources. Producers tend to substitute the production of more profitable products for that of less profitable products. So the decrease in the price in the wheat market has caused an increase in supply (a rightward shift) in the cotton market, as seen in Exhibit 2(b).

If the price of wheat, a substitute in production, increases, then that crop becomes more profitable. This leads to an increase in the quantity supplied of wheat. Consequently, farmers will shift their resources out of the relatively lower-priced crop (cotton); the result is a decrease in supply of cotton.

Other examples of substitutes in production include automobile producers that have to decide between producing sedans and pick-ups or construction companies that have to choose between building single residential houses or commercial buildings.

Some goods are *complements in production*. Producing one good does not prevent the production of the other, but actually enables production of the other. For example, leather and beef are complements in production. Suppose the price of a beef rises and as a result cattle ranchers increase the quantity supplied of beef, moving up the supply curve for beef, as seen in Exhibit 2(c). When cattle ranchers produce more beef they automatically produce more leather. Thus, when the price of beef increases, the supply of the related good, leather, shifts to the right, as seen in Exhibit 2(d). Suppose the price of beef falls, and as a result, the quantity supplied of beef falls; this leads to a decrease (a leftward shift) in the supply of leather.

Other examples of complements in production where goods are produced simultaneously from the same resource include: a lumber mill that produces lumber and sawdust or an oil refinery that can produce gasoline or heating oil from the same resource—crude oil.

Expectations

Another factor shifting supply is suppliers' expectations. If producers expect a higher price in the future, they will supply less now than they otherwise would have, preferring to wait and sell when their goods will be more valuable. For example, if a cotton producer expected the future price of cotton to be higher next year, he might decide to store some of his current production of cotton for next year when the price will be higher. Similarly, if producers expect now that the price will be lower later, they will supply more now. Oil refiners will often store some of their spring supply of gasoline for summer because gasoline prices typically peak in summer. In addition, some of the heating oil for the fall is stored to supply it in the winter when heating oil prices peak.

Number of Suppliers

We are normally interested in market demand and supply (because together they determine prices and quantities) rather than in the behavior of individual consumers and firms. As we discussed earlier in the chapter, the supply

section 4.5 exhibit 1 Supply Shifts

An increase in supply shifts the supply curve to the right. A decrease in supply shifts the supply curve to the left.

section 4.5 exhibit 2 — Substitutes and Complements in Production

If land can be used for either wheat or cotton, a decrease in the price of wheat causes a decease in the quantity supplied; a movement down along the supply curve in Exhibit 2(a). This may cause some farmers to shift out of the production of wheat and into the substitute in production—cotton—shifting the cotton supply curve to the right in Exhibit 2(b). If the price of the complement in production increases (cattle), it becomes more profitable and and as a result cattle ranchers increase the quantity supplied of beef, moving up the supply curve for beef, as seen in Exhibit 2 (c). When cattle ranchers produce more beef they also produce more leather. Thus, when the price of beef increases, the supply of the related good, leather, shifts to the right, as seen in Exhibit 2(d).

curves of individual suppliers can be summed horizontally to create a market supply curve. An increase in the number of suppliers leads to an increase in supply, denoted by a rightward shift in the supply curve. For example, think of the number of gourmet coffee shops that have sprung up over the last 15 to 20 years, shifting the supply curve of gourmet coffee to the right. An exodus of suppliers has the opposite impact, a decrease in supply, which is indicated by a leftward shift in the supply curve.

Technology

Technological change can lower the firm's costs of production through productivity advances. These changes allow the firm to spend less on inputs and produce the same level of output. Human creativity works to find new ways to produce goods and services using fewer or less costly inputs of labor, natural resources, or capital. Because the firm can now produce the good at a lower cost it will supply more of the good at each and every price—the supply curve shifts to the right.

Government (Regulation, Taxes, and Subsidies)

Supply may also change because of changes in the legal and regulatory environment in which firms operate. Government regulations can influence the costs of production to a firm, leading to cost-induced supply changes similar to those just discussed. For example, if new safety or clean air requirements increase labor and capital costs, the increased cost will result, other things being equal, in a decrease in supply, shifting the supply curve to the left, or up. However, deregulation can shift the supply curve to the right.

Certain types of taxes can also alter the costs of production borne by the supplier, causing the supply curve to shift to the left at each price. A subsidy, the opposite of a tax, can lower a firm's costs and shift the supply curve to the right. For example, the government sometimes provides farmers with subsidies to encourage the production of certain agricultural products.

Weather

In addition, weather can sometimes dramatically affect the supply of certain commodities, particularly agricultural products and transportation services. A drought or freezing temperatures will almost certainly cause the supply curves for many crops to shift to the left, while exceptionally good weather can shift a supply curve to the right. For example, unusually cold weather in California during the winter of 2006 destroyed billions of dollars worth of citrus fruit. Hurricane Rita disrupted oil and refining processes. Both events shifted the supply curve for those products to the left.

For example, if production costs rise because of a wage increase or higher fuel costs, other things remaining constant, we would expect a decrease in supply—that is, a leftward shift in the supply curve. Alternatively, if some variable, such as lower input prices, causes the costs of production to fall, the supply curve will shift to the right. Exhibit 3 illustrates the effects of some of the determinants that cause shifts in the supply curve.

A major disaster such as a flood or hurricane can reduce the supply of crops and livestock. Occasionally, floods have spilled over the banks of the Mississippi River—bursting through levees and destroying crops and animals.

Change in Supply Versus Change in Quantity Supplied—Revisited

If the price of a good changes, it leads to a change in the quantity supplied. If one of the other factors influences sellers' behavior, we say it results in a change in supply.

section 4.5 exhibit 3 Possible Supply Shifts

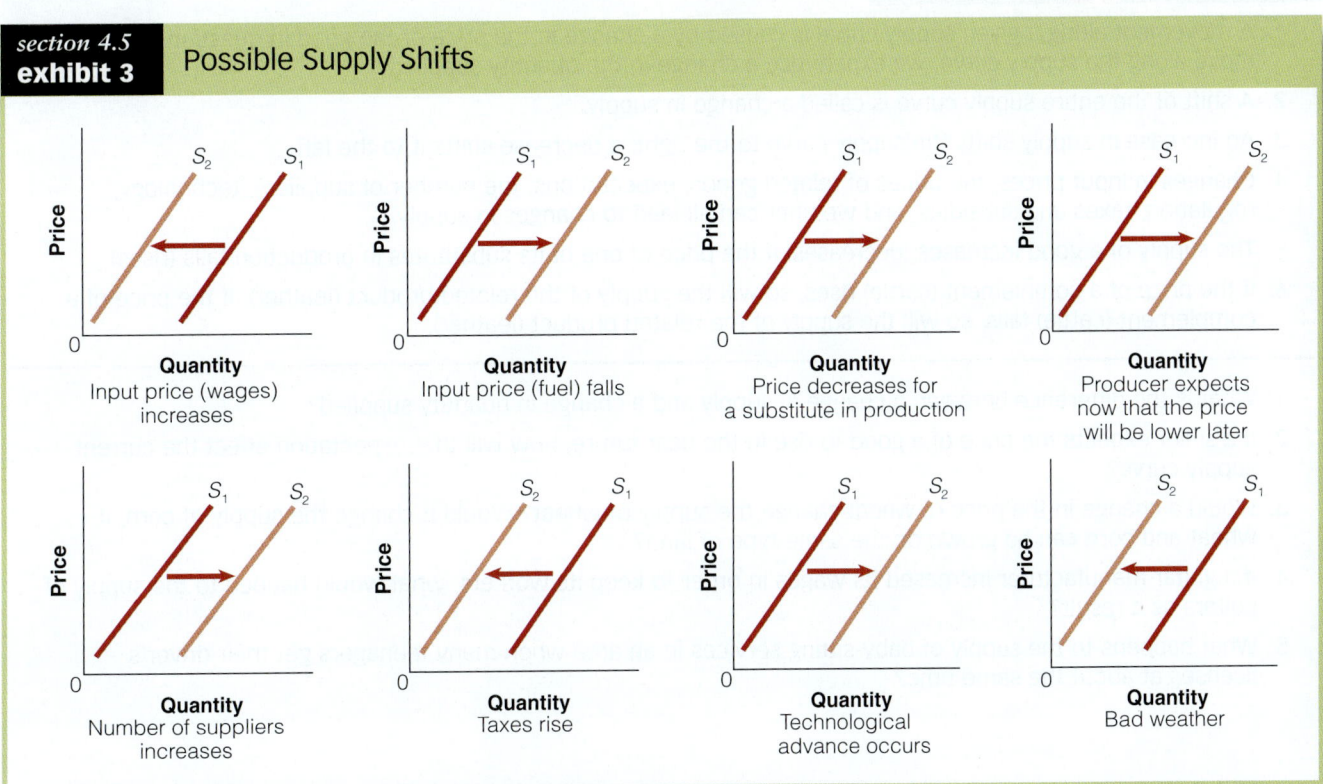

Use what you've LEARNED
CHANGE IN SUPPLY VERSUS CHANGE IN QUANTITY SUPPLIED

Q How would you graph the following two scenarios: (1) the price of cotton rises; and (2) good weather causes an unusually abundant cotton harvest?

A In the first scenario, the price of cotton increases, so the quantity supplied changes (i.e., a movement along the supply curve). In the second scenario, the good weather causes the supply curve for cotton to shift to the right, which is called a change in supply (not quantity supplied). A shift in the whole supply curve is caused by one of the other variables, not by a change in the price of the good in question.

As shown in Exhibit 4, the movement from A to B is called an increase in quantity supplied, and the movement from B to A is called a decrease in quantity supplied. However, the change from B to C is called an increase in supply, and the movement from C to B is called a decrease in supply.

section 4.5 exhibit 4 Change in Supply vs Change in Quantity Supplied

A ↔ B Change in quantity supplied

B ↔ C Change in supply

SECTION CHECK

1. A movement along a given supply curve is caused by a change in the price of the good in question. As we move along the supply curve, we experience a change in the quantity supplied.
2. A shift of the entire supply curve is called a change in supply.
3. An increase in supply shifts the supply curve to the right; a decrease shifts it to the left.
4. Changes in input prices, the prices of related goods, expectations, the number of suppliers, technology, regulation, taxes and subsidies, and weather can all lead to changes in supply.
5. The supply of a good increases (decreases) if the price of one of its substitutes in production falls (rises).
6. If the price of a complement (cattle) rises, so will the supply of the related product (leather). If the price of a complement (cattle) falls, so will the supply of the related product (leather).

---

1. What is the difference between a change in supply and a change in quantity supplied?
2. If a seller expects the price of a good to rise in the near future, how will that expectation affect the current supply curve?
3. Would a change in the price of wheat change the supply of wheat? Would it change the supply of corn, if wheat and corn can be grown on the same type of land?
4. If a guitar manufacturer increased its wages in order to keep its workers, what would happen to the supply of guitars as a result?
5. What happens to the supply of baby-sitting services in an area when many teenagers get their driver's licenses at about the same time?

Interactive Chapter Summary

Fill in the blanks:

1. A(n) _____ is the process of buyers and sellers _____ goods and services.

2. The important point about a market is what it does—it facilitates _____.

3. _____, as a group, determine the demand side of the market. _____, as a group, determine the supply side of the market.

4. A(n) _____ market consists of many buyers and sellers, no single one of whom can influence the market price.

5. According to the law of demand, other things being equal, when the price of a good or service falls, the _____ increases.

6. An individual _____ curve reveals the different amounts of a particular good a person would be willing and able to buy at various possible prices in a particular time interval, other things being equal.

7. The _____ curve for a product is the horizontal summing of the demand curves of the individuals in the market.

8. A change in _____ leads to a change in quantity demanded, illustrated by a(n) _____ demand curve.

9. A change in demand is caused by changes in any of the other factors (besides the good's own price) that would affect how much of the good is purchased: the _____, _____, the _____ of buyers, _____, and _____.

10. An increase in demand is represented by a _____ shift in the demand curve; a decrease in demand is represented by a _____ shift in the demand curve.

11. Two goods are called _____ if an increase in the price of one causes the demand curve for another good to shift to the _____.

12. For normal goods an increase in income leads to a(n) _____ in demand, and a decrease in income leads to a(n) _____ in demand, other things being equal.

13. An increase in the expected future price of a good or an increase in expected future income may _____ current demand.

14. According to the law of supply, the higher the price of the good, the greater the _____, and the lower the price of the good, the smaller the _____.

15. The quantity supplied is positively related to the price because firms supplying goods and services want to increase their _____ and because increasing _____ costs mean that the suppliers will require _____ prices to induce them to increase their output.

16. An individual supply curve is a graphical representation that shows the _____ relationship between the price and the quantity supplied.

17. The market supply curve is a graphical representation of the amount of goods and services that suppliers are _____ and _____ to supply at various prices.

18. Possible supply determinants (factors that determine the position of the supply curve) are _____ prices; _____; _____ of suppliers; and _____, _____, _____, and _____.

19. A fall in input prices will _____ the costs of production, causing the supply curve to shift to the _____.

20. The supply of a good _____ if the price of one of its substitutes in production falls.

21. The supply of a good _____ if the price of one of its substitutes in production rises.

Answers: 1. market; exchanging 2. trade 3. Buyers; Sellers 4. competitive 5. quantity demanded 6. demand 7. market demand 8. a good's price; movement along 9. prices of related goods; income; number; tastes; expectations 10. rightward; leftward 11. substitutes; right 12. increase; decrease 13. increase 14. quantity supplied; quantity supplied 15. profits; production; higher 16. positive 17. willing; able 18. input; expectations; number; technology; regulation; taxes and subsidies; weather 19. lower; right 20. increases 21. decreases

Key Terms and Concepts

market 93
competitive market 94
law of demand 94
individual demand schedule 95
individual demand curve 95

market demand curve 95
change in quantity demanded 97
change in demand 98
substitutes 99
complements 99

normal good 100
inferior good 100
law of supply 104
individual supply curve 105
market supply curve 105

Section Check Answers

4.1 Markets

1. **Why is it difficult to define a market precisely?**
   Every market is different. An incredible variety of exchange arrangements arise for different types of products, different degrees of organization, different geographical extents, and so on.

2. **Why do you get your produce at a supermarket rather than directly from farmers?**
   Supermarkets act as middlepersons between growers of produce and consumers of produce. You hire them to do this task for you when you buy produce from them, rather than directly from growers, because they conduct those transactions at lower costs than you could (if you could do it more cheaply than supermarkets, you would buy directly rather than from supermarkets).

3. **Why do the prices people pay for similar items at garage sales vary more than for similar items in a department store?**
   Items for sale at department stores are more standardized, easier to compare, and more heavily advertised, which makes consumers more aware of the prices at which they could get a particular good elsewhere, reducing the differences in price that can persist among department stores. Garage sale items are nonstandardized, costly to compare, and not advertised, which means people are often quite unaware of how much a given item could be purchased for elsewhere, so that price differences for similar items at different garage sales can be substantial.

4.2 Demand

1. **What is an inverse relationship?**
   An inverse, or negative, relationship is one where one variable changes in the opposite direction from the other—if one increases, the other decreases.

2. **How do lower prices change buyers' incentives?**
   A lower price for a good means that the opportunity cost to buyers of purchasing it is lower than before, and self-interest leads buyers to buy more of it as a result.

3. **How do higher prices change buyers' incentives?**
   A higher price for a good means that the opportunity cost to buyers of purchasing it is higher than before, and self-interest leads buyers to buy less of it as a result.

4. **What is an individual demand schedule?**
   An individual demand schedule reveals the different amounts of a good or service a person would be willing to buy at various possible prices in a particular time interval.

5. **What is the difference between an individual demand curve and a market demand curve?**
   The market demand curve shows the total amounts of a good or service all the buyers as a group are willing to buy at various possible prices in a particular time interval. The market quantity demanded at a given price is just the sum of the quantities demanded by each individual buyer at that price.

6. **Why does the amount of dating on campus tend to decline just before and during final exams?**
   The opportunity cost of dating—in this case, the value to students of the studying time forgone—is higher just before and during final exams than during most of the rest of an academic term. Because the cost is higher, students do less of it.

4.3 Shifts in the Demand Curve

1. **What is the difference between a change in demand and a change in quantity demanded?**
   A change in demand shifts the entire demand curve, while a change in quantity demanded refers to a movement along a given demand curve, caused by a change in the good's price.

2. **If the price of zucchini increases, causing the demand for yellow squash to rise, what do we call the relationship between zucchini and yellow squash?**
   Whenever an increased price of one good increases the demand for another, they are substitutes. The fact that some people consider zucchini an alternative to yellow squash explains in part why zucchini becomes more costly. Therefore, some people substitute into buying relatively cheaper yellow squash now instead.

3. **If incomes rise and, as a result, demand for jet skis increases, how do we describe that good?**
   If income rises and, as a result, demand for jet skis increases, we call jet skis a normal good, because for most (or normal) goods, we would rather have more of them than less, so an increase in income would lead to an increase in demand for such goods.

4. **How do expectations about the future influence the demand curve?**
   Expectations about the future influence the demand curve because buying a good in the future is an alternative to buying it now. Therefore, the higher

future prices are expected to be compared to the present, the less attractive future purchases become, and the greater the current demand for that good, as people buy more now when it is expected to be cheaper, rather than later, when it is expected to be more costly.

5. **Would a change in the price of ice cream cause a change in the demand for ice cream? Why or why not?**
   No. The demand for ice cream represents the different quantities of ice cream that would be purchased at different prices. In other words, it represents the relationship between the price of ice cream and the quantity of ice cream demanded. Changing the price of ice cream does not change this relationship, so it does not change demand.

6. **Would a change in the price of ice cream likely cause a change in the demand for frozen yogurt, a substitute?**
   Yes. Changing the price of ice cream, a substitute for frozen yogurt, would change the quantity of frozen yogurt demanded at a given price. This change in price means that the whole relationship between the price and quantity of frozen yogurt demanded has changed, which means the demand for frozen yogurt has changed.

7. **If plane travel is a normal good and bus travel is an inferior good, what will happen to the demand curves for plane and bus travel if people's incomes increase?**
   The demand for plane travel and all other normal goods will increase if incomes increase, while the demand for bus travel and all other inferior goods will decrease if incomes increase.

4.4 Supply

1. **What are the two reasons why a supply curve is positively sloped?**
   A supply curve is positively sloped because (1) the benefits to sellers from selling increase as the price they receive increases, and (2) the opportunity costs of supplying additional output rise with output (the law of increasing opportunity costs), so it takes a higher price to make increasing output in the self-interest of sellers.

2. **What is the difference between an individual supply curve and a market supply curve?**
   The market supply curve shows the total amounts of a good all the sellers as a group are willing to sell at various prices in a particular time period. The market quantity supplied at a given price is just the sum of the quantities supplied by each individual seller at that price.

4.5 Shifts in the Supply Curve

1. **What is the difference between a change in supply and a change in quantity supplied?**
   A change in supply shifts the entire supply curve, while a change in quantity supplied refers to a movement along a given supply curve.

2. **If a seller expects the price of a good to rise in the near future, how will that expectation affect the current supply curve?**
   Selling a good in the future is an alternative to selling it now. Therefore, the higher the expected future price relative to the current price, the more attractive future sales become, and the less attractive current sales become. This will lead sellers to reduce (shift left) the current supply of that good, as they want to sell later, when the good is expected to be more valuable, rather than now.

3. **Would a change in the price of wheat change the supply of wheat? Would it change the supply of corn, if wheat and corn can be grown on the same type of land?**
   The supply of wheat represents the different quantities of wheat that would be offered for sale at different prices. In other words, it represents the relationship between the price of wheat and the quantity of wheat supplied. Changing the price of wheat does not change this relationship, so it does not change the supply of wheat. However, a change in the price of wheat changes the relative attractiveness of raising wheat instead of corn, which changes the supply of corn.

4. **If a guitar manufacturer increased its wages in order to keep its workers, what would happen to the supply of guitars as a result?**
   An increase in wages, or any other input price, would decrease (shift left) the supply of guitars, making fewer guitars available for sale at any given price, by raising the opportunity cost of producing guitars.

5. **What happens to the supply of baby-sitting services in an area when many teenagers get their driver's licenses at about the same time?**
   When teenagers get their driver's licenses, their increased mobility expands their alternatives to baby-sitting substantially, raising the opportunity cost of baby-sitting. This change decreases (shifts left) the supply of baby-sitting services.

CHAPTER 4 STUDY GUIDE

True or False:

1. When economists talk of markets, they are only referring to organized markets such as the London Stock Exchange.
2. High transportation costs can make markets local rather than global.
3. The relationship between price and quantity demanded is direct, or positive.
4. The market demand curve is the horizontal summation of individual demand curves.
5. A change in a good's price does changes its demand in the same direction.
6. A decrease in demand is illustrated by a rightward shift in the demand curve.
7. Goods that are complements for one person may not be complements for another person.
8. If an increase in the price of one good causes an increase in the demand for another good, those two goods are substitutes.
9. Those goods for which falling income leads to increased demand are called inferior goods.
10. Either an increase in the number of buyers or an increase in the price of a complementary good will increase the market demand for a good or service.
11. A decrease in the price of ice cream increases the quantity of ice cream demanded and decreases the demand for frozen yogurt, a substitute.
12. Other things being equal, the quantity of a good or service supplied will vary in the opposite direction from the price of the good or service.
13. The market supply curve for a product is the horizontal summation of the supply curves for individual firms.
14. A decrease in the price of a good leads to a decrease in supply, other things equal.
15. An increase in supply leads to a movement up along the supply curve.
16. A decrease in supply shifts the supply curve downward.
17. Demanders will demand more now if the price of a good is expected to rise in the near future, but sellers will supply less now if the price of a good is expected to rise in the near future.
18. Both technological progress and reduced input prices will increase the supply of a good or service.

Multiple Choice:

1. In a competitive market, which of the following is not true?
    a. There are a number of buyers and sellers.
    b. No single buyer or seller can appreciably affect the market price.
    c. Sellers offer substantially different products.
    d. All of the above are true of a competitive market.

2. Which of the following is not a market?
    a. An eBay auction.
    b. A restaurant.
    c. The New York Stock Exchange.
    d. A garage sale.
    e. All of the above are examples of markets.

3. According to the law of demand, a decrease in the price of milk will result in a(n)
    a. increase in the demand for milk.
    b. decrease in the demand for milk.
    c. increase in the quantity of milk demanded.
    d. decrease in the quantity of milk demanded.
    e. decrease in the supply of milk.

4. Which of the following would increase the demand for cheese?
   a. An increase in the price of crackers, which are consumed with cheese.
   b. An increase in the income of cheese consumers.
   c. A decrease in the population of cheese lovers.
   d. A decrease in the price of cheese.
   e. Either b. or d. would increase the demand for cheese.

5. Which of the following would likely decrease the demand for jelly?
   a. An increase in the price of peanut butter, which is often used with jelly.
   b. An increase in income, because jelly is a normal good.
   c. An increase in the price of jelly.
   d. Medical research that finds that daily consumption of jelly makes people live 10 years longer, on average.

6. Other things equal, an increase in the price of Blu-Ray DVD players would tend to
   a. decrease the demand for Blu-Ray DVD players.
   b. decrease the demand for Blu-Ray DVDs.
   c. increase the price of televisions, a complement to Blu-Ray DVD players.
   d. increase the demand for Blu-Ray DVD players.
   e. decrease the demand for both Blu-Ray DVD players and Blu-Ray DVDs.

7. Whenever the price of Good A decreases, the demand for Good B decreases as well. Goods A and B are
   a. normal goods.
   b. inferior goods.
   c. substitutes.
   d. complements.
   e. inverse goods.

8. Whenever the price of Good A increases, the demand for Good B decreases. Goods A and B are
   a. substitutes.
   b. complements.
   c. normal goods.
   d. inferior goods.

9. Which of the following is true?
   a. A change in demand is caused by a change in a good's own price, while a change in quantity demanded is caused by a change in some other variable, such as income, tastes, or expectations.
   b. A change in quantity demanded is caused by a change in a good's own price, while a change in demand is caused by a change in some other variable, such as income, tastes, or expectations.
   c. A change in quantity demanded is a change in the amount people actually buy, while a change in demand is a change in the amount they want to buy.
   d. A change in demand and a change in quantity demanded are the same thing.

10. Suppose the Weather Channel forecasts unusually good weather in Central America has greatly increased the growing cocoa bean crop, so that the price of chocolate is expected to fall soon. As a result,
    a. the current market demand for chocolate will decrease.
    b. the current market demand for chocolate will increase.
    c. the current quantity of chocolate demanded will decrease.
    d. no change will occur in the current market for chocolate.

11. An upward-sloping supply curve shows that
    a. buyers are willing to pay more for particularly scarce products.
    b. the more of a good that is produced, the more valuable each unit becomes.
    c. suppliers expand production to make up for lost revenue as the product price falls.
    d. suppliers are willing to bear higher costs to produce their goods if they receive higher prices for them.

12. Along a supply curve,
    a. supply changes as technology changes.
    b. supply changes as price changes.
    c. quantity supplied changes as price changes.
    d. quantity supplied changes as technology changes.

13. Which of the following will not increase the supply of leather shoes?
    a. An increase in consumer income.
    b. A technological improvement that reduces the amount of leather wasted in shoe production.
    c. Lower prices for leather.
    d. Lower wages for shoe factory workers.

14. Which of the following is correct?
    a. A change in supply and a change in the quantity supplied are the same thing.
    b. A change in quantity supplied is a change in the amount people want to sell, while a change in supply is a change in the amount they actually sell.
    c. A change in supply is caused by a change in a good's own price, while a change in the quantity supplied is caused by a change in some other variable, such as input prices, prices of related goods, expectations, or taxes.
    d. A change in quantity supplied is caused by a change in a good's own price, while a change in supply is caused by a change in some other variable, such as input prices, prices of related goods, expectations, or taxes.

15. Crusty's Pizzeria delivers pizza to all the dorms around campus. Last week, Crusty's supplier of pepperoni announced a 25% decrease in its price. What effect will that change have on the supply of pizza?
    a. Supply decreases because an input price decreases.
    b. Supply increases because an input price decreases.
    c. Supply decreases because the price of pizza will fall.
    d. Supply increases because the price of pizza will rise.

16. Which of the following will not increase current supply?
    a. A fall in input prices.
    b. An advance in technology.
    c. The expectation that prices in the near future will be lower.
    d. The prices of substitute goods go up.
    e. All of the above will increase current supply.

17. If incomes are rising, in the market for an inferior good,
    a. demand will rise, and in response, so will supply.
    b. demand will fall, and in response, so will supply.
    c. demand will increase, but supply will not change.
    d. demand will decrease, but supply will not change.

18. If a farmer were choosing between growing wheat and growing soybeans on his own land,
    a. an increase in the price of soybeans would not change his supply of either wheat or soybeans.
    b. an increase in the price of soybeans would decrease his supply of wheat.
    c. an increase in the price of soybeans would decrease his supply of soybeans.
    d. an increase in the price of soybeans would increase his supply of wheat.
    e. an increase in the price of soybeans would increase his supply of soybeans.

19. A supply curve illustrates a(n) _____ relationship between _____ and _____.
    a. direct; price; quantity supplied.
    b. inverse; price; quantity supplied.
    c. direct; price; quantity demanded.
    d. inverse; price; quantity demanded.
    e. direct; price; supply.

20. A decrease in the market supply of a good could be caused by
    d. a fall in the price of inputs to the industry.
    c. some firms leaving the industry.
    b. a decrease in income.
    a. an improvement in productive technology.

Problems:

1. Ben moves to New York City, where he lives in a small condominium, from rural Minnesota, where he had a large house on several acres of land. If his choices reflect the law of demand, what do you expect is true of land prices in New York relative to those in rural Minnesota?

2. Is the market for cement best considered global? What about laptop computers?

3. Draw the demand curves for the following goods. When the price of the first good rises, what will happen to the demand for the second good? Why?
   a. Golf clubs and golf balls.
   b. Skateboards and razor scooters.
   c. Hamburger and ketchup.
   d. Coca-Cola and Pepsi.
   e. Camera and film.

4. Using the demand curve, show the effect of the following events on the market for beef:
   a. The price of chicken (a substitute) increases.
   b. The price of barbecue grills (a complement) increases.
   c. Consumer income increases.
   d. The price of beef increases.
   e. An outbreak of "mad cow" disease occurs.

5. Shown below is Hillary's demand schedule for Cherry Blossom Makeup. Graph her demand curve.

Price (dollars per ounce)	Quantity Demanded (ounces per week)
$15	5 oz.
12	10
9	15
6	20
3	25

6. Below are Cherry Blossom Makeup demand schedules for Hillary's friends, Barbara and Nancy. If Hillary, Barbara, and Nancy constitute the whole market for Cherry Blossom Makeup, complete the market demand schedule and graph the market demand curve.

Price (dollars per ounce)	Quantity Demanded (ounces per week)			
	Hillary	Barbara	Nancy	Market
$15	5	0	15	
12	10	5	20	
9	15	10	25	
6	20	15	30	
3	25	20	35	

7. Show the impact of each of the following events on the oil market.
   a. Electric and hybrid cars become subsidized and their prices fall.
   b. New oil discoveries occur in Alaska.
   c. The price for natural gas (a substitute for heating oil) rises.
   d. OPEC becomes less effective in limiting the supply of oil.
   e. OPEC becomes more effective in limiting the supply of oil.

8. Which of the following will cause an increase in the quantity of cell phones demanded? In the demand for cell phones?
   a. The price of cell phone service (a complement) increases.
   b. The prices of cell phones fall.
   c. Your income increases.
   d. The price of pagers (a substitute) falls.

9. If the price of ice cream increased,
   a. what would be the effect on the demand for ice cream?
   b. what would be the effect on the demand for frozen yogurt?

10. What would be the effect of each of the following on the demand for Chevrolets in the United States? In each case, identify the responsible determinant of demand.
    a. The price of Fords plummets.
    b. Consumers believe that the price of Chevrolets will rise next year.
    c. The incomes of Americans rise.
    d. The price of gasoline falls dramatically.

11. Using the graph above, answer the following questions:
    a. What is the movement from a to b called?
    b. What is the shift from D_1 to D_2 called?
    c. What is the movement from b to a called?
    d. What is the shift from D_2 to D_1 called?

12. What would be the effects of each of the following on the demand for hamburger in an area. In each case, identify the responsible determinant of demand.
    a. The price of chicken increases.
    b. The price of hamburger buns falls.
    c. Scientists find that eating hamburger shortens people's lives substantially.
    d. The population of the area falls.

13. The graph below shows three market demand curves for cantaloupe. Beginning at point A,
    a. Which point represents a decrease in quantity demanded?
    b. Which point represents a decrease in demand?
    c. Which point represents an increase in demand?
    d. Which point represents an increase in quantity demanded?

14. Which curve (supply or demand) would shift which way in the following cases?
    a. An increase in the price of a substitute and an increase in income, for an inferior good.
    b. Producers' expectations that prices will soon fall, and increasingly costly government regulations.
    c. An increase in income and a decreasing price of a complement, for a normal good.
    d. A technological advance and lower input prices.

15. Using the graph above, answer the following questions:
    a. What is the shift from S_1 to S_2 called?
    b. What is the movement from a to b called?
    c. What is the movement from b to a called?
    d. What is the shift from S_2 to S_1 called?

16. If the price of corn rose,
    a. what would be the effect on the supply of wheat?
    b. what would be the effect on the supply of corn?

17. Felix is a wheat farmer who has two fields he can use to grow wheat. The first field is right next to his house and the topsoil is rich and thick. The second field is 10 miles away in the mountains and the soil is rocky. At current wheat prices, Felix just produces from the field next to his house because the market price for wheat is just high enough to cover his costs of production including a reasonable profit. What would have to happen to the market price of wheat for Felix to have the incentive to produce from the second field?

18. Below is the supply schedule for Rolling Rock Oil Co. Plot Rolling Rock's supply curve on a graph.

Price (dollars per barrel)	Quantity Supplied (barrels per month)
$5	10,000
10	15,000
15	20,000
20	25,000
25	30,000

19. Below are the supply schedules for Rolling Rock and two other petroleum companies, Armadillo Oil and Pecos Petroleum. Assuming these three companies make up the entire supply side of the oil market, complete the market supply schedule and draw the market supply curve on a graph.

Price (dollars per barrel)	Quantity Supplied (barrels per month)			
	Rolling Rock	Armadillo	Pecos	Market
$5	10,000	8,000	2,000	_____
10	15,000	10,000	5,000	_____
15	20,000	12,000	8,000	_____
20	25,000	14,000	11,000	_____
25	30,000	16,000	14,000	_____

20. Below are three market supply curves for cantaloupe. Compared to point A, which point represents:
    a. A decrease in supply?
    b. A decrease in quantity supplied?
    c. An increase in supply?
    d. An increase in quantity supplied?

21. What would be the effect of each of the following on the supply of salsa in the United States? In each case, identify the responsible determinant of supply.
    a. Tomato prices skyrocket.
    b. Congress places a 26 percent tax on salsa.
    c. Ed Scissorhands introduces a new, faster vegetable chopper.
    d. Elton John, Madonna, and Paul Newman each introduce a new brand of salsa.

22. What would be the effects of each of the following on the worldwide supply of coffee. In each case, identify the responsible determinant of supply.
    a. Freezing temperatures wipe out half of Brazil's coffee crop.
    b. Wages of coffee workers in Latin America rise as unionization efforts succeed.
    c. Indonesia offers big subsidies to its coffee producers.
    d. Genetic engineering produces a super coffee bean that grows faster and needs less care.
    e. Coffee suppliers expect prices to be higher in the future.

Bringing Supply and Demand Together

5

5.1 Market Equilibrium Price and Quantity

5.2 Changes in Equilibrium Price and Quantity

5.3 Price Controls

In the words of the great economist Alfred Marshall, "Like scissors that function by the interaction of two distinct blades, supply and demand interact to determine the price and quantity exchanged."

In this chapter, we bring the market supply and demand curves together. It is market demand and supply that determine the quantity of each good that is produced and the price at which it is sold. In this chapter, we learn how markets with many buyers and sellers adjust to temporary shortages and surpluses, as prices move back to equilibrium. In addition, we will study the impact of a change in one or more of the determinants of supply and demand and see how it impacts the market price and quantity exchanged. That is, if you want to know how an event or policy may affect the economy, you must know supply and demand. We will then explore the impact of price controls, which are government mandates to set a price above or below the equilibrium price. We will also see that policies can have unintended effects—adverse effects that the policymakers did not anticipate.

SECTION 5.1 Market Equilibrium Price and Quantity

- What is the equilibrium price?
- What is the equilibrium quantity?
- What is a shortage?
- What is a surplus?

Enough has been said for now about supply and demand separately. We now bring the market supply and demand together.

Equilibrium Price and Quantity

The **market equilibrium** is found at the point at which the market supply and market demand curves intersect. The price at the intersection of the market supply curve and the market demand curve is called the **equilibrium price,** and the quantity is called the **equilibrium quantity.** At the equilibrium price, the amount that buyers are willing and able to buy is exactly equal to the amount that sellers are willing and

market equilibrium
the point at which the market supply and market demand curves intersect

equilibrium price
the price at the intersection of the market supply and demand curves; at this price, the quantity demanded equals the quantity supplied

equilibrium quantity
the quantity at the intersection of the market supply and demand curves; at the equilibrium quantity, the quantity demanded equals the quantity supplied

able to produce. The equilibrium market solution is best understood with the help of a simple graph. Let's return to the coffee example we used in our earlier discussions of supply and demand. Exhibit 1 combines the market demand curve for coffee with the market supply curve. At $3 per pound, buyers are willing to buy 5,000 pounds of coffee and sellers are willing to supply 5,000 pounds of coffee. Neither may be "happy" about the price; the buyers would probably like a lower price and the sellers would probably like a higher price. But both buyers and sellers are able to carry out their purchase and sales plans at the $3 price. At any other price, either suppliers or demanders would be unable to trade as much as they would like.

Equilibrium is not some mythical notion. It is very real. Every morning fishermen bring in their fresh catch. Along the pier, they negotiate with fish brokers—sellers find buyers and buyers find sellers. Equilibrium is reached when the quantity demanded equals the quantity supplied.

section 5.1 exhibit 1 Market Equilibrium

The equilibrium is found at the intersection of the market supply and demand curves. The equilibrium price is $3 per pound, and the equilibrium quantity is 5,000 pounds of coffee. At the equilibrium quantity, the quantity demanded equals the quantity supplied.

Shortages and Surpluses

What happens when the market price is not equal to the equilibrium price? Suppose the market price is above the equilibrium price, as seen in Exhibit 2(a). At $4 per pound, the quantity of coffee demanded would be 3,000 pounds, but the quantity supplied would be 7,000 pounds. At this price, a **surplus**, or excess quantity supplied, would exist. That is, at this price, growers would be willing to sell more coffee than demanders would be willing to buy. To get rid of the unwanted surplus, frustrated suppliers would cut their price and cut back on production. And as price falls, consumers would buy more, ultimately eliminating the unsold surplus and returning the market to the equilibrium level.

What would happen if the market price of coffee were below the equilibrium price? As seen in Exhibit 2(b), at $2 per pound, the yearly quantity demanded of 8,000 pounds would be greater than the 3,000 pounds that producers would be willing to supply at that low price. So at $2 per pound, a **shortage** or excess quantity demanded of 5,000 pounds would exist. Because of the coffee shortage, frustrated buyers would be forced to compete for the existing supply, bidding up the price. The rising price would have two effects: (1) Producers would be willing to increase the quantity supplied, and (2) the higher price would decrease the quantity demanded. Together, these two effects would ultimately eliminate the shortage, returning the market to equilibrium.

> **surplus**
> a situation where quantity supplied exceeds quantity demanded
>
> **shortage**
> a situation where quantity demanded exceeds quantity supplied

Scarcity and Shortages

People often confuse scarcity with shortages. Remember most goods are scarce—desirable but limited. A shortage occurs when the quantity demanded is greater than the quantity supplied at the current price. We can eliminate shortages by increasing the price but we cannot eliminate scarcity.

section 5.1 exhibit 2 Markets in Temporary Disequilibrium

In (a), the market price is above the equilibrium price. At this price, $4, the quantity supplied (7,000 pounds) exceeds the quantity demanded (3,000 pounds), resulting in a surplus of 4,000 pounds. To get rid of the unwanted surplus, suppliers cut their prices. As prices fall, consumers buy more, eliminating the surplus and moving the market back to equilibrium. In (b), the market price is below the equilibrium price. At this price, $2, the quantity demanded (8,000 pounds) exceeds the quantity supplied (3,000 pounds), and a shortage of 5,000 pounds is the result. The many frustrated buyers compete for the existing supply, offering to buy more and driving the price up toward the equilibrium level. Therefore, with both shortages and surpluses, market prices tend to pull the market back to the equilibrium level.

Use what you've LEARNED: SHORTAGES

Q Imagine that you own a butcher shop. Recently, you have noticed that at about noon, you run out of your daily supply of chicken. Puzzling over your predicament, you hypothesize that you are charging less than the equilibrium price for your chicken. Should you raise the price of your chicken? Explain using a simple graph.

A If the price you are charging is below the equilibrium price (P_E), you can draw a horizontal line from that price straight across Exhibit 3 and see where it intersects the supply and demand curves. The point where this horizontal line intersects the demand curve indicates how much chicken consumers are willing to buy at the below-equilibrium price (P_1). Likewise, the intersection of this horizontal line with the supply curve indicates how much chicken producers are willing to supply at P_1. From this, it is clear that a shortage (or excess quantity demanded) exists, because consumers want more chicken (Q_D) than producers are willing to supply (Q_S) at this relatively low price. This excess quantity demanded results in competition among buyers, which will push prices up and reduce or eliminate the shortage. That is, it would make sense to raise your price on chicken. As the price moves up toward the equilibrium price, consumers will be willing to purchase less (some will substitute fish, steak, or ground round), and producers will have an incentive to supply more chicken.

section 5.1 exhibit 3 Shortages

in the news: Scalping and the Super Bowl

The Super Bowl is a high demand, limited supply sports event. The face value on most Super Bowl tickets is in the $700 to $900 range. Many of the recipients of the tickets are corporate sponsors or are affiliated with the teams playing in the game. There are also some tickets that are allocated through a lottery. However, at the face value for the tickets at P_1, the quantity demanded far exceeds the quantity supplied as seen in Exhibit 4. In other words, the National Football League (NFL) has not priced their tickets equal to what the market will bear. Consequently, some fans are willing to pay much more, sometimes $6,000 to $7,000, for these tickets from scalpers, who buy the tickets at face value and try to sell them for a higher price. While ticket scalping is illegal in many states, scalpers will still descend on the host city to make a profit, even though the probability of arrest and conviction are substantial.

But is ticket scalping for athletic events and concerts really so objectionable? Could scalpers be transferring tickets into the hands of those who value them the most? The buyer must value attending the event more than the scalped price of the ticket or he would not buy the ticket. The seller would not sell her ticket unless she valued the money from the ticket more than attending the event. That is, the scalper has helped transfer tickets from those placing lower values on them to those placing higher values on them. The sponsors of the event are the losers, in the form of lost profits, for failing to charge the higher equilibrium market price. Why would the NFL not charge the higher price? Perhaps it sends a sign of goodwill to NFL fans, even if they have no appreciable chance of getting a ticket. That is, maybe the NFL is willing to take a hit on short-run profits to make sure they keep their base of fans (long-run profits).

section 5.1 exhibit 4 — The Market for Super Bowl Tickets

At the face value for Super Bowl tickets (P_1), there is a shortage. That is, at P_1, the quantity demanded (Q_D) is greater than the quantity supplied (Q_S).

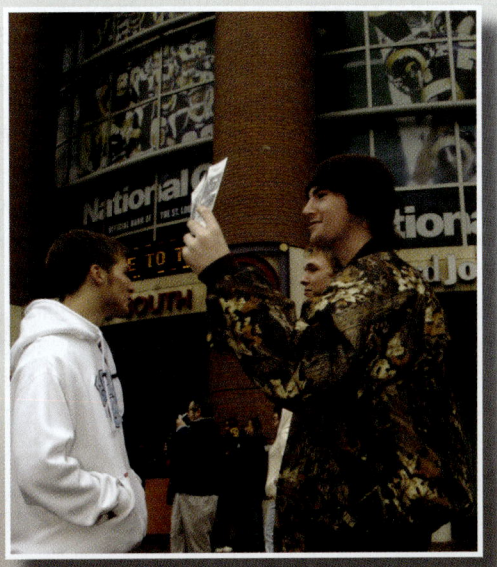

in the news — The Role of Prices in the Aftermath of Hurricane Katrina

The fallout from Hurricane Katrina has featured a lot of ignorance and demagoguery about prices. Let's look at some of it. One undeniable fact is that the hurricane disaster changed scarcity conditions. There are fewer stores, fewer units of housing, less gasoline and a shortage of many other goods and services used on a daily basis. Rising prices are not only a manifestation of these changed scarcity conditions, they help us cope, adjust and get us on the road to recovery.

Here's a which-is-better question for you. Suppose a hotel room rented for $79 a night prior to Hurricane Katrina's devastation. Based on that price, an evacuating family of four might rent two adjoining rooms. When they arrive at the hotel, they find the rooms rent for $200; they decide to make do with one room. In my book, that's wonderful. The family voluntarily opted to make a room available for another family who had to evacuate or whose home was

(continued)

in the news: The Role of Prices in the Aftermath of Hurricane Katrina (cont.)

destroyed. Demagogues will call this price-gouging, but I ask you, which is preferable: a room available at $200 or a room unavailable at $79? Rising prices get people to voluntarily economize on goods and services rendered scarcer by the disaster.

After Hurricane Katrina struck, gasoline prices shot up almost a dollar nearly overnight. Some people have been quick to call this price-gouging, particularly since wholesalers and retailers were charging the higher price for gasoline already purchased and in their tanks prior to the hurricane. The fact of business is that what a seller paid for something doesn't necessarily determine its selling price. Put in a bit more sophisticated way: Historical costs have nothing to do with selling price. For example, suppose you maintained a 10-pound inventory of coffee in your cupboard. When I ran out, you'd occasionally sell me a pound for $2. Suppose there's a freeze in Brazil destroying much of the coffee crop, driving coffee prices to $5 a pound. Then I come around to purchase coffee. Are you going to charge me $2 a pound, what you paid for it, or $5, what it's going to cost you to restock your coffee inventory?

What about the house that you might have purchased for $50,000 in 1970 that you're selling today? If you charged me $250,000 for it, today's price for its replacement, as opposed to what you paid for it, are you guilty of price-gouging?

Recovering from Katrina means resources will have to be moved to the Gulf Coast. I ask you, how does one get electricians, plumbers and other artisans to give up their comfortable homes and livelihoods in Virginia and Pennsylvania and travel to Mobile and New Orleans to help in the recovery? If you said pay them higher prices, go to the head of the class. Higher prices, along with windfall profits, are economic signals of unmet human wants. As such, they encourage producers to meet those human wants....

— BY WALTER E. WILLIAMS
SEPTEMBER 14, 2005, TOWNHALL.COM

SECTION CHECK

1. The intersection of the supply and demand curves shows the equilibrium price and equilibrium quantity in a market.
2. A surplus is a situation where quantity supplied exceeds quantity demanded.
3. A shortage is a situation where quantity demanded exceeds quantity supplied.
4. Shortages and surpluses set in motion actions by many buyers and sellers that will move the market toward the equilibrium price and quantity unless otherwise prevented.

---

1. How does the intersection of supply and demand indicate the equilibrium price and quantity in a market?
2. What can cause a change in the supply and demand equilibrium?
3. What must be true about the price charged for a shortage to occur?
4. What must be true about the price charged for a surplus to occur?
5. Why do market forces tend to eliminate both shortages and surpluses?
6. If tea prices were above their equilibrium level, what force would tend to push tea prices down? If tea prices were below their equilibrium level, what force would tend to push tea prices up?

SECTION 5.2
Changes in Equilibrium Price and Quantity

- What happens to equilibrium price and quantity when the demand curve shifts?
- What happens to equilibrium price and quantity when the supply curve shifts?
- What happens when both supply and demand shift in the same time period?
- What is an indeterminate solution?

When one of the many determinants of demand or supply (input prices, prices of related products, number of suppliers, expectations, technology, and so on) changes, the demand and/or supply curves will shift, leading to changes in the equilibrium price and equilibrium quantity. We first consider a change in demand.

A Change in Demand

A shift in the demand curve—caused by a change in the price of a related good (substitutes or complements), income, the number of buyers, tastes, or expectations—results in a change in both equilibrium price and equilibrium quantity, assuming the supply curve has not changed. But how and why does this relationship happen? The answer can be most clearly explained by means of an example. Suppose a new study claimed that two cups of coffee per day had significant health benefits. We would expect an increase in the demand for coffee. An increase in demand, *ceteris paribus*, will lead to a higher equilibrium price and a higher equilibrium quantity, as shown in Exhibit 1. The rightward shift of the demand curve results in an increase in both equilibrium price and quantity, *ceteris paribus*.

A Change in Supply

Like a shift in demand, a shift in the supply curve will also influence both equilibrium price and equilibrium quantity, assuming that demand for the product has not changed. For example, what impact would unfavorable weather conditions have in coffee-producing countries? Such conditions could cause a reduction in the supply of coffee. A decrease in supply, *ceteris paribus*, will lead to a higher equilibrium price and a lower equilibrium quantity, as shown in Exhibit 2.

section 5.2 exhibit 1 An Increase in Demand

An increase in demand leads to a higher equilibrium price and a greater equilibrium quantity, *ceteris paribus*.

section 5.2 exhibit 2 A Decrease in Supply

A decrease in supply leads to an increase in equilibrium price and a decrease in equilibrium quantity.

Use what you've LEARNED
CHANGE IN DEMAND

Q In ski resorts such as Aspen and Sun Valley, hotel prices are higher in February (in-season when more skiers want to ski) than in May (off-season when fewer skiers want to ski). If the May hotel prices were charged in February, what problem would arise? What if we charged February's price in May?

A In the (likely) event that supply is not altered significantly, demand is chiefly responsible for the higher prices in the prime skiing months. In Exhibit 3(a), if prices were maintained at the off-season rates (P_{May}) all year long, a shortage would exist—the difference between points A and B in Exhibit 3(a). This excess demand at the off-peak prices causes prime-season rates to be higher. After all, why would a self-interested resort owner rent you a room for less than its opportunity cost (what someone else would be willing to pay)? For example, at the Hotel Jerome in Aspen, the price per night of a Deluxe King room is almost 6 times higher in late December (in-season) than it is in mid May (off-season). In Exhibit 3(b), we see that if hotels

What would happen if the Hotel Jerome, pictured above, charged the lower out-of-season rate for resort rentals during peak ski season?

were to charge the in-season price (P_{Feb}) during the off-season (May), a surplus would result—the difference between points C and D. Now, it would be this excess supply during the off-season (at in-season prices) that would cause the price to fall. Who needs all the empty rooms?

section 5.2 exhibit 3 The Market for Aspen Rentals

a. Charging May (Off-Season) Prices in February (In-Season)

b. Charging February (In-Season) Prices in May (Off-Season)

Changes in Both Supply and Demand

We have discussed that, as part of the continual process of adjustment that occurs in the marketplace, supply and demand can each shift in response to many different factors, with the market then adjusting toward the new equilibrium. We have, so far, only considered what happens when just one such change occurs at a time. In these cases, we learned that the results of the adjustments in supply and demand on the equilibrium price and quantity are predictable. However, both supply and demand will often shift in the same time period. Can we predict what will happen to equilibrium prices and equilibrium quantities in these situations?

As you will see, when supply and demand move at the same time, we can predict the change in one variable (price or quantity), but we are unable to predict the direction of the effect on the other variable with any certainty. The change in the second variable, then, is said to be *indeterminate*, because it cannot be determined without additional information about the size of the relative shifts in supply and demand. This concept will become clearer to you as we work through the following example.

An Increase in Supply and a Decrease in Demand

In Exhibits 4(a) and 4(b), we have an increase in supply and a decrease in demand. These changes will clearly result in a decrease in the equilibrium price, because both the increase in supply and the decrease in demand work to push this price down. This drop in equilibrium price (from P_1 to P_2) is shown in the movement from E_1 to E_2 in Exhibits 4(a) and 4(b).

The effect of these changes on equilibrium price is clear, but how does the equilibrium quantity change? The impact on equilibrium quantity is indeterminate because the increase in supply increases the equilibrium quantity and the decrease in demand decreases it. In this scenario, the change in the equilibrium quantity

section 5.2 exhibit 4 — Shifts in Supply and Demand

a. A Small Increase in Supply and a Large Decrease in Demand

If the decrease in demand (leftward shift) is greater than the increase in supply (rightward shift), the equilibrium price and equilibrium quantity will fall.

b. A Large Increase in Supply and a Small Decrease in Demand

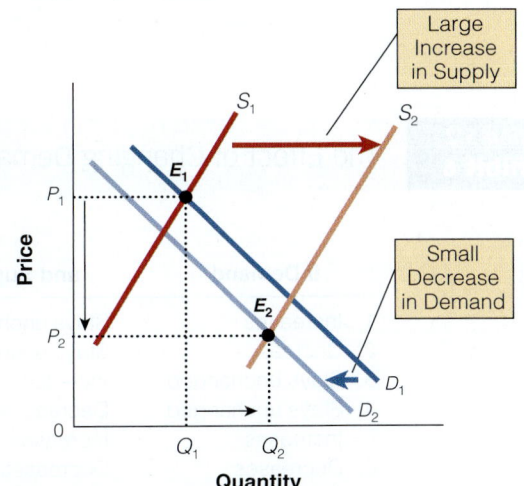

If the increase in supply (rightward shift) is greater than the decrease in demand (leftward shift), the equilibrium price will fall and the equilibrium quantity will rise.

will vary depending on the relative changes in supply and demand. If, as shown in Exhibit 4(a), the decrease in demand is greater than the increase in supply, the equilibrium quantity will decrease. If, however, as shown in Exhibit 4(b), the increase in supply is greater than the decrease in demand, the equilibrium quantity will increase.

section 5.2 exhibit 5 An Increase in the Demand and Supply of HD Televisions

The increase in supply and demand caused an increase in the equilibrium quantity. Price is the indeterminate variable. Because the supply of HD televisions shifted more than the demand for HD televisions, the price of HD televisions has fallen.

An Increase in Demand and Supply

It is also possible that both supply and demand will increase (or decrease). This situation, for example, has happened with flat screen televisions (and with DVDs, laptops, cell phones, high definition (HD) televisions, digital cameras, and other electronic equipment, too). As a result of technological breakthroughs and new factories manufacturing HD televisions, the supply curve for HD televisions shifted to the right. That is, at any given price, more HD televisions were offered than before. But with rising income and an increasing number of buyers in the market, the demand for HD televisions increased as well. As shown in Exhibit 5, both the increased demand and the increased supply caused an increase in the equilibrium quantity—more HD televisions were sold. The equilibrium price could have gone either up (because of increased demand) or down (because of increased supply), depending on the relative sizes of the demand and supply shifts. In this case, price is the indeterminate variable. However, in the case of HD televisions, we know that the supply curve shifted more than the demand curve, so that the effect of increased supply pushing prices down outweighed the effect of increased demand pushing prices up. As a result, the equilibrium price of HD televisions has fallen (from P_1 to P_2) over time.

The Combinations of Supply and Demand Shifts

The eight possible changes in demand and/or supply are presented in Exhibit 6, along with the resulting changes in equilibrium quantity and equilibrium

section 5.2 exhibit 6 The Effect of Changing Demand and/or Supply

If Demand	and Supply	Then Equilibrium Quantity	and Equilibrium Price
1. Increases	Stays unchanged	Increases	Increases
2. Decreases	Stays unchanged	Decreases	Decreases
3. Stays unchanged	Increases	Increases	Decreases
4. Stays unchanged	Decreases	Decreases	Increases
5. Increases	Increases	Increases	Indeterminate*
6. Decreases	Decreases	Decreases	Indeterminate*
7. Increases	Decreases	Indeterminate*	Increases
8. Decreases	Increases	Indeterminate*	Decreases

*May increase, decrease, or remain the same, depending on the size of the change in demand relative to the change in supply.

price. Even though you could memorize the impact of the various possible changes in demand and supply, it would be more profitable to draw a graph, as shown in Exhibit 7, whenever a situation of changing demand and/or supply arises. Remember that an increase in either demand or supply means a rightward shift in the curve, while a decrease in either means a leftward shift. Also, when both demand and supply change, one of the two equilibrium values, price or quantity, will change in an indeterminate manner (increase or decrease), depending on the relative magnitude of the changes in supply and demand.

section 5.2
exhibit 7 — The Combination of Supply and Demand Shifts

Use what you've LEARNED
COLLEGE ENROLLMENT AND THE PRICE OF GOING TO COLLEGE

Q How is it possible that the price of a college education has increased significantly over the past 37 years, yet many more students are attending college? Does this relationship defy the law of demand?

A If we know the price of a college education (adjusted for inflation) and the number of students enrolled in college for the two years 1970 and 2010, we can tell a plausible story using the analysis of
(continued)

Use what you've LEARNED
COLLEGE ENROLLMENT AND THE PRICE OF GOING TO COLLEGE (cont.)

supply and demand. In Exhibit 8(a), suppose that we have data for points A and B; the price of a college education and the quantity (the number of college students enrolled in the respective years, 1970 and 2010). In Exhibit 8(b), we connect the two points with supply and demand curves and see a decrease in supply and an increase in demand. Demand increased between 1970 and 2010 for at least two reasons. First, on the demand side, as population grows, a greater number of buyers want a college education. Second, a college education is a normal good; as income increases, buyers increase their demand for a college education. On the supply side, several factors caused the supply curve for education to shift to the left: the cost of maintenance (hiring additional staff and increasing faculty salaries), new equipment (computers, lab equipment, and library supplies), and buildings (additional classrooms, labs, cafeteria expansions, and dormitory space).

This situation does not defy the law of demand that states that there is an inverse relationship between price and quantity demanded, *ceteris paribus*. The truth is that supply and demand curves are shifting constantly. In this case, the demand (increasing) and supply (decreasing) caused price and quantity to rise.

section 5.2 exhibit 8 — Market for College Education

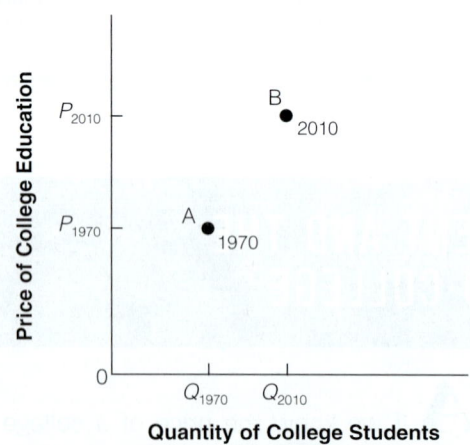

a. Price of College Education and Quantity of College Students

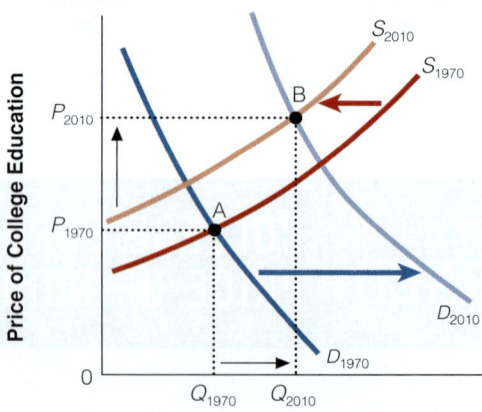

b. Simultaneous Increase in Demand and Decrease in Supply

Use what you've LEARNED: SUPPLY AND DEMAND APPLICATIONS

Q During the second half of the twentieth century, demand for chicken increased because of rising income and the purported health benefits. However, as the demand for chicken increased, the price fell. Why? (*Hint:* Remember it is supply and demand.)

A Even though the demand for chicken did increase (a small rightward shift), the supply of chicken increased even more—technological advances in the poultry industry and many new suppliers caused the supply curve to shift rightward. In order for the price to fall, the supply must have shifted further to the right than the demand curve. The result is more chickens consumed at a lower price.

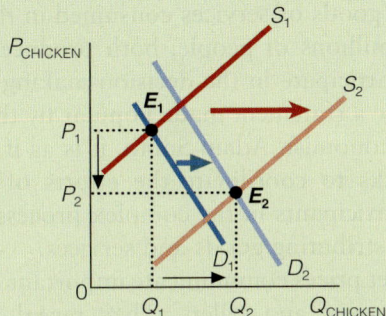

Q Suppose the demand of gasoline increases because of world economic growth and higher incomes. At the same time, supply decreases because of hostilities in the Middle East and refinery problems. What can we predict would happen to the price and quantity of gasoline?

A The increase in demand (rightward shift) and the decrease in supply (leftward shift) would lead to an increase in price. We are not sure about the quantity of gasoline consumed—it depends on the magnitude of the shifts in the demand and supply curves. That is, quantity is indeterminate.

Q Suppose the demand for air travel decreases because of air safety concerns. At the same time, the price of jet fuel increases. What do you think will happen to the price and quantity of air travel?

A The decrease in demand (leftward shift) for air travel and the decrease in supply (leftward shift) result from the higher input cost of jet fuel. These factors reduce the quantity of air travel. The price change will depend on the magnitude of the shifts in the demand and supply curves. That is, price is indeterminate.

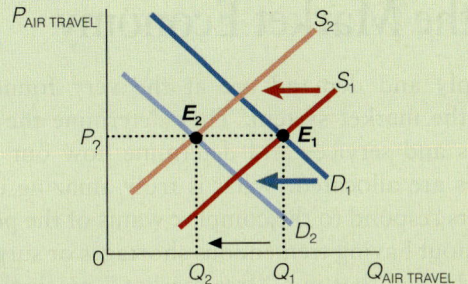

Q Hypothetically, suppose a new study reveals that sugar can have "huge" negative health consequences, causing a large decrease in demand. In addition, a slight reduction in the sugar yield occurs because of bad weather in sugar-producing areas. What do you think will happen to the price and quantity of sugar?

A A large decrease in demand (leftward shift) for sugar and a small decrease in supply (leftward shift) because of bad weather lead to a reduction in price and a large reduction in quantity.

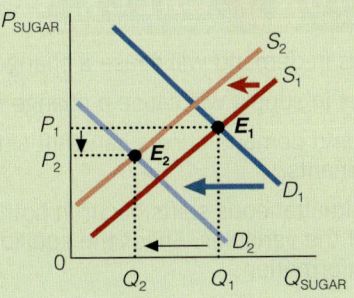

(continued)

Use what you've LEARNED
SUPPLY AND DEMAND APPLICATIONS (cont.)

Q As the price of oil rises, many may switch to burning natural gas to save money. Can buyers of natural gas expect any surprises?

A If oil and natural gas are substitutes, then the higher price for oil will cause an increase in demand for natural gas (rightward shift). As a result, the price and quantity of natural gas will rise.

Supply, Demand, and the Market Economy

Supply and demand are at the very foundation of the market system. They determine the prices of goods and services and determine how our scarce resources are allocated. What is truly amazing is how producers respond to the complex wants of the population without having tremendous shortages or surpluses, despite the fact that in a "free market," no single individual or agency makes decisions about what to produce. The market system provides a way for millions of producers and consumers to allocate scarce resources. Buyers and sellers indicate their wants through their actions and inactions in the marketplace, and this collective "voice" determines how resources are allocated. But how is this information communicated? Market prices serve as the language of the market system.

We often say the decision is made by "the market" or "market forces," but this is of little help in pinpointing the name and the place of the decision maker. In fact, no single person makes decisions about the quantity and quality of television, cars, beds, or any other goods or services consumed in the economy. Literally millions of people, both producers and consumers, participate in the decision-making process. To paraphrase a statement made popular by the first great modern economist, Adam Smith, it is as if an invisible hand works to coordinate the efforts of millions of diverse participants in the complex process of producing and distributing goods and services.

Market prices communicate important information to both buyers and sellers. They reveal information about the relative availability of products to buyers and they provide sellers with critical information about the relative value that consumers place on those products. In effect, market prices provide a way for both buyers and sellers to communicate about the relative value of resources. This communication results in a shifting of resources from those uses that are less valued to those that are more valued.

SECTION CHECK

1. Changes in demand will cause a change in the equilibrium price and/or quantity, *ceteris paribus*.
2. Changes in supply will cause a change in the equilibrium price and/or quantity, *ceteris paribus*.
3. Supply and demand curves can shift simultaneously in response to changes in both supply and demand determinants.
4. When simultaneous shifts occur in both supply and demand curves, we will be able to determine one, but not both, of the variables. Either the equilibrium price or the equilibrium quantity will be indeterminate without more information.

1. Does an increase in demand create a shortage or surplus at the original price?
2. What happens to the equilibrium price and quantity as a result of a demand increase?
3. Does an increase in supply create a shortage or surplus at the original price?
4. Assuming the market is already at equilibrium, what happens to the equilibrium price and quantity as a result of a supply increase?
5. Why do heating oil prices tend to be higher in the winter?
6. Why are evening and weekend long-distance calls cheaper than weekday long-distance calls?
7. What would have to be true for both supply and demand to shift in the same time period?
8. When both supply and demand shift, what added information do we need to know in order to determine in which direction the indeterminate variable changes?
9. If both buyers and sellers of grapes expect grape prices to rise in the near future, what will happen to grape prices and sales today?
10. If demand for peanut butter increases and supply decreases, what will happen to equilibrium price and quantity?

SECTION 5.3 Price Controls

- What are price controls?
- What are price ceilings?
- What are price floors?
- What is the law of unintended consequences?

Price Controls

Although nonequilibrium prices can occur naturally in the private sector, reflecting uncertainty, they seldom last for long. Governments, however, may impose nonequilibrium prices for significant periods. Price controls involve the use of the power of the state to establish prices different from the equilibrium prices that would otherwise prevail. The motivations for price controls vary with the market under consideration. For example, a **price ceiling**, a legal maximum price, is often set for goods deemed important to low-income households, such as housing. Or a **price floor**, a legal minimum price, may be set on wages because wages are the primary source of income for most people.

Price controls are not always implemented by the federal government. Local governments (and more rarely, private companies) can and do impose local price controls. One fairly well-known example is rent control. The inflation of the late 1970s meant rapidly rising rents; and some communities, such as Santa Monica, California, decided to do something about it. In response, they limited how much landlords could charge for rental housing.

price ceiling
a legally established maximum price

price floor
a legally established minimum price

Price Ceilings: Rent Controls

Rent control experiences can be found in many cities across the country. San Francisco, Berkeley, and New York City all have had some form of rent control. Although the rules may vary from city to city and over time, generally the price (or rent) of an apartment remains fixed over the tenure of an occupant, except for allowable annual increases tied to the cost of living or some other price index. When an occupant moves out, the owners can usually, but not always, raise the rent to a near-market level for the next occupant. The controlled rents for existing occupants, however, are generally well below market rental rates.

Results of Rent Controls

Most people living in rent-controlled apartments are getting a good deal, one that they would lose by moving as their family circumstances or income changes. Tenants thus are reluctant to give up their governmentally granted right to a below-market-rent apartment. In addition, because the rents received by landlords are constrained and below market levels, the

global WATCH: ZIMBABWE PRICE CONTROLS SPARK FOOD SHORTAGES

—BY MACDONALD DZIRUTWE

ZIMBABWE'S government and the country's businesses have clashed over prices of basic commodities, now blamed for widespread shortages days after disputed polls won by President Robert Mugabe's ruling party.

Prices shot up by as much as 100 percent after the March 31 parliamentary elections in which Mugabe's ZANU-PF government defeated the opposition Movement for Democratic Change (MDC), but the government swiftly moved in, ordering businesses to reverse the increases.

"Increases were actually delayed to avoid harsh criticism of the government ahead of the elections but now the government is saying you can not increase prices without consulting us . . . that's not what we agreed," a spokesman for the Confederation of Zimbabwe Industries told Reuters.

The staple maize-meal, sugar and cooking oil have disappeared from most shops in Harare's city centre and suburbs while most pumps at fuel stations have run dry, forcing motorists to brace for long queues.

Maize-meal supplies were already erratic in the country in recent months with supermarkets out of stocks for days on end and long queues quickly form where the commodity is available.

SOURCE: newzimbabwe.com, retrieved 12/01/2008. © newzimbabwe.com.

AP PHOTO/KAREL PRINSLOO

consider this:

In July of 2007, Zimbabwe's government threatened to seize any business that did not roll their prices back. But many shop-keepers and manufacturers threatened to shut down and lay off workers rather than produce at a loss. Gasoline was disappearing from the pumps and many workers were forced to walk to work. Shoppers were told to queue (wait in line) for whatever products were left on the shelf. Police were sent in to enforce the price controls which resulted in hundreds of shop owners being arrested for not lowering prices enough. In short, price controls and the resulting shortages can turn into social unrest. This is not the first time Zimbabwe has tried price controls; they are usually short-lived and poorly enforced. In 2009, the finance minister Patrick Chinamasa announced the government is abandoning price controls. Mr. Chinamasa told parliament "that price controls would be abandoned because they had "unintentionally" harmed businesses and added to Zimbabwe's hyperinflation."

rate of return (roughly, the profit) on housing investments falls compared with that on other forms of real estate not subject to rent controls, such as office rents or mortgage payments on condominiums. Hence, the incentive to construct new housing is reduced.

Further, when landlords are limited in the rents they can charge, they have little incentive to improve or upgrade apartments—by putting in new kitchen appliances or new carpeting, for instance. In fact, rent controls give landlords some incentive to avoid routine maintenance, thereby lowering the cost of apartment ownership to a figure approximating the controlled rental price, although the quality of the housing stock will deteriorate over time.

Another impact of rent controls is that they promote housing discrimination. Where rent controls do not exist, prejudiced landlords might willingly rent to people they believe are undesirable simply because the undesirables are the only ones willing to pay the requested rents (and the landlords are not willing to lower their rents substantially to get desirable renters because of the possible loss of thousands of dollars in income). With rent controls, each rent-controlled apartment is likely to attract many possible renters, some desirable and some undesirable as judged by the landlord, simply because the rent is at a below-equilibrium price. Landlords can indulge in their "taste" for discrimination without any additional financial loss beyond that required by the controls. Consequently, they will be more likely to choose to rent to desirable people, perhaps a family without children or pets, rather than to undesirable ones, perhaps a family with lower income and so a greater risk of nonpayment.

Exhibit 1 shows the impact of rent controls. If the price ceiling (P_{RC}) is set below the equilibrium price (P_E), consumers are willing to buy Q_D, but producers are only willing to supply Q_S. The rent control policy will therefore create a persistent shortage, the difference between Q_D and Q_S.

Price Floors: The Minimum Wage

The argument for a minimum wage is simple: Existing wages for workers in some types of labor markets do not allow for a very high standard of living, and a minimum wage allows those workers to live better than before. Ever since 1938, when the first minimum wage was established (at 25 cents per hour), the federal government has, by legislation, made it illegal to pay most workers an amount below the current legislated minimum wage. As of July of 2009, the federal minimum wage was set at $7.25. A number of states also have minimum wage laws. In cases where an employee is subject to both state and federal minimum wage laws, the employee is entitled to the higher minimum wage.

Let's examine graphically the impact of a minimum wage on low-skilled workers. In Exhibit 2, suppose the government sets the minimum wage, W_{MIN}, above the market equilibrium wage, W_E. In Exhibit 2, we see that the price floor is binding. That is, there is a surplus of low-skilled workers at W_{MIN}, because the quantity of labor supplied is greater than the quantity of labor demanded. The reason for the surplus of low-skilled workers (unemployment) at W_{MIN} is that more people are willing to work than employers are willing and able to hire.

section 5.3 exhibit 1 Rent Controls

The impact of a rent ceiling set below the equilibrium price is a persistent shortage.

section 5.3 exhibit 2 Unemployment Effects of a Minimum Wage on Low-Skilled Workers

The impact of a price floor (a minimum wage) set above the equilibrium price is a surplus—in this case, a surplus of low-skilled workers.

section 5.3 exhibit 3: Unemployment Effects of a Minimum Wage on Skilled Workers

There is no impact of a price floor on the market for skilled workers. In this market, the price floor (the minimum wage) is not binding.

In 1974, the government imposed price ceilings on gasoline. The result was shortages. In some cities, such as Chicago, Portland, and New York, drivers waited over an hour to fill up their tanks. As you know, the value of your time has an opportunity cost.

Notice that not everyone loses from a minimum wage. Workers who continue to hold jobs have higher incomes—those between 0 and Q_D in Exhibit 2. However, many low-skilled workers suffer from a minimum wage—those between Q_D and Q_S in Exhibit 2—because they either lose their jobs or are unable to get them in the first place. Although studies disagree somewhat on the precise magnitudes, they largely agree that minimum wage laws do create some unemployment and that the unemployment is concentrated among teenagers—the least-experienced and least-skilled members of the labor force.

Most U.S. workers are not affected by the minimum wage because in the market for their skills, they earn wages that exceed the minimum wage. For example, a minimum wage will not affect the unemployment rate for physicians. In Exhibit 3, we see the labor market for skilled and experienced workers. In this market, the minimum wage (the price floor) is not binding because these workers are earning wages that far exceed the minimum wage—W_E is much higher than W_{MIN}.

This analysis does not "prove" that minimum wage laws are "bad" and should be abolished. First, consider the empirical question of how much unemployment is caused by minimum wages. Economists David Card and Alan Kreuger published a controversial study on the increase in minimum wage in the fast food industry in New Jersey and Pennsylvania. They found the effect on employment to be quite small. However, other researchers using similar data have found the effect on employment to be much larger. In fact, most empirical studies indicate that a 10 percent increase in the minimum wage would reduce employment of teenagers between 1 and 3 percent. Second, some might believe that the cost of unemployment resulting from a minimum wage is a reasonable price to pay for ensuring that those with jobs get a "decent" wage. However, opponents of minimum wage argue that it might induce teenagers to drop out of school. Less than one-third of minimum wage earners are from families with incomes below the poverty line. In fact, many recipients of the minimum wage are part-time teenage workers from middle income families. More efficient methods transfer income to low-wage workers; perhaps a wage subsidy like a earned income tax credit. This is a government program that supplements low wage-workers. Of course, there are no free lunches so subsidies in the form of wages, income, or rent ultimately cost taxpayers. We will revisit this topic in upcoming chapters.

However, the analysis does point out there is a cost to having a minimum wage: The burden of the minimum wage falls not only on low-skilled workers and employers but also on consumers of products made more costly by the minimum wage.

Price Ceilings: Price Controls on Gasoline

Another example of price ceilings leading to shortages is the price controls imposed on gasoline in 1974. In 1973, the Organization of Petroleum Exporting Nations (OPEC) reduced the supply of oil. Because crude oil is the most important input in the production of gasoline, this reduction in the supply of oil caused a shift in the supply curve for gasoline leftward from S_1 to S_2 in Exhibit 4. In an effort to prevent sharply rising prices, the government

section 5.3 exhibit 4 Gasoline Price Ceiling

The higher price of crude oil (a major input for gasoline) caused the supply curve to shift leftward from S_1 to S_2. Without price controls, the price would have risen to P_2. However, with the binding price ceiling consumers were able and willing to buy Q_D but producers were able and willing to sell Q_S. Therefore, a shortage of $Q_D - Q_S$ occurred at P_C.

What do you think would happen to the number of teenagers getting jobs if we raised the minimum wage to $50 an hour?

imposed price controls on gasoline in 1974. The government told gasoline stations they could not charge more than P_C for gasoline. But people wanted to buy more gasoline than was available at the controlled price, P_C. That is, a shortage developed at P_C, as you can see in Exhibit 4. Some customers were lucky enough to get their gasoline at P_C (0 to Q_S), but others were left wanting (Q_S to Q_D). The price ceiling was binding. Consequently, people wasted hours waiting in line for gasoline. Some gas stations sold their gas on a first-come, first-served basis. Some states implemented an even/odd license plate system. If your license plate ended in an odd number, you could buy gas on only odd numbered days. In addition, quantity restrictions meant that some stations would only allow you to buy a few gallons a day; when they ran out of gas, they closed for the day. Many gas stations were closed in the evenings and on weekends.

A number of government officials wanted to put the blame on OPEC, but if prices were allowed to rise to their equilibrium at E_2, shortages would have been avoided. Instead, it would have meant higher prices at P_2 and a greater quantity sold, Q_2 rather than Q_S. Of course, not everybody was unhappy with the price ceiling. Recall our discussion of opportunity cost in Chapter 2. People place different values on their time. People with a low opportunity cost of time but who cannot as easily afford the higher price per gallon (e.g., poor retired senior citizens) would be more likely to favor the controls. Surgeons, lawyers, and others who have high hourly wages and salaries would view the controls less favorably, because the time spent waiting in line may be worth more to them than paying the higher price for gasoline.

Unintended Consequences

When markets are altered for policy reasons, it is wise to remember that actions do not always have the results that were initially intended—in other words, actions can have **unintended consequences**. As economists, we must always look for the secondary effects of an action, which may occur along with the initial effects. For example, the government is often well intentioned when it adopts price controls to help low-skilled workers or tenants in search of affordable housing; however, such policies may also cause unintended consequences that could completely undermine the intended effects. For example, rent controls may have the immediate effect of lowering rents, but secondary effects may well include low vacancy rates, discrimination against low-income and large families, deterioration of the quality of rental units, and black markets. Similarly, a sizable increase in the minimum wage may help many low-skilled workers or apprentices but may also result in higher unemployment and/or a reduction in fringe benefits, such as vacations and discounts to employees. Society has to make tough decisions, and if the government subsidizes some programs or groups of people in one area, then something must always be given up somewhere else. The "law of scarcity" cannot be repealed!

unintended consequences the secondary effects of an action that may occur after the initial effects

in the news

Rent Control: New York's Self-Destruction

"[R]ent control appears to be the most efficient technique presently known to destroy a city—except for bombing," Swedish economist Assar Lindbeck observed in a 1972 book. Rent control is a big cause of New York City's chronic financial mess, a huge cause of its notorious housing scarcity and a neat illustration of its political unreality. Ending it would be a big step toward unleashing a construction boom and boosting its economy to offset destructive tax increases.

New York has maintained price controls on rent since World War II....William Tucker, the writer who has studied the costs most closely, estimates the direct costs of rent control at $2 billion a year, exclusive of the effect of shrinking the property tax base.

Rent control . . . has inhibited construction in the city. During the recession of 1990–91, the city actually lost more housing units than it gained. . . .

The Manhattan Institute chartered an elaborate study by Henry O. Pollakowski, an MIT housing expert. He concluded, "tenants in low- and moderate-income areas receive little or no benefit from rent stabilization, while tenants in more affluent locations are effectively subsidized for a substantial portion of their rent."

SOURCE: Robert L. Bartley, "Rent Control: New York's Self-Destruction," *Wall Street Journal*, May 19, 2003, p. A17.

Use what you've LEARNED: BINDING PRICE CONTROLS

Q If binding price controls are imposed by the government at levels that are either above or below the equilibrium price, is the quantity of goods bought (and sold) less than the equilibrium quantity?

A If a price ceiling (a legally established maximum price) is set below the equilibrium price, quantity demanded will be greater than quantity supplied, resulting in a shortage at that price. Because producers will only increase the quantity supplied at higher prices, *ceteris paribus*, only Q_1 will be bought and sold. Alternatively, if a price floor (a legally established minimum price) is set above the equilibrium price, quantity supplied will be greater than quantity demanded, causing a surplus at that price. Because consumers will only increase their quantity demanded, *ceteris paribus*, at lower prices, only Q_1 will be bought and sold.

SECTION CHECK

1. Price controls involve government mandates to keep prices above or below the market-determined equilibrium price.
2. Price ceilings are government-imposed maximum prices.
3. If price ceilings are set below the equilibrium price, shortages will result.
4. Price floors are government-imposed minimum prices.
5. If price floors are set above the equilibrium price, surpluses will result.
6. The law of unintended consequences states that the results of certain actions may not always be as clear as they initially appear.

1. How is rent control an example of a price ceiling?
2. What predictable effects result from price ceilings such as rent control?
3. How is the minimum wage law an example of a price floor?
4. What predictable effects result from price floors such as the minimum wage?
5. What may happen to the amount of discrimination against groups such as families with children, pet owners, smokers, or students when rent control is imposed?
6. Why does rent control often lead to condominium conversions?
7. What is the law of unintended consequences?
8. Why is the law of unintended consequences so important in making public policy?

Interactive Chapter Summary

Fill in the blanks:

1. The price at the intersection of the market demand curve and the market supply curve is called the _____ price, and the quantity is called the _____ quantity.
2. A situation where quantity supplied is greater than quantity demanded is called a(n) _____.
3. A situation where quantity demanded is greater than quantity supplied is called a(n) _____.
4. At a price greater than the equilibrium price, a(n) _____, or excess quantity supplied, would exist. Sellers would be willing to sell _____ than demanders would be willing to buy. Frustrated suppliers would _____ their price and _____ on production, and consumers would buy _____, returning the market to equilibrium.
5. An increase in demand results in a(n) _____ equilibrium price and a(n) _____ equilibrium quantity.
6. A decrease in supply results in a(n) _____ equilibrium price and a(n) _____ equilibrium quantity.
7. If demand decreases and supply increases, but the decrease in demand is greater than the increase in supply, the equilibrium quantity will _____.
8. If supply decreases and demand increases, the equilibrium price will _____ and the equilibrium quantity will be _____.
9. A price _____ is a legally established maximum price; a price _____ is a legally established minimum price.
10. Rent controls distort market signals and lead to _____ of rent-controlled apartments.
11. The quality of rent-controlled apartments would tend to _____ over time.
12. An increase in the minimum wage would tend to create _____ unemployment for low-skilled workers.
13. The secondary effects of an action that may occur after the initial effects are called _____.

Answers: 1. equilibrium; equilibrium 2. surplus 3. shortage 4. surplus; more; lower; cut back; more 5. greater; greater 6. higher; lower 7. decrease 8. increase; indeterminate 9. ceiling; floor 10. shortages 11. decline 12. additional 13. unintended consequences

Key Terms and Concepts

market equilibrium 122
equilibrium price 122
equilibrium quantity 122
surplus 123
shortage 123
price ceiling 135
price floor 135
unintended consequences 139

Section Check Answers

5.1 Market Equilibrium Price and Quantity

1. **How does the intersection of supply and demand indicate the equilibrium price and quantity in a market?**
   The intersection of supply and demand indicates the equilibrium price and quantity in a market because at higher prices, sellers would be frustrated by their inability to sell all they would like, leading sellers to compete by lowering the price they charge; at lower prices, buyers would be frustrated by their inability to buy all they would like, leading buyers to compete by increasing the price they offer to pay.

2. **What can cause a change in the supply and demand equilibrium?**
   Changes in any of the demand curve shifters or the supply curve shifters will change the supply and demand equilibrium.

3. **What must be true about the price charged for a shortage to occur?**
   The price charged must be less than the equilibrium price, with the result that buyers would like to buy more at that price than sellers are willing to sell.

4. **What must be true about the price charged for a surplus to occur?**
   The price charged must be greater than the equilibrium price, with the result that sellers would like to sell more at that price than buyers are willing to buy.

5. **Why do market forces tend to eliminate both shortages and surpluses?**
   Market forces tend to eliminate both shortages and surpluses because of the self-interest of the market participants. A seller is better off successfully selling at a lower equilibrium price than not being able to sell at a higher price (the surplus situation) and a buyer is better off successfully buying at a higher equilibrium price than not being able to buy at a lower price (the shortage situation). Therefore, we expect market forces to eliminate both shortages and surpluses.

6. **If tea prices were above their equilibrium level, what force would tend to push tea prices down? If tea prices were below their equilibrium level, what force would tend to push tea prices up?**
   If tea prices were above their equilibrium level, sellers frustrated by their inability to sell as much tea as they would like at those prices would compete the price of tea down, as they tried to make more attractive offers to tea buyers. If tea prices were below their equilibrium level, buyers frustrated by their inability to buy as much tea as they would like at those prices would compete the price of tea up, as they tried to make more attractive offers to tea sellers.

5.2 Changes in Equilibrium Price and Quantity

1. **Does an increase in demand create a shortage or surplus at the original price?**
   An increase in demand increases the quantity demanded at the original equilibrium price, but it does not change the quantity supplied at that price, meaning that it would create a shortage at the original equilibrium price.

2. **What happens to the equilibrium price and quantity as a result of a demand increase?**
   Frustrated buyers unable to buy all they would like at the original equilibrium price will compete the market price higher, and that higher price will induce suppliers to increase their quantity supplied. The result is a higher market price and a larger market output.

3. **Does an increase in supply create a shortage or surplus at the original price?**
   An increase in supply increases the quantity supplied at the original equilibrium price, but it does not change the quantity demanded at that price, meaning that it would create a surplus at the original equilibrium price.

4. **Assuming the market is already at equilibrium, what happens to the equilibrium price and quantity as a result of a supply increase?**
   Frustrated sellers unable to sell all they would like at the original equilibrium price will compete the market price lower, and that lower price will induce demanders

to increase their quantity demanded. The result is a lower market price and a larger market output.

5. **Why do heating oil prices tend to be higher in the winter?**
The demand for heating oil is higher in cold weather winter months. The result of this higher winter heating oil demand, for a given supply curve, is higher prices for heating oil in the winter.

6. **Why are evening and weekend long-distance calls cheaper than weekday long-distance calls?**
The demand for long-distance calls is greatest during weekday business hours, but far lower during other hours. Because the demand for "off-peak" long-distance calls is lower, for a given supply curve, prices during those hours are lower.

7. **What would have to be true for both supply and demand to shift in the same time period?**
For both supply and demand to shift in the same time period, one or more of both the supply curve shifters and the demand curve shifters would have to change in that same time period.

8. **When both supply and demand shift, what added information do we need to know in order to determine in which direction the indeterminate variable changes?**
When both supply and demand shift, we need to know which of the shifts is of greater magnitude, so we can know which of the opposing effects in the indeterminate variable is larger; whichever effect is larger will determine the direction of the net effect on the indeterminate variable.

9. **If both buyers and sellers of grapes expect grape prices to rise in the near future, what will happen to grape prices and sales today?**
If grape buyers expect grape prices to rise in the near future, it will increase their current demand to buy grapes, which would tend to increase current prices and increase the current quantity of grapes sold. If grape sellers expect grape prices to rise in the near future, it will decrease their current supply of grapes for sale, which would tend to increase current prices and decrease the current quantity of grapes sold. Because both these effects tend to increase the current price of grapes, grape prices will rise. However, the supply and demand curve shifts tend to change current sales in opposing directions, so without knowing which of these shifts was of a greater magnitude, we do not know what will happen to current grape sales. They could go up, go down, or even stay the same.

10. **If demand for peanut butter increases and supply decreases, what will happen to equilibrium price and quantity?**
An increase in the demand for peanut butter increases the equilibrium price and quantity of peanut butter sold. A decrease in the supply of peanut butter increases the equilibrium price and decreases the quantity of peanut butter sold. The result is an increase in peanut butter prices and an indeterminate effect on the quantity of peanut butter sold.

5.3 Price Controls

1. **How is rent control an example of a price ceiling?**
A price ceiling is a maximum price set below the equilibrium price by the government. Rent control is an example because the controlled rents are held below the market equilibrium rent level.

2. **What predictable effects result from price ceilings such as rent control?**
The predictable effects resulting from price ceilings include shortages, reduced amounts of the controlled good being made available by suppliers, reductions in the quality of the controlled good, and increased discrimination among potential buyers of the good.

3. **How is the minimum wage law an example of a price floor?**
A price floor is a minimum price set above the equilibrium price by the government. The minimum wage law is an example because the minimum is set above the market equilibrium wage level for some low-skill workers.

4. **What predictable effects result from price floors such as the minimum wage?**
The predictable effects resulting from price floors include surpluses, reduced amounts of the controlled good being purchased by demanders, increases in the quality of the controlled good, and increased discrimination among potential sellers of the good.

5. **What may happen to the amount of discrimination against groups such as families with children, pet owners, smokers, or students when rent control is imposed?**
Rent control laws prevent prospective renters from compensating landlords through higher rents for any characteristic landlords find less attractive, whether it is bothersome noise from children or pets, odors from smokers, increased numbers of renters per unit, risks of nonpayment by lower income tenants such as students, and so on. As a result, it lowers the cost of discriminating against anyone with what landlords consider unattractive characteristics, because other prospective renters without those characteristics are willing to pay the same controlled rent.

6. **Why does rent control often lead to condominium conversions?**
   Rent control applies to rental apartments, but not to apartments owned by their occupants. Therefore, one way to get around rent control restrictions on apartment owners' ability to receive the market value of their apartments is to convert those apartments to condominiums by selling them to tenants instead (what was once a controlled rent becomes part of an uncontrolled mortgage payment).

7. **What is the law of unintended consequences?**
   The law of unintended consequences is the term used to remind us that the results of actions are not always as clear as they appear, because the secondary effects of an action may cause its results to include many consequences that were not part of what was intended.

8. **Why is the law of unintended consequences so important in making public policy?**
   It is impossible to change just one incentive to achieve a particular result through a government policy. A policy will change the incentives facing multiple individuals making multiple decisions, and changes in all those affected choices will result. Sometimes, the unintended consequences can be so substantial that they completely undermine the intended effects of a policy.

CHAPTER 5 STUDY GUIDE

True or False:

1. If the quantity demanded does not equal the quantity supplied, a shortage will always occur.
2. At the equilibrium price, the quantity demanded equals the quantity supplied.
3. A decrease in demand results in a lower equilibrium price and a higher equilibrium quantity.
4. An increase in supply results in a lower equilibrium price and a higher equilibrium quantity.
5. An increase in supply, combined with a decrease in demand, will decrease the equilibrium price but result in an indeterminate change in the equilibrium quantity.
6. If supply increases and demand decreases, but the increase in supply is greater than the decrease in demand, the equilibrium quantity will decrease.
7. An increase in both demand and supply increases the equilibrium quantity.
8. Neither a price ceiling at the equilibrium price nor a price floor at the equilibrium price would have any effect on the market price or quantity exchanged.
9. A price ceiling decreases the quantity of a good exchanged, but a price floor increases the quantity of a good exchanged.
10. A minimum wage (price floor) is likely to be binding in the market for experienced and skilled workers.

Multiple Choice:

1. A market will experience a _____ in a situation where quantity supplied exceeds quantity demanded and a _____ in a situation where quantity demanded exceeds quantity supplied.
    a. shortage; shortage
    b. surplus; surplus
    c. shortage; surplus
    d. surplus; shortage

2. The price of a good will tend to rise when
    a. a temporary shortage at the current price occurs (assuming no price controls are imposed).
    b. a temporary surplus at the current price occurs (assuming no price controls are imposed).
    c. demand decreases.
    d. supply increases.

3. Other things equal, a decrease in consumer income would
    a. increase the price and increase the quantity of autos exchanged.
    b. increase the price and decrease the quantity of autos exchanged.
    c. decrease the price and increase the quantity of autos exchanged.
    d. decrease the price and decrease the quantity of autos exchanged.

4. An increase in the expected future price of a good by consumers would, other things equal,
    a. increase the current price and increase the current quantity exchanged.
    b. increase the current price and decrease the current quantity exchanged.
    c. decrease the current price and increase the current quantity exchanged.
    d. decrease the current price and decrease the current quantity exchanged.

5. Assume that airline travel is a normal good and intercity bus travel is an inferior good. Higher incomes would
    a. increase both the price and the quantity of airline travel.
    b. decrease both the price and quantity of airline travel.
    c. increase the price and decrease the quantity of intercity bus travel.
    d. decrease the price and increase the quantity of intercity bus travel.

6. If you observed the price of a good increasing and the quantity exchanged decreasing, it would be most likely caused by
   a. an increase in demand.
   b. a decrease in demand.
   c. an increase in supply.
   d. a decrease in supply.

7. If you observed the price of a good increasing and the quantity exchanged increasing, it would be most likely caused by
   a. an increase in demand.
   b. a decrease in demand.
   c. an increase in supply.
   d. a decrease in supply.

8. If you observed the price of a good decreasing and the quantity exchanged increasing, it would be most likely caused by
   a. an increase in demand.
   b. a decrease in demand.
   c. an increase in supply.
   d. a decrease in supply.

9. If you observed the price of a good decreasing and the quantity exchanged decreasing, it would be most likely caused by
   a. an increase in demand.
   b. a decrease in demand.
   c. an increase in supply.
   d. a decrease in supply.

10. If many cooks consider butter and margarine to be substitutes, and the price of butter rises, then in the market for margarine
    a. the equilibrium price will rise, while the change to equilibrium quantity is indeterminate.
    b. the equilibrium price will rise, and the equilibrium quantity will fall.
    c. both the equilibrium price and equilibrium quantity will rise.
    d. both the equilibrium price and equilibrium quantity will fall.
    e. the equilibrium price will fall, and the equilibrium quantity will rise.

11. If you observed that the market price of a good rose while the quantity exchanged fell, which of the following could have caused the change?
    a. an increase in supply
    b. a decrease in supply
    c. an increase in demand
    d. a decrease in demand
    e. none of the above

12. If both supply and demand decreased, but supply decreased more than demand, the result would be
    a. a higher price and a lower equilibrium quantity.
    b. a lower price and a lower equilibrium quantity.
    c. no change in the price and a lower equilibrium quantity.
    d. a higher price and a greater equilibrium quantity.
    e. a lower price and a greater equilibrium quantity.

13. If the equilibrium price of wheat is $3 per bushel and then a price floor of $2.50 per bushel is imposed by the government,
    a. there will be no effect on the wheat market.
    b. there will be a shortage of wheat.
    c. there will be a surplus of wheat.
    d. the price of wheat will decrease.

14. If both supply and demand for a good shifted the same amount to the right, then we would expect that
    a. both the price and quantity exchanged would increase.
    b. price would not change and quantity exchanged would increase.
    c. the price would increase and quantity exchanged would not change.
    d. neither the price nor the quantity exchanged would change.

15. If, in a given market, the price of inputs increases and income increases (assuming it is a normal good), then
    a. price would increase but the change in quantity exchanged would be indeterminate.
    b. price would decrease but the change in quantity exchanged would be indeterminate.
    c. quantity exchanged would increase but the change in price would be indeterminate.
    d. quantity exchanged would decrease but the change in price would be indeterminate.

16. Which of the following is true?
    a. A price ceiling reduces the quantity exchanged in the market, but a price floor increases the quantity exchanged in the market.
    b. A price ceiling increases the quantity exchanged in the market, but a price floor decreases the quantity exchanged in the market.
    c. Both price floors and price ceilings reduce the quantity exchanged in the market.
    d. Both price floors and price ceilings increase the quantity exchanged in the market.

17. If a price floor was set at the current equilibrium price, which of the following would cause a surplus as a result?
    a. an increase in demand
    b. a decrease in demand
    c. an increase in supply
    d. a decrease in supply
    e. either b or c

18. The quantity exchanged on a market tends to
    a. increase for both price floors and price ceilings.
    b. decrease for both price floors and price ceilings.
    c. increase for price floors and decrease for price ceilings.
    d. decrease for price floors and increase for price ceilings.

19. A current shortage is due to a price ceiling. If the price ceiling is removed,
    a. price would increase, quantity supplied would increase, and quantity demanded would decrease.
    b. price would increase, quantity supplied would decrease, and quantity demanded would increase.
    c. price would decrease, quantity supplied would increase, and quantity demanded would decrease.
    d. price would decrease, quantity supplied would decrease, and quantity demanded would increase.

20. A current surplus is due to a price floor. If the price floor is removed,
    a. price would increase, quantity demanded would increase, and quantity supplied would increase.
    b. price would increase, quantity demanded would decrease, and quantity supplied would decrease.
    c. price would decrease, quantity demanded would increase, and quantity supplied would decrease.
    d. price would decrease, quantity demanded would decrease, and quantity supplied would increase.

21. Which of the following will most likely occur with a 20 percent increase in the minimum wage?
    a. higher unemployment rates among experienced and skilled workers
    b. higher unemployment rates among young and low-skilled workers
    c. lower unemployment rates for young and low-skilled workers
    d. the price floor (minimum wage) will be binding in the young and low-skilled labor market but not in the experienced and skilled labor market
    e. both b and d

Problems:

1. The following table shows the hypothetical monthly demand and supply schedules for cans of macadamia nuts in Hawaii.

Price	Quantity Demanded (cans)	Quantity Supplied (cans)
$6	700	100
7	600	200
8	500	300
9	400	400
10	300	500

    a. What is the equilibrium price of macadamia nuts in Hawaii?
    b. At a price of $7 per can, is there equilibrium, a surplus, or a shortage? If it is a surplus or shortage, how large is it?
    c. At a price of $10, is there equilibrium, a surplus, or a shortage? If it is a surplus or shortage, how large is it?

2. When asked about the reason for a lifeguard shortage that threatened to keep one-third of the city's beaches closed for the summer, the Deputy Parks Commissioner of New York responded that "Kids seem to want to do work that's more in tune with a career. Maybe they prefer carpal tunnel syndrome to sunburn." What do you think is causing the shortage? What would you advise the Deputy Parks Commissioner to do in order to alleviate the shortage?

3. Using supply and demand curves, show the effect of each of the following events on the market for wheat.
    a. The midwestern United States (a major wheat-producing area) suffers a flood.
    b. The price of corn decreases (assume that many farmers can grow either corn or wheat).
    c. The Midwest has great weather.
    d. The price of fertilizer declines.
    e. More individuals start growing wheat.

4. If a price is above the equilibrium price, explain the forces that bring the market back to the equilibrium price and quantity. If a price is below the equilibrium price, explain the forces that bring the market back to the equilibrium price and quantity.

5. Beginning from an initial equilibrium, draw the effects of the changes in the following list in terms of the relevant supply and demand curves.
    a. an increase in the price of hot dogs on the hamburger market
    b. a decrease in the number of taxicab companies in New York City on cab trips
    c. effect of El Niño rain storms destroying the broccoli crop in two California counties

6. Use supply and demand curves to show:
    a. simultaneous increases in supply and demand, with a large increase in supply and a small increase in demand.
    b. simultaneous increases in supply and demand, with a small increase in supply and a large increase in demand.
    c. simultaneous decreases in supply and demand, with a large decrease in supply and a small decrease in demand.
    d. simultaneous decrease in supply and demand, with a small decrease in supply and a large decrease in demand.

7. The market for baseball tickets at your college stadium, which seats 2,000, is the following:

Price	Quantity Demanded	Quantity Supplied
$2	4,000	2,000
4	2,000	2,000
6	1,000	2,000
8	500	2,000

    a. What is the equilibrium price?
    b. What is unusual about the supply curve?
    c. At what prices would a shortage occur?
    d. At what prices would a surplus occur?
    e. Suppose that the addition of new students (all big baseball fans) next year will add 1,000 to the quantity demanded at each price. What will this increase do to next year's demand curve? What is the new equilibrium price?

8. What would be the impact of a rental price ceiling set above the equilibrium rental price for apartments? Below the equilibrium rental price?

9. What would be the impact of a price floor set above the equilibrium price for dairy products? Below the equilibrium price?

10. Giving in to pressure from voters who charge that local theater owners are gouging their customers with ticket prices as high as $10 per movie, the city council of a Midwestern city imposes a price ceiling of $2 on all movies. What effect is this likely to have on the market for movies in this particular city? What will happen to the quantity of tickets demanded? What will happen to the quantity supplied? Who gains? Who loses?

11. Why do price floors and price ceilings both reduce the quantity of goods traded in those markets?

12. Why do 10 A.M. classes fill up before 8 A.M. classes during class registration? Use supply and demand curves to help explain your answer.

13. What would happen to the equilibrium price and quantity exchanged in the following cases?
    a. an increase in income and a decreasing price of a complement, for a normal good
    b. a technological advance and lower input prices
    c. an increase in the price of a substitute and an increase in income, for an inferior good
    d. producers' expectations that prices will soon fall, and increasingly costly government regulations

14. Assume the following information for the demand and supply curves for good Z.

Demand		Supply	
Price	Quantity Demanded	Price	Quantity Supplied
$10	10	$1	10
9	20	2	15
8	30	3	20
7	40	4	25
6	50	5	30
5	60	6	35
4	70	7	40
3	80	8	45
2	90	9	50
1	100	10	55

a. Draw the corresponding supply and demand curves.
b. What are the equilibrium price and quantity traded?
c. Would a price of $9 result in a shortage or a surplus? How large?
d. Would a price of $3 result in a shortage or a surplus? How large?
e. If the demand for Z increased by 15 units at every price, what would the new equilibrium price and quantity traded be?
f. Given the original demand for Z, if the supply of Z were increased by 15 units at every price, what would the new equilibrium price and quantity traded be?

15. Refer to the following supply and demand curve diagram.

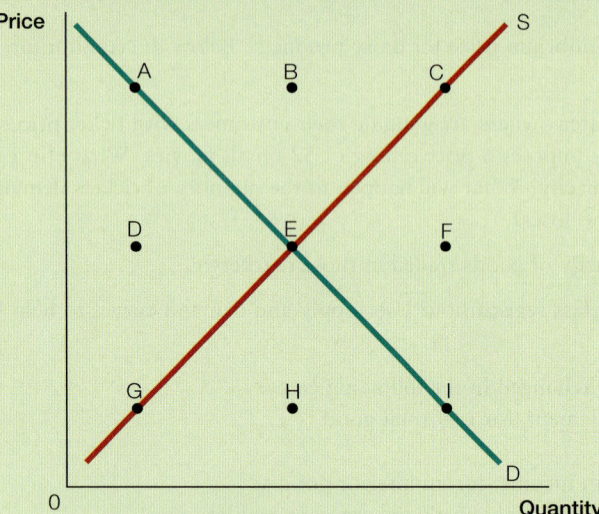

a. Starting from an initial equilibrium at E, what shift or shifts in supply and/or demand could move the equilibrium price and quantity to each of points A through I?
b. Starting from an initial equilibrium at E, what would happen if both a decrease in the price of a substitute in production and an increase in income occurred, if it is a normal good?
c. Starting from an initial equilibrium at E, what would happen if both an increase in the price of an input and an advance in technology occurred?
d. If a price floor is imposed above the equilibrium price, which of A through I would tend to be the quantity supplied, and which would tend to be the quantity demanded? Which would be the new quantity exchanged?
e. If a price ceiling is imposed below the equilibrium price, which of A through I would tend to be the quantity supplied, and which would tend to be the quantity demanded? Which would be the new quantity exchanged?

Elasticities

6

- 6.1 Price Elasticity of Demand
- 6.2 Total Revenue and the Price Elasticity of Demand
- 6.3 Other Types of Demand Elasticities
- 6.4 Price Elasticity of Supply

If a rock group increases the price it charges for concert tickets, what impact would that have on ticket sales? More precisely, would ticket sales fall a little or a lot?

Will the group make more money by lowering the price or by raising the price? This chapter will allow you to answer these types of questions and more.

Some of the results in this chapter may surprise you. A huge flood in the Midwest that destroyed much of this year's wheat crop would leave some wheat farmers better off. Ideal weather that led to a bountiful crop of wheat everywhere might leave most wheat farmers worse off. As you will soon find out, these issues hinge importantly on the tools of elasticity.

In this chapter, we will also see the importance of elasticity in determining the effects of taxes. If a tax is levied on the seller, will the seller pay all of the taxes? If the tax were levied on the buyer—who pays the larger share of taxes? We will see that elasticity is critical in the determination of tax burden. Elasticities will also help us to more fully understand many policy issues—from illegal drugs to luxury taxes. If Congress were to impose a large tax on yachts, what do you think would happen to yacht sales? What would happen to employment in the boat industry? ■

SECTION 6.1 Price Elasticity of Demand

- What is price elasticity of demand?
- How do we measure consumers' responses to price changes?
- What determines the price elasticity of demand?

In learning and applying the law of demand, we have established the basic fact that quantity demanded changes inversely with change in price, *ceteris paribus*. But how much does quantity demanded change? The extent to which a change in price affects quantity demanded may vary considerably from product to product and over the various price ranges for the same product. The **price elasticity of demand** measures the responsiveness of quantity demanded to a change in price. Specifically, price elasticity is defined as the percentage change in quantity demanded divided by the percentage change in price, or

$$\text{Price elasticity of demand}(E_D) = \frac{\text{Percentage change in quantity demanded}}{\text{Percentage change in price}}$$

Note that, following the law of demand, price and quantity demanded show an inverse relationship. For this reason, the price elasticity of demand is, in theory, always negative. But in practice and for simplicity, this quantity is always expressed in absolute value terms—that is, as a positive number.

Is the Demand Curve Elastic or Inelastic?

It is important to understand the basic intuition behind elasticities, which requires a focus on the percentage changes in quantity demanded and price.

Think of elasticity as an elastic rubber band. If the quantity demanded is responsive to even a small change in price, we call it elastic. On the other hand, if even a huge change in price results in only a small change in quantity demanded, then the demand is said to be inelastic. For example, if a 10 percent increase in the price leads to a 50 percent reduction in the quantity demanded, we say that demand is elastic because the quantity demanded is sensitive to the price change.

$$E_D = \frac{\%\Delta Q_D}{\%\Delta P} = \frac{50\%}{10\%} = 5$$

Demand is elastic in this case because a 10 percent change in price led to a larger (50 percent) change in quantity demanded.

Alternatively, if a 10 percent increase in the price leads to a 1 percent reduction in quantity demanded, we say that demand is *inelastic* because the quantity demanded did not respond much to the price reduction.

$$E_D = \frac{\%\Delta Q_D}{\%\Delta P} = \frac{1\%}{10\%} = 0.10$$

Demand is inelastic in this case because a 10 percent change in price led to a smaller (1 percent) change in quantity demanded.

Types of Demand Curves

Economists refer to a variety of demand curves based on the magnitude of their elasticity. A demand curve, or a portion of a demand curve, can be elastic, inelastic, or unit elastic.

Demand is **elastic** when the elasticity is greater than 1 ($E_D > 1$)—the quantity demanded changes proportionally more than the price changes. In this case, a given percentage increase in price, say 10 percent, leads to a larger percentage change in quantity demanded, say 20 percent, as seen in Exhibit 1(a). If the curve is *perfectly elastic*, the demand curve is horizontal. The elasticity coefficient is infinity because even the slightest change in price will lead to a huge change in quantity demanded—for example, a tiny increase in price will cause the quantity demanded to fall to zero. In Exhibit 1(b), a *perfectly elastic* demand curve (horizontal) is illustrated.

Demand is **inelastic** when the elasticity is less than 1; the quantity demanded changes proportionally less than the price changes. In this case, a given percentage (for example, 10 percent) change in price is accompanied by a smaller (for example, 5 percent) reduction in quantity demanded, as seen in Exhibit 2(a). If

---

price elasticity of demand the measure of the responsiveness of quantity demanded to a change in price

elastic when the quantity demanded is greater than the percentage change in price ($E_D > 1$)

inelastic when the quantity demanded is less than the percentage change in price ($E_D < 1$)

section 6.1 exhibit 1 — Elastic Demand

a. Elastic Demand ($E_D > 1$)

b. Perfectly Elastic Demand ($E_D = \infty$)

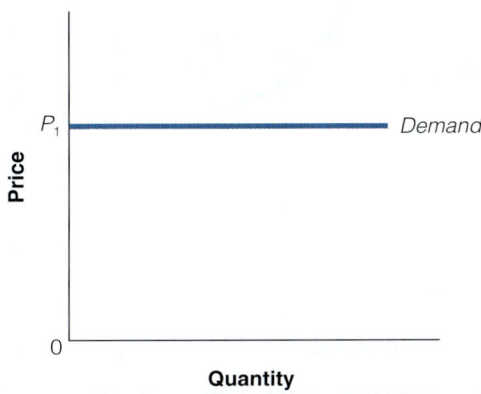

A small percentage change in price leads to a larger percentage change in quantity demanded.

A small percentage change in price will change quantity demanded by an infinite amount.

section 6.1 exhibit 2 — Inelastic Demand

a. Inelastic Demand ($E_D < 1$)

b. Perfectly Inelastic Demand ($E_D = 0$)

A change in price leads to a smaller percentage change in quantity demanded.

The quantity demanded does not change regardless of the percentage change in price.

---

the demand curve is *perfectly inelastic*, the quantity demanded is the same regardless of the price. The elasticity coefficient is zero because the quantity demanded does not respond to a change in price. This relationship is illustrated in Exhibit 2(b).

Goods for which E_D equals one ($E_D = 1$) are said to have **unit elastic demand.** In this case, the quantity demanded changes proportionately to price changes. For example, a 10 percent increase in price will lead to a 10 percent reduction in quantity demanded. This relationship is illustrated in Exhibit 3.

The price elasticity of demand is closely related to the slope of the demand curve. Generally speaking, the flatter the demand curve passing through a given point, the more elastic the demand. The steeper the demand curve passing through a given point, the less elastic the demand.

unit elastic demand demand with a price elasticity of 1; the percentage change in quantity demanded is equal to the percentage change in price section 6.1 exhibit 3   Unit Elastic Demand

The percentage change in quantity demanded is the same as the percentage change in price that caused it ($E_D = 1$).

section 6.1 exhibit 4   Calculating the Price Elasticity of Demand

The price elasticity of demand is found with the formula
$$\frac{\Delta Q_D / Q_{D\,ave}}{\Delta P / P_{ave}}$$

Calculating the Price Elasticity of Demand: The Midpoint Method

To get a clear picture of exactly how the price elasticity of demand is calculated, consider the case for the compact disc (CD) market. Say the price of CDs increases from $19 to $21. If we take an average between the old price, $19, and the new price, $21, we can calculate an average price of $20. Exhibit 4 shows that as a result of the increase in the price of CDs, the quantity demanded has fallen from 82 million CDs to 78 million CDs per year. If we take an average between the old quantity demand, 82 million, and the new quantity demanded, 78 million, we have an average quantity demanded of 80 million CDs per year. That is, the $2 increase in the price of CDs has led to a 4-million-CD reduction in quantity demanded. How can we figure out the price elasticity of demand?

You might ask why we are using the average price and average quantity. The answer is that if we did not use the average amounts, we would come up with different values for the elasticity of demand depending on whether we moved up or down the demand curve. When the change in price and quantity are of significant magnitude, the exact meaning of the term *percentage change* requires clarification, and the terms *price* and *quantity* must be defined more precisely. The issue thus is, should the percentage change be figured on the basis of price and quantity before or after the change has occurred? For example, a price rise from $10 to $15 constitutes a 50 percent change if the original price ($10) is used in figuring the percentage ($5/$10), or a 33 percent change if the price after the change ($15) is used ($5/$15). For small changes, the distinction is not important, but for large changes, it is. To avoid this confusion, economists often use this average technique. Specifically, we are actually calculating the elasticity at a midpoint between the old and new prices and quantities.

Now to figure out the price elasticity of demand, we must first calculate the percentage change in price. To find the percentage change in price, we take the change in price (ΔP) and divide it by the average price (P_{ave}). (Note: The Greek letter delta, Δ, means "change in.")

Percentage change in price $= \Delta P / P_{ave}$

In our CD example, the original price was $19, and the new price is $21. The change in price (ΔP) is $2, and the average price (P_{ave}) is $20. The percentage change in price can then be calculated as

Percentage change in price $= \$2/\$20$
$= 1/10 = 0.10 = 10$ *percent*

Next, we must calculate the percentage change in quantity demanded. To find the percentage change in quantity demanded, we take the change in quantity demanded (ΔQ_D) and divide it by the average quantity demanded ($Q_{D\,ave}$).

Percentage change in quantity demanded
$= \Delta Q_D / Q_{D\,ave}$

In our CD example, the original quantity demanded was 82 million, and the new quantity demanded is 78 million. The change in quantity demanded (ΔQ_D) is 4 million, and the average quantity demanded ($Q_{D\,ave}$) is 80 million. The percentage change in quantity demanded can then be calculated as

Percentage change in quantity demanded =
4 million/80 million = 1/20 = 0.05 = 5 percent

Because the price elasticity of demand is equal to the percentage change in quantity demanded divided by the percentage change in price, the price elasticity of demand for CDs between point A and point B can be shown as

$$E_D = \frac{\text{Percentage change in quantity demanded}}{\text{Percentage change in price}}$$
$$= \frac{\Delta Q_D / Q_{D\,ave}}{\Delta P / P_{ave}} = \frac{4 \text{ million}/80 \text{ million}}{\$2/\$20}$$
$$= \frac{1/20}{1/10} = \frac{5\%}{10\%} = 0.5$$

The Determinants of the Price Elasticity of Demand

As you have learned, the elasticity of demand for a specific good refers to movements along its demand curve as its price changes. A lower price will increase quantity demanded, and a higher price will reduce quantity demanded. But what factors will influence the magnitude of the change in quantity demanded in response to a price change? That is, what will make the demand curve relatively more elastic (where Q_D is responsive to price changes), and what will make the demand curve relatively less elastic (where Q_D is less responsive to price changes)?

For the most part, the price elasticity of demand depends on three factors: (1) the availability of close substitutes, (2) the proportion of income spent on the good, and (3) the amount of time that has elapsed since the price change.

Availability of Close Substitutes

Goods *with* close substitutes tend to have more elastic demands. Why? Because if the price of such a good increases, consumers can easily switch to other now relatively lower priced substitutes. In many examples, such as one brand of root beer as opposed to another, or different brands of gasoline, the ease of substitution will make demand quite elastic for most individuals.

If bus fares increase, will ridership fall a little or a lot? It all depends on the price elasticity of demand. If the price elasticity of demand is elastic, a 50-cent price increase will lead to a relatively large reduction in bus travel as riders find viable substitutes. If the price elasticity of demand is inelastic, a 50-cent price increase will lead to a relatively small reduction in bus ridership as riders are not able to find good alternatives to bus transportation.

Unlike most tangible items (such as specific types of food or cars), there are few substitutes for a physician and medical care when you have an emergency. Because the number of available substitutes is limited, the demand for emergency medical care is relatively inelastic.

Goods *without* close substitutes, such as insulin for diabetics, cigarettes for chain smokers, heroin for addicts, or emergency medical care for those with appendicitis or broken legs, tend to have inelastic demands. The demand for an antivenom shot after a rattle snake bite is another example. Once bitten, that demand curve becomes extremely inelastic.

The degree of substitutability can also depend on whether the good is a necessity or a luxury. Goods that are necessities, such as food, have no ready substitutes and thus tend to have lower elasticities than do luxury items, such as jewelry.

When the good is broadly defined, it tends to be less elastic than when it is narrowly defined. For example, the elasticity of demand for food, a broad category, tends to be inelastic because few substitutes are available for food. But for a certain type of food, such as pizza, a narrowly defined good, it is much easier to find a substitute—perhaps tacos, burgers, salads, burritos, or chili fries. That is, the demand for a particular type of food is more elastic because more and better substitutes are available than for food as an entire category.

Proportion of Income Spent on the Good

The smaller the proportion of income spent on a good, the lower its elasticity of demand. If the amount spent on a good relative to income is small, then the impact of a change in its price on one's budget will also be small. As a result, consumers will respond less to price changes for small-ticket items than for similar percentage changes in large-ticket items, where a price change could potentially have a large impact on the consumer's budget. For example, a 50 percent increase in the price of salt will have a much smaller impact on consumers' behavior than a similar percentage increase in the price of a new automobile. Similarly, a 50 percent increase in the cost of private university tuition will have a greater impact on students' (and sometimes parents') budgets than a 50 percent increase in textbook prices.

Time

For many goods, the more time that people have to adapt to a new price change, the greater the elasticity of demand. Immediately after a price change, consumers may be unable to locate good alternatives or easily change their consumption patterns. But as time passes, consumers have more time to find or develop suitable substitutes and to plan and implement changes in their patterns of consumption. For example, drivers may not respond immediately to an increase in gas prices, perhaps believing it to be temporary. However, if the price persists over a longer period, we would expect people to drive less, buy more fuel-efficient cars, move closer to work, carpool, take the bus, or even bike to work. So for many goods, especially nondurable goods

Some studies show that a 10 percent increase in the price of cigarettes will lead to a 7 percent reduction in the quantity demanded of youth smoking. In this price range, however, demand is still inelastic at −0.7. Of course, proponents of higher taxes to discourage underage smoking would like to see a more elastic demand, where a 10 percent increase in the price of cigarettes would lead to a reduction in quantity demanded of more than 10 percent.

section 6.1 exhibit 5 — Short-Run and Long-Run Demand Curves

For many goods, such as gasoline, price is much more elastic in the long run than in the short run because buyers have more time to find suitable substitutes or change their consumption patterns. In the short run, the increase in price from P_1 to P_2 has only a small effect on the quantity demanded for gasoline. In the long run, the effect of the price increase will be much larger.

(goods that do not last a long time), the short-run demand curve is generally less elastic than the long-run demand curve, as illustrated in Exhibit 5.

Estimated Price Elasticities of Demand

Because of shifts in supply and demand curves, researchers have a difficult task when trying to estimate empirically the price elasticity of demand for a particular good or service. Despite this difficulty, Exhibit 6 presents some estimates for the price elasticity of demand for certain goods. As you would expect, certain goods like medical care, air travel and gasoline are all relatively price inelastic in the short run because buyers have fewer substitutes. On the other hand, air travel in the long run is much more sensitive to price (elastic) because the available substitutes are much more plentiful. Exhibit 6 shows that the price elasticity of demand for air travel is 2.4, which means that a 1 percent increase in price will lead to a 2.4 percent reduction in quantity demanded. Notice, in each case where the data are available, the estimates of the long-run price elasticities of demand are greater than the short-run price elasticities of demand. In short, the price elasticity of demand is greater when the price change persists over a longer time periods.

section 6.1 exhibit 6 Price Elasticities of Demand for Selected Goods

Good	Short Run	Long Run
Salt	—	0.1
Air travel	0.1	2.4
Gasoline	0.2	0.7
Medical care and hospitalization	0.3	0.9
Jewelry and watches	0.4	0.7
Physician services	0.6	—
Alcohol	0.9	3.6
Movies	0.9	3.7
China, glassware	1.5	2.6
Automobiles	1.9	2.2
Chevrolets	—	4.0

SOURCES: Adapted from Robert Archibald and Robert Gillingham, "An Analysis of the Short-Run Consumer Demand for Gasoline Using Household Survey Data," *Review of Economics and Statistics* 62 (November 1980): 622–628; Hendrik S. Houthakker and Lester D. Taylor, Consumer Demand in the United States: Analyses and Projections (Cambridge, Mass.: Harvard University Press, 1970), pp. 56–149; Richard Voith, "The Long-Run Elasticity of Demand for Commuter Rail Transportation," *Journal of Urban Economics* 30 (November 1991): 360–372.

SECTION CHECK

1. Price elasticity of demand measures the percentage change in quantity demanded divided by the percentage change in price that caused it, moving along a demand curve.
2. The elasticity of demand is calculated using the midpoint formula = $\dfrac{\Delta Q_D / Q_{D\,ave}}{\Delta P / P_{ave}}$.
3. If the demand for a good is price elastic in the relevant range, quantity demanded is very responsive to a price change. If the demand for a good is relatively price inelastic, quantity demanded is not very responsive to a price change.
4. The price elasticity of demand depends on: (1) the availability of close substitutes, (2) the proportion of income spent on the good, and (3) the amount of time that buyers have to respond to a price change.

1. What question is the price elasticity of demand designed to answer?
2. How is the price elasticity of demand calculated?
3. What is the difference between a relatively price elastic demand curve and a relatively price inelastic demand curve?
4. What is the relationship between the price elasticity of demand and the slope at a given point on a demand curve?
5. What factors tend to make demand curves more price elastic?
6. Why would a tax on a particular brand of cigarettes be less effective at reducing smoking than a tax on all brands of cigarettes?
7. Why is the price elasticity of demand for products at a 24-hour convenience store likely to be lower at 2 A.M. than at 2 P.M.?
8. Why is the price elasticity of demand for turkeys likely to be lower, but the price elasticity of demand for turkeys at a particular store likely to be greater, at Thanksgiving than at other times of the year?

SECTION 6.2
Total Revenue and the Price Elasticity of Demand

* What is total revenue?
* What is the relationship between total revenue and the price elasticity of demand?
* Does the price elasticity of demand vary along a linear demand curve?

How Does the Price Elasticity of Demand Impact Total Revenue?

The price elasticity of demand for a good also has implications for total revenue. **Total revenue (TR)** is the amount sellers receive for a good or service. Total revenue is simply the price of the good (P) times the quantity of the good sold (Q): $TR = P \times Q$. The elasticity of demand will help to predict how changes in the price will impact total revenue earned by the producer for selling the good. Let's see how this works.

In Exhibit 1, we see that when the demand is price elastic ($E_D > 1$), total revenues will rise as the price declines, because the percentage increase in the quantity demanded is greater than the percentage reduction in price. For example, if the price of a good is cut in half (say from $10 to $5) and the quantity demanded more than doubles (say from 40 to 100), total revenue will rise from $400 ($10 × 40 = $400) to $500 ($5 × 100 = $500). Equivalently, if the price rises from $5 to $10 and the quantity demanded falls from 100 to 40 units, then total revenue will fall from $500 to $400. As this example illustrates, if the demand curve is relatively elastic, total revenue will vary inversely with a price change.

You can see from the following what happens to total revenue when demand is price elastic. (*Note:* The size of the price and quantity arrows represents the size of the percentage changes.)

When Demand Is Price Elastic

$$\downarrow TR = \uparrow P \times \downarrow Q$$

or

$$\uparrow TR = \downarrow P \times \uparrow Q$$

On the other hand, if demand for a good is relatively inelastic ($E_D < 1$), the total revenue will be lower at lower prices than at higher prices because a given

total revenue (TR)
the amount sellers receive for a good or service, calculated as the product price times the quantity sold

price reduction will be accompanied by a proportionately smaller increase in quantity demanded. For example, as shown in Exhibit 2, if the price of a good is cut (say from $10 to $5) and the quantity demanded less than doubles (say it increases from 30 to 40), then total revenue will fall from $300 ($10 × 30 = $300) to $200 ($5 × 40 = $200). Equivalently, if the price increases from $5 to $10 and the quantity demanded falls from 40 to 30, total revenue will increase from $200 to $300. To summarize, then: If the demand curve is inelastic, total revenue will vary directly with a price change.

When Demand Is Price Inelastic

$$\downarrow TR = \uparrow P \times \downarrow Q$$

or

$$\uparrow TR = \downarrow P \times \uparrow Q$$

section 6.2 exhibit 1 Elastic Demand and Total Revenue

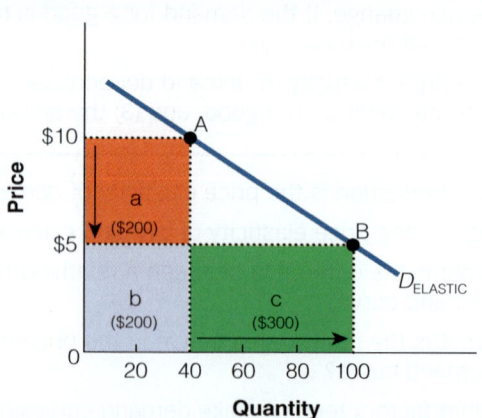

At point A, total revenue is $400 ($10 × 40 × $400), or area a + b. If the price falls to $5 at point B, the total revenue is $500 ($5 × 100 = $500), or area b + c. Total revenue increased by $100. We can also see in the graph that total revenue increased, because the area b + c is greater than area a + b, or c > a.

section 6.2 exhibit 2 — Inelastic Demand and Total Revenue

At point A, total revenue is $300 ($10 × 30 = $300), or area a + b. If the price falls to $5 at point B, the total revenue is $200 ($5 × 40 = $200), or area b + c. Total revenue falls by $100. We can also see in the graph that total revenue decreases, because area a + b is greater than area b + c, or a > c.

In this case, the "net" effect on total revenue is reversed but easy to see. (Again, the size of the price and quantity arrows represents the size of the percentage changes.)

Price Elasticity Changes Along a Linear Demand Curve

As already shown (Section 6.1, Exhibit 1), the slopes of demand curves can be used to estimate their *relative* elasticities of demand: The steeper one demand curve is relative to another, the more inelastic it is relative to the other. However, except for the extreme cases of perfectly elastic and perfectly inelastic curves, great care must be taken when trying to estimate the degree of elasticity of one demand curve from its slope. In fact, as we will soon see, a straight-line demand curve with a constant slope will change elasticity continuously as you move up or down it. It is because the slope is the ratio of changes in the two variables (price and quantity) while the elasticity is the ratio of percentage changes in the two variables.

We can easily demonstrate that the elasticity of demand varies along a linear demand curve by using what we already know about the interrelationship between price and total revenue. Exhibit 4 shows a linear (constant slope) demand curve. In Exhibit 4(a), we see that when the price falls on the upper half of the demand curve from P_1 to P_2, and quantity demanded increases from Q_1 to Q_2, total revenue increases. That is, the new area of total revenue (area b + c) is larger than the old area of total revenue (area a + b). It is

Use what you've LEARNED
ELASTICITIES AND TOTAL REVENUE

Q Is a poor wheat harvest bad for all farmers and is a great wheat harvest good for all farmers? (Hint: Assume that demand for wheat is inelastic—the demand for food is generally inelastic.)

A Without a simultaneous reduction in demand, a reduction in supply from a poor harvest results in higher prices. With that, if demand for the wheat is inelastic over the pertinent portion of the demand curve, the price increase will cause farmers' total revenues to rise. As shown in Exhibit 3(a), if demand for the crop is inelastic, an increase in price will cause farmers to lose the revenue indicated by area c. They will, however, experience an increase in revenue equal to area a, resulting in an overall increase

in total revenue equal to area a–c. Clearly, if some farmers lose their entire crop because of, say, bad weather, they will be worse off; but collectively,

(continued)

Use what you've LEARNED: ELASTICITIES AND TOTAL REVENUE (cont.)

farmers can profit from events that reduce crop size—and they do, because the demand for most agricultural products is inelastic. Interestingly, if all farmers were hurt equally, say losing one-third of their crop, each farmer would be better off. Of course, consumers would be worse off, because the price of agricultural products would be higher. Alternatively, what if phenomenal weather led to record wheat harvests or a technological advance led to more productive wheat farmers? Either event would increase the supply from S_1 to S_2 in Exhibit 3(b). The increase in supply leads to a decrease in price, from P_1 to P_2. Because the demand for wheat is inelastic, the quantity sold of wheat rises less than proportionately to the fall in the price. That is, in percentage terms, the price falls more than the quantity demanded rises. Each farmer is selling a few more bushels of wheat, but the price of each bushel has fallen even more, so collectively wheat farmers will experience a decline in total revenue despite the good news.

The same is also true for the many government programs that attempt to help farmers by reducing production—crop restriction programs. These programs, like droughts or floods, tend to help farmers because the demand for food is relatively inelastic. But it hurts consumers who now have to pay a higher price for less food. Farm technology may be good for consumers because it shifts the supply curve to the right and lowers prices. However it may be bad for some small farmers because it could put them out of business. See Exhibit 3(b).

section 6.2 exhibit 3 Elasticities and Total Revenue

a. Total Revenue and Inelastic Demand: A Reduction in Supply (Poor Harvest)

b. Total Revenue and Inelastic Demand: An Increase in Supply (Good Harvest)

also true that if price increased in this region (from P_2 to P_1), total revenue would fall, because b + c is greater than a + b. In this region of the demand curve, then, there is a negative relationship between price and total revenue. As we discussed earlier, this is characteristic of an elastic demand curve ($E_D > 1$).

Exhibit 4(b) illustrates what happens to total revenue on the lower half of the same demand curve. When

section 6.2 exhibit 4
Price Elasticity Along a Linear Demand Curve

The slope is constant along a linear demand curve, but the elasticity varies. Moving down along the demand curve, the elasticity is elastic at higher prices and inelastic at lower prices. It is unit elastic between the inelastic and elastic ranges.

the price falls from P_3 to P_4 and the quantity demanded increases from Q_3 to Q_4, total revenue actually decreases, because the new area of total revenue (area e + f) is less than the old area of total revenue (area d + e). Likewise, it is clear that an increase in price from P_4 to P_3 would increase total revenue. In this case, there is a positive relationship between price and total revenue, which, as we discussed, is characteristic of an inelastic demand curve ($E_D < 1$). Together, parts (a) and (b) of Exhibit 4 illustrate that, although the slope remains constant, the elasticity of a linear demand curve changes along the length of the curve—from relatively elastic at higher price ranges to relatively inelastic at lower price ranges.

SECTION CHECK

1. Total revenue is the price of the good times the quantity sold ($TR = P \times Q$).
2. If demand is price elastic ($E_D > 1$), total revenue will vary inversely with a change in price.
3. If demand is price inelastic ($E_D < 1$), total revenue will vary in the same direction as a change in price.
4. A linear demand curve is more price elastic at higher price ranges and more price inelastic at lower price ranges, and it is unit elastic at the midpoint: $E_D = 1$.

1. Why does total revenue vary inversely with price if demand is relatively price elastic?
2. Why does total revenue vary directly with price if demand is relatively price inelastic?
3. Why is a linear demand curve more price elastic at higher price ranges and more price inelastic at lower price ranges?
4. If demand for some good was perfectly price inelastic, how would total revenue from its sales change as its price changed?
5. Assume that both you and Art, your partner in a picture-framing business, want to increase your firm's total revenue. You argue that in order to achieve this goal, you should lower your prices; Art, on the other hand, thinks that you should raise your prices. What assumptions are each of you making about your firm's price elasticity of demand?

Use what you've LEARNED
ELASTICITY VARIES ALONG A LINEAR DEMAND CURVE

Q Why do economists emphasize elasticity at the current price?

A Because for most demand (and supply) curves, the price elasticity varies along the curve. Thus, for most goods we usually refer to a particular point or a section of the demand (or supply) curves. In Exhibit 5, we see that the upper half of the straight-line demand curve is elastic and the lower half is inelastic. Notice on the lower half of the demand curve, a higher (lower) price increases (decreases) total revenue—that is, in this lower region, demand is inelastic. However, on the top half of the demand curve, a lower (higher) price increases (decreases) total revenue—that is, in this region demand is elastic.

For example, when the price increases from $2 to $3, the total revenue increases from $32 to $42—an increase in price increases total revenue, so demand is inelastic in this portion of the demand curve. But when the price increases from $8 to $9, the total revenue falls from $32 to $18—an increase in price lowers total revenue, so demand is elastic in this portion of the demand curve.

Specifically, when the price is high and the quantity demanded is low, this portion of the demand curve is elastic. Why? It is because a $1 reduction in price is a smaller percentage change when the price is high than when it is low. Similarly, an increase in 2 units of output is a larger percentage change when quantity demanded is lower. So we have a relatively small change in price leading to a proportionately greater change in quantity demanded—that is, demand is elastic on this portion of the demand curve. Of course, the opposite is true when the price is low and the quantity demanded is high. Why? It is because a $1 change in price is a larger percentage change when the price is low and an increase in 2 units of output is a smaller percentage change when the quantity demanded is larger. That is, a relatively larger percentage change in price will lead to a relatively smaller change in quantity demanded—demand is relatively inelastic on this portion of the demand curve.

section 6.2 exhibit 5 Elasticity Varies Along a Linear Demand Curve

SECTION 6.3 Other Types of Demand Elasticities

* What is the cross-price elasticity of demand?
* What is the income elasticity of demand?

The Cross-Price Elasticity of Demand

The price of a good is not the only factor that affects the quantity consumers will purchase. Sometimes the quantity of one good demanded is affected by the price of a related good. For example, if the price of potato chips falls, what is the impact, if any, on the demand for soda (a complement)? Or if the price of soda increases, to what degree will the demand for iced tea (a substitute) be affected? The cross-price elasticity of demand measures both the direction and magnitude of the impact that a price change for one good will have on the demand for another good. Specifically, the **cross-price elasticity of demand** is defined as the percentage change in the demand of one good (good A) divided by the percentage change in price of another good (good B), or

cross-price elasticity of demand the measure of the impact that a price change of one good will have on the demand of another good.

$$\text{Cross-price elasticity demand} = \frac{\text{\% change in the demand for Good A}}{\text{\% change in the price for Good B}}$$

The cross-price elasticity of demand indicates not only the degree of the connection between the two variables but also whether the goods in question are substitutes or complements for one another.

Calculating the Cross-Price Elasticity of Demand

Let's calculate the cross-price elasticity of demand between soda and iced tea, where a 10 percent increase in the price of soda results in a 20 percent increase in the demand for iced tea. In this case, the cross-price elasticity of demand would be +2 (+20 percent ÷ +10 percent = +2).

Consumers responded to the soda price increase by buying less soda (moving along the demand curve for soda) and increasing the demand for iced tea (shifting the demand curve for iced tea). In general, if the cross-price elasticity is positive, we can conclude that the two goods are substitutes because the price of one good and the demand for the other move in the same direction.

As another example, let's calculate the cross-price elasticity of demand between potato chips and soda, where a 10 percent decrease in the price of potato chips results in a 30 percent increase in the demand for soda. In this case, the cross-price elasticity of demand is −3 (+30 percent ÷ −10 percent = −3). The demand for chips increases as a result of the price decrease, as consumers then purchase additional soda to wash down those extra bags of salty chips. Potato chips and soda, then, are complements. In general, if the cross-price elasticity is negative, we can conclude that the two goods are complements because the price of one good and the demand for the other move in opposite directions.

Cross-Price Elasticity and Sodas

According to economist Jean-Pierre Dube, Coca-Cola is a good substitute for Pepsi—the cross-price elasticity is a 0.34. In other words, a 10 percent increase in the price of a Pepsi 12 pack will lead to an increase in the sales of Coca-Cola 12 packs by 3.4 percent. But six packs of Coca-Cola and Diet Coke are even a better substitute with a cross-price elasticity of 1.15; a 10 percent increase in the price of a six pack of Diet Coke will lead to a 15 percent increase in the sales of six packs of Coca-Cola. And a 10 percent increase in the price of a 12 pack of Mountain Dew will lead to a 7.7 percent increase in the sales of 12 packs of Pepsi.

The Income Elasticity of Demand

Sometimes it is useful to measure how responsive demand is to a change in income. The income elasticity of demand is a measure of the relationship between a relative change in income and the consequent relative change in demand, *ceteris paribus*. The income elasticity of demand coefficient not only expresses the degree of the connection between the two variables, but it also indicates whether the *good in question is normal or inferior*. Specifically, the **income elasticity of demand** is defined as the percentage change in the demand divided by the percentage change in income, or

Income elasticity of demand

$$= \frac{\% \Delta \text{ in demand}}{\% \Delta \text{ in income}}$$

Calculating the Income Elasticity of Demand

Let's calculate the income elasticity of demand for lobster, where a 10 percent increase in income results in a 15 percent increase in the demand for lobster. In this case, the income elasticity of demand is +1.5 (+15 percent ÷ +10 percent = +1.5). Lobster, then, is a normal good because an increase in income results in an increase in demand. In general, if the income elasticity is positive, then the good in question is a normal good because income and demand move in the same direction.

income elasticity of demand the percentage change in demand divided by the percentage change in consumer's income

---

global WATCH: ENDANGERED SPECIES GET A LIFT FROM VIAGRA

—BY KATE MELVILLE

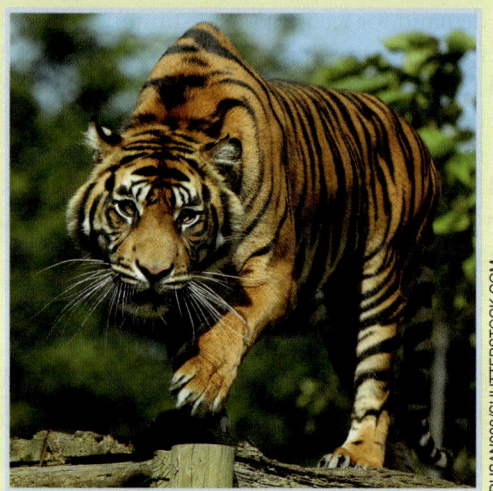

Much to the dismay of Western conservationists, traditional Chinese medicine has often relied on a bizarre mix of animal parts to cure ailments ranging from gout to erectile dysfunction. But that may be changing, and the beneficiaries are a wide range of animal species that have traditionally been sought for their virility-enhancing properties. A study, in the journal *Environmental Conservation*, suggests that Chinese men are switching from traditional Chinese medicine remedies to the drug Viagra to treat erectile dysfunction.

The researchers, from the University of New South Wales (UNSW) and the University of Alaska, say they predicted the trend at the advent of Viagra's release in 1998, but at the time were pooh-poohed by conservationists. "When we proposed that Viagra might make inroads into traditional Chinese medicine treatments for impotence, conservationists told us we were naïve and that consumers were unwilling to use a product outside their own medical tradition," said UNSW researcher Bill von Hippel.

The study was based on data from men attending a large traditional Chinese medicine clinic in Hong Kong. They were questioned about their use of traditional and Western treatments of arthritis, indigestion, gout, and impotence. The findings were unambiguous, said von Hippel. "First, significantly more men had formerly used a traditional Chinese medicine treatment for impotence than were current users. Second, they were significantly more likely to be using a Western treatment for impotence than a traditional treatment. Finally, among men who formerly used either Western or traditional treatments for impotence, they were more likely to switch from a traditional treatment to Western drug than vice versa. In fact, nobody had switched from a Western drug to a traditional treatment for impotence."

"The fact is that prior to the commercial availability of Viagra in 1998, no product in any medical tradition had been proven to be an effective and non-intrusive treatment of erectile dysfunction. So despite their history of using traditional medicines and their alleged suspicions of Western medicine, the men we interviewed chose the product that works best," von Hippel added. . .

consider this:
It looks like the cross-price elasticity between Viagra and traditional Chinese medicine from a mix of animal parts is positive. This may be very good news for endangered species.

In comparison, let's calculate the income elasticity of demand for beans, where a 10 percent increase in income results in a 15 percent decrease in the demand for beans. In this case, the income elasticity of demand is −1.5 (−15 percent ÷ +10 percent = −1.5). In this example, then, beans are an inferior good because an increase in income results in a decrease in the demand for beans. If the income elasticity is negative, then the good in question is an inferior good because the change in income and the change in demand move in opposite directions.

SECTION CHECK

1. The cross-price elasticity of demand is the percentage change in the demand of one good divided by the percentage change in the price of another related good.
2. If the sign on the cross-price elasticity is positive, the two goods are substitutes; if it is negative, the two goods are complements.
3. The income elasticity of demand is the percentage change in demand divided by the percentage change in income.
4. If the income elasticity is positive, then the good is a normal good; if it is negative, the good is an inferior good.

---

1. How does the cross-price elasticity of demand tell you whether two goods are substitutes? Complements?
2. How does the income elasticity of demand tell you whether a good is normal? Inferior?
3. If the cross-price elasticity of demand between potato chips and popcorn was positive and large, would popcorn makers benefit from a tax imposed on potato chips?
4. As people's incomes rise, why will they spend an increasing portion of their incomes on goods with income elasticities greater than 1 (DVDs) and a decreasing portion of their incomes on goods with income elasticities less than 1 (food)?
5. If people spent three times as much on restaurant meals and four times as much on DVDs as their incomes doubled, would restaurant meals or DVDs have a greater income elasticity of demand?

SECTION 6.4 Price Elasticity of Supply

* What is the price elasticity of supply?
* How does time affect the supply elasticity?
* How does the relative elasticity of supply and demand determine the tax burden?

What Is the Price Elasticity of Supply?

ccording to the law of supply, there is a positive relationship between price and quantity supplied, *ceteris paribus*. But by how much does quantity supplied change as price changes? It is often helpful to know the degree to which a change in price changes the quantity supplied.

price elasticity of supply
the measure of the sensitivity of the quantity supplied to changes in price of a good

The **price elasticity of supply** measures how responsive the quantity sellers are willing and able to sell is to changes in price. In other words, it measures the relative change in the quantity supplied that results from a change in price. Specifically, the price elasticity of supply (E_s) is defined as the percentage change in the quantity supplied divided by the percentage change in price, or

$$E_s = \frac{\% \, \Delta \text{ in the quantity supplied}}{\% \, \Delta \text{ in price}}$$

Calculating the Price Elasticity of Supply

The price elasticity of supply is calculated in much the same manner as the price elasticity of demand. Consider, for example, the case in which it is determined that a 10 percent increase in the price of artichokes results in a 25 percent increase in the quantity of artichokes supplied after, say, a few harvest seasons. In this case, the price elasticity is +2.5 (+25 percent ÷ +10 percent = +2.5). This coefficient indicates that each 1 percent increase in the price of artichokes induces a 2.5 percent increase in the quantity of artichokes supplied.

Types of Supply Curves

As with the elasticity of demand, the ranges of the price elasticity of supply center on whether the elasticity coefficient is greater than or less than 1. Goods with a supply elasticity that is greater than 1 ($E_S > 1$) are said to be relatively elastic in supply. With that, a 1 percent change in price will result in a greater than 1 percent change in quantity supplied. In our example, artichokes were elastic in supply because a 1 percent price increase resulted in a 2.5 percent increase in quantity supplied. An example of an *elastic supply curve* is shown in Exhibit 1(a).

Goods with a supply elasticity that is less than 1 ($E_S < 1$) are said to be inelastic in supply. In other words, a 1 percent change in the price of these goods will induce a proportionately smaller change in the quantity supplied. An example of an *inelastic supply curve* is shown in Exhibit 1(b).

Finally, two extreme cases of price elasticity of supply are perfectly inelastic supply and perfectly elastic supply. In a condition of *perfectly inelastic supply*, an increase in price will not change the quantity supplied. In this case the elasticity of supply is zero. For example, in a sports arena in the short run (that is, in a period too brief to adjust the structure), the number of seats available will be almost fixed, say at 20,000 seats. Additional portable seats might be available, but for the most part, even if a higher price is charged, only 20,000 seats will be available. We say that the elasticity of supply is zero, which describes a perfectly inelastic supply curve. Famous paintings, such as Van Gogh's *Starry Night*, provide another example: Only one original exists; therefore, only one can be supplied, regardless of price. An example of this condition is shown in Exhibit 1(c).

At the other extreme is a perfectly elastic supply curve, where the elasticity equals infinity, as shown in Exhibit 1(d). In a condition of *perfectly elastic supply*, the price does not change at all. It is the same regardless of the quantity supplied, and the elasticity of supply is infinite.

Firms would supply as much as the market wants at the market price (P_1) or above. However, firms would supply nothing below the market price because they would not be able to cover their costs of production. Most cases fall somewhere between the two extremes of perfectly elastic and perfectly inelastic.

How Does Time Affect Supply Elasticities?

Time is usually critical in supply elasticities (as well as in demand elasticities), because it is more costly for sellers to bring forth and release products in a shorter period. For example, higher wheat prices may cause farmers to grow more wheat, but big changes cannot occur until the next growing season. That is, immediately after harvest season, the supply of wheat is relatively inelastic, but over a longer time extending over the next growing period, the supply curve becomes much more elastic. Thus, supply tends to be more elastic in the long run than in the short run, as shown in Exhibit 2.

Another example of a good whose supply is completely inelastic in the short run is rental units in most urban areas without rent controls. There is generally only a fixed amount of rental units available in the short run. Thus, in the short run, an increase in demand will only lead to higher prices (rents). However, in the long run, the higher prices (rents) provide an incentive to renovate and build new rental units.

In the short run, firms can increase output by using their existing facilities to a greater capacity, paying workers to work overtime, and hiring additional workers. However, firms will be able to change output much more in the long run when firms can build new factories or close existing ones. In addition, some firms can enter as others exit. In other words, the quantity supplied will be much more elastic in the long run than in the short run.

Elasticities and Taxes: Combining Supply and Demand Elasticities

Who pays the tax? Someone may be legally required to send the check to the government but that is not necessarily the party that bears the burden of the tax.

The relative elasticity of supply and demand determines the distribution of the tax burden for a good.

section 6.4 exhibit 1 — The Price Elasticity of Supply

a. Elastic Supply ($E_s > 1$)

A change in price leads to a larger percentage change in quantity supplied.

b. Inelastic Supply ($E_s < 1$)

A change in price leads to a smaller percentage change in quantity supplied.

c. Perfectly Inelastic Supply ($E_s = 0$)

The quantity supplied does not change regardless of the change in price.

d. Perfectly Elastic Supply ($E_s = \infty$)

Even a small percentage change in price will change quantity supplied by an infinite amount.

As we will see, if demand is relatively less elastic than supply in the relevant tax region, the largest portion of the tax is paid by the consumer. However, if demand is relatively more elastic than supply in the relevant tax region, the largest portion of the tax is paid by the producer.

In Exhibit 3(a), the pre-tax equilibrium price is $1.00 and the pre-tax equilibrium quantity is Q_{BT}—the quantity before tax. If the government imposes a $0.50 tax on the seller, the supply curve shifts vertically by the amount of the tax (just as if an input price rose $0.50).

When demand is relatively less elastic than supply in the relevant region, the consumer bears more of the burden of the tax. For example, in Exhibit 3(a), the demand curve is relatively less elastic than the supply curve. In response to the tax, the consumer pays $1.40 per unit, $0.40 more than the consumer paid before the tax increase. The producer, however, receives $0.90 per unit, which is $0.10 less than the producer received before the tax.

In Exhibit 3(b), demand is relatively more elastic than the supply in the relevant region. Here we see that the greater burden of the same $0.50 tax falls on the producer. That is, the producer is now responsible for $0.40 of the tax, while the consumer only pays $0.10. In general, then, the tax burden falls on the side of the market that is relatively less elastic.

section 6.4 exhibit 2 — Short-Run and Long-Run Supply Curves

For most goods, supply is more elastic in the long run than in the short run. For example, if the price of a certain good increases, firms have an incentive to produce more but are constrained by the size of their plants. In the long run, they can increase their capacity and produce more.

Yachts, Taxes, and Elasticities

In 1991, Congress levied a 10 percent luxury tax. The tax applied to the "first retail sale" of luxury goods with sales prices above the following thresholds: automobiles $30,000; boats, $100,000; private planes, $250,000; and furs and jewelry, $10,000. The Congressional Budget Office forecasted that the luxury tax would raise about $1.5 billion over five years. However, in 1991, the luxury tax raised less than $30 million in tax revenues. Why? People stopped buying items subject to the luxury tax.

Let's focus our attention on the luxury tax on yachts. Congress passed this tax thinking that the demand for yachts was relatively inelastic and that the tax would have only a small impact on the sale of new yachts. However, the people in the market for new boats had plenty of substitutes—used boats, boats from other countries, new houses, vacations, and so on. In short, the demand for new yachts was more elastic than Congress thought. Remember, when demand is relatively more elastic than supply, most of the tax is passed on to the seller—in this case, the boat industry (workers and retailers). And supply was relatively inelastic because boat factories are not easy to change in the short run. So sellers received a lower price for their boats, and sales fell. In the first year after the tax, yacht retailers reported a 77 percent drop in sales, and approximately 25,000 workers were laid off. The point is that incorrectly predicting elasticities can lead to huge social, political, and economic problems. After intense lobbying by industry groups, Congress repealed the luxury tax on boats in 1993, and on January 1, 2003, the tax on cars finally expired.

section 6.4 exhibit 3 — Elasticity and the Burden of Taxation

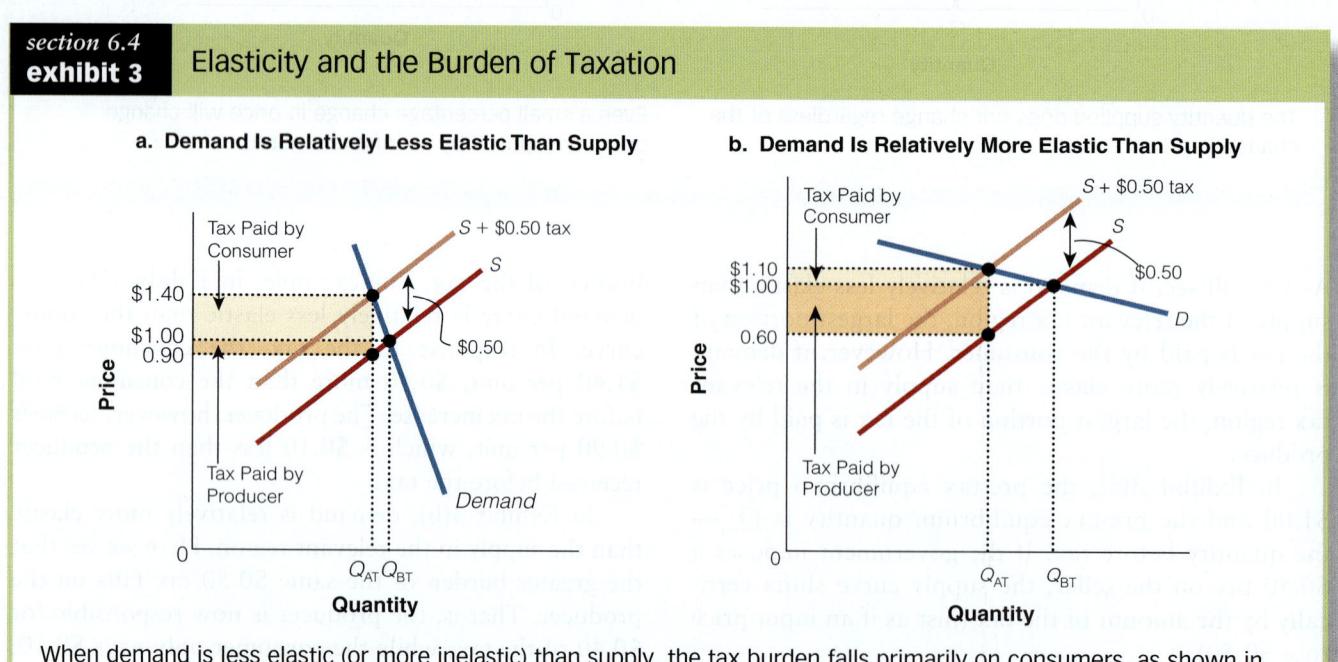

When demand is less elastic (or more inelastic) than supply, the tax burden falls primarily on consumers, as shown in (a). When demand is more elastic than supply, as shown in (b), the tax burden falls primarily on producers.

Use what you've LEARNED
FARM PRICES FALL OVER THE LAST HALF-CENTURY

Q In the last half-century, farm prices experienced a steady decline—roughly 2 percent per year. Why?

A The demand for farm products grew more slowly than supply. Productivity advances in agriculture caused large increases in supply. And because of the inelastic demand for farm products, farmers' incomes fell considerably. That is, the total revenues ($P \times Q$) that farmers collected at the higher price, P_1, was much greater, area $0P_1E_1Q_1$, than the total revenue collected by farmers now when prices are lower, P_2, at area $0P_2E_2Q_2$.

in the news
Drugs Across the Border

The United States spends billions of dollars a year to halt the importation of illegal drugs across the border. Although these efforts are clearly targeted at suppliers, who really pays the higher enforcement and evasion costs? The government crackdown has increased the probability of apprehension and conviction for drug smugglers. That increase in risk for suppliers increases their cost of doing business, raising the cost of importing and distributing illegal drugs. This would shift the supply curve for illegal drugs to the left, from S_1 to S_2, as seen in Exhibit 4. For most drug users—addicts, in particular—the price of drugs such as cocaine and heroin lies in the highly inelastic region of the demand curve. Because the demand for drugs is

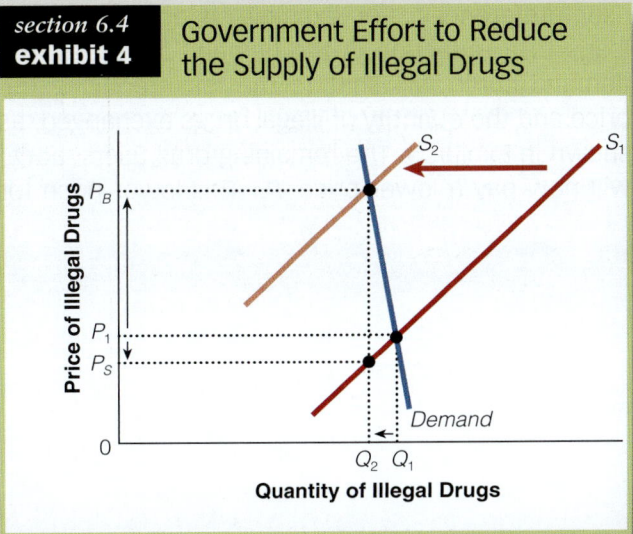

section 6.4 exhibit 4 Government Effort to Reduce the Supply of Illegal Drugs

(continued)

in the news: Drugs Across the Border (cont.)

relatively inelastic in this region, the seller would be able to shift most of this cost onto the consumer (think of it as similar to the tax shift just discussed). The buyer now has to pay a much higher price, P_B, and the seller receives a slightly lower price, P_S. That is, enforcement efforts increase the price of illegal drugs, but only a small reduction in quantity demanded results from this price increase. Increased enforcement efforts may have unintended consequences due to the fact that buyers bear the majority of the burden of this price increase. Tighter smuggling controls may, in fact, result in higher levels of burglary, muggings, and white-collar crime, as more cash-strapped buyers search for alternative ways of funding their increasingly expensive habit. In addition, with the huge financial rewards in the drug trade, tougher enforcement and higher illegal drug prices could lead to even greater corruption in law enforcement and the judicial system.

These possible reactions do not mean we should abandon our efforts against illegal drugs. Illegal drugs can impose huge personal and social costs—billions of dollars of lost productivity and immeasurable personal tragedy. However, solely targeting the supply side can have unintended consequences. Policy makers may get their best results by focusing on a reduction in demand—changing user preferences. For example, if drug education leads to a reduction in the demand for drugs, the demand curve will shift to the left—reducing the price and the quantity of illegal drugs exchanged, as shown in Exhibit 5. The remaining drug users, at Q_2, will now pay a lower price, P_2. This lower price for drugs will lead to fewer drug-related crimes, *ceteris paribus*.

It is also possible that the elasticity of demand for illegal drugs may be more elastic in the long run than the short run. In the short run, as the price rises, the quantity demanded falls less than proportionately because of the addictive nature of illegal drugs (this relationship is also true for goods such as tobacco and alcohol). However, in the long run, the demand for illegal drugs may be more elastic; that is, the higher price may deter many younger, and poorer, people from experimenting with illegal drugs.

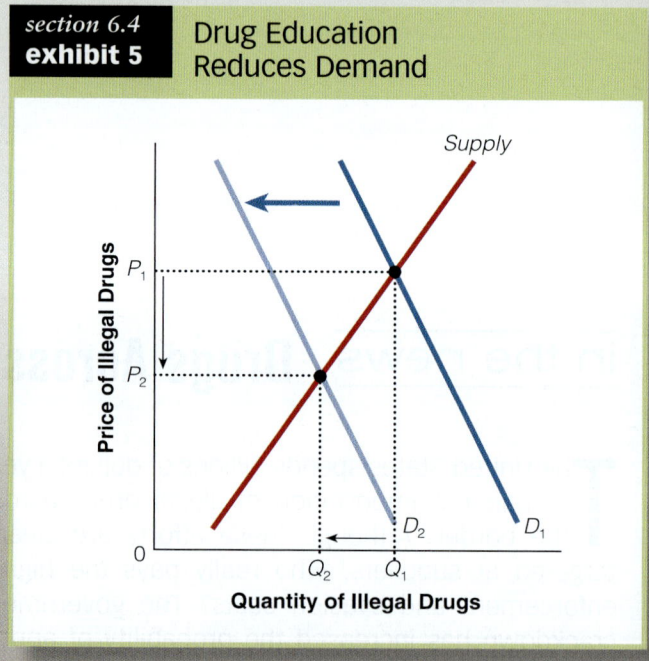

section 6.4 exhibit 5 Drug Education Reduces Demand

Use what you've LEARNED: OIL PRICES

One reason that small changes in supply (or demand) lead to large changes in oil prices and small changes in quantity is because of the inelasticity of demand (and supply) in the short run. Because bringing the production of oil to market takes a long time, the elasticity of supply is relatively low—supply is inelastic. Few substitutes for oil products (e.g., gasoline) are available in the short run as seen in (a).

However, in the long run, demand and supply are more elastic. At higher prices, consumers will replace gas guzzlers with more fuel-efficient cars, and non-OPEC oil producers will expand exploration and production. Thus, in the long run, when supply and demand are much more elastic, a reduction in supply will have a smaller impact on price, as seen in (b).

section 6.4 exhibit 6

a. Oil Prices in the Short Run

section 6.4 exhibit 7

b. Oil Prices in the Long Run

SECTION CHECK

1. The price elasticity of supply measures the relative change in the quantity supplied that results from a change in price.
2. If the supply price elasticity is greater than 1, it is elastic; if it is less than 1, it is inelastic.
3. Supply tends to be more elastic in the long run than in the short run.
4. The relative elasticity of supply and demand determines the distribution of the tax burden for a good. If demand is more elastic than supply, producers bear the greater burden of the tax; if the supply is more elastic than the demand, consumers bear the greater burden.

1. What does it mean to say the elasticity of supply for one good is greater than that for another?
2. Why does supply tend to be more elastic in the long run than in the short run?
3. How do the relative elasticities of supply and demand determine who bears the greater burden of a tax?

Interactive Chapter Summary

Fill in the blanks:

1. The price elasticity of demand measures the responsiveness of quantity _____ to a change in price.

2. The price elasticity of demand is defined as the percentage change in _____ divided by the percentage change in _____.

3. If the price elasticity of demand is elastic, it means the quantity demanded changes by a relatively _____ amount than the price change.

4. If the price elasticity of demand is inelastic, it means the quantity demanded changes by a relatively _____ amount than the price change.

5. A demand curve or a portion of a demand curve can be relatively _____, _____, or relatively _____.

6. For the most part, the price elasticity of demand depends on the availability of _____, the _____ spent on the good, and the amount of _____ people have to adapt to a price change.

7. The elasticity of demand for a Ford automobile would likely be _____ elastic than the demand for automobiles, because there are more and better substitutes for a certain type of car than for a car itself.

8. The smaller the proportion of income spent on a good, the _____ its elasticity of demand.

9. The more time that people have to adapt to a new price change, the _____ the elasticity of demand. The more time that passes, the more time consumers have to find or develop suitable _____ and to plan and implement changes in their patterns of consumption.

10. When demand is price elastic, total revenues will _____ as the price declines because the percentage increase in the _____ is greater than the percentage reduction in price.

11. When demand is price inelastic, total revenues will _____ as the price declines because the percentage increase in the _____ is less than the percentage reduction in price.

12. When the price falls on the _____ half of a straight-line demand curve, demand is relatively _____. When the price falls on the lower half of a straight-line demand curve, demand is relatively _____.

13. The cross-price elasticity of demand is defined as the percentage change in the _____ _____ of good A divided by the percentage change in _____ of good B.

14. The income elasticity of demand is defined as the percentage change in the _____ by the percentage change in _____.

15. The price elasticity of supply measures the sensitivity of the quantity _____ to changes in the price of the good.

16. The price elasticity of supply is defined as the percentage change in the _____ divided by the percentage change in _____.

17. Goods with a supply elasticity that is greater than 1 are called relatively _____ in supply.

18. When supply is inelastic, a 1 percent change in the price of a good will induce a _____ 1 percent change in the quantity supplied.

19. Time is usually critical in supply elasticities because it is _____ costly for sellers to bring forth and release products in a shorter period of time.

20. The relative _____ determines the distribution of the tax burden for a good.

21. If demand is relatively _____ elastic than supply in the relevant region, the largest portion of a tax is paid by the producer.

Answers: 1. demanded 2. quantity demanded, price 3. larger 4. smaller 5. elastic, unit elastic, inelastic 6. close substitutes, proportion of income, time 7. more 8. lower 9. greater; substitutes 10. rise; quantity demanded 11. fall; quantity supplied 12. upper; elastic; inelastic 13. demand, price 14. demand, income 15. supplied 16. quantity supplied, price 17. elastic 18. less than 19. more 20. elasticity of supply and demand 21. more

Key Terms and Concepts

price elasticity of demand 152
elastic 152
inelastic 152
unit elastic demand 153
total revenue (TR) 158
cross-price elasticity of demand 163
income elasticity of demand 164
price elasticity of supply 165

Section Check Answers

6.1 Price Elasticity of Demand

1. **What question is the price elasticity of demand designed to answer?**
   The price elasticity of demand is designed to answer the question: How responsive is quantity demanded to changes in the price of a good?

2. **How is the price elasticity of demand calculated?**
   The price elasticity of demand is calculated as the percentage change in quantity demanded, divided by the percentage change in the price that caused the change in quantity demanded.

3. **What is the difference between a relatively price elastic demand curve and a relatively price inelastic demand curve?**
   Quantity demanded changes relatively more than price along a relatively price elastic segment of a demand curve, while quantity demanded changes relatively less than price along a relatively price inelastic segment of a demand curve.

4. **What is the relationship between the price elasticity of demand and the slope at a given point on a demand curve?**
   At a given point on a demand curve, the flatter the demand curve, the more quantity demanded changes for a given change in price, so the greater is the elasticity of demand.

5. **What factors tend to make demand curves more price elastic?**
   Demand curves tend to become more elastic, the larger the number of close substitutes available for the good, the larger proportion of income spent on the good, and the greater the amount of time that buyers have to respond to a change in the good's price.

6. **Why would a tax on a particular brand of cigarettes be less effective at reducing smoking than a tax on all brands of cigarettes?**
   A tax on one brand of cigarettes would allow smokers to avoid the tax by switching brands rather than by smoking less, but a tax on all brands would raise the cost of smoking any cigarettes. A tax on all brands of cigarettes would therefore be more effective in reducing smoking.

7. **Why is the price elasticity of demand for products at a 24-hour convenience store likely to be lower at 2 A.M. than at 2 P.M.?**
   Fewer alternative stores are open at 2 A.M. than at 2 P.M., and with fewer good substitutes, the price elasticity of demand for products at 24-hour convenience stores is greater at 2 P.M.

8. **Why is the price elasticity of demand for turkeys likely to be lower, but the price elasticity of demand for turkeys at a particular store likely to be greater, at Thanksgiving than at other times of the year?**
   For many people, far fewer good substitutes are acceptable for turkey at Thanksgiving than at other times, so that the demand for turkeys is more inelastic at Thanksgiving. But grocery stores looking to attract customers for their entire large Thanksgiving shopping trip also often offer and heavily advertise turkeys at far better prices than normally, which means shoppers have available more good substitutes and a more price elastic demand curve for buying a turkey at a particular store than normally.

6.2 Total Revenue and the Price Elasticity of Demand

1. **Why does total revenue vary inversely with price if demand is relatively price elastic?**
   Total revenue varies inversely with price if demand is relatively price elastic, because the quantity demanded (which equals the quantity sold) changes relatively more than price along a relatively elastic demand curve. Therefore, total revenue, which equals price times quantity demanded (sold) at that price, will change in the same direction as quantity demanded and in the opposite direction from the change in price.

2. **Why does total revenue vary directly with price, if demand is relatively price inelastic?**
   Total revenue varies in the same direction as price, if demand is relatively price inelastic, because the quantity demanded (which equals the quantity sold) changes relatively less than price along a relatively inelastic demand curve. Therefore, total revenue, which equals price times quantity demanded (and sold) at that price, will change in the same direction as price and in the opposite direction from the change in quantity demanded.

3. **Why is a linear demand curve more price elastic at higher price ranges and more price inelastic at lower price ranges?**
   Along the upper half of a linear (constant slope) demand curve, total revenue increases as the price falls, indicating that demand is relatively price elastic. Along the lower half of a linear (constant slope) demand curve, total revenue decreases as the price falls, indicating that demand is relatively price inelastic.

4. **If demand for some good was perfectly price inelastic, how would total revenue from its sales change as its price changed?**

   A perfectly price inelastic demand curve would be one where the quantity sold did not vary with the price. In such an (imaginary) case, total revenue would increase proportionately with price—a 10 percent increase in price with the same quantity sold would result in a 10 percent increase in total revenue.

5. **Assume that both you and Art, your partner in a picture-framing business, want to increase your firm's total revenue. You argue that in order to achieve this goal, you should lower your prices; Art, on the other hand, thinks that you should raise your prices. What assumptions are each of you making about your firm's price elasticity of demand?**

   You are assuming that a lower price will increase total revenue, which implies you think the demand for your picture frames is relatively price elastic. Art is assuming that an increase in your price will increase your total revenue, which implies he thinks the demand for your picture frames is relatively price inelastic.

6.3 Other Types of Demand Elasticities

1. **How does the cross-price elasticity of demand tell you whether two goods are substitutes? Complements?**

   Two goods are substitutes when an increase (decrease) in the price of one good causes an increase (decrease) in the demand for another good. Substitutes have a positive cross-price elasticity. Two goods are complements when an increase (decrease) in the price of one good decreases (increases) the demand for another food. Compliments have a negative cross-price elasticity.

2. **How does the income elasticity of demand tell you whether a good is normal? Inferior?**

   If demand for a good increases (decreases) when income rises (falls), it is a normal good and has a positive income elasticity. If demand for a good decreases (increases) when income rises (falls), it is an inferior good and has a negative income elasticity.

3. **If the cross-price elasticity of demand between potato chips and popcorn was positive and large, would popcorn makers benefit from a tax imposed on potato chips?**

   A large positive cross-price elasticity of demand between potato chips and popcorn indicates that they are close substitutes. A tax on potato chips, which would raise the price of potato chips as a result, would also substantially increase the demand for popcorn, increasing the price of popcorn and the quantity of popcorn sold, increasing the profits of popcorn makers.

4. **As people's incomes rise, why will they spend an increasing portion of their incomes on goods with income elasticities greater than 1 (DVDs) and a decreasing portion of their incomes on goods with income elasticities less than 1 (food)?**

   An income elasticity of 1 would mean people spent the same fraction or share of their income on a particular good as their incomes increase. An income elasticity greater than 1 would mean people spent an increasing fraction or share of their income on a particular good as their incomes increase, and an income elasticity less than 1 would mean people spent a decreasing fraction or share of their income on a particular good as their incomes increase.

5. **If people spent three times as much on restaurant meals and four times as much on DVDs as their incomes doubled, would restaurant meals or DVDs have a greater income elasticity of demand?**

   DVDs would have a higher income elasticity of demand (4) in this case than restaurant meals (3).

6.4 Price Elasticity of Supply

1. **What does it mean to say the elasticity of supply for one good is greater than that for another?**

   For the elasticity of supply for one good to be greater than for another, the percentage increase in quantity supplied that results from a given percentage change in price will be greater for the first good than for the second.

2. **Why does supply tend to be more elastic in the long run than in the short run?**

   Just as the cost of buyers changing their behavior is lower, the longer they have to adapt, leading to long-run demand curves being more elastic than short-run demand curves, the same is true of suppliers. The cost of producers changing their behavior is lower, the longer they have to adapt, leading to long-run supply curves being more elastic than short-run supply curves.

3. **How do the relative elasticities of supply and demand determine who bears the greater burden of a tax?**

   When demand is more elastic than supply, the tax burden falls mainly on producers; when supply is more elastic than demand, the tax burden falls mainly on consumers.

CHAPTER 6 STUDY GUIDE

True or False:

1. If a small change in quantity demanded results from a huge change in price, then demand is said to be elastic.
2. A segment of a demand curve has an elasticity less than 1 if the percentage change in quantity demanded is less than the percentage change in price that caused it.
3. A perfectly elastic demand curve would be horizontal, but a perfectly inelastic demand curve would be vertical.
4. Using the formula, the same elasticity results whether going from a higher (lower) price to a lower (higher) price.
5. Along a segment of a demand curve that is unit elastic, quantity demanded would change by 10 percent as a result of a 10 percent change in the price.
6. Goods with close substitutes tend to have more elastic demands, while goods without close substitutes tend to have less elastic demands.
7. We would expect that the elasticity of demand for Ford automobiles would be greater than the demand for insulin by diabetics.
8. Based on the percentage of a person's budget devoted to a particular item, you would expect that the elasticity of demand for salt would be greater than the elasticity of demand for attending a university.
9. The short-run demand curve is generally more elastic than the long-run demand curve.
10. Along a demand curve, if the price rises and total revenue falls as a result, then demand must be relatively elastic along that range of the demand curve.
11. If demand is inelastic, the price and total revenue will move in opposite directions along the demand curve.
12. A straight-line demand curve will have a constant elasticity of demand along its length.
13. The price elasticity of supply measures the relative change in the quantity supplied that results from a change in price.
14. When supply is relatively elastic, a 10 percent change in price will result in a greater than 10 percent change in quantity supplied.
15. A perfectly elastic supply curve would be vertical, but a perfectly inelastic supply curve would be horizontal.
16. Goods with a supply elasticity that is less than 1 are called relatively inelastic in supply.
17. Unlike demand, supply tends to be more elastic in the long run than in the short run.
18. If demand has a lower elasticity than supply in the relevant region, the largest portion of a tax is paid by the producer.
19. Who bears the burden of a tax has nothing to do with who actually pays the tax at the time of the purchase.

Multiple Choice:

1. Price elasticity of demand is defined as the _____ change in quantity demanded divided by the _____ change in price.
    a. total; percentage
    b. percentage; marginal
    c. marginal; percentage
    d. percentage; percentage
    e. total; total
2. Demand is said to be _____ when the quantity demanded is not very responsive to changes in price.
    a. independent
    b. inelastic
    c. unit elastic
    d. elastic

3. For a given decrease in price, the greater the elasticity of demand, the greater the resulting
   a. increase in quantity demanded.
   b. increase in demand.
   c. decrease in quantity demanded.
   d. decrease in demand.

4. When demand is inelastic,
   a. price elasticity of demand is less than 1.
   b. consumers are not very responsive to changes in price.
   c. the percentage change in quantity demanded resulting from a price change is less than the percentage change in price.
   d. all of the above are correct.

5. Using the midpoint formula for the elasticity of demand, if a price increase from $57 to $63 reduces quantity demanded from 66 units to 54 units, the elasticity of demand
   a. equals 0.5.
   b. equals 1.
   c. equals 2.
   d. cannot be determined from the information given.

6. Which of the following will not tend to increase the elasticity of demand for a good?
   a. an increase in the availability of close substitutes
   b. an increase in the amount of time people have to adjust to a change in the price
   c. an increase in the proportion of income spent on the good
   d. all of the above will increase the elasticity of demand for a good

7. Which of the following would tend to have the most elastic demand curve?
   a. automobiles
   b. Chevrolet automobiles
   c. a and b would be the same
   d. none of the above

8. Iron Mike's steel mill finds that a 10 percent increase in its price leads to a 14 percent decrease in the quantity it is able to sell. The demand curve for the mill's output is
   a. elastic.
   b. inelastic.
   c. unit elastic.
   d. perfectly elastic.

9. Price elasticity of demand is said to be greater
   a. the shorter the period of time consumers have to adjust to price changes.
   b. the longer the period of time consumers have to adjust to price changes.
   c. when there are fewer available substitutes.
   d. when the elasticity of supply is greater.

10. If recent sharp increases in the price of insulin have had only a small effect on the amount of insulin purchased, then the demand for insulin is
    a. elastic.
    b. inelastic.
    c. unit elastic.
    d. perfectly elastic.

11. The price-elasticity-of-demand coefficient for herbal tea is estimated to be equal to 0.5. It is expected, therefore, that a 10 percent decrease in price would lead to _____ in the quantity of herbal tea demanded.
    a. a 5 percent decrease
    b. a 5 percent increase
    c. a 10 percent decrease
    d. a 10 percent increase
    e. a 0.5 percent increase

12. The long-run demand curve for gasoline is likely to be
    a. more elastic than the short-run demand curve for gasoline.
    b. more inelastic than the short-run demand curve for gasoline.
    c. the same as the short-run demand curve for gasoline.
    d. more inelastic than the short-run supply of gasoline.

13. Demand curves for goods tend to become more inelastic
    a. when more good substitutes for the good are available.
    b. when the good makes up a larger portion of a person's income.
    c. when people have less time to adapt to a given price change.
    d. when any of the above is true.
    e. in none of the above situations.

14. When the local symphony recently raised the ticket price for its summer concerts in the park, the symphony was surprised to see that its total revenue had actually decreased. The reason was that the elasticity of demand for tickets was
    a. unit elastic.
    b. unit inelastic.
    c. inelastic.
    d. elastic.

15. For a given increase in price, the greater the elasticity of supply, the greater the resulting
    a. decrease in quantity supplied.
    b. decrease in supply.
    c. increase in quantity supplied.
    d. increase in supply.

16. If the demand for gasoline is highly inelastic and the supply is highly elastic, and then a tax is imposed on gasoline, it will be paid
    a. largely by the sellers of gasoline.
    b. largely by the buyers of gasoline.
    c. equally by the sellers and buyers of gasoline.
    d. by the government.

17. An increase in demand will increase the price but not the quantity sold in a market if
    a. supply is perfectly elastic.
    b. supply is perfectly inelastic.
    c. supply is relatively elastic.
    d. supply is relatively inelastic.

18. A straight-line demand curve would
    a. have the same elasticity along its entire length.
    b. have a higher elasticity of demand near its top than near its bottom.
    c. have a lower elasticity of demand near its bottom than near its top.
    d. be relatively inelastic at high prices, but relatively elastic at low prices.

19. The longer the time horizon, a permanent increase in demand will tend to increase the quantity traded _____, and increases the price _____.
    a. more; more
    b. more; less
    c. less; more
    d. less; less

20. If you observed that price increased 20 percent when the quantity traded increased by 10 percent, then
    a. the elasticity of demand is 2.0.
    b. the elasticity of demand is 0.5.
    c. the elasticity of supply is 2.0.
    d. the elasticity of supply is 0.5.

21. If the cross-price elasticity of demand between two goods is negative, we know that
    a. they are substitutes.
    b. they are complements.
    c. they are both inferior goods.
    d. they are both normal goods.

22. If the income elasticity of demand for good A is 0.5 and the income elasticity of demand for good B is 1.5, then
    a. both A and B are normal goods.
    b. both A and B are inferior goods.
    c. A is a normal good, but B is an inferior good.
    d. A is an inferior good, but B is a normal good.

23. If good X has a negative cross-price elasticity of demand with good Y and good X also has a negative income elasticity of demand, then
    a. X is a substitute for Y, and X is a normal good.
    b. X is a substitute for Y, and X is an inferior good.
    c. X is a complement for Y, and X is a normal good.
    d. X is a complement for Y, and X is an inferior good.

Problems:

1. In each of the following cases, indicate which good you think has a relatively *more* price elastic demand and identify the most likely reason, in terms of the determinants of the elasticity of demand (more substitutes, greater share of budget, or more time to adjust).
   a. cars or Chevrolets
   b. salt or housing
   c. going to a New York Mets game or a Cleveland Indians game
   d. natural gas this month or over the course of a year

2. How might your elasticity of demand for copying and binding services vary if your work presentation is next week versus in two hours?

3. The San Francisco Giants want to boost revenues from ticket sales next season. You are hired as an economic consultant and asked to advise the Giants whether to raise or lower ticket prices next year. If the elasticity of demand for Giants game tickets is estimated to be −1.6, what would you advise? If the elasticity of demand equals −0.4?

4. For each of the following pairs, identify which one is likely to exhibit more elastic demand:
   a. shampoo; Paul Mitchell Shampoo
   b. air travel prompted by an illness in the family; vacation air travel
   c. paper clips; an apartment rental
   d. prescription heart medication; generic aspirin

5. Using the midpoint formula for calculating the elasticity of demand, if the price of a good fell from $42 to $38, what would be the elasticity of demand if the quantity demanded changed from:
   a. $19 to $21?
   b. $27 to $33?
   c. $195 to $205?

6. Explain why using the midpoint formula for calculating the elasticity of demand gives the same result whether price increases or decreases, but using the initial price and quantity instead of the average does not.

7. Why is a more narrowly defined good (pizza) likely to have a greater elasticity of demand than a more broadly defined good (food)?

8. If the elasticity of demand for hamburgers equals −1.5 and the quantity demanded equals 40,000, predict what will happen to the quantity demanded of hamburgers when the price increases by 10 percent. If the price falls by 5 percent, what will happen?

9. Evaluate the following statement: "Along a downward-sloping linear demand curve, the slope and therefore the elasticity of demand are both 'constant.'"

10. If the midpoint on a straight-line demand curve is at a price of $7, what can we say about the elasticity of demand for a price change from $12 to $10? What about from $6 to $4?

11. Assume the following weekly demand schedule for Sunshine DVD Rentals in Cloverdale.

   a. When Sunshine DVD Rentals lowers their rental price from $4 to $3, what happens to its total revenue?
   b. Between a price of $4 and a price of $3, is the demand for Sunshine DVD Rentals in Cloverdale elastic or inelastic?
   c. Between a price of $2 and a price of $1, is the demand for Sunshine DVD Rentals in Cloverdale elastic or inelastic?

12. The Cowtown Hotel is the only first-class hotel in Fort Worth. The hotel owners hired economics advisors for advice about improving the hotel's profitability. They suggested the hotel could increase this year's revenue by raising prices. The owners asked, "Won't raising prices reduce the quantity of hotel rooms demanded and increase vacancies?" What do you think the advisors replied? Why would they suggest increasing prices?

13. A movie production company faces a linear demand curve for its film, and it seeks to maximize total revenue from the film's distribution. At what level should the price be set? Where is demand elastic, inelastic, or unit elastic? Explain.

14. Isabella always spends $50 on red roses each month and simply adjusts the quantity she purchases as the price changes. What can you say about Isabella's elasticity of demand for roses?

15. If taxi fares in a city rise, what will happen to the total revenue received by taxi operators? If the fares charged for subway rides, a substitute for taxi rides, do not change, what will happen to the total revenue earned by the subway as a result?

16. Mayor George Henry has a problem. He doesn't want to anger voters by taxing them because he wants to be reelected, but the town of Gapville needs more revenue for its schools. He has a choice between taxing tickets to professional basketball games or taxing food. If the demand for food is relatively inelastic while the supply is relatively elastic, and if the demand for professional basketball games is relatively elastic while the supply is relatively inelastic, in which case would the tax burden fall primarily on consumers? In which case would the tax burden fall primarily on producers?

17. Indicate whether a pair of products are substitutes, complements, or neither based upon the following estimates for the cross-price elasticity of demand:
   a. 0.5
   b. −0.5

18. Using the midpoint formula for calculating the elasticity of supply, if the price of a good rose from $95 to $105, what would be the elasticity of supply if the quantity supplied changed from:
   a. 38 to 42?
   b. 78 to 82?
   c. 54 to 66?

19. Why is an increase in price more likely to decrease the total revenue of a seller in the long run than in the short run?

20. If both supply curves and demand curves are more elastic in the long run than in the short run, how does the incidence of a tax change from the short run to the long run as a result? What happens to the revenue raised from a given tax over time, *ceteris paribus*?

21. Assume you had the following observations on U.S. intercity rail travel: Between 1990 and 1993 rail travel increased from 17.5 passenger miles per person to 19 passenger miles per person. At the same time neither per-mile railroad price or incomes changed but the per-mile price of intercity airline travel increased by 7.5 percent. Between 1995 and 1998 per capita incomes rose by approximately 13 percent while the price of travel by rail and plane stayed constant. Intercity rail travel was 20 passenger miles per person in 1995 and 19.5 in 1998. Assuming the demand for travel didn't change between these periods:
    a. calculate the income elasticity of demand for intercity rail travel.
    b. calculate the cross-price elasticity of demand for intercity rail travel.
    c. are air travel and rail travel substitutes or complements? Is intercity rail travel a normal or an inferior good?

PART 3 MARKET EFFICIENCY, MARKET FAILURE, AND THE PUBLIC SYSTEM

Chapter 7 Market Efficiency and Welfare *182*
Chapter 8 Market Failure *209*
Chapter 9 Public Sector and Public Choice *233*

7 Market Efficiency and Welfare

7.1 Consumer Surplus and Producer Surplus

7.2 The Welfare Effects of Taxes, Subsidies, and Price Controls

In earlier chapters, we saw how the market forces of supply and demand allocate society's scarce resources. However, we did not discuss whether this outcome was desirable or to whom.

Are the price and output that result from the equilibrium of supply and demand right from society's standpoint?

Using the tools of consumer and producer surplus, we can demonstrate the *efficiency* of a competitive market. In other words, we can show that the equilibrium price and quantity in a competitive market maximize the economic welfare of consumers and producers. Maximizing total surplus (the sum of consumer and producer surplus) leads to an efficient allocation of resources. Efficiency makes the size of the economic pie as large as possible. How we distribute that economic pie (equity) is the subject of future chapters. Efficiency can be measured on objective, positive grounds while equity involves normative analysis.

We can also use the tools of consumer and producer surplus to study the *welfare effects* of government policy—rent controls, taxes, and agricultural support prices. To economists, *welfare* does not mean a government payment to the poor; rather, it is a way that we measure the impact of a policy on a particular group, such as consumers or producers. By calculating the changes in producer and consumer surplus that result from government intervention, we can measure the impact of such policies on buyers and sellers. For example, economists and policymakers may want to know how much a consumer or producer might benefit or be harmed by a tax or subsidy that alters the equilibrium price and quantity.

Let's begin by presenting the most widely used tool for measuring consumer and producer welfare. ■

SECTION 7.1 Consumer Surplus and Producer Surplus

* What is consumer surplus?
* What is producer surplus?
* How do we measure the total gains from trade?

Consumer Surplus

In a competitive market, consumers and producers buy and sell at the market equilibrium price. However, some consumers will be willing and able to pay more for the good than they have to. But they would never knowingly buy something that is worth less to them. That is, what a consumer actually pays for a unit of a good is usually less than the amount she is *willing* to pay. For example, you would be willing and able to pay far more than the market price for a rope ladder to get out of a burning building. You would be willing to pay more than the market price for a tank of gasoline if you had run out of gas on a desolate highway in the desert. **Consumer surplus** is the monetary difference between the amount a consumer is willing and able to pay for an additional unit of a good and what the consumer actually pays—the market price. Consumer surplus for the whole market is the sum of all the individual consumer surpluses for those consumers who have purchased the good.

Imagine it is 115 degrees in the shade. Do you think you would get more consumer surplus from your first glass of iced tea than you would from a fifth glass?

Marginal Willingness to Pay Falls as More Is Consumed

consumer surplus
the difference between the price a consumer is willing and able to pay for an additional unit of a good and the price the consumer actually pays; for the whole market, it is the sum of all the individual consumer surpluses

Suppose it is a hot day and iced tea is going for $1 per glass, but Julie is willing to pay $4 for the first glass (point a), $2 for the second glass (point b), and $0.50 for the third glass (point c), reflecting the law of demand. How much consumer surplus will Julie receive? First, it is important to note the general fact that if the consumer is a buyer of several units of a good, the earlier units will have greater marginal value and therefore create more consumer surplus, because *marginal willingness to pay* falls as greater quantities are consumed in any period. In fact, you can think of the demand curve as a marginal benefit curve—the additional benefit derived from consuming one more unit. Notice in Exhibit 1 that Julie's demand curve for iced tea has a step-like shape. This is demonstrated by Julie's willingness to pay $4 and $2 successively for the first two glasses of iced tea. Thus, Julie will receive $3 of consumer surplus for the first glass ($4 − $1) and $1 of consumer surplus for the second glass ($2 − $1), for a total consumer surplus of $4, as seen in Exhibit 1. Julie will not be willing to purchase the third glass, because her willingness to pay is less than its price ($0.50 versus $1.00).

In Exhibit 2, we can easily measure the consumer surplus in the market by using a market demand curve rather than an individual demand curve. In short, the market consumer surplus is the area under the market demand curve and above the market price (the shaded area in Exhibit 2). The market for chocolate contains millions of potential buyers, so we will get a smooth demand curve. Because the demand curve represents the *marginal benefits* consumers receive from consuming an additional unit, we can conclude that all buyers of chocolate receive at least some consumer surplus in the market because the marginal benefit is greater than the market price—the shaded area in Exhibit 2.

section 7.1 exhibit 1 — Julie's Consumer Surplus for Iced Tea

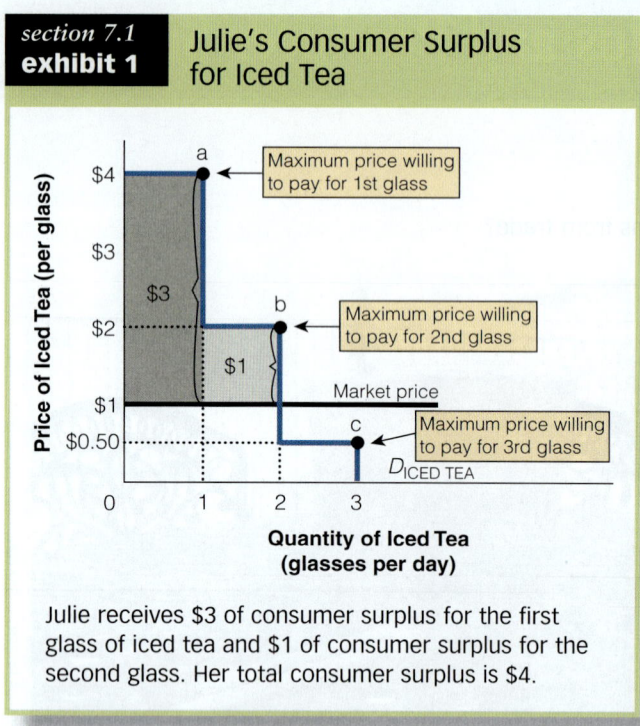

Julie receives $3 of consumer surplus for the first glass of iced tea and $1 of consumer surplus for the second glass. Her total consumer surplus is $4.

section 7.1 exhibit 3 — Impact of an Increase in Supply on Consumer Surplus

As a result of the increase in supply, the price falls from P_1 to P_2. The initial consumer surplus at P_1 is the area P_1AB. The increase in the consumer surplus from the fall in price is from P_1 to P_2.

section 7.1 exhibit 2 — Consumer Surplus

The area below the market demand curve but above the market price is called consumer surplus. It is represented by the shaded area. The market demand curve is smooth because many buyers purchase chocolate each year.

increase your consumer surplus for each unit you were already consuming and will also increase your consumer surplus from additional purchases at the lower price. Conversely, a decrease in supply and increase in price will lower your consumer surplus.

Exhibit 3 shows the gain in consumer surplus associated with, say, a technological advance that shifts the supply curve to the right. As a result, equilibrium price falls (from P_1 to P_2) and quantity rises (from Q_1 to Q_2). Consumer surplus then increases from area P_1AB to area P_2AC, or a gain in consumer surplus of P_1BCP_2. The increase in consumer surplus has two parts. First, there is an increase in consumer surplus, because Q_1 can now be purchased at a lower price; this amount of additional consumer surplus is illustrated by area P_1BDP_2 in Exhibit 3. Second, the lower price makes it advantageous for buyers to expand their purchases from Q_1 to Q_2. The net benefit to buyers from expanding their consumption from Q_1 to Q_2 is illustrated by area BCD.

Price Changes and Changes in Consumer Surplus

Imagine that the price of your favorite beverage fell because of an increase in supply. Wouldn't you feel better off? An increase in supply and a lower price will

Producer Surplus

As we have just seen, the difference between what a consumer would be willing and able to pay for a given quantity of a good and what a consumer actually has to pay is called consumer surplus. The parallel concept for producers is called producer surplus. **Producer surplus** is the difference between what a producer is paid for a good and the cost of producing one unit of that good. Producers would never knowingly sell a good that is worth more to them than the asking price. Imagine selling coffee for half of what it cost to produce—you won't be in business very long with that pricing strategy. The supply curve shows the minimum amount that sellers must receive to be willing to supply any given quantity; that is, the supply curve reflects the marginal cost to sellers. The **marginal cost** is the cost of producing one more unit of a good. In other words, the supply curve is the marginal cost curve, just like the demand curve is the marginal benefit curve. Because some units can be produced at a cost that is lower than the market price, the seller receives a surplus, or a net benefit, from producing those units. For example, in Exhibit 4, the market price is $5. Say the firm's marginal cost is $2 for the first unit, $3 for the second unit, $4 for the third unit, and $5 for the fourth unit. Because producer surplus for a particular unit is the difference between the market price and the seller's cost of producing that unit, producer surplus would be as follows: The first unit would yield $3; the second unit would yield $2; the third unit would yield $1; and the fourth unit would add no more to producer surplus, because the market price equals the seller's cost.

producer surplus
the difference between what a producer is paid for a good and the cost of producing that unit of the good; for the market, it is the sum of all the individual sellers' producer surpluses—the area above the market supply curve and below the market price

marginal cost
the cost of producing one more unit of a good

When there are a lot of producers, the supply curve is more or less smooth, like in Exhibit 5. Total producer surplus for the market is obtained by summing all the producer surpluses of all the sellers—the area above the market supply curve and below the market price up to the quantity actually produced—the shaded area in Exhibit 5. Producer surplus is a measurement of how much sellers gain from trading in the market.

Suppose an increase in market demand causes the market price to rise, say from P_1 to P_2; the seller now receives a higher price per unit, so additional producer surplus is generated. In Exhibit 6, we see the additions to producer surplus. Part of the added surplus (area P_2DBP_1) is due to a higher price for the quantity already being produced (up to Q_1) and part (area DCB) is due to the expansion of output made profitable by the higher price (from Q_1 to Q_2).

Market Efficiency and Producer and Consumer Surplus

With the tools of consumer and producer surplus, we can better analyze the total gains from exchange. The demand curve represents a collection of maximum prices that consumers are willing and able to pay for

section 7.1 exhibit 4 A Firm's Producer Surplus

The firm's supply curve looks like a staircase. The marginal cost is under the stair and the producer surplus is above the red stair and below the market price for each unit.

section 7.1 exhibit 5 Market Producer Surplus

The market producer surplus is the shaded area above the supply curve and below the market price up to the quantity produced, 50,000 units.

section 7.1 exhibit 6: Impact of an Increase in Demand on Producer Surplus

A higher market price due to an increase in market demand will increase total producer surplus. The initial producer surplus at P_1 is the area ABP_1. The increase in producer surplus from the higher price is area P_2CBP_1.

section 7.1 exhibit 7: Consumer and Producer Surplus

Increasing output beyond the competitive equilibrium output, 4 million units, decreases welfare, because the cost of producing this extra output exceeds the value the buyer places on it ($MC > MB$)—producing 5 million units rather than 4 million units leads to a deadweight loss of area ECD. Reducing output below the competitive equilibrium output level, 4 million units, reduces total welfare, because the buyer values the extra output by more than it costs to produce that output—producing 3 million units rather than 4 million units leads to a deadweight loss of area EAB, $MB > MC$, only at equilibrium, E, is $MB = MC$.

additional quantities of a good or service. It also shows the marginal benefits derived by consumers. The supply curve represents a collection of minimum prices that suppliers require to be willing and able to supply each additional unit of a good or service. It also shows the marginal cost of production. Both are shown in Exhibit 7. For example, for the first unit of output, the buyer is willing to pay up to $7, while the seller would have to receive at least $1 to produce that unit. However, the equilibrium price is $4, as indicated by the intersection of the supply and demand curves. It is clear that the two would gain from getting together and trading that unit, because the consumer would receive $3 of consumer surplus ($7 − $4), and the producer would receive $3 of producer surplus ($4 − $1). Both would also benefit from trading the second and third units of output—in fact, both would benefit from trading every unit up to the market equilibrium output. That is, the buyer purchases the good, except for the very last unit, for less than the maximum amount she would have been willing to pay; the seller receives for the good, except for the last unit, more than the minimum amount for which he would have been willing to supply the good. Once the equilibrium output is reached at the equilibrium price, all the mutually beneficial trade opportunities between the demander and supplier will have taken place, and the sum of consumer surplus and producer surplus is maximized. This is where the marginal benefit to buyers is equal to the marginal cost to producers. Both buyer and seller are better off from each of the units traded than they would have been if they had not exchanged them.

It is important to recognize that, in this case, the **total welfare gains** to the economy from trade in this good is the sum of the consumer and producer surpluses created. That is, consumers benefit from additional amounts of consumer surplus, and producers benefit from additional amounts of producer surplus. Improvements in welfare come from additions to both consumer and producer surpluses. In competitive markets with large numbers of buyers and sellers, at the market equilibrium price and quantity, the net gains to society are as large as possible.

> **total welfare gains** the sum of consumer and producer surpluses

in the news   Is Santa a Deadweight Loss?

In America, retailers make 25% of their yearly sales and 60% of their profits between Thanksgiving and Christmas. Even so, economists find something to worry about in the nature of the purchase being made.

Much of the holiday spending is on gifts for others. At the simplest level, giving gifts involves the giver thinking of something that the recipient would like—he tries to guess her preferences, as economists say—and then buying the gift and delivering it. Yet this guessing of preferences is no mean feat; indeed, it is often done badly. Every year, ties go unworn and books unread. And even if a gift is enjoyed, it may not be what the recipient would have bought had she spent the money herself.

Intrigued by this mismatch between wants and gifts, in 1993 Joel Waldfogel, then an economist at Yale University, sought to establish the disparity in dollar terms. In a paper that has proved seminal in the literature on the issue, he asked students two questions at the end of the holiday season: first, estimate the total amount paid (by givers) for all holiday gifts you received; second, apart from sentimental value of the items, if you did not have them, how much would you be willing to pay to get them? His results were gloomy: on average, a gift was valued by the recipient well below the price paid by the giver.

The most conservative estimate put the average receiver's valuation at 90% of the buying price. The missing 10% is what economists call a deadweight loss: a waste of resources that could be averted without making anyone worse off. In other words, if the giver gave the cash value of the purchase instead of the gift itself, the recipient could then buy what she really wants, and be better off for no extra cost.

Perhaps not surprisingly, the most effective gifts (those with the smallest deadweight loss) were those from close friends and relations, while non-cash gifts from extended family were the least efficient. As the age difference between giver and recipient grew, so did the inefficiency. All of which suggests what many grandparents know: when buying gifts for someone with largely unknown preferences, the best present is one that is totally flexible (cash) or very flexible (gift vouchers).

If the results are generalized, a waste of one dollar in ten represents a huge aggregate loss to society. It suggests that in America, where givers spend $40 billion on Christmas gifts, $4 billion is being lost annually in the process of gift giving. Add in birthdays, weddings, and non-Christian occasions and the figure would balloon. So should economists advocate an end to gift giving, or at least press for money to become the gift of choice?

Sentimental Value

There are a number of reasons to think not. First, recipients may not know their own preferences very well. Some of the best gifts, after all, are the unexpected items that you would never have thought of buying but turn out to be especially well picked. And preferences can change. So by giving a jazz CD, for example, the giver may be encouraging the recipient to enjoy something that was shunned before. This, and a desire to build skills, is presumably the hope held by the many parents who ignore their children's pleas for video games and give them books instead.

(continued)

in the news Is Santa a Deadweight Loss? (cont.)

Second, the giver may have access to items—because of travel or an employee discount, for example—that the recipient does not know existed, cannot buy, or can only buy at a higher price. Finally, there are items that a recipient would like to receive but not purchase. If someone else buys them, however, they can be enjoyed guilt-free. This might explain the high volume of chocolate that changes hands over the holidays.

But there is a more powerful argument for gift giving, deliberately ignored by most surveys. Gift giving, some economists think, is a process that adds value to an item over and above what it would otherwise be worth to the recipient. Intuition backs this up, of course. A gift's worth is not only a function of its price but also of the giver and the circumstances in which it is given.

Hence, a wedding ring is more valuable to its owner than to a jeweler, and the imprint of a child's hand on dried clay is priceless to a loving grandparent. Moreover, not only can gift giving add value for the recipient, but it can be fun for the giver, too. It is good, in other words, to give as well as to receive.

The lesson then, for gift givers? Try hard to guess the preferences of each person on your list and then choose a gift that will have high sentimental value. As economists have studied hard to tell you, it's the thought that counts.

SOURCE: From "Economics Focus: Is Santa a Deadweight Loss?", 'The Economist', December 20, 2001. © The Economist Newspaper Limited, London 2001. Reprinted with permission.

Why would it be inefficient to produce only 3 million units? The demand curve in Exhibit 7 indicates that the buyer is willing to pay $5 for the 3 millionth unit. The supply curve shows that it only costs the seller $3 to produce that unit. That is, as long as the buyer values the extra output by more than it costs to produce that unit, total welfare would increase by expanding output. In fact, if output is expanded from 3 million units to 4 million units, total welfare (the sum of consumer and producer surpluses) will increase by area AEB in Exhibit 7.

What if 5 million units are produced? The demand curve shows that the buyer is only willing to pay $3 for the 5 millionth unit. However, the supply curve shows that it would cost about $5.50 to produce that 5 millionth unit. Thus, increasing output beyond equilibrium decreases total welfare, because the cost of producing this extra output is greater than the value the buyer places on it. If output is reduced from 5 million units to 4 million units, total welfare will increase by area ECD in Exhibit 7.

> **deadweight loss**
> net loss of total surplus that results from an action that alters a market equilibrium

Not producing the efficient level of output, in this case 4 million units, leads to what economists call a **deadweight loss.** A deadweight loss is the reduction in both consumer and producer surpluses—it is the net loss of total surplus that results from the misallocation of resources.

In a competitive equilibrium, supply equals demand at the equilibrium. This means that the buyers value the last unit of output consumed by exactly the same amount that it cost to produce. If consumers valued the last unit by more than it cost to produce, welfare could be increased by expanding output. If consumers valued the last unit by less than it cost to produce, then welfare could be increased by producing less output.

In sum, *market efficiency* occurs when we have maximized the sum of consumer and producer surplus, when the margin of benefits of the last unit consumed is equal to the marginal cost of productivity, $MB = MC$.

GREAT ECONOMIC THINKERS

ALFRED MARSHALL (1842–1924)

Alfred Marshall was born outside of London in 1842. His father, a domineering man who was a cashier for the Bank of England, wanted nothing more than for Alfred to become a minister. But the young Marshall enjoyed math and chess, both of which were forbidden by his authoritarian father. When he was older, Marshall turned down a theological scholarship to Oxford to study at Cambridge, with the financial support of a wealthy uncle. Here he earned academic honors in mathematics. Upon graduating, Marshall set upon a period of self-discovery. He traveled to Germany to study metaphysics, later adopting the philosophy of agnosticism, and moved on to studying ethics. He found within himself a deep sorrow and disgust over the condition of society. He resolved to use his skills to lessen poverty and human suffering, and, in wanting to use his mathematics in this broader capacity, Marshall soon developed a fascination with economics.

Marshall became a fellow and lecturer in political economy at Cambridge. He had been teaching for nine years when, in 1877, he married a former student, Mary Paley. Because of the university's celibacy rules, Marshall had to give up his position at Cambridge. He moved on to teach at University College at Bristol and at Oxford. But in 1885, the rules were relaxed and Marshall returned to Cambridge as the Chair in Political Economy, a position that he held until 1908, when he resigned to devote more time to writing.

Before this point in time, economics was grouped with philosophy and the "moral sciences." Marshall fought all of his life for economics to be set apart as a field all its own. In 1903, Marshall finally succeeded in persuading Cambridge to establish a separate economics course, paving the way for the discipline as it exists today. As this event clearly demonstrates, Marshall exerted a great deal of influence on the development of economic thought in his time. Marshall popularized the heavy use of illustration, real-world examples, and current events in teaching, as well as the modern diagrammatic approach to economics. Relatively early in his career, it was being said that Marshall's former students occupied half of the economic chairs in the United Kingdom. His most famous student was John Maynard Keynes.

Marshall is most famous for refining the marginal approach. He was intrigued by the self-adjusting and self-correcting nature of economic markets, and he was also interested in time—how long did it take for markets to adjust? Marshall coined the analogy that compares the tools of supply and demand to the blades on a pair of scissors—that is, it is fruitless to talk about whether it was supply or demand that determined the market price; rather, one should consider both in unison. After all, the upper blade is not of more importance than the lower when using a pair of scissors to cut a piece of paper. Marshall was also responsible for refining some of the most important tools in economics—elasticity and consumer and producer surplus. Marshall's book *Principles of Economics* was published in 1890; immensely popular, the book went into eight editions. Much of the content in *Principles* is still at the core of microeconomics texts today.

SECTION CHECK

1. The difference between how much a consumer is willing and able to pay and how much a consumer has to pay for a unit of a good is called consumer surplus.
2. An increase in supply will lead to a lower price and an increase in consumer surplus; a decrease in supply will lead to a higher price and a decrease in consumer surplus.
3. Producer surplus is the difference between what a producer is paid for a good and the cost of producing that good.
4. An increase in demand will lead to a higher market price and an increase in producer surplus; a decrease in demand will lead to a lower market price and a decrease in producer surplus.

(continued)

5. We can think of the demand curve as a marginal benefit curve and the supply curve as a marginal cost curve.
6. Total welfare gains from trade to the economy can be measured by the sum of consumer and producer surpluses.

1. What is consumer surplus?
2. Why do the earlier units consumed at a given price add more consumer surplus than the later units consumed?
3. Why does a decrease in a good's price increase the consumer surplus from consumption of that good?
4. Why might the consumer surplus from purchases of diamond rings be less than the consumer surplus from purchases of far less expensive stones?
5. What is producer surplus?
6. Why do the earlier units produced at a given price add more producer surplus than the later units produced?
7. Why does an increase in a good's price increase the producer surplus from production of that good?
8. Why might the producer surplus from sales of diamond rings, which are expensive, be less than the producer surplus from sales of far less expensive stones?
9. Why is the efficient level of output in an industry defined as the output where the sum of consumer and producer surplus is maximized?
10. Why does a reduction in output below the efficient level create a deadweight loss?
11. Why does an expansion in output beyond the efficient level create a deadweight loss?

SECTION 7.2 The Welfare Effects of Taxes, Subsidies, and Price Controls

* What are the welfare effects of a tax?
* What is the relationship between a deadweight loss and price elasticities?
* What are the welfare effects of subsidies?
* What are the welfare effects of price controls?

In the previous section we used the tools of consumer and producer surplus to measure the efficiency of a competitive market—that is, how the equilibrium price and quantity in a competitive market lead to the maximization of aggregate welfare (for both buyers and sellers). Now we can use the same tools, consumer and producer surplus, to measure the welfare effects of various government programs—taxes and price controls. When economists refer to the **welfare effects** of a government policy, they are referring to the gains and losses associated with government intervention. This use of the term should not be confused with the more common reference to a welfare recipient who is getting aid from the government.

welfare effects
the gains and losses associated with government intervention in markets

Using Consumer and Producer Surplus to Find the Welfare Effects of a Tax

To simplify the explanation of elasticity and the tax incidence, we will not complicate the illustration by shifting the supply curve (tax levied on sellers) or demand curve (tax levied on buyers) as we did in Section 6.4. We will simply show the result a tax must cause. The tax is illustrated by the vertical distance between the supply and demand curves at the new after-tax output—shown as the bold vertical line in

section 7.2 exhibit 1 — Supply and Demand of a Tax

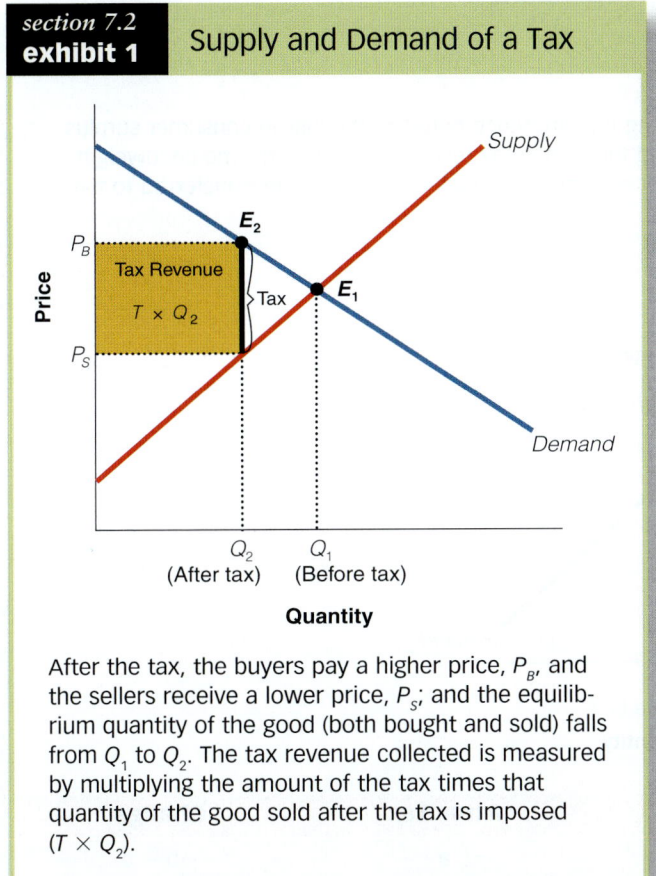

After the tax, the buyers pay a higher price, P_B, and the sellers receive a lower price, P_S; and the equilibrium quantity of the good (both bought and sold) falls from Q_1 to Q_2. The tax revenue collected is measured by multiplying the amount of the tax times that quantity of the good sold after the tax is imposed ($T \times Q_2$).

Exhibit 1. After the tax, the buyers pay a higher price, P_B, and the sellers receive a lower price, P_S; and the equilibrium quantity of the good (both bought and sold) falls from Q_1 to Q_2. The tax revenue collected is measured by multiplying the amount of the tax times the quantity of the good sold after the tax is imposed ($T \times Q_2$).

In Exhibit 2, we can now use consumer and producer surpluses to measure the amount of welfare loss associated with a tax. First, consider the amounts of consumer and producer surplus before the tax. Before the tax is imposed, the price is P_1 and the quantity is Q_1; at that price and output, the amount of consumer surplus is area a + b + c, and the amount of producer surplus is area d + e + f. To get the total surplus, or total welfare, we add consumer and producer surpluses, area a + b + c + d + e + f. Without a tax, tax revenues are zero.

After the tax, the price the buyer pays is P_B, the price the seller receives is P_S, and the output falls to Q_2. As a result of the higher price and lower output from the tax, consumer surplus is smaller—area a. After the tax, sellers receive a lower price, so producer surplus is smaller—area f. However, some of the loss in consumer and producer surpluses is transferred in the form of tax revenues to the government, which can be used to reduce other taxes, fund public projects, or be redistributed to others in society. This transfer of society's resources is not a loss from society's perspective. The net loss to society can be found by measuring the difference between the loss in consumer surplus (area b + c) plus the loss in producer surplus (area d + e) and the gain in tax revenue (area b + d). The reduction in total surplus is area c + e, or the shaded area in Exhibit 2. This deadweight loss from the tax is the reduction in producer and consumer surpluses minus the tax revenue transferred to the government.

Deadweight loss occurs because the tax reduces the quantity exchanged below the original output level, Q_1, reducing the size of the total surplus realized from trade. The problem is that the tax distorts market incentives: The price to buyers is higher than before the tax, so they consume less; and the price to sellers is lower than before the tax, so they produce less. These effects lead to deadweight loss, or market inefficiencies—the waste associated with not producing the efficient level of output. That is, the tax causes a deadweight loss because it prevents some mutual beneficial trade between buyers and sellers.

Use what you've LEARNED: SHOULD WE USE TAXES TO REDUCE DEPENDENCY ON FOREIGN OIL?

Q What if we placed a $0.50 tax on gasoline to reduce dependence on foreign oil and to raise the tax revenue?

A If the demand and supply curves are both equally elastic, as in Exhibit 2, both consumers and producers will share the burden equally. The tax collected would be b + d, but total loss in consumer surplus (b + c) and producer surplus (d + e) would be greater than the gains in tax revenue. Not surprisingly, both consumers and producers fight such a tax every time it is proposed.

section 7.2 exhibit 2 — Welfare Effects of a Tax

The net loss to society due to a tax can be found by measuring the difference between the loss in consumer surplus (area b + c) plus the loss in producer surplus (area d + e) and the gain in tax revenue (area b + d). The deadweight loss from the tax is the reduction in the consumer and producer surpluses minus the tax revenue transferred to the government, area c + e.

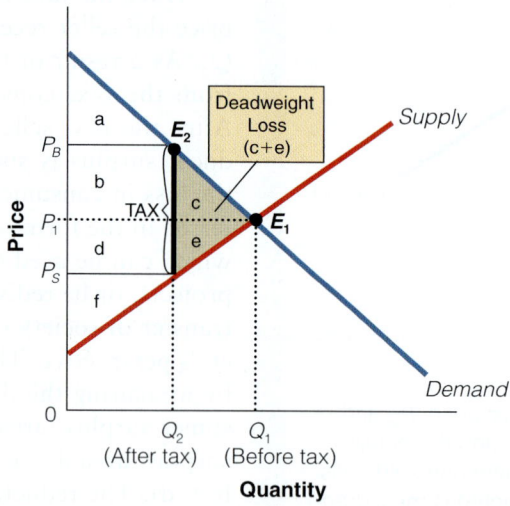

	Before Tax	After Tax	Change
Consumer Surplus	a + b + c	a	−b − c
Producer Surplus	d + e + f	f	−d − e
Tax Revenue ($T \times Q_2$)	zero	b + d	b + d
Total Welfare	a + b + c + d + e + f	a + b + d + f	−c − e

All taxes lead to deadweight loss. The deadweight loss is important because if the people are to benefit from the tax, then more than $1 of benefit must be produced from $1 of government expenditure. For example, if a gasoline tax leads to $100 million in tax revenues and $20 million in deadweight loss, then the government needs to provide a benefit to the public of more than $120 million with the $100 million revenues.

Elasticity and the Size of the Deadweight Loss

The size of the deadweight loss from a tax, as well as how the burdens are shared between buyers and sellers, depends on the price elasticities of supply and demand. In Exhibit 3(a) we can see that, other things being equal, the less elastic the demand curve, the smaller the deadweight loss. Similarly, the less elastic the supply curve, other things being equal, the smaller the deadweight loss, as shown in Exhibit 3(b). However, when the supply and/or demand curves become more elastic, the deadweight loss becomes larger, because a given tax reduces the quantity exchanged by a greater amount, as seen in Exhibit 3(c). Recall that elasticities measure how responsive buyers and sellers are to price changes. That is, the more elastic the curves are, the greater the change in output and the larger the deadweight loss.

Elasticity differences can help us understand tax policy. Goods that are heavily taxed, such as alcohol, cigarettes, and gasoline, often have a relatively inelastic demand curve in the short run, so the tax burden falls primarily on the buyer. It also means that the deadweight loss to society is smaller for the tax revenue raised than if the demand curve were more elastic. In other words, because consumers cannot find many close substitutes in the short run, they reduce their consumption only slightly at the higher after-tax price. Even though the deadweight loss is smaller, it is still positive, because the reduced after-tax price received by sellers and the increased after-tax price paid by buyers reduces the quantity exchanged below the previous market equilibrium level.

section 7.2 exhibit 3 — Elasticity and Deadweight Loss

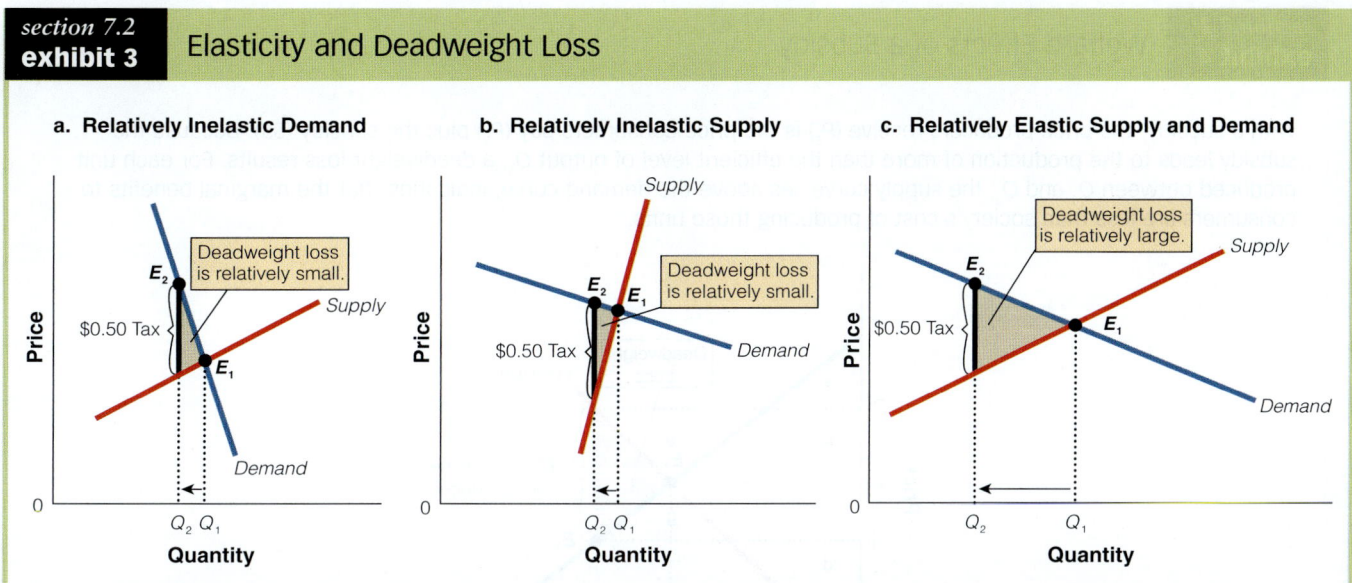

In (a) and (b), we see that when one of the two curves is relatively price inelastic, the deadweight loss from the tax is relatively small. However, when the supply and/or demand curves become more elastic, the deadweight loss becomes larger, because a given tax reduces the quantity exchanged by a greater amount, as seen in (c). The more elastic the curves are, the greater the change in output and the larger the deadweight loss.

The Welfare Effects of Subsidies

If taxes cause deadweight or welfare losses, do subsidies create welfare gains? For example, what if a government subsidy (paid by taxpayers) was provided in a particular market? Think of a subsidy as a negative tax. Before the subsidy, say the equilibrium price was P_1 and the equilibrium quantity was Q_1, as shown in Exhibit 4. The consumer surplus is area a + b, and the producer surplus is area c + d. The sum of producer and consumer surpluses is maximized (a + b + c + d), with no deadweight loss.

In Exhibit 4, we see that the subsidy lowers the price to the buyer to P_B and increases the quantity exchanged to Q_2. The subsidy results in an increase in consumer surplus from area a + b to area a + b + c + g, a gain of c + g. And producer surplus increases from area c + d to area c + d + b + e, a gain of b + e. With gains in both consumer and producer surpluses, it looks like a gain in welfare, right? Not quite. Remember that the government is paying for this subsidy, and the cost to government (taxpayers) of the subsidy is area b + e + f + c + g (the subsidy per unit times the number of units subsidized). That is, the cost to government (taxpayers), area b + e + f + c + g, is greater than the gains to consumers, c + g, and the gains to producers, b + e, by area f. Area f is the deadweight or welfare loss to society from the subsidy because it results in the production of more than the competitive market equilibrium, and the market value of that expansion to buyers is less than the marginal cost of producing that expansion to sellers. In short, the market overproduces relative to the efficient level of output, Q_1.

Price Ceilings and Welfare Effects

As we saw in Chapter 5, price controls involve the use of the power of the government to establish prices different from the equilibrium market price that would otherwise prevail. The motivations for price controls vary with the markets under consideration. A maximum, or ceiling, is often set for goods deemed important, such as housing. A minimum price, or floor, may be set on wages because wages are the primary source of income for most people, or on agricultural products, in order to guarantee that producers will get a certain minimum price for their products.

If a price ceiling (that is, a legally established maximum price) is binding and set below the equilibrium price at P_{MAX}, the quantity demanded will be greater than the quantity supplied at that price, and a shortage will occur. At this price, buyers will compete for the limited supply, Q_2.

We can see the welfare effects of a price ceiling by observing the change in consumer and producer surpluses from the implementation of the price ceiling in Exhibit 5. Before the price ceiling, the buyer receives area a + b + c of consumer surplus at price P_1 and

section 7.2 exhibit 4 — Welfare Effects of a Subsidy

With a subsidy, the price producers receive (P_S) is the price consumers pay (P_B) plus the subsidy ($\$S$). Because the subsidy leads to the production of more than the efficient level of output Q_1, a deadweight loss results. For each unit produced between Q_1 and Q_2, the supply curve lies above the demand curve, indicating that the marginal benefits to consumers are less than society's cost of producing those units.

	Before Tax Subsidy	After Tax Subsidy	Change
Consumer Surplus	a + b	a + b + c + g	c + g
Producer Surplus	c + d	c + d + b + e	b + e
Government (Taxpayers)	zero	−b − e − f − c − g	−b − e − f − c − g
Total Welfare (CS + PS − G)	a + b + c + d	a + b + c + d − f	−f

quantity Q_1. However, after the price ceiling is implemented at P_{MAX}, consumers can buy the good at a lower price but cannot buy as much as before (they can only buy Q_2 instead of Q_1). Because consumers can now buy Q_2 at a lower price, they gain area d of consumer surplus after the price ceiling. However, they lose area c of consumer surplus because they can only purchase Q_2 rather than Q_1 of output. Thus, the change in consumer surplus is d − c. In this case, area d is larger than area e and area c and the consumer gains from the price ceiling.

The price the seller receives for Q_2 is P_{MAX} (the ceiling price), so producer surplus falls from area d + e + f before the price ceiling to area f after the price ceiling, for a loss of area d + e. That is, any possible gain to consumers will be more than offset by the losses to producers. The price ceiling has caused a deadweight loss of area c + e.

There is a deadweight loss because less is sold at Q_2 than at Q_1; and consumers value those units between Q_2 and Q_1 by more than it cost to produce them. For example, at Q_2, consumers will value the unit at P_2, which is much higher than it cost to produce it—the point on the supply curve at Q_2.

Applications of Consumer and Producer Surplus

Rent Controls

If consumers use no additional resources, search costs, or side payments for a rent controlled unit, the consumer surplus is equal to a + b + d in Exhibit 5. If landlords were able to extract P_2 from renters, consumer surplus would be reduced to area a. Landlords are able to collect higher "rent" using a variety of methods. They might have the tenant slip them a couple hundred dollars each month; they might charge a high rate for parking in the garage; they might rent used furniture at a high rate; or they might charge an exorbitant key price—the price for changing the locks for a new tenant. These types of arrangements take place in so-called

section 7.2 exhibit 5 — Welfare Effects of a Price Ceiling

	Before Price Ceiling	After Price Ceiling	Change
Consumer Surplus	a + b + c	a + b + d	d − c
Producer Surplus	d + e + f	f	−d − e
Total Welfare (CS + PS)	a + b + c + d + e + f	a + b + d + f	−c − e

If area d is larger than area c, consumers in the aggregate would be better off from the price ceiling. However, any possible gain to consumers will be more than offset by the losses to producers, area d + e. Price ceiling causes a deadweight loss of c + e.

black markets—markets where goods are transacted outside the boundaries of the law. One problem is that law-abiding citizens will be among those least likely to find a rental unit. Other problems include black market prices that are likely to be higher than the price would be if restrictions were lifted and the inability to use legal means to enforce contracts and resolve disputes.

If the landlord is able to charge P_2, then the area b + d of consumer surplus will be lost by consumers and gained by the landlord. This redistribution from the buyer to the seller does not change the size of the deadweight loss; it remains area c + e.

The measure of the deadweight loss in the price ceiling case may underestimate the true cost to consumers. At least two inefficiencies are not measured. One, consumers may spend a lot of time looking for rental units because vacancy rates will be very low—only Q_2 is available and consumers are willing to pay as much as P_2 for Q_2 units. Two, someone may have been lucky to find a rental unit at the ceiling price, P_{MAX}, but someone who values it more, say at P_2, may not be able to find a rental unit.

It is important to distinguish between deadweight loss, which measures the overall efficiency loss, and the distribution of the gains and losses from a particular policy. For example, as a rent control tenant, you may be pleased with the outcome—a lower price than you would ordinarily pay (a transfer from landlord to tenant) providing that you can find a vacant rent-controlled unit.

Rent Controls—Short Run Versus Long Run

In the absence of rent control (a price ceiling), the equilibrium price is P_1 and the equilibrium quantity is Q_1, with no deadweight loss. However, a price ceiling leads to a deadweight loss, but the size of the deadweight loss depends on elasticity: The deadweight loss is greater in the short run (less elastic supply) than the long run (more elastic supply). Why? A city that enacts a rent control program will not lose many rental units in the next week. That is, even at lowered legal prices, roughly the same number of units will be available this week as last week; thus, in the short run the supply of rental units is virtually fixed—relatively inelastic, as seen in Exhibit 6(a). In the long run, however, the supply of rental units is much more elastic; landlords respond to the lower rental prices by allowing rental

section 7.2 exhibit 6: Deadweight Loss of Rent Control: Short Run vs. Long Run

The reduction in rental units in response to the rent ceiling price P_C is much smaller in the short run (Q_1 to Q_{SR}) than in the long run (Q_1 to Q_{LR}). The deadweight loss is also much greater in the long run than in the short run, as indicated by the shaded areas in the two graphs. In addition, the size of the shortage is much greater in the long run than in the short run.

units to deteriorate and building fewer new rental units. In the long run, then, the supply curve is much more elastic, as seen in Exhibit 6(b). It is also true that demand becomes more elastic over time as buyers respond to the lower prices by looking for their own apartment (rather than sharing one) or moving to the city to try to rent an apartment below the equilibrium rental price. What economic implications do these varying elasticities have on rent control policies?

In Exhibit 6(a), only a small reduction in rental unit availability occurs in the short term as a result of the newly imposed rent control price—a move from Q_1 to Q_{SR}. The corresponding deadweight loss is small, indicated by the shaded area in Exhibit 6(a). However, the long-run response to the rent ceiling price is much larger: The quantity of rental units falls from Q_1 to Q_{LR}, and the size of the deadweight loss and the shortage are both larger, as seen in Exhibit 6(b). Hence, rent controls are much more harmful in the long run than the short run, from an efficiency standpoint.

Price Floors

Since the Great Depression, several agricultural programs have been promoted as assisting small-scale farmers. Such a price-support system guarantees a minimum price—promising a dairy farmer a price of $4 per pound for cheese, for example. The reasoning is that the equilibrium price of $3 is too low and would not provide enough revenue for small-volume farmers to maintain a "decent" standard of living. A price floor sets a minimum price that is the lowest price a consumer can legally pay for a good.

The Welfare Effects of a Price Floor When the Government Buys the Surplus

Who gains and who loses under price-support programs when the government buys the surplus? In Exhibit 7, the equilibrium price and quantity without the price floor are at P_1 and Q_1, respectively. Without the price floor, consumer surplus is area a + b + c, and producer surplus is area e + f, for a total surplus of area a + b + c + e + f.

After the price floor is in effect, price rises to P_2; output falls to Q_2; consumer surplus falls from area a + b + c to area a, a loss of b + c; and producer surplus increases from area e + f to area b + c + d + e + f, a gain of area b + c + d. If those changes were the end of the story, we would say that producers gained (area b + c + d) more than consumers lost (area b + c), and, on net, society would benefit

Use what you've LEARNED: QUANTIFYING CONSUMER AND PRODUCER SURPLUSES

You may recall from your geometry class that the area of a triangle is ½ base × height. Suppose the government imposes a price ceiling on wheat at $2 per bushel. Use the graph to answer the following questions: What would be the change in consumer surplus? In producer surplus? In the deadweight loss?

	No Ceiling	Ceiling	Change ($ millions)
Consumer Surplus	a + b + c	a + b + d	d − c = $47.50 ($70 − $22.50)
Producer Surplus	d + e + f	f	− d − e = − $85 (−$70 − $15)
Total Welfare (CS + PS)	a + b + c + d + e + f	a + b + d + f	− c − e = −$32.50

Suppose the government imposes a $0.50 per gallon gasoline tax. Use the graph to answer the following questions: How much is the annual revenue from the tax? How much is the loss to consumers and producers? How much is the deadweight loss?

The total revenue from the tax is $45 billion ($0.50 × 90 billion gallons). This amount is also a cost to consumers and producers of $45 billion in tax revenues. The total loss to producers and consumers is larger than the revenues raised because consumers lose (a + b) and producers lose (c + d) and the government gains (a + c), so society is out the deadweight loss, or $2.5 billion per year [(½)($0.50) × 10 billion gallons per year].

section 7.2 exhibit 7 — Welfare Effects of a Price Floor When Government Buys the Surplus

	Before Price Floor	After Price Floor	Change
Consumer Surplus	a + b + c	a	−b − c
Producer Surplus	e + f	b + c + d + e + f	b + c + d
Government (Taxpayers)	zero	−c − d − f − g − h − i	−c − d − f − g − h − i
Total Welfare	a + b + c + e + f	a + b + e − g − h − i	−c − f − g − h − i

After the price floor is implemented, the price rises to P_2 and output falls to Q_2; the result is a loss in consumer surplus of area b + c but a gain in producer surplus of area b + c + d. However, these changes are not the end of the story, because the cost to the government (taxpayers), area c + d + f + g + h + i, is greater than the gain to producers, area d, so the deadweight loss is area c + f + g + h + i.

by area d from the implementation of the price floor. However, those changes are not the end of the story. The government (taxpayers) must pay for the surplus it buys, area c + d + f + g + h + i. That is, the cost to government, area c + d + f + g + h + i, is greater than the gain to producers, area d. Assuming no alternative use of the surplus the government purchases, the result is a deadweight loss from the price floor of area c + f + g + h + i. Why? Consumers are consuming less than the previous market equilibrium output, eliminating mutually beneficial exchanges, while sellers are producing more than is being consumed, with the excess production stored, destroyed, or exported.

Deficiency Payment Program

Another possibility is the deficiency payment program. In Exhibit 8, if the government sets the target price at P_2, producers will supply Q_2 and sell all they can at the market price, P_M. The government then pays the producers a deficiency payment (DP)—the vertical distance between the price the producers receive, P_M, and the price they were guaranteed, P_2. Producer surplus increases from area c + d to area c + d + b + e, which is a gain of area b + e, because producers can sell a greater quantity at a higher price. Consumer surplus increases from area a + b to area a + b + c + g, which is a gain of area c + g, because consumers can buy a greater quantity at a lower price. The cost to government (Q_2 × DP), area b + e + f + c + g, is greater than the gains in producer and consumer surpluses (area b + e + c + g), and the deadweight loss is area f. The deadweight loss occurs because the program increases the output beyond the efficient level of output, Q_1. From Q_1 to Q_2, the marginal cost to sellers for producing the good (the height of the supply curve) is greater than the marginal benefit to consumers (the height of the demand curve).

Compare area f in Exhibit 8 with the much larger deadweight loss for price supports in Exhibit 7. The deficiency payment program does not lead to the production of crops that will not be consumed, or to the storage problem we saw with the previous price-support program in Exhibit 8.

section 7.2 exhibit 8 — Welfare Effects of a Deficiency Payment Plan

	Before Plan	After Plan	Change
Consumer Surplus	a + b	a + b + c + g	c + g
Producer Surplus	c + d	c + d + b + e	b + e
Government (Taxpayers)	zero	−b − e − f − c − g	−b − e − f − c − g
Total Welfare (CS + PS − G)	a + b + c + d	a + b + c + d − f	−f

The cost to government (taxpayers), area b + e + f + c + g, is greater than the gains to producer and consumer surplus, area b + e + c + g. The deficiency payment program increases the output level beyond the efficient output level of Q_1. From Q_1 to Q_2, the marginal cost of producing the good (the height of the supply curve) is greater than the marginal benefit to the consumer (the height of the demand curve)—area f.

SECTION CHECK

1. Taxes distort market incentives—the price to buyers is higher than before the tax, so they are able to consume less and the price to sellers is lower than before the tax, so they produce less. This situation leads to deadweight loss, or market inefficiencies—the waste associated with not producing the efficient output.
2. The size of the deadweight loss from a tax, as well as how the burdens are shared between buyers and sellers, depends on the elasticities of supply and demand.
3. A price ceiling causes a deadweight loss because the efficient level of output is not produced.
4. A price floor causes a deadweight loss because consumers are consuming less than the efficient output, eliminating mutually beneficial exchanges, and sellers are producing more than is being consumed.

1. Could a tax be imposed without a welfare cost?
2. How does the elasticity of demand represent the ability of buyers to "dodge" a tax?
3. If both supply and demand were highly elastic, how large would the effect be on the quantity exchanged, the tax revenue, and the welfare costs of a tax?
4. What impact would a larger tax have on trade in the market? What will happen to the size of the deadweight loss?
5. What would be the effect of a price ceiling?
6. What would be the effect of a price floor if the government does not buy up the surplus?
7. What causes the welfare cost of subsidies?
8. Why does a deficiency payment program have the same welfare cost analysis as a subsidy?

Interactive Chapter Summary

Fill in the blanks:

1. The monetary difference between the price a consumer is willing and able to pay for an additional unit of a good and the price the consumer actually pays is called _____.

2. We can think of the demand curve as a _____ curve.

3. Consumer surplus for the whole market is shown graphically as the area under the market _____ (willingness to pay for the units consumed) and above the _____ (what must be paid for those units).

4. A lower market price due to an increase in supply will _____ consumer surplus.

5. A _____ is the difference between what a producer is paid for a good and the cost of producing that unit of the good.

6. We can think of the supply curve as a _____ curve.

7. Part of the added producer surplus when the price rises as a result of an increase in demand is due to a higher price for the quantity _____ being produced, and part is due to the expansion of _____ made profitable by the higher price.

8. The demand curve represents a collection of _____ prices that consumers are willing and able to pay for additional quantities of a good or service, while the supply curve represents a collection of _____ prices that suppliers require to be willing to supply additional quantities of that good or service.

9. The total welfare gain to the economy from trade in a good is the sum of the _____ and _____ created.

10. In competitive markets, with large numbers of buyers and sellers at the market equilibrium price and quantity, the net gains to society are _____ as possible.

11. After a tax is imposed, consumers pay a(n) _____ price and lose the corresponding amount of consumer surplus as a result. Producers receive a _____ price after tax and lose the corresponding amount of producer surplus as a result. The government _____ the amount of the tax revenue generated, which is transferred to others in society.

12. The size of the deadweight loss from a tax, as well as how the burdens are shared between buyers and sellers, depends on the relative _____.

13. When there is a subsidy, the market _____ relative to the efficient level of output.

14. Because the _____ leads to the production of more than the efficient level of output, a _____ results.

15. With a _____, any possible gain to consumers will be more than offset by the losses to producers.

16. With a price floor where the government buys up the surplus, the cost to the government is _____ than the gain to _____.

17. With no alternative use of the government purchases from a price floor, a _____ will result because consumers are consuming _____ than the previous market equilibrium output and sellers are producing _____ than is being consumed.

18. With a deficiency payment program, the deadweight loss is _____ than with an agricultural price support program when the government buys the surplus.

Answers: 1. consumer surplus 2. marginal benefit 3. demand curve; market price 4. increase 5. producer surplus 6. marginal cost 7. already; output 8. maximum; minimum 9. consumer surplus; producer surplus 10. as large 11. higher; lower; gains 12. elasticities of supply and demand 13. overproduces 14. subsidy; deadweight loss 15. price ceiling 16. greater; producers 17. deadweight loss; less; more 18. smaller

Key Terms and Concepts

consumer surplus 183
producer surplus 185

marginal cost 185
total welfare gains 186

deadweight loss 188
welfare effects 190

Section Check Answers

7.1 Consumer Surplus and Producer Surplus

1. **What is consumer surplus?**
   Consumer surplus is defined as the monetary difference between what a consumer is willing to pay for a good and what the consumer is required to pay for it.

2. **Why do the earlier units consumed at a given price add more consumer surplus than the later units consumed?**
   Because what a consumer is willing to pay for a good declines as more of that good is consumed, the difference between what he is willing to pay and the price he must pay also declines for later units.

3. **Why does a decrease in a good's price increase the consumer surplus from consumption of that good?**
   A decrease in a good's price increases the consumer surplus from consumption of that good by lowering the price for those goods that were bought at the higher price and by increasing consumer surplus from increased purchases at the lower price.

4. **Why might the consumer surplus from purchases of diamond rings be less than the consumer surplus from purchases of far less expensive stones?**
   Consumer surplus is the difference between what people would have been willing to pay for the amount of the good consumed and what they must pay. Even though the marginal value of less expensive stones is lower than the marginal value of a diamond ring to buyers, the difference between the total value of the far larger number of less expensive stones purchased and what consumers had to pay may well be larger than that difference for diamond rings.

5. **What is producer surplus?**
   Producer surplus is defined as the monetary difference between what a producer is paid for a good and the producer's cost.

6. **Why do the earlier units produced at a given price add more producer surplus than the later units produced?**
   Because the earlier (lowest cost) units can be produced at a cost that is lower than the market price, but the cost of producing additional units rises, the earlier units produced at a given price add more producer surplus than the later units produced.

7. **Why does an increase in a good's price increase the producer surplus from production of that good?**
   An increase in a good's price increases the producer surplus from production of that good because it results in a higher price for the quantity already being produced and because the expansion in output in response to the higher price also increases profits.

8. **Why might the producer surplus from sales of diamond rings, which are expensive, be less than the producer surplus from sales of far less expensive stones?**
   Producer surplus is the difference between what a producer is paid for a good and the producer's cost. Even though the price, or marginal value, of a less expensive stone is lower than the price, or marginal value of a diamond ring to buyers, the difference between the total that sellers receive for those stones in revenue and the producer's cost of the far larger number of less expensive stones produced may well be larger than that difference for diamond rings.

9. **Why is the efficient level of output in an industry defined as the output where the sum of consumer and producer surplus is maximized?**
   The sum of consumer surplus plus producer surplus measures the total welfare gains from trade in an industry, and the most efficient level of output is the one that maximizes the total welfare gains.

10. **Why does a reduction in output below the efficient level create a deadweight loss?**
    A reduction in output below the efficient level eliminates trades whose benefits would have exceeded their costs; the resulting loss in consumer surplus and producer surplus is a deadweight loss.

11. **Why does an expansion in output beyond the efficient level create a deadweight loss?**
    An expansion in output beyond the efficient level involves trades whose benefits are less than their costs; the resulting loss in consumer surplus and producer surplus is a deadweight loss.

7.2 The Welfare Effects of Taxes, Subsidies, and Price Controls

1. **Could a tax be imposed without a welfare cost?**
   A tax would not impose a welfare cost only if the quantity exchanged did not change as a result—only when supply was perfectly inelastic or in the nonexistent case

where the demand curve was perfectly inelastic. In all other cases, a tax would create a welfare cost by eliminating some mutually beneficial trades (and the wealth they would have created) that would otherwise have taken place.

2. **How does the elasticity of demand represent the ability of buyers to "dodge" a tax?**

   The elasticity of demand represents the ability of buyers to "dodge" a tax, because it represents how easily buyers could shift their purchases into other goods. If it is relatively low cost to consumers to shift out of buying a particular good when a tax is imposed on it—that is, demand is relatively elastic—they can dodge much of the burden of the tax by shifting their purchases to other goods. If it is relatively high cost to consumers to shift out of buying a particular good when a tax is imposed on it—that is, demand is relatively inelastic—they cannot dodge much of the burden of the tax by shifting their purchases to other goods.

3. **If both supply and demand were highly elastic, how large would the effect be on the quantity exchanged, the tax revenue, and the welfare costs of a tax?**

   The more elastic are supply and/or demand, the larger the change in the quantity exchanged that would result from a given tax. Given that tax revenue equals the tax per unit times the number of units traded after the imposition of a tax, the smaller after-tax quantity traded would reduce the tax revenue raised, other things equal. Because the greater change in the quantity traded wipes out more mutually beneficial trades than if demand and/or supply was more inelastic, the welfare cost in such a case would also be greater, other things equal.

4. **What impact would a larger tax have on trade in the market? What will happen to the size of the deadweight loss?**

   A larger tax creates a larger wedge between the price including tax paid by consumers and the price net of tax received by producers, resulting in a greater increase in prices paid by consumers and a greater decrease in price received by producers, and the laws of supply and demand imply that the quantity exchanged falls more as a result. The number of mutually beneficial trades eliminated will be greater and the consequent welfare cost will be greater as a result.

5. **What would be the effect of a price ceiling?**

   A price ceiling reduces the quantity exchanged, because the lower regulated price reduces the quantity sellers are willing to sell. This lower quantity causes a welfare cost equal to the net gains from those exchanges that no longer take place. However, that price ceiling would also redistribute income, harming sellers, increasing the well-being of those who remain able to buy successfully at the lower price, and decreasing the well-being of those who can no longer buy successfully at the lower price.

6. **What would be the effect of a price floor if the government does not buy up the surplus?**

   Just as in the case of a tax, a price floor where the government does not buy up the surplus reduces the quantity exchanged, thus causing a welfare cost equal to the net gains from the exchanges that no longer take place. However, that price floor would also redistribute income, harming buyers, increasing the incomes of those who remain able to sell successfully at the higher price, and decreasing the incomes of those who can no longer sell successfully at the higher price.

7. **What causes the welfare cost of subsidies?**

   Subsidies cause people to produce units of output whose benefits (without the subsidy) are less than the costs, reducing the total gains from trade.

8. **Why does a deficiency payment program have the same welfare cost analysis as a subsidy?**

   Both tend to increase output beyond the efficient level, so that units whose benefits (without the subsidy) are less than the costs, reducing the total gains from trade in the same way; further, the dollar cost of the deficiency payments are equal to the dollar amount of taxes necessary to finance the subsidy, in the case where each increases production the same amount.

CHAPTER 7 STUDY GUIDE

True or False:

1. A lower price will increase your consumer surplus for each of the units you were already consuming and will also increase your consumer surplus from increased purchases at the lower price.
2. Because some units can be produced at a cost that is lower than the market price, the seller receives a surplus, or net benefit, from producing those units.
3. Producer surplus is shown graphically as the area under the demand curve and above the supply curve.
4. If the market price of a good falls as a result of a decrease in demand, additional producer surplus is generated.
5. At the market equilibrium, both consumers and producers benefit from trading every unit up to the market equilibrium output.
6. Once the equilibrium output is reached at the equilibrium price, all of the mutually beneficial trade opportunities between the suppliers and the demanders will have taken place, and the sum of consumer and producer surplus is maximized.
7. The deadweight loss of a tax is the difference between the lost consumer and producer surpluses and the tax revenue generated.
8. The deadweight loss of a tax occurs because the tax reduces the quantity exchanged below the original output level, reducing the size of the total surplus realized from trade.
9. Other things being equal, the more elastic the demand curve or the more elastic the supply curve, the smaller the deadweight loss of a tax.
10. If either the supply or demand curve becomes more inelastic, a given tax will reduce the quantity exchanged by a greater amount.
11. Those goods that are heavily taxed often have a relatively inelastic demand curve in the short run, so the burden falls mainly on the buyer, and the deadweight loss to society is smaller than if the demand curve were more elastic.
12. Consumers never benefit from a binding price ceiling.
13. Any possible gains to consumers are more than offset by losses to producers when a binding price ceiling is in place.
14. With an agricultural price-support program where the government buys up the surplus, a net benefit is realized because the benefits to producers are greater than the cost to consumers.
15. The deadweight loss is greater in an agricultural price-support program than in a deficiency payment plan.

Multiple Choice:

1. In a supply and demand graph, the triangular area under the demand curve but above the market price is
   a. the consumer surplus.
   b. the producer surplus.
   c. the marginal cost.
   d. the deadweight loss.
   e. the net gain to society from trading that good.

   Use the following demand schedule to answer questions 2 and 3.
   Fred's demand schedule for DVDs is as follows: At $30 each, he would buy 1; at $25, he would buy 2; at $15, he would buy 3; and at $10, he would buy 4.

2. If the price of DVDs is $20, the consumer surplus Fred receives from purchasing two DVDs would be
   a. $10.
   b. $15.
   c. $20.
   d. $55.
   e. $90.

3. If the price of DVDs is $25, the consumer surplus Fred receives from purchasing one DVD would be
   a. $0.
   b. $5.
   c. $25.
   d. $55.
   e. $70.
4. Which of the following is not true about consumer surplus?
   a. Consumer surplus is the difference between what consumers are willing to pay and what they actually pay.
   b. Consumer surplus is shown graphically as the area under the demand curve but above the market price.
   c. An increase in the market price due to a decrease in supply will increase consumer surplus.
   d. A decrease in market price due to an increase in supply will increase consumer surplus.
5. Which of the following is not true about producer surplus?
   a. Producer surplus is the difference between what sellers are paid and their cost of producing those units.
   b. Producer surplus is shown graphically as the area under the market price but above the supply curve.
   c. An increase in the market price due to an increase in demand will increase producer surplus.
   d. All of the above are true about producer surplus.
6. At the market equilibrium price and quantity, the total welfare gains from trade are measured by
   a. the total consumer surplus captured by consumers.
   b. the total producer surplus captured by producers.
   c. the sum of consumer surplus and producer surplus.
   d. the consumer surplus minus the producer surplus.
7. In a supply and demand graph, the triangular area under the demand curve but above the supply curve is
   a. the consumer surplus.
   b. the producer surplus.
   c. the marginal cost.
   d. the deadweight loss.
   e. the net gain to society from trading that good.
8. In a supply and demand graph, the triangular area between the demand curve and the supply curve lost because of the imposition of a tax, price ceiling, or price floor is
   a. the consumer surplus.
   b. the producer surplus.
   c. the marginal cost.
   d. the deadweight loss.
   e. the net gain to society from trading that good.
9. Taxes on goods with _____ demand curves will tend to raise more tax revenue for the government than taxes on goods with _____ demand curves.
   a. elastic; unit elastic
   b. elastic; inelastic
   c. inelastic; elastic
   d. unit elastic; inelastic
10. After the imposition of a tax,
    a. consumers pay a higher price, including the tax.
    b. consumers lose consumer surplus.
    c. producers receive a lower price after taxes.
    d. producers lose producer surplus.
    e. all of the above occur.

11. Other things being equal, for a given tax, if the demand curve is less elastic,
    a. the greater the tax revenue raised and the greater the deadweight cost of the tax.
    b. the greater the tax revenue raised and the smaller the deadweight cost of the tax.
    c. the less the tax revenue raised and the greater the deadweight cost of the tax.
    d. the less the tax revenue raised and the smaller the deadweight cost of the tax.

12. An increase in a subsidy will increase
    a. consumer surplus.
    b. producer surplus.
    c. the deadweight loss.
    d. all of the above.

13. With a subsidy,
    a. the price producers receive is the price consumers pay plus the subsidy.
    b. the subsidy leads to the production of more than the efficient level of output.
    c. there is a deadweight loss.
    d. all of the above are true.

14. The longer the time people have to adjust to a tax, the _____ revenue it will raise and the _____ quantity traded will fall.
    a. more; more
    b. more; less
    c. less; more
    d. less; less

15. A permanent increase in price would tend to decrease the consumer surplus by _____ or increase the producer surplus by _____ in the long run than in the short run.
    a. more; more
    b. more; less
    c. less; more
    d. less; less

16. In the case of a price floor, if the government buys up the surplus,
    a. consumer surplus decreases.
    b. producer surplus increases.
    c. a greater deadweight loss occurs than with a deficiency payment system.
    d. all of the above are true.

17. The longer a price ceiling is left below the equilibrium price in a market, the _____ is the reduction in the quantity exchanged and the _____ is the resulting deadweight loss.
    a. greater; greater
    b. greater; smaller
    c. smaller; greater
    d. smaller; smaller

18. With a deficiency payment program,
    a. the government sets the target price at the equilibrium price.
    b. producer and consumer surplus falls.
    c. there is a deadweight loss because the program increases the output beyond the efficient level of output.
    d. all of the above are true.

Problems:

1. Refer to the following exhibit.

   a. If the price of each karate lesson is P_0, the consumer surplus is equal to what area?
   b. If the price falls from P_0 to P_1, the change in consumer surplus is equal to what area?

2. Steve loves potato chips. His weekly demand curve is shown in the following exhibit.

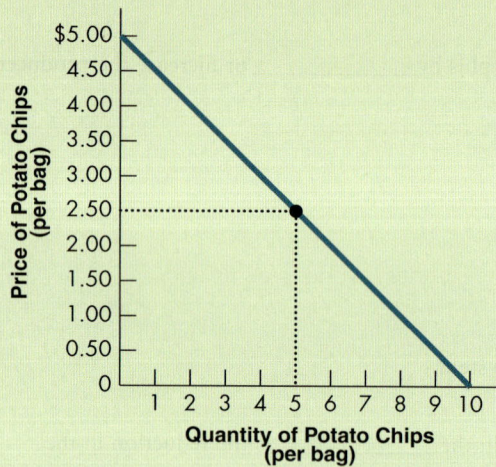

   a. How much is Steve willing to pay for one bag of potato chips?
   b. How much is Steve willing to pay for a second bag of potato chips?
   c. If the actual market price of potato chips is $2.50, and Steve buys five bags as shown, what is the value of his consumer surplus?
   d. What is Steve's total willingness to pay for five bags?

3. If a freeze ruined this year's lettuce crop, show what would happen to consumer surplus.

4. If demand for apples increased as a result of a news story that highlighted the health benefits of two apples a day, what would happen to producer surplus?

5. How is total surplus (the sum of consumer and producer surpluses) related to the efficient level of output? Using a supply and demand curve, demonstrate that producing less than the equilibrium output will lead to an inefficient allocation of resources—a deadweight loss.

6. If the government's goal is to raise tax revenue, which of the following are good markets to tax?
   a. luxury yachts
   b. alcohol
   c. movies
   d. gasoline
   e. grapefruit juice

7. Which of the following do you think are good markets for the government to tax if the goal is to boost tax revenue? Which will lead to the least amount of deadweight loss? Why?
   a. luxury yachts
   b. alcohol
   c. motor homes
   d. cigarettes
   e. gasoline
   f. pizza

8. Elasticity of demand in the market for one-bedroom apartments is 2.0, elasticity of supply is 0.5, the current market price is $1,000, and the equilibrium number of one-bedroom apartments is 10,000. If the government imposes a price ceiling of $800 on this market, predict the size of the resulting apartment shortage.

9. Use the diagram to answer the following questions (a–d).

   a. At the equilibrium price before the tax is imposed, what area represents consumer surplus? What area represents producer surplus?
   b. Say that a tax of $T per unit is imposed in the industry. What area now represents consumer surplus? What area represents producer surplus?
   c. What area represents the deadweight cost of the tax?
   d. What area represents how much tax revenue is raised by the tax?

10. Use consumer and producer surplus to show the deadweight loss from a subsidy (producing more than the equilibrium output). (*Hint:* Remember that taxpayers will have to pay for the subsidy.)

11. Use the diagram to answer the following questions (a–c).

a. At the initial equilibrium price, what area represents consumer surplus? What area represents producer surplus?
b. After the price ceiling is imposed, what area represents consumer surplus? What area represents producer surplus?
c. What area represents the deadweight loss cost of the price ceiling?

12. Use the diagram to answer the following questions (a–c).

a. At the competitive output, Q_1, what area represents the consumer surplus? What area represents the producer surplus?
b. At the larger output, Q_2, what area represents the consumer surplus? What area represents the producer surplus?
c. What area represents the deadweight loss of producing too much output?

13. The 2000–2001 California energy crisis produced brownouts, utility company bankruptcies, and worries about high prices. The California electric power regulatory program imposed price ceilings on electricity sold to consumers. The following exhibit describes the California situation with P_S as the price ceiling. Answer the following questions referring to this exhibit.

a. What was the loss imposed on consumers by this price ceiling?
b. What was the loss imposed on producers by this price ceiling?
c. What was the total loss imposed on California by this price ceiling?
d. Using this exhibit, explain the brownouts in California.
e. What would have to be true for consumers to support market set prices? Use the exhibit to explain why there might not be support among consumers for raising prices.

Market Failure

8.1 Externalities
8.2 Public Goods
8.3 Asymmetric Information

In the last several chapters, we concluded that markets are efficient. But we made some assumptions about how markets work. If these assumptions do not hold, our conclusion about efficiency may be flawed.

What are the assumptions?

First, in our model of supply and demand, we assumed that markets are perfectly competitive—many buyers and sellers exchanging similar goods in an environment where buyers and sellers can easily enter and exit the market. This is not always true. In some markets, few firms may have control over the market price. When firms can control the market price, we say that they have market power. This market power can cause inefficiency because it will lead to higher prices and lower quantities than the competitive solution.

Sometimes the market system fails to produce efficient outcomes because of side effects economists call *externalities*. With *positive externalities*, the private market supplies too little of the good in question (such as education). In the case of *negative externalities* (such as pollution), the market supplies too much.

Another possible source of market failure is that competitive markets provide less than the efficient quantity of public goods. A public good is a good or service that someone can consume simultaneously with everyone else even if he or she doesn't pay for it. For example, everyone enjoys the benefits of national defense and yet it would be difficult to exclude anyone from receiving these benefits. The problem is that if consumers know it is too difficult to exclude them, then they could avoid paying their share of the public good (take a free ride), and producers would find it unprofitable to provide the good. Therefore, the government provides important public goods such as national defense.

Many economists believe that asymmetric information can cause market failures. *Asymmetric information* is a situation where some people know what other people don't know. This can lead to adverse selection where an informed party benefits in an exchange by taking advantage of knowing more than the other party. ■

SECTION 8.1 Externalities

- What is a negative externality?
- How are negative externalities internalized?
- What is a positive externality?
- How are positive externalities internalized?

Even if the economy is competitive, it is still possible that the market system fails to produce the efficient level of output because of side effects economists call **externalities**. With **positive externalities**, the private market supplies too little of the good in question (such as education). In the case of **negative externalities** (such as pollution), the market supplies too much. Both types of externalities are caused by economic agents—producers and consumers—receiving the wrong signals. That is, the free market works well in providing most goods but does less well without regulations, taxes, and subsidies in providing others.

externality
a benefit or cost from consumption or production that spills over onto those who are not consuming or producing the good

positive externality
occurs when benefits spill over to an outside party who is not involved in producing or consuming the good

negative externality
occurs when costs spill over to an outside party who is not involved in producing or consuming the good

Negative Externalities in Production

The classic example of a negative externality in production is air pollution from a factory, such as a steel mill. If the firm uses clean air in production and returns dirty air to the atmosphere, it creates a negative externality. The polluted air "spills over" to outside parties. Now people in the neighboring communities may experience higher incidences of disease, dirtier houses, and other property damage. Such damages are real costs; but because no one owns the air, the firm does not have to pay for its use, unlike the other resources the firm uses in production. A steel mill pays for labor, capital, energy, and raw materials because it must compensate the owners of those inputs for their use. If a firm can avoid paying the costs it imposes on others—the external costs—it has lowered its own costs of production, but not the true costs to society.

Examples of negative externalities are numerous: the roommate who plays his stereo too loud at 2:00 A.M., the neighbor's dog that barks all night long or leaves "messages" on your front lawn, or the gardener who runs her leaf blower on full power at 7:00 A.M. on a Saturday. Driving our cars may be another area in which people don't bear the full costs of their choices. We pay the price to purchase cars, as well as to maintain, insure, and fuel them—those are the private costs. But do we pay for all of our external costs such as emissions, congestion, wear and tear on our highways, and the possible harm to those driving in cars smaller than ours?

Graphing Negative External Costs in Production

Let's take a look at the steel industry. In Exhibit 1, we see the market for steel. Notice that at each level of output, the first supply curve, $S_{PRIVATE}$, is lower than the second, S_{SOCIAL}. The reason is simple: $S_{PRIVATE}$ only includes the private costs to the firm—the capital, entrepreneurship, land, and labor for which it must pay. However, S_{SOCIAL} includes all of these costs, plus the external costs that production imposes on others. If the firm could somehow be required to compensate society for the damage it causes, the cost of production for the firm would increase and would shift the supply curve to the left. That is, the true social cost of producing steel is represented by S_{SOCIAL} in Exhibit 1. The equilibrium at P_2 and Q_2 is efficient. The market equilibrium is not efficient because the true supply curve is above the demand curve at Q_1. At Q_1 the marginal benefits (point a) are less than the marginal cost (point b) and society would be better off if the firm produced less steel. The deadweight loss from overproduction is measured by the shaded area in Exhibit 1. From society's standpoint, Q_2 is the efficient level of output because it represents all the costs (private plus external costs) associated with the production of this good. If the suppliers of steel are not aware of or not responsible for the external costs, they will tend to produce too much, Q_1 from society's standpoint and efficiency would be improved if less were produced.

section 8.1 exhibit 1: Negative Externalities in Production

When a negative externality in production is present, firms do not bear the full cost of their actions, and they will produce more than the efficient level of output: Q_1 rather than Q_2. $S_{PRIVATE}$ reflects the private cost of the firm. S_{SOCIAL} reflects the private costs plus the external (or spillover) costs that the steel production imposes on others. If the supply curve is $S_{PRIVATE}$, the market equilibrium is at P_1 and Q_1. This level is not efficient and leads to a deadweight loss—the shaded area. However, when the supply curve is S_{SOCIAL}, then the equilibrium occurs at P_2 and Q_2, which is the efficient equilibrium.

In the United States, people deposit large amounts of solid waste as litter on beaches, campgrounds, highways, and vacant lots. Some of this litter is removed by government agencies, and some of it biodegrades over many years. Several solutions are possible for the litter problem. Stiffer fines and penalties and more aggressive monitoring could be employed. Alternatively, through education and civic pride, individuals and groups could be encouraged to pick up trash.

What Can the Government Do to Correct for Negative Externalities?

The government can intervene in market decisions in an attempt to take account of these negative externalities. It may do this by estimating the amount of those external costs and then taxing the manufacturer by that amount, forcing the manufacturer to internalize (bear) the costs.

Pollution Taxes

Pollution taxes are designed to internalize negative externalities. If government could impose a pollution tax equal to the exact size of the external cost, then the firm would produce the efficient level of output, Q_2. That is, the tax would shift the supply curve for steel leftward to S_{SOCIAL} and would provide an incentive for the firm to produce at the socially optimum level of output. Additionally, tax revenues would be generated that could be used to compensate those who had suffered damage from the pollution or in some other productive way.

Regulation

Alternatively, the government could use regulation. The government might simply prohibit certain types of activities that cause pollution or force firms to adopt a specific technology to reduce their emissions. However, regulators, would have to know the best available technology for each and every industry. The purchase and use of new pollution-control devices will increase the cost of production and shift the supply curve to the left, from $S_{PRIVATE}$ to S_{SOCIAL}.

Which Is Better—Pollution Tax or Regulation?

Most economists agree that a pollution tax, or a corrective tax, is more efficient than regulation. The pollution tax is good because it gets rid of the externality and moves society closer to the efficient level of output. The tax also gives firms an incentive to find and apply new technology to further reduce pollution levels in their plant and consequently lower the tax they would have to pay. Under regulation, a firm has little incentive to further reduce emissions once it reaches the predetermined level set by the regulated standard.

For example, a gas tax is a form of pollution tax: It helps reduce the externalities of pollution and congestion. The higher the tax, the fewer the vehicles on the road, the fewer miles driven, and the more fuel efficient

global WATCH: LONDON TOLLS ARE A TAXING PROBLEM FOR DRIVERS

The mayor of London [recently set a fee of over $8.00 for driving in the city center] on weekdays between 7 A.M. and 6:30 P.M. The aim of the plan... is to ease congestion, not drive all the cars from the road.

Consider the following:

* Vehicles in central London move no faster today than horse-drawn vehicles did 100 years ago....
* Estimates of the economic costs—in lost time, wasted fuel, and increased vehicle operating costs—tend to be in the range of 2 to 4 percent of the gross domestic product.

No city has attempted a scheme with anything like the size, scale, and complexity of the London congestion charge:

* About 50 million vehicle miles are traveled in London every day.
* Motorists will have to pay to drive into or inside an area roughly 10 square miles around the City (the financial district) and the West End.
* The zone will be policed by hundreds of fixed mobile cameras, which will automatically pick up vehicles' license plates.
* Computers will match the registrations with a database of drivers who have paid in advance....

[Hopefully,] the scheme will cut traffic in the zone by 10–15 percent, reduce delays by 20–30 percent, and raise about $210,700,000 a year to invest in public transport and road schemes.

SOURCE: National Center for Policy Analysis, "London Tolls Are a Taxing Problem for Drivers," synopsis of "Economists Agree That the Best Way to Tackle the Growing Problem of Overcrowded Roads Is to Introduce Tolls at Peak Times," by Chris Giles and Juliette Joweit (*Financial Times*, 13 February 2003). 14 February 2003; http://ncpa.org/iss/pri/2003/pd021403d.html

consider this:

If a road is crowded, it creates a negative externality. That is, when one person enters a road, all other people must drive a little more slowly. Highway space is overused because we pay so little for it. At least at some particular times—at rush hours, for example—if we charge a zero money price, a shortage of highway space will result. A toll raises the price and brings the market closer to equilibrium as seen in Exhibit 2.

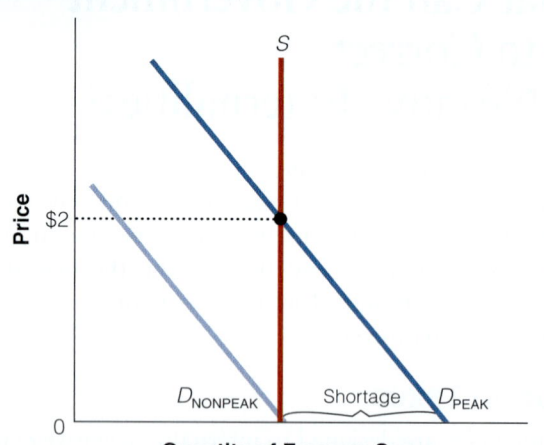

section 8.1 exhibit 2 A Shortage of Freeway Space During Peak Hours

The supply of highway space is fixed in the short run, so the supply curve is perfectly inelastic. The demand varies during the day considerably. For example, the demand at peak hours (7 A.M.–8:30 A.M. and 4:00 P.M.–6:30 P.M.) is much higher than at nonpeak hours. At some price, the shortage during peak hours will disappear. In this example, it is at $2.

vehicles purchased, each of which leads to less congestion and pollution. Therefore, the pollution tax, unlike other taxes, can enhance economic efficiency while generating revenue for the government.

Positive Externalities in Consumption

Unlike negative externalities, positive externalities benefit others. For some goods, the individual consumer receives all the benefits. If you buy a hamburger, for example, you get all its benefits. On the other hand, consider education. This is a positive externality in consumption whose benefits extend beyond the individual consumer of education. Certainly, when you "buy" an education, you receive many of its benefits: greater future income, more choice of future occupations, and the consumption value of knowing more about life as a result of classroom (and extracurricular) learning. However, these benefits, great as they may be, are not all the benefits associated with your education. You may be less likely to be unemployed or commit crimes; you may end up curing cancer or solving some other social problem. These nontrivial benefits are the positive external benefits of education.

Many economists like the gas tax because it is easy to collect, difficult for users to avoid, and encourages fuel economy. It puts the tax on highway users. But completely internalizing the externality may cost an additional $2 a gallon; the national average gas tax is $0.50. In England, the gas tax is over $3 per gallon. It is much more efficient to pay for transportation improvements by using a gas tax than a sales tax because it associates the tax with those who are creating the externality.

The government frequently subsidizes education. Why? Presumably because the private market does not provide enough. It is argued that the education of a person benefits not only that person but all society, because a more informed citizenry can make more intelligent collective decisions, which benefits everyone. Public health departments sometimes offer "free" inoculations against certain communicable diseases, such as influenza, because by protecting one group of citizens, everyone gets some protection; if one citizen is prevented from getting the disease, that person cannot pass it on to others. Many governmental efforts in the field of health and education are justified on the basis of positive externalities. Of course, because positive externalities are often difficult to measure, it is hard to demonstrate empirically whether many governmental education and health programs achieve their intended purposes.

In short, the presence of positive externalities interferes with reaching economic efficiency because of the tendency for the market to underallocate (produce too little) of this good.

Graphing Positive External Benefits of Consumption

Let's take the case of a new vaccine against the common cold. The market for the vaccine is shown in Exhibit 3. The demand curve, $D_{PRIVATE}$, represents the prices and quantities that buyers would be willing to pay in the private market to reduce their probability of catching the common cold. The supply curve shows the amounts that suppliers would offer for sale at different prices. However, at the equilibrium market output, Q_1, the output of vaccinations falls far short of the efficient level, Q_2. Why? Many people benefit from the vaccines, including those who do not have to pay for them; they are now less likely to be infected because others took the vaccine. If we could add the benefits derived by nonpaying consumers, the demand curve would shift to the right, from $D_{PRIVATE}$ to D_{SOCIAL}. The greater level of output, Q_2, that would result if D_{SOCIAL} were the observed demand reflects the efficient output level.

The market equilibrium at P_1 and Q_1 is not efficient because D_{SOCIAL} is above $D_{PRIVATE}$ for all levels of output between Q_1 and Q_2. That is, at Q_1 the marginal benefits (D_{SOCIAL}) at point b are greater than the marginal cost (S_{SOCIAL}) at point a. Consequently, a deadweight loss is associated with the underproduction. In short, too little of the good is produced. Because producers are unable to collect payments from all those who benefit

section 8.1 exhibit 3 Positive Externalities in Consumption

The private demand curve plus external benefits is presented as the demand curve D_{SOCIAL}. This demand curve is to the right of the private demand curve, $D_{PRIVATE}$. At Q_1 the marginal benefits (point b) are greater than the marginal cost (point a) leading to a deadweight loss—the shaded area. The market equilibrium output, Q_1, falls short of the efficient level of output, Q_2. The market produces too little of the good or service.

from the good or service, the market has a tendency to underproduce. In this case, the market is not producing enough vaccinations from society's standpoint and an *underallocation* of resources occurs.

What Can the Government Do to Correct for Positive Externalities?

How could society correct for this market failure? Two particular methods of achieving the higher preferred output are subsidies and regulation.

Subsidies

Government could provide a subsidy—either give refunds to individuals who receive an inoculation or provide an incentive for businesses to give their employees "free" inoculations at the office. If the subsidy was exactly equal to the external benefit of inoculation, the demand curve would shift from $D_{PRIVATE}$ to D_{SOCIAL}, resulting in an efficient level of output, Q_2.

Regulation

The government could also pass a regulation requiring each person to get an inoculation. This approach would also shift the demand curve rightward toward the efficient level of output.

In summary, with positive externalities, the private market supplies too little of the good in question (such as education or inoculations for communicable diseases). In the case of negative externalities, the market supplies too much. In either case, buyers and sellers are receiving the wrong signals. The producers and consumers are not doing what they do because they are evil; rather, whether well-intentioned or ill-intentioned, they are behaving according to the incentives they face. The free market, then, works fine in providing most goods, but it functions less well without regulations, taxes, and subsidies in providing others.

Nongovernmental Solutions to Externalities

Sometimes the externality problems can be handled by individuals without the intervention of government, and people may decide to take steps on their own

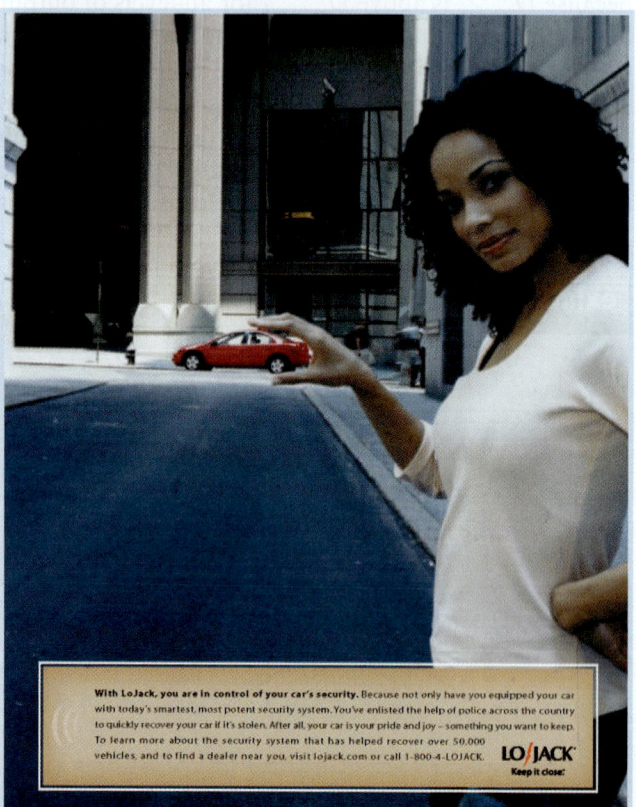

These types of systems use a hidden radio transmitter to help owners retrieve their stolen cars. If the devices also help law enforcement break up rings of car thieves, they will have spillover benefits (positive externalities) for car owners who do not own the devices, because they will reduce the probability of their cars being stolen.

Sometimes it is difficult to enforce statutes that are designed to reduce negative externalities such as drunk driving. In this case, police officers are soliciting the public's help. However, the sign is a bit confusing. Perhaps the sign should say "To Report a Drunk Driver—Call 911."

in the news

Outlawing Text Messaging While Driving— Legislators in Several States Respond to Safety Concerns

—BY BRET SCHULTE

Suddenly, those drivers talking on their cellphones seem relatively harmless, at least when compared to drivers who are staring at their cellphones, texting. An estimated 20 percent of drivers are sending or receiving text messages while behind the wheel, according to a Nationwide Insurance study. And, according to another poll, that number skyrockets to 66 percent when drivers 18 to 24 are isolated. The practice, especially popular among young people, is exacting a deadly toll.

No one knows how many vehicular crashes are related to drivers distracted by text messaging, but anecdotal evidence is mounting. A fiery crash made headlines in June when five female friends died in a collision with a tractor trailer just a week after graduating from their suburban Rochester, N.Y., high school. Police discovered the teenage driver had been texting moments before the crash. Similar accidents are happening with increasingly regularity nationwide.

Now, at least 16 states are considering legislation that would outlaw or restrict the practice. "Certainly, texting is the issue du jour this year in the legislatures," says Matt Sundeen of the National Conference of State Legislatures. That means another fight over the role of National Conference of State Legislatures. That means another fight over the role of government in regulating cellphone use, but it's one that proponents of new laws expect to win. Indeed, a Harris Interactive Poll from August shows 9 out of 10 American adults believe that sending text messages or E-mails while driving is "distracting, dangerous, and should be outlawed."

Only two states expressly prohibit texting while driving. Washington banned the practice last May, and New Jersey followed suit in November. Similar bills are now in the works in Delaware, Florida, Hawaii, Iowa, Kansas, Kentucky, Maryland, Massachusetts, Michigan, New Hampshire, New York, Ohio, Rhode Island, Tennessee, Virginia, and West Virginia.

Sundeen cites two reasons for the proposed legislation: the growing sophistication of cellphones that are increasingly catered to texting and, perhaps more important, the growing number of "high-profile accidents—and those always tend to translate into legislation."

In Iowa, Democratic Rep. McKinley Bailey proposed a texting ban that would target only beginning drivers, ages 16 and 17. He wrote the bill because of several text-related accidents after the last legislative session ended. Not everyone was for it. The ACLU called it discriminatory against young people, and Bailey received some phone calls from people who saw the ban as "an erosion of freedom," he says. Some Republicans are also trying to muster opposition. But, he notes, "overall, the response was positive." In fact, party leaders liked it so well that they're rewriting the bill to include a texting ban on drivers of all ages.

Experts say anti-texting laws are following on the heels of a wave of more general bans on the use of cellphones while driving. Five states already prohibit all drivers from using hand-held phones, and 24 more have considered similar legislation. Several states have such restrictions for younger drivers.

consider this:

Many would consider that texting while driving creates a negative externality—distracting and dangerous for other drivers. The dangers of multitasking behind the wheel are well documented. Of course, if you pull over to the side of the road and use your cell phone to report a crime or an accident, the use of the phone may provide a positive externality.

to minimize negative externalities. Moral and social codes may prevent some people from littering, driving gas-guzzling cars, or using gas-powered mowers and log-burning fireplaces. The same self-regulation also applies to positive externalities. Philanthropists, for example, frequently donate money to public and private schools. In part, this must be because they view the positive externalities from education as a good buy for their charitable dollars.

> **SECTION CHECK**
>
> 1. When the action of one party poses a cost on another party, it is called a negative externality.
> 2. The government can use taxes or other forms of regulation to correct the overallocation problem associated with negative externalities.
> 3. When the action of one party benefits another party, it is called a positive externality.
> 4. The government can provide subsidies or other forms of regulation to correct the underallocation problem associated with positive externalities.
>
> ---
>
> 1. Why are externalities also called spillover effects?
> 2. How do external costs affect the price and output of a polluting activity?
> 3. How can the government intervene to force producers to internalize external costs?
> 4. How do external benefits affect the output of an activity that causes them?
> 5. How can the government intervene to force external benefits to be internalized?
> 6. Why do most cities have more stringent noise laws for the early morning and late evening hours than for during the day?

SECTION 8.2 Public Goods

- What is a public good?
- What is the free-rider problem?
- Why does the government provide public goods?
- What is a common resource good?
- What is the tragedy of the commons?

Private Goods Versus Public Goods

Externalities are not the only culprit behind resource misallocation. A **public good** is another source of market failure. As used by economists, this term refers not to how these particular goods are purchased—by a government agency rather than some private economic agent—but to the properties that characterize them. In this section, we learn the difference between private goods, public goods, and common resources.

public good
a good that is nonrivalrous in consumption and nonexcludable

private good
a good with rivalrous consumption and excludability

Private Goods

A **private good** such as a cheeseburger has two critical properties in this context; it is rival and excludable. First, a cheeseburger is rival in consumption because if one person eats a particular cheeseburger, nobody else can eat the same cheeseburger. Second, a cheeseburger is excludable. It is easy to keep someone from eating your cheeseburger by not giving it to him. Most goods in the economy like food, clothing, cars, and houses are private goods that are rival and excludable.

Public Goods

The consumption of public goods, unlike private goods, is neither rival nor excludable. A public good is not rival because everyone can consume the good simultaneously; that is, one person's use of it does not diminish another's ability to use it. A public good is likewise *not excludable* because once the good is produced, it is prohibitively costly to exclude anyone from consuming the good. Consider national defense. Everyone enjoys the benefits of national defense (not rival) and it would be too costly to exclude anyone from those benefits (not excludable). That is, once the military has its defense in place, everyone is protected simultaneously (not rival) and it would be prohibitively costly to exclude anyone from consuming national defense (not excludable).

Another example of a public good is a flood control project. A flood control project would allow all the people who live in the flood plain area to enjoy the protection of the new program simultaneously. It would also be very difficult to exclude someone who lived in the middle of the project who said she did not want to pay. Like national defense, the good is nonrival in consumption—everyone within the flood project enjoys the protection simultaneously. Other examples of public goods include outdoor fireworks (not stadium) displays and tornado sirens in small towns. You cannot easily keep someone from seeing the fireworks or hearing the siren (not excludable). Also, when one person gets the benefits of the fireworks display or the siren warning it does not reduce the benefits to anyone else (not rival).

Voters may disagree on whether we have too much or too little, but most agree that we must have national defense. If national defense were provided privately and people were asked to pay for the use of national defense, many would be free riders, knowing they could derive the benefits of the good without paying for it. For this reason, the government provides important public goods, such as national defense.

free rider
deriving benefits from something not paid for

Public Goods and the Free-Rider Problem

The fact that a public good is not rival and not excludable makes the good difficult to produce privately. Some would know they could derive the benefits from the good without paying for it, because once it is produced, it is too difficult to exclude them. Some would try to take a *free ride*—derive benefits from something they did not pay for. Let's return to the example of national defense. Suppose the private protection of national defense is actually worth $100 to you. Assume that 100 million households in the United States are willing to make a $100 contribution for national defense. These contributions would add up to $10 billion. You might write a check for $100, or you might reason as follows: "If I don't give $100 and everybody else does, I will be equally well protected plus derive the benefits of $100 in my pocket." Taking the latter course represents a rational attempt to be a free rider. The rub is that if everyone attempts to take a free ride, the ride will not exist.

The free-rider problem prevents the private market from supplying the efficient amounts of public goods. That is, no private firm would be willing to supply national defense because people can consume it without paying for it—the free rider problem. Therefore, the government provides important public goods such as national defense.

The Government and Benefit-Cost Analysis

Everything the government provides has an opportunity cost. What is the best level of national defense? More national defense means less of something else that society may value more, like health care or Social Security. To be efficient, additional goods from the public sector must also follow the rule of rational choice—pursue additional government activities if and only if the expected marginal benefits exceed the expected marginal costs. It all comes back to the adage—there are no free lunches.

In addition, there is also the problem of assessing the value of these goods. Consider the case of a new highway. Before it builds the highway, the appropriate government agency will undertake a benefit-cost analysis of the situation. In this case, it must evaluate consumers' willingness to pay for the highway against the costs that will be incurred for construction and maintenance. However, those individuals that want the highway have an incentive to exaggerate their desire for it. At the same time, individuals who will be displaced or otherwise harmed by the highway have an incentive to exaggerate the harm that will be done to them. Together, these elements make it difficult for the government to accurately assess need. Ultimately, their evaluations are reduced to educated guesses about the net impact, weighing both positive and negative effects, of the highway on all parties concerned.

Common Resources and the Tragedy of the Commons

In many cases we do not have exclusive private property rights to things such as the air around us or the fish in the sea. They are common resources—goods that are owned by everyone and therefore not owned by anyone. When a good is not owned by anyone, individuals feel little incentive to conserve or use the resource efficiently.

in the news: The Tragedy of the Commons

—BY DANIEL MCFADDEN

Immigrants to New England in the 17th century formed villages in which they had privately owned homesteads and gardens, but they also set aside community-owned pastures, called commons, where all of the villagers' livestock could graze. Settlers had an incentive to avoid overuse of their private lands, so they would remain productive in the future. However, this self-interested stewardship of private lands did not extend to the commons. As a result, the commons were overgrazed and degenerated to the point that they were no longer able to support the villagers' cattle. This failure of private incentives to provide adequate maintenance of public resources is known to economists as "the tragedy of the commons."

Contemporary society has a number of current examples of the tragedy of the commons: the depletion of fish stocks in international waters, congestion on urban highways, and the rise of resistant diseases due to careless use of antibiotics. However, the commons that is likely to have the greatest impact on our lives in the new century is the digital commons, the information available on the Internet through the portals that provide access. The problem with digital information is the mirror image of the original grazing commons: Information is costly to generate and organize, but its value to individual consumers is too dispersed and small to establish an effective market. The information that is provided is inadequately catalogued and organized. Furthermore, the Internet tends to fill with low-value information: The products that have high commercial value are marketed through revenue-producing channels, and the Internet becomes inundated with products that cannot command these values. Self-published books and music are cases in point....

The solutions that resolve the problem of the digital commons are likely to be ingenious ways to collect money from consumers with little noticeable pain, and these should facilitate the operation of the Internet as a market for goods and services. Just don't expect it to be free.

SOURCE: Daniel McFadden, "The Tragedy of the Commons," *Forbes*, 10 September 2001, pp. 61–63. Daniel McFadden won the Nobel Prize for economics in 2000.

A **common resource** is a rival good that is nonexcludable; that is, nonpayers cannot be easily excluded from consuming the good, and when one unit is consumed by one person, it means that it cannot be consumed by another. Fish in the vast ocean waters are a good example of a common resource. They are rival because fish are limited—a fish taken by one person is not available for others. They are nonexcludable because it is prohibitively costly to keep anyone from catching them—almost anyone with a boat and a fishing rod could catch one. Common resources can lead to tragedy—see the In the News story.

common resource
a rival good that is nonexcludable

SECTION CHECK

1. A public good is both nonrivalrous in consumption (one person's usage of it does not diminish another's ability to use it) and nonexclusive (no one can be excluded from using it).
2. A free rider is someone who attempts to enjoy the benefits of a good without paying for it.
3. The free-rider problem prevents the private market from supplying the efficient amount of public goods.
4. A common resource good is rival in consumption but nonexcludable.
5. The failure of private incentives to maintain public resources leads to the tragedy of the commons.

1. How are public goods different from private goods?
2. Why does the free-rider problem arise in the case of public goods?
3. In what way can government provision of public goods solve the free-rider problem?
4. What is a common resource?
5. What is the tragedy of the commons?

SECTION 8.3 Asymmetric Information

* What is asymmetric information?
* What is adverse selection?
* What is moral hazard?

What Is Asymmetric Information?

When the available information is initially distributed in favor of one party relative to another, **asymmetric information** is said to exist. Suppose you bought a new car for $25,000 and about a month later you decide that you would be much happier with your old car and the money. So you call your salesperson and ask what your car is worth—perfect condition and less than 1,000 miles on the odometer. The salesperson tells you about $20,000. Why did your "new" car depreciate $5,000 in just one month? The problem is that a potential buyer is going to be skeptical. Why is that new car being sold? Is it a lemon?

asymmetric information
occurs when the available information is initially distributed in favor of one party relative to another in an exchange

Sellers are at an information advantage over potential buyers when selling a car because they have more information about the car than does the potential buyer. However, potential buyers know that sellers are more likely to sell a lemon. As a result, potential buyers will offer a lower price than they would if they could be certain of the quality. This is known as the lemon problem. Without incurring significant quality detection costs, such as having it inspected by a mechanic, the potential buyer is at an informational disadvantage relative to the seller. It is rational for the seller to claim that the car is in good shape and has no known defects, but the potential buyer cannot detect whether the car is a lemon or not

When players get traded from one team to another, a potential asymmetric information and adverse selection problem occurs—especially with pitchers. The team that is trading the pitcher knows more about his medical past, his pitching mechanics, his demeanor on and off the field, and so on, than the team that is trading for him. Even though trades are not finalized until the player passes a physical, many ailments or potential problems may go undetected.

without incurring costs. If the quality detection costs are sufficiently high, a solution is to price all used cars as if they are average quality. That is, used cars of the same year, make, and model generally will be offered at the same price, regardless of their known conditions. The seller of a lemon will then receive a payment that is more than the car is worth, and the seller of a relatively high-quality car will receive less than the car is worth. However, if a seller of a high-quality car does *not* receive what the car would sell for if the potential buyer knew its quality, the seller will rationally withdraw the offer to sell the car. Given the logical response of sellers of higher-than-average quality cars, the average quality of used cars on the market will fall, and consequently, many people will avoid buying in the used car market. In other words, the bad cars will drive the good cars out of the market. Thus, fewer used cars are bought and sold because fewer good cars are offered for sale. That is, information problems reduce economic efficiency. A situation where an informed party benefits in an exchange by taking advantage of knowing more than the other party is called **adverse selection**.

This distortion in the used car market resulting from adverse selection can be reduced by the buyer acquiring more information so that the buyer and seller have equal information. In the used car example, it might mean that an individual buyer would demand that an independent mechanic do a detailed inspection of the used car or that the dealership provide an extended warranty. A warranty provides a credible signal that this dealer is not selling lemons. In addition, new services such as carfax.com allow you to pay to find the history of a used car before you buy it. These services help in eliminating the adverse selection problem because buyers would have more information about the product they are buying.

The least-cost solution would have sellers reveal their superior information to potential buyers. The problem is that it is not individually rational for the seller to provide a truthful and complete disclosure, a point that is known by a potential buyer. Only if the seller is punished for not truthfully revealing exchange-relevant information will a potential buyer perceive the seller's disclosure as truthful.

Adverse selection also occurs in the insurance market. Imagine an auto insurance company that has a one-size-fits-all policy for their insurance premiums. Careful drivers would be charged the same premium as careless drivers. The company would assess the average risk of accidents for all drivers and then set the premium. Of course, this would be very appealing to careless drivers, who are more likely to get in an accident; but not very appealing to careful drivers who have a much lower probability of getting in an accident. Under this pricing scheme, the bad drivers would drive the good drivers out of the market. Good drivers would be less likely to buy a policy, thinking that they are paying too much, since they are less likely to get in an accident than a careless driver. Many good drivers would exit the market, leaving a disproportionate share of bad drivers—exactly what the insurance companies do not want—people with a higher risk of getting in accidents. So what do they do?

Insurance companies set premiums according to the risk associated with particular groups of drivers, so good drivers do not exit the market. One strategy they use for dealing with adverse selection is called *screening*, where they use observable information about people to reveal private information. For example, a 17-year-old male driving a sports car will be charged a much higher premium than a 40-year-old female driving a minivan, even if he is a careful driver. Or someone with a good driving record or good grades gets a discount on his insurance. Insurance companies have data on different types of drivers and the probability of

adverse selection
a situation where an informed party benefits in an exchange by taking advantage of knowing more than the other party

those drivers being in accidents, and they use this data to set insurance premiums. They may be wrong on an individual case (the teenager may be accident-free for years), but they are likely to be correct on average.

Reputation and Standardization

Asymmetric information is also present in other markets like rare stamps, coins, paintings, and sports memorabilia where the dealer (seller) knows more about the product than does the potential buyer. Potential buyers want to be assured that these items are authentic, not counterfeits. Unless the seller can successfully provide evidence of the quality of the product, bad products will tend to drive good products out of the market, resulting in a market failure.

One method that sellers can use to convince potential buyers that their products are high quality is *reputation*. For example, if a supermarket has a reputation of selling fresh produce, you are more likely to shop there. The same is true when you choose an electrician, plumber, or physician. In the used car market, the dealer might advertise how long he has been in business. This provides a signal that he has many satisfied customers. Therefore, he is likely to sell more used cars at a higher price. In short, if there is a reputation of high quality, it will minimize the market failure problem.

However, there may be cases where it is difficult to develop a reputation. For example, take a restaurant or a motel on a desolate highway. These establishments may not receive repeat customers. Customers have little idea of the quality of food, the probability of bedbugs, and so on. In this case, *standardization* is important. A national restaurant or a motel chain provides standardization. While you may not frequent McDonald's when you are at home, when confronted with the choice between a little known restaurant and McDonald's, you may pick the McDonald's because of the standardized products backed by a large corporation.

Asymmetric Information and Job Market Signaling

Why does non-job-related schooling raise your income? Why would salaried workers work longer hours—putting in 60 to 70 hours a week? The reason is this behavior provides a useful signal to the employer about the person's intelligence and work ethic.

Signaling is important because it reduces information costs associated with asymmetric information; the seller of labor (potential employee) has more information about her work ethic and reliability than the buyer of labor (potential employer). Imagine how costly it would be to try out 150 potential employees for a job. In short, signals provide a measure that can help reduce asymmetric information and lower hiring costs.

There are strong signals and weak signals. Wearing a nice suit to work would be a weak signal because it does not necessarily distinguish a high productivity worker from a low productivity worker—a lazy worker can dress well too. To provide a strong signal, it must be harder for a low productivity worker to give the signal than a high productivity worker. Education is a strong signal in labor markets because it requires effort that many low productivity workers may find too difficult to obtain. The education signal is also relatively easy to measure—years of education, grade point average, highest degree attained, reputation of the university of college, rigor of courses attempted, and so on. Education can clearly improve a person's productivity; even if it did not, however, it would be a useful signal because more productive people find it easier to obtain education than lazy people. Furthermore, productive people are more likely to attain more education in order to signal to their employer that they are productive. So it may not just be the knowledge obtained from a college education, it may be the effort that you are signaling—something you presumably already had before you entered college. So according to the signaling model, workers go to college, not for the knowledge gained, but to send the important signal that they are highly productive.

In all likelihood, education provides knowledge and enhances productivity. However, it also sends an important signal. For example, many firms will not hire managers without an MBA because of the knowledge potential employees gained in courses like finance and economics, but also because an MBA sends a powerful signal that the worker is disciplined and hard working.

Durable Goods, Signals, and Warranties

Why are people reluctant to buy durable goods like televisions, refrigerators, and cameras without a warranty? Warranties are a signal. Honest and reliable firms find it less expensive to provide a warranty than dishonest firms. The dilemma for consumers is that they are trying to distinguish the good brands from the bad brands. One way to do this is to see what kind of warranty the producer offers. Low-quality items would require more frequent and expensive servicing than high-quality items. Thus, producers of low-quality items will tend to not offer extensive warranties. In short, extensive warranties signal high quality, while low-quality items without extensive warranties signal poor quality. With this knowledge, consumers will pay more for high-quality products with good warranties.

Asymmetric information occurs when the available information is initially distributed in favor of one party relative to another. In the used car market, the problem of asymmetric information can be reduced if a private seller can show records of regular maintenance and service and dealers can offer extended warranties.

to detect if a product failure was the consequence of a manufacturing defect or the abuse of the owner-user.

Adverse Selection versus Moral Hazard

Don't confuse adverse selection and moral hazard. Adverse selection is the phenomenon that occurs when one party in the exchange takes advantage of knowing more than the other party. Moral hazard involves the action taken *after* the exchange, such as if you were a nonsmoker who had just bought a life insurance policy and then started smoking heavily.

Winner's Curse

Suppose you and five other classmates were asked to bid on a jar of pennies. Nobody knows how many pennies are in the jar and you are not allowed to open the jar. The winner gets the jar of pennies. Let's say there are 500 pennies ($5) in the jar and you win by bidding $7. You are happy you won the bid until they count the pennies and you realize you just paid $7 for $5 worth of pennies. A common-value auction is where the auctioned item has the same value for all buyers but the value is unknown prior to the bidding. We call this a **winner's curse** because in this case the "winner" is overly optimistic and bids more for an item than its worth. Therefore, the winner could end up being worse off (cursed) than the loser.

What Is Moral Hazard?

Another information problem is associated with the insurance market and is called moral hazard. If an individual is fully insured for fire, theft, auto, life, and so on, what incentives will this individual have to take additional precautions from risk? For example, a person with auto insurance may drive less cautiously than would a person without auto insurance.

Insurance companies do, however, try to remedy the adverse selection problem by requiring regular checkups, discounts for nonsmokers, charging different deductibles and different rates for different age and occupational groups, and so on.

Additionally, those with health insurance may devote less effort and resources to staying healthy than those who are not covered. The problem, of course, is that if the insured are behaving more recklessly than they would if they were not insured, the result might be much higher insurance rates. The **moral hazard** arises from the fact that it is costly for the insurer to monitor the behaviors of the insured party. Suppose an individual knew that his car was protected with a "bumper to bumper" warranty. He might have less incentive to take care of the car, despite the manufacturer's contract specifying that the warranty was only valid under "normal wear and tear." It would be too costly for the manufacturer

moral hazard
taking additional risks because you are insured

winner's curse
a situation that arises in certain auctions where the winner is worse off than the loser because of an overly optimistic value placed on the good

The problem also occurs because value is subjective. In some cases bidders have a difficult time establishing an item's value. Without complete information, participants with limited skill in establishing valuation may overpay for an item. Historically, we have seen this when speculative bubbles in the stock or real estate markets occur. Then, investors with little skill in valuation and incomplete information tend to push prices beyond their true value.

However, an actual overpayment will generally occur only if the winner fails to account for the winner's curse when bidding. So despite its dire-sounding name, the winner's curse does not necessarily have ill effects.

The severity of the winner's curse tends to increase with the number of bidders. This is because the more bidders, the more likely it is that some of them have overestimated the auctioned item's value. The more serious your error of overbidding, the more likely you are to win. However, if you win you probably made a serious error. The best strategy may be to underbid. If the winner normally overestimates the true value by 20 percent then you might offer 80 percent of what you

Use what you've LEARNED: ADVERSE SELECTION

Q If individuals know a lot more about their health condition than an insurance company, do we have a case of adverse selection?

A Yes. Even after a medical examination, individuals will know more about their health than the insurance company. That is, the buyers of health insurance have a better idea about their overall body conditions and nutritional habits than the seller, the insurance company. People with greater health problems tend to buy more health insurance than those who are healthy. This tendency drives up the price of health insurance to reflect the costs of sicker-than-average people, which drives people of average health out of the market. So the people who end up buying insurance will be the riskiest group.

---

think the item is worth. That way, if you happen to win by overbidding you won't "get taken to the cleaners." You might also choose not to participate in auctions likely to generate a winner's curse.

There is often confusion that winner's curse applies to the winners of all auctions. However, it is worth repeating here that for auctions based on the private value someone places on a good (i.e., when the item is desired independent of its value in the market), the winner's curse does not arise.

The winner's curse can also occur with underbidding, where people offer to do a job for less than other bidders. Imagine you need to hire a landscaper, so you get estimates from various landscapers. Who is likely to win? Probably, the landscaper with the lowest estimate. However, he may not think he won if he underestimated the amount of work required in your yard.

Use what you've LEARNED: THE WINNER'S CURSE—OIL FIELD ECONOMICS AND BASEBALL

It's the middle of winter. Right now baseball General Managers (GMs) are hitting the phones talking to player agents, trying to sign the men they think will push them over the top next season. The fans enter the season with great expectations. Yet so many times the player thought to be a savior to the team ends up not being worth the money it took to sign him. Is it because free agents lose their edge after signing their big-money contracts? Seeing as many of these guys were set for life before they switched teams, this explanation doesn't seem to work. To find the real answer, we have to drill for oil.

Back in the 1950s the players in the American petroleum industry turned their eyes to the Gulf of Mexico. With newer technology it was possible to drill offshore. So the race began and the oil companies bid for drilling rights and set up operations. There was only one problem. These offshore oil wells weren't turning a profit. Is drilling on the seabed harder than drilling on dry land? Sure, but that wasn't the difficulty. The real problem was the bidding process

(continued)

Use what you've LEARNED: THE WINNER'S CURSE—OIL FIELD ECONOMICS AND BASEBALL (cont.)

given the uncertainties in information available to the oil companies. This was explained in an article published in the Journal of Petroleum Technology titled "Competitive bidding in high risk situations," by Capen, Clapp and Campbell of the Atlantic Richfield Company (ARCO) in 1971. Here they coined the term "winner's curse."

Suppose you have four oil companies all interested in the same patch of offshore property. Back in the 1950s the methods available for determining the amount of liquid gold under a few hundred feet of water were primitive. This led to a large spread in the estimations of the value of the oil, and hence the drilling rights. Suppose that after all the costs of drilling were accounted for there was $10M worth of oil in the ground. Company A might determine that there was only $5M worth of oil. On the other hand, Company B might nail it at $10M, Company C could value the oil at $12M and Company D could make a gross overestimation and believe that there was $20M worth of oil in the ground.

Now we come to the bidding for the drilling rights. At $5M, Company A drops out of the competition. At $10M, we lose Company B. At $12M Company C bows out, and Company D is very happy because they have paid $12M for property they believe is worth $20M. But since there is only $10M worth of oil in the ground, Company D is in the red for $2M. They have suffered the winner's curse. In an auction, the prize goes to whoever has the most optimistic view of the value of the object being bid upon. In many cases, this also means that the winner is the person who has overestimated the most.

Is a baseball player really like an oil well? He is in that some estimation to his value can be made with the data available, but his future value (what the owners are bidding on) is in many cases an open question. How much will a thirty-year-old outfielder with a .280 batting average and 30 homers a year be worth over the span of his next contract? $5M a year? $7M a year? It's hard to guess, especially when the future free-market value of his competition is factored in. How fast will the average salary rise over the next three years? (Note that the oil companies need to make a similar calculation—they need to not only estimate the amount of oil in the ground, but they also have to make an estimation of the future price of oil.) It's easy to see how several different teams could make very different estimations of the value of this player. And the team that signs him in the end is the team that was the most optimistic about his value. Like an oil company, this optimism could leave them well in the red.

So what solutions exist to the winner's curse? Information and caution are two big factors. Improving technology allowed oil companies to get a better grasp on how much oil is in the ground. Obviously a company that had better information made smarter bids, and was less likely to overbid. After the winner's curse phenomenon became better understood, oil companies were more cautious and started bidding fractions of what they thought the drilling rights were worth in order to avoid the curse. If all of the oil companies were bidding .75 what they thought the true value of the drilling rights were worth, they were much less likely to be bitten. A higher-risk operator might be willing to bid .8 the estimated value, whereas a more conservative player might only bid .65. The problem that quickly surfaced is that newcomers to the industry often did not factor in the fractional weighting when making their bids. Well, these newcomers were often bitten by the winner's curse, and while the newcomers might have annoyed the older companies, in the long run it was mainly the newcomers that were hurt.

In baseball more information will also lead to a better bid. A team that understands statistics will probably realize that a certain slugger's gaudy RBI (Runs Batted In) totals are due to his high-OBP (on base percentage) table-setters, while a team that doesn't analyze the situation as well will drool over the RBIs and adjust their bid accordingly. A team that understands how aging affects performance is less likely to overbid for the thirty-five-year-old shortstop. Caution also comes into play. A GM can estimate a player's value, discount it by a fraction as would an oil executive, and then bid accordingly. The problem is the newcomers. How often do we

Use what you've LEARNED
THE WINNER'S CURSE–OIL FIELD ECONOMICS AND BASEBALL (cont.)

see a new owner come in and make a big splash in the free agent market? This is the case of the new oil company that hasn't figured out how the modified bidding works to fight against the winner's curse.

Sadly, the baseball owners can't just sit back and watch the new guy squirm under the burden of his foolish purchases. Because of the salary arbitration process the winner's curse becomes everyone's curse. The grossly overpaid shortstop can be used as evidence against all the other teams in baseball when the arbitration process sets the next year's salaries. Perhaps when new owners are initiated into baseball and taught the secret handshake, they also need to be given a short course on the history of oil field economics.

SOURCE: From http://economics.about.com/cs/baseballeconomics/a/winnerscurse.htm. Used by permission of the author.

SECTION CHECK

1. Asymmetric information occurs when the available information is initially distributed in favor of one party relative to another in an exchange.
2. Adverse selection is a situation where an informed party benefits in an exchange by taking advantage of knowing more than the other party.
3. Moral hazard occurs when one party to a contract passes on the cost of its behavior to the other party.
4. Asymmetric information, adverse selection, and moral hazard are information problems that can distort market signals.
5. Asymmetric information leads to signaling behavior.
6. Auctions for goods of uncertain value may suffer from the winner's curse. In the winner's curse the most optimistic buyer wins, but may overpay as a result, leaving the winner worse off.

---

1. How do substantial warranties offered by sellers of used cars act to help protect buyers from the problem of asymmetric information and adverse selection? Why might too extensive a warranty lead to a moral hazard problem?
2. If where you got your college degree acted as a signaling device to potential employers, why would you want the school from which you graduated to raise its academic standards after you leave?
3. Why might withdrawals in several classes send a poor signal to potential employers?
4. Why is the winner's curse less likely for repeat-purchase items?

Interactive Chapter Summary

Fill in the blanks:

1. Sometimes the market system fails to produce efficient outcomes because of side effects economists call _____.

2. Whenever an activity has physical impacts on individuals not directly involved in the activity, if the impact on the outside party is negative, it is called a _____; if the impact is positive, it is called a _____.

3. If a firm can avoid paying the external costs it imposes on others, it _____ its own costs of production but not the _____ cost to society.

4. If the government taxed a manufacturer by the amount of those external costs it imposes on others, it would force the manufacturer to _____ the costs.

5. The benefits of a product or service that spill over to an outside party not involved in producing or consuming the good are called _____.

6. If suppliers are unaware of or not responsible for the external costs created by their production, the result is a(n) _____ of scarce resources to the production of the good.

7. Because producers are unable to collect payments from all who are benefiting from the good or service, the market has a tendency to _____ goods with external benefits.

8. In the case of either external benefits or external costs, buyers and sellers are receiving the wrong signals: The apparent benefits or costs of some actions differ from the _____ benefits or costs.

9. Unlike the consumption of private goods, the consumption of public goods is both _____ and _____.

10. If once a good is produced it is prohibitively costly to exclude anyone from consuming the good, consumption of that good is called _____.

11. If everyone can consume a good simultaneously, it is _____.

12. When individuals derive the benefits of a good without paying for it, it is called a(n) _____.

13. The government may be able to overcome the free-rider problem by _____ the public good and imposing taxes to pay for it.

14. Goods that are owned by everyone and therefore not owned by anyone are called _____ resources.

15. A common resource is a _____ good that is _____.

16. Fish in the vast ocean are a good example of a _____ resource.

17. The failure of private incentives to provide adequate maintenance of public resources is known to economists as the _____.

18. When the available information is initially distributed in favor of one party relative to another, _____ is said to exist.

19. The existence of _____ may give rise to signaling behavior.

20. When one party enters into an exchange with another party that has more information, we call it _____ selection.

21. A college education can provide a _____ about a person's intelligence and perseverance.

22. Good warranties are an example of _____ behavior that takes place because the _____ may know the actual quality of durable goods better than the _____.

23. _____ arises from the cost involved for the insurer to monitor the behaviors of the insured party.

24. The _____ occurs when the winner of an auction overpays.

25. The winner's curse is less likely for items that are purchased _____/infrequently and where there is a larger/_____ number of bidders.

Answers: 1. externalities 2. negative externality; positive externality 3. lowers; true 4. internalize (bear) 5. positive externalities 6. overallocation 7. underproduce 8. true social 9. nonexcludable; nonrivalous 10. nonexcludable 11. nonrivalous 12. free ride 13. providing 14. common 15. rival; nonexcludable 16. common 17. tragedy of the commons 18. asymmetric information 19. asymmetric information 20. adverse 21. signal 22. signaling; sellers; buyers 23. Moral hazard 24. winner's curse 25. frequently; smaller

Key Terms and Concepts

externality 210
positive externality 210
negative externality 210
public good 216
private good 216
free rider 217
common resource 219
asymmetric information 219
adverse selection 220
moral hazard 222
winner's curse 222

Section Check Answers

8.1 Externalities

1. **Why are externalities also called spillover effects?**
   An externality exists whenever the benefits or costs of an activity impact individuals outside the market mechanism. That is, some of the effects spill over to those who have not voluntarily agreed to bear them or compensate others for them, unlike the voluntary exchange of the market.

2. **How do external costs affect the price and output of a polluting activity?**
   If the owner of a firm that pollutes does not have to bear the external costs of pollution, she can ignore those real costs of pollution to society. The result is that the private costs she must pay are less than the true social costs of production, so that the market output of the polluting activity is greater, and the resulting market price less, than it would be if producers did have to bear the external costs of production.

3. **How can the government intervene to force producers to internalize external costs?**
   If the government could impose on producers a tax or fee, equal to the external costs imposed on people without their consent, producers would have to take into account those costs. The result would be that those costs were no longer external costs, but internalized by producers.

4. **How do external benefits affect the output of an activity that causes them?**
   External benefits are benefits that spill over to others, because the party responsible need not be paid for those benefits. Therefore, some of the benefits of an activity to society will be ignored by the relevant decision makers in this case, and the result will be a smaller output and a higher price for goods that generate external benefits to others.

5. **How can the government intervene to force external benefits to be internalized?**
   Just as taxes can be used to internalize external costs imposed on others, subsidies can be used to internalize external benefits generated for others.

6. **Why do most cities have more stringent noise laws for the early morning and late evening hours than for during the day?**
   The external costs to others from loud noises in residential areas early in the morning and late in the evening are higher, because most residents are home and trying to sleep, than when many people are gone at work or are already awake in the daytime. Given those higher potential external costs, most cities impose more restrictive noise laws for nighttime hours to reduce them.

8.2 Public Goods

1. **How are public goods different from private goods?**
   Private goods are rival in consumption (we can't both consume the same unit of a good) and exclusive (nonpayers can be prevented from consuming the good unless they pay for it). Public goods are nonrival in consumption (more than one person can consume the same good) and nonexclusive (nonpayers can't be effectively kept from consuming the good, even if they don't voluntarily pay for it).

2. **Why does the free-rider problem arise in the case of public goods?**
   The free-rider problem arises in the case of public goods because people cannot be prevented from enjoying the benefits of public goods once they are provided. Therefore, people have an incentive to not voluntarily pay for those benefits, making it difficult or even impossible to finance the efficient quantity of public goods through voluntary market arrangements.

3. **In what way can government provision of public goods solve the free-rider problem?**
   The government can overcome the free-rider problem by forcing people to pay for the provision of a public good through taxes.

4. **What is a common resource?**
   A common resource good is rival in consumption but nonexcludable.

5. **What is the tragedy of the commons?**
   Common resource goods often lead to overuse because if no one owns the resource, they are not likely to

consider the cost of their use of the resource on others. This is the so-called tragedy of the commons. This problem has led to overfishing. Of course, you could remove the common and make the resource private property, but assigning private property rights to a vast ocean area would be virtually impossible.

8.3 Asymmetric Information

1. **How do substantial warranties offered by sellers of used cars act to help protect buyers from the problem of asymmetric information and adverse selection? Why might too extensive a warranty lead to a moral hazard problem?**

   In the used car market, the seller has superior information about the car's condition, placing the buyer at an information disadvantage. It also increases the chance that the car being sold is a "lemon." A substantial warranty can provide the buyer with valuable additional information about the condition of the car, reducing both asymmetric information and adverse selection problems.

   Too extensive a warranty (e.g., an unlimited "bumper to bumper" warranty) will give the buyer less incentive to take care of the car, because the buyer is effectively insured against the damage that lack of care would cause.

2. **If where you got your college degree acted as a signaling device to potential employers, why would you want the school from which you graduated to raise its academic standards after you leave?**

   If an employer used your college's academic reputation as a signal of your likely "quality" as a potential employee, you want the school to raise its standards after you graduate, because it would improve the average quality of its graduates, improving the quality it signals about you to an employer.

3. **Why might withdrawals in several classes send a poor signal to potential employers?**

   It would indicate a failure to stick to difficult tasks relative to other students.

4. **Why is the winner's curse less likely for repeat-purchase items?**

   Repeat purchases reveal good information on the actual value of items.

CHAPTER 8 STUDY GUIDE

True or False:

1. A negative externality is when the action of one party imposes a cost on another party.
2. A positive externality is when the action of one party benefits another party.
3. In the case of external costs, firms tend to produce too little from society's standpoint, causing an efficiency loss due to an underallocation of scarce resources to the production of the good.
4. If government could impose a pollution tax equal to the exact size of the external costs imposed by a firm, then the firm would produce at the socially desired level of output.
5. The tax revenues raised by a pollution tax could be used to compensate those who have suffered damages from the pollution.
6. Alternatives to pollution taxes include the government prohibiting certain types of activities that cause pollution and forcing firms to clean up their emissions.
7. Because the decision makers involved ignore some of the real social benefits, the private market does not provide enough of goods that generate external benefits.
8. In the case of external benefits, if we could add the benefits that are derived by nonpaying consumers, the demand curve would shift to the right, increasing output.
9. In the case of external benefits, a tax equal to external benefits would result in an efficient level of output.
10. Externality problems always require the intervention of government.
11. In the case of goods where all those affected benefit simultaneously and it is prohibitively costly to exclude anyone from consuming them, market failures tend to arise.
12. In the case of public goods, when people act as free riders, some goods having benefits greater than costs will not be produced.
13. If quality detection costs are high, high-quality products will tend to be withdrawn from the market, and the average quality will rise.
14. Asymmetric information exists when the available information is initially distributed in favor of one party to a transaction relative to another.
15. In adverse selection situations, it is rational for a seller with more information about a product to provide a truthful and complete disclosure and make that fact known to a potential buyer.
16. Warranty agreements that limit the responsibility of the insurer in certain situations can be one method of controlling moral hazard problems.
17. In the market for insurance, the adverse selection problem leads those most likely to collect on insurance to buy it.
18. In the market for insurance, moral hazard can lead those who buy insurance to take fewer precautions to avoid the insured risk.
19. The winner's curse is more likely when a large number of bidders is involved.
20. Repeat purchasers are less likely to suffer from the winner's curse than one-time purchasers.

Multiple Choice:

1. The presence of negative externalities leads to a misallocation of societal resources because
    a. whenever external costs are imposed on outside parties, the good should not be produced at all.
    b. less of the good than is ideal for society is produced.
    c. some costs are associated with production that the producer fails to take into consideration.
    d. the government always intervenes in markets when negative externalities are present, and the government is inherently inefficient.
2. A tax equal to the external cost on firms that emit pollutants would
    a. provide firms with the incentive to increase the level of activity creating the pollution.
    b. provide firms with the incentive to decrease the level of activity creating the pollution.
    c. provide firms with little incentive to search for less environmentally damaging production methods.
    d. not reduce pollution levels at all.

3. In the case of a good whose production generates negative externalities,
   a. those not directly involved in the market transactions are harmed.
   b. internalizing the externality would tend to result in a greater output of the good.
   c. too little of the good tends to be produced.
   d. a subsidy would be the appropriate government corrective action.
   e. all of the above are true.

4. If firms were required to pay the full social costs of the production of goods, including both private and external costs, other things being equal, there would probably be
   a. an increase in production.
   b. a decrease in production.
   c. a greater misallocation of resources.
   d. a decrease in the market price of the product.

5. Which of the following will most likely generate positive externalities of consumption?
   a. a hot dog vendor
   b. public education
   c. an automobile
   d. a city bus
   e. a polluting factory

6. Assume that production of a good imposes external costs on others. The market equilibrium price will be _____ and the equilibrium quantity _____ for efficient resource allocation.
   a. too high; too high
   b. too high; too low
   c. too low; too high
   d. too low; too low

7. Assume that production of a good generates external benefits of consumption. The market equilibrium price of the good will be _____ and the equilibrium quantity _____ for efficient resource allocation.
   a. too high; too high
   b. too high; too low
   c. too low; too high
   d. too low; too low

8. Socially inefficient outcomes may occur in markets that have
   a. free riders.
   b. negative externalities.
   c. asymmetric information problems.
   d. positive externalities.
   e. any of the above.

9. In the case of externalities, appropriate government corrective policy would be
   a. taxes in the case of external benefits and subsidies in the case of external costs.
   b. subsidies in the case of external benefits and taxes in the case of external costs.
   c. taxes in both the case of external benefits and the case of external costs.
   d. subsidies in both the case of external benefits and the case of external costs.
   e. none of the above; the appropriate thing to do would be to do nothing.

10. The market system fails to provide the efficient output of public goods because
    a. people place no value on public goods.
    b. private firms cannot restrict the benefits from those goods to consumers who are willing to pay for them.
    c. public enterprises can produce those goods at lower cost than private firms.
    d. public goods create widespread spillover costs.

11. Public goods, like national defense, are usually funded through government because
    a. no one cares about them, because they are public.
    b. it is prohibitively difficult to withhold national defense from someone unwilling to pay for it.

c. they cost too much for private firms to produce them.
d. they provide benefits only to individuals, and not firms.

12. Adverse selection refers to
    a. the phenomenon that occurs when one party in an exchange takes advantage of knowing more than another party.
    b. the tendency for individuals to alter their behavior once they are insured against loss.
    c. the tendency for individuals to engage in insurance fraud.
    d. both b and c.

13. Which of the following is not true of adverse selection?
    a. It can result when both parties to a transaction have little information about the quality of the goods involved.
    b. It can cause the quality of goods traded to fall, if quality detection costs are high.
    c. It can be a difficult problem to overcome, because it is not individually rational for the transactor with the superior information to provide a truthful and complete disclosure.
    d. All of the above are true.

14. If a company offers a medical and dental care plan that offers benefits to all of the members of each employee's family for a given monthly premium, an employee who is a mother of five children and who has bad teeth who elects that plan would be an illustration of
    a. the moral hazard problem.
    b. the free-rider problem.
    c. the adverse selection problem.
    d. the "lemon" problem.

15. If, after you buy a car with air bags, you start to drive recklessly, it would be an illustration of
    a. the moral hazard problem.
    b. the free-rider problem.
    c. the adverse selection problem.
    d. the "lemon" problem.

16. In the market for insurance, the moral hazard problem leads
    a. those most likely to collect on insurance to buy it.
    b. those who buy insurance to take fewer precautions to avoid the insured risk.
    c. those with more prior insurance claims to be charged a higher premium.
    d. to none of the above.

17. The winner's curse
    a. is more likely the fewer the bidders.
    b. is more likely the more frequently a good is purchased.
    c. is more likely when a good is being purchased because of its expected future market value.
    d. is a myth.

18. In the analysis of the winner's curse
    a. a bidder who realizes he might be in a winner's curse situation may bid less as a result.
    b. it can be better to lose an auction than to win it.
    c. a good bought for its value to the bidder is less likely to be subject to the winner's curse than a good bought for its expected future market value.
    d. all of the above are true.

Problems:

1. Indicate which of the following activities create a positive externality, a negative externality, or no externality at all:
   a. During a live theater performance, an audience member's cell phone loudly rings.
   b. You are given a flu shot.
   c. You purchase and drink a soda during a break from class.
   d. A college fraternity and sorority clean up trash along a two-mile stretch on the highway.
   e. A firm dumps chemical waste into a local water reservoir.
   f. The person down the hall in your dorm plays loud music while you are trying to sleep.

2. Draw a standard supply and demand diagram for televisions, and indicate the equilibrium price and output.
    a. Assuming that the production of televisions generates external costs, illustrate the effect of the producers being forced to pay a tax equal to the external costs generated, and indicate the equilibrium output.
    b. If instead of generating external costs, television production generates external benefits, illustrate the effect of the producers being given a subsidy equal to the external benefits generated, and indicate the equilibrium output.
3. For each of the following goods, indicate whether they are nonrival and/or nonexclusive. Indicate whether they are private or public goods.
    a. hot dogs
    b. cable TV
    c. broadcast TV
    d. automobiles
    e. national defense
    f. pollution control
    g. parking in a parking structure
    h. a sunset
    i. admission to a theme park
4. Is a lighthouse a public good if it benefits many ship owners? What if it primarily benefits ships going to a port nearby?
5. Why do you think buffaloes became almost completely extinct on the Great Plains but cattle did not? Why is it possible that you can buy a buffalo burger in a store or diner today?
6. What kind of problems does the government face when trying to perform a cost-benefit analysis of whether or how much of a public project to produce?
7. How does a TV broadcast have characteristics of a public good? What about cable services such as HBO?
8. In order to get a license to practice in the United States, foreign-trained veterinarians must take an exam given by the American Veterinary Association. Only 48 people per year are allowed to take the exam, which is administered at only two universities. The fee for the exam, which must be booked at least 18 months in advance, was recently raised from $2,500 to $6,000. What effects does this clinical competency exam have on the number of veterinarians practicing in the United States? Do you think it improves the quality of veterinary services?
9. How would the adverse selection problem arise in the insurance market? How is it like the "lemon" used-car problem?
10. In terms of signaling behavior:
    a. Why is wearing a suit a weaker signal of ability than higher educational achievement?
    b. Why do some majors in college provide more powerful signals to future employers than others?
    c. Why could double-majoring provide a more powerful labor market signal than having a single major?
    d. How would you explain why students might be said to "overinvest" in grades as opposed to learning course material?
11. In terms of winner's curse:
    a. Why is the winner's curse unlikely for frequently purchased goods?
    b. Why would the winner's curse be more likely as the number of bidders increases?
    c. Why would we except there to be no winner's curse for goods desired for their own private value, unlike the case of purchases based on a good's market value to others?
12. In terms of moral hazard:
    a. Why does someone's willingness to pay a large deductible on an insurance policy tell an insurer something valuable about the seriousness of the moral hazard problem they might expect from the policyholder?
    b. Why does car insurance which explicitly excludes insuring the car for commercial use act to reduce moral hazard?
    c. Why does vehicle insurance based in part on miles driven reduce moral hazard problems?
    d. Why would a GPS monitor that can record the location and the speed a rental car is driven help reduce the moral hazard problem that rental companies are exposed to?

Public Sector and Public Choice

9

9.1 Other Functions of Government
9.2 Government Spending and Taxation
9.3 Public Choice

In the last chapter, we discussed the role of government in the case of externalities and public goods. We argued that the government can sometimes improve economic well-being by remedying externalities through pollution taxes, regulation and subsidies, and providing public goods.

However, in this chapter, we cover other important facets of the public sector—protecting property rights, providing a legal system, intervention in cases of insufficient competition, income redistribution, and promoting stability and growth in the economy. In this chapter, we will see how the government obtains revenues through taxation to provide these goods and services. We also examine the different types of taxation. The last section of the chapter is on public choice economics, the application of economic principles to politics. ∎

SECTION 9.1 Other Functions of Government

* What are private property rights?
* What is the role of the legal system?
* How does government discourage insufficient competition?
* What tools does the government use to redistribute income?

Property Rights and the Legal System

In a market economy, private individuals and firms own most of the resources. For example, when consumers buy houses, cars, or pizzas, they have purchased the right to use these goods in ways they, not someone else, see fit. These rights are called **private property rights.** Property rights are the rules of our economic game. If well-defined, property rights give individuals the incentive to use their property efficiently. That is, owners with property rights have a greater incentive to maintain, improve, and even conserve their property to preserve or increase its value.

Markets, just like baseball, need umpires. It is the government that plays this role when it defines and protects the rights of people and their property through the legal system and police protection. That is, by providing rules and regulations, government makes markets work more efficiently. Private enforcement is possible, but as economic life becomes more complex, political institutions have become the major instrument for defining and enforcing property rights.

The government defines and protects property rights through the legal system and policy protection. The legal system ensures the rights of private ownership, the enforcement of contracts, and the legal status for businesses. The legal system serves as the referee and imposes penalties on violators of our legal rules. Property rights also include intellectual property—the property rights that an owner receives through patents, copyrights, and trademarks. These rights give the owner long-term protection that encourages individuals to write books, music, and software programs and invent new products (see the In the News story on song swapping on the Net). In short, well-defined property rights encourage investment, innovation, exchange, conservation, and economic growth.

> **private property rights**
> consumers' right to use their property as they see fit

Insufficient Competition in Markets

Another justification given for government intervention is to correct cases of insufficient competition that arise in the marketplace. As we discussed in Chapter 2, monopoly, or one-supplier, situations result in higher prices and lower quantities traded than in a competitive market. When such conditions of restricted competition arise, the communication system of the marketplace is disrupted, causing the market to function inefficiently, to the detriment of consumers. For this reason, since the 1880s, the federal government has engaged in antitrust activities designed to encourage competition and discourage monopoly conditions. Specifically, the Antitrust Division of the Department of Justice and the Federal Trade Commission attempt to increase competition by attacking monopolistic practices.

Income Redistribution

Not only does the market determine what goods are going to be produced, and in what quantities, but it also determines, through the interaction of demand and supply for productive resources, the distribution of output among members of society. Some argue that the market distribution of income may produce disparities

in the news: Song Swapping on the Net

If you were a rock star, would you want to put a stop to bootlegged music on the Internet?

* Yes, it violates copyright laws and cheats the artist.
* Yes, but unlicensed music sharing is inevitable.
* No, it will only increase the size of my audience.
* No, it hurts only record companies, which charge too much anyway.

Song swapping on the Net allows you to search for almost any song you can think of, find the song on a fellow enthusiast's hard drive, and then download it for yourself, right now—for the unbeatable cost of zero, free, nada, gratis.

consider this:

Song swapping on the Net has set the stage for an interesting battle over copyright laws and intellectual property rights. Is sharing songs with others on the Internet underground piracy, or is it sharing someone's purchased possession? Is it a "personal use" right to share music online—like sharing a CD with a friend?

Napster and Grokster may be gone, but "free" music and videos are alive and well. The network is still wide open. It is a tough war to win, and the people trading music illegally online have little chance of being caught. Also, many young music lovers do not see downloading music without paying the copyright as a crime. The industry must innovate its way out. One reason that illegal downloading took off was because the industry did not keep up with the technology. The music industry continued to sell CDs and tapes when buyers had the technology to download songs.

A 2007 study by the Institute for Policy Innovation concludes that the "piracy" of recorded music costs the U.S. recording industries billions of dollars annually in lost revenue and profits. In addition, the study states that recorded music piracy costs American workers significant losses in jobs and earnings, and lost tax revenues to the government.

Incentives play an important part in this story, too. If the price is zero, the probability of being caught is close to zero, and people do not view it as illegal, then you would expect many to download music illegally rather than purchase. However, the flipside of the story is that when talented producers and artists do not get royalties for their artistic work, you will see a lot less of it—especially quality music. Incentives matter.

SOURCE: From 'Newsweek', June 5, 2000, "The Noisy War Over Napster" by Steven Levy, pp. 46, 49. Copyright © 2005 Newsweek, Inc. All rights reserved. Used by permission and protected by the Copyright Laws of the United States. The printing, copying, redistribution, or retransmission of the Material without express written permission is prohibited.

that violate a common sense of equity or fairness and government should intervene to reduce income inequality. Others argue that high incomes are a result of hard work and greater skills. They believe that higher taxes designed to redistribute income only reduce incentives to work hard, save, and invest. Ultimately, the decision on how much redistribution will occur is a normative issue. Economists can estimate the benefits and costs of these efforts, but society must decide.

Government redistributes income in three major ways: taxes, subsidies, and transfer payments. We will now briefly examine each of these methods in turn.

Taxes

In addition to being one of the primary ways that the government finances its activities, taxes are an important tool for redistributing income. Specifically, one type of tax, a progressive tax, is designed to take a larger percentage of higher incomes as compared to lower incomes. In this way, progressive taxes help to reduce income disparities. The federal income tax is an example of a progressive tax. The progressive tax and other types of taxes will be discussed in greater detail in the next section.

Government Subsidies

A second way that governments can help the less affluent is by the use of governmental revenues to provide low-cost public services. Inexpensive public housing, subsidized public transport, and even public parks are services that probably serve the poor to a greater extent than the rich. "Free" public education is viewed by many as an equalizing force in that it opens opportunities for children of less prosperous members of society to obtain the skills necessary for employment that could improve their economic status.

Transfer Payments

A third means by which income redistribution can be carried out by government is through direct transfer payments. Cash transfer payments are made by the government, particularly to the poor and aged, for which no goods or services are exchanged. Transfer payments include Social Security, unemployment compensation benefits, welfare (temporary assistance for needy families, or TANF), and veteran payments.

Noncash transfers, such as food stamps, Medicaid, school lunch programs, and housing subsidies, for example, are designed to raise the living standards of the poor.

SECTION CHECK

1. The government defines and protects property rights through the legal system and police protection.
2. Well-defined property rights encourage investment, innovation, exchange, conservation, and economic growth.
3. Government encourages competition and discourages monopoly, or one-supplier conditions, through its antitrust activities.
4. The government redistributes income through taxes, subsidies, and transfer payments.

1. Why do owners with clear property rights have incentives to use their property efficiently?
2. How does the government use taxes, subsidies, and transfer payments to redistribute income toward lower-income groups?
3. Why would the government want to prevent market conditions of insufficient competition?

SECTION 9.2 Government Spending and Taxation

- How does government finance its spending?
- On what does the public sector spend its money?
- What are progressive and regressive taxes?
- What is a flat tax?
- What is the ability to pay principle?
- What is vertical equity?
- What is the benefits received principle?
- What is a consumption tax?

Growth in Government

Government plays a large role in the economy; and its role increased markedly from 1929 to 1975, as may be seen in Exhibit 1. Although it is true that federal spending has changed little since 1960, the composition of government spending has changed considerably. National defense spending fell from roughly 9 percent of GDP in 1960 to 2.9 percent in 2000. However, the aftermath of the terrorist attacks of September 11, 2001, and the wars in Iraq and Afghanistan, led to increases in defense spending. It rose to 4.7 percent of GDP in 2009. Areas of government growth can be identified at least in part by looking at statistics on the types of government spending.

section 9.2 exhibit 1 Growth of Government Expenditures as a Percentage of GDP in the United States, 1929–2008

Government plays a large role in the economy, a role that has increased over time.

SOURCE: *Economic Report of the President*, 2009.

section 9.2 exhibit 2 — Government Expenditures

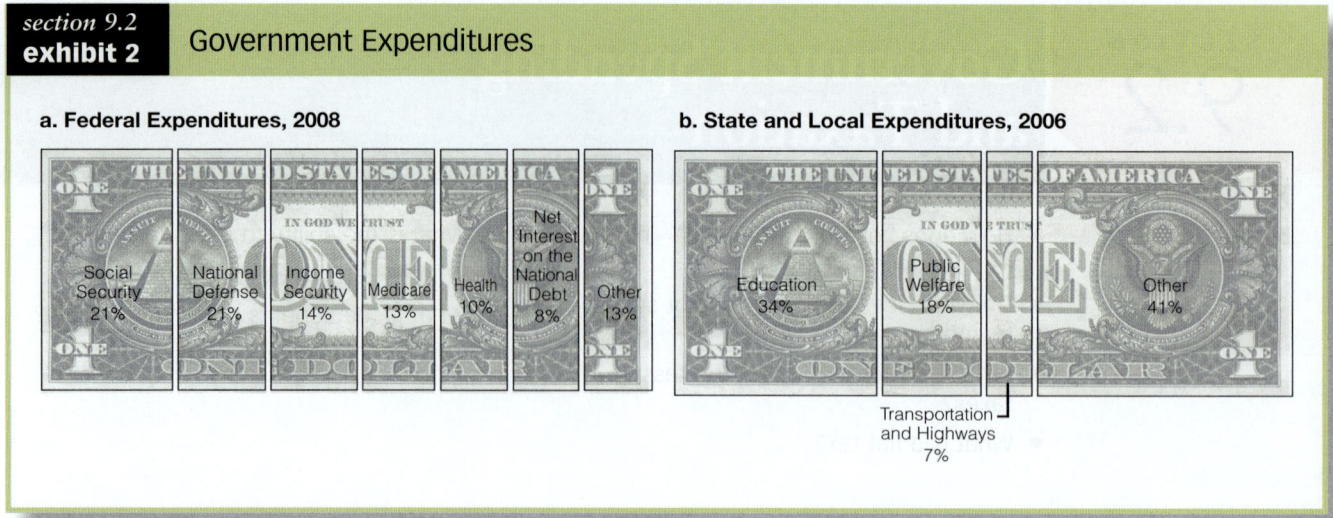

a. Federal Expenditures, 2008: Social Security 21%, National Defense 21%, Income Security 14%, Medicare 13%, Health 10%, Net Interest on the National Debt 8%, Other 13%.

b. State and Local Expenditures, 2006: Education 34%, Public Welfare 18%, Transportation and Highways 7%, Other 41%.

SOURCE: *Economic Report of the President,* 2009.

The share of GDP devoted to Social Security and Medicare rose from about 2.5 percent in 1960 to more than 7 percent today. Exhibit 2(a) shows that 35 percent of federal government spending in 2008 went to Social Security and income security programs. Another 23 percent was spent on health care and Medicare (for the elderly). The remaining federal expenditures were national defense, 21 percent; interest on the national debt, 8 percent; and miscellaneous items such as foreign aid, agriculture, transportation, and housing, 13 percent.

Exhibit 2(b) shows that state and local spending differs greatly from federal spending. Education and public welfare account for 52 percent of state and local expenditures. Other significant areas of state and local spending include highways, utilities, and police and fire protection.

Generating Government Revenue

Governments have to pay their bills like any person or institution that spends money. But how do they obtain revenue? In most years, a large majority of government activity is financed by taxation. What kinds of taxes are levied on the American population?

section 9.2 exhibit 3 — Tax Revenues

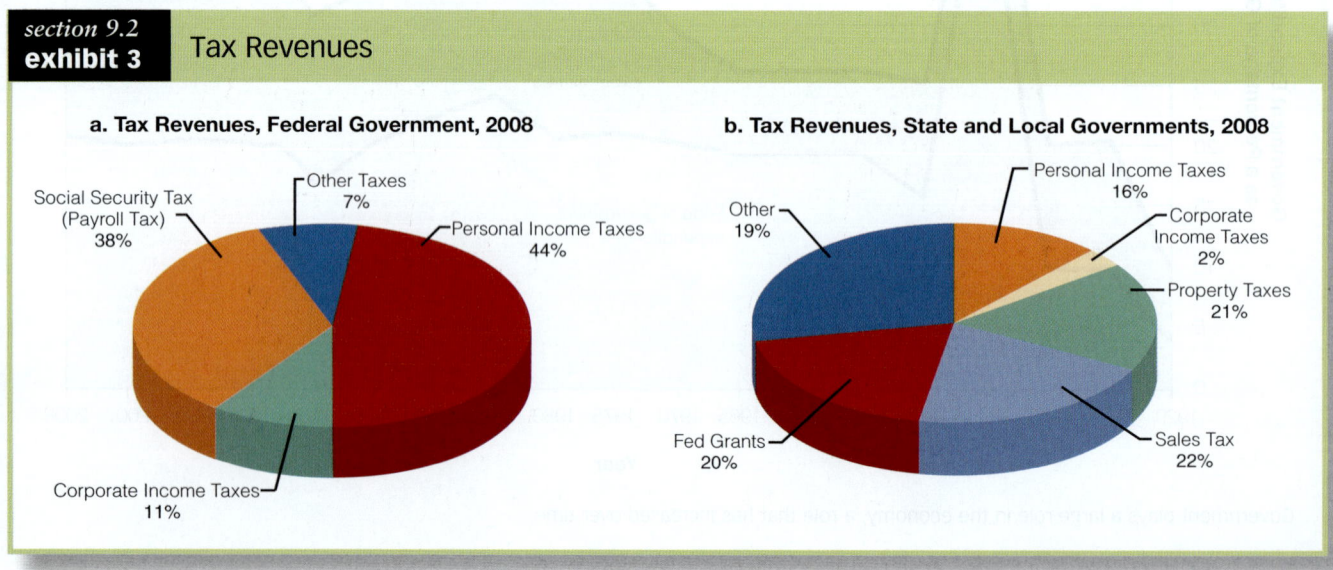

a. Tax Revenues, Federal Government, 2008: Social Security Tax (Payroll Tax) 38%, Other Taxes 7%, Personal Income Taxes 44%, Corporate Income Taxes 11%.

b. Tax Revenues, State and Local Governments, 2008: Other 19%, Personal Income Taxes 16%, Corporate Income Taxes 2%, Property Taxes 21%, Sales Tax 22%, Fed Grants 20%.

SOURCE: *Economic Report of the President and Bureau of Economic Analysis,* 2009.

At the federal level, most taxes or levies are on income. Exhibit 3 shows that 55 percent of tax revenues come in the form of income taxes on individuals and corporations, called personal income taxes and corporate income taxes, respectively. Most of the remaining revenues come from payroll taxes, which are levied on work-related income, that is, payrolls. These taxes are used to pay for Social Security and compulsory insurance plans such as Medicare. Payroll taxes are split between employees and employers. The Social Security share of federal taxes has steadily risen as the proportion of the population over age 65 has grown and as Social Security benefits have been increased. Consequently, payroll taxes have risen significantly in recent years. Other taxes, on such items as gasoline, liquor, and tobacco products, provide for a small proportion of government revenues, as do customs duties, estate and gift taxes, and some minor miscellaneous taxes and user charges.

The U.S. federal government relies more heavily on income-based taxes than nearly any other government in the world. Most other governments rely more heavily on sales taxes, excise taxes, and customs duties.

A Progressive Tax

One effect of substantial taxes on income is that the "take home" income of Americans is significantly altered by the tax system. **Progressive taxes,** of which the federal income tax is one example, are designed so that those with higher incomes pay a greater proportion of their income in taxes. A progressive tax is one tool that the government can use to redistribute income. It should be noted, however, that certain types of income are excluded from income for taxation purposes, such as interest on municipal bonds and income in kind—food stamps or Medicare, for example.

A Regressive Tax

Payroll taxes, the second most important source of income for the federal government, are actually **regressive taxes;** that is, they take a greater proportion of the income of lower-income groups than of higher-income groups. The reasons for this are simple. Social Security, for example, is imposed as a fixed proportion (now 6.2 percent on employees and an equal amount on employers) of wage and salary income up to $106,800 as of 2009. Also, wealthy persons have relatively more income from sources such as dividends and interest that

progressive tax
tax designed so that those with higher incomes pay a greater proportion of their income in taxes

regressive tax
as a person's income rises, the amount his or her tax as a proportion of income falls

excise tax
a sales tax on individual products such as alcohol, tobacco, and gasoline

are not subject to payroll taxes, and earnings above a certain level are not subject to some payroll taxes.

At first glance it appears that employers and employees split the burden of Social Security tax (called the Federal Insurance Contribution Act, or FICA). However, recall our discussion of elasticity and its burden of taxation. Most labor economists believe the labor supply curve is relatively inelastic compared to the demand curve for labor, so employers will pass on most of the tax in the form of lower wages to employees. So, if workers are relatively unresponsive to a decrease in the wage rate (they have a relatively inelastic labor supply curve), then employers can pass most of the tax on in the form of lower wages, as seen in Exhibit 4. Congress may have intended a 50-50 split on the payroll tax between workers and firms. However, we have learned that the burden of the tax does not depend whether it is levied on the buyer or the seller but rather it depends on the price elasticity of supply and demand.

An Excise Tax

Some consider an **excise tax**—a sales tax on individual products such as alcohol, tobacco, and gasoline—to be the most unfair type of tax because it is generally the most regressive. Excise taxes on specific items impose a far greater burden, as a percentage of income, on the poor and middle classes than on the wealthy, because low-income families generally spend a greater proportion of their income on these items than do high-income families.

In addition, excise taxes may lead to economic inefficiencies. By isolating a few products and subjecting them to discriminatory taxation, excise taxes subject economic choices to political manipulation, which leads to inefficiency.

Financing State and Local Government Activities

Historically, the primary source of state and local revenue has been property taxes. In recent decades, state and local governments have relied increasingly on sales and income taxes for revenues (see Exhibit 3). Today, sales taxes account for roughly 19 percent of revenues, property taxes account for 17 percent, and personal and corporate income taxes account for another 14 percent. Approximately 22 percent of state and local revenues come from the federal government

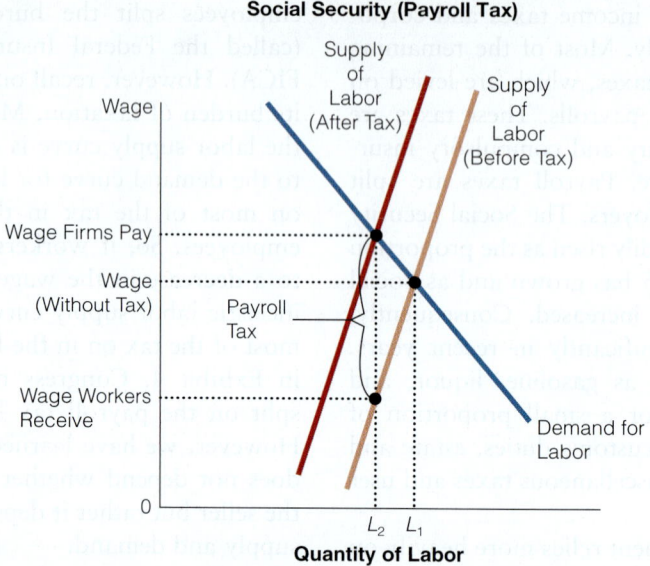

section 9.2 exhibit 4 Payroll Tax

A payroll (FICA) tax puts "a wedge" between the wage firms pay and the wage workers receive. The wedge does not depend on whether the tax was imposed on the buyers or sellers. But the effects depend on elasticity of supply and demand. If, as most labor economists believe the supply of labor is less elastic than the demand for labor. The worker (not the firm) bears most of the burden of the payroll tax.

as grants. The remaining share of revenues comes from license fees and user charges (e.g., payment for utilities, occupational license fees, tuition fees) and other taxes.

Should We Have a Flat Tax?

Some politicians and individuals believe that we should scrap the current progressive income tax and replace it with a **flat tax.** A flat tax, also called a proportional tax, is designed so that everybody would be charged the same percentage of their income. How would a flat tax work? What do you think would be the advantages and disadvantages of a flat tax?

With a flat tax, a household could simply report its income, multiply it by the tax rate, and send in the money. Because no deductions are involved, the form could be a simple page! But most flat tax proposals call for exempting income to a certain level—say, the poverty line.

Actually, if the flat tax plan allowed individuals to deduct a standard allowance of, say, $20,000 from their wages, the tax would still be progressive. Here's how it would work: If you were earning less than $20,000 a year, you would not have to pay any income taxes.

flat tax
a tax that charges all income earners the same percentage of their income

However, if you earned $50,000 a year, and the flat tax rate was 15 percent, after subtracting your $20,000 allowance you would be paying taxes on $30,000. In this system, you would have to pay $4,500 in taxes (0.15 × $30,000) and your average tax rate would be 9 percent ($4,500/$50,000 = 0.09). Now, say you made $100,000 a year. After taking your $20,000 allowance, you would have to pay a 15 percent tax on $80,000, and you would owe the government $12,000. Notice, however, that your average tax rate would be higher: 12 percent ($12,000/$100,000 = 0.12) as opposed to 9 percent. So if the flat tax system allows individual taxpayers to take a standard allowance, like most flat tax proposals, then the tax is actually progressive. That is, lower- and middle-income families will pay, on average, a smaller average tax rate, even though everyone has the same tax rate over the stipulated allowance.

The advantages of the flat tax are that all of the traditional exemptions, like entertainment deductions, mortgage interest deductions, business travel expenses, and charitable contribution deductions, would be out the door, along with the possibilities of abuses and misrepresentations that go with tax deductions. Taxpayers could fill out tax returns in the way they did in the old days, in a space about the size of a postcard. Advocates

in the news: Social Security: A Ponzi Scheme?

The offer to double your money in 90 days seemed too good to be true. But once the first people to sign up were paid the promised return on their investment, more and more punters queued up in Boston to put their money into the "Securities Exchange Company." Charles Ponzi had devised a classic fraud: extravagant payouts to the first investors were easily financed by the growing numbers of those who followed. But not indefinitely. Once the fraud was uncovered in 1920, Ponzi was sent to jail.

Fifteen years later the American president of the day, Franklin Roosevelt, signed the law establishing Social Security, the name America gives to its public pension system. The first pensioner to benefit was Ida May Fuller, a spinster from Vermont, who had paid the grand sum of $24.75 in contributions. Her first monthly Social Security check in January 1940 was for almost as much. Miss Fuller lived to be 100 and received benefits totaling $22,889.

As it happens, the pension scheme that proved so beneficial to Miss Fuller relies on much the same principle as the Ponzi scam. America's Social Security scheme is the pay-as-you-go [PAYG] sort in which today's workers pay for today's pensioners. The first few generations of pensioners received much more in benefits than they had paid in contributions. These windfall gains arguably continued until quite recently because the PAYG system was extended to cover more and more workers, and contribution rates kept going up.

Paul Samuelson, a Nobel-prize-winning economist, pinpointed the Ponzi characteristics of pay-as-you-go pensions back in 1967. "The beauty of social insurance is that it is actuarially unsound. Everyone who reaches retirement age is given benefit privileges that far exceed anything he has paid in. . . . Always there are more youths than old folks in a growing population. More important, with real incomes growing at some 3% a year, the taxable base upon which benefits rest in any period are much greater than the taxes paid historically by the generation now retired. . . . A growing nation is the greatest Ponzi game ever contrived."

Prosperous Ponzi

After the second world war, politicians in most developed countries joined in the game with gusto. In the 1960s and 1970s, they made state PAYG pensions even more unsound by introducing big hikes in benefits. To this day, PAYG schemes remain the main form of pension provision the world over. They are especially important in the EU, where they account for nearly 90% of total pension income. Even in Britain, where the PAYG scheme is much less generous than in most of continental Europe, it accounts for 60% of total pension income.

Yet all the while the foundations of PAYG schemes were being undermined. As Mr. Samuelson had pointed out, the underlying return from this kind of pension comes from the growth in the workforce and its real earnings. But in the 1970s, the post-war baby boom gave way to a baby bust that put an end to the indefinite prospect of "more youths than old folks." Besides, those "old folks" were living longer because of an unprecedented rise in life expectancy at older ages. At the same time the postwar surge in productivity and hence real wages gave way to much more pedestrian growth rates.

What has saved PAYG schemes so far is that demographic developments take a long time to work their way through the system. The schemes are still benefiting from the large number of post-war baby boomers in the working-age population, most of whom won't reach retirement for another decade or so.

(continued)

in the news: Social Security: A Ponzi Scheme? (cont.)

Today's problems arise largely from overgenerous increases in pension benefits that have already pushed contribution rates to the limit.

The worst is yet to come. Over the next 30 years, western populations will age at a record rate. The ratio of the over-65s to those aged 20–64 will double. Japan's working-age population, already declining, will shrink drastically. Something will have to give. Either benefits must halve in relation to average incomes; or contribution rates—already oppressively high in many countries—must double; or the retirement age must go up.

If governments were to leave matters as they are, they would eventually have to borrow to bridge the gap between future pension outlays and tax revenue. . . .

consider this:

Rumor has it that most young people believe that there is a greater chance that they will see an unidentified flying object (UFO) in their lifetime than a Social Security payment.

We are often told that Social Security is a retirement program. However, it is really a tax plan that transfers money from workers to the elderly. Social Security is a pay-as-you-go system—payments to current retirees are derived from payroll taxes imposed on current workers.

SOURCE: From "Snares and Delusions", 'The Economist', February 14, 2002 © The Economist Newspaper Limited, London 2002. Reprinted with permission.

The Social Security Trust Fund is slowly going broke, and if it is not fixed, it is predicted to go belly up by 2037 (and some say serious problems could occur as soon as 2016). At that point, retirees would only get 75 percent of their promised benefits. The problem is that many baby boomers will begin to retire in the next several years, and simply not enough workers are contributing part of their incomes to pay for these new retirees. Currently, the system has 3.3 workers for each Social Security beneficiary. By 2031, that ratio changes to only an estimated 2.2 workers for each beneficiary. In addition, demographers' forecasts of declining birth rates and longer life expectancies only make matters worse.

In 1940, the life expectancy of a 65-year-old was 12.5 years; today it is 17.5 years. According to the Social Security Administration, in 30 years, the number of older Americans will be nearly twice what it is today—an increase from 36 million to almost 74 million in 2034. Another serious problem stems from indexing initial benefits to wages rather than prices. Wages rise almost 1 percent per year faster than prices. According to Greg Mankiw, former chair of the Council of Economic Advisers, "A person, with average wages, retiring at age 65 this year gets an annual benefit of about $14,000, but a similar person retiring in 2050 is scheduled to get over $20,000 in today's dollars. In other words, even after adjusting for inflation, a typical person's benefits are scheduled to rise by over 40 percent."

argue that the government could collect the same amount of tax revenues, but the tax would be much more efficient, as many productive resources would be released from looking for tax loopholes to doing something productive from society's standpoint.

Of course, some versions of the flat tax will hurt certain groups. Not surprisingly, realtors and homeowners, who like the mortgage interest deductions, and tax accountants, who make billions every year preparing tax returns, will not be supportive of a flat tax with no deductions. And, of course, many legitimate questions would inevitably arise, such as: What would happen to the size of charitable contributions if the charitable contribution deduction was eliminated? And how much will the housing sector be hurt if the mortgage interest deduction was eliminated or phased out? After all, the government's intent of the tax break was to increase home ownership. And the deductions for hybrid cars are intended to get drivers into cleaner, more fuel-efficient cars. These deductions could be gone in most flat tax proposals. In addition, the critics of the flat tax believe that the tax is not progressive enough to eliminate the inequities in income and are skeptical of the tax-revenue–raising capabilities of a flat tax.

Taxes: Efficiency and Equity

In the last few chapters, we talked about efficiency—getting the most out of our scarce resources. However, taxes for the most part are *not* efficient (except for internalizing externalities and providing public goods) because they change incentives and distort the values that buyers and sellers place on goods and services. That is, decisions made by buyers and sellers are different from what they would be without the tax. Taxes can be inefficient because they may lead to less work, less saving, less investment, and lower output.

Economists spend a lot of time on issues of efficiency, but policymakers (and economists) are also concerned about other goals, such as fairness. Income redistribution through taxation may also lead to greater productivity for low-income workers through improvements in health and education. Even though what is fair to one person may not be fair to another, most people would agree that we should have a fair tax system based on either ability to pay or benefits received.

Ability to Pay Principle and Vertical Equity The **ability to pay principle** is simply that those with the greatest ability to pay taxes (richer people) should pay more than those with the least ability to pay taxes (poorer people). This concept is known as **vertical equity**—people with different levels of income should be treated differently. The federal income tax is a good example of the ability to pay principle because the rich pay a larger percentage of their income in taxes. That is, high-income individuals will pay a higher percentage of their income in taxes than low-income individuals. The richest 20 percent of households in the United States make slightly more than 60 percent of the income but pay roughly 85 percent of the federal income tax; the poorest 40 percent actually have a negative tax (many in the group receive tax credits). When you add payroll taxes (Social Security) and Medicare, the tax system becomes less progressive than the federal income tax: 40 percent of the low-income taxpayers pay about 3 percent and the

ability to pay principle
belief that those with the greatest ability to pay taxes should pay more than those with less ability to pay

vertical equity
different treatment based on level of income and the ability to pay principle

---

Use what you've LEARNED
THE BURDEN OF THE CORPORATE INCOME TAX

Corporate income taxes are generally popular among voters because they think the tax comes from the corporation. Of course, it does write the check to the IRS, but that does not mean that the corporation (and its stockholders) bears the burden of the tax. Some of the tax burden (perhaps a great deal) is passed on to consumers in the form of higher prices. It will also impact investors' rates of return. Less investment leads to less capital for workers which lowers workers' productivity and wages. The key here is to be careful to distinguish between who pays the tax and who incurs the burden of the tax.

POLICY application: A CONSUMPTION TAX?

Some economists believe the current system of taxation creates a disincentive to save. They would replace the income tax with a **consumption tax**: that is, tax the amount that is spent rather than what is earned. Under a consumption tax, saved income is not taxed. Europeans tax consumption more than the United States. Former chair of the Federal Reserve, Alan Greenspan, encouraged policymakers to look at consumption taxes rather than income taxes because of its positive impact on saving and capital formation.

The theory behind a consumption tax is that people are taxed based on what they take out of the economy, not on what they put in. The reason: When they save and invest, those dollars add to the capital stock and raise workers' productivity. A consumption tax, such as a sales tax, provides more incentive to save and invest than does an income tax. Saving provides the funds that business uses to engage in investment, which in turn leads to more capital stock, greater output and productivity, and higher real wages.

According to UC Berkeley economist, Alan Auerbach, a consumption tax could raise the same amount of revenue as the current tax system and increase GDP by 9 percent in the long run, as production increases with increased saving and capital formation.

consumption tax tax collected based on a taxpayer's spending

SOURCE: Alan Auerbach, "A Consumption Tax," *Wall Street Journal*, August 25, 2005.

> **consider this:**
>
> Although many economists believe that a consumption tax is a good idea, the transition from an income tax to a consumption tax would be challenging. Others argue that low-income individuals save a small percentage of their income and spend a large fraction of their income, so they would benefit little from a consumption tax. Moving from an income tax to a consumption tax would also shift tax burdens to older generations that would have to pay a consumption tax on spending with income on which they had already paid income taxes. In addition, individual retirement accounts (IRAs) are already similar to a consumption tax. With IRA accounts, taxpayers can put a limited amount of their savings away and not have it taxed until retirement.

top 20 percent of income earners pay slightly less than 70 percent. Sales taxes are not a good example of the ability to pay principle, because low-income individuals pay a larger percentage of their income in such taxes.

Benefits Received Principle

The *benefits received principle* means that the individuals receiving the benefits are those who pay for them. Take the gasoline tax: the more miles one drives on the highway, the more gasoline used and the more taxes collected. The tax revenues are then used to maintain the highways. Or those who benefit from a new airport or an opera house should be the ones who pay for such public spending. Although this principle may work for some private goods, it does not work well for public goods such as national defense and the judicial system. Because we collectively consume national defense, it is not possible to find out who benefits and by exactly how much.

Administration Burden of Taxation

The administration burden of the income tax also leads to another deadweight loss. Imagine if everyone filled out a one-page tax form that took no more than 5 minutes. Instead the opportunity cost of the hours of time and services used in tax preparation is in the billions of dollars. The government also spends a great deal to enforce these taxes. A simplified tax system would reduce the deadweight loss.

Social Policy of Taxes

Taxes and subsidies can be efficiency enhancing when used to correct for externalities. For example, the government may view it as good social policy to subsidize cleaner, more efficient hybrid vehicles. Or they may want to put a high tax on cigarettes in an attempt to reduce teen smoking. In other words, taxes on alcohol and cigarettes may be used to discourage these activities—sometimes we call these "sin taxes."

SECTION CHECK

1. Over a third of federal spending goes toward pensions and income security programs.
2. A progressive tax takes a greater proportion of the income of higher-income groups than of lower-income groups.
3. A regressive tax takes a greater proportion of the income of lower-income groups than of higher-income groups.
4. A flat tax charges all income earners the same percentage of their income.
5. The ability to pay principle is the belief that those with the greatest ability to pay taxes should pay more than those with less ability.
6. Vertical equity is the concept that people with different levels of income should be treated differently.
7. The benefits received principle means that individuals receiving the benefits are those who pay for them.
8. A consumption tax is a tax collected based on the taxpayer's spending.

---

1. Has federal government spending as a fraction of GDP changed much since the 1960s?
2. What finances the majority of federal government spending?
3. What happens to the proportion of income paid as taxes when income rises, for a progressive tax? What is an example of such a progressive tax?
4. Why are excise taxes on items such as alcohol, tobacco, and gasoline considered regressive taxes?
5. How could a flat tax also be a progressive tax?
6. Why is the federal income tax an example of the ability to pay principle?
7. How is a gas tax an example of the benefits received principle?

SECTION 9.3 Public Choice

* What is public choice theory?
* What is the median voter model?
* What is rational ignorance?
* Why do special interest groups arise?

When the market fails, as in the case of an externality or public good, it may be necessary for the government to intervene and make public choices. However, it is possible for government actions in response to externalities to make matters worse. That is, just because markets have failed to generate efficient results does not necessarily mean that government can do a better job—see Exhibit 1. One explanation for this outcome is presented by public choice theory.

behavior of individuals in politics, as in the marketplace, will be influenced by self-interest. Bureaucrats, politicians, and voters make choices that they believe will yield them expected marginal benefits that will be greater than their expected marginal costs. Of course, the private sector and the public sector differ when it comes to the "rules of the game" that they must follow. The self-interest assumption is, however, central to the analysis of behavior in both arenas.

What Is Public Choice Theory?

Public choice theory is the application of economic principles to politics. Public choice economists believe that government actions are an outgrowth of individual behavior. Specifically, they assume that the

Scarcity and the Public Sector

The self-interest assumption is not the only similarity between the market and public sectors. For example, scarcity is present in the public sector as well as in the private sector. Public schools and public libraries come at the

section 9.3 exhibit 1	Do People in Government Waste Tax Money? 1970–2004 (percent of population agreeing)																	
	'70	'72	'74	'76	'78	'80	'82	'84	'86	'88	'90	'92	'94	'96	'98	'00	'02	'04
A Lot	69	66	74	74	77	78	66	65	**	63	67	67	70	59	61	59	48	61
Some	26	30	22	20	19	18	29	29	**	33	30	30	27	39	34	38	49	37
Not Very Much	4	2	1	3	2	2	2	4	**	2	2	2	2	1	4	3	3	2
Don't Know	1	2	2	3	2	2	3	2	**	2	1	1	1	0	1	1	0	1

**No data available for 1986 and 2006.

SOURCE: The American National Election Studies, 2009, http://www.electionstudies.org.

expense of something else. Competition is also present in the public sector, as different government agencies compete for government funds and lobbyists compete with each other to get favored legislation through Congress.

The Individual Consumption-Payment Link

In private markets, when a shopper goes to the supermarket to purchase groceries, the shopping cart is filled with many different goods that the consumer presumably wants and is willing to pay for; the shopping cart reflects the individual consumption-payment link. The link breaks down when an assortment of political goods is decided on by majority rule. These political goods might include such items as additional national defense, additional money for the space program, new museums, new public schools, increased foreign aid, and so on. Even though an individual may be willing to pay for some of these goods, it is unlikely that she will want to consume or pay for everything placed in the political shopping cart. However, if the majority decides that these political goods are important, the individual will have to purchase the goods through higher taxes, whether she values the goods or not.

Majority Rule and the Median Voters

In a two-party system, the candidate with the most votes wins the election. Because voters are likely to vote for the candidate who holds views similar to theirs, candidates must pay close attention to the preferences of the majority of voters.

For example, in Exhibit 2, we assume a normal distribution, with a continuum of voter preferences from the liberal left to the conservative right. We can see from the figure that only a few are extremely liberal or extremely conservative. A successful campaign would have to address the concerns of the median voters (those in the middle of the distribution in Exhibit 2), resulting in moderate policies. For example, if one candidate ran a fairly conservative campaign, attracting voters at and to the right of V_1, an opponent could win by a landslide by taking a fairly conservative position just to the left of this candidate. Alternatively, if the candidate takes a liberal position, say V_2, then the

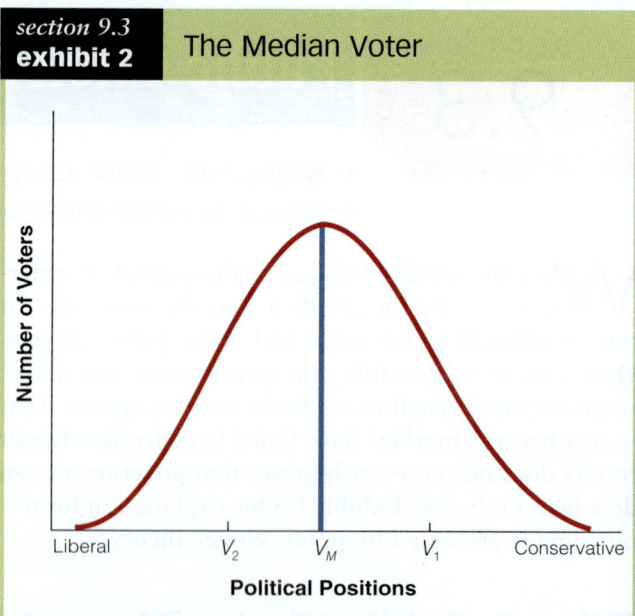

section 9.3 exhibit 2 — The Median Voter

The median voter model predicts a strong tendency for both candidates to pick a position in the middle of the distribution, such as V_M, and that the election will be close.

Is this person selecting the items she wants? Do taxpayers always want what they have to pay for?

opponent can win by campaigning just to the right of that position. In this case, it is easy to see that the candidate who takes the median position, V_M, is least likely to be defeated. Of course, the distribution does not have to be normal or symmetrical; it could be skewed to the right or left. Regardless of the distribution, however, the successful candidate will still seek out the median voters. In fact, the **median voter model** predicts a strong tendency for both candidates to choose a position in the middle of distribution, and therefore the election will be close.

Of course, this model does not mean that all politicians will find or even attempt to find the median. Politicians, for example, may take different positions because they have arrived at different predictions of voter preferences or have merely misread public sentiment; or they may think they have the charisma to change voter preferences.

median voter model a model that predicts candidates will choose a position in the middle of the distribution

rational ignorance lack of incentive to be informed

Voters and Rational Ignorance

Representative democracy provides a successful mechanism for making social choices in many countries. But some important differences are evident in the way democracy is ideally supposed to work and how it actually works.

One of the keys to an efficiently working democracy is a concerned and informed electorate. Everyone is supposed to take time to study the issues and candidates and then carefully weigh the relevant information before deciding how to vote. Although an informed citizenry is desirable from a social point of view, it is not clear that individuals will find it personally desirable to become politically informed.

Obtaining detailed information about issues and candidates is costly. Many issues are complicated, and a great deal of technical knowledge and information is necessary to make an informed judgment on them. To find out what candidates are really going to do requires a lot more than listening to their campaign slogans. It requires studying their past voting records, reading a great deal that has been written either by or about them, and asking them questions at public meetings. Taking the time and trouble to do these things—and more—is the cost that each eligible voter has to pay personally for the benefits of being politically informed. These costs may help to explain why the majority of Americans cannot identify their congressional representatives and are unlikely to be acquainted with their representatives' views on Social Security, health care, tariffs, and agricultural policies.

For many people the costs of becoming politically informed are high, whereas the benefits are low. As a result, they limit their quest for political information to listening to the radio on the way to work, talking with friends, casual reading, and other things they would normally do anyway. Even though most people in society might be better off if everyone became more informed, it isn't worth the cost for most individuals to make the requisite effort to become informed themselves. Public choice economists refer to this lack of incentive to become informed as **rational ignorance**. People will generally make much more informed decisions as buyers than as voters. For example, you are likely to gather more information when making a decision on a car purchase than when you are deciding between candidates in an upcoming election. An uninformed decision on a car purchase will most likely affect your life much more than an uninformed decision on a candidate, especially when your vote will most likely not alter the outcome of the election.

The fact that one vote, especially in a state or national election, is highly unlikely to affect the outcome of the election may explain why some citizens choose not to vote. Many factors may determine the net benefits for voting, including candidates and issues on the ballot, weather, and distance to the polling booths. For example, we would certainly expect fewer voters to turn out at the polls on the day of a blizzard; the blizzard would change the net benefits. We would also expect more voters at the polls if the election were predicted to be a close one, with emotions running higher and voter perception that their individual vote is more significant.

If the cost of being an informed voter is high and the benefits low, why do people vote? Many people vote for reasons other than to affect the outcome of the election. They vote because they believe in the democratic process and because of civic pride. In other words, they perceive that the benefits they derive from being involved in the political process outweigh the costs.

Furthermore, rational ignorance does not imply that people should not vote; it is merely one explanation for why some people do not vote. The point that public choice economists are making is that some people will vote only if they think that their vote will make a difference; otherwise, they will not vote.

special interest groups groups with an intense interest in particular voting issues that may be different from that of the general public

Special Interest Groups

Even though many voters may be uninformed about specific issues, others may feel a strong need to be politically informed. Such individuals may be motivated to organize a **special interest group.** These groups may have intense feelings about and a degree of interest in particular issues that is at variance with the general public. However, as a group these individuals are more likely to influence decision makers and have a far greater impact on the outcome of a political decision than they would with their individual votes.

If a special interest group is successful in getting everyone else to pay for a project that benefits them, the cost will be spread over so large a number of taxpayers that the amount any one person will have to pay is negligible. Hence, the motivation for an individual citizen to spend the necessary time and effort to resist an interest group is minimal, even if she had a guarantee that this resistance would be effective.

For example, many taxpayers and consumers are unaware of the federal subsidy to sugar growers. The subsidy is estimated to cost consumers more than $1 billion a year, which is less than $5 per person. However, the gain from the subsidy is estimated to be over $100,000 per sugar grower. At that price, few customers are going to invest the time and money to fight this issue. However, the effort to keep the subsidy is surely enough to get sugar growers to make trips to Washington, D.C., and help in political campaigns.

SECTION CHECK

1. Public choice theory holds that the behavior of individuals in politics, as in the marketplace, is influenced by self-interest.
2. The median voter model predicts that a candidate will choose a position in the middle of the distribution.
3. Rational ignorance is the condition in which voters tend to be relatively uninformed about political issues because of the high information costs and low benefits of being politically informed.
4. A special interest group is a political pressure group formed by individuals with a common political objective.
5. Special interest groups are more likely to have an impact on the outcome of a social decision than their members would if they voted individually.

---

1. What principles does the public choice analysis of government behavior share with the economic analysis of market behavior?
2. Why is the tendency strong for candidates to choose positions in the middle of the distribution of voter preferences?
3. Why is it rational to be relatively less informed about most political choices than about your own market choices?
4. Why can't the majority of citizens effectively counter the political power of special interest groups?

Interactive Chapter Summary

Fill in the blanks:

1. _____ are the rules of our economic game.
2. Government redistributes income in three ways: _____, _____, and _____.
3. The market mechanism does not always assure fulfillment of some macroeconomic goals: _____, _____, and _____.
4. Governments obtain revenue through two major avenues: _____ and _____.
5. The government share of GDP changed _____ between 1970 and 2000, but its composition has changed _____.
6. From 1968 to 2005, national defense spending as a fraction of GDP _____.
7. By the mid-1970s, for the first time in history, roughly half of government spending in the United States was for _____.
8. Income transfer payments _____ in the 1980s and 1990s.
9. _____ and _____ account for roughly half of state and local government expenditures.
10. At the federal level, _____ half of taxes are from personal income taxes and corporate income taxes.
11. The United State relies _____ heavily on income-based taxes than most other developed countries in the world.
12. If a higher-income person paid the same taxes as a lower-income person, that tax would be considered _____.
13. Excise taxes are considered regressive because lower-income people spend a _____ fraction of their incomes on such taxes than do higher-income people.
14. Sales taxes account for _____ state and local tax revenue than property taxes.
15. Most people agree that the tax system should be based on either _____ or _____.
16. When people with different levels of income are treated differently, it is called _____ equity.
17. Federal income tax is a good example of the _____ principle.
18. The _____ principle means that the individuals receiving the benefits are those who pay for them.
19. The _____ burden of a tax leads to a deadweight loss.
20. With a _____ tax, individuals are taxed on what they take out of the economy, not on what they put in.
21. Public choice theory is the application of _____ principles to politics.
22. Public choice economists believe that the behavior of individuals in politics, as in the marketplace, will be influenced by _____.
23. The amount of information that is necessary to make an efficient decision is much _____ in political markets than in private markets.
24. In private markets, an individual _____ link indicates that the goods consumers get reflect what they are willing to pay for.
25. Even though actors in both the private and public sectors are _____, the _____ are different.

26. A successful political campaign would have to address the concerns of the _____ voters.

27. _____ implies that most private-sector buyers will tend to be more informed than voters on a given issue.

28. If voters were _____ informed, special-interest groups would have less influence on political results, other things being equal.

29. Compared to private-sector decisions, acquiring information to make public-sector decisions will tend to have _____ benefits and _____ costs.

30. _____ positions tend to win in elections decided by majority votes.

Answers: 1. Property rights 2. taxes; subsidies; transfer payments 3. full employment; stable prices; economic growth 4. taxation; borrowing 5. little; considerably 6. fell 7. social concerns 8. increased 9. Education; public welfare 10. more than 11. more 12. regressive 13. larger 14. more 15. ability to pay; benefits received 16. vertical 17. ability to pay 18. benefits received 19. administrative 20. consumption 21. economic 22. self-interest 23. greater 24. consumption-payment 25. self-interested; "rules of the game" 26. median 27. Rational ignorance 28. more 29. smaller; larger 30. Middle-of-the-road

Key Terms and Concepts

private property rights 234
progressive tax 239
regressive tax 239
excise tax 239

flat tax 240
ability to pay principle 243
vertical equity 243
consumption tax 244

median voter model 247
rational ignorance 247
special interest groups 248

Section Check Answers

9.1 Other Functions of Government

1. **Why do owners with clear property rights have incentives to use their property efficiently?**

   Private property rights mean that owners will capture the benefits and bear the costs of their choices with regard to their property, making it in their self-interest to use it efficiently, in ways for which the benefits are expected to exceed the costs.

2. **How does the government use taxes, subsidies, and transfer payments to redistribute income toward lower-income groups?**

   Taxes, particularly progressive ones such as the individual income tax, are borne more heavily by higher-income citizens than lower-income citizens, while most subsidy and transfer payment programs are primarily focused on lower-income citizens.

3. **Why would the government want to prevent market conditions of insufficient competition?**

   When there is insufficient or restricted competition, outputs are lower and prices paid by consumers are higher than they would be with more effective competition. By encouraging competition and discouraging monopoly, then, consumers can benefit.

9.2 Government Spending and Taxation

1. **Has federal government spending as a fraction of GDP changed much since the 1960s?**

   Overall federall government spending as a fraction of GDP has not changed much since the 1960s. However, the composition of federal government spending has changed, with substantial decreases in national defense spending and substantial increases in income security spending, such as for Social Security and Medicare.

2. **What finances the majority of federal government spending?**

   The majority of federal government spending is financed by taxes on personal and corporate incomes, although payroll taxes have risen substantially in recent years.

3. **What happens to the proportion of income paid as taxes when income rises, for a progressive tax? What is an example of such a progressive tax?**

   A progressive tax is one that takes an increasing proportion of income as income rises. The personal income tax is an example because higher-income earners pay a larger proportion of their incomes than lower-income earners.

4. **Why are excise taxes on items such as alcohol, tobacco, and gasoline considered regressive taxes?**

   Lower-income people pay a larger fraction of their incomes for such items, so that they pay a larger fraction of their incomes for taxes on those items, even though all users pay the same tax rate on them.

5. **How could a flat tax also be a progressive tax?**

   With a standard allowance or deduction amount, a proportional tax on taxable income would represent a larger fraction of total income for a high-income earner than for a low-income earner.

6. **Why is the federal income tax an example of the ability to pay principle?**

   Higher-income people, with a greater ability to pay, pay a larger fraction of their income in taxes.

7. **How is a gas tax an example of the benefits received principle?**

   Those who drive more benefit more from the highway system, but they also pay more in total gasoline taxes.

9.3 Public Choice

1. **What principles does the public choice analysis of government behavior share with the economic analysis of market behavior?**

   Public choice analysis of government behavior is based on the principle that the behavior of individuals in politics, just like that in the marketplace, is influenced by self-interest. That is, it applies basic economic theory to politics, looking for differences in incentives to explain people's behavior.

2. **Why is the tendency strong for candidates to choose positions in the middle of the distribution of voter preferences?**

   This is what we would predict from the median voter model, because the candidate closer to the median is likely to attract a majority of the votes.

3. **Why is it rational to be relatively less informed about most political choices than about your own market choices?**

   It is rational to be relatively less informed about most political choices because the costs of becoming more informed about political issues tend to be higher and the benefits of becoming more informed about political choices tend to be lower than for your own market choices.

4. **Why can't the majority of citizens effectively counter the political power of special interest groups?**

   The majority of citizens can't effectively counter the political power of special interest groups because even if a special interest group is successful in getting everyone else to pay for a project that benefits that group, the cost to each citizen will be small. In fact, this cost is very likely to be far smaller than the cost to a member of the majority of becoming sufficiently informed and active to successfully oppose it.

CHAPTER 9 STUDY GUIDE

True or False:

1. Government spending as a percentage of GDP has changed little since 1970, but the composition of government spending has changed considerably.
2. The composition of state and local spending is different from that of federal spending.
3. A large majority of government activity is financed by borrowing.
4. Neither the composition of U.S. federal government spending nor its share of GDP has changed much since 1970.
5. Taxpayers in other parts of the developed world have heavier tax burdens than those in the United States.
6. Taxes on gasoline, liquor, and tobacco products provide a substantial portion of federal tax revenues.
7. The share of federal taxes going to Social Security and Medicare has risen significantly in recent years.
8. Most other countries rely less heavily on income-based taxes than the United States.
9. If a higher-income person pays more in total taxes than a lower-income person, those taxes would be considered progressive.
10. Excise taxes, such as those on alcohol, tobacco, and gasoline, tend to be the most regressive taxes.
11. Excise taxes can lead to economic inefficiency.
12. A larger share of state and local government revenues are from the federal government in grants than from state and local personal and corporate income taxes.
13. For the most part taxes are inefficient because they change incentives and alter the true value buyers and sellers place on goods and services.
14. Most taxes provide incentives for individuals to work hard, save, and invest.
15. The ability to pay principle states that those with the least ability to pay taxes should pay more than those with the greatest ability to pay taxes.
16. The gasoline tax is a good example of the benefits received principle.
17. In public choice analysis, bureaucrats, politicians, and voters are assumed to make choices that they believe will yield to the public expected marginal benefits greater than their expected marginal costs.
18. Scarcity and competition are present in the public sector as well as in the private sector.
19. The individual consumption-payment link breaks down when goods are decided on by majority rule.
20. The median voter result implies that when those with extreme political views become more extreme, it will have a large effect on the majority voting outcome.
21. The majority of Americans cannot identify their congressional representatives.
22. The benefits of casting a well-informed vote are generally far greater than the cost of doing so for most voters.
23. An election that is expected to be close would tend to increase voter turnout.

Multiple Choice:

1. Which of the following are important roles of the government?
    a. protecting property rights
    b. providing a legal system
    c. intervention when insufficient competition occurs in the marketplace
    d. promoting stability and economic growth
    e. all of the above

2. Social Security and Medicare are financed by
   a. personal income taxes.
   b. payroll taxes.
   c. excise taxes.
   d. corporation income taxes.
   e. none of the above taxes.

3. Who must legally pay Social Security and Medicare taxes?
   a. employers
   b. employees
   c. both employers and employees
   d. neither employers nor employees

4. Expenditures on _____ comprise the largest component of state and local government budgets.
   a. education
   b. public safety
   c. public infrastructure (such as roads and water works)
   d. public welfare (such as food stamps and income supplemental programs)

5. _____ taxes are designed to take a larger percentage of high incomes as compared to lower incomes.
   a. Progressive
   b. Regressive
   c. Proportional
   d. Negative

6. An example of a proportional tax would be
   a. a state sales tax.
   b. a local property tax.
   c. a flat rate income tax.
   d. the current U.S. income tax.

7. The largest single source of revenue for the federal government is the
   a. corporate income tax.
   b. federal excise tax.
   c. personal income tax.
   d. Social Security tax.

8. Which is the largest single component of federal expenditures?
   a. interest on the national debt
   b. defense spending
   c. Social Security
   d. foreign aid

9. The U.S. federal income tax is an example of a
   a. progressive tax.
   b. proportional tax.
   c. regressive tax.
   d. value-added tax.

10. The gasoline tax is an example of
    a. progressive taxation.
    b. neutral taxation.
    c. proportional taxation.
    d. regressive taxation.

11. The ability to pay principle states:
    a. Those with the greatest ability to pay taxes should pay more.
    b. Those with the least ability to pay taxes should pay more.
    c. Individuals receiving the benefits should pay for them.
    d. All of the above are true.

12. The amount of information that is necessary to make an efficient choice is generally _____ in the public sector than in the private sector.
    a. less
    b. more
    c. the same
    d. None of the above is true.
13. Voters will tend to be _____ informed about their political choices than their private market choices, other things being equal.
    a. more
    b. equally
    c. less
    d. Any of the above are equally likely to be true.
14. The median voter result implies that
    a. elections will often be very close.
    b. elections will usually be landslides for the same party year after year.
    c. elections will usually be landslides, with victories alternating between parties each year.
    d. when the preferences of most voters change substantially, winning political positions will also tend to change.
    e. both a and d are true.
15. For a voter to become more informed on a political issue is likely to have _____ benefits and _____ costs than for similar market decisions, other things being equal.
    a. smaller; larger
    b. smaller; smaller
    c. larger; larger
    d. larger; smaller
16. Which of the following would tend to raise voter turnout?
    a. a blizzard or heavy rainstorm on election day
    b. an election that is expected to be a landslide
    c. the longer the wait is expected to be at the voting locations
    d. a feeling that the candidates are basically running on the same platforms
    e. None of the above would tend to raise voter turnout.
17. If there are far fewer sugar growers than sugar consumers,
    a. the growers are likely to be more informed and influential on policy than voters.
    b. the consumers are likely to be more informed and influential on policy than voters.
    c. individual sugar growers are likely to have more at stake than individual sugar consumers.
    d. individual sugar consumers are likely to have more at stake than individual sugar growers.
    e. a is likely to be true because c is likely to be true.

Problems:

1. Why does favoring market mechanisms over command and control mechanisms *not* mean that a person wants no government whatsoever?
2. Why would means-tested transfer payments (such as food stamps, in which benefits are reduced as income rises) act like an income tax facing recipents?
3. Why are income taxes more progressive than excise taxes such as those on alcohol, tobacco, and gasoline?
4. Why is the Social Security payroll tax considered regressive?
5. Could the burdens of a regulation be either progressive or regressive, like the effects of a tax?
6. Is a gas tax better described as reflecting the ability to pay principle or the benefits received principle? What about the federal income tax?

7. Why would the benefits received principle be difficult to apply to national defense and the provision of the justice system?
8. Illustrate the median voter model graphically and explain it.
9. Why would a candidate offering "a choice, not an echo," run a risk of losing in a landslide?
10. Why might the party favorites at a political convention sometimes be harder to elect than more moderate candidates?
11. How can you be forced to pay for something you do not want to "buy" in the political sector? Is this sometimes good?
12. Why does the creation of a government program create a special interest group, which makes it difficult to reduce or eliminate it in the future?
13. Why are college students better informed about their own teachers' and schools' policies than about national education issues?
14. Why do you think news reporters are more informed than average citizens about public policy issues?

PART 4 HOUSEHOLDS AND MARKET STRUCTURE

Chapter 10 Consumer Choice Theory *258*

Appendix: A More Advanced Theory of Consumer Choice *279*

Chapter 11 The Firm: Production and Costs *289*

Appendix: Using Isoquants and Isocosts *320*

Chapter 12 Firms in Perfectly Competitive Markets *328*

Chapter 13 Monopoly and Antitrust *361*

Chapter 14 Monopolistic Competition and Product Differentiation *400*

Chapter 15 Oligopoly and Strategic Behavior *421*

10 Consumer Choice Theory

10.1 Consumer Behavior

10.2 The Consumer's Choice

APPENDIX: A More Advanced Theory of Consumer Choice

In this chapter, we discuss how individuals allocate their income between different bundles of goods. This decision involves trade-offs—if you buy more of one good, you cannot afford as much of other goods.

Why do consumers buy more of a product when the price falls and less of a product when the price rises? How do consumers respond to rising income? Falling income? How do we as consumers choose certain bundles of goods with our available budget to fit our desires? We address these questions in this chapter to strengthen our understanding of the law of demand. ■

SECTION 10.1 Consumer Behavior

* What is the substitution effect?
* What is the income effect?
* Can we make interpersonal utility comparisons?
* What is diminishing marginal utility?

As you may recall from Chapter 4, the law of demand is intuitive. Put simply, at a higher price, consumers will buy less (a decrease in the quantity demanded); at a lower price, consumers will buy more (an increase in quantity demanded), *ceteris paribus*. However, the downward-sloping demand curve has three other explanations: (1) the income and substitution effects of a price change, (2) the law of diminishing marginal utility, and (3) an interpretation using indifference curves and budget lines (in the appendix).

Let's start with out first explanation of a downward-sloping demand curve—the substitution and income effects of a price change. For example, if the price of pizza increases, the quantity of pizza demanded will fall because some consumers might switch out of pizza into hamburgers, tacos, burritos, submarine sandwiches, or some other foods that substitute for pizza. This behavior is called the **substitution effect** of a price change. In addition, a price increase for pizza will reduce the quantity of pizza demanded because it reduces a buyer's purchasing power. The buyer cannot buy as many pieces of pizza at higher prices as she could at lower prices, which is called the **income effect** of a price change.

The second explanation for the negative relationship between price and quantity demanded is what economists call **diminishing marginal utility**. In a given time period, a buyer will receive less satisfaction from each successive unit consumed. For example, a second ice cream cone will yield less satisfaction than the first, a third less satisfaction than the second, and so on. It follows from diminishing marginal utility that if people are deriving less satisfaction from successive units, consumers would buy added units only if the price were reduced. Let's now take a closer look at utility theory.

substitution effect
a consumer's switch to another similar good when the price of the preferred good increases

income effect
reduction in quantity demanded of a good when its price increases because of a consumer's decreased purchasing power

diminishing marginal utility
a good's ability to provide less satisfaction with each successive unit consumed

Economists conducted an experiment with rats to see how they would respond to changing prices of different drinks (changing the number of times a rat had to press a bar). Rats responded by choosing more of the beverage with a lower price, showing they were willing to substitute when the price changed. That is, even rats seem to behave rationally—responding to incentives and opportunities to make themselves better off.

Wants Versus Needs

The law of demand puts the concept of basic human "needs," at least as an analytical tool, to rest. Needs are those things that you must have at any price. That is, there are no substitutes. There are usually plenty of substitutes for any good, some better than others. The law of demand, with its inverse relationship between price and quantity demanded, implies that even so-called needs can be more or less urgent, depending on the circumstances (opportunity costs). Whenever you hear somebody say, "I need a new car," "I need a new laptop" or "I need new clothes," always be sure to ask: What does the person really mean? At what price does that person "need" the good? What is someone willing to give up to buy a new car—a trip to Hawaii? tuition? rent? That is, the cost of the new car is the items that you could have purchased if you did not buy the car. There are many substitutes for a new car—a used car, the bus, a motorcycle, carpooling, or moving within walking distance to work. The relevant question is whether the marginal benefits of buying a new car exceed the marginal cost, which is very different than saying you need a new car.

Economic goods are scarce and the amount people consume depends on the prices they are willing and able to pay. To need a good implies that we are willing to give up anything for it; need as a concept ignores scarcity and the fact that choices may change with circumstances and trade-offs.

Do We Need More Freeways?

Commuters are constantly complaining about how long it takes to drive to work. Do we *need* more freeways?

Perhaps many commuters would like to see more taxpayer dollars going toward freeways instead of museums, schools, or parks. Remember, the concept of need implies some type of urgency and conveys the message: "I will give up anything to get it." The real question is: At what price do we want more freeways? Would we need more freeways if the price of downtown parking was $1,000 a day? Probably not. Train yourself to think that we want different amounts of goods and services at different opportunity costs and that costs are more than just dollars and cents. For example, a person who normally does not speed while driving may do so if the relevant benefit of speed rises—for example, if he is late for his final exam or wedding, or if she is on her way to the hospital to deliver her baby.

Should There Be a Lane Reserved for Urgent Needs on Our Freeways?

During rush hour there are often very congested freeways. Perhaps we should have an express lane for people who have urgent needs. What do you think of this idea? Imagine the number of people that would develop what they felt were urgent needs if the "urgent need" lane was much shorter than the other lanes. It would be inevitable that the system would fall apart. In fact, it would be fun to guess what might be defined as an urgent need. It might include: "I am really in a hurry because I have to get home to clean up my apartment" or "I need to get back to the dorm to type my overdue term paper." "Oh shoot, I left the dog in the house." Many people would perceive their needs as more urgent than other people's urgent needs. This is a reason that the concept of needs falls apart as a means of explaining behavior. It is impossible to make the concept of need useful analytically when it is so hard to define or compare those "needs" among people.

Utility

To more clearly define the relationship between consumer choice and resource allocation, economists developed the concept of **utility**—a measure of the relative levels of satisfaction that consumers get from the consumption of goods and services. Defining one **util** as equivalent to one unit of satisfaction, economists can indicate relative levels of consumer satisfaction that result from alternative choices. For example, for a java junkie who wouldn't dream of starting the day without a strong dose of caffeine, a cup of coffee might generate 150 utils of satisfaction while a cup of herb tea might only generate 10 utils.

Inherently, utility varies from individual to individual depending on specific preferences. For example, Jason might get 50 utils of satisfaction from eating his first piece of apple pie, while Brittany may only derive 4 utils of satisfaction from her first piece of apple pie.

In fact, a whole school of thought called utilitarianism, based on utility theory, was developed by Jeremy Bentham. Bentham believed that society should seek the greatest happiness for the greater number. (See Bentham's biography on page 259.)

> **utility**
> a measure of the relative levels of satisfaction consumers get from consumption of goods and services
>
> **util**
> one unit of satisfaction

Utility Is a Personal Matter

Economists recognize that it is not really possible to make interpersonal utility comparisons. That is, they know that it is impossible to compare the relative satisfactions of different persons. The relative

GREAT ECONOMIC THINKERS: JEREMY BENTHAM (1748–1832)

Jeremy Bentham was born in London in 1748. He was a gifted child, reading history and other "serious" books at age 3, playing the violin at age 5, and studying Latin and French when he was only 6. At 12, he entered Queens College, Oxford, where he studied law. In his late teens, Bentham decided to concentrate on his writings. With funding provided by his father, he wrote a series of books on philosophy, economics, and politics. He would often write for 8 to 12 hours a day, a practice that continued through his life, leaving scholars material to compile for years to come. Most of his writings were not published until well over a century after his death.

According to Bentham, "pain and pleasure are the sovereign masters governing man's conduct": People will tend to pursue things that are pleasurable and avoid things that are painful. To this day, the rule of rational choice—weighing marginal benefits against marginal costs—has its roots in the earlier works of Jeremy Bentham. That is, economists predict human behavior on the basis of people's responses to changing incentives; people make choices on the basis of their expected marginal benefits and their expected marginal costs.

Although Bentham was most well known for utilitarianism, a philosophy stemming from his rational-choice ideas, he also had much to say on the subjects of prison reform, religion, relief to the poor, international law, and animal welfare. He was an ardent advocate of equality. Good humored, meditative, and kind, he was thought to be a visionary and ahead of his time, and he attracted the leading thinkers of the day to his company.

Bentham died in London in 1832. He left behind a strange legacy. At his request, his body was dissected, his skeleton padded and fully clothed, and his head preserved in the manner of South American headhunters. He asked that this "auto-icon," as it is now called, be seated in a glass case at the University College in London, and that his remains should be present at all meetings for the board. The auto-icon is still there today, although the mummified head, which did not preserve well, has been replaced by a wax head. The real head became an easy target for students and one story has the head being used at soccer practice! No one is quite sure why Bentham desired such an odd afterlife for his body; explanations range from it being a testament to an inflated sense of self-worth to a statement about religion or a practical joke.

COURTESY OF ROBERT L. SEXTON

---

satisfactions gained by two people drinking cups of coffee, for example, simply cannot be measured in comparable terms. Likewise, although we might be tempted to believe that a poorer person would derive greater utility from finding a $100 bill than would a richer person, we should resist the temptation. We simply cannot prove it. The poorer person may be "monetarily" poor because money and material things are not important to her, and the rich person may have become richer because of his lust for the things money can buy.

Total Utility and Marginal Utility

Economists recognize two different dimensions of utility: total utility and marginal utility. **Total utility** is the total amount of satisfaction derived from the

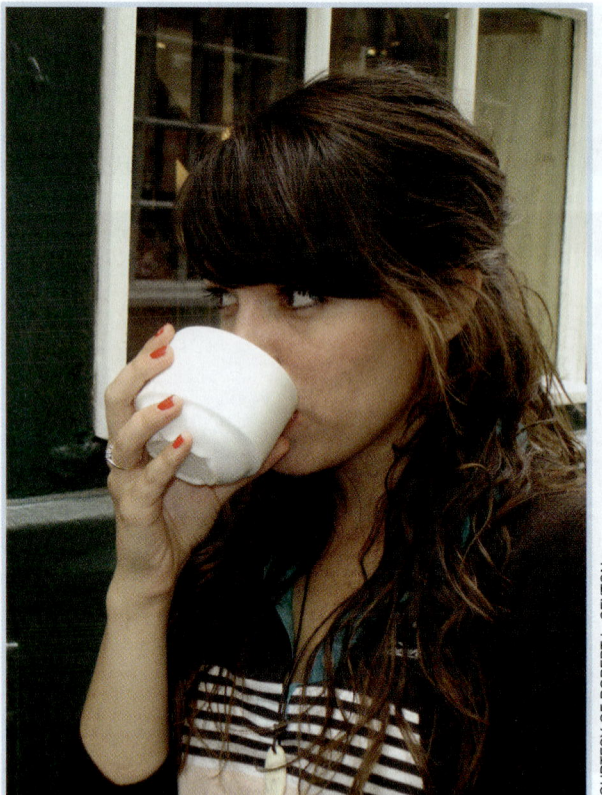

How many utils is this woman deriving from this cup of coffee? Can we accurately compare her satisfaction of a cup of coffee with another person's?

section 10.1 exhibit 1 — Total and Marginal Utility

As you can see in (a), the total utility from pizza increases as consumption increases. In (b) marginal utility decreases as consumption increases. That is, as you eat more pizza, your satisfaction from each additional slice diminishes.

Slices of Pizza (per day)	Total Utility (utils)	Marginal Utility (utils)
0	0	
1	10	10
2	18	8
3	24	6
4	28	4
5	30	2
6	30	0
7	28	−2

consumption of a certain number of units of a good or service. In comparison, **marginal utility** is the extra satisfaction generated by an additional unit of a good that is consumed in a particular time period. For example, eating four slices of pizza in an hour might generate a total of 28 utils of satisfaction. The first three slices of pizza might generate a total of 24 utils, while the last slice generates only 4 utils. In this case, the total utility of eating four slices of pizza is 28 utils, and the marginal utility of the fourth slice is 4 utils. Notice in Exhibit 1(a) how total

total utility
total amount of satisfaction derived from the consumption of a certain number of goods or services

marginal utility
extra satisfaction generated by consumption of an additional good or service during a specific time period

Use what you've LEARNED
DIMINISHING MARGINAL UTILITY

Q Why do most individuals take only one newspaper from covered, coin-operated newspaper racks when it would be so easy to take more? Do you think potato chips, candy, or sodas could be sold profitably in the same kind of dispenser? Why or why not?

A Although ethical considerations keep some people from taking additional papers, the law of diminishing marginal utility is also at work here. The second newspaper adds practically zero utility to most individuals on most days, so they typically feel no incentive to take more than one. The exception to this case might be on Sundays, when supermarket coupons are present. In that instance, while the marginal utility is still lower for the second paper than for the first, the marginal utility of the second paper may be large enough to tempt some individuals to take additional copies.

On the other hand, if putting money in a vending machine gave access to many bags of potato chips, candy bars, or sodas, the temptation to take more than one might be too great for some people. After all, the potato chip bags would still be good tomorrow. Therefore, vending machines with foods and drinks only dispense one item at a time, because it is likely that, for most people, the marginal utility gained from another unit of food or drink is higher than for a second newspaper.

Why are newspaper racks different from vending machines?

utility increases as consumption increases (we see more total utility after the fourth slice of pizza than after the third). But notice, too, that the increase in total utility from each additional unit (slice) is less than the unit before, which indicates the marginal utility. In Exhibit 1(b) we see how the marginal utility falls as consumption increases.

Diminishing Marginal Utility

Although economists believe that total utility increases with additional consumption, they also argue that the incremental satisfaction—the marginal utility—that results from the consumption of additional

diminishing marginal utility
the concept that states that as an individual consumes more and more of a good, each successive unit generates less and less utility (or satisfaction)

units tends to decline as consumption increases. In other words, each successive unit of a good that is consumed generates less satisfaction than did the previous unit. This concept is traditionally referred to as the **diminishing marginal utility.** Exhibit 1(b) demonstrates this graphically, where the marginal utility curve has a negative slope.

It follows from the law of diminishing marginal utility that as a person uses more and more units of a good to satisfy a given want, the intensity of the want, and the utility derived from further satisfying that want, diminishes. Think about it: If you are starving, your desire for that first piece of pizza will be great, but as you eat, you gradually become more and more full, reducing your desire for yet another piece.

Use what you've LEARNED
THE DIAMOND-WATER PARADOX: MARGINAL AND TOTAL UTILITY

"Nothing is more useful than water: but it will not purchase scarce anything. . . . Diamond, on the contrary, has scarce any value in use; but a very great quantity of other goods may frequently be had in exchange for it."
—ADAM SMITH, *Wealth of Nations*, 1776

Q Use the concept of marginal utility to evaluate the social value of water versus diamonds.

A The classic diamond-water paradox is the observation that sometimes those things that are necessary for life, like water, are inexpensive, and those items that are not necessary for life, like diamonds, are expensive. This paradox puzzled philosophers for centuries. The answer lies in making the distinction between total utility and marginal utility. The amount of total utility is indeed higher for water than for diamonds because of its importance for survival. But price is not determined by total utility, it is determined by marginal utility. Total utility measures the total amount of satisfaction someone derives from a good, whereas marginal utility determines the price. Market value—the value of the last, or marginal, unit traded—depends on both supply and demand. Thus, the limited supply of diamonds relative to the demand generates a high price, but an abundant supply of water relative to the demand results in a low price. The total utility (usefulness) for water is very large compared to the marginal utility. Because the price of water is so low, we use so much water that the marginal utility we receive from the last glass of water is small. Diamonds have a much smaller total utility (usefulness) relative to water, but because the price of diamonds is so high, we buy so few diamonds that they have a high marginal utility. Could water ever have a higher marginal utility than diamonds? Yes, if you had no water and no diamonds, your first cup of water would give you a much higher marginal value than your first cup of diamonds. Furthermore, if diamonds were very plentiful and water was very scarce, which would have the higher marginal utility? In this case, water would be expensive and diamonds would be inexpensive.

Why is water, which is so critical to life, priced lower than diamonds which are less useful?

in the news

What Can "Neuroeconomics" Teach Us About How We Shop?

This morning, I had a remarkable experience: I strolled into a delicatessen and bought some delicious Stilton [a cheese produced in England]. What made the shopping trip unusual was that I was wearing a brain scanner while I did it. My costume consisted of an electroencephalograph cap, which looks like a polka-dot shower cap with wires plugged into it; a pair of wraparound glasses with a tiny video camera attached; a clothes peg on one finger to measure my heart rate; two other finger monitors that function like a lie detector; a thermometer patch on a fourth finger; and a satchel to hold a computer gathering the data.

Most of these devices, or their equivalent, can be hidden under clothes or baseball caps so that the wearer looks as if they are sporting only shades and an iPod, but in my case the boffins hadn't bothered, and so I entered the deli looking like an extra from a 1970s episode of Doctor Who.

This was all part of my efforts to understand "neuroeconomics," a new, controversial, and eclectic marriage between economics, marketing, and various branches of physiology and brain science. With very different aims, economists and marketers are attempting to tap into the dramatic advances in our understanding of the brain that have taken place over the past 15 years. Their tools encompass mood-altering drugs, tests for hormone levels, animal studies, and fMRI scans (which use immobile scanners to measure blood flows deep inside the brain).

"Neuromarketing" is the simplest application, and the one in which I was participating. David Lewis, a neurophysiologist at the Mind Lab, a spinoff from the University of Sussex, showed me how the physiological readings could be viewed alongside output from my camera to provide a simple but—presumably—useful demonstration of what really grabbed my attention in the deli. Among Lewis' findings are that eating chocolate is more exciting than making out (at least, making out in an electrical shower cap while surrounded by men with clipboards) and that, subconsciously, young men are more interested in sneakers than in the wares on display in an Ann Summers sex shop.

While the possible applications for marketers are obvious enough, such trials are hardly unlocking the deepest secrets of thought. It remains to be seen whether neuroscience has much to contribute to economics itself, a subject that has long focused on the decisions people make, without relying on any particular theory of how they make them. It is also hard to point to anything terribly interesting that the neuroeconomists have discovered, although neuroeconomics may contribute more as time goes by.

Neuroeconomics may provide more shape to the older and more famous field of behavioral economics. A mixture of economics and psychology, behavioral economics has used laboratory experiments to expose a bewildering number of exceptions to the traditional economic theory of rational choice. At present, though, there is little pattern to what the behavioral economists are observing, and it's possible that a greater understanding of how the brain works might help to provide one.

Yet neuroscience might also help reinforce the traditionalists. Wolfram Schultz, a neuroscientist at Cambridge who studies how the brain processes risk and reward, says that just as the brain registers sensations such as sight, he can now see it registering rewards. There was no reason to expect that the mathematically convenient economists' fantasy of "utility" had any real analogue in the brain—but it seems that it might, after all. There's a thought.

SOURCE: *State* Magazine Tim Harford Posted Saturday, Nov. 1, 2008, at 7:55 A.M. Tim Harford is a columnist for the *Financial Times*. He is the author of *The Undercover Economist*, and his latest book is *The Logic of Life*.

SECTION CHECK

1. A substitution effect occurs when a consumer switches to another similar good when the price of the preferred good increases.
2. The income effect occurs when there is a reduction in quantity demanded of a good when its price increases because of a consumer's decreased purchasing power.
3. Utility is the amount of satisfaction an individual receives from consumption of a good or service.
4. Economists recognize that it is not possible to make interpersonal utility comparisons.
5. Total utility is the amount of satisfaction derived from all units of goods and services consumed. Total utility increases as consumption increases.
6. Marginal utility is the change in utility from consuming one additional unit of a good or service.
7. According to the law of diminishing marginal utility, as a person consumes additional units of a given good, marginal utility declines.

---

1. What is the substitution effect of a price change?
2. What is the income effect of a price change?
3. How do economists define utility?
4. Why can't interpersonal utility comparisons be made?
5. What is the relationship between total utility and marginal utility?
6. Why could you say that a millionaire gets less marginal utility from a second piece of pizza than from the first piece, but you couldn't say that the millionaire derives more or less marginal utility from a second piece of pizza than someone else who has a much lower level of income?
7. Are you likely to get as much marginal utility from your last piece of chicken at an all-you-can-eat restaurant as at a restaurant where you pay $2 per piece of chicken?

SECTION 10.2 The Consumer's Choice

* How do consumers maximize satisfaction?
* What is the connection between the law of demand and the law of diminishing marginal utility?

What Is the "Best" Decision for Consumers?

We established the fact that marginal utility diminishes as additional units of a good are acquired. But what significance does this idea have for consumers? Remember, consumers try to add to their own total utility, so when the marginal utility generated by the purchase of additional units of one good drops too low, it can become rational for the consumer to purchase other goods rather than purchase more of the first good. In other words, a rational consumer will avoid making purchases of any one good beyond the point at which other goods will yield greater satisfaction for the amount spent—the "bang for the buck."

Marginal utility, then, is an important concept in understanding and predicting consumer behavior, especially when combined with information about prices. By comparing the marginal utilities generated by units of the goods that they desire as well as the prices, rational consumers seek the combination of goods that maximizes their satisfaction for a given amount spent. In the next section, we will see how this concept works.

Consumer Equilibrium

To reach consumer equilibrium, consumers must allocate their incomes in such a way that the marginal utility per dollar's worth of any good is the same for every good. That is, the "bang for the buck" must be equal for all goods at consumer equilibrium. When this goal is realized, one dollar's worth of additional gasoline will yield the same marginal utility as one dollar's worth of additional bread or apples or movie tickets or soap. This concept will become clearer to you as we work through an example illustrating the forces present when consumers are not at equilibrium.

Given a fixed budget, if the marginal utilities per dollar spent on additional units of two goods are not the same, you can increase total satisfaction by buying more of one good and less of the other. For example, assume that the price of a loaf of bread is $1, the price of a bag of apples is $1, the marginal utility of a dollar's worth of apples is 1 util, and the marginal utility of a dollar's worth of bread is 5 utils. In this situation, your total satisfaction can be increased by buying more bread and fewer apples, because bread is currently giving you greater satisfaction per dollar than apples—5 utils versus 1 util, for a net gain of 4 utils to your total satisfaction. By buying more bread, though, you alter the marginal utility of both bread and apples. Consider what would happen if, next week, you buy one more loaf of bread and one less bag of apples. Because you are consuming more of it now, the marginal utility for bread will fall, say to 4 utils. On the other hand, the marginal utility for apples will rise, perhaps to 2 utils, because you now have fewer apples.

A comparison of the marginal utilities for these goods in week 2 versus week 1 would look something like this:

Week 1

$MU_{bread}/\$1 > MU_{apples}/\$1$

5 utils/$1 > 1 util/$1

Week 2

$MU_{bread}/\$1 > MU_{apples}/\$1$

4 utils/$1 > 2 utils/$1

Notice that although the marginal utilities of bread and apples are now closer, they are still not equal. Because of this difference, it is still in the consumer's interest to purchase an additional loaf of bread rather than the last bag of apples; in this case, the net gain would be 2 utils (3 utils for the unit of bread added at a cost of 1 util for the apples given up). By buying yet another loaf of bread, you once again push further down your marginal utility curve for bread, and as a result, the marginal utility for bread falls. With that change, the relative value to you of apples increases again, changing the ratio of marginal utility to dollar spent for both goods in the following way:

consumer equilibrium allocation of consumer income that balances the ratio of marginal utility to the price of goods purchased

Week 3

$MU_{bread}/\$1 = MU_{apples}/\$1$

3 utils/$1 = 3 utils/$1

What this example shows is that, to achieve maximum satisfaction—**consumer equilibrium**—consumers have to allocate income in such a way that the ratio of the marginal utility to the price of the goods is equal for all goods purchased. In other words, in a state of consumer equilibrium,

$MU_1/P_1 = MU_2/P_2 = MU_3/P_3 = \cdots MU_N/P_N$

In this situation, each good provides the consumer with the same level of marginal utility per dollar spent.

The Law of Demand and the Law of Diminishing Marginal Utility

The law of demand states that when the price of a good is reduced, the quantity of that good demanded will increase. But why is this the case? By examining the law of diminishing marginal utility in action, we can determine the basis for this relationship between price and quantity demanded. Indeed, the demand curve merely translates marginal utility into dollar terms.

For example, let's say that you are in consumer equilibrium when the price of a personal-sized pizza is $4 and the price of a hamburger is $1. Further, in equilibrium, the marginal utility on the last pizza consumed is 40 utils, and the marginal utility on the last hamburger is 10 utils. So in consumer equilibrium, the MU/P ratio for both the pizza and the hamburger is 10 utils per dollar:

MU_{pizza} (40 utils)/$4 = $MU_{hamburger}$ (10 utils)/$1

Now suppose the price of the personal-sized pizza falls to $2, *ceteris paribus*. Instead of the MU/P ratio of the pizza being 10 utils per dollar, it is now 20 utils per dollar (40 utils/$2). This calculation implies, *ceteris paribus*, that you will now buy more pizza at the lower price because you are getting relatively more satisfaction for each dollar you spend on pizza.

MU_{pizza} (40 utils)/$2 > $MU_{hamburger}$ (10 utils)/$1

In other words, because the price of the personal-sized pizza fell, you are now willing to purchase more pizzas and fewer hamburgers.

Use what you've LEARNED
MARGINAL UTILITY

A consumer is faced with choosing between hamburgers and milkshakes that are priced at $2 and $1, respectively. He has $11 to spend for the week. The marginal utility derived from each of the two goods is as follows:

If you did not have a budget constraint, you would choose 5 hamburgers and 5 milkshakes because you would maximize your total utility (68 + 34 = 102); that is, adding up all the marginal utilities for all hamburgers (68 utils) and all milkshakes (34 utils). And that would cost you $15; $10 for the 5 hamburgers and $5 for the 5 milkshakes. However, you can only spend $11; so what is the best way to spend it? Remember economic decisions are made at the margin. This idea is the best "bang for the buck" principle, we must equalize the marginal utility per dollar spent. Looking at the table, we accomplish this at 4 hamburgers and 3 milkshakes per week.

Or

$$MU_H/P_H = MU_M/P_M$$
$$10/\$2 = 5/\$1$$
$$(Q_H \times P_H) + (Q_M \times P_M) = \$11$$
$$(4 \times \$2) + (3 \times \$1) = \$11$$

Marginal Utility from Last Hamburger	Quantity of Hamburgers Consumed Each Week	(MU_H/P_H)
20	1	10
16	2	8
14	3	7
10	4	5
8	5	4

Marginal Utility from Last Milkshake	Quantity of Milkshakes Consumed Each Week	(MU_M/P_M)
12	1	12
10	2	10
5	3	5
4	4	4
3	5	3

SECTION CHECK

1. To maximize consumer satisfaction, income must be allocated so that the ratio of the marginal utility to the price is the same for all goods purchased.
2. If the marginal utility per dollar of additional units is not the same, a person can increase total satisfaction by buying more of some goods and less of others.

1. What do economists mean by consumer equilibrium?
2. How could a consumer raise his total utility if the ratio of his marginal utility to the price for good A was greater than that for good B?
3. What must be true about the ratio of marginal utility to the price for each good consumed in consumer equilibrium?
4. How does the law of demand reflect the law of diminishing marginal utility?
5. Why doesn't consumer equilibrium imply that the ratio of total utility per dollar is the same for different goods?
6. Why does the principle of consumer equilibrium imply that people would tend to buy more apples when the price of apples is reduced?
7. Suppose the price of walnuts is $6 per pound and the price of peanuts is $2 per pound. If a person gets 20 units of added utility from eating the last pound of peanuts she consumes, how many utils of added utility would she have to get from eating the last pound of walnuts in order to be in consumer equilibrium?

in the news
Behavioral Economics

Today there is a growing school of economists who are drawing on a vast range of behavioural traits identified by experimental psychologists which amount to a frontal assault on the whole idea that people, individually or as a group, mostly act rationally.

A quick tour of the key observations made by these psychologists would make even Mr. Spock's head spin. For example, people appear to be disproportionately influenced by the fear of feeling **regret**, and will often pass up even benefits within reach to avoid a small risk of feeling they have failed. They are also prone to **cognitive dissonance**: holding a belief plainly at odds with the evidence, usually because the belief has been held and cherished for a long time. Psychiatrists sometimes call this "denial."

And then there is **anchoring**: people are often overly influenced by outside suggestion. People can be influenced even when they know that the suggestion is not being made by someone who is better informed. In one experiment, volunteers were asked a series of questions whose answers were in percentages—such as what percentage of African countries is in the United Nations? A wheel with numbers from one to 100 was spun in front of them; they were then asked to say whether their answer was higher or lower than the number on the wheel, and then to give their answer. These answers were strongly influenced by the randomly selected, irrelevant number on the wheel. The average guess when the wheel showed 10 was 25%; when it showed 65 it was 45%.

Experiments show that most people apparently also suffer from **status quo bias**: they are willing to take bigger gambles to maintain the status quo than they would be to acquire it in the first place. In one common experiment, mugs are allocated randomly to some people in a group. Those who have them are asked to name a price to sell their mug; those without one are asked to name a price at which they will buy. Usually, the average sales price is considerably higher than the average offer price.

Expected-utility theory assumes that people look at individual decisions in the context of the big picture. But psychologists have found that, in fact, they tend to **compartmentalize**, often on superficial grounds. They then make choices about things in one particular mental compartment without taking account of the implications for things in other compartments.

There is also a huge amount of evidence that people are persistently, and irrationally, **overconfident**. Asked to answer a factual question, then asked to give the probability that their answer was correct, people typically overestimate this probability. This may be due to a **representativeness heuristic**: a tendency to treat events as representative of some well-known class or pattern. This gives people a sense of familiarity with an event and thus confidence that they have accurately diagnosed it. This can lead people to "see" patterns in data even where there are none. A closely related phenomenon is the **availability heuristic**: people focus excessive attention on a particular fact or event, rather than the big picture, simply because it is more visible or fresher in their mind.

Another delightfully human habit is **magical thinking**: attributing to one's own actions something that had nothing to do with them, and thus assuming that one has a greater influence over events than is actually the case. For instance, an investor who luckily buys a share that goes on to beat the market may become convinced that he is a skillful investor rather than a merely fortunate one. He may also fall prey to **quasi-magical thinking**—behaving as if he believes his thoughts can influence events, even though he knows that they can't.

Most people, say psychologists, are also vulnerable to **hindsight bias**: once something happens, they overestimate the extent to which they could have predicted it. Closely related to this is memory bias: when something happens people often persuade themselves that they actually predicted it, even when they didn't.

Finally, who can deny that people often become **emotional**, cutting off their noses to spite their faces. One of the psychologists' favorite experiments is the

(continued)

in the news: Behavioral Economics (cont.)

"ultimatum game" in which one player, the proposer, is given a sum of money, say $10, and offers some portion of it to the other player, the responder. The responder can either accept the offer, in which case he gets the sum offered and the proposer gets the rest, or reject the offer in which case both players get nothing. In experiments, very low offers (less than 20% of the total sum) are often rejected, even though it is rational for the responder to accept any offer (even one cent!) which the proposer makes. And yet responders seem to reject offers out of sheer indignation at being made to accept such a small proportion of the whole sum, and they seem to get more satisfaction from taking revenge on the proposer than in maximizing their own financial gain. Mr. Spock would be appalled if a Vulcan made this mistake.

The psychological idea that has so far had the greatest impact on economics is "prospect theory." This was developed by Daniel Kahneman of Princeton University and the late Amos Tversky of Stanford University. It brings together several aspects of psychological research and differs in crucial respects from expected-utility theory—although, equally crucially, it shares its advantage of being able to be modeled mathematically. It is based on the results of hundreds of experiments in which people have been asked to choose between pairs of gambles.

What Messrs Kahneman and Tversky claim to have found is that people are "loss averse": they have an asymmetric attitude to gains and losses, getting less utility from gaining, say, $100 than they would lose if they lost $100. This is not the same as "risk aversion," any particular level of which can be rational if consistently applied. But those suffering from loss aversion do not measure risk consistently. They take fewer risks that might result in suffering losses than if they were acting as rational utility maximizers. Prospect theory also claims that people regularly miscalculate probabilities: they assume that outcomes which are very probable are less likely than they really are, that outcomes which are quite unlikely are more likely than they are, and that extremely improbable, but still possible, outcomes have no chance at all of happening. They also tend to view decisions in isolation, rather than as part of a bigger picture.

Several real-world examples of how this theory can explain human decisions are reported in a forthcoming paper, "Prospect Theory in the Wild," by Colin Camerer, an economist at the California Institute of Technology. Many New York taxi drivers, points out Mr. Camerer, decide when to finish work each day by setting themselves a daily income target, and on reaching it they stop. This means that they typically work fewer hours on a busy day than on a slow day. Rational labor-market theory predicts that they will do the opposite, working longer on the busy day when their effective hourly wage-rate is higher, and less on the slow day when their wage-rate is lower. Prospect theory can explain this irrational behavior: failing to achieve the daily income target feels like incurring a loss, so drivers put in longer hours to avoid it, and beating the target feels like a win, so once they have done that, there is less incentive to keep working.

Racing and the Equity Premium
People betting on horse races back long-shots over favorites far more often than they should. Prospect theory suggests this is because they attach too low a probability to likely outcomes and too high a probability to quite unlikely ones. Gamblers also tend to shift their bets away from favorites towards long-shots as the day's racing nears its end. Because of the cut taken by the bookies, by the time later races are run most racegoers have lost some money. For many of them, a successful bet on an outsider would probably turn a losing day into a winning one. Mathematically, and rationally, this should not matter. The last race of

the day is no different from the first race of the next day. But most racegoers close their "mental account" at the end of each racing day, and they hate to leave the track a loser.

Perhaps the best-known example of prospect theory in action is in suggesting a solution to the "equity-premium puzzle." In America, shares have long delivered much higher returns to investors relative to bonds than seems justified by the difference in riskiness of shares and bonds. Orthodox economists have ascribed this simply to the fact that people have less appetite for risk than expected. But prospect theory suggests that if investors, rather like racegoers, are averse to losses during any given year, this might justify such a high equity premium. Annual losses on shares are much more frequent than annual losses on bonds, so investors demand a much higher premium for holding shares to compensate them for the greater risk of suffering a loss in any given year.

A common response of believers in homo economicus is to claim that apparently irrational behaviour is in fact rational. Gary Becker, of the University of Chicago, was doing this long before behavioral economics came along to challenge rationality. He has won a Nobel prize for his work, which has often shed light on topics from education and family life to suicide, drug addiction and religion. Recently, he has developed "rational" models of the formation of emotions and of religious belief.

Rationalists such as Mr. Becker often accuse behavioralists of picking whichever psychological explanation happens to suit the particular alleged irrationality they are explaining, rather than using a rigorous, consistent scientific approach. Caltech's Mr. Camerer argues that rationalists are guilty of exactly the same error. For instance, rationalists explain away people's fondness for betting on long-shots in horse races by claiming that most are simply more risk-loving than expected, and then claim precisely the opposite about investors to explain the equity premium. Both are possible, but as explanations they leave something to be desired.

Being irrational may even be rational, according to some rationalists. Irrationality can be a good to be consumed like any other, argues Bryan Caplan, an economist at George Mason University—in the sense that the less it costs a person, the more of it they buy. A peculiar feature of beliefs about politics and religion, he says, is that the costs to an individual of error are "virtually non-existent, setting the private cost of irrationality at zero; it is therefore in these areas that irrational views are most apparent." Maybe, although Mr. Caplan may grow sick of having those views read back to him for eternity should he ever end up in hell.

In his book, "Alchemies of the Mind: Rationality and the Emotions," Jon Elster of New York's Columbia University prefers to look at the other side of the same coin. Observing that "those who are most likely to make unbiased cognitive assessments are the clinically depressed," he argues that the "emotional price to pay for cognitive rationality may be too high."

In fact, the battle between rationalists and behavioralists may be largely in the past. Those who believe in homo economicus no longer routinely ignore his emotional and spiritual dimensions. Nor do behavioralists any longer assume people are wholly irrational. Instead, most now view them as "quasi-rational": trying as hard as they can to be rational but making the same mistakes over and over.

Robert Shiller, an economist at Yale who is writing a book on psychology and the stockmarket, and is said to have prompted Mr. Greenspan's "irrational exuberance" remark, argues that "conventional efficient-markets theory is not completely out the window. . . . Doing research that is sensitive to lessons from behavioral research does not mean entirely abandoning research in the conventional expected-utility framework."

Mr. Kahneman, the psychologist who inspired much of the economic research on irrationality, goes further: "as a first approximation, it makes sense to assume rational behaviour." He believes that economists cannot give up the rational model entirely. "They will be doing it one assumption at a time. Otherwise the analysis will very soon become intractable; the great strength of the rational model is that it is very tractable."

Rational Taxi Drivers!
What seems certain is that economics will increasingly embrace the insights of other disciplines, from

(continued)

in the news Behavioral Economics (cont.)

psychologists to biologists. Andrew Lo, an economist at Massachusetts Institute of Technology, is hopeful that natural scientists will help social scientists by discovering the genetic basis for different attitudes to risk-taking. Considerable attention will be paid to discoveries about how people form their emotions, tastes and beliefs. Understanding better how people learn will also be a priority. Strikingly, even New York taxi drivers seem to become less irrational over time: with experience, they learn to do more work on busy days and less when things are slow. But how representative are they of the rest of humanity?

Richard Thaler was an almost lone pioneer in the use of psychology in financial economics during the 1980s and early 1990s. Today he is a professor at the University of Chicago, the high temple of rational economics. He believes that in the future, "economists will routinely incorporate as much 'behaviour' into their models as they observe in the real world. After all, to do otherwise would be irrational." Mr. Spock could not have said it better.

consider this:
Henry Farber, an economist at Princeton University, has analyzed data for New York taxicab drivers and shows that traditional economic models offer important insights into taxicab drivers behavior. In short, he found that daily income and hitting one's target had only a *small* effect on a driver's decisions. Drivers responded positively to the prospect of higher pay. He found that drivers put in more hours when the pickings are rich, say during a convention or a theater season, and take more leisure when business is slow. What was important was the cumulative number of hours already worked that day, which is a vastly different result than the conclusions of the behavioral economists.

SOURCE: From "Rethinking Thinking", 'The Economist', December 16, 1999. © The Economist Newspaper Limited, London 1999. Reprinted with permission.

Interactive Chapter Summary

Fill in the blanks:

1. The _____ effect explains why the quantity of pizza demanded decreases as its price goes up, because some people switch to substitute goods that become relatively cheaper as a result.

2. The _____ effect explains why the quantity of pizza demanded decreases as its price goes up, because it reduces buyers' purchasing power.

3. _____ utility implies that people will derive less satisfaction from successive units.

4. You would expect a third ice cream cone to provide _____ additional utility, or satisfaction, on a given day, than the second ice cream cone the same day.

5. _____ is the satisfaction or enjoyment derived from consumption.

6. The relative satisfaction gained by two people drinking cups of coffee _____ be measured in comparable terms.

7. _____ is the total amount of satisfaction derived from the consumption of a certain number of units of a good.

8. _____ utility is the extra satisfaction generated by an additional unit of a good that is consumed in a given time period.

9. If the first of three slices of pizza generates 24 utils and four slices of pizza generates 28 utils, then the marginal utility of the fourth slice of pizza is _____ utils.

10. Marginal utility _____ as consumption increases, which is called the law of _____.

11. Market prices of goods and services are determined by _____ utility.

12. If total utility fell for consuming one more unit of a good, the marginal utility for that good would be _____.

13. To reach _____, consumers must allocate their incomes in such a way that the marginal utility per dollars' worth of any good is the same for every good.

14. If the last dollar spent on good A provides more marginal utility per dollar than the last dollar spent on good B, total satisfaction would increase if _____ was spent on good A and _____ was spent on good B.

15. As an individual approaches consumer equilibrium, the ratio of marginal utility per dollar spent on different goods gets _____ apart across goods.

16. In consumer equilibrium, if the price of good A is three times that of the price of good B, then the marginal utility from the last unit of good A will be _____ times the marginal utility from the last unit of good B.

17. Starting in consumer equilibrium, when the price of good A falls, it makes the marginal utility per dollar spent on good A _____ relative to that of other goods, leading to a _____ quantity of good A purchased.

Answers: 1. substitution 2. income 3. Diminishing marginal 4. less 5. Utility 6. cannot 7. Total utility 8. Marginal 9. 4 10. declines; diminishing marginal utility 11. marginal 12. negative 13. consumer equilibrium 14. more; less 15. less far 16. three 17. rise; larger

Key Terms and Concepts

substitution effect 259
income effect 259
diminishing marginal utility 259
utility 260
util 260
total utility 262
marginal utility 262
diminishing marginal utility 263
consumer equilibrium 267

Section Check Answers

10.1 Consumer Behavior

1. **What is the substitution effect of a price change?**
   The substitution effect of a price change occurs when a consumer switches to another similar good when the price of the preferred good increases.

2. **What is the income effect of a price change?**
   The income effect of a price change occurs when there is a reduction in the quantity demanded of a good when its price increases because of a consumer's decreased purchasing power.

3. **How do economists define utility?**
   Economists define utility as the level of satisfaction or well-being an individual receives from consumption of a good or service.

4. **Why can't interpersonal utility comparisons be made?**
   We can't make interpersonal utility comparisons because it is impossible to measure the relative satisfaction of different people in comparable terms.

5. **What is the relationship between total utility and marginal utility?**
   Marginal utility is the increase in total utility from increasing consumption of a good or service by one unit.

6. **Why could you say that a millionaire gets less marginal utility from a second piece of pizza than from the first piece, but you couldn't say that the millionaire derives more or less marginal utility from a second piece of pizza than someone else who has a much lower level of income?**
   Both get less marginal utility from a second piece of pizza than from the first piece because of the law of diminishing marginal utility. However, it is impossible to measure the relative satisfaction of different people in comparable terms, even when we are comparing rich and poor people, so we cannot say who got more marginal utility from a second slice of pizza.

7. **Are you likely to get as much marginal utility from your last piece of chicken at an all-you-can-eat restaurant as at a restaurant where you pay $2 per piece of chicken?**
   No. If you pay $2 per piece, you only eat another piece as long as it gives you more marginal utility than spending the $2 on something else. But at an all-you-can-eat restaurant, the dollar price of one more piece of chicken is zero, so you consume more chicken and get less marginal utility out of the last piece of chicken you eat.

10.2 The Consumer's Choice

1. **What do economists mean by consumer equilibrium?**
   Consumer equilibrium means that a consumer is consuming the optimum, or utility maximizing, combination of goods and services, for a given level of income.

2. **How could a consumer raise his total utility if the ratio of his marginal utility to the price for good A was greater than that for good B?**
   Such a consumer would raise his total utility by spending less on good B, and more on good A, because a dollar less spent on B would lower his utility less than a dollar more spent on A would increase it.

3. **What must be true about the ratio of marginal utility to the price for each good consumed in consumer equilibrium?**
   In consumer equilibrium, the ratio of marginal utility to price for each good consumed must be the same, otherwise the consumer could raise his total utility by changing his consumption pattern to increase consumption of those goods with higher marginal utility per dollar and decrease consumption of those goods with lower marginal utility per dollar.

4. **How does the law of demand reflect the law of diminishing marginal utility?**
   In consumer equilibrium, the marginal utility per dollar spent is the same for all goods and services consumed. Starting from that point, reducing the price of one good increases its marginal utility per dollar, resulting in increased consumption of that good. But that is what the law of demand states—that the quantity of a good demanded will increase, the lower its price, *ceteris paribus*.

5. **Why doesn't consumer equilibrium imply that the ratio of total utility per dollar is the same for different goods?**
   It is the additional, or marginal, utility per dollar spent for different goods, not the total utility you get per dollar spent, that matters in determining whether consuming more of some goods and less of others will increase total utility.

6. **Why does the principle of consumer equilibrium imply that people would tend to buy more apples when the price of apples is reduced?**
   A fall in the price of apples will increase the marginal utility per dollar spent on the last apple a person was willing to buy before their price fell. This means a person could increase his or her total utility for a given income by buying more apples and less of some other goods.

7. **Suppose the price of walnuts is $6 per pound and the price of peanuts is $2 per pound. If a person gets 20 units of added utility from eating the last pound of peanuts she consumes, how many utils of added utility would she have to get from eating the last pound of walnuts in order to be in consumer equilibrium?**
   Since consumer equilibrium requires that the marginal utility per dollar spent must be the same across goods that are consumed, the last pound of walnuts would have to provide 60 units of added or marginal utility in this case (60/6 = 20/2).

CHAPTER 10 STUDY GUIDE

True or False:

1. Utility is the satisfaction or enjoyment derived from consumption.
2. Economists do *not* think it is possible to compare the relative satisfaction derived from consumption across individuals.
3. Marginal utility is the satisfaction received from all units of a good that are consumed.
4. When marginal utility begins to diminish, total utility always diminishes.
5. If a consumer is maximizing utility, she will purchase quantities of output to the point where the marginal utility per dollar spent on consumption is equal across all goods.
6. As long as the marginal utility of the last unit consumed is positive, total utility will fall if a person consumes less of a good.
7. As long as a person had to pay a positive price for a good, he would never consume to the point where his marginal utility was falling with additional consumption.
8. A person could receive a higher marginal utility from the last diamond she purchases than from the last ounce of water she purchases, yet receive less total utility from diamonds than from water.
9. If total utility from consuming five cups of cocoa is 13, 25, 35, 44, and 52 utils, respectively, the marginal utility of the fourth cup of coffee is 9.
10. If Phil says, "You would have to pay me to eat another cookie now," it would imply that his marginal utility from consuming one more cookie now was negative.

Multiple Choice:

1. The increase in total utility that one receives from eating an additional piece of sushi is called
    a. marginal utility.
    b. interpersonal utility.
    c. marginal cost.
    d. average utility.
    e. average cost.

2. Marginal utility is
    a. the total satisfaction derived from consuming all goods.
    b. always the total satisfaction derived from consuming the first unit of a good.
    c. always positive.
    d. always negative.
    e. the change in total satisfaction derived from consuming one more unit of a particular good.

3. As one eats more and more oranges
    a. his total utility falls, but the marginal utility of each orange rises.
    b. his marginal utility rises as long as the total utility derived from the oranges remains positive.
    c. his total utility rises, as does the marginal utility of each orange.
    d. his total utility rises as long as the marginal utility of the oranges is positive, but the marginal utility of each additional orange likely falls.

4. The marginal utility from a hot fudge sundae
    a. is always increasing.
    b. is always greater than the average utility derived from all hot fudge sundaes consumed.
    c. generally depends on how many hot fudge sundaes the consumer has already consumed.
    d. is always equal to the price paid for the hot fudge sundae.

5. Total utility will decline when
    a. marginal utility is falling.
    b. marginal utility is rising.
    c. marginal utility equals zero.
    d. marginal utility is constant.
    e. marginal utility is negative.

275

6. When total utility is at its maximum
   a. marginal utility is negative.
   b. marginal utility is positive.
   c. marginal utility is at its maximum.
   d. marginal utility equals zero.
   e. marginal utility stops decreasing and starts increasing.

7. The total utility from consuming five slices of pizza is 11, 18, 24, 29, and 32 utils, respectively. The marginal utility of the third slice of pizza is
   a. 11.
   b. 7.
   c. 18.
   d. 6.
   e. 53.

8. The total utility from consuming five sushi rolls is 12, 23, 33, 42, and 45 utils, respectively. Marginal utility begins to diminish *after* consuming the _____ sushi roll.
   a. first
   b. second
   c. third
   d. fourth
   e. None of the above are correct; marginal utility does not diminish.

9. The law of diminishing marginal utility implies that the more of a commodity you consume, the
   a. more you value additional units of output.
   b. less you value additional units of output.
   c. happier you are.
   d. higher the price that is paid for the commodity.

10. When a consumer spends her income on goods and services in such a way that her utility is maximized, she reaches
    a. monetary equilibrium.
    b. market equilibrium.
    c. consumer equilibrium.
    d. marginal equilibrium.

11. Hamburgers cost $2 and hot dogs cost $1, and Juan is in consumer equilibrium. What must be true about the marginal utility of the last hamburger Juan consumes?
    a. The marginal utility of the last hamburger consumed must be less than that of the last hot dog.
    b. The marginal utility of the last hamburger consumed must be equal to that of the last hot dog.
    c. The marginal utility of the last hamburger consumed must be greater than that of the last hot dog.
    d. The marginal utility of the last hamburger consumed must be equal to zero.

12. Melissa spent the week at an amusement park and used all of her money on rides and popcorn. Both rides and bags of popcorn are priced at $1 each. Melissa realizes that the last bag of popcorn she consumed increased her utility by 40 utils, while the marginal utility of her last ride was only 20 utils. What should Melissa have done differently to increase her satisfaction?
    a. reduced the number of bags of popcorn she consumed and increased the number of rides
    b. increased the number of bags of popcorn she consumed and reduced the number of rides
    c. decreased both the number of bags of popcorn and rides consumed
    d. increased both the number of bags of popcorn and rides consumed
    e. nothing, as her utility was maximized

13. The fact that a gallon of gasoline commands a higher market price than a gallon of water indicates that
    a. gasoline is a scarce good but water is not.
    b. the total utility of gasoline exceeds the total utility of water.
    c. the marginal utility of a gallon of gasoline is greater than the marginal utility of a gallon of water.
    d. the average utility of a gallon of gasoline is greater than the average utility of a gallon of water.

14. The total utility derived from consuming scoops of ice cream can be found by
    a. multiplying the marginal utility of the last scoop consumed by the number of scoops consumed.
    b. multiplying the marginal utility of the last scoop consumed by the price of a scoop of ice cream.
    c. dividing the marginal utility of the last scoop consumed by its price.
    d. summing the marginal utilities of each scoop consumed.
    e. multiplying together the marginal utilities of each scoop of ice cream consumed.

15. In consumer equilibrium
    a. the marginal utility from consumption is the same across all goods.
    b. individuals consume so as to maximize their total satisfaction, given limited income.
    c. the ratio of the marginal utility of each good divided by its price is equal across all goods consumed.
    d. all of the above are true.
    e. all of the above are generally true except a.

Problems:

1. Why can we *not* say that two people who chose to buy the same quantity of a good at the same price have the same marginal utility?

2. If someone said, "You would have to pay me to eat one more bite," what do we know about her marginal utility? What do we know about her total utility?

3. Why would you not continue to consume a good in the range where there was diminishing total utility?

4. The following table shows Rene's total utility from eating escargot. Fill in the blanks that show the marginal utility that Rene derives from eating escargot.

Escargot Per Day	Total Utility	Marginal Utility
1	10	_____
2	18	_____
3	24	_____
4	28	_____
5	30	_____
6	30	_____

5. Plot both Rene's total and marginal utility curves on graphs.

   a. Total Utility

   b. Marginal Utility

6. Suppose it is "All You Can Eat" Night at your favorite restaurant. Once you've paid $9.95 for your meal, how do you determine how many helpings to consume? Should you continue eating until your food consumption has yielded $9.95 worth of satisfaction? What happens to the marginal utility from successive helpings as consumption increases?

7. Suppose you currently spend your weekly income on movies and video games such that the marginal utility per dollar spent on each activity is equal. If the price of a movie ticket rises, how will you reallocate your fixed income between the two activities? Why?

8. Brandy spends her entire weekly budget of $20 on soda and pizza. A can of soda and a slice of pizza are priced at $1 and $2, respectively. Brandy's marginal utility from soda and pizza consumption is 6 utils and 4 utils, respectively. What advice could you give Brandy to help her increase her overall satisfaction from the consumption of soda and pizza? What will happen to the marginal utility per dollar from soda consumption if Brandy follows your advice? What will happen to the marginal utility per dollar from pizza consumption?

9. Suppose you were studying late one night and you were craving a Papa John's pizza. How much marginal utility would you receive? How much marginal utility would you receive from a pizza that was delivered immediately after you finished a five-course Thanksgiving dinner? Where would you be more likely to eat more pizza in a single setting, at home or at a crowded party (particularly if you are not sure how many pizzas have been ordered)? Use marginal utility analysis to answer the last question.

10. The Consumer Price Index (CPI) measures changes in the cost of living by comparing the cost of buying a certain bundle of goods and services over time. The quantities of each commodity remain the same from year to year but their prices change, so changes in the index reflect the weighted average of changes in the prices of goods and services. Explain how the behavior assumed in the CPI conflicts with the way consumers actually respond to price changes. Do you think the CPI overestimates or underestimates the effect of price changes on consumers?

11. A restaurant offers a free dinner with a six-pound steak, potatoes, and all the trimmings, but only if the patron can eat it all. Otherwise, he must pay $80 for the steak dinner. What does this say about the likely marginal utility most people expect to get from the sixth pound of steak during that dinner?

12. How does the water-diamond paradox explain why there is such a poor correlation between the price of a good and the total utility a person receives from it?

13. Explain the income and substitution effects of a price reduction of a good.

14. Explain the book's distinction between newspaper racks, where the price allows you access to multiple papers, and food vending machines, where you can only get one of the items purchased. Would you expect the policy used by newspaper racks to change if each newspaper routinely included hundreds of dollars of valuable coupons?

APPENDIX
A More Advanced Theory of Consumer Choice

In this appendix, we will develop a slightly more advanced set of tools using indifference curves and budget lines to aid in our understanding of the theory of consumer choice. These approaches allow us to express our total utility as a function of two goods. The tools developed here allow us to see how the optimal combination changes in response to changing prices and income. Let's begin with indifference curves.

Indifference Curves

On the basis of their tastes and preferences, consumers must subjectively choose the bundle of goods and services that yield the highest level of satisfaction given their money income and prices.

What Is an Indifference Curve?

A consumer's indifference curve, shown in Exhibit 1, contains various combinations of two commodities, and each combination of goods (like points A, B, and C) on the indifference curve will yield the same level of total utility to this consumer. The consumer is said to be indifferent between any combination of the two goods along an individual indifference curve because she receives the same level of satisfaction from each bundle.

The Properties of the Indifference Curve

Indifference curves have the following three properties: (1) Higher indifference curves represent greater satisfaction, (2) they are negatively sloped, and (3) they are convex from the origin.

Higher Indifference Curves Represent Greater Satisfaction

Although consumers are equally happy with any bundle of goods along the indifference curve, they prefer to be on the highest indifference curve possible. This preference follows from the assumption that more of a good is preferred to less of a good. For example, in Exhibit 2, the consumer would prefer I_2 to I_1. The higher indifference curve represents more satisfaction. As you can see in Exhibit 2, bundle D gives the consumer more of both goods than does bundle C, which is on a lower indifference curve. Bundle D is also preferred to bundle A because there is more than enough extra food to compensate the consumer for the loss of clothing; total utility has risen because the consumer is now on a higher indifference curve.

appendix **exhibit 1** An Indifference Curve

appendix **exhibit 2** Indifference Curves

Indifference Curves Are Negatively Sloped

Indifference curves must slope downward from left to right if the consumer views both goods as desirable. If the quantity of one good is reduced, the quantity of the other good must be increased to maintain the same level of total satisfaction.

Indifference Curves Are Convex from the Origin

The slope of an indifference curve at a particular point measures the marginal rate of substitution (MRS), the rate at which the consumer is willing to trade one good to gain one more unit of another good. If the indifference curve is steep, the marginal rate of substitution is high. The consumer would be willing to give up a large amount of clothing for a small amount of food because she would still maintain the same level of satisfaction; she would remain on the same indifference curve, as at point A in Exhibit 3. If the indifference curve is flatter, the marginal rate of substitution is low. The consumer is only willing to give up a small amount of clothing in exchange for an additional unit of food to remain indifferent, as seen at point B in Exhibit 3. A consumer's willingness to substitute one good for another depends on the relative quantities he consumes. If he has lots of something, say food relative to clothing, he will not value the prospect of getting even more food very highly, which is just the law of demand, which is based on the law of diminishing marginal utility.

Complements and Substitutes

As we learned in Chapter 4, many goods are complements to each other; that is, the use of more units of one encourages the acquisition of additional units of the other. Gasoline and automobiles, baseballs and baseball bats, snow skis and bindings, bread and butter, and coffee and cream are examples of complementary goods. When goods are complements, units of one good cannot be acquired without affecting the want-satisfying power of other goods. Some goods are substitutes for one another; that is, the more you have of one, the less you desire the other. (The relationship between substitutes is thus the opposite of the relationship between complements.) Examples of substitutes include coffee and tea, sweaters and jackets, and home-cooked and restaurant meals.

The degree of convexity of an indifference curve—that is, the extent to which the curve deviates from a straight line—depends on how easily the two goods can be substituted for each other. If two commodities are perfect substitutes—one $10 bill and two $5 bills, for example—the indifference curve is a straight line (in this case, the line's slope is -1). As depicted in Exhibit 4(a), the marginal rate of substitution is the same regardless of the extent to which one good is replaced by the other.

At the other extreme are two commodities that are not substitutes but are perfect complements, such as left and right shoes. For most people, these goods are never used separately but are consumed only together. Because it is impossible to replace units of one with units of the other and maintain satisfaction, the marginal rate of substitution is undefined; thus, the indifference curve is a right angle, as shown in Exhibit 4(b). Because most people only care about pairs of shoes, 4 left shoes and 2 right shoes (bundle B) would yield the same level of satisfaction as 2 left shoes and 2 right shoes (bundle A). Two pairs of shoes (bundle A) are also as good as 4 right shoes and 2 left shoes (bundle C). That is, bundles A, B, and C all lie on the same indifference curve and yield the same level of satisfaction. But the combination of three right shoes and three left shoes (bundle D) is preferred to any combination of bundles on indifference curve I_1.

If two commodities can easily be substituted for one another, the nearer the indifference curves will approach a straight line; in other words, it will maintain more closely the same slope along its length throughout. The greater the complementarity between the two goods, the nearer the indifference curves will approach a right angle.

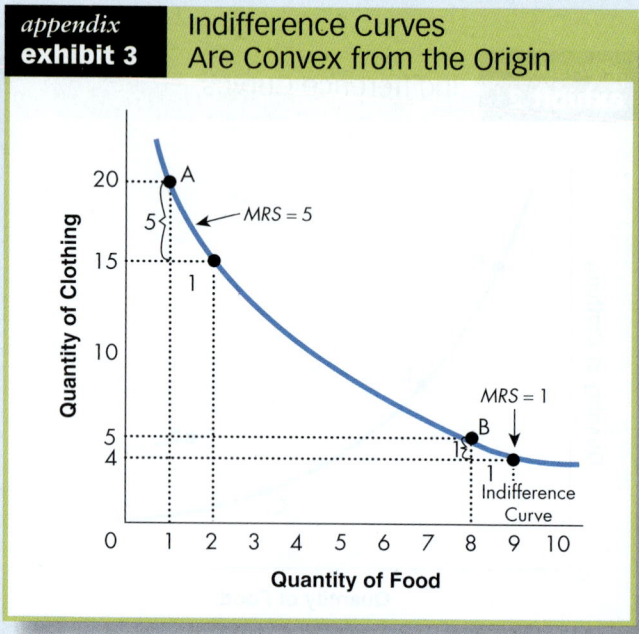

appendix exhibit 3 — Indifference Curves Are Convex from the Origin

appendix exhibit 4 Perfect Substitutes and Perfect Complements

The Budget Line

A consumer's purchase opportunities can be illustrated by a budget line. More precisely, a budget line represents the various combinations of two goods that a consumer can buy with a given income, holding the prices of the two goods constant. For simplicity, we only examine the consumer's choices between two goods. We recognize that this example is not completely realistic, as a quick visit to the store shows consumers buying a variety of different goods and services. However, the two-good model allows us to focus on the essentials, with a minimum of complication.

First, let's look at a consumer who has $50 of income a week to spend on two goods—food and clothing. The price of food is $10 per unit, and the price of clothing is $5 per unit. If the consumer spends all her income on food, she can buy 5 units of food per week ($50/$10 = 5). If she spends all her income on clothing, she can buy 10 units of clothing per week ($50/$5 = 10). However, it is likely that she will spend some of her income on each. Six of the affordable combinations are presented in the table in Exhibit 5. In the graph in Exhibit 5, the horizontal axis measures the quantity of food and the vertical axis measures the quantity of clothing. Moving along the budget line we

appendix exhibit 5 The Budget Line

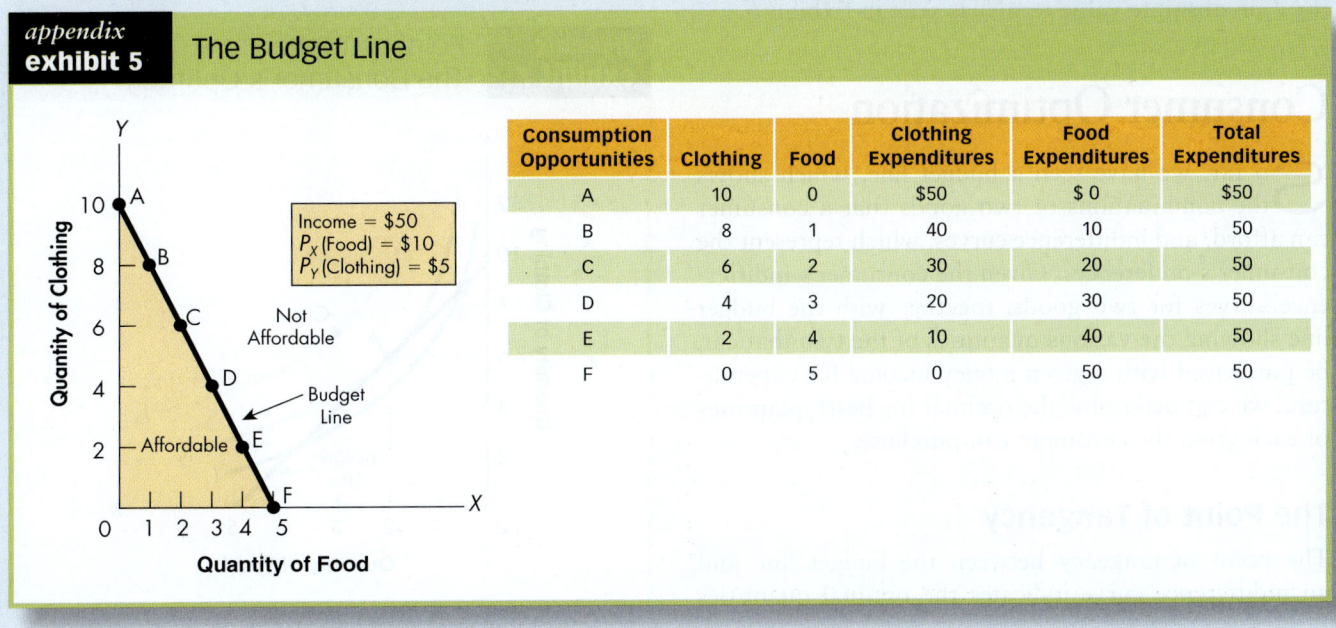

Consumption Opportunities	Clothing	Food	Clothing Expenditures	Food Expenditures	Total Expenditures
A	10	0	$50	$ 0	$50
B	8	1	40	10	50
C	6	2	30	20	50
D	4	3	20	30	50
E	2	4	10	40	50
F	0	5	0	50	50

can see the various combinations of food and clothing the consumer can purchase with her income. For example, at point A, she could buy 10 units of clothing and 0 units of food; at point B, 8 units of clothing and 1 unit of food; and so on.

Of course, any other combination along the budget line is also affordable. However, any combination of goods beyond the budget line is not feasible.

Finding the X- and Y-Intercepts of the Budget Line

The intercept on the vertical Y-axis (the clothing axis) and the intercept on the horizontal X-axis (the food axis) can easily be found by dividing the total income available for expenditures by the price of the good in question. For example, if the consumer has a fixed income of $50 a week and clothing costs $5 per unit, we know that if he spends all his income on clothing, he can afford 10 (Income/P_Y = $50/$5 = 10); so 10 is the intercept on the Y-axis. Now if he spends all his $50 on food and food costs $10 per unit, he can afford to buy 5 (Income/P_X = $50/$10 = 5); so 5 is the intercept on the X-axis, as shown in Exhibit 6.

Finding the Slope of the Budget Line

The slope of the budget line is equal to $-P_X/P_Y$. The negative coefficient of the slope indicates that the budget line is negatively sloped (downward sloping), reflecting the fact that you must give up some of one good to get more of the other. For example, if the price of X (food) is $10 and the price of Y (clothing) is $5, then the slope is equal to −10/5, or −2. That is, 2 units of Y can be obtained by forgoing the purchase of 1 unit of X; hence, the slope of the budget line is said to be −2 (or 2, in absolute value terms) as seen in Exhibit 6.

Consumer Optimization

So far, we have seen a budget line, which shows the combinations of two goods that a consumer can afford, and indifference curves, which represent the consumer's preferences. Given the consumer's indifference curves for two goods, together with the budget line showing the various quantities of the two that can be purchased with a given money income for expenditure, we can determine the optimal (or best) quantities of each good the consumer can purchase.

The Point of Tangency

The point of tangency between the budget line and an indifference curve indicates the optimal quantities

appendix **exhibit 6** The Budget Line: Intercepts and Slopes

of each good that will be purchased to maximize total satisfaction. At that point of tangency, −MRS (the slope of the indifference curve) will be equal to −P_X/P_Y (the slope of the budget line). Exhibit 7 shows the consumer's optimal combination of clothing and food. The optimum occurs where the budget line is tangent to indifference curve I_2, at point A: The consumer will acquire 2 units of food and 6 units of clothing.

To maximize satisfaction, the consumer must acquire the most preferred attainable bundle—that is, reach the highest indifference curve that can be reached with a given level of income. The highest curve that can be reached is the one to which the budget line is tangent, at point A. Any other possible combination of the two

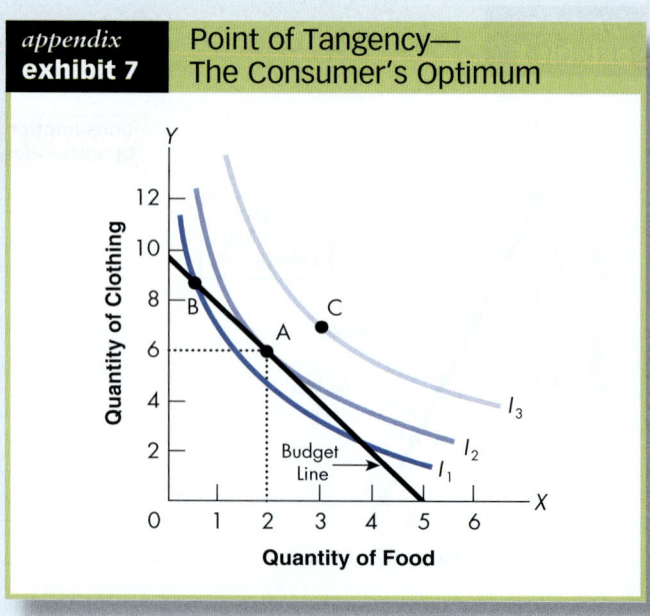

appendix **exhibit 7** Point of Tangency—The Consumer's Optimum goods either would be on a lower indifference curve and thus yield less satisfaction or would be unobtainable with the given income. For example, point B is affordable but would place the consumer on a lower indifference curve. In other words, if the consumer were at point B, she could be made better off moving to point A by consuming less clothing and more food. How about point C? That move would be nice because it is on a higher indifference curve and would yield greater total utility, but unfortunately it is unattainable with the current budget line.

Changes in the Budget Line

So far, we have seen how the prices of goods along with a consumer's income determine a budget line. Now let us examine how the budget line can change as a result of a change in the income level or the price of either good.

The Position of the Budget Line If Income Rises

An increase in income, holding relative prices constant, will cause the curve to shift outward, parallel to the old curve. As seen in Exhibit 8, a richer person can afford more of both goods than a poorer person because of the higher budget line. Suppose you just received an inheritance from a relative; this money will allow you to now buy more of the things that you want. The change in income, holding relative prices constant, is

appendix **exhibit 8** Change in Income

called the income effect and it causes this parallel shift in the budget line.

With a given pattern of indifference curves, larger amounts available for spending will result in an income-consumption curve (*ICC*) connecting the best consumption points (tangencies) at each income level.

Consider what happens to consumer purchases with a rise in income. In Exhibit 9(a), the rise in income shifts the budget line outward. If both goods, clothing and food, are normal goods in this range, then the consumer will buy more of both goods as seen in Exhibit 9(a). If income rises and the consumer buys less of one good, we say that good is an inferior good. In Exhibit 9(b), we

appendix **exhibit 9** Change in Income

a. Both goods are normal

b. Low-quality meat is the inferior good

see that the consumer buys more clothing (normal good) but less liver (inferior good). In this example, as income rises, the consumer may choose to consume fewer units of liver—the lower quality meat. Other examples of inferior goods include secondhand clothing or do-it-yourself haircuts, which consumers generally buy only because they cannot afford more expensive substitutes.

In Exhibit 9(a), both goods are normal goods, so the consumer responds to the increase in income by buying more of both clothing and food. In Exhibit 9(b), clothing is normal and hamburger is an inferior good, so the consumer responds to the increase in income by buying more clothing and less hamburger.

The Budget Line Reflects Price Changes

Purchases of goods and services depend on relative prices as well as a consumer's level of income. However, when the price of one good changes, holding income and the price of the other good constant, it causes a relative price effect. Relative prices affect the way consumers allocate their income among different goods. For example, a change in the price of the good on either the Y- or X-axis will cause the budget line to rotate inward or outward from the budget line's intercept on the other axis.

Let's return to our two-good example—clothing and food. Say the price of food falls from $10 to $5. This decrease in price comes as good news to consumers because it expands their buying opportunities—rotating the budget line outward, as seen in Exhibit 10. Thus, a consumer who spends all his income on food can now buy 10 units of food, as Income/P_X = $50/$5 = 10. If the price per unit of food rose from $10 to $25, it would contract the consumer's buying opportunities and rotate the budget line inward; so the consumer who spends all his income on food would be able to buy only 2 units of food, as Income/P_X = $50/$25 = 2.

The tangency relationship between the budget line and the indifference curve indicates the optimal amounts of each of the two goods the consumer will purchase, given the prices of both goods and the consumer's total available income for expenditures. At different possible prices for one of the goods, given the price of the other and given total income, a consumer would optimally purchase different quantities of the two goods.

A change in the price of one of the goods will alter the slope of the budget line because a different amount of the good can be purchased with a given level of income. If, for example, the price of food falls, the budget line becomes flatter because the consumer can purchase more food with a given income than she previously could. As shown in Exhibit 11, the new budget line rotates outward, from L_1 to L_2, as a result of the price reduction. Thus, the new point of tangency with an indifference curve will be on a higher indifference curve. In Exhibit 11(a), the point of tangency moves from point A to point B as a result of the decline in price of food from $10 to $5; the equilibrium quantity of food purchased increases from 2 to 5 units.

A relation known as the price-consumption curve (PCC) may be drawn through these points of tangency, indicating the optimum quantities of food (and clothing) at various possible prices of food (given the price of clothing). From this price-consumption curve, we can derive the usual demand curve for the good. Thus, Exhibit 11(a) shows that if the price of food is $10, the consumer will purchase 5 units. These data may be plotted, as in Exhibit 11(b), to derive a demand curve of the usual form. Notice that in Exhibit 11(b) the price of food is measured on the vertical axis and the quantity purchased on the horizontal axis, whereas the axes of Exhibit 11(a) refer to quantities of the two goods. Notice also that the quantities demanded, as shown in Exhibit 11(b), are those with the consumer's expenditures in equilibrium (at her optimum) at the various prices. Essentially, the demand curve is made up of various price and quantity optimum points.

appendix **exhibit 10** Change in the Relative Price of Food

The Income and Substitution Effects of a Price Change

With indifference curves, we can easily see the two ways in which a price reduction influences the quantity demanded. When the price of a good falls, the

appendix exhibit 11 The Price-Consumption Curve

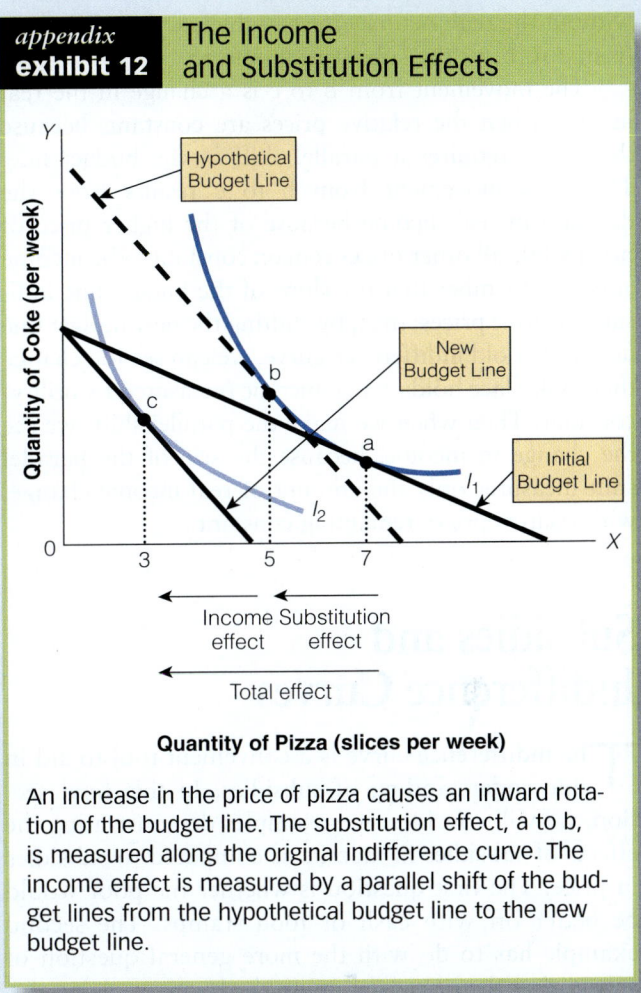

appendix exhibit 12 The Income and Substitution Effects

An increase in the price of pizza causes an inward rotation of the budget line. The substitution effect, a to b, is measured along the original indifference curve. The income effect is measured by a parallel shift of the budget lines from the hypothetical budget line to the new budget line.

income effect enables the person to buy more of this good (or other goods) with a given income; the price reduction has the same effect as an increase in money income. That is, the consumer can now move onto a higher indifference curve.

The second influence of the price decline on the quantity demanded is the substitution effect. The lower price encourages the consumer to buy larger quantities of this good. *The substitution effect is always negative.* That is, price and quantity demanded are negatively correlated; lower prices mean higher quantities demanded, and vice versa.

Exhibit 12 shows the income and substitution effects for an *increase* in the price of pizza. Because the relative price of pizza increases, the budget line rotates inward. (Note that the Y-intercept did not change, because neither income nor the price of pizza changed.

Hence if all income is spent on Coke before and after the price increase of pizza, the same amount of Coke can be purchased). The total effect of the increase in the price of pizza is indicated by point c; that is, a reduction in the quantity of pizza from 7 slices of pizza to 3 slices of pizza.

Within the total effect are the substitution effect and the income effect. First consider how much of the total effect is substituting away from the now higher-priced good, pizza. This comparison can easily be made by taking the new budget line and drawing a new hypothetical budget line parallel to the new budget line but tangent to the old indifference curve I_1. Why? It shows the effect of the new relative price on the old indifference curve—in effect, the consumer is compensated for the loss of welfare associated with the price rise by enough income to return to the original indifference curve, I_1. Remember that as long as the new budget line and the hypothetical budget line are parallel, the relative prices are the same; the only difference is the level of income. Thus, we are able to isolate the one effect—the amount of substitution that would prevail without the real income effect—which is the movement from a to b, or the substitution effect.

The movement from b to c is a change in the real income when the relative prices are constant, because this move requires a parallel shift in the budget line. Thus, the movement from b to c results from the decrease in real income because of the higher price of pizza while all other prices remain constant—the income effect. Remember that the slope of the budget line indicates relative prices; thus, by shifting the new budget line next to the old indifference curve, we can see the change that took place holding real income (measured by utility) constant. Then when we make the parallel shift, we see the change in income, because the size of the parallel shift measures only the amount of real income change, with relative prices remaining constant.

Subsidies and Indifference Curves

The indifference curve is a convenient tool to aid in our understanding of subsidies. In this final section, we will consider two examples demonstrating the effects of subsidies in income as compared to subsidies in price. The first question is whether the poor would be better off with cash or food stamps. The second example has to do with the more general question of subsidizing the price of a good like buses or trains.

Using the indifference curve approach, we can show that the poor would be at least equally as well off receiving cash rather than a subsidy like food stamps.

In Exhibit 13, if the individual's initial position is at bundle a (consuming F_1 amount of food, an amount deemed insufficient by society), the introduction of a food stamp program that allowed the recipient to spend an additional $100 per month exclusively on food would make the consumer better off (bundles of indifference curve I_2 are preferred to those on I_1). However, for the same expense, this individual might be made even better off by receiving $100 in cash. The reason is that the shaded triangle is unobtainable to the recipient of food stamps but not to those receiving a cash payment. Unless the individual intended to spend *all* of the next $100 of additional income on food, he or she would be better off with a choice.

Similarly, subsidizing the price of a good (like education, postal services, mass transportation, or medical services) is usually *not* the best method to assure that society's scarce resources are properly allocated. If the price of a good is subsidized, it distorts market signals and results in output levels of the subsidized

appendix **exhibit 13** Cash Grants Versus Food Stamp Income Subsidy

With no government assistance, the consumer chooses bundle a. The availability of food stamps increases the budget and allows the buyer to purchase bundle b, consuming more food and more other goods and attaining a higher level of utility. A cash grant, however, expands the budget set further. The recipient would purchase bundle c, which contains more nonfood items and less food than bundle b. The consumer reaches a higher level of utility with a cash grant than with food stamps.

good that are inefficiently large. In other words, the opportunity cost of forgone other goods that could have been produced with those resources is greater than the (marginal) value of the subsidized good. (Recall the ordinary supply and demand diagram for a subsidy from your elementary economics course.) Exhibit 14 shows that if the whole budget constraint is shifted parallel by an amount equivalent to the price subsidy, ab (ab = cd), then a higher indifference curve can be reached, I_2 rather than I_1. Because reaching the highest indifference curve subject to the budget constraint maximizes consumer satisfaction, this simple diagram shows that it is better to subsidize income (parallel shift) than to subsidize price (altering the slope), if one is interested in making some group better off. Of course, if you want certain groups (say, the poor) to consume more of *particular goods* (housing or food), rather than just raising their utility, you may not wish to give unconstrained income subsidies. Recall that economists can never, in their role as economists, recommend one approach over the other but they can point out the implications of alternative choices.

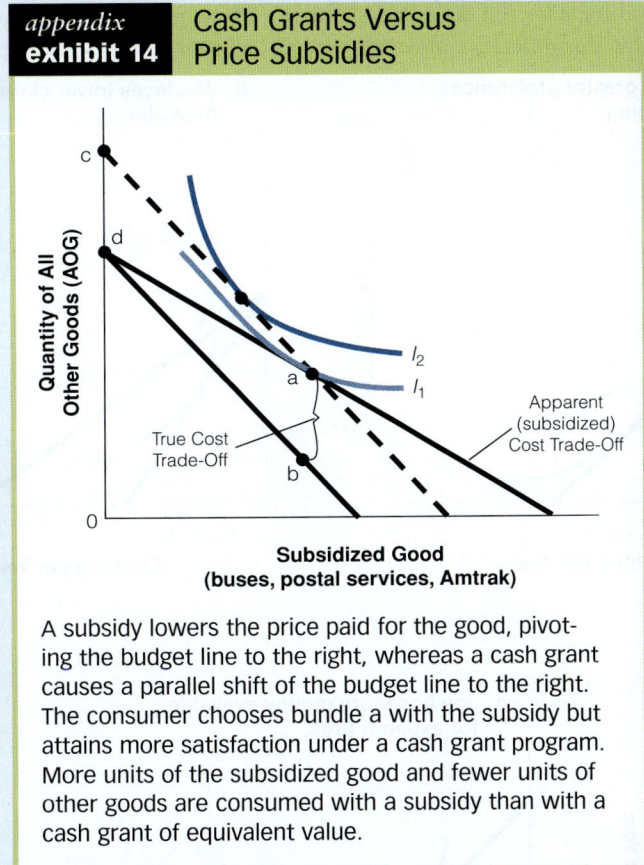

appendix **exhibit 14** Cash Grants Versus Price Subsidies

A subsidy lowers the price paid for the good, pivoting the budget line to the right, whereas a cash grant causes a parallel shift of the budget line to the right. The consumer chooses bundle a with the subsidy but attains more satisfaction under a cash grant program. More units of the subsidized good and fewer units of other goods are consumed with a subsidy than with a cash grant of equivalent value.

Problems:

1. If you had a budget of $200, and the P_Y is $5 and the P_X is $10, draw the budget line. Draw the budget lines when the P_X falls to $8. Show the budget line when the money available for expenditures increases to $400. What is the slope of the budget line when P_Y is $5 and P_X is $10? How about when P_X falls to $8?

2. Joe buys more clothes than Jim.
   a. Using indifference curves, show how Jim's consumption of clothing and food may differ from Joe's because they have different tastes, *ceteris paribus*.
   b. Suppose that Jim and Joe have the same tastes and income. Joe's father manages a clothing store, and Joe is able to buy all his clothes at wholesale prices. Show why Jim's choices of food and clothing differ from Joe's in this situation.

c. Now suppose that Jim and Joe have the same tastes and face the same prices, but that Joe has more money to spend than Jim. Demonstrate how this difference affects Joe's consumption pattern compared with Jim's.

3. Cigarette taxes are imposed to discourage consumption of so-called "undesirable goods." Using indifference curves, show the effect of an increase in taxes on cigarettes. What is the total effect? How much of the change is due to the income effect? How much is due to the substitution effect?

The Firm: Production and Costs

11

- 11.1 Firms and Profits: Total Revenues Minus Total Costs
- 11.2 Production in the Short Run
- 11.3 Costs in the Short Run
- 11.4 The Shape of the Short-Run Cost Curves
- 11.5 Cost Curves: Short-Run Versus Long-Run
- APPENDIX: Using Isoquants and Isocosts

Costs exist because resources are scarce and have competing uses—to produce more of one good means forgoing the production of another good. The cost of producing a good is measured by the worth of the most valuable alternative that was given up to obtain the resource, which is called the *opportunity cost*.

In Chapter 3, the production possibilities curve highlighted this trade-off. Recall that the opportunity cost of producing additional shelter was the units of food that had to be sacrificed. Other examples of opportunity costs abound: Paper used in this book could have been used in newspapers or magazines; the steel used in the construction of a new building could have been used in the production of an automobile or a washing machine.

In this chapter, we examine the firm's costs in more detail—what really lies behind the firm's supply curve? A firm's costs are a key determinant in pricing and production decisions. A caveat to this chapter—it is a very important building block for the theory of the firm.

But what exactly makes up a firm's cost of production? Let's begin by looking at the two distinct components of a firm's total cost: explicit costs and implicit costs. ■

SECTION 11.1 Firms and Profits: Total Revenues Minus Total Costs

- What are explicit and implicit costs?
- What are accounting profits?
- What are economic profits?
- What are sunk costs?

Explicit Costs

Explicit costs are the input costs that require a monetary payment—the out-of-pocket expenses that pay for labor services, raw materials, fuel, transportation, utilities, advertising, and so on. It is important to note that the explicit costs are opportunity costs to the firm. For example, money spent on electricity cannot be used for advertising. Remember that in a world of scarcity we are always giving up something to get something else.

explicit costs
the opportunity costs of production that require a monetary payment

implicit costs
the opportunity costs of production that do not require a monetary payment

profits
the difference between total revenues and total costs

Trade-offs are pervasive. The costs discussed so far are relatively easy to measure, and an economist and an accountant would most likely arrive at the same figures. However, that will not always be the case.

What explicit and implicit costs might the owner of this salon incur? His explicit costs include chairs, rent for the shop, scissors, the rinse sinks, electricity, blow dryers, and so on. The implicit costs include the salary he could make at another job or the leisure he could enjoy if he retired.

Implicit Costs

Some of the firm's (opportunity) costs of production are implicit. Implicit costs do not require an outlay of money. Here is where the economist's and accountant's ideas of costs diverge, because accountants do not include implicit costs. For example, whenever an investment is made, opportunities to invest elsewhere are forgone. This lost opportunity is an implicit cost that economists include in the firm's total cost even though no money is expended. A typical farmer or small business owner may perform work without receiving formal wages, but the value of the alternative earnings forgone represents an implicit opportunity cost to the individual. Because other firms could have used the resources, what the resources could have earned elsewhere is an implicit cost to the firm. It is important to emphasize that whenever we are talking about costs—explicit or implicit—we are talking about opportunity costs.

Profits

Economists generally assume that the ultimate goal of every firm is to maximize its profits. In other words, firms try to maximize the difference between what they give up for their inputs—their total costs (explicit and implicit)—and the amount they receive for their goods and services—their total revenues. Like revenues and costs, profits refer to flows over time. When we say that a firm earned $5 million in profit, we must specify the period in which the profit was earned—a week, month, year, and so on.

Are Accounting Profits the Same as Economic Profits?

A firm can make profits in the sense that the total revenues it receives exceed the explicit costs it incurs in the process of doing business. We call

Use what you've LEARNED: EXPLICIT AND IMPLICIT COSTS

Q True or false? If a company owns its own building in a growing urban area, it can protect itself from rising rents.

A False. The company cannot avoid implicit costs. If the company owned the building and rents increased, so would the opportunity cost of owning the building. That is, by occupying the building, the company is giving up the new, higher rents it could receive from renters if it leased out the space. Even though the firm pays zero rent by owning the building, the rent it could receive by leasing it to another company is a real economic cost (but not an accounting cost) to the firm.

these profits **accounting profits**. Profits as accountants record them are based on total revenues and explicit costs and do not include implicit costs.

Economists prefer an alternative way of measuring profits; they are interested in total revenues minus total costs (both explicit and implicit).

accounting profits
total revenues minus total explicit costs

Economists include the implicit costs—as well as the explicit costs—when calculating the total costs of the firm.

Summing up, measured in terms of accounting profits such as those reported in real-world financial statements, a firm has a profit if its

Use what you've LEARNED: ACCOUNTING PROFITS AND ECONOMIC PROFITS

Q Emily, an energetic 10-year-old, set up a lemonade stand in front of her house. One Saturday, she sold 50 cups of lemonade at 50 cents apiece to her friends, who were hot and thirsty from playing. These sales generated $25 in total revenues for Emily. Emily was pleased because she knew her total costs—for lemonade, mix, cups, and so on—was only $5. As she was closing up shop for the day, her neighbor, an accountant, stopped by to say hello. Emily told him about her successful day. He said, "What a great job! You made a $20 profit!" Excited, Emily rushed into the house to tell her mother, an economist, the great news. Will Emily's mother agree with the accountant's calculation of Emily's profits? If not, why?

A No, Emily's mother will not agree with the accountant, because he forgot to include the implicit costs when calculating Emily's profits. That is, he neglected to take into account what Emily could have been doing with her time if she had not been selling lemonade. For example, she could have been playing with her friends, cleaning her room, or perhaps helping her friends make money at their garage sale. These lost opportunities are implicit costs that should be included in the calculation of Emily's economic profits.

section 11.1 exhibit 1 — Accounting Profits Versus Economic Profits

Economic profits equal total revenues minus economic costs (explicit plus implicit costs). Accounting profits equal total revenues minus accounting costs (explicit costs).

total revenues exceed its explicit costs. In terms of **economic profits,** a firm has profits if its total revenues exceed its total opportunity costs—both its explicit costs and implicit costs. Exhibit 1 illustrates the difference between accounting profits and economic profits.

A Zero Economic Profit Is a Normal Profit

As we just discussed, an economic profit is less than an accounting profit because an economic profit includes implicit as well as explicit costs. In fact, an economist considers a zero economic profit a normal profit. A zero economic profit means that the firm is covering both explicit and implicit costs—the total opportunity costs of its resources. In other words, the firm's total revenues are sufficient to compensate for the time and money that owners put in the business. This view is clearly different from making a zero accounting profit, when revenues would not cover the implicit costs.

economic profits
total revenues minus explicit and implicit costs

sunk costs
costs that have been incurred and cannot be recovered

Sunk Costs

We just saw how opportunity costs are often hidden, as in the case of implicit costs, and that economists believe they should be taken into account when making economic decisions. Another type of cost should also be discussed: sunk costs. **Sunk costs** have already been incurred and cannot be recovered. These costs are visible but should be ignored when making economic decisions. Suppose, for example, that you buy a DVD that sounds interesting but when you get home and play it, you regret your purchase. Now your friend comes over and says he likes that DVD and will buy it from you for $5. You say "no way" because you paid $15 for the DVD. Are you acting rationally? Economists believe that what you paid for the DVD is now irrelevant. Now you must simply decide whether you would rather have the $5 or the DVD. If you decide to keep the DVD, the cost is the $5 you could have received from your friend—the rest is sunk.

Or suppose a donut shop has a one-year lease, but after three months the owner decides that the shop would do much better by relocating to a new mall that just opened. Should the donut shop just stay put until the end of the year because it is legally obligated to pay the 12-month lease? No, the nonrefundable lease payment is sunk and irrelevant to the decision to relocate. The decision to relocate should be based on the prospects of future profits, regardless of the length of the current lease.

In short, sunk costs are irrelevant for any future action because they have already been incurred and cannot be recovered.

SECTION CHECK

1. Total cost consists of explicit costs and implicit costs.
2. Explicit costs are the opportunity costs of production that require a monetary payment.
3. Some opportunity costs of the firm are implicit, and they do not represent an outlay of money or a contractual obligation.
4. Profits are the difference between the total revenues of a firm and its total costs.
5. Accounting profits are total revenues minus explicit costs.

6. Economic profits are total revenues minus total opportunity costs—both explicit and implicit costs.
7. Sunk costs have already been incurred and cannot be recovered.

1. What is the difference between explicit costs and implicit costs?
2. Why are both explicit costs and implicit costs relevant in making economic decisions?
3. How do we measure profits?
4. Why is it important to look at all the opportunity costs of production?
5. If you turn down a job offer of $45,000 per year to work for yourself, what is the opportunity cost of working for yourself?

SECTION 11.2 Production in the Short Run

* What is the difference between the short run and the long run?
* What is a production function?
* What is diminishing marginal product?

The Short Run Versus the Long Run

Of fundamental importance for cost and production behavior is the extent to which a firm is able to adjust inputs as it varies output. Because it takes more time to vary some inputs than others, we must distinguish between the short run and the long run. The **short run** is defined as a period too brief for some inputs to be varied. For example, a firm cannot alter the current size of its plant in a day, and it cannot obtain new equipment overnight. If demand increases for the firm's product and the firm chooses to produce more output in the short run, it must do so with its existing equipment and factory. Inputs such as buildings and equipment that do not change with output are called *fixed* inputs.

The **long run** is a period in which a firm can adjust all inputs. That is, in the long run, all inputs to the firm are *variable,* changing as output changes. The long run can vary considerably from industry to industry. For a chain of coffeehouses that wants to add a few more stores, the long run may only be a few months. In other industries, such as automobiles or steel, the long run might be a couple of years, as a new plant or factory in this type of industry takes much longer to build.

short run
a period too brief for some production inputs to be varied

long run
a period over which all production inputs are variable

production function
the relationship between the quantity of inputs and the quantity of outputs

total product (TP)
the total output of a good produced by the firm

Production in the Short Run

Exhibit 1 shows how the quantity of bagels produced by Moe's Bagel Shop per hour varies with the number of workers. This relationship between the quantity of inputs (workers) and the quantity of outputs (bagels) is called the **production function**. Suppose that Moe's has just one input that is variable (labor) and the size of the bagel shop is fixed in the short run. What will happen to **total product (TP),** the total amount of output (bagels) generated by Moe's, as the level of the variable input, labor, rises? Common sense suggests that total product will start at a low level and increase—perhaps rapidly at first and then more slowly—as the amount of the variable input increases. It will continue to increase until the quantity of the variable input (labor) becomes so large in relation to the quantity of other inputs—the size of the bagel shop, for example—that further increases in output become more and more difficult or even impossible. In the second column of Exhibit 1, we see that as Moe increases the number of workers in his bagel shop, the number of bagels Moe is able to produce increases. The addition of the first worker results in a total output of

section 11.2 exhibit 1: Moe's Production Function with One Variable, Labor

Variable Input Labor (Workers)	Total Output (Bagels per hour) Q	Marginal Product of Labor (Bagels per hour) ΔQ/ΔV
0	0	
1	10	10
2	24	14
3	36	12
4	46	10
5	50	4
6	51	1

Diminishing Marginal Product

The **marginal product (MP)** of any single input is defined as the change in total product resulting from a small change in the amount of input used. This concept is shown in the final column in Exhibit 1 and is illustrated by the MP curve in Exhibit 2(b). As you can see in Exhibit 2(b), the MP curve first rises and then falls.

The Rise in Marginal Product

The initial rise in the marginal product is the result of more effective use of fixed inputs as the number of workers increases. For example, certain types of capital equipment may require a minimum number of workers for efficient operation, or perhaps any operation at all. With a small number of workers (the variable input), some machines cannot operate at all, or only at a low level of efficiency. As additional workers are added, machines are brought into efficient operation and thus the marginal product of the workers rises. Similarly, if one person tried to operate a large department store alone—doing all the types of work necessary in the store—her energies would

10 bagels per hour. When Moe adds a second worker, bagel output climbs to 24, an increase of 14 bagels per hour. Total product continues to increase even with the sixth worker hired; but you can see that it has slowed considerably, with the sixth worker only increasing total product by 1 bagel per hour. Beyond this point, additional workers may even result in a decline in total bagel output as workers bump into each other in the small bagel shop. This outcome is evident both

> **marginal product (MP)**
> the change in total output of a good that results from a one-unit change in input

section 11.2 exhibit 2: Total Product and Marginal Product

In (a), we see that total output increases as the amount of the variable input, labor, is increased—usually more rapidly at first and then more slowly. In (b), we see that the marginal product first rises (increasing marginal product) as workers are added to the fixed input (a machine, for example), which is thus used more efficiently. Then the marginal product falls; the crowding of the fixed input with more and more workers causes marginal product to fall. Finally, negative marginal product occurs as additional inputs cause output to fall.

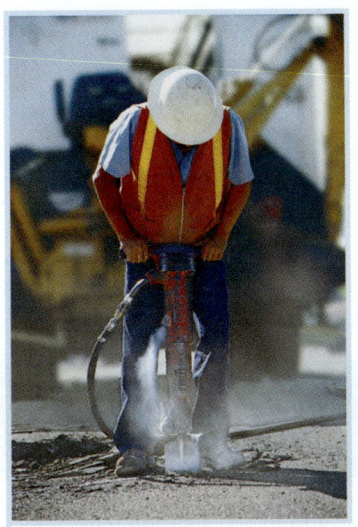

How many workers could be added to this jackhammer and still be productive (not to mention safe)? If more workers were added, how much output would be derived from each additional worker? Slightly more total output might be realized from the second worker, because the second worker would be using the jackhammer while the first worker was taking a break from "the shakes." However, the fifth or sixth worker would clearly not create any additional output, as workers would just be standing around for their turn. That is, the marginal product (additional output) would eventually fall because of diminishing marginal product.

lead to **diminishing marginal product.** Specifically, as the amount of a variable input is increased, with the amount of other (fixed) inputs held constant, a point will ultimately be reached beyond which marginal product will decline. Beyond this point, output increases but at a decreasing rate. It is the crowding of the fixed input with more and more workers that causes the decline in the marginal product.

The point of this discussion is that production functions conform to the same general pattern as that shown by Moe's Bagel Shop in the third column of Exhibit 1 and illustrated in Exhibit 2(b). In the third column of Exhibit 1, we see that as the number of workers in Moe's Bagel Shop increases, Moe is able to produce more bagels. The first worker is able to produce 10 bagels per hour. When Moe adds a second worker, total bagel output climbs to 24, an increase of 14 bagels per hour. When Moe hires a third worker, bagel output still increases. However, a third worker's marginal production (12 bagels per hour) is less than that of the second worker. In fact, the marginal product continues to drop as more and more workers are added to the bagel shop. This example shows diminishing marginal product at work. Note that it is not because the third worker is not as "good" as the second worker that marginal product falls. Even with identical workers, the increased "crowding" of the fixed input eventually causes marginal output to fall.

A firm never *knowingly* allows itself to reach the point where the marginal product becomes negative—the situation in which the use of additional variable input units actually reduces total product. In such a situation, having so many units of the variable input—inputs with positive opportunity costs—actually impairs efficient use of the fixed input units. In such a situation, *reducing* the number of workers would actually *increase* total product.

be spread so thin in so many directions that total output (sales) might be less than if she were operating a smaller store (working with less capital). As successive workers are added, up to a certain number, each worker adds more to total product than the previous one, and the marginal product rises. This relationship is seen in the shaded area of Exhibit 2(b) labeled "Increasing Marginal Product."

diminishing marginal product

as a variable input increases, with other inputs fixed, a point will be reached where the additions to output will eventually decline

The Fall in Marginal Product

Too many workers in a store make it more difficult for customers to shop; too many workers in a factory get in each other's way. Adding more and more of a variable input to a fixed input will eventually

SECTION CHECK

1. The short run is defined as a period too brief for some inputs to be varied. Inputs such as buildings and equipment that do not change with output are called fixed inputs.
2. The long run is a period of time long enough to allow the firm to adjust all inputs. That is, in the long run, all costs are variable and will change as output changes.
3. The production function is the relationship between the quantity of inputs and the quantity of outputs.
4. A diminishing marginal product occurs when the amount of a variable input keeps increasing while the amount of fixed inputs holds constant; eventually, the marginal product declines.

(continued)

1. What is the difference between fixed and variable inputs?
2. Why are all inputs variable in the long run?
3. What relationship does a production function represent?
4. What is diminishing marginal product? What causes it?

SECTION 11.3 Costs in the Short Run

* What are fixed costs?
* What are variable costs?
* What are marginal costs?
* What are average fixed, average variable, and average total costs?

In the last section, we discussed the relationship between a firm's inputs and its level of output. But that relationship is only one part of the discussion; we must also consider how much it will cost the firm to use each of these inputs in production. In this section, we examine the short-run costs of the firm—what they are and how they vary with the output levels that are produced. The short-run total costs of a business fall into two distinct categories: fixed costs and variable costs.

Fixed Costs, Variable Costs, and Total Costs

Fixed costs are those costs that do not vary with the level of output. For example, the rent on buildings or equipment is usually fixed, at least for some period; whether the firm produces lots of output or little output, the rent stays the same. Insurance premiums, property taxes, and interest payments on debt used to finance capital equipment are other examples of fixed costs; they have to be paid even if no output is produced. In the short run, fixed costs cannot be avoided. The sum of the firm's fixed costs is called the **total fixed cost (TFC)**.

Variable costs vary with the level of output. As more variable inputs such as labor and raw materials are added, output increases. The variable cost (expenditures for wages and raw materials) increases as output increases. The sum of the firm's variable costs is called the **total variable cost (TVC)**. The sum of the total fixed costs and total variable costs is called the firm's **total cost (TC)**.

fixed costs
costs that do not vary with the level of output

total fixed cost (TFC)
the sum of the firm's fixed costs

variable costs
costs that vary with the level of output

total variable cost (TVC)
the sum of the firm's variable costs

total cost (TC)
the sum of the firm's total fixed costs and total variable costs

average total cost (ATC)
a per-unit cost of operation; total cost divided by output

average fixed cost (AFC)
a per-unit measure of fixed costs; fixed costs divided by output

average variable cost (AVC)
a per-unit measure of variable costs; variable costs divided by output

Average Total Costs

Although we are often interested in the total amount of costs incurred by the firm, sometimes we find it convenient to discuss these costs on a per-unit-of-output, or an average, basis. For example, if Pizza Shack Company has a total fixed cost of $1,600 and a total variable cost of $2,400, its total cost is $4,000. If it produces 800 pizzas in the period in question, its total cost per unit of output equals $5 ($4,000 total cost ÷ 800 units of output = $5). We call this per-unit cost the **average total cost (ATC)**. Likewise, we might talk about the fixed cost per unit of output, or **average fixed cost (AFC)**. In the case of Pizza Shack, the average fixed cost, or AFC, would equal $2 ($1,600 fixed cost ÷ 800 units of output = $2). Similarly, we can speak of the per-unit variable cost, or **average variable cost (AVC)**. In this example, the average variable cost would equal $3 ($2,400 variable cost ÷ 800 units of output = $3).

Use what you've LEARNED
TRUE OR FALSE

Q If a baseball team signs a superstar free agent, they will have to increase their ticket prices to cover the costs.

A False. Whether the team sells 1,000 tickets or 1,000,000 tickets during the season, their fixed cost (which includes the superstar and other player's salary) remains the same. However, they might be able to charge more because people want to see this superstar play. But in that case demand is affecting the price, *not* costs.

Marginal Costs

Up to this point, six different short-run cost concepts have been introduced: total cost, total fixed cost, total variable cost, average total cost, average fixed cost, and average variable cost. All these concepts are relevant to a discussion of firm behavior and profitability. However, the most important single cost concept has yet to be mentioned: marginal (or additional) cost. You may recall this concept from Chapter 2, where we highlighted the importance of using marginal analysis—that is, analysis that focuses on *additional* or marginal choices. Specifically, **marginal cost (MC)** shows the change in total cost (TC) associated with a change in output (Q) by one unit ($\Delta TC/\Delta Q$). Put a bit differently,

> **marginal cost (MC)**
> the change in total costs resulting from a one-unit change in output

Use what you've LEARNED
MARGINAL COST VERSUS AVERAGE TOTAL COST

Q Suppose an oil producer's average cost of producing a barrel of oil has been $60 a barrel, and the oil producer can sell the oil to a distributor for $68 a barrel. On average, this seems like a profitable business. Given this profitability, should the oil producer expand production?

A Not necessarily. It is marginal cost that is critical. The next barrel of oil might cost $75 to produce because the well may be drying up, or the company might have to drill deeper to get additional oil, making it even more costly to retrieve. It is possible that the marginal cost of the additional barrels of oil would be greater than the market price and thus no longer profitable.

marginal cost is the cost of producing one more unit of output. As such, looking at marginal cost is a useful way to view variable cost—cost that varies as output varies. Marginal cost represents the added labor, raw materials, and miscellaneous expenses incurred in making an additional unit of output. Marginal cost is the additional, or incremental, cost associated with the "last" unit of output produced.

How Are These Costs Related?

Exhibit 1 summarizes the definitions of the seven different short-run cost concepts introduced in this chapter. To further clarify these concepts and to illustrate the relationships between them, let's return to our discussion of the costs faced by Pizza Shack.

Exhibit 2 presents the costs incurred by Pizza Shack at various levels of output. Notice that the total fixed cost is the same at all output levels and that at low output levels (four or fewer units in the example), total fixed cost is the dominant portion of total costs. At high output levels (eight or more units in the example), total fixed cost becomes quite small relative to total variable cost. As the firm increases its output, it spreads its total fixed cost across more units; as a result, the average fixed cost declines continuously.

It is often easier to understand these cost concepts by examining graphs that show the levels of the various

section 11.3 exhibit 1 A Summary of the Short-Run Cost Concept

Concept	Abbreviation	Definition
Total fixed cost	TFC	Costs that are the same at all output levels (e.g., insurance, rent)
Total variable cost	TVC	Costs that vary with the level of output (e.g., hourly labor, raw materials)
Total cost	TC	Sum of the firm's total fixed costs and total variable costs at a level of output (TC = TFC + TVC)
Marginal cost	MC	Added cost of producing one more unit of output; change in TC associated with one more unit of output ($\Delta TC/\Delta Q$)
Average total cost	ATC	TC per unit of output; TC divided by output (TC/Q)
Average fixed cost	AFC	TFC per unit of output; TFC divided by output (TFC/Q)
Average variable cost	AVC	TVC per unit of output; TVC divided by output (TVC/Q)

section 11.3 exhibit 2 Cost Calculations for Pizza Shack Company

(1) Hourly Output (Q)	(2) Total Fixed Cost (TFC)	(3) Total Variable Cost (TVC)	(4) Total Cost (TC = TVC + TFC)	(5) Average Fixed Cost (AFC = TFC/Q)	(6) Average Variable Cost (AVC = TVC/Q)	(7) Average Total Cost (ATC = TC/Q or AFC + AVC)	(8) Marginal Cost (MC = $\Delta TC/\Delta Q$)
0	$40	$0	$40	—	—	—	—
1	40	10	50	$40.00	$10.00	$50.00	$10
2	40	18	58	20.00	9.00	29.00	8
3	40	25	65	13.33	8.33	21.66	7
4	40	33	73	10.00	8.25	18.25	8
5	40	43	83	8.00	8.60	16.60	10
6	40	56	96	6.67	9.33	16.00	13
7	40	73	113	5.71	10.43	16.14	17
8	40	94	134	5.00	11.75	16.75	21
9	40	120	160	4.44	13.33	17.77	26
10	40	152	192	4.00	15.20	19.20	32

section 11.3 exhibit 3 — Total and Fixed Costs

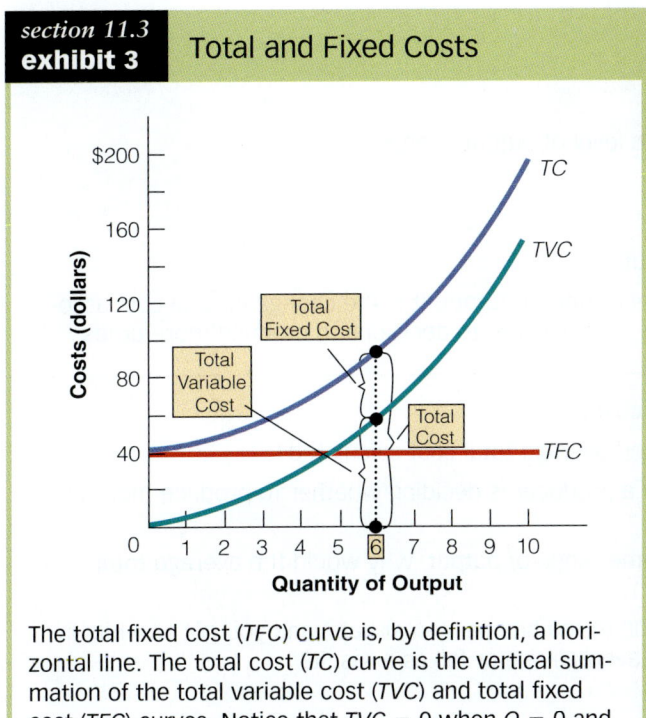

The total fixed cost (TFC) curve is, by definition, a horizontal line. The total cost (TC) curve is the vertical summation of the total variable cost (TVC) and total fixed cost (TFC) curves. Notice that $TVC = 0$ when $Q = 0$ and that $TFC = \$40$ even when no output is being produced.

costs at different output levels. The graph in Exhibit 3 shows the first three cost concepts: fixed, variable, and total costs. The total fixed cost (TFC) curve is always a horizontal line because, by definition, fixed costs are the same at all output levels—even at zero level of output. In Exhibit 3, notice that $TVC = 0$ when $Q = 0$; if no output is being produced, no variable costs are incurred.

The total cost (TC) curve is the summation of the total variable cost (TVC) and total fixed cost (TFC) curves. Because the total fixed cost curve is horizontal, the total cost curve lies above the total variable cost curve by a fixed (vertical) amount.

Exhibit 4 shows the average fixed cost curve, the average variable cost curve, the average total cost curve, and the associated marginal cost curve. In this exhibit, notice how the average fixed cost (AFC) curve constantly declines, approaching but never reaching zero. Remember, AFC is simply TFC/Q, so as output expands, AFC declines, because the total fixed cost is being spread over successively larger volumes of output. Also observe how the marginal cost (MC) curve crosses the average variable cost (AVC) and average total cost (ATC) curves at their lowest points. At higher output levels, high marginal costs pull up the average variable cost and average total cost curves, while at low output levels, low marginal costs pull the curves down. In the next section, we will explain why the marginal cost curve intersects the average variable cost curve and the average total cost curve at their minimum points.

section 11.3 exhibit 4 — Average and Marginal Costs

The marginal cost (MC) curve always intersects the average total cost (ATC) and average variable cost (AVC) curves at those curves' minimum points. Average fixed cost (AFC) curves always decline and approach—but never reach—zero. The ATC curve is the vertical summation of the AFC and AVC curves; it reaches its minimum (lowest unit cost) point at a higher output than the minimum point of the AVC curve.

SECTION CHECK

1. Fixed costs do not change with the level of output.
2. Variable costs are not fixed. Variable costs change as the level of output changes.
3. Average total cost (*ATC*) is total cost divided by output.
4. Average fixed cost (*AFC*) is fixed cost divided by output.
5. Average variable cost (*AVC*) is variable cost divided by output.
6. Marginal cost (*MC*) is the added cost of producing one more unit of output; it is the change in total cost associated with one more unit of output. Marginal cost is the cost relevant to decisions to produce more or less.

1. What is the difference between fixed costs and variable costs?
2. How are the average fixed cost, average variable cost, and average total cost calculated?
3. Why is marginal cost the relevant cost to consider when a producer is deciding whether to produce more or less of a product?
4. If the average variable cost curve were constant over some range of output, why would the average total cost be falling over that range of output?
5. If your season batting average going into a game was .300 (three hits per ten at bats) and you got two hits in five at bats during the game, would your season batting average rise or fall as a result?

SECTION 11.4 The Shape of the Short-Run Cost Curves

* What is the relationship between marginal costs and marginal product?
* Why is the average total cost curve U-shaped?
* When marginal cost is greater than average cost, what happens to the average?

The Relationship Between Marginal Costs and Marginal Product

The behavior of marginal costs bears a definite relationship to marginal product (*MP*). Say, for example, that the variable input is labor. Initially, as the firm adds more workers, the marginal product of labor tends to rise. When the marginal product of labor is rising, marginal costs are falling, because each additional worker adds more to the total product than the previous worker. Thus, the increase in total cost resulting from the production of another unit of output—marginal cost—falls. However, when marginal product of labor is declining, marginal costs are rising, because additional workers are adding less to total output. In sum, if an additional worker's marginal product is lower (higher) than that of previous workers, marginal costs increase (decrease), as seen in Exhibit 1. In area a of the two graphs in Exhibit 1, we see that as marginal product rises, marginal costs fall; in area b, we see that as marginal product falls, marginal costs rise. For example, if we are only producing a few bagels in our bagel shop we have some idle resources like the equipment; toasters, cash registers and so on. At this point, the marginal product of an extra worker is large and the marginal cost of producing one more bagel is small. However, when the bagel shop is crowded, producing many bagels with many workers and the equipment is being used to capacity, the marginal product of hiring another worker is low. Why? Because the new worker has to work in crowded conditions where she may be bumping into other workers as she waits to use the toasters and cash register. In short, when the number of bagels produced is high, the marginal product of another worker is low and the marginal cost of an additional bagel is large.

section 11.4 exhibit 1 — Marginal Product and Marginal Costs

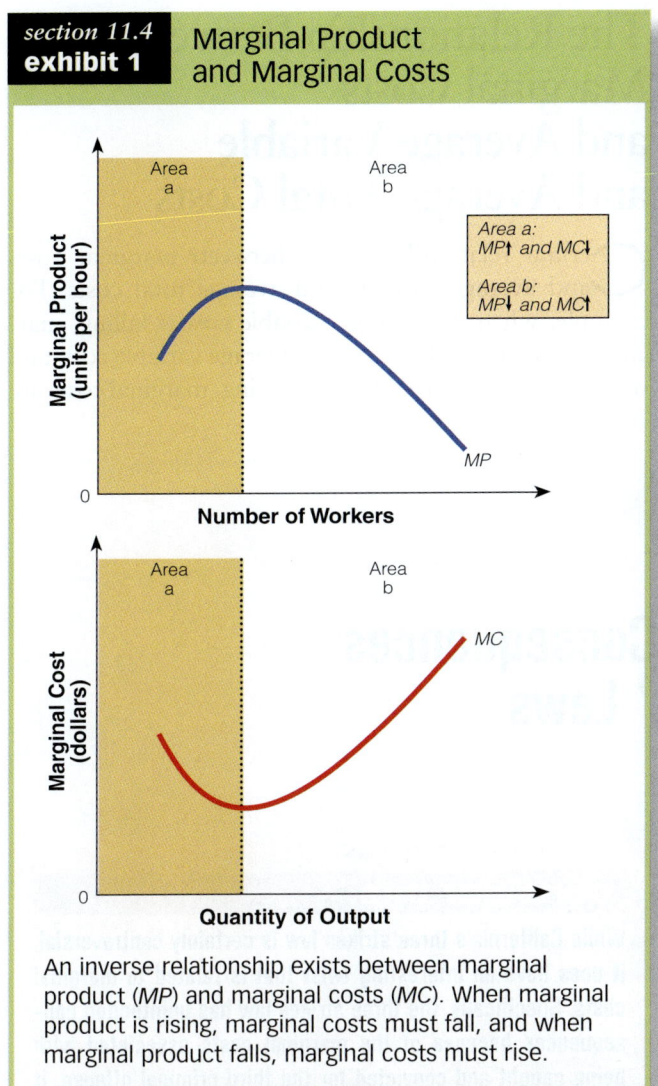

An inverse relationship exists between marginal product (*MP*) and marginal costs (*MC*). When marginal product is rising, marginal costs must fall, and when marginal product falls, marginal costs must rise.

section 11.4 exhibit 2 — U-Shaped Average Total Cost Curve

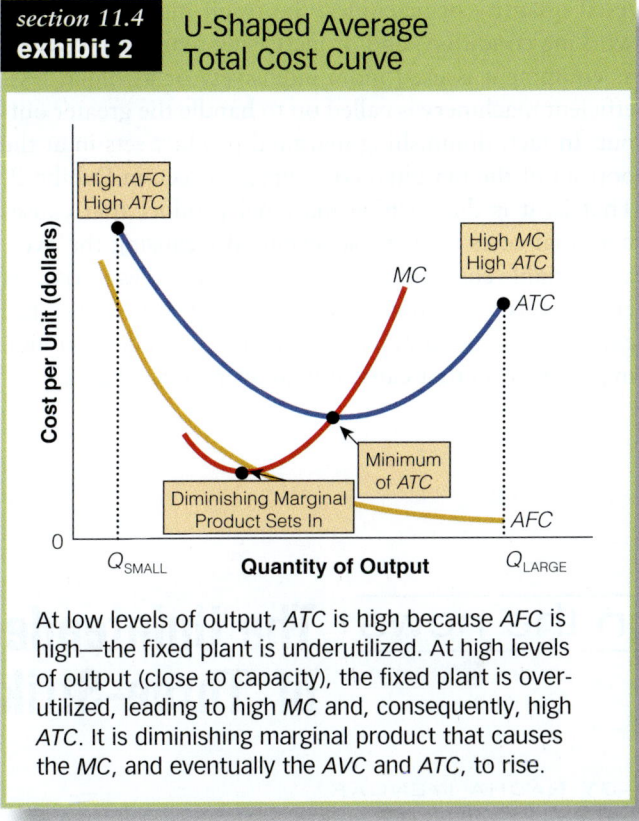

At low levels of output, *ATC* is high because *AFC* is high—the fixed plant is underutilized. At high levels of output (close to capacity), the fixed plant is over-utilized, leading to high *MC* and, consequently, high *ATC*. It is diminishing marginal product that causes the *MC*, and eventually the *AVC* and *ATC*, to rise.

The Relationship Between Marginal and Average Amounts

The relationship between the marginal and the average is simply a matter of arithmetic; when a number (the marginal cost) being added into a series is smaller than the previous average of the series, the new average will be lower than the previous one. Likewise, when the marginal number is larger than the average, the average will rise. For example, if you have taken two economics exams and received a 90 percent on your first exam and an 80 percent on your second exam, you have an 85 percent average. If, after some serious studying, you get a 100 percent on the third exam (the marginal exam), what happens to your average? It rises to 90 percent. Because the marginal is greater than the average, it "pulls" the average up. However, if the score on your third (marginal) exam is lower—a 70 percent—your average will fall to 80 percent, because the marginal is below the average. Or a baseball or softball player will improve on their batting average if the next trip to the plate is a hit or the average will fall if they strike out.

Why Is the Average Total Cost Curve U-Shaped?

Why is the average total cost curve usually U-shaped, as seen in Exhibit 2? At very small levels of output and very large levels of output, average total cost is very high. The reason for the high average total cost when the firm is producing a very small amount of output is the high average fixed cost—when the output rate of the plant is small relative to its capacity, the plant is being underutilized. But as the firm expands output beyond this point, the average total cost falls. Why? Remember that $ATC = AFC + AVC$, and average fixed cost always falls when output expands, because the fixed costs are being spread over more units of output. Thus, it is the declining *AFC* that is primarily responsible for the falling *ATC*.

The average total cost rises at high levels of output because of diminishing marginal product. For example, as more and more workers are put to work using a fixed quantity of machines, the result may be crowded working conditions and/or increasing maintenance costs as equipment is used more intensively or as older, less-efficient machinery is called on to handle the greater output. In fact, diminishing marginal product sets in at the bottom of the marginal cost curve, as seen in Exhibit 2. That is, it is diminishing marginal product that causes marginal costs to increase, eventually causing the average variable cost and average total cost curves to rise. At large levels of output, where the plant approaches full capacity, the fixed plant is overutilized, leading to high marginal costs that cause a high average total cost.

The Relationship Between Marginal Costs and Average Variable and Average Total Costs

Certain relationships exist between marginal costs and average variable and average total costs. For example, when the average variable cost is falling, marginal costs must be less than the average variable cost; and when the average variable cost is rising, marginal costs are

---

in the news: The Unintended Consequences of 'Three-Strikes' Laws

—BY RADHA IYENGAR

Strong sentences are common "tough on crime" tool[s] used to reduce the incentives for individuals to participate in criminal activity. However, the design of such policies often ignores other margins along which individuals interested in participating in crime may adjust. I use California's Three Strikes law to identify several effects of a large increase in the penalty for a broad set of crimes. Using criminal records data, I estimate that Three Strikes reduced participation in criminal activity by 20 percent for second-strike eligible offenders and a 28 percent decline for third-strike eligible offenders. However, I find two unintended consequences of the law. First, because Three Strikes flattened the penalty gradient with respect to severity, criminals were more likely to commit more violent crimes. Among third-strike eligible offenders, the probability of committing violent crimes increased by 9 percentage points. Second, because California's law was more harsh than the laws of other nearby states, Three Strikes had a beggar-thy-neighbor effect increasing the migration of criminals with second and third-strike eligibility to commit crimes in neighboring states. The high cost of incarceration combined with the high cost of violent crime relative to non-violent crime implies that Three Strikes may not be a cost-effective means of reducing crime.

consider this:

While California's three strikes law is certainly controversial, it does have an interesting twist that is related to marginal costs. Specifically, the three strikes law has unintended consequences because of the marginal costs associated with being caught and convicted for the third criminal offense. It is the third offense, no matter what it is, violent or nonviolent, that will put the convicted two-striker away for 25 years to life. Because the marginal cost of the third crime is so high, two-striker might take extreme actions to avoid being caught—perhaps even murdering a witness or a police officer to go undetected. The Fresno Police Department reported a 48 percent increase in assaults on police officers after the passage of the three strikes law. In addition, the number of high-speed chases has increased. There is even the possibility that prisons may become less safe, because three-striker will not be paroled for good behavior. This puts prison staff and fellow prisoners at higher risk.

NBER Working Paper No. W13784

SOURCE: Iyengar, Radha, I'd Rather Be Hanged for a Sheep than a Lamb: The Unintended Consequences of 'Three-Strikes' Laws (February 2008). NBER Working Paper No. W13784. Available at SSRN: http://ssrn.com/abstract=1091419.

greater than the average variable cost. Marginal costs are equal to the average variable cost at the lowest point of the average variable cost curve, as seen in Exhibit 3. In the left-hand (shaded) portion of Exhibit 3, marginal costs are less than the average variable cost, and the average is falling. On the right side, marginal costs are greater than the average variable cost, and the average is rising. The same relationship holds for the marginal cost curve and the average total cost curve. In the left-hand (shaded) portion of Exhibit 4, marginal costs are less than the average total cost, and the average is falling. On the right side, marginal costs are greater than the average total cost, and the average is rising. So it is the marginal cost curve that determines the U-shape of the AVC and ATC curves.

section 11.4 exhibit 3 Marginal Cost and Average Variable Cost

The marginal cost curve crosses the average variable cost curve at its minimum point.

section 11.4 exhibit 4 Marginal Cost and Average Total Cost

The marginal cost curve crosses the average total cost curve at its minimum point.

Use what you've LEARNED — MARGINAL VERSUS AVERAGE AMOUNTS

Q If a small horse-racing jockey decided to join your economics class of 10 students, what would happen to the *average* height of the class?

A The marginal addition, the jockey, would presumably be smaller than the average person in the class, so the average height of the class would fall. Now, if the star seven-foot center on the basketball team joined your class, the average height would rise, because the newer marginal member would presumably be taller than the average person. In sum, if the margin is greater (less) than the average, the average will rise (fall).

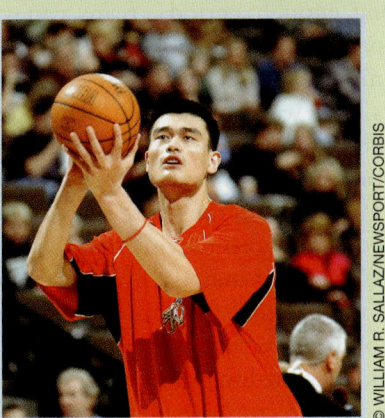

If Yao Ming (7'5") joined your class of 10 students, what would happen to the average class height?

SECTION CHECK

1. Average total cost declines as output expands but then increases again as output expands still further beyond a certain point.
2. Declining AFC is primarily responsible for the ATC. The ATC rises at high levels of output because of the diminishing marginal product.
3. When marginal costs are less than the average variable cost, the average variable cost must be falling; when marginal costs are less than the average total cost, the average total cost must be falling.
4. When marginal costs are greater than the average variable cost, the average variable cost must be rising; when marginal costs are greater than the average total cost, the average total cost must be rising.

1. What is the primary reason that the average total cost falls as output expands over low output ranges?
2. Why does the average total cost rise at some point as output expands further?
3. If marginal costs are less than the average total cost, why does ATC fall? If MC is greater than ATC, why does ATC rise?

SECTION 11.5 Cost Curves: Short-Run Versus Long-Run

* Why are long-run costs different than short-run costs?
* What are economies of scale?
* What are diseconomies of scale?
* What are constant returns to scale?

Why Are Long-Run Cost Curves Different from Short-Run Cost Curves?

Over long enough periods, firms can vary all of their productive inputs. That is, time provides an opportunity to substitute lower-cost capital, like larger plants or newer, more sophisticated equipment, for more expensive labor inputs. However, in the short run a firm cannot alter its plant size and equipment. These inputs are fixed in the short run, so the firm can only expand output by employing more variable inputs (e.g., workers and raw materials) in order to get extra output from the existing factory. If a company has to pay many workers overtime wages to expand output in the short run, over the long run firms may opt to invest in new equipment to conserve on expensive labor. That is, in the long run, the firm can expand its factories, build new ones, or shut down unproductive ones. Of course, the time it takes for a firm to get to the long run varies from firm to firm. For example, it may take only a couple of months to build a new coffee shop,

Larger plants may be built in the long run.

while it may take a few years to build a new automobile plant.

In Exhibit 1, we see that the long-run average total cost (LRATC) curve lies equal to or below the short-run average total cost (SRATC) curves. The reason for the difference between the firm's long-run total cost curve and the short-run total cost curve is that in the long run,

section 11.5 exhibit 1 — Short- and Long-Run Average Total Costs

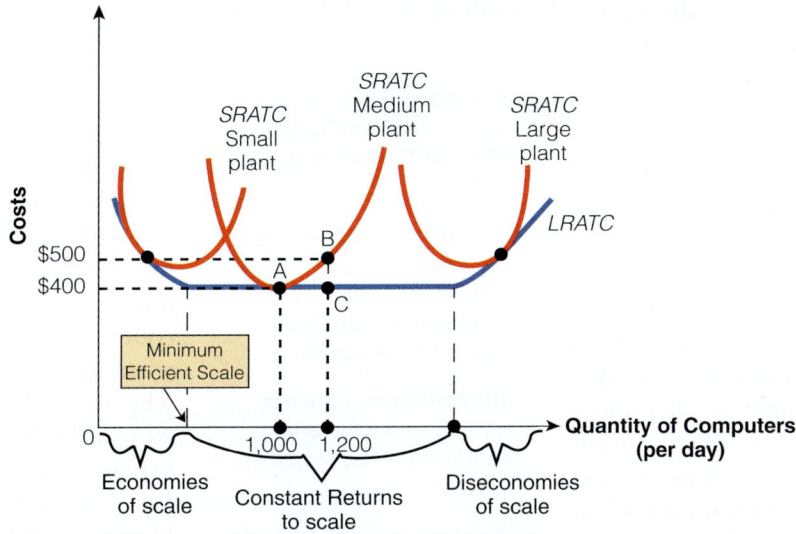

In the long run, firms can increase their capital inputs (fixed in the short run) as well as their inputs that are variable in the short run, in some cases lowering average costs per unit and overcoming the cost-increasing effects of the law of diminishing marginal product. The long-run average total cost curve is thus less U-shaped than short-run average total cost curves. Still, at very low output levels, some reduction of average costs per unit are obtainable by expanding output and productive capacity; in those output ranges, economies of scale exist. At high output ranges, average costs per unit may start rising if the firm enters an output range characterized by diseconomies of scale.

Large automobile manufacturers can produce at a lower average total cost as a result of economies of scale considerations.

costs are lower because firms have greater flexibility in changing inputs that are fixed in the short run. Exhibit 1 presents three short-run average total cost curves, representing small, medium, and large plant sizes.

It also shows the long-run average total cost curve. In the *short run*, the firm is restricted to the current plant size, but in the long run it can choose the short-run cost curve for the level of production it is planning on producing. As the firm moves along the long-run average total cost curve, it is adjusting the size of the factory to the quantity of production.

For example, in Exhibit 1, if Apple computer wanted to expand output in the medium plant size from 1,000 computers per day to 1,200 computers per day it has no choice but to hire more workers in the short run, moving from point A to point B. Because of diminishing marginal product (adding more workers to fixed plant size), the short-run average total cost rises from $400 to $500. However, in the long run, Apple can expand its factory size and workforce and the average total cost returns to $400, moving from point A to point C.

What Are Economies of Scale?

By examining the long-run average total cost curve for a firm, we can see three possible production patterns. In Exhibit 1, we see that extremely small firms experience **economies of scale,** falling per-unit costs as output expands. These firms, then, are functioning inefficiently from a long-run perspective. The **minimum efficient scale** is the output level in which the economies of scale are exhausted and the long-run average total costs are minimized. Similarly, firms that expand beyond a certain point encounter **diseconomies of scale;** that is, they incur rising per-unit costs as their output grows. In more intermediate output ranges, firms of varying sizes can compete on a roughly equal basis as far as costs are concerned because they all exhibit approximately **constant returns to scale.** That is, their per-unit costs remain stable as output grows. In this example Apple computers have economies of scale at low levels of output, construct returns to scale at intermediate levels of output, and diseconomies of very high levels of output.

> **economies of scale**
> occur in an output range where LRATC falls as output increases
>
> **minimum efficient scale**
> the output level where economies of scale are exhausted and constant returns to scale begin
>
> **diseconomies of scale**
> occur in an output range where LRATC rises as output expands
>
> **constant returns to scale**
> occur in an output range where LRATC does not change as output varies

producing at lower levels of output. For example, workers might experience greater proficiency gains if they concentrated on a few specific tasks rather than on many different tasks. That is, people who try to do everything may end up doing nothing very well.

Recall that diseconomies of scale exist when there is an increase in the firm's long-run average costs as output expands. This may occur as the firm finds it increasingly difficult to handle the complexities of large-scale management. For example, information and coordination problems tend to increase when a firm becomes very large. This is why the *LRATC* is usually U-shaped. At low levels of output, firms generally benefit from increased size because they can take advantage of specialization. However, at high levels of output, the gains from specialization have already occurred but coordination and bureaucratic problems increase.

Why Do Economies and Diseconomies of Scale Occur?

As we have just seen, economies of scale exist when there is a reduction in the firm's long-run average costs as output expands. This may occur because the firm can capture gains from specialization that might not be possible if the firm were

By having several screens in one complex, the cinema company can cut down on advertising and employee costs as well as rent. Because of economies of scales, it may be less expensive to have eight screens in one building with one concession area than eight separate theaters, each with one screen and a concession area.

SECTION CHECK

1. At low output levels, when all inputs can be varied, some firms will experience economies of scale, where their per-unit costs are decreasing as output increases.
2. Firms that expand all inputs beyond a certain point will encounter diseconomies of scale, incurring rising per-unit costs as output grows in the long-run.
3. In intermediate output ranges, firms may exhibit roughly constant returns to scale; in this range, their per-unit costs remain stable as output increase.

---

1. What are economies of scale, diseconomies of scale, and constant returns to scale?
2. How might cooking for a family dinner be subject to falling average total cost in the long run as the size of the family grows?
3. What may cause economies or diseconomies of scale?

Interactive Chapter Summary

Fill in the blanks:

1. Profits are defined as _____ minus _____.
2. The cost of producing a good is measured by the worth of the _____ alternative that was given up to obtain the resource.
3. Explicit costs are input costs that require a(n) _____ payment.
4. Whenever we talk about cost—explicit or implicit—we are talking about _____ cost.
5. Economists generally assume that the ultimate goal of a firm is to _____ profits.
6. Accounting profits equal actual revenues minus actual expenditures of cash (explicit costs), so they do not include _____ costs.
7. Economists consider a zero economic profit a normal profit because it means that the firm is covering both _____ and _____ costs—the total opportunity cost of its resources.
8. _____ costs are costs that have already been incurred and cannot be recovered.
9. Because it takes more time to vary some inputs than others, we must distinguish between the _____ run and the _____ run.
10. The long run is a period of time in which the firm can adjust _____ inputs.
11. In the long run, all costs are _____ costs and will change as output changes.
12. The total product schedule shows the total amount of _____ generated as the level of the variable input increases.
13. The marginal product of any single input is the change in total product resulting from a(n) _____ change in the amount of that input used.
14. As the amount of a variable input is increased, the amount of other fixed inputs being held constant, a point will ultimately be reached beyond which marginal product will decline. This point is called _____.
15. The short-run total costs of a business fall into two distinct categories: _____ costs and _____ costs.
16. Fixed costs are costs that _____ with the level of output.
17. In the short run, fixed costs cannot be avoided without _____.
18. The sum of a firm's fixed costs is called its _____.
19. Costs that are not fixed are called _____ costs.
20. The sum of a firm's variable costs is called its _____.
21. The sum of a firm's total _____ costs and total _____ costs is called its total cost.
22. Average total cost equals _____ divided by the _____ produced.
23. Average fixed cost equals _____ divided by the _____ produced.
24. _____ equals total variable cost divided by the level of output produced.
25. Marginal costs are the _____ costs associated with the "last" unit of output produced.
26. A fixed cost curve is always a(n) _____ line because, by definition, fixed costs are the same at all output levels.
27. The reason for high average total costs when a firm is producing a very small amount of output is the high _____ costs.
28. The average total cost curve rises at high levels of output because of _____ product.
29. When AVC is falling, MC must be _____ than AVC; and when AVC is rising, MC must be _____ than AVC.
30. In the _____ run, a company cannot vary its plant size and equipment, so the firm can only expand output by employing more _____ inputs.
31. The $LRATC$ curve is often called a(n) _____ curve because it represents the cost data relevant to a firm when it is planning policy relating to scale of operations, output, and price over a long period of time.

32. When *LRATC* falls as output expands, _____ of scale occur. When the *LRATC* does not vary with output, the firm faces _____ to scale. When the *LRATC* rises as output expands, _____ of scale occur.

33. At the _____ scale, a plant has exhausted its economies of scale and the long-run average total costs are minimized.

34. Any particular cost curve is based on the assumption that _____ prices and _____ are constant.

35. _____ may occur as a firm finds it increasingly difficult to handle the complexities of large-scale management.

Answers: 1. total revenues; total costs 2. most valuable 3. monetary 4. opportunity 5. maximize 6. implicit 7. implicit; explicit 8. Sunk 9. short; long 10. all 11. variable 12. output 13. small 14. diminishing marginal product 15. fixed; variable 16. do not vary 17. going out of business 18. total fixed cost 19. variable 20. total variable cost 21. fixed; variable 22. total cost; level of output 23. total fixed cost; level of output 24. Average variable cost 25. additional 26. horizontal 27. average fixed 28. diminishing marginal 29. less; more 30. short; variable 31. planning 32. economies; constant returns; diseconomies 33. minimum efficient 34. input; technology 35. Diseconomies of scale

Key Terms and Concepts

explicit costs 290
implicit costs 290
profits 290
accounting profits 291
economic profits 292
sunk costs 292
short run 293
long run 293
production function 293

total product (TP) 293
marginal product (MP) 294
diminishing marginal product 295
fixed costs 296
total fixed cost (TFC) 296
variable costs 296
total variable cost (TVC) 296
total cost (TC) 296
average total cost (ATC) 296

average fixed cost (AFC) 296
average variable cost (AVC) 296
marginal cost (MC) 297
economies of scale 306
minimum efficient scale 306
diseconomies of scale 306
constant returns to scale 306

Section Check Answers

11.1 Firms and Profits: Total Revenues Minus Total Costs

1. **What is the difference between explicit costs and implicit costs?**
   Explicit costs are those costs readily measured by the money spent on the resources used, such as wages. Implicit costs are those that do not represent an explicit outlay of money, but do represent opportunity costs, such as the opportunity cost of your time when you work for yourself.

2. **Why are both explicit costs and implicit costs relevant in making economic decisions?**
   In making economic decisions, where expected marginal benefits must be weighed against expected marginal costs, all relevant costs must be included, whether they are explicit or implicit.

3. **How do we measure profits?**
   Profit is measured as total revenue minus total cost.

4. **Why is it important to look at all the opportunity costs of production?**
   Economic profit equals total revenue minus both explicit and implicit costs, including the opportunity cost (forgone earnings) of financial resources invested in the firm. All of your owned inputs—including your own time, equipment, structures, land, and so on—have opportunity costs that aren't revealed in explicit dollar payments. Correctly assigning implicit costs to all these owned inputs is necessary so that a correct measure of economic profits can be made. To be earning economic profits means that a firm is earning an above-normal rate of return.

5. **If you turn down a job offer of $45,000 per year to work for yourself, what is the opportunity cost of working for yourself?**
   Other things being equal, you incur a $45,000 per year implicit cost of working for yourself in this case, because it is what you give up when you choose to turn down the alternative job offer. If you turned down even better offers, your opportunity cost of working for yourself would be even higher.

11.2 Production in the Short Run

1. **What is the difference between fixed and variable inputs?**
   Fixed inputs are those, such as plants and equipment, that cannot be changed in the short run, while variable

inputs are those, such as hourly labor, that can be changed in the short run.

2. **Why are all inputs variable in the long run?**
   All inputs are variable in the long run by definition, because the long run is defined as that time period necessary to allow all inputs to be varied.

3. **What relationship does a production function represent?**
   A production function represents the relationship between different combinations of inputs and the maximum output of a product that can be produced with those inputs, with given technology.

4. **What is diminishing marginal product? What causes it?**
   Diminishing marginal product means that as the amount of a variable input is increased—the amount of other inputs being held constant—a point will ultimately be reached beyond which marginal product will decline. It is caused by reductions in the amount of fixed inputs that can be combined with each unit of a variable input, as the amount of that variable input used increases.

11.3 Costs in the Short Run

1. **What is the difference between fixed costs and variable costs?**
   Fixed costs are the expenses associated with fixed inputs (that therefore only exist in the short run), which are constant regardless of output. Variable costs are the expenses associated with variable inputs, which change as the level of output changes.

2. **How are the average fixed cost, average variable cost, and average total cost calculated?**
   For a given level of output, any average cost is calculated as the relevant total cost divided by the level of output. Average fixed cost is therefore total fixed cost divided by output; average variable cost is total variable cost divided by output; and average total cost is total cost (fixed cost plus variable cost) divided by output.

3. **Why is marginal cost the relevant cost to consider when a producer is deciding whether to produce more or less of a product?**
   Marginal cost is the additional cost of increasing output by one unit. That is, it is the cost relevant to the choice of whether to produce and sell one more unit of a good. For producing and selling one more unit of a product to increase profits, the addition to revenue from selling that output (marginal revenue) must exceed the addition to cost from producing it (marginal cost).

4. **If the average variable cost curve were constant over some range of output, why would the average total cost be falling over that range of output?**
   Average total cost is the sum of average variable cost and average fixed cost. Average fixed costs fall over the entire possible range of output. Therefore, if the average variable cost curve were constant over a range of output, the average total cost curve must be falling over that range of output.

5. **If your season batting average going into a game was .300 (three hits per ten at bats) and you got two hits in five at bats during the game, would your season batting average rise or fall as a result?**
   Your "marginal" batting average in the game was .400 (two hits per five at bats), which was higher than your previous batting average. As a consequence, because that game's marginal results were above your previous average, it raises your season batting average as a result.

11.4 The Shape of the Short-Run Cost Curves

1. **What is the primary reason that the average total cost falls as output expands over low output ranges?**
   The primary reason average total cost falls as output expands over low output ranges is that average fixed cost declines sharply with output at low levels of output.

2. **Why does the average total cost rise at some point as output expands further?**
   Average total cost begins to rise at some point as output expands further, because of the law of diminishing marginal product, also called the law of increasing costs. Over this range of output, adding more variable inputs does not increase output by the same proportion, so the average cost of production increases over this range of output.

3. **If marginal costs are less than the average total cost, why does *ATC* fall? If *MC* is greater than *ATC*, why does *ATC* rise?**
   When the marginal cost of a unit of output is less than its average total cost, including the lower-cost unit will lower the average (just as getting lower marginal grades this term will decrease your GPA). When the marginal cost of a unit of output exceeds its average total cost, including the higher-cost unit will raise the average (just as getting higher marginal grades this term will increase your GPA).

11.5 Cost Curves: Short-Run Versus Long-Run

1. **Why does the *LRATC* curve have a shallower U-shape than the *SRATC*?**

   In the short run, some inputs are fixed, like the size of the physical plant or certain machinery. Once a firm has chosen its plant size it is fixed in the short run. In the long run, firms can increase their capital inputs (fixed in the short run) as well as their inputs that are variable in the short run. So the short-run costs are at least as high as the long-run costs and higher if the wrong level of capital is chosen in the short run. Thus, the long-run curve has a shallower U-shape curve than the short run. Remember, the firm can adjust all factors in the long run which allows it to keep its costs lower.

2. **What are economies of scale, diseconomies of scale, and constant returns to scale?**

   Each of these terms refers to average or per-unit costs as output expands. Economies of scale means that long-run average cost falls as output expands; diseconomies of scale means that long-run average cost rises as output expands; and constant returns to scale means that long-run average cost is constant as output expands.

3. **How might cooking a family dinner be subject to falling average total cost in the long run as the size of the family grows?**

   Once the appropriate larger-scale cooking technology has been adopted (i.e., in the long run, when all inputs can be varied), such as larger cooking pots, pans, and baking sheets, larger ovens, dishwashers, and so on, and more family members can be involved, each specializing in fewer tasks, this larger scale can reduce the average cost per meal served.

4. **What may cause economies or diseconomies of scale?**

   Economies of scale can result when expanding output allows the use of mass production techniques such as assembly lines or allows gains from further labor specialization that may not be possible at lower levels of output. Diseconomies of scale can result when a firm finds it increasingly difficult to handle the complexity as well as the information and coordination problems of large-scale management.

CHAPTER 11 STUDY GUIDE

True or False:

1. Explicit costs exclude the opportunity cost of using one's own land, labor, or capital.
2. Implicit costs are opportunity costs.
3. When economists say firms try to maximize profits, they mean that firms try to maximize the difference between what they receive for their goods and services in total revenue and what they give up for their inputs in total explicit costs.
4. Economic profits equal actual revenues minus all implicit costs.
5. Economists consider a zero economic profit a normal profit rate.
6. Earning zero economic profit is equivalent to earning zero accounting profit.
7. Sunk costs are opportunity costs.
8. The short run is simply defined as the present.
9. In the short run, the inputs that do not change with output are called fixed inputs or fixed factors of production.
10. The long run is the same length of time in every industry.
11. Total product will typically start at a low level and increase rapidly at first, but will eventually increase more slowly as the amount of the variable input increases.
12. Marginal product first rises as the result of increasing amounts of fixed inputs, but then at some point it falls.
13. Diminishing marginal product occurs when the crowding of the fixed inputs with more and more of the variable input lowers total output.
14. A firm with positive marginal costs will chose to produce where the marginal product becomes zero.
15. A firm should produce as long as the marginal product of its inputs are positive.
16. Fixed costs for a given period have to be paid whether or not a firm produces output in that period.
17. Variable costs vary with output, while fixed costs do not.
18. Marginal cost is the cost of producing one more unit of output.
19. Marginal costs are a useful way to view changes in variable costs as output changes.
20. The total cost curve is the summation of the marginal cost and total fixed cost curves.
21. The average fixed cost curve always decreases with output in the short run.
22. The marginal cost curve crosses the average variable cost and average fixed cost curves at those curves' lowest points.
23. At output levels where average total cost is falling, marginal cost must be falling.
24. The average fixed cost curve declines only as long as the marginal cost curve falling.
25. The average variable cost and average total cost curves are usually U-shaped.
26. It is the declining average fixed cost curve that is primarily responsible for the falling segment of the average total cost curve.
27. Diminishing marginal product first sets in at the minimum point of the marginal cost curve.
28. Diminishing marginal product causes the marginal cost curve to increase, eventually causing the average variable cost and average total cost curves to rise.
29. *MC* is equal to *AVC* at the lowest point on the *AVC* curve, and it is equal to *ATC* at the lowest point on the *ATC* curve.
30. Even over long time periods, firms cannot vary all of their fixed inputs.
31. As we move along the *LRATC*, factory size is held constant.
32. A typical firm experiences economies of scale at low levels of output, constant returns to scale at higher levels of output, and diseconomies of scale at still higher levels of output.

33. Economies of scale may exist because a firm can use mass production techniques or capture gains from further labor specialization not possible at lower levels of output.
34. When either input prices rises or technology advances, the cost curves of a firm will shift upward.

Multiple Choice:

1. An explicit cost
    a. is an opportunity cost.
    b. does not require an outlay of money.
    c. is an out-of-pocket expense.
    d. is characterized by both a and b.
    e. is characterized by both a and c.

2. Which of the following is false?
    a. Explicit costs are input costs that require a monetary payment.
    b. Implicit costs do not represent an explicit outlay of money.
    c. Both implicit and explicit costs are opportunity costs.
    d. Sunk costs are opportunity costs.
    e. All of the above are *true*.

3. Which of the following is true?
    a. Profits are a firm's total revenue minus its total costs.
    b. Accounting profits are actual revenues minus actual expenditures of money.
    c. Economic profits are actual revenues minus all explicit and implicit costs.
    d. If a firm has any implicit costs, its economic profits will be less than its accounting profits.
    e. All of the above are true.

4. The crucial difference between how economists and accountants analyze the profitability of a business has to do with whether or not are included when calculating total production costs.
    a. sunk costs.
    b. cash payments.
    c. implicit costs.
    d. explicit costs.

5. Which of the following is true?
    a. If a firm's implicit costs are zero, accounting profits equal economic profits.
    b. If a firm's implicit costs are positive, economic profits exceed accounting profits.
    c. If a firm's implicit costs are positive, accounting profits exceed economic profits.
    d. Both a. and b. are true.
    e. Both a. and c. are true.

6. Marjorie produces and sells 300 jars of homemade jelly each month for $3 each. Each month, she pays $300 for jars, pays $200 for ingredients, and uses her own time, with an opportunity cost of $250. Her economic profits each month are
    a. $450.
    b. $400.
    c. $150.
    d. minus $150.
    e. minus $450.

7. Sunk costs
    a. have already been incurred and are not relevant for present decisions.
    b. should be included when weighing the marginal costs of production against the marginal benefits received.
    c. plus variable costs equal the total costs of production.
    d. are relevant to future decisions and should be carefully considered.

8. The short run
   a. is a period too brief for fixed inputs to be varied.
   b. is a period that involves no fixed costs.
   c. is normally a period of one year.
   d. is none of the above.

9. The long run
   a. is a period in which a firm can adjust all its inputs.
   b. can vary in length from industry to industry.
   c. is a period in which all costs are variable costs.
   d. is characterized by all of the above.

10. The long-run production period
    a. is a time when all inputs are variable.
    b. varies in length according to how specialized the capital goods involved are.
    c. is likely to be longer for a steel manufacturer than for a retailer who sells watches off a cart at the local mall.
    d. is characterized by all of the above.
    e. is characterized by a. and b., but not c.

11. Which of the following most accurately describes the long-run period?
    a. The long run is of sufficient length to allow a firm to transform economic losses into economic profits.
    b. The long run is of sufficient length to allow a firm to alter its plant capacity and all other factors of production.
    c. In the long run, a firm is able to expand output by utilizing additional workers and raw materials, but not physical capital.
    d. The long run is a period of time in which a firm is unable to vary some of its factors of production.
    e. Both a. and b. accurately describe the long-run period.

12. Production in the short run
    a. is subject to the law of diminishing marginal product.
    b. involves only variable factors of production.
    c. can be increased by employing another unit of a fixed input, as long as the marginal product of that input is positive.
    d. is characterized by all of the above.
    e. is characterized by none of the above.

13. A production function shows the relationship between
    a. costs and output.
    b. variable inputs and fixed inputs.
    c. variable inputs and output.
    d. inputs and costs.
    e. production and sales revenue.

14. Diminishing marginal product
    a. occurs both in the long run and the short run.
    b. occurs in the long run but not in the short run.
    c. occurs in the short run but not in the long run.
    d. occurs in neither the long run nor the short run.

15. Diminishing marginal productivity in a frozen-pizza company means that
    a. hiring additional workers adds fewer and fewer pizzas to total output.
    b. hiring additional workers causes the total output of pizza to fall.
    c. hiring additional workers does not change the total output of pizza produced.
    d. the average total cost of production must be decreasing.

16. If the marginal product of a firm's only variable input is positive,
    a. its total product is growing at a decreasing rate.
    b. it will use more of the variable input until its marginal product is zero.
    c. it will reduce its use of the variable input.
    d. all of the above are true.
    e. none of the above are true.

17. Total fixed costs
    a. do not vary with the level of output.
    b. cannot be avoided in the short run without going out of business.
    c. do not exist in the long run.
    d. are characterized by all of the above.

18. Which of the following is most likely a variable cost for a business?
    a. the lease payment on a warehouse used by the business.
    b. the opportunity cost of the heavy equipment installed in a factory.
    c. the loan payment on funds borrowed when a new building is constructed.
    d. payments for electricity.

19. The change in total cost that results from the production of one additional unit of output is called
    a. marginal cost.
    b. average fixed cost.
    c. average variable cost.
    d. average total cost.
    e. marginal revenue.

20. Which short-run cost curve begins to rise first as output expands?
    a. average variable cost
    b. average total cost.
    c. average fixed cost.
    d. marginal cost.
    e. total cost.

21. Which of the following is true?
    a. The short-run *AFC* is always falling with increased output, whether the short-run *MC* curve is greater or less than short-run *AFC*.
    b. The short-run *ATC* exceeds the short-run *AVC* at any given level of output.
    c. If the short-run *ATC* curve is rising, the short-run *AVC* curve is also rising.
    d. If short-run *MC* is less than short-run *AVC*, short-run *AVC* is falling.
    e. All of the above are true.

22. Which of the following is true in the short run?
    a. *ATC* is usually U-shaped.
    b. Declining *AFCs* are the primary reason *ATC* decreases at low levels of output.
    c. *ATC* increases at high levels of output because of diminishing marginal product.
    d. Diminishing marginal product sets in at the minimum point of *MC*.
    e. All of the above are true in the short run.

23. Typically, what is the shape of the average total cost curve for a firm in the short run?
    a. Typically, an average total cost curve constantly slopes upward as output expands and eventually approaches an infinite dollar amount at high rates of output.
    b. Typically, an average total cost curve is U-shaped.
    c. Typically, an average total cost curve is a vertical line.
    d. Typically, an average total cost curve slopes downward as output expands and approaches the *X*-axis when output is very large.

24. Which of the following is false in the short run?
    a. *MC* equals *ATC* at the lowest point of *ATC*.
    b. *MC* equals *AVC* at the lowest point of *AVC*.
    c. When *AVC* is falling, *ATC* must be falling.
    d. When *ATC* is falling, *AVC* must be falling.
    e. All of the above are true.

25. Which of the following is true?
    a. When marginal cost is less than average total cost, average total cost is decreasing.
    b. The fact that average fixed cost is falling tells us nothing about the shape of the marginal cost curve.
    c. When average variable cost is falling, marginal cost must be less than average variable cost.
    d. When marginal cost is greater than average total cost, average total cost is increasing.
    e. All of the above are true.

26. When marginal product is increasing,
    a. marginal cost is decreasing.
    b. marginal cost is increasing.
    c. average variable cost is increasing.
    d. average total cost is increasing.
    e. total cost is decreasing.

27. If a producer is operating in the region of diminishing marginal product and more variable inputs are added in the short run, what is true of the marginal cost of providing the additional service?
    a. Marginal cost will be decreasing.
    b. Marginal cost will be increasing.
    c. Marginal cost will stay the same.
    d. It is impossible to say anything about marginal cost with the information provided.

28. If the city permit to operate Widgets R Us rose by $3,000 per year,
    a. its *MC*, *AVC*, and *ATC* curves would shift upward.
    b. its *MC* curve would shift upward.
    c. its *AVC* curve would shift upward.
    d. its *ATC* curve would shift upward.

29. Over the range where a firm's *ATC* is falling in the long run,
    a. output is subject to diseconomies of scale.
    b. output is subject to economies of scale.
    c. output is subject to constant return to scale.
    d. output has reached the minimum efficient scale of production.
    e. both c and d are true.

30. In the short run,
    a. the average fixed cost curve is U-shaped.
    b. average fixed cost generally exceeds the average variable cost of production.
    c. all costs are variable.
    d. all costs are fixed.
    e. none of the above is correct.

31. When a firm experiences economies of scale in production,
    a. the marginal product of an input diminishes with increased utilization.
    b. marginal cost increases as output expands.
    c. long-run average total cost increases as output expands.
    d. long-run average total cost declines as output expands.

32. The lowest level of output at which a firm's goods are produced at minimum long-run average total cost is called
    a. the minimum efficient scale.
    b. the point of zero marginal cost.
    c. the point of diminishing returns.
    d. the minimum total product.
    e. plant capacity.

Problems:

1. As a farmer, you work for yourself using your own tractor, equipment and farm structures, and you cultivate your own land. Why might it be difficult to calculate your profits from farming?

2. The salmon fishery in Alaska's Bristol Bay has historically been one of the world's richest. Over the past few years, poor returns of salmon to the Bay and competition from farm-raised salmon have reduced the economic returns to the fishermen. One response to lower revenues has been for fishermen to use family members instead of hiring crew "in order to reduce their costs." Evaluate this business strategy. Will employing relatives really keep profits from falling? Under what conditions is this a good strategy?

3. What happens to the cost of growing onions on your own land if a housing developer offers you twice what you thought your land was worth?

4. Say that your firm's total product curve includes the following data: one worker can produce 16 units of output; two workers, 40 units; three workers, 68 units; four workers, 100 units; five workers, 120 units; six workers, 140 units; seven workers, 152 units; eight workers, 156 units; and nine workers, 154 units.
   a. When does the law of diminishing product set in?
   b. What is the marginal product of the seventh worker?
   c. Under these conditions, would you ever choose to employ nine workers?

5. Whitewater Park Short-Run Production Function

Labor (workers)	Total Product (visitors per hour)	Marginal Product
0	____	
1	____	30
2	____	36
3	____	27
4	____	24
5	____	12
6	____	−6

   a. Fill in the Total Product column.
   b. Whitewater Park experiences diminishing marginal product beginning with which worker?
   c. Whitewater Park experiences diminishing total product beginning with which worker?

6. Harry's Hat Company makes hats using the technology described below:

	With 3 Machines			With 4 Machines	
Labor	Total Product (hats)	Marginal Product (hats)	Labor	Total Product (hats)	Marginal Product (hats)
1 day	8	____	1 day	9	____
2 days	18	____	2 days	20	____
3 days	30	____	3 days	35	____
4 days	45	____	4 days	55	____
5 days	57	____	5 days	76	____
6 days	67	____	6 days	88	____
7 days	72	____	7 days	95	____

a. Fill in the Marginal Product columns of these tables.
b. At what point does diminishing marginal product set in with three machines? With four?
c. Why is the point of diminishing marginal product different in each case?

7. The Lighthouse Safety Vest Co. makes flotation vests for recreational boaters. They currently employ 50 people and produce 12,000 vests per month. Lighthouse managers know that when they hire one more person, monthly vest production will increase by 200 vests. They pay workers $1600 per month.
   a. What is the marginal product of the 51st worker?
   b. What is the marginal cost to produce one more vest? (*Hint:* Think of the marginal cost as the additional worker's pay divided by the changes in output.)
   c. If labor is the only variable factor of production, will the average variable cost of production rise or fall as a result of hiring a 51st worker? Why?
   d. What happens to the marginal cost of a vest when the fifty-second worker is added and the marginal product drops to 160 vests per month?

8. Fill in the rest of the production function for Sue's Sweets from the information provided.

Labor (workers)	Total Product (pounds)	Marginal Product (pounds)
0	___	
1	40	___
2	88	___
3	124	___
4	___	24
5	___	12
6	78	___

   a. Sue's Sweets begins to experience diminishing marginal product with which worker?
   b. Does Sue's Sweets ever experience negative marginal product? If so, with the addition of which worker?

9. Draw a typically shaped total product curve and the marginal product curve derived from it, and indicate the ranges of increasing, diminishing, and negative marginal product.

10. Why does the law of diminishing marginal product imply the law of increasing costs?

11. A one-day ticket to visit the Screaming Coasters theme park costs $108, but you can also get a two-consecutive-day ticket for $120. What is the average cost per day for the two-day ticket? What is the marginal cost of the second consecutive day?

12. If your university pays lecture note takers $30 per hour to take notes in your economics class and then sells subscriptions for $20 per student, is the cost of the lecture note taker a fixed or variable cost of selling an additional subscription?

13. As a movie exhibitor, you can choose between paying a flat fee of $4,000 to show a movie for a week and paying a fee of $3 per customer. Will your choice affect your fixed and variable costs? How?

14. What is likely to happen to your marginal costs when adding output requires working beyond an eight-hour day, if workers must be paid time-and-a-half wages beyond an eight-hour day?

15. Use the graph to answer the following questions.

a. Curve A represents which cost curve?
b. Curve B represents which cost curve?
c. Curve C represents which cost curve?
d. Curve D represents which cost curve?
e. Why must curve D pass through the minimum points of both curve B and curve C?
f. What significance does the point where curve A intersects curve D have?

16. Complete the following table describing the short-run daily costs of the Attractive Magnet Co. for 2011.

Total Product (magnets)	Total Fixed Costs	Total Variable Costs	Total Costs	Average Fixed Costs	Average Variable Costs	Average Total Costs	Marginal Costs
1	$100	$ 30	$130	$100	$30	$130	$30
2	___	___	___	___	25	___	___
3	___	___	___	___	20	___	___
4	___	___	___	___	16	___	___
5	___	___	___	___	18	___	___
6	___	___	___	___	21	___	___
7	___	___	___	___	24	___	___
8	___	218	318	___	___	___	___

17. How might a university cafeteria cooking for 600 students rather than for 5 students be subject to economies of scale in the long run?

18. Illustrate how the shape of the marginal product curve relates to the shape of the marginal cost curve.

19. Fill in the rest of the cost function for Bob's Bowling Balls.

Output	Total Fixed Costs	Total Variable Costs	Total Costs	Average Fixed Cost	Average Variable Cost	Average Total Cost	Marginal Cost
1	$200	$ 60	$_____	$_____	$_____	$_____	$_____
2	_____	100	_____	_____	_____	_____	_____
3	_____	120	_____	_____	_____	_____	_____
4	_____	128	_____	_____	_____	_____	_____
5	_____	180	_____	_____	_____	_____	_____
6	_____	252	_____	_____	_____	_____	_____
7	_____	316	_____	_____	_____	_____	_____
8	_____	436	_____	_____	_____	_____	_____

20. You have the following information about long run total cost for the following firms:

Quantity	Arnold's Apples LRTC	Belle's Bananas LRTC	Cam's Cantaloupes LRTC
1	120	33	42
2	140	72	68
3	160	117	98
4	180	168	132
5	200	225	170
6	220	288	212
7	240	357	258

a. Do any of these firms experience constant returns to scale? How do you know?
b. Do any of these firms experience diseconomies of scale? How do you know?
c. Do any of these firms experience economies of scale? How do you know?

21. Refer to the cost curve in exhibit 3:

a. What is the lowest level of output at which the efficient scale of production is reached in the long run?
b. In the short described by *SRATC*, what is the efficient output level?
c. When the firm is producing at the level of output described by D, will it be experiencing constant returns to scale, economies of scale or diseconomies of scale?

22. Buffalo Bill has a potato chip company, Buffalo's Chips. He is currently losing money on every bag of chips he sells. Mrs. Bill, who has just completed an economics class, tells Bill he could make a profit if he adds more machines and produces more chips. How could this be possible? What is Mrs. Bill assuming about the output range in which Bill is currently producing?

APPENDIX
Using Isoquants and Isocosts

Optimal Factor Combinations: Two Variable Inputs

If the production manager had to deal with just one variable input, decision problems would be relatively easy. Given the output target, the production manager would purchase the minimum quantity of input needed to produce the assigned output and would inform the output manager of the costs incurred. However, the production manager's job becomes much more complicated when the output can be produced with several alternative combinations of inputs. For the sake of simplicity, we shall confine ourselves to two variable inputs, capital and labor.

isoquant
curve showing the various factor combinations that can produce a given level of output

The Isoquant

The various combinations of two factors that allow the firm to produce a given quantity of output can be illustrated graphically. The curve showing the various factor combinations that can produce a given level of output is known as an **isoquant**. Exhibit 1 shows that units of capital are measured on the vertical axis, and units

appendix exhibit 1 — Isoquant Showing Various Combinations of Labor and Capital That Can Be Used to Produce 20 Units of Output per Day

Combination	Labor (L)	Capital (K)	Marginal Rate of Technical Substitution
A	1	10	
B	2	6	4
C	3	3	3
D	4	1	2
E	5	1/4	3/4

The isoquant q indicates that 20 units of output can be produced with 10 units of capital and 1 unit of labor (combination A), or 3 units of capital and 3 units of labor (combination C). All other combinations of capital and labor capable of producing 20 units of output are also charted along isoquant q.

of labor on the horizontal axis; isoquant q shows the various combinations of capital and labor that allow the firm to produce a given level (20 units) of output.

Isoquants, like indifference curves, have several important properties. Isoquants are negatively sloped, nonintersecting, convex, and they increase in value as we move in a northeast direction from the origin. However, unlike indifference curves, isoquants are measured cardinally. That is, an output of 40 is twice as large as an output of 20.

The Marginal Rate of Technical Substitution

Explanation of the optimal factor combination can be facilitated by discussing the concept of the **marginal rate of technical substitution of labor for capital (MRTS)** (to distinguish it from the marginal rate of substitution along an indifference curve). The slope of the isoquant is the number of units of one factor necessary to replace a unit of another factor, in order to maintain the same level of output, $-\Delta K/\Delta L$. If we remove the negative sign on the slope we have the *MRTS*.

Suppose that various combinations of labor and capital (together with given quantities of other factors) are used to produce a given level of output, as illustrated in Exhibit 1. Various combinations will produce 20 units of output per day; for example, if 2 units of labor are used, 6 units of capital will be needed (Combination B); and if 3 units of labor are used, then 3 units of capital will be required (Combination C). Note that the various combinations are alternative possibilities for the production of a given quantity of the product, 20 units of output per day in this example.

The *MRTS* measures the quantity of capital that can be given up by using one additional unit of labor, while still producing the same level of output. For example, if 2 units of labor (and 6 units of capital) are now being used, 3 units of capital can be given up by using 1 additional unit of labor.

As the data in Exhibit 1 illustrate, the isoquants are convex. That is, the *MRTS* diminishes as we move down along the isoquant. We also see that labor becomes more abundant and capital more scarce. Hence, it becomes increasingly difficult to substitute even more labor for capital.

As the quantity of one factor, say labor, is increased relative to the quantity of the other, say capital, output being constant, the number of units of capital that can be replaced by one unit of labor falls. In other words, the marginal product of labor falls as we use more of it, and the marginal product of capital rises as we use less of it.

Under ordinary circumstances, the isoquant will be convex to the point of origin, because of the principle of diminishing marginal rate of technical substitution. The greater the quantity of labor used, the smaller is the quantity of the capital needed to replace a unit of labor and maintain output. Thus, the right-hand portion of the isoquant is almost parallel to the horizontal axis, while the left-hand portion is almost parallel to the vertical axis.

The marginal rate of technical substitution is equal to $-\Delta K/\Delta L$, which is the slope of the isoquant. Recall that all combinations on a given isoquant yield the same level of output. Thus, if labor is substituted for capital, with output remaining constant, we know that:

$$(\Delta K)(MP_K) + (\Delta L)(MP_L) = 0$$

Rearranging the terms in this equation we have:

$$MRTS = -(\Delta K)/(\Delta L) = MP_L/MP_K$$

That is, the slope of the isoquant at any point is equal to the ratio of the marginal product of labor to the marginal product of capital.

The *MRTS* is a measure of the extent to which the two factors are substitutes for each other. If they are perfect substitutes—that is, if either factor can be used equally well to produce the product—the marginal rate of technical substitution will be a constant. If capital and labor can be used equally well, the *MRTS* will remain unchanged, regardless of the extent to which substitution is carried in either direction, as seen in Exhibit 2. For example, a woven rug or a sweater could either be done almost exclusively by machine or with a few tools and hand labor.

At the other extreme, two factors may not be substitutes for a particular purpose (such as carpenters and hammers or taxicab drivers and taxicabs). Here, the *MRTS* is undefinable, because output cannot be maintained if one factor is replaced by the other. If this relationship exists between all factors the firm uses, the factor combination the firm employs is dictated entirely by technological conditions, and no substitution is possible. The curve in Exhibit 3 is a right angle indicating that the same output would be forthcoming if more of either (but not more of both!) of the inputs were used. That is, you are equally well off producing q_1 output using factor combination A as you would be using factor combination B. However, you can clearly produce more output, q_2, if you increase both labor and capital, a move from A to C. This type of

> **marginal rate of technical substitution of labor for capital (MRTS)**
> the quantity of capital that can be given up by using one additional unit of labor while producing the same level of output

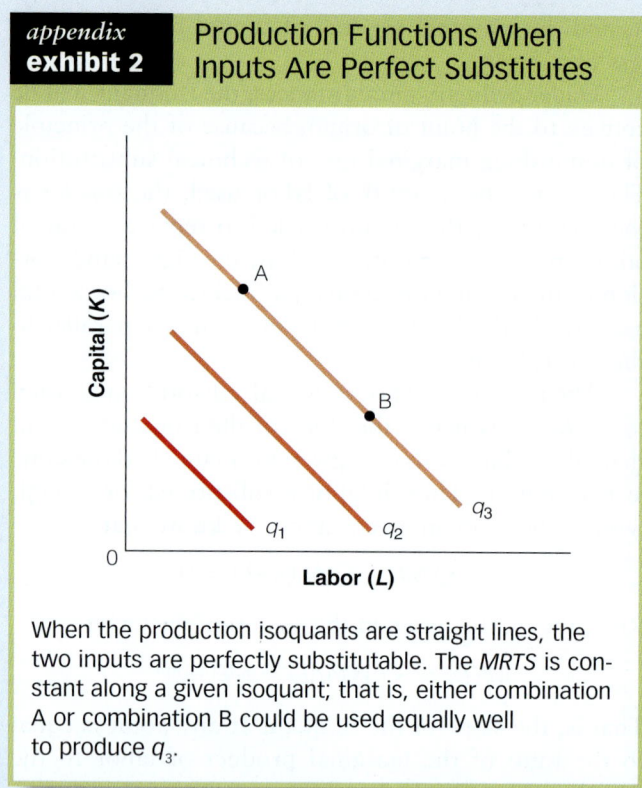

appendix exhibit 2 Production Functions When Inputs Are Perfect Substitutes

When the production isoquants are straight lines, the two inputs are perfectly substitutable. The *MRTS* is constant along a given isoquant; that is, either combination A or combination B could be used equally well to produce q_3.

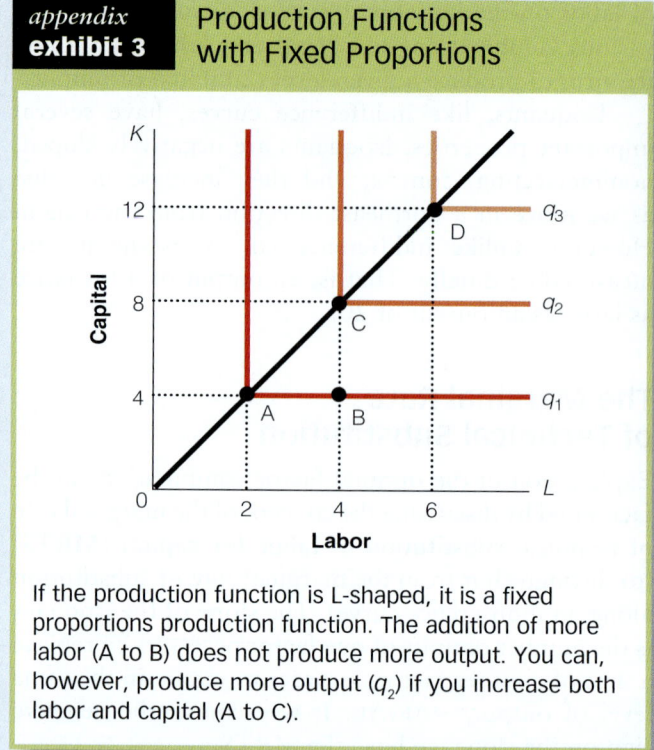

appendix exhibit 3 Production Functions with Fixed Proportions

If the production function is L-shaped, it is a fixed proportions production function. The addition of more labor (A to B) does not produce more output. You can, however, produce more output (q_2) if you increase both labor and capital (A to C).

production relationship is called **fixed-proportions production function**.

Cost Schedules with Long-Run Adjustments Completed

The long-run period has been defined as a period sufficiently long for a firm to adjust all factors of production. The long run, as emphasized earlier, is always a *planning period*, because at any moment, firms are inevitably in some short-run situation. In the long run, however, a firm can choose any short-run plant configuration. The actual time interval depends on the nature of the production processes and particularly on the extent to which specialized capital equipment, requiring a substantial period to construct and having a certain lifespan, are used. The time a firm needs to adjust all factors is much greater for a steel mill or a railroad than for a service station or a grocery store. Over a long-run period, because all factors are adjustable, all costs are variable.

In the long run, the firm can alter all its inputs. Thus, the manager must choose among alternative inputs that minimize the cost of producing a given output. In addition we need to obtain information on long-run costs and output levels.

Isocost Lines and the Optimum Factor Combination

The optimal factor combination can be shown graphically by combining isoquants with **isocost (equal cost) lines**, each of which shows the various possible quantities of the two factors that can be purchased with a given outlay of money. Exhibit 4 shows isoquants when isocost lines are added. Specifically, Exhibit 4 shows the various quantities of capital and labor that can be purchased with a given outlay of money, assuming that the prices of labor and capital are $5 and $10 per hour, respectively. If the given outlay is $600, for example, the isocost line is represented in Exhibit 4 by line B, which indicates that 60 units of capital can be purchased if only capital is purchased, 120 units of labor if only labor is purchased, and 60 units of labor if 30 units of capital are used. The isocost relation is a straight line as a matter of mathematical necessity as long as prices paid for factor units are the same regardless of the quantities purchased.

fixed-proportions production function when it is impossible to substitute one input for another so inputs must be used in fixed proportions

isocost (equal cost) lines graphical display of the various possible quantities of the two factors that can be purchased with a given outlay of money

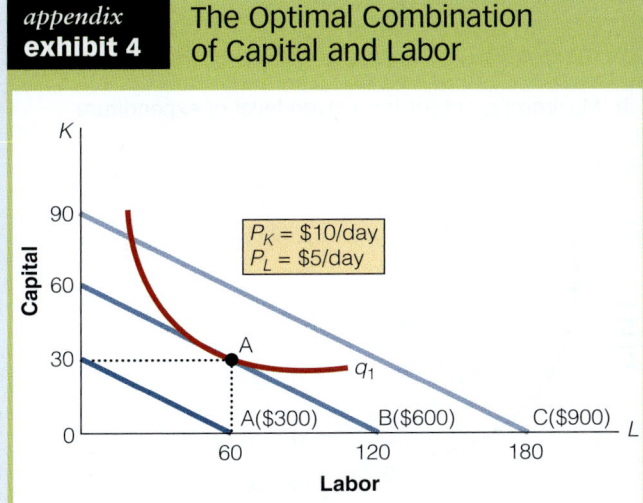

appendix exhibit 4: The Optimal Combination of Capital and Labor

The isocost lines contain factor combinations that can be hired at the same expense. Minimizing the cost of producing q_1 output involves choosing a factor combination that coincides with q_1 output. The optimum input combination occurs at point A, where 60 units of labor and 30 units of capital are utilized to produce q_1 output.

The various possible isocost lines, one for each potential level of outlay on factors, are parallel to each other (see lines A, B, and C in Exhibit 4). The farther to the right an isocost line is located, the higher is the level of outlay that it represents.

Minimum cost is achieved when the firm chooses the least expensive combination of factor inputs for a given level of output. This combination is represented graphically by the lowest isocost line (the farthest one to the left) that touches the isoquant representing the quantity to be produced. Thus, the **optimum factor combination** is represented by a point of tangency between the given isoquant and the lowest possible isocost line, point A in Exhibit 4.

The isocost line that is just tangent to the isoquant allows a firm to acquire the necessary factor units with the lowest possible outlay.* Any lower line would not allow the firm to purchase enough factors to produce the desired output, while any higher isocost line would entail unnecessarily high factor costs. At any point on the isoquant other than the point of tangency, the outlay on the factors to produce the given output would be higher than that at the tangency point. At the tangency, the slope of the isoquant (which represents the marginal rate of technical substitution between the two factors) is equal to the slope of the isocost line (which represents the ratio of the prices of the two factors), and thus the marginal rate of technical substitution is equal to the ratio of the factor prices.

Therefore at the tangency points, the isoquant and the isocost line will have identical slopes. The slope of the MRTS is equal to the ratio of the factor prices:

$$MRTS_{LK} = w/r.$$

where

w = wages (the price of labor)
r = rental rate of capital

For example, in Exhibit 5(a), to minimize the cost of producing 100 units of output, the firm should produce at point A, where the isoquant is tangent to the isocost line. Point B is an input combination that can produce 100 units of output. However, B costs more than A. Point C represents a cheaper factor combination, but it is impossible to produce 100 units of output with so few inputs. Exhibit 5(b) illustrates the alternative optimization process, maximizing output for a given level of costs. The producer attempts to reach the highest isoquant for a given isocost line. Again point A, the tangency point between the isoquant and the isocost line, gives the optimum factor combination. Point B is feasible, but produces a lower level of output. Greater output is attained at point C, but costs are too high. Hence, both strategies result in the same optimization conditons: the isoquant and the isocost line are tangent, and the MRTS equals the ratio of input prices.

Recall that MRTS is a measure of the extent to which the two factors are substitutes for each other. Also recall that the MRTS is equal to the ratio of the marginal product of labor to capital. So we can rewrite our previous equation as:

$$(\text{slope of the isoquant}) - MP_L/MP_K = -w/r \, (\text{slope of the isocost line})$$

or

$$MP_L/MP_K = w/r$$

Rearranging our terms, we find that

$$MP_{L/w} = MP_{K/r}$$

In other words, at the tangency solution, the ratio of the marginal product to input price must be the same for all inputs used in production.

optimum factor combination
a point of tangency between the given isoquant and the lowest possible isocost line

The Expansion Path

In Exhibit 6, the optimal factor bundles are presented for different levels of output. For example,

---

*Remember that an isoquant shows the various quantities of the two factors necessary to produce a given output, while each isocost line shows the various quantities of two factors which can be acquired with the expenditure of a given sum of money.

appendix exhibit 5: Equivalent Optimization Solutions

the least-cost method for producing 100 units of output is using L_1 units of labor and K_1 units of capital, while the least-cost method of producing 120 units of output would be combining L_2 units of labor and K_2 units of capital. The

expansion path shows the least-cost input solutions for providing a given output

expansion path is the line that connects these least-cost input combinations, holding input prices constant.

The **expansion path** provides us information regarding the long-run total cost curve. Specifically, it shows

appendix exhibit 6: The Expansion Path

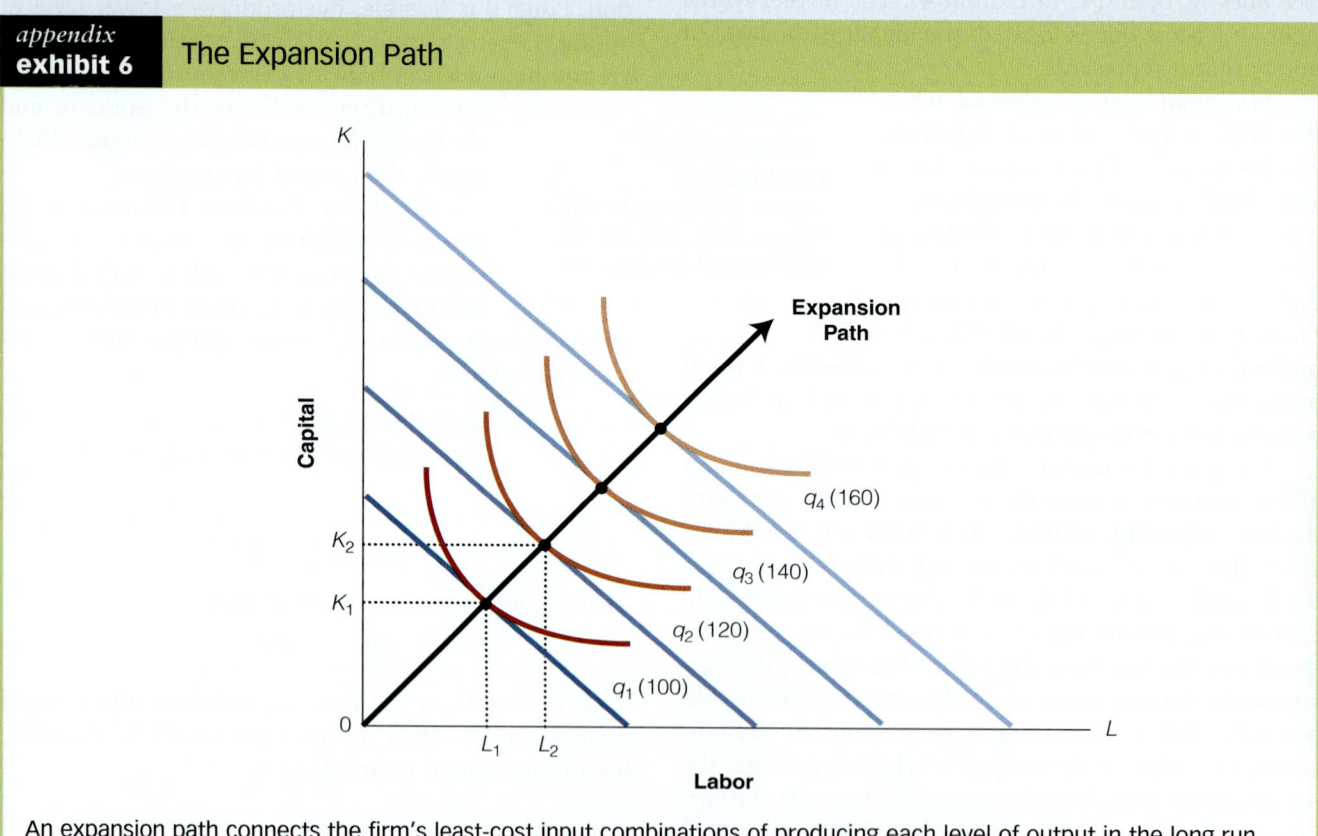

An expansion path connects the firm's least-cost input combinations of producing each level of output in the long run, when all inputs can be varied. The least-cost input combination for producing 120 units of output is K_2 units of capital and L_2 units of labor.

appendix exhibit 7: Deriving *LRTC* from an Isoquant-Isocost Map

the least-cost input solutions for providing a given output, or equivalently, the lowest long-run total cost for producing each level of output. The connection between long-run total cost and the expansion path is seen in Exhibit 7. Points A, B, and C are the cost minimizing input combinations along the expansion path in part (a). The corresponding points on the long-run total cost curve are A, B, and C in part (b). Long-run total cost is simply the optimum amount of labor times the wage plus the optimum amount of capital times the price of capital.

Key Terms and Concepts

isoquant 320
marginal rate of technical substitution of labor for capital (MRTS) 321
fixed-proportions production function 322
isocost (equal cost) lines 322
optimum factor combination 323
expansion path 324

Problems:

1. Would a firm ever choose a factor combination on a positively sloped portion of an isoquant? Explain.

    Answer

    The following figure reveals two isoquants with positively sloped sections. If the amount of input V_2 is fixed at V_2, 1 unit of output can be produced at either V_1 or V_1''. The input combination at point C would clearly be less efficient than at point A because C uses more of input V_1 and would be more costly. Note that the positively sloped segment of an isoquant corresponds to stage three of production because an increase in V_1 from V_1' to V_1'' when V_2 is fixed at $\overline{V}_2$ results in a lower quantity of output (q falls from 2 to 1).

Isoquants with Positively Sloped Segments

2. If two factors are partial substitutes for one another, will the marginal rate of substitution vary as factor proportions are altered, ranging from infinity to values of, or equal to, zero? Explain.

Answer

Suppose, for example, that in the production of DVDs, either metal or plastic can be used for most purposes, but metal is essential for some purposes because plastic lacks sufficient strength for performing the task. In this case, once the quantity of metal has been reduced to the minimum amount required, the MRTS will become infinite, because output cannot be maintained if substitution is carried further.

3. A firm is producing 50 units of output. The marginal rate of technical substitution at the current usage rates of V_1 and V_2 is 1. The price of V_1 = \$8 per unit, and the price of V_2 = \$9 per unit. Should the firm change its purchases of V_1 and V_2?

Answer

The firm can substitute one unit of V_1 for one unit of V_2 and still produce the same output level, but the price of V_1 is less than the price of V_2. Thus, the firm should decrease the amount of V_2 and increase the amount of V_1. The situation is depicted in the following graph. The input price ratio, 8/9, is less than the MRTS, 1, which is demonstrated by the flatter slope of the isocost than the isoquant at point A, the current factor combination. The firm can, however, lower its expenditure by moving to point B and hiring more V_1 and less V_2.

4. Suppose a union raises earnings for workers, and management decides to continue to produce the same output level. How will the firm's optimum combination of labor and capital change, assuming only two inputs? Illustrate graphically. Under what conditions will the effect be large?

Answer

The original factor combination is L and K at point A in the figure. A pay raise increases the slope of the isocost line, the price of labor divided by the price of capital. If the firm continues to produce along the same isoquant, the new quantities of labor and capital are L' and K''. If labor and capital are roughly equally good substitutes over a wide range of input combinations the isoquant will have little curvature, and the substitution of capital for labor will be great.

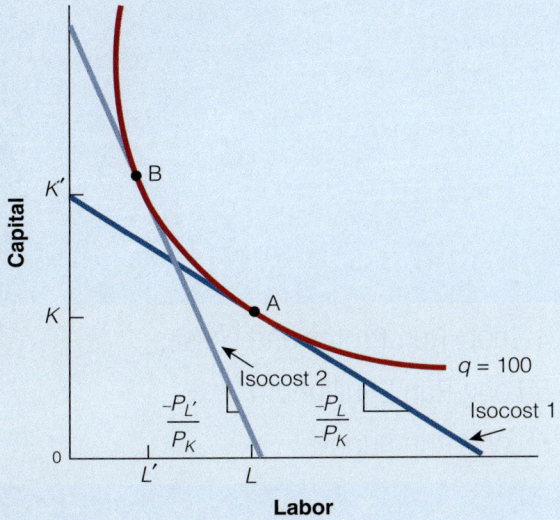

5. Use isoquants to demonstrate how a technological advance allows a firm to produce the same level of output with fewer inputs.

Answer

In the following figure, a technological advance is illustrated by the inward shift of the isoquant from $q = 100$ to $q' = 100$. Both isoquants represent the same level of output, but q' demonstrates that the new technology requires fewer inputs to do so. Thus, the same level of output can be produced at lower costs.

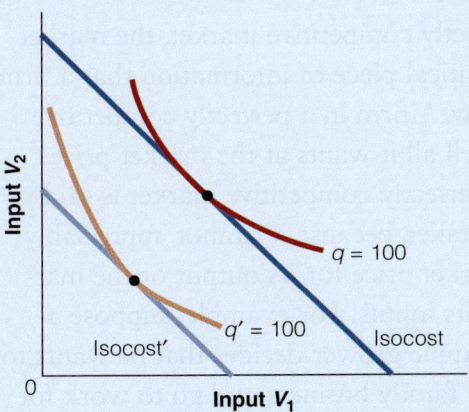

12 Firms in Perfectly Competitive Markets

12.1 A Perfectly Competitive Market
12.2 An Individual Price Taker's Demand Curve
12.3 Profit Maximization
12.4 Short-Run Profits and Losses
12.5 Long-Run Equilibrium
12.6 Long-Run Supply

A firm must answer two critical questions: What price should we charge for the goods and services we sell, and how much should we produce? The answers to these two questions will depend on the market structure.

The behavior of firms will depend on the number of firms in the market, the ease with which firms can enter and exit the market, and the ability of firms to differentiate their products from those of other firms. There is no typical industry. An industry might include one firm that dominates the market, or it might consist of thousands of smaller firms that each produce a small fraction of the market supply. Between these two end points are many other industries. However, because we cannot examine each industry individually, we break them into four main categories: perfect competition, monopoly, monopolistic competition, and oligopoly.

In a perfectly competitive market, the market price is the critical piece of information that a firm needs to know. A firm in a perfectly competitive market can sell all it wants at the market price. A firm in a perfectly competitive market is said to be a price taker, because it cannot appreciably affect the market price for its output or the market price for its inputs. For example, suppose a Washington apple grower decides that he wants to get out of the family business and go to work for Microsoft. Because he may be one of 50,000 apple growers in the United States, his decision will not appreciably change the price of the apples, the production of apples, or the price of inputs. ■

SECTION 12.1 A Perfectly Competitive Market

* What are the characteristics of a firm in a perfectly competitive market?
* What is a price taker?

A Perfectly Competitive Market

This chapter examines perfect competition, a market structure characterized by (1) many buyers and sellers, (2) identical (homogeneous) products, and (3) easy market entry and exit. Let's examine these characteristics in greater detail.

Many Buyers and Sellers

In a perfectly competitive market, there are *many buyers and sellers;* perhaps thousands or conceivably millions. Because each firm is so small in relation to the industry, its production decisions have no impact on the market—each regards price as something over which it has little control. For this reason, perfectly competitive firms are called price takers: They must take the price given by the market because their influence on price is insignificant. If the price of apples in the apple market is $2 a pound, then individual apple farmers will receive $2 a pound for their apples. Similarly, no single buyer of apples can influence the price of apples, because each buyer purchases only a small amount of the apples traded. We will see how this relationship works in more detail in Section 12.2.

Identical (Homogeneous) Products

Consumers believe that all firms in perfectly competitive markets *sell identical (or homogeneous) products.* For example, in the wheat market, it is not possible to determine any significant and consistent qualitative differences in the wheat produced by different farmers. Wheat produced by Farmer Jones looks, feels, smells, and tastes like that produced by Farmer Smith. In short, a bushel of wheat is a bushel of wheat. The products of all the firms are considered to be perfect substitutes.

Easy Entry and Exit

Product markets characterized by perfect competition *have no significant barriers to entry or exit.* Therefore it is fairly easy for entrepreneurs to become suppliers of the product or, if they are already producers, to stop supplying the product. "Fairly easy" does not mean that any person on the street can instantly enter

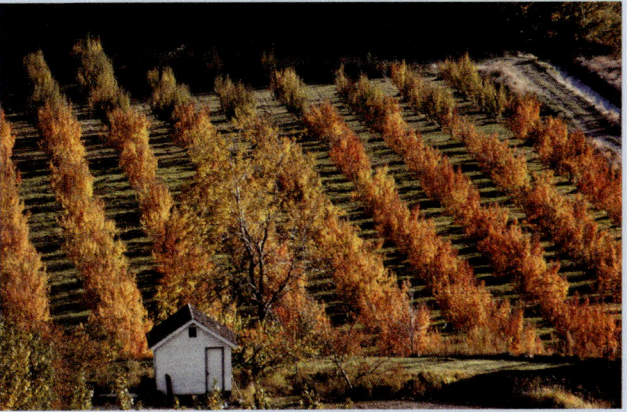

Can the owner of this orchard charge a noticeably higher price for apples of similar quality to those sold at the orchard down the road? What if she charges a lower price for apples of similar quality? How many apples can she sell at the market price?

the business but rather that the financial, legal, educational, and other barriers to entering the business are modest, enabling large numbers of people to overcome the barriers and enter the business if they so desire in any given period. If buyers can easily switch from one seller to another and sellers can easily enter or exit the industry, then they have met the perfectly competitive condition of easy entry and exit. Because of this easy market entry, perfectly competitive markets generally consist of a large number of small suppliers.

A perfectly competitive market is approximated most closely in highly organized markets for securities and agricultural commodities, such as the New York Stock Exchange or the Chicago Board of Trade. Wheat, corn, soybeans, cotton, and many other agricultural products are sold in perfectly competitive markets. Although all the criteria for a perfectly competitive market are rarely met, a number of markets come close to satisfying them. Even when all the assumptions don't hold, it is important to note that studying the model of perfect competition is useful because many markets resemble perfect competition—that is, markets in which firms face highly elastic (flat) demand curves and relatively easy entry and exit. The model also gives us a standard of comparison. In other words, we can make comparisons with the perfectly competitive model to help us evaluate what is going on in the real world.

PART 4 Households and Market Structure

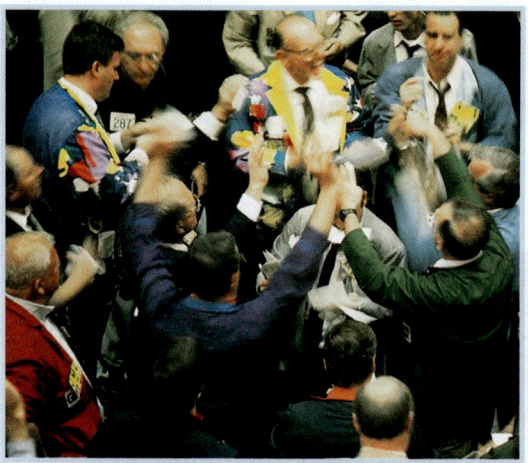

At the Chicago Board of Trade (CBOT), prices are set by thousands of buyers interacting with thousands of sellers. The goods in question are typically standardized (e.g., grade A winter wheat), and information is readily available. Every buyer and seller in the market knows the price, the quantity, and the quality of the wheat. Transaction costs are negligible. For example, if a news story breaks on an infestation in the cotton crop, the price of cotton will rise immediately. CBOT price information is used to determine the value of a particular commodity all over the world.

SECTION CHECK

1. A perfectly competitive market is characterized by many buyers and sellers, an identical (homogeneous) product, and easy market entry and exit.
2. Consumers believe that all firms in perfectly competitive markets sell virtually identical (homogeneous) products. The products of all firms are considered to be perfect substitutes.
3. In markets with so many buyers and so many sellers, neither buyers nor sellers have any control over price in perfect competition. They must take the going price and hence are called price takers.
4. Firms in perfectly competitive markets have no significant barriers to entry. That is, the barriers are significantly modest, so that many sellers can enter or exit the industry.

---

1. Why do firms in perfectly competitive markets involve homogeneous goods?
2. Why does the absence of significant barriers to entry tend to result in a large number of suppliers?
3. Why does the fact that perfectly competitive firms are small relative to the market make them price takers?

SECTION 12.2 An Individual Price Taker's Demand Curve

* Why won't individual price takers raise or lower their prices?
* Can individual price takers sell all they want at the market price?
* Will the position of individual price takers' demand curves change when market price changes?

An Individual Firm's Demand Curve

Perfectly competitive firms are **price takers;** that is, they must sell at the market-determined price, where the market price and output are determined

price takers
a perfectly competitive firm that takes the price it is given by the intersection of the market demand and market supply curves

by the intersection of the market supply and demand curves, as seen in Exhibit 1(b). Individual wheat farmers know that they cannot dispose of their wheat at any figure higher than the current market price; if they attempt to charge a higher price, potential buyers will simply make their purchases from

section 12.2 exhibit 1 — Market and Individual Firm Demand Curves in a Perfectly Competitive Market

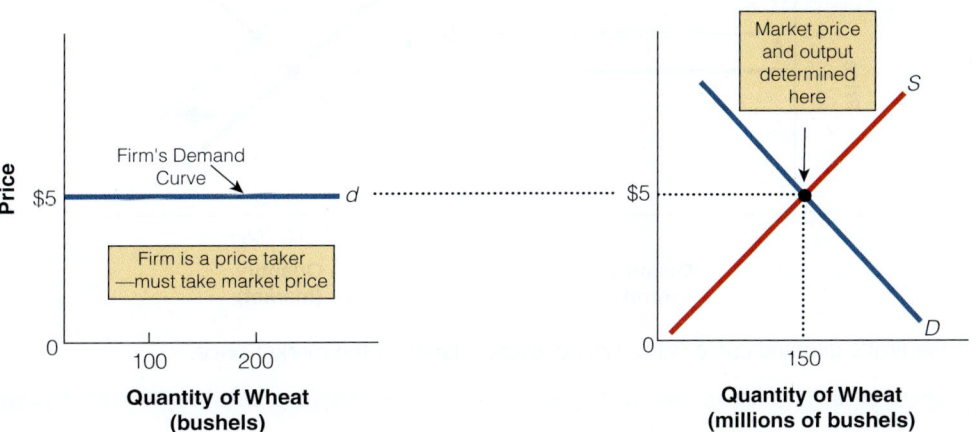

At the market price for wheat, $5, the individual farmer can sell all the wheat he wishes. Because each producer provides only a small fraction of industry output, any additional output will have an insignificant impact on market price. The firm's demand curve is perfectly elastic at the market price.

other wheat farmers. Further, the farmers certainly would not knowingly charge a lower price, because they could sell all they want at the market price.

Likewise, in a perfectly competitive market, individual sellers can change their outputs, and it will not alter the market price. The large number of sellers who are selling identical products make this situation possible. Each producer provides such a small fraction of the total supply that a change in the amount he offers does *not* have a noticeable effect on market equilibrium price. In a perfectly competitive market, then, an individual firm can sell as much as it wishes to place on the market at the prevailing price; the demand, as seen by the seller, is perfectly elastic.

It is easy to construct the demand curve for an individual seller in a perfectly competitive market. Remember, she won't charge more than the market price because no one will buy it, and she won't charge less because she can sell all she wants at the market price. Thus, the farmer's demand curve is horizontal over the entire range of output that she could possibly produce. If the prevailing market price of the product is $5, the farmer's demand curve will be represented graphically by a horizontal line at the market price of $5, as shown in Exhibit 1(a).

A Change in Market Price and the Firm's Demand Curve

To say that producers under perfect competition regard price as a given is not to say that price is constant. The *position* of the firm's demand curve varies with every change in the market price. In Exhibit 2, we see that when the market price for wheat increases, say as a result of an increase in market demand, the price-taking firm will receive a higher price for all its output. Or when the market price decreases, say as a result of a decrease in market demand, the price-taking firm will receive a lower price for all its output.

In effect, sellers are provided with current information about market demand and supply conditions as a result of price changes. It is an essential aspect of the perfectly competitive model that sellers respond to the signals provided by such price movements, so they must alter their behavior over time in the light of actual experience, revising their production decisions to reflect changes in market price. In this respect, the perfectly competitive model is straightforward; it does not assume any knowledge on the part of individual buyers and sellers about market demand and supply—they only have to know the price of the good they sell.

section 12.2 exhibit 2: Market Prices and the Position of a Firm's Demand Curve

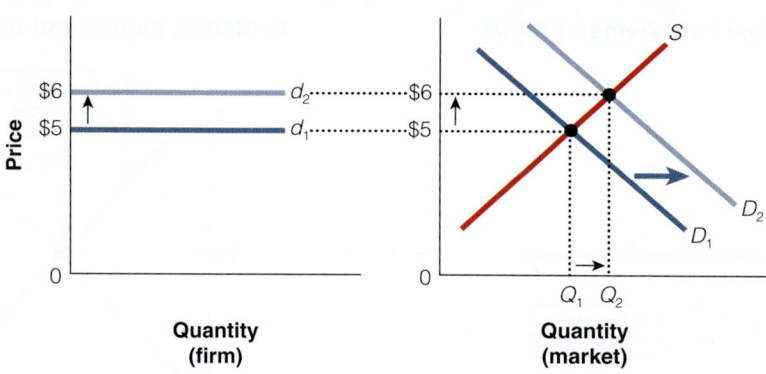

The position of the firm's demand curve will vary with every change in the market price.

SECTION CHECK

1. An individual seller won't sell at a higher price than the going price, because buyers can purchase the same good from someone else at the going price.
2. Individual sellers won't sell for less than the going price, because they are so small relative to the market that they can sell all they want at the going price.
3. The position of the individual firm's demand curve varies directly with the market price.

---

1. Why would a perfectly competitive firm not try to raise or lower its price?
2. Why can we represent the demand curve of a perfectly competitive firm as perfectly elastic (horizontal) at the market price?
3. How does an individual perfectly competitive firm's demand curve change when the market price changes?
4. If the marginal cost facing every producer of a product shifted upward, would the position of a perfectly competitive firm's demand curve be likely to change as a result? Why or why not?

SECTION 12.3 Profit Maximization

* What is total revenue?
* What is average revenue?
* What is marginal revenue?
* Why does the firm maximize profits where marginal revenue equals marginal costs?

Revenues in a Perfectly Competitive Market

The objective of the firm is to maximize profits. To maximize profits, the firm wants to produce the amount that maximizes the difference between its total revenues and total costs. In this section, we will examine the different ways to look at revenue in a perfectly competitive market: total revenue, average revenue, and marginal revenue.

Total Revenue

Total revenue (TR) is the revenue that the firm receives from the sale of its products. Total revenue from a product equals the price of the good (P) times the quantity (q) of units sold ($TR = P \times q$). For example, if a farmer sells 10 bushels of wheat a day for $5 a bushel, his total revenue is $50 ($5 × 10 bushels). (*Note:* We will use the lowercase letter q to denote the single firm's output and reserve the uppercase letter Q for the output of the entire market. For example, q would be used to represent the output of one lettuce grower, while Q would be used to represent the output of all lettuce growers in the lettuce market.)

> **total revenue (TR)**
> the product price times the quantity sold
>
> **average revenue (AR)**
> total revenue divided by the number of units sold
>
> **marginal revenue (MR)**
> the increase in total revenue resulting from a one-unit increase in sales

Average Revenue and Marginal Revenue

Average revenue (AR) equals total revenue divided by the number of units sold of the product ($TR \div q$, or $[P \times q] \div q$). For example, if the farmer sells 10 bushels at $5 a bushel, total revenue is $50 and average revenue is $5 per bushel ($50 ÷ 10 bushels). Thus, in perfect competition, average revenue is equal to the price of the good.

Marginal revenue (MR) is the additional revenue derived from the production of one more unit of the good. In other words, marginal revenue represents the increase in total revenue that results from the sale of one more unit ($MR = \Delta TR \div \Delta q$). In a perfectly competitive market, because additional units of output can be sold without reducing the price of the product, marginal revenue is constant at all outputs and equal to average revenue. For example, if the price of wheat per bushel is $5, the marginal revenue is $5. Because total revenue is equal to price multiplied by quantity ($TR = P \times q$), as we add one additional unit of output, total revenue will always increase by the amount of the product price, $5. Marginal revenue facing a perfectly competitive firm is equal to the price of the good.

In perfect competition, then, we know that marginal revenue, average revenue, and price are all equal: $P = MR = AR$. These relationships are clearly illustrated in the calculations presented in Exhibit 1.

How Do Firms Maximize Profits?

Now that we have discussed the firm's cost curves (in Chapter 11) and its revenues, we are ready to see how a firm maximizes its profits. A firm's profits equal its total revenues minus its total costs. However, at what output level must a firm produce and sell to maximize profits? In all types of market environments, the firm will maximize its profits at the output that maximizes the difference between total revenue and total cost, which is at the same output level at which marginal revenue equals marginal cost.

Equating Marginal Revenue and Marginal Cost

The importance of equating marginal revenue and marginal cost is seen in Exhibit 2. As output expands beyond zero up to q^*, the marginal revenue derived from each unit of the expanded output exceeds the marginal cost of that unit of output; so

section 12.3 exhibit 1 Revenues for a Perfectly Competitive Firm

Quantity (q)	Price (P)	Total Revenue (TR = P × q)	Average Revenue (AR = TR/q)	Marginal Revenue (MR = ΔTR/Δq)
1	$5	$5	$5	$5
2	5	10	5	5
3	5	15	5	5
4	5	20	5	5
5	5	25	5	

section 12.3 exhibit 2 — Finding the Profit-Maximizing Level of Output

At any output below q^*—at q_1, for example—the marginal revenue (MR) from expanding output exceeds the added costs (MC) of that output, so additional profits can be made by expanding output. Beyond q^*—at q_2, for example—marginal costs exceed marginal revenue, so output expansion is unprofitable and output should be reduced. The profit-maximizing level of output is at q^*, where the profit-maximizing output rule is followed—the firm should produce the level of output where $MR = MC$.

at q^*, where $MR = MC$, is the output level just right—not too large, not too small. Further expansion of output beyond q^* will lead to losses on the additional output (i.e., decrease the firm's overall profits), because $MC > MR$. For example, if the firm produces q_2, the firm incurs losses on the output produced beyond q^*; the firm should reduce its output. Only at output q^*, where $MR = MC$, can we find the **profit-maximizing level of output**.

Be careful not to make the mistake of focusing on profit per unit rather than total profit. That is, you might think that at q_1, if MR is much greater than MC, the firm should not produce more because the profit per unit is high at this point. However, that would be a mistake because a firm can add to its total profits as long as $MR > MC$—that is, all the way to q^*.

The Marginal Approach

We can use the data from the table in Exhibit 3 to find Farmer Jones's profit-maximizing position. Columns 5 and 6 show the marginal revenue and marginal cost, respectively. We see that output levels of 1 and 2 bushels produce outputs that have marginal revenues that exceed marginal cost—Farmer Jones wants to produce those units and more. That is, as long as marginal revenue exceeds marginal cost, producing and selling those units add more to revenues than to costs; in other words, they add to profits. However, once he expands production beyond four units of output, Farmer Jones's costs are less than his marginal revenues, and his profits begin to fall. Clearly, Farmer Jones should not produce beyond 4 bushels of wheat.

Let's take another look at profit maximization, using the table in Exhibit 3. Comparing columns 2 and 3—the calculations of total revenue and total cost, respectively—we

the expansion of output creates additional profits. This addition to profit is shown as the leftmost shaded section in Exhibit 2. As long as marginal revenue exceeds marginal cost, profits continue to grow. For example, if the firm decides to produce q_1, the firm sacrifices potential profits, because the marginal revenue from producing more output is greater than the marginal cost. Only

profit-maximizing level of output
a firm should always produce at the output where $MR = MC$

section 12.3 exhibit 3 — Cost and Revenue Calculations for a Perfectly Competitive Firm

Quantity (1)	Total Revenue (2)	Total Cost (3)	Profit (TR − TC) (4)	Marginal Revenue ($\Delta TR/\Delta q$) (5)	Marginal Cost ($\Delta TC/\Delta q$) (6)	Change in Profit (MR − MC) (7)
0	$0	$2	$−2			
1	5	4	1	$5	$2	$3
2	10	7	3	5	3	2
3	15	11	4	5	4	1
4	20	16	4	5	5	0
5	25	22	3	5	6	−1

see that Farmer Jones maximizes his profits at output levels of 3 or 4 bushels, where he will make profits of $4. In column 4—profit—you can see that there is no higher level of profit at any of the other output levels. Producing 5 bushels would reduce profits by $1, because marginal revenue, $5, is less than the marginal cost, $6. Consequently, Farmer Jones would not produce this bushel of output. If $MR > MC$, Farmer Jones should increase production; if $MR < MC$, Farmer Jones should decrease production.

In the next section we will use the profit-maximizing output rule to see what happens when changes in the market cause the price to fall below average total cost and even below average variable costs. We will introduce the three-step method to determine whether the firm is making an economic profit, minimizing its losses, or should be temporarily shut down.

SECTION CHECK

1. Total revenue is price times the quantity sold ($TR = P \times q$).
2. Average revenue is total revenue divided by the quantity sold ($AR = TR/q = P$).
3. Marginal revenue is the change in total revenue from the sale of an additional unit of output ($MR = \Delta TR/\Delta q$). In a competitive industry, the price of the good equals both the average revenue and the marginal revenue.
4. As long as the marginal revenue exceeds marginal costs, the seller should expand production, because producing and selling those units adds more to revenues than to costs; that is, it increases profits. However, if the marginal revenue is less than the marginal cost, the seller should decrease production.
5. The profit-maximizing output rule says a firm should always produce where $MR = MC$.

1. How is total revenue calculated?
2. How is average revenue derived from total revenue?
3. How is marginal revenue derived from total revenue?
4. Why is marginal revenue equal to price for a perfectly competitive firm?

SECTION 12.4 Short-Run Profits and Losses

* How do we determine whether a firm is generating an economic profit?
* How do we determine whether a firm is experiencing an economic loss?
* How do we determine whether a firm is making zero economic profits?
* Why doesn't a firm produce when price is below average variable cost?

In the previous section, we discussed how to determine the profit-maximizing output level for a perfectly competitive firm. How do we know whether a firm is actually making economic profits or losses?

The Three-Step Method

What Is the Three-Step Method?
Determining whether a firm is generating economic profits, economic losses, or zero economic profits at the profit-maximizing level of output, q^*, can be done in three easy steps. First, we will walk through these steps, and then we will apply the method to three situations for a hypothetical firm in the short run in Exhibit 1.

1. Find where marginal revenue equals marginal cost and proceed straight down to the horizontal quantity axis to find q^*, the profit-maximizing output level.
2. At q^*, go straight up to the demand curve and then to the left to find the market price, P^*. Once you have identified P^* and q^*, you can find total revenue at the profit-maximizing output level, because $TR = P \times q$.

section 12.4 exhibit 1 — Short-Run Profits, Losses, and Zero Economic Profits

In (a), the firm is earning short-run economic profits of $120. In (b), the firm is suffering losses of $80. In (c), the firm is making zero economic profits, with the price just equal to the average total cost in the short run.

3. The last step is to find the total cost. Again, go straight up from q^* to the average total cost (ATC) curve and then left to the vertical axis to compute the average total cost *per unit*. If we multiply average total cost by the output level, we can find the total cost ($TC = ATC \times q$).

If total revenue is greater than total cost at q^*, the firm is generating economic profits. If total revenue is less than total cost at q^*, the firm is generating economic losses. If total revenue is equal to total cost at q^*, there are zero economic profits (or a normal rate of return).

Alternatively, to find total economic profits, we can take the product price at P^* and subtract the average total cost at q^*. This will give us per-unit profit. If we multiply this by output, we will arrive at total economic profit. Or $(P^* - ATC) \times q^* =$ total economic profit.

Remember, the cost curves include implicit and explicit costs—that is, we are covering the opportunity costs of our resources. Therefore, even with zero economic profits, no tears should be shed, because the firm is covering both its implicit and explicit costs. Because firms are also covering their implicit costs, or what they could be producing with these resources in another endeavor, economists sometimes call this zero economic profit *a normal rate of return*. That is, the owners are doing as well as they could elsewhere, in that they are getting the normal rate of return on the resources they invested in the firm.

The Three-Step Method in Action

Exhibit 1 shows three different short-run equilibrium positions; in each case, the firm is producing at a level where marginal revenue equals marginal cost. Each of these alternatives shows that the firm is maximizing profits or minimizing losses in the short run.

Assume that three alternative prices—$6, $5, and $4—are available for a firm with given costs. In Exhibit 1(a), the firm receives $6 per unit at an equilibrium level of output ($MR = MC$) of 120 units. Total revenue ($P \times q^*$) is 6×120, or $720. The average total cost at 120 units of output is $5, and the total cost ($ATC \times q^*$) is $600. Following the three-step method, we can calculate that this firm is earning a total economic profit of $120. Or we can calculate total economic profit by using the following equation: $(P^* - ATC) \times q^* = (\$6 - \$5) \times 120 = \$120$.

In Exhibit 1(b), the market price has fallen to $4 per unit. At the equilibrium level of output, the firm is now producing 80 units of output at an average total cost of $5 per unit. The total revenue is now $320 ($4 \times 80$), and the total cost is $400 ($5 \times 80$). We can see that the firm is now incurring a total economic loss of $80. Or we can calculate total economic profit by using the following equation: $(P^* - ATC) \times q^* = (\$4 - \$5) \times 80 = -\$80$.

In Exhibit 1(c), the firm is earning zero economic profits, or a normal rate of return. The market price is $4.90, and the average total cost is $4.90 per unit for 100 units of output. In this case, economic profits are zero, because total revenue, $490, minus total cost, $490, is equal to zero. This firm is just covering all its costs, both implicit and explicit. Or we can calculate total economic profit by using the following equation: $(P^* - ATC) \times q^* = \$4.90 - \$4.90 \times 100 = \$0$.

Evaluating Economic Losses in the Short Run

A firm generating an economic loss faces a tough choice: Should it continue to produce or should it shut down its operation? To make this decision, we need to add another variable to our discussion of economic profits and losses: average variable cost. Variable costs are costs that vary with output—for example, wages, raw material, transportation, and electricity. If a firm cannot generate enough revenues to cover its variable costs, it will have larger losses if it operates than if it shuts down (when losses are equal to fixed costs). That is, the firm will shut down if its total revenue ($p \times q$) is less than its variable costs (VC). If we divide $p \times q$ by q, we get p, and if we divide VC by q we get AVC, so if $p < AVC$, a profit-maximizing firm will shut down. Thus, a firm will not produce at all unless the price is greater than its average variable cost.

Operating at a Loss

At price levels greater than or equal to the average variable cost, a firm may continue to operate in the short run even if its average total cost—variable and fixed costs—is not completely covered. That is, the firm may continue to operate even though it is experiencing an economic loss. Why? Because fixed costs continue whether the firm produces or not; it is better to earn enough to cover a portion of fixed costs than to earn nothing at all.

In Exhibit 2, price is less than average total cost but more than average variable cost. In this case, the firm produces in the short run, but at a loss. To shut down would make this firm worse off, because it can cover at least *some* of its fixed costs with the excess of revenue over its variable costs.

The Decision to Shut Down

Exhibit 3 illustrates a situation in which the price a firm is able to obtain for its product is below its average variable cost at all ranges of output. In this case, the firm is unable to cover even its variable costs in the short run. Because the firm is losing even more than the fixed costs it would lose if it shut down, it is more logical for the firm to cease operations. Hence, if $P < AVC$, the firm can cut its losses by shutting down.

The Short-Run Supply Curve

As we have just seen, at all prices above the minimum AVC, a firm produces in the short run even if average total cost (ATC) is not completely covered;

section 12.4 exhibit 2 Short-Run Losses: Price Above AVC But Below ATC

In this case, the firm operates in the short run but incurs a loss because $P < ATC$. Nevertheless, $P > AVC$, and revenues cover variable costs and partially defray fixed costs. This firm will leave the industry in the long run unless prices are expected to rise in the near future; but in the short run, it continues to operate at a loss as long as $P > AVC$, the shutdown point.

section 12.4 exhibit 3 Short-Run Losses: Price Below AVC

Because its average variable cost exceeds price at all levels of output, this firm would cut its losses by discontinuing production.

and at all prices below the minimum AVC, the firm shuts down. The firm produces above the minimum AVC even if it is incurring economic losses because it can still earn enough in total revenues to cover all

Because the demand for summer camps will be lower during the off-season, it is likely that revenues may be too low for the camp to cover its variable costs and the owner will choose to shut down. Remember, the owner will still have to pay the fixed costs: property tax, insurance, the costs associated with the building and land. However, if the camp is not in operation during the off-season, the owner will at least not have to pay the variable costs: salaries for the camp staff, food, and electricity.

section 12.4 exhibit 4 — The Firm's Short-Run Supply Curve

If price is less than average variable cost, the firm's losses would be smaller if it shut down and stopped producing. That is, if $P < AVC$, the firm is better off producing zero output. Hence, the firm's short-run supply curve is the marginal cost curve above average variable cost.

its average variable cost and a portion of its fixed costs, which is better than not producing and earning nothing at all.

In graphical terms, the **short-run supply curve** of an individual competitive seller is identical to the portion of the MC curve that lies above the minimum of the AVC curve. As a cost relation, this curve shows the marginal cost of producing any *given output*; as a supply curve, it shows the *equilibrium output* that the firm will supply at various prices in the short run. The thick line in Exhibit 4 is the firm's supply curve—the portion of MC above its intersection with AVC. The declining portion of the MC curve has no significance for supply, because if the price falls below the average variable cost, the firm is better off shutting down—producing no output. The shutdown point is at the minimum point on the average variable cost curve where the output level is $q_{SHUT\ DOWN}$. Beyond the point of lowest AVC, the marginal costs of successively larger amounts of output are progressively greater, so the firm will supply larger and larger amounts only at higher prices. The absolute maximum that the firm can supply, regardless of price, is the maximum quantity that it can produce with the existing plant.

short-run supply curve
the portion of the MC curve above the AVC curve

short-run market supply curve
the horizontal summation of the individual firms' supply curves in the market

Deriving the Short-Run Market Supply Curve

The **short-run market supply curve** is the summation of all the individual firms' supply curves (that is, the portion of the firms' MC above AVC) in the market. Because the short run is too brief for new firms to enter the market, the market supply curve is the summation of *existing* firms. For example, in Exhibit 5, at P_1, each of the 1,000 identical firms in the industry produces 500 bushels of wheat per day at point a, in Exhibit 5(a); and the quantity supplied in the market is 500,000 bushels of wheat, point A, in Exhibit 5(b). We can again sum horizontally at P_2; the quantity supplied for each of the 1,000 identical firms is 800 bushels of wheat per day at point b in Exhibit 5(a), so the quantity supplied for the industry is 800,000 bushels of wheat per day, point B in Exhibit 5(b). Continuing this process gives us the market supply curve for the wheat market. In a market of 1,000 identical wheat farmers, the market supply curve is 1,000 times the quantity supplied by each firm, as long as the price is above AVC.

section 12.4 exhibit 5 — Deriving the Short-Run Market Supply Curve

a. Individual Firm Supply Curve for Wheat

b. Market Supply Curve for Wheat

The short-run supply curve is the horizontal summation of the individual firms' supply curves (each firm's marginal cost curve above AVC), shown in (a). In a market of 1,000 identical wheat farmers, the market supply curve is 1,000 times the quantity supplied by each firm, shown in (b).

Use what you've LEARNED: REVIEWING THE SHORT-RUN OUTPUT DECISION

Exhibit 6 shows the firm's short-run output at these various market prices: P_1, P_2, P_3, and P_4.

At the market price of P_1, the firm would not cover its average variable cost—the firm would produce zero output, because the firm's losses would be smaller if it shut down and stopped producing. At the market price of P_2, the firm would produce at the loss-minimizing output of q_2 units. It would operate rather than shut down, because it could cover all its average variable costs and some of its fixed costs. At the market price of P_3, the firm would produce q_3 units of output and make zero economic profit (a normal rate of return). At the market price of P_4, the firm would produce q_4 units of output and be making short-run economic profits.

section 12.4 exhibit 6 — The Short-Run Output Decision

Use what you've LEARNED
EVALUATING SHORT-RUN ECONOMIC LOSSES

Q Lei-ann is one of many florists in a medium-size urban area. That is, we assume that she works in a market similar to a perfectly competitive market and operates, of course, in the short run. Lei-ann's cost and revenue information is shown in Exhibit 6. Based on this information, what should Lei-ann do in the short run, and why?

A Fixed costs are unavoidable unless the firm goes out of business. Lei-ann really has two decisions in the short run—either to operate or to shut down temporarily. In Exhibit 6, we see that Lei-ann makes $2,000 a day in total revenue, but her daily costs (fixed and variable) are $2,500. She has to pay her workers, pay for fresh flowers, and pay for the fuel used by her drivers in picking up and delivering flowers. She must also pay the electricity bill to heat her shop and keep her refrigerators going to protect her flowers. That is, every day, poor Lei-ann is losing

If Lei-ann cannot cover her fixed costs, will she continue to operate?

section 12.4 exhibit 7 Lei-ann's Daily Revenue and Cost Schedule

Total Revenue	$2,000
Total Costs	2,500
Variable Costs	1,500
Fixed Costs	1,000

$500; but she still might want to operate the shop despite the loss. Why? Lei-ann's average variable cost (comprising flowers, transportation, fuel, daily wage earners, and so on) amounts to $1,500 a day; her fixed costs (insurance, property taxes, rent for the building, and refrigerator payments) are $1,000 a day. Now, if Lei-ann does not operate, she will save on her variable cost—$1,500 a day—but she will be out the $2,000 a day she makes in revenue from selling her flowers. Thus, every day she operates, she is better off than if she had not operated at all. That is, if the firm can cover the average variable cost, it is better off operating than not operating. But suppose Lei-ann's VC were $2,100 a day. Then Lei-ann should not operate, because every day she does, she is $100 worse off than if she shut down altogether. In short, a firm will shut down if $TR < VC$ or $(P \times q) < VC$. If we divide both sides by q, the firm will shut down if $P < AVC$ or $(P \times q)/q < VC/q$.

Why does Lei-ann even bother operating if she is making a loss? Perhaps the economy is in a recession and the demand for flowers is temporarily down, but Lei-ann thinks things will pick up again in the next few months. If Lei-ann is right and demand picks up, her prices and marginal revenue will rise, and she may have a chance to make short-run economic profits.

SECTION CHECK

1. The profit-maximizing output level is found by equating *MR* to *MC* at q^*. If at that output the firm's price is greater than its average total costs, it is making an economic profit.
2. If at the profit-maximizing output level, q^*, the price is less than the average total cost, the firm is incurring an economic loss.
3. If at the profit-maximizing output level, q^*, the price is equal to average total cost, the firm is making zero economic profits; that is, the firm is covering both its implicit and explicit costs (making a normal rate of return).
4. If the price falls below average variable cost, the firm is better off shutting down than operating in the short run, because it would incur greater losses from operating than from shutting down.

1. How is the profit-maximizing output quantity determined?
2. How do we determine total revenue and total cost for the profit-maximizing output quantity?
3. If a profit-maximizing perfectly competitive firm is earning a profit because total revenue exceeds total cost, why must the market price exceed average total cost?
4. If a profit-maximizing perfectly competitive firm is earning a loss because total revenue is less than total cost, why must the market price be less than average total cost?
5. If a profit-maximizing perfectly competitive firm is earning zero economic profits because total revenue equals total cost, why must the market price be equal to the average total cost for that level of output?
6. Why would a profit-maximizing perfectly competitive firm shut down rather than operate if price was less than its average variable cost?
7. Why would a profit-maximizing perfectly competitive firm continue to operate for a period of time if price was greater than average variable cost but less than average total cost?

SECTION 12.5 Long-Run Equilibrium

* When an industry is earning profits, will it encourage the entry of new firms?
* Why do perfectly competitive firms make zero economic profits in the long run?

Economic Profits and Losses Disappear in the Long Run

If farmers are able to make economic profits producing wheat, what will their response be in the long run? Farmers will increase the resources that they devote to the lucrative business of producing wheat. Suppose Farmer Jones is making an economic profit (he is earning an above-normal rate of return) producing wheat. To make even more profits, he may take land out of producing other crops and plant more wheat. Other farmers or people who are holding land for speculative purposes may also decide to plant wheat on their land.

As word gets out that wheat production is proving profitable, it will cause a supply response—the market supply curve will shift to the right as more firms enter the industry and existing firms expand as shown in Exhibit 1(b). With this shift, the quantity of wheat supplied at any given price is greater than before. It may take a year or even longer, of course, for the complete supply response to take place, simply because it takes some time for information on profit opportunities to spread and still more time to plant, grow, and harvest the wheat. Note that the effect of increasing supply, other things being equal, is a reduction in the equilibrium price of wheat.

Suppose that, as a result of the supply response, the price of wheat falls from P_1 to P_2. The impact of the change in the market price of wheat, over which Farmer Jones has absolutely no control, is simple. If his costs don't change, he moves from making a profit ($P_1 > ATC$) to zero economic profits ($P_2 = ATC$), as shown in Exhibit 1(a). In long-run equilibrium, perfectly competitive firms make zero economic profits.

Remember, a zero economic profit means that the firm actually earns a normal return on the use of its capital. Zero economic profit is an equilibrium or stable situation because any positive economic (above-normal) profit signals resources into the industry, beating down prices and therefore revenues to the firm.

Any economic losses signal resources to leave the industry, causing supply reductions that lead to increased prices and higher firm revenues for the remaining firms. For example, in Exhibit 2 we see a firm that continues to operate despite its losses—ATC is greater than P_1 at q_1. With losses, however, some

section 12.5 exhibit 1 — Profits Disappear with Entry

As the industry-determined price of wheat falls in (b), Farmer Jones's marginal revenue curve shifts downward from mr_1 to mr_2 in (a). A new profit-maximizing ($MC = MR$) point is reached at q_2. When the price is P_1, Farmer Jones is making a profit, because $P_1 > ATC$. When the market supply increases, causing the market price to fall to P_2, Farmer Jones's profits disappear, because $P_2 = ATC$.

section 12.5 exhibit 2 — Losses Disappear with Exit

When firms in the industry suffer losses, some firms will exit in the long run, shifting the market supply curve to the left from S_1 to S_2. This shift causes market price to rise from P_1 to P_2 and market output to fall from Q_1 to Q_2. When the price is P_1, the firm is incurring a loss, because ATC is greater than P_1 at q_1. When the market supply increases from S_1 to S_2, it causes the market price to rise and the firm's losses disappear, because $P_2 = ATC$.

firms will exit the industry, causing the market supply curve to shift from S_1 to S_2 and driving up the market price to P_2. This price increase reduces the losses for the firms remaining in the industry, until the losses are completely eliminated at P_2. The remaining firms will maximize profits by producing at q_2 units of output, where profits and losses are zero. Only at zero economic profits is there no tendency for firms to either enter or leave the industry.

The Long-Run Equilibrium for the Competitive Firm

The long-run competitive equilibrium for a perfectly competitive firm is illustrated graphically in Exhibit 3. At the equilibrium point, e (where $MC = MR$), short-run and long-run average total costs are also equal. The average total cost curves touch the marginal cost and marginal revenue (demand) curves at the equilibrium output point. Because the marginal revenue curve is also the average revenue curve, average revenue and average total cost are equal at the equilibrium point. The long-run equilibrium in perfect competition depicted in Exhibit 3 has an interesting feature. Note that the equilibrium output occurs at the lowest point on the average total cost curve. As you may recall, this occurs because the marginal cost curve must intersect the average total cost curve at the latter curve's lowest point. Hence, the equilibrium condition in the long run in perfect competition is for each firm to produce at the output that minimizes average total cost—that is, the firm is operating at its minimum efficient scale. At this long-run equilibrium, all firms in the industry earn zero economic profit; consequently, new firms have no incentive to enter the market, and existing firms have no incentive to exit the market.

section 12.5 exhibit 3 The Long-Run Competitive Equilibrium

In the long run in perfect competition, a stable situation or equilibrium is achieved when economic profits are zero. In this case, at the Profit-maximizing point where $MC = MR$, short-run and long-run average total costs are equal. Industrywide supply shifts would change prices and average revenue, wiping out any losses or profits that develop in the short run and leading to the situation depicted in the exhibit.

SECTION CHECK

1. Economic profits encourage the entry of new firms, which shift the market supply curve to the right.
2. Any positive economic profits signal resources into the industry, driving down prices and revenues to the firm.
3. Any economic losses signal resources to leave the industry, leading to supply reduction, higher prices, and increased revenues.
4. Only at zero economic profits is there no tendency for firms to either enter or exit the industry.

---

1. Why do firms enter profitable industries?
2. Why does entry eliminate positive economic profits in a perfectly competitive industry?
3. Why do firms exit unprofitable industries?
4. Why does exit eliminate economic losses in a perfectly competitive industry?
5. Why is a situation of zero economic profits a stable long-run equilibrium situation for a perfectly competitive industry?

SECTION 12.6 Long-Run Supply

- What are constant-cost industries?
- What are increasing-cost industries?
- What are decreasing-cost industries?
- What is productive efficiency?
- What is allocative efficiency?

The preceding sections considered the costs for an individual, perfectly competitive firm as it varies output, on the assumption that the prices it pays for inputs (costs) are given. However, when the output of an entire industry changes, the likelihood is greater that changes in costs will occur. How will the changes in the number of firms in an industry affect the input costs of individual firms? In this section, we develop the long-run supply (*LRS*) curve. As we will see, the shape of the long-run supply curve depends on the extent to which input costs change with the entry or exit of firms in the industry. We will look at three possible types of industries when considering long-run supply: constant-cost industries, increasing-cost industries, and decreasing-cost industries.

A Constant-Cost Industry

In a **constant-cost industry**, the prices of inputs do not change as output is expanded. The industry may not use inputs in sufficient quantities to affect input prices. For example, say the firms in the industry use a lot of unskilled labor but the industry is small. Therefore, as output expands, the increase in demand for unskilled labor will not cause the market wage for unskilled labor to rise. Similarly, suppose a paper clip maker decides to double its output. It is highly unlikely that its demand for steel will have an impact on steel prices, because its demand for the input is so small.

Once long-run adjustments are complete, by necessity each firm operates at the point of lowest long-run average total cost, because supply shifts with entry and exit, eliminating profits. Therefore, each firm supplies the market with the quantity of output that it can produce at the lowest possible long-run average total cost.

In Exhibit 1, we can see the impact of an unexpected increase in market demand. Suppose that recent reports show that blueberries can lower cholesterol, lower blood pressure, and significantly reduce the risk of all cancers. The increase in market demand for blueberries leads to a price increase from P_1 to P_2 as the firm increases output from q_1 to q_2, and blueberry industry output increases from Q_1 to Q_2, as seen in Exhibit 1(b). The increase in market demand generates a higher price and positive profits for existing firms in the short run. The existence of economic profits will attract new firms into the industry, causing the short-run supply curve to shift from S_1 to S_2 and lowering price until excess profits are zero. This shift results in a new equilibrium, point C in Exhibit 1(c). Because the industry is one with constant costs, industry expansion does not alter firms' cost curves, and the industry long-run supply curve is horizontal. That is, the long-run equilibrium price is at the same level that prevailed before demand increased; the only long-run effect of the increase in demand is an increase in industry output, as more firms enter that are just like existing firms [shown in Exhibit 1(c)]. The long-run supply curve is horizontal when the market has free entry and exit, there is a large number of firms with identical costs and input prices are constant. Because these strong assumptions do not generally hold, we will now discuss when the long run supply curve has a positive or negative slope.

> **constant-cost industry**
> an industry where input prices (and cost curves) do not change as industry output changes
>
> **increasing-cost industry**
> an industry where input prices rise (and cost curves rise) as industry output rises

An Increasing-Cost Industry

In an **increasing-cost industry**, a more likely scenario, the cost curves of individual firms rise as the total output of the industry increases. Increases in input prices (upward shifts in cost curves) occur as larger quantities of factors are employed in the industry. When an industry utilizes a large portion of an input whose total supply is not huge, input prices will rise when the industry uses more of the input.

Increasing cost conditions are typical of "extractive" industries, such as agriculture, fishing, mining, and lumbering, which utilize large portions of the total supply of specialized natural resources such as land or mineral deposits. As the output of such an industry expands, the increased demand for the resources raises the prices that must be paid for their use. Because additional resources of giving quality cannot be produced, greater supplies can be obtained (if at all) only by luring them away

section 12.6 exhibit 1 — Demand Increase in a Constant-Cost Industry

a. Initial Equilibrium

b. Short-Run Profits

c. Long-Run Entry and No Economic Profits

An unexpected increase in market demand for blueberries leads to an increase in the market price in (b). The new market price leads to positive profits for existing firms, which attracts new firms into the industry, shifting market supply from S_1 to S_2 in (c). This increased short-run industry supply curve intersects D_2 at point C. Each firm (of a new, larger number of firms) is again producing at q_1 and earning zero economic profits.

from other industries, or by using lower-quality (and less-productive, thus higher-cost) resources.

Wheat production is a typical example of an increasing-cost industry. As the output of wheat increases, the demand for land suitable for the production of wheat rises, and thus the price paid for the use of land of any given quality increases.

If there were a construction boom in a fully employed economy, would it be more costly to get additional resources like skilled workers and raw materials? Yes, if this is an increasing-cost industry, the industry can only produce more output if it gets a higher price because the firm's costs of production rise as output expands. As new firms enter and output expands, the increase in demand for inputs causes the price of inputs to rise—the cost curves of all construction firms shift upward as the industry expands. Or consider a downtown building boom where the supply of workers that are willing to work on tall skyscrapers is very small; a very steep supply of labor curve. The high demand for these few workers causes their wages to rise sharply and the cost of skyscrapers to rise. The industry can produce more output but only at a higher price, enough to compensate the firm for the higher input costs. In an increasing-cost industry, the long-run supply curve is upward sloping.

For example, in Exhibit 2, we see that an unexpected increase in the market demand for wheat will shift the market demand curve from D_1 to D_2, in panel (b). Consequently, price will increase from P_1 to P_2 in the short run and the industry output increases from Q_1 to Q_2. The typical firm (farm) will have positive short-run profits and expand output from q_1 to q_2 as seen in panel (a). With the presence of short-run economic profits, new firms will enter the industry, shifting the short-run market supply curve to the right from S_1 to S_2. The prices of inputs, like farm land, fertilizer, seed, farm machinery, and so on, will be bid up by competing farmers, causing the firm's marginal and long-run average cost curves to rise.

Another example is provided by the airlines. Growth in the airline industry results in more congestion of airports and airspace. That is, as the output of the airline industry increases, the firm's cost increases, *ceteris paribus*. This situation of an upward sloping long-run industry supply curve is what economists call *external diseconomies of scale*—factors that are beyond, the firm's control (that is, external) raise the firm's costs as industry output expands. In contrast, recall the discussion of diseconomies of scale in the last chapter where the costs were internal to the firm—increased costs due to managing a larger firm.

A Decreasing-Cost Industry

It is also possible that an expansion in the output of an industry can lead to a reduction in input costs and shift the MC and ATC curves downward, and

section 12.6 exhibit 2 Increasing-Cost Industry

a. Individual Firm

b. Industry

In (b) the unexpected increase in demand for wheat shifts the demand curve from D_1 to D_2. The increase in demand leads to higher prices from P_1 to P_2. In (a) firms increase output from q_1 to q_2 and experience short-run economic profits ($P_2 >$ LRATC$_1$ at q_2). The short-run economic profits induce other firms to enter the industry. This causes the short-run supply curve to shift right, from S_1 to S_2. As new firms enter and output expands, the increase in demand for inputs causes the price of inputs to rise, leading to higher cost curves for the firm—SMC$_1$ to SMC$_2$ and LRATC$_1$ to LRATC$_2$. The new long-run equilibrium is at P_3 and q_1. The LRS is positively sloped. This means the industry must receive a higher market price to produce more output, Q_3, because the increased output causes input prices to rise.

the market price falls because of *external economies of scale*. We use the term external because the cost decreases are external to the firm; no one firm can gain by its own expansion. That is, the gains occurs when the total industry's output expands. The new long-run market equilibrium has more output at a lower price—that is, the long-run supply curve for a *decreasing-cost industry* is downward sloping (not shown).

Consider a new mining region, developed in an area remote from railroad facilities back in the days before motor vehicles. So long as the total output of the mines was small, the ore was hauled by wagon, an extremely expensive form of transportation. But when the number of mines increased, and the total output of the region rose substantially, it became feasible to construct a railroad to serve the area. The railroad lowered transportation costs and reduced the costs of all firms in the industry. As a practical matter, decreasing-cost industries are rarely encountered, at least over a large range of output. However, some industries may operate under decreasing-cost conditions in the short intervals of output expansion when continued growth makes possible the supply of materials or services at reduced cost. A larger industry might benefit from improved transportation or financial services, for example.

This situation might occur in the computer industry. The firms in the industry may be able to acquire computer chips at a lower price as the industry's demand for computer chips rises. Why? Perhaps it is because the computer chip industry can employ cost-saving techniques that become more economical at higher levels of output. That is, the marginal and average costs of the firm fall as input prices fall because of expanded output in the industry.

Perfect Competition and Economic Efficiency

In this chapter, we have seen that a firm in a perfectly competitive market produces at the minimum of the ATC curve in the long run and charges a price consistent with that cost. Because competitive firms are producing using the least-cost method, the minimum amount of resources is being used to produce a given level of output. This leads to lower product prices for consumers. In short, **productive efficiency** requires that firms produce goods and services in the least costly way, where P = Minimum ATC, as seen in Exhibit 3 in section 12.5 on page 341. However, productive efficiency alone does not guarantee that

productive efficiency where a good or service is produced at the lowest possible cost

---

section 12.6 exhibit 3 Allocative Efficiency and Perfect Competition

a. Producing Less Than the Competitive Level of Output Lowers Welfare

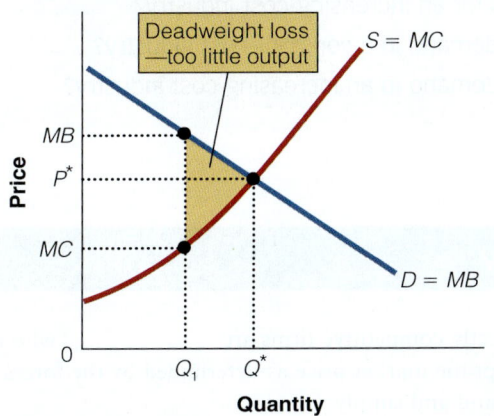

b. Producing More Than the Competitive Level of Output Lowers Welfare

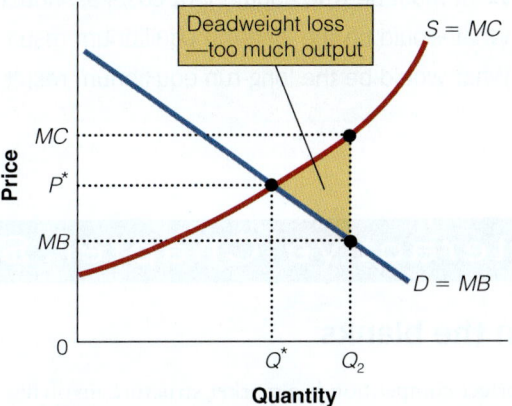

The demand curve measures the marginal benefits to the consumer and the supply curve measures the marginal cost to the sellers. At P^* and Q^*, resources are being allocated efficiently—the marginal benefits of these resources are equal to the marginal cost of these resources. If Q_1 is produced, then the marginal benefits from producing additional units are greater than the marginal costs. Society gains from expending output up to the point where $MB = MC$ at Q^*. If output is expanded beyond Q^* ($MC > MB$) society gains from a reduction in output back to Q^*.

markets are operating efficiently—society must also produce the goods and services that society wants most. This leads us to what economists call allocative efficiency.

We say that the output that results from equilibrium conditions of market demand and market supply in perfectly competitive markets achieve an efficient allocation of resources.

At the intersection of market supply and market demand, we find the competitive equilibrium price, P^*, and the competitive equilibrium output, Q^*. In competitive markets, market supply equals market demand, and $P = MC$. When $P = MC$, buyers value the last unit of output by the same amount that it cost sellers to produce it. If buyers value the last unit by more than the marginal cost of production, resources are not being allocated efficiently, as at Q_1 in Exhibit 3(a). Think of the demand curve as the marginal benefit curve ($D = MB$) and the supply curve as the marginal cost curve ($S = MC$). According to the rule of rational choice, we should pursue an activity as long as the expected marginal benefits are greater than the expected marginal costs. For example, in Exhibit 3(a), if Q_1 is produced, then the marginal benefits from producing additional units are greater than the marginal costs. The shaded area is deadweight loss. That is, at Q_1, resources are not being allocated efficiently, and output should be expanded.

allocative efficiency
where $P = MC$ and production will be allocated to reflect consumer preferences

We can also produce too much output. For example, if output is expanded beyond Q^* in Exhibit 3(b), the cost to sellers for producing the good is greater than the marginal benefit to consumers. The shaded area is deadweight loss. Society would gain from a reduction in output back to Q^*. Once the competitive equilibrium is reached, the buyers' marginal benefit equals the sellers' marginal cost. That is, in a competitive market, producers efficiently use their scarce resources (labor, machinery, and other inputs) to produce what consumers want. In this sense, perfect competition achieves **allocative efficiency.**

SECTION CHECK

1. In constant-cost industries, the cost curves of the firm are not affected by changes in the output of the entire industry. Such industries must be small demanders of resources in the market.
2. In an increasing-cost industry, the cost curves of the individual firms rise as total output increases. This case is the most typical.
3. A decreasing-cost industry has a downward-sloping long-run supply curve. Firms experience lower cost as industry expands.
4. Productive efficiency occurs in perfect competition because the firm produces at the minimum of the *ATC* curve.
5. Allocative efficiency occurs when $P = MC$; production is allocated to reflect consumers' wants.

---

1. What must be true about input costs as industry output expands for a constant-cost industry?
2. What must be true about input costs as industry output expands for an increasing-cost industry?
3. What would be the long-run equilibrium result of an increase in demand in a constant-cost industry?
4. What would be the long-run equilibrium result of an increase in demand in an increasing-cost industry?

Interactive Chapter Summary

Fill in the blanks:

1. Perfect competition is a market structure involving a(n) _____ number of buyers and sellers, a(n) _____ product, and _____ market entry and exit.

2. Perfectly competitive firms are _____, who must accept the market price as determined by the forces of demand and supply.

3. Because perfectly competitive markets have _____ buyers and sellers, each firm is so

_____ in relation to the industry that its production decisions have no impact on the market.

4. Because consumers believe that all firms in a perfectly competitive market sell _____ products, the products of all the firms are perfect substitutes.

5. Because of _____ market entry and exit, perfectly competitive markets generally consist of a(n) _____ number of small suppliers.

6. In a perfectly competitive industry, each producer provides such a(n) _____ fraction of the total supply that a change in the amount he or she offers does not have a noticeable effect on the market price.

7. Because perfectly competitive sellers can sell all they want at the market price, their demand curve is _____ at the market price over the _____ range of output that they could possibly produce.

8. The objective of a firm is to maximize profits by producing the amount that maximizes the difference between its _____ and _____.

9. Total revenue for a perfectly competitive firm equals the _____ times the _____.

10. _____ equals total revenue divided by the number of units of the product sold.

11. _____ is the additional revenue derived from the sale of one more unit of the good.

12. In perfect competition, we know that _____ and price are equal.

13. In all types of market environments, firms will maximize profits at that output which maximizes the difference between _____ and _____, which is the same output level where _____ equals _____.

14. At the level of output chosen by a competitive firm, total cost equals _____ times quantity, while total revenue equals _____ times quantity.

15. If total revenue is greater than total costs at its profit-maximizing output level, a firm is generating _____. If total revenue is less than total costs, the firm is generating _____. If total revenue equals total costs, the firm is earning _____.

16. If a firm cannot generate enough revenues to cover its _____ costs, then it will have larger losses if it operates than if it shuts down in the short run.

17. The loss a firm would bear if it shuts down would be equal to _____.

18. When price is less than _____ but more than _____, a firm produces in the short run, but at a loss.

19. The short-run supply curve of an individual competitive seller is identical with that portion of the _____ curve that lies above the minimum of the _____ curve.

20. The short-run market supply curve is the horizontal summation of the individual firms' supply curves, providing that _____ are not affected by increased production by existing firms.

21. If perfectly competitive producers are currently making economic profits, the market supply curve will shift to the right over time as more firms _____ and existing firms _____.

22. As entry into a profitable industry pushes down the market price, producers will move from a situation where price _____ average total cost to one where price _____ average total cost.

23. Only at _____ is the tendency for firms either to enter or leave the business eliminated.

24. The long-run equilibrium output in perfect competition occurs at the lowest point on the average total cost curve, so the equilibrium condition in the long run in perfect competition is for firms to produce at that output that minimizes the _____.

25. The shape of the long-run supply curve depends on the extent to which _____ change with the entry or exit of firms in the industry.

26. In a constant-cost industry, the prices of inputs _____ as output is expanded.

27. In an increasing-cost industry, the cost curves of the individual firms _____ as the total output of the industry increases.

28. There is a _____ efficiency in perfect competition because the firm produces at the minimum of the ATC curve.

29. There is _____ efficiency in perfect competition because $P = MC$ and production is allocated to reflect consumers' wants.

30. Once the competitive equilibrium is reached, the buyers' _____ equals the sellers' _____.

Answers: 1. large; homogeneous (standardized); easy 2. price takers 3. many; small 4. identical (homogeneous) 5. easy 6. large 7. horizontal; entire 8. total revenues; total costs 9. market price; quantity of units sold 10. Average revenue 11. Marginal revenue 12. marginal revenue 13. total revenues; total costs; marginal revenue; marginal costs 14. average total cost; the market price 15. economic profits; economic losses; zero economic profits 16. variable 17. fixed costs 18. average total costs; average variable costs 19. marginal cost; average variable cost 20. input prices 21. enter the industry; expand 22. exceeds; equals 23. zero economic profits 24. average total cost curve 25. input costs 26. do not change 27. rise 28. productive 29. allocative 30. marginal benefit; marginal cost

Key Terms and Concepts

price takers 330
total revenue (TR) 333
average revenue (AR) 333
marginal revenue (MR) 333
profit-maximizing level of output 334
short-run supply curve 338
short-run market supply curve 338
constant-cost industry 344
increasing-cost industry 344
productive efficiency 347
allocative efficiency 348

Section Check Answers

12.1 A Perfectly Competitive Market

1. **Why do firms in perfectly competitive markets involve homogeneous goods?**
   For there to be a large number of sellers of a particular good, so that no seller can appreciably affect the market price (i.e., sellers are price takers), the goods in question must be the same, or homogeneous.

2. **Why does the absence of significant barriers to entry tend to result in a large number of suppliers?**
   With no significant barriers to entry, it is fairly easy for entrepreneurs to become suppliers of a product. With such easy entry, as long as an industry is profitable it will attract new suppliers, typically resulting in large numbers of sellers.

3. **Why does the fact that perfectly competitive firms are small relative to the market make them price takers?**
   If a perfectly competitive firm sells only a small amount relative to the total market supply, even sharply reducing its output will make virtually no difference in the market quantity supplied; therefore, it will make virtually no difference in the market price. In this case, a firm is able to sell all it wants at the market equilibrium price but is unable to appreciably affect that price; therefore, it takes the market equilibrium price as given—that is, it is a price taker.

12.2 An Individual Price Taker's Demand Curve

1. **Why would a perfectly competitive firm not try to raise or lower its price?**
   A perfectly competitive firm is able to sell all it wants at the market equilibrium price. Therefore, it has no incentive to lower prices (sacrificing revenues and therefore profits) in an attempt to increase sales. Because other firms are willing to sell perfect substitutes for each other's product (because goods are homogeneous) at the market equilibrium price, trying to raise price would lead to the firm losing all its sales. Therefore, it has no incentive to try to raise its price, either.

2. **Why can we represent the demand curve of a perfectly competitive firm as perfectly elastic (horizontal) at the market price?**
   If a perfectly competitive firm can sell all it would like at the market equilibrium price, the demand curve it faces for its output is perfectly elastic (horizontal) at that market equilibrium price.

3. **How does an individual perfectly competitive firm's demand curve change when the market price changes?**
   If a perfectly competitive firm can sell all it would like at the market equilibrium price, it faces a perfectly elastic demand curve at the market equilibrium price. Therefore, anything that changes the market equilibrium price (any of the market demand curve shifters or the market supply curve shifters) will change the price at which each perfectly competitive firm's demand curve is perfectly elastic (horizontal).

4. **If the marginal cost facing every producer of a product shifted upward, would the position of a perfectly competitive firm's demand curve be likely to change as a result? Why or why not?**
   Yes. If the marginal cost curves facing each producer shifted upward, a decrease (leftward shift) would occur in the industry supply curve. This shift would result in a higher market price that each producer takes as given, which would shift each producer's horizontal demand curve upward to that new market price.

12.3 Profit Maximization

1. **How is total revenue calculated?**
   Total revenue is equal to the price times the quantity sold. However, because the quantity sold at that price must equal the quantity demanded at that price (to sell a product you need a willing buyer), it can also be described as price times quantity demanded at that price.

2. **How is average revenue derived from total revenue?**

   Average or per-unit revenue for a given quantity of output is just the total revenue from that quantity of sales divided by the quantity sold.

3. **How is marginal revenue derived from total revenue?**

   Marginal revenue is the change in total revenue from the sale of one more unit of output. It can be either positive (total revenue increases with output) or negative (total revenue decreases with output).

4. **Why is marginal revenue equal to price for a perfectly competitive firm?**

   If a perfectly competitive seller can sell all it would like at the market equilibrium price, it can sell one more unit at that price without having to lower its price on the other units it sells (which would require sacrificing revenues from those sales). Therefore, its marginal revenue from selling one more unit equals the market equilibrium price, and its horizontal demand curve therefore is the same as its horizontal marginal revenue curve.

12.4 Short-Run Profits and Losses

1. **How is the profit-maximizing output quantity determined?**

   The profit-maximizing output is the output where marginal revenue equals marginal cost (because profits increase for every unit of output for which marginal revenue exceeds marginal cost).

2. **How do we determine total revenue and total cost for the profit-maximizing output quantity?**

   At the profit-maximizing quantity, total revenue is equal to average revenue (price) times quantity (because average revenue is total revenue divided by quantity), and total cost is equal to average cost times quantity (because average cost equals total cost divided by quantity).

3. **If a profit-maximizing perfectly competitive firm is earning a profit because total revenue exceeds total cost, why must the market price exceed average total cost?**

   If total revenue exceeds total cost, total revenue divided by the quantity of output, which is average revenue or price, must also exceed total cost divided by the same quantity of output, which is average total cost, for that level of output.

4. **If a profit-maximizing perfectly competitive firm is earning a loss because total revenue is less than total cost, why must the market price be less than average total cost?**

   If total revenue is less than total cost, total revenue divided by the quantity of output, which is average revenue or price, must also be less than total cost divided by the same quantity of output, which is average total cost, for that level of output.

5. **If a profit-maximizing perfectly competitive firm is earning zero economic profits because total revenue equals total cost, why must the market price be equal to the average total cost for that level of output?**

   If total revenue equals total cost, total revenue divided by the quantity of output, which is average revenue or price, must also be equal to total cost divided by the same quantity of output, which is average total cost, for that level of output.

6. **Why would a profit-maximizing perfectly competitive firm shut down rather than operate if price was less than its average variable cost?**

   If a firm shuts down, its losses will equal its fixed costs (because it has no revenue or variable costs). If a firm operates, and revenues exactly cover variable costs, it will also suffer losses equal to fixed costs. But if a firm cannot cover even all its variable costs with its revenues, it will lose its fixed costs plus part of its variable costs. But because these losses are greater than the losses from shutting down, a firm would choose to shut down rather than continue to operate in this situation.

7. **Why would a profit-maximizing perfectly competitive firm continue to operate for a period of time if price was greater than average variable cost but less than average total cost?**

   If price was greater than average variable cost but less than average total cost, a firm would be earning losses and would eventually go out of business if that situation continued. However, in the short run, as long as revenues more than covered variable costs, losses from operating would be less than the losses from shutting down (these losses equal total fixed cost), as at least part of fixed costs would be covered by revenues; so a firm would continue to operate in the short run in this situation.

12.5 Long-Run Equilibrium

1. **Why do firms enter profitable industries?**

   Profitable industries generate a higher rate of return to productive assets than other industries. Therefore, firms will enter such industries in their search for more profitable uses for their assets.

2. **Why does entry eliminate positive economic profits in a perfectly competitive industry?**

   Entry eliminates positive economic profits (above-normal rates of return) in a perfectly competitive industry because entry will continue as long as economic profits remain positive (rates of return are higher than in other industries); that is, until no more positive economic profits can be earned.

3. **Why do firms exit unprofitable industries?**
Unprofitable industries generate lower rates of return to productive assets than other industries. Therefore, firms will exit such industries in their search for more profitable uses for their assets elsewhere.

4. **Why does exit eliminate economic losses in a perfectly competitive industry?**
Exit eliminates negative economic profits (below-normal rates of return) in a perfectly competitive industry because exit will continue as long as economic profits remain negative (rates of return are lower than in other industries); that is, until no firms are experiencing economic losses.

5. **Why is a situation of zero economic profits a stable long-run equilibrium situation for a perfectly competitive industry?**
A situation of zero economic profits is a stable long-run equilibrium situation for a perfectly competitive industry because that situation offers no profit incentives for firms to either enter or leave the industry.

12.6 Long-Run Supply

1. **What must be true about input costs as industry output expands for a constant-cost industry?**
Input costs remain constant as industry output expands for a constant-cost industry (which is why it is a constant-cost industry).

2. **What must be true about input costs as industry output expands for an increasing-cost industry?**
Input costs increase as industry output expands for an increasing-cost industry (which is why it is an increasing-cost industry).

3. **What would be the long-run equilibrium result of an increase in demand in a constant-cost industry?**
The long-run equilibrium result of an increase in demand in a constant-cost industry is an increase in industry output with no change in price, because output will expand as long as price exceeds the constant level of long-run average cost.

4. **What would be the long-run equilibrium result of an increase in demand in an increasing-cost industry?**
The long-run equilibrium result of an increase in demand in an increasing-cost industry is an increase in industry output (but a smaller increase than in the constant-cost case) and a higher price. Output will expand as long as price exceeds long-run average cost; but that expansion of output increases costs by raising input prices, so in the long run prices just cover the resulting higher costs of production.

CHAPTER 12 STUDY GUIDE

True or False:

1. In perfect competition, no single firm produces more than an extremely small proportion of output, so no firm can influence the market price.
2. Perfectly competitive firms are price takers because their influence on price is insignificant.
3. It is difficult for entrepreneurs to become suppliers of a product in a perfectly competitive market structure.
4. A perfectly competitive market is approximated most closely in highly organized markets for securities and agricultural commodities.
5. A perfectly competitive firm cannot sell at any figure higher than the current market price and would not knowingly charge a lower price, because it could sell all it wants at the market price.
6. In a perfectly competitive market, individual sellers can change their output without altering the market price.
7. In a perfectly competitive industry, the market demand curve is perfectly elastic at the market price.
8. Because perfectly competitive firms are price takers, each firm's demand curve remains unchanged even when the market price changes.
9. The perfectly competitive model does not assume any knowledge on the part of individual buyers and sellers about market demand and supply—they only have to know the price of the good they sell.
10. In a perfectly competitive market, marginal revenue is constant and equal to the market price.
11. For a perfectly competitive firm, as long as the price derived from expanded output exceeds the marginal cost of that output, the expansion of output creates additional profits.
12. Producing at the profit-maximizing output level means that a firm is actually earning economic profits.
13. A competitive firm earning zero economic profits will be unable to continue in operation over time.
14. A firm will not produce at all unless the price is greater than its average variable costs.
15. A perfectly competitive firm will operate in the short run only at price levels greater than or equal to average total costs.
16. The MC curve above minimum AVC shows the marginal cost of producing any given output, as well as the equilibrium output that the firm will supply at various prices in the short run.
17. Because the short run is too brief for new firms to enter the market, the market supply curve is the vertical summation of the supply curves of existing firms.
18. As new firms enter an industry where sellers are earning economic profits, the result will include a reduction in the equilibrium price.
19. In long-run equilibrium, perfectly competitive firms make zero economic profits, earning a normal return on the use of their capital.
20. For a perfectly competitive firm, the long-run equilibrium will be the point at which price equals marginal cost as well as short-run average total cost and long-run average cost.
21. In a constant-cost industry, the industry does not use inputs in sufficient quantities to affect input prices.
22. In a constant-cost competitive industry, industry expansion does not alter a firm's cost curves, and the industry long-run supply curve is upward sloping.
23. In a constant-cost competitive industry, the only long-run effect of an increase in demand is an increase in industry output.
24. When an industry utilizes a large portion of an input, input prices will rise when the industry uses more of that input as it expands output.

Multiple Choice:

1. Which of the following is false about perfect competition?
   a. Perfectly competitive firms sell homogeneous products.
   b. A perfectly competitive industry allows easy entry and exit.
   c. A perfectly competitive firm must take the market price as given.
   d. A perfectly competitive firm produces a substantial fraction of the industry output.
   e. All of the above are true.

2. An individual perfectly competitive firm
   a. may increase its price without losing sales.
   b. is a price maker.
   c. has no perceptible influence on the market price.
   d. sells a product that is differentiated from those of its competitors.

3. When will a perfectly competitive firm's demand curve shift?
   a. never
   b. when the market demand curve shifts
   c. when new producers enter the industry in large numbers
   d. when either b or c occurs

4. In a market with perfectly competitive firms, the market demand curve is _____ and the demand curve facing each individual firm is _____.
   a. upward sloping; horizontal
   b. downward sloping; horizontal
   c. horizontal; downward sloping
   d. horizontal; upward sloping
   e. horizontal; horizontal

5. The marginal revenue of a perfectly competitive firm
   a. decreases as output increases.
   b. increases as output increases.
   c. is constant as output increases and is equal to price.
   d. increases as output increases and is equal to price.

6. A perfectly competitive firm seeking to maximize its profits would want to maximize the difference between
   a. its marginal revenue and its marginal cost.
   b. its average revenue and its average cost.
   c. its total revenue and its total cost.
   d. its price and its marginal cost.
   e. either a or d.

7. If a perfectly competitive firm's marginal revenue exceeded its marginal cost,
   a. it would cut its price in order to sell more output and increase its profits.
   b. it would expand its output but not cut its price in order to increase its profits.
   c. it is currently earning economic profits.
   d. both a and c are true.
   e. both b and c are true.

8. A perfectly competitive firm maximizes its profit at an output in which
   a. total revenue exceeds total cost by the greatest dollar amount.
   b. marginal cost equals the price.
   c. marginal cost equals marginal revenue.
   d. all of the above are true.

9. In perfect competition, at a firm's short-run profit-maximizing output,
   a. its marginal revenue equals zero.
   b. its average revenue could be greater or less than average cost.
   c. its marginal revenue will be falling.
   d. both b and c will be true.

10. In perfect competition, at the firm's short-run profit-maximizing output, which of the following need *not* be true?
    a. Marginal revenue equals marginal cost.
    b. Price equals marginal cost.
    c. Average revenue equals average cost.
    d. Average revenue equals marginal revenue.
    e. All of the above would have to be true.

11. The minimum price at which a firm would produce in the short run is the point at which
    a. price equals the minimum point on its marginal cost curve.
    b. price equals the minimum point on its average variable cost curve.
    c. price equals the minimum point on its average total cost curve.
    d. price equals the minimum point on its average fixed cost curve.

12. A profit-maximizing perfectly competitive firm would never operate at an output level at which
    a. it would lose more than its total fixed costs.
    b. it was not earning a positive economic profit.
    c. it was not earning a zero economic profit.
    d. it was not earning an accounting profit.

13. If a perfectly competitive firm finds that price is greater than AVC but less than ATC at the quantity where its marginal cost equals the market price,
    a. the firm will produce in the short run but may eventually go out of business.
    b. the firm will produce in the short run, and new entrants will tend to enter the industry over time.
    c. the firm will immediately shut down.
    d. the firm will be earning economic profits.
    e. both b and d are true.

Use the following diagram to answer questions 14–17.

14. When the market price equals P_1, the firm should produce output
    a. Q_1.
    b. Q_2.
    c. Q_3.
    d. Q_4.
    e. none of the above.

355

15. When the market price equals P_3, the firm should produce output
    a. Q_3, operating at a loss.
    b. Q_4, operating at a loss.
    c. Q_4, earning an economic profit.
    d. Q_5, operating at a loss.
    e. Q_5, earning a normal profit.

16. When the market price equals P_4, the firm should produce output
    a. Q_4, operating at a loss.
    b. Q_4, earning an economic profit.
    c. Q_5, operating at a loss.
    d. Q_5, earning a normal profit.
    e. Q_5, earning a positive economic profit.

17. When the market price equals P_5, the firm should produce output
    a. Q_5, operating at a loss.
    b. Q_5, earning an economic profit.
    c. Q_6, operating at a loss.
    d. Q_6, earning a normal profit.
    e. Q_6, earning a positive economic profit.

18. The short-run supply curve of a perfectly competitive firm is
    a. its MC curve.
    b. its MC curve above the minimum point of AVC.
    c. its MC curve above the minimum point of ATC.
    d. none of the above.

19. Darlene runs a fruit-and-vegetable stand in a medium-sized community where many such stands operate. Her weekly total revenue equals $3,000. Her weekly total cost of running the stand equals $3,500, consisting of $2,500 of variable costs and $1,000 of fixed costs. An economist would likely advise Darlene to
    a. shut down as quickly as possible in order to minimize her losses.
    b. keep the stand open because it is generating an economic profit.
    c. keep the stand open for a while longer because she is covering all of her variable costs and some of her fixed costs.
    d. keep the stand open for a while longer because she is covering all of her fixed costs and some of her variable costs.

20. The entry of new firms into an industry will likely
    a. shift the industry supply curve to the right.
    b. cause the market price to fall.
    c. reduce the profits of existing firms in the industry.
    d. do all of the above.

21. Which of the following statements concerning equilibrium in the long run is incorrect?
    a. Firms will exit the industry if economic profits equal zero.
    b. Firms are able to vary their plant sizes in the long run.
    c. Economic profits are eliminated as new firms enter the industry.
    d. The market price equals both marginal cost and average total cost.

22. In long-run equilibrium under perfect competition, price does not equal which of the following?
    a. long-run marginal cost
    b. minimum average total cost
    c. average fixed cost
    d. marginal revenue
    e. average revenue

23. If the domino-making industry is a constant-cost industry, one would expect the long-run result of an increase in demand for dominos to include
    a. a greater number of firms and a higher price.
    b. a greater number of firms and the same price.
    c. the same number of firms and a higher price.
    d. the same number of firms and the same price.

24. In an increasing-cost industry, an unexpected increase in demand would lead to what result in the long run?
    a. higher costs and a higher price
    b. higher costs and a lower price
    c. no change in costs or prices
    d. impossible to determine from the information given

Problems:

1. Which of the following are most likely to be perfectly competitive?
   a. Chicago Board of Trade
   b. fast-food industry
   c. computer software industry
   d. New York Stock Exchange
   e. clothing industry

2. Using the following information, which of the industries described are perfectly competitive? Check the perfectly competitive market characteristics each industry possessed and determine whether it is a perfectly competitive industry.

Industry	Many Firms and Buyers	Identical Products	Ease of Entry and Exit	Perfectly Competitive Market?
New York taxi business: City issues a limited number of permits.	☐	☐	☐	____
Commercial aircraft industry: The costs of starting such a business are significant.	☐	☐	☐	____
Window washing business: Low cost of entry and limited specialized training.	☐	☐	☐	____
Fast-food business: Restaurant chains produce meals that are distinct	☐	☐	☐	____
Broccoli farming: There are many producers of broccoli, which requires no special growing conditions.	☐	☐	☐	____

3.

Output	Total Cost	Total Revenue
0	$ 30	$ 0
1	45	25
2	65	50
3	90	75
4	120	100
5	155	125

Given these data, determine AR, MR, P, and the short-run profit-maximizing (loss-minimizing) level of output.

4. Illustrate the *SRATC, AVC, MC,* and *MR* curves for a perfectly competitive firm that is operating at a loss. What is the output level that minimizes losses? Why is it more profitable to continue producing in the short run rather than shut down?

5. Industry councils promote the consumption of particular types of farm products. These groups urge us to "Drink Milk" or "Eat Apples." Very little advertising is done by individual farmers. Using your understanding of the perfectly competitive market, explain this advertising strategy.

6. Complete the following table and identify the profit-maximizing output.
   a.

Quantity	Price	Total Revenue	Marginal Revenue	Marginal Cost	Total Profit
10	$12	$120	$12	$8	$25
11	12	___	___	9	___
12	12	___	___	11	___
13	12	___	___	12	___
14	12	___	___	14	___

   b. What is true about marginal revenue and marginal costs when profit is maximized?
   c. What would be the profit-maximizing level of output if price fell to $9?

7. Explain why the following conditions are typical under perfect competition in the long run.
   a. $P = MC$
   b. $P = $ minimum ATC

8. Discuss the following questions.
   a. Why must price cover *AVC* if firms are to continue to operate?
   b. If the firm is covering its *AVC* but not all its fixed costs, will it continue to operate in the short run? Why or why not?
   c. Why is it possible for price to remain above the average total cost in the short run but not in the long run?

9. At a price of $5 the profit-maximizing output for a perfectly competitive firm is 1,000 units per year. If the average total cost is $3 per unit, what will be the firm's profit? If the average total cost is $6 per unit, what will be the firm's profit? What is the relationship between profit, price, and average total cost?

10. Use the following diagram to answer a, b, and c.

   a. Illustrate the relationship between a perfectly competitive firm's demand curve and the market supply and demand curve.
   b. Illustrate the effects of an increase in market demand on a perfectly competitive firm's demand curve.
   c. Illustrate the effects of a decrease in market demand on a perfectly competitive firm's demand curve.

11. Complete the following table for a perfectly competitive firm, and indicate its profit-maximizing output.

Quantity	Price	Total Revenue	Marginal Revenue	Total Cost	Marginal Cost	Total Profit
6	$10	$___	$___	$30	$3	$30
7	___	___	___	35	___	___
8	___	___	___	42	___	___
9	___	___	___	51	___	___
10	___	___	___	62	___	___
11	___	___	___	75	___	___
12	___	___	___	90	___	___

12. Use the following diagram to answer a–d.

a. How much would a perfectly competitive firm produce at each of the indicated prices?
b. At which prices is the firm earning economic profits? Zero economic profits? Negative economic profits?
c. At which prices would the firm shut down?
d. Indicate what this firm's supply curve would be.

13. Use the following diagram to answer a–d.

a. How much would a perfectly competitive firm produce at each of the indicated prices?
b. At which prices is the firm earning economic profits? Zero economic profits? Negative economic profits?
c. At which prices would the firm shut down?
d. Indicate what this firm's supply curve would be.

14. Use the following diagrams to answer a and b.

   a. Show the effect of an increase in demand on the perfectly competitive firm's price, marginal revenue, output, and profits in the short run.
   b. Show the long-run effects of an increase in demand for the industry, and the effects on a perfectly competitive firm's price, marginal revenue, output, and profits for a constant-cost industry.

15. In The *Wealth of Nations*, Adam Smith wrote, "Every individual endeavors to employ his capital so that its produce may be of greatest value. He generally neither intends to promote the public interest, nor knows how much he is promoting it. He intends only his own security, only his own gain. And he is led by an invisible hand to promote an end which was no part of his intention. By pursuing his own interest he frequently promotes that of society more effectively than when he really intends to promote it." How does the story of long-run equilibrium in a perfectly competitive industry illustrate Adam Smith's invisible hand?

16. Graph and explain the adjustments to long-run equilibrium when market demand decreases in a constant-cost industry.

17. Evaluate the following statements. Determine whether each is true or false and explain your answer.
    a. If economic profits are zero, firms will exit the industry in the long run.
    b. A firm cannot maximize profits without minimizing costs.
    c. If a firm is minimizing costs, it must be maximizing profits.

18. Describe what would happen to the industry supply curve and the economic profits of the firms in a competitive industry if those firms were currently earning economic profits. What if they were currently earning economic losses?

19. Given the industry description, identify each of the following as an increasing- or constant-cost industry.
    a. Major League Baseball: Uses the majority of pitchers. As the number of pitchers used increased, the quality declines.
    b. Fast-food restaurants: Uses a relatively small share of land and unskilled labor in most cities.
    c. Trucking industry: Uses a large portion of the trained and experienced drivers, especially long-distance drivers.

Monopoly and Antitrust

13

13.1 Monopoly: The Price Maker
13.2 Demand and Marginal Revenue in Monopoly
13.3 The Monopolist's Equilibrium
13.4 Monopoly and Welfare Loss
13.5 Monopoly Policy
13.6 Price Discrimination and Peak Load Pricing

Monopoly is at the other end of the spectrum from perfect competition. Pure monopoly is a market with a single seller. Because it is the sole supplier, a monopoly faces the market demand curve for its product.

Consequently, the monopolist has control over the market price—it is a price maker. The monopolist can choose any combination of price and quantity along its market demand curve. But do not confuse ability with incentive. The monopolist, just like the perfectly competitive firm, will maximize profits (or minimize losses) by producing at the output level where $MR = MC$.

A pure monopoly, with literally one seller, is rare in the real world. But situations in which a few firms compete with each other are quite common. For example, Microsoft's Windows system, certain patented prescription drugs, the DeBeers diamond company, and your cable company are all examples of near monopolies. All of these firms have some monopoly power—control over prices and output.

In this chapter, we will see how a monopolist determines the profit-maximizing price and output. We will also compare monopoly and perfect competition to see which is more efficient. Does the monopoly equilibrium solution lead to higher prices and lower output levels than the perfectly competitive equilibrium solution? If so, what can the government do about it?

Monopoly: The Price Maker

* What is a monopoly?
* Why is pure monopoly rare?
* What are the sources of monopoly power?
* What is a natural monopoly?

What Is a Monopoly?

A true or pure **monopoly** exists when a market consists of only one seller of a product with no close substitute and natural or legal barriers to prevent entry competition. The reason a monopoly is the only firm in the market is because other firms cannot enter—there are barriers to entry. In monopoly, the firm and "the industry" are one and the same. Consequently, the firm sets the price of the good, because the firm faces the industry demand curve and can pick the most profitable point on that demand curve. Monopolists are price makers (rather than price takers) that try to pick the price that will maximize their profits.

Pure Monopoly Is a Rarity

Few goods and services truly have only one producer. One might think of a small community with a single bank, a single newspaper, or even a single grocery store. Even in these situations, however, most people can bank out of town, use a substitute financial institution, buy out-of-town newspapers or read them on the Web, go to a nearby town to buy groceries, and so on. Near-monopoly conditions exist, but absolutely pure monopoly is unusual.

One market in which there is typically only one producer of goods and services within an area is public utilities. In any given market, usually only one company provides natural gas or supplies water. Moreover, governments themselves provide many services for which they are often the sole provider—sewer services, fire and police protection, and military protection. Most of these situations resemble a pure monopoly. However, for most of these goods and services, substitute goods and services are available. People heating their homes with natural gas can switch to electric heat (or vice versa). In some areas, residents can even substitute home-collected rainwater or well water for what the local water company provides.

Even though the purist may correctly deny the existence of monopoly, the number of situations where monopoly conditions are closely approximated is numerous enough to make the study of monopoly more than a theoretical abstraction; moreover, the study of monopoly is useful in clarifying certain desirable aspects of perfect competition.

Barriers to Entry

A monopolist can use several ways to make it virtually impossible for other firms to overcome barriers to entry. For example, a monopolist might prevent potential rivals from entering the market by establishing legal barriers, taking advantage of economies of scale, or controlling important inputs.

Legal Barriers

In the case of legal barriers, the government might franchise only one firm to operate an industry, as is the case for postal services in most countries. The government can also provide licensing designed to ensure a certain level of quality and competence. Workers in many trade industries must obtain government licensing—hair stylists, bartenders, contractors, electricians, and plumbers, for instance.

Also, the government could award patents that encourage inventive activity. It can cost millions of dollars to develop a new drug or computer chip, for example, and without a patent to recoup some of the costs, a company would certainly be less motivated to pursue inventive activity. As long as the patent is in effect, the company has the potential to enjoy monopoly profits for many years. After all, why would a firm engage in costly research if any company could take a free ride on their discovery and produce and sell the new drug or computer chip?

Economies of Scale

The situation in which one large firm can provide the output of the market at a lower cost than two or more smaller firms is called a **natural monopoly.** With a natural monopoly, it is more efficient to have one firm produce the good. The reason for the cost advantage

> **monopoly**
> the single supplier of a product that has no close substitute
>
> **natural monopoly**
> a firm that can produce at a lower cost than a number of smaller firms can

is economies of scale; that is, ATC falls as output expands throughout the relevant output range, as seen in Exhibit 1. Public utilities, such as water, gas, and electricity, are examples of natural monopoly. It is less costly for one firm to lay down pipes and distribute water than for competing firms to lay down a maze of competing pipes. That is, a single water company can supply the town water more efficiently than a large number of competing firms.

Control Over an Important Input

Another barrier to entry could exist if a firm had control over an important input. For example, from the late nineteenth century to the early 1940s, the Aluminum Company of America (Alcoa) had a monopoly in the production of aluminum. Its monopoly power was guaranteed because of its control over an important ingredient in the production of aluminum—bauxite. Similarly, the DeBeers diamond company of South Africa has monopoly power because it controls roughly 75 percent of the world's output of diamonds.

section 13.1 exhibit 1 — Economies of Scale

The firm has economies of scale over the relevant range of output with declining average total costs. When one firm can produce the total output at a lower cost than several small firms, it is called a natural monopoly.

SECTION CHECK

1. A pure monopoly exists in a market with only one seller of a product for which no close substitute is available.
2. Pure monopolies are rare because few goods and services have only one existing producer.
3. Sources of monopoly power include legal barriers, economies of scale, and control over important inputs.
4. A natural monopoly occurs when one firm can provide the good or service at a lower cost than two or more smaller firms.

---

1. Why does monopoly depend on the existence of barriers to entry?
2. Why is a pure monopoly a rarity?
3. Why does the government grant some companies, such as public utilities, monopoly power?

SECTION 13.2 — Demand and Marginal Revenue in Monopoly

* How does the demand curve for a monopolist differ from that for a perfectly competitive firm?
* Why is marginal revenue less than price in monopoly?

In monopoly, the market demand curve may be regarded as the demand curve for the firm's product because the monopoly firm *is* the market for that particular product. The demand curve indicates the quantities that the firm can sell at various possible prices. In monopoly, the demand curve for the firm's product declines as

section 13.2 exhibit 1 — Comparing Demand Curves: Perfect Competition Versus Monopoly

The demand curve for a perfectly competitive firm is perfectly elastic; competitive firms can sell all they want at the market price. The firm is a price taker. The demand curve for a monopolist is downward sloping; if the monopolist raises its price it will lose some but not all of its customers. The monopolist is a *price maker*. Because a monopoly has no close competitors, it can change the product price by adjusting its output.

additional units are placed on the market—the demand curve is downward sloping. In monopoly, the firm cannot set both its price and the quantity it sells. That is, a monopolist would love to sell a larger quantity at a high price, but it can't. If the monopolist raises the price, the amount sold will fall; if the monopolist lowers the price, the amount sold will rise.

Recall that in perfect competition, many buyers and sellers of homogeneous goods (resulting in a perfectly elastic demand curve) mean that competitive firms can sell all they want at the market price. They face a horizontal demand curve. The firm takes the price of its output as determined by the market forces of supply and demand. Monopolists, and all other firms that are price makers, face a downward-sloping demand curve. If the monopolist raises its price, it will lose some—but not all—of its customers. The two demand curves are displayed side by side in Exhibit 1.

In Exhibit 2, we see the price of the good, the quantity of the good, the *total revenue*, which is the quantity sold times the price ($TR = P \times Q$), and the *average revenue*, that is, the amount of revenue the firm receives per unit sold ($AR = TR \div Q$). The average revenue is simply the price per unit sold, which is exactly equal to the market demand curve, and the *marginal revenue* (MR)—the amount of revenue the firm receives from selling an additional unit—is equal to $\Delta TR \div \Delta Q$.

Taking the information from Exhibit 2, we can create the demand and marginal revenue curves as seen in Exhibit 3. We see that the marginal revenue is always less than the price of the good. To understand why, suppose the firm cuts its price from $4 to $3.

To induce a third daily customer to purchase the good, the firm must cut its price to $3. In doing so, it gains $3 in revenue from the newest customer—the output effect. However, it loses $2 in revenue because each of the first

section 13.2 exhibit 2 — Total, Marginal, and Average Revenue

Price	Quantity	Total Revenue ($TR = P \times Q$)	Average Revenue ($AR = TR/Q$)	Marginal Revenue ($MR = \Delta TR/\Delta Q$)
$6	0	—	—	—
5	1	$5	$5	$3
4	2	8	4	1
3	3	9	3	−1
2	4	8	2	−3
1	5	5	1	

section 13.2 exhibit 3: Demand and Marginal Revenue for the Monopolist

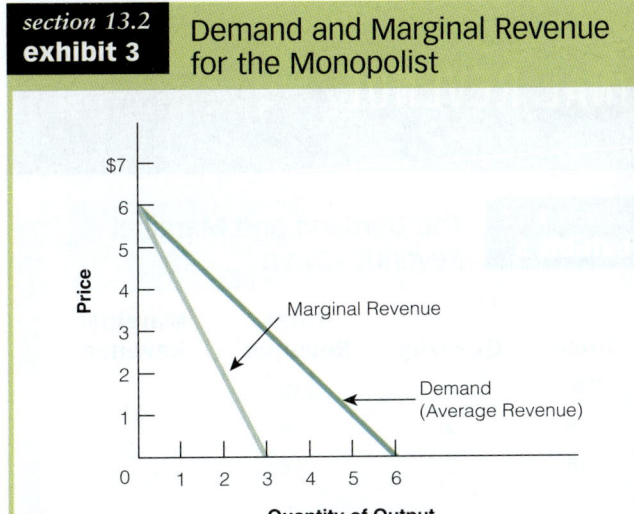

To sell more output, the monopolist must accept a lower price on all units sold—the price effect; the monopolist receives additional revenue from the new unit sold—the output effect, but less revenue on all the units it was previously selling. Thus, the marginal revenue curve for the monopolist always lies below the demand curve.

two customers are now paying $1 less than previously—the price effect. The marginal revenue is $1 ($3 − $2), which is less than the price of the good ($3).

Exhibit 3 graphs the relationship between the demand curve and the marginal revenue curve for a monopolist. Because *a monopolist's marginal revenue is always less than the price*, the marginal revenue curve will always lie below the demand curve, as shown in Exhibit 3. Recall that in perfect competition, the firm could sell all it wanted at the market price, and the price was equal to marginal revenue. However, in monopoly, if the seller wants to expand output, it will have to lower the price on *all* units; the monopolist receives additional revenue from the new unit sold—the output effect, but will receive less revenue on all the units it was previously selling—the price effect. Thus, when the monopolist cuts the price to attract new customers, the old customers benefit.

In Exhibit 4, we can compare marginal revenue for the competitive firm with marginal revenue for the monopolist. The firm in perfect competition can sell another unit of output without lowering its price; hence, the marginal revenue from selling its last unit of output is the market price. However, the monopolist

section 13.2 exhibit 4: Marginal Revenue—Competitive Firm Versus Monopolist

a. Perfect Competitive Firm's Demand Curve

b. Monopolist's Demand Curve

Area b in (a) represents the marginal revenue from an extra unit of output ($q + 1$) for the firm in perfect competition. The competitive firm's marginal revenue (area b) is equal to the market price, P_1 ($P_1 \times 1$). In (b), we see that the monopolist's marginal revenue from an extra unit ($Q + 1$) is less than the price by area b minus area c, because the monopolist must lower its price to sell another unit of output. That is, area b is the gain in revenue from the output effect and area c is the loss in revenue from the price effect. Notice there is no price effect for the perfectly competitve firm.

Use what you've LEARNED
DEMAND AND MARGINAL REVENUE

Q Using the concepts of total revenue and marginal revenue, show why marginal revenue is less than price in a monopoly situation. Suppose a monopolist wants to expand output from one unit to two units. To sell two units rather than one, the monopolist must lower its price from $10 to $8, as shown in Exhibit 5. Will the marginal revenue be less than the price?

A In Exhibit 5, we see that to sell two units, the monopolist will have to lower the price on both units to $8. That is, the seller doesn't receive $10 for unit one and $8 for unit two but receives $8 for both units. Therefore, what happens to marginal revenue? This answer involves two parts: First, a loss in revenue, $2, occurs from selling the first unit at $8 instead of $10. Second, the gain in revenue from the additional output—the second unit—is $8. Thus, the marginal revenue is $6 ($8 − $2), which is less than the price of the good, $8. The monopolist's marginal revenue will always be less than the price of the downward-sloping demand curve.

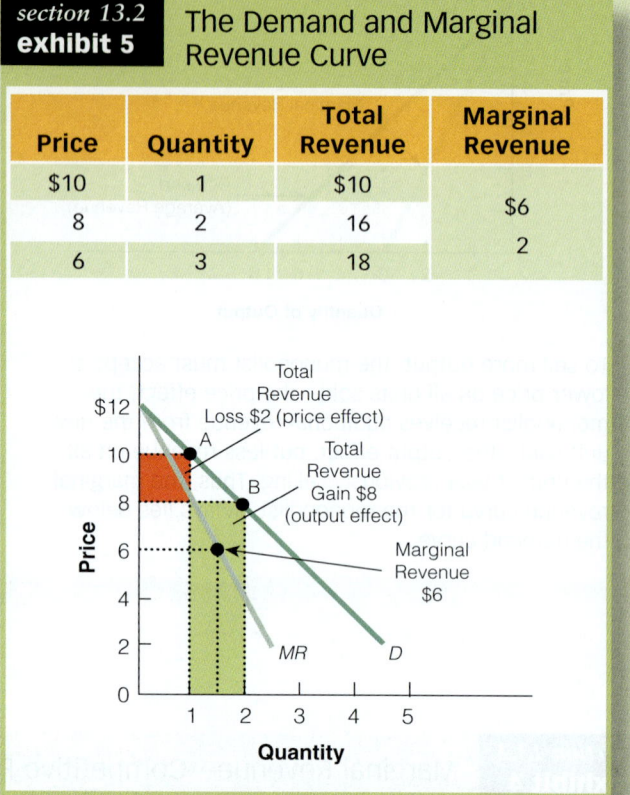

section 13.2 exhibit 5 The Demand and Marginal Revenue Curve

Price	Quantity	Total Revenue	Marginal Revenue
$10	1	$10	
8	2	16	$6
6	3	18	2

has a downward-sloping demand curve. To sell an extra unit of output, the price falls from P_1 to P_2, and the monopolist loses area c in Exhibit 4(b).

It is important to note that even though a monopolist can set its price anywhere it wants, it will not set its price as high as possible—be careful not to confuse ability with incentive. As we will see in the next section, some prices along the demand curve will not be profitable for a firm. In other words, the monopolist can enhance profits by either lowering the price or raising it, depending on the circumstances.

The Monopolist's Price in the Elastic Portion of the Demand Curve

The relationships between the elasticity of demand and the marginal and total revenue are shown in Exhibit 6. In Exhibit 6(a), elasticity varies along a linear demand curve. Recall from Chapter 6 that above the midpoint, the demand curve is elastic ($E_D > 1$); below the midpoint, it is inelastic ($E_D < 1$); and at the midpoint, it is unit elastic ($E_D = 1$). How does elasticity relate to total and marginal revenue? In the elastic portion of the curve shown in Exhibit 6(b), when the price falls, total revenue rises and marginal revenue is positive. In the inelastic region of the demand curve, when the price falls, total revenue falls, and marginal revenue is negative. At the midpoint of the linear demand curve in Exhibit 6(b), the total revenue curve reaches its highest point and $MR = 0$.

For example, suppose the price falls on the top half of the demand curve in Exhibit 6(a) from $90 to $80; total revenue increases from $90 ($90 × 1) to $160 ($80 × 2), and marginal revenue is positive at $70. Because a reduction in price leads to an increase in total revenue, the demand curve is elastic in this region. Now suppose the price falls from $20 to $10 on the lower portion of the demand curve; total revenue falls from $160 ($20 × 8) to $90 ($10 × 9), and marginal

section 13.2 exhibit 6 — The Relationship Between the Elasticity of Demand and Total and Marginal Revenue

a. Demand and Marginal Revenue

b. Total Revenue

In (a), we see that along a linear demand curve, the elastic segment lies above the midpoint, the inelastic segment lies below the midpoint, and at the midpoint the demand is unit elastic. When demand is elastic, a decline in price will increase total revenue; when demand is inelastic, a decline in price will lead to a decrease in total revenue. In (b), we see that over the range from 0 to 5 units, total revenue is rising, so marginal revenue is positive. Over the range from 5 units to 10 units, total revenue is falling, so marginal revenue is negative. At 5 units of output, total revenue is maximized at $250 ($50 × 5), so marginal revenue is zero.

revenue is negative at −$70. Because a reduction in price leads to a decrease in total revenue, the demand curve is inelastic in this region.

A monopolist will never knowingly operate on the inelastic portion of its demand curve, because increased output will lead to lower total revenue in this region. Not only are total revenues falling, but total costs will rise as the monopolist produces more output. Similarly, if the monopolist were to lower its output, it could increase its total revenue and lower its total costs (because it costs less to produce fewer units), leading to greater economic profits.

SECTION CHECK

1. The monopolist's demand curve is downward sloping because it is the market demand curve. To produce and sell another unit of output, the firm must lower its price on *all* units sold. As a result, the marginal revenue curve lies below the demand curve.
2. The monopolist cannot set both the price and the quantity it sells. If the monopolist reduces output, the price will rise, and if the monopolist expands output, the price will fall.
3. The monopolist's marginal revenue will always be less than the price because of its downward-sloping demand curve. In order to sell more output, the monopolist must accept a lower price on all units sold; the monopolist will receive additional revenue from the new unit sold but will receive less revenue on all of the units it was previously selling.
4. The monopolist will operate on the elastic portion of its demand curve.

1. Why are the market and firm demand curves the same for a monopoly?
2. Why is a monopoly a price maker, but a perfectly competitive firm a price taker?
3. Why is marginal revenue less than price for a profit-maximizing monopolist?
4. Why would a monopolist never knowingly operate in the inelastic portion of its demand curve?

SECTION 13.3 The Monopolist's Equilibrium

* How does the monopolist decide what output to produce?
* How does the monopolist decide what price to charge?
* How do we know whether the monopolist is making a profit?
* How do we know whether the monopolist is incurring a loss?
* Can the monopolist's economic profits last into the long run?

How Does the Monopolist Determine the Profit-Maximizing Output?

In the preceding section, we saw how a monopolist could choose any point along a demand curve. However, the monopolist's decision as to what level of output to produce depends on more than the marginal revenue derived at various outputs. The firm faces production costs; and the monopolist, like the perfect competitor, will maximize profits at that output where $MR = MC$. This point is demonstrated graphically in Exhibit 1.

As you can see in Exhibit 1, at output level Q_1, the marginal revenue exceeds the marginal cost of production, so it is profitable for the monopolist to expand output. Profits continue to grow until output Q_M is reached. Beyond that output, say at Q_2, the marginal cost of production exceeds the marginal revenue from production, so profits decline. The monopolist should cut production back to Q_M. Therefore, the equilibrium output is Q_M. At this output, marginal cost and marginal revenue are equal.

Three-Step Method for the Monopolist

Let's return to the three-step method we used in Chapter 12. Determining whether a firm is generating positive economic profits, economic losses, or zero economic profits at the profit-maximizing level of output, Q_M, can be done in three easy steps.

1. Find where marginal revenue equals marginal cost and proceed straight down to the horizontal (quantity) axis to find Q_M, the profit-maximizing output level for the monopolist.
2. At Q_M, go straight up to the demand curve and then to the left to find the market price, P_M. Once you have identified P_M and Q_M, you can find total revenue at the profit-maximizing output level, because $TR = P \times Q$.
3. The last step is to find total cost. Again, go straight up from Q_M to the average total cost (ATC) curve and then left to the vertical axis to compute the average total cost at Q_M. If we multiply average total cost by the output level, we can find the total cost ($TC = ATC \times Q$).

section 13.3 exhibit 1 — Equilibrium Output and Price for a Monopolist

The monopolist maximizes profits at that quantity where $MR = MC$, that is, at Q_M. At Q_M the monopolist finds P^* by extending a vertical line up to the demand curve and over to the vertical axis to find the price. Rather than charging a price equal to marginal cost or marginal revenue at their intersection, however, the monopolist charges the price that customers are willing to pay for that quantity as indicated on the demand curve at P_M. At Q_1, $MR > MC$, and the firm should expand output. At Q_2, $MC > MR$, and the firm should cut back production.

Profits for a Monopolist

Exhibit 1 does not show what profits, if any, the monopolist is actually making. This missing information is found in Exhibit 2, which shows the

section 13.3 exhibit 2: A Monopolist's Profits

The intersection of MR and MC determines Q_M, the profit-maximizing level of output. The demand curve shows the price that can be charged for Q_M. Total profits equal the area DABC—the difference between total revenues (DAQ_M0) and total costs (CBQ_M0).

section 13.3 exhibit 3: A Monopolist's Losses

Total loss equals CBAD—the difference between total cost (CBQ_M0) and total revenue (DAQ_M0).

equilibrium position for a monopolist, this time adding an average total cost (*ATC*) curve. As we just discussed, the firm produces where $MC = MR$, at output Q_M. At output Q_M (100) and price P_M ($6) the firm's total revenue is equal to DAQ_M0, which is $P_M \times Q_M$ ($600). At output Q_M, the firm's total cost is CBQ_M0, which is $ATC \times Q_M$ ($400). In Exhibit 2, we see that total revenue is greater than total cost, so the firm has a total profit of area DABC. Or, $P_M - ATC$ (price minus average total cost) is the per-unit profit, $2. The width of the box (segment CB) is the quantity sold (0 to Q_M), 100 units. Hence, the area of the box is the monopoly firm's total profit, $200 (per-unit profit × quantity sold).

In perfect competition, profits in an economic sense will persist only in the short run. In the long run, new firms will enter the industry and increase industry supply, thereby driving down the price of the good and eliminating profits. In monopoly, however, profits are not eliminated, because one of the conditions for monopoly is that barriers to entry exist. Other firms cannot enter, so economic profits persist in the long run.

Losses for the Monopolist

It is easy to imagine a monopolist ripping off consumers by charging prices that result in long-run economic profits. However, many companies with monopoly power have gone out of business. Imagine that you received a patent on a bad idea such as a roof ejection seat for a helicopter, or that you had the sole rights to turn an economics textbook into a screenplay for a motion picture. Although you may be the sole supplier of a product, you are not guaranteed that consumers will demand your product. Even without a close substitute for your product, you will always face competition for the consumer dollar, and other goods may provide greater satisfaction.

Exhibit 3 illustrates loss in a monopoly situation. In this graph, notice that the demand curve is below the average total cost curve. In this case, the monopolist will incur a loss, because of insufficient demand to cover the average total cost at any price and output combination along the demand curve. At Q_M, total cost, CBQ_M0, is greater than total revenue, DAQ_M0, so the firm incurs a total loss of CBAD. Or, total revenue is $600 ($P_M \times Q_M = \$6 \times 100$) and total cost is $700 ($ATC \times Q_M = \$7 \times 100$), for an economic loss of $100. Notice that the total revenue is great enough to cover the variable costs of $400 ($TVC = \$4 \times 100$). That is, the firm can reduce its losses by operating rather than shutting down in the short run. However, in monopoly as in perfect competition, a firm will go out of business in the long run if it cannot generate enough revenue to cover its total costs.

In summary, if total revenue is greater than total cost at Q_M, the firm generates a total economic profit;

and if total revenue is less than total cost at Q_M, the firm generates a total economic loss. If total revenue is equal to total cost at Q_M, the firm earns zero economic profit. Remember, the cost curves include implicit and explicit costs, so in this case, the monopolist is covering the total opportunity costs of its resources and earning a normal profit or rate of return.

Patents

Governments confer one form of monopoly power through patents and copyrights. A patent puts the government's police power behind the patent-holder's exclusive right to make a product for a specified period (up to 20 years) without anyone else being able to make an identical product. As Exhibit 4 suggests, the patent gives the supplier at least temporary monopoly power over that good or service. The firm with the patent can then price its product well above marginal costs, at P_M. Notice that the marginal cost curve is flat. The reason is that most of the cost of drugs is in the development stage. Once the drug is available for the market, the marginal costs are close to constant—flat. When the patent expires, the price of the patented good or service usually falls substantially with the entry of competing firms into the market. The price will fall toward the perfectly competitive price P_{PC}, and the output will increase toward Q_{PC}.

Why does the government give inventors this limited monopoly power, raising the prices of pharmaceutical drugs and other "vital" goods? The rationale is simple. Without patents, inventors would have little incentive to incur millions of dollars in research and development expenses to create new products (e.g., lifesaving drugs), because others could immediately copy the idea and manufacture the products without incurring the research expenses. Similarly, copyrights stimulate creative activity of other kinds, giving writers the incentive to write books that earn royalties and are not merely copied for free. The enormous number of computer programs written for home computers reflects the fact that program writers receive royalties from the sale of each copy sold; that is why they and the firms they work for vehemently oppose unauthorized copying of their work.

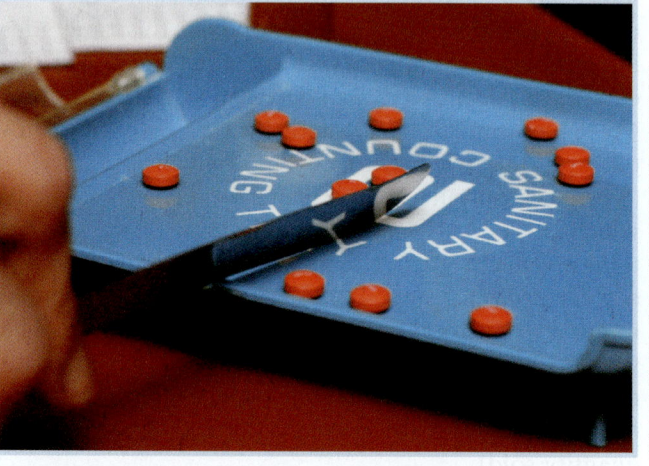

Without patents, would some lifesaving drugs have been invented? Some drugs cost millions of dollars in research. Without the protection of a patent, the firm might not have been able to make profits from its inventive activity for very long, which is why the government issues patents that last up to 20 years. However, after the patent expires, many popular drugs soon lose their protection; Prozac lost its patent in February 2001 and Claritin lost its patent in April 2004. In most cases, less costly generic drugs hit the market soon after patent expiration; and prices then move closer to the competitive price, although perhaps not all the way to the competitive level, as some companies are able to keep customers through brand loyalty.

section 13.3 exhibit 4: Impact of Patent Protection on Equilibrium Price and Quantity

Patent power allows the firm to charge the higher monopoly price, P_M, which is well above the marginal cost of producing that good. However, when the patent expires, the price falls to a position closer to the perfectly competitive price, P_{PC}.

SECTION CHECK

1. The monopolist, like the perfect competitor, maximizes profits at that output where marginal revenue equals marginal cost.
2. The monopolist sets the price according to the demand for the product at the profit-maximizing output.
3. Monopoly profits can be found by comparing the price per unit and average total cost per unit at Q^*. If $P > ATC$, a firm realizes economic profits. If $P < ATC$, it has economic losses.
4. Monopolists' profits can last into the long run, because of a monopoly's barriers to entry.

---

1. What is a monopolist's principle for choosing the profit-maximizing output?
2. How do you find the profit-maximizing price for a monopolist?
3. For a monopolist making positive economic profits, what must be true about the relationship between price and average total cost?
4. For a monopolist making negative economic profits, what must be true about the relationship between price and average total cost?
5. Why, unlike perfectly competitive firms, can a monopolist continue to earn positive economic profits in the long run?

SECTION 13.4 Monopoly and Welfare Loss

* How does monopoly lead to inefficiencies?
* What is the welfare loss in monopoly?
* Does monopoly retard innovation?

Does Monopoly Promote Inefficiency?

onopoly is often considered to be bad. Two main objections form the basis for concerns about the establishment of monopoly power. First, on equity grounds, many people feel that it is not "fair" for monopoly owners to have persistent economic profits when they work no harder than other firms. However, to most economists, the more serious objection is that monopolies result in market inefficiencies. That is, monopoly leads to a lower output and higher prices than would exist under perfect competition. Exhibit 1 demonstrates why. In monopoly, the firm produces output Q_M and charges price P_M. Suppose, however, that perfect competition exists and the industry is characterized by many small firms that could produce output with the same efficiency (at the same cost) as one large firm. Then the marginal cost curve shown in Exhibit 1 is the sum of all the individual marginal cost curves of the individual firms, which is the industry supply curve.

In the perfectly competitive market, the equilibrium price and quantity would be determined where the marginal cost (or supply) curve intersects with the demand curve, at output Q_{PC} and price P_{PC}. Thus, the competitive equilibrium solution provides for more output and lower prices than the solution prevailing in monopoly, which leads to the major efficiency objection to monopoly: Monopolists charge higher prices and produce less output. This situation may also be viewed as "unfair," in that consumers are burdened more than under the alternative competitive arrangement.

Welfare Loss in Monopoly

In addition to the monopolist producing lower levels of output at higher prices, notice that the monopolist produces at an output where the price (P_M) is greater than the marginal cost (MC_M). Because $P > MC$, the value to society from the last unit produced is greater than its costs (MC_M). That is, the monopoly is *not* producing enough of the good from society's perspective. We call the area c + e in Exhibit 1 the welfare or deadweight loss due to monopoly. In perfect competition, the equilibrium is P_{PC} and the equilibrium quantity is Q_{PC}. Consumer surplus is area a + b + c, and the product surplus is area d + e + f. In monopoly, the equilibrium

section 13.4 exhibit 1 Perfect Competition Versus Monopoly

Compared with perfect competition, the monopolist's equilibrium price is higher, P_M, and its equilibrium output is lower, Q_M. Also notice that P_M is greater than MC_M, which means that the value of the last unit produced by the monopolist (P_M) is greater than the cost (MC_M), so from society's point of view the monopolist is producing too little output. Under monopoly, consumer surplus is area a, producer surplus is area b + d + f, and the deadweight loss of monopoly is c + e.

	Perfect Competition	Monopoly	Change
Consumer Surplus	a + b + c	a	− b − c
Producer Surplus	d + e + f	b + d + f	b − e
Welfare	a + b + c + d + e + f	a + b + d + f	− c − e

Use what you've LEARNED
THE WELFARE COST OF MONOPOLY

Q The output level set by the monopolist is inefficient from society's standpoint, but the profits are not. Why?

A The net loss resulting from lower output is what economists call the welfare cost of monopoly. However, society as a whole does not lose from monopoly profits. Why? Because the income is not lost, but it is transferred from consumers to producers (stockholders and workers). The monopolist gains at the expense of consumers who pay a higher price for a monopolist's product than they would if the product were produced by a perfectly competitive firm. This situation is depicted in Exhibit 2.

The welfare loss is graphically represented by area cde. It is the difference between how much consumers value quantity Q_1 minus Q_0, which is $Q_0 ce Q_1$, and how much they would have to give up for it, $Q_0 de Q_1$. You may recall from Chapter 7 that this area represents *consumer surplus*. Under perfectly competitive conditions, however, area abdc would also be part of the consumer's surplus. In sum, the loss to society from monopoly is area cde, and area abdc is merely a transfer of consumer surplus to monopoly profits.

section 13.4 exhibit 2 The Welfare Cost of Monopoly

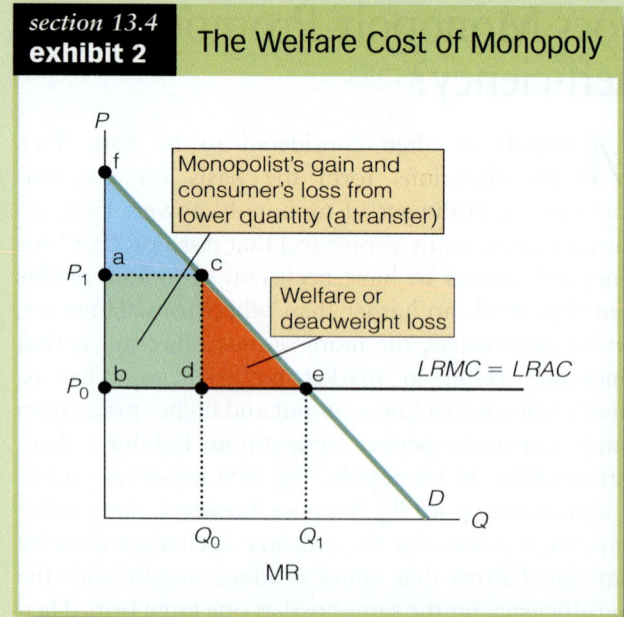

price is higher at P_M and the equilibrium quantity is lower at Q_M. Under monopoly, consumer surplus is area a, producer surplus is area b + d + f, and lost welfare or the deadweight loss of monopoly is c + e.

The actual amount of the welfare loss in monopoly is of considerable debate among economists. Estimates vary from between one-tenth of 1 percent to 6 percent of national income. The variation depends on the researchers' estimates of elasticity of demand, whether firm or industry data were used, whether adjustments for profits were made (for the inclusion of royalties and intangibles), and whether the researcher included some proxy for scarce resources used in attempting to create the monopoly.

Does Monopoly Retard Innovation?

Another argument against monopoly is that a lack of competition tends to retard technological advancement. Monopolists become comfortable, reaping their monopolistic profits, so they do not work hard at product improvement, technical advances designed to promote efficiency, and so forth. The American railroad is sometimes cited as an example of this situation. Early in the last century, railroads had strong monopoly power, but they did not spend much on research or development; they did not aggressively try to improve rail transport. Consequently, technical advances in substitute modes of transportation—like cars, trucks, and airplanes—led to a loss of monopoly power for the railroads.

However, the notion that monopoly retards all innovation can be disputed. Many near monopolists are, in fact, important innovators. Companies such as Microsoft, International Business Machines (IBM), Polaroid, and Xerox have all, at one time or another, had strong market positions, in some instances approaching monopoly secured by patent protection, but they were also important innovators. Indeed, innovation helps firms initially obtain a degree of monopoly status, because patents can give a monopoly to new products and/or cost-saving technology. Even the monopolist wants more profits, and any innovation that lowers costs or expands revenues creates profits for the monopolist. In addition, because patents expire, a monopolist may be expected to innovate in order to obtain additional patents and preserve its monopoly power. Therefore, the incentive to innovate might well exist in monopolistic market structures.

SECTION CHECK

1. Monopoly results in smaller output and a higher price than would be the case under perfect competition.
2. The monopolist produces at an output where P > MC and the value to society of the last unit produced is greater than its cost. In other words, the monopoly is not producing enough output from society's standpoint.
3. Monopoly may lead to greater concentration of economic power and could retard innovation.

---

1. Why does the reduced output under monopoly cause inefficiency?
2. Does monopoly power retard innovation? Why or why not?
3. What does the welfare cost of monopoly represent? How is it measured?
4. How can economies of scale lead to monopoly? How could it result in monopoly increasing rather than decreasing market output, relative to the competitive market structure?
5. Can monopoly be the result of a new innovation that leaves consumers better off than before? Why or why not?

SECTION 13.5 Monopoly Policy

* What is the objective of antitrust policy?
* What is regulation?
* What is average cost pricing?

Because monopolies pose certain problems with respect to efficiency, equity, and power, the public, through its governments, must decide how to deal with the phenomenon. Two major approaches to dealing with such problems are commonly employed: antitrust policies and regulation. It should be pointed

Policy application: COLLUSION

Ivy League schools have been charged with illegally colluding to fix the price of scholarships. Ivy League schools wanted to make sure they did not get into a "scholarship war," so the participating schools collectively met and fixed scholarship packages. Students would then pick their schools on the basis of academic quality, not the size of the scholarship package. These activities guaranteed that any student applying to more than one of these schools would be offered the same financial package. The Justice Department charged the eight Ivy League schools and MIT with an illegal conspiracy to set prices and required these schools to stop their collusion on tuition, salaries, and financial aid by signing a consent order.

out that in these discussions, the word *monopoly* is sometimes used in a loose, general sense to refer to imperfectly competitive markets, not just to "pure" monopoly.

Antitrust Policies

Perhaps the most obvious way to deal with monopoly is to make it illegal. The government can bring civil lawsuits or even criminal actions against businesspeople or corporations engaged in monopolistic practices. By imposing costs on monopolists that can be either monetary or nonmonetary (such as the fear of lawsuits or even jail sentences), antitrust policies reduce the profitability of monopoly.

Antitrust Laws

The first important law regulating monopoly was the Sherman Antitrust Act. The Sherman Act prohibited "restraint of trade"—price fixing and collusion—but narrow court interpretation of the legislation led to a number of large mergers, such as U.S. Steel. Some important near-monopolies were broken up, however. For example, in 1911, the Standard Oil Trust, which controlled most of the country's oil refining, and the American Tobacco Co., which had similar dominance in tobacco, were both forcibly divided up into smaller companies.

Antitrust Acts Strengthened

Antitrust efforts were strengthened by subsequent legislation, the most important of which was the Clayton Act in 1914. Additional legislation in the same year created the Federal Trade Commission (FTC), which became the second government agency concerned with antitrust actions. The Clayton Act made it illegal to engage in predatory pricing—setting prices to drive out competitors or deter potential entrants in order to ensure higher prices in the future. The Clayton Act also prohibited mergers if it led to weakened competition. Not all of the later legislation actually served to enhance competition. A case in point is the Robinson-Patman Act of 1936 (forbidding most forms of price discrimination) and the Cellar-Kefauver Act in 1950, legislation that toughened restrictions on mergers that reduced competition.

However, antitrust laws may have costs as well as benefits because mergers may lead to lower costs and greater efficiency. A number of banks recently merged, lowering costs. So, good antitrust policy must be able to recognize which mergers are desirable and which are not.

Promoting More Price Competition

Many professional associations restrict the promotion of price competition by prohibiting advertising among their members. Recently, both the FTC and the Justice Department successfully attacked these types of restrictions on the grounds that they violate the antitrust laws. They have been spurred on in their efforts by consumer groups who noticed that prices tend to be much lower

in the news: Is Microsoft a Monopoly?

Government prosecutors argued that Microsoft engaged in a pattern of using its monopoly power to crush its rivals and prevent real competition from developing. In June 2001, a federal appeals court unanimously threw out a lower court order to break Microsoft into two companies. However, the appeals court did find that the company repeatedly abused its monopoly power in the software business.

According to competitor Larry Ellison, "They repeatedly broke the law. They said to Compaq: If you want to get a good price for Windows, you better not put Netscape on that computer. That is using an existing monopoly, Windows, to obtain a new monopoly in browsers. That's an explicit violation of the Sherman Antitrust Act. They did it over and over again."

A settlement was finally reached in November 2002 that led to some restrictions on Microsoft's business practices.

SOURCE: Staff, "Is Microsoft a Monopoly," *Business Week*, 26 February 2001.

consider this:
It appears that the Microsoft case has less to do with the degree of monopoly power and more to do with the abuse of that power. Specifically, antitrust is about actions taken to form, extend, or maintain the monopoly. However, we have to ask the question: Are consumers necessarily worse off as a result of a few powerful computer companies that temporarily dominate the industry? Because of potential economies of scale in production and technology, the monopoly may be short lived. Are the barriers to entry in the computer industry insurmountable? The history of the computer industry includes several success stories of individuals with great ideas who have successfully broken into the industry. In addition, Microsoft and Intel are at least partially responsible for making computer power what it is today—providing consumers with low-priced, innovative products. By bundling its internet browser (Internet Explorer) into its Windows operating system the government claimed that Microsoft was expanding its market power in the computer industry. This apparently allowed Windows to win the browser wars knocking out Netscape Navigator and in the office suite market knocking out Word Perfect. The government believed there would have been more competition if Microsoft had not bundled their package and given their browser away for "free." Every Windows user had a copy of Internet Explorer.

When the dust settled Microsoft had to agree to some business restrictions but was allowed to keep their browser as part of their operating system.

In 2005, European Union cracked down on Microsoft because they bundled their media player with its Windows operation system. They were fined and required to offer both bundled and unbundled versions of their operating system.

---

when price competition is allowed to flourish. Thus, optometrists were prodded to advertise the price of eyeglasses; pharmacists, the price of commonly prescribed drugs; and even lawyers, the price of a divorce.

Have Antitrust Policies Been Successful?

The success of antitrust policies can be debated. It is true that few giant monopolies were disbanded as a consequence of antitrust policies. Studies showed little change in the degree of monopoly/oligopoly power in the first 100 years or so of U.S. antitrust legislation. Manufacturing, as a whole, actually became more concentrated; that is, fewer firms are now in the industry. However, it is likely that at least some anticompetitive practices were prevented simply by the existence of laws prohibiting monopoly-like practices. Although the laws were probably enforced in an imperfect fashion, on balance they impeded monopoly influences to some degree, at least.

Government Regulation

Government regulation is an alternative approach to dealing with monopolies. Under regulation, a company would not be allowed to charge any price it wants. Suppose the government does not want to break up a natural monopoly in the water or power industry. Remember that natural monopolies occur when one large firm can produce as much output as many smaller firms but at a lower average cost per unit. The government may decide to regulate the monopoly price; but what price does it let the firm charge? The goal is to achieve the efficiency of large-scale production without permitting the high monopoly prices and low output that can promote allocative *inefficiency*.

The basic policy dilemma that regulators often face in attempting to fix maximum prices can be illustrated rather easily. Consider Exhibit 1. Without regulation, say the profit-maximizing monopolist operates at point A—at output Q_M and price P_M. At this output, the price exceeds the average total cost, so economic profits exist, as seen in Exhibit 1. However, the monopolist is producing relatively little output and is charging a relatively high price; and it is producing at a point where price is above marginal cost. This point is not the best from society's perspective.

Allocative Efficiency

From society's point of view, what would be the best price and output position? As we discussed in Chapter 12, the best position is at the competitive equilibrium output, where $P = MC$, because the equilibrium price represents the marginal value of output. The marginal cost represents society's opportunity costs of making the good as opposed to something else. Where price equals marginal cost, society matches marginal value and marginal cost—that is, it achieves allocative efficiency, as seen at point C in Exhibit 1.

Can the Regulated Monopolist Operate at $P = MC$?

Unfortunately, the natural monopoly cannot operate profitably at the allocative efficient point, where $P = MC$, indicated as point C in Exhibit 1. At point C, the intersection of the demand and marginal cost curves, average total cost is greater than price. The optimal output, then, is an output that results in losses for the producer. Any regulated business that produced for long at this "optimal" output would go bankrupt; it would be impossible to attract new capital to the industry.

Therefore, the "optimal" output from a welfare perspective is not really viable, because firms incur losses. The regulators cannot force firms to price their products at P_{MC} and to sell Q_{MC} output, because they would go out of business. Indeed, in the long run, the industry's capital would deteriorate as investors failed to replace old capital as it became worn out or

section 13.5 exhibit 1 Marginal Cost Pricing Versus Average Cost Pricing

The marginal cost (MC) curve is less than the average total cost (ATC) curve for the natural monopolist as the average cost falls. If the monopolist is unregulated, it could produce a relatively small level of output, Q_M, at a relatively high price, P_M, and make an economic profit. If regulators require the natural monopolist to use marginal cost pricing, the monopoly will lose money, because P_{MC} is less than ATC. Average cost pricing (at point B) would permit firms to make a normal rate of return, where $P_{AC} = ATC$. The monopolist's unregulated output at point A is not optimal from society's standpoint, and the optimal output at point C is not feasible.

obsolete. If the monopolist's unregulated output at point A is not optimal from society's standpoint, and the short-run optimal output at point C is not feasible from the monopolist's standpoint, where should the regulated monopolist be allowed to operate?

One possible solution to the problem is for the government to subsidize the losses associated with marginal cost pricing. However, the burden of this solution would ultimately fall on the taxpayers, as the government would have to raise the money to pay for the losses.

The Compromise: Average Cost Pricing

A compromise between monopoly pricing and marginal cost pricing is found at point B in Exhibit 1, at output Q_{AC}, which is somewhere between the excessively low output and high prices of an unregulated monopoly and the excessively high output and low prices achieved when prices are equated with marginal cost pricing. At point B, price equals average total cost. The monopolist is permitted to price the product where economic profit is zero, earning a normal economic profit or rate of return, such as firms experience in perfect competition in the long run. This compromise is called **average cost pricing.**

In the real world, regulators often permit utilities to receive a "fair and reasonable" return that is a rough approximation to that suggested by average cost pricing, at point B. Point B would seem "fair" in that the monopolist is receiving rewards equal to those that a perfect competitor would ordinarily receive—no more, no less. Point B permits more output at a significantly lower price than is possible at point A, where the monopolist is unregulated, even though output is still somewhat less and price somewhat more than that suggested by point C, the socially optimum or best position.

average cost pricing
setting price equal to average total cost

Difficulties in Average Cost Pricing

Inaccurate Calculations of Costs

The actual implementation of a rate (price) that permits a "fair and reasonable" return is more difficult than the analysis suggests. The calculations of costs and values are difficult. In reality, the firm may not know exactly what its demand and cost curves look like, which forces regulatory agencies to use profits, another somewhat ambiguous target, as a guide. If profits are "too high," lower the price; if profits are "too low," raise the price. In addition, what if the regulated firm has more information than the regulators about its firm, workers and technology—asymmetric information? If the firm can persuade regulators that its average cost is higher than it actually is; the regulated price could be set higher, closer to the monopoly price.

No Incentives to Keep Costs Down

Another problem is that average cost pricing offers the monopolist no incentive to reduce costs. That is, if the firm's costs rise from ATC_1 to ATC_2 in Exhibit 2, the price will rise from P_1 to P_2. If costs fall, the firm's price will fall. In either scenario, the firm will still be earning a normal rate of return. In other words, if the regulatory agency sets the price at any point where the ATC curve intersects the demand curve, the firm will earn a normal rate of return. Thus, if the agency is going to set the price wherever ATC intersects the demand curve, the firm might just think, Why not let average costs rise? Why not let employees fly first class and dine in the finest restaurants? Why not buy concert tickets and season tickets to sporting events? And if the regulated monopolist knows that the regulators will reduce prices if costs fall, the regulated monopolist does not benefit from lower costs. Regulators have tackled this problem by allowing the regulated firm to keep some of the profits that come from lower costs; that is, they do not adhere strictly to average cost pricing.

Special Interest Groups

In the real world, consumer groups are constantly battling for lower utility rates, while the utilities themselves are lobbying for higher rates so they can approach the monopoly profits indicated by point A in Exhibit 1. Decisions are not always made in a calm, objective, dispassionate atmosphere free from outside involvement. It is precisely the political economy of rate setting that disturbs some critics of this approach to dealing with the monopoly problem. For example, a rate-making commissioner could become friendly with a utility company, believing that he could obtain a nice job after his tenure as a regulator expires. The temptation would be great for the commissioner to be generous to the utilities. On the other hand, the tendency might be for regulators to bow to pressure from consumer groups. A politician who wants to win votes can almost always succeed by attacking utility rates and promising rate "reform" (lower rates). If zealous rate regulators listen too closely to consumer groups and push rates down to a level indicated by point C

section 13.5 exhibit 2 Changes in Average Costs

An increase in average total cost leads to a higher price and lower output (P_2Q_2); lower average total cost leads to a lower price and greater output (P_1Q_1). However, both situations lead to a normal rate of return. Because the regulated firm has little incentive to minimize costs, average total cost would have a tendency to rise.

in Exhibit 1, the industry might be too unstable to attract capital for expansion.

In recent years, we have seen a trend away from regulation toward competition; for example, after AT&T was broken up by the courts in 1982, the long-distance market became very competitive, and local telephone service is much more competitive now than in the past. Technological advances now allow us to separate the production of electronic power or natural gas from the distributor, which will ultimately lead to greater competition in these markets. Some states have already started deregulation in the electricity market.

SECTION CHECK

1. Antitrust policies are government policies designed to reduce the profitability of a monopoly and push production closer to the social optimum.
2. Privately owned monopolies may be allowed to operate if under regulation by a government agency.
3. Average cost pricing sets price equal to average total cost, where the demand curve intersects average total costs.

---

1. What alternative ways of dealing with the monopoly problem are commonly used?
2. How do antitrust laws promote greater price competition?
3. What price and output are ideal for allocative efficiency for a regulated natural monopolist? Why is an unregulated natural monopolist unlikely to pick this solution?
4. What is average cost pricing? How is it different from marginal cost pricing?
5. What are some difficulties encountered when regulators try to implement average cost pricing for natural monopolies?
6. Why might a job with a regulated natural monopolist that is allowed to earn a "fair and reasonable" return have more perks (noncash forms of compensation) than a comparable job in a nonregulated firm?

SECTION 13.6 Price Discrimination and Peak Load Pricing

* What is price discrimination?
* Why does price discrimination exist?
* Does price discrimination work when reselling is easy?
* What is peak load pricing?

Price Discrimination

Sometimes sellers will charge different customers different prices for the same good or service when the cost of providing that good or service does not differ among customers. This practice is called **price discrimination**. Under certain conditions, the monopolist finds it profitable to discriminate among various buyers, charging higher prices to those who are more willing to pay and lower prices to those who are less willing to pay.

price discrimination
the practice of charging different consumers different prices for the same good or service

Conditions for Price Discrimination

The ability to practice price discrimination is not available to all sellers. To practice price discrimination, the following three conditions must hold:

Monopoly Power

Price discrimination is possible only with monopoly or where members of a small group of firms (firms that are not price takers) follow identical pricing policies. In cases with a large number of competing firms, discrimination is less likely because competitors tend to undercut the high prices charged by the firms that are engaging in price discrimination.

Market Segregation

Price discrimination can only occur if the demand curves for markets, groups, or individuals are different. If the demand curves are not different, a profit-maximizing monopolist would charge the same price in both markets. In short, price discrimination requires the ability to separate customers according to their willingness to pay.

No Resale

For price discrimination to work, the person buying the product at a discount must have difficulty in reselling the product to customers being charged more. Otherwise, those getting the items cheaply would want to buy extra amounts of the product at the discounted price and sell it at a profit to others. Price differentials between groups erode if reselling is easy.

Why Does Price Discrimination Exist?

Price discrimination results from the profit-maximization motive. Our graphical analysis of monopoly described the demand curve for the product and the corresponding marginal revenue curve. Sometimes, however, different groups of people have different demand curves and therefore react differently to price changes. A producer can make more money by charging these different buyers different prices. For example, if the price of a movie is increased from $7 to $10, many kids who would attend at $7 may have to stay home at $10, as they (and perhaps their parents) balk at paying the higher price. The impact of raising prices on attendance may be less, however, for adults, who have higher incomes in the first place and for whom the ticket price may represent a smaller part of the expenses of an evening out.

Thus, a different demand curve applies for those, say, under 2, as opposed to those who are older. Specifically, the elasticity of demand with respect to price is greater for children than for adults, meaning that the demand and marginal revenue curves for children is different from the curves for adults. Assume, for simplicity, that the marginal cost is constant. The

Disneyland practices price discrimination. During the off-season, locals are charged less than out-of-town visitors. If nonlocals have a greater willingness to pay (a less elastic demand curve) for the park hopper ticket (which is good for both Disneyland and its next door neighbor, California Adventure) than locals do, Disneyland can increase its profits with this pricing strategy as long as it can prevent reselling.

profit-maximizing movie theater owner will price where the constant marginal costs equal marginal revenue for each group. As you can see in Exhibit 1(a), the demand curve for children is relatively elastic—firms will charge these customers a lower price. The adult demand curve, shown in Exhibit 1(b), is less elastic; firms will charge adult customers a higher price. But in order for price discrimination to be feasible, the seller must be able to successfully distinguish members of targeted groups.

Examples of Price Discrimination

Other examples of price discrimination in the United States are plentiful. Here are just a few.

section 13.6 exhibit 1 — Price Discrimination in Movie Ticket Prices

If the movie theaters in the area have some monopoly power and if children have a lower willingness to pay than adults, then movie theaters can increase profits by price discriminating. Because the demand curve for children is relatively more elastic than the demand curve for adults, the firm finds it profitable to charge the two different groups a different price. To maximize profit, the firm charges the group with the less elastic demand curve (adults) a higher price and the group with the more elastic demand curve (children) a lower price.

Airline Tickets

Seats on airplanes usually go for different prices. They sell high-priced, no-strings-attached fares, and they sell restricted fares—tickets that require Saturday night layovers or must be purchased weeks in advance. This airline pricing strategy allows the airlines to discriminate against business travelers, who usually have little advance warning, travel on the weekdays, and are not as willing to spend their weekends away from home and family. Because business travelers have a high willingness to pay (a relatively inelastic demand curve), the airlines can charge them higher prices. If the airlines were to cut prices for these clients, their revenues would fall. On the other hand, the personal traveler (perhaps a vacationer) can choose among many substitutes, such as other modes of transportation and different times. In short, the personal traveler has a lower willingness to pay (a relatively elastic demand curve). Thus, the airlines can clearly make more money by charging a higher price to those who have a higher willingness to pay (less elastic demand) and a lower price to those who have a lower willingness to pay (more elastic demand)—those who are willing to book in advance and stay over on Saturday nights. If the airlines charged a higher single price to everyone, those with a lower willingness to pay would not travel; if they charged a lower single price to everyone, they would lose profits by receiving less revenue from those who were willing to pay more.

Coupons

The key to price discrimination is observing the difference in demand curves for different customers. The coupon cutter, who spends an hour looking through the Sunday paper for coupons, will probably have a relatively more elastic demand curve than, say, a busy and wealthy physician or executive. Consequently, firms charge a lower price to customers with a lower willingness to pay (more elastic demand)—the coupon cutter—and a higher price to those who don't use coupons (less elastic demand).

College and University Tuition

Another example of price discrimination is the financial aid packages given by many colleges and universities. That is, even though colleges do not charge different tuitions to different students, they do offer different financial aid packages. Furthermore, to receive financial aid, parents must disclose their family income and wealth. In short, students who are well off financially tend to pay more for their education than do students who are less well off.

Quantity Discounts

Another form of price discrimination occurs when customers buy in large quantities, as with public utilities and wholesalers. But even stores will sell a six-pack

Use what you've LEARNED
PRICE DISCRIMINATION OVER TIME

Q Why do people pay a lot more for a hardcover book than a paperback book?

A Sometimes firms engage in price discrimination over time to increase their profits. Although a hardcover book is only slightly more expensive to publish, the real reason for the price differential between hardcover and paperback books is the price elasticity of demand. Some people are willing to pay a higher price to be among the first to read a book; the demand curve is relatively inelastic for these devoted fans. Other individuals have a more elastic demand curve for these goods and are willing to wait for the book to come out in paperback. Other customers, such as libraries, find that paperbacks are not durable enough to be good substitutes for hardbacks. Sellers are able to profit from this difference in elasticities of demand by charging more to those who are more willing to pay and charging a lower price to those who are less willing to pay. Thus, book publishers are able to profit.

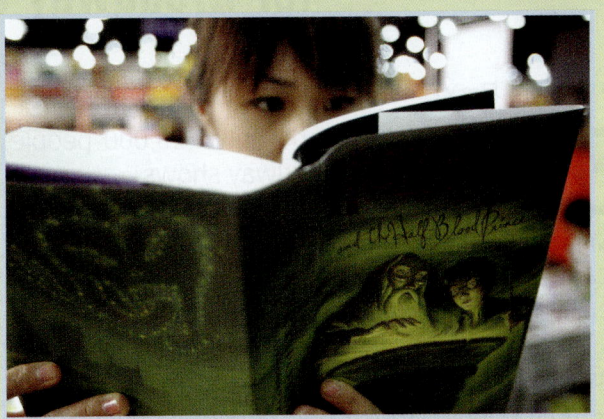

Why do hardcover texts come out before the paperback version?

of soda for less than six single cans. For example, the local bagel shop might sell you a baker's dozen, where you get 13 bagels for the price of 12. This type of price discrimination allows the producer to charge a higher price for the first unit than for, say, the 20th. This form of price discrimination is effective because a buyer's willingness to pay declines as additional units are purchased.

The Welfare Effects of Price Discrimination

In Exhibit 2 on page 384, we analyze the welfare effects of perfect price discrimination using consumer and producer surplus and then compare this with perfect competition and single-price monopoly. When the firm is able to perfectly price discriminate, each unit is sold at its **reservation price**; that is, the firm sells each unit at the maximum amount that the customer would be willing to pay. Because

reservation price the maximum amount a customer would be willing to pay for a unit of output

Why is the price a lot higher to launder a woman's blouse than a man's shirt? Why are women charged more for haircuts than are men? Are these differences based on costs—perhaps it is more costly to launder a delicate blouse or cut longer hair? Or is it a form of price discrimination where one group may have a greater willingness to pay than the other group?

in the news

The Dynamics of Pricing Tickets for Broadway Shows

—BY HAL R. VARIAN

EVERY night in New York, about 25,000 people, on average, attend Broadway shows.

As avid theatergoers know, ticket prices have been rising inexorably. The top ticket price for Broadway shows has risen 31 percent since 1998. But the actual price paid has gone up by only 24 percent.

The difference is a result of discounting. Savvy fans know that there are deals available for even the most popular shows, with the most popular discounts being offered through coupons, two-for-one deals, special prices for students, and through the TKTS booth in Times Square.

Why so much discounting? The value of a seat in a theater, like a seat on an airplane, is highly perishable. Once the show starts or the plane takes off, a seat is worth next to nothing.

In both industries, sellers use a variety of strategies to try to ensure that the seats are sold to those who are willing to pay the most.

This phenomenon was examined recently by a Stanford economist, Phillip Leslie, in an article, "Price Discrimination in Broadway Theater," published in the autumn 2004 issue of the RAND Journal of Economics.

Mr. Leslie was able to collect detailed data on a 1996 Broadway play, "Seven Guitars." Over 140,000 people saw this play, and they bought tickets in 17 price categories. Some price variation was due to the quality of the seats—orchestra, mezzanine, balcony and so on—while other price differences were a result of various forms of discounting.

The combination of quality variation and discounts led to widely varying ticket prices. The average difference of two tickets chosen at random on a given night was about 40 percent of the average price. This is comparable to the price variation in airline tickets.

The highest price, for full-price orchestra seats, was about $55, while the lowest-price balcony seats were about $17. The average price over all performances was about $36.

The ticket promotions also varied over the 199 performances of the show. Targeted direct mail was used early on, while two-for-one tickets were not introduced until about halfway through the run.

The tickets offered for sale at the TKTS booth in Times Square are typically orchestra seats, the best category of seats available. But the discounted tickets at TKTS tend to be the lower-quality orchestra seats. They sell at a fixed discount of 50 percent, but are offered only for performances that day.

Mr. Leslie's goal was primarily to model the behavior of the theatergoer. The audience for Broadway shows is highly diverse. About 10 percent, according to a 1991 survey conducted by Broadway producers, had household incomes of $25,000 or $35,000 while an equal number had incomes over $150,000 (in 1990 dollars).

The prices and discounting policy set by the producers of Broadway shows try to use this heterogeneity to get people to sort themselves by their willingness to pay for tickets.

You probably will not see Donald Trump waiting in line at TKTS; presumably, those in his income class do not mind paying full price. But a lot of students, unemployed actors and tourists do use TKTS.

Yes, it is inconvenient to wait in line at TKTS. But that is the point. If it weren't inconvenient, everyone would do it, and this would result in substantially lower revenues for Broadway shows.

Mr. Leslie uses some advanced econometric techniques to estimate the values that different income groups put on the various categories of tickets. He finds that Broadway producers do a pretty good job, in general, at maximizing revenue. The average price set—which is different than the average price paid—was about $55. According to Mr. Leslie's estimates, the best price to maximize revenue would be about $60.

Mr. Leslie was also able to examine what would happen if the producers changed the way tickets were sold. For example, suppose the producers moved to flat-rate pricing, where they sold every ticket at the same price. In this case, his model predicts that the average price set would be about $50.

Mr. Leslie also looked at various possibilities involving the TKTS booth. He found that the current

50 percent discount is too low if the goal is to maximize revenue. He calculates that a 30 percent discount would raise revenue by about 7 percent, albeit at the cost of reducing attendance by about 1.6 percent.

Of course, this estimate is based on data from only one show.

The availability of the TKTS booth stimulates attendances at dozens of shows. Even though any single show might wish for a lower discount and higher revenue, the overall industry could easily benefit from the low prices and the variety of choice offered by the Times Square booth.

There are other variations in ticket pricing that could be considered. For example, rather than sell good orchestra seats at full prices and not-so-good seats at half price at the TKTS booth, why not split these seats into two categories? It is difficult to estimate the impact of such a change with the data Mr. Leslie used, but theater owners might want to consider such an experiment.

We are likely to see more and more goods and services sold using the same sort of differential pricing. As more and more transactions become computer-mediated, it becomes easier for sellers to collect data, to experiment with pricing and to analyze the results of those experiments.

This, of course, makes life more complicated for us consumers. The flip side is that pricing variations make those good deals more likely.

Last time I was in New York, I was pleased that I managed to get a ticket to "The Producers" for half price. It almost made up for the fact that I had to book my airline ticket two weeks in advance and stay over a Saturday night.

SOURCE: From Hal R. Varian, "The Dynamics of Pricing Tickets for Broadway Shows", 'New York Times', January 13, 2005. Copyright © 2005 The New York Times. All rights reserved.

Used by permission and protected by the Copyright Laws of the United States. The printing, copying, redistribution, or retransmission of the Material without express written permission is prohibited.

each customer pays exactly the amount he is willing to pay, the marginal revenue is the same as the demand curve.

In Exhibit 2, we see that the firm sells its first unit at P_1 to the customer who is willing to pay the most. The marginal cost for producing that good is MC, so the firm makes $P_1 - MC$ on that unit. For each successive unit, the firm receives a lower price (moving down the demand curve) and has a higher marginal cost (moving up the marginal cost curve). The firm will continue to sell units as long as price exceeds marginal cost. Perfect price discrimination leads to an economically efficient level of output because price equals marginal cost on the last unit sold. However, what is efficient may not always be viewed as fair. In particular, consumers may not be happy with the outcome because the entire surplus (a + b + c + d + e) goes to the monopolist in the form of producer surplus. Consumer surplus is zero because each consumer pays exactly the amount she is willing to pay—her reservation price.

In Exhibit 2, we see that in the competitive market, the equilibrium is established at the intersection of the demand curve and the marginal cost curve, where the equilibrium price is P_{PC} and the equilibrium quantity is Q_{PC}. The perfectly competitive market is efficient because price equals marginal cost. Consumer surplus is a + b + c, producer surplus is d + e, and total welfare is maximized (a + b + c + d + e). The deadweight loss is zero.

We can also see in Exhibit 2 that if the monopolist charges a single price (the monopoly price), deadweight loss is area c + e; that is, some potential buyers value

Use what you've LEARNED
PRICE DISCRIMINATION AND COUPONS

Q Bill loves to go through the Sunday paper and cut out supermarket coupons. How do you think Bill's coupon-clipping habits apply to the concept of price discrimination?

A Often the key to price discrimination is observing the differences in customers' demand curves. For example, Bill, a full-time student who finds it relaxing to look through the Sunday paper for coupons, may have a relatively more elastic demand curve than, say, a wealthy neurosurgeon who enjoys sailing and golfing on Sundays.

section 13.6 exhibit 2 — The Welfare Effects of Perfect Price Discrimination

In perfect competition, the market equilibrium price is P_{PC} and the market equilibrium quantity is Q_{PC}. Consumer surplus is area a + b + c, producer surplus is area d + e, and there is no deadweight loss. In a single-price monopoly, the monopoly equilibrium price is P_M and the equilibrium quantity is Q_M. Compared with perfect competition, consumer surplus falls to area a, producer surplus is area b + d, and the deadweight loss is area c + e. In perfect price discrimination, the monopolist sells each unit at the buyer's reservation price—the consumer surplus falls to zero, producer surplus increases to area a + b + c + d + e, and there is no deadweight loss.

	Perfect Competition	Single Price Monopoly	Perfect Price Discrimination
Customer Surplus	a + b + c	a	0
Producer Surplus	d + e	b + d	a + b + c + d + e
Total Welfare	a + b + c + d + e	a + b + d	a + b + c + d + e
Deadweight Loss	0	c + e	0

Use what you've LEARNED
PERFECT PRICE DISCRIMINATION

Q Why does no social-welfare loss occur when a monopolist practices perfect price discrimination?

A A perfect price discriminating monopolist obtains the maximum price along the demand curve for each unit of output. For example, in Exhibit 3, the monopolist charges $10 for the first unit of output, $9 for the second, $8 for the third, and so on. The demand curve represents the firm's marginal revenue curve, and profits are maximized at the output level at which the *LRMC* equals *MR,* or in this case, *LRMC* equals *P.* (Constant costs are assumed for simplicity.) The marginal social benefits, represented by the demand price of the last unit sold ($5), equal marginal social costs, *LRMC,* and social welfare cannot be improved by increasing or decreasing output. Thus, the perfect price discriminating monopolist charges the competitive price, $5, on only the last unit sold and produces the competitive output level, 6 units. The consumer surplus that would have arisen in perfect competition, area ABC (the difference between what consumers are willing to pay and what they actually pay), is transferred to the monopolist as a profit.

section 13.6 exhibit 3 Perfect Price Discrimination

---

the good at more than the marginal cost but are not able to buy the good at the monopoly price. The market is not efficient because $P > MC$ at Q_M. In this market, the consumer surplus is area a, and the producer surplus is area b + d. While consumers receive the most consumer surplus from perfect competition, they are better off with the single-price monopoly than with perfect price discrimination, where consumer surplus is totally eliminated.

Market conditions obviously do not permit perfect price discrimination to be carried out to any significant extent. It is much too difficult to know each consumer's demand curve. However, rough approximations of perfect price discrimination are possible. Lawyers, accountants, and doctors might try to figure out whether their customers are rich or poor and charge accordingly. Car dealers might try to figure out how much a prospective buyer is willing to pay. We do know that price discrimination increases the monopolist's profits;

peak load pricing
when producers charge different prices during different periods because the demand and the cost of producing a product vary over time

otherwise, it would simply charge a single uniform price to all its customers.

Peak Load Pricing

In our earlier discussion of price discrimination, we assumed that the marginal costs associated with selling output over time were constant, but this assumption is not always true. Sometimes producers will charge different prices during different periods because the demand and the cost of producing the product vary over time. For a number of goods and services, demand peaks at particular times—bridges, roads, and tunnels during rush hour traffic; telephone services during business hours; electricity during late summer afternoons; movie theaters on weekend evenings; and amusement parks and ski resorts during holidays.

In price discrimination, we saw that prices reflected different demands from buyers. With **peak load pricing**, demand levels and costs are different. Peak load pricing leads to greater efficiency because consumer prices reflect the higher marginal costs of production during peak periods. That is, buyers pay higher prices for goods and services during peak periods and lower prices during nonpeak periods.

Suppose a regulatory agency for an electric utility company is deciding whether to change its pricing strategy from constant pricing to peak load pricing. In Exhibit 4, the utility company is presently charging 4 cents per kilowatt-hour 24 hours a day. This constant price is based on the average cost to the electricity company in the combined peak and nonpeak periods. Notice, however, that a separate demand curve applies for each of two different times of day. Let's look at the nonpeak demand curve first. During nonpeak hours, at a price of 4 cents, customers will purchase 200,000 kilowatts. If we look at the marginal cost of producing 200,000 kilowatts (by looking at the supply curve), we see that it costs less than 3 cents per kilowatt-hour. This solution is clearly not efficient because society would be better off if the marginal benefit (demand curve) was equal to the marginal cost (supply curve), which is where supply intersects demand—at a price of 3 cents and a quantity of 300,000 kilowatt-hours (point C).

Now let's look at the demand curve during peak hours. Notice that if the company stuck with its price of 4 cents per kilowatt-hour, it would sell 600,000 kilowatts. However, how much does it cost to produce 600,000 kilowatts? Looking at the supply curve, we see that the marginal cost is more than 6 cents per kilowatt-hour. This solution is not efficient because, once again, society would be better off if the marginal benefit (demand curve) equaled the marginal cost (supply curve), which is where supply intersects

section 13.6
exhibit 4 **Peak Load Pricing**

Demand for some goods and services fluctuates considerably and predictably between peak and nonpeak periods. It is more efficient to charge a higher price, 5 cents, during peak periods (when marginal costs are higher) and a lower price, 3 cents, during nonpeak periods (when marginal costs are lower) compared with charging a single price, 4 cents, at all times.

demand—at a price of 5 cents and a quantity of 500,000 kilowatt-hours (point D).

In sum, the most economically efficient solution is to charge the lower price during the nonpeak period and the higher price during the peak period. The gain from peak load pricing, compared with constant pricing, can be seen graphically as the sum of the two shaded triangles in Exhibit 4. With this pricing strategy, consumers have an incentive to give their appliances a rest during the peak period when the cost of providing electricity is the highest.

SECTION CHECK

1. When producers charge different prices for the same good or service when no cost difference exists, it is called price discrimination.
2. Price discrimination occurs if demand differs among buyers and the seller can successfully identify group members, because producers can make profits by charging different prices to each group.
3. Price discrimination would not work well if the person buying the product could easily resell the product to another customer at a higher profitable price.

1. How do we define price discrimination?
2. Why does price discrimination arise from the profit-maximization motive?
3. Why is preventing resale the key to successful price discrimination?
4. Why is it generally easier to price discriminate for services than for goods?

5. What principle will a profit-maximizing monopolist use in trying to price discriminate among different groups of customers?
6. How can offering quantity discounts increase a producer's profits?
7. Why does perfect price discrimination lead to the economically efficient level of output while reducing consumer surplus to zero?
8. What does perfect price discrimination do to the deadweight cost of monopoly?
9. Why is peak load pricing more efficient than constant pricing for a good with sharp swings in demand over time?

Interactive Chapter Summary

Fill in the blanks:

1. A true or pure monopoly exists in cases of only _____ seller of a product for which no close substitute is available.
2. Monopolists are _____ rather than price takers.
3. A monopolist's barriers to entry can include _____, _____, and _____.
4. _____ include franchising, licensing, and patents.
5. The situation in which one large firm can provide the output of the market at a lower cost than two or more smaller firms is called a(n) _____.
6. A barrier to entry is control over an important _____, such as Alcoa's control over bauxite in the 1940s and DeBeers' control over much of the world's output of diamonds.
7. In monopoly, the market demand curve may be regarded as the demand curve for the _____ because it is the market for that particular product.
8. If a monopolist reduces output, the price will _____; if the monopolist expands output, the price will _____.
9. In monopoly, if the seller wants to expand output, it will have to lower its price on _____ units.
10. The monopolist, like the perfect competitor, will maximize profits at that output where _____ = MC.
11. The monopolist, unlike the perfect competitor, will not maximize profits at that output where _____ = MC.
12. If at a monopolist's profit-maximizing price and output, the price is less than _____, the monopolist is generating economic losses.
13. In monopoly, economic profits are not eliminated by entry, because one of the conditions for monopoly is that _____ exist.
14. Patents and copyrights are examples of _____ power designed to provide an incentive to develop new products.
15. The major efficiency objection to monopoly is that a monopolist charges _____ prices and produces _____ output than would exist under perfect competition.
16. A monopolist produces at an output where the price is _____ than its marginal cost, so the value to society from the last unit produced is _____ than its marginal cost.
17. An argument against monopoly is that a lack of competition tends to retard _____ advance; but, in fact, many near monopolists are important innovators.
18. Three major approaches to dealing with the monopoly problem are commonly used: _____ policies, _____, and _____ ownership.
19. It is likely that at least some anticompetitive practices have been prevented by _____ policies simply by their prohibition of monopoly-like practices.
20. The goal of government regulation as an alternative approach to dealing with monopolies is to achieve the efficiency of large-scale production without permitting the _____ monopoly prices and _____ output that can cause allocative inefficiency.
21. From society's point of view, allocative efficiency occurs where the price of the good is equal to _____. But with natural monopoly, at the "optimal" level of output for allocative efficiency, _____ are incurred.
22. A compromise between unregulated monopoly and marginal cost pricing is _____ pricing, where

the monopolist is permitted to price the product where price equals _____.

23. Average cost pricing _____ the incentives for a monopolist to find ways to reduce its costs.

24. _____ occurs when sellers charge different customers different prices for the same good or service when the cost does not differ.

25. In the case of a number of competing firms, price discrimination is _____ likely because competitors tend to undercut the _____ prices charged.

26. A profit-maximizing seller will charge a(n) _____ price for more inelastic demanders and a(n) _____ price for more elastic demanders.

27. The profit-maximizing rule for a price discriminating monopolist is to price where _____ equals _____ for each different group of demanders.

28. For price discrimination to work, the person buying the product at a discount must have difficulty in _____ the product to customers being charged more.

29. _____, which allow sellers to charge a higher price for the first unit than for later units, are another form of price discrimination.

Answers: 1. one 2. price makers 3. legal barriers; economies of scale; control of important inputs 4. Legal barriers to entry 5. natural monopoly 6. input 7. firm 8. rise; fall 9. all 10. MR 11. P 12. average total cost 13. barriers to entry 14. barriers to entry 15. higher; less 16. greater; greater 17. technological 18. antitrust regulation; public 19. antitrust; losses 22. marginal cost; average cost; average total cost 23. reduces 24. Price discrimination 25. less; high 26. higher; lower 27. marginal revenue; marginal cost 28. reselling 29. Quantity discounts

Key Terms and Concepts

monopoly 362
natural monopoly 362
average cost pricing 377
price discrimination 378
reservation price 381
peak load pricing 385

Section Check Answers

13.1 Monopoly: The Price Maker

1. **Why does monopoly depend on the existence of barriers to entry?**
   If a monopoly were unusually profitable (earning a higher than normal rate of return), entry by other firms would occur, driving its economic profits down and increasing the number of sellers, unless some barrier to entry prevented it.

2. **Why is a pure monopoly a rarity?**
   Pure monopolies are a rarity because there are very few goods or services for which there are no close substitutes and for which there is only one producer.

3. **Why does the government grant some companies, such as public utilities, monopoly power?**
   In some industries, it is inherently inefficient to have more than one firm producing the good or service (i.e., the good or service is a natural monopoly).

13.2 Demand and Marginal Revenue in Monopoly

1. **Why are the market and firm demand curves the same for a monopoly?**
   The market and firm demand curves are the same for a monopoly because a monopoly is the only seller of the product under consideration. Since a monopolist is the only seller in the industry, its demand curve is the industry or market demand curve.

2. **Why is a monopoly a price maker, but a perfectly competitive firm a price taker?**
   A perfectly competitive firm is a price taker because it cannot appreciably change the quantity offered for sale on a market, and therefore it cannot change the equilibrium market price appreciably. However, since a monopoly controls the quantity offered for sale, it can alter the price by changing its output—it "makes" the price through its decision of how much to produce.

3. **Why is marginal revenue less than price for a profit-maximizing monopolist?**
   For a monopolist, selling an additional unit requires it to reduce its price, and reducing its price reduces its revenues from units it was selling before at its previous higher price. Therefore, the monopolist's marginal revenue equals price minus this lost revenue from the reduced price on other units, and is less than price as a result.

4. **Why would a monopolist never knowingly operate in the inelastic portion of its demand curve?**
   To maximize its profits, a monopolist will produce the output where marginal revenue equals marginal cost. But since marginal cost will be positive, this requires that marginal revenue is also positive at the profit-maximizing

level. Since a positive marginal revenue means that total revenue increases as quantity sold increases along a demand curve, and this only occurs if demand is relatively elastic (the elasticity of demand is greater than one), this means that a monopolist will always choose to operate on the elastic portion of its demand curve.

13.3 The Monopolist's Equilibrium

1. **What is a monopolist's principle for choosing the profit-maximizing output?**
   A monopolist's principle for choosing the profit-maximizing output is the same as for a perfectly competitive firm: Produce all those units for which marginal revenue exceeds marginal cost, resulting in a profit-maximizing equilibrium quantity where marginal revenue equals marginal cost. The differences between a monopoly and a perfectly competitive firm arise because marginal revenue also equals price for a perfectly competitive firm, but marginal revenue is less than price for a monopolist.

2. **How do you find the profit-maximizing price for a monopolist?**
   A monopolist produces the quantity where marginal revenue equals marginal cost. The height of its demand curve at that quantity indicates the price at which that profit-maximizing quantity can be sold.

3. **For a monopolist making positive economic profits, what must be true about the relationship between price and average total cost?**
   Just as with a perfectly competitive firm, for a monopoly to be earning economic profits, its total revenue must exceed total cost at the profit-maximizing output. But this means that price (average revenue) must also exceed average cost at the profit-maximizing output level for positive economic profits to be earned.

4. **For a monopolist making negative economic profits, what must be true about the relationship between price and average total cost?**
   Just as with a perfectly competitive firm, for a monopoly to be earning negative economic profits, its total revenue must be less than its total cost at the profit-maximizing output. But this means that price (average revenue) must also be less than average cost at the profit-maximizing output level for negative economic profits to be earned.

5. **Why, unlike perfectly competitive firms, can a monopolist continue to earn positive economic profits in the long run?**
   Unlike perfectly competitive firms, a monopolist can continue to earn positive economic profits in the long run, because barriers to entry keep entrants, whose entry would erode those economic profits, from entering the industry.

13.4 Monopoly and Welfare Loss

1. **Why does the reduced output under monopoly cause inefficiency?**
   The reduced output and higher prices under monopoly cause inefficiency because some units for which the marginal value (indicated by willingness to pay along the demand curve) exceeds the marginal cost are no longer exchanged (unlike in perfect competition), eliminating the net gains that such trades would have generated.

2. **Does monopoly power retard innovation? Why or why not?**
   Monopoly has been claimed to retard innovation, but many near-monopolists are important innovators. Therefore the incentive to innovate exists in monopolistic as well as competitive market structures.

3. **What does the welfare cost of monopoly represent? How is it measured?**
   The welfare cost of monopoly represents the net gains from trade (the difference between the marginal values of those goods indicated by the demand curve and the marginal costs of producing them) from those units of a good that would have been traded, but are no longer traded because of the output restriction of monopoly. It is measured by the area between the demand curve and the marginal cost curve for those units that are no longer traded because of the monopoly output restriction.

4. **How can economies of scale lead to monopoly? How could it result in monopoly increasing rather than decreasing market output, relative to the competitive market structure?**
   Economies of scale can lead to monopoly because output can be produced at lower costs on a larger scale than on a smaller scale, and this efficiency (cost) advantage can result in a larger firm outcompeting smaller firms. Industries with economies of scale over the entire range of industry output therefore tend toward monopoly. But if the production cost savings are greater than the price increasing effect of monopoly output restriction, the result of such a monopoly would be a lower price and a higher quantity than would be the case with a larger number of firms (i.e., a more competitive market structure).

5. **Can monopoly be the result of a new innovation that leaves consumers better off than before? Why or why not?**
   A new innovation may result in its innovator having a monopoly on it, which would give its creator incentives to raise prices and reduce outputs like any other monopoly. But for that monopoly innovator to attract customers away from the products customers currently purchase, those customers must expect to be made

better off buying the product at the price charged. This means that such a monopoly has no ability to harm consumers compared to their earlier situation, but can make them better off.

13.5 Monopoly Policy

1. **What alternative ways of dealing with the monopoly problem are commonly used?**
   The monopoly problem (with respect to efficiency, equity, and power) is commonly dealt with through antitrust policies, regulation, and public ownership.

2. **How do antitrust laws promote greater price competition?**
   Antitrust laws promote more price competition by making monopolistic practices and restrictions on price competition illegal.

3. **What price and output are ideal for allocative efficiency for a regulated natural monopolist? Why is an unregulated natural monopolist unlikely to pick this solution?**
   The efficient price and output are where demand (marginal value) equals marginal cost, since this guarantees that every mutually beneficial trade takes place. However, with economies of scale (falling average cost curves), marginal cost is less than average cost for a natural monopolist, so that marginal cost prices would result in economic losses. An unregulated natural monopolist would not choose such a solution.

4. **What is average cost pricing? How is it different from marginal cost pricing?**
   Average cost pricing is a regulatory approach to natural monopoly that permits the regulated natural monopolist to earn a normal rate of return on capital investment (zero economic profits). Zero economic profits requires that total revenues equal total (opportunity) costs, which requires that average revenue, or price, equals average cost. Forcing such a natural monopolist to charge prices equal to marginal cost would require a price below average cost, because marginal cost is less than average cost for a natural monopolist, implying losses to the producer, which is not sustainable over the long run.

5. **What are some difficulties encountered when regulators try to implement average cost pricing for natural monopolies?**
   Difficulties encountered when regulators try to implement average cost pricing include difficulties in calculating costs, eroded incentives for regulated firms to keep costs down, and the risk that the regulatory agency will make decisions on a political rather than on an economic basis.

6. **Why might a job with a regulated natural monopolist that is allowed to earn a "fair and reasonable" return have more perks (noncash forms of compensation) than a comparable job in a nonregulated firm?**
   A regulated natural monopolist that is allowed to earn a "fair and reasonable" rate of return has little or no incentive to keep costs down, since reducing costs won't allow them to earn higher profits as a result. Those potential profits the monopolist is not allowed to keep get converted instead into business expenses that benefit the management, such as lavish perks (first class air travel, hotels, meals, etc.).

13.6 Price Discrimination and Peak Load Pricing

1. **How do we define price discrimination?**
   Price discrimination is defined as charging different customers different prices for the same good or service.

2. **Why does price discrimination arise from the profit-maximization motive?**
   Price discrimination arises from the profit-maximization motive because different customers react differently to price changes (i.e., they have different elasticities of demand). Therefore, profit-maximization implies treating these different customers differently.

3. **Why is preventing resale the key to successful price discrimination?**
   If customers who are being charged different prices for the same goods can resell the goods among themselves, the lower price group will resell to the higher price group, undermining the seller's ability to charge a higher price to the groups with more inelastic demand curves.

4. **Why is it generally easier to price discriminate for services than for goods?**
   Preventing resale is a key to successful price discrimination, and it is typically easier to prevent resale of services provided directly to customers than for goods sold to them (e.g., it is harder to resell a gall bladder surgery or plumbing repairs than to resell a computer).

5. **What principle will a profit-maximizing monopolist use in trying to price discriminate among different groups of customers?**
   A profit-maximizing monopolist will attempt to charge higher prices to those who are more willing to pay (more inelastic demanders), and lower prices to those who are less willing to pay (more elastic demanders).

6. **How can offering quantity discounts increase a producer's profits?**
   Quantity discounts can allow a producer to charge a lower price for additional units, without having

to reduce the price on the earlier units; it is effective because a buyer's willingness to pay declines as additional units are purchased.

7. **Why does perfect price discrimination lead to the economically efficient level of output while reducing consumer surplus to zero?**
Perfect price discrimination allows a seller to sell each unit for a price equal to the buyer's reservation price, which eliminates any consumer surplus. But since a perfect price discriminating monopolist need not lower its price on previous units when it sells more, its marginal revenue is the same as its price, so when it produces to the output level where marginal revenue equals marginal cost, it also produces to the output level where price equals marginal cost, which is the efficient level of output.

8. **What does perfect price discrimination do to the deadweight cost of monopoly?**
Since perfect price discrimination makes marginal revenue equal to price for each unit sold, such a monopolist has no reason to restrict output to increase profits; with no incentive to reduce output below the efficient level, there would be no deadweight cost.

9. **Why is peak load pricing more efficient than constant pricing for a good with sharp swings in demand over time?**
A constant price would result in price being too low in the peak demand period, and too high in the low demand period; both of these pricing "errors" would cause a deadweight cost that could be avoided by peak load pricing.

CHAPTER 13 STUDY GUIDE

True or False:

1. For firm to qualify as a pure monopoly, if must have over 50% of the market.
2. Pure monopolies are common.
3. As long as market demand curves are downward sloping, the demand curves faced by monopolists will be downward sloping.
4. Monopoly is at the other end of the spectrum from perfect competition, in terms of the number of firms in an industry.
5. A monopoly firm is a price maker, and it will pick a price that corresponds to the quantity where marginal revenue equals marginal cost.
6. While firms in perfect competition face horizontal firm demand curves, in monopoly, the demand curve for the firm's product is downward sloping.
7. For a monopoly who charges the same price to everyone to get revenue from marginal customers, the firm has to lower the price so that marginal revenue is always less than price.
8. When a monopolist cuts its price to attract new customers, its existing customers are unaffected.
9. The marginal revenue curve for a monopolist lies below, and is parallel, to, the demand curve.
10. For a monopolist, the profit-maximizing price is indicated by the price at which marginal revenue equals marginal cost.
11. Along the elastic portion of the demand curve, when the quantity sold falls, total revenue rises, so that marginal revenue is positive.
12. Along the inelastic portion of the demand curve, when the price falls, total revenue falls, so that marginal revenue is negative.
13. For a monopolist who had zero marginal cost, profit maximization imply operating where the elasticity of demand equals one.
14. Having monopoly does not guarantee economic profits.
15. A monopolist will incur a loss if demand is insufficient to cover average total costs at any price and output combination along its demand curve.
16. If at a monopolist's profit-maximizing price and output, the price is greater than average total cost, the monopolist is generating economic profits.
17. Economic profits could persist in the long run for a monopolist.
18. Monopoly creates a welfare loss because a monopoly does not produce enough of a good from society's perspective.
19. Economists disagree about the size of the welfare loss from monopoly.
20. Perfect competition leads to higher output and lower prices than would exist under monopoly.
21. Government regulation of monopolies aims to achieve the efficiency of large-scale production without permitting the monopolists to charge monopoly prices, which would reduce output.
22. The cost advantage of a natural monopoly is due to economies of scale throughout the relevant output range.
23. With natural monopoly, regulators who impose average cost pricing aim at producing zero economic profits for the producer.
24. By imposing monetary and nonmonetary costs on monopolists, antitrust policies aim to reduce the profitability of monopoly.
25. Under average cost pricing, a regulated monopoly is permitted to earn zero accounting profits such as firms experience in perfect competition in the long run.
26. Any regulated business producing at the optimal, or efficient, output would earn a normal rate of return.
27. When different groups of customers have predictably different willingness to pay, a monopolist could earn higher profits by charging those different buyers different prices, if it could prevent resale of the product among customers.
28. Price discrimination is possible only with monopoly or where members of a small group of firms follow identical pricing policies.
29. Price differentials between groups will erode if reselling is easy, which is why price discrimination is usually limited to services and to some goods where it is inherently difficult to resell or where the producer can effectively prevent resale.

Multiple Choice Questions:

1. For a true, or pure, monopoly, which of the following is not true?
   a. There is only one seller of the product.
   b. No close substitutes are available.
   c. The firm and the industry are the same.
   d. Barriers to entry are low.
   e. all of the above are true.

2. Pure monopoly is defined as
   a. a market structure consisting of a single buyer.
   b. a market structure that involves many substitute products.
   c. a market in which many rival firms compete for sales.
   d. an industry consisting of a single seller.

3. Which of the following is inconsistent with monopoly?
   a. A single seller.
   b. Free entry and exit.
   c. Marginal revenue is less than price.
   d. Economies of scale.
   e. Selling in the elastic portion of the demand curve in order to maximize profits.

4. Which of the following is potentially a barrier to entry into a product market?
   a. Patent protection on the design of the product
   b. Economies of scale in the product market
   c. Government licensing of the product's producers
   d. The control of a crucial input necessary to produce the product
   e. All of the above are potentially barriers to entry into a product market.

5. For a natural monopoly, which of the following is true?
   a. It is more efficient to have a single firm produce the good.
   b. Production of the good must involve economies of scale throughout the relevant output range.
   c. It could result from a firm's possession of an exclusive patent.
   d. One large firm can produce at lower cost than two or more smaller firms.
   e. All of the above are true.

6. For a monopolist, which of the following is false?
   a. Its demand curve is downward sloping.
   b. Its marginal revenue is less than price.
   c. Entry will eliminate any existing economic profits.
   d. All of the above are true.

7. A profit-maximizing monopolist sets
   a. the product price where marginal cost equals marginal revenue.
   b. output where marginal cost equals average revenue.
   c. output where marginal cost equals marginal revenue.
   d. output where demand equals average total cost.
   e. price equal to the highest dollar amount that any customer is willing to pay.

8. If a profit-maximizing monopolist is currently charging a price on the inelastic portion of its demand curve, to increase economic profits, it should
   a. hold output constant and raise price.
   b. lower price and increase output.
   c. reduce both output and price.
   d. raise price and decrease output.
   e. do none of the above.

9. Rick owns the only race-car track in the entire region. When he lowers his price, the track attracts more customers and its total revenue rises. Which of the following is true of Rick?
    a. He is a monopolist operating in the inelastic region of his demand curve.
    b. He is a monopolist operating in the elastic region of his demand curve.
    c. He would not choose to lower his price in such a situation.
    d. He is a price taker.
    e. Both a. and c. are true of Rick.
10. Which of the following is *not* true about a profit-maximizing monopolist?
    a. A monopolist faces the downward-sloping market demand curve.
    b. A monopolist could earn negative economic profits.
    c. Its price exceeds marginal revenue.
    d. Ahe monopolist chooses output where marginal revenue equals marginal cost.
    e. All of the above are true.
11. Which of the following is true for a firm that is a monopolist?
    a. The firm could make either economic profits or losses in the short run.
    b. The firm will produce a smaller quantity of output than what would be best from the viewpoint of ideal economic efficiency.
    c. The additional revenue that can be generated from an increase in output will be less than the firm's price.
    d. All of the above are true.
12. If a monopolist had a zero marginal cost of production, it would maximize profits by choosing to produce a quantity where
    a. demand was unit elastic.
    b. demand was elastic.
    c. demand was inelastic.
    d. It is impossible to determine where along a demand curve such a monopolist would choose to produce.
13. Arnold is the monopoly provider of a town's TV cable service, whose current subscription price is $30.00 per month. In order to attract one more subscriber, he has to lower his price to $29.95. What is true of Arnold's marginal revenue from that additional subscriber?
    a. Arnold's marginal revenue is greater than $29.95.
    b. Arnold's marginal revenue is less than $29.95.
    c. Arnold's marginal revenue equals $29.95.
    d. Arnold's marginal revenue is between $29.95 and $30.00.
14. Monopoly is like perfect competition in that
    a. They both charge prices greater than marginal cost.
    b. There are no barriers to entry into either type of industry.
    c. Both types of firms earn economic profits only if their price is greater than ATC.
    d. Monopoly is like perfect competition in all of the preceding ways.
15. Monopolists are unlike perfectly competitive firms in that
    a. monopolists maximize profits at the output level where marginal revenue equals marginal cost.
    b. monopolists could be earning either profits or losses in the short run.
    c. they face firm demand curves that are downward sloping.
    d. both a. and c. are true of monopolists but not perfectly competitive firms.
16. A price-taking firm and a monopolist are alike in that
    a. marginal revenue equals marginal cost for both.
    b. both maximize profits by choosing an output where marginal revenue equals marginal cost when price is less than average variable cost.
    c. price exceeds marginal cost at the profit-maximizing level of output for both.
    d. in the long run, both earn zero economic profits.

17. Which of the following is true of perfect competition but not true of monopoly?
    a. A shift on market demand leaves the firm's demand curve unchanged.
    b. A profit-maximizing firm chooses output where marginal revenue equals marginal cost.
    c. Marginal revenue is equal to price.
    d. Profits may exist in the short run.
    e. Both c. and d. are true of perfectly competitive firms but not monopolies.

18. Objections to monopolies do *not* include which of the following?
    a. They reduce output below the efficient level of output that would be produced in perfect competition.
    b. They increase the price above what would be charged in perfect competition.
    c. They charge a price that is greater than marginal cost.
    d. They create a welfare cost.
    e. All of the preceding are objections that have been made to monopolies.

19. A natural monopoly is defined as an industry in which
    a. a single firm controls crucial inputs to the production process.
    b. one firm can produce the entire industry output at a lower average cost than can two or more firms.
    c. one firm is especially large relative to other firms that could enter the industry.
    d. a single seller exists as a result of patent protection.

20. Average cost pricing for a natural monopoly will
    a. result in a less than socially efficient level of output.
    b. result in the socially efficient level of output.
    c. result in a greater than socially efficient level of output.
    d. result in the firm suffering economic losses.
    e. result in the firm earning economic profits.

21. If regulators set a price according to marginal cost pricing, the firm will
    a. earn positive economic profits.
    b. make zero economic profits.
    c. earn the same level of profits as it would absent regulation.
    d. suffer an economic loss.
    e. Both a. and c. are true.

22. Which of the following is not a limitation that regulators face when they implement average cost pricing?
    a. Average cost pricing provides little or no incentive for firms to keep costs down.
    b. The accurate calculation of a firm's costs is difficult.
    c. Decisions are political and often influenced by special interests.
    d. All of the preceding are limitations faced by regulators implementing average cost pricing.

23. Under average cost pricing by a natural monopoly,
    a. price is greater than marginal cost.
    b. a welfare cost will be incurred.
    c. the producer will earn a normal rate of return.
    d. a producer experiences little or no incentive to hold down costs.
    e. all of the preceding are true.

24. A price-discriminating monopolist will
    a. price where marginal revenue equals marginal cost for each different group of demanders.
    b. charge a higher price to those with a greater willingness to pay (the more inelastic demanders).
    c. have to face customers who have a difficult time reselling the good to others who were charged more.
    d. do all of the above.

25. Which of the following is *not* true of successful price discriminators?
    a. They must have monopoly power.
    b. Their customers must differ in their willingness to pay.
    c. Their customers must have difficulty reselling the good to other customers.
    d. They could make greater profits by charging everyone a higher, uniform price.

26. Price discrimination may be a rational strategy for a profit-maximizing monopolist when
    a. consumers are unable to be segmented into identifiable markets.
    b. consumers have a substantial ability to resell across market segments.
    c. consumers have no opportunity to resell across market segments.
    d. the willingness to pay is the same across all customers.

27. A price-discriminating monopolist would tend to charge a higher price to students if it believed that student demand is
    a. more elastic than that of other demanders.
    b. more inelastic than that of other demanders.
    c. unit elastic.
    d. graphically represented by a vertical curve.

Problems:

1. Barriers to entry are important in the creation of monopolies because they keep competitors out of the industry. Although many types of barriers exist, historically, ownership of an essential resource, government patents and licenses, and large entry costs have served as the primary barriers to entry. For each of the following cases, indicate which type of barrier created the monopoly.
    a. In the 1940s, Aluminum Company of America owns all of the world's known bauxite deposits.
    b. The local cable TV company has the only government issued license to supply services in the area.
    c. The pharmaceutical company, MAXCO, invented and patented a new baldness drug.
    d. In the 1950s, AT&T provided long-distance telephone service by stringing millions of miles of copper wiring across the United States.

2. Which of the following could be considered a monopoly?
    a. DeBeers diamond company.
    b The only doctor in a small town.
    c. The Ford Motor Company.
    d. Kate Hudson (an actress).

3. The Mobile Phone Company has served Mobile, Alabama, since the 1930s as a government-authorized natural monopoly. Exhibit 1 describes a portion of the demand curve for long-distance service facing Mobile Phone.
    a. Complete the table.

EXHIBIT 1 MOBILE PHONE COMPANY DEMAND FOR PHONE HOURS

Quantity	Price	Total Revenue	Marginal Revenue	Elastic or Inelastic?
30	$3.65	_____	_____	_____
31	3.58	_____	_____	_____
32	3.50	_____	_____	_____
33	3.43	_____	_____	_____
34	3.35	_____	_____	_____
35	3.27	_____	_____	_____
36	3.20	_____	_____	_____
37	3.12	_____	_____	_____
38	3.05	_____	_____	_____
39	2.97	_____	_____	_____
40	2.89	_____	_____	_____
41	2.82	_____	_____	_____
42	2.74	_____	_____	_____
43	2.67	_____	_____	_____
44	2.59	_____	_____	_____
45	2.51	_____	_____	_____
46	2.44	_____	_____	_____
47	2.36	_____	_____	_____
48	2.29	_____	_____	_____
49	2.21	_____	_____	_____
50	2.13	_____	_____	_____

b. How does the company's marginal revenue change as the price changes? What is the relationship between marginal revenue and price?
c. At what price does demand become inelastic?
d. What will happen to the elasticity of demand when a new company, Mobile Phones of Mobile, starts a competing wireless phone company?

4. Is it optimal for the monopolist to operate on the inelastic portion of the demand curve? Why or why not?

5. If economic profits were zero, would a monopolist ever stay in business? Why might it be possible for a monopolist to earn positive economic profits in the long run?

6. Below is the demand for water and cost conditions for the New South Springdale Water Utility, a pure monopoly.
   a. Complete the table.

Quanity (gallons)	Price (per gallon)	Total Revenue	Marginal Revenue	Marginal Costs	Average Total Costs	Profit
100	$1.28	_____	_____	$0.15	$1.252	_____
101	$1.27	_____	_____	$0.18	$1.241	_____
102	$1.26	_____	_____	$0.21	$1.231	_____
103	$1.25	_____	_____	$0.23	$1.221	_____
104	$1.24	_____	_____	$0.26	$1.212	_____

   b. What is true about the relationship between marginal revenue and marginal costs when profit is the greatest?
   c. Suppose the government imposed a tax on the firm of $103, which the firm had to pay even if it went out of business. What would be the profit-maximizing level of output? What would happen to profits? Would the firm stay in business?

7. What is meant by the welfare loss of monopoly? Why does no welfare loss occur if a monopolist successfully practices perfect price discrimination?

8. A simple monopolist with these fixed and variable cost schedules maximizes profits at what level of output? Explain why.

Price	Quantity	Fixed Cost	Variable Cost
$100	0	$60	$0
90	1	60	25
80	2	60	40
70	3	60	50
60	4	60	70
50	5	60	100
40	6	60	140
30	7	60	190
20	8	60	250

9. A patent gives a firm a monopoly in production of the patented good. While the monopoly profits provide an incentive for firms to innovate, the monopoly power imposes a cost on consumers. Why do consumers suffer a cost? Is it greater than the profits earned by the monopolist?

10. Suppose an industry experiences decreasing average costs of production over the relevant range of market demand. Discuss the merits of a regulation requiring the natural monopolist to price where demand equals marginal cost and to service all willing customers. What about where demand equals average cost? Are any practical difficulties likely to be encountered with either regulatory program?

11. Governments around the world are allowing competition in the production of goods and services that have historically been considered natural monopolies. Competition has been introduced in industries such as the local telephone service and electricity provision. Why might the introduction of competition increase the efficiency of these industries?

12. In October of 1999, Coca-Cola announced that it was considering testing a new vending machine that was temperature sensitive. The price of the soft drinks in the machines would be higher on hot days. The *Miami Herald* story read "Soda jerks." How is this practice a form of price discrimination? How can the placement of the vending machines create a monopoly? What if other vending machines are close by and are not owned by Coca-Cola?

13. Explain how each of the following is a form of price discrimination.
    a. a senior citizen breakfast discount at a local restaurant.
    b. coupon discounts on laundry detergent.
    c. a student discount at the movie theater.
    d. long-distance phone service that costs 15 cents per minute for the first 10 minutes and 5 cents per minute after 10 minutes.
    e. a psychic who charges each customer his or her maximum reservation price for palm readings.

14. Compare the size of the welfare (deadweight) loss under monopoly in the case of perfect price discrimination and under the standard case of simple monopoly. Explain.

15. Fill in the missing data in the following table for a monopolist.

Quantity	Price	Total Revenue	Marginal Revenue	Demand Elastic or Inelastic?
1	$11	_____	_____	_____
2	10	_____	_____	_____
3	9	_____	_____	_____
4	8	_____	_____	_____
5	7	_____	_____	_____
6	6	_____	_____	_____
7	5	_____	_____	_____
8	4	_____	_____	_____
9	3	_____	_____	_____
10	2	_____	_____	_____
11	1	_____	_____	_____

16. Assume that the monopolist in problem 15 had fixed costs of $10 and a constant marginal cost of $4 per unit. Add columns to the above table for Total Cost, Marginal Cost, and Profit.

17. Use the accompanying diagram to answer the questions.

a. Assuming the monopolist indicated in the diagram produced at all, indicate its profit-maximizing quantity and price.
b. Add an *ATC* curve that would show this monopolist earning an economic profit.
c. Add an *ATC* curve that would show this monopolist experiencing an economic loss.

18. Use the following diagram to answer the questions.

a. Indicate the efficient result on the graph.
b. Illustrate the profits or losses from the efficient result in a.
c. Show the average cost-pricing solution. What profits are earned with that approach?

19. The Mississippi Bridge Authority operates a toll bridge that crosses the river near St. Louis. Traffic over the bridge includes tourist traffic and commercial traffic. It also includes commuters who work in St. Louis but live on the Illinois side of the river.
a. Would you expect demand for bridge use to differ at different times during the day? Why?
b. How might costs differ in these time periods?
c. What would be the effects of charging a higher toll to cross the bridge during busy times?

14 Monopolistic Competition and Product Differentiation

14.1 Monopolistic Competition

14.2 Price and Output Determination in Monopolistic Competition

14.3 Monopolistic Competition Versus Perfect Competition

14.4 Advertising

Restaurants, clothing stores, beauty salons, video stores, hardware stores, and coffee houses have elements of both competitive and monopoly markets.

Recall that the perfectly competitive model includes many buyers and sellers; coffee houses can be found in almost every town in the country. You can even find Starbucks in Barnes & Noble bookstores and grocery stores. In addition, the barriers to entry of owning an individual coffee shop are relatively low. However, monopolistically competitive firms sell a differentiated product and thus each firm has an element of monopoly power. Each coffee store is different. It might be different because of its location or décor. It might be different because of its products. It might be different because of the service it provides. Monopolistically competitive markets are common in the real world. They are the topic of this chapter. ■

SECTION 14.1 Monopolistic Competition

* What are the distinguishing features of monopolistic competition?
* How can a firm differentiate its product?

What Is Monopolistic Competition?

Monopolistic competition is a market structure where many producers of somewhat different products compete with one another. For example, a restaurant is a monopoly in the sense that it has a unique name, menu, quality of service, location, and so on; but it also has many competitors—others selling prepared meals. That is, monopolistic competition has features in common with both monopoly and perfect competition, even though this explanation may sound like an oxymoron—like "jumbo shrimp" or "civil war." As with monopoly, individual sellers in monopolistic competition believe that they have some market power. But monopolistic competition is probably closer to competition than monopoly. Entry into and exit out of the industry is unrestricted, and consequently, the industry has many independent sellers. In virtue of the relatively free entry of new firms, the long-run price and output behavior, and zero long-run economic profits, monopolistic competition is similar to perfect competition. However, the monopolistically competitive firm produces a product that is different (that is, *differentiated* rather than identical or homogeneous) from others, which leads to some degree of monopoly power. In a sense, sellers in a monopolistically competitive market may be regarded as "monopolists" of their own particular brands; but unlike firms with a true monopoly, competition occurs among the many firms selling similar (but not identical) brands. For example, a buyer living in a city of moderate size and in the market for books, CDs, toothpaste, furniture, shampoo, video rentals, restaurants, eyeglasses, running shoes, movie theaters, super markets, and music lessons has many competing sellers from which to choose.

monopolistic competition
a market structure with many firms selling differentiated products

product differentiation
goods or services that are slightly different, or perceived to be different, from one another

The Three Basic Characteristics of Monopolistic Competition

The theory of monopolistic competition is based on three characteristics: (1) product differentiation, (2) many sellers, and (3) free entry.

Product Differentiation

One characteristic of monopolistic competition is **product differentiation**—the accentuation of unique product qualities, real or perceived, to develop a specific product identity.

The significant feature of differentiation is the buyer's belief that various sellers' products are not the same, whether the products are actually different or not. Aspirin and some brands of over-the-counter cold medicines are examples of products that are similar

Restaurants can be very different. A restaurant that sells tacos and burritos competes with other Mexican restaurants, but it also competes with restaurants that sell burgers and fries. Monopolistic competition has some elements of competition (many sellers) and some elements of monopoly power (differentiated products).

in the news: Is a Beer a Beer?

To show that some differentiation is perceived rather than real, blind taste tests on beer were conducted on 250 participants.

Four glasses of identical beer, each with different labels, were presented to the subjects as four different brands of beer. In the end, all the subjects believed that the brands of beer were different and that they could tell the difference between them. Another interesting result came out of the taste tests—most of the participants commented that at least one of the beers was unfit for human consumption.

SOURCE: Russell L. Ackoff and James R. Emshoff, "Advertising Research at Anheuser-Busch, Inc. (1963–1968)," *Sloan Management Review* 16 (Winter 1975): 1–15.

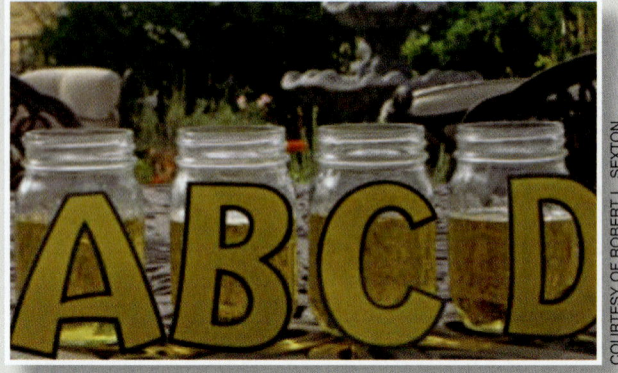

consider this:

Product differentiation, whether perceived or real, can be effective. Take another example: In blind taste testing, few people can consistently distinguish between Coca-Cola and Pepsi, yet each brand has many loyal customers. Sometimes the key to product differentiation is that consumers believe they are different.

---

or identical but have different brand names. Product differentiation leads to preferences among buyers dealing with or purchasing the products of particular sellers.

Physical Differences Physical differences constitute a primary source of product differentiation. For example, brands of ice cream (such as Dreyer's and Breyers), running shoes (such as Nike and Asics), or fast-food Mexican restaurants (such as Taco Bell and Del Taco) differ significantly in taste to many buyers.

Prestige Prestige considerations also differentiate products to a significant degree. Many people prefer to be seen using the currently popular brand, while others prefer the "off" brand. Prestige considerations are particularly important with gifts—Cuban cigars, Montblanc pens, beluga caviar, Godiva chocolates, Dom Perignon champagne, Rolex watches, and so on.

Location Location is a major differentiating factor in retailing. Shoppers are not willing to travel long distances to purchase similar items, which is one reason for the large number of convenience stores and service station mini-marts. Most buyers realize brands of gasoline do not differ significantly, which means the location of a gas station might influence their choice of gasoline. Location is also important for restaurants. Some restaurants can differentiate their products with beautiful views of the city lights, ocean, or mountains.

Service Service considerations are likewise significant for product differentiation. Speedy and friendly service or lenient return policies are important to many people. Likewise, speed and quality of service may significantly influence a person's choice of restaurants.

The Impact of Many Sellers

When many firms compete for the same customers, any particular firm has little control over or interest in what other firms do. That is, a restaurant may change prices or improve service without a retaliatory move on the part of other competing restaurants, because the time and effort necessary to learn about such changes may have marginal costs that are greater than the marginal benefits.

The Significance of Free Entry

Entry in monopolistic competition is relatively unrestricted in the sense that new firms may easily start the production of close substitutes for existing products, as happens with restaurants, styling salons, barber shops, and many forms of retail activity. Because of relatively free entry, economic profits tend to be eliminated in the long run, as is the case with perfect competition.

> **SECTION CHECK**
>
> 1. The theory of monopolistic competition is based on three primary characteristics: product differentiation, many sellers, and free entry.
> 2. The many sources of product differentiation include physical differences, prestige, location, and service.
>
> ---
>
> 1. How is monopolistic competition a mixture of monopoly and perfect competition?
> 2. Why is product differentiation necessary for monopolistic competition?
> 3. What are some common forms of product differentiation?
> 4. Why are many sellers necessary for monopolistic competition?
> 5. Why is free entry necessary for monopolistic competition?

SECTION 14.2 Price and Output Determination in Monopolistic Competition

* How are short-run economic profits and losses determined?
* Why is marginal revenue less than price?
* How is long-run equilibrium determined?

The Firm's Demand and Marginal Revenue Curve

Suppose the Coffee Bean decides to raise its price on caffè lattes from $2.75 to $3.00, as seen in Exhibit 1. The Coffee Bean is one of many places to get caffè lattes in town (Starbucks, Diedrich's, Peet's, and others). At the higher price, $3.00, a number of Coffee Bean customers will switch to other places in town for their caffè lattes, but not everyone. Some may not switch; perhaps because of the location, the ambience, the selection of other drinks, or the quality of the coffee. Because there are many substitutes and the fact that some will not change, the demand curve will be very elastic (flat) but not horizontal, as seen in Exhibit 1. That is, unlike the perfectly competitive firm, a monopolistically competitive firm faces a downward-sloping demand curve. The increase in price from $2.75 to $3.00 leads to a reduction in caffè lattes sold from 2,400 per month to 800 per month.

Let's continue our example with the Coffee Bean. In the table in Exhibit 2, we will show how a monopolistically competitive firm must cut its price to sell more and why its marginal revenue will therefore lie below its demand curve. For simplicity, we will use caffè lattes sold per hour. The first two columns in the table show the demand schedule. If the Coffee Bean charges $4.00 for a caffè latte, no one will buy it and will buy their caffè lattes at another store. If it charges $3.50, it will sell one caffè latte per hour. And if the Coffee Bean wants to sell 2 caffè lattes, it must lower the price to

section 14.2 exhibit 1 Downward-Sloping Demand for Caffè Lattes at the Coffee Bean

The Coffee Bean faces a downward-sloping demand curve. If the price of coffee increases at the Coffee Bean, some but not all of its customers will leave. In this case, an increase in its price from $2.75 to $3.00 leads to a reduction in caffè lattes sold from 2,400 per month to 800 per month.

$3.00, and so on. If we were to graph these numbers, we would get a downward-sloping demand curve.

The third column presents the *total revenue*—the quantity sold (column 1) times the price (column 2). The fourth column shows the firm's *average revenue*—the amount of revenue the firm receives per unit sold. We compute average revenue by dividing total revenue (column 3) by output (column 1) or $AR = TR/q$. In the last column, we show the marginal revenue the firm receives for each additional caffè latte. We find this by looking at the change in total revenue when output changes by 1 unit. For example, when the Coffee Bean sells 2 caffè lattes its total revenue is $6.00. Increasing output to 3 caffè lattes will increase total revenue to $7.50. Thus, the marginal revenue is $1.50; $7.50 − $6.00.

It is important to notice in Exhibit 3 that the marginal revenue curve is below the demand curve. That is, the price on all units must fall if the firm increases its production; consequently, marginal revenue must be less than price. This is true for all firms that face a downward-sloping demand curve. Recall from the Monopoly chapter, when the firm sells more output there are two effects; the output effect and the price effect. For example, in Exhibit 4, we see that if the Coffee Bean wants to sell 4 caffè lattes rather than 3 caffè lattes it will have to lower its price on all 4 caffè lattes from $2.50 to $2.00. This is the *price effect*; the lower price leads to a loss in total revenue ($0.50 × 3 = $1.50). There is also an *output effect*; more output is sold when the Coffee Bean lowers its price ($2 × 1 = $2). That is, more output is sold which increases total revenue. It is the price effect that leads to lower revenue; consequently, marginal revenue is less than price for all firms that face a downward-sloping demand curve. Marginal revenue can become negative when the price effect on revenue is greater than the output effect. Recall, there is no price effect in perfectly competitive markets because the firm can sell all it wants at the going market price.

Determining Short-Run Equilibrium

Because monopolistically competitive sellers are price makers rather than price takers, they do not regard price as a given by market conditions like perfectly competitive firms.

section 14.2 exhibit 2 Demand and Marginal Revenue for Caffè Lattes at the Coffee Bean

Caffè Lattes Sold (q)	Price (P)	Total Revenue (TR = P × q)	Average Revenue (AR = TR/q)	Marginal Revenue (MR = ΔTR/Δq)
0	$4.00	$ 0	—	
				$ 3.50
1	3.50	3.50	$3.50	
				2.50
2	3.00	6.00	3.00	
				1.50
3	2.50	7.50	2.50	
				0.50
4	2.00	8.00	2.00	
				−0.50
5	1.50	7.50	1.50	
				−1.50
6	1.00	6.00	1.00	

section 14.2 exhibit 3 — The Demand Curve and Marginal Revenue Curve for a Monopolistically Competitive Firm

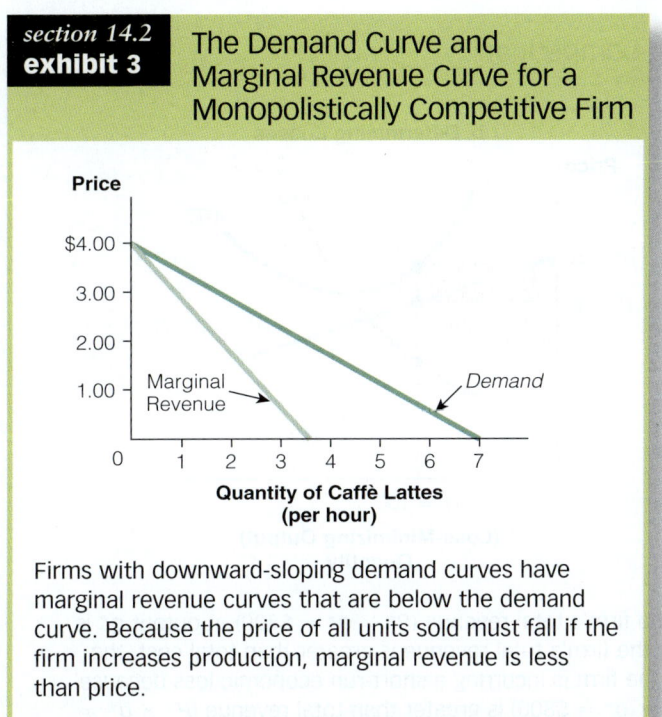

Firms with downward-sloping demand curves have marginal revenue curves that are below the demand curve. Because the price of all units sold must fall if the firm increases production, marginal revenue is less than price.

section 14.2 exhibit 4 — The Price and Output Effect of a Decrease in Price

When a firm with a downward-sloping demand curve increases output, it has two effects on total revenue ($P \times q$)—the output effect (or gain in total revenue because more is sold) and the price effect (a loss in total revenue because the price falls on all units sold).

The cost and revenue curves of a typical seller are shown in Exhibit 5; the intersection of the marginal revenue and marginal cost curves indicates that the short-run profit-maximizing output will be q^*. Now, by observing how much will be demanded at that output level, we find our profit-maximizing price, P^*. That is, at the equilibrium quantity, q^*, we go vertically to the demand curve and read the corresponding price on the vertical axis, P^*.

Three-Step Method for Monopolistic Competition

Let us return to the same three-step method we used in Chapters 12 and 13. Determining whether a firm is generating economic profits, economic losses, or zero economic profits at the profit-maximizing level of output, q^*, can be done in three easy steps.

1. Find where marginal revenues equal marginal costs and proceed straight down to the horizontal quantity axis to find q^*, the profit-maximizing output level.
2. At q^*, go straight up to the demand curve then to the left to find the market price, P^*. Once you have identified P^* and q^*, you can find total revenue at the profit-maximizing output level, because $TR = P \times q$.
3. The last step is to find total costs. Again, go straight up from q^* to the average total cost (ATC) curve then left to the vertical axis to compute the average total cost *per unit*. If we multiply average total costs by the output level, we can find the total costs ($TC = ATC \times q$).

If total revenue is greater than total costs at q^*, the firm is generating total economic profits. And if total revenue is less than total costs at q^*, the firm is generating total economic losses.

Or, if we take the product price at P^* and subtract the average cost at q^*, this will give us per-unit profit. If we multiply this by output, we will arrive at total economic profit, that is, $(P^* - ATC) \times q^* =$ total profit.

Remember, the cost curves include implicit and explicit costs—that is, even at zero economic profits the firm is covering the total opportunity costs of its resources and earning a normal profit or rate of return.

Short-Run Profits and Losses in Monopolistic Competition

Exhibit 5(a) shows the equilibrium position of a monopolistically competitive firm. As we just discussed, the firm produces where $MC = MR$, or output

section 14.2 exhibit 5 — Short-Run Equilibrium in Monopolistic Competition

In (a) the firm is making short-run economic profits because the firm's total revenue ($P^* \times q^* = \$800$) at output q^* is greater than the firm's total cost ($ATC \times q^* = \$700$). Because the firm's total revenue is greater than total cost, the firm has a total profit of \$100; $TR - TC = \$800 - \$700$. In (b) the firm is incurring a short-run economic loss because at q^*, price is below average total cost. At q^*, total cost ($ATC \times q^* = \$800$) is greater than total revenue ($P^* \times q^* = \$700$), so the firm incurs a total loss ($TR - TC = \$700 - \$800 = -\$100$).

q^*. At output q^* and price P^*, the firm's total revenue is equal to $P^* \times q^*$, or \$800. At output q^*, the firm's total cost is $ATC \times q^*$, or \$700. In Exhibit 5(a), we see that total revenue is greater than total cost so the firm has a total economic profit. That is, $TR\ (\$800) - TC\ (\$700) = $ total economic profit (\$100) or $P^*\ (\$8) - ATC\ (\$7) \times q^*\ (100) = \$100$.

In Exhibit 5(b), at q^*, price is below average total cost, so the firm is minimizing its economic loss. At q^*, total cost (\$800) is greater than total revenue (\$700). So the firm incurs a total loss (\$100) or $P^*\ (\$7) - ATC\ (\$8) \times q^*\ (100) = $ total economic losses ($-\$100$).

Determining Long-Run Equilibrium

The short-run equilibrium situation, whether involving profits or losses, will probably not last long, because entry and exit occur in the long run. If market entry and exit are sufficiently free, new firms will have an incentive to enter the market when there are economic profits, and exit when there are economic losses.

What Happens to Economic Profits When Firms Enter the Industry?

In Exhibit 6(a), we see the market impact as new firms enter to take advantage of the economic profits. The result of this influx is more sellers of similar products, which means that each new firm will cut into the demand of the existing firms. That is, the demand curve for each of the existing firms will fall. With entry, not only will the firm's demand curve move inward but it also becomes relatively more elastic due to each firm's products having more substitutes (more choices for consumers). We see this situation in Exhibit 6(a) when demand shifts leftward from D_{SR} to D_{LR}. This decline in demand continues to occur until the average total cost (ATC) curve becomes tangent with the demand curve, and economic profits are reduced to zero.

What Happens to Losses When Some Firms Exit?

When firms are making economic losses, some firms will exit the industry. As some firms exit, it means fewer firms in the market, which increases the demand for the remaining firms' product, shifting their demand curves to the right, from D_{SR} to D_{LR} as seen in

section 14.2 exhibit 6 — Market Entry and Exit in the Long Run

In (a), excess profits attract new firms into the industry. As a result, the firm's share of the market declines and demand shifts down. Profits are eliminated when $P_{LR} = ATC$, that is, when the ATC curve is tangent to D_{LR}. In (b), some firms exit because of economic losses. Their exit increases the demand for existing firms, shifting D_{SR} to D_{LR}, where all losses have been eliminated.

Exhibit 6(b). When firms exit not only will the firm's demand curve move outward but it also becomes relatively more inelastic due to each firm's products having fewer substitutes (less choices for consumers). The higher demand results in smaller losses for the existing firms until all losses finally disappear where the ATC curve is tangent to the demand curve.

Achieving Long-Run Equilibrium

Long-run equilibrium will occur when demand is equal to average total costs for each firm at a level of output at which each firm's demand curve is just tangent to its ATC curve. The point of tangency will always occur at the same level of output as that at which marginal cost is equal to marginal revenue, as seen in Exhibit 7. At this equilibrium point, there are zero economic profits and there are no incentives for firms to either enter or exit the industry.

However, complete adjustment toward equality of price with average cost may be checked by the strength of reputation built up by established firms. Those firms that are particularly successful in their selling efforts may create such strong consumer preferences that newcomers—even though they are able to enter the industry freely and cover their own costs—will not take sufficient business away from the well-established firms to eliminate their excess profits.

section 14.2 exhibit 7 — Long-Run Equilibrium for a Monopolistically Competitive Firm

Long-run equilibrium occurs at q^*, where $D_{LR} = ATC$ and $MR_{LR} = MC$.

Thus, a restaurant that has been particularly successful in promoting customer goodwill may continue to earn excess profits long after the entry of new firms has brought about equality of price and average cost for the others, or even losses. Adjustments toward a final equilibrium situation involving equality of price and average cost do not proceed with the certainty that is supposed to be characteristic of perfect competition.

SECTION CHECK

1. Firms that face downward-sloping demand curves have marginal revenue curves that are below the demand curve because the price on all units sold must fall if the firm increases production. Therefore, marginal revenue must be less than price.
2. A monopolistic competitive firm is making short-run economic profits when the equilibrium price is greater than average total costs at the equilibrium output; when equilibrium price is below average total cost at the equilibrium output, the firm is minimizing its economic loss.
3. In the long run, equilibrium price equals average total costs. With that, economic profits are zero, eliminating incentives for firms to either enter or exit the industry.

1. What is the short-run profit-maximizing policy of a monopolistically competitive firm?
2. How is the choice of whether to operate or shut down in the short run the same for a monopolistic competitor as for a perfectly competitive firm?
3. How is the long-run equilibrium of monopolistic competition like that of perfect competition?
4. How is the long-run equilibrium of monopolistic competition different from that of perfect competition?

SECTION 14.3 Monopolistic Competition Versus Perfect Competition

* What are the differences and similarities between monopolistic competition and perfect competition?
* What is excess capacity?
* Why does the monopolistically competitive firm fail to meet productive efficiency?
* Why does the monopolistically competitive firm fail to meet allocative efficiency?

We have seen that both monopolistic competition and perfect competition have many buyers and sellers and relatively free entry. However, product differentiation enables a monopolistic competitor to have some influence over price. Consequently, a monopolistically competitive firm has a downward-sloping demand curve, but because of the large number of good substitutes for its product, the curve tends to be much more elastic than the demand curve for a monopolist.

The Significance of Excess Capacity

Because in monopolistic competition the demand curve is downward sloping, its point of tangency with the *ATC* curve will not and cannot be at the lowest level of average cost. What does this statement mean? It means that even when long-run adjustments are complete, firms are not operating at a level that permits the lowest average cost of production—the efficient scale of the firm. The existing plant, even though optimal for the equilibrium volume of output, is not used to capacity; that is, **excess capacity** exists at that level of output. Excess capacity occurs when the firm produces below the level where average total cost is minimized.

excess capacity
occurs when the firm produces below the level where average total cost is minimized

Unlike a perfectly competitive firm, a monopolistically competitive firm could increase output and lower its average total cost, as shown in Exhibit 1(a). However, any attempt to increase output to attain lower average cost would be unprofitable,

section 14.3 exhibit 1 — Comparing Long-Run Perfect Competition and Monopolistic Competition

Comparing the differences between perfect competition and monopolistic competition, we see that the monopolistically competitive firm fails to meet both productive efficiency, minimizing costs in the long run, and allocative efficiency, producing output where $P = MC$.

because the price reduction necessary to sell the greater output would cause marginal revenue to fall below the marginal cost of the increased output. As we can see in Exhibit 1(a), to the right of q^*, marginal cost is greater than marginal revenue. Consequently, in monopolistic competition, the tendency is too many firms in the industry, each producing a volume of output less than what would allow lowest cost. Economists call this tendency a failure to reach productive efficiency. For example, the market may have too many grocery stores or too many service stations, in the sense that if the total volume of business were concentrated in a smaller number of sellers, average cost, and thus price, could in principle be less.

Failing to Meet Allocative Efficiency, Too

Productive inefficiency is not the only problem with a monopolistically competitive firm. Exhibit 1(a) shows a firm that is not operating where price is equal to marginal costs. In the monopolistically competitive model, at the intersection of the MC and MR curves (q^*), we can clearly see that price is greater than marginal cost. Society is willing to pay more for the product (the price, P^*) than it costs society to produce it (MC at q^*). In this case, the firm is failing to reach allocative efficiency, where price equals marginal cost. Because the price is greater than the marginal cost, it would be profitable for the monopolistically competitive firm to sell to another customer. If it were a perfectly competitive firm it would not care because price is equal to marginal cost and the extra profit from another customer would be zero.

In short, firms are not producing at the minimum point of ATC, failing to meet productive efficiency and firms are not charging a price equal to marginal cost; failing to meet allocative efficiency. Note that in Exhibit 1(b), the perfectly competitive firm has reached both productive efficiency ($P = ATC$ at the minimum point on the ATC curve) and allocative efficiency ($P = MC$).

However, in defense of monopolistic competition, the higher average cost and the slightly higher price and lower output may simply be the price firms pay for differentiated products—variety. That is, just because monopolistically competitive firms have not met the conditions for productive and allocative efficiency, it is not obvious that society is not better off.

What Are the Real Costs of Monopolistic Competition?

We just argued that perfect competition meets the tests of allocative and productive efficiency and that monopolistic competition does not. Can we "fix" a monopolistically competitive firm to look more like an efficient, perfectly competitive firm? One remedy might entail using government regulation, as in the case of a natural monopoly. However, this process would be costly because a monopolistically competitive firm makes no economic profits in the long run. Therefore, asking monopolistically competitive firms to equate price and marginal cost would lead to economic losses, because long-run average total cost would be greater than price at $P = MC$. Consequently, the government would have to subsidize the firm. Living with the inefficiencies in monopolistically competitive markets might be easier than coping with the difficulties entailed by regulations and the cost of the necessary subsidies.

We argued that the monopolistically competitive firm does not operate at the minimum point of the ATC curve while the perfectly competitive firm does. However, is this comparison fair? A monopolistic competition involves differentiated goods and services, while a perfect competition does not. In other words, the excess capacity that exists in monopolistic competition is the price we pay for product differentiation. Have you ever thought about the many restaurants, movies, and gasoline stations that have "excess capacity"? Can you imagine a world where all firms were working at full capacity? After all, choice is a good, and most of us value some choice.

In short, the inefficiency of monopolistic competition is a result of product differentiation. Because consumers value variety—the ability to choose from competing products and brands—the loss in efficiency must be weighed against the gain in increased product variety. The gains from product diversity can be large and may easily outweigh the inefficiency associated with a downward-sloping demand curve. Remember, firms differentiate their products to meet consumers' demand.

Are the Differences Between Monopolistic Competition and Perfect Competition Exaggerated?

The significance of the difference between the relationship of marginal cost to price in monopolistic competition and in perfect competition can easily be exaggerated. As long as preferences for various brands are not extremely strong, the demand for a firm's products will be highly elastic (flat). Accordingly, the points of tangency with the ATC curves are not likely to be far above the point of lowest cost, and excess capacity will be small, as illustrated in Exhibit 2. Only if differentiation is strong will the difference between the long-run

section 14.3 exhibit 2 The Impact of Product Differentiation

Strong preferences for various brands result in more excess capacity than when the preferences are weak.

price level and the price that would prevail under perfectly competitive conditions be significant.

Remember this little caveat: The theory of the firm is like a road map that does not detail every gully, creek, and hill but does give directions to get from one geographic point to another. Any particular theory of the firm may not tell precisely how an individual firm will operate, but it does provide valuable insight into the ways firms will tend to react to changing economic conditions such as entry, demand, and cost changes.

SECTION CHECK

1. Both the competitive firm and the monopolistically competitive firm may earn short-run economic profits, but these profits will be eliminated in the long run.
2. Because monopolistically competitive firms face a downward-sloping demand curve, average total cost is not minimized in the long run, after entry and exit have eliminated profits. Monopolistically competitive firms fail to reach productive efficiency, producing at output levels less than the efficient output.
3. The monopolistically competitive firm does not achieve allocative efficiency, because it does not operate where the price is equal to marginal costs, which means that society is willing to pay more for additional output than it costs society to produce additional output.

1. Why is a monopolistic competitor's demand curve relatively elastic (flat)?
2. Why do monopolistically competitive firms produce at less than the efficient scale of production?
3. Why do monopolistically competitive firms operate with excess capacity?
4. Why does the fact that price exceeds marginal cost in monopolistic competition lead to allocative inefficiency?
5. What is the price we pay for differentiated goods under monopolistic competition?
6. Why is the difference between the long-run equilibriums under perfect competition and monopolistic competition likely to be relatively small?

SECTION 14.4 Advertising

* Why do firms advertise?
* Is advertising good or bad from society's perspective?
* Will advertising always increase costs?
* Can advertising increase demand?

Why Do Firms Advertise?

Advertising is an important nonprice method of competition that is commonly used in industries where the firm has market power. It would make little sense for a perfectly competitive firm to advertise its products. Recall that the perfectly competitive firm sells a homogeneous product and can sell all it wants at the market price—so why spend money to advertise to encourage consumers to buy more of its product? Why do some firms advertise? The reason is simple: By advertising, firms hope to increase the demand and create a less elastic demand curve for their products, thus enhancing revenues and profits. In short, this is how monopolistically competitive firms can differentiate their products to appeal to consumers. Advertising is part of our life, whether we are watching television, listening to the radio, reading a newspaper or magazine, or simply driving down the highway. Firms that sell differentiated products can spend between 10 and 20 percent of their revenue on advertising. Advertising to differentiate products is also important in oligopoly, as we will see in the next chapter.

Use what you've LEARNED: ADVERTISING

Q Why is it so important for monopolistically competitive firms to advertise?

A Owners of fast-food restaurants must compete with many other restaurants, so they often must advertise to demonstrate that their restaurant is different. Advertising may convince customers that a firm's products or services are better than others, which then may influence the shape and position of the demand curve for the products and potentially increase profits. Remember, monopolistically competitive firms are different from competitive firms because of their ability, to some extent, to set prices.

Is Advertising "Good" or "Bad" from Society's Perspective?

What Is the Impact of Advertising on Society?

This question elicits sharply different responses. Some have argued that advertising manipulates consumer tastes and wastes billions of dollars annually creating "needs" for trivial products. Advertising helps create a demonstration effect, whereby people have new urges to buy products previously unknown to them. In creating additional demands for private goods, the ability to provide needed public goods (for which little advertising is needed to create demand) is potentially reduced. Moreover, sometimes advertising is based on misleading claims, so people find themselves buying products that do not provide the satisfaction or results promised in the ads. Finally, advertising itself requires resources that raise average costs and increase prices.

On the other hand, who is to say that the purchase of any product is frivolous or unnecessary? If one believes that people are rational and should be permitted freedom of expression, the argument against advertising loses some of its force. In addition, advertisers might be focusing in on what consumer's want rather than what producers want to sell.

Furthermore, defenders of advertising argue that firms use advertising to provide important information about the price and availability of a product, the location and hours of store operation, and so on. For example, a real estate ad might state when a rental unit is available, the location, the price, the number of bedrooms and bathrooms, wood floors, and proximity to mass transit, freeways, or schools. This information allows for customers to make better choices and allows markets to function more efficiently. An expensive ad on television or in the telephone book *may signal* to consumers that this product may come from a relatively large and successful company. Finally, a nationally recognized *brand name* will provide consumers with confidence about the quality of its product. It will also distinguish its product from others. For example, brand names such as Ritz-Carlton, Double Tree, or Motel 6 will provide the buyer with information about the quality of the accommodations more so than the No-Tell Motel. Or consider a national chain restaurant such as McDonald's or Burger King versus the Greasy Spoon Coffee Shop—consumers expect consistent quality from a chain restaurant. The chain name may also send a *signal* to the buyer that the company expects repeat business and, therefore, it has an important reputation to uphold. This aspect may help it assume even greater quality in the consumers' eyes.

Will Advertising Always Increase Costs?

Even though it is true that advertising may raise the average total cost, it is possible that when substantial economies of scale exist, the average production cost will decline more than the amount of the per-unit cost of advertising. In other words, average total cost, in some situations, actually declines after extensive advertising, because advertising may allow the firm to operate closer to the point of minimum cost on its *ATC* curve. Specifically, notice in Exhibit 1 that the average total cost curve before advertising is $ATC_{BEFORE\ ADVERTISING}$. After advertising, the curve shifts upward to $ATC_{AFTER\ ADVERTISING}$. If the increase in demand resulting from advertising is significant, economies of scale from higher output levels may offset the advertising costs. Average total cost may fall from C_1 to C_2, a movement from point A to point B, and allow the firm to sell its product at a lower price. Therefore, it is possible for the decline in production costs (through specialization and division of labor in the short run and/or economies of scale in the long run) to exceed the added advertising cost, per unit of output, thus allowing the firm to sell its product at a lower price; Toys"R"Us versus a smaller, owner-operated toy store provides an example.

However, it also is possible that an advertising war between two firms, say Burger King and McDonald's, will result in higher advertising costs for both and no gain in market share (increased output) for either. This possibility is shown as a movement from point A to point C in Exhibit 2. Output remains at q_1, but average total cost rises from C_1 to C_3.

Firms in monopolistic competition are not likely to experience substantial cost reductions as output increases. Therefore, they probably will not be able to offset advertising costs with lower production costs, particularly if advertising costs are high. Even if advertising does add to total cost, however, it is true that advertising conveys information. Through advertising, customers become aware of the options available to them in terms of product choice. Advertising helps customers choose products that best meet their needs, and it informs price-conscious customers about the costs of products. In this way, advertising lowers information costs, which is one reason that the Federal Trade Commission opposes bans on advertising.

What If Advertising Increases Competition?

The idea that advertising reduces information costs leads to some interesting economic implications. For example, say that as a result of advertising, we know about more products that may be substitutes for the products we have been buying for years. That is, the more goods that are advertised, the more consumers are aware of "substitute" products, which leads to increasingly competitive markets. Studies in the eyeglass,

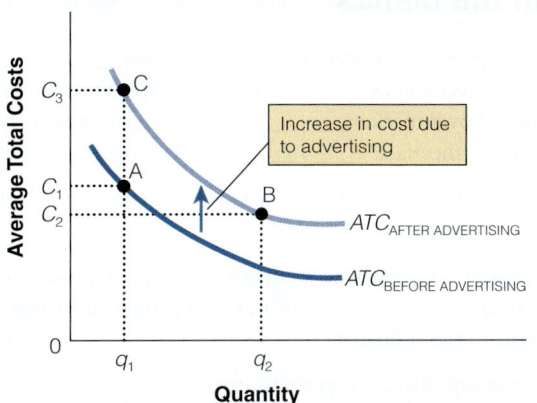

section 14.4 exhibit 1 Advertising and Economies of Scale

The average total cost before advertising is shown as $ATC_{BEFORE\ ADVERTISING}$. After advertising, the curve shifts to $ATC_{AFTER\ ADVERTISING}$. If the increase in demand resulting from advertising is significant, economies of scale from higher output levels may offset the advertising costs, lowering average total cost. The movement from point A to point B allows the firm to sell its product at a lower price. However, when two firms engage in an advertising war, it is possible that neither will gain market share (increased output) but each will incur higher advertising costs. This possibility is shown as a movement from point A to point C—output remains at q_1, but average total cost rises from C_1 to C_3.

toy, and drug industries have shown that advertising increases competition and leads to lower prices in these markets. In short, critics of advertising argue that impedes competition, alters consumer's tastes and may lead to "irrational" brand loyalty. But defenders believe it can increase competition and quality and often provides valuable product and service information.

SECTION CHECK

1. With advertising, a firm hopes it can alter the elasticity of the demand for its product, making it more inelastic and causing an increase in demand that will enhance profits.
2. To some, advertising manipulates consumer tastes and creates "needs" for trivial products. However, if one believes that people act rationally, this argument loses some of its force.
3. Where substantial economies of scale exist, it is possible that average production costs will decline more than the amount of per-unit costs of advertising in the long run. Even in the short run, specialization and division of labor may cause advertising to decrease average costs.
4. By making consumers aware of different "substitute" products, advertising may lead to more competitive markets and lower consumer prices.

1. How can advertising make a firm's demand curve more inelastic?
2. What are the arguments made against advertising?
3. What are the arguments made for advertising?
4. Can advertising actually result in lower costs? How?

Interactive Chapter Summary

Fill in the blanks:

1. Monopolistic competition is similar to both _____ and perfect competition. As in monopoly, firms have some control over market _____, but as in perfect competition, they face _____ from many other sellers.

2. Due to the free entry of new firms, long-run economic profits in monopolistic competition are _____.

3. Firms in monopolistic competition produce products that are _____ from those produced by other firms in the industry.

4. In monopolistic competition, firms use _____ names to gain some degree of control over price.

5. The theory of monopolistic competition is based on three characteristics: (1) product _____, (2) many _____, and (3) free _____.

6. Product differentiation is the accentuation of _____ product qualities to develop a product identity.

7. Monopolistic competitive sellers are price _____ and they do not regard price as given by the market. Because products in the industry are slightly different each firm faces a(n) _____ sloping demand curve.

8. In the short run, equilibrium output is determined where marginal revenue equals marginal _____. The price is set equal to the _____ the consumer will pay for this amount.

9. When price is greater than average total costs, the monopolistic competitive firm will make an economic _____.

10. Barriers to entry do not protect monopolistic competitive firms in the _____ run. Economic profits will _____ new firms to the industry. Similarly, firms will leave when there are economic _____.

11. Long-run equilibrium in a monopolistic competitive industry occurs when the firm experiences _____ economic profits or losses, which eliminates incentive for firms to _____ or _____ the industry.

12. Because it faces competition, a monopolistically competitive firm has a(n) _____ sloping demand curve that tends to be more _____ than the demand curve for a monopolist.

13. Even in the long run, monopolistically competitive firms do not operate at levels that permit the full realization of _____ of scale.

14. Unlike a perfectly competitive firm in long-run equilibrium, a monopolistically competitive firm will produce with _____ capacity. The firm could lower average costs by increasing output, but this move would reduce _____.

15. In monopolistic competition the tendency is toward too _____ firms in the industry. Monopolistically competitive industries will not reach _____ efficiency, because firms in the industry do not produce at the _____ per-unit cost.

16. In monopolistic competition, firms operate where price is _____ than marginal cost, which means that consumers are willing to pay _____ for the product than it costs society to produce it. In this case, the firm fails to reach _____ efficiency.

17. Although average costs and prices are higher under monopolistic competition than they are under perfect competition, society gets a benefit from monopolistic competition in the form of _____ products.

18. Advertising is an important type of _____ competition that firms use to _____ the demand for their products.

19. Advertising may not only increase the demand facing a firm, it may also make the demand facing the firm more _____ if it convinces buyers the product is truly different. A more inelastic demand curve means price changes will have relatively _____ effects on the quantity demanded of the product.

20. Critics of advertising assert that it _____ average total costs while manipulating consumers' tastes. However, if people are _____, this argument loses some of its force.

21. When advertising is used in industries with significant economies of _____, per-unit costs may decline by more than per-unit advertising costs.

22. An important function of advertising is to lower the cost of acquiring _____ about the availability of substitutes and the _____ of products.

23. By making information about substitutes and prices less costly to acquire, advertising will increase the _____ in industries, which is good for consumers.

Answers: 1. monopoly; price; competition 2. zero 3. differentiated 4. brand 5. differentiation; sellers; entry 6. unique 7. makers; negatively 8. cost; maximum 9. profit 10. long; attract; losses 11. zero; enter; exit 12. downward; elastic 13. economies 14. excess; profits 15. many; productive; lowest 16. greater; more; allocative 17. differentiated 18. nonprice; increase 19. inelastic; smaller 20. raises; rational 21. scale 22. information; prices 23. competition

Key Terms and Concepts

monopolistic competition   401   product differentiation   401   excess capacity   408

Section Check Answers

14.1 Monopolistic Competition

1. **How is monopolistic competition a mixture of monopoly and perfect competition?**
   Monopolistic competition is like monopoly in that sellers' actions can change the price. It is like competition in that it is characterized by competition from substitute products, many sellers, and relatively free entry.

2. **Why is product differentiation necessary for monopolistic competition?**
   Product differentiation is the source of the monopoly power each monopolistically competitive seller (a monopolist of its own brand) has. If products were homogeneous, others' products would be perfect substitutes for the products of any particular firm, and such a firm would have no market power as a result.

3. **What are some common forms of product differentiation?**
   Forms of product differentiation include physical differences, prestige differences, location differences, and service differences.

4. **Why are many sellers necessary for monopolistic competition?**
   Many sellers are necessary in the monopolistic competition model because it means that a particular firm has little control over what other firms do; with only a few firms in an industry, they would begin to consider competitors as individuals (rather than only as a group) whose policies will be influenced by their own actions.

5. **Why is free entry necessary for monopolistic competition?**
   Free entry is necessary in the monopolistic competition model because entry in this type of market is what tends to eliminate economic profits in the long run, as in perfect competition.

14.2 Price and Output Determination in Monopolistic Competition

1. **What is the short-run profit-maximizing policy of a monopolistically competitive firm?**
   A monopolistic competitor maximizes its short-run profits by producing the quantity (and corresponding price along the demand curve) at which marginal revenue equals marginal cost.

2. **How is the choice of whether to operate or shut down in the short run the same for a monopolistic competitor as for a perfectly competitive firm?**
   Because a firm will lose its fixed costs if it shuts down, it will shut down if price is expected to remain below average variable cost, regardless of market structure, because operating in that situation results in even greater losses than shutting down.

3. **How is the long-run equilibrium of monopolistic competition like that of perfect competition?**
   The long-run equilibrium of monopolistic competition is like that of perfect competition in that entry, when the industry makes short-run economic profits, and exit, when it makes short-run economic losses, drives economic profits to zero in the long run.

4. **How is the long-run equilibrium of monopolistic competition different from that of perfect competition?**
   For zero economic profits in long-run equilibrium at the same time each seller faces a downward-sloping demand curve, a firm's downward-sloping demand curve must be just tangent to its average cost curve (because that is the situation where a firm earns zero economic profits and that is the best the firm can do), resulting in costs greater than the minimum possible average cost. This same tangency to long-run cost curves characterizes the long-run zero economic profit equilibrium in perfect competition; but because firm demand curves are horizontal in perfect competition, that tangency comes at the minimum point of firm average cost curves.

14.3 Monopolistic Competition Versus Perfect Competition

1. **Why is a monopolistic competitor's demand curve relatively elastic (flat)?**
   A monopolistic competitor has a downward-sloping demand curve because of product differentiation; but because of the large number of good substitutes for its product, its demand curve is very elastic.

2. **Why do monopolistically competitive firms produce at less than the efficient scale of production?**

   Because monopolistically competitive firms have downward-sloping demand curves, their long-run zero-profit equilibrium tangency between demand and long-run average total cost must occur along the downward-sloping part of the long-run average total cost curve. Because this level of output does not allow the full realization of all economies of scale, it results in a less than efficient scale of production.

3. **Why do monopolistically competitive firms operate with excess capacity?**

   Monopolistically competitive firms operate with excess capacity because the zero-profit tangency equilibrium occurs along the downward-sloping part of a firm's short-run average cost curve, so the firm's plant has the capacity to produce more output at lower average cost than it is actually producing.

4. **Why does the fact that price exceeds marginal cost in monopolistic competition lead to allocative inefficiency?**

   The fact that price exceeds marginal cost in monopolistic competition leads to allocative inefficiency because some goods for which the marginal value (measured by willingness to pay along a demand curve) exceeds their marginal cost are not traded and the net gains that would have resulted from those trades are therefore lost. However, the degree of that inefficiency is relatively small because firms face a very elastic demand curve so the resulting output restriction is small.

5. **What is the price we pay for differentiated goods under monopolistic competition?**

   Under monopolistic competition, excess capacity can be considered the price we pay for differentiated goods, because it is the "cost" we pay for the value we get from the additional choices and variety offered by differentiated products.

6. **Why is the difference between the long-run equilibriums under perfect competition and monopolistic competition likely to be relatively small?**

   Even though monopolistically competitive firms face downward-sloping demand curves, which is the cause of the excess capacity and higher than necessary costs in these markets, those demand curves are likely to be highly elastic because of the large number of close substitutes. Therefore, the deviation from perfectly competitive results is likely to be relatively small.

14.4 Advertising

1. **How can advertising make a firm's demand curve more inelastic?**

   Advertising is intended to increase a firm's demand curve by increasing consumer awareness of the firm's products and improving its image. It is intended to make its demand curve more inelastic by convincing buyers that its products are truly different (better) than alternatives (remember that the number of good substitutes is the primary determinant of a firm's elasticity of demand).

2. **What are the arguments made against advertising?**

   Some people argue that advertising manipulates consumer tastes and creates artificial "needs" for unimportant products, taking resources away from more valuable uses.

3. **What are the arguments made for advertising?**

   The essential argument for advertising is that it conveys valuable information to potential customers about the products and options available to them and the prices at which they are available, helping them to make choices that better match their situations and preferences.

4. **Can advertising actually result in lower costs? How?**

   Advertising can lower costs by increasing sales, thereby lowering production costs if a company can realize economies of scale. Overall costs and prices may be lowered as a result, if the savings in production costs are greater than the additional costs of advertising.

CHAPTER 14 STUDY GUIDE

True or False:

1. Monopolistic competition is a mixture of monopoly and perfect competition.
2. All firms in monopolistically competitive industries earn economic profits in the long run.
3. By differentiating their products and promoting brand-name loyalty, firms in monopolistic competition can raise prices without losing all their customers.
4. In monopolistic competition, as in perfect competition, all firms in an industry charge the same price.
5. Competitive firms and monopolistic competitive firms follow the same general rule when deciding how much to produce.
6. A monopolistic competitor's demand curve is relatively inelastic (steep).
7. Unlike perfectly competitive firms, firms in monopolistic competition will operate with excess capacity, even in the long run.
8. Although certain inefficiencies are associated with monopolistic competition, society receives a benefit from monopolistic competition in the form of differentiated goods and services.
9. Even though advertising will add to the cost of production, it may lead to significant economies of scale that may lower the per-unit total cost.
10. Misleading claims and preposterous bragging about products are a type of advertising that will result in increased demand for a firm's products.

Multiple Choice:

1. Which of the following is *not* a source of product differentiation?
   a. physical differences in products
   b. differences in quantities that firms offer for sale
   c. differences in service provided by firms
   d. differences in location of sales outlets

2. Which of the following characteristics do monopolistic competition and perfect competition have in common?
   a. Individual firms believe that they can influence market price.
   b. Firms sell brand-name products.
   c. Firms are able to earn long-run economic profits.
   d. Competing firms can enter the industry easily.

3. Firms in monopolistically competitive industries cannot earn economic profits in the long run because
   a. government regulators, whose first interest is the public good, will impose regulations that limit economic profits.
   b. the additional costs of product differentiation will eliminate long-run economic profits.
   c. economic profits will attract competitors whose presence will eliminate profits in the long run.
   d. whenever one firm in the industry begins making economic profits, others will lower their prices, thus eliminating long-run economic profits.

4. Maria's West Side Bakery is the only bakery on the west side of the city. She is a monopolistic competitor and she is open for business. Which of the following *cannot* be true of Maria's profits?
   a. She is making an economic profit.
   b. She is making neither an economic profit nor a loss.
   c. She is making an economic loss that is less than her fixed cost.
   d. She is making an economic loss that is greater than her fixed cost.

5. Claire is considering buying the only Hungarian restaurant in Boise, Idaho. The restaurant's unique food means that it faces a negatively sloped demand curve and is currently earning an economic profit. Why shouldn't Claire assume that the current profits will continue when she makes her decision?
   a. Claire will not earn those profits right away because she doesn't know much about cooking.
   b. The firm is a monopolist, which attracts government regulation.
   c. Current economic profits will be eliminated by the entry of competitors.
   d. While economic profits are positive, accounting profits may be negative.

Use the accompanying diagram to answer questions 6–7.

6. Which of the demand curves represents a long-run equilibrium for the firm?
   a. D_0
   b. D_1
   c. D_2
   d. D_3

7. Which of the demand curves will result in the firm shutting down in the short run?
   a. D_0
   b. D_1
   c. D_2
   d. D_3

8. In the long run, firms in monopolistic competition do not attain productive efficiency because they produce
   a. at a point where economic profits are positive.
   b. at a point where marginal revenue is less than marginal cost.
   c. at a point to the left of the low point of their long-run average total cost curve.
   d. where marginal cost is equal to long-run average total cost.

9. In the long run, firms in monopolistic competition do not attain allocative efficiency because they
   a. operate where price equals marginal cost.
   b. do not operate where price equals marginal cost.
   c. produce more output than society wants.
   d. charge prices that are less than production costs.

10. Compared to perfect competition, firms in monopolist competition in the long run produce
    a. less output at a lower cost.
    b. less output at a higher cost.
    c. more output at a lower cost.
    d. more output at a higher cost.

11. If Rolf wants to use advertising to reduce the elasticity of demand for his chiropractic services, he must make sure the advertising
    a. clearly states the prices he charges.
    b. shows that he is producing a product like that of the other chiropractors in town.

c. shows why his services are truly different from the other chiropractors in town.
d. explains the hours and days that he is open for business.

12. Advertising about prices by firms in an industry will make an industry more competitive because it
    a. reduces the cost of finding a substitute when one producer raises his price.
    b. assures the consumers that prices are the same everywhere.
    c. increases the cost for all firms because of the existence of economies of scale.
    d. reduces the number of firms because of the existence of economies of scale.

Problems:

1. Which of the following markets are perfectly competitive or monopolistically competitive. Why?
    a. soy market
    b. retail clothing stores
    c. Spago's Restaurant Beverly Hills

2. List three ways in which a grocery store might differentiate itself from its competitors.

3. What might make you choose one gas station over another?

4. If Frank's hot dog stand was profitable when he first opened, why should he expect those profits to fall over time?

5. Draw a graph showing a monopolistically competitive firm in a short-run equilibrium where it is earning positive economic profits. What must be true of price versus average total cost for such a firm? What will happen to the firm's demand curve as a result of the short-run profits?

6. Draw a graph showing a monopolistically competitive firm in a short-run equilibrium where it is earning economic losses. What must be true of price versus average total cost for such a firm? What will happen to the firm's demand curve as a result of the short-run losses?

7. How are monopolistically competitive firms and perfectly competitive firms similar? Why don't monopolistically competitive firms produce the same output in the long run as perfectly competitive firms, which face similar costs?

8. Can you explain why some restaurants are highly profitable while other restaurants in the same general area are going out of business?

9. Suppose that half the restaurants in a city are closed so that the remaining eateries can operate at full capacity. What "cost" might restaurant patrons incur as a result?

10. How is price related to marginal and average total cost for monopolistically competitive firms in the following situations?
    a. a short-run equilibrium where it is earning positive economic profits
    b. a short-run equilibrium where it is earning negative economic profits
    c. a short-run equilibrium where it is earning zero economic profits
    d. a long-run equilibrium

11. What is meant by the price of variety? Graph and explain.

12. How does Starbucks differentiate its product? Why does Starbucks stay open until late at night but a donut or bagel shop might close at noon?

13. How are monopolistically competitive firms and perfectly competitive firms similar? Why don't monopolistically competitive firms produce the same output in the long run as perfectly competitive firms, which face similar costs?

14. Why is advertising more important for the success of chains such as Toys "R" Us and Office Depot than for the corner barbershop?

15. Think of your favorite ads on television. Do you think that these ads have an effect on your spending? These ads are expensive; do you think they are a waste from society's standpoint?

16. Product differentiation is a hallmark of monopolistic competition, and the text lists four sources of such differentiation: physical differences, prestige, location, and service. How do firms in the industries listed here differentiate their products? How important is each of the four sources of differentiation in each case? Give the most important source of differentiation in each case.
    a. fast-food restaurants
    b. espresso shops/carts
    c. hair stylists
    d. soft drinks
    e. wine

17. As you know, perfect competition and monopolistic competition differ in important ways. Show your understanding of these differences by listing the following terms under either "perfect competition" or "monopolistic competition."

		Perfect Competition	Monopolistic Competition
standardized product	productive efficiency	_____	_____
differentiated product	horizontal demand curve	_____	_____
allocative efficiency	downward-sloping demand curve	_____	_____
excess capacity	no control over price	_____	_____

18. In what way is the use of advertising another example of Adam Smith's "Invisible Hand," according to which entrepreneurs pursuing their own best interest make consumers better off?

19. How does advertising intend to shift demand? How does it intend to change the elasticity of demand?

15

Oligopoly and Strategic Behavior

15.1 Oligopoly

15.2 Collusion and Cartels

15.3 Other Oligopoly Models

15.4 Game Theory and Strategic Behavior

Oligopoly is a market structure where a few large firms dominate an industry. Examples of oligopolistic markets include commercial airlines, oil, automobiles, steel, breakfast cereals, computers, cigarettes, tobacco, and sports drinks.

In all of these instances, the market is dominated by anywhere from a few to several big companies, although they may have many different brands (e.g., General Motors, General Foods, Apple Computers). In this chapter, we will learn about the unique characteristics of firms in this industry. ■

Section 15.1 Oligopoly

- What is oligopoly?
- What is mutual interdependence?
- Are economies of scale a major barrier to entry?
- Why is it so difficult for the oligopolist to determine its profit-maximizing price and output?

What Is Oligopoly?

As we discussed in Chapter 12, oligopolies exist, by definition, where relatively few firms control all or most of the production and sale of a product ("oligopoly" = few sellers). The products may be homogeneous or differentiated, but the barriers to entry are often high, which makes it difficult for firms to enter into the industry. Consequently, long-run economic profits may be earned by firms in the industry.

Mutual Interdependence

mutual interdependence when a firm shapes its policy with an eye to the policies of competing firms

Oligopoly is characterized by **mutual interdependence** among firms; that is, each firm shapes its policy with an eye to the policies of competing firms. Oligopolists must strategize, much like good chess or bridge players who are constantly observing and anticipating the moves of their rivals. Oligopoly is likely to occur whenever the number of firms in an industry is so small that any change in output or price by one firm appreciably impacts the sales of competing firms. In this situation, it is almost inevitable that competitors will respond directly to these actions in determining their own policy.

Why Do Oligopolies Exist?

Primarily, oligopoly is a result of the relationship between the technological conditions of production and potential sales volume. For many products, a firm cannot obtain a reasonably low cost of production unless it is producing a large fraction of the market output. In other words, substantial economies of scale are present in oligopoly markets. Automobile and steel production are classic examples of this. Because of legal concerns such as patents, large start-up costs, and the presence of pronounced economies of scale, the barriers to entry are quite high in oligopoly.

Measuring Industry Concentration

The extent of oligopoly power in various industries can be measured by means of concentration ratios. A concentration ratio indicates the proportion of total industry shipments (sales) of goods produced by a specified number of the largest firms in the industry, or the proportion of total industry assets held by these largest firms. We can use four-firm or eight-firm concentration ratios; most often, concentration ratios are for the four largest firms.

The extent of oligopoly power is indicated by the four-firm concentration ratio for the United States shown in Exhibit 1. Note that for breakfast cereals, to take an example, the four largest firms produce 87 percent of all breakfast cereals produced in the United

section 15.1 exhibit 1 Four-Firm Concentration Ratios, U.S. Manufacturing

Industry	Share of Value of Shipments by the Top Four Firms (%)
Tobacco products	96
Breweries	91
Motor vehicles	90
Electric lightbulbs	89
Small arms ammunition	89
Refrigerators	88
Breakfast cereals	87
Aircraft	85
Soaps, detergents	73
Tires	69
Motorcycles and bicycles	68
Lawn and garden equipment	65
Coffee and tea	58

SOURCE: U.S. Census Bureau.

States. Concentration ratios of 70 to 100 percent are common in oligopolies. That is, a high concentration ratio means that a few sellers dominate the market.

Concentration ratios, however, are not a perfect guide to industry concentration. One problem is that they do not take into consideration foreign competition. For example, the U.S. auto industry is highly concentrated but faces stiff competition from foreign automobile producers. The same is true for motorcycles and bicycles.

Economies of Scale as a Barrier to Entry

Economies of large-scale production make operation on a small scale during a new firm's early years extremely unprofitable. A firm cannot build up

section 15.1 exhibit 2 Economies of Scale as a Barrier to Entry

Economies of large-scale production make operation on a small scale more costly, *ceteris paribus*.

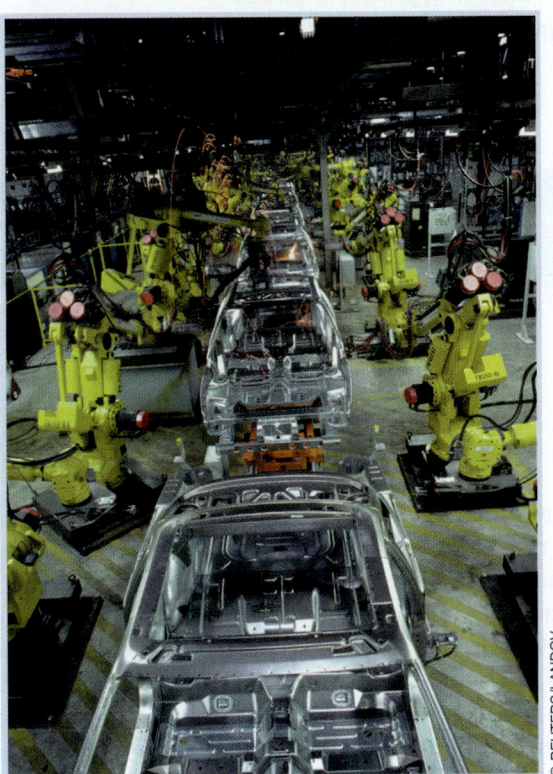

Do you think economies of scale are important in this industry? Unlike home-cooked meals, few cars are "homemade." The barriers to entry in the auto industry are formidable. A new entrant would have to start out as a large producer (investing billions of dollars in plant, equipment, and advertising) to compete with existing firms, which have lower average total costs per unit because of economies of large-scale production.

a large market overnight; in the interim, average total cost is so high that losses are heavy. Recognition of this fact discourages new firms from entering the market, as illustrated in Exhibit 2. We can see that if an automobile company produces quantity Q_{LARGE} rather than Q_{SMALL}, it will be able to produce cars at a significantly lower cost. If the average total cost to a potential entrant is equivalent to point A on the ATC curve and the price of automobiles is less than P_1, a new firm would be deterred from entering the industry.

Equilibrium Price and Quantity in Oligopoly

It is difficult to predict how firms will react in situations of mutual interdependence. No firm knows what its demand curve looks like with any degree of certainty, and therefore it has a limited knowledge of its marginal revenue curve. To know anything about its demand curve, the firm must know how other firms will react to its prices and other policies. In the absence of additional assumptions, then, equating marginal revenue and expected marginal cost is relegated to guesswork. Thus, it is difficult for an oligopolist to determine its profit-maximizing price and output.

SECTION CHECK

1. Oligopolies exist where relatively few firms control all or most of the production and sale of a product. The products may be homogeneous or differentiated, but the barriers to entry are often very high and, consequently, they may be able to realize long-run economic profits.
2. When firms are mutually interdependent, each firm shapes its policy with an eye to the policies of competing firms.
3. Economies of large-scale production make operation on a small scale extremely unprofitable. Recognition of this fact discourages new firms from entering the market.
4. Because in oligopoly the pricing decision of one firm influences the demand curve of competing firms, the oligopolist faces considerable uncertainty as to the location and shape of its demand and marginal revenue curves. Thus, it is difficult for an oligopolist to determine its profit-maximizing price and output.

---

1. How can concentration ratios indicate the extent of oligopolies' power?
2. Why is oligopoly characterized by mutual interdependence?
3. Why do economies of scale result in few sellers in oligopoly models?
4. How do economies of scale result in barriers to entry in oligopoly models?
5. Why does an oligopolist have a difficult time finding its profit-maximizing price and output?
6. Why would an automobile manufacturer be more likely than the corner baker to be an oligopolist

SECTION 15.2 Collusion and Cartels

* Why do firms collude?
* What is joint profit maximization?
* Why does collusion break down?

Uncertainty and Pricing Decisions

The uncertainties of pricing decisions are substantial in oligopoly. The implications of misjudging the behavior of competitors could prove to be disastrous. An executive who makes the wrong pricing move may force the firm to lose sales or, at a minimum, be forced himself to back down in an embarrassing fashion from an announced price increase. Because of this uncertainty, some believe that oligopolists change their prices less frequently than perfect competitors, whose prices may change almost continually. The empirical evidence, however, does not clearly indicate that prices are in fact always slow to change in oligopoly situations.

Collusion

Because the actions and profits of oligopolists are so dominated by mutual interdependence, the temptation is great for firms to **collude**—to get together and agree to act jointly in pricing and other matters. If firms believe they can increase their profits by coordinating their actions, they will be tempted to collude. Collusion reduces uncertainty and increases the potential for economic profits. From society's point of view, collusion creates a situation in which goods very likely become overpriced and underproduced, with consumers losing out as the result of a misallocation of resources.

collude
when firms act together to restrict competition

cartel
a collection of firms that agree on sales, pricing, and other decisions

Joint Profit Maximization

Agreements between or among firms on sales, pricing, and other decisions are usually referred to as cartel agreements. A **cartel** is a collection of firms making an agreement.

Cartels may lead to what economists call **joint profit maximization:** Price is based on the marginal revenue function, which is derived from the product's total (or market) demand schedule and the various firms' marginal cost schedules, as shown in Exhibit 1. With outright agreements—necessarily secret because of antitrust laws (in the United States, at least)—firms that make up the market will attempt to estimate demand and cost schedules and then set optimum price and output levels accordingly.

joint profit maximization determination of price based on the marginal revenue derived from the market demand schedule and marginal cost schedule of the firms in the industry

Equilibrium price and quantity for a collusive oligopoly are determined according to the intersection of the marginal revenue curve (derived from the market demand curve) and the horizontal sum of the short-run marginal cost curves for the oligopolists. As shown in Exhibit 1, the resulting equilibrium quantity is Q^* and the equilibrium price is P^*. Collusion facilitates joint profit maximization for the oligopoly. If the oligopoly is maintained in the long run, it charges a

section 15.2 exhibit 1 Collusion in Oligopoly

In collusive oligopoly, the producers would restrict joint output to Q^*, setting their price at P^*. The members of the collusive oligopoly would share the profits in the shaded area.

in the news: The Crash of an Airline Collusion

Mr. Crandall: I think it's dumb as @#$% for !@#$%* sake, . . . to sit here and pound the @#$% out of each other and neither one of us making a #!@!$&* dime. I mean, you know, @!#$, what the @#$!, is the point of it.

Mr. Putnam: Do you have a suggestion for me?

Mr. Crandall: Yes, I have a suggestion for you. Raise your @#$&!$% fares 20 percent. I'll raise mine the next morning. . . . You'll make more money and I will, too.

Mr. Putnam: We can't talk about pricing!

Mr. Crandall: Oh @#$% we can talk about any @#$%&*# thing we want to talk about.

consider this:
At the time of this conversation, Crandall was the president of American Airlines and Putnam was the president of Braniff Airlines. According to the Sherman Antitrust Act, it is illegal for corporate leaders to talk about and propose price fixing with their competitors. Putnam turned the tapes of this conversation over to the Justice Department. After reviewing the tapes, the Justice Department ruled that attempts to fix prices could monopolize the airline industry. American Airlines promised they would not engage in this type of activity again.

SOURCE: Staff, "American Air Accused of Bid to Fix Prices," *The Wall Street Journal*, February 24, 1983, pp. 2, 23.

global WATCH: THE OPEC CARTEL

The most spectacularly successful example of a collusive oligopoly able to earn monopoly-type profits is the Organization of Petroleum Exporting Countries (OPEC) cartel. Although organized in 1960, it only became successful as a collusive oligopoly in 1973.

OPEC began acting as a cartel in part because of political concern over U.S. support for Israel. For 20 years before 1973, the price of crude oil had hovered around $2 a barrel. In 1973, OPEC members agreed to quadruple oil prices in nine months; later price increases pushed the cost of a barrel of oil to more than $20. Prices then stabilized, falling in real terms (adjusted for inflation) between 1973 and 1978 as OPEC sought the profit-maximizing price and politics remained relatively calm. By the early 1980s, however, prices were approaching $40 per barrel. Exhibit 2 illustrates the relative impact of the OPEC cartel on the supply and price of oil.

section 15.2 exhibit 2 The Impact of the OPEC Cartel

The OPEC nations were successful with their pricing policies between 1973 and the early 1980s for several reasons. First, the worldwide demand for petroleum was highly inelastic with respect to price in the short run. Second, OPEC's share of total world oil output had steadily increased, from around 20 percent of total world output in the early 1940s to about 70 percent by 1973, when OPEC became an effective cartel. Third, the price elasticity of supply of petroleum from OPEC's competitors was low in the short run: Ability to increase production from existing wells is limited, and it takes time to drill new ones.

From the mid-1980s to the mid-1990s, OPEC oil prices hovered around $20 per barrel because of increases in non-OPEC production and the uncertain willingness of key suppliers (such as Saudi Arabia) to restrict supply. Moreover, at the higher prices of the 1970s, long-run substitution possibilities caused oil consumption to fall almost 5 percent per year, with conservation and alternative energy easing the demand for OPEC oil. After adjusting for inflation, oil prices during most of the 1990s was roughly the same as it was before OPEC formed.

OPEC now controls less than one-third of world oil production and surprisingly it still has some clout as a cartel. However, it is not just OPEC. High oil prices still emerge because of growing world demand and the political instability in the Middle East. By July 2006, oil prices had reached $78 per barrel. However, in real terms (adjusted for inflation), a barrel would have to reach $90 to beat the mark it set in 1980. In 2008, in the midst of a worldwide recession, the price of oil fell below $40, despite OPEC's attempts to keep prices higher.

higher price, produces less output, and fails to maximize social welfare, relative to perfect competition, because $P^* > MC$ at Q^*.

The manner in which total profits are shared among firms in the industry depends in part on the relative costs and sales of the various firms. Firms with low costs and large supply capabilities will obtain the largest profits, because they have greater bargaining power. Sales, in turn, may depend in large measure on consumer preferences for various brands if there is product differentiation. With outright collusion, firms may agree on market shares and the division of profits. The division of total profits will depend on the relative bargaining strength of each firm, influenced by its relative financial strength, ability to inflict damage (through price wars) on other firms if an agreement is not reached, ability to withstand similar actions on the part of other firms, relative costs, consumer preferences, and bargaining skills.

Why Are Most Collusive Oligopolies Short Lived?

Collusive oligopolies are potentially highly profitable for participants but detrimental to society. Fortunately, most strong collusive oligopolies are rather short lived, for two reasons. First, in the United States and in some other nations, collusive oligopolies are strictly illegal under antitrust laws. Second, for collusion to work, firms must agree to restrict output to a level that will support the profit-maximizing price. At that price, firms can earn positive economic profits. Yet a great temptation is for firms to cheat on the agreement of the collusive oligopoly; and because collusive agreements are illegal, the other parties have no way to punish the offender. Why do they have a strong incentive to cheat? Because any individual firm could lower its price slightly and thereby increase sales and profits, as long as it goes undetected. Undetected price cuts could bring in new customers, including rivals' customers. In addition, nonprice methods of defection include better credit terms, rebates, prompt delivery service, and so on.

SECTION CHECK

1. A price leader sends a signal to competing firms about a price change. Competitors that go along with the pricing decisions of the price leader are known as price followers.
2. The mutual interdependence of oligopolists tempts them to collude in order to reduce uncertainty and increase potential for economic profits.
3. Joint profit maximization requires the determination of price based on the market demand for the product and the marginal costs of the various firms.
4. Most strong collusive oligopolies are rather short lived for primarily two reasons: (1) Collusive oligopolies are strictly illegal under U.S. antitrust laws, and (2) there is a great temptation for firms to cheat on the agreement of the collusive oligopoly.

1. Why are collusive agreements typically unstable and short lived?
2. Why is the temptation to collude greater when the industry's demand curve is more inelastic?

SECTION 15.3 Other Oligopoly Models

* What is the kinked demand curve model?
* What happens to the oligopolists' profits if entry is easy?
* How can existing firms deter potential entrants?

The Kinked Demand Curve Model—Price Rigidity

As we have seen, collusion tends to be fragile in oligopoly markets. Prices in some oligopolistic industries tend to be quite stable, or rigid. That is, even if demand or cost changes, firms will be reluctant to change their prices. For example, if demand or costs were to increase, a firm might be tempted to increase its prices but may not because it fears that rivals will not raise their prices and the firm will lose customer sales. The firm may also be reluctant to lower its prices in fear of setting off a round of price warfare. That is, once the collusion outcome has been reached, individual producers have an incentive to be cautious about changing their output—or price.

This idea of price rigidity in oligopoly is the basis of the **kinked demand curve** model. According to the kinked

kinked demand curve indicates the price rigidity in oligopoly when competitors show a greater tendency to follow price reductions than price increases

section 15.3 exhibit 1 — The Kinked Demand Curve

If the firm increases its price from P^*, most firms will not follow, and its demand curve is said to be relatively elastic (that is, a slight increase in price will lead to a more than proportionate fall in the quantity demanded). Conversely, below P^*, demand is relatively inelastic; a slight decrease in price will not lead to a large increase in the quantity demanded because rivals will also lower prices to hold onto their market share. Even if the marginal cost increases from MC_1 to MC_2, the firm will produce the same at the same price, P^*, and at the same output, q^*.

demand curve model, each firm faces a demand curve that is kinked at the collusive market price (P^*) and output (q^*). This kinked demand curve, illustrated in Exhibit 1, is produced by the greater tendency of competitors to follow price reductions than price increases. A price reduction takes business away from other firms and forces them to cut prices in order to protect their sales. A price increase does not necessitate a readjustment because other firms gain customers if one increases its price. At the point of the kink, the MR curve is discontinuous.

The profit-maximizing price, P^*, is indicated in Exhibit 1 by the point at which the demand curve changes slope. At prices higher than P^*, the firm's demand curve is very elastic. The reason for this elasticity is that a price increase would significantly cut revenues, as other rival firms fail to follow the price increase, causing the firm to lose sales and market share. If it lowers the price below P^*, reductions would yield little additional business because most of the other firms are presumed to follow price cuts. That is, sales will only increase if the total market quantity demanded increases due to the lower price. Below P^*, the firm does not capture many rivals' clients as rival firms match the price reduction, so the demand curve tends to be relatively inelastic below P^*. A slight decrease in price will not lead to a large increase in quantity demanded because rivals will lower their price to maintain their market share.

One important consequence of the kink in the demand curve is that the firm may be slow to adjust price in response to cost changes. Because of the kink in the demand curve, the marginal revenue curve is discontinuous. Therefore, the MC curve can move up or down over a substantial range without affecting the optimum level of output or price. For example, as the marginal cost increases from MC_1 to MC_2 in Exhibit 1, the firm will continue to produce at the same price, P^*, and at the same output, q^*.

The key feature of the kinked demand curve is that the shape of the firm's demand curve is dependent on the action of competing firms. In the real world, of course, when a firm raises its price, anticipating that other firms will also raise prices but they do not, then the price-raising firm will face the prospect of a major sales decline, and the firm that initiated the price increase will usually retreat from the price increase originally announced. The explanation for the price rigidity comes from the idea that firms do not want to engage in destructive price competition. Game theory is useful in this situation. We will discuss game theory in the context of prisoners' dilemma in Section 15.4.

Not all oligopolies experience price rigidity. For example, during the high inflationary periods of the 1970s, some oligopolists increased their prices frequently. Oligopolists are more likely to experience price rigidity in situations of excess capacity—during a business downturn or a recession, for instance. In such cases, firms are likely to match a price cut but not a price hike—that is, they face a kinked demand curve. Also, if an oligopolist believes that other firms are faced with rising cost, then all the firms in the industry would respond to the change in marginal cost by adjusting their price and output accordingly to maintain their collusive position.

price leader
a large firm in an oligopoly that unilaterally makes changes in its product prices that competitors tend to follow

Price Leadership

Over time, an implied understanding may develop in an oligopoly market that a large firm is the **price leader**, sending a signal to competitors, perhaps through a press release, that they have increased their prices. This approach is not outright collusion because no formal cartel arrangement or formal meetings are used to determine price and output; but this is what

Oligopolists may initiate pricing policies that reduce the entry incentive for new firms, or they may try to drive a competitor out of the industry. For example, it is possible that a small-town drug store might be run out of town by Wal-Mart's "falling prices."

section 15.3 exhibit 2 Long-Run Equilibrium and Deterring Entry

With barriers to entry, oligopolists may earn excess profits in the long run. Theoretically, profit maximization occurs at P^* and q^* in the short run. Empirical work, however, suggests that oligopolists often actually charge a lower price than the short-run profit-maximizing price (such as P_1). This strategy discourages entry because newcomers may have costs higher than P_1.

is called tacit collusion. Any competitor that goes along with the pricing decision of the price leader is called a **price follower**.

Price leadership is most likely to develop when one firm, the so-called dominant firm, produces a large portion of the total output. The dominant firm sets the price that maximizes its profits and the smaller firms, which would have little influence over price anyway, act as if they are perfect competitors—selling all they want at that price. In the past, a number of firms have been price leaders: U.S. Steel and Bethlehem Steel, RJ Reynolds (tobacco), General Motors (automobiles), Kellogg's (breakfast cereals), and Goodyear (tires). In the banking industry, various dominant banks have taken turns being the dominant firm in announcing changes in the prime interest rate—the interest rate that banks charge large corporate clients. Because the prime rate is widely cited in newspapers, it makes it easy for other banks to follow the lead and avoid frequent changes and competitive warfare.

> **price follower**
> a competitor in an oligopoly that goes along with the pricing decision of the price leader
>
> **price leadership**
> when a dominant firm that produces a large portion of the industry's output sets a price that maximizes its profits, and other firms follow

What Happens in the Long Run If Entry Is Easy?

Mutual interdependence is, in itself, no guarantee of economic profits, even if the firms in the industry succeed in maximizing joint profits. The extent to which economic profits disappear depends on the ease with which new firms can enter the industry. When entry is easy, excess profits attract newcomers. New firms may break down existing price agreements by undercutting prices in an attempt to establish themselves in the industry. In response, older firms may reduce prices to avoid excessive sales losses; as a result, the general level of prices will begin to approach average total cost.

How Do Oligopolists Deter Market Entry?

If most firms reach a scale of plant and firm size great enough to allow lowest-cost operation, their long-run positions will be similar to that shown in Exhibit 2. To simplify, we have drawn MC and ATC constant. The equilibrium, or profit-maximizing, price in an established oligopoly is represented by P^*. Typically, the rate of profit in these industries is high, which would encourage entry. However, empirical research indicates that oligopolists often initiate pricing policies that reduce the entry incentive for new firms. Established firms may deliberately hold prices below the maximum profit point at P^*, charging a price of, say, P_1. This lower than profit-maximizing price may discourage newcomers from entering. Because new firms would likely have higher costs than existing firms, the lower price may not be high enough to cover their costs. However, once the threat of entry subsides, the market price may return to the profit-maximizing price, P^*.

Antitrust and Mergers

In the beginning of this chapter, we introduced a method for determining an industry's market structure called a concentration ratio. However, the Justice Department and the Federal Trade Commission (FTC) both prefer to use a measure called the Herfindahl-Hirshman Index (HHI). The HHI is measured by taking the square for each firm's share of market sales summed over the firms in the industry. For example, if the industry has three firms and their market share is 50 percent, 30 percent, 20 percent, respectively, the HHI would be:

$$HHI = 50^2 + 30^2 + 20^2 = 3,800$$

By squaring, the HHI produces a much larger number when industry is dominated by a few firms. According to the Justice Department, an HHI below 1,000 is very competitive, an HHI between 1,000 and 1,800 is somewhat competitive, and an HHI over 1,800 indicates an oligopoly. The HHI takes into account the relative size and distribution of the firms in a market. The HHI is lowest when a market consists of a large number of firms of relatively equal size. The HHI increases both as the number of firms in the market decreases and as the disparity in size between those firms increases.

A potential merger resulting in an HHI over 1,000 will receive close scrutiny. In 2007, for example, Whole Foods made a takeover bid for Wild Oats. Both were organic grocery stores. The FTC argued that the takeover would increase prices and limit competition in the organic food market. Whole Foods argued that it competes with many grocery stores that carry healthy food and organic products. The merger is still in appeal at the time of this writing. Another interesting case is the merger of Ticketmaster and Live Nation (see the In the News box).

predatory pricing
setting a price deliberately low in order to drive out competitors

Three Types of Mergers

There are three different types of mergers.

1. A *horizontal merger* combines firms that sell similar products; for example, if Motel 6 merges with Holiday Inn or GM merges with Chrysler.
2. A *vertical merger* combines firms at different stages of production; for example, Pepsi merged with Pizza Hut and Taco Bell. Similarly, a hotel chain may merge with a mattress company.
3. A *conglomerate merger* combines firms in different industries. For example, an automobile company might merge with a pharmaceutical company.

Since vertical mergers are not often a threat to competition, they are not usually subject to antitrust probes. They do not reduce competition in other markets. This is also true of conglomerate mergers—when an auto company merges with a pharmaceutical company, neither increases market share. Most of the problems occur with horizontal mergers. For example, an attempted merger between Office Depot and Staples was blocked.

Antitrust and Pricing Strategies

Most economists agree that price fixing should be illegal. However, there are antitrust laws that forbid other types of activities where the effects are not as obvious—predatory pricing, price discrimination, and tying.

Predatory Pricing

If the price is deliberately kept low (below average variable cost) to drive a competitor out of the market, it is called **predatory pricing**. However, both economists and the courts have a difficult time deciding whether or not the price is truly predatory or not. Even if the price is driven down below average variable cost (recall from Chapter 11, that when price is below AVC it is the shutdown point of a firm), the courts still have to determine whether the low price destroyed the rival and kept it out of business. And did the firm raise its price to the monopoly level once the rival had been driven out of the industry? Microsoft, American Airlines, and other companies have been accused of predatory pricing, but not convicted because it is so difficult to distinguish predatory pricing from vigorous competition.

Price Discrimination

Price discrimination, as we studied in Chapter 13, is a common pricing strategy for many businesses. It generally does not reduce competition unless it is part of a strategy to block entry or force a competitor out of the market; therefore, it is not normally challenged by antitrust authorities. However, it can be challenged under the Robinson-Patman Act, which places restrictions on allowable price discrimination.

in the news

Live Nation, Ticketmaster Merger Risks Antitrust Scrutiny

—BY ELIOT VAN BUSKIRK

[T]wo of the biggest forces in live music today—Live Nation and Ticketmaster—are set to merge into a single behemoth of ticketing and promotion that will call itself "Live Nation Entertainment."

The new powerhouse may be able to run from an unpopular brand—"Ticketmaster" is for many synonymous with niggling "convenience" fees and the stress-inducing process of vying for limited supplies of concert tickets, especially since no method of matching supply with demand seems particularly fair.

But it cannot hide from the antitrust scrutiny the deal is virtually certain to attract from governmental agencies since the combination could reduce competition and result in higher ticket prices.

Update: The Justice Department says it will in fact investigate the merger between Live Nation and Ticketmaster.

For Ticketmaster, this is familiar territory: It attracted a healthy dose of interest from antitrust regulators in the '90s for its domination of the concert ticket market. But now it is merging with the largest concert promoter in the world. The combined entity, which would control aspects of booking, promotion, primary ticket sales, secondary (fan-to-fan, or scalped) ticket sales, merchandising, direct marketing and even album sales in some cases, will be doubly attractive as a target for regulators.

"From an antitrust perspective, I do think it's going to get an extensive and thorough investigation by one of the two antitrust agencies—maybe more likely the Justice Department than the FTC, because the Justice Department did a monopoly investigation of Ticketmaster in the '90s," said Marc Schildkraut, a former assistant director of the Federal Trade Commission's Bureau of Competition and partner at merger clearance firm Howrey, LLP, by phone.

The Justice Department closed that investigation in 1999 for undisclosed reasons. Schildkraut said the likely cause was that the government didn't find a sufficient barrier to entry to other companies entering the music-ticketing space, even despite Ticketmaster's exclusive, multiyear venue contracts.

But Live Nation Entertainment would be a completely different animal. The world's largest promoter doubling as its largest ticket seller presents challenges Ticketmaster did not face during its '90s antitrust travails.

"This is both a horizontal and a vertical merger," explained Shildkraut. "Horizontal means they're competitors to each other [due to Live Nation's recent entry into the ticketing market, two years of development] and vertical means they are in adjacent spaces in the market."

By the latter, he's referring to synergy between the company's ticketing and promotion departments. The combined effort could present a barrier to entry to promoters, who would likely have to work with Live Nation Entertainment's ticketing division—not to mention other potential ticket sellers, who would be prevented from ticketing Live Nation Entertainment-promoted shows.

Why merge, if it's going to mean this much scrutiny? According to Live Nation CEO Michael Rapino (who would be CEO of Live Nation Entertainment if the merger goes through) the idea here is merely to sell more tickets, more efficiently. "As every industry observer knows, too many tickets go unsold and too many fans are frustrated with their ticket-buying experiences," he said, adding, "the better job we do of getting the right fan in the right seat at the right time, the more money our clients are going to make."

AP PHOTO/HENNY RAY ABRAMS

Use what you've LEARNED
MUTUAL INTERDEPENDENCE IN OLIGOPOLY

Q Suppose that Firm A is a member of a naive oligopoly, meaning that neither Firm A nor its competitors recognize the mutual interdependence that exists between them. Firm A decides to lower its price to capture a greater market share. What will happen to profits in this market in the long run?

A If an oligopolist believes that its rivals will not respond to pricing policies, it will expect to capture market share by reducing price. In response, rivals will cut prices as well, and if they do not understand the mutual interdependence among firms in oligopoly, they will attempt to undercut prices, as shown in Exhibit 3 in the movement from P_1 to P_2, and so on. This exchange would result in a price war, which could continue until economic profits were zero and price equaled average cost.

section 15.3 exhibit 3 — Mutual Interdependence in Oligopoly

Tying

Tie-in-sales *require* that a customer who buys one product (the tying good) must also buy another product (the tied good) that a customer needs to use the first product. Two companies that followed this practice were Xerox and IBM. When Xerox was the largest photocopier producer, they required companies that rented their machines to also buy paper from them. Similarly, IBM required that users of its computers buy IBM computer cards. IBM charged more for the computer cards than other firms would have charged.

Antitrust authorities look for dominant firms that use types of pricing discrimination policies. For example, the Supreme Court ruled that studios could not force theaters to buy an entire package of films in order to get the rights to show a blockbuster movie. That is, tying a blockbuster movie together with a package of not-so-good B movies could allow studios to expand their market power. To economists, the "jury" is still out on whether various forms of price discrimination really impede competition.

SECTION CHECK

1. In the kinked demand curve model, if one firm cuts its price, rivals will follow, but rival firms will not follow the firm if it raises its price.
2. When market entry is easy, excess profits attract newcomers. They may break down existing price agreements, causing older firms to reduce their prices and, ultimately, drive the general level of prices toward average total cost.
3. Firms in an oligopoly may deliberately hold prices below the short-run profit-maximizing point in order to discourage newcomers from entering the market.
4. The Herfindahl-Hirshman Index (HHI), which equals the sum of the squares of the market shares, is a measure of the competitiveness of a market structure, where a lower number indicates a more competitive structure.
5. There are three types of mergers: horizontal (merging firms that produce similar products), vertical (merging firms at different stages of a production process), and conglomerate (merging firms in different industries).
6. Price discrimination, allegations of predatory pricing, and tying sales are also subject to antitrust laws.

1. What explains the kink in the kinked demand curve?
2. What impact does easy entry have on the profitability of oligopolies?
3. Why are barriers to entry necessary for successful, ongoing collusion?
4. Why might oligopolists charge less than their short-run profit-maximizing price when threatened by entry?
5. A group of colluding oligopolists incurs costs of $10 per unit, and their profit-maximizing price is $15. If they know that potential market entrants could produce at a cost of $12 per unit, what price are the colluders likely to charge?
6. Why is price leadership also called tacit collusion?
7. What two factors increase the Herfindahl-Hirshman Index (HHI)?
8. Why do horizontal mergers tend to concern antitrust authorities more than vertical or conglomerate mergers?
9. For someone to be engaged in predatory pricing, what must happen to prices after their predation? Why would potential entry undermine the strategy?

SECTION 15.4 Game Theory and Strategic Behavior

- What is game theory?
- What are cooperative and noncooperative games?
- What is a dominant strategy?
- What is Nash equilibrium?

Some Strategies for Noncollusive Oligopolies

In some respects, noncollusive oligopoly resembles a military campaign or a poker game. Firms take certain actions not because they are necessarily advantageous in themselves but because they improve the position of the oligopolist relative to its competitors and may ultimately improve its financial position. For example, a firm may deliberately cut prices, sacrificing profits either to drive competitors out of business or to discourage them from undertaking actions contrary to the interests of other firms.

What Is Game Theory?

Some economists have suggested that the entire approach to oligopoly equilibrium price and output should be recast. They replace the analysis that assumes that firms attempt to maximize profits with one that examines firm behavior in terms of a strategic game. This point of view, called **game theory**, stresses the tendency of various parties in such circumstances to act in a way that minimizes damage from opponents. This approach involves a set of alternative actions (with respect to price and output levels, for example); the action that would be taken in a particular case depends on the specific policies followed by each firm. The firm may try to figure out its competitors' most likely countermoves to its own policies and then formulate alternative defense measures.

Each firm will react to the price, quantity, and quality of rival firms. Because each firm is interdependent, each must observe the moves of its rivals.

game theory
firms attempt to maximize profits by acting in ways that minimize damage from competitors

cooperative game
collusion by two firms in order to improve their profit maximizations

noncooperative game
each firm sets its own price without consulting other firms

Cooperative and Noncooperative Games

Games, in interactions between oligopolists, can either be cooperative or noncooperative. An example of a **cooperative game** would be two firms that decide to collude in order to improve their profit-maximization position. However, as we discussed earlier, enforcement costs are usually too high to keep all firms from cheating on collusive agreements. Consequently, most games are **noncooperative games,** in which each firm sets its own price without consulting other firms. The primary difference between cooperative and noncooperative games is the contract.

For example, players in a cooperative game can talk and set binding contracts, while those in noncooperative games are assumed to act independently, with no communication and no binding contracts. Because antitrust laws forbid firms to collude, we will assume that most strategic behavior in the marketplace is noncooperative.

dominant strategy
strategy that will be optimal regardless of opponents' actions

prisoners' dilemma
the basic problem facing noncolluding oligopolists in maximizing their own profit

payoff matrix
a summary of the possible outcomes of various strategies

The Prisoners' Dilemma

A firm's decision makers must map out a pricing strategy based on a wide range of information. They must also decide whether their strategy will be effective and whether it will be affected by competitors' actions. A strategy that will be optimal regardless of the opponents' actions is called a **dominant strategy**. A famous game that has a dominant strategy and demonstrates the basic problem confronting noncolluding oligopolists is known as the **prisoners' dilemma**.

Imagine that a bank robbery occurs and two suspects are caught. The suspects are placed in separate cells in the county jail and are not allowed to talk with each other. Four results are possible in this situation: both prisoners confess, neither confesses, Prisoner A confesses but Prisoner B doesn't, or Prisoner B confesses but Prisoner A doesn't. In Exhibit 1, we see the **payoff matrix**, which summarizes the possible outcomes from the various strategies. Looking at the payoff matrix, we can see that if each prisoner confesses to the crime, each will serve two years in jail. However, if neither confesses, each prisoner may only get one year because of insufficient evidence. Now, if Prisoner A confesses and Prisoner B does not, Prisoner A will get six months (because of his cooperation with the authorities and his evidence) and Prisoner B six years. Alternatively, if Prisoner B confesses and Prisoner A does not, Prisoner B will get six months and Prisoner A six years. As you can see, then, the prisoners have a dilemma. What should each prisoner do?

Looking at the payoff matrix, we can see that if Prisoner A confesses, it is in the best interest for Prisoner B to confess. If Prisoner A confesses, he will

section 15.4 exhibit 1 The Prisoners' Dilemma Payoff Matrix

		Prisoner B Confesses	Prisoner B Doesn't Confess
Prisoner A	Confesses	2 years (A) / 2 years (B)	6 months (A) / 6 years (B)
	Doesn't Confess	6 years (A) / 6 months (B)	1 year (A) / 1 year (B)

The sentence depends on the prisoner's decision to confess or remain silent and on the decision made by the other prisoner. When the prisoners follow their dominant strategy and confess, both will be worse off than if each had remained silent—hence, the "prisoners' dilemma."

A pitcher wants to throw a pitch that will surprise this batter. The batter knows that the pitcher wants to fool him. So what does the pitcher throw, knowing the batter expects the pitcher to fool him? Is this a game with strategic interaction?

get either two years or six months, depending on what Prisoner B does. However, Prisoner B knows the temptation to confess facing Prisoner A, so confessing is also the best strategy for Prisoner B. A confession would mean a lighter sentence for Prisoner B—two years rather than six years.

It is clear that both would be better off confessing *if* they knew for sure that the other was going to remain silent, because that would lead to a six-month sentence for each. However, in each case, can the prisoner take the chance that the co-conspirator will not talk? The dominant strategy, although it may not lead to the best joint outcome, is to confess. That is, the prisoners know that confessing is the way to make the best of a bad situation. No matter what their counterpart does, the maximum sentence will be two years for each, and each understands the possibility of being out in six months. In summary, when the prisoners follow their dominant strategy and confess, both will be worse off than if each had remained silent—hence, the "prisoners' dilemma."

Firms in oligopoly often behave like the prisoners in the prisoners' dilemma, carefully anticipating the moves of their rivals in an uncertain environment. For example, should a firm cut its prices and try to gain more sales by luring customers away from its competitors? What if the firm keeps its price stable and competitors lower theirs? Or what if the firm and its competitors all lower their prices? What if all of the firms decide to raise their prices? Each of these situations will have vastly different implications for an oligopolist, so it must carefully watch and anticipate the moves of its competitors.

Profits Under Different Pricing Strategies

To demonstrate how the prisoners' dilemma can shed light on oligopoly theory, let us consider the pricing strategy of two firms. In Exhibit 2, we present the payoff matrix—the possible profits that each firm would earn under different pricing strategies. Assume that each firm has total production costs of $1 per unit. When both firms set their price at $10 and each sells 1,000 units per week, then each earns a profit of $9,000 a week. If each firm sets its price at $9, each sells 1,100 units per week for a profit of $8,800 [($9 − $1) × 1,100]. However, what if one firm charges $10 and the other firm charges $9? The low-price firm increases its profits through additional sales. It now sells, say, 1,500 units for a profit of $12,000, while the high-price firm sells only 600 units per week for a profit of $5,400.

When the two firms each charge $9 per unit, they are said to have reached a Nash equilibrium (named after Nobel Prize–winning economist and mathematician John Nash). At a Nash equilibrium, each firm is said to be doing as well as it can *given the actions of its competitor*. For example, if each firm believes the other is going to charge $9, then the best strategy for both firms is to charge $9. In this scenario, if Firm A charges $9, the worst possible outcome is a profit of $8,800. However, if Firm A prices at $10 and Firm B prices at $9, Firm A will have a profit of only $5,400. Hence, the choice that minimizes the risk of the worst scenario is $9. The same is true for Firm B; it too

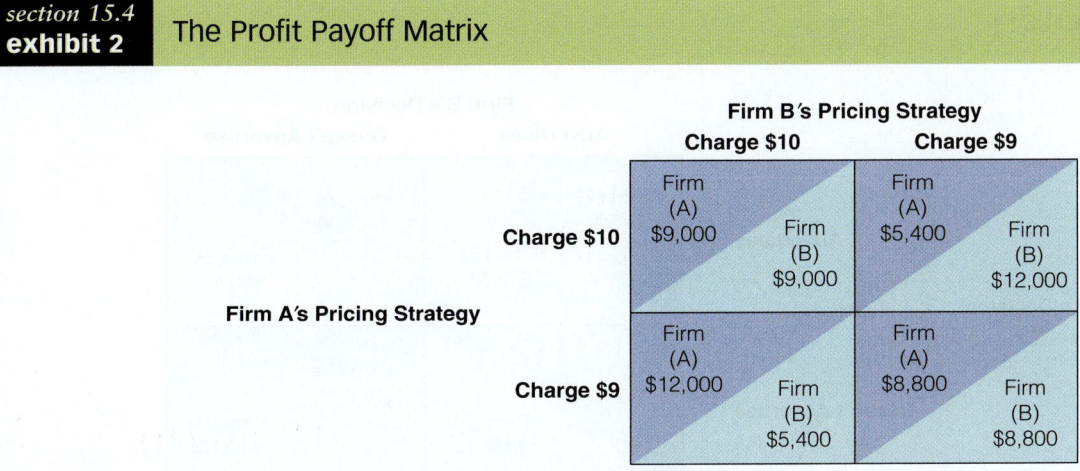

section 15.4 exhibit 2 The Profit Payoff Matrix

If both firms defect by lowering their prices from the level of joint profit maximization, both will be worse off than if they had colluded, but at least each will have minimized its potential loss if it cannot trust its competitor. This situation is the oligopolists' dilemma.

minimizes the risk of the worst scenario by choosing to price at the Nash equilibrium, $9. In this case, the Nash equilibrium is also the dominant strategy. The Nash equilibrium takes on particular importance because it is a self-enforcing equilibrium. That is, once this equilibrium is established, neither firm has an incentive to move.

In sum, we see that if the two firms were to collude and set their price at $10, it would be in their best interest. However, each firm has a strong incentive to lower its price to $9 if this pricing strategy goes undetected by its competitor. However, if both firms defect by lowering their prices from the level of joint profit maximization, both will be worse off than if they had colluded, but at least each will have minimized its potential loss if it cannot trust its competitor. This situation is the oligopolists' dilemma.

Advertising

Advertising can lead to a situation like the prisoners' dilemma. For example, perhaps the decision makers of a large firm are deciding whether to launch an advertising campaign against a rival firm. According to the payoff matrix in Exhibit 3, if neither company advertises, the two companies split the market, each making $100 million in profits. They also split the market if they both advertise, but their net profits are smaller, $75 million, because they would both incur advertising costs that are greater than any gains in additional revenues from advertising. However, if one advertises and the other does not, the company that advertises takes customers away from the rival. Profits for the company that advertises would be $125 million, and profits for the company that does not advertise would be $50 million.

The dominant strategy—the optimal strategy regardless of the rival's actions—is to advertise. In this game, both firms will choose to advertise, even though both would be better off if no one advertised. But one company can't take a chance and not advertise, because if its competitor then elects to advertise, the competitor could have a big year, primarily at the expense of the firm that doesn't advertise.

Arms Race

The arms race provides a classic example of prisoners' dilemma. During the Cold War (mid 1940s to the early 1990s), the United States and the former Soviet Union were engaged in costly military expansion that hampered both economies. It exacted a greater toll on the Soviets because their economy was not as economically productive as the United States and may have ultimately led to their decline. The United States' power was based on economic and military strength; the USSR's was based solely on military strength. Each country raced to produce more military goods than the other. Representatives from both sides would periodically meet to discuss arms reduction but to no avail. Neither party was willing to risk losing its military superiority.

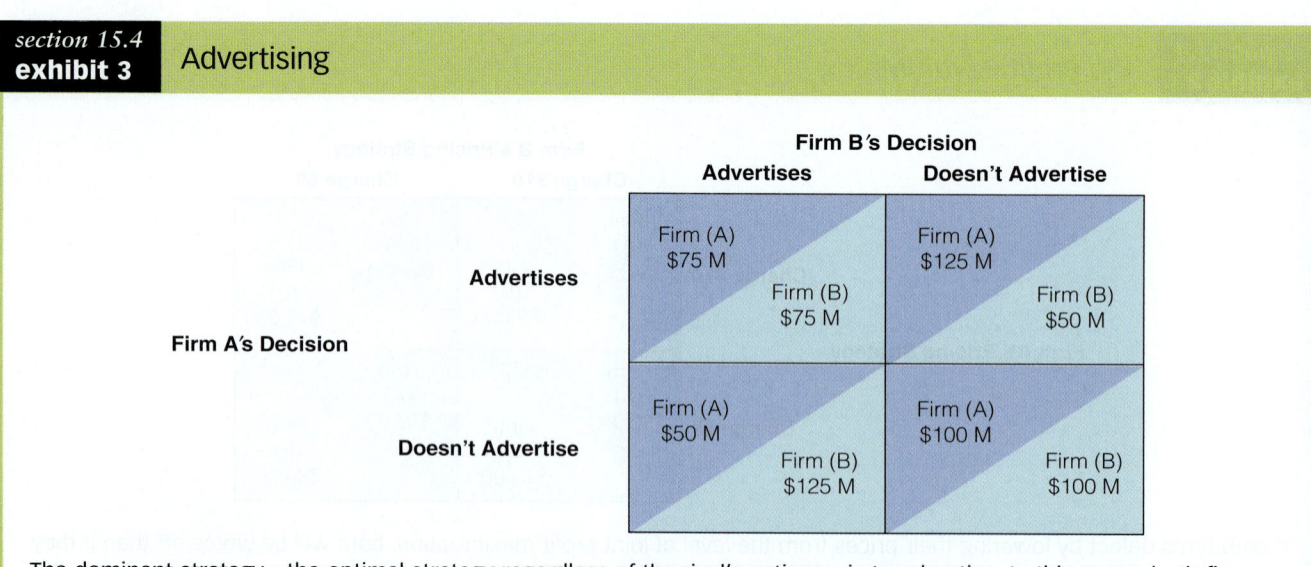

section 15.4 exhibit 3 Advertising

The dominant strategy—the optimal strategy regardless of the rival's actions—is to advertise. In this game, both firms will choose to advertise, even though both would be better off if no one advertised.

in the news: The Game Theory of the Bar Scene Problem from *A Beautiful Mind*

The Problem

You and three male friends are at a bar trying to pick up women. Suddenly one blonde and four brunettes enter in a group. What's the individual strategy?

Here are the rules. Each of you wants to talk to the blonde. If more than one of you tries to talk to her, however, she will be put off and talk to no one. At that point it will also be too late to talk to a brunette, as no one likes being second choice. Assume anyone who starts out talking to a brunette will succeed.

The Movie

Nash suggests the group should cooperate. If everyone goes for the blonde, they block each other and no one wins. The brunettes will feel hurt as a second choice and categorically reject advances. Everyone loses.

But what if everyone goes for a brunette? Then each person will succeed, and everyone ends up with a good option.

It's a good thought, except for one question: what about the blonde?

The Equilibrium

The movie is directed so well that it sounds persuasive. But it's sadly incomplete. It misses the essence of noncooperative game theory.

A Nash equilibrium is a state where no one person can improve *given what others are doing*. This means you are picking the best possible action in response to others—the formal term is you are picking a *best response*.

As an example, let's analyze whether everyone going for a brunette is a Nash equilibrium. You are *given* that three of your friends go for brunettes. What is your best response?

You can either go for the brunette or the blonde. With your friends already going for brunettes, you have no competition to go for the blonde. The answer is clear that you would talk to the blonde. That's your best response. Incidentally, this is a Nash equilibrium. You are happy, and your friends cannot do better. If your friends try to talk to the blonde, they end up with nothing and give up talking to a brunette. So you see, when Nash told his friends to go for the brunettes in the movie, it really does sound like he was leaving the blonde for himself.

The lesson: advice that sounds good for you might really be better for someone else. Be skeptical of the strategic implications.

Now, in practical matters it will be hard to achieve the equilibrium that one person goes for a blonde. There is going to be competition and someone in the group will surely sabotage the mission. So there are two ways you might go about it using strategies outside the game. One is to ignore the current group and wait for another group of blondes (the classic "wait and see" strategy). The second is to let a random group member go for the blonde as the others distract the brunettes (also practiced as "wingman theory").

section 15.4 exhibit 4 — Arms Race

		Country A	
		Spend More on Arms	Spend Less on Arms
Country B	Spend More on Arms	At risk (A) / At risk (B)	At risk (A) / Safe (B)
	Spend Less on Arms	Safe (A) / At risk (B)	Safe (A) / Safe (B)

For each country the dominant strategy is to build arms. Self interest drives each participant into a noncooperative game that is worse for both.

The dilemma was that each country wanted to achieve military superiority, and building more arms could make that possible, for a given level of arms spending by the other. Each would prefer less spending on the military but each rationally chose to spend more to avoid the risk of becoming militarily inferior. They were trapped in a spending war. Of course, negotiations to spend less would be the preferred outcome for both, if they could be assured the other party would not cheat.

As you can see in the payoff matrix in Exhibit 4, if Country A spends more money on arms, then Country B better do the same or risk military inferiority. If Country A chooses to spend less on arms, then Country B gains military superiority by not following. For each country, the dominant strategy is to build arms, which leads to an inferior outcome—a less safe world. This is similar to the collusion game we examined earlier where self-interest drives each participant to a noncooperative outcome that is worse for both parties.

Repeated Games

In the one-shot, prisoners' dilemma game in Exhibit 1, we saw that the best strategy is to confess regardless of what your opponent does—your behavior does not influence the other player's behavior. In one-shot prisoners' dilemma games, self-interest prevents cooperative behavior and leads to an inferior joint outcome for the participants.

However, cooperation is not impossible because most oligopolistic interactions are not one-shot games. Instead they are repeated games. Most firms assume that they will have repeat customers. For example, if a grocery store fails to provide fresh produce, customers can punish the store by shopping elsewhere in the future. These future consequences change the incentives from those in a one-shot game. All stores might have gained short-run profits from low-quality (and cost) produce, but all may offer high-quality produce because of the adverse future effects of offering lower quality produce. In a repeated game, cooperation occurs as long as others continue to cooperate.

Suppose two firms are both going to be in business for many years. Several studies have shown that, in this type of situation, the best strategy is to do what your opponent did to you earlier. This type of response tends to elicit cooperation rather than competition. This form of strategic behavior is called a **tit-for-tat strategy**.

tit-for-tat strategy *strategy used in repeated games where one player follows the othe player's move in the previous round; leads to greater cooperation*

A repeated game allows the firm to establish a reputation of cooperation. Cooperation may mean maintaining a high price or a certain advertising budget, provided that the other firm did the same in the previous round. In short, a firm has an incentive to cooperate now so there is greater cooperation in the future. However, if your opponent cheats, you cheat in the next round to punish your opponent for a lack of cooperation. You do what your opponent did in the previous round. In the tit-for-tat game, both firms will be better off if they stick to the plan rather than cheating—that is, failing to cooperate. Many cartels appear to employ the tit-for-tat strategy.

Use what you've LEARNED: NASH AT THE BEACH

Two ice cream vendors on the beach are selling identical ice cream at the same price. The demanders are uniformly distributed along the beach. To minimize transportation costs, each vendor might strategically set up at the 1/4-mile mark and 3/4-mile mark, each with an advantage of being halfway to its rival. However, the situation in Exhibit 5 is not a stable equilibrium, because if vendor A thinks vendor B is going to stay put, then vendor A will move to the right, closer to vendor B, and capture three-fourths of the market, and vendor B will have the remaining one-fourth. Vendor B would then want to move to the left of vendor A. They would continue to leap frog until they reached the center. That is, a Nash equilibrium will lead to both vendors locating in the middle—doing the best they can given what the competitor is doing.

Recall the discussion of the median voter model in Chapter 8, where the prediction was that the candidates will pick a political position in the middle of the distribution of voters. The ice cream vendor model helps us understand this phenomenon as well as why fast-food restaurants, car dealerships, and motels are often found in close proximity to each other.

section 15.4 exhibit 5 — Vendors at the Beach

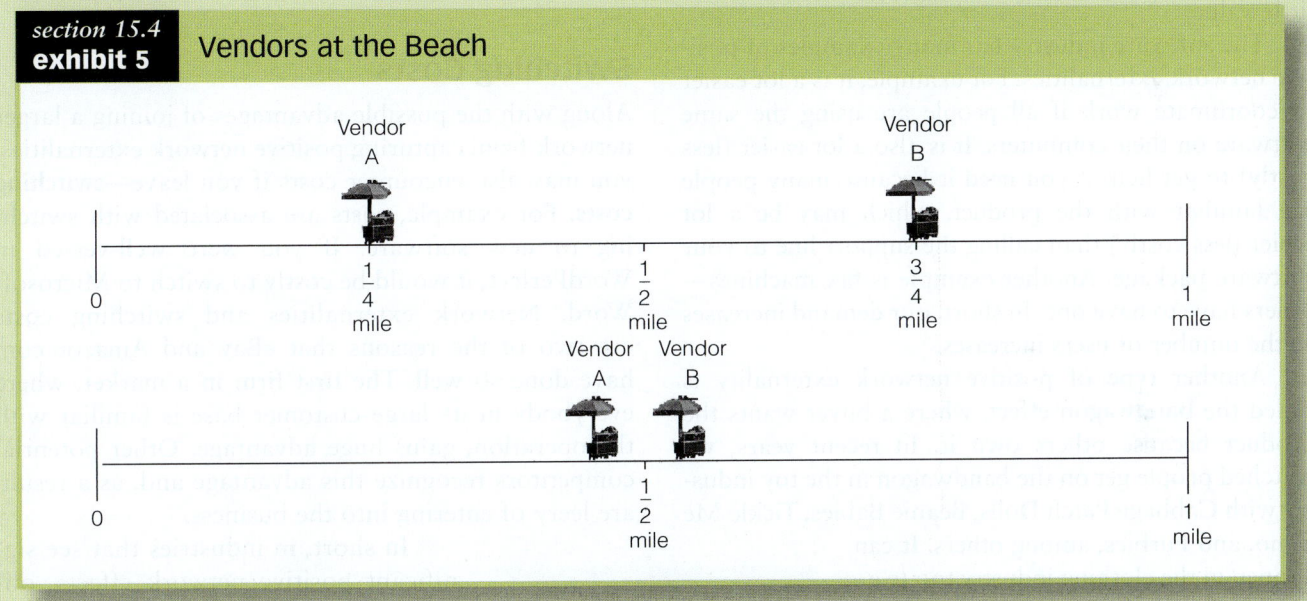

In short, the most effective strategy to promote cooperation is tit-for-tat.

Network Externalities

In our discussion of supply and demand (Chapter 4), we assumed that demand was a function of the price of the good (a change in quantity demanded) and the determinants of demand (the shifters that cause changes in demand). For example, the amount of ice cream we are willing and able to buy is a function of the price of ice cream, the price of related goods—substitutes like yogurt and complements like hot fudge—income, the number of buyers, tastes, and expectations. However, we did not mention that for some goods, the quantity demanded depends on how many other people purchase the good. This factor is called a **network externality**. A **positive network externality** occurs

network externality
when the number of other people purchasing the good influences quantity demanded

positive network externality
increase in a consumer's quantity demanded for a good because a greater number of other consumers are purchasing the good

when a consumer's quantity demanded for a good increases because a greater number of consumers purchase the same good. A **negative network externality** occurs if the consumer's quantity demanded for a good increases because fewer consumers are purchasing the same good. In other words, sometimes an individual's demand curve is influenced by the other people purchasing the good.

Positive Network Externalities

Many examples of network externalities can be found in the communications area, such as with fax machines, telephones, and the Internet. Imagine you had a telephone, but nobody else did; it would be relatively worthless without others with whom to talk. It is also true that if you were the only one to own a compact disc player, it would make little sense for manufacturers to make discs and your CD player would be of little value.

The software industry has many examples of positive network externalities. For example, it is a lot easier to coordinate work if all people are using the same software on their computers. It is also a lot easier (less costly) to get help if you need it because many people are familiar with the product, which may be a lot easier (less costly) than calling the support line to your software package. Another example is fax machines—others have to have one. In short, our demand increases as the number of users increases.

Another type of positive network externality is called the **bandwagon effect,** where a buyer wants the product because others own it. In recent years, we watched people get on the bandwagon in the toy industry with Cabbage Patch Dolls, Beanie Babies, Tickle Me Elmo, and Furbies, among others. It can happen in the clothing industry too (e.g., Tommy Bahama or Ugg boots).

Negative Network Externalities

Other goods and services are subject to negative network externalities, which may be a result of the snob effect. The snob effect is a negative network externality where a consumer wants to own a unique good. For example, a rare baseball card of Shoeless Joe Jackson, a Model T car (a tin lizzy), a Vincent Van Gogh painting, a Rolex watch, or an expensive sports car may qualify as snob goods where the quantity that a particular individual demanded of a good increases when fewer other people own it. Firms seek to achieve a snob effect through marketing and advertising, knowing that if they can create a less elastic demand curve for their product they can raise prices.

Negative network externalities can arise from congestion too. For example, if you are a member of a health club, a negative network externality may occur because too many people are in the gym working out at the same time. Even though I may prefer a ski resort with shorter lift lines, others may view these goods as a positive externality and would increase their quantity demanded if more people were in the gym, on the beach, or at the ski slopes. Perhaps they do not want to work out alone, hang out on a lonely beach, or ride up on the chair lift by themselves. That is, whether it is a positive or negative network externality may depend on the consumer's tastes and preferences.

Switching Costs

Along with the possible advantages of joining a larger network from capturing positive network externalities, you may also encounter costs if you leave—**switching costs.** For example, costs are associated with switching to new software. If you were well-versed in WordPerfect, it would be costly to switch to Microsoft Word. Network externalities and switching costs are two of the reasons that eBay and Amazon.com have done so well. The first firm in a market, where everybody in its large customer base is familiar with the operation, gains huge advantage. Other potential competitors recognize this advantage and, as a result, are leery of entering into the business.

In short, in industries that see significant positive network effects, oligopoly is likely to be present. That is, a small number of firms may be able to secure most of the market. Consumers tend to choose the products that everyone else is using. Thus, behavior may allow these firms to increase their output and achieve economics of scale that smaller firms cannot obtain. Hence, the smaller firms will go out of business or be bought out by larger firms.

You might legitimately ask the question: If perfectly competitive and monopolistic firms are rare and monopolistically competitive and oligopoly firms are common, why did we study the former first? What we

> **negative network externality**
> increase in a consumer's demand for a good because fewer consumers are purchasing the same good
>
> **bandwagon effect**
> a positive network externality in which a consumer's demand for a product increases because other consumers own it
>
> **switching costs**
> the costs involved in changing from one product to another brand or in changing suppliers

learned from the perfectly competitive model about costs, entry, exit, and efficiency are still important concepts for imperfectly competitive firms. In addition, the applications of oligopoly and monopolistic competition theory are still somewhat controversial among economists—so we started with what we know best. Exhibit 6 provides an overview of the various types of market structures.

section 15.4 exhibit 6: Characteristics of the Four Major Market Structures

Characteristic	Perfect Competition	Monopoly	Monopolistic Competition	Oligopoly
Number of firms	Very many	One	Many	A few
Firm role in determining price	No role; price taker	Major role; price maker	Some role	Some role
Close substitutes available	Perfect substitutes	No	Yes	Usually but not always
Barriers to entry or exit from industry	No substantial ones	Extremely great	Minor barriers	Considerable barriers
Type of product	Homogeneous	Homogeneous	Differentiated	Homogeneous or differentiated
Key characteristic	Firms are price takers	Only one firm	Product differentiation	Mutual interdependence

SECTION CHECK

1. Game theory stresses the tendency of various parties to minimize damage from opponents. A firm may try to figure out its competitors' most likely countermoves to its own policies and then formulate alternative defense measures.
2. Players in cooperative games can talk and set binding contracts, while those in noncooperative games are assumed to act independently with no communications and no binding contracts.
3. The prisoners' dilemma is an example of a noncooperative game.
4. A dominant strategy is optimal regardless of the opponents' actions.
5. At a Nash equilibrium, each player is said to be doing as well as it can, given the actions of its competitor.
6. In one-shot games, the participants' self-interest tends to prevent cooperative behavior, but in repeated games, cooperation occurs as long as others continue to cooperate (a tit-for-tat strategy).
7. The arms race is a classic example of prisoners' dilemma.
8. Positive (negative) network externality occurs when a consumer's quantity demanded increases (decreases) because a greater (smaller) number of consumers purchase the same good.
9. In industries with significant positive network externalities, oligopoly is likely to be present.

---

1. How is noncollusive oligopoly like a military campaign or a poker game?
2. What is the difference between cooperative and noncooperative games?
3. How does the prisoners' dilemma illustrate a dominant strategy for noncolluding oligopolists?
4. What is a Nash equilibrium?
5. In the prisoners' dilemma, if each prisoner believed that the other prisoner would deny the crime, would each choose to deny the crime?
6. Why are repeated games more likely to lead to cooperative results than one-shot games?
7. How does a tit-for-tat strategy work?
8. Why would industries with substantial positive network externalities tend to be oligopolies?

Interactive Chapter Summary

Fill in the blanks:

1. Oligopolies exist when only a (n) _____ firms control all or most of the production and sale of a product.

2. In oligopoly, products may be either homogeneous or _____.

3. In oligopoly, _____ to entry are often high, preventing competing firms from entering the market.

4. In oligopoly, firms can earn long-run _____ profits.

5. Oligopoly is characterized by mutual _____ among firms. Oligopolists must _____ because the number of firms in the industry is so small that changes in one firm's price of output will affect the sales of competing firms.

6. In oligopoly, barriers to entry in the form of large start-up costs, economies of scale, or _____ are usually present.

7. The economy of large-scale production _____ new firms from entering a market, because high initial average total costs impose heavy losses on new entrants.

8. Mutual interdependence means that no firm knows with _____ what its demand curve looks like. The demand curve and the profit-maximizing price and output will depend on how others _____ to the firm's policies.

9. Because they are mutually interdependent, oligopolists are tempted to get together and agree to act jointly, or to _____, in order to reduce uncertainty and raise profits.

10. From society's point of view, collusion creates a situation where goods are priced too _____ and outputs too _____.

11. International agreements between firms regarding sales, pricing, and other decisions are called _____ agreements.

12. Although collusive oligopolies may be profitable for participants, they are often short lived because firms have a great temptation to _____ on their fellow colluders.

13. In oligopoly, an understanding may develop under which one large firm will play the role of price_____, sending signals to competitors that they have changed their prices.

14. Competitors that go along with the pricing decisions of a price leader are called price _____.

15. Collusive behavior is no guarantee of economic profits in the _____ run.

16. Without _____ to entry, new firms will be attracted by the economic profits earned when firms act to maximize joint profits.

17. New firms will lower _____ and break down existing pricing agreements. Price competition will result in prices approaching the level of average total _____.

18. Oligopolists may charge a price lower than the profit-maximizing price to _____ new firms from entering the market. This strategy will be effective when new firms face _____ costs than existing firms in the industry do.

19. The idea of price _____ in oligopoly is the basis of the kinked demand curve model.

20. The kinked oligopoly firm's demand curve is produced by the greater tendency of competitors to follow price _____ than price _____.

21. Under the assumptions of the kinked demand curve model, a firm's demand curve is _____ elastic for price increases than for price decreases.

22. The kinked demand curve model implies that firms may be slow to adjust price in response to changes in _____.

23. In some respects, _____ oligopoly resembles a military campaign or poker game.

24. Oligopoly interdependence is often analyzed in terms of _____ theory.

25. Collusion is an example of a _____ game.

26. In _____, each firm sets its policy without consulting other firms.

27. The primary difference between cooperative games and noncooperative games lies in the players' ability to make _____.

28. In game theory, a strategy that will be optimal regardless of one's opponents' actions is called a _____ strategy.

29. In the traditional prisoners' dilemma, a _____ matrix is used to illustrate the various possibilities and results for the two parties.

30. A _____ equilibrium is reached in game theory when each firm is doing as well as it can, given the actions of its competitor.

31. A Nash equilibrium is _____, because once it is established, neither firm has an incentive to change behavior.

32. Repeated games are _____ likely to lead to cooperative results than one-shot games.
33. In a _____ strategy, a game participant does whatever the other participant did during the previous play.
34. A _____ externality occurs when a consumer's quantity demanded increases because a greater number of consumers purchase the same good.
35. Positive network externalities are particularly common in the area of _____.
36. The _____ effect refers to the case where a buyer wants a product because others also own it.
37. Congestion can cause _____ network externalities by overcrowding.
38. Switching costs can give an advantage to the _____ firms in an industry.

Answers: 1. few 2. differentiated 3. barriers 4. economic 5. interdependence; strategize 6. patents 7. discourages 8. certainty; react 9. collude 10. high; low 11. cartel 12. cheat 13. leader 14. followers 15. long 16. barriers 17. prices; costs 18. discourages; higher 19. rigidity 20. reductions; increases 21. more 22. marginal cost 23. noncollusive 24. game 25. cooperative 26. noncooperative games 27. contracts 28. dominant 29. payoff 30. Nash 31. self-enforcing 32. more 33. tit-for-tat 34. positive network 35. communications 36. bandwagon 37. negative 38. first

Key Terms and Concepts

mutual interdependence 422
collude 424
cartel 424
joint profit maximization 425
kinked demand curve 427
price leader 428
price follower 429

price leadership 429
predatory pricing 430
game theory 433
cooperative game 433
noncooperative game 433
dominant strategy 434
prisoners' dilemma 434

payoff matrix 434
tit-for-tat strategy 438
network externality 439
positive network externality 439
negative network externality 440
bandwagon effect 440
switching costs 440

Section Check Answers

15.1 Oligopoly

1. **How can concentration ratios indicate the extent of oligopolies' power?**
   Concentration ratios indicate the fraction of total industry output produced by the largest firms in the industry, which is a guide to their ability to increase prices. However, they are imperfect indicators; for instance, they do not reflect foreign competition.

2. **Why is oligopoly characterized by mutual interdependence?**
   Because an oligopoly includes few sellers, any change in output or price by one of them is likely to appreciably impact the sales of competing firms. Each of the sellers recognizes this fact, so what each firm should do to maximize its profits depends on what other firms do. Their choices and policies therefore reflect this mutual interdependence.

3. **Why do economies of scale result in few sellers in oligopoly models?**
   Where substantial economies of scale are available relative to market demand, reasonably low costs of production cannot be obtained unless a firm produces a large fraction of the market output. If each firm, to produce at low costs, must supply a substantial fraction of the market, the industry has room for only a few firms to produce efficiently.

4. **How do economies of scale result in barriers to entry in oligopoly models?**
   Low-cost entry must take place on a large scale in industries with substantial economies of scale. Therefore, existing firms could be profitable at their current prices and outputs without leading to entry. The great increase a large-scale entrant would cause in market output and the resulting decrease in market price could make that entrant unprofitable at those lower post-entry prices, even if current firms are profitable at current prices.

5. **Why does an oligopolist have a difficult time finding its profit-maximizing price and output?**
   An oligopolist has a difficult time finding its profit-maximizing price and output because its demand curve is dramatically affected by the price and output policies of each of its rivals. This difficulty causes a great deal of uncertainty about the location and shape of its demand and marginal revenue curves, because they depend on what policies rivals actually adopt.

6. **Why would an automobile manufacturer be more likely than the corner baker to be an oligopolist?**
   The automobile industry realizes substantial economies of scale relative to market demand, so lower-cost automobile production can be obtained by a firm that produces a substantial fraction of the market output. As a result, the automobile industry only has room for relatively few efficient-scale producers. In contrast, the bakery industry does not have substantial economies of scale relative to market demand, so the industry has room for a large number of efficient-scale bakeries.

15.2 Collusion and Cartels

1. **Why are collusive agreements typically unstable and short lived?**
   Collusive agreements are typically unstable and short lived because they are strictly illegal under antitrust laws in the United States and many other countries and because firms experience a great temptation to cheat on collusive agreements by increasing their output and decreasing prices, which undermines any collusive agreement.

2. **Why is the temptation to collude greater when the industry's demand curve is more inelastic?**
   The more inelastic the demand curve, the greater the increase in profits from colluding to jointly restrict output below its current level and raise prices in the industry; and hence the greater the temptation to collude.

15.3 Other Oligopoly Models

1. **What explains the kink in the kinked demand curve?**
   The kink is produced by the greater tendency of competitors to follow price reductions than price increases. If a price increase is not met by rivals, a competitor would lose a substantial number of sales to rivals, resulting in a relatively elastic demand for price increases. If, on the other hand, a price decrease is met by rivals, a competitor would not be able to take a substantial number of sales from rivals, resulting in a more inelastic demand curve for price decreases.

2. **What impact does easy entry have on the profitability of oligopolies?**
   Economic profits in oligopolistic industries will attract entrants, if entry is easy. Entrants may break down existing price agreements by cutting prices in an attempt to establish themselves in the industry, forcing existing firms to reduce their prices and suffer reduced market shares and thus undermining the profitability of the oligopoly.

3. **Why are barriers to entry necessary for successful, ongoing collusion?**
   Because easy entry erodes economic profits where they are positive, barriers to entry are necessary for oligopolists to continue to earn economic profits in the long run.

4. **Why might oligopolists charge less than their short-run profit-maximizing price when threatened by entry?**
   When entry threatens to undermine the economic profits of an oligopolistic industry, firms in the industry may lower their prices below the level that would maximize their short-run profits in order to deter entry by making it less profitable.

5. **A group of colluding oligopolists incurs costs of $10 per unit, and their profit-maximizing price is $15. If they know that potential market entrants could produce at a cost of $12 per unit, what price are the colluders likely to charge?**
   If the colluding oligopolists are afraid of attracting entrants who will expand market output and reduce market prices and the colluders' profits, they might price below their short-run profit-maximizing price in order to make it unprofitable for new entrants. In this case, colluding oligopolists might well charge $12 or just below rather than the $15 they would otherwise charge.

6. **Why is price leadership also called tacit collusion?**
   Price leadership, where one (typically dominant) firm signals how it intends to change its price and other firms follow suit, does not involve explicit agreements to restrict output and raise price. However, it can potentially be used to coordinate firms' behavior to achieve the same ends.

7. **What two factors increase the Herfindahl-Hirshman Index (HHI)?**
   The HHI increases as either the number of firms in an industry decreases or the disparity in firm sizes increases.

8. **Why do horizontal mergers tend to concern antitrust authorities more than vertical or conglomerate mergers?**
   Only horizontal mergers between makers of similar products increase market shares in a particular market, triggering changes in the HHI.

9. **For someone to be engaged in predatory pricing, what must happen to prices after the predation? Why would potential entry undermine the strategy?**
   To reap monetary profits after predatory pricing, a firm would have to raise its prices substantially afterward. Easy entry would tend to make such a price increase unprofitable, as it would attract new competitors.

15.4 Game Theory and Strategic Behavior

1. **How is noncollusive oligopoly like a military campaign or a poker game?**
   Noncollusive oligopoly is like a military campaign, a poker game, or other strategic games in that firms take certain actions, not because they are necessarily advantageous in themselves, but because they improve the position of the oligopolist relative to its competitors, with the intent of improving its ultimate position. Firm actions take into account the likely countermoves rivals will make in response to those actions.

2. **What is the difference between cooperative and noncooperative games?**
   Noncooperative games are those where actions are taken independently, without consulting others; cooperative games are those where players can communicate and agree to binding contracts with each other.

3. **How does the prisoners' dilemma illustrate a dominant strategy for noncolluding oligopolists?**
   The prisoners' dilemma illustrates a dominant strategy for noncolluding oligopolists because it is in each player's interest to make the same choice regardless of the choice of the other player. Where a strategy is optimal regardless of opponents' actions, that strategy will dominate (be chosen over) others.

4. **What is a Nash equilibrium?**
   A Nash equilibrium is one where each firm is doing as well as it can, given the actions of its competitors. It is self-enforcing because once it is established, there is no incentive for any firm to change its policies or its actions.

5. **In the prisoners' dilemma, if each prisoner believed that the other prisoner would deny the crime, would each choose to deny the crime?**
   The prisoners' dilemma illustrates a dominant strategy in which it is in the interest of each of the two prisoners to confess, regardless of whether the other prisoner confesses—Prisoner A gets a lighter sentence if he confesses (2 years) than if he does not (6 years) if Prisoner B confesses, but he also gets a lighter sentence if he confesses (6 months) than if he does not (1 year) when Prisoner B does not confess; and the same is true for Prisoner B. The result is that, given the payoff matrix, each prisoner will confess regardless of what he expects the other prisoner will do.

6. **Why are repeated games more likely to lead to cooperative results than one-shot games?**
   While there are no adverse future consequences from "cheating" in a one-shot game, repeated games introduce these effects into the analysis by influencing the results of future games.

7. **How does a tit-for-tat strategy work?**
   In the first round, you cooperate. Then, in each successive round, you do what the other player did in the previous round. This "rewards" the opponent's current cooperation and "punishes" any choice the opponent makes not to cooperate.

8. **Why would industries with substantial positive network externalities tend to be oligopolies?**
   Consumers' demands are greater the larger the number of consumers. This could allow the more successful firms to grow and increase their output more, letting them achieve economies of scale that others cannot attain.

CHAPTER 15 STUDY GUIDE

True or False:

1. Under oligopoly, individual firms produce only an infinitesimal share of total output.
2. The auto industry is an example of oligopoly.
3. Under oligopoly, as in perfect competition and monopolistic competition, firms cannot earn economic profits in the long run.
4. When firms in an oligopolistic industry collude, in the long run they fail to maximize social welfare.
5. When firms collude to set prices, their individual demand curves become relatively more elastic.
6. Although they are difficult to establish, most collusive oligopolies last indefinitely.
7. The new diamond industry in northern Canada will not threaten the economic profits earned by members of the international diamond cartel.
8. By the year 2050 the moon travel business consists of three international firms that create the International Moon Cartel, which restricts output and raises prices. Because this industry is an oligopoly, the existing firms' economic profits will be guaranteed for the long run.
9. Collusion tends to be quite durable in oligopoly markets.
10. In the kinked demand curve model, other firms are assumed to match price reductions because price reductions take business away from rivals, forcing them to cut price to protect their sales.
11. In the kinked demand curve model, an oligopoly firm's marginal revenue is discontinuous (has a gap in it).
12. The kinked demand curve model illustrates how costs can change for some oligopolists without leading to a change in price, even without collusion.
13. Oligopolists are less likely to experience price rigidity when they have excess capacity than when they are near full capacity.
14. The Herfindahl-Hirshman Index (HHI) increases when the number of firms in an industry increases.
15. Horizontal, vertical, and conglomerate mergers all increase a firm's market shares in the industries involved.
16. For predatory pricing to work, a firm would have to be able to raise its prices substantially afterward.
17. In noncooperative games, each firm sets its policy without consulting other firms.
18. A dominant strategy is one that will be optimal regardless of one's opponent's actions.
19. A Nash equilibrium is an example of a game that does not have a dominant strategy.
20. Repeated games are more likely to produce cooperative results than one-shot games.
21. Firms always cooperate in repeated games.
22. All network externalities act to increase consumer demands for products.
23. The area of communications often exhibits positive network externalities.
24. The bandwagon effect can apply to the "hot" toy during the Christmas shopping season.
25. Whether a good is subject to positive or negative network externalities from congestion can depend on a consumer's preferences.
26. Switching costs can be a significant barrier to new entrants in an industry.
27. When significant positive network effects are present, oligopoly is a common market structure.

Multiple Choice:

1. Which of the following is *not* a characteristic of oligopoly?
   a. A few firms control most of the production and sale of a product.
   b. Firms in the industry make price and output decisions with an eye to the decisions and policies of other firms in the industry.
   c. Competing firms can enter the industry easily.
   d. Substantial economies of scale are present in production.

2. Under oligopoly, a few large firms control most of the production and sale of a product because
   a. economies of scale make it difficult for small firms to compete.
   b. diseconomies of scale make it difficult for small firms to compete.
   c. average total costs rise as production expands.
   d. marginal costs rise as production expands.

3. In an oligopoly such as the U.S. domestic airline industry, a firm such as United Airlines would
   a. carefully anticipate Delta, American, and Southwest's likely responses before it raised or lowered fares.
   b. pretty much disregard Delta, American, and Southwest's likely responses when raising or lowering fares.
   c. charge the lowest fare possible in order to maximize market share.
   d. schedule as many flights to as many cities as possible without regard to what competitors do.

4. One of the reasons that collusive oligopolies are usually short lived is that
   a. they are unable to earn economic profits in the long run.
   b. they do not set prices where marginal cost equals marginal revenue.
   c. they set prices below long-run average total costs.
   d. parties to the collusion often cheat on one another.

5. In a collusive oligopoly, joint profits are maximized when a price is set based on
   a. its own demand and cost schedules.
   b. the market demand for the product and the summation of marginal costs of the various firms.
   c. the price followers' demand schedules and the price leader's marginal costs.
   d. the price leader's demand schedule and the price followers' marginal costs.

6. During the 1950s, many profitable manufacturing industries in the United States, such as steel, tires, and autos, were considered oligopolies. Why do you think such firms work hard to keep imports from other countries out of the U.S. market?
   a. Without import barriers, excess profits in the United States would attract foreign firms, break down existing price agreements, and reduce profits of U.S. firms.
   b. Without import barriers, foreign firms would be attracted to the United States and cause the cost in the industry to rise.
   c. Without import barriers, foreign firms would buy U.S. goods and resell them in the United States, causing profits to fall.
   d. Without import barriers, prices of goods would rise, so consumers would buy less of the products of these firms.

7. Over the past 20 years, Dominator, Inc., a large firm in an oligopolistic industry, has changed prices a number of times. Each time it does so, the other firms in the industry follow suit. Dominator, Inc., is a
   a. monopoly.
   b. perfect competitor.
   c. price leader.
   d. price follower.

8. In the kinked demand curve model, starting from the initial price, the demand curve assumed to face a firm is relatively _____ for price increases and relatively _____ for price decreases.
   a. elastic; elastic
   b. elastic; inelastic
   c. inelastic; elastic
   d. inelastic; inelastic

9. The kinked demand curve model illustrates
   a. how price rigidity could characterize some oligopoly firms, despite changing marginal costs.
   b. how price increases and price decreases can elicit different responses from rival firms, in oligopoly.
   c. why price rigidity may be more common when firms have excess capacity than when operating near capacity.
   d. the importance of expectations about rival behavior in oligopoly.
   e. all of the above.

10. The Herfindahl-Hirshman Index (HHI) increases as the number of firms _____ or the disparity of firm sizes _____.
    a. increases; increases
    b. increases; decreases
    c. decreases; increases
    d. decreases; decreases

11. The Herfindahl-Hirshman Index (HHI) will increase the most in an industry when
    a. one large firm merges with another large firm.
    b. one large firm merges with a small firm.
    c. two small firms merge.
    d. a large firm separates into two firms.

12. Which kind of merger increases the HHI and thus triggers concerns about competitiveness?
    a. horizontal mergers
    b. vertical mergers
    c. conglomerate mergers
    d. all of the above

13. In game theory
    a. there is not always a dominant strategy.
    b. a Nash equilibrium is a dominant strategy.
    c. collusion is an example of a cooperative game.
    d. all of the above are true.

14. In game theory
    a. cooperative strategies are more likely in repeated games than one-shot games.
    b. cooperative strategies are more likely in one-shot games than repeated games.
    c. cooperative strategies are equally likely in one-shot and repeated games.
    d. we do not know whether cooperative strategies are more likely in one type of game or another.

15. In game theory
    a. a dominant strategy in a noncooperative game does not yield the same result as if players cooperate.
    b. a tit-for-tat strategy is a way to reward cooperation and punish noncooperation in a repeated game.
    c. in a Nash equilibrium, neither firm has an incentive to change behavior.
    d. all of the above are true.

16. Which of the following areas illustrates positive network externalities?
    a. telephones
    b. software
    c. fax machines
    d. the Internet
    e. all of the above

Problems:

1. Which of the following markets are oligopolistic?
   a. corn
   b. funeral services
   c. airline travel
   d. hamburgers
   e. oil
   f. breakfast cereals

2. Which of the following are characteristic of oligopolistic industries?
   a. a large number of firms
   b. few firms
   c. a high degree of product differentiation
   d. high barriers to entry
   e. free entry and exit
   f. mutual interdependence

3. Suppose Farmer Smith from Kansas and Farmer Jones from Missouri agree to restrict their combined output of wheat in an attempt to increase the price and profits. How likely do you think the Smith–Jones cartel is to succeed? Explain.

4. Explain how the joint profit-maximizing price of colluding firms under oligopoly is determined. How about output?

5. Explain how the long-run equilibrium under oligopoly differs from that of perfect competition.

6. Important differences exist between perfect competition and oligopoly. Show your understanding of these differences by listing the following terms under either "perfect competition" or "oligopoly."

		Perfect Competition	Oligopoly
allocative efficiency	large economies of scale	_____	_____
many small firms	productive efficiency	_____	_____
high barriers to entry	horizontal demand curve	_____	_____
few large firms	mutual interdependence	_____	_____
downward-sloping demand curve	no control over price	_____	_____

7. One of the world's most successful cartels has been the Central Selling Organization (CSO), which controls about three-quarters of the world's diamonds. This collusive oligopoly has kept diamond prices high by restricting supply. The CSO has also promoted the general consumption of diamonds through advertising and marketing. New supplies of diamonds have been found in Canada and Russia. These new mines, which are outside the direct control of the CSO, want to sell their diamonds on the open market.
   a. What would you predict will happen in the market for diamonds if these new mines do not cooperate with the cartel?
   b. What do you think will happen to CSO diamond advertising?

8. The U.S. Justice Department has been worried that the nation's four largest air carriers—Delta, Northwest, American, and United—use low prices to limit competition at the busiest airports. Predatory pricing exists when the dominant carrier at an airport matches the low prices of any new low-fare competitor and sells more low-fare seats. The major carrier holds these low prices until the new competition folds. The dominant carrier recovers any short-term losses with increased fares once the competition is eliminated.

   The government thinks that this pricing response is an anticompetitive strategy. The dominant carriers claim that this response is simply a part of competition. Which is it? How would each of the following pieces of information affect your decision as to whether it is an anticompetitive strategy or a competitive response? Check the appropriate column.

	Anticompetitive Strategy	Competitive Response
Large, unrecoverable start-up costs for new airlines.	_____	_____
Many airlines serve the airport.	_____	_____
Dominant airline drops price below average variable cost.	_____	_____
Dominant airline flights have excess capacity before the new airline enters the market.	_____	_____

9. In the kinked demand model, what is assumed about rival responses to price increases? Price decreases? What does that imply about anticipated elasticities of demand as a result?

10. What would the Herfindahl-Hirshman Index (HHI) be in each of the following situations:
    a. 10 firms, each with 10 percent of the market
    b. 4 firms, each with 25 percent of the market
    c. 2 firms, each with 50 percent of the market
    d. 1 firm with a monopoly in the market

11. Why would someone consider how broadly or narrowly the relevant market is considered to be so critical to the results when HHI values are used to evaluate mergers?

12. Assume there are initially 10 firms, each with a 10 percent market share.
    a. What is the initial HHI?
    b. What will the HHI become if two firms merge?
    c. What will the HHI become if three firms merge?

13. Answer questions a–c on HHI.
    a. What would the HHI be for an industry made up of one firm with 30 percent of the market, and 14 firms, each with 5 percent of the market?
    b. What would the HHI be if two of the firms with 5 percent of the market merge?
    c. What would the HHI be if the large (30 percent share) firm merged with one of the smaller (5 percent share) firms?

14. Are the following mergers horizontal, vertical, or conglomerate?
    a. *Newsweek* magazine and *Time* magazine
    b. Tyson Chicken and Popeye's Chicken restaurants
    c. CBS TV and Jerry Bruckheimer Productions (TV show producer)
    d. Alcoa and McDonald's
    e. Alcoa and an aluminum siding company
    f. Sealy Mattress Company and Beautyrest Mattress Company
    g. a bakery and a sandwich chain

15. Two firms compete in the breakfast cereal industry producing Rice Krinkles and Wheat Krinkles cereal, respectively. Each manufacturer must decide whether to promote its product with a large or small advertising budget. The potential profits for these firms are as follows (in millions of dollars):

		Firm A Wheat Krinkles Cereal	
		Small Advertising Budget	Large Advertising Budget
Firm B Rice Krinkles Cereal	Small Advertising Budget	Firm (A) $50 M Firm (B) $50 M	Firm (A) $30 M Firm (B) $100 M
	Large Advertising Budget	Firm (A) $140 M Firm (B) $20 M	Firm (A) $150 M Firm (B) $150 M

Describe the nature of the mutual interdependence between the two firms. Is a Nash equilibrium evident?

16. Suppose Pepsi is considering an ad campaign aimed at rival Coca-Cola. What is the dominant strategy if the payoff matrix is similar to the one shown in Exhibit 3 in Section 15.4?

17. Suppose your professor announces that each student in your large lecture class who receives the highest score (no matter how high) on the take-home final exam will get an A in the course. The professor points out that if the entire class colludes successfully everyone could get the same score. Is it likely that everyone in the class will get an A?

18. The following payoff matrix shows the possible sentences that two suspects, who are arrested on suspicion of car theft, could receive. The suspects are interrogated separately and are unable to communicate with one another.

    Use the following information to answer the question below.

		Suspect 2	
		Confess	Don't Confess
Suspect 1	Confess	1: 6 years / 2: 6 years	1: 1 year / 2: 10 years
	Don't Confess	1: 10 years / 2: 1 year	1: 2 years / 2: 2 years

    For the information given in the payoff matrix above:
    a. Is there is a dominant strategy?
    b. What is the dominant strategy? How do you know?
    c. Is there a Nash equilibrium? How do you know?

19. Why are repeated games more likely to be cooperative than one-shot games?

20. Why might shirking on a team project in school be a dominant strategy, but not shirking on a team project at work?

PART 5 INPUT MARKETS AND MICROECONOMIC POLICY ISSUES

Chapter **16 The Markets for Labor, Capital, and Land** *454*

Chapter **17 Income and Poverty** *482*

Chapter **18 The Environment** *513*

Chapter **19 Health Care** *539*

16 The Markets for Labor, Capital, and Land

16.1 Input Markets
16.2 Supply and Demand in the Labor Market
16.3 Labor Market Equilibrium
16.4 Labor Unions
16.5 The Markets for Land and Capital

Approximately 75 percent of national income goes to wages and salaries for labor services. So, how are salary levels among those individuals determined?

After laborers take their share, the remaining 25 percent of national income is compensation received by the owners of land and capital and the entrepreneurs who employ these resources to produce valued goods and services.

In labor markets, actor Johnny Depp can make more than $20 million acting in one film. Baseball player Alex Rodriguez of the New York Yankees makes $25 million a year. Singer Madonna's income is many times larger than that of the average college professor or medical doctor. Female models make more than male models, yet male basketball players make more than female basketball players. Why do these differences occur? To understand the reasons for the wide variation in compensation workers receive for their labors, we must focus on the workings of supply and demand in the labor market.

In this chapter, we also study the relationship between productivity and wages, labor unions, and the markets for land and capital. ▪

SECTION 16.1 Input Markets

- How is income distributed among workers, landowners, and the owners of capital?
- What is derived demand?

Determining the Price of a Productive Factor: Derived Demand

derived demand
the demand for an input derived from consumers' demand for the good or service produced with that input

Input markets are the markets for the factors of production used to produce output. Output (goods and services) markets and input markets have one major difference. In input or factor markets, the demand for an input derived from consumers' demand for the good or service produced with that input is called a **derived demand.** That is, the demand for an input such as labor is derived from the demand for the good

in the news: Demand, Not Higher Salaries, Drives Up Baseball Ticket Prices

Teams that blame escalating salaries for escalating ticket prices are simply using players as a handy scapegoat, University of Chicago economist Allen Sanderson says. . . . "Player salaries have virtually no impact on ticket prices. Ticket prices are set by what the market will bear. After that, it's a matter of who gets the money, [the owners or the players]. . . ."

Remember supply and demand from your economics class? A team would raise ticket prices, regardless of player salaries, only if it believed fans would pay the higher prices. In economic jargon, a team would raise ticket prices only if it believed a demand would remain strong at the higher prices for a fixed supply of seats.

"If I'm an owner and I have to justify this to my season-ticket holders, I have to blame somebody," Sanderson said. "I can't stand up and say, 'The ticket prices are going up 19% next year because you'll pay it. . . .'"

Virtually all economists would support this application of the basic economic theory of supply and demand.

"Anyone who has studied the industry would tell you this is what's going on," said [Roger] Noll [a Stanford economist and a specialist on sports economics]. . . . "Revenues drive everything, including the degree of vitriol in collective bargaining."

So owners, defending price increases, point fingers at players. But when three national theater chains increased movie prices recently, executives did not point fingers at actors. "There was certainly no reference to . . . we have to do this because Jack Nicholson and Tom Cruise and Michelle Pfeiffer have such high salaries," Sanderson said. "I've never heard anyone say, 'If Tom Cruise would work for $10 million [a movie] instead of $20 million, my ticket would be $6 instead of $7. . . .'"

"Every sports fan, if he wants to see why player salaries are so high should go look in the mirror," Noll said. "If fans were not willing to pay a lot, salaries would not be so high. Everything starts with what consumers are willing to pay."

SOURCE: Bill Shaikin, "Face Value," *Los Angeles Times*, April 1, 1999, p. D1. Copyright © 1999 Los Angeles Times. Reprinted with permission.

consider this:

Baseball salaries are a derived demand. It is the customers' demand for a baseball game that drives baseball salaries. This same reason explains why top women's tennis players make more than top women (and men) professional bowlers.

or service. Thus, consumers do *not* demand the labor directly—it is the goods and services the labor produces that consumers demand. For example, the chef at a restaurant is paid and her skills are in demand because she produces what customers want—great-tasting meals. The "price" of any productive factor is directly related to consumer demand for the final good or service.

> **SECTION CHECK**
>
> 1. Supply and demand determine the prices paid to workers, landowners, and capital owners.
> 2. In factor or input markets, demand is derived from consumers' demand for the final good or service that the input produces.
>
> ---
>
> 1. Why is the demand for productive inputs derived from the demand for the outputs those inputs produce?
> 2. Why is the demand for tractors and fertilizer derived from the demand for agricultural products?

SECTION 16.2 Supply and Demand in the Labor Market

* What is the marginal revenue product for an input?
* What is the marginal resource cost of hiring another worker?
* Why is the demand curve for labor downward sloping?
* What is the shape of the supply curve of labor?

Will Hiring That Input Add More to Revenue Than Costs?

Because firms are trying to maximize their profits, they try (by definition) to make the *difference* between total revenue and total cost as large as possible. An input's attractiveness, then, varies with what the input can add to the firm's revenues relative to what the input adds to costs. In a competitive labor market, the demand for labor is determined by its **marginal revenue product (MRP)**, which is the additional revenue that a firm obtains from one more unit of input. Why? Suppose a worker adds $500 per week to a firm's sales by his productivity; he produces 100 units that add $5 each to firm revenue. To determine whether the worker adds to the firm's profits, we would need to calculate the marginal resource cost associated with the worker. The **marginal resource cost (MRC)** is the amount that an extra input adds to the firm's total costs. In this case, the marginal resource cost is the wage the employer has to pay to entice an extra worker. Assume that the marginal resource cost of the worker, the market wage, is $350 per worker per week. In our example, the firm would find its profits growing by adding one more worker, because the marginal benefit (MRP) associated with the worker, $500, would exceed the marginal cost (MRC) of the worker, $350. So we can see that just by adding another worker to its labor force, the firm would increase its weekly profits by $150 ($500 − $350). Even if the market wage were $490 per week, the firm could slightly increase its profits by hiring the employee, because the marginal revenue product, $500, is greater than the added labor cost, $490. At wage payments greater than $500, however, the firm would not be interested in the worker, because the marginal resource cost would exceed the marginal revenue product, making additional hiring unprofitable.

> **marginal revenue product (MRP)**
> marginal product times the price of the product
>
> **marginal resource cost (MRC)**
> the amount that an extra input adds to the firm's total cost

The Demand Curve for Labor Slopes Downward

The downward-sloping demand curve for labor indicates a negative relationship between wage and the quantity of labor demanded. Higher wages will decrease the quantity of labor demanded, while lower wages will increase the quantity of labor demanded. But why does this relationship exist?

The major reason for the downward-sloping demand curve for labor (illustrated in Exhibit 1) is the law of diminishing marginal product. Remember that the law of diminishing marginal product states that as increasing quantities of some variable input (say, labor) are added to fixed quantities of another input (say, land or capital), output will rise, but at some point it will increase by diminishing amounts.

Consider a farmer who owns a given amount of land. Suppose the farmer is producing wheat, and the relationship between output and labor force requirements is that indicated in Exhibit 2. Output expands as more workers are hired to cultivate the land, but the growth in output steadily slows, meaning that the added output associated with one more worker declines as more workers are added. For example, in Exhibit 2, when a third worker is hired, total wheat output increases from 5,500 bushels to 7,000 bushels, an increase of 1,500 bushels in terms of marginal product. However, when a fourth worker is added, total wheat output only increases from 7,000 bushels to 8,000 bushels, or a marginal increase of 1,000 bushels. Note that the reason for the decline in marginal product is *not* that the workers being added are steadily inferior in terms of ability or quality relative to the first workers. Indeed, for simplicity, we assume that each worker has exactly the same skills and productive capacity. But as more workers are added, each additional worker has fewer of the fixed resources with which to work, and marginal product falls. For example, the fifth worker might merely cultivate the same land more intensively. The work of the fifth worker, then, might only slightly improve output. That is, the **marginal product (MP)**—the number of physical units of added output from the addition of one additional unit of input—falls.

marginal product (MP)
the change in total output of a good that results from a one-unit change in input

As we discussed earlier, the marginal revenue product (*MRP*) is the change in total revenue associated with an additional unit of input. The marginal revenue product is equal to the marginal product (that is, the units of output added by a worker) multiplied by marginal revenue (*MR*) (that is, the price of the output):

$$MRP = MP \times MR$$

The *MRP* curve takes on different characteristics depending on whether the output market is competitive or imperfectly competitive. In this chapter, we are assuming the product, or output markets, are competitive. Recall from Chapter 12, that in competitive output markets, the firm will sell all its output at the market price. Consequently, the marginal revenue from the sale of an additional unit is also equal to the market price. Therefore, when output markets are perfectly

section 16.2 exhibit 2 — Diminishing Marginal Productivity on a Hypothetical Farm

Units of Labor Input (workers)	Total Wheat Output (bushels per year)	Marginal Product of Labor (bushels per year)
0	—	
		3,000
1	3,000	
		2,500
2	5,500	
		1,500
3	7,000	
		1,000
4	8,000	
		500
5	8,500	
		300
6	8,800	
		200
7	9,000	

section 16.2 exhibit 1 — The Marginal Revenue Product of Labor

The value of the marginal revenue product of labor shows how the marginal revenue product depends on the number of workers employed. The curve is downward sloping because of the diminishing marginal product of labor.

section 16.2 exhibit 3 — Marginal Revenue Product, Output, and Labor Inputs

Quantity of Labor	Total Output (bushels per week)	Marginal Product of Labor (bushels per week)	Product Price (dollars per bushel)	Marginal Revenue Product of Labor	Wage Rate (MRC) (dollars per week)	Marginal Profit (MRP − W)
0	0					
		100	$10	$1,000	$550	$450
1	100					
		90	10	900	550	350
2	190					
		80	10	800	550	250
3	270					
		70	10	700	550	150
4	340					
		60	10	600	550	50
5	400					
		50	10	500	550	−50
6	450					
		40	10	400	550	−150
7	490					
		30	10	300	550	−250
8	520					

competitive, the marginal revenue product of a factor is equal to the marginal product times the price of the product the firm is selling:

$$MRP = MP \times P$$

For example, if an additional worker adds 10 bushels of wheat per day (marginal product) and each of these 10 bushels sells for $10 (price of the product), then the worker's marginal revenue product is $100 per day.

The marginal revenue product of labor declines because of the diminishing marginal product of labor when additional workers are added. This decline in MRP is illustrated in Exhibit 3, which shows various output and revenue levels for a wheat farmer using different quantities of labor. We see in Exhibit 3 that the marginal product, or the added physical volume of output, declines as the number of workers grows, because of diminishing marginal product. Thus, the fifth worker adds only 60 bushels of wheat per week compared with 100 bushels for the first worker.

How Many Workers Will an Employer Hire?

Profits are maximized if the firm hires only to the point where the wage equals the expected marginal revenue product; that is, the firm will hire up to the last unit of input for which the marginal revenue product is expected to exceed the wage. Because the demand curve for labor and the value of the marginal revenue product show the quantity of labor that a firm demands at a given wage in a competitive market, we say that the marginal revenue product (MRP) is the same as the demand curve for labor for a competitive firm.

Using the data in Exhibit 3, if the market wage is $550 per week, it would pay for the wheat farmer to employ five workers. The fifth worker's marginal revenue product ($600) exceeds the wage, so profits are increased $50 by adding the worker. Adding a sixth worker would be unprofitable, however, as that worker's marginal revenue product of $500 is less than the wage of $550. Hiring the sixth worker would reduce profits by $50.

But what if the market wage increases from $550 to $650? In this case, hiring the fifth worker becomes unprofitable, because the marginal resource cost, $650, is now greater than the marginal revenue product of $600. That is, a higher wage rate, *ceteris paribus*, lowers the employment levels of individual firms.

In a competitive labor market, many firms are competing for workers, and no single firm is big enough by itself to have any significant effect on the level of wages. The intersection of the market supply of labor and the market demand for labor determines the competitive market wage, as shown in Exhibit 4(a). The firm's ability to hire all the workers it wishes at the prevailing wage is analogous to perfect competition in output markets, where a firm can sell all it wants at the going price.

In Exhibit 4(b), when the firm hires less than q^* workers, the marginal revenue product exceeds the market wage, so adding workers expands profits. With more than q^* workers, however, the "going wage" exceeds marginal revenue product, and hiring additional workers lowers profits. With q^* workers, profits are maximized.

In this chapter, we assume that labor markets are competitive, with many buyers and sellers of labor,

section 16.2 exhibit 4 — The Competitive Firm's Hiring Decision

a. Market Supply and Demand for Labor

b. Firm's Supply and Demand for Labor

A competitive firm can hire any number of potential workers at the market-determined wage; it is a price (wage) taker. At employment levels less than q^*, additional workers add profits. At employment levels beyond q^*, additional workers are unprofitable. At q^*, profits are maximized.

and no individual worker having an impact on wages. It is generally a realistic assumption because in most labor markets firms compete with each other to attract workers, and workers can choose from many possible employers.

The Market Labor Supply Curve

How much work effort individuals are collectively willing and able to supply in the marketplace is the essence of the market supply curve. Just as was the case in our earlier discussion of the law of supply, a positive relationship exists between the wage rate and the quantity of labor supplied. As the wage rate rises, the quantity of labor supplied increases, *ceteris paribus*; as the wage rate falls, the quantity of labor supplied falls, *ceteris paribus*. This positive relationship is consistent with the evidence that the total quantity of labor supplied by *all* workers increases as the wage rate increases, as shown in Exhibit 5.

An Individual's Labor Supply Curve

Will the quantity of labor supplied by an individual be greater at higher wages than at lower wages? The answer is by no means obvious because workers have another use for their time—namely, leisure. Furthermore, wage increases have two conflicting effects on the quantity of labor supplied:

section 16.2 exhibit 5 — The Market Supply Curve of Labor

An increase in the wage rate, from A to B, leads to an increase in the quantity of labor supplied, *ceteris paribus*. A decrease in the wage rate, from B to A, leads to a decrease in the quantity of labor supplied, *ceteris paribus*.

1. *Substitution effect:* At a higher wage rate, the cost of forgoing labor time to gain greater leisure time increases, producing a tendency to substitute labor for leisure. In other words, a higher wage rate makes leisure more expensive—its opportunity cost rises.

2. *Income effect:* At a higher wage rate, the quantity of labor supplied tends to decrease because many individuals consider leisure a normal good. So when income increases, people demand more leisure. That is, at some wage rate, some workers feel that they can afford more leisure.

backward-bending labor supply curve
above a certain wage rate, a worker may prefer to enjoy more leisure and less work to meet his or her own personal preferences (the income effect dominates the substitution effect)

Thus, the individual's labor supply curve might be backward bending. At a lower wage rate, as wages increase, the worker might supply more hours of work to obtain as much money income as possible (the substitution effect dominates the income effect), an upward-sloping labor supply curve. However, above a certain wage rate, a worker might prefer to enjoy more leisure and less work to meet personal preferences (the income effect dominates the substitution effect), a **backward-bending labor supply curve.** That is, if the substitution effect is stronger than the income effect, the individual's labor supply curve is upward sloping. If the income effect is stronger than the substitution effect, the individual's labor supply curve is backward bending. For example, a student working during the summer to earn money for the school year might quit her job once she has reached a certain level of earnings; she then concentrates on leisure for the rest of the summer. The great American writer Henry David Thoreau worked a couple of months each year to make enough money to spend the rest of the year at Walden Pond, pursuing his pastime of writing and observing nature. In both these cases, the individual's labor supply curve might appear as shown in Exhibit 6. Actually, the market supply curve might actually bend backwards too but at a much higher wage rate than what currently exists. In the rest of this chapter, therefore, we will assume that the market supply curve is upward sloping, at least in the relevant range.

section 16.2 exhibit 6 An Individual's Backward-Bending Labor Supply Curve

B→C The income effect is stronger than the substitution effect.

A→B The substitution effect is stronger than the income effect.

SECTION CHECK

1. The demand curve for labor is downward sloping because of diminishing marginal product. That is, if additional labor is added to a fixed quantity of land or capital equipment, output will increase, but eventually by smaller amounts.
2. The value of the marginal product of labor is the marginal product times the price of the output.
3. Along a market supply curve, a higher wage rate will increase the quantity supplied of labor and a lower wage rate will decrease the quantity supplied of labor.
4. An individual labor supply curve can be backward bending. When higher wages are offered, the cost of forgoing labor time to gain greater leisure time becomes greater; thus, workers tend to substitute labor for leisure—the substitution effect. At higher wage levels, the income from a given quantity of labor is greater, and a worker may feel that he or she can afford more leisure—the income effect. If the substitution effect is stronger than the income effect, the individual's labor supply curve is upward sloping. If the income effect is stronger than the substitution effect, the individual's labor supply curve is backward bending.

1. What is marginal revenue product?
2. Would a firm hire another worker if the marginal revenue product of labor exceeded the market wage rate? Why or why not?
3. Why does the marginal product of labor eventually fall?
4. Why does diminishing marginal product mean that the marginal revenue product will eventually fall?
5. Why is a firm hiring in a competitive labor market a price (wage) taker for a given quality of labor?
6. What is responsible for a backward-bending individual supply curve for labor?

SECTION 16.3 Labor Market Equilibrium

- How are the equilibrium wage and employment determined in labor markets?
- What shifts the labor demand curve?
- What shifts the labor supply curve?

Determining Equilibrium in the Competitive Labor Market

The equilibrium wage and quantity in competitive markets for labor is determined by the intersection of labor demand and labor supply. As shown in Exhibit 1, the equilibrium wage, W^*, and equilibrium employment level, Q^*, are found at that point where the quantity of labor demanded equals the quantity of labor supplied. At any wage higher than W^*—at W_1, for example—the quantity of labor supplied exceeds the quantity of labor demanded, resulting in a surplus of labor. In this situation, unemployed workers are willing to undercut the established wage in order to get jobs, pushing the wage down and returning the market to equilibrium. At a wage below the equilibrium level—at W_2, for example—quantity demanded exceeds quantity supplied, resulting in a labor shortage. In this situation, employers are forced to offer higher wages in order to hire as many workers as they would like. Note that only at the equilibrium wage are both suppliers and demanders able to exchange the quantity of labor they desire.

Shifts in the Labor Demand Curve

In Chapter 4, we demonstrated that the determinants of demand can shift the demand curve for a good or service. In the case of an input such as labor, two important factors can shift the demand curve: increases in labor productivity—caused by technological advances, for instance—or changes in the output price of the good—caused by, say, an increased demand for the firm's product. Exhibit 2 highlights the impact of these changes.

Changes in Labor Productivity

Workers can increase productivity if they have more capital or land with which to work, if technological improvements occur, or if they acquire additional skills or experience (human capital). This increase in productivity will increase the marginal product of the labor and shift the demand curve for labor to the right from D_1 to D_2 in Exhibit 2(a). However, if labor productivity falls, then marginal product will fall, and the demand curve for labor will shift to the left [see Exhibit 2(b)].

Changes in the Demand for the Firm's Product

The greater the demand for the firm's product, the greater the firm's demand for labor or any other variable input (the *derived demand* discussed earlier). The reason for this is that the higher demand for the firm's product increases the firm's marginal revenue, which increases marginal revenue product. That is, the greater

section 16.3 exhibit 1 — Supply and Demand in the Competitive Labor Market

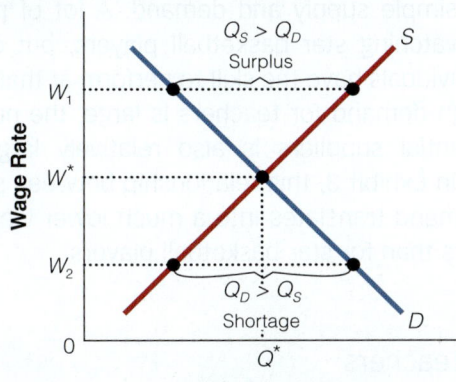

Equilibrium prices and quantities in the competitive labor market are determined in the same way prices and quantities of goods and services are determined: by the intersection of demand and supply. At wages above the equilibrium wage—at W_1, for example—quantity supplied exceeds quantity demanded, and potential workers are willing to supply their labor services for an amount lower than the prevailing wage. At a wage lower than W^*—at W_2, for example—potential demanders overcome the resulting shortage of labor by offering workers a wage greater than the prevailing wage. In both cases, wages are pushed toward the equilibrium value.

section 16.3 exhibit 2 — Shifts in the Labor Demand Curve

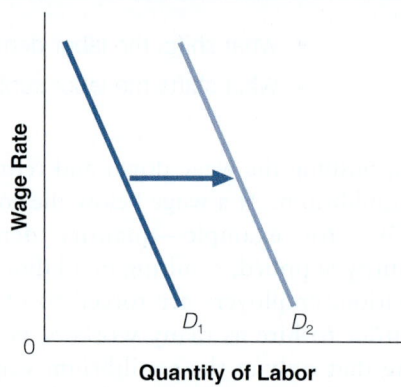

a. Increase in Labor Demand

b. Decrease in Labor Demand

An increase in labor demand will shift the demand curve for labor to the right. A decrease in labor demand will shift the demand curve for labor to the left.

Use what you've LEARNED: LABOR SUPPLY AND DEMAND

Q Why do teachers, who provide a valuable service to the community, make millions and millions of dollars less than star basketball players?

A It is the marginal revenue product of additional teachers and the supply of teachers that determine the market wage (regardless of how important we consider the job). A teacher's marginal revenue product is likely to be well below $5 million a year. Most people probably think that teachers are more important than star basketball players, yet teachers make a lot less money. Of course, the reason for this is simple supply and demand. A lot of people enjoy watching star basketball players, but only a few individuals have the skill to perform at that level. Although demand for teachers is large, the number of potential suppliers is also relatively large. As shown in Exhibit 3, this relationship between supply and demand translates into a much lower wage for teachers than for star basketball players.

section 16.3 exhibit 3 — Labor Markets for Basketball Players and Teachers

a. Labor Market for Star Basketball Players

b. Labor Market for Teachers

demand for the product causes prices to rise, and the price of the product is part of the value of the labor to the firm ($MRP = MP \times P$). Therefore, the rising product price shifts the labor demand curve to the right. Of course, if demand for the firm's product falls, the labor demand curve will shift to the left as marginal revenue product falls.

Shifting the Labor Supply Curve

In Chapter 4, we learned that changes in the determinants of supply can shift the supply curve for goods and services to the right or left. Likewise, several factors can cause the labor supply curve to shift. These factors include immigration and population growth, the number of hours workers are willing to work at a given wage (worker tastes or preferences), nonwage income, and amenities. Exhibit 4 illustrates the impact of these factors on the labor supply curve.

Immigration and Population Growth

If new workers enter the labor force, the labor supply curve will shift to the right—from S_1 to S_2 in Exhibit 4(a). Of course, if workers leave the country—and thus the labor force—or the relevant population declines, the supply curve will shift to the left, as shown in Exhibit 4(b).

Number of Hours People Are Willing to Work (Worker Preferences)

If people become willing to work more hours at a given wage (due to changes in worker tastes or preferences), the labor supply curve will shift to the right, as shown in the movement from S_1 to S_2 in Exhibit 4(a). If they become willing to work fewer hours at a given wage, the labor supply curve will shift to the left, as shown in Exhibit 4(b).

Nonwage Income

Increases in income from other sources than employment can cause the labor supply curve to shift to the left. For example, if you just won $20 million in your state's Super Lotto, you might decide to take yourself out of the labor force. Likewise, a decrease in nonwage income might push a person back into the labor force, thus shifting the labor supply curve to the right.

Amenities

Amenities associated with a job or location—such as good fringe benefits, safe and friendly working conditions, a child-care center, and so on—will make for a more desirable work environment, *ceteris paribus*. These amenities will cause an increase in the supply of labor, resulting in a rightward shift of the labor supply curve—from S_1 to S_2 in Exhibit 4(a). If job conditions deteriorate, the labor supply will decrease, shifting the labor supply curve to the left, as shown in Exhibit 4(b).

section 16.3
exhibit 4 Shifts in the Labor Supply Curve

An increase in labor supply shifts the supply curve to the right. A decrease in labor supply shifts the curve to the left.

Monopsony

So far our discussion assumed that the labor market is competitive—many buyers of labor and many sellers of labor with no one having a marked impact on wages. Recall that, in the case of a single seller of a product or input, we say a monopoly exists. When the market involves a single buyer, however, we say a **monopsony** exists. While monopsony could exist in any single buyer situation, the situation considered most relevant in the real world is the labor market. Monopsony usually refers, then, to circumstances where only one employer is bidding for the services of many laborers. Where monopsony is present, the buyer of labor may have market power and may be able to affect wages. However, pure monopsony, like pure monopoly, is rare. For example, monopsony may arise because a person within a given locality has only a relatively few choices of where to work. However, if the individual was willing to move, or the number of buyers of services potentially is enlarged, then the role of a monopsony is diminished. So monopsony power is more likely to be present where movement and search costs impede workers from seeking employment in different locales.

In the nineteenth century, one or two textile mills often dominated New England mill towns; in other areas, a single mining or manufacturing firm dominated the community to the point that it might be called a company town. Monopsony power existed in such situations and increased the opportunities for monopsonistic exploitation. Even though no fences around the town kept workers from leaving, high transportation and information costs made it expensive, sometimes prohibitively so, for workers to overcome exploitation by moving. The theory suggests that where monopsony exists, fewer workers will be hired at lower wages than if perfect competition prevailed in labor markets. That is, the monopsony firm moves down along the positively sloped labor supply curve it faces, lowering the wages it pays and increasing its profits. In short, workers will work for less than their marginal revenue product—they are in this sense exploited.

monopsony
a market with a single buyer

Today, an example of monopsony power would include the only auto repair shop in a small town—if workers do not want to move. In some professional sports, players are drafted and are assigned to teams until they are eligible to be free agents (after six years in baseball). Because other teams cannot compete for these players, the outcome is lower salaries, as teams exercise their monopsony power. However, for the most part, in most occupations, many potential employers in many different locations compete for workers.

SECTION CHECK

1. The intersection of the labor demand curve and the labor supply curve determines wages in the labor market.
2. The labor demand curve can shift when a change in productivity or a change in the demand for the final product occurs.
3. The labor supply curve can shift when changes in immigration or population growth, workers' preferences, nonwage income, or amenities occur.

---

1. If wages were above their equilibrium level, why would they tend to fall toward the equilibrium level?
2. If wages were below their equilibrium level, why would they tend to rise toward the equilibrium level?
3. Why do increases in technology or increases in the amounts of capital or other complementary inputs increase the demand for labor?
4. Why do any of the demand shifters for output markets shift the demand for labor and other inputs used to produce that output in the same direction?
5. Why do increases in immigration or population growth, increases in workers' willingness to work at a given wage, decreases in nonwage income, or increases in workplace amenities increase the supply of labor?
6. What would happen to the supply of labor if nonwage incomes increased and workplace amenities also increased over the same period?
7. Why are wages in different fields not necessarily related to how important people think those jobs are?
8. If the private-market wage of engineers was greater than that of sociologists, what would happen if a university tried to pay its engineering faculty and its sociology faculty the same salary?

SECTION 16.4
Labor Unions

- Why do labor unions exist?
- What is the impact of unions on wages?
- Can unions increase productivity?

Labor Unions in the United States

Before the Civil War, when the country was still largely rural and agricultural, labor unions were few, weak, and short-lived. After the Civil War, industrialization grew rapidly. The proportion of the labor force in manufacturing went from 10 percent in 1860 to nearly 30 percent by 1920. Union membership rose after 1880. The rise in labor unions was partially due to the horrendous working conditions in factories—women and children as young as 5 were operating dangerous machinery for 14 hours a day, 7 days a week. In short, early union demands were not only for higher wages but for shorter workweeks and better working conditions too. In the last 60 years, the percentage of workers in union jobs has fallen sharply from 33 percent to 12.4 percent as seen in Exhibit 1. The percentage of workers in the public sector remains high—almost 40 percent of public sector workers are members of a union. In private industry, less than 8 percent are union members. In education, teachers' organizations such as the National Education Association (NEA) have become powerful labor unions.

Several possible reasons explain the recent decline in labor union membership. First, a shift of U.S. workers shows them moving out of manufacturing into the service sector, where unions typically have a smaller presence. Second, in recent years the federal government deregulated heavily unionized industries such as trucking, railroad, and the airline industry. This deregulation led to increased competition at home and abroad, and consequently, firms hired fewer expensive non-union workers. Third, global competition means many firms must close down plants and lay off workers. This "downsizing" makes it more difficult for unions to gain concessions from firms. Fourth, the federal government passed new laws regarding safer workplaces.

Labor Legislation

Worker alienation and dissatisfaction grew with the rapidly rising unemployment of the early 1930s. Previous depressions in economic activity were accompanied by

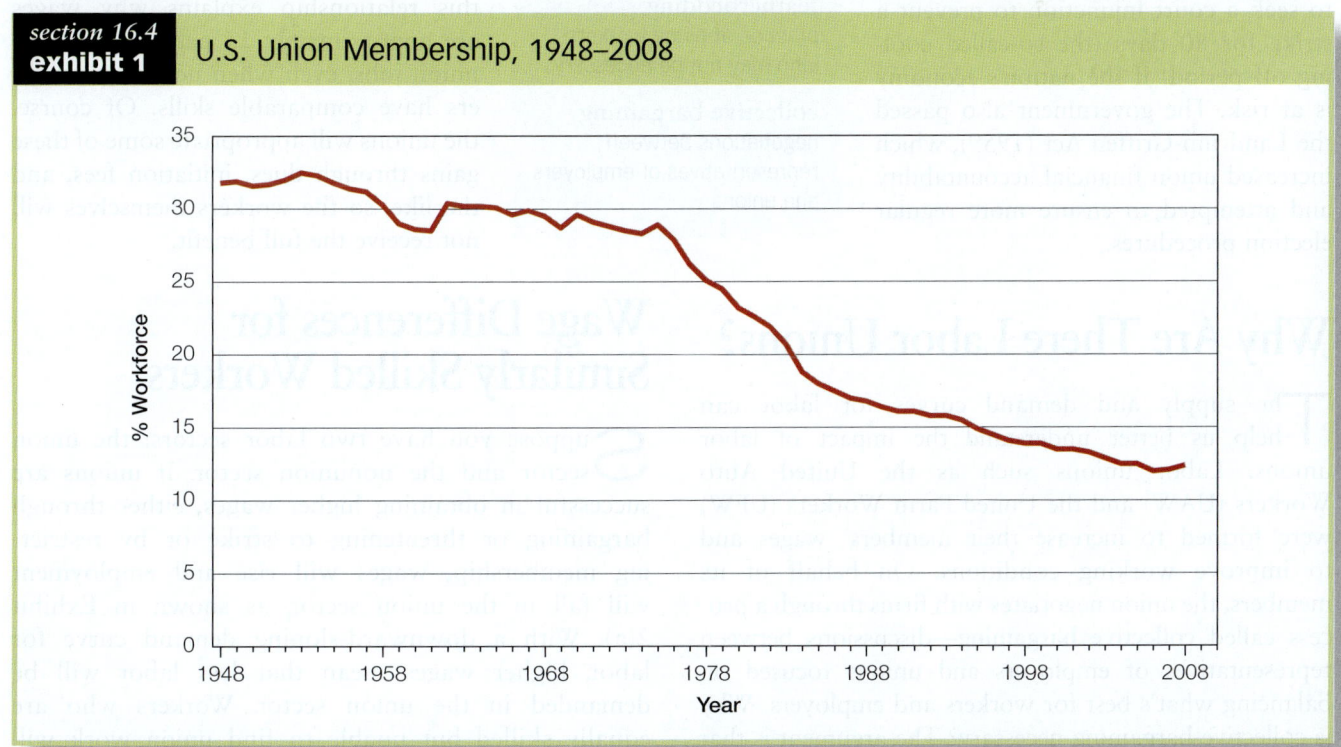

section 16.4 exhibit 1 U.S. Union Membership, 1948–2008

SOURCES: *Union Sourcebook* 1947–1983; U.S. Bureau of Labor Statistics.

a decline in union membership, as unemployed workers dropped their memberships and even employed workers were afraid to stay in unions knowing that the employer could readily "break" the union given the large pool of unemployed. But in the 1930s, the deteriorating economy provided a setting for pro-labor legislation. Several laws were passed that restricted the practices of employers in fighting unions and created a right for employees to engage in collective bargaining.

By far the most important of the labor law reforms of the 1930s was the National Labor Relations Act of 1935, more popularly known as the Wagner Act. The **Wagner Act** protected the right of workers to organize and bargain collectively. In the late 1930s and early 1940s, most of the heavy mass production industries, such as steel and automobiles, unionized for the first time.

The **Taft-Hartley Act** (1947) restricted somewhat the power of unions granted by the Wagner Act. The closed shop that required union membership before employment could be obtained was outlawed. The union shop, which permitted nonunion workers to be hired but required them to join the union within 30 days, was permissible. **Featherbedding,** the practice of adding workers who may not be necessary, was also prohibited by the 1947 law, but it has been difficult to enforce. However, the most famous provision of the Taft-Hartley Act is that it allows the president to seek a court injunction to prevent a strike for 80 days (the so-called cooling off period) if the nation's economy is at risk. The government also passed the Landrum-Griffen Act (1959), which increased union financial accountability and attempted to ensure more regular election procedures.

> **Wagner Act**
> legislation enacted in 1935 that protected workers' rights to organize and bargain collectively
>
> **Taft-Hartley Act**
> legislation enacted in 1947 to somewhat restrict the power of unions granted by the Wagner Act
>
> **featherbedding**
> practice of hiring workers who may not be necessary
>
> **collective bargaining**
> negotiations between representatives of employers and unions

more distant from the workers. In small shops or on farms, workers usually have a close relationship with an owner/employer; but in larger enterprises, the workers may only know a supervisor and have no direct contact with either the owner or upper management. Workers realize that acting together, as a union of workers, they have more power in the collective bargaining process than they would acting individually.

Union Impact on Labor Supply and Wages

Labor unions influence the quantity of union labor hired and the wages at which they are hired, primarily through their ability to alter the supply of labor services from what would exist if workers acted independently. One way of influencing supply, of course, is by raising barriers to entry into a given occupation. For example, by restricting membership, unions can reduce the quantity of labor supplied to industry employers from what it otherwise would be. As a result, wages in that occupation will increase, as shown in Exhibit 2(a), from W_1 to W_2. As you can see in the shift from Q_1 to Q_2, some union workers will consequently receive higher wages, but others will become unemployed. Many economists believe that this relationship explains why wages are approximately 15 percent higher in union jobs, even when nonunion workers have comparable skills. Of course, the unions will appropriate some of these gains through dues, initiation fees, and the like, so the workers themselves will not receive the full benefit.

Why Are There Labor Unions?

The supply and demand curves for labor can help us better understand the impact of labor unions. Labor unions such as the United Auto Workers (UAW) and the United Farm Workers (UFW) were formed to increase their members' wages and to improve working conditions. On behalf of its members, the union negotiates with firms through a process called **collective bargaining**—discussions between representatives of employers and unions focused on balancing what's best for workers and employers. Why is collective bargaining necessary? The argument is that when economies begin to industrialize and urbanize, firms become larger, and often the "boss" becomes

Wage Differences for Similarly Skilled Workers

Suppose you have two labor sectors: the union sector and the nonunion sector. If unions are successful in obtaining higher wages, either through bargaining or threatening to strike or by restricting membership, wages will rise and employment will fall in the union sector, as shown in Exhibit 2(a). With a downward-sloping demand curve for labor, higher wages mean that less labor will be demanded in the union sector. Workers who are equally skilled but unable to find union work will seek nonunion work, thus increasing supply and, in turn, lowering wages in the nonunion sector.

section 16.4 exhibit 2 — The Effect of Unions on Wages

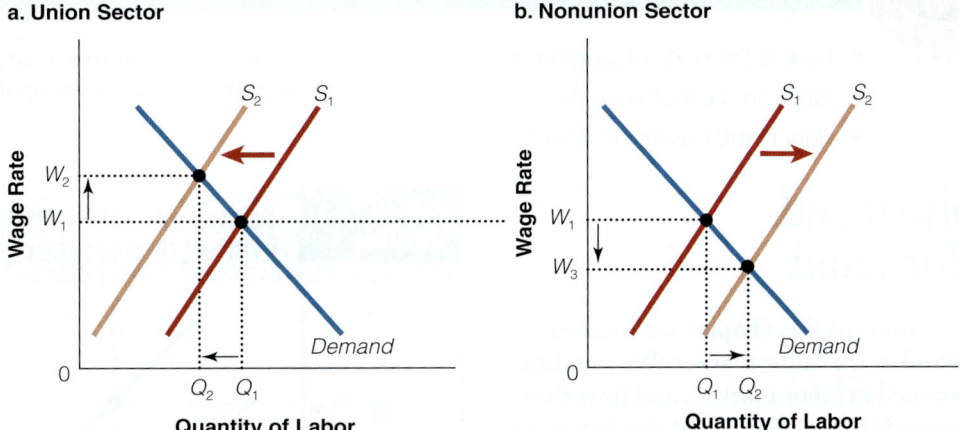

Through restrictive membership practices and other means, a union can reduce the labor supply in its industry, thereby increasing the wage rate they can earn (from W_1 to W_2) but reducing employment (from Q_1 to Q_2), as shown in (a). However, as workers unable to get jobs in the union sector join the nonunion sector, the supply of labor in the nonunion sector increases (from Q_1 to Q_2), lowering wages in those industries (from W_1 to W_3), as shown in (b).

This effect is shown in Exhibit 2(b). Thus, comparably skilled workers will experience higher wages in the union sector (W_1) than in the nonunion sector (W_2).

Can Unions Lead to Increased Productivity?

Harvard economists Richard Freeman and James Medoff argue that unions might actually increase worker productivity by increasing marginal productivity. Their argument is that unions provide a collective voice that workers can use to communicate their discontents more effectively, thereby lowering the number of union workers who quit their jobs. Resignations can be particularly costly for firms that invest in training their employees in job-specific skills. In addition, by handling worker's grievances, unions may increase worker motivation and morale. The combined impact of fewer resignations and improved morale could boost productivity.

However, this improvement in worker productivity in the labor sector should show up on the bottom line—the profit statement of the firm. Although the evidence is still preliminary, it appears that unions tend to lower the profitability of firms, not raise it.

SECTION CHECK

1. Workers realize that acting together gives them collective bargaining power.
2. Labor unions try to increase their members' wages and improve working conditions.
3. Through restrictive membership, a union can reduce the labor supply in the market for union workers, thus reducing employment and raising wages. This union "restriction" increases the supply of workers in the nonunion sector and shifts supply to the right, lowering wages for nonunion workers.

---

1. How can acting together as a group increase workers' bargaining power?
2. Why are service industries harder to unionize than manufacturing industries?
3. How do union restrictions on membership or other barriers to entry affect the wages of members?
4. What would increasing unionization do to the wages of those who are not in unions?
5. How can unions potentially increase worker productivity?
6. Why do data indicating that unionization tends to lower firm profits weaken the argument that unions might actually increase worker productivity?

SECTION 16.5 The Markets for Land and Capital

- How is the price of land determined?
- What are economic rents?
- How is the price of capital determined?
- How does a potential investor decide whether to purchase capital or not?

The Supply of and Demand for Land

In the first four sections of this chapter we focused on supply and demand in the labor market. We saw how wages were determined in labor markets and how firms determined how much labor to use and the forces of supply and demand in the union market for workers. However, firms must also decide on the other inputs of production—land and capital: how much capital to employ or how much land to acquire.

You might think of the term *rent* as something you pay at the beginning of the month to compensate the owner for the use of a house or an apartment. But economists use this term in a narrower sense. **Economic rent** is the price paid for land or any other factor that has a fixed supply—a perfectly inelastic supply curve. For example, for the most part, the total supply of land in the country can be viewed as fixed—that is, the supply of land is perfectly inelastic and not at all responsive to prices. The same amount of land will be available at zero price as at a high price. The supply curve does not shift. Only so much land is available.

In Exhibit 1, we see that the price of using land is determined by demand and supply considerations. Because the supply curve is completely inelastic, demand determines the price of the land. If the demand is high, D_{High}, the rental price of the land is high, at R_{High}; if the demand for the land is low, D_{Low}, the rental price of the land is low at R_{Low}. Only changes in the demand for land will change the price of land.

section 16.5 exhibit 1 Supply and Demand in the Land Market

Because the supply of land is perfectly inelastic, demand determines the amount paid to landowners.

economic rent
the payment for the use of any resource above its opportunity cost

What Causes High Rents?

Rents are high because of a high demand for land, but what causes the demand for land to be high? It is derived from the demand for the products being produced. Suppose an effective advertising campaign promises that cotton is going to keep us looking and feeling cooler. That is, the price of cotton is now higher because of the higher demand for cotton as a result of the advertising campaign. If the supply of land suitable for raising cotton is fixed, an increase in the demand for cotton raises the demand (or the MRP) of land, driving up rents.

That same reason explains why rents are high for stores in trendy locations. Rents are bid up as prospective tenants compete with each other for the desirable location. The reason for the bidding wars for the busy locations is that each prospective tenant sees the potential for greater revenue there than elsewhere.

Supply and Demand in the Capital Market

Capital (buildings, machines, and equipment) can be "leased" or "rented" for some stipulated period of time. For example, an airline might lease an airplane or a firm might rent a warehouse. Suppose a company were in the market for a certain type of machine that can be used in making chocolate. Following the law of demand, the lower the rental price of a chocolate-making machine (which would lower the cost of making chocolate), the greater the quantity of chocolate

Why is the price of land so expensive in Malibu? The supply of land is fixed in the short run. That is, no matter whether the price is high or low, only so much land is available in Malibu. It is the demand for living on the beach, good air quality, and closeness to the city of Los Angeles that is high. These features, in turn, increase the demand for land, which drives up the price of land. In Malibu, summer rents of $100,000 a month are not uncommon.

section 16.5 exhibit 2 — The Supply and Demand for Capital Goods

The intersection of the upward-sloping supply curve for capital and the downward-sloping demand curve for capital determines the rental price of capital.

machines demanded. Following the law of supply, the greater the rental price of the machine, the more willing owners of chocolate machines are to supply them to entrepreneurs.

Rather than renting a chocolate machine, the company may borrow funds and buy its own machine. In this case, the manufacturer is borrowing funds for the purpose of acquiring capital. The cost of the borrowed funds is usually called **interest.** At lower interest rates, the cost of financing the purchase of the chocolate machine is lower. If a machine costs $1,000 and the interest rate being charged is 10 percent, the interest cost of a chocolate machine is $100 a year ($1,000 × 0.10); if the relevant interest rate is 8 percent, interest costs are only $80 a year ($1,000 × 0.08). At lower interest rates, then, capital costs are lower, and the quantity of funds demanded is greater. Likewise, fund lenders will derive greater income the greater the interest rate, so the benefits to them of making a loan increase as interest rates (the "price" of funds) rise. Thus, the quantity of funds supplied is positively related to interest rates.

The graph in Exhibit 2 is virtually the same whether we are renting the capital equipment or borrowing to pay for that capital. The demand for capital, just like labor, is a derived demand. When a firm increases its capital, the value it receives equals the increase in revenue the firm receives from selling another unit of output by employing the machine. The marginal revenue product curve is the demand curve for capital.

The demand curve for capital is downward sloping, reflecting the fact that as more capital is employed, the value of the marginal product of capital falls. The supply curve for capital is upward sloping, implying that owners of capital face increasing marginal costs and will be more willing to supply at higher prices. The rental price of capital is found at the intersection of the supply and demand curves. At equilibrium, suppliers receive a rental price equal to the marginal revenue product of capital. That is, in equilibrium: The rental price of capital is equal to: the marginal product of capital.

interest — the cost of borrowed funds

The Interdependence of Input Markets

For simplicity, we treated the labor, capital, and land markets independently. In reality, these markets are interconnected. For example, if wages rise or the rental price of capital falls, machines might be substituted for some workers.

Income Distribution and Marginal Productivity

marginal productivity theory of income distribution
income is distributed according to marginal revenue product of the factors of production individuals own

As we have seen, in competitive equilibrium labor, land, and capital receive a price that equals its marginal revenue product. Because marginal revenue product equals the value of each factor's marginal contribution to the productivity of a good or service, it can be used to explain the distribution of income. For example, workers will receive compensation/wages plus other "fringe benefits" that are equal to their marginal contribution to output. That is, workers are paid for the value of their contribution to output. This is also true of owners of capital and land. The greater quantity and quality an owner of a factor of production possesses, the greater that owner's income. That is, each person receives income for what he or she creates—the marginal revenue product. This theory is called the **marginal productivity theory of income distribution.**

SECTION CHECK

1. The intersection of the supply and demand curves for land determines the price of land, the compensation to land owners.
2. At the profit-maximizing level, the price of land will equal the value of the marginal product of land.
3. Economic rent represents the payment that the resource owner receives beyond its opportunity cost.
4. The demand and supply curves for capital determine the compensation paid to the owners of capital.
5. In equilibrium, the rental price of capital equals the marginal revenue product of capital.

---

1. If the supply of land was perfectly inelastic, how much would the price of land rise if the price of crops raised on the land doubled, other things equal? What if the supply of land was less than perfectly inelastic?
2. Why is the demand curve for capital downward sloping?
3. Why is the supply curve for capital upward sloping?

Interactive Chapter Summary

Fill in the blanks:

1. In input or factor markets, the demand for an input is a _____ demand—_____ from consumers' demand for the good or service.
2. The demand for labor is determined by its _____, which is the additional revenue that a firm obtains from one more unit of input.
3. The _____ is the amount that an extra input adds to a firm's total costs.
4. A firm would find its profits growing by adding one more worker when the _____ associated with the worker exceeds the _____ of the worker.
5. The law of diminishing marginal product reflects the fact that by adding increasing quantities of a(n) _____ input (e.g., labor) to fixed quantities of another input, output will rise, but at some point it will increase by _____ amounts.
6. Profits are maximized if a firm hires only to the point where the wage equals the expected _____.
7. As the wage rate rises, the quantity of labor supplied _____, ceteris paribus; as the wage falls, the quantity of labor supplied _____, ceteris paribus.
8. At a wage below the equilibrium level, quantity _____ would exceed quantity _____, resulting in a labor _____. In this situation, employers would be forced to offer higher wages in order to hire as many workers as they would like.
9. Increases in the demand curve for labor may arise from _____ in labor productivity or from _____ in the price of the good.

10. Workers can increase productivity if they have more _____ or land with which to work, if _____ improvements occur, or if they acquire additional _____ or experience.

11. If labor productivity falls, then the demand curve for labor will shift to the _____.

12. If new workers enter the labor force, the labor supply curve will shift to the _____.

13. If unions are successful in raising union wages, the result will be _____ wages in the nonunion sector.

14. When a market consists of a single buyer, we say _____ exists.

15. Monopsony power is more likely to be present when high _____ and _____ costs are involved.

16. Under monopsony, _____ workers will be hired at _____ wages than if perfect competition prevailed in a labor market.

17. Monopsony tends to result in _____ profits for a firm.

18. The percentage of workers in the public sector that are unionized is far _____ than average in the economy.

19. The most important labor law reform of the 1930s was the _____, also known as the Wagner Act.

20. The Taft-Hartley Act outlawed a _____ shop, which required union membership before employment could be obtained.

21. Unions have a much _____ presence in other industrial countries than in the United States.

22. _____ is the price paid for land or any other factor that has a fixed supply.

23. The supply of land is perfectly _____.

24. An increase in the demand for land will _____ the quantity supplied and _____ the price of land.

25. For a given supply of land capable of growing cotton, an increase in the demand for cotton will _____ rents.

26. Economic rent is the payment to a resource in excess of its _____.

27. The cost of borrowed funds is called _____.

28. At _____ interest rates, capital costs are lower.

29. The quantity of funds supplied is _____ related to the interest rate.

30. The intersection of the supply of capital and the demand for capital determines the rental _____ of capital.

31. At equilibrium suppliers of capital receive a rental price equal to the _____.

Answers: 1. derived; derived 2. marginal revenue product 3. marginal resource cost 4. marginal benefit; marginal cost 5. variable; diminishing 6. marginal revenue product 7. increases; decreases 8. demanded; supplied shortage 9. increases; changes 10. capital; technological; skills 11. left 12. right 13. lower 14. monopsony 15. movement; search 16. fewer; higher 17. lower 18. larger 19. National Labor Relations Act 20. closed 21. larger 22. Economic rent 23. inelastic 24. not change; increase 25. increase 26. opportunity cost 27. interest 28. lower 29. positively 30. price 31. marginal revenue product of capital

Key Terms and Concepts

derived demand 455
marginal revenue product (MRP) 456
marginal resource cost (MRC) 456
marginal product (MP) 457
backward-bending labor supply curve 460

monopsony 464
Wagner Act 466
Taft-Hartley Act 466
featherbedding 466
collective bargaining 466

economic rent 468
interest 469
marginal productivity theory of income distribution 470

Section Check Answers

16.1 Input Markets

1. **Why is the demand for productive inputs derived from the demand for the outputs those inputs produce?**
   The demand for productive inputs is derived from the demand for the outputs those inputs produce because the value to a firm of the services of a productive input depends on the value of the outputs produced, and the value of the output depends on the demand for that output.

2. **Why is the demand for tractors and fertilizer derived from the demand for agricultural products?**
   The reason farmers demand tractors and fertilizer is that they increase the output of crops they grow. But the value to farmers of the additional crops they can grow as a result is greater, the higher the price of those crops. Therefore, the greater the demand for those crops, other things equal, the higher the price of those crops, which increases the demand for tractors and fertilizer by increasing the value to farmers of the added output they make possible.

16.2 Supply and Demand in the Labor Market

1. **What is marginal revenue product?**
   Marginal revenue product is the additional revenue that a firm obtains from employing one more unit of an input. It is equal to the marginal product multiplied by marginal revenue.

2. **Would a firm hire another worker if the marginal revenue product of labor exceeded the market wage rate? Why or why not?**
   A firm would hire another worker if the marginal revenue product of labor exceeded the market wage rate, because doing so would add more to its total revenue than it would add to its total costs, raising profits.

3. **Why does the marginal product of labor eventually fall?**
   As more and more units of the variable input labor are added to a given quantity of the fixed input, land or capital, the additional output from each additional unit of labor must begin to fall at some point. This is the law of diminishing marginal product.

4. **Why does diminishing marginal product mean that the marginal revenue product will eventually fall?**
   Since marginal revenue product equals marginal product times marginal revenue, the eventually falling marginal product means that the marginal revenue product must also eventually fall, even if the price of the output did not fall with increasing output. If the marginal revenue falls with increasing output, that will also cause marginal revenue product to fall with additional output.

5. **Why is a firm hiring in a competitive labor market a price (wage) taker for a given quality of labor?**
   A perfectly competitive seller cannot by its output choices appreciably affect the market quantity, and thereby the market price of that output, and so it takes the output market price as given. In just the same way, a firm hiring in a competitive labor market cannot by its input (hiring) choices appreciably affect the quantity of that input employed, and therefore the market price of that input, and so it takes the input (labor) market price (wage) as given.

6. **What is responsible for a backward-bending individual supply curve for labor?**
   A backward-bending individual supply curve for labor would result when the income effect of a higher wage (since leisure is a normal good, a higher income leads to a reduction in labor supplied as a result) dominates the substitution effect of a higher wage (at a higher wage, the cost of forgoing labor time for leisure becomes greater, leading to an increase in labor supplied).

16.3 Labor Market Equilibrium

1. **If wages were above their equilibrium level, why would they tend to fall toward the equilibrium level?**
   If wages were above their equilibrium level, the quantity of labor supplied at that price would exceed the quantity of labor demanded at that price. The resulting surplus of labor would lead workers frustrated by their inability to get jobs to compete the wage for those jobs down toward the equilibrium level.

2. **If wages were below their equilibrium level, why would they tend to rise toward the equilibrium level?**
   If wages were below their equilibrium level, the quantity of labor demanded at that price would exceed the quantity of labor supplied at that price. The resulting shortage of labor would lead employers frustrated by their ability to find workers to compete the wage for those jobs up toward the equilibrium level.

3. **Why do increases in technology or increases in the amounts of capital or other complementary inputs increase the demand for labor?**
   Increases in technology or increases in the amounts of capital or other complementary inputs increase the demand for labor by increasing the productivity of labor; as labor productivity increases, the marginal revenue product of labor (the demand for labor) increases.

4. **Why do any of the demand shifters for output markets shift the demand for labor and other inputs used to produce that output in the same direction?**
   When any of the demand shifters for output markets change the price of that output, it changes the marginal revenue product (marginal product times price) of labor and other inputs used to produce that output in the same direction.

5. **Why do increases in immigration or population growth, increases in workers' willingness to work at a given wage, decreases in nonwage income, or increases in workplace amenities increase the supply of labor?**
   Increases in immigration or population growth increase the number of potential workers; increases in willingness to work at a given wage increase hours worked; decreases in nonwage income lower workers' incomes, increasing their willingness to work at any given wage; and an increase in workplace amenities makes working more desirable (less undesirable), also increasing workers' willingness to work at a given wage.

6. **What would happen to the supply of labor if nonwage incomes increased and workplace amenities also increased over the same period?**
   Higher nonwage incomes would reduce the supply of labor, but better workplace amenities would increase the supply of labor. The net effect would depend on which of these effects was of greater magnitude.

7. **Why are wages in different fields not necessarily related to how important people think those jobs are?**
   Wages are determined by the marginal revenue product of labor, and that marginal value which results from the forces of supply and demand does not bear any necessary relationship to how important or critical people consider that job to be in some absolute sense.

8. **If the private-market wage of engineers was greater than that of sociologists, what would happen if a university tried to pay its engineering faculty and its sociology faculty the same salary?**
   Say the university based its salaries on the average salaries elsewhere for all fields. Other things being equal, the resulting salaries would be below the equilibrium salary level for engineers, resulting in a shortage of engineering professors at that university (e.g., they would lose current engineering faculty and have a hard time hiring new engineering faculty), but above the equilibrium salary level for sociologists, resulting in a surplus of sociology professors at that university (who would never voluntarily leave or retire).

16.4 Labor Unions

1. **How can acting together as a group increase workers' bargaining power?**
   Workers acting together to reduce the competition between them for jobs reduces competition among workers, and therefore gives them increased bargaining power.

2. **Why are service industries harder to unionize than manufacturing industries?**
   Service industries tend to be harder to unionize than manufacturing industries because service industry jobs tend to be less standardized and service industry firms tend to be smaller.

3. **How do union restrictions on membership or other barriers to entry affect the wages of members?**
   Union restrictions on membership or other barriers to entry reduce the quantity of labor services offered to employers, reducing the number of such jobs and increasing their wages.

4. **What would increasing unionization do to the wages of those who were not in unions?**
   Increasing unionization would reduce the number of jobs in industries that became more unionized, increasing the supply of workers in industries that were non-union, and lowering the wages those jobs pay.

5. **How can unions potentially increase worker productivity?**
   Unions can potentially increase worker productivity by providing a collective voice that workers can use to communicate their discontents more effectively, which can reduce the number of workers that quit, reducing employee training costs. They could also improve worker motivation and morale by better handling worker grievances.

6. **Why do data indicating that unionization tends to lower firm profits weaken the argument that unions might actually increase worker productivity?**
   If increased worker productivity was the primary effect of unionization, unionized firms should have lower costs and therefore higher profits than non-union firms. But the data seem to indicate that the opposite is true.

16.5 The Market for Land and Capital

1. **If the supply of land was perfectly inelastic, how much would the price of land rise if the price of crops raised on the land doubled, other things equal? What if the supply of land was less than perfectly inelastic?**

   Because the demand for land is derived from the demand for the products produced on the land, a doubling of the price of the crops raised on land would double the demand for the land. If the supply of land was perfectly inelastic, this would double the price of the land. If the supply of land was less than perfectly elastic, the higher demand would increase the quantity of land supplied, and the doubling of demand would lead the price to rise, but less than double.

2. **Why is the demand curve for capital downward sloping?**

   The demand curve for capital is downward sloping because the lower the interest rate, the lower the opportunity cost of borrowed funds, and the more projects that can profitably be pursued with those funds (there are more capital investment projects with higher rates of return than the opportunity cost of borrowing).

3. **Why is the supply curve for capital upward sloping?**

   The interest rate represents the benefit savers get from saving (deferring consumption). A higher interest rate means an increase in the benefits of saving, resulting in increased saving and therefore an increase in the supply of funds available for capital investment projects.

CHAPTER 16 STUDY GUIDE

True or False:

1. By far the largest fraction of national income goes to wages and salaries for labor services.
2. The "price" of a productive factor is directly related to consumer demand for the final good or service.
3. In a competitive labor market, a firm's marginal resource cost is the market wage.
4. Hiring an additional worker would lower profits when the marginal revenue product is greater than the marginal resource cost.
5. The law of diminishing marginal product states that as increasing quantities of a variable input (e.g., labor) are added to fixed quantities of another input, output will rise, but at some point it will increase by diminishing amounts.
6. The marginal revenue product of labor declines, even in the case of competitive output markets, because of the diminishing marginal product of labor.
7. A profit-maximizing firm will hire up to the last unit of input for which the wage is expected to exceed the marginal revenue product.
8. In a competitive labor market, a firm can hire all the labor it wishes at the prevailing wage.
9. Only at the equilibrium wage are both suppliers (workers) and demanders (employers) of labor able to exchange the quantity of labor they desire.
10. Decreases in the demand curve for labor may arise from decreases in labor productivity or from increases in the price of the good produced by that labor.
11. An increase in the demand for a good will increase the demand for labor.
12. A decrease in the nonwage income of workers would shift the labor supply curve to the right.
13. The wage premium paid to union workers shows that all workers benefit from the activity of unions.
14. If unions are successful in obtaining higher wages, it causes employment to rise in the union sector but fall in the nonunion sector.
15. Monopsony as a market structure is considered most relevant to the labor market, in the real world.
16. If a person is willing to move, any employers' monopsony power will be reduced, other things equal.
17. Monopsony power tends to increase wages in a market.
18. Monopsony power tends to reduce output in a market.
19. Before the Civil War, labor unions were few, weak, and short-lived.
20. Early union demands were primarily for higher wages.
21. The Wagner Act protected the rights of workers to organize and bargain collectively.
22. Economic rent arises when a factor of production has a perfectly inelastic supply curve.
23. Because the supply of land is perfectly inelastic, the demand curve for land determines its price.
24. An increase in the demand for land will increase both its price and the quantity of land supplied.
25. The concept of economic rent applies only to land.
26. Economic rent is the payment to a resource above the amount necessary to induce the resource to be supplied.
27. At lower interest rates, the quantity of funds demanded will be greater.
28. At higher interest rates, the quantity of funds supplied will be greater.
29. If the interest rate rose, it would increase the present value of a given flow of future benefits.
30. Falling interest rates lead to greater investment, other things equal.

Multiple Choice:

1. Which of the following is false about input markets?
   a. The greatest fraction of national income goes to wages and salaries for labor services.
   b. The price and quantity of an input traded depends on its supply and demand.
   c. The demand for an input is a derived demand.
   d. The price of an input tends to increase when the demand for the output produced by the input increases.
   e. All of the preceding are true.

2. Marginal revenue product
   a. is the additional revenue that a firm obtains by employing one more unit of an input.
   b. will increase if an input's productivity increases.
   c. will decrease if the price of the output produced by the input falls.
   d. is characterized by all of the preceding.

3. The marginal resource cost of an input
   a. is the amount an added unit of an input adds to a firm's total cost.
   b. exceeds the market wage in a competitive industry.
   c. is less than the market wage in a competitive industry.
   d. is characterized by both a and b.
   e. is characterized by both a and c.

4. If an additional salesclerk is hired to work in a furniture store, the clerk's sales efforts will contribute $700 to the store's total revenue. The store's profits will rise if the additional salesclerk is hired whenever the cost of hiring the clerk is _____ in wages and other costs.
   a. $700
   b. less than $700
   c. more than $700
   d. Not enough information is given to make a determination.

5. A firm will increase its profits by adding one more unit of an input when
   a. $MRP < MRC$.
   b. $MRP = MRC$.
   c. $MRP > MRC$.
   d. none of the above.

6. Assuming competitive markets, a worker's contribution to revenue is given by
   a. the production function.
   b. the marginal revenue product of labor.
   c. the marginal resource cost of labor.
   d. the marginal product minus marginal cost.

7. In a competitive labor market,
   a. a firm is a wage taker.
   b. a firm can hire all the labor it wishes to at the market wage.
   c. a firm hires a small fraction of the total market quantity of labor supplied.
   d. all of the preceding are true.

8. *MRP* falls as more labor is hired in a competitive labor market because
   a. *MRC* increases as more labor is hired.
   b. workers that are added are steadily inferior in terms of ability.
   c. of the law of diminishing marginal product.
   d. of all of the preceding.

9. In a competitive labor market in equilibrium,
   a. a firm's $MRP = MP \times MR$.
   b. a firm's $MRP = MP \times P$.
   c. a firm's $MRP = MRC$.
   d. a firm's wage $= MRC$.
   e. all of the preceding are true.

10. At any wage higher than the equilibrium wage, the quantity of labor supplied _____ the quantity of labor demanded, resulting in a _____ of labor.
    a. exceeds; surplus
    b. exceeds; shortage
    c. is less than; surplus
    d. is less than; shortage

11. An increase in the demand for labor can result from
    a. increases in the price of the good produced by the labor.
    b. technological improvements.
    c. improvements in labor productivity.
    d. an increase in the amount of capital available for use by workers.
    e. all of the preceding.

12. Which of the following results in a rightward shift of the market demand curve for labor?
    a. an increase in labor productivity
    b. an increase in demand for the firm's product
    c. an increase in a firm's product price
    d. all of the preceding

13. The market supply of labor resources is affected by
    a. the number of hours workers are willing to work.
    b. the amount of immigration allowed.
    c. changes in a nation's working-age population.
    d. all of the preceding.

14. Differences in monetary wages across jobs may result from
    a. differences in job amenities.
    b. differences in on-the-job hazards.
    c. differences in working conditions.
    d. differences in fringe benefits.
    e. all of the preceding.

15. If labor unions successfully negotiate wage increases for their members,
    a. the wages of nonunion workers increase as well.
    b. the wages in nonunion sectors decrease.
    c. employment likely falls in the union sector.
    d. both a and c occur.
    e. both b and c occur.

16. Monopsony in a market would tend to increase an employer's
    a. wages paid.
    b. profits earned.
    c. output produced.
    d. employment level.

17. Monopsony power will *not* be reduced,
    a. the lower are search costs.
    b. the lower are movement costs.
    c. the more potential employers there are in an area.
    d. by any of these changes.

18. Labor union membership has declined in part due to
    a. a shift in workers from manufacturing to the service sector.
    b. deregulation in unionized industries.
    c. increasing global competition.
    d. all of the preceding.

19. The distinguishing feature of the land market is that
    a. the supply curve is highly inelastic.
    b. the supply curve is highly elastic.
    c. the demand curve is highly inelastic.
    d. the demand curve is highly elastic.

20. The rent paid for land currently used to graze cattle would increase if
    a. the productivity of the land in cattle grazing increased.
    b. people decided to eat more red meat.
    c. oil deposits were discovered under the land.
    d. any of the preceding occurred.

21. An increase in the demand for land will
    a. increase the price of land and increase the quantity of land supplied.
    b. increase the price of land but not change the quantity of land supplied.
    c. increase the quantity of land supplied but not change the price of land.
    d. do none of the preceding.

22. Economic rent
    a. applies as a concept to land.
    b. is the payment to a resource in excess of its opportunity cost.
    c. will increase when the demand for input increases, if supply is perfectly inelastic.
    d. does all of the preceding.

23. At low levels of interest, borrowers will want to borrow _____ and suppliers of funds will want to supply _____.
    a. more; less
    b. less; more
    c. more; more
    d. less; less

Problems:

1. The following table shows the Total Output each week of workers on a perfectly competitive cherry farm. The equilibrium price of a pound of cherries is $4. Complete the Marginal Product of Labor and the Marginal Revenue Product of Labor columns in the table.

Quantity of Labor	Total Output	Marginal Product of Labor	Marginal Revenue Product of Labor
0			
1	250	_____	_____
2	600	_____	_____
3	900	_____	_____
4	1,125	_____	_____
5	1,300	_____	_____
6	1,450	_____	_____
7	1,560	_____	_____

2. Using the table in Problem 1, how many workers will the farmer hire if the equilibrium wage rate is $550 per week? $650 per week?

3. What happens to the demand curve for labor when the equilibrium price of output increases?
4. Which of the following groups are likely to benefit from legislation substantially increasing the minimum wage? Explain why.
   a. unskilled workers seeking jobs but lacking experience and education
   b. skilled workers whose current wages are above the minimum wage
   c. manufacturers of machines that save labor in industries employing large amounts of unskilled labor
   d. unskilled workers who have criminal records
   e. a teenager seeking his or her first job
   f. unskilled workers who retain employment after the minimum wage is raised
   g. regions where almost everybody already earns substantially more than the minimum wage
5. If a competitive firm is paying $8 per hour (with no fringe benefits) to its employees, what would tend to happen to its equilibrium wage if the company began to give on-the-job training or free health insurance to its workers? What would happen to the firm's on-the-job training and workers' health insurance if the government mandated a minimum wage of $9 an hour?
6. Would the owner of University Pizza Parlor hire another worker for $60 per day if that worker added 40 pizzas a day and each pizza added $2 to University Pizza Parlor's revenues? Why or why not?
7. What would happen to the demand for unskilled labor if the demand for hamburgers and fries increased?
8. If all individuals have backward-bending labor supply curves, is the labor supply curve for a particular industry or occupation also backward bending?
9. Professional athletes command and receive higher salaries than teachers. Yet teachers, not athletes, are considered essential to economic growth and development. Why then do athletes receive higher salaries than teachers?
10. The availability of jobs at higher real wages motivates many people to migrate—legally or illegally—to the United States. Other things being equal, what impact would a large influx of immigrants have on real wages? What impact would it have on real wages in the immigrant's home country?
11. The dean at Middle State University knows that poets generally earn less than engineers in the private market; that is, the equilibrium wage for engineers is higher than that for poets. Suppose that all colleges and universities except for Middle State University pay their professors according to their potential private market wage. The administration at Middle State believes that salaries should be equal across all disciplines because its professors work equally hard and because all of the professors have similar degrees—PhDs. As a result, Middle State opts to pay all its professors a mid-range wage, W_{MS}. What do you think is likely to happen to the engineering and poetry programs at Middle State?
12. An entrepreneur considers the following investment opportunity: For an investment of $500 today, he can earn a return of $200 per year over the next three years. Should he undertake the investment if the interest rate is 8 percent? 10 percent?
13. Indicate which point could correspond to the equilibrium wage and quantity hired

   a. at the initial equilibrium.
   b. if the price of the output produced by the labor increased.

c. if the price of the output produced by the labor decreased.
d. if worker productivity increased and workers' nonwage incomes increased.
e. if worker productivity decreased and population decreased.
f. if the price of output produced by the labor increased and the number of hours workers were willing to work increased.
g. if the price of output produced by the labor decreased and workers' nonwage incomes decreased.

14. Using supply and demand curves, show how each of the following would affect the demand or supply of workers. In each case, label the new equilibrium wage and quantity.
    a. Immigration increases dramatically.

    b. Demand for U.S. manufactured goods declines.

    c. New computerized technology increases productivity of U.S. workers.

480

d. U.S. firms increase job amenities for workers.

e. U.S. workers choose more leisure.

15. Use the following diagrams to answer a–c:

   a. If unions are unable to have any effect on wages, draw the supply curve for the nonunion market.
   b. If unions become able to restrict the supply of labor in the union sector, indicate what would happen in both the union and nonunion sectors.
   c. What happens to the union wage and the number of union workers hired in b? What happens to the nonunion wage and the number of nonunion workers hired in b?

16. If the marginal revenue product for capital increased, what would it do to the demand for capital, the rental price of capital, and the quantity of capital supplied?

17. What is the marginal productivity theory of income distribution?

17 Income and Poverty

17.1 Income Distribution

17.2 Income Redistribution

17.3 The Economics of Discrimination

17.4 Poverty

The ultimate purpose of producing goods and services is to satisfy the material wants of people. Up to this point, we examined the process by which society decides which wants to satisfy in a world characterized by scarcity; we examined the question of how goods are produced; and we examined the question of how society can fully utilize its productive resources. We did not, however, look carefully into two equally important questions: For whom does society produce consumer goods and services? Why are some people able to consume much more than others?

SECTION 17.1 Income Distribution

- What happened to income distribution since 1935?
- Are income distribution statistics accurate?
- How significant is income mobility?
- How much income inequality exists in other countries?

In many economies, some individuals will have high income and others will have low income. How unequal is the U.S. income distribution? And why do some individuals earn more than others? We will address these and other questions regarding income distribution and poverty in this chapter.

Measuring Income Inequality

Exhibit 1 shows a breakdown of average annual family income by groups of five (or quintiles): the bottom fifth, the second fifth, the third fifth, the fourth fifth, and the top fifth.

Exhibit 2 illustrates the changing distribution of measured income in the United States since 1935. As you can see in this table, the proportion of income received by the richest Americans (top 5 percent) declined sharply after 1935 but has been edging back up since the 1980s. The proportion received by the poorest Americans (the lowest 20 percent) remained virtually unchanged since 1935. Most of the observed changes occurred between 1935 and 1950, probably reflecting the impact of the Great Depression and new government programs in the 1930s, as well as World War II. From 1950 to 1980, there was little change in the overall distribution of income. Two significant changes occurred since the 1980s: The lowest one-fifth of families have seen their share of measured income fall from 5.3 percent to 4.0 percent of all income, and the top one-fifth of families have seen their share of measured income rise from 41.1 to 47.8 percent of all income.

section 17.1 exhibit 1 Income Distribution of the United States, 2008

Group	Household Income (Average)
Bottom Fifth	$ 11,656
Second Fifth	$ 29,517
Third Fifth	$ 50,132
Fourth Fifth	$ 79,760
Top Fifth	$171,057

SOURCE: U.S. Bureau of the Census.

section 17.1 exhibit 2 Income Inequality in the United States

Year	Lowest Fifth	Second Fifth	Third Fifth	Fourth Fifth	Highest Fifth	Highest 5%
1935	4.1%	9.2%	14.1%	20.9%	51.7%	26.5%
1950	4.5	12.0	17.4	23.4	42.7	17.3
1960	4.8	12.2	17.8	24.0	41.3	15.9
1970	5.4	12.2	17.6	23.8	40.9	15.6
1980	5.3	11.6	17.6	24.4	41.1	14.6
1990	4.6	10.8	16.6	23.8	44.3	17.4
2000	4.3	9.8	15.5	22.8	47.4	20.8
2005	4.0	9.6	15.3	22.9	48.1	21.1
2008	4.0	9.6	15.5	23.1	47.8	20.5

SOURCE: U.S. Bureau of the Census, 2009.

The Lorenz Curve

Economists sometimes use a graphical representation of the distribution of income called the Lorenz curve. The Lorenz curve gives us a visual picture of the difference between the actual distribution of income and perfect equality. In Exhibit 3, we see that along the vertical axis we measure the cumulative percentage of total income and along the horizontal axis we measure the cumulative percentage of households. Moving along the horizontal axis from the left-hand corner to the right-hand corner, we move from 0 percent of the households to 100 percent of the households.

Along the 45-degree line—the line of perfect income equality—the poorest 20 percent of the families would receive 20 percent of total income, 40 percent of the families would receive 40 percent of total income, 60 percent of the families would receive 60 percent of total income, and so on. The curved line on this graph—the Lorenz curve—represents the actual distribution of income. The greater the distance between the Lorenz curve and the 45-degree line—the greater the amount of inequality. In Exhibit 3, we plot some of the points that make up the Lorenz curve from U.S. data for 1980 and 2008. For example, in 2008, we see the poorest 20 percent of all households received 4 percent of the income, point a′ on the graph. The first 40 percent received 14 percent (4 percent + 10 percent), point b′ on the graph. At point c′ the first 60 percent of households earn 30 percent of the income. At point d′ the first 80 percent of households receive 53 percent of the income or flipping it around—the richest 20 percent receive 47 percent of the income. Notice that the distribution of income was more equal in 1980 because the Lorenz curve is closer to the line of perfect equality.

In Exhibit 4, the shaded area A between the line of perfect income equality and the Lorenz curve measures the amount of income inequality. We derive a Gini coefficient, G, by dividing area A by area A + B. G varies from zero to one. If G is zero, it represents perfect income equality—that is, area A would be zero and the Lorenz curve would overlap the line of perfect income equality. $G = 1$ means perfect income inequality—if one household earned all the income.

section 17.1 exhibit 3 — The Lorenz Curve

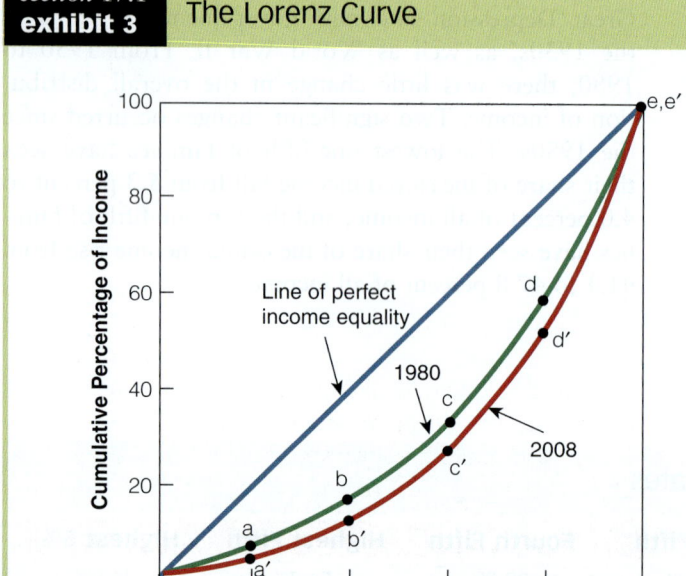

The Lorenz curve is a graphical presentation of the distribution of income. The horizontal axis measures the cumulative percentage of households and the vertical axis measures the cumulative percentage of income. The 45-degree line represents the line of perfect income equality. The further the Lorenz curve is from the line of perfect income equality the more unequal is the distribution of income.

	Households			Income 1980			Income 2008	
Point	Percentage	Cumulative Percentage	Point	Percentage	Cumulative Percentage	Point	Percentage	Cumulative Percentage
a	Lowest 20	20%	a	5.3%	5.3%	a′	4%	4%
b	Second 20	40	b	11.6	16.9	b′	10	14
c	Third 20	60	c	17.6	34.5	c′	16	30
d	Fourth 20	80	d	24.4	58.9	d′	23	53
e	Highest 20	100	e	41.1	100.0	e′	47	100

section 17.1 exhibit 4 Gini Coefficient

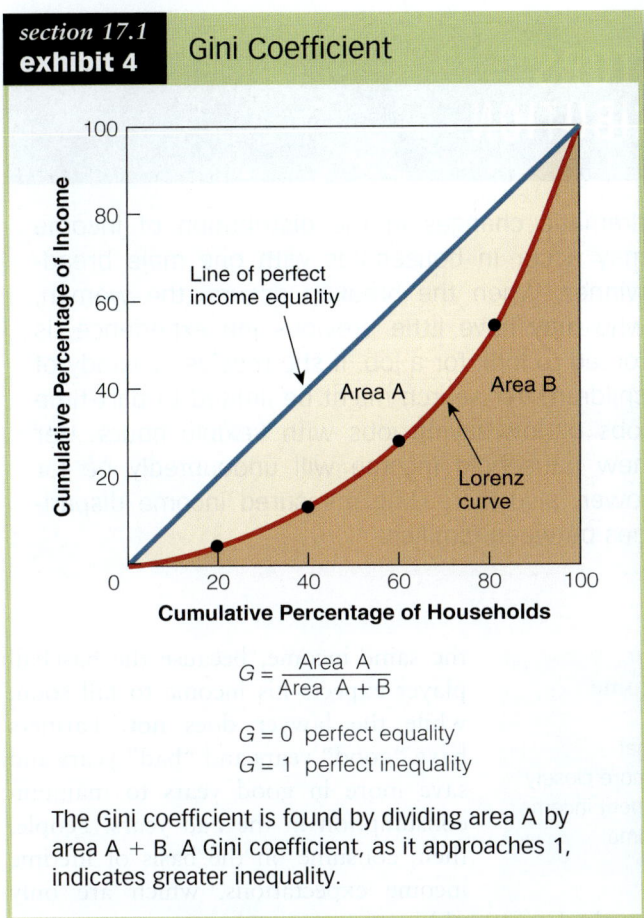

$$G = \frac{\text{Area A}}{\text{Area A} + \text{B}}$$

G = 0 perfect equality
G = 1 perfect inequality

The Gini coefficient is found by dividing area A by area A + B. A Gini coefficient, as it approaches 1, indicates greater inequality.

That is, the closer G is to 1 the greater the degree of income inequality; consequently, area A becomes larger. In the United States, the Gini coefficient was 0.403 in 1980 and 0.466 in 2008, indicating that the distribution of income has become less equal over the last 30 years.

Are We Overstating the Disparity in the Distribution of Income?

Failing to take into consideration differences in age, certain demographic factors, institutional factors, and government redistributive activities have all been identified as elements that influence income distribution data and may suggest that we might be overstating inequality.

Differences in Age

At any moment in time, middle-age people tend to have higher incomes than both younger and older people. Middle age is when most people are at their peak in terms of productivity and participate in the labor force to a greater extent than do the very old or very young. Put differently, if every individual earned exactly the same total income over his or her lifetime, we would still observe some inequality at any given moment in time simply because people usually earn more in middle age.

Inequality resulting from this demographic difference overstates the true inequality in the lifetime earnings of people. A typical 50-year-old male earns nearly twice the income of a male in his early 20s and nearly one-third more than workers over 65. Since 1950, the proportion of individuals who are either very young or very old has grown, meaning that in a relative sense, more people are in lower-income age groups.

Other Demographic Trends

Other demographic trends, such as the increased number of divorced couples and the rise of two-income families, also cause the measured distribution of income (which is measured in terms of household income) to appear more unequal. For example, in the 1950s, the overwhelming majority of families had single incomes. Today, many households have two breadwinners instead of one. Suppose their incomes rise from $50,000 a year to roughly $100,000; thus, these households move into a higher-income quintile and create greater apparent income inequality. At the same time, divorces create two households instead of one, lowering income per household for divorced couples; thus, they move into lower-income quintiles, also creating greater apparent income inequality.

Government Activities

Some economists argue that the impact of increased government activity should be considered in evaluating the measured income distribution. Government-imposed taxes burden different income groups in different ways. Also, government programs benefit some groups of income recipients more than others. For example, state-subsidized higher education seems to benefit the high- and middle-income groups more than the poor (because far more students from the higher-income groups go to college), as have such things as government subsidies to airports and airlines, operas, and art museums. Some programs, though, clearly aid the poor more than the rich. Food stamps, school lunch programs, housing subsidies, Medicaid, and several other programs provide recipients with **in-kind transfers**. In-kind transfers are given in the form of goods and services rather than money. When in-kind transfers are included in income distribution data, many economists conclude that they have served to

in-kind transfers
in-kind transfers are transfers in the form of goods and services instead of money. In-kind transfers include food stamps, school lunch programs, housing subsidies, and Medicaid, among others.

Use what you've LEARNED: DEMOGRAPHIC FACTORS AND INCOME DISTRIBUTION

Q What impact do you think higher divorce rates will have on income inequality?

A As you would probably imagine, when one family with two incomes turns into two families with one income each, more families will report less income per family. Often, this situation causes one high-income household to become two middle-income households in the data. However, the most dramatic changes in the distribution of income may occur in households with one male breadwinner. When the breakup occurs, the woman, who may have little previous job experience, is forced to look for a job. If she receives custody of children, her search might be limited to part-time jobs or low-paying jobs with flexible hours. Her new household income will undoubtedly be far lower, also increasing measured income disparities between families.

reduce levels of inequality significantly from the levels suggested by aggregate income statistics.

On balance, the evidence suggests that inequality of money income in the United States declined from 1935 to 1950 and then remained rather stable until 1980. Since then, the distribution of income has become less equal. However, if we consider age distribution, institutional factors, and in-kind transfer programs, it is safe to say that the income distribution is more equal than it appears in Exhibit 2.

permanent income hypothesis
the hypothesis that consumption is more closely related to permanent income than current income

Permanent Income Hypothesis

Milton Friedman, a Nobel laureate in economics who taught for many years at the University at Chicago, observed that consumption is related to permanent income rather than to current income levels. This is called the **permanent income hypothesis.** Studies show, for example, that college students often consume more than their total income; the same is true of very old persons. These groups *dissave*. On the other hand, people in their 30s and 40s tend to save quite a bit and consume relatively less of their income (even so, though, a higher-income person of 40 is likely to consume more than a low-income person of 20 or 70). Why? College-age persons expect to earn more income later, and gauge their consumption in part by their expectations of future (lifetime) income. Likewise middle-age persons expect to retire at some future date on a lower income and save for that eventuality. Older, retired persons expect to die and, accordingly, feel justified in drawing down their savings. A highly paid 35-year-old baseball player may consume less than a 35-year-old lawyer with the same income, because the baseball player expects his income to fall soon, while the lawyer does not. Farmers have "good" years and "bad" years and save more in good years to maintain consumption in the bad years. People, then, consume on the basis of lifetime income expectations, which are only partly determined by current income.

If standard of living depends on lifetime income rather than current income, people can borrow to smooth out the transitory changes in income that affect all individuals over their "life cycle." Thus, if people save in good years and borrow from their savings in bad years, they can avoid the transitory income changes that can impact standard of living.

That is, to measure inequality it may be more relevant to observe permanent income than current income. The relationship between permanent income and consumption is much more equal because it is less affected by transitory income—wide changes in income that vary from year to year. That is, using permanent income smoothes out the life cycle variation in income and thus leads to less inequality than using the wide variations associated with current income.

How Much Movement Happens on the Economic Ladder?

A study of income mobility during the decade of 1985–1995 found that less than 50 percent of individuals who began in the poorest quintile ended up there a decade later, and almost 30 percent of those in the poorest quintile moved up to the top three quintiles. Although roughly 80 percent of individuals in the richest quintile were still there a decade later, the research does not show that people moving into the top quintile tended to stay there. The middle quintiles appear to experience considerable movement up and down the income ladder. Generational studies also suggest a considerable income mobility—that is, incomes of fathers and sons tend to be only slightly positively correlated. If a father had lifetime income earnings 20 percent above his generation, his son could expect to earn income about 8 percent above his generation. Virtually no positive correlation could be made between the earnings of grandchildren and grandparents. In short, high-income and low-income earners will always be with us, but more than likely they will be different people.

In sum, most Americans experience significant fluctuations in their economic well-being from one year to the next. According to a Census Bureau study in the mid-1990s, about three-fourths of the population see their economic well-being go either up or down by at least 5 percent from one year to the next. Economic well-being can be affected by changes in personal and family circumstances, such as work experience, marital status, and household composition, as well as changes in earnings.

Why Do Some Earn More than Others?

Many reasons explain why some people earn more income than others. Some reasons for income differences include differences in age, skill, human capital (education and training), and preferences toward risk and leisure.

Age

The amount of income people earn varies over their lifetimes. Younger people with few skills tend to make little income when they begin their working careers. Income rises as workers gain experience and on-the-job training. As productivity increases, workers can command higher wages. These wage earnings generally increase up to the age of 50 and fall dramatically at retirement age, around 65.

Skills and Human Capital

Some workers are just more productive than others and therefore earn higher wages. Greater productivity can be a result of innate skills or of improvements in human capital, such as training and education. In Exhibit 5, we

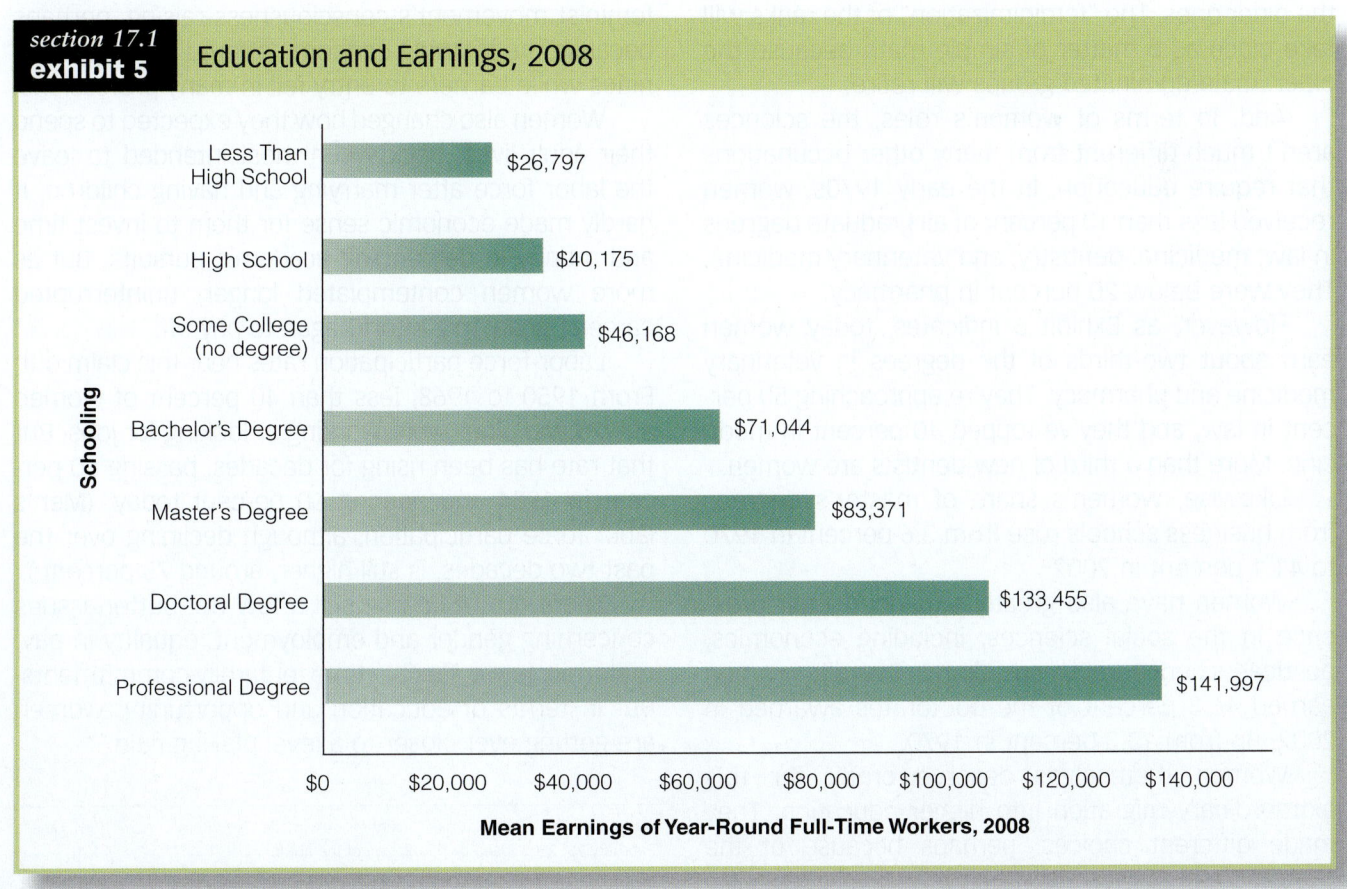

section 17.1 exhibit 5 Education and Earnings, 2008

Schooling	Mean Earnings
Less Than High School	$26,797
High School	$40,175
Some College (no degree)	$46,168
Bachelor's Degree	$71,044
Master's Degree	$83,371
Doctoral Degree	$133,455
Professional Degree	$141,997

Mean Earnings of Year-Round Full-Time Workers, 2008

Census Bureau, Current Population Survey, 2009.

in the news Scientists Are Made, Not Born

—BY MICHAEL COX AND RICHARD ALM

Dallas—Do women have what it takes to become scientists?

In our effort to create more female scientists, what matters are the choices and opportunities open to young women at our universities.

Until the last 30 or so years, few women studied the sciences, so there was little mystery about why most people in those professions were men. Over the past generation, however, our research shows, there has been a truly stunning change. As an illustration of the gains by women in historically male disciplines, consider how the percentages of women receiving bachelor's degrees, master's degrees, and doctorates in the sciences increased from 1970 to 2002.

Clearly debating whether women are intellectually equipped for sciences makes little sense. Women themselves have already settled the issue, one degree at a time. The younger generations within the science professions are decidedly more female than the older ones. The "feminization" of the ranks will take place as a matter of simple math because the older, male-dominated groups will retire.

And, in terms of women's roles, the sciences aren't much different from many other occupations that require education. In the early 1970s, women received less than 10 percent of all graduate degrees in law, medicine, dentistry, and veterinary medicine. They were below 20 percent in pharmacy.

However, as Exhibit 6 indicates, today women earn about two-thirds of the degrees in veterinary medicine and pharmacy. They're approaching 50 percent in law, and they've topped 40 percent in medicine. More than a third of new dentists are women.

Likewise, women's share of master's degrees from business schools rose from 3.6 percent in 1970 to 41.1 percent in 2002.

Women have also greatly expanded their presence in the social sciences, including economics, political science, and sociology. Overall, women earned 46.3 percent of the doctorates awarded in 2002, up from 13.3 percent in 1970.

Women themselves deserve credit for this extraordinary migration into higher education. They made different choices, perhaps because of the feminist movement's consciousness-raising, perhaps because the growing economy offered new opportunities while barriers to entry fell in many professions.

Women also changed how they expected to spend their adult lives. Back when most intended to leave the labor force after marrying and having children, it hardly made economic sense for them to invest time and money in demanding academic pursuits. But as more women contemplated longer, uninterrupted careers, academic effort began to pay off.

Labor-force participation rates bear this claim out: From 1950 to 1968, less than 40 percent of women age 20 and older were working or looking for jobs. But that rate has been rising for decades, passing 50 percent in 1984 and nearing 60 percent today. (Men's labor force participation, although declining over the past two decades, is still higher, around 75 percent.)

There are of course still a few hot-button issues concerning gender and employment: equality in pay, maternity leave, flexible time for family commitments. But in terms of education and opportunity, women are getting ever closer to a level playing field.

section 17.1 exhibit 6 Percentage Share of Professional Degrees Awarded to Women, 1950–2000

SOURCE: From Michael Cox, "Scientists Are Made, Not Born", 'New York Times', February 28, 2005. Used by permission of the author.

see that college graduates' average earnings are 81 percent greater than high school graduates. The financial rewards for attending college are higher than ever. Why is the gap widening between skilled and unskilled workers? One possibility is that increasing international trade over the last 30 years prompted an increase in domestic demand for skilled workers and a decrease in demand for domestic unskilled workers (unskilled workers are relatively cheap and plentiful in developing countries). That is, the United States tends to import goods produced with unskilled workers and export goods produced with skilled workers. In addition, technological changes to more sophisticated equipment can lead to an increase in demand for skilled workers. Other workers, such as star athletes and rock stars, have specialized talents that are in huge demand, so they make more money than those with fewer skills or with skills that are in less demand.

Worker Preferences

Aside from differences in age, skills, education, and training, people have different attitudes about and preferences regarding their work. Because workaholics (by definition) work longer hours, they earn more than others with comparable skills. Some workers earn more because they work more intensely than others. Still others may choose jobs that pay less but have more amenities—flexible hours, favorable job locations, generous benefit programs, child care, and so on. Some people choose to work less and spend more time pursuing leisure activities, such as traveling, hobbies, or spending time with family and friends. It is not for us to say that one preference is better than another but simply to recognize that these choices lead to differences in earnings.

Job Preferences

Finally, some of the differences in income are the result of the risks or undesirable features of some occupations. Police officers and firefighters are paid higher wages because of the dangers associated with their jobs. The same would be true for window washers on skyscrapers and painters on the Golden Gate bridge. Coal miners and garbage collectors are paid more than other workers with comparable skill levels because of the unpleasantness of the jobs. In short, some workers have higher earnings because they are compensated for the difficult, risky, or unappealing nature of their jobs.

Income Distribution in Other Countries

Is the United States typical of advanced, industrial nations with respect to the distribution of income among its population? This question is difficult to answer with absolute certainty, given international differences in defining income, difficulties in measuring the impact of taxes, the problem of nonmonetary payments, and so on. Despite these hurdles, international comparisons of income distribution have been made.

Exhibit 7, constructed with data from the World Bank, shows that income inequality is greater in the United States and the United Kingdom than in Sweden and Japan. Japan's ratio of 4.5 means that the richest 10 percent of the population makes 4.5 times as much income as the bottom ten percent. In Brazil, the richest ten percent of the population make 51.3 times as much income as the bottom 10 percent. The table shows that some of the greatest disparities in income are found in developing countries such as Mexico, South Africa, and Brazil.

Although income inequality within nations is often substantial, it is far less than income inequality among nations. A majority of income inequality on Earth reflects differences in living standards among countries rather than disparities within nations. This conclusion is borne out by statistics.

section 17.1 exhibit 7 Global Income Inequalities

Income Inequality	Country	Gap between Rich and Poor (Ratio)
Most Equal ↑	Japan	4.5
	Sweden	6.2
	Germany	6.9
	India	8.6
	France	9.1
	Canada	9.4
	Russia	12.7
	United Kingdom	13.8
	United States	15.9
	Nigeria	17.8
	China	21.6
	Mexico	24.6
	Chile	33.0
	South Africa	33.1
↓	Argentina	40.9
Least Equal	Brazil	51.3

NOTE: The ratio of the richest 10% to the poorest 10% gives us the gap between rich and poor. The smaller the ratio the greater the equality.

SOURCE: World Bank

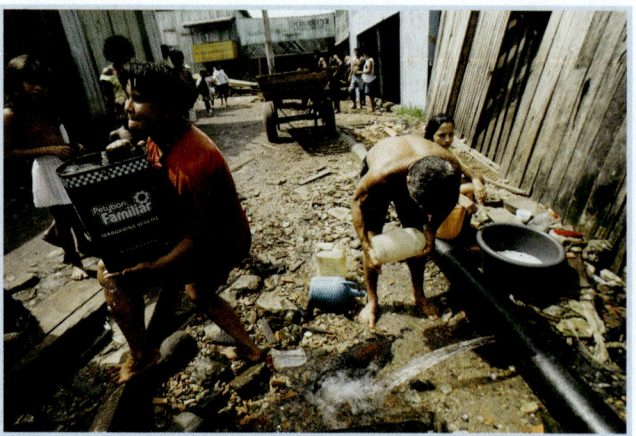

The contrasts between rich and poor are more extreme in Brazil than in almost any other country in the world. According to the UN Development Program, nearly half of Brazil's population lives in absolute poverty. Those who are unable to make a living as vendors of newspapers or lottery tickets, shoeshine boys, guards for parked cars, or the like are often forced to earn a living illegally. The number of children who work on the streets, or even live there permanently, is estimated to have reached 10 million.

> **SECTION CHECK**
>
> 1. From 1935 to 1980, the distribution of income became more equal. However, since 1980, inequality has increased.
> 2. Nonmonetary income and privileges to the well-to-do may understate the disparity in income inequality, while demographics, institutional factors, measuring current income rather than permanent income, and government programs may overstate the disparity in income inequality.
> 3. High-income and low-income earners will always be with us, but they will likely be different people.
> 4. The level of income inequality differs from country to country.
>
> ---
>
> 1. Why might patterns in the measured income distribution give an inaccurate impression?
> 2. Why might income distribution statistics understate the degree of income inequality?
> 3. Why might measured income shares overstate the degree of income inequality?
> 4. How does the fraction of the population that is middle-aged, rather than young or old, affect measurements of income inequality?
> 5. How does the growth of both two-earner families and divorced couples increase measured income inequality?
> 6. Why is it important to take account of the substantial mobility of families within the income distribution over time when evaluating the degree of income inequality in America?

SECTION 17.2 Income Redistribution

* What is the case for redistribution on the grounds of fairness?
* What is the case for efficiency and productivity?

The emphasis to this point has been on describing the amount of income inequality present in the United States and the rest of the world. Little has been said about the impact that inequality has on human welfare. Because of the difficulty of measuring welfare or of comparing the welfare of one person with another, it is impossible to "prove" that a given income distribution is better than another.

At the same time, however, it is clear that political and social changes in the past century or two have generally worked to reduce income inequality. In some cases, revolutions have been fought with income redistribution as a paramount motive—such was the case with the Russian Revolution and probably the French Revolution, not to mention many more recent upheavals in less-developed countries. Why is it generally felt that justice, fairness, and happiness would all be improved by increasing the income of the poor relative to the well-to-do or rich?

Equality

The economic theory supporting policies of income redistribution is derived from the principle of diminishing marginal utility. According to this principle, increases in income generate less additional happiness (utility) at higher levels of income.

Consider Exhibit 1. Suppose a family with an income of $300,000 a year has $30,000 taken from it in the form of a tax on income. The family accordingly reduces its consumption spending, forcing it to cut out some spending on luxuries—perhaps taking less-expensive vacations, forgoing a vacation home, and so on. This lowers the family's daily utility, say, from 27 utils to 25 utils. The marginal utility of the income given up is 2 utils (27 − 25). Now, suppose the income of some family making $10,000 a year is increased by the $30,000 taken from the first, well-to-do family. The poor family was formerly unable to purchase cars or appliances or take vacations. Now their utility is positively influenced by the transfer payment of $30,000, as it increases from 6 to 15 utils a week. The marginal utility to the poor family of the $30,000 in transfer payments is 9 utils (15 − 6). Using the Robin Hood approach—taking from the rich and giving to the poor—could possibly increase society's total utility in this case, because the rich family loses only 2 utils a week while the poor family gains 9 utils.

Thus, a theoretical argument favors income redistribution. Note, however, that the argument is based on the critical assumption that people are alike in how they experience diminishing marginal utility from increasing income, a proposition impossible to prove (economists assume that interpersonal utility comparisons are not possible). Many people believe it is a plausible assumption, but it is merely an assumption nonetheless. It is possible, however, that someone making $20 million a year after taxes would lose little utility if that income was cut to $17 million compared with the gains of the many poor families who could have their income doubled or tripled by receiving a portion of that income.

From time to time, groups have conducted polls asking people, "Are you happy?" Evidence from these polls suggests that, at a moment in time within a country, happiness is positively correlated with income—rich people are generally happier than poor people. This does not necessarily support the existence of diminishing marginal utility, but it might be evidence used by those who argue that income ought to be redistributed simply on the grounds of economic justice and fairness. Many people are able to command high incomes simply because of some inherited physical or mental talents that they develop or because they were, in some other way, "lucky." Why should these people be happier than others simply because of fate? If you believe society should try to equalize happiness among its members, you could argue that some income redistribution makes sense.

section 17.2 exhibit 1 — Diminishing Marginal Utility of Income

As income rises, the happiness associated with that income also rises, but the principle of diminishing marginal utility of income means it rises by diminishing amounts. Assuming the two groups have identical marginal utility curves, the decrease in utility that results from taking some income from high-income groups may be less than the increase in utility generated by giving this income to low-income groups. Such redistribution would enhance total utility in society if people have similar preferences for income. The exact utility-income relationship is impossible to state, however, because of our inability to measure utility or to make utility comparisons among individuals.

Income Redistribution Can Reduce Incentives to Work, Invest, and Save

Even if one agreed that income redistribution from the rich to the poor would both tend to equalize happiness and, in the short run, increase the total utility received by the population, one might legitimately oppose some income redistribution on other grounds. If some income redistribution is good, why not go all the way and completely equalize everyone's income, taxing the rich extremely heavily and giving massive subsidies to the poor? Nearly everyone opposes that scenario because our incomes would all be equal but much smaller, providing little incentive to work, invest, and save. Why help make the economic pie (total output) if they will give you a piece if you don't work? Who would take on the risky jobs if everyone were paid the same? Why would you go to school if your investment in human capital was so low? Most of us believe, for efficiency and equity (fairness) reasons, that there ought to be some limits on redistributive efforts. The principal disagreement is not over whether we should have some redistribution, but rather over at what point we should stop in our redistributive efforts. Some believe we should go further than we have, while others think we have already gone too far in attempts to alter the distribution of income in favor of the poor and less affluent.

"Fair" May or May Not Be Fair

What are the arguments against a radical redistribution of income that would eliminate virtually all inequality? The first argument is an equity one. Is it "fair" to take most of the income of hard-working, talented people who earn high incomes, particularly when some of it is given to people who perhaps may be perceived as shiftless and lazy? Not all poor people are automatically good and deserving, nor are all rich people greedy and selfish. Related to that, some income inequality would seem desirable, because consumption needs may well vary with family size, age of family members, and other factors. Total equality of *family* income, for example, would penalize those who choose to have big families, while total equality in *individual* incomes would perhaps penalize those who choose to have small families or live alone.

Indeed, it is possible that the rich are rich largely because of their high marginal utility of income, while many poor may be poor because they care less about goods relative to nonwork activities. As you can see by comparing the shaded areas of Exhibit 2, the rich lose more than the poor gain from the transfer of income. In this situation, then, transferring income from rich to poor actually makes society worse off!

section 17.2 exhibit 2 Differences in Marginal Utility of Income

The rich may have a higher marginal utility of income. Therefore, transferring income from rich to poor could make society worse off.

Revisiting Marginal Productivity Theory

Income derived from payments according to marginal productivity may sound fair, but it may lead to very unequal incomes because ownership of resources is initially divided unequally. For example, individuals have different opportunities to obtain education and training. Some individuals inherit property; in contrast, others may have physical or mental disabilities. In addition, imperfections in labor markets (e.g., unions and licensing restrictions) can lead to factory owners not receiving income according to their marginal productivity. Discrimination can also distort the linkage between income and marginal contribution to output.

SECTION CHECK

1. If the happiness or utility derived from additional income is subject to diminishing marginal utility, then it is possible that income taken from the very rich and given to the very poor might increase total utility. However, this argument is based on the assumption that people are alike in how they experience diminishing marginal utility from increasing income, a proposition that is impossible to prove.
2. Too much income redistribution provides fewer incentives to work, invest, and save.

---

1. How is the principle of diminishing marginal utility used to justify income redistribution?
2. Why is it not possible to prove the idea that redistributing income from rich to poor will increase society's utility?
3. What are the fairness and incentive arguments against government redistribution of income?
4. If high-income individuals must pay increased income tax rates in order to provide subsidies for low-income individuals (and the subsidies are phased out as income increases), are the productive incentives of both high- and low-income people reduced? Why or why not?

SECTION 17.3 The Economics of Discrimination

* What is job-entry discrimination?
* What is wage discrimination?
* Do earnings differences reflect discrimination or differences in productivity?
* How can we remedy discrimination?

When a worker is denied employment on the basis of some biological feature, such as sex or race, without any regard to productivity, it is called **job-entry discrimination**. **Wage discrimination** occurs when a worker is given employment at a wage lower than that of other workers, based on something other than productivity.

Job-Entry Discrimination

In a world where sex and race have absolutely no bearing whatsoever on the employment circumstances of people (e.g., talent, education, willingness and ability to work, move, etc.), every occupation would, apart from random variations, have a workforce with the same sex and race proportions as the population at large. Thus, on average, 51 percent of employees in each occupation would be expected to be female, if women comprised 51 percent of the population, and approximately 12 percent or so would be blacks and other racial minorities, reflecting the proportion of nonwhites to the total population.

In fact, the proportion of females working (46 percent) is slightly less than the proportion of men. Likewise, the proportion of blacks in the workforce is lower than would be expected given the general population percentages. Looking first at females, their less-than-proportionate presence in the workforce might be viewed as a matter of choice; some women may prefer to be engaged in full-time household production rather than work outside the home. On the other hand, others argue that this attitude reflects ingrained sexism; no inherent reason says that the adult male member of the household should not stay at home with the kids as much as the female member. In any case, the proportion of women to men in the workforce has dramatically increased over time—women were only 38 percent of the labor force in 1970, and now they are more than 46 percent.

Job-entry discrimination is further evidenced by the higher proportion of white males with relatively high-paying jobs compared with females and non-whites who make up a relatively larger proportion of employees working in unskilled jobs with low pay and relatively little prestige.

job-entry discrimination
a worker is denied employment on the basis of some biological feature, such as sex or race, without any regard to productivity

wage discrimination
when a worker is given employment at a wage lower than that of other workers, based on something other than productivity

Wage Discrimination

A strong statistical correlation exists between lifetime earnings and years of schooling. High-school graduates earn roughly two-thirds of the salary of college graduates.

Overall, white women make 25 percent to 30 percent less than white men. White males also typically earn 25 percent to 30 percent more than black males. At least part of this wage differential can be explained by differences in educational attainment and does not simply reflect racial prejudice on the part of employers. Blacks and women on average may have acquired fewer years of schooling, less training, and fewer years of experience. For example, although almost 25 percent of whites have college degrees, less than 14 percent of blacks and 10 percent of Hispanics have completed four years of college. Also, compared with 26 percent of men, less than 22 percent of women have completed four years of college. Among females, black women earn 10 percent less than white women. While a major reason women and nonwhites earn less than white males is that they occupy jobs that are lower paying due to their lower skills, it is also possible that they earn less because of wage discrimination—being paid less, strictly because of their race or sex.

Discrimination or Differences in Productivity?

Merely demonstrating that wages are lower for blacks and females does not in itself prove wage discrimination, although it is consistent with the notion

Education level has a great impact on earnings potential. Young adults who have completed bachelor's degrees earn substantially more than those with high school diplomas.

that discrimination occurs. However, if occupational and wage differentials are not caused by discrimination, what are the causes?

Several scholars developed statistical models that argue that a great deal of the earnings differentials across the sexes and races can be explained by differences in productivity. In other words, employers hire and pay workers roughly an amount equal to their perceived contributions (marginal revenue product). Now, if the marginal revenue product of blacks and women happens to be lower on average than that of white men, even within occupational groups, then one could argue that employers are not discriminating on the basis of race or sex but rather on the basis of expected productivity. Assuming this reasoning is at least partly true, why might white male workers be more productive than other workers?

Productivity Differences: An Environmental Explanation

The first explanation is that various environmental factors have prevented blacks, Hispanics, and females from gaining the training and skills necessary to achieve high productivity. In the past, blacks and Hispanics often received less schooling than did whites, and the quality of that schooling has often been lower—discrimination in the acquisition of human capital. Even if blacks and Hispanics were to attend school as long as whites, their quality of schooling is less because of the lack of resources in schools populated with minorities.

Females, because they are far more likely to interrupt their careers to have and care for children, often have less work experience than their male counterparts. This factor may also lower their productivity relative to males. Women may also be more likely to take jobs, such as teaching, that may pay less but have more flexible hours that make it easier to raise children. In other words, some of the wage differences may be job preferences. Also, women who have never been married and have not had any job interruptions earn roughly 10 percent less than their male counterparts. White married women earn roughly 40 percent less than married men. This environmental explanation of productivity differences does not rule out discrimination but rather argues that past discrimination's perverse influences on the environment of females and nonwhites has caused them to have an inferior endowment of human capital now, even if present-day employers were color and sex blind in terms of paying workers. However, unexplained differences between whites and minorities and males and females lead us to believe discrimination is a factor in the labor market.

Why Do People Discriminate?

Why would any employer want to discriminate against an employee on the basis of race or sex? It might appear that discrimination is totally inconsistent with the economist's view of the rational utility-maximizing person. After all, if a firm really wants to maximize profits, it should hire the best person available per dollar of wage expenditure, regardless of age, sex, race, or other attribute of the worker.

Let's take a look at some reasons why discrimination occurs.

Reducing Information Costs

To some extent, discrimination may reflect information costs. Suppose an employer has previously hired 10 green workers and 10 blue workers for a certain type of work, and eight of the green workers performed well while only two of the blue workers did. (The poorer blue worker performance may have reflected poorer training and educational backgrounds.) In this situation, the employer might prefer to hire a green employee for the next job opening, because past experience suggests that the probability is greater that the green worker will perform well. In this case, the color of the worker is used as a screening device, a means of narrowing the list of job candidates.

It costs money and time to evaluate the prospects of every applicant, and race is an imperfect but cheap way of doing some of the screening. A profit-maximizing employer is not overly concerned that by screening workers by color, he discriminates against good blue workers. To this employer, the reduction in information costs achieved by hiring on the basis of color may exceed the perceived benefits from the identification of good blue workers.

Personal Preferences

It is a fact that some people prefer association with others with certain racial and/or sexual attributes. These people may have acquired these preferences out of an ignorance that fosters bigotry and racism, but the preferences are there nonetheless. The utility gained from having the desired racial mix might exceed the loss in income from not having the best employees. For example, a racially prejudiced business owner might prefer making $900,000 a year in profits from a business with, say, an all-white labor force to making $1,000,000 with a racially mixed force. In the words of the pioneer in the economics of discrimination, Nobel laureate Gary Becker of the University of Chicago, the person has acquired a "taste" for discrimination, just as one might acquire a taste for certain goods. That is, an employer may be willing to trade away some income to satisfy an acquired taste for discrimination.

The Costs of Discrimination

It is also true that in competitive industries, firms that discriminate may lose out ultimately to firms that do not. The nondiscriminating firm can hire the unfavored but equally competent workers and have a cost advantage over firms that discriminate. This cost advantage may allow the nondiscriminating firm to undercut its discriminating competitors' prices and either force them out of business or make them change their hiring practices. That is, in the long run, competition has the potential to reduce discrimination.

SECTION CHECK

1. If a worker is denied employment on the basis of some noneconomic factor like race, religion, sex, or ethnic origin, it is called job-entry discrimination.
2. If a worker is hired at a wage lower than that of other workers on some basis other than productivity differences, it is called wage discrimination.
3. If a firm really wants to maximize its profits, it should minimize costs by hiring the best persons available per dollar of wage expenditure, regardless of age, sex, race, or other attribute of the worker.
4. Discrimination may occur because of information costs or because some workers may prefer to associate with persons with certain racial or sexual attributes.

---

1. What is the difference between job-entry discrimination and wage discrimination?
2. Explain how earnings differences could reflect either discrimination or productivity differences.
3. What is the environmental explanation for differences in earnings across the sexes and races?
4. How do firms' incentives to maximize profits tend to reduce the extent of discrimination?
5. How can discrimination reflect imperfect information and the costs of acquiring more information about potential employees?
6. Say you only hire purple workers. If purple workers strongly prefer to work with one another instead of with other groups, why might you prefer to hire a less productive purple worker than a more productive nonpurple worker at the same wage?
7. Why would subsidizing employers for hiring minority workers rather than imposing implicit quotas give employers greater incentives to expand minority job opportunities?

SECTION 17.4 Poverty

- How do we define poverty?
- How many people live in poverty?
- What is relative income?

At several points in the previous discussion, the words *rich* and *poor* have been used without being defined. Of particular interest is the question of poverty. Our concern over income distribution largely arises because most people believe that those with low incomes have lower satisfaction than those with higher incomes. Thus, the "poor" people are those who, in a material sense, suffer relative to other people. It is desirable, therefore, to define and measure the extent of poverty in the United States.

Defining Poverty

The federal government measures poverty by using a set of money income thresholds that vary by family size to detect who is poor. If the family's total income is less than the established family threshold, then that family, and every individual in it, is considered poor. The poverty thresholds are adjusted annually for inflation. The **poverty rate** is the percentage of the population who fall below this absolute level, called the **poverty line**. The official poverty rate for the United States is currently set at three times the cost of providing a nutritionally adequate diet—roughly $20,000 for a family of four. The official poverty definition may overstate the level of poverty because it does not include noncash benefits (such as public housing, Medicaid, and food stamps).

The amount of poverty fell steadily in the 1960s, was steady in the 1970s, and rose during the recession in the early 1980s. The poverty rate then fell slightly during the rest of the 1980s and rose again during the recessions of 1990–1991 and the recessions of 2001 and 2008–09. As you would expect, when the economy is in a recession, unemployment rises and poverty tends to increase. Exhibit 1 provides some statistics on the U.S. poverty rate.

poverty rate
the percentage of the population who fall below the poverty line

poverty line
a set of money income thresholds, established by the federal government, that vary by family size and are used to detect who is poor; if a family's total income is less than the established family threshold, then that family, and every individual in it, is considered poor

Poverty rates vary considerably among different races. Exhibit 2 shows that poverty rates for blacks and Hispanics were much higher than for whites. However, poverty rates fell markedly for blacks and Hispanics during the 1990s. Household status also influences poverty. A family headed by a female with no husband present is about five times more likely to experience poverty than a family headed by a married couple. Children are also more likely than average to be members of poor families—see Exhibit 2.

With a definition of poverty that is determined at some fixed, real-income level (that is, an income that has been adjusted for inflation), poverty over time should decline and, indeed, largely disappear, because real incomes generally rise over time with economic growth. Unless lower income groups do not share at all in the rising incomes of the population, some reduction in poverty is inevitable. Thus, one cure for poverty, as defined by some absolute income or standard of living criterion, is economic growth. The greater the rate of economic growth, the more rapidly poverty will be eradicated.

An Alternative Definition of Poverty

Many "poor" individuals in the United States, using the official definition, would be considered well off, even "rich," in many less-developed countries. For example, $15,000 of income a year, while not much in the United States, would make you very rich in a country such as Ethiopia. On the other hand, many Americans with incomes now considered just above the poverty line might be considered poor a generation or two from now, even though their incomes will permit them to buy far more than what today are considered to be the necessities of life. Why?

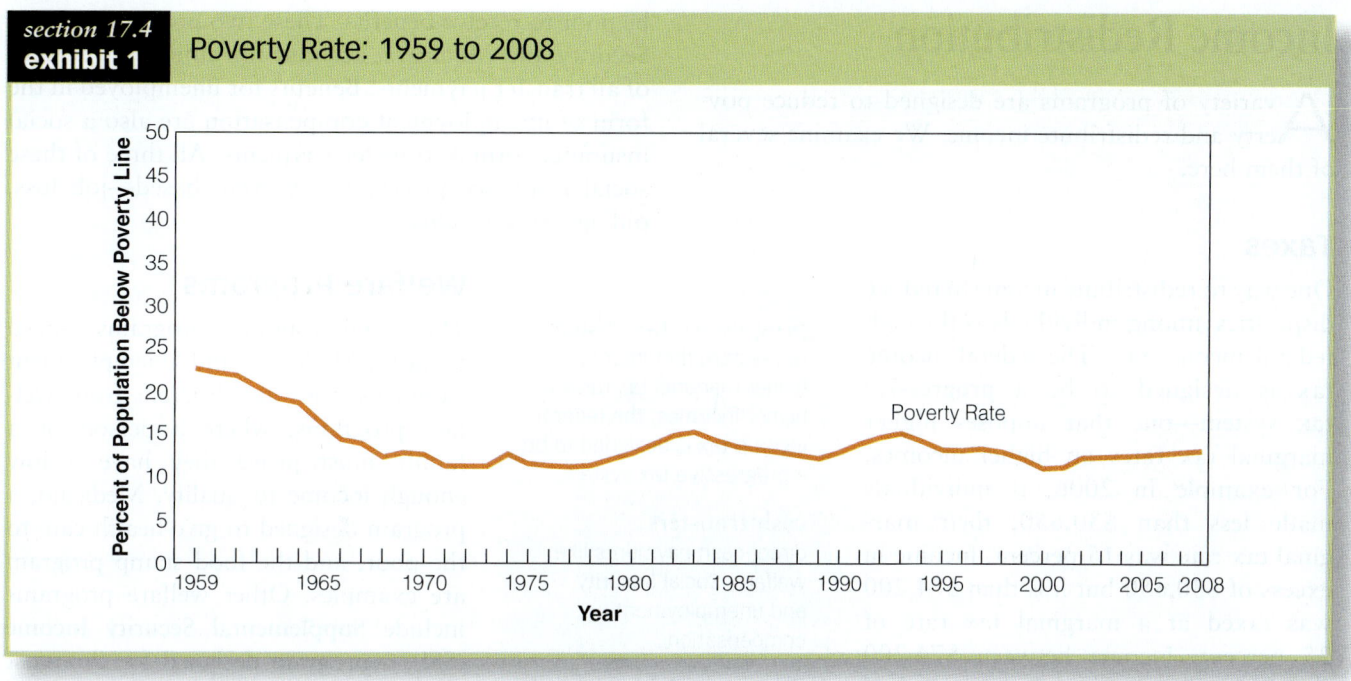

section 17.4 exhibit 1 Poverty Rate: 1959 to 2008

SOURCE: U.S. Census Bureau, Current Population Survey, 2009.

section 17.4 exhibit 2 Poverty Among Different Groups, 2008

Group	Below Poverty Rate
Female household, no husband present	28.7
Black	24.7
Hispanic	23.2
Children (under age 18)	19.0
Male household, no wife present	13.8
All Persons	13.2
Asian	11.8
Elderly (over age 65)	9.7
White, not Hispanic	8.6
Married-couple families	5.5

SOURCE: U.S. Census Bureau.

To most people, being poor means having less income and purchasing power than most other people living in the same community or nation. A person is poor if her income is low relative to the incomes of most other people in the same geographical area, and she is rich if her income exceeds that of most other people in the area. Poverty is therefore often thought of as a relative income concept, rather than being determined by some ability to buy a specific fixed basket of goods and services.

Alternative definitions of poverty have been suggested based on relative income measures. For instance, families that earn less than one-half the median (or middle) family income could be considered poor. Over time, as economic growth proceeds, the income necessary to avoid being considered poor by this measure increases. Using this definition, then, poverty cannot be eradicated by economic growth but only by income redistribution. Even from an equity or fairness point of view, few people favor total income equality, because income needs presumably vary with family size and possibly with the ages of the family members and the cost of living in different cities. It is clear, then, that "poverty," in a relative income sense, will always be with us. We can perhaps reduce the consequences of being poor by policies that raise the incomes of society's lowest-income members to levels closer to the median, but we cannot raise everyone's income to a level equal to or above that median; that is an economic, as well as a statistical, impossibility.

Income Redistribution

A variety of programs are designed to reduce poverty and redistribute income. We examine several of them here.

Taxes

One way to redistribute income to reduce disparities among individuals is through federal income tax. The federal income tax is designed to be a **progressive tax system**—one that imposes higher marginal tax rates on higher incomes. For example in 2006, if individuals made less than $30,650, their marginal tax rate was 15 percent. Income in excess of $30,650 but less than $74,200 was taxed at a marginal tax rate of 25 percent; income between $74,200 and $154,800 was taxed at a marginal tax rate of 28 percent; and income in the range of $154,800 to $336,500 was taxed at a marginal tax rate of 33 percent. Any income earned by an individual over $336,500 was taxed at a marginal tax rate of 35 percent.

Transfer Payments

A second means by which income redistribution can be carried out by the government is through direct transfer payments to the lower part of the income distribution. Transfer payments are payments made to individuals for which goods or services are exchanged. They come in the form of in-kind transfers—direct transfers of goods or services such as food stamps, housing subsidies, and Medicaid—and **cash transfers** of direct cash payments such as welfare, Social Security, and unemployment compensation.

Social Security, Medicare, and Unemployment Compensation

Social Security is a cash transfer program that provides income primarily to older persons. Social Security accounts for almost 45 percent of all federal transfer payments. Medicare is an in-kind transfer—a health insurance subsidy program that pays many of the doctor and hospital bills for those over the age of 65. Neither of these programs are considered welfare programs because one does not have to be poor to receive benefits. These two programs, Social Security and Medicare, account for almost 70 percent of all transfer payments. Benefits for unemployed in the form of unemployment compensation are also a social insurance form of transfer payments. All three of these social insurance programs are event based—job loss, old age, or disability.

> **progressive tax system**
> tax system that imposes higher marginal tax rates on higher incomes; the federal income tax is designed to be a progressive tax system
>
> **cash transfers**
> direct cash payments like welfare, Social Security, and unemployment compensation
>
> **Supplemental Security Income (SSI)**
> a welfare program designed for the most needy, elderly, disabled, and blind
>
> **Temporary Assistance for Needy Families (TANF)**
> a welfare program designed to help families that have few financial resources
>
> **Earned Income Tax Credit (EITC)**
> a welfare program that allows the working poor to receive income refunds that can be greater than the taxes they paid during the last year
>
> **means-tested income transfer program**
> program in which eligibility is dependent on low income; food stamps, Medicaid, and housing subsidies are examples of means-tested income transfer programs

Welfare Programs

The social insurance programs (Social Security, Medicare, and Unemployment Compensation) are different from welfare programs, where a person or a family must prove they have a low enough income to qualify. Medicaid, a program designed to give health care to the poor, and the food stamp program are examples. Other welfare programs include **Supplemental Security Income (SSI)**, a program designed for the most needy, elderly, disabled, and blind, and **Temporary Assistance for Needy Families (TANF)**, designed to help families that have few financial resources. The **Earned Income Tax Credit (EITC)** is a program that allows the working poor to receive income refunds that can be greater than the taxes they paid during the last year. It is a **means-tested income transfer program** (eligibility is dependent on low income) like food stamps, Medicaid, and housing subsidies.

Negative Income Tax

A negative income tax collects taxes from high-income families and gives subsidies to low-income families. Thus, it is a tax and a transfer program. It uses the personal income tax system to set up a series of payments to citizens and tax receipts by the U.S. Treasury according to a schedule based on family size and actual income earned. The plan would not require setting up a new system. It could be an extension of the fully computerized system that already exists.

How Does it Work? High-income families would pay a tax; low-income families would receive a subsidy. For example, suppose the government formula for a negative tax is Tax = (25 percent × income) − $10,000. So, if a family earned $100,000 a year it would pay $15,000 in taxes (0.25 × $100,000 = $25,000 − $10,000 =

$15,000). A family that earned $40,000 a year would pay $0.00 in taxes (0.25 × $40,000 = $10,000 − $10,000 = $0). And a family that earned $20,000 would owe −$5,000 (0.25 × $20,000 = $5,000 − $10,000 = −$5,000). That is, this family would get $5,000 in return.

The Case for a Negative Income Tax Many economists favor a negative income tax. They point out that it would not require the massive bureaucracy that now exists for administering public assistance, food stamp, and other programs. Hence, many of the resources now spent for this huge bureaucracy could be spent on other priorities, or used to provide the negative tax (the government payment) to needy families. No one would have to demonstrate need. It would not encourage illegitimate births, family break-ups, or many claims the current welfare system does.

The Case Against a Negative Income Tax On the other hand, many economists oppose a negative income tax, pointing out that it might cost "too much." In particular, if for political reasons such current welfare programs as food stamps and subsidized housing cannot be dismantled, then the negative income tax would just be one more facet of the welfare system.

They also contend that any effective negative income tax would have a *work disincentive effect*. That is, the payoff for returning to work would be smaller with an effective negative income tax program, so that many who could work might nevertheless decide not to do so. There is also concern that cash assistance, rather than in-kind welfare (food stamps, housing subsidies, etc.) would lead to poor consumption choices—perhaps drugs and alcohol. However, recipients would substitute food stamps for cash purchases, allowing them to buy whatever they wanted. And some critics say while it subsidizes the unfortunate, it also subsidizes the lazy and undeserving.

Government Subsidies

A third way that governments can help the less affluent is by using government revenues to provide low-cost public services. Inexpensive public housing, subsidized public transport, and even public parks are services that probably serve the poor to a greater extent than the rich. "Free" public education is viewed by many as an equalizing force in that it opens opportunities for children of less prosperous members of society to obtain employment that could improve their economic status. Of course, not all government programs benefit the relatively poor at the expense of the rich. For example, federal government subsidies to commuter railroads primarily lower the cost to affluent suburbanites of getting to work in the central city. Support for public universities may help the middle or even upper income groups more than the poor. In addition, agricultural subsidies often provide large benefits to farmers who already have large incomes.

global WATCH: WHAT'S THE BEST WAY TO REDUCE EXTREME POVERTY? GOOD NEWS ABOUT POVERTY

—BY DAVID BROOKS

I hate to be the bearer of good news, because only pessimists are regarded as intellectually serious, but we're in the 11th month of the most prosperous year in human history. Last week, the World Bank released a report showing that global growth "accelerated sharply" this year to a rate of about 4 percent.

Best of all, the poorer nations are leading the way. Some rich countries, like the U.S. and Japan, are doing well, but the developing world is leading this economic surge. Developing countries are seeing their economies expand by 6.1 percent this year—an unprecedented rate—and, even if you take China,

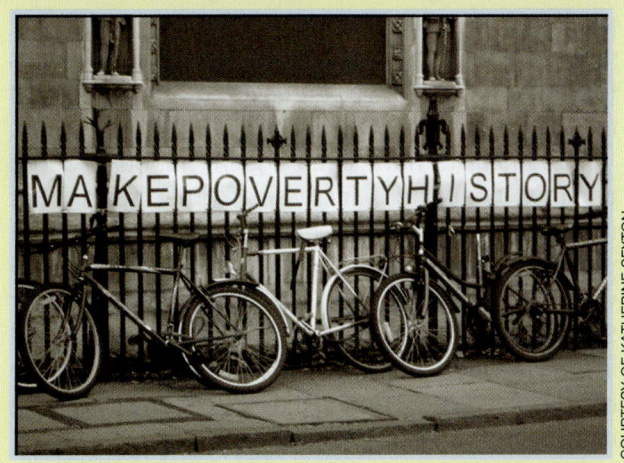

(continued)

global WATCH: WHAT'S THE BEST WAY TO REDUCE EXTREME POVERTY? GOOD NEWS ABOUT POVERTY (cont.)

India and Russia out of the equation, developing world growth is still around 5 percent. As even the cautious folks at the World Bank note, all developing regions are growing faster this decade than they did in the 1980's and 90's.

This is having a wonderful effect on world poverty, because when regions grow, that growth is shared up and down the income ladder. In its report, the World Bank notes that economic growth is producing a "spectacular" decline in poverty in East and South Asia. In 1990, there were roughly 472 million people in the East Asia and Pacific region living on less than $1 a day. By 2001, there were 271 million living in extreme poverty, and by 2015, at current projections, there will only be 19 million people living under those conditions.

Less dramatic declines in extreme poverty have been noted around the developing world, with the vital exception of sub-Saharan Africa. It now seems quite possible that we will meet the United Nations' Millennium Development Goals, which were set a few years ago: the number of people living in extreme poverty will be cut in half by the year 2015. As Martin Wolf of The Financial Times wrote in his recent book, "Why Globalization Works": "Never before have so many people—or so large a proportion of the world's population—enjoyed such large rises in their standard of living."

As other research confirms, these rapid improvements at the bottom of the income ladder are contributing to and correlating with declines in illiteracy, child labor rates and fertility rates. The growth in the world's poorer regions also supports the argument that we are seeing a drop in global inequality.

Economists have been arguing furiously about whether inequality is increasing or decreasing. But it now seems likely that while inequality has grown within particular nations, it is shrinking among individuals worldwide. The Catalan economist Xavier Sala-i-Martin looked at eight measures of global inequality and found they told the same story: after remaining constant during the 70's, inequality among individuals has since declined.

What explains all this good news? The short answer is this thing we call globalization. Over the past decades, many nations have undertaken structural reforms to lower trade barriers, shore up property rights and free economic activity. International trade is surging. The poor nations that opened themselves up to trade, investment and those evil multinational corporations saw the sharpest poverty declines. Write this on your forehead: Free trade reduces world suffering.

Of course, all the news is not good. Plagued by bad governments and AIDS, sub-Saharan Africa has not joined in the benefits of globalization. Big budget deficits in the U.S. and elsewhere threaten stable growth. High oil prices are a problem. Trade produces losers as well as winners, especially among less-skilled workers in the developed world.

But especially around Thanksgiving, it's worth appreciating some of the things that have gone right, and not just sweeping reports like the one from the World Bank under the rug.

It's worth reminding ourselves that the key task ahead is spreading the benefits of globalization to Africa and the Middle East. It's worth noting this perhaps not too surprising phenomenon: As free trade improves the lives of people in poor countries, it is viewed with suspicion by more people in rich countries.

Just once, I'd like to see someone like Bono or Bruce Springsteen stand up at a concert and speak the truth to his fan base: that the world is complicated and there are no free lunches. But if you really want to reduce world poverty, you should be cheering on those guys in pinstripe suits at the free-trade negotiations and those investors jetting around the world. Thanks, in part, to them, we are making progress against poverty. Thanks, in part, to them, more people around the world have something to be thankful for.

SOURCE: From David Brooks, "Good News About Poverty", 'New York Times', November 27, 2004. Copyright © 2004 The New York Times. All rights reserved. Used by permission and protected by the copyright laws of the United States. The printing, copying, redistribution, or retransmission of the material without express written permission is prohibited.

POLICY application
TEACH YOUR CHILDREN WELL
THE ECONOMIC CASE FOR PRESCHOOL

—BY JOEL WALDFOGEL

Softhearted people always advocate spending more on kids. But according to a new and authoritative synthesis of available evidence, there's a hardheaded case for investing more in young kids over older ones.

In the United States, we've spent trillions of dollars over decades on K–12 schooling in the hopes of making young people more productive, or at least less criminally delinquent. The results have been mixed. About 20 percent of the American workforce is essentially illiterate (compared with 5 to 10 percent in Sweden or Germany), creating a major drag on our international competitiveness. And an astronomical 5.6 million adults in the United States have served time in state or federal prison, with 1.3 million there currently. Their incarceration, along with other costs of crime, costs us around $1.3 trillion a year.

Why doesn't all our spending on education buy better results? Nobel Prize winner James Heckman of the University of Chicago and Dimitriy Masterov of the University of Michigan argue that by waiting until kindergarten, we throw money at kids when it's too late. Their evidence urges shifting educational spending to younger children.

The early investment is needed, the authors argue, to supplement the role of the family. Recent developments in neuroscience have shown that the early years are vital to cognitive development, which in turn is important to subsequent success and productivity in school, life, and work. Early-Childhood nurturing has traditionally been the province of families. But families are deteriorating. Roughly one in six kids was born into poverty or single parenthood or both in 1970. In 2000, the rate was about one in four. What's more, almost 10 percent of children were born to unmarried teenage mothers in 1999; these kids tend to receive especially low levels of emotional and intellectual support and cognitive stimulation. They arrive at kindergarten cognitively disadvantaged, and the gap widens as they get older, eventually leading to early babies, lousy jobs, and elevated crime.

Heckman and Masterov look at a number of pilot programs in early-childhood education that have targeted high-risk kids in disadvantaged families, and studied them into adulthood. These programs are like Head Start, only more intensive. For example, between 1962 and 1967, the Perry Project in Ypsilanti, Mich., provided two years of intensive preschool to a group of disadvantaged 3-year-old black children, chosen from an eligible pool by a coin flip. The program consisted of a daily session of two and a half hours and a weekly 90-minute teacher home visit. In today's dollars, it would cost $10,000 per child per year.

Perry participants have been followed through age 40, and the program has shown substantial benefits in educational achievement and other social outcomes. Participants achieved greater literacy and higher grades, and they were more likely to graduate high school. Later in life, they were more likely to be employed—and to earn more—and less likely to be on welfare. They also committed less crime and had lower rates of teen pregnancy.

The authors estimate the rate of return for programs like the Perry Project to be a substantial 16 percent. While some of this payback accrues directly to the kids, in the form of higher earnings when they're grown up, about three-quarters of it goes to the rest of us in the form of lower crime and savings on prison spending. Heckman and Masterov compare the return from investing in preschool kids with the returns from lower class size in high school (smaller than the return to preschool) and to GED programs (smaller still). They propose that the return on investment declines with age, although they don't offer a ton of quantitative evidence on this point.

The big economic return for intensive preschool for disadvantaged kids has two implications. First, while many people advocate spending on these kids for reasons of fairness or justice, Heckman and Masterov make a different case. They're saying this preschool spending is a sound economic investment. Each dollar we spend on targeted, intensive preschool returns more than a dollar invested in, say, a pretty good mutual fund.

(continued)

POLICY application: TEACH YOUR CHILDREN WELL THE ECONOMIC CASE FOR PRESCHOOL (CONT.)

Many families already make this investment on their own, either by spending time with their kids or by purchasing high-quality child care. Why involve governments? Well, Heckman and Masterov show that if *your* kid goes to one of these programs, *the rest of us* get most of the benefit. Economists assume that even if parents of disadvantaged kids are rational and forward-looking—as if they didn't have enough to worry about—they will invest in preschool only to boost their kids' earnings and not to reduce crime and prison costs, which are borne by the rest of us. As a result, even conscientious parents will under-invest. So, Economics 101 tells you—granted, in an end-of-semester lecture that you probably skipped—that clearly this is a job for government.

The hardheaded case for Perry-like preschool extends beyond higher pay and reduced crime. Unlike many efforts to boost productivity—think trickle-down—this one would reduce inequality as well, by raising the incomes of the disadvantaged. Investing in preschools can also enhance international competitiveness. Much of the growth in American standards of living over the past half-century has flowed from our population's ever-increasing educational attainment. But for the generations born since 1950, the growth has stopped. The problem is not that a college education costs too much, but rather that many disadvantaged kids aren't academically ready for college when they finish high school. And Heckman and Masterov argue that it stems from the academic deficits they bring to kindergarten. If preschool whips them into shape, they'll be better prepared for all the other steps along the way.

A sales problem remains: These programs invade the traditional province of the family, and in Heckman and Masterov's conception, they would target disadvantaged populations that are disproportionately minority. Wanted: a credible and sympathetic pitchman. Paging Barack Obama.

SOURCE: Joel Waldfogel is the Ehrenkranz Family Professor of business and public policy at the Wharton School of the University of Pennsylvania. His new book is The Tyranny of the Market: Why you Can't Always Get What You Want.

SECTION CHECK

1. One method of defining poverty is to determine an absolute income level that is necessary to provide the basic necessities of life in minimum quantities. The poverty rate, then, would be the proportion of persons who fail to earn the minimum income standard.
2. An alternative definition of poverty is a relative income measure. For instance, families that earn less than one-half the median (or middle) family income are considered poor. Using this definition, poverty cannot be eradicated by economic growth, but only by income redistribution.
3. A negative income tax (NIT) is a tax and transfer program that collects taxes from higher income families and gives subsidies to lower income families.

---

1. How are absolute and relative measures of poverty different?
2. Why could economic growth potentially eliminate absolute measures of poverty but not relative measures of poverty?
3. Some people argue that poverty could be eliminated by "rich" countries. Can both absolute and relative poverty be eliminated by rich countries? Why or why not?
4. What are some of the programs designed to reduce poverty and redistribute income?

Interactive Chapter Summary

Fill in the blanks:

1. Since the 1980s, the share of measured income received by the top 5 percent has _____ and that of the lowest fifth of families has _____.

2. People are at their peak in terms of productivity when they are _____.

3. At any moment in time, middle-aged people tend to have _____ incomes than both younger and older people do.

4. An increase in the divorce rate has caused the measured distribution of income in the United States to appear more _____.

5. If we consider age distribution, institutional factors, and in-kind transfer programs, the income distribution is likely considerably more _____ than it appears from measured income.

6. The greater the distance between the Lorenz curve and the 45-degree line, the _____ the amount of inequality.

7. The Gini coefficient, which measures income inequality, varies from _____ for perfect equality to _____ for perfect inequality.

8. Political and social changes in the past century or two have worked to _____ income inequality.

9. The permanent income hypothesis (PIH) indicates that consumption would be _____ likely to exceed income, when one is middle-aged rather than when one is young or old.

10. The economic theory supporting policies of income redistribution is derived from the principle of _____.

11. Diminishing marginal utility implies that increases in income generate _____ additional happiness or utility at higher levels of income.

12. Arguments to justify income redistribution based on diminishing marginal utility must assume that people are _____ in how they experience diminishing marginal utility from increasing income.

13. Heavy taxes on the rich, combined with large subsidies for the poor, would result in little incentive to _____ or _____.

14. Large-scale redistribution from high-income individuals to low-income individuals would likely _____ the level of human capital (education) in society.

15. When a person is denied employment without regard to productivity, it is called _____ discrimination.

16. When a person is given employment at a wage lower than that of other workers, based on something other than productivity, it is called _____ discrimination.

17. The proportion of women to men in the labor force has dramatically _____ over time.

18. A _____ statistical correlation exists between lifetime earnings and years of schooling.

19. The _____ explanation of productivity differences focuses on past discrimination's perverse effect on the environment of females and nonwhites.

20. Discrimination sometimes reflects _____ costs, based on past experiences.

21. Using race or sex is an _____ but cheap way of screening applicants for some jobs.

22. Nondiscriminating firms have a cost _____ compared with firms that discriminate.

23. Differences in _____, certain _____ factors, _____ factors, and government _____ activities have all been identified as elements that influence the income distribution data and suggest that we might be overstating inequality.

24. At any moment in time, middle-aged persons tend to have _____ incomes than younger and older persons because they are at an age when their _____ is at a peak and they are participating in the _____ to a greater extent.

25. The earnings of children of fathers with lifetime earnings 20 percent greater than the average tend to be _____ average.

26. Reasons that some people make more money than others include differences in _____, _____, _____, _____, and _____ towards risk and leisure.

27. A majority of the income inequality on Earth reflects differences in living standards _____ nations rather than disparities _____ nations.

28. _____ discrimination occurs when a worker is denied employment on the basis of some factor without regard to his or her productivity.

29. A great deal of the earnings differentials across the sexes and races can be explained by differences in _____.

30. In competitive industries, firms that do not discriminate can hire the unfavored but equally competent workers and have a(n) _____ advantage, allowing them to _____ discriminating competitors' prices.

31. The poverty rate for the United States is currently set at _____ the cost of providing a nutritionally adequate diet.

32. The greater the rate of economic growth, the _____ rapidly poverty will be eradicated.

33. Using a relative definition of poverty, poverty cannot be eradicated by economic growth but only by _____.

34. Because the federal income tax is _____, it tends to redistribute income in a way that reduces income disparities.

35. Social Security accounts for almost _____ of federal transfer payments and, along with Medicare, accounts for almost _____.

Answers: 1. risen; fallen 2. middle-aged 3. higher 4. unequal 5. equal 6. greater 7. zero; one 8. reduce 9. less 10. diminishing marginal utility 11. less 12. alike 13. works; invest 14. reduce 15. job-entry 16. wage 17. increased 18. strong 19. environmental 20. information 21. imperfect 22. advantage 23. age; demographic; institutional; redistributive 24. higher; productivity; labor force 25. above 26. age; skill; education; training; preferences 27. among; within 28. Job-entry 29. productivity 30. costs; undercut 31. three times 32. more 33. income redistribution 34. progressive 35. 45 percent; 70 percent

Key Terms and Concepts

in-kind transfers 485
permanent income hypothesis 486
job-entry discrimination 493
wage discrimination 493
poverty rate 496
poverty line 496

progressive tax system 498
cash transfers 498
Supplemental Security Income (SSI) 498
Temporary Assistance for Needy Families (TANF) 498

Earned Income Tax Credit (EITC) 498
means-tested income transfer program 498

Section Check Answers

17.1 Income Distribution

1. **Why might patterns in the measured income distribution give an inaccurate impression?**
   The measured income distribution may give an inaccurate impression because it does not include all forms of income. For instance, it does not include nonmonetary income.

2. **Why might income distribution statistics understate the degree of income inequality?**
   These statistics may understate the degree of income inequality because they do not include the nonmonetary income and privileges of the relatively well-to-do.

3. **Why might measured income shares overstate the degree of income inequality?**
   Measured income shares may overstate the degree of income inequality because they don't adjust for predictable differences in incomes by age, demographic trends such as the growth of both divorce and two-earner families, taxes, in-kind income from the government (e.g., food stamps), the benefits of government programs, or movement within the income distribution over time.

4. **How does the fraction of the population that is middle-aged, rather than young or old, affect measurements of income inequality?**
   The more people are in their peak earning middle-age years, the higher their earnings appear relative to their lifetime incomes; the more people who are young or old, in their low earning years, the lower their earnings appear relative to their lifetime income.

5. **How does the growth of both two-earner families and divorced couples increase measured income inequality?**
   Combining two incomes as the income of one family and increasing the number of lower-income female-headed households due to divorce increase the number of families counted at both the upper and lower ends of the income distribution, increasing measured income inequality.

6. **Why is it important to take account of the substantial mobility of families within the income distribution over time when evaluating the degree of income inequality in America?**
   The substantial income mobility within the income distribution means that someone who has a low income

today will not necessarily have a low income for a long period of time; there may continue to be low-income people, but they are likely to be different people.

17.2 Income Redistribution

1. **How is the principle of diminishing marginal utility used to justify income redistribution?**
   The idea that the marginal utility of income falls with income has been used to argue that by taking income from those with higher incomes (and therefore low marginal utility of income) and giving it to those with lower incomes (and therefore high marginal utility of income), total utility in society could be increased.

2. **Why is it not possible to prove the idea that redistributing income from rich to poor will increase society's utility?**
   Utility is not comparable between people. Even if an individual's marginal utility of income falls with income, that means his marginal utility is lower for higher incomes than for lower incomes; it does not mean that a higher-income person's marginal utility of income is lower than the marginal utility of income of a different person with a lower income.

3. **What are the fairness and incentive arguments against government redistribution of income?**
   The fairness argument against government redistribution of income is that it is unfair to take a substantial part of someone's income (given to him or her voluntarily by others) to give to others. The incentive argument is that there is no way for the government to redistribute income without undermining the incentives to earn income of both those taxed and those subsidized.

4. **If high-income individuals must pay increased income tax rates in order to provide subsidies for low-income individuals (and the subsidies are phased out as income increases), are the productive incentives of both high- and low-income people reduced? Why or why not?**
   Increased income tax rates on high-income people reduce their take-home (after tax) pay from the marginal hours of work involved, giving them less incentive to work those hours. Subsidies to low-income people whose benefits are phased out as their incomes grow act as income taxes (benefit reductions) on low-income people, giving them less incentive to work as well.

17.3 The Economics of Discrimination

1. **What is the difference between job-entry discrimination and wage discrimination?**
   Job-entry discrimination refers to a worker denied employment due to discrimination; wage discrimination refers to those who are employed, but at lower wages, due to discrimination.

2. **Explain how earnings differences could reflect either discrimination or productivity differences.**
   If employers discriminated among workers for reasons other than productivity, that would result in earnings differences. But employers are also willing to pay more to more productive workers (e.g., those with more education), resulting in earnings differences. The difficulty is determining how much each accounts for differences in earnings.

3. **What is the environmental explanation for differences in earnings across the sexes and races?**
   The environmental explanation for differences in earnings across the sexes and races is that women and minorities are not as productive because they have been prevented from gaining the necessary training and skills and because women are more likely to interrupt their careers to have and care for children.

4. **How do firms' incentives to maximize profits tend to reduce the extent of discrimination?**
   A firm that chose not to hire an employee that has a higher marginal revenue product than his or her wage, because of some preference for discrimination, sacrifices profits as a result. Those sacrificed profits make discriminating costly, reducing its extent.

5. **How can discrimination reflect imperfect information and the costs of acquiring more information about potential employees?**
   If an employer's past experience with a particular group has been worse than that with other groups, he or she might prefer not to hire people from that group because the probability that they will perform well is lower. But this use of past experience as a screening device for new employees only makes sense if it is costly for employers to discover the productivity of individual potential employees, rather than the average of some group, prior to hiring them.

6. **Say you only hire purple workers. If purple workers strongly prefer to work with one another instead of with other groups, why might you prefer to hire a less productive purple worker than a more productive nonpurple worker at the same wage?**
   Say each of your 20 current purple workers would demand $1 more per hour to work with a non-purple worker than with another purple worker. You would then have to compare how much more productive your prospective nonpurple worker was at a given wage than a purple worker, or how much less he would have to be paid for a given level of productivity, against how much more you would have to pay your other workers to work next to him. In this case, if the productivity

or wage difference exceeds $20 per hour of work, the nonpurple worker would be hired, but if it were less than $20 per hour of work, he would not be hired.

7. Why would subsidizing employers for hiring minority workers rather than imposing implicit quotas give employers greater incentives to expand minority job opportunities?

An implicit minority hiring quota would raise employers' costs by making them hire workers they find less productive than those they would otherwise have hired. This reduces the profits of those firms, tending to reduce their size and number, and the number of job opportunities they offer. Subsidizing the hiring of minority workers, however, lowers the cost to employers (they would not hire them unless the subsidy more than compensated them for any reduction in productivity) of hiring minority workers, increasing their profits and expanding the number of job opportunities for minority workers.

17.4 Poverty

1. How are absolute and relative measures of poverty different?

An absolute measure of poverty is one based on whether income is sufficient to provide the basic necessities of life (food, clothing, etc.) in minimum quantities; a relative measure of poverty is based on having lower incomes relative to others (e.g., earning half the median income).

2. Why could economic growth potentially eliminate absolute measures of poverty but not relative measures of poverty?

Economic growth increases output, making it possible to bring every citizen up to some minimal absolute level of income. It does not, however, eliminate the fact that some will still have relatively lower incomes than others.

3. Some people argue that poverty could be eliminated by "rich" countries. Can both absolute and relative poverty be eliminated by rich countries? Why or why not?

Absolute poverty could possibly be eliminated—providing all citizens the basic necessities of life in minimum quantities—by "rich" countries. However, unless a country completely equalized incomes of all its citizens, some would continue to have lower incomes than others, and such relative poverty would persist to some degree.

4. What are some of the programs designed to reduce poverty and redistribute income?

These programs include progressive income taxes; transfer payments such as Social Security, Medicare, and unemployment compensation; welfare programs such as Supplementary Security Income and Temporary Assistance to Needy Families; the Earned Income Tax Credit; government subsidies; and minimum wage laws.

CHAPTER 17 STUDY GUIDE

True or False:

1. The proportion of income received by the top 5 percent of Americans declined after 1935, but it has been increasing since the 1980s.
2. Differences in age among a population can lead to differences in the distribution of income.
3. Since 1950, the proportion of the population that is very young or very old has fallen.
4. If every individual earned the same total income over his or her lifetime, there would still be observed income inequality because people earn more when they are middle-aged.
5. Inequalities in annual incomes observed at one point in time overstate the degree of income inequality over lifetimes.
6. The distribution of income is more equal when the Lorenz curve is closer to the 45-degree line of perfect equality.
7. The closer the Gini coefficient is to one, the smaller the degree of income inequality.
8. The permanent income hypothesis (PIH) indicates that both college students and the elderly tend to dissave.
9. The PIH indicates that, in recessions, consumption will tend to fall more than proportionately to the fall in current income.
10. It is impossible to prove that a given income distribution is better than another.
11. According to the principle of diminishing marginal utility, increases in income generate greater additional happiness or utility at higher levels of income.
12. Economists assume that interpersonal utility comparisons are not possible.
13. If each person had diminishing marginal utility of income, income redistribution would increase utility in a society.
14. Within a country at a moment in time, happiness is positively correlated with income.
15. If we taxed the rich heavily and gave large subsidies to the poor, our incomes would be more equal but smaller.
16. Large-scale redistribution from high-income people to low-income people would likely result in less overtime being worked in a society.
17. Total equality of family income would result in total equality of individual income.
18. People agree that we should increase the degree of income redistribution in society.
19. Only a weak statistical correlation exists between lifetime earnings and years of schooling.
20. Discovering that wages are lower for blacks and females does not prove wage discrimination.
21. The environmental explanation of productivity differences assumes that there has been no discrimination.
22. Discrimination may reflect information costs, where group characteristics are used as a low-cost screening device.
23. Nondiscriminating firms will have a cost disadvantage over firms that discriminate.
24. If employers can hire equally productive female employees at a lower wage than males, the profit motive will give them a strong incentive to do so.
25. Even if every individual earned exactly the same income over his or her lifetime, there would still be inequality at any given moment in time.
26. The increased proportion of the U.S. population that is either very young or very old has tended to decrease the observed inequality in the distribution of income.
27. Both the increased number of divorced couples and the rise of two-income families have caused the measured distribution of income to appear more unequal.
28. There is virtually no positive correlation between the earnings of grandparents and grandchildren.
29. Other things being equal, workers who prefer more amenities at work or more time for leisure earn less.
30. Income inequality is less in the United States and the United Kingdom than in Sweden and Japan.

31. Some of the greatest disparities in income are found in developing nations.
32. Wage discrimination occurs when workers are given employment at wages lower than other workers on some basis other than productivity differences.
33. The poverty rate reflects a percentage of the population that falls below an absolute value.
34. Economic growth could eliminate poverty in an absolute sense but not poverty in a relative sense.
35. Many "poor" individuals in the United States, using the official definition, would be considered well off, even "rich," in many developing countries.
36. A progressive income tax imposes higher marginal tax rates on individuals with higher incomes.
37. Transfer payments include in-kind transfers but not cash transfers.
38. One argument for a negative income tax is that it would not require any added bureaucracy, unlike other forms of public assistance.
39. The fact that average wages are lower for blacks and females proves wage discrimination.
40. To some extent, discrimination may reflect information costs.
41. In the long run, competition has the potential to reduce discrimination.
42. If poverty is defined as earning less than one-half of the median income, then it cannot be eradicated through economic growth.
43. Poverty can be defined in two ways: using an absolute concept of poverty or a relative concept of poverty.
44. If poverty is defined using an absolute measure, then poverty can never be eliminated.

Multiple Choice:

1. The proportion of income received by the richest 5 percent of Americans has
   a. edged upward since the 1980s.
   b. held steady since the 1980s.
   c. decreased slightly since the 1980s.
   d. decreased significantly since the 1980s.

2. The measured distribution of income may appear more unequal as a result of
   a. an increase in the proportion of young people in the population.
   b. an increase in the number of two-income families.
   c. an increase in the number of divorced couples.
   d. an increase in the proportion of retired older people in the population.
   e. all of the above.

3. Which of the following are over-represented among those with low incomes?
   a. college students working toward their graduate degrees
   b. single-parent families
   c. young, inexperienced workers
   d. all of the above

4. American income inequality data indicate that
   a. most poor families never significantly rise above poverty, but rich families get poorer over time.
   b. most rich families remain rich, but poor families move up substantially through the income distribution over time.
   c. there is substantial movement over time among income groups in America.
   d. rich families stay rich and poor families stay poor in America.

5. Which of the following is false?
   a. The poverty line varies with the size of the family.
   b. The poverty rate is adjusted for inflation.
   c. The poverty rate is set at three times the cost of a nutritionally adequate diet.
   d. The receipt of food stamps cannot lift a recipient family from below the poverty line to above the poverty line.
   e. None of the above is false; all are true.

6. Large-scale income redistribution would make incomes _____ and _____.
   a. more equal; larger
   b. more equal; smaller
   c. less equal; larger
   d. less equal; smaller

7. Large-scale income redistribution would tend to reduce the level of
   a. income inequality.
   b. savings and investment.
   c. human capital (education).
   d. the number of overtime hours worked in society.
   e. all of the above.

8. Which of the following is true?
   a. There is substantial income inequality in the United States, and there has been little change in the distribution of measured income in the past few decades.
   b. There is substantial income inequality in the United States, but there have been appreciable changes in the distribution of measured income in the past few decades.
   c. There is very little income inequality in the United States, and there has been little change in the distribution of measured income in the past few decades.
   d. There is very little income inequality in the United States, but there have been appreciable changes in the distribution of measured income in the past few decades.

9. As more women prepare for careers as professionals,
   a. their level of human capital will more closely approach that of men.
   b. the ratio of female to male earnings will increase.
   c. their number of years of work experience will more closely approach that of men.
   d. all of the above are likely to occur.

10. Evidence suggests that levels of inequality of income _____ from 1935 to 1950, then _____ until 1980, and have since _____.
    a. increased; decreased; increased
    b. increased; remained relatively stable; decreased
    c. decreased; increased; decreased
    d. decreased; remained relatively stable; increased
    e. increased; decreased; remained relatively stable

11. Differences in monetary wages across jobs may result from
    a. differences in job amenities.
    b. differences in on-the-job hazards.
    c. differences in working conditions.
    d. differences in fringe benefits.
    e. all of the above.

12. Diminishing marginal utility
    a. implies that increases in income will give less utility to a rich person than to a poor person.
    b. implies that a given amount of added income would tend to provide less utility to a given individual at higher levels of income than at lower levels of income.
    c. implies that income redistribution from higher- to lower-income persons will give more utility to the lower-income persons than it will take from the higher-income persons.
    d. implies that all of the above are true.

13. The principle of diminishing marginal utility is not enough to guarantee that transferring income from the rich to the poor will increase society's utility because
    a. the total utility of the rich will still be greater.
    b. the rich get richer and the poor get poorer.
    c. it is impossible to make utility comparisons between individuals.
    d. diminishing marginal utility does not hold for everyone.

14. If complete equality of income was legislated, which of the following would be expected to occur?
    a. People, on average, would become richer.
    b. Society would become happier.
    c. Individuals would work longer hours.
    d. The incentive to produce would be largely eliminated.

15. Women earn less on average than men. Which of the following can we conclude as a result?
    a. Women must be less productive.
    b. Men must be highly motivated and productive.
    c. Women must be the victim of discrimination by employers.
    d. Without considering preferences and productivity factors, differences in average earnings do not necessarily imply employment discrimination.

16. Women are more likely than men to
    a. move in order to take a higher-income job.
    b. take jobs with out-of-town travel.
    c. interrupt their careers.
    d. take jobs with uncertain schedules and long hours.

17. Economic theory suggests that when discrimination is based on the personal prejudices of employers
    a. the wages of those who are discriminated against will rise.
    b. it will make no difference to an employer's costs.
    c. profit incentives will tend to reduce discrimination.
    d. it will reduce production costs.

18. Women tend to earn less than men because
    a. women tend to work fewer hours, on average, than men.
    b. women tend to have fewer years of schooling, on average, than men.
    c. women are more likely to prefer jobs that give them flexible hours.
    d. all of the above are true.

19. As more women prepare for careers as professionals,
    a. their level of human capital will more closely approach that of men.
    b. the ratio of female to male earnings will increase.
    c. their number of years of work experience will more closely approach that of men.
    d. all of the above are likely to occur.

20. The poverty rate
    a. is the proportion of persons who fall below the poverty line.
    b. is set at the cost of providing a nutritionally adequate diet.
    c. has been rising since 1960.
    d. All of the above are true.
    e. None of the above is true.

21. Social Security and Medicare
    a. are considered welfare programs.
    b. are only received by senior citizens with low incomes.
    c. together make up the majority of all federal transfer payments.
    d. are both considered in-kind transfer payments.
    e. are characterized by none of the above.

22. Which of the following is *not* a means-tested income transfer program?
    a. Medicare
    b. Food stamps
    c. Temporary Assistance for Needy Families
    d. All of the above are considered means-tested income transfer programs.

23. Which of the following is true?
    a. Job-entry discrimination occurs when a person is denied employment on some basis other than productivity, while wage discrimination involves paying equally productive workers different wages.
    b. Wage discrimination occurs when a person is denied employment on some basis other than productivity, while job-entry discrimination involves paying equally productive workers different wages.
    c. Both wage and job-entry discrimination involve denying some persons employment on some basis other than productivity.
    d. Both wage and job-entry discrimination involve paying equally productive workers different wages.
    e. None of the above is true.

24. The official poverty rate for the United States is currently set at _____ times the cost of providing a nutritionally adequate diet.
    a. two
    b. three
    c. five
    d. eight
    e. ten

25. The official poverty definition may _____ the level of poverty because it does not include _____.
    a. overstate; cash benefits
    b. overstate; noncash benefits
    c. understate; cash benefits
    d. understate; noncash benefits

26. Economic growth has the potential to eliminate:
    a. all unemployment.
    b. relative poverty.
    c. absolute poverty.
    d. both a and b.
    e. both a and c.

27. Because the poverty line is an absolute standard
    a. more families are pushed above the poverty line as economic growth moves the entire distribution of income upward.
    b. the poverty rate has been fairly stable over the last 50 years.
    c. an increase in the price of food will not have an effect on the poverty rate.
    d. the poverty rate increases as an economy grows.

Problems:

1. How might each of the following affect the distribution of income in the near term?
    a. There is a massive influx of low-skilled immigrants.
    b. A new baby boom occurs.
    c. The new baby boomers enter their 20s.
    d. The new baby boomers reach age 65 or older.
    e. There is an increase in cash transfer payments, such as Supplemental Security Income.
    f. There is an increase in in-kind transfer payments, such as food stamps.

2. Using the axes from a Lorenz curve, draw
    a. the Lorenz curve for perfect equality.
    b. the Lorenz curve for perfect inequality.
    c. a Lorenz curve for some inequality.
    d. For the curve used in c, show which ratio of areas equals the Gini coefficient.

3. a. If every individual earned the same total income over his or her lifetime, why would we still see inequality at a given point in time?
   b. Why could means-tested income redistribution be described, at least in part, as redistributing from you to yourself?
4. If the permanent income hypothesis is true, why would inequality measured by current consumption tend to be smaller than inequality measured by current income?
5. If the marginal utility of income falls with added income, why can't we be sure that redistribution from higher to lower income individuals would increase total utility?
6. What factors might explain the differential in average income between males and females?
7. How might a significant reduction in the divorce rate affect the distribution of income?
8. a. How could in-kind transfers, such as food stamps, not reduce measured poverty or inequality?
   b. How could food stamp benefit reductions as income rises cause the program to actually decrease measured incomes of the poor and raise official poverty rates?
9. Consider two economies: one in which there is no redistribution of income by government and one in which the government enforces equality of income among everyone. Evaluate the advantages and disadvantages of each system. Which of these two alternatives would you prefer? Given the choice, would you prefer a system of redistribution of income that lies somewhere between these two extremes?
10. Why would large-scale government redistribution tend to reduce hours worked, savings and investment, and human capital (education)?
11. Why might a regulated utility, which is restricted to keeping profits for less than they could have earned, be more likely to discriminate than if its profits were not limited?
12. If a negative income tax was Tax = (30 percent × income) − $15,000:
    a. What would be the tax/refund for a family earning $100,000 a year?
    b. What would be the tax/refund for a family earning $50,000 a year?
    c. What would be the tax/refund for a family earning $40,000 a year?
    d. What would be the tax/refund for a family earning $10,000 a year?

The Environment

18

18.1 Negative Externalities and Pollution
18.2 Public Policy and the Environment
18.3 Property Rights

In the 1960s, fish were mysteriously disappearing from thousands of lakes in the northeastern portion of the United States. The culprit was the acid rain from coal-burning power plants that were releasing sulfur dioxide and nitric oxide into the atmosphere; when combined with water, it created acid rain. Acid rain was not only killing fish but destroying crops and trees as well. Today, acid rain is not the problem it was in the 1960s. The Acid Rain Program introduced an allowance trading system (cap and trade) which is a dramatic departure from traditional command and control regulatory methods. In this chapter, we will examine the economics of pollution: How much pollution should we allow? Why does a market produce too much pollution? What policies can be used to reduce pollution? What are private market solutions to pollution? ∎

SECTION 18.1 Negative Externalities and Pollution

* What are social costs?
* How are negative externalities internalized?
* What is the optimal level of pollution?

What Are Social Costs?

As we learned in Chapter 8, whenever an economic activity has benefits or costs that are shared by individuals other than the demanders or suppliers of a good or service, an externality is involved. If the activity imposes costs on individuals other than the demanders or suppliers of a good or service, it is said to have negative externalities. Put another way, negative externalities exist any time the social costs of producing a good or service exceed the private costs. Social costs refer to costs that spill over to other members of society. Private costs refer to costs incurred only by the producer of the good or service.

Negative Externalities and Pollution

The classic example of a negative externality is pollution. When a steel mill puts soot and other forms of "crud" into the air as a by-product of making steel, it imposes costs on others not connected with the steel mill or with buying or selling steel. The soot requires nearby homeowners to paint their houses more often, entailing costs. Studies show that respiratory diseases are greater in areas with high air pollution, imposing substantial costs, often the shortening of life itself. In addition, the steel mill might discharge chemicals or overheated water into a stream, thus killing wildlife, ruining business for those who make a living fishing, spoiling recreational activities for the local population, and so on.

In deciding how much to produce, the steel makers are governed by demand and supply. They do not worry (unless forced to) about the external costs imposed on members of society, and in all likelihood, the steel makers would not even know the full extent of those costs.

section 18.1 exhibit 1 The Effect of a Negative Externality

The industry would normally produce where demand equals supply (where supply is equal to the marginal private costs), at output $Q_{PRIVATE}$ and charging price $P_{PRIVATE}$. If, however, the industry were forced to also pay those external costs imposed on others, the industry would produce where demand equals marginal social costs, at output Q_{SOCIAL} and price P_{SOCIAL}. Where firms are not forced to pay for negative externalities, output tends to be larger and prices lower than at the optimal output, where the marginal benefits to society (as measured by demand) equal the marginal costs to society.

Consider the hypothetical steel industry in Exhibit 1. It produces where demand and supply intersect, at output $Q_{PRIVATE}$ and $P_{PRIVATE}$. Let us assume that the marginal social cost of producing the product is indicated by the marginal social cost (MSC) curve, lying above the supply curve, which represents the industry's marginal private costs (MPC). The marginal social costs of production are higher at all output levels, as those costs include all of the industry's private costs plus the costs that spill over to other members of society from the pollution produced by the industry—that is, the external costs.

Chapter 18 The Environment

This factory is clearly polluting the water downstream, creating a negative externality for those who fish downstream. It is possible that the people who fish could try to bargain with the factory, perhaps even pay it to pollute less. However, sometimes private bargaining does not work and the government can provide a solution through regulation or pollution taxes.

were somehow forced to compensate people who endure the costs of its pollution, the firm would produce at output Q_{SOCIAL} and price steel at P_{SOCIAL}. In that case, we would say that the externalities were **internalized,** because each firm in the industry would now be paying the entire cost to society of making steel. When negative externalities are internalized, steel firms produce less output (Q_{SOCIAL} instead of $Q_{PRIVATE}$) and charge higher prices (P_{SOCIAL} instead of $P_{PRIVATE}$). Optimal output occurs where the marginal social costs are equal to the marginal social benefits. When firms do not pay all of the social costs they incur, and therefore produce too much output, the result is too much pollution. The output of pollution is directly related to the output of the primary goods produced by the firm.

Measuring Externalities

It is generally accepted that in the absence of intervention, the market mechanism will underproduce goods and services with positive externalities, such as education, and overproduce those with negative externalities, such as pollution. But the exact extent of these market misallocations is quite difficult to establish in the real world, because the divergence

At output Q_{SOCIAL}, the marginal social costs to society equal the marginal social benefits (as indicated by the demand curve) from the sale of the last unit of steel. At that output, the price of steel is P_{SOCIAL}. If the firm

internalized externalities when an industry is forced to compensate those enduring some negative externality caused by its production

Use what you've LEARNED

NEGATIVE EXTERNALITIES

Q After months of looking at houses he could not afford, Dean recently bought a home near the airport. After living in his house for only a week, Dean was so fed up with the noise that he decided to organize a group of local homeowners in an effort to stop the noise pollution. Should Dean be compensated for bearing this negative externality?

A Because few people want to live in noisy areas, housing prices and rents in those areas are lower, reflecting the cost of the noise in the area. As a result, fewer people competed with Dean for the purchase of his house relative to houses in quieter neighborhoods, so it is likely he did not pay as much as he might have in another area. Because Dean

paid a lower price for living in a noisier area, he has already been compensated for the noise pollution.

between social and private costs and benefits is often difficult to measure. For example, exactly how much damage at the margin does a steel mill's air pollution do to nonconsumers of the steel? No one really knows, because no market fully measures those costs. Indeed, the costs are partly nonpecuniary, meaning that no outlay of money occurs. Even though we pay dollars to see the doctor for respiratory ailments and pay dollars for paint to repair pollution-caused peeling, we do not make explicit money payments for the visual pollution and undesirable odors that the mill might produce as a by-product of making steel. Nonpecuniary costs are real costs and potentially have a monetary value that can be associated with them, but assessing that value in practical terms is immensely difficult. You might be able to decide how much you would be willing to pay to live in a pollution-free world, but no current mechanism allows anyone to express the perceived monetary value of having clear air to breathe and smell. Even some pecuniary, or monetary, costs are difficult to truly measure: How much respiratory disease is caused by pollution and how much by other factors such as secondhand cigarette smoke? Environmental economists continue to make progress in valuing these difficult damages.

SECTION CHECK

1. Social costs are those costs that accrue to the total population; private costs are incurred only by the producer of the good or service.
2. If the industry were somehow forced to compensate people who endure the costs of pollution, we would say that the industry had internalized the externality.
3. When negative externalities are internalized, the industry produces less output at a higher price.
4. Optimal output occurs when marginal social benefits are equal to marginal social costs.

1. What is the difference between private and social costs?
2. Why do decision makers tend to ignore external costs?
3. How can internalizing the external costs of production move us closer to the efficient level of output?
4. Why is it particularly difficult to measure the value of external costs or benefits?
5. How does pollution control lead to both rising marginal costs and falling marginal benefits?
6. How is the optimal amount of pollution control determined, in principle?

SECTION 18.2 Public Policy and the Environment

* What is the "best" level of pollution?
* What are command and control regulations?
* What is a pollution tax?
* What are transferable pollution rights?

Why Is a Clean Environment Not Free?

In many respects, a clean environment is no different from any other desirable good. In a world of scarcity, we can increase our consumption of a clean environment only by giving up something else. The problem that we face is choosing the combination of goods that does the most to enhance human well-being. Few people would enjoy a perfectly clean environment if they were cold, hungry, and generally destitute. On the other hand, an individual choking to death in smog is hardly to be envied, no matter how great his or her material wealth.

Only by considering the additional cost as well as the additional benefit of increased consumption of all goods, including clean air and water, can decisions on the desirable combination of goods to consume be made properly.

The Costs and Benefits of Pollution Control

It is possible, even probable, that pollution elimination, like nearly everything else, is subject to diminishing returns. Initially, a large amount of pollution can be eliminated fairly inexpensively, but getting rid of still more pollution may prove more costly. Likewise, it is also possible that the benefits from eliminating "crud" from the air might decline as more and more pollution is eliminated. For example, perhaps some pollution elimination initially would have a profound impact on health costs, home repair expenses, and so on, but as pollution levels fall, further elimination of pollutants brings fewer marginal benefits.

The cost-benefit trade-off just discussed is illustrated in Exhibit 1, which examines the marginal social benefits and marginal social costs associated with the elimination of air pollution. In the early 1960s, we had few regulations as a nation on pollution control, and as a result, private firms had little incentive to eliminate the problem. In the context of Exhibit 1, we may have spent Q_1 on controls, meaning that the marginal social benefits of greater pollution control expenditures exceeded the marginal costs associated with having the controls. Investing more capital and labor to reduce pollution is efficient in such a situation.

Optimum pollution control occurs when Q^* of pollution is eliminated. Up to that point, the benefits from the elimination of pollution exceed the marginal costs, both pecuniary and nonpecuniary, of the pollution control. Overly stringent compliance levels force companies to control pollution to the level indicated by Q_2 in Exhibit 1, where the additional costs from the controls far outweigh the environmental benefits. It should be stated, however, that increased concerns about pollution have probably caused the marginal social benefit curve to shift to the right over time, increasing the optimal amount of pollution control. Because of measurement problems, however, it is difficult to state whether we are generally below, at, or above the optimal pollution level.

section 18.2 exhibit 1 — Costs and Benefits of Pollution Controls

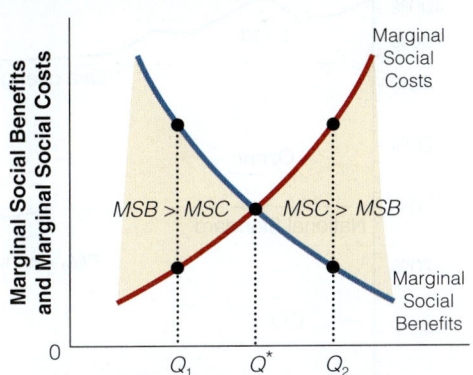

With the principles of diminishing marginal utility and increasing marginal cost at work, the marginal benefits of further expenditures on pollution control will, at some point, fall below the added costs to society imposed by still stricter controls. At output Q_1, pollution control is inadequate; on the other hand, elimination of Q_2 pollution will entail costs that exceed the benefits. Only at Q^* is pollution control expenditure at an optimum level. Of course, in practice, it is difficult to know exactly the position and slope of these curves.

in the news: Levels of Six Common Pollutants Continue to Decline

- Cleaner cars, industries, and consumer products have contributed to cleaner air for much of the U.S.
- Since 1990, nationwide air quality for six air pollutants for which there are national standards has improved significantly. These air pollutants are ground-level ozone (O_3), particle pollution ($PM_{2.5}$ and PM_{10}), lead (Pb), nitrogen dioxide (NO_2), carbon monoxide (CO), and sulfur dioxide (SO_2). Nationally, air pollution was lower in 2007 than 1990 for:
  - 8-hour ozone, by 9 percent
  - annual $PM_{2.5}$ (since 2000), by 11 percent
  - PM_{10}, by 28 percent
  - Lead, by 80 percent
  - NO_2, by 35 percent
  - 8-hour CO, by 67 percent
  - SO_2, by 54 percent
- Despite clean air progress, in 2007, 158.5 million people lived in counties that exceeded any national ambient air quality standard (NAAQS). Ground-level ozone and particle pollution still present challenges in many areas of the country.
- Though $PM_{2.5}$ concentrations were higher in 2007 than in 2006, partly due to weather conditions, annual $PM_{2.5}$ concentrations were nine percent lower in 2007 than in 2001.
- 8-hour ozone concentrations were five percent lower in 2007 than in 2001. Ozone levels did not improve in much of the East until 2002, after which there was a significant decline. This decline is largely due to reductions in oxides of nitrogen (NO_x) emissions required by EPA's rule to reduce ozone in the East, the NO_x SIP Call. EPA tracks progress toward meeting these reductions through its NO_x Budget Trading Program.

section 18.2 exhibit 2: National Levels of Six Common Pollutants, 1990-2007

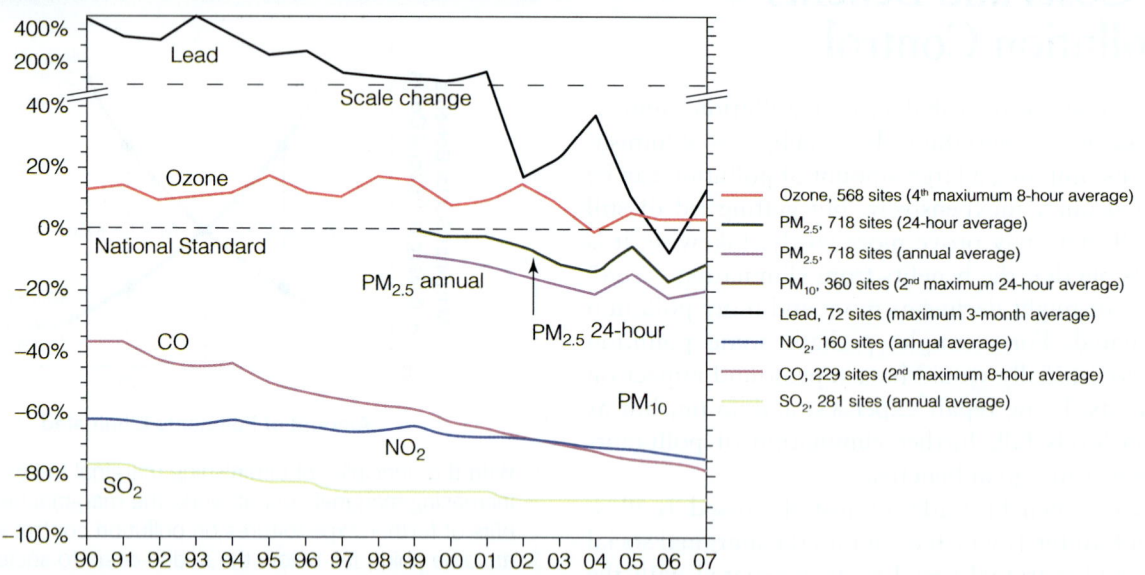

Comparison of national levels of the six common pollutants to national ambient air quality standards, 1990–2007. National levels are averages across all sites with complete data for the time period.

Use what you've LEARNED
RELATIVE COSTS AND BENEFITS OF POLLUTION CONTROL

Q Pete drives a 1948 pickup truck that has no smog equipment and gets poor gas mileage. He lives and does most of his driving in a sparsely populated area of Wyoming. Do you think Pete should be required to install the same smog equipment on his car as someone with a similar vehicle living in downtown Los Angeles or Denver?

A The economic benefits of pollution control vary by location. In the wide-open, low population density areas of Wyoming, the marginal benefit of pollution cleanup is lower than it would be in a large metropolitan area that already has a large amount of smog. Why? Wyoming has so much space and so few people that the marginal benefit of pollution abatement is quite low. The same would certainly not be true in Los Angeles, where the air is already more polluted by cars and factories. Because so many people are affected and the air is already

so saturated with pollutants, the marginal benefit of pollution elimination is much higher in Los Angeles than it would be in rural Wyoming. That is, if a uniform standard is applied, regardless of location, then the car in Wyoming would be overcontrolled and the car in Los Angeles would be undercontrolled. Unfortunately, many of our environmental laws contain this "uniformity" flaw.

Even though measuring externalities, both negative and positive, is often nearly impossible, it does not necessarily mean that it is better to ignore the externality and allow the market solution to operate. As already explained, the market solution will almost certainly result in excessive output by polluters unless some intervention occurs. What form should the intervention take?

Command and Control Policies: Regulation

One approach to dealing with externalities is to require private enterprise to produce their outputs in a manner that would reduce negative externalities below the amounts that would persist in the absence of regulation. For example, the Environmental Protection Agency (EPA) was established by the Clean Air Act of 1970 to serve as a watchdog over the production of goods and services in areas where externalities, especially negative externalities, exist. The EPA's main duty is to enforce environmental standards.

However, the EPA might also require a firm to use a certain technology to reduce emissions. In order to design good policies, the government regulators need information on specific industries and the technologies they could employ. This is not easy information for the government to obtain.

For example, the EPA may identify and then enforce a standard equal to the maximum amount of pollution that firms can produce per unit of output per year. To be effective in pollution reduction, of course, these standards must result in less pollution than would exist in the absence of regulation. The regulations, then, force companies to find less pollution-intensive ways of producing goods and services. Or in the case of consumer products that pollute—such as automobiles, for example—manufacturers have been forced to reduce the emissions from the products themselves. In 1984, the federal government required that auto producers install catalytic converters in new cars to reduce auto emissions.

Pollution (Pigovian) Taxes: A Market-Based Policy

Another means of solving the misallocation problem (relatively too many polluting goods) posed by the existence of externalities is for the government to create incentives for firms to internalize the external costs or benefits resulting from their activities. For example, returning to the case of pollution, suppose that the marginal private cost of making steel was $150 a ton. Suppose further that at the margin, each ton of steel caused $40 in environmental damages per ton. If the government were then to levy a **pollution tax**—a tax levied on a firm for environmental pollution—on the steel maker equal to $40 per ton, the manufacturer's marginal private cost would rise from $150 to $190; the $190 figure would then be equal to the true marginal social cost of making steel. The firm would accordingly alter its output and pricing decisions to take into account its higher marginal cost, leading ultimately to reduced output (and pollution) and higher prices. The firm also has an incentive to seek new, less pollution-intensive methods of making steel.

Using taxes to internalize external costs is appealing because it allows the relatively efficient private sector to operate according to market forces in a manner that takes socially important spillover costs into account. A major objection to the use of such taxes and subsidies is that, in most cases, it is difficult to measure externalities with any precision. Choosing a tax rate involves some guesswork, and poor guessing might lead to a solution that is far from optimal. But it is likely to be better than ignoring the problem. In spite of the severe difficulties in measurement, however, many economists would like to see greater effort made to force internalization of externalities through taxes rather than using alternative approaches. Why? We know that firms will seek out the least-expensive (in terms of using society's scarce resources) approaches to cleanup because they want more profits. This plan is good for them and good for society, because we can have more of everything that way, including environmental quality.

pollution tax tax levied by government on a firm for environmental pollution

transferable pollution rights a right given to a firm to discharge a specified amount of pollution; its transferable nature creates incentive to lower pollution levels

Transferable Pollution Rights

Economists see an opportunity to control pollution through a government-enforced system of property rights. In this system, the government issues **transferable pollution rights** that give the holder the right to discharge a specified amount (smaller than the uncontrolled amount) of pollution into the air. In this plan, firms have an incentive to lower their levels of pollution because they can sell their permits if they go unused. Specifically, firms that can lower their emissions at the lowest costs will do so and trade their pollution

Pulp and paper mills pollute our environment. The pulp and paper industry is one of the largest and most polluting industries in North America. One of the primary environmental concerns is the use of chlorine-based bleaches and resultant toxic emissions to air, water, and soil.

rights to firms that cannot reduce their pollution levels as easily. That is, each polluter—required either to reduce pollution to the level allowed by the number of rights it holds or buy more rights—will be motivated to eliminate all pollution that is cheaper than the price of pollution rights. The crucial advantage to the pollution rights approach comes from the fact that the rights are private property and can be sold.

It is worth emphasizing that this least-cost pattern of abatement does not require any information about the techniques of pollution abatement on the part of the government—more specifically, the EPA. The EPA does not need to know the cheapest abatement strategy for each and every polluter. Faced with a positive price for pollution rights, each polluter has every motivation to discover and use the cheapest way to reduce pollution. Nor does the EPA need to know anything about the differences in abatement costs among polluters. Each polluter is motivated to reduce pollution as long as the cost of reducing one more unit is less than the price of pollution rights. The information and incentives generated by private ownership and market exchange of these pollution rights automatically leads to the desirable pattern of pollution abatement—namely, having those best at cleaning up doing all the cleanup.

The pollution rights approach also creates an incentive for polluters to develop improved pollution abatement technologies.

The prospect of buying and selling pollution permits would allow firms to move into an area that is already as polluted as allowed by EPA standards. Under the tradable permits policy, the firm can set up operation by purchasing pollution permits from an existing polluter in the area. This type of exchange allows the greatest value to be generated with a given amount of pollution. It also encourages polluters to come up with cheaper ways of reducing pollution, because the firm that reduces pollution is able to sell its pollution credits to others, making pollution reduction profitable.

What Is an Ideal Pollution Control Policy?

What would be the objectives of an ideal pollution control policy? First, and most obviously, we want pollution reduced to the efficient level—the level that maximizes the value of all of our resources. This goal would involve continuing to reduce pollution by one more unit only as long as the value of the improved environmental quality is greater than the value of ordinary goods that are sacrificed.

A second related objective is to reduce pollution as cheaply as possible. Two separate considerations are important here. If pollution is to be reduced as cheaply as possible, it is obvious that each pollution source has to abate at minimum cost. Of the many ways to cut back on pollution, not all are equally costly. But even if all polluters are abating as cheaply as possible, it does not necessarily mean that pollution overall is being reduced at least cost.

The pattern of pollution abatement over all sources is of great importance here. Because some polluters will be more efficient at pollution reduction than others, the least-cost abatement pattern will require some polluters to clean up more than others.

A third objective of a pollution control policy is to establish incentives that will motivate advances in pollution abatement technology. Over the long run, this objective may be even more important than the first two. For example, the cost of controlling pollution can be significantly reduced over time, even if the second objective is not fully realized, if consistent advances are made in the technology of pollution control.

It should be clear that these three objectives—(1) achieving the efficient level of pollution, (2) achieving pollution reduction at least cost, and (3) motivating advances in abatement technology—may never be fully realized, especially the first objective.

global WATCH
ONE ANSWER TO GLOBAL WARMING: A NEW TAX

—BY N. GREGORY MANKIW

In the debate over global *climate change*, there is a yawning gap that needs to be bridged. The gap is not between environmentalists and industrialists, or between Democrats and Republicans. It is between policy wonks and political consultants.

Among policy wonks like me, there is a broad consensus. The scientists tell us that world temperatures are rising because humans are emitting carbon into the atmosphere. Basic economics tells us that when you tax something, you normally get less of it. So if we want to reduce global emissions of carbon, we need a global carbon tax. Q.E.D.

The idea of using taxes to solve problems, rather than merely raise government revenue, has a long history. The British economist Arthur Pigou advocated such corrective taxes to deal with pollution in the early 20th century. In his honor, economics textbooks now call them "Pigovian taxes."

Using a Pigovian tax to address global warming is also an old idea. It was proposed as far back as 1992 by Martin S. Feldstein on the editorial page of *The Wall Street Journal*. Once chief economist to Ronald Reagan, Mr. Feldstein has devoted much of his career to studying how high tax rates distort incentives and impede economic growth. But like most other policy wonks, he appreciates that some taxes align private incentives with social costs and move us toward better outcomes.

Those vying for elected office, however, are reluctant to sign on to this agenda. Their political consultants are no fans of taxes, Pigovian or otherwise. Republican consultants advise using the word "tax" only if followed immediately by the word "cut." Democratic consultants recommend the word "tax" be followed by "on the rich."

Yet this natural aversion to carbon taxes can be overcome if the revenue from the tax is used to reduce other taxes. By itself, a carbon tax would raise the tax burden on anyone who drives a car or uses electricity produced with fossil fuels, which means just about everybody. Some might fear this would be particularly hard on the poor and middle class.

But Gilbert Metcalf, a professor of economics at Tufts, has shown how revenue from a carbon tax could be used to reduce payroll taxes in a way that would leave the distribution of total tax burden approximately unchanged. He proposes a tax of $15 per metric ton of carbon dioxide, together with a rebate of the federal payroll tax on the first $3,660 of earnings for each worker.

The case for a carbon tax looks even stronger after an examination of the other options on the table. Lawmakers in both political parties want to require carmakers to increase the fuel efficiency of the cars they sell. Passing the buck to auto companies has a lot of popular appeal.

Increased fuel efficiency, however, is not free. Like a tax, cost of complying with more stringent regulation will be passed on to consumers in the form of higher car prices. But the government will not raise any revenue that it can use to cut other taxes to compensate for these higher prices. (And don't expect savings on gas to compensate consumers in a meaningful way: Any truly cost-effective increase in fuel efficiency would already have been made.)

More important, enhancing fuel efficiency by itself is not the best way to reduce energy consumption. Fuel use depends not only on the efficiency of the car fleet but also on the daily decisions that people make—how far from work they choose to live and how often they carpool or use public transportation.

A carbon tax would provide incentives for people to use less fuel in a multitude of ways. By contrast, merely having more efficient cars encourages more driving. Increased driving not only produces more carbon, but also exacerbates other problems, like accidents and road congestion.

Another popular proposal to limit carbon emissions is a cap-and-trade system, under which carbon emissions are limited and allowances are bought and sold in the marketplace. The effect of such a system depends on how the carbon allowances are allocated. If the government auctions them off, then the price of a carbon allowance is effectively a carbon tax.

global WATCH: ONE ANSWER TO GLOBAL WARMING: A NEW TAX (cont.)

But the history of cap-and-trade systems suggests that the allowances would probably be handed out to power companies and other carbon emitters, which would then be free to use them or sell them at market prices. In this case, the prices of energy products would rise as they would under a carbon tax, but the government would collect no revenue to reduce other taxes and compensate consumers.

The international dimension of the problem also suggests the superiority of a carbon tax over cap-and-trade. Any long-term approach to global climate change will have to deal with the emerging economies of China and India. By some reports, China is now the world's leading emitter of carbon, in large part simply because it has so many people. The failure of the Kyoto treaty to include these emerging economies is one reason that, in 1997, the United States Senate passed a resolution rejecting the Kyoto approach by a vote of 95 to zero.

Agreement on a truly global cap-and-trade system, however, is hard to imagine. China is unlikely to be persuaded to accept fewer carbon allowances per person than the United States. Using a historical baseline to allocate allowances, as is often proposed, would reward the United States for having been a leading cause of the problem.

But allocating carbon allowances based on population alone would create a system in which the United States, with its higher standard of living, would buy allowances from China. American voters are not going to embrace a system of higher energy prices, coupled with a large transfer of national income to the Chinese. It would amount to a massive foreign aid program to one of the world's most rapidly growing economies.

A global carbon tax would be easier to negotiate. All governments require revenue for public purposes. The world's nations could agree to use a carbon tax as one instrument to raise some of that revenue. No money needs to change hands across national borders. Each government could keep the revenue from its tax and use it to finance spending or whatever form of tax relief it considered best.

Convincing China of the virtues of a carbon tax, however, may prove to be the easy part. The first and more difficult step is to convince American voters, and therefore political consultants, that "tax" is not a four-letter word.

consider this:

One potentially serious problem with using cap and trade permits that are not auctioned off is that they may be allocated to specific industries in exchange for political support.

SOURCE: From N. Gregory Mankiw, "One Answer to Global Warming: A New Tax", 'New York Times', September 16, 2007. Copyright © 2007 The New York Times. All rights reserved. Used by permission and protected by the Copyright Laws of the United States. The printing, copying, redistribution, or retransmission of the Material without express writtten permission is prohibited.

Use what you've LEARNED
INCENTIVES AND POLLUTION

Q Brad and Angelina were horrified with the number of abandoned automobiles in their community. Attempting to come up with a solution for this form of visual pollution, they thought maybe something along the line of deposits on bottles might work. Can you help? How would deposits on autos work? How would it affect the incentives of the litterer and the recoverer?

A It is estimated that 15 percent of all automobiles in this country are abandoned at the end of their useful lives along streams, fields, highways, and streets. However, mandatory deposits would provide incentives for both recovery and against the littering of abandoned automobiles. That is, if the deposit is set sufficiently high, people would be less likely to abandon their autos because they would lose their deposits. On the other hand, if someone did decide to abandon an auto, someone else has the incentive to tow it to a recycling center and receive

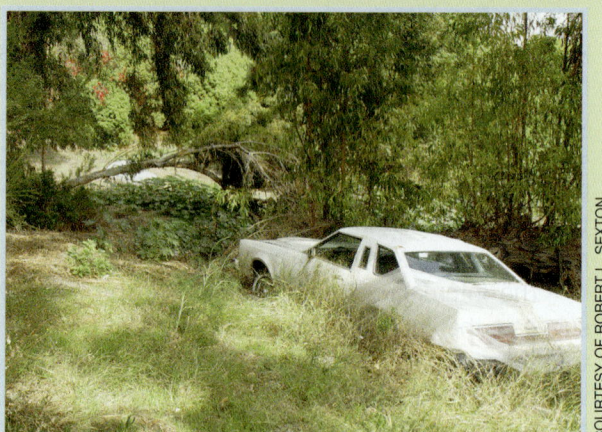

the deposit. This example emphasizes the essential economic reasoning that incentives matter.*

---

*For more details, see D. Lee, P. Graves, and R. Sexton, "Controlling the Abandonment of Automobiles: Mandatory Deposits Versus Fines," *Journal of Urban Economics* 31, no. 1 (January 1992).

SECTION CHECK

1. As with other goods, rational choices about environmental quality involve comparing the marginal benefits to the marginal costs.
2. Command and control policies force companies to find less pollution-intensive ways of producing goods and services.
3. Pollution taxes can be used to force firms to internalize externalities and allow the relatively efficient private sector to operate according to market forces in a manner that takes socially important spillover costs into account.
4. Transferable pollution rights create incentives for the firms that are best at cleaning up to do so.
5. The transferable pollution rights policy encourages polluters to come up with cheaper ways of reducing pollution, because the firm that reduces pollution is able to sell its remaining pollution credits to others.
6. The objectives of pollution control policies are achieving the efficient level of pollution, achieving pollution reduction at least cost, and motivating advances in abatement technology.

---

1. How do command and control policies act to internalize external costs?
2. How could transferable pollution rights lead to pollution being reduced at the lowest possible opportunity cost?
3. What are the objectives of an ideal pollution control policy from the perspective of economists interested in resource allocation?
4. Why might an efficient pollution tax be lower in Fargo, North Dakota, than in Los Angeles, California?

SECTION 18.3 Property Rights

- What is the relationship between externalities and property rights?
- What is the Coase theorem?

Property Rights and the Environment

The existence of externalities and the efforts to deal with them in a manner that will enhance the social good can be considered a question of the nature of property rights. If the EPA limits the soot that a steel company emits from "its" smokestack, then the property rights of the steel company with respect to its smokestack have been altered or restricted. Similarly, zoning laws restrict how property owners can use their property. Sometimes, to deal with externalities, governments radically alter arrangements of property rights.

Indeed, the entire matter of dealing with externalities ultimately evolves into a question of how property rights should be altered. If no externalities existed in the world, reasons for prohibiting property owners from using their property in any manner they voluntarily chose would be few. Ultimately, then, externalities involve an evaluation of the legal arrangements under which we operate our economy and thus illustrate one area where law and economics merge.

If a rancher lives downstream from a polluting factory and the courts have given the rights to the factory to pollute, economists say that the property rights to pollute are well defined. However, the rancher may be able to negotiate privately and pay the polluting firm to reduce the amount of pollution—and make both parties better off.

The Coase Theorem

In a classic paper, Nobel laureate Ronald Coase observed that when the benefits are greater than the costs for some course of action (say, environmental cleanup), potential transactions can make some people better off without making anyone worse off. This idea is known as the **Coase theorem**. To appreciate this important insight, consider the following problem: A cattle rancher lives downstream from a paper mill. The paper mill dumps waste into the stream, which injures the rancher's cattle. If the rancher is not compensated, an externality exists. The question is, why does the externality persist? Suppose the courts have established (perhaps because the paper mill was there first) that the property rights to use (or abuse) the stream reside with the mill. If the benefits of cleanup are greater than the costs, the rancher should be willing to pay the mill owner to stop polluting. Let's assume that the rancher's benefits (say $10,000) from the cleanup undertaken by the mill are greater than the cost (say $5,000). If the rancher were to offer $7,500 to the mill owner to clean up the stream, both the rancher and the mill owner would be better off than with continued pollution. If, on the other hand, the rancher had the property rights to the stream, and the mill owner received a sufficiently high benefit from polluting the river, then it would be rational for the mill owner to pay the rancher up to the point where the marginal benefit to the mill owner of polluting equaled the marginal damage to the rancher from pollution.

Coase theorem states that where property rights are defined in a clear-cut fashion, externalities are internalized

Transaction Costs and the Coase Theorem

The mill owner and rancher example hinges critically on low transaction costs. Transaction costs are the costs of negotiating and executing an exchange, excluding the cost of the good or service bought. For

Policy application: PIGOU ON FACEBOOK?

An Old Debate Gets a Makeover in Cyberspace

Arthur Pigou, an early-20th-century British economist, might well have shuddered at the thought of Facebook.com, a student networking site. A hermetic academic, awkward in the company of women, he surely would have balked at the dating and the picture uploads. But what would he have made of the "Pigou Club," which has surfaced on Facebook and is giving him unprecedented—even cultish—exposure?

His appearance on the Internet is due to a contemporary economist clearly at home in cyberspace: Greg Mankiw of Harvard University. For months, Mr. Mankiw, a former adviser to George Bush, has been blogging away in support of "Pigovian taxes" on petrol, believing that a levy of $1 a gallon would not only bring America $100 billion of extra revenue but might also reduce global warming.

With his Pigou Club, Mr. Mankiw has whipped up a following behind an economist whose theories on unemployment came under attack from his colleague, John Maynard Keynes. On Facebook, 600 people have signed up to the Pigou Club. Mostly students, they join other Pigovians such as Larry Summers, Gary Becker, and Kenneth Rogoff.

Pigou advocated taxation as a way to combat the negative externalities, or side-effects, associated with certain activities. These have been used to justify levies on cigarettes, alcohol, and even traffic congestion. Their advocates argue that they could be used to wean Americans off their dependence on petrol, which degrades the environment, props up unsavory regimes, and clogs traffic.

But governments are not perfect arbiters, say opponents of the Pigou Club. In the spirit of Ronald Coase, an intellectual nemesis of Pigou, a NoPigou Club has taken shape on the Internet, with its own Facebook following (though with only 59 supporters so far). Coase claimed that a Pigovian tax would penalize producers and consumers and might have other undesirable side-effects. People should be able to negotiate among themselves when there are side-effects, he said. Terence Corcoran, editor of Canada's *Financial Post*, writes a NoPigou blog, arguing that such taxes are blunt instruments and governments have insufficient information about them to wield them properly.

Pigou did indeed accept that point, albeit rather late in life, so it is unclear how he would have felt about petrol and global warming. One thing, however, is certain: the reclusive outdoorsman would have found the effects of Internet fame decidedly taxing.

SOURCE: From "Pigou or NoPigou? An old debate gets a makeover in cyberspace", 'The Economist', November 9, 2006. © The Economist Newspaper Limited, London 2006. Reprinted with permission.

consider this:

Taxes, like pollution taxes, that are enacted to correct the effects of a negative externality are called Pigovian taxes, after the economist Arthur Pigou (1877–1959). Pigovian taxes are not just pollution taxes but can be used to reduce any negative externality. Unlike other taxes that distort incentives, Pigovian taxes have the potential to actually move the allocation of resources closer to the social optimum. In short, they could raise revenue and enhance economic efficiency.

---

example, when buying a car, it is usually rational for the buyer to spend some time searching for the "right" car and negotiating a mutually agreeable price.

Suppose instead that the situation involved 1,000 ranchers and 10 mill owners. Trying to coordinate the activity between the ranch owners and mill owners would be almost impossible. Now imagine the complexities of more realistic cases: 12 million people live within 60 miles of downtown Los Angeles. Each of them is damaged a little by a large number of firms and other consumers (for example, automobile drivers) in Los Angeles.

It thus becomes apparent why the inefficiencies resulting from pollution control are not eliminated by private negotiations. First is the issue of ambiguity regarding property rights in air, water, and other environmental media. Firms that have historically polluted resent controls, giving up their rights to pollute only if bribed, yet consumers feel they have the right to breathe clean air and use clean bodies of water. These conflicting positions must be resolved in court, with the winner being, of course, made wealthier. Second, transaction costs increase greatly with the number of transactors, making it next to impossible for individual firms and citizens to negotiate private agreements. Finally, the properties of air or water quality (and similar public goods) are such that additional people can enjoy the benefits at no additional cost and cannot be excluded from doing so. Hence, in practice, private agreements are unlikely to solve many problems of market failure.

It is, however, too easy to jump to the conclusion that governments should solve any problems that cannot be solved by private actions. No solution may be possible, or all solutions may involve costs that exceed benefits. In any event, the ideas developed in this chapter should enable you to think critically about such problems and the difficulties in formulating appropriate policies.

SECTION CHECK

1. In a world with no externalities, property owners with only a few exceptions, could use their property in any manner they desired. Ultimately, then, externalities involve an evaluation of the legal arrangements in which we operate our economy.
2. The Coase theorem states that where property rights are defined in a clear-cut fashion, externalities are internalized. This condition holds where information and transaction costs are close to zero.

---

1. Why can externalities be considered a property rights problem?
2. Why, according to the Coase theorem, will externalities tend to be internalized when property rights are clearly defined and information and transaction costs are low?
3. How do transaction costs limit the market's ability to efficiently solve externality problems?

Interactive Chapter Summary

Fill in the blanks:

1. _____ are costs imposed on people other than the suppliers or demanders of a good or service.

2. When a factory puts "crud" in the air as a by-product of its production, it is imposing _____ on others.

3. With external costs, the marginal _____ costs of production are greater than the marginal _____ costs of production.

4. Pollution policy from an efficiency perspective largely seeks ways for external costs to be _____ by decision makers.

5. Where firms are not forced to pay for negative externalities, their output is _____ and their prices are _____ than they would otherwise be.

6. Forcing producers to internalize external costs would _____ their costs of production.

7. Many of the costs of negative externalities are _____ to measure, especially the _____ costs that have no market prices.

8. The goal of compliance standards is to force companies to find less _____-intensive ways to produce.

9. Air quality has _____ in most U.S. cities since 1970.

10. Pollution reduction, like other forms of production, is subject to _____ returns.

11. The marginal cost of pollution abatement _____ with increasing levels of abatement.

12. The optimal quantity of pollution is where the _____ of pollution abatement equals the _____ from pollution abatement.

13. Compliance standards should be stricter where the marginal benefit from pollution reduction is _____.

14. Eliminating nearly all pollution would be economically _____, because the marginal _____ would exceed the marginal _____.

15. The economically ideal tax to impose on a polluter would be _____ the marginal external costs imposed on others by its production.

16. Compared to compliance standards, pollution taxes lead to abatement by firms who can do so at the _____ cost.

17. The imposition of per-unit pollution taxes would likely be _____ costly than compliance standards for the same degree of pollution abatement.

18. Firms buy and sell rights to pollute under a system of _____ rights.

19. Transferable pollution rights _____ work when the EPA does not know the cheapest way for polluters to reduce their emissions, because they make it in polluters' interests to reduce pollution the cheapest way.

20. Under a system of transferable pollution rights, firms with high costs of abatement would likely be _____, and firms with low costs of abatement would be _____.

21. Problems of external costs are largely a question of how _____ should be assigned.

22. _____, the costs of negotiating and executing exchanges, must be low for well-defined property rights to allow externalities to be internalized.

23. According to the Coase theorem, markets can internalize externalities as long as _____ are well-defined and _____ costs are low.

24. When large numbers of individuals are affected by an external cost, the transaction costs of using voluntary negotiation to internalize it is likely to be _____.

Answers: 1. Negative externalities 2. external costs 3. social; private 4. internalized 5. larger; lower 6. raise 7. difficult; nonpecuniary 8. pollution 9. improved 10. diminishing 11. rises 12. marginal benefit; marginal cost 13. greater 14. inefficient; costs; benefits 15. equal to 16. lowest 17. less 18. transferable pollution 19. can 20. buyers; sellers 21. property rights 22. Transaction costs 23. property rights; transaction 24. large

Key Terms and Concepts

internalized externalities 515
pollution tax 520

transferable pollution rights 520

Coase theorem 525

Section Check Answers

18.1 Negative Externalities and Pollution

1. **What is the difference between private and social costs?**
   Social costs include all the relevant opportunity costs of production, whether they must be paid for by the decision maker or not. Private costs include only those social costs that must be borne by the decision maker.

2. **Why do decision makers tend to ignore external costs?**
   Decision makers pay attention to their private costs because they are forced to compensate others for those costs; they tend to ignore external costs because they are not forced to compensate those who bear the costs.

3. **How can internalizing the external costs of production move us closer to the efficient level of output?**
   A decision maker will produce the quantity where the marginal benefit of production (the price he sells his output for) equals his marginal private costs, in order to maximize profits. But the marginal social costs of those last units, which equal the sum of marginal private and marginal external costs, must exceed their marginal benefits. Internalizing external costs will make the private and social cost of production the same, and will lead profit-maximizing decision makers to reduce their output to the efficient level.

4. **Why is it particularly difficult to measure the value of external costs or benefits?**
   Since there is no market (where people's behavior reveals the relative values they place on goods and services) on which externalities are traded, there are no market prices to reveal those values to us. Therefore, estimating the values of external costs or benefits is much more difficult than for goods traded on markets.

5. **How does pollution control lead to both rising marginal costs and falling marginal benefits?**
   The marginal costs of pollution control rise for the same reason it is true of other goods. Pollution will be reduced in the lowest cost manner first. Once lower cost pollution control methods are exhausted, if we wish to reduce pollution further, we will have to turn to progressively more costly methods. The marginal benefits from pollution controls will fall, because the value of reducing crud in the atmosphere is higher, the more crud there is. As controls reduce the level of crud in the air, the marginal benefit of further crud reductions will fall.

6. **How is the optimal amount of pollution control determined, in principle?**
   In principle, the optimal amount of pollution control is the amount at which the marginal social benefit of pollution reduction equals the marginal cost of pollution reduction. But there is no clear agreement about what those marginal benefits or costs are, leading to disagreements about the optimal amount of pollution.

18.2 Public Policy and the Environment

1. **How do command and control policies act to internalize external costs?**
   By forcing companies to find less pollution-intensive ways of production rather than imposing the costs of additional pollution on others, they are forced to internalize those costs formerly imposed on others.

2. **How could transferable pollution rights lead to pollution being reduced at the lowest possible opportunity cost?**
   Transferable pollution rights would create a market for pollution reduction. Every polluter would then find it profitable to reduce pollution as long as they could do it more cheaply than the price of a pollution right. Therefore, producers would employ the lowest cost pollution control methods for a given amount of pollution reduction.

3. **What are the objectives of an ideal pollution control policy from the perspective of economists interested in resource allocation?**
   An ideal pollution control strategy from the perspective of economists interested in resource allocation would reduce pollution to the efficient level, it would do so at the lowest possible opportunity cost, and it would create incentives to motivate advances in pollution abatement technology.

4. **Why might an efficient pollution tax be lower in Fargo, North Dakota, than in Los Angeles, California?**

    The more polluted an area already is and the more people there are breathing that pollution, the greater the marginal social cost of an additional unit of pollution. Therefore, the marginal social benefit from pollution reduction is greater, and therefore the optimal pollution tax will also be greater, in such circumstances.

18.3 Property Rights

1. **Why can externalities be considered a property rights problem?**

    If the rights to clean air, water, and so on, were clearly owned, those that infringe on those rights would be forced to compensate the owners. Such costs would be internalized, rather than external, to the relevant decision makers. Therefore, externalities are the result of the absence of clear and enforceable property rights in certain goods.

2. **Why, according to the Coase theorem, will externalities tend to be internalized when property rights are clearly defined and information and transaction costs are low?**

    When property rights are clearly defined and information and transaction costs are low, whoever wants to exercise their right faces an opportunity cost of what others would pay for that right. That opportunity cost, represented by the potential payment from others to sell the right, is what forces decision makers to internalize what would otherwise be an externality.

3. **How do transaction costs limit the market's ability to efficiently solve externality problems?**

    Transaction costs limit the ability of the market mechanism to internalize externalities, because trading becomes more difficult. The free-rider problem—where those who benefit from some action cannot be forced to pay for it—also hinders the ability for voluntary trade across markets to generate efficient levels of goods such as cleaner air.

CHAPTER 18 STUDY GUIDE

True or False:

1. Activities that impose costs on people other than the suppliers or demanders of a good or service are negative externalities.
2. In markets where negative externalities are created, the marginal social cost of production exceeds the marginal private cost of production.
3. In markets where negative externalities are created, the marginal private cost of production exceeds the marginal social cost of production.
4. The marginal social cost of production equals the marginal private cost of production plus the marginal external cost of production.
5. A poultry packing firm breeds, raises, and slaughters chickens for market. The firm's chicken yards and processing plant emit foul odors into the air, which affects surrounding residential neighborhoods. If the poultry packing firm is a perfectly competitive firm producing at a level of output such that the price of a pound of chicken equals the firm's marginal cost, it will produce a socially optimal quantity of chicken.
6. The nonpecuniary (or nonmonetary) costs associated with negative externalities are, in practice, very difficult to assess.
7. The goal of EPA compliance standards is to force companies to find less pollution-intensive ways of producing goods and services.
8. Available evidence suggests that since 1970, compliance standards have not succeeded in reducing U.S. pollution levels.
9. Compliance standards can create situations where the marginal cost of eliminating pollution exceeds the marginal benefit from doing so.
10. Eliminating nearly all pollution would lead to economic efficiency and healthier lifestyles for all.
11. Economists believe that pollution reduction is likely subject to diminishing returns.
12. In practice, it is very difficult to determine the appropriate pollution tax to levy to correct for a negative externality.
13. Under a system of transferable pollution rights, firms with relatively high abatement costs will sell rights to pollute to firms with relatively low abatement costs.
14. In order for a transferable pollution rights system to work, the EPA needs to know the cheapest way for each polluter to reduce pollution.
15. Transaction costs must be low for well-defined property rights to lead to the internalization of externalities.
16. The problem of externalities can be viewed as a question of how property rights should be assigned.
17. According to the Coase theorem, if transaction costs are high it is unlikely that private negotiations can resolve an externality problem and achieve social efficiency.

Multiple Choice:

1. If the production of a good generates a negative externality, then in equilibrium in a perfectly competitive market,
    a. marginal private cost > price.
    b. price > marginal private cost.
    c. marginal private cost > marginal social cost.
    d. marginal social cost > price.

2. Many harmful externalities occur because
   a. persons do not pay the full social cost of using a resource.
   b. persons do not pay the full private cost of using a resource.
   c. companies do not pay the market price for natural resources.
   d. companies pay more than the full social cost of using a resource.

3. A firm is generating harmful externalities when
   a. marginal social cost is less than marginal private cost.
   b. marginal social cost is the same as marginal private cost.
   c. marginal social cost is greater than marginal private cost.
   d. the firm is not producing at the level of output where the *MPC* is minimized.

4. Pollution
   a. is an example of a positive externality.
   b. should be reduced to zero, the socially efficient level.
   c. is not an economic problem.
   d. is an example of a negative externality.
   e. is characterized by both b and d.

5. Pollution control costs lead to
   a. lower prices for goods and services produced by polluting firms.
   b. higher prices for goods and services produced by polluting firms.
   c. a decrease in the cost of production by polluting firms.
   d. an increase in production of output by polluting firms.

6. Which of the following statements is true?
   a. The phasing out of leaded gasoline, which began in 1984, has not had a measurable impact on the levels of lead in our atmosphere.
   b. The EPA's main duty is to collect tax revenue to fund miscellaneous government programs.
   c. Using a compliance standards approach, the EPA identifies and then enforces a standard equal to the maximum amount of pollution that firms can produce per unit of output per year.
   d. Nonpecuniary costs are the out-of-pocket costs of medical bills and environmental cleanup imposed on third parties by polluters.

7. If emissions standards are made more stringent, the privately borne
   a. costs of production would decrease.
   b. costs of production would not be affected.
   c. costs of production would increase.
   d. output prices would decrease.

8. The true extent of a negative externality may be difficult to measure because
   a. firms often keep poor records of their cash outlays.
   b. of the intricacies of accounting rules.
   c. certain costs may be nonpecuniary.
   d. none of the above.

9. If the government were able to force a firm to internalize the external cost of its production, we would expect
   a. the firm to produce more to make up for incurring a higher private cost.
   b. the marginal social cost curve to shift up and the firm to produce more and charge a higher price as a result.
   c. the firm to produce less and charge a higher price as a result of incurring higher marginal private costs.
   d. the firm to lower its price to compensate for incurring a higher private cost.

10. If significant external costs are imposed on third parties by a polluting firm,
    a. the marginal private cost curve overstates the relative importance of the product to society and output should increase.
    b. the marginal private cost curve understates the relative importance of the product to society and output should increase.
    c. the marginal private cost curve overstates the cost to society and output should increase.
    d. the marginal private cost curve understates the cost to society and output should decrease.
    e. the marginal private cost curve accurately reflects the cost to society and output should not change.

11. External costs created by polluting firms
    a. are paid by no one in society.
    b. are typically paid by the consumer purchasing the product.
    c. may be paid by society in the form of nonpecuniary costs, higher medical bills, and/or cleanup costs.
    d. are typically paid by the producer of the pollution.
    e. are typically paid for by the government.

12. It is likely that the marginal cost of pollution abatement
    a. falls the more pollution is reduced.
    b. rises the more pollution is reduced.
    c. is constant as pollution is reduced more.
    d. equals zero.

13. Compliance standards for air pollution
    a. should be the same in Wyoming as in California, since pollution is harmful everywhere.
    b. should probably be stricter in Wyoming, where the marginal benefit of pollution reduction is likely greater than in California.
    c. should probably be stricter in California, where the marginal benefit of pollution reduction is likely greater than in Wyoming.
    d. have not been at all effective in reducing pollution levels.

14. Which of the following is the best example of a nonpecuniary external cost?
    a. wages paid to workers in a steel mill
    b. the medical costs associated with increased asthma caused by steel mill pollution
    c. the cost of repainting cars because of steel mill pollution damage
    d. the cost to steel mill neighbors of suffering from the obnoxious odors from the pollution
    e. Both b and c are good examples of nonpecuniary external costs.

15. There has been a downward trend in the United States since 1980 in the air pollution concentrations of
    a. sulfur dioxide.
    b. carbon monoxide.
    c. lead.
    d. all of the above.

16. Which of the following makes it difficult to achieve the efficient level of pollution reduction?
    a. Property rights are not always well-defined.
    b. It is difficult to accurately measure the costs and benefits of pollution.
    c. It is difficult to determine the level of pollution that is socially optimal.
    d. All of the above.

17. Taxes on the emissions of polluting firms are primarily intended to
    a. encourage firms to reduce product prices.
    b. encourage firms to increase production of output.
    c. raise revenue for general spending needs.
    d. encourage firms to pollute less.

18. An ideal pollution tax
    a. does not affect the quantity of the good produced.
    b. forces a firm to internalize the externality.
    c. causes a polluting firm to increase production to the socially efficient level of output.
    d. leads to a reduction in price to the consumer of the polluting firm's output.

19. Compliance standards that impose emissions limits on polluters
    a. are a fair and efficient way to reduce pollution since all firms are treated equally.
    b. are likely to reduce pollution at a higher cost than would the imposition of per-unit pollution taxes.
    c. are more efficient than the use of pollution taxes since large polluters are less likely to respond to such taxes than are small polluters.
    d. are likely to reduce pollution at a lower cost than would the use of transferable pollution rights.

20. The reason why cleanup costs are lower when the government mandates pollution taxes rather than compliance standards is that
    a. the biggest polluters reduce emissions the most, which is always the lowest cost.
    b. all firms reduce pollution an equal amount.
    c. emissions are reduced most by firms that can do so at the lowest cost.
    d. the smallest polluters reduce emissions the most, which is more cost effective than if large polluters reduce emissions.

21. If compliance standards are too stringent,
    a. the marginal social benefit of pollution reduction may outweigh the marginal social cost of pollution reduction.
    b. the marginal social cost of pollution reduction may outweigh the marginal social benefit of pollution reduction.
    c. the marginal social cost of pollution reduction will just equal the marginal social benefit from pollution reduction.
    d. none of the above is correct.

22. An advantage that emission taxes and tradable emissions permits have over compliance standards is that the former
    a. work well even if pollution output cannot be accurately measured.
    b. result in equal levels of pollution abatement across all firms.
    c. make it in the interests of firms to reduce pollution in the most efficient manner possible.
    d. reduce pollution to zero.

23. A transferable pollution right
    a. would command a price of zero in the free market since pollution is "bad" for society.
    b. could never be resold.
    c. gives a firm the right to emit a certain quantity of pollution.
    d. gives a firm the right to emit an unlimited amount of pollution.

24. Which of the following is *not* an advantage of transferable pollution rights?
    a. They create incentives for polluters to develop cheaper ways to reduce pollution.
    b. They allow the greatest value of output to be produced with a given amount of pollution.
    c. They require polluters to reduce emissions, regardless of the cost.
    d. The rights are private property and may be bought or sold freely.

25. Under a system in which the government grants a fixed number of transferable pollution rights, an increase in demand for the output of firms would
    a. decrease the resale price of pollution rights.
    b. increase the resale price of pollution rights.
    c. increase overall pollution levels.
    d. decrease overall pollution levels.

26. Achieving a 25 percent reduction in pollution is likely to be most costly under
    a. a system of transferable pollution rights.
    b. a compliance standard.
    c. a per-unit pollution tax system.
    d. Costs are the same under all three pollution control policies.

27. Pollution in a free market is more likely when
    a. property rights are not well-defined.
    b. property rights are difficult to enforce.
    c. transaction costs of negotiating private market solutions are high.
    d. any of the above is true.

28. According to the Coase theorem, one way to deal with an externality problem when transaction costs are low is
    a. for the government to impose pollution taxes.
    b. for the government to make certain that property rights are well-defined.
    c. for the government to issue transferable pollution permits.
    d. for the government to impose compliance standards.

29. The Coase theorem suggests that private solutions to externality problems
    a. can lead to an optimal allocation of resources if private parties can bargain at relatively low cost.
    b. result in the efficient outcome under all conditions.
    c. will result in the same distribution of wealth no matter how property rights are assigned.
    d. will result in different efficiency levels of production, depending crucially on how property rights are assigned.

30. In the case of a private solution to the externality problem, the distribution of rights
    a. restricts the ability of private parties to properly price the externalities.
    b. enhances the market incentive to reach an efficient solution.
    c. determines who bears the cost of the solution but does not affect the efficient result.
    d. affects the efficiency of the outcome, but does not determine who bears the cost.

31. It is difficult to identify the efficient level of air pollution because
    a. private ownership of different portions of air is not possible.
    b. there is no way to precisely determine the price that should be paid for fouling an individual's air.
    c. there are no private market transactions over air for politicians to look to when determining the appropriate level of pollution.
    d. of all of the above.

32. Pollution reduction will be achieved for the least cost when
    a. large polluters are required to reduce pollution by a greater extent than small polluters.
    b. small polluters are required to reduce pollution by a greater extent than large polluters.
    c. all firms are required to reduce pollution by a proportionate amount.
    d. all firms are required to reduce pollution by an equal absolute amount.
    e. the cost of reducing pollution by an additional unit is the same for all polluting firms.

33. If the rivers, lakes, and air in the United States could all be privately owned, then
    a. there would be less pollution.
    b. costs of production for many firms would rise.
    c. externalities would be internalized.
    d. a market for the pollution rights would not be needed.
    e. all of the above are correct.

34. Which of the following does not inhibit the ability of voluntary exchange to internalize external costs?
    a. high transaction costs
    b. clear property rights
    c. large numbers of people affected by the external cost, but by a small amount each
    d. the free-rider problem
    e. All of the above do inhibit the ability of voluntary exchange to internalize external costs

35. If there were well-defined property rights in all goods, but positive transaction costs,
    a. there would be no external costs.
    b. external costs would be reduced but not eliminated.
    c. there would be no effect on the magnitude of external costs.
    d. the amount of external costs imposed would increase.

Problems:

1. Say that the last ton of steel produced by a steel company imposes three types of costs: labor costs of $25; additional equipment costs of $10; and the cost of additional "crud" dumped into the air of $15. What costs will the steel company consider in deciding whether to produce another ton of steel?

2. Why can a homeowner make a better argument for compensation for noise pollution if a local airport was built after he moved in than if it was already there when he moved in? Would it matter whether or not he knew it was going to be built?

3. A newly released study demonstrates that populated areas with significant air pollution caused by diesel engines experience a much higher incidence of cancer. If diesel engines were then banned, what sorts of results would you expect?

4. Discuss the incentive effects of each of these policies to reduce air pollution:
    a. a higher tax on gasoline
    b. an annual tax on automobiles based on average emissions
    c. an annual tax on total emissions from a particular model of car

5. Draw a standard supply and demand diagram for widgets, and indicate the equilibrium price and output.

   a. Assuming that the production of widgets generates external costs, illustrate the effect of the producer being forced to pay a tax equal to the external costs generated, and indicate the equilibrium output.
   b. If instead of generating external costs, widget production generates external benefits, illustrate the effect of the producer being given a subsidy equal to the external benefits generated, and indicate the equilibrium output.

6. a. Why does internalizing externalities with taxes or subsidies sometimes increase the prices of goods and sometimes decrease them?
   b. When would workers in an industry benefit from internalizing its externalities?

7. Many communities have launched programs to collect recyclable materials but have been unable to find buyers for the salvaged materials. If the government were to offer a subsidy to firms using recycled materials, how might this affect the market for recycled materials? Illustrate using a demand and supply diagram.

8. What would be the result of taxing an industry that produces external benefits? Subsidizing an industry that produces external cost?

9. If a firm can reduce its sulfur dioxide emissions for $30 per ton, but it owns tradable emissions permits that are selling for $40 per ton, what will the firm want to do if it is trying to maximize profits?

10. A chemical factory dumps pollutants into a nearby river (permissible under the existing laws). In lieu of dumping into the river, the factory could pay for the pollution to be hauled to a toxic waste dump site at a cost of $125,000 per year. A vacation resort located downstream from the factory suffers damages estimated at $200,000 per year. Evaluate whether a change in law is necessary to achieve an efficient outcome in this situation.

11. A factory releases air pollutants that have a negative impact on the adjacent neighborhood (populated by 2,000 households). If the government could assign property rights to the air to either the factory or to the residents of the neighborhood, would this make a difference in the quantity of pollution generated? Explain.

12. Compare a pollution reduction program that permits a certain level of pollution using emissions standards with one that permits the same level of pollution using tradable emissions permits.

13. Evaluate the following toll charges for a stretch of highway frequented by commuters: a $2 toll between 7 A.M. and 10 A.M. and between 3 P.M. and 6 P.M., and a $4 toll at all other times of the day. Do you think these toll charges will help reduce traffic congestion?

14. Evaluate the following statement: "Public health is at stake when drinking water is contaminated by pollution. Local governments should take all measures necessary to ensure that zero pollutants contaminate the water supply."

15. Evaluate the following statement: "If people do not use paper or if they recycle paper, there is less incentive for lumber companies to plant trees on private land."

16. Why does the text argue that lower air pollution taxes should be charged to drivers in less-populated areas? What if air pollution quickly spread throughout the world?

17. If an industry created both external benefits and external cost, would a tax or subsidy be appropriate? Why would someone be hurt by either one?

Health Care

19

19.1 The Rising Cost of Health Care

19.2 The Health Care Market

There have been many modern-day successes made possible by tremendous advances in medical knowledge. The twenty-first century will lead to technological progress at a rapid rate, helping to prolong and improve the quality of life of many patients.

Like the production of any other good or service, however, health care involves the use of scarce resources. Not only must the health care sector compete with other sectors for resources, but those resources must also be allocated across patients facing vastly different circumstances.

Where health and survival may be at stake, the question as to how to best allocate limited resources is a particularly complex one. Considerations of ethics and equity cannot be disentangled from decisions as to what quantity and quality of health care to provide and how that care is distributed. How much should be spent to save a life? Is it ethical to deny care on the basis of inability to pay? These questions are difficult to answer. ■

SECTION 19.1 The Rising Cost of Health Care

* How much does the United States spend on health care?
* What are the benefits of investment in health care?

The United States spends more money on health care per person and as a percentage of national income than any other industrialized nation (see Exhibit 1). In 2007, health care expenditures (which includes spending on physician, hospital, nursing home, home care, dental, vision, and other services) in the United States made up approximately 16.2 percent of the total value of the output of goods and services produced in the economy, GDP. This figure is up from 13.3 percent in 2000.

Exhibit 2 shows how health care expenditures as a percentage of GDP varied since 1960. Notice that spending on health care increased significantly over the last several decades, averaging more than 14 percent of GDP since 2000 compared with only 5.1 percent in 1960. Health care spending is roughly 4 times the amount spent on national defense.

Health care is often regarded as if it were a basic "human right." However, it is important to recognize that, as with the consumption of other goods and services, the utilization of medical care involves trade-offs. Scarce resources allocated toward the production of health services cannot be used in the production of other goods and services.

section 19.1 exhibit 1 — Health Care Spending in Selected Countries

Country	Percent of GDP Spent on Health Care
United States	16.2%
Switzerland	11.3
Germany	10.5
France	11
Canada	10
Italy	8.9
United Kingdom	8.4
Japan	8.0
Mexico	6.6

Among industrialized countries, the United States has the highest health care spending as a percentage of GDP.

SOURCES: OECD, 2009; and Center for Medicare and Medicaid Services.

section 19.1 exhibit 2 — U.S. Health Care Expenditures as a Percentage of GDP Since 1960

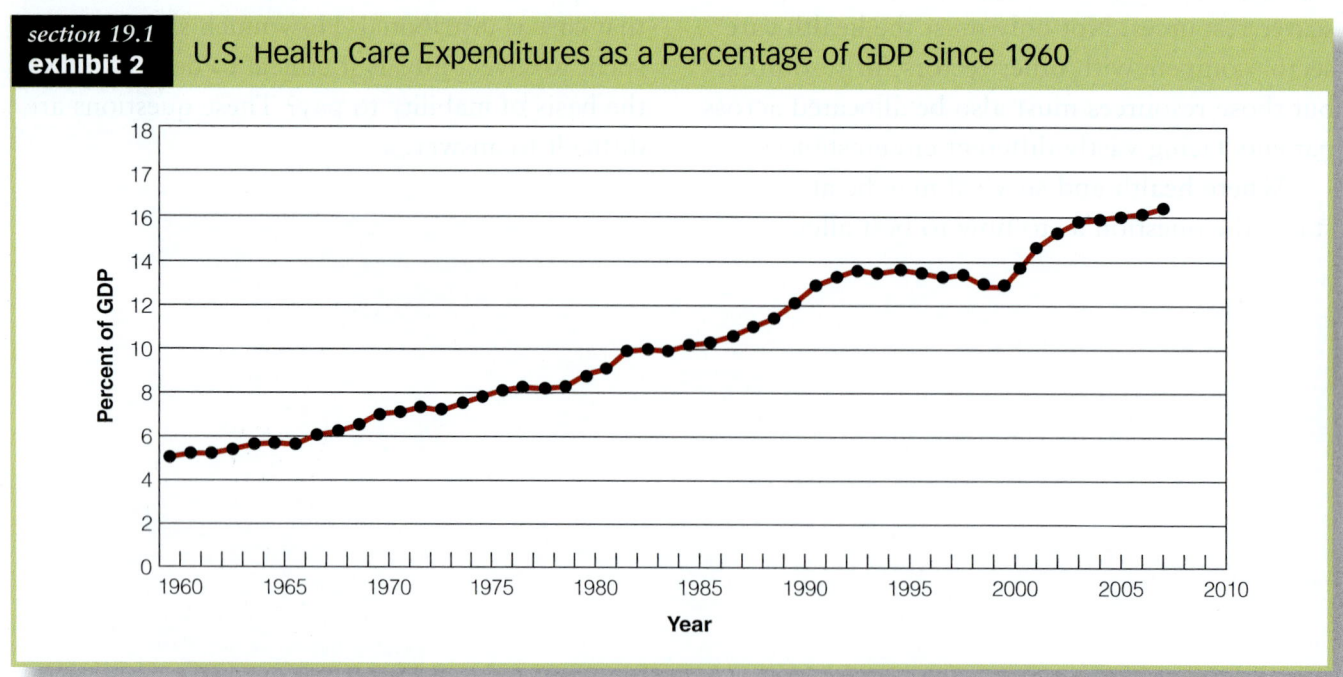

SOURCE: Center for Medicare and Medicaid Services, 2009.

section 19.1 exhibit 3 **Production Possibilities Curve Between Health Care and All Other Goods**

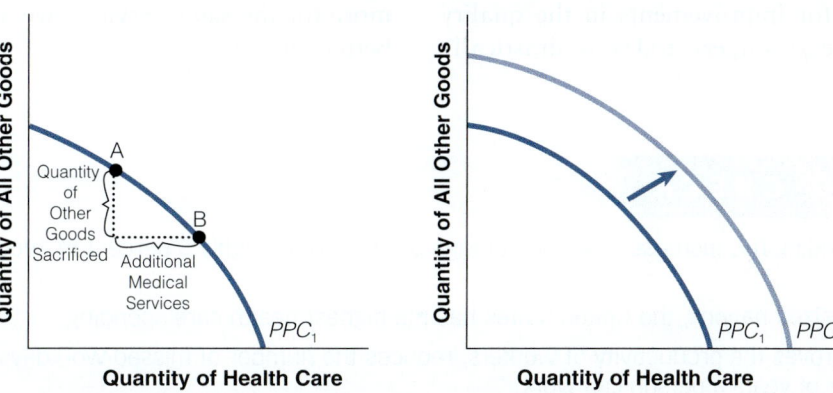

Moving along the production possibilities curve between health care and all other goods from A to B requires sacrificing other goods and services to acquire additional medical care. Over time, however, the production possibilities curve could shift outward from PPC_1 to PPC_2, if worker productivity and/or the labor force increases due to improved health.

Investment in health care, however, does bear similarities to investment in human or physical capital. By promoting health and removing disabilities, medical care can (1) improve the productivity of workers on the job and reduce missed workdays and (2) extend the average number of years that people can participate in the labor force. Increases in the quality and quantity of labor available due to better health care will shift an economy's production possibilities curve outward, as seen in Exhibit 3.

The sources and uses of health care expenditures in the United States during 2007 are illustrated in Exhibit 4(a). Only 12 percent of the nation's health care expenditures are financed by consumers out-of-pocket. Private insurance funds 35 percent of the cost of health care. Public health care expenditures (both federal and state) add up to 47 percent of total U.S. health care expenditures. Health care spending averaged $8,000 per person in 2009. In Exhibit 4(b), most expenditures are for hospital care (31 percent) and physician and clinical services (21 percent).

Part of the increase in health care costs over the last couple of decades may be a measurement problem.

section 19.1 exhibit 4 **The U.S. Health Dollar, 2007**

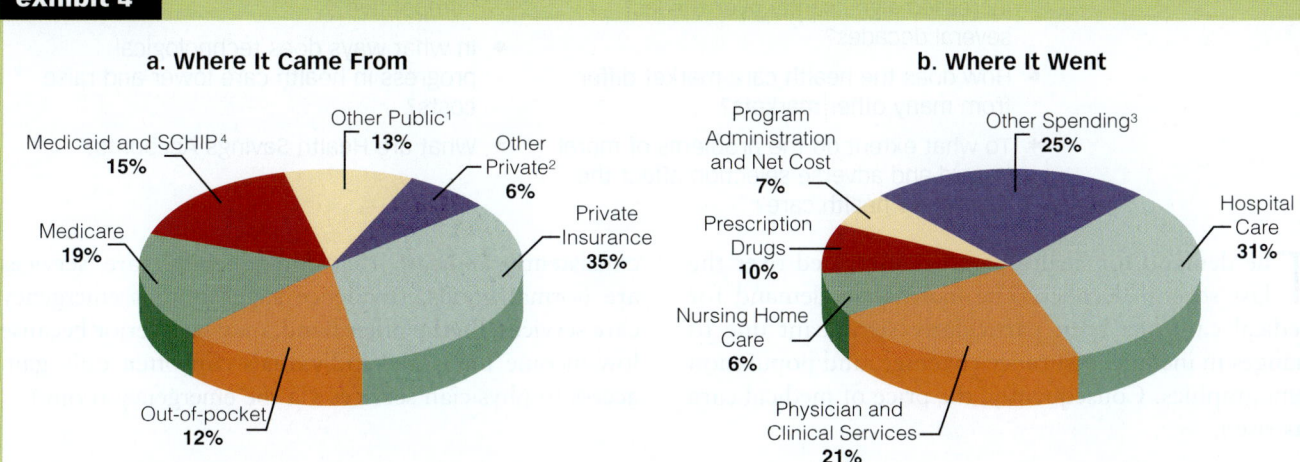

[1] "Other Public" includes programs such as workers' compensation, public health activity, Department of Defense, Department of Veterans Affairs, Indian health services, and state and local hospitals and school health.
[2] "Other Private" includes industrial implant, privately funded construction, and nonpatient revenues including philanthropy.
[3] "Other Spending" includes dental services, other professional services, home health, durable medical products, over-the-counter medicines and sundries, public health, research, and construction.
[4] SCHIP is the State Children's Health Insurance Program designed to help uninsured children for families with low incomes.

SOURCE: Center for Medicare and Medicaid Services, Office of the Actuary, National Health Statistics Group, 2009.

In particular, CPI (the consumer price index which measures the inflation rate) may overestimate the increase in the price of health care because it may not adequately account for improvements in the quality of health care. A heart surgery today is drastically different from one 20 years ago, with fewer complications and a longer and higher-quality life after the operation. In other words, we are not merely paying more for the same service—we are paying more for a better service.

SECTION CHECK

1. Health care spending has increased as a percentage of GDP from roughly 5 percent in 1960 to 16.2 percent in 2007.
2. Among industrialized nations, the United States has the highest health care spending.
3. Health care improves the productivity of workers, reduces the number of missed workdays, and extends the average number of years a person can work.
4. Only 12 percent of health care expenditures are financed by consumers out of pocket.
5. Part of the increase in health care costs may be a measurement problem with the consumer price index (CPI), which may overstate the increase in the price of health care because it may not accurately account for all of the improvements in the quality of health care.

1. How is investment in health care like investments in human and physical capital?
2. Who pays for most of the health care?
3. Where are most of the health care dollars spent?
4. Why is it possible that some of the increases in health care costs may be a measurement problem?

SECTION 19.2 The Health Care Market

* Why have expenditures on health care increased significantly over the last several decades?
* How does the health care market differ from many other markets?
* To what extent do the problems of moral hazard and adverse selection affect the market for health care?
* Why are health care markets imperfectly competitive?
* In what ways does technological progress in health care lower and raise costs?
* What are Health Savings Accounts?

The demand for health care has increased over the last several decades. The increase in demand for medical care has been particularly significant due to changes in income, insurance coverage, and population demographics. Consequently, the price of medical care has risen.

Income

Rising U.S. real income has contributed to the increase in demand for medical services. Estimates of the income elasticity of health care vary but consistently indicate that most health care services are normal goods. (Evidence suggests that emergency care services, on the other hand, may be inferior because low-income uninsured individuals can often only gain access to physician services via the emergency room.)

Price Elasticity of Demand

Estimates of the price elasticity of demand for health care are as low as 0.2, indicating significant inelasticity of demand for medical services. That is, a 10 percent increase in price would reduce quantity demanded by only 2 percent. The quantity of medical care demanded appears to be quite insensitive to changes in price. For example, it is hard to imagine that anyone suffering a life-threatening injury would travel from emergency room to emergency room shopping for the lowest-priced care.

Health care is considered a necessity with few good substitutes, particularly when it comes to serious illness. Although vitamins and homeopathic therapies are available to treat minor ailments, few good alternatives to hospital- or physician-guided care are available to treat serious disease or injury. Additionally, many patients in the United States establish long-term relationships with primary care physicians and are reluctant to search for new physicians even if fees increase significantly. Physician services are, in this regard, "experience goods." Average consumers are "brand loyal," often preferring the physician they know and trust to an untried physician (even one with lower fees).

Insurance and Third-Party Payers

The health services market differs from many others in that, because of insurance, the consumer often pays only a fraction of the direct cost of care. Third-party payers, such as insurance companies or health maintenance organizations, play significant roles in this industry. In fact, the structure of the health care payment system has important incentive effects and can alter the behavior of both patients and providers.

In Exhibit 1, we see that approximately 85 percent of the U.S. population is covered by some kind of medical insurance policy. Most of that coverage (59.3 percent) is sponsored through employers. Despite the fact that the United States spends more on health care per capita than any other nation in the world, over 15 percent of the U.S. population remain uninsured. However, the health care system does provide a safety net whereby the cost of unreimbursed care is shifted to other health care payers. Many of the uninsured are able to receive some care, particularly from public hospitals and clinics.

In Exhibit 2, we see that insurance lowers the price of health care to consumers and increases the quantity of services demanded—a movement down the demand curve. An insurance policy requiring consumers to pay, say, a $20 copayment induces patients to visit physicians more frequently and raises the marginal cost of producing the larger quantity ($150 in Exhibit 2). Total expenditure on office visits increases from $100 million ($100 × 1 million) to $240 million (150 × 1.6 million) as a result.

Moral Hazard

In addition to increasing the quantity demanded of health care by reducing prices, insurance alters the incentive of patients in other ways. Insurance reduces the cost to the insured of undertaking risky activities. In the event of an accident or illness, the burden of health care costs are borne by the insurer. This situation creates what economists call a "moral hazard" problem.

Moral hazard in health care exists whenever insurance makes a person more likely to engage in risky behavior (which could lead to an accident or illness) and less likely to undertake preventative measures against illness. For example, a person covered by a generous insurance plan may be more likely to smoke

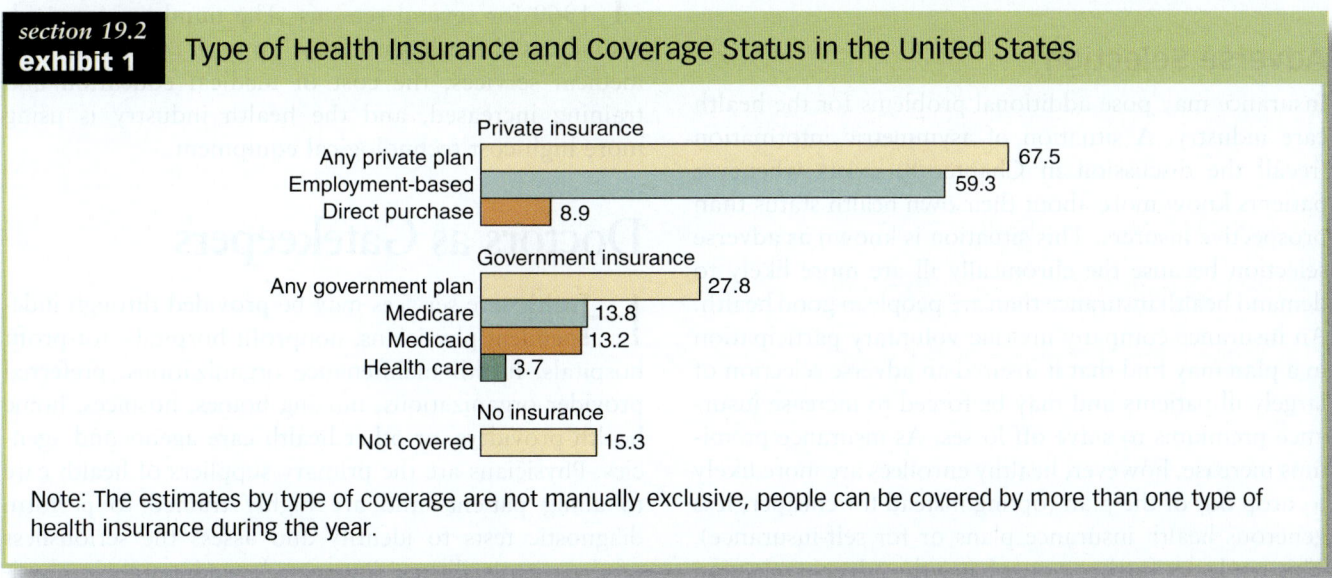

section 19.2 exhibit 1 Type of Health Insurance and Coverage Status in the United States

Note: The estimates by type of coverage are not manually exclusive, people can be covered by more than one type of health insurance during the year.

SOURCE: U.S. Census Bureau, Current Population Survey, 2008

section 19.2
exhibit 2 Demand for Physician Services

Insurance lowers the price of health care to consumers and increases the quantity of services demanded. An insurance policy requiring consumers to pay only $20 per office visit lowers the price of each visit enough to induce patients to visit physicians more frequently. Total expenditure on office visits increases from $100 million to $240 million as a result. Because the marginal cost (MC) is greater than the marginal benefit (MB) at 1.6 million office visits, an overallocation of resources is made to the health care sector.

cigarettes or take up motocross racing or skydiving and less likely to eat a healthy diet and exercise regularly.

Insurance companies or third-party payers attempt to reduce moral hazard problems by requiring patients to pay higher deductibles or copayments (thereby compelling the insured to share a greater proportion of incurred costs).

Adverse Selection

Insurance may pose additional problems for the health care industry. A situation of asymmetric information (recall the discussion in Chapter 8) exists whenever patients know more about their own health status than prospective insurers. This situation is known as adverse selection because the chronically ill are more likely to demand health insurance than are people in good health. An insurance company inviting voluntary participation in a plan may find that it insured an adverse selection of largely ill patients and may be forced to increase insurance premiums to stave off losses. As insurance premiums increase, however, healthy enrollees are more likely to drop out of the plan (opting instead for cheaper, less generous health insurance plans or for self-insurance). This tendency further exacerbates the adverse selection problem.

Insurers can reduce adverse selection risk by limiting the period of open enrollment in health insurance plans, requiring physical exams (so that an individual cannot purchase insurance after serious illness strikes), and insuring entire groups (such as all members of a large employer or union), thereby ensuring a diversity of health statuses.

Demographic Changes

The aging of the U.S. population is an additional factor that explains the increase in demand for health care. In 2007, the elderly composed 12.4 percent of the U.S. population versus 9 percent in 1960. The elderly segment of the U.S. population is expected to expand as millions of baby boomers approach retirement age.

The elderly consume a disproportionate share of health care services (three to four times as much as the rest of the population). Illnesses that used to end life fairly quickly (infections, heart disease, and some cancers, for example) can now be treated effectively using expensive new procedures. Thus, the elderly are living longer, increasingly experiencing chronic disease (such as emphysema or Alzheimer's disease), and consuming larger total quantities of health care as a result. However, recent research shows that the aging U.S. population can only account for roughly 10 percent of the growth in health care spending.

The Supply of Health Care

The supply of health care increased slowly since 1960 for several reasons: The number of providers increased but has not kept up with the demand for medical services, the cost of medical education and training increased, and the health industry is using more high-cost technological equipment.

Doctors as Gatekeepers

Health care services may be provided through independent physicians, nonprofit hospitals, for-profit hospitals, health maintenance organizations, preferred provider organizations, nursing homes, hospices, home health providers, or other health care agents and agencies. Physicians are the primary suppliers of health care to ailing patients and are highly trained to perform diagnostic tests to identify and assess the seriousness of a patient's illness. Patients depend on their physicians' recommendations as to the appropriate courses of treatment, leading to a situation of asymmetric information: Doctors are better informed than their patients about health status and appropriate remedies. Primary care physicians act as gatekeepers, controlling access to prescription drugs, hospitals, surgeries, and other treatments. Acting in this capacity, physicians induce demand for additional medical services. If physicians are paid on a fee-for-service basis (as is common), incentives exist for doctors to err on the side of recommending too many services. The suppliers themselves help increase the demand for health care.

Traditional Insurance

Traditional health insurance in the United States provides **indemnity coverage** (security in the event of illness or injury) on a fee-for-service basis. Patients can freely choose physicians and treatment options in the event of illness. Individuals covered by fee-for-service plans typically pay an annual deductible and a small percentage of all health care costs incurred (called co-insurance) up to an annual limit.

Escalating health care costs over the past decade, however, led to a greater emphasis on cost containment. The result was a proliferation of organizations offering managed care, including health maintenance organizations and preferred provider organizations.

Health Maintenance Organizations

Health maintenance organizations (HMOs) combine two traditionally separated functions: the provision of comprehensive health care and its financing. HMOs seek to contain health care costs by exerting control over patients' treatment options. Patients are often limited to seeking treatment from plan doctors only, whose utilization of services is subject to review. Doctors are typically paid a salary and not reimbursed on a fee-for-service basis. Physicians are generally required to prescribe drugs from an approved list, or formulary, to encourage the substitution of cheaper alternatives for expensive branded products. In some instances, doctors are also provided with financial incentives to limit the utilization of plan services and thereby minimize costs.

Preferred Provider Organizations

A **preferred provider organization (PPO)** is a network of doctors who agree to provide services to a health plan's enrollees at discounted fees. Patients can choose from any of the doctors within the plan. Unlike those enrolled in an HMO, patients in a PPO can generally opt for nonparticipating physicians, but they can do so only by incurring much higher out-of-pocket costs.

> **indemnity coverage** compensation toward the cost of medical services in the event of illness or injury
>
> **health maintenance organization (HMO)** an organization that contracts with physicians, medical facilities, employers, and individuals to provide medical care to a group of individuals. Health care services are usually provided at a fixed price per patient. The cost of providing care is contained through the rationing of health care resources.
>
> **preferred provider organization (PPO)** a network of doctors who agree to provide services to a health plan's enrollees at discounted fees

Technological Progress and Quality of Care

Medical research and technological progress have vastly improved the quality of medical care. Innovative therapies help reduce disability, improve health, and prolong life. Some innovations undoubtedly reduce the overall cost of health care. For example, cholesterol-reducing drugs can save thousands of dollars in surgical and hospitalization costs while reducing the likelihood of death from coronary heart disease. Other innovations, however, significantly add to the cost of health care. For example, many cancer patients can now be saved through surgery, bone marrow transplants, radiation, and chemotherapy treatments. The availability of these treatment options (where previously little but comfort care would have been provided) adds many thousands of dollars per patient to the cost of treating disease. Magnetic resonance imaging (MRI) scans typically cost from $1,000 to $1,500. Such exams, like an MRI, add cost to a patient's treatment when a cheaper CAT scan ($250 to $300) or X-ray ($100 or less) may suffice.

Technological advances, through interaction with insurance, lead to a significant increase in the demand for medical care. Insured patients who bear a small fraction of health care costs naturally desire the best possible care, contributing to rising health care costs that far exceeds the average level of inflation.

Imperfect Competition

Health care markets are imperfectly competitive for several reasons, including the presence of legal or administrative barriers to entry, economies of scale, collusion, and restrictions on advertising.

Barriers to Entry

Laws requiring the compulsory licensing of physicians help restrict entry into the health care market. Likewise, hospitals sometimes limit privileges to certain physicians. Licensing requirements and limitations on hospital privileges are justified as a means to protect patients from inferior-quality medical care by certifying that physicians possess a certain level of competency. (A voluntary certification program would likely serve the same purpose, however, so it is not clear that compulsory licensing is necessary.) By restricting the supply of physicians, licensing programs and hospital privilege requirements no doubt restrict the quantity of services provided and lead to higher medical prices, as seen in Exhibit 3. In addition, some major metropolitan areas have been dominated by a few hospital systems. The reduced competition can lead to higher prices (as physicians and hospitals leverage market power) and a reduction in quality.

Economies of Scale

Economies of scale are often associated with the provision of health care. Specialty services, such as organ transplants, brain surgery, or treatments of rare diseases, may be used infrequently, which means that even areas with a large population may be served by only a few providers. Likewise, cities and towns are often unable to support a large number of hospitals. Except in densely populated metropolitan areas, it may not be economical for numerous hospitals to compete. Conditions may be such that "natural health care monopolies" exist in many areas.

Collusion Among Sellers

Health care providers possess significant market power, making price discrimination and collusive behavior (such as price fixing) more likely to occur. For example, price discrimination is commonly practiced by the pharmaceutical industry, where large favored buyers (such as hospital networks or health maintenance organizations) are offered drugs at significant discounts. The Federal Trade Commission recently settled four cases against associations of physicians, dentists, surgeons, and chiropractors that had each agreed to boycott health care payers in order to extract higher reimbursement rates.

Advertising Restrictions

Legal restrictions on advertising eyeglasses were shown to reduce price competition. In states that permit price advertising, the prices of glasses were markedly lower. In states with prohibitions against the advertising of eyeglass prices, consumers are less aware of substitute products (due to the high cost of information gathering) and pay on average higher prices for glasses.

Shortages

In Canada, where a national health care program controls prices and strictly rations care, conditions of excess demand for surgery prevail. In 2001, the median waiting time between visiting a primary physician and finally receiving treatment from a specialist was 16.5 weeks, and in 2002, the waiting time was 77 percent higher than in 1995. Consequently, some Canadians travel to the United States and pay for treatment themselves, rather than wait for insurance covered care. Medical referral brokers help match frustrated Canadians with surgical providers in the United States (where fees can vary drastically). In addition, research by Statistics Canada shows that for every one doctor permanently migrating from the United States to Canada, 18 Canadian doctors are migrating permanently to the United States. (The migration to the United States, across all occupations, is found to be grossly disproportionate among those earning $150,000 or more—the most highly skilled.)

Likewise, shortages prevail in the market for organ transplants at zero price, as we can see in Exhibit 4. Ethical considerations leave policymakers reluctant to raise the price of organ transplantation or provide remuneration for organ donations. Trade in body parts is illegal, and few organs become available. Donated organs are rationed according to strict criteria.

section 19.2 exhibit 3 The Market for Physician Services

The market supply of physicians is restricted due to education and licensing requirements, causing the supply curve to shift leftward, ceteris paribus. Compared to a market with fewer restrictive licensing requirements, physicians are able to command higher fees. Fewer physician services are used as a result.

section 19.2 exhibit 4: The Market for Human Organs

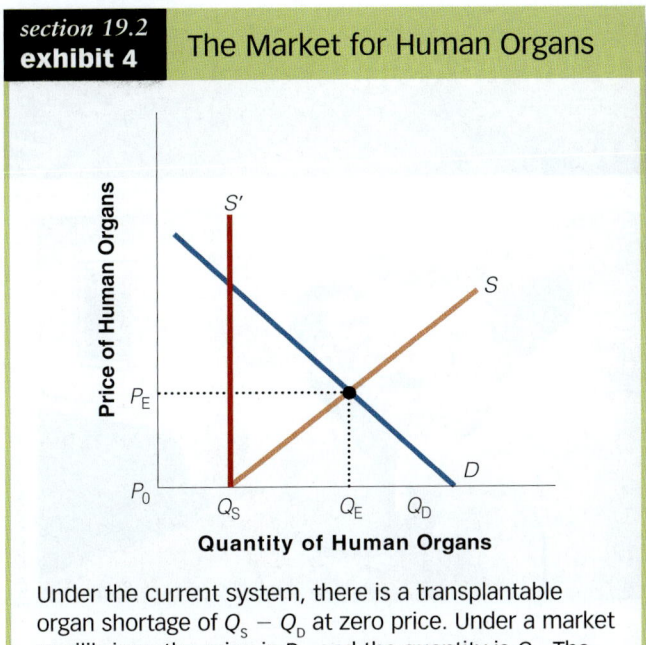

Under the current system, there is a transplantable organ shortage of $Q_S - Q_D$ at zero price. Under a market equilibrium, the price is P_E, and the quantity is Q_E. The demand for transplantable organs far exceeds the supply of organs available at the current price of transplantation services, zero. Because federal law prohibits the sale of organs, no upward pressure is exerted on the price of organs. The result is a persistent shortage of organs for transplant.

The Market for Human Organs

The demand curve for human organs is downward sloping, as seen in Exhibit 4. That is, the quantity demanded for human organs is lower at higher prices and higher at lower prices. Currently, the supply curve for human organs is perfectly inelastic (S' in Exhibit 4)—a fixed quantity of organs is available in the United States because all organs are required to be donated. Notice that in Exhibit 4, at a zero money price, P_0, for human organs, there will be a shortage—donors will supply Q_S organs per year but Q_D will be demanded; resulting in a shortage of $Q_S - Q_D$. That is, many people who want transplantable kidneys, livers, or hearts will not be able to obtain them because of lack of donors.

In 2005, roughly 28,000 organ transplants were made, but 100,000 people remained on the waiting lists. Shortages are so severe that thousands die each year waiting for needed organs. In 1998, 4,557 patients in the United States awaited lung transplants; 485 died. The same year, of the 17,983 U.S. patients waiting for a liver, 1,317 died. The average waiting period for an 18- to 34-year-old needing a lung or a liver transplant in 1997 was 800 days or 273 days, respectively.

Advocates of allowing people to sell their own body parts argue that it would save roughly 6,000 lives a year. In addition, they argue that artificial legs, hips, joints, and hearts are sold, so why not live organs?

Suppose you signed a legal document stating that upon your death you would like to make your organs available for sale. Perhaps you could specify that the proceeds from the sale could go to a loved one, a charity, or a university. We would expect to see an upward-sloping supply curve for human organs—at higher prices, we would expect more people to allow their organs to be sold at death. In Exhibit 4, we present a hypothetical market where S is upward sloping, the market price rises to P_E and the quantity exchanged increases from Q_S to Q_E. In short, the price and quantity would rise, and the shortage would disappear. However, there are several problems with the sale of human organs. First, there may be an asymmetric information problem. When people receive money for their organs, they might hide "adverse" information about their health history. For example, a blood donor might not reveal that he or she has hepatitis, AIDS, or some other virus. However, screening may resolve this problem. After all, there is a market for blood so the problem could not be insurmountable. However, it may be more difficult to detect good kidneys, livers, and hearts than blood. Second, there is the equity issue of allocating human organs on the basis of willingness to pay. But you might ask why are artificial limbs, hearts, and other body parts for sale but kidneys are not? Third, it is also likely to increase health care spending as patients and insurance companies would have to pay a higher price. And increasing demand will only send that price even higher in the future.

Advocates of allowing the sale of human organs argue that the current system is just sending the market underground. Over $1 billion of body parts are purportedly exchanged in the global market. In November 2006, after years of denial, China acknowledged that most of the human organs used in China are taken from executed prisoners. According to rules adopted in 1984, a prisoner's organs can be taken if the relatives of the prisoner are unwilling to take the corpse or if the prisoner or his family agrees to the organ donation. Many of the recipients are foreigners (including those from the United States) who come to China, and pay a hefty sum to avoid the long wait in their home countries for organs.

Health Saving Account (HSA)

The biggest health care problems include the roughly 40 million people who are uninsured and the absence of incentives to cut down on health spending.

Some policies could make health care better. One possibility is a combination of a high-deductible health

global WATCH: PAYING WORKERS TO GO ABROAD FOR HEALTH CARE

With an estimated 750,000 Americans traveling abroad for in-patient and out-patient procedures, insurance plans are beginning to cover treatment overseas. To make travel abroad even more attractive, these plans often throw in a bonus for employees if they agree to undergo elective surgeries abroad, or they offer to split the cost savings between the employer and worker, says the *Wall Street Journal*.

Among the employers jumping on the medical tourism bandwagon are:

* Maine-based supermarket chain Hannaford Bros. Co., which began allowing its 18,000 insured workers and dependents to travel to an internationally accredited hospital in Singapore for surgical hip and knee replacements; the company's self-funded plan, administered by Aetna Inc., waives out-of-pocket expenses, saving patients up to $3,000, and reimburses all travel costs.
* Corporate Synergies Group Inc., which advises companies on worker benefits, says at least a dozen of its clients with 250 to 2,000 employees are considering adding medical tourism programs in the next few years.
* Blue Cross & Blue Shield of South Carolina created a subsidiary for medical tourism called Companion Global Healthcare Inc., which maintains a network of international doctors and hospitals.
* Some individual policies offer medical tourism options; however, labor unions have opposed some efforts to set up medical tourism plans and Medicare generally doesn't cover treatments abroad.

While medical tourism isn't expected to be a solution to the country's soaring health-care costs, the practice is intended to produce savings for insurers, employers and workers. Open-heart surgery, which can cost roughly $100,000 in the United States, can be done at an internationally accredited hospital in India for just $8,500, for instance.

Proponents note that many international hospitals are staffed with American and European-trained physicians. Many facilities also are accredited by an affiliate of the Joint Commission, a nonprofit group that is the main accrediting body for U.S. hospitals.

SOURCE: M. P. McQueen, "Paying Workers to Go Abroad for Health Care," *Wall Street Journal*, September 30, 2008.

---

care policy and a *health saving account (HSA)* that could replace a traditional health care policy. Health saving accounts allow people to set aside tax-free dollars to pay for medical expenses. People with high health insurance annual deductibles of $1,050 or $2,100 per family would be able to open up an HSA account. Employers can also offer a high-deductible plan that will cover medical expenses once the employee hits the deductible of $1,050 for an individual or $2,100 for a family. Once the employees reach their deductible, they have a copayment. The good news is that the premium is lower.

The HSA account can be used to help pay the high deductible prior to the point when benefits kick in. Money in the tax-free account must be used for medical expenses or a penalty fee is assessed, plus taxes.

This type of a program is not a panacea, but could help control health care costs because it changes the incentive structure. In short, people will have to spend more of their own money. The plan would require that consumers cover more routine costs out of pocket, and their insurance coverage would primarily protect them against catastrophic expenses. Consequently, health consumers would be more cost conscious and curtail their use of health services.

This system would create incentives for employees to spend less on frivolous medical expenses. As health economist Victor Fuchs states, "When people are

Use what you've LEARNED: HEALTH CARE RATIONING

Q As technological advances continue at a rapid pace, the resulting increased medical costs have forced policymakers to scramble to figure out how to pay for new therapies. How can scarce resources be allocated while equity considerations remain balanced?

A In 1989, the government of the state of Oregon proposed a health care scheme that highlighted the nature of scarcity in the health care market and the rationing problem. The Oregon Basic Health Services Act provided Medicaid health care coverage for all the poorest citizens (nearly doubling the number eligible) but aimed to limit covered services to those offering the greatest cost-benefit ratio. The Oregon plan was an attempt to carefully ration health care by weighing social benefits and costs. The Oregon Health Services Commission produced a list of health services ranked according to relative importance, based on extensive research, surveys, and public hearings. Ailments with the highest priority were acute but potentially fatal; ailments for which treatment would likely result in full recovery. Oregon estimated that it had enough funding to cover the top 587 ailments on the list. Those unfortunate enough to suffer from ailment 588 or below (including congenital birth defects) were to be denied funding for treatment by the state. Although ultimately a less controversial state health plan was adopted, the Oregon plan raised many ethical concerns and brought to the forefront of debate the necessity of making choices when faced with scarcity, even when it comes to medical care.

---

spending their own money they will tend to use less health care than if somebody else is paying for it."

Critics claim that higher deductibles may lead people to postpone critically needed care or preventive care that could become even more costly if not addressed. Critics also contend that high deductibles and copayments will lead employers to shift health care costs to workers. However, proponents believe that the savings from this policy may be passed on in higher wages to employees. Others, such as MIT professor Jonathan Gruber, believe that the best strategy is through large copayments, not high deductibles, because this strategy reduces the risk of forgoing important health care yet at the same time provides an incentive to be vigilant about costs.

Another benefit of HSAs is that they are portable. Many people lose their company-based health coverage when they become unemployed, which reduces job turnover. This insurance factor results in a less flexible and efficient labor market. In a dynamic economy, when a good job opens up, some qualified applicants might be reluctant to apply because their insurance is not portable.

The Debate over Health Care Reform

At the time of this writing, policy makers, government officials and their constituents are debating health care reform. Most agree that something must be done but they disagree on the best way to control the escalating health costs.

The Congressional Budget Office estimates that the current House health care proposal will require government medical insurance subsidies of $773 billion from 2013–2019.

On the President's official web page it states that his plan, "will not restrict you to just national health care or private health care. Obama's plan is to make both of these options accessible to you.... Health care available to everyone, same coverage as members of congress and no American will be turned down because of their pre-existing conditions. Obama also plans to make premiums, deductibles and co-pays more affordable.... You can also choose to purchase private insurance. There will be new rules and practices set forth to help control the private sector.... If an employer does not help their employees out with a helpful contribution towards health coverage, they will have to contribute a percentage of their payroll towards the national plan. Some smaller business may be exempt from this part of the plan. Obama's plan will also protect you if you switch jobs. If you switch jobs you will not have to worry about jeopardizing your existing coverage.

Obama's plan will protect private insurers from catastrophic health expenditures that have been the cause of high medical expenses in recent years. The plan would help out these insurers by reimbursing them for a portion of the catastrophic costs that come about, if they promise to reduce the cost of premiums.... In order to keep

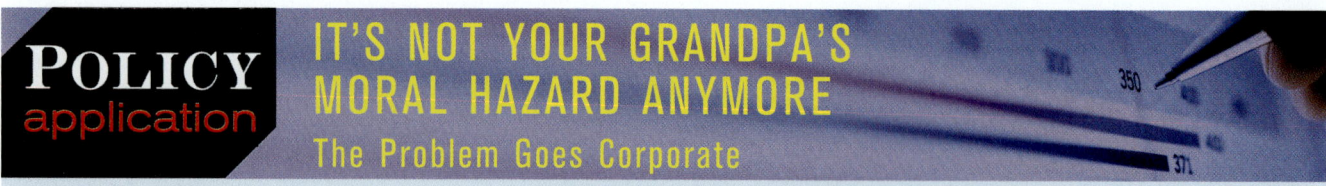

POLICY application

IT'S NOT YOUR GRANDPA'S MORAL HAZARD ANYMORE
The Problem Goes Corporate

—BY AUSTAN GOOLSBEE

To the despair of almost every informed economist, by New Year's Day, Medicare recipients who want coverage for 2006 will have chosen a prescription drug plan. Even the former chairman of the president's Council of Economic Advisers, R. Glenn Hubbard, says that the costs of the prescription drug benefit are unsustainable in the long term, and perhaps even in the next five years. Meanwhile, a health-care program that many economists love, the Flexible Savings Account, is also approaching a New Year's deadline. By Jan. 1, anyone with an FSA—a tax-free spending account for health care—must spend the money he or she has accumulated in that account or else lose it.

Most economists feel differently about the Medicare drug benefit and FSAs (called Health Savings Accounts in another form) because the two policies represent opposing views of the health market. The FSAs were designed to address what economists call the moral-hazard problem—that if you subsidize people's expenses for something, they will increase the amount they want to spend on it. To contain costs in health care, economists generally argue, we should raise the direct costs that people pay for medicine so they'll feel that they are spending their own money and have more incentive to be frugal. The Medicare benefit, on the other hand, tends to ignore economics and instead embodies a political idea about the social compact: that as a society we should subsidize the expenses of the elderly. A natural fear of that benefit is that the more drugs people can get for free, the more drugs they will take—regardless of how much they really need them—and as a result, spending will spiral out of control. In other words, FSAs were meant to solve the problems created by programs like the Medicare drug benefit.

While the budget analysts panic, though, health economists have begun to disagree over how important moral hazard really is in influencing people's decisions about when to go to the doctor. Older surveys, like the RAND Health Insurance Experiment in the 1970s and 1980s, suggested that patients who don't pay out-of-pocket expenses sought care much more frequently than patients who have to make co-payments—but alas were not any healthier despite the added expense. Those studies have greatly influenced experts' opinions about the merits of big subsidies like the new Medicare benefit. Some newer studies, however, have downgraded the importance of moral hazard for the choices that individual patients make. A good example is a study by David Grabowski at Harvard and Jon Gruber at MIT. The two economists found that the Medicaid payment rates had no impact on the share of people who went into nursing homes. That means there was no evidence of a moral-hazard problem in this massive segment of the health-care market (it accounted for 7 percent of all health-care spending in the United States in 2000). The traditional economics view would hold that if patient choices aren't driven by more hazard, then we might not have to worry that subsidies like the Medicare drug benefit will impose huge costs.

Unfortunately, the moral-hazard problem isn't gone. It has merely morphed into something more pernicious. The last decade has seen a dramatic consolidation of ownership in much of the health-care industry. Increasingly, it is the few companies left standing, rather than the patients, that are the source of the rapid escalation of health-care costs. With regard to the Medicare prescription drug benefit, the new fear isn't that costs will skyrocket as grandpa goes on a Lipitor buying spree. It's that Medicare spending will skyrocket because Pfizer jacks up Lipitor's price. The moral-hazard problem is more and more about corporations rather than individuals.

The evidence shows that companies are particularly likely to raise prices when the government is footing the bill. Economists Mark Duggan at the University of Maryland and Fiona Scott Morton at Yale studied the prices of the top 200 drugs in the United States from 1997 to 2002. They found that drug makers gamed the government procurement rules that forbid companies from billing Medicaid more for a drug than they bill private consumers. When private-sector demand for a drug is small compared with the demand of Medicaid patients (as is the case, for example, with antipsychotics), drug companies massively inflate the price of the drug for private buyers. Sure, they lose some business from

POLICY application: IT'S NOT YOUR GRANDPA'S MORAL HAZARD ANYMORE
The Problem Goes Corporate (cont.)

that part of the market. But they more than make up for that loss by being able to bill the government at a vastly higher price for the medical patients. Similarly, as the *Wall Street Journal* reported last week, some drug makers are donating money to charities that help patients make their co-pays for expensive drugs. The donations help ensure that the patients will be able to keep taking the drugs—and also keep the official prices high when the bill goes out to insurance companies.

As the moral-hazard problem for medical expenses becomes a corporate rather than individual matter, the solution that economists currently favor—Flexible Savings Accounts—will fail to rein in costs. The FSAs won't fix things because they change the incentives of individuals, not companies. Indeed, as more people get FSAs, we may very well see the companies raise prices even further to capture the tax-free savings in people's accounts. That would be exactly analogous to what has happened with "529" college savings programs. In 2001, Congress passed a tax break for college savings accounts. As I wrote three years ago, the plans were "supposed to be an enormous federal tax subsidy for education." But the small number of financial firms that are approved to manage the 529 accounts have basically captured that subsidy by raising their investment fees to levels well above those in the regular investment market.

So, as Jan. 1 approaches, we should certainly worry about the potential escalation in drug spending from the new Medicare benefit. But don't think the problem can be solved by forcing Medicare recipients to pay into Flexible Savings Accounts. It's not your grandpa's moral hazard anymore.

SOURCE: Austan Goolsbee is an economics professor at the University of Chicago Graduate School of Business and a senior research fellow at the American Bar Foundation.

---

our people healthy and provide more efficient treatment we need to promote smart preventative care, like cancer screenings and better nutrition, and make critical investments in electronic health records, technology that can reduce errors while ensuring privacy and saving lives."

Skeptics of a government run health plan want to know if it will have access to taxpayer dollars. Private plans cover expenses with their premiums; shouldn't the government's plan do the same? If it ran into difficulty, would it receive help, like government-sponsored mortgage companies Freddy Mac and Fannie Mae? Further, subsidies to the government plan would not just insure those without previous insurance coverage; it could induce many people to switch from their private insurance to capture the benefits. In addition, critics point to the history of government programs such as Medicaid, Medicare and Social Security, whose multi-trillion dollar unfunded liabilities are a major reason for current government financial problems. Gregory Mankiw of Harvard University writes, "the health care of the future won't come cheap, but a public option won't make it better."

Recall that living in a world of scarcity requires giving up something to get something else. In order to get more or better health care, we have to sacrifice other goods and services we value. Health care is not free. So the question is whether we value the additional health care more than what we have to give up to obtain it.

SECTION CHECK

1. Factors contributing to the rapid rise in health care costs in recent decades include rising national income, more extensive health insurance coverage, and an aging population.
2. Unlike most other markets, consumers in the health care market often pay only a small fraction of health care costs because of insurance coverage. Insurance essentially lowers the price of care, leading consumers to increase utilization of medical services.
3. Ill consumers are more likely to purchase health insurance than are healthy individuals. Insured individuals may be less likely to take preventive measures against illness. These are problems faced by insurance companies known as adverse selection and moral hazard, respectively.

(continued)

4. Health care markets are imperfectly competitive for several reasons: barriers to entry, economies of scale, collusion among sellers, and advertising restrictions.
5. Health Saving Accounts (HSA) allow people to set aside tax-free dollars to pay for medical expenses.

1. Evaluate the following statement: "People are concerned with safety first. Therefore, automobile insurance is unlikely to affect the care with which people drive."
2. What do you think happens to health insurance premiums as a person ages? Why?
3. Why does co-insurance increase the quantity of medical care demanded by a consumer? Why does it increase the demand faced by a physician?
4. If it became easier to sue your doctor, what do you think would happen to the supply and demand curves for medical care? Why? What would happen to the price of medical care?
5. Suppose physicians charge patients $200 per office visit. What is the marginal cost of a physician consultation to a patient who pays no deductible but 20 percent co-insurance? To a patient who pays no deductible but a $10 fee per office visit? Which insurance alternative is likely to exhibit the highest patient utilization of physician services, other things equal?
6. It is often argued that lawyers create demand for more lawyers by filing lawsuits. How do suppliers create their own demand in the medical care market?

Interactive Chapter Summary

Fill in the blanks:

1. Considerations of _____ and _____ cannot be disentangled from decisions about health care provision and distributions.
2. The United States spends approximately _____ percent of GDP on health care, which is _____ than any other industrialized nation.
3. The demand for health care and health care spending have both _____ significantly over the past several decades.
4. Investment in health care would be likely to _____ a society's production possibilities curve over time.
5. The demand for medical care increased because of changes in _____, _____, and _____.
6. When incomes rise, the demand for health care _____, because health care is a _____ good.
7. The demand curve for most health care is relatively _____ with respect to price.
8. Insurance _____ the price of health care to consumers and _____ the quantity of health care services demanded.
9. _____ exists in health care when insurance makes a person more likely to engage in more risky behavior and less likely to take preventative measures against illness.
10. Third-party payers attempt to reduce moral hazard problems with _____ and _____.
11. Asymmetric information, where patients know more about their health status than insurers, leads to the problem of _____.
12. Health insurers try to reduce _____ problems by insuring entire groups.
13. The chronically ill are _____ likely to demand insurance than people in good health.
14. The _____ cause a disproportionate share of health care expenses.
15. The supply of health care has _____ slowly since 1960.
16. Primary care physicians act as _____ to health care.
17. Escalating health care costs have led to a greater emphasis on _____ containment.
18. The interaction of _____ advances and _____ significantly increased the demand for medical care.
19. Health care markets are imperfectly competitive because of legal and administrative barriers to _____, economies of _____, _____, and restrictions on _____.

20. Compulsory _____ of physicians limits entry into the health care market.

21. In countries where medical care prices are controlled and health care is rationed, we would expect _____ of medical care.

22. With health savings accounts, people would have to pay _____ of their own money for health care, making them _____ cost conscious.

23. Because health savings accounts are portable, unlike most employer-provided health insurance, they would _____ flexibility in the job market.

Answers: 1. ethics; equity 2. 16; greater 3. increased 4. increase 5. income; insurance coverage; demographics 6. rises; normal 7. inelastic 8. lowers; increases 9. Moral hazard 10. deductibles; copayments 11. adverse selection 12. adverse selection 13. more 14. elderly 15. increased 16. gatekeepers 17. cost 18. technological; health insurance 19. entry scale; collusion; advertising 20. licensing 21. shortages 22. more 23. increase

Key Terms and Concepts

indemnity coverage 545

health maintenance organization (HMO) 545

preferred provider organization (PPO) 545

Section Check Answers

19.1 The Rising Cost of Health Care

1. **How is investment in health care like investments in human and physical capital?**
   Improvements in medical care can improve worker productivity, reduce absenteeism, and extend the average number of years that a worker participates in the workforce.

2. **Who pays for most of the health care?**
   Nearly 80 percent of the health care spending is financed by insurance. Private insurance accounts for 36 percent of the funding. Public insurance (Medicare, Medicaid, and Other Public—like workers' compensation, veterans, school health, and state and local hospitals) account for 44 percent of health care spending.

3. **Where are most of the health care dollars spent?**
   Roughly 30 percent of health care dollars is spent on hospitals. Another 21 percent is spent on physician services, while 24 percent is spent on services such as dental services, home care, and eye care.

4. **Why is it possible that some of the increases in health care costs may be a measurement problem?**
   The price of health care over the last couple of decades may not adequately take into account the vast improvements in the quality of health care.

19.2 The Health Care Market

1. **Evaluate the following statement: "People are concerned with safety first. Therefore, automobile insurance is unlikely to affect the care with which people drive."**
   The statement implies that when it comes to safety, the law of demand does not apply. However, safety, as with other goods, involves trade-offs. This statement assumes that people's safety-related behavior is not affected, even at the margin, by the costs to them of an accident. In fact, we would expect people to drive less safely when the cost to them of doing so is lower—the moral hazard problem.

2. **What do you think happens to health insurance premiums as a person ages? Why?**
   The elderly consume a disproportionate share of health care services. Since health insurance premiums are determined by the expected costs of the care provided to members of a group, health insurance premiums increase as a person ages.

3. **Why does co-insurance increase the quantity of medical care demanded by a consumer? Why does it increase the demand faced by a physician?**
   Co-insurance lowers the cost to a patient of physician services for a given market price, increasing the quantity of physician services they demand (moving

them down along their demand curve for physician services). However, that increases the quantity of physician services demanded at any given market price, increasing the demand as seen by physicians.

4. **If it became easier to sue your doctor, what do you think would happen to the supply and demand curves for medical care? Why? What would happen to the price of medical care?**

   If it became easier to sue your doctor, the demand curve for medical care would increase, as the benefits of seeing him increase (services otherwise not provided may be provided as a result) and/or the costs fall (some of the costs to patients could be reduced via lawsuits or the threat of lawsuits). However, it would increase the cost to doctors of providing medical care, decreasing the supply curve of medical care. Both of these effects would tend to increase the price of medical care.

5. **Suppose physicians charge patients $200 per office visit. What is the marginal cost of a physician consultation to a patient who pays no deductible but 20 percent co-insurance? To a patient who pays no deductible but a $10 fee per office visit? Which insurance alternative is likely to exhibit the highest patient utilization of physician services, other things equal?**

   The first patient bears a marginal cost of $40 per visit—20 percent of $200. The second patient bears a marginal cost of $10 per visit—their fee. The second alternative is likely to exhibit the highest patient utilization of physician services, other things equal, because the marginal cost to the patient is lower, increasing the quantity of physician services that will be demanded.

6. **It is often argued that lawyers create demand for more lawyers by filing lawsuits. How do suppliers create their own demand in the medical care market?**

   Physicians, particularly primary care physicians, act as gatekeepers, controlling access to prescription drug, hospital, surgical, and other treatments, inducing demand for additional medical services. Especially where physicians are paid on a fee-for-service basis, incentives exist for doctors to err on the side of recommending too many services.

CHAPTER 19 STUDY GUIDE

True or False:

1. The United States spends a larger fraction of national income on health care than any other country.
2. Investment in health care, like investment in human and physical capital, can shift a country's production possibilities curve outward over time.
3. If the CPI does not adequately adjust for the increasing quality of medical care, it will result in overestimating increases in the cost of health care.
4. The quality of medical care demanded is quite sensitive to its price.
5. The majority of Americans do not have some kind of medical insurance.
6. Private insurance and public health care expenditures each account for a larger proportion of health care spending than that by consumers paid out of pocket.
7. Insurance coverage is likely to increase the total expenditures on health care from all sources.
8. The chronically ill are more likely to demand insurance than healthy people, because of adverse selection.
9. The chronically ill are more likely to demand insurance than healthy people, because of moral hazard.
10. Physical exams are one way insurers try to reduce their adverse selection risks from health insurance.
11. An increasing share of older people in the population would tend to increase the demand for health care spending.
12. The supply of health care has decreased in recent decades.
13. The demand for health care has increased faster than supply in recent decades.
14. When doctors are paid on a fee-for-service basis, they are more liable to err by recommending too many health care services rather than too few.
15. Because of long-term relationships with primary physicians, people are often reluctant to search for new physicians even when fees increase significantly.
16. The incentives of HMO doctors to provide medical care are greater than those of traditional fee-for-service doctors.
17. Technological advances in providing health care have generally decreased total health care spending in those areas.
18. Insurance lowers the cost to patients of getting "the best possible" care.
19. Economies of scale in health care can limit the number of health care providers in an area.
20. Far more Canadian doctors migrate to the United States than the number of American doctors migrating to Canada.
21. Price controls on medical care cause surpluses of health care.
22. Health savings accounts allow people to set aside tax-free dollars to pay for medical care.
23. Traditional insurance, unlike health savings accounts, is portable, so that workers can take it with them when they change jobs.
24. The demand for health care is thought to be highly elastic.
25. Only about 5 million people in the United States have no health insurance.

Multiple Choice:

1. Investing in health care can
   a. improve worker productivity.
   b. reduce the number of missed workdays.
   c. extend people's working lives.
   d. shift a society's production possibilities curve outward over time.
   e. do all of the above.

2. The largest proportion of health care expenditures comes from which of the following sources?
   a. private insurance funds
   b. public health care expenditures
   c. out-of-pocket expenditures from consumers
   d. emergency room care

3. The demand for health care has increased in recent decades due to
   a. increased income.
   b. increased levels of insurance coverage.
   c. an aging population.
   d. all of the above.

4. Health insurance tends to
   a. reduce the price of health care services to consumers.
   b. increase the quantity of health care services demanded.
   c. increase the total expenditures on health care.
   d. do all of the above.

5. A person covered by more generous health insurance, other things equal, would be
   a. more likely to smoke cigarettes.
   b. more likely to eat a healthy diet.
   c. more likely to exercise regularly.
   d. more likely to do all of the above.

6. Health insurers attempt to reduce the risk from adverse selection by
   a. limiting periods of open enrollment in health care plans.
   b. requiring physical exams.
   c. ensuring large groups.
   d. doing all of the above.

7. Reasons for restricted competition in the health care market do not include
   a. compulsory licensing, which restricts entry into the health care market.
   b. economies of scale in the provision of certain health care services.
   c. collusion among sellers.
   d. the high cost of advertising health care products.

8. Which of the following is not true of health care expenditures over the past few decades?
   a. The share paid for by private insurance companies has fallen.
   b. The share paid for by health care consumers out of pocket has fallen.
   c. The share of health care expenditures spent on the elderly has risen.
   d. Total expenditures on health care from all sources have risen.

9. In the decades following the passage of Medicare and Medicaid, which of the following has not risen?
   a. the share of expenditures on health care in proportion to the economy
   b. the prices of health care services relative to the prices of other goods and services
   c. the share of health care expenditures financed by consumers out of pocket
   d. the share of health care expenditures that are from third-party payers

10. Growth in payments for health care services that come from third-party payers has not tended to be accompanied by
    a. increased incentives for consumers to demand "the best" health care providers.
    b. increased incentives for suppliers to find ways to provide health care at low prices.
    c. decreased sensitivity of health care consumers to the prices of health care services.
    d. increases in the level of medical technology.

11. Given current U.S. health care policy, the growth in the proportion of the population that is elderly will tend to _____ health care demand and _____ the share of health care services financed by third parties.
    a. increase; increase
    b. increase; decrease
    c. decrease; increase
    d. decrease; decrease

12. Which of the following would assist in controlling the growth of future health care expenditures?
    a. an increase in the share of the population that has private health insurance with low copayments
    b. expanding Medicare to include discounts for drugs in the program
    c. an increase in the share of health care paid for by consumers through health savings accounts
    d. a decrease in copayments for the elderly under Medicare

13. Special accounts that people pay into to be used for medical expenses are called
    a. comprehensive insurance plans.
    b. national health insurance plans.
    c. health savings accounts.
    d. health maintenance organizations.

14. Advantages of health savings accounts from an efficiency standpoint include
    a. guaranteeing that no one will every be forced to pay for another medical bill.
    b. giving medical care consumers substantial incentives to economize on their expenditures.
    c. requiring employers to pay a larger fraction of their employees' health care bills.
    d. increasing the flexibility of the labor market by allowing employees to take the accounts with them when they change jobs.
    e. both b and d.

15. _____ spends more money on health care per person than any other industrialized nation.
    a. Canada
    b. The United States
    c. Sweden
    d. France
    e. Germany

16. Spending on health care in the United States over the last several decades has
    a. increased significantly.
    b. decreased significantly.
    c. remained steady.
    d. increased slightly.
    e. decreased slightly.

17. Health care
    a. can be provided to everyone without requiring sacrifices.
    b. improves the productivity of workers.
    c. can extend the number of years a person is able to participate in the labor force.
    d. is characterized by all of the above.
    e. is characterized by b and c only.

18. Over the last several decades, the price of medical care has _____, while the utilization of health care services has _____.
    a. increased; increased
    b. increased; decreased
    c. decreased; decreased
    d. decreased; increased

19. Evidence suggests that the demand for health care
    a. is relatively elastic.
    b. is relatively inelastic.
    c. has decreased over the last decade.
    d. is characterized by both a and b.
    e. is characterized by both b and c.

20. Which of the following statements about health insurance in the United States is true?
    a. Most health insurance policies in the United States are sponsored by the government.
    b. Most health insurance policies in the United States are sponsored through employers.
    c. Over 80 million Americans have no health insurance.
    d. Only 60 percent of the U.S. population is covered by some kind of medical insurance policy.
    e. Both c and d are correct.

21. The safety net in the U.S. health care system is that
    a. anyone without private insurance coverage is automatically covered by Medicaid.
    b. all employers are required to offer employees basic health insurance coverage.
    c. many of the uninsured are able to receive care, for which the cost is often shifted to other health care payers.
    d. physicians are required to provide free services in public clinics to low-income patients in order to renew their medical licenses.

22. Insurance
    a. increases the price of health care to patients and decreases the quantity of services demanded.
    b. decreases the price of health care to patients and decreases the quantity of services demanded.
    c. increases the price of health care to patients and increases the quantity of services demanded.
    d. decreases the price of health care to patients and increases the quantity of services demanded.

23. When insurance increases the likelihood that an individual will engage in risky behavior, it is known as
    a. moral hazard.
    b. adverse selection.
    c. risk selection.
    d. the lemon problem.
    e. both b and d.

24. To reduce the problem of moral hazard, health insurance companies could
    a. decrease required deductible payments.
    b. increase required deductible payments.
    c. increase required copayments.
    d. do both b and c.

25. Adverse selection
    a. arises in situations where there is asymmetric information.
    b. arises because the unhealthy are more likely to purchase health insurance than are the healthy.
    c. problems can be reduced by insuring entire employee groups, rather than individual applicants.
    d. is characterized by all of the above.

26. Health insurers can reduce adverse selection problems by
    a. insuring entire groups.
    b. requiring physical exams as a condition of purchase.
    c. limiting the period of open enrollment in health insurance.
    d. doing all of the above.

27. Since 1960 the elderly proportion of the population has _____ and in the next two decades is expected to _____.
    a. increased; decrease
    b. increased; increase
    c. decreased; decrease
    d. decreased; increase

28. With traditional indemnity insurance coverage,
    a. patients must choose physicians from a limited network.
    b. patients can freely choose physicians.
    c. patients typically pay nothing out of pocket for medical care.
    d. both a and c are correct.
    e. both b and c are correct.

29. Physicians are least likely to limit the utilization of health care services if
    a. they are paid an annual salary for their services.
    b. they are paid on a fee-for-service basis.
    c. they are restricted to choosing treatment options on an approved list.
    d. they are required to contain health care costs as a condition of membership in a physicians' network.

30. Technological advances in medical care
    a. always lead to reductions in the overall cost of treating a disease.
    b. always lead to increases in the overall cost of treating a disease.
    c. can either increase or decrease the overall cost of treating a disease.
    d. decrease the supply of health care.

31. Technological advances in medical care
    a. increase the supply of health care.
    b. increase the demand for health care, since the quality of care increases.
    c. can either increase or decrease the overall cost of treating a disease.
    d. are characterized by all of the above.

32. The supply of health care services is restricted by
    a. the compulsory licensing of physicians.
    b. limitations on hospital privileges of physicians.
    c. a reduction in the wages of health care employees.
    d. all of the above.
    e. only a and b.

33. Natural monopolies may arise in health care
    a. when the government grants exclusive licenses for hospitals to operate in a local area.
    b. when cities and towns are sufficiently small that they are unable to support a large number of hospitals.
    c. when a health care provider holds crucial patents over new medical technologies.
    d. in metropolitan areas with large populations.

34. It has been shown that in states where restrictions are placed on the advertising of eyeglasses
    a. price competition between eyeglass manufacturers increases.
    b. consumers pay, on average, lower prices.
    c. consumers pay, on average, higher prices.
    d. the prices of eyeglasses are unaffected.
    e. both a and b occur.

35. When the price of health care is controlled,
    a. shortages are likely to result.
    b. it may be necessary to ration health care services.
    c. patients may die while waiting for treatment.
    d. all of the above may occur.

Problems:

1. Why would calling health care a basic "human right" make it difficult to effectively analyze health care?
2. How can health care expenditures be viewed as similar to other investments in capital equipment and education (human capital)?
3. Why would the percentage that health care consumers pay out of pocket be an important determinant of how much care they receive?
4. Why would the welfare cost of insurance be smaller, the more inelastic the demand for that type of health care?
5. How does an insurance company inviting voluntary participation in a plan face an adverse selection problem?
6. How can better care for potentially fatal diseases sharply increase the cost of health care?
7. Are the chronically ill more likely to demand health insurance because of moral hazard or adverse selection?
8. Do health care innovations raise or lower the overall cost of health care?
9. If the selling of kidneys were legalized, predict the impact on the market for organ transplants using supply and demand analysis. Why might the quantity supplied increase?
10. Who is most likely to purchase a kidney? Who is most likely to sell a kidney? Would either party be harmed?
11. Decisions as to the allocation of human organs for transplant are based on characteristics such as "blood type, weight, and age; urgency of need; and length of time on the waiting list" (quoted from the Transplant Resource Center of Maryland, http://www.mdtransplant.org/topicsa2.htm). Suppose you were on a transplant committee that was permitted to consider other factors. Do you think that the life of a person who is beloved by many family members and friends should be given greater weight than a person with few friends? Should the chief executive officer of a major corporation be given preferential treatment over someone who is a cook at McDonald's? How about Mickey Mantle, a famous baseball player who battled alcoholism? Do these queries fall into the realm of normative or positive economic analysis?
12. Is it inefficient that the United States spends a larger fraction of income on health care than the fraction spent by other countries?
13. How do higher deductibles act to reduce moral hazard problems, especially for small medical expenses?
14. Why do both adverse selection and moral hazard mean that "lunch insurance," which would pay for lunch if you choose to eat it, is never likely to be a commercial success?
15. How does insuring all the workers at a given firm tend to reduce adverse selection problems? How does requiring physical exams have a similar effect?
16. Why does health insurance increase demand for the highest quality of care?
17. If genetic testing becomes widely practiced, is there an economic reason to fear the discovery of a genetic predisposition toward a serious illness?

PART 6
MACROECONOMIC FOUNDATIONS

Chapter 20 Introduction to Macroeconomics: Unemployment, Inflation, and Economic Fluctuations *562*

Chapter 21 Measuring Economic Performance *607*

Chapter 22 Economic Growth in the Global Economy *631*

Chapter 23 Financial Markets, Saving, and Investment *653*

Appendix: Calculating Present Value *684*

20 Introduction to Macroeconomics: Unemployment, Inflation, and Economic Fluctuations

20.1 Macroeconomic Goals
20.2 Employment and Unemployment
20.3 Types of Unemployment
20.4 Reasons for Unemployment
20.5 Inflation
20.6 Economic Fluctuations

Now we focus our attention on macroeconomics and, in particular, on two key concepts that are at the heart of macroeconomics and economic policymaking—unemployment and inflation.

To those who have just lost a job, unemployment ranks high on the stress meter. To an elderly person who is living on a fixed income, inflation and the loss of purchasing power may be just as threatening.

In this chapter, we see how economists define unemployment and inflation and consider the problems associated with each. In the last section of the chapter, we examine the short-run fluctuations in the economy—the so-called business cycle.

SECTION 20.1 Macroeconomic Goals

* What are the most important macroeconomic goals in the United States?
* How has the United States shown its commitment to these goals?

Three Major Macroeconomic Goals

Recall from Chapter 1 that macroeconomics is the study of the whole economy—the study of the forest, not the trees. Nearly every society has been interested in three major macroeconomic goals: (1) maintaining employment of human resources at relatively high levels, meaning that jobs are relatively plentiful and financial suffering from lack of work and income is relatively uncommon; (2) maintaining prices at a relatively stable level so that consumers and producers can make better decisions; and (3) achieving a high rate of economic growth, meaning a growth in output per person over time. We use the term **real gross domestic product (RGDP)** to measure output or production. The term *real* is used to indicate that the output is adjusted for the general increase in prices over time. Technically, gross domestic product (GDP) is defined as the total value of all final goods and services produced in a given period of time, such as a year or a quarter. Accomplishing smooth, rapid economic growth in an environment of stable prices and low unemployment is no easy task. Sometimes the cure for one problem comes at the expense of another. In the coming chapters we will discuss the causes and possible remedies for high inflation, high unemployment and sluggish economic growth.

real gross domestic product (RGDP)
the total value of all final goods and services produced in a given period, such as a year or a quarter, adjusted for inflation

Employment Act of 1946
a commitment by the federal government to hold itself accountable for short-run economic fluctuations

Acknowledging Our Goals: The Employment Act of 1946

Many economic problems—particularly those involving unemployment, price instability, and economic stagnation—are pressing concerns for the U.S. government. The **Employment Act of 1946** and the Full Employment and Balanced Growth Act of 1978 (the Humphrey–HawkinsAct) commit the U.S. government to pursuing unemployment policies that are also consistent with price stability. This legislation was the first formal acknowledgment of these primary macroeconomic goals.

SECTION CHECK

1. The most important U.S. macroeconomic goals are full employment, price stability, and economic growth.
2. The United States showed its commitment to the major macroeconomic goals with the Employment Act of 1946 and the Full Employment and Balanced Growth Act of 1978 (the Humphrey–Hawkins Act).

1. What are the three major economic goals of most societies?
2. What is the Employment Act of 1946? Why was it significant?

SECTION 20.2: Employment and Unemployment

- What are the consequences of unemployment?
- What is the unemployment rate?
- Does unemployment affect everyone equally?
- What causes unemployment?
- How long are people typically unemployed?

The Consequences of High Unemployment

Unemployment figures are reported by the U.S. Department of Labor on a monthly basis. The news of lower unemployment usually sends stock prices higher; and the news of higher unemployment usually sends stock prices lower. Politicians are also concerned about the unemployment figures because elections often hinge precariously on whether unemployment has been rising or falling.

Nearly everyone agrees that it is unfortunate when a person who wants a job cannot find one. A loss of a job can mean financial insecurity and a great deal of anxiety. High rates of unemployment in a society can increase tensions and despair. A family without income from work undergoes great suffering; as a family's savings fade, family members wonder where they are going to obtain the means to survive. Society loses some potential output of goods when some of its productive resources—human or nonhuman—remain idle, and potential consumption is reduced. Clearly, then, a loss in efficiency occurs when people willing to work and equipment able to produce remain idle. That is, other things being equal, relatively high rates of unemployment are viewed almost universally as undesirable.

What Is the Unemployment Rate?

When discussing unemployment, economists and politicians refer to the **unemployment rate.** To calculate the unemployment rate, you must first understand another important concept—the **labor force.** The labor force is the number of people over the age of 16 who are available for employment, as shown in Exhibit 1. The civilian labor force figure excludes people in the armed services and those in prisons or mental hospitals. Other people regarded as outside the labor force include homemakers, retirees, and

unemployment rate
the percentage of the population aged 16 and older who are willing and able to work but are unable to obtain a job

labor force
the number of people aged 16 and over who are available for employment

section 20.2 exhibit 1 — The U.S. Labor Force, 2009

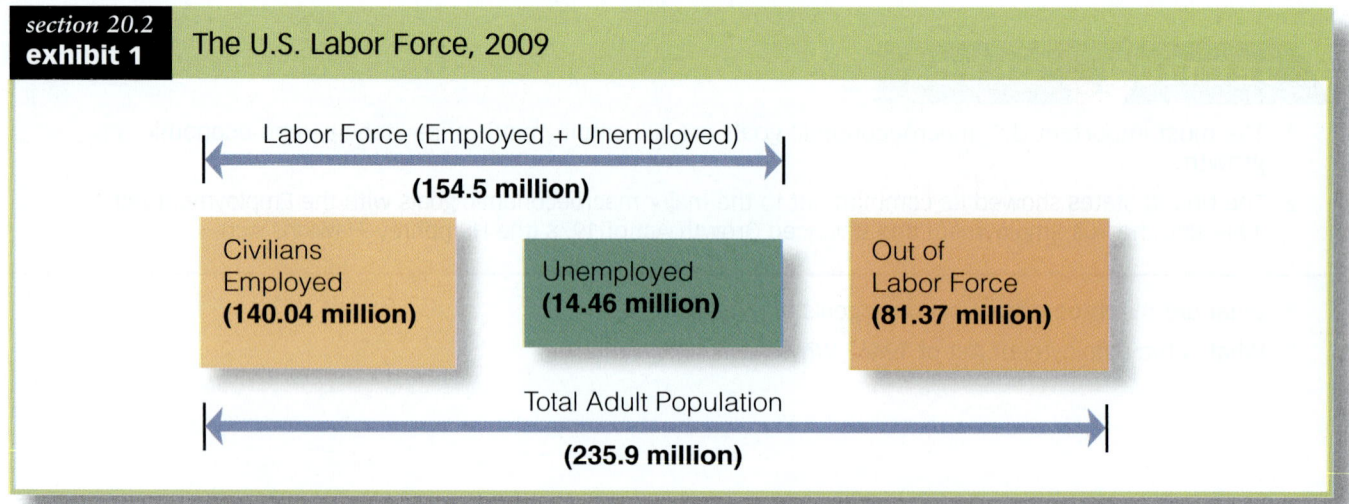

SOURCE: Bureau of Labor Statistics, August 2009.

full-time students. These groups are excluded from the labor force because they are not considered currently available for employment.

When we say that the unemployment rate is 5 percent, we mean that 5 percent of the population over the age of 16 who are willing and able to work are unable to get jobs. This 5 percent means that 5 out of 100 people in the total labor force are unemployed. To calculate the unemployment rate, we simply divide the number of unemployed by the number in the civilian labor force:

$$\text{Unemployment rate} = \frac{\text{Number of unemployed}}{\text{Civilian labor force}}$$

In August 2009, the number of civilians unemployed in the United States was 14.46 million, and the civilian labor force totaled 154.5 million. Using these data, we can calculate that the unemployment rate in August 2009 was 9.4 percent:

$$\text{Unemployment rate} = 14.46 \text{ million}/154.5 \text{ million}$$
$$= 0.094 \times 100 = 9.4 \text{ percent}$$

The Worst Case of U.S. Unemployment

By far, the worst employment downturn in U.S. history occurred during the Great Depression, which began in late 1929 and continued until 1941. Unemployment rose from only 3.2 percent of the labor force in 1929 to more than 20 percent in the early 1930s, and double-digit unemployment persisted through 1941. The debilitating impact of having millions of productive people out of work led Americans (and people in other countries as well) to say, "Never again." Some economists would argue that modern macroeconomics, with its emphasis on the determinants of unemployment and its elimination, truly began in the 1930s.

Variations in the Unemployment Rate

Exhibit 2 shows U.S. unemployment rates over the last 49 years. Unemployment since 1960 ranged from a low of 3.5 percent in 1969 to a high of 10.8 percent in 1982. The financial crisis of 2008 led to unemployment rates of 9.4 percent by mid-2009. Unemployment in the worst years is two or more times what it is in good years. Before 1960, variations in unemployment were more pronounced.

Are Unemployment Statistics Accurate Reflections of the Labor Market?

In periods of prolonged recession, some individuals think that the chances of landing a job are so bleak that they quit looking. These people are called

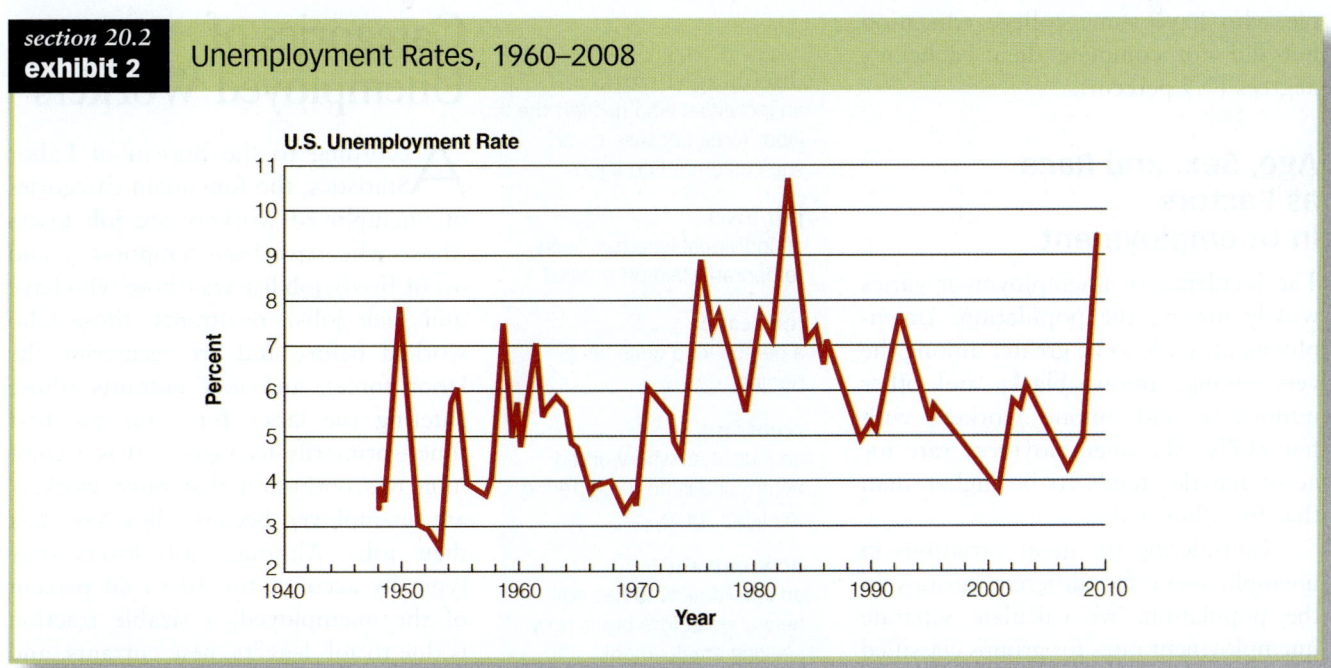

section 20.2 exhibit 2 — Unemployment Rates, 1960–2008

SOURCE: Bureau of Labor Statistics, August 2009.

discouraged workers. Individuals who have not actively sought work for four weeks are not counted as unemployed; instead, they fall out of the labor force. Also, people looking for full-time work who grudgingly settle for part-time jobs are counted as "fully" employed, even though they are only "partly" employed. At least partially balancing these two biases in government employment statistics, however, is the number of people who are overemployed—that is, working overtime or at more than one job. Also, a number of jobs in the underground economy (e.g., drug dealing, prostitution, gambling, and so on) are not reported. In addition, many people may claim they are seeking work when, in fact, they may just be going through the motions so they can continue to collect unemployment compensation or receive other government benefits.

Teenagers have the highest rates of unemployment. Do you think it would be easier for them to find jobs if they had more experience and higher skill levels?

Who Are the Unemployed?

Unemployment usually varies greatly across different segments of the population and over time.

Education as a Factor in Unemployment

According to the Bureau of Labor Statistics, the unemployment rate across the sexes and races among college graduates is significantly lower than for those who do not complete high school. In July 2009, the unemployment rate for individuals without high school diplomas was 15.4 percent, compared with 4.7 percent for those with bachelor's degrees and higher. Further, college graduates have lower unemployment rates than people who have some college education but did not complete their bachelor's degrees (7.9 percent).

Age, Sex, and Race as Factors in Unemployment

The incidence of unemployment varies widely among the population. Unemployment tends to be greater among the very young, among blacks and other minorities, and among workers with few skills. The unemployment rate for adult females tends to be higher than that for adult males.

Considering the great variations in unemployment for different groups in the population, we calculate separate unemployment rates for groups classified by sex, age, race, family status, and type of occupation. Exhibit 3 shows unemployment rates for various groups. Note that the variation around the average unemployment rate for the total population of 9.4 percent was considerable. The unemployment rate for blacks was much higher than the rate for whites, a phenomenon that has persisted throughout the post–World War II period. Unemployment among teenagers was much higher than adult unemployment, at 23.8 percent. Some would regard teenage unemployment a lesser evil than unemployment among adults, because most teenagers have parents or guardians on whom they can rely for subsistence.

discouraged worker
an individual who has left the labor force because he or she could not find a job

job loser
an individual who has been temporarily laid off or fired

job leaver
a person who quits his or her job

reentrant
an individual who worked before and is now reentering the labor force

new entrant
an individual who has not held a job before but is now seeking employment

Categories of Unemployed Workers

According to the Bureau of Labor Statistics, the four main categories of unemployed workers are **job losers** (those who have been temporarily laid off or fired), **job leavers** (those who have quit their jobs), **reentrants** (those who worked before and are reentering the labor force), and **new entrants** (those entering the labor force for the first time—primarily teenagers). It is a common misconception that most workers are unemployed because they have lost their jobs. Although job losers may typically account for 50 to 60 percent of the unemployed, a sizable fraction is due to job leavers, new entrants, and reentrants, as seen in Exhibit 4.

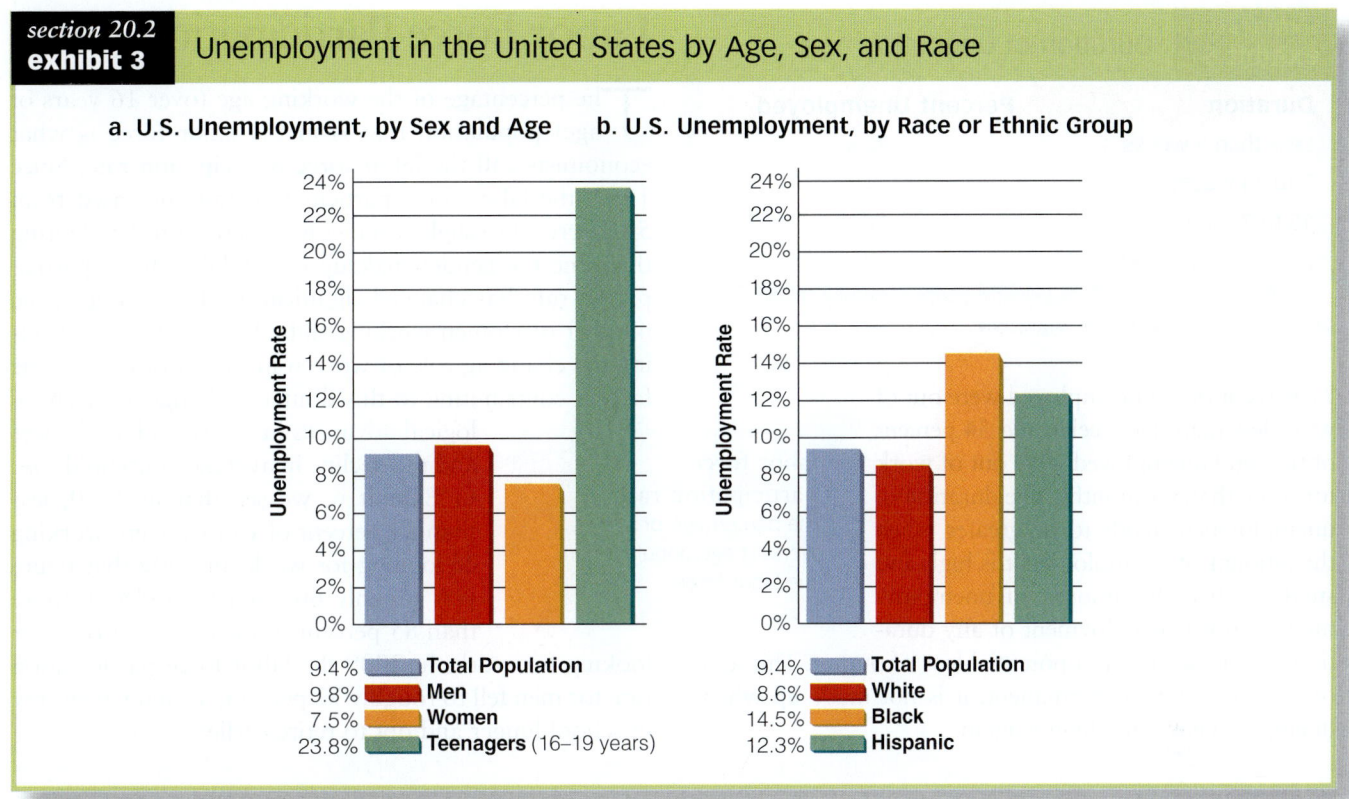

section 20.2 exhibit 3 Unemployment in the United States by Age, Sex, and Race

a. U.S. Unemployment, by Sex and Age
- 9.4% Total Population
- 9.8% Men
- 7.5% Women
- 23.8% Teenagers (16–19 years)

b. U.S. Unemployment, by Race or Ethnic Group
- 9.4% Total Population
- 8.6% White
- 14.5% Black
- 12.3% Hispanic

SOURCE: Bureau of Labor Statistics, August 2009.

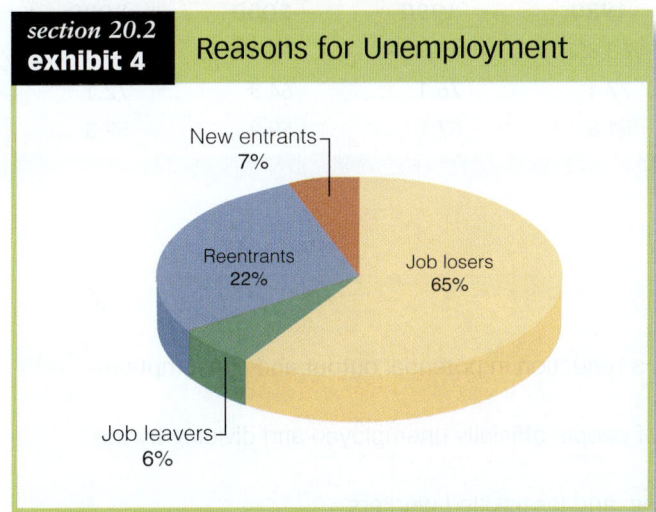

section 20.2 exhibit 4 Reasons for Unemployment

- New entrants 7%
- Reentrants 22%
- Job losers 65%
- Job leavers 6%

SOURCE: Bureau of Labor Statistics, August 2009.

How Much Unemployment?

Even though unemployment is painful to those who have no source of income, reducing unemployment is not costless. In the short run, a reduction in unemployment may come at the expense of a higher rate of inflation, especially if the economy is close to full capacity, where resources are almost fully employed. Moreover, trying to match employees with jobs can quickly lead to significant inefficiencies, because of mismatches between a worker's skill level and the level of skill required for a job. For example, the economy would be wasting resources subsidizing education if people with PhDs in biochemistry were driving taxis or tending bars. That is, the skills of the employee may be higher than those necessary for the job, resulting in what economists call **underemployment.** Another source of inefficiencies is placing employees in jobs beyond their abilities.

How Long Are People Usually Unemployed?

The duration of unemployment is equally as important as the amount of unemployment. The financial consequences of a head of household's being unemployed for four or five weeks are usually not extremely serious, particularly if the individual is covered by an unemployment compensation system. The impact becomes much more serious if that person is unemployed for several months. Therefore, it is useful to look at the average duration of unemployment to discover what percentage of the labor force is unemployed longer than a certain period, say 15 weeks. Exhibit 5 presents data on the duration of unemployment. As you can see in this table,

underemployment a situation in which a worker's skill level is higher than necessary for a job

section 20.2 exhibit 5 — Duration of Unemployment

Duration	Percent Unemployed
Less than 5 weeks	22%
5 to 14 weeks	24
15 to 26 weeks	20
27 weeks and over	34

SOURCE: Bureau of Labor Statistics, August 2009.

22 percent of the unemployed were out of work less than five weeks, and 34 percent of the total unemployed were out of work for more than six months. The duration of unemployment tends to be greater when the amount of unemployment is high and smaller when the amount of unemployment is low. Unemployment of any duration, of course, means a potential loss of output. This loss of current output is permanent; it is not made up when unemployment starts falling again.

labor force participation rate
the percentage of the working age population in the labor force

Labor Force Participation Rate

The percentage of the working age (over 16 years of age) population that is in the labor force is what economists call the **labor force participation rate.** Since 1950, the labor force participation rate increased from 59.2 percent to slightly under 65.5 percent today. During this time the gender makeup of the labor force participation rate has changed significantly. For example, the number of women working shifted dramatically, reflecting the changing role of women in the workforce. Some factors contributing to this dramatic change are technological advances in household appliances and the decline in average household size. In Exhibit 6, we see that in 1950, less than 34 percent of women were working or looking for work. In 2009 that figure was roughly 60 percent. In 1950, more than 85 percent of men were working or looking for work. In 2009 the labor force participation rate for men fell to roughly 72 percent, as many men stay in school longer and opt to retire earlier.

section 20.2 exhibit 6 — Labor Force Participation Rates for Men and Women

	1950	1960	1970	1980	1990	2000	2009
Total	59.2%	59.4%	60.4%	63.8%	66.4%	67.1%	65.5%
Men	86.4	83.3	79.7	77.4	76.1	64.8	72.1
Women	33.9	37.7	43.3	51.5	57.5	59.9	59.3

SOURCE: Bureau of Labor Statistics, August 2009.

SECTION CHECK

1. The consequences of unemployment for society include a reduction in potential output and consumption—a decrease in efficiency.
2. The unemployment rate is found by taking the number of people officially unemployed and dividing by the number in the civilian labor force.
3. Unemployment rates are highest for minorities, the young, and less-skilled workers.
4. The four main categories of unemployed workers are job losers, job leavers, reentrants, and new entrants.
5. The duration of unemployment tends to be greater (smaller) when the amount of unemployment is high (low).

---

1. What happens to the unemployment rate when the number of unemployed people increases, *ceteris paribus*? When the labor force grows, *ceteris paribus*?
2. How might the official unemployment rate understate the "true" degree of unemployment? How might it overstate it?
3. Why might the fraction of the unemployed who are job leavers be higher in a period of strong labor demand?
4. Suppose you live in a community of 100 people. If 80 people are over 16 years old and 72 people are willing and able to work, what is the unemployment rate in this community?

5. What would happen to the unemployment rate if a substantial group of unemployed people started going to school full time? What would happen to the size of the labor force?

6. What happens to the unemployment rate when officially unemployed people become discouraged workers? Does anything happen to employment in this case?

Types of Unemployment

* What are the three types of unemployment?
* What is frictional unemployment?
* What is structural unemployment?
* What is cyclical unemployment?
* What is the natural rate of unemployment?

In examining the status of and changes in the unemployment rate, it is important to recognize that unemployment can take several forms. In this section, we will examine the three types of unemployment—frictional, structural, and cyclical—and evaluate the relative effects of each on the overall unemployment rate.

Frictional Unemployment

In a dynamic economy where people are constantly losing or leaving their jobs, some frictional unemployment is always present. **Frictional unemployment** is the temporary unemployment that results from the search time that occurs when people are searching for suitable jobs and firms are looking for suitable workers. People seeking work do not usually take the first job offered to them. Likewise, firms do not usually take the first person they interview. People and firms engage in a search to match up skills and interests. While the unemployed are looking, they are frictionally unemployed.

For example, consider an advertising executive who was fired in Chicago on March 1 and is now actively looking for similar work in San Francisco. Of course, not all unemployed workers were fired; some may have voluntarily quit their jobs. In either case, frictional unemployment is short term and results from normal turnover in the labor market, as when people change from one job to another.

Some unemployment occurs because certain types of jobs are seasonal in nature. This type of unemployment is called *seasonal unemployment*. For example, a ski instructor in Aspen might become seasonally unemployed at the end of April when ski season is over. Or a roofer in

> **frictional unemployment**
> the unemployment that results from workers searching for suitable jobs and firms looking for suitable workers

Minnesota may become seasonally unemployed during the harsh winter months. In agricultural areas, employment increases during harvest season and falls after the season is over. Even a forest firefighter in a national park might only be employed during the summer and fall, when forest fires peak. Occupations that experience either sharp seasonal shifts in demand or are subject to changing weather conditions may lead to seasonal unemployment—like in agriculture where employment increases during harvest season. Because this type of unemployment can make the unemployment rate higher in the off-season and lower during the in-season, the Bureau of Labor Statistics (BLS) publishes a seasonally adjusted unemployment rate as well. These figures are more accurate because they take into account the effects of seasonal unemployment.

Should We Worry About Frictional Unemployment?

Geographic and occupational mobility are considered good for the economy because they generally lead human resources to go from activities of relatively low productivity or value to areas of higher productivity, increasing output in society as well as the wage income of the mover. Indeed, some of this frictional unemployment involving searches by firms and workers to find *more* suitable matchups is obviously beneficial to the economy. Even though the amount of frictional unemployment varies somewhat over time, it is unusual for it to be much less than 2 percent of the labor force. Actually, frictional unemployment tends to be somewhat greater in periods of low unemployment, when job opportunities are plentiful. This high level of job opportunity stimulates mobility, which, in turn, creates some frictional unemployment.

Structural Unemployment

A second type of unemployment is structural unemployment. Like frictional unemployment, **structural unemployment** is related to occupational movement or mobility—in this case, to a lack of mobility. Structural unemployment occurs when workers lack the necessary skills for jobs that are available or have particular skills that are no longer in demand. For example, if a machine operator in a manufacturing plant loses his job, he could still remain unemployed despite the openings for computer programmers in his community. The quantity of unemployed workers conceivably could equal the number of job vacancies, with the unemployment persisting because the unemployed lack the appropriate skills. Given the existence of structural unemployment, it is wise to look at both unemployment and job vacancy statistics in assessing labor market conditions. Structural unemployment, like frictional unemployment, reflects the dynamic dimension of a changing economy. Over time, new jobs open up that require new skills, while old jobs that required different skills disappear. It is not surprising, then, that many people advocate government-subsidized retraining programs as a means of reducing structural unemployment.

structural unemployment the unemployment that results from workers not having the skills to obtain long-term employment

cyclical unemployment unemployment due to short-term cyclical fluctuations in the economy

Another reason for structural unemployment is that low-skilled workers are frequently unable to find desirable long-term employment. Some of these low-skilled jobs do not last long and involve little job training, so a worker may soon be looking for a new job. Because they acquired no new skill from the old job, they may be stuck without long-term secure work. That is, structural workers cannot be said to be "in-between jobs" like those who are frictionally unemployed. Structural unemployment is more long term and serious than frictional unemployment because these workers do not have marketable skills.

The dimensions of structural unemployment are debatable, in part because of the difficulty in precisely defining the term in an operational sense. Structural unemployment varies considerably—sometimes it is low and at other times, as in the 1970s and early 1980s, it is high. To some extent, in the latter period, jobs in the traditional sectors such as automobile manufacturing and oil production were giving way to jobs in the computer and biotechnology sectors. Consequently, structural unemployment was higher.

Some Unemployment Is Unavoidable

Some unemployment is actually normal and important to the economy. Frictional and structural unemployment are simply unavoidable in a vibrant economy. To a considerable extent, we can view both frictional and structural unemployment as phenomena resulting from imperfections in the labor market. For example, if individuals seeking jobs and employers seeking workers had better information about each other, the amount of frictional unemployment would be considerably lower. It takes time for suppliers of labor to find the demanders of labor services, and it takes time and money for labor resources to acquire the necessary skills. But because information and job search are costly, bringing together demanders and suppliers of labor services does not occur instantaneously.

Cyclical Unemployment

Often, unemployment is composed of more than just frictional and structural unemployment. In years of relatively high unemployment, some joblessness may result from short-term cyclical fluctuations in the economy. We call this type **cyclical unemployment**.

What type of unemployment would occur if these coal miners lost their jobs as a result of a permanent reduction in demand for coal and needed retraining to find other employment? Usually, structural unemployment occurs because of workers' lack of skills or long-term changes in demand. Consequently, it generally lasts for a longer period than does frictional unemployment.

Whenever the unemployment rate is greater than normal, such as during a recession, it is due to cyclical unemployment. Most attempts to solve the cyclical unemployment problem emphasized increasing aggregate demand to counter recession.

The Cost of Cyclical Unemployment

When the unemployment rate is high, numerous economic and social hardships result. The economic costs are the forgone output when the economy is not producing at its potential level. According to Okun's Law (really, a rule of thumb), a 1 percent increase in cyclical unemployment reduces output by 2 percentage points. Thus, we can actually estimate the economic costs of not producing at our potential output. The costs are particularly high for those groups with the least skills—the poorly educated and teenagers with little work experience.

The Natural Rate of Unemployment

It is interesting to observe that over the period in which annual unemployment data are available, the median, or "typical," annual unemployment rate has been at or slightly above 5 percent. Some economists call this typical unemployment rate the **natural rate of unemployment.** When unemployment rises well above 5 percent, we have abnormally high unemployment; when it falls well below 5 percent, we have abnormally low unemployment. The natural rate of unemployment of approximately 5 percent roughly equals the sum of frictional and structural unemployment when they are at their maximums. Thus, we can view unemployment rates below the natural rate as reflecting the existence of below-average levels of frictional and structural unemployment. When unemployment rises above the natural rate, however, it reflects the existence of cyclical unemployment. In short, the natural rate of unemployment is the unemployment rate when the economy is experiencing neither a recession nor a boom. The natural rate of unemployment is also called the *full employment rate of unemployment.*

The natural rate of unemployment can change over time as technological, demographic, institutional, and other conditions vary. For example, as baby boomers age, the natural rate falls because middle-aged workers generally experience lower unemployment rates than do younger workers. In addition, the Internet and job placement agencies have improved access to employment information and allowed workers to find jobs more quickly. Also, the new work requirements of the welfare laws increased the number of people with jobs. Thus, the natural rate is not fixed, because it can change with demographic changes over time.

Full Employment and Potential Output

When all the resources of an economy—labor, land, and capital—are fully employed, the economy is said to be producing its **potential output.** Literally, *full employment of labor* means that the economy is providing employment for all who are willing and able to work with no cyclical unemployment. It also means that capital and land are fully employed. That is, at the natural rate of unemployment, all resources are fully employed, the economy is producing its potential output, and no

> **natural rate of unemployment**
> the median, or "typical," unemployment rate, equal to the sum of frictional and structural unemployment when they are at a maximum
>
> **potential output**
> the amount of real output the economy would produce if its labor and other resources were fully employed, that is, at the natural rate of unemployment

---

Use what you've LEARNED: CYCLICAL UNEMPLOYMENT

Q Are layoffs more prevalent during a recession than a recovery? Do most resignations occur during a recovery?

A Layoffs are more likely to occur during a recession. When times are bad, employers are often forced to let workers go. Resignations are relatively more prevalent during good economic times because more job opportunities are available to those seeking new jobs.

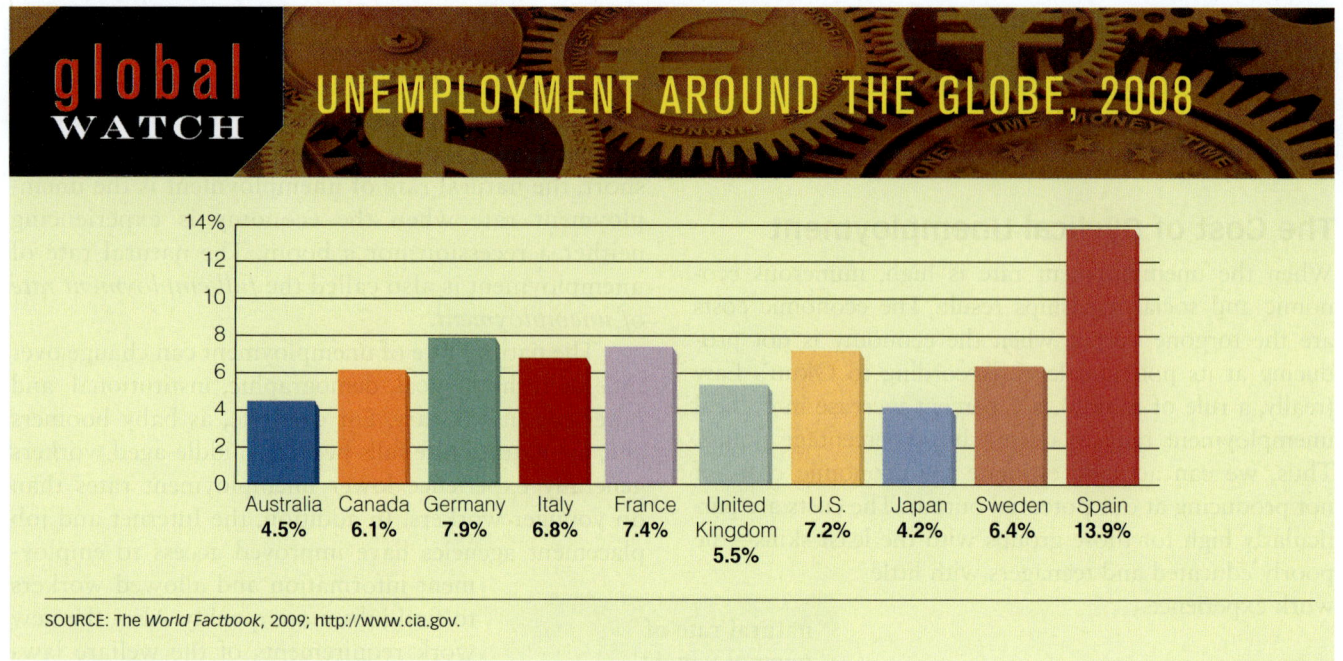

global WATCH — UNEMPLOYMENT AROUND THE GLOBE, 2008

Australia	Canada	Germany	Italy	France	United Kingdom	U.S.	Japan	Sweden	Spain
4.5%	6.1%	7.9%	6.8%	7.4%	5.5%	7.2%	4.2%	6.4%	13.9%

SOURCE: The *World Factbook*, 2009; http://www.cia.gov.

cyclical unemployment is present. It does not mean the economy will always be producing at its potential output of resources. For example, when the economy is experiencing cyclical unemployment, the unemployment rate is greater than the natural rate. It is also possible for the economy to temporarily exceed the natural rate, as workers put in overtime or moonlight by taking on extra employment.

SECTION CHECK

1. The three types of unemployment are frictional unemployment, structural unemployment, and cyclical unemployment.
2. Frictional unemployment results when a person moves from one job to another as workers search for suitable jobs and firms look for suitable workers.
3. Structural unemployment results when people who are looking for jobs lack the required skills for the jobs that are available or a long-term change in demand occurs.
4. Cyclical unemployment is caused by a recession.
5. Imperfections in the labor market and institutional factors result in higher rates of unemployment.
6. When cyclical unemployment is almost completely eliminated, our economy is said to be operating at full employment, or at a natural rate of unemployment.

---

1. Why do we want some frictional unemployment?
2. Why might a job retraining program be a more useful policy to address structural unemployment than to address frictional unemployment?
3. What is the traditional government policy "cure" for cyclical unemployment?
4. What types of unemployment are present at full employment (at the natural rate of unemployment)?
5. Why might frictional unemployment be higher in a period of plentiful jobs (low unemployment)?
6. If the widespread introduction of the automobile caused a productive buggy whip maker to lose his job, would he be structurally unemployed?
7. If a fall in demand for domestic cars causes auto workers to lose their jobs in Michigan, while plenty of jobs are available for lumberjacks in Montana, what kind of unemployment results?

SECTION 20.4 Reasons for Unemployment

- How does a higher minimum wage lead to greater unemployment among the young and unskilled?
- Can unions cause higher rates of unemployment?
- How does an efficiency wage cause a higher rate of unemployment?
- How do changes in job search costs affect the unemployment rate?
- Does unemployment insurance increase the unemployment rate?

In this section, we look at the causes of frictional and structural unemployment. In later chapters, we discuss the causes of cyclical unemployment.

Why Does Unemployment Exist?

In many markets, prices adjust to the market equilibrium price and quantity, and no prolonged periods of shortage or surplus occur. However, in labor markets, obstacles prevent wages from adjusting and balancing the quantity of labor supplied and the quantity of labor demanded. In Exhibit 1, we see that W_1 is higher than the market equilibrium wage that equates the quantity demanded of labor with the quantity supplied of labor. At W_1, the quantity of labor supplied is greater than the quantity of labor demanded, resulting in an excess quantity supplied of labor—unemployment. That is, more people want to work at the going (nonequilibrium) wage than employers want to hire, and those who are not able to find work are "unemployed." Why? Economists cite three reasons for the failure of wages to balance the labor demand and labor supply equilibrium—minimum wages, unions, and the efficiency wage theory.

minimum wage rate
an hourly wage floor set above the equilibrium wage

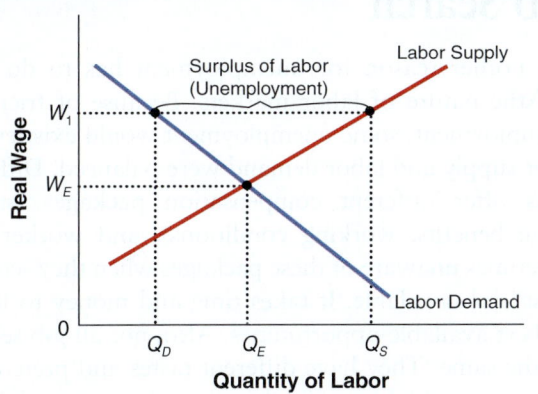

section 20.4 exhibit 1 Wages Above Equilibrium Lead to Greater Unemployment

The labor market is in equilibrium where the quantity demanded of labor is equal to the quantity supplied of labor, at W_E and Q_E. If the wage persists above the equilibrium wage, a surplus of labor or unemployment of $Q_S \times Q_D$ exists. That is, at W_1, the quantity of labor supplied is greater than the quantity of labor demanded; we can think of this surplus of labor as unemployment.

Minimum Wages and Unemployment

Many different types of labor markets exist for different types of workers. The labor market for workers with little experience and job skills is called the unskilled labor market. Suppose the government decided to establish a **minimum wage rate** (an hourly wage floor) for unskilled workers above the equilibrium wage, W_E. At the minimum wage, the quantity of labor supplied grows because more people are willing to work at a higher wage. However, the quantity of labor demanded falls because some employers would find it unprofitable to hire low-skilled workers at the higher wage. At W_1, a gap exists between the quantity of labor demanded and the quantity supplied, representing a surplus of unskilled workers—unemployment, as seen in Exhibit 1.

Because minimum wage earners, a majority of whom are 25 years or younger, are a small portion of the labor force, most economists believe the effect of minimum wage on unemployment is small.

The Impact of Unions on the Unemployment Rate

Unions negotiate their wages and benefits collectively through their union officials, a process called collective bargaining. If, through this process of collective bargaining, union officials are able to increase wages, then unemployment will rise in the union sector. If the bargaining raises the union wage above the equilibrium level, the quantity of union labor demanded will decrease, and the quantity of union labor supplied will increase—that is, union workers will be unemployed. The union workers who still have their jobs will be better off, but some who are equally skilled will be unemployed and will either seek nonunion work or wait to be recalled in the union sector. Many economists believe that is why wages are approximately 15 percent higher in union jobs, even when nonunion workers have comparable skills. On the other hand, even though wages in the union sector are typically higher than the market wage, the presence of unions does not necessarily lead to greater unemployment because workers can find jobs in the nonunion sector. Less than 10 percent of private sector jobs are unionized.

Efficiency Wage

In economics, it is generally assumed that as productivity rises, wages rise, and workers can raise their productivity through investments in human capital like education and on-the-job training. However, some economists follow the **efficiency wage model,** which is based on the belief that *higher wages lead to greater productivity.*

In the efficiency wage model, employers pay their employees more than the equilibrium wage to be more efficient. Proponents of this theory suggest that it may lead to attracting the most productive workers, fewer job turnovers, and higher morale, which in turn can lead to lower hiring and training costs. In addition, higher paid workers may be healthier (better diets) and therefore more productive. This is particularly true in developing countries. In Exhibit 1, suppose workers are paid W_E. Why wouldn't they shirk at their current job if someone else will hire them almost immediately at the same wage? In short, there are few adverse consequences to shirking. One option for firms is to pay an efficiency wage. However, if all firms pay an efficiency wage, like W_1 in Exhibit 1, then why can't they just shirk and if fired, find another firm that will pay them W_1? The reason is because at W_1, firms are paying higher than the equilibrium wage reducing the number of jobs, so fired workers might face a prolonged period of unemployment.

In 1914, Henry Ford increased his workers' wages from $3 to $5 per day—roughly twice the going wage rate for unskilled workers. This wage rate led to long lines of workers seeking jobs at the Ford plant—that is, quantity supplied greatly exceeded quantity demanded at the efficiency wage rate. Ford knew that assembly line work was boring, and to overcome the problem he was having with morale and absenteeism, he decided to increase daily wages to $5 a day. At the time, many business leaders were skeptical because this put Ford's labor costs at nearly twice that of his rivals. However, Ford profits continued to mount. Historical records suggest that the efficiency wage led to lower turnover, less absenteeism, better hires, and less shirking—in short, greater worker productivity. Even though the higher wages led to higher labor costs, the costs were more than offset by the increase in worker productivity.

Some scholars have argued that the positive effects of the efficiency wage are unique to assembly line production and its high degree of worker interdependence. However, it is costly for firms to pay an efficiency wage. Consequently, firms must monitor their workers' efforts. If enough firms resort to paying the efficiency wage rate it leads to a surplus of workers who want jobs and cannot find them. This, like a binding minimum wage, leads to unemployment.

> **efficiency wage model** theory stating that higher wages lead to greater productivity

Job Search

Another reason for unemployment has to do with the nature of labor markets. Because of frictional unemployment, some unemployment would exist even if labor supply and labor demand were balanced. Different firms offer different compensation packages (salary, fringe benefits, working conditions), and workers are sometimes unaware of these packages when they seek the "best" job available. It takes time and money to locate the best available opportunities. Also, not all job seekers are the same: They have different tastes and preferences about types of jobs and job locations. Sometimes it is difficult to get the information about particular jobs to the right job candidate. These search activities prolong the duration of unemployment. However, the search goes on because the job seeker hopes to find a better offer.

The labor demand and supply curves are constantly shifting. That is, labor markets are constantly in flux—people losing jobs, leaving jobs, reentering jobs. In a growing and dynamic economy, jobs are constantly being destroyed and created, leading to temporary unemployment as workers search for the best jobs for their skills.

Unemployment Insurance

Losing a job can lead to considerable hardships, and unemployment insurance is designed to partially offset the severity of the unemployment problem. The program does not cover those who were fired or quit their jobs. To qualify, recipients must have worked a certain length of time and lost their jobs because the employer no longer needed their skills. The typical compensation is half salary for 26 weeks. Although the program is intended to ease the pain of unemployment, it also leads to prolonged periods of unemployment, as job seekers stay unemployed for longer periods searching for new jobs.

For example, some unemployed people may show little drive in seeking new employment, because unemployment insurance lowers the opportunity cost of being unemployed. Say a worker making $400 a week when employed receives $220 in compensation when unemployed; as a result, the cost of losing the job is not $400 a week in forgone income but only $180. It has been estimated that the existence of unemployment compensation programs may raise overall unemployment rates by as much as 1 percent.

Without unemployment insurance, a job seeker would be more likely to take the first job offered, even if the job did not match the job seeker's preferences or skill levels. A longer job search might mean a better match, but it comes at the expense of lost production and greater amounts of tax dollars.

Does New Technology Lead to Greater Unemployment?

The widespread belief that technological advances inevitably result in the displacement of workers is not necessarily true. Generally, new inventions are cost saving, and these cost savings usually generate higher incomes for producers and lower prices and better products for consumers—benefits that ultimately result in the growth of other industries. If the new equipment is a substitute for labor, it might displace workers. For example, many fast-food restaurants installed self-service beverage bars to replace workers. However, new capital equipment requires new workers to manufacture and repair the new equipment. The most famous example of this trade-off is the computer, which was supposed to displace thousands of workers. Instead, the computer generated a whole new growth industry that created jobs. The problem is that it is easy to see only the initial effect of technological advances (displaced workers) but difficult to recognize the implications of that invention throughout the whole economy over time.

Some economists believe that some of the real wage differentials between skilled and unskilled workers in the last couple of decades are due to technical changes that are biased toward skilled workers. New machines, with highly sophisticated computerization, require highly skilled workers. Consequently, the new machines make these workers more productive and

section 20.4 exhibit 2: Skill-Biased Technical Change and Wage Inequality

When a skill-biased technical change occurs, it increases the productivity of skilled workers. Consequently, the increase in demand for skilled workers shifts the curve from D_1 to D_2 in (a). The increase in demand leads to higher real wages from W_1 to W_2 and a greater quantity of skilled labor, Q_1 to Q_2. In (b) we see a reduction in demand for unskilled workers from D_1 to D_2, because these workers cannot use the new technology that increases productivity. The result is lower wages, W_1 to W_2, and lower employment, Q_1 to Q_2.

therefore they receive higher real wages. In Exhibit 2(a), we graph the labor market for skilled workers. Because of the increase in demand for skilled labor—skilled workers can produce more with the new machines—their real wages and employment are higher. At the same time, the demand is lower for workers who do not have the technical training to work with specialized machinery, and the demand for unskilled workers falls as seen in Exhibit 2(b). As a result of the decrease in demand for unskilled workers, real wages and employment fall. Thus, skill-biased technical change tends to create even greater disparities between the wages of skilled and unskilled workers. The message: stay in school (vocational or traditional).

SECTION CHECK

1. Economists have cited three reasons why wages have failed to bring the quantity of labor demanded into balance with the quantity of labor supplied—minimum wage, unions, and the efficiency wage theory.
2. At the minimum wage, the quantity of labor supplied grows because more people are willing to work at a higher wage. However, the quantity of labor demanded falls because some employers would find it unprofitable to hire low-skilled workers at the higher wage. That is, a higher minimum wage can lead to higher rates of unemployment—particularly among unskilled teenagers.
3. If the efficiency wage rate is greater than the equilibrium wage rate, the quantity of labor supplied is greater than the quantity of labor demanded, resulting in greater amounts of unemployment.
4. Sometimes it is difficult to get the information about particular jobs to the right job candidate. These search activities prolong the duration of unemployment.
5. Some unemployed persons may show little drive in seeking new employment, given the existence of unemployment compensation. Unemployment compensation lowers the opportunity cost of being unemployed.

---

1. What are the three reasons for wages to fail to balance labor supply and labor demand?
2. What is an efficiency wage?
3. How do search costs lead to prolonged periods of unemployment?
4. Why would higher unemployment compensation in a country like France lead to higher rates of unemployment?
5. Does new technology increase unemployment?

SECTION 20.5 Inflation

* Why is the overall price level important?
* How did price level behave during the previous century?
* What is the purpose of a price-level index?
* What problems are inherent with a price-level index?
* Who are the winners and losers during inflation?
* Can wage earners avoid the consequences of inflation?

Stable Price Level as a Desirable Goal

Just as full employment brings about one kind of economic security, an overall stable **price level** increases another form of economic security. Most prices in the U.S. economy tend to rise over time. The continuing rise in the *overall* price level is called **inflation**. Even when the level of prices is stable, some prices will be rising while others are falling. However, when inflation is present, the goods and services with rising prices will outweigh the goods

price level
the average level of prices in the economy

inflation
a rise in the overall price level, which decreases the purchasing power of money

and services with lower prices. Without stability in the price level, consumers and producers will experience more difficulty in coordinating their plans and decisions. When the *overall* price level is falling, it is called **deflation.** The average price level in the U.S. economy fell throughout the late nineteenth century.

In general, the only thing that can cause a *sustained* increase in the rate of inflation is a high rate of growth in money, a topic we will discuss thoroughly in upcoming chapters.

Measuring Inflation

We often use the term *purchasing power* when we discuss how much a dollar can buy of goods and services. In times of inflation, a dollar cannot buy as many goods and services. Thus, the higher the inflation rate, the greater the rate of decline in purchasing power.

In periods of high and variable inflation, households and firms have a difficult time distinguishing between changes in the **relative price** of individual goods and services (the price of a specific good compared to the prices of other goods) and changes in the general price level of all goods and services. Suppose the price of milk rises by 5 percent between 2010 and 2011, but the overall price level (inflation rate) increases by only 2 percent during that period. Then we could say that between 2010 and 2011, the relative price of milk rose only 3 percent (5−2 percent). The next year, the price of milk might increase 5 percent again, but the general inflation rate might be 6 percent. That is, between 2011 and 2012, the relative price of milk might actually fall by 1 percent (5−6 percent). Remember, the relative price is the price of a good relative to all other goods and services.

deflation
a decrease in the overall price level, which increases the purchasing power of money

relative price
the price of a specific good compared to the price of other goods

Use what you've LEARNED: BABE RUTH'S SALARY ADJUSTED FOR INFLATION

Q To many baseball purists, Babe Ruth was the greatest player of the game, but how does his salary compare with the highest salary in baseball today? When Babe Ruth made $80,000 a year in 1931, he was asked by the press if he knew that his salary exceeded that of President Herbert Hoover. Ruth said, "Yes, I know. But I had a better year than President Hoover did."

A The Bureau of Labor Statistics computes CPI all the way back to 1913. The average CPI for 1931, the year Babe Ruth made $80,000, was 15.2. The average CPI for 2008 was 215.3. We can easily convert the Babe's salary into current dollars by performing the following calculation:

Babe's salary in 1931

$$\$80{,}000 \times \frac{\text{Price level in 2008}}{\text{Price level in 1931}}$$

$$= \$80{,}000 \times \frac{215.3}{15.2} = \$1{,}133{,}158$$

Therefore, the Babe would be making $1,133,158 a year if he were paid the same in 2008 as he was paid in 1931. Not bad, but not even close to what today's stars of the game are paid. At $27 million a year, Alex Rodriguez makes roughly 25 times Babe's adjusted salary.

Because of this difficulty in establishing relative prices, inflation distorts the information that flows from price signals. Does the good have a higher price because it has become relatively more scarce and therefore more valuable relative to other goods, or did the price rise along with all other prices because of inflation? This muddying of price information undermines good decision making.

Thus, we need a method to measure inflation. We adjust for the changing purchasing power of the dollar by constructing a **price index.** Essentially, a price index attempts to provide a measure of the prices paid for a certain bundle of goods and services over time.

The Consumer Price Index and the GDP Deflator

There are many different types of price indices. The most well-known index, the **consumer price index (CPI),** measures the trend in the prices of certain goods and services purchased for consumption purposes—see Exhibit 1. The CPI may be most relevant to households trying to evaluate their changing financial positions over time.

The **GDP deflator** corrects for changing prices in even broader terms. The GDP deflator measures the average level of prices of all final goods and services produced in the economy.

How Is a Price Index Created?

Constructing a price index is complicated. First, literally thousands of goods and services are in our economy; attempting to include all of them in an index would be cumbersome and make the index expensive to compute, and it would take a long time to gather the necessary data. Therefore, a "bundle" or "basket" of representative goods and services is selected by the index calculators (the Bureau of Labor Statistics of the U.S. Department of Labor for consumer and wholesale price indices;

price index
a measure of the trend in prices paid for a certain bundle of goods and services over a given period

consumer price index (CPI)
a measure of the cost of a market basket that represents the consumption of a typical household

GDP deflator
a price index that helps measure the average price level of all final consumer goods and services produced

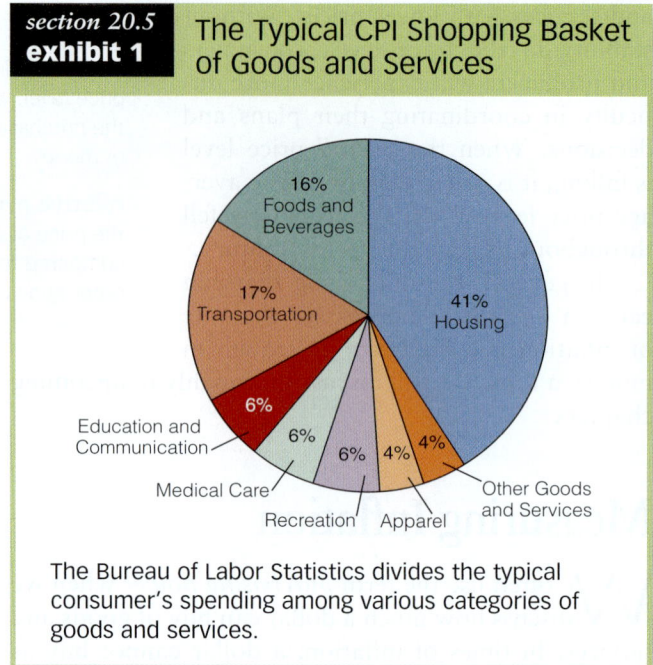

section 20.5 exhibit 1 The Typical CPI Shopping Basket of Goods and Services

The Bureau of Labor Statistics divides the typical consumer's spending among various categories of goods and services.

SOURCE: U.S. Bureau of Labor Statistics.

the Office of Business Economics of the Department of Commerce for the GDP deflator).

Calculating a Simple Price Index

Suppose a consumer typically buys 24 loaves of bread and 12 gallons of milk in a year. The following table lists the prices of bread and milk and the cost of the consumer's typical market basket in the years 2010–2012.

Year	Price of Bread	Price of Milk	Cost of Market Basket
2010	$1.00	$2.00	(24 × $1.00) + (12 × $2.00) = $48.00
2011	1.15	2.10	(24 × $1.15) + (12 × $2.10) = $52.80
2012	1.40	2.20	(24 × $1.40) + (12 × $2.20) = $60.00

Using the numbers from the table and the following formula, we can calculate a price index to measure the inflation rate.

$$\text{Price index} = \frac{\text{Cost of market basket in current year}}{\text{Cost of market basket in base year}} \times 100$$

The year 2010 is designated as the base year, so its value is set equal to 100.

Year	Price Index
2010	$48/$48 × 100 = 100
2011	$52.80/$48 × 100 = 110
2012	$60/$48 × 100 = 125

A comparison of the price indices shows that between 2010 and 2011, prices increased an average of 10 percent. In addition, between 2010 and 2012, 25 percent inflation occurred.

$$\text{Price index} = \frac{\text{Cost of market basket in 2012}}{\text{Cost of market basket in 2010}} \times 100$$
$$= \frac{\$60}{\$48} \times 100 = 125$$

That is, the price index for 2012 compared with 2010 is 125. Therefore, using the price index formula, we can say that prices are 25 percent higher in 2012 than they were in 2010, the base year.

Unfortunately, not all prices move by the same amount or in the same direction. Consequently, we need to calculate an average of the many price changes. This calculation is complicated by several factors. First, goods and services change in quality over time, so the observed price change may, in reality, reflect a quality change in the product rather than the purchasing power of the dollar. A $300 television set today is dramatically better than a television set in 1950. Second, new products come on the market and old products occasionally disappear. For example, color TV sets did not exist in 1950 but are a major consumer item now. How can we calculate changes in prices over time when some products did not even exist in the earlier period?

Clearly, calculating a price index is not a simple, direct process. As you can see from the *In the News* article ("A Better CPI"), many factors can potentially distort the CPI.

producer price index
a measure of the cost of goods and services bought by firms

Producer Price Index

Economists also calculate the **producer price index**—a measure of the cost of goods and services bought by firms. Because firms often pass on part of their costs to consumers, this measure is useful in predicting changes in the CPI.

GDP Deflator Versus CPI

Is the CPI or the GDP deflator a better indicator of inflation? Or does it not really matter which one we use? In Exhibit 2, we see that the two mea-

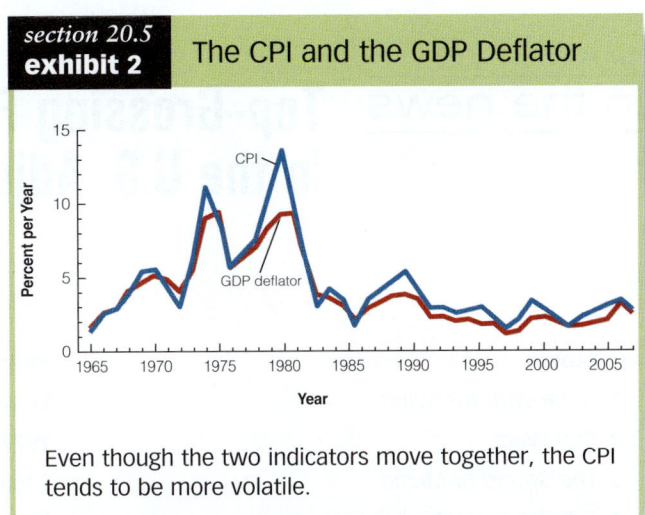

section 20.5 exhibit 2 The CPI and the GDP Deflator

Even though the two indicators move together, the CPI tends to be more volatile.

SOURCES: U.S. Department of Labor; U.S. Department of Commerce, and International Monetary Fund.

sures tend to move in the same direction but that the CPI tends to be much more volatile—it bounces around more than the GDP deflator. However, both measures probably overstate the inflation rate. One important difference between them that can yield different results is that the GDP deflator measures the price of all goods and services that are *produced domestically*, while the CPI measures the goods and services *bought by consumers*. For example, a Porsche produced in Stuttgart, Germany, will show up in the CPI, but it will not show up in the GDP deflator because it was not produced in the U.S. economy. More important, the same is true for the price of oil, because much of U.S. oil is imported. Consequently, oil price increases are fully captured in the CPI but only partially captured in the GDP deflator—partially captured because those increases do add to the cost of production.

However, suppose the price of an airplane or aircraft carrier being produced domestically for the military increases. Because it is produced domestically, its price will show up in the GDP deflator but not in the typical consumer basket—the CPI.

The Price Level over the Years

Unanticipated and sharp changes in the price level are almost universally considered to be "bad" and to require a policy remedy. What is the historical record of changes in the overall U.S. price level? Exhibit 3 shows changes in the consumer price index (CPI), the standard measure of inflation, from 1914 to 2008. Can you believe that in 1940, stamps were

in the news: Top-Grossing Films of All Time in the U.S. Adjusted for Inflation

Movie	Year	Gross Domestic Receipts (millions)	Inflation Adjusted Gross Receipts (millions)
1. Gone with the Wind	1939	$198.7	$1,454.7
2. Star Wars	1977	$461.0	$1,282.5
3. The Sound of Music	1965	$158.7	$1,025.4
4. E.T. The Extra-Terrestrial	1982	$435.1	$1,021.4
5. The Ten Commandments	1956	$65.5	$943.2
6. Titanic	1997	$600.8	$924.1
7. Jaws	1975	$260.0	$922.2
8. Doctor Zhivago	1965	$111.7	$893.8
9. The Exorcist	1973	$232.7	$796.1
10. Snow White and the Seven Dwarfs	1937	$184.9	$784.8

SOURCE: The Movie Times, http://www.the-movie-times.com/thrsdir/alltime.mv?adjusted+ByAG+1.

section 20.5 exhibit 3 The Inflation in the United States, 1914–2008

SOURCE: Bureau of Labor Statistics, 2009.

3 cents per letter, postcards were a penny, the median price of a house was $2,900, and the price of a new car was $650? However, the problem with comparing prices today with prices in the past is that it focuses on the number of dollars it takes to buy something rather than the purchasing power of the dollar. For example, if prices and wages both doubled overnight, raising the price of a quart of milk from $1 to $2, you would be no worse off because you would still work the same number of minutes to buy a quart of milk.

in the news

A Better CPI

The monthly consumer price index (CPI) is the most oft-cited measure of inflation and one of the most important and closely watched statistics in the U.S. economy. It is an indicator of how well the Federal Reserve is doing in achieving and maintaining low inflation, and it also is used to determine cost-of-living adjustments for many government programs, collective bargaining contracts, and individual income tax brackets.

Since 1995, the Bureau of Labor Statistics (BLS) has been eliminating biases that cause the index to overstate inflation. . . . These changes are expected to create a more reliable index. . . . Although this may seem like a small change, the effect of these changes is permanent so that measured inflation will be lower by this amount in all future years.

It is important that the CPI should measure inflation accurately or that the degree of bias be known. Macroeconomic policymakers such as the Fed then can take appropriate steps to keep inflation low, and the public can be informed about their successes and failures in achieving their goal. Also, if the CPI does not measure inflation correctly, cost-of-living adjustments based on it will have different effects from those desired when the commitments to make these adjustments were made. For example, adjusting Social Security benefits based on an upwardly biased CPI may shift spending power from the young toward the old.

The BLS has been studying possible biases in the CPI for a long time. The issue gained national prominence in 1996 when the Congress commissioned a panel of experts on price measurement issues, chaired by Michael Boskin of Stanford University, to examine biases in the CPI. Their report, "Toward a More Accurate Measure of the Cost of Living," identified four major sources of bias and estimated that they caused the CPI to overstate inflation by 1.1 percentage points per year at that time.

If people prefer buying in bulk at discount stores, will the CPI accurately measure inflation? The success of discount stores has grown over the last few years, indicating that for some customers, the reduction in customer service often associated with these megastores does not offset the lower prices, introducing an upward bias into the index.

Substitution Bias

Substitution bias occurs because the CPI measures the price changes of a fixed basket of goods and services and thus does not capture the savings that households enjoy when they change their spending in response to relative price changes of goods and services. For example, a rise in the price of beef leads people to buy more chicken in order to keep their food costs down. . . .

Outlet Bias

This type of bias is similar to substitution bias, but refers to where households shop rather than to what they purchase. Over the past 15 years, for example, the growth of discount stores has helped consumers lower their expenditures by offering high-volume purchases at reduced prices. The expansion of these establishments has not been adequately represented in the CPI, thus creating an upward bias of prices estimated at 0.1 percentage point per year. A similar problem may arise in the future as shopping online becomes more widespread.

New Product Bias

This bias occurs because new products, such as VCRs and cellular phones, are not introduced into

(continued)

in the news A Better CPI (cont.)

the index until they are commonplace items. This means that the substantial price decreases and quality increases that occur during the early years following introduction are not captured by the index. A problem of dealing with this bias is that the BLS can never know in advance which of the many new products introduced each year will be successful and hence worthy of inclusion in the CPI.

Quality Bias

This bias arises because some of any increase in the price of an item may be due to an improvement in quality, rather than being a pure price increase. For example, when car prices rise, this may be due to the addition of seat belts, air bags, or anti-smog devices, or to pure price inflation. In the case of cars, the BLS often uses the price of the new item as an optional feature before it becomes standard equipment as an indicator of what the improvement is worth to consumers. Quality improvements in other areas—such as medical care—are more difficult to measure so that bias is more likely to occur. And features of a product that become mandatory—such as seat belts, which buyers are forced to purchase even if they would prefer not to—are particularly difficult to handle.

The BLS began to address the bias in the CPI even before the Boskin Commission was convened. For example, in 1995 the BLS introduced a new sampling procedure to determine which outlets to visit to obtain price data for specific items and what weights to apply to those item prices. The old procedure put too much weight on items that were temporarily cheap at that outlet, so when their prices rose back to their normal level, this registered as an increase in inflation. That same year, the BLS also revised sampling methods to remove the effects of substituting between brand drugs and generic drugs. . . . Spurred by the work of the Boskin Commission, the BLS introduced further changes to confront substitution and outlet bias.

Since the Fed uses the CPI as an indicator of price inflation, a more accurate index should make anti-inflationary monetary policy more effective. The public will have a better indicator to check how well the Fed is doing its job. If we want our tax and transfer system to be invariant to inflation, an accurate CPI is essential so that the task of adjusting tax and transfer payments to price changes can be done quickly, easily, and without undue dispute.

Ongoing research is necessary to identify biases in the CPI. Changes to this index are ongoing as the BLS strives to maintain an accurate measure of inflation in our dynamic economy. The BLS has reduced the size of the substitution bias and the new product bias by updating the market basket every 2 years rather than every 10 years. Other improvements have also been implemented. Many economists believe that the BLS improvements have cut the inflationary bias in half and it is now less than 1 percent.

SOURCE: Alison Wallace and Brian Motley, "A Better CPI," *Economic Letter*, The Federal Reserve Bank of San Francisco, February 5, 1999. http://www.frbsf.org. Reprinted from the Federal Reserve Bank of San Francisco *Economic Letter* 99–05. The opinions expressed in this article do not necessarily reflect the views of the management of the Federal Reserve Bank of San Francisco, or of the Board of Governors of the Federal Reserve System.

Who Loses with Inflation?

Inflation brings about changes in peoples' purchasing power, and these changes may be either desirable or undesirable. Suppose you retire on a fixed pension of $2,000 per month. Over time, that $2,000 will buy less and less if prices generally rise. Your real income—your income adjusted to reflect changes in purchasing power—falls. Inflation lowers income in real terms for people on fixed-dollar incomes. Likewise, inflation can hurt creditors. For example, suppose a bank loaned someone money for a house, at a 4 percent fixed rate for 20 years, in the early 1960s (a period of low inflation). However, the 1970s was a period of high inflation rates (roughly 10 percent per year). Under this scenario, because the lender did not correctly anticipate the higher rate of inflation, the lender is the victim of unanticipated inflation. That is, the borrower is paying back with dollars that have much less purchasing power than those dollars they borrowed in the early 1960s. Another group that sometimes loses from inflation, at least temporarily, comprises people whose incomes are tied to long-term contracts. If inflation begins shortly after a labor union signs a three-year wage agreement, it may completely eat up the wage gains provided by the contract. The same applies to businesses that agree to sell quantities of one thing, say coal, for a fixed price for a given number of years.

If some people lose because of changing prices, others must gain. Debtors pay back dollars worth less in purchasing power than those borrowed. Corporations that can quickly raise the prices on their goods may have revenue gains greater than their increases in costs, providing additional profits. Wage earners sometimes lose from inflation because wages may rise at a slower rate than the price level. The redistributional impact of inflation is not the result of conscious public policy; it just happens.

The uncertainty that inflation creates can also discourage investment and economic growth. When inflation rates are high, they also tend to vary considerably, which creates a lot of uncertainty. This uncertainty complicates planning for businesses and households, which is vital to capital formation, as well as adding an inflation risk premium to long-term interest rates.

Moreover, inflation can raise one nation's price level relative to price levels in other countries. In turn, this shift can make financing the purchase of foreign goods difficult, or it can decrease the value of the national currency relative to that of other countries.

Costs of High Inflation

Predictably low rates of inflation, while still a problem, are considerably better than high and variable inflation rates. A slow predictable rate of inflation makes predicting future price increases relatively easy. Consequently, setting interest rates will be an easier task and the redistribution effects of inflation will be minimized. In addition, high and variable inflation rates make it almost impossible to set long-term contracts because prices and interest rates may be changing by the day, or even by the hour in the case of **hyperinflation**—extremely high rates of inflation for sustained periods of time.

In its extreme form, inflation can lead to a complete erosion of faith in the value of the pieces of paper we commonly call money. In Germany, after both world wars, prices rose so fast that people in some cases finally refused to take paper money, insisting instead on payment in goods or metals, whose prices tend to move predictably with inflation. Unchecked inflation can feed on itself and may ultimately lead to hyperinflation of 300 percent or more per year. We saw these rapid rates of inflation in Argentina in the 1980s and Brazil in the 1990s. Most economists believe we can live quite well in an environment of low, steady inflation, but no economist believes we can prosper with high, variable inflation.

hyperinflation
extremely high rates of inflation for sustained periods of time

menu costs
the costs imposed on a firm from changing listed prices

shoe-leather cost
the cost incurred when individuals reduce their money holdings because of inflation

Other Costs of Inflation

Another cost of inflation is the cost incurred by firms as a result of being forced to change prices more frequently. For example, a restaurant might have to print new menus, or a department or mail-order store may have to print new catalogs, to reflect changing prices. These costs are called **menu costs;** they are the costs of changing posted prices. In some South American economies in the 1980s, inflation increased at more than 300 percent per year, with prices changing on a daily, or even hourly, basis in some cases. Imagine how large the menu costs could be in an economy such as that!

The **shoe-leather cost** of inflation is the cost of going to and from the bank to check on your assets (so often that you wear out the leather on your shoes). Specifically, high rates of inflation erode the value of a currency, which means that people will want to hold less currency—perhaps going to the ATM once a week rather than twice a month. That is, the higher inflation rates lead to higher nominal interest rates, which may induce more individuals to put money in the bank rather than allowing it to depreciate in their pockets. So, the cost is really the time and convenience sacrificed to keep less money on hand than you would if inflation were not a factor. The effects of shoe-leather costs of inflation, like those of menu costs, are modest in countries with low inflation rates but can be quite large in countries where inflation is substantial.

Inflation and Interest Rates

The interest rate is usually reported as the **nominal interest rate,** which means it is not adjusted for inflation. We determine the **real interest rate** by taking the nominal rate of interest and subtracting the inflation rate:

Real interest rate = Nominal interest rate − Inflation rate

For example, if the nominal interest rate was 5 percent, and the inflation rate was 3 percent, the real interest rate would be 2 percent.

If people can correctly anticipate inflation, they will behave in a manner that will largely protect them against loss. However, if the inflation is not correctly anticipated (it is not an easy task to predict inflation), inflation will still redistribute income. Consider the creditor who believes that the overall price level will rise 6 percent a year, based on experience in the immediate past. Would that creditor lend money to someone at a 5 percent rate of interest? No. A 5 percent rate of interest means that a person borrowing $1,000 now will pay back $1,050 ($1,000 plus 5 percent of $1,000) one year from now. But if prices go up 6 percent, it will take $1,060 to buy what $1,000 does today ($1,060 is 6 percent more than $1,000). Thus, the creditor lending at 5 percent will get paid back an amount ($1,050) less than the purchasing power of the original loan ($1,060) at the time it was paid back. The real interest rate would actually be negative. To protect themselves, creditors will demand a rate of interest large enough to compensate for the deteriorating value of money.

Failure to understand the difference between nominal and real interest rates is critical. In most economic decisions, it is the real rate of interest that matters because it is this rate that shows how much borrowers pay and lenders receive in terms of purchasing power—goods and services money can buy. Investors and lenders will do best when the real interest rates are high.

When the nominal interest rate is high, the inflation rate tends to be high; and when the nominal interest rate is low, the inflation rate tends to be low. Why? The reason is that when inflation is high, borrowers offer and lenders demand higher nominal interest rates to compensate for the falling value of money in the future. When the inflation rate is low, borrowers offer and lenders demand lower nominal interest rates because the value of money (purchasing power) is falling less quickly. Therefore, the tendency is for nominal interest rates and inflation rates to move together—high inflation rates mean high nominal interest rates, and low inflation rates mean low nominal interest rates.

> **nominal interest rate**
> the reported interest rate that is not adjusted for inflation
>
> **real interest rate**
> the nominal interest rate minus the inflation rate; also called the inflation-adjusted interest rate

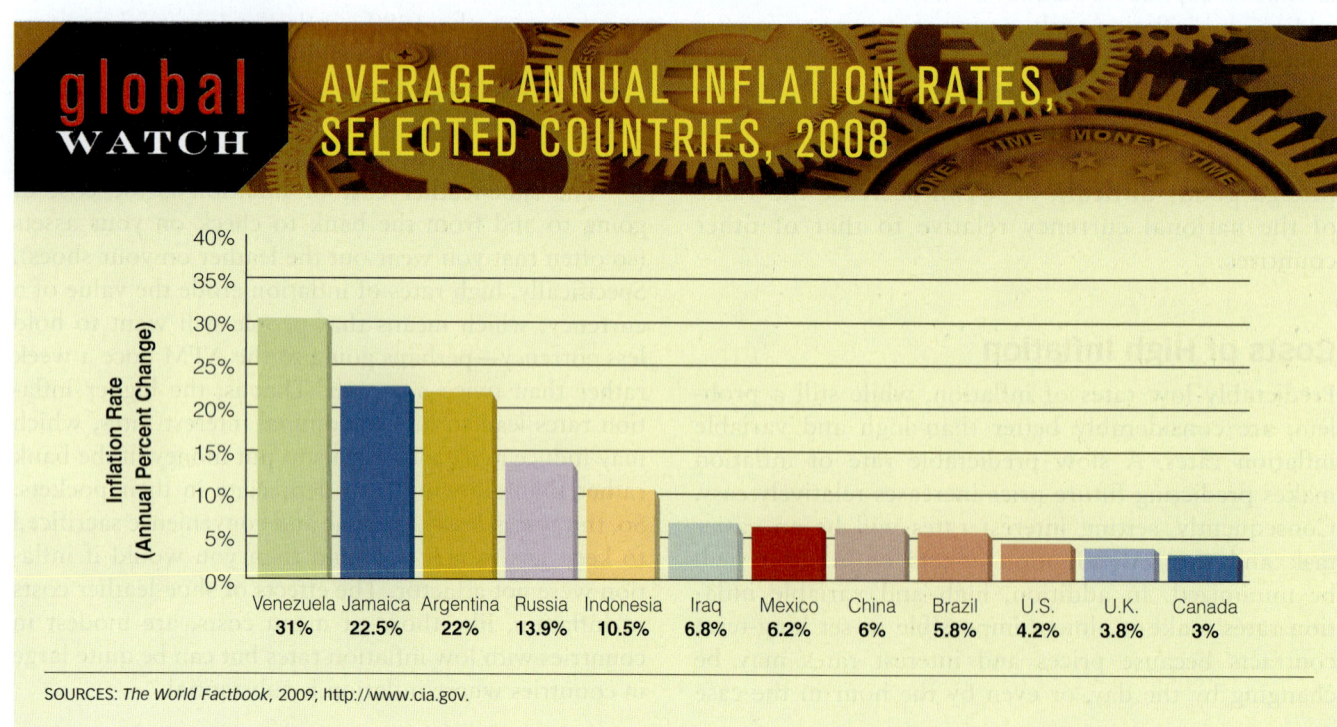

global WATCH — AVERAGE ANNUAL INFLATION RATES, SELECTED COUNTRIES, 2008

Country	Inflation Rate
Venezuela	31%
Jamaica	22.5%
Argentina	22%
Russia	13.9%
Indonesia	10.5%
Iraq	6.8%
Mexico	6.2%
China	6%
Brazil	5.8%
U.S.	4.2%
U.K.	3.8%
Canada	3%

SOURCES: *The World Factbook*, 2009; http://www.cia.gov.

Use what you've LEARNED: INFLATION

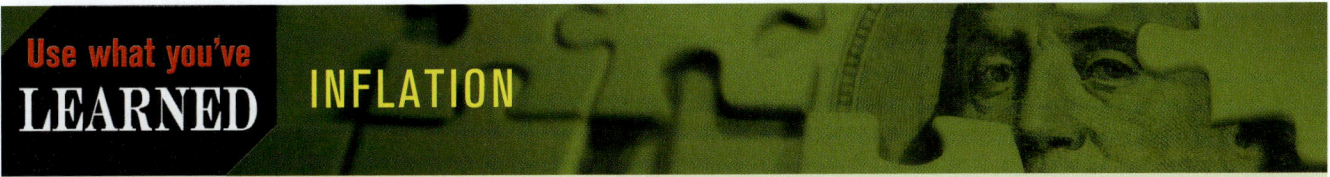

Q Evaluate the following three statements regarding what happens during inflation: (1) People have less money to spend, (2) fewer goods are available, and (3) people must pay more money for goods purchased.

A Of the three statements, only one is correct: With inflation, we must, on average, pay more money for the goods we purchase. Inflation does not necessarily mean we have fewer goods but rather that, on net, these goods have higher price tags. Inflation does not necessarily mean that people have less money to spend. Employees and unions will bargain for higher wages when inflation is a factor.

Do Creditors Always Lose During Inflation?

Usually, lenders are able to anticipate inflation with reasonable accuracy. For example, in the late 1970s, when the inflation rate was more than 10 percent a year, nominal interest rates on a 90-day Treasury bill were relatively high. In 2002, with low inflation rates, the nominal interest rate was relatively low. If the inflation rate is anticipated accurately, new creditors will not lose nor will debtors gain from a change in the inflation rate. However, nominal interest rates and real interest rates do not always run together. For example, in periods of high *unexpected* inflation, the nominal interest rates can be high when the real interest rates are low or even negative.

Protecting Ourselves from Inflation

Increasingly, groups try to protect themselves from inflation by means of cost-of-living clauses in contracts. Many long-term contracts between firms and unions include a cost of living allowance (COLA) that automatically increases when the consumer price index (CPI) increases. With these clauses, laborers automatically get wage increases that reflect rising prices. The same is true of many pensioners, including those on Social Security. Personal income taxes likewise are now indexed (adjusted) for inflation. However, some of the tax code is still not indexed for inflation. These factors affect the incentives to work, save, and invest.

Use what you've LEARNED: INFLATION AND CAPITAL GAINS TAXES

In an environment of inflation, the tax code can distort market signals and may lead to a reduction in saving, lending, and investment. To many economists, the problem stems from *capital gains tax* (a tax on a person's assets) being taxed in nominal terms rather than in real terms (adjusted for inflation). For example, suppose you sold a stock in 1980 for $50,000 that you bought in 1970 for $40,000. In real terms, adjusted for inflation, you would have lost money because the 25 percent increase in the stock price would be less than the percentage change in the inflation rate (over 100%). In fact, inflation was so high in the 1970s you would have lost money on your stock in real terms and then have to pay capital gains tax on the nominal gains—$10,000 ($50,000−$40,000)—ouch! Thus, many economists believe capital gains should be taxed on real gains. In this case, you could write off capital losses because you actually lost money on your investment in real terms. These costs are not just a redistribution cost but can impact economic growth if the taxes are discouraging saving and investment.

Use what you've LEARNED
ANTICIPATED INFLATION AND INTEREST RATES

Q Suppose you had a 30-year fixed-interest mortgage on a home you purchased six years ago. In the meantime, the inflation rate has fallen considerably and probably will not reach that higher level again. Did you get a good interest rate on your loan?

A No. You will be paying a higher interest rate to borrow money than others who borrowed money more recently. Of course, you could refinance to get a lower interest rate, but you would need to calculate how much you would save on your loan and compare it to the cost of refinancing to determine whether it would be worthwhile.

Some economists argue that we should go one step further and index everything, meaning that all contractual arrangements would be adjusted frequently to take account of changing prices. Such an arrangement might reduce the impact of inflation, but it would also entail additional contracting costs (and not every good—most notably, currency—can be indexed). An alternative approach has been to try to stop inflation through various policies relating to the amount of government spending, tax rates, and the amount of money created. **Wage and price controls**—legislation limiting wage and price increases—offer still another approach to the inflation problem.

wage and price controls
legislation used to combat inflation by limiting changes in wages and prices

SECTION CHECK

1. Unanticipated inflation causes unpredictable transfers of wealth and reduces the efficiency of the market system by distorting price signals.
2. A price-level index allows us to compare prices paid for goods and services over time by creating a measure of how many dollars it would take to maintain a constant purchasing power over time. The consumer price index (CPI) is the best-known index.
3. The GDP deflator is a price index that measures the average level of prices of all final goods and services produced in the economy.
4. The consumer price index fails to account for increased quality of goods, introduction of new goods, or changes in the relative quantities of goods purchased.
5. Inflation generally hurts creditors and those on fixed incomes and pensions; debtors generally benefit from inflation.
6. The nominal interest rate is the actual amount of interest you pay. The real interest rate is the nominal rate minus the inflation rate.
7. Wage earners attempt to keep pace with inflation by demanding higher wages each year or by indexing their annual wage to inflation.

1. How does price level stability reduce the difficulties buyers and sellers have in coordinating their plans?
2. Why does the consumer price index tend to overstate inflation if the quality of goods and services is rising over time?
3. Why would the CPI take into account some goods imported from other countries, but not take into account some goods produced domestically, unlike the GDP deflator?
4. Why doesn't the consumer price index accurately adjust for the cost-of-living effects of a tripling in the price of bananas relative to the prices of other fruits?

5. What will happen to the nominal interest rate if the real interest rate rises, *ceteris paribus*? What if inflation increases, *ceteris paribus*?
6. Say you owe money to Big River Bank. Will you gain or lose from an unanticipated decrease in inflation?
7. How does a variable interest rate loan "insure" the lender against unanticipated increases in inflation?
8. Why will neither creditors nor debtors lose from inflation if it is correctly anticipated?
9. How could inflation make people turn to exchange by barter?

SECTION 20.6 Economic Fluctuations

- What are short-term economic fluctuations?
- What are the four stages of a business cycle?
- What is the difference between a recession and a depression?

Short-Term Fluctuations in Economic Growth

The aggregate amount of economic activity in the United States and most other nations has increased markedly over time, even on a per capita basis, indicating economic growth. Short-term fluctuations in the level of economic activity also occur. We sometimes call these short-term fluctuations **business cycles.** Exhibit 1 illustrates the distinction between long-term economic growth and short-term economic fluctuations. Over a long period, the line representing economic activity slopes upward, indicating increasing real output. Over short periods, however, downward, as well as upward, output changes occur. Business cycles refer to the short-term ups and downs in economic activity, not to the long-term trend in output, which in modern times has been upward.

The Phases of a Business Cycle

A business cycle has four phases—expansion, peak, contraction, and trough—as illustrated in Exhibit 2. The period of **expansion** is when output (real GDP) is rising significantly. Usually, during the expansion phase, unemployment is falling and both consumer and business confidence are high. Thus, investment is rising, as are expenditures for expensive durable consumer goods, such as automobiles and household appliances. The **peak** is the point in time when the expansion comes to an end, when output is at the highest point in the cycle. The **contraction** is a period of

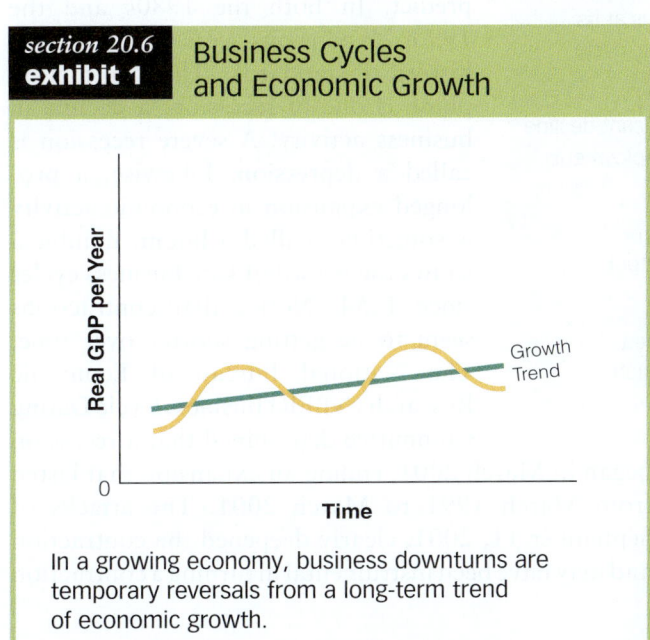

section 20.6 exhibit 1 Business Cycles and Economic Growth

In a growing economy, business downturns are temporary reversals from a long-term trend of economic growth.

business cycles
short-term fluctuations in the economy relative to the long-term trend in output

expansion
when output (real GDP) is rising significantly—the period between the trough of a recession and the next peak

peak
the point in time when expansion comes to an end, that is, when output is at the highest point in the cycle

contraction
when the economy is slowing down—measured from the peak to the trough

section 20.6 exhibit 2 — Four Phases of a Business Cycle

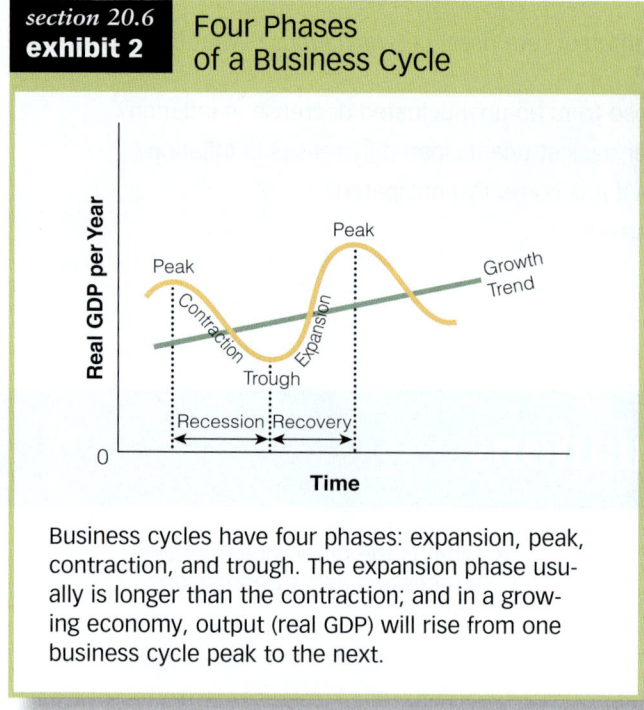

Business cycles have four phases: expansion, peak, contraction, and trough. The expansion phase usually is longer than the contraction; and in a growing economy, output (real GDP) will rise from one business cycle peak to the next.

section 20.6 exhibit 3 — A Historical Record of U.S. Recessions, 1921–2008

Peak	Trough	Length of Recession
January 1920	July 1921	18
May 1923	July 1924	14
October 1926	November 1927	13
August 1929	March 1933	43
May 1937	June 1938	13
February 1945	October 1945	8
November 1948	October 1949	11
July 1953	May 1954	10
August 1957	April 1958	8
April 1960	February 1961	10
December 1969	November 1970	11
November 1973	March 1975	16
January 1980	July 1980	6
July 1981	November 1982	16
July 1990	March 1991	8
March 2001	November 2001	8
December 2007	—	—

SOURCES: National Bureau of Economic Research, Inc., http://www.nber.org/cycles.html; and U.S. Department of Commerce.

falling real output and is usually accompanied by rising unemployment and declining business and consumer confidence. The contraction phase is measured from the peak to the **trough**—the point in time when output stops declining and business activity is at its lowest point in the cycle. Investment spending and expenditures on consumer durable goods fall sharply in a typical contraction. The contraction phase is also called **recession,** a period of significant decline in output and employment (lasting more than a few months). Unemployment is relatively high at the trough, although the actual maximum amount of unemployment may not occur exactly at the trough. Often, unemployment remains fairly high well into the expansion phase. The expansion phase is measured from the trough to the peak.

trough
the point in time when output stops declining, that is, when business activity is at its lowest point in the cycle

recession
a period of significant decline in output and employment

depression
severe recession or contraction in output

boom
period of prolonged economic expansion

How Long Does a Business Cycle Last?

The length of any given business cycle is not uniform. Because it does not have the regularity that the term *cycle* implies, economists often use the term *economic fluctuation* rather than *business cycle.* In addition, economic fluctuations are almost impossible to predict. In both the 1980s and the 1990s, expansions were quite long by historical standards. The contraction phase is one of recession, a decline in business activity. A severe recession is called a **depression.** Likewise, a prolonged expansion in economic activity is sometimes called a **boom.** Exhibit 3 shows the record of U.S. business cycles since 1854. Notice that contractions seem to be getting shorter over time. The National Bureau of Economic Research (NBER) Business Cycle Dating Committee determined that a recession began in March 2001, ending an expansion that lasted from March 1991 to March 2001. The attacks of September 11, 2001, clearly deepened the contraction and may have been instrumental in turning a contraction into a recession. The committee met in November of 2008 and determined that the economy peaked in December 2007, marking the end of a 73-month expansion and the beginning of a recession. There is a delay before the NBER announces the beginning or end of a recession, because of the complexities involved in gathering and evaluating the data. So the official beginning and end dates of a recession are not known until many months later.

Seasonal Fluctuations Affect Economic Activity

The determinants of cyclical fluctuations in the economy are the major thrust of the next several chapters, and some fluctuation in economic activity reflects seasonal patterns. Business activity, whether measured by production or by the sale of goods, tends to be high in the two months before the winter holidays and somewhat lower in summertime, when many families are on vacation. Within individual industries, of course, seasonal fluctuations in output often are extremely pronounced, agriculture being the best example. Often, key economic statistics, such as unemployment rates, are seasonally adjusted, meaning the numbers are modified to account for normal seasonal fluctuations. Thus, seasonally adjusted unemployment rates in summer months are below actual unemployment rates, because employment is normally high in summertime due to the inflow of school-age workers into the labor force.

> **leading economic indicators**
> factors that economists at the Commerce Department have found typically change before changes in economic activity

Forecasting Cyclical Changes

The farmer and the aviator rely heavily on weather forecasters for information on climatic conditions in planning their activities. Similarly, businesses, government agencies, and, to a lesser extent, consumers rely on economic forecasts to learn of forthcoming developments in the business cycle. If it looks as if the economy will continue in an expansionary phase, businesses may expand production to meet a perceived forthcoming need; if it looks as if contraction is coming, businesses may decide to be more cautious.

Forecasting Models

Using theoretical models, which will be discussed in later chapters, economists gather statistics on economic activity in the immediate past, including, for example, consumer expenditures, business inventories, the supply of money, governmental expenditures, tax revenues, and so on. Using past historical relationships between these factors and the overall level of economic activity (which form the basis of the economic theories), they formulate *econometric models*. Statistics from the immediate past are plugged into the model, and forecasts are made. Because human behavior changes, and our assumptions about certain future developments may not be correct, our numbers are imperfect, and our econometric models are not always accurate. But like the weather forecasts, although the econometric models are not perfect, they are helpful.

Leading Economic Indicators

One less sophisticated but useful forecasting tool is watching trends in **leading economic indicators.** Some types of economic activity change before the economy as a whole changes. If in March these activities show an increase after having declined for several months, past experience suggests that the entire output will start rising after a few months, perhaps in July or August. About a dozen such leading indicators exist, including the lengths of the average workweek, the size of the nation's money supply, prices of common stocks, the number of new businesses formed, and new orders for plants and equipment. The Department of Commerce combines all these into an index of leading indicators. If the index rises sharply for two or three months, it is likely (but not certain) that increases in the overall level of activity will follow.

Since the development of the leading economic indicators, the composite index of leading economic indicators has never failed to give some warning of an economic downturn. Unfortunately, the lead time has varied widely. The composite index turned down 23 months prior to the 1957–1958 recession but gave only a three-month warning before the 1981–1982 slump. This variance in lead time can cause particular policy problems. Specifically, the use of leading economic indicators to predict future trends can make policy decisions less accurate. For example, if the federal government responds with policies to combat the recession as soon as the leading economic indicators begin predicting a recession, then the recession that would have occurred may fail to materialize. On the other hand, a self-fulfilling prophecy may result if businesses respond with cutbacks in orders for plants and equipment as soon as the leading economic indicators begin predicting a recession.

The economic indicators do provide a warning of a likely downturn, but they do not provide accurate information on the depth or duration of the downturn.

SECTION CHECK

1. Business cycles (or economic fluctuations) are short-term fluctuations in the amount of economic activity, relative to the long-term growth trend in output.
2. The four phases of a business cycle are expansion, peak, contraction, and trough.
3. Recessions occur during the contraction phase of a business cycle. Severe, long-term recessions are called depressions.
4. The economy often goes through short-term contraction even during a long-term growth trend.

1. Why would you expect unemployment to fall during an economy's expansionary phase and to rise during a contractionary phase?
2. Why is the output of investment goods and durable consumer goods more sensitive to the business cycle than that of most goods?
3. Why might the unemployment rate fall after output starts recovering during the expansion phase of the business cycle?

Interactive Chapter Summary

Fill in the blanks:

1. Three major macroeconomic goals are maintaining employment at _____ levels; maintaining prices at a(n) _____ level; and achieving a(n) _____ rate of economic growth.
2. Concern over both unemployment and price instability led to the passage of the _____, in which the United States committed itself to policies designed to reduce unemployment in a manner consistent with price stability.
3. With high rates of unemployment, society loses some potential _____ of goods and services.
4. The unemployment rate is the number of people officially _____ divided by _____.
5. The labor force is the number of people over the age of 16 who are either _____ or _____.
6. _____ workers, who have not actively sought work for four weeks, are not counted as unemployed; instead, they fall out of the _____.
7. Some people working overtime or extra jobs might be considered to be _____ employed.
8. The four main categories of unemployed workers include job _____ (temporarily laid off or fired), job _____ (quit), _____ (worked before and now reentering the labor force), and _____ (entering the labor force for the first time).
9. _____ typically account for the largest fraction of those unemployed.
10. In the short run, a reduction in unemployment may come at the expense of a higher rate of _____, especially if the economy is close to full capacity.

11. Trying to match employees with jobs quickly may lead to significant inefficiencies because of _____ between a worker's skill level and the level of skill required for a job.

12. The duration of unemployment tends to be greater when the amount of unemployment is _____ and smaller when the amount of unemployment is _____.

13. The percentage of the population that is in the labor force is called the _____ rate.

14. Frictional unemployment is _____ term and results from the _____ turnover in the labor market.

15. Frictional unemployment tends to be somewhat _____ in periods of low unemployment, when job opportunities are plentiful.

16. If individuals seeking jobs and employers seeking workers had better information about each other, the amount of frictional unemployment would be considerably _____.

17. _____ unemployment reflects the existence of persons who lack the necessary skills for jobs that are available.

18. _____ unemployment is the most volatile form of unemployment.

19. Most of the attempts to solve the unemployment problem have placed an emphasis on increasing _____.

20. Job retraining programs have the potential to reduce _____ unemployment.

21. The natural rate of unemployment roughly equals the sum of _____ and _____ unemployment when they are at a maximum.

22. One can view unemployment rates below the _____ rate as reflecting the existence of a below-average level of frictional and structural unemployment.

23. The natural rate of unemployment is the median, or "typical," unemployment rate, equal to the sum of _____ and _____ unemployment when they are at a maximum.

24. The natural rate of unemployment may change over time as _____, _____, _____, and other conditions vary.

25. When all of the economy's labor resources and other resources, such as capital, are fully employed, the economy is said to be producing its _____ level of output.

26. When the economy is experiencing cyclical unemployment, the unemployment rate is _____ than the natural rate.

27. The economy can _____ exceed potential output as workers put in overtime or moonlight by taking on extra employment.

28. Without price stability, consumers and producers will experience more difficulty in _____ their plans and decisions.

29. In general, the only thing that can cause a sustained increase in the rate of inflation is a(n) _____ rate of growth in money.

30. The _____ is the standard measure of inflation.

31. We must adjust for the changing purchasing power of the dollar by constructing a price _____.

32. The best-known price index is the _____, which provides a measure of the trend in the prices of goods and services purchased for consumption purposes.

33. The GDP deflator measures the average level of prices of all _____ goods and services produced in the economy.

34. The CPI is the price index that is most relevant to _____ trying to evaluate their changing financial position over time.

35. A price index is equal to the cost of the chosen market basket in the _____ year, divided by the cost of the same market basket in the _____ year, times 100.

36. While the CPI and the GDP deflator move together, the CPI tends to be _____ volatile.

37. Retirees on fixed pensions, creditors, and those whose incomes are tied to long-term contracts can be hurt by inflation because inflation _____ the purchasing power of the money they receive.

38. The _____ that inflation creates can discourage investment and economic growth.

39. Inflation can _____ one nation's price level relative to price levels in other countries, which can lead to difficulties in financing the purchase of foreign goods or to a decline in the value of the national currency relative to that of other countries.

40. In periods of high and variable inflation, households and firms have a difficult time distinguishing changes in _____ prices from changes in the general price level, distorting the information that flows from price signals.

41. _____ costs are the costs of changing posted prices.

42. _____ costs are the costs of checking on your assets.

43. The real interest rate equals the _____ interest rate minus the _____ rate.

44. In most economic decisions, it is the _____ rate of interest that matters, because it shows how much borrowers pay and lenders receive in terms of purchasing power.

45. The _____ the interest rate, the greater the quantity of funds people will demand, *ceteris paribus*; the _____ the interest rate, the greater the quantity of loanable funds supplied, *ceteris paribus*.

46. When creditors start expecting future inflation, there will be a(n) _____ shift in the supply curve of loanable funds. Likewise, demanders of funds (borrowers) are more anxious to borrow because they think they will pay their loans back in dollars of lesser purchasing power than the dollars they borrowed. Thus, the demand for funds increases.

47. If the inflation rate is _____ anticipated, new creditors do not lose, nor do debtors gain, from inflation.

48. Groups try to protect themselves from inflation by using _____ clauses in contracts.

49. The tendency is for nominal interest rates and inflation rates to move in the _____ direction.

50. Business cycles refer to the _____ fluctuations in economic activity, not to the _____ trend in output.

51. A business cycle has four phases: _____, _____, _____, and _____.

52. Expansion occurs when output is _____ significantly, unemployment is _____, and both consumer and business confidence are _____.

53. The _____ is when an expansion comes to an end, that is, when output is at the highest point in the business cycle; while the _____ is the point in time when output stops declining, that is, when business activity is at its lowest point in the business cycle.

54. Seasonally adjusted unemployment rates in summer months are _____ actual unemployment rates because unemployment is normally _____ in summertime as a result of the inflow of school-age workers into the labor force.

55. Businesses, government agencies, and, to a lesser extent, consumers rely on economic _____ to learn of forthcoming developments in the business cycles.

56. If the index of _____ increases sharply for two or three months, it is likely (but not certain) that increases in the overall level of activity will follow.

57. Even though the leading economic indicators do provide a warning of a likely downturn, they do not provide accurate information on the _____ or _____ of the downturn.

Answers: 1. high; stable; high 2. Employment Act of 1946 3. output 4. unemployed; the civilian labor force 5. employed; unemployed 6. Discouraged; labor force 7. over 8. losers; leavers; reentrants; new entrants 9. Job losers 10. inflation 11. mismatches 12. high; low 13. labor force participation 14. short; normal 15. greater 16. lower 17. Structural 18. Cyclical 19. aggregate demand 20. structural 21. frictional; structural 22. natural 23. frictional; structural 24. technological; demographic; institutional 25. potential 26. greater 27. temporarily 28. coordinating 29. high 30. consumer price index 31. index 32. consumer price index 33. final 34. households 35. current; base 36. more 37. erodes 38. uncertainty 39. raise 40. relative 41. Menu 42. Shoe-leather 43. nominal; inflation 44. real 45. lower; higher 46. leftward 47. accurately 48. cost-of-living 49. same 50. short-term; long-term 51. expansion; peak; contraction; trough 52. rising; falling; high 53. peak; trough 54. below 55. forecasts 56. leading indicators 57. depth; duration

Key Terms and Concepts

real gross domestic product (RGDP) 563
Employment Act of 1946 563
unemployment rate 564
labor force 564
discouraged worker 566
job loser 566
job leaver 566
reentrant 566
new entrant 566
underemployment 567
labor force participation rate 568
frictional unemployment 569
structural unemployment 570
cyclical unemployment 570
natural rate of unemployment 571
potential output 571
minimum wage rate 573
efficiency wage model 574
price level 576
inflation 576
deflation 577
relative price 577
price index 578

consumer price index (CPI) 578
GDP deflator 578
producer price index 579
hyperinflation 583
menu costs 583
shoe-leather cost 583

nominal interest rate 584
real interest rate 584
wage and price controls 586
business cycles 587
expansion 587
peak 587

contraction 587
trough 588
recession 588
depression 588
boom 588
leading economic indicators 589

Section Check Answers

20.1 Macroeconomic Goals

1. **What are the three major economic goals of most societies?**

   The three major economic goals of most societies are (1) maintaining employment at high levels, so that jobs are relatively plentiful and financial suffering from lack of income is relatively uncommon; (2) price stability, so consumers and producers can make better decisions; and (3) achieving a high rate of economic growth, so output, and therefore income and consumption, increases over time.

2. **What is the Employment Act of 1946? Why was it significant?**

   The Employment Act of 1946 was a law that committed the federal government to policies designed to reduce unemployment in a manner consistent with price stability. It was significant as the first formal government acknowledgment of these primary macroeconomic goals.

20.2 Employment and Unemployment

1. **What happens to the unemployment rate when the number of unemployed people increases, *ceteris paribus*? When the labor force grows, *ceteris paribus*?**

   The unemployment rate is defined as the number of people officially unemployed divided by the labor force. Therefore, the unemployment rate rises as the number of unemployed people increases and it falls when the labor force grows, *ceteris paribus*.

2. **How might the official unemployment rate understate the "true" degree of unemployment? How might it overstate it?**

   The official unemployment rate understates the "true" degree of unemployment by not including discouraged workers as unemployed, by counting part-time workers who cannot find full-time jobs as "fully" employed, and by counting those employed in jobs that underutilize worker skills as "fully" employed.

   It overstates the "true" degree of unemployment by not counting those working overtime or multiple jobs as "overemployed," by counting those employed in the underground economy as unemployed, and by including those just "going through the motions" of job search to maintain unemployment benefits or other government benefits as unemployed.

3. **Why might the fraction of the unemployed who are job leavers be higher in a period of strong labor demand?**

   In a period of strong labor demand, people would be more confident of their ability to find other jobs, and therefore they would be more likely to leave (quit) their current jobs.

4. **Suppose you live in a community of 100 people. If 80 people are over 16 years old and 72 people are willing and able to work, what is the unemployment rate in this community?**

   The unemployment rate in this community is the number unemployed (8) divided by the labor force (80), or 10 percent.

5. **What would happen to the unemployment rate if a substantial group of unemployed people started going to school full time? What would happen to the size of the labor force?**

   Full-time students are not considered part of the labor force, so the labor force, the number officially unemployed, and the unemployment rate would all fall if a substantial group of unemployed people became full-time students.

6. **What happens to the unemployment rate when officially unemployed people become discouraged workers? Does anything happen to employment in this case?**

   When officially unemployed workers become discouraged workers, they stop seeking jobs and are no longer counted as either part of the labor force or as unemployed, reducing the unemployment rate. However, since they do not find jobs, there is no effect on employment as a result.

20.3 Types of Unemployment

1. **Why do we want some frictional unemployment?**
   We want some frictional unemployment because we want human resources employed in areas of higher productivity, and some period of job search (frictional unemployment), rather than taking the first job offered, can allow workers to find more productive employment.

2. **Why might a job retraining program be a more useful policy to address structural unemployment than to address frictional unemployment?**
   Structural unemployment reflects people who lack the necessary skills for the jobs available, rather than a temporary period of search between jobs. A job retraining program to develop skills to match the jobs available addresses such structural unemployment, not frictional unemployment.

3. **What is the traditional government policy "cure" for cyclical unemployment?**
   The traditional government policy "cure" for cyclical unemployment is to adopt policies designed to increase aggregate demand for goods and services.

4. **What types of unemployment are present at full employment (at the natural rate of unemployment)?**
   At full employment (at the natural rate of unemployment), both frictional and structural unemployment, but not cyclical unemployment, are present.

5. **Why might frictional unemployment be higher in a period of plentiful jobs (low unemployment)?**
   In a period of plentiful jobs, frictional unemployment can be higher because job opportunities are plentiful, which stimulates mobility between jobs, which, in turn, increases frictional unemployment.

6. **If the widespread introduction of the automobile caused a productive buggy whip maker to lose his job, would he be structurally unemployed?**
   If the buggy whip maker's skills were not in demand in other industries and they learned no new transferable skills from the old job, this would result in structural unemployment.

7. **If a fall in demand for domestic cars causes auto workers to lose their jobs in Michigan, while plenty of jobs are available for lumberjacks in Montana, what kind of unemployment results?**
   This would be an example of structural unemployment, resulting from skills mismatched to the jobs available.

20.4 Reasons for Unemployment

1. **What are the three reasons for wages to fail to balance labor supply and labor demand?**
   Minimum wages, unions, and efficiency wages can each lead to a failure to balance labor supply and demand, by leading to wages for some workers that are above their opportunity costs, and increasing unemployment.

2. **What is an efficiency wage?**
   An efficiency wage is a wage that is greater than the equilibrium wage. Its intent is to reduce the costs of turnover, absenteeism, and shirking, and increase worker quality and morale, thereby increasing productivity and reducing costs. If the increased productivity and reduced costs that result outweigh the higher wage costs, producers' profits will rise.

3. **How do search costs lead to prolonged periods of unemployment?**
   Because employers offer different jobs, compensation packages, and working conditions, and workers differ in skills and preferences, matching up workers to appropriate jobs requires a great deal of information. The search for this information entails frictional unemployment, which can also be thought of as employment in gathering information, which, in some cases, can lead to prolonged periods of unemployment.

4. **Why would higher unemployment compensation in a country like France lead to higher rates of unemployment?**
   Unemployment insurance lowers the opportunity cost to a worker from being unemployed, increasing the duration of unemployment and the unemployment rate. Higher unemployment insurance payments will decrease the opportunity cost of remaining unemployed, tending to induce the duration of unemployment and raise the unemployment rate.

5. **Does new technology increase unemployment?**
   New technology can increase unemployment among those whose skills are replaced by that technology. However, it also creates new jobs manufacturing, servicing, and repairing the new equipment, and, by lowering costs, new technology frees up more income to demand other goods and services, creating jobs in those industries.

20.5 Inflation

1. How does price level stability reduce the difficulties buyers and sellers have in coordinating their plans?

Price level instability increases the difficulties buyers and sellers have in coordinating their plans by reducing their certainty about what price changes mean—do they reflect changes in relative prices or changes in inflation? Eliminating this uncertainty makes the meaning of price changes clearer, allowing buyers and sellers to better coordinate their plans through the price system. High and variable rates of inflation also interact with the tax code in ways which distort incentives and lead people to invest resources trying to protect themselves against inflation rather than in socially productive activities.

2. Why does the consumer price index tend to overstate inflation if the quality of goods and services is rising over time?

The consumer price index does not adjust for most quality increases that take place in goods and services. Therefore, higher prices that actually reflect increased quality are counted as higher prices for a given quality, and as a result the consumer price index overstates increases in the cost of living.

3. Why would the CPI take into account some goods imported from other countries, but not take into account some goods produced domestically, unlike the GDP deflator?

The CPI measures the prices of goods and services bought by U.S. consumers, and some goods consumed by U.S. consumers are imported from other countries. The CPI also fails to take into account those goods produced domestically that are not purchased by U.S. consumers, such as investment goods purchased by businesses and military goods bought by the government. The GDP deflator, on the other hand, takes into account all the goods produced in the United States, whether purchased directly by consumers or not.

4. Why doesn't the consumer price index accurately adjust for the cost-of-living effects of a tripling in the price of bananas relative to the prices of other fruits?

The consumer price index assumes that people continue to consume the same number of bananas as in the base year (survey period). Therefore, the cost of the banana component of the consumer price index triples when the price of bananas triples. However, in fact, consumers will substitute other fruits that become relatively cheaper as a result of the banana price increase; so this component of their cost of living has not actually increased as fast as banana prices.

5. What will happen to the nominal interest rate if the real interest rate rises, *ceteris paribus*? What if inflation increases, *ceteris paribus*?

The real interest rate is the nominal interest rate minus the inflation rate. Alternatively, the nominal interest rate is the sum of the desired real interest rate and the expected inflation rate. If either the real interest rate or the rate of inflation increases, nominal interest rates will also increase.

6. Say you owe money to Big River Bank. Will you gain or lose from an unanticipated decrease in inflation?

An unanticipated decrease in inflation will mean that the dollars you must pay back on your loan will be worth more than you expected, raising the real interest rate you must pay on that loan, which makes you worse off.

7. How does a variable interest rate loan "insure" the lender against unanticipated increases in inflation?

With a variable interest rate loan, an unanticipated increase in inflation does not reduce the real interest rate received by the lender, but instead increases the nominal interest rate on the loan to compensate for the increased inflation.

8. Why will neither creditors nor debtors lose from inflation if it is correctly anticipated?

Correctly anticipated inflation will be accurately reflected in the terms creditors and debtors agree to, so that neither will lose from inflation. Only unexpected rates of inflation can redistribute wealth between debtors and creditors.

9. How could inflation make people turn to exchange by barter?

If inflation is very rapid, people lose faith in the value of their monetary unit, and this can lead to exchange by barter, because goods can then have a more predictable value than their country's money.

20.6 Economic Fluctuations

1. Why would you expect unemployment to fall during an economy's expansionary phase and to rise during a contractionary phase?

Output increases during an economy's expansion phase. To produce that increased output in the short term requires more workers, which increases employment and reduces the unemployment rate, other things equal.

2. **Why is the output of investment goods and durable consumer goods more sensitive to the business cycle than that of most goods?**

   When output is growing and business confidence is high, investment rises sharply because it appears highly profitable; when incomes and consumer confidence are high, durable goods, whose purchases are often delayed in less prosperous times, rise sharply in demand. In recessions, investment and consumer durables purchases fall sharply, as such projects no longer appear profitable, and plans are put on hold until better times.

3. **Why might the unemployment rate fall after output starts recovering during the expansion phase of the business cycle?**

   Often unemployment remains fairly high well into the expansion phase, because it takes a period of recovery before businesses become convinced that the increasing demand for their output is going to continue, making it profitable to hire added workers.

CHAPTER 20 STUDY GUIDE

True or False:

1. Economic growth is not considered to be positive by all individuals.
2. Economic growth means a growth in per capita dollar output over time.
3. Individuals, because they may differ considerably in their evaluation of the relative importance of certain issues, may disagree about whether certain so-called problems are really problems after all.
4. The unemployment rate is the number of people officially unemployed divided by a country's labor force.
5. Other things being equal, relatively high rates of unemployment are almost universally viewed as bad.
6. The civilian labor force figure includes homemakers, retirees and full-time students.
7. Discouraged workers, who have not actively sought work for four weeks, are not counted as unemployed.
8. By far, the worst employment downturn in U.S. history was the Great Depression.
9. Since 1960, variations in unemployment have tended to be more pronounced than before 1960.
10. People working in the underground economy are counted in labor statistics as unemployed.
11. People looking for full-time work who grudgingly settle for a part-time job are not counted as employed.
12. In the short run, a reduction in unemployment may come at the expense of a higher rate of inflation.
13. Unemployment rates usually differ across different segments of the population, and they vary substantially over time.
14. The duration of unemployment tends to be greater when the amount of unemployment is high and smaller when the amount of unemployment is low.
15. Unemployment means a loss of potential output.
16. When the baby-boom generation began entering the labor force, it raised the labor force participation rate.
17. Frictional unemployment, while not good in itself, is a by-product of a healthy phenomenon; and because it is short lived, it is not generally viewed as a serious problem.
18. Frictional unemployment results from persons being temporarily between jobs.
19. Structural employment can arise from persons being temporarily between jobs.
20. Structural unemployment is difficult to measure.
21. Cyclical unemployment may result because jobs that require particular skills disappear.
22. Given the volatility and dimensions of unemployment, governments often view it as the result of inadequate demand, which is especially correctable through government policies.
23. The natural rate of unemployment roughly equals the sum of frictional and structural unemployment when they are at a maximum.
24. The natural rate of unemployment can change over time.
25. At the natural rate of unemployment, the economy is producing its potential output.
26. When unemployment rises above the natural rate, it reflects the existence of higher frictional unemployment.
27. When the economy is experiencing cyclical unemployment, the unemployment rate is greater than the natural rate.
28. Unanticipated and sharp price changes are almost universally considered to be a "bad" thing that needs to be remedied by some policy.
29. Inflation causes a country's unit of currency to increase in purchasing power.
30. A price index can be used to deflate current dollar GDP to real GDP expressed in dollars of constant purchasing power.
31. The GDP deflator measures the average level of prices of all final goods and services produced in the economy.
32. Many factors can potentially distort the CPI.

33. Our ability to calculate inflation accurately is complicated by changing qualities of goods and services over time and the creation of new products.
34. Chain weighting reduces the downward bias of the GDP deflator.
35. The PPI is often useful in predicting changes in the CPI.
36. A Porsche produced in Germany and purchased in the United States would not be reflected in the GDP deflator.
37. Debtors gain from unanticipated inflation.
38. Wage earners will lose from inflation only if wages rise at a faster rate than the price level.
39. Uncertainty about inflation can increase long-term interest rates by adding an inflation risk premium.
40. Anticipated changes in inflation redistribute income from lenders to borrowers.
41. Menu costs and shoe-leather costs are modest at low rates of inflation.
42. The real interest rate equals the nominal interest rate minus the inflation rate.
43. As long as nominal interest rates cannot be negative, real interest rates cannot be negative.
44. Real interest rates can be negative.
45. When people start expecting future inflation, creditors become less willing to lend funds at any given interest rate because they fear they will be repaid in dollars of lesser value than those they loaned.
46. If people correctly anticipate inflation, they will behave in a manner that will largely protect them against loss.
47. When both suppliers and demanders of funds begin to expect inflation, it will push up the real interest rate to a new, higher equilibrium level.
48. In periods of high unexpected inflation, the nominal interest rate can be high while the real interest rate is low or even negative.
49. When borrowers of funds start expecting future inflation, the demand for funds increases.
50. In an expansion, investment and expenditures for expensive durable consumer goods are rising.
51. In a growing economy, real GDP will tend to rise from one business cycle peak to the next.
52. A contraction is a period of falling real output and is usually accompanied by rising unemployment and inflation.
53. Unemployment is usually slow to fall substantially in the expansion phase of the business cycle.
54. The lengths of business cycles are uniform.
55. The performance of the economy and the fate of an incumbent's bid for reelection show a very weak correlation.
56. Econometric forecasts often inaccurate at forecasting turning points in the business cycle.
57. Since the development of the index of leading economic indicators, it has failed several to give some warning of an economic downturn several times.
58. The lead time between a change in the index of economic indicators and changes in business conditions has been very stable.

Multiple Choice:

1. The three major macroeconomic goals of nearly every society are
   a. maintaining stable prices, maintaining high levels of employment, and achieving high rates of economic growth.
   b. achieving high rates of economic growth, reducing unemployment, and reducing interest rates.
   c. maintaining stable prices, reducing interest rates, and achieving a high rate of economic growth.
   d. maintaining high levels of employment, increasing the supply of money, and achieving a high rate of economic growth.

2. With regard to macroeconomic goals, which is *not* true?
   a. Individuals differ considerably in their evaluation of the relative importance of certain issues.
   b. Virtually everyone views economic growth positively.
   c. Individuals disagree on whether certain "problems" are really problems.
   d. Some individuals disagree about the appropriate distribution of income.
   e. All of the above are true.

3. Which is *not* one of society's major economic goals?
   a. maintaining employment at high levels
   b. maintaining prices at a stable level
   c. maintaining a high rate of economic growth
   d. All of the above are major economic goals of society.

4. Economic growth is best measured by changes in
   a. nominal GDP.
   b. nominal GDP per capita.
   c. real GDP.
   d. real GDP per capita.

5. The unemployment rate is the number of people officially unemployed divided by
   a. the total population.
   b. the noninstitutional population.
   c. the civilian labor force.
   d. the number of people employed.
   e. none of the above.

6. High rates of unemployment
   a. reduce the possible level of consumption in society.
   b. result in the loss of some potential output in society.
   c. can lead to increased tensions and despair.
   d. represent a loss of efficiency in society.
   e. All of the above are true.

7. The civilian labor force excludes which of the following groups?
   a. those in the armed forces
   b. those who are currently working part time
   c. full-time students
   d. retirees
   e. all of the above except b.

8. The labor force consists of
   a. all persons over the age of 16 who are working or actively seeking work.
   b. all persons over the age of 16 who are able to work.
   c. all persons over the age of 16 who are working, plus those not working.
   d. discouraged workers, part-time workers, and full-time workers.
   e. discouraged workers, employed workers, and those actively seeking work.

9. Discouraged workers
   a. are considered unemployed.
   b. are considered as both unemployed and in the labor force.
   c. are considered as in the labor force.
   d. are considered as not in the labor force.
   e. are considered as unemployed but not in the labor force.

10. The largest fraction of those counted as unemployed is due to
    a. job leavers.
    b. job losers.
    c. new entrants.
    d. reentrants.

11. Which of these groups tends to have the lowest unemployment rate?
    a. teenagers.
    b. those with some college education.
    c. college graduates.
    d. those with a high school diploma but no college experience.

12. The unemployment rate may underestimate the true extent of unemployment if
    a. many people become discouraged and cease looking for work.
    b. employees increase the number of hours they work overtime.
    c. a large number of people are working in the underground economy.
    d. any of the above occur.

13. In Littletown, the population includes 3,000 people over the age of 16; 2,400 are in the labor force, and 1,800 are employed. The unemployment rate is
    a. 33 percent.
    b. 20 percent.
    c. 25 percent.
    d. 75 percent.
    e. none of the above.

14. The official unemployment rate may overstate the extent of unemployment because
    a. it includes those who claim to be looking for work as unemployed, even if they are just going through the motions in order to get government benefits.
    b. it excludes discouraged workers.
    c. it does not count those with jobs in the underground economy as employed.
    d. it counts part-time workers as fully employed.
    e. of both a. and c.

15. Persons who do not have jobs and who do not look for work are considered
    a. out of the labor force.
    b. unemployed.
    c. underemployed.
    d. overemployed.
    e. part of the underground economy.

16. If unemployment benefits increase, leading more people to claim to be seeking work when they are not really seeking work, the measured unemployment rate will
    a. be unaffected.
    b. fall.
    c. rise.
    d. change in an indeterminate direction.

17. After looking for a job for more than eleven months, Fred became frustrated and stopped looking. Economists view Fred as
    a. unemployed.
    b. a discouraged worker.
    c. part of the labor force, but neither employed nor unemployed.
    d. cyclically unemployed.
    e. both b and c.

18. If the unemployment rate is 6 percent and the number of persons unemployed is 12 million, the number of people employed is equal to
    a. 200 million.
    b. 188 million.
    c. 212 million.
    d. 12 million.
    e. none of the above.

19. According to the Bureau of Labor Statistics, the four main categories of unemployed workers are
    a. discouraged workers, part-time workers, the cyclically unemployed, and the frictionally unemployed.
    b. new entrants, job losers, job leavers, and reentrants.
    c. discouraged workers, job losers, new entrants, and the underemployed.
    d. job losers, job leavers, the structurally unemployed, and the frictionally unemployed.

20. Frictional unemployment is
    a. unemployment caused by automation in the workplace.
    b. unemployment caused by lack of training and education.
    c. unemployment that is due to normal turnover in the labor market.
    d. unemployment that is due to the friction of competing ideological systems.
    e. all of the above.

21. Unemployment caused by a contraction in the economy is called
    a. cyclical unemployment.
    b. frictional unemployment.
    c. structural unemployment.
    d. seasonal unemployment.

22. A federal program aimed at retraining the unemployed workers of the declining auto and steel industries is designed to reduce which type of unemployment?
    a. Seasonal.
    b. Cyclical.
    c. Frictional.
    d. Structural.

23. When unemployment rises above the natural rate, it reflects the existence of _____ unemployment.
    a. frictional
    b. cyclical
    c. seasonal
    d. structural

24. If a nation's labor force receives a significant influx of young workers,
    a. the natural rate of unemployment is likely to decrease.
    b. the natural rate of unemployment is unlikely to change.
    c. the natural rate of unemployment is likely to increase.
    d. frictional unemployment will likely decrease to zero.

25. When an economy is operating at full employment,
    a. the unemployment rate will equal zero.
    b. frictional unemployment will equal zero.
    c. cyclical and frictional unemployment will equal zero.
    d. structural unemployment will equal zero.
    e. cyclical unemployment will be zero.

26. The natural rate of unemployment would increase when which of the following increases?
    a. Frictional unemployment.
    b. Structural unemployment.
    c. Cyclical unemployment.
    d. Either frictional or structural unemployment.

27. When would consumers and producers experience increased difficulty in coordinating their plans and decisions?
    a. In a period of inflation.
    b. In a period of deflation.
    c. In a period of either inflation or deflation.
    d. None of the above.

28. Which of the following is true?
    a. At the natural rate of unemployment, the economy is considered to be at full employment.
    b. At full employment, the economy is producing at its potential output.
    c. If unemployment is greater than its natural rate, the economy is producing at less than its potential output.
    d. If we are at less than full employment, some cyclical unemployment exists.
    e. All of the above are true.

29. Inflation will be least harmful if
    a. interest rates are not adjusted accordingly when inflation occurs.
    b. it is correctly anticipated and interest rates adjust accordingly.
    c. worker wages are set by long-term contracts.
    d. it is not fully anticipated.

30. The CPI is a measure of
    a. the overall cost of inputs purchased by a typical producer.
    b. the overall cost of goods and services produced in the economy.
    c. the overall cost of stocks on the New York Stock Exchange.
    d. the overall cost of goods and services bought by a typical consumer.

31. The CPI overestimates changes in the cost of living because
    a. the growth of discount stores where consumers can obtain goods at discount prices has not been adequately represented in the construction of the CPI.
    b. the CPI does not adequately deal with changes in the quality of products over time.
    c. the CPI deals with a fixed market basket and doesn't capture the savings households enjoy when they substitute cheaper alternatives in response to a price change.
    d. of all of the above.

32. If the consumer price index was 110 in the base year and 121 in the following year, the inflation rate was
    a. 121 percent.
    b. 21 percent.
    c. 11 percent.
    d. 10 percent.

33. The current cost of a market basket of goods is $12,000. The cost of the same basket of goods in the base year was $4,000. The current price index is
    a. 300.
    b. 200.
    c. 150.
    d. 66.7.
    e. 33.3

34. Which measures of inflation tend to overstate it?
    a. Both the GDP deflator and the CPI.
    b. The CPI, but not the GDP deflator.
    c. The GDP deflator, but not the CPI.
    e. neither the GDP deflator nor the CPI.

35. The cost of an aircraft carrier produced domestically would be included in
    a. the CPI, but not the GDP deflator.
    b. neither the GDP deflator nor the CPI.
    c. the GDP deflator, but not the CPI.
    d. both the GDP deflator and the CPI.

36. Unexpected inflation generally benefits
    a. lenders.
    b. people on fixed incomes.
    c. the poor.
    d. borrowers.

37. The costs of inflation include
    a. menu costs.
    b. shoe-leather costs.
    c. a distortion of price signals.
    d. all of the above.

38. Inflation can harm
    a. retirees on fixed pensions.
    b. wage earners whose incomes grow slower than inflation.
    c. borrowers who have long-term fixed interest rate loans.
    d. either a. or c.
    e. all of the above.

39. If people correctly anticipate inflation, it will
    a. harm both borrowers and lenders.
    b. benefit neither borrowers nor lenders.
    c. benefit lenders.
    d. benefit borrowers.

40. If the nominal interest rate is 12 percent and the inflation rate is 3 percent, the real interest rate is
    a. 3 percent.
    b. 6 percent.
    c. 9 percent.
    d. 15 percent.
    e. 36 percent.

41. What is the nominal interest rate paid on a loan earning 7 percent real interest per year if the inflation rate is 6 percent?
    a. 13 percent.
    b. 7 percent.
    c. 6 percent.
    d. 1 percent.

42. An increase in the expected future rate of inflation will lead to
    a. a decrease in the supply of funds.
    b. an increase in the supply of funds.
    c. an increase in the demand for funds.
    d. an increase in the demand for funds.
    e. both a. and c.

43. The contractionary phase of the business cycle is characterized by
    a. increased output and increased unemployment.
    b. reduced output and reduced unemployment.
    c. reduced output and increased unemployment.
    d. increased output and reduced unemployment.

44. A business cycle reflects changes in economic activity, particularly real GDP. The stages of a business cycle in order are
    a. expansion, peak, contraction, and trough.
    b. expansion, trough, contraction, and peak.
    c. contraction, recession, expansion, and boom.
    d. trough, expansion, contraction, and peak.

45. In the expansion phase of the business cycle,
    a. output is rising.
    b. unemployment is falling.
    c. consumer and business confidence are high.
    d. investment is rising.
    e. all of the above are true.

Problems:

1. Which of the following individuals would economists consider unemployed?
    a. A factory worker is temporarily laid off but expects to be called back to work soon.
    b. A receptionist, who works only 20 hours per week, would like to work 40 hours per week.
    c. A high school graduate is spending the summer backpacking across the country rather than seeking work.
    d. Sam looked for work for several weeks but has now given up his search and is going back to college.
    e. A 14-year-old wants to mow lawns for extra cash but is unable to find neighbors willing to hire her.

2. Answer the following questions about unemployment:
    a. If a country has a noninstitutional population of 100 million and a labor force of 80 million, and 70 million people were employed, what is its labor force participation rate and its unemployment rate?
    b. If 5 million new jobs were created in the country, and it attracted 10 million of the people previously not in the labor force into the labor force, what would the new labor force participation rate and new unemployment rate be?
    c. Beginning with the situation in part (a), if 5 million unemployed people became discouraged and stopped looking for work, what would the new labor force participation rate and new unemployment rate be?
    d. Beginning with the situation in part (a), if 10 million current workers retired but their jobs were filled by others still in the labor force, what would the new labor force participation rate and new unemployment rate be?

3.
    a. What would be the labor force participation rate if the non-institutional adult population was 200 million, the labor force was 160 million, and employment was 140 million?
    b. What would be the labor force participation rate if the non-institutional adult population was 200 million, the labor force was 140 million, and employment was 120 million?
    c. Starting from the situation in a., what would happen to the labor force participation rate if 30 million people lost their jobs and all of them exited the labor force?
    d. Starting from the situation in a., what would happen to the labor force participation rate if employment rose from 140 million to 150 million?

4. Answer the following questions about unemployment:
    a. In a severe recession, what would tend to happen to the number of people in each of the following categories?
       job losers   reentrants
       job leavers   new entrants
    b. In good economic times, why might the number of job leavers, reentrants, and new entrants all increase?

5. Identify whether each of the following reflects seasonal, structural, frictional, or cyclical unemployment.
    a. A salesperson quits a job in California and seeks a new sales position after moving to New York.
    b. A sales employee is laid off due to slow business after consumer spending falls.
    c. An employee is fired due to poor job performance and searches the want ads each day for work.
    d. An automotive worker is replaced by robotic equipment on the assembly line.

6. Which type of unemployment would be affected by the following changes? Would that type of unemployment rise or fall?
    a. More people have been retrained to develop new skills.
    b. Online job search becomes more effective.
    c. Unemployment benefits increase.
    d. There is a sharp fall in demand for goods and services in the economy.
    e. There is a large, permanent reduction in the demand for coal.
    f. There is massive snowstorm in Minnesota that closes down much of the state.

7. How can unions result in higher unemployment rates? How would the results differ for someone who wants to be employed in the union sector as compared with someone who currently has a job in the union sector?

8. Unemployment benefits in many European countries tend to be both more generous and available for longer periods than those in the United States. What impact do you think this is likely to have on the unemployment rate in a European country? Why?

9.
   a. What is the relationship between the natural rate of unemployment and frictional, structural and cyclical unemployment?
   b. What would happen to both the actual and the natural rate of unemployment if:
      i. cyclical unemployment increases?
      ii. frictional unemployment decreases?
      iii. structural unemployment rises and cyclical unemployment falls by the same amount?
      iv. structural unemployment falls and cyclical unemployment rises by a larger amount?
      v. frictional unemployment rises and structural unemployment falls by the same amount?

10. Why isn't the belief that technological advances inevitably displace workers true?

11. Answer the following questions about inflation:
    a. What would be the effect of unexpected inflation on each of the following?
       Menu costs.   Retirees on fixed incomes.
       Shoe-leather costs.   Debtors.
       Creditors.   Workers.
    b. How would your answers change if the inflation was expected?

12. Say that the bundle of goods purchased by a typical consumer in the base year consisted of 20 gallons of milk at a price of $1 per gallon and 15 loaves of bread at a price of $2 per loaf. What would the price index be in a year in which
    a. milk cost $2 per gallon and bread cost $4 per loaf? 200
    b. milk cost $3 per gallon and bread cost $2 per loaf? 180
    c. milk cost $2 per gallon and bread cost $1 per loaf? 110

13. Calculate a price index for 2011, 2012, and 2013 using the following information about prices. Let the market basket consist of one pizza, two sodas, and three video rentals. Let the year 2011 be the base year (with an index value of 100).

Year	Price of a Pizza	Price of a Soda	Price of a Video Rental
2011	$9.00	$0.50	$2.00
2012	$9.50	$0.53	$2.24
2013	$10.00	$0.65	$2.90

How much inflation occurred between 2011 and 2012? Between 2011 and 2013?

14. Indicate which of the following are true of the CPI and the GDP deflator:

	CPI	GDP Deflator
Will reflect the cost of building an aircraft carrier domestically.		
Reflects the cost of imported consumer goods.		
Chain weighted.		
Tends to overstate inflation.		
More volatile.		
Reflects prices charged in the underground economy.		

15. You borrow money at a fixed rate of interest to finance your college education. If the rate of inflation unexpectedly slows down between the time you take out the loan and the time you begin paying it back, is there a redistribution of income? Do you gain or lose? What if you already expected the inflation rate to slow at the time you took out the loan? Explain.

16. How does an adjustable rate mortgage agreement protect lenders against inflation? Who bears the inflation risk?

17. Answer the following questions about the nominal and real interest rates:
    a. What would be the real interest rate if the nominal interest rate were 12 percent and the inflation rate were 9 percent? If the nominal interest rate were 10 percent and the inflation rate were 5 percent?
    b. What would happen to the real interest rate if the nominal interest rate went from 9 percent to 12 percent when the inflation rate went from zero to 6 percent?
    c. What would happen if the nominal interest rate went from 12 percent to 8 percent when the inflation rate went from 8 percent to 4 percent?

18. In 2000, a proposal was made in Santa Monica, California, to raise the minimum wage in the hotel and shopping district to a "living" wage of $10.69 per hour. Predict the effect of such legislation on unemployment in the hotel and shopping industries in Santa Monica. What would you expect to happen to the unemployment rate in neighboring areas?

Measuring Economic Performance

21

21.1 National Income Accounting: A Standardized Way to Measure Economic Performance

21.2 Measuring Total Production

21.3 Other Measures of Total Production and Total Income

21.4 Problems in Calculating an Accurate GDP

21.5 Problems with GDP as a Measure of Economic Welfare

The desire to measure the success, or performance, of our national economy is significant. Is it getting "bigger" (and, we hope, better) or "smaller" (and worse) over time?

Aside from intellectual curiosity, the need to evaluate the magnitude of the country's economic performance is important to macroeconomic policymakers, who want to know how well the economy is performing so that they can set goals and develop policy recommendations.

Measurement of the economy's performance is also important to private businesses because inaccurate measurement can lead to bad decision making. Traders in stocks and bonds are continually checking economic statistics—buying and selling in response to the latest economic data.

To fulfill the need for a reliable method of measuring economic performance, **national income accounting** was born early in the twentieth century. The establishment of a uniform means of accounting for economic performance was such an important accomplishment that one of the first Nobel prizes in economics was given to the late Simon Kuznets, a pioneer of national income accounting in the United States.

Several measures of aggregate national income and output have been developed, the most important of which is gross domestic product (GDP). We will examine GDP and other indicators of national economic performance in detail in this chapter. ∎

national income accounting
a uniform means of measuring economic performance

SECTION 21.1
National Income Accounting: A Standardized Way to Measure Economic Performance

★ What is gross domestic product? ★ Why must expenditures equal income?

What Is Gross Domestic Product?

The measure of aggregate economic performance that gets the most attention in the popular media is **gross domestic product (GDP)**, which is defined as the value of all final goods and services produced within a country during a given period. By convention, that period is almost always one year. But let's examine the rest of this definition. What is meant by "final good or service" and "value"?

Measuring the Value of Goods and Services

Value is determined by the market prices at which goods and services sell. Underlying the calculations, then, are the various equilibrium prices and quantities for the multitude of goods and services produced.

What Is a Final Good or Service?

The word *final* means that the good is ready for its designated ultimate use. Many goods and services are intermediate goods or services—that is, used in the production of other goods. For example, suppose U.S. Steel Corporation produces some steel that it sells to General Motors Corporation for use in making an automobile. If we counted the value of steel used in making the car as well as the full value of the finished auto in the GDP, we would be engaging in **double counting**—adding the value of the steel in twice, first in its raw form and second in its final form, the automobile.

Production, Income, and the Circular Flow Model

When we calculate GDP in the economy, we are measuring the value of total production—our total expenditures, $C + I + G + (X - M)$. However, we are also measuring the value of total income. Why? It is because every dollar of spending by some buyer ends up being a dollar of income for some seller. In short, expenditures (spending) must equal income. And this is true whether it is a household, firm, or the government that buys the good or service. The main point is that when we spend (the value of total expenditure) it ends up as someone's income (the value of total income). Buyers have sellers.

In Exhibit 1, we reintroduce the circular flow model to show the flow of money in the economy. For example, households use some of their income to buy domestic goods and services and some to buy foreign goods and services (imports). Households also use some of their income to pay taxes and invest in financial markets (stocks, bonds, saving accounts, and other financial assets). When income flows into the financial system as saving, it makes it possible for consumers, firms, and government to borrow. This market for saving and borrowing is vital to a well-functioning economy.

Firms sell their goods and services to domestic and foreign consumers and foreign firms and government. Firms use their factors of production (labor, land, capital, and entrepreneurship) to produce goods and services. Firms pay wages to workers, interest for the use of capital, and rent for land. Profits are the return to entrepreneurs for taking the risk of producing the goods and services. Wages, rent, interest, and profit comprise aggregate income in the economy. Government provides transfer payments such as Social Security and unemployment insurance payments. Whether we add up the aggregate expenditure on final goods and services, $C + I + G + (X - M)$, or the value of aggregate income (wages, rent, interest, and profit) we get the same GDP. For an economy as a whole, expenditures and income are the same. Actually, while the two should be exactly the same—there may be a slight variation because of data issues.

gross domestic product (GDP) the measure of economic performance based on the value of all final goods and services produced within a country during a given period

double counting adding the value of a good or service twice by mistakenly counting the intermediate goods and services in GDP

section 21.1 exhibit 1 — The Expanded Circular Flow Model

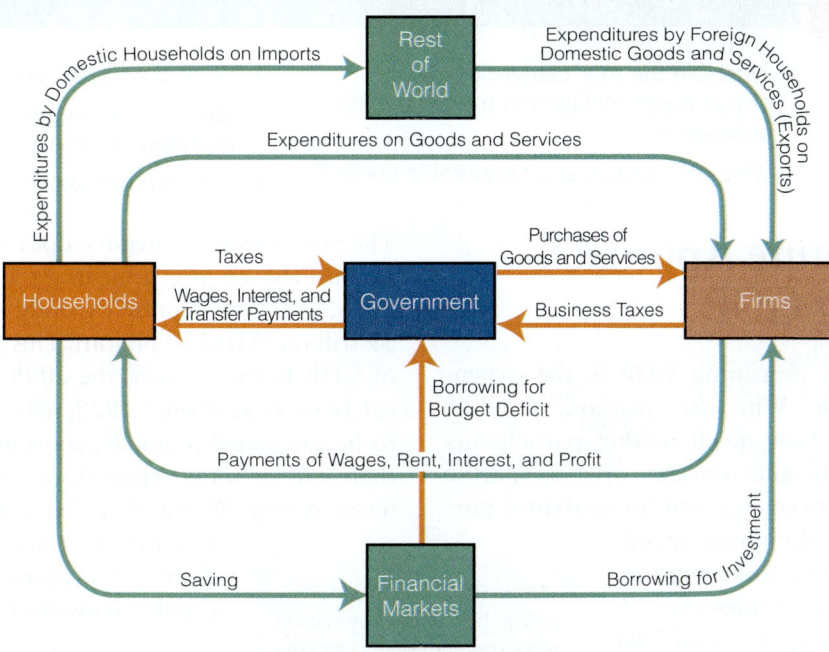

In the circular flow model of income and expenditures, we can measure GDP either by calculating the total value of expenditures or the total value of aggregate income because for the economy as a whole expenditures must equal income. GDP equals the total amount spent by households in the market—to buy goods and services, to pay taxes and save. To produce goods and services, the firm uses the factors of production (labor, land, capital, and entrepreneurship), and it pays these factors wages, rent, interest, and profit. These payments are total income, which is also equal to GDP. The government and firms borrow the funds that flow into the financial system from households.

SECTION CHECK

1. We measure our economy's status in order to see how its performance has changed over time. These economic measurements are important to government officials, private businesses, and investors.
2. National income accounting, pioneered by Simon Kuznets, provides a uniform means of measuring national economic performance.
3. Gross domestic product (GDP) is the value of all final goods and services produced within a country during a given time period.
4. When we spend (the value of total expenditure) it ends up as someone's income (the value of total income). Buyers have sellers.

---

1. Why does GDP measure only final goods and services produced, rather than all goods and services produced?
2. Why aren't all of the expenditures on used goods in an economy included in current GDP?
3. Why do GDP statistics include real estate agents' commissions from selling existing homes and used car dealers' profits from selling used cars, but not the value of existing homes or used cars when they are sold?
4. Why are sales of previously existing inventories of hula hoops not included in the current year's GDP?

SECTION 21.2 Measuring Total Production

- What are the four categories of purchases included in the expenditure approach?
- What are durable and nondurable goods?
- What are fixed investments?
- What types of government purchases are included in the expenditure approach?
- How are net exports calculated?

The Expenditure Approach to Measuring GDP

One approach to measuring GDP is the **expenditure approach.** With this method, GDP is calculated by adding how much market participants spend on final goods and services over a specific period of time. For convenience and for analytical purposes, economists usually group spending into four categories: consumption, designated by the letter C; investment, I; government purchases, G; and net exports, which equals exports (X) minus imports (M), or $X - M$. According to the expenditure method, then,

$$GDP = C + I + G + (X - M)$$

Consumption (C)

Consumption refers to the purchase of consumer goods and services by households. For most of us, a large percentage of our income in a given year goes for consumer goods and services.

expenditure approach
calculation of GDP by adding the expenditures by market participants on final goods and services over a given period

consumption
purchases of final goods and services

nondurable goods
tangible items consumed in a short period of time, such as food

durable goods
longer-lived consumer goods, such as automobiles

The consumption category does not include purchases by business or government. As Exhibit 1 indicates, in 2008, U.S. consumption expenditures totaled more than $9 trillion ($10,130 billion). This figure was 70 percent of GDP. In this respect, the 2008 data were fairly typical. In every year since 1929, when GDP accounts began to be calculated annually, consumption has been more than half of total expenditures on goods and services (even during World War II). Consumption spending, in turn, is usually broken down into three subcategories: nondurable goods, durable consumer goods, and services.

What Are Nondurable and Durable Goods?

Nondurable goods include tangible consumer items that are typically consumed or used up in a relatively short period. Food and clothing are examples, as are such quickly consumable items as drugs, toys, magazines, soap, razor blades, light bulbs, and so on. Nearly everything purchased in a supermarket or drug store is a nondurable good.

Durable goods include longer-lived consumer goods, the most important single category of which is automobiles

section 21.2 exhibit 1 — GDP: The Expenditure Approach

Category	Amount (billions of current dollars)	Percent of GDP
Consumption (C)	$10,130	70%
Investment (I)	2,136	15
Government purchases (G)	2,883	20
Net exports of goods and services (X − M)	−708	−5
Gross domestic product	$14,441	100%

SOURCE: U.S. Bureau of Economic Analysis, *Survey of Current Business*, August 2009.

and other consumer vehicles. Appliances, stereos, and furniture are also included in the durable goods category. On occasion, it is difficult to decide whether a good is durable or nondurable; the definitions are, therefore, somewhat arbitrary.

The distinction between durables and nondurables is important because consumers' buying behavior is somewhat different for each of these categories of goods. In boom periods, when GDP is rising rapidly, expenditures on durables often increase dramatically, while in years of stagnant or falling GDP, sales of durable goods often plummet. By contrast, sales of nondurables such as food tend to be more stable over time because purchases of such goods are more difficult to shift from one period to another. You can "make do" with your car for another year, but not your lettuce.

What Are Services?

Services are intangible items of value, as opposed to physical goods. Education, health care, domestic housekeeping, professional football, legal help, automobile repair, haircuts, airplane transportation—all these items are services. In recent years, U.S. service expenditures grew faster than spending on goods; the share of total consumption of services increased from 35 percent in 1950 to 66 percent by 2008. As incomes rise, service industries such as health, education, financial, and recreation grow dramatically.

Investment (*I*)

Investment, according to economists, refers to the creation of capital goods—inputs such as machines and tools whose purpose is to produce other goods. This definition of *investment* differs from the popular use of that term. It is common for people to say that they have invested in stocks, meaning that they have traded money for pieces of paper, called stock certificates, that say they own shares in certain companies. Such transactions are not investments as defined by economists (i.e., increases in capital goods), even though they might provide the enterprises selling the stocks the resources to buy new capital goods, which *would* be counted as investment purchases by economists.

The two categories of investment purchases measured in the expenditures approach are fixed investment and inventory investment.

services
intangible items of value provided to consumers, such as education

investment
the creation of capital goods to augment future production

fixed investment
all new spending on capital goods by producers

producer goods
capital goods that increase future production capabilities

inventory investment
purchases that add to the stocks of goods kept by the firm to meet consumer demand

Fixed Investment

Fixed investment includes all spending on capital goods—sometimes called **producer goods**—such as machinery, tools, and factory buildings. All these goods increase future production capabilities. Residential construction is also included as an investment expenditure in GDP calculations. The construction of a house allows for a valuable consumer service—shelter—to be provided and is thus considered an investment. Residential construction is the only part of investment tied directly to household expenditure decisions.

Inventory Investment

Inventory investment includes all purchases by businesses that add to their inventories—stocks of goods kept on hand by businesses to meet customer demands. Every business needs inventory and, other things being equal, the greater the inventory, the greater the amount of goods and services that can be sold to a consumer in the future. Thus, inventories are considered a form of investment. For example, if a grocery store expands and increases the quantity and variety of goods on its shelves, future sales can rise. An increase in inventories, then, is presumed to increase the firm's future sales, which is why we say it is an investment.

How Stable Are Investment Expenditures?

In recent years, investment expenditures generally hovered around 15 percent of gross domestic product. Investment spending is the most volatile category of GDP, however, and tends to fluctuate considerably with changing business conditions. When the economy is booming, investment purchases tend to increase dramatically. In downturns, the reverse happens. In the first year of the Great Depression, investment purchases declined by 37 percent. In recent years, expenditures on capital goods have been a smaller proportion of GDP in the United States than in many other developed nations. This fact worries some people who are concerned about GDP growth in the United States compared to that in other countries, because investment in capital goods is directly tied to a nation's future production capabilities.

Government Purchases (G)

The portion of government purchases included in GDP is expenditures on goods and services. For example, a government must pay the salaries of its employees, and it must also make payments to the private firms with which it contracts to provide various goods and services, such as highway construction companies and weapons manufacturers. All these payments would be included in GDP. However, *transfer payments* (such as Social Security, farm subsidies, and welfare) are not included in government purchases, because this spending does not go to purchase newly produced goods or services but is merely a transfer of income among the country's citizens (which is why such expenditures are called transfer payments).

Exports (X − M)

Some of the goods and services produced in the United States are exported for use in other countries. The fact that these goods and services were made in the United States means that they should be included in a measure of U.S. production. Thus, we include the value of exports when calculating GDP. At the same time, however, some of our expenditures in other categories (consumption and investment, in particular) were for foreign-produced goods and services. These imports must be excluded from GDP to obtain an accurate measure of U.S. production. Thus, GDP calculations measure net exports, which equals total exports (X) minus total imports (M). Net exports are a small proportion of GDP and are often negative for the United States.

SECTION CHECK

1. The expenditure approach to measuring GDP involves adding up the purchases of final goods and services by market participants.
2. Four categories of spending are used in the GDP calculation: consumption (C), investment (I), government purchases (G), and net exports (X − M).
3. Consumption includes spending on nondurable consumer goods (tangible items that are usually consumed in a short period of time); durable consumer goods (longer-lived consumer goods); and services (intangible items of value that do not involve physical production).
4. Fixed investment includes all spending on capital goods, such as machinery, tools, and buildings. Inventory investment includes the net expenditures by businesses to increase their inventories.
5. Purchases of goods and services are the only part of government spending included in GDP. Transfer payments are not included in these calculations, because that spending is not a payment for a newly produced good or service.
6. Net exports are calculated by subtracting total imports from total exports.

---

1. What would happen to GDP if consumption purchases (C) and net exports (X − M) both rose, holding other things equal?
2. Why do you think economic forecasters focus so much on consumption purchases and their determinants?
3. Why are durable goods purchases more unstable than nondurable goods purchases?
4. Why does the investment component of GDP include purchases of new capital goods but not purchases of company stock?
5. If Mary received a welfare check this year, would that transfer payment be included in this year's GDP? Why or why not?
6. Can inventory investment or net exports ever be negative?

SECTION 21.3 Other Measures of Total Production and Total Income

- How is national income calculated?
- What does personal income measure?

In addition to computing the gross domestic product, the Bureau of Economic Analysis (BEA) also computes five additional measures of production and income: gross national product, net national product, national income, personal income, and disposable personal income.

Incomes received by people providing goods and services are actually payments to the owners of productive resources. These payments are sometimes called **factor payments**. Factor payments include wages for the use of labor services, rent for land, payments for the use of capital goods in the form of interest, and profits for entrepreneurs who put labor, land, and capital together. Before we can measure national income, we must make three adjustments to GDP. First, we must look at the net income of foreigners—that is, we add any income earned abroad by U.S. citizens or firms and we subtract any income earned in the United States by foreign firms and citizens. This difference between net income of foreigners and GDP is called **gross national product (GNP)**. For example, we would add to GDP the profits sent back to the United States from Wal-Mart stores in Canada and Mexico. However, the profits Toyota earns in the United States are sent back to Japan and are subtracted from U.S. GDP, so GNP becomes the income earned worldwide by U.S. firms and residents. In the United States, the difference between GDP and GNP is small because net income of foreigners is a small percentage of GDP.

The second adjustment we make to find national income is to deduct depreciation from GNP. **Depreciation** payments are annual allowances set aside for the replacement of worn-out plant and equipment. After we subtract depreciation, we have **net national product (NNP)**.

The final adjustment is to subtract **indirect business taxes**. The best example of an indirect business tax is a sales tax. For example, a compact disc might cost $14.95 plus a tax of $1.20 for a total of $16.15. The retail distributor (record store), record producer, and others will share $14.95 in proceeds, even though the actual equilibrium price is $16.15. In other words, the output (compact disc) is valued at $16.15, even though recipients only get $14.95 in income. Besides sales taxes, other important indirect business taxes include excise taxes (e.g., taxes on cigarettes, automobiles, and liquor) and gasoline taxes.

Now we can measure **national income (NI)**, which is a measure of the income earned by owners of resources—factor payments. Accordingly, national income includes payments for labor services (wages, salaries, and fringe benefits), payments for use of land and buildings (rent), money lent to finance economic activity (interest), and payments for use of capital resources (profits). To obtain GDP, we add indirect business taxes, depreciation, and net income of foreigners.

We should keep in mind that not all income can be used by those who earn it. **Personal income (PI)** measures the amount of income received by households (including transfer payments) before income taxes. **Disposable personal income** is the personal income available to individuals after taxes.

---

factor payments
wages (salaries), rent, interest payments, and profits paid to the owners of productive resources

gross national product (GNP)
the difference between net income of foreigners and GDP

depreciation
annual allowance set aside to replace worn-out capital

net national product (NNP)
GNP minus depreciation

indirect business taxes
taxes, such as sales tax, levied on goods and services sold

national income (NI)
a measure of income earned by owners of the factors of production

personal income (PI)
the amount of income received by households before personal taxes

disposable personal income
the personal income available after personal taxes

SECTION CHECK

1. To find national income, we must subtract from GDP: (1) indirect business taxes, such as sales taxes; (2) depreciation—payments set aside for the replacement of worn-out capital; and (3) net income of foreigners in the United States.
2. National income (NI) is measured by adding together the payments to the factors of production—wages, rent, interest, and profit.
3. Personal income (PI) measures the amount of income received by households (including transfer payments) before personal taxes.
4. Disposable personal income is the personal income available after personal taxes.

1. How is personal income different from national income?
2. What is the difference between GDP and national income?

SECTION 21.4 Problems in Calculating an Accurate GDP

* What are the problems with using GDP to measure output?
* What is per capita GDP?

Problems in Calculating an Accurate GDP

The primary problem in calculating accurate GDP statistics becomes evident when attempts are made to compare the GDP over time. Between 1970 and 1978, a period of relatively high inflation, GDP in the United States rose more than 100 percent. What great progress! Unfortunately, however, the "yardstick" used in adding the values of different products, the U.S. dollar, also changed in value over this period. A dollar in 1979, for example, would certainly not buy as much as a dollar in 1970, because the *overall* price level for goods and services increased.

How Do We Solve This Problem?

One solution to this problem would be to use physical units of output—which, unlike the dollar, do not change in value from year to year—as the measure of total economic activity. The major problem with this approach is that different products have different units of measurement. How can anyone add tons of steel to bushels of wheat, kilowatts of electricity, gallons of paint, cubic feet of natural gas, miles of air passenger travel, and number of magazines sold? To compare GDP values over time, the calculations must use a common, or standardized, unit of measure, which only money can provide.

A Price-Level Index

The dollar, then, is the yardstick of value we can use to correct the inflation-induced distortion of the GDP. We must adjust for the changing purchasing power of the dollar by using a price index. As we discussed in the last chapter, a price index attempts to provide a measure of the prices paid for a certain bundle of goods and services over time. The price index can be used to deflate the nominal or current dollar GDP values to a real GDP expressed in dollars of constant purchasing power.

Real GDP

Once the price index has been calculated, the actual procedure for adjusting nominal, or current dollar, GDP to get real GDP is not complicated. For convenience, an index number of 100 is assigned to some base year. The base year is arbitrarily chosen—it can be any year.

The formula for converting any year's nominal GDP into real GDP (in base year dollars) is as follows:

$$\text{Real GDP} = \frac{\text{Nominal GDP}}{\text{Price-level index}} \times 100$$

Suppose the GDP deflator (price-level index) was expressed in terms of 2000 prices (2000 = 100), and the price index figure for 2010 was 122.42. The increase in the figure means that prices were 22 percent higher in 2010 than they were in 2000. To correct the 2010 nominal GDP, we take the nominal GDP figure for 2010—say, $14,264.6 billion—and divide it by the price-level index (122.42), which results in a quotient of $116.52 billion. We then multiply this number by 100, giving us $11,652.18 billion, which would be the 2010 GDP in 2000 dollars (that is, 2010 real GDP, in terms of a 2000 base year).

In Exhibit 1, notice that in years after the base year (2000), real GDP is greater than nominal GDP. This means the price level has risen since 2000, lowering the purchasing power of the dollar. Prior to 2000, nominal GDP was less than real GDP; the purchasing power of the dollar was higher relative to the base year (2000). Also, notice that nominal GDP rises more rapidly than real GDP because inflation is included in the nominal GDP figures.

real gross domestic product per capita real output of goods and services per person

with a declining price level was 1955. Therefore, the adjustment of nominal (money) GDP to real GDP will tend to reduce the growth in GDP suggested by nominal GDP figures. Given the distortions introduced by inflation, most news reports about GDP today speak of real GDP changes, although this distinction is not always made explicit.

Is Real GDP Always Less Than Nominal GDP?

In modern times, inflation has been prevalent. For many readers of this book, the price level (as measured by the consumer price index and the GDP deflator) has risen in every year of their lifetime, because the last year

Real GDP per Capita

The measure of economic well-being, or standard of living, most often used is **real gross domestic product per capita.** We use a measure of real GDP for reasons already cited. To calculate real GDP per capita, we divide the real GDP by the total population to get the value of real output of final goods and services per person. *Ceteris paribus,* people prefer more goods to fewer, so a higher GDP per capita would seemingly make people better off, improving their standard of living. Economic growth, then, is usually considered to have occurred anytime the real GDP per capita has risen. In Exhibit 2 (on page 655), we see that in the United States the real gross domestic product per capita has grown sharply from 1958 to 2008. Real GDP per capita is almost three times larger in 2008 than it was in 1958. However, the growth in real GDP per capita is not steady, as seen by the shaded areas that represent recessions in Exhibit 2. Falling real GDP per capita can bring on many human hardships, such as rising unemployment, lower profits, stock market losses, and bankruptcies.

section 21.4 exhibit 1 Nominal and Real GDP 1960–2008 (2000 Base Year)

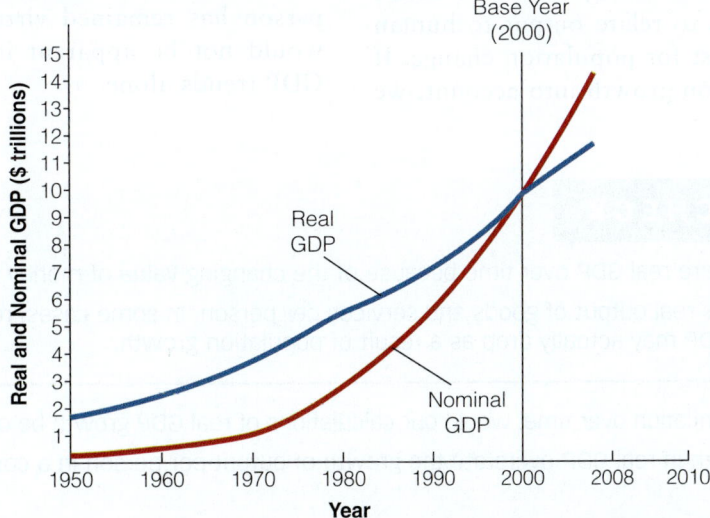

The gap between the real GDP and the nominal GDP represents price-level changes. The base year is 2000 where real GDP and nominal GDP are equal.

section 21.4 exhibit 2 | Real GDP per Capita

NOTE: Shaded areas represent recessions.
SOURCE: U.S. Bureau of Economic Analysis, July 2009.

Why Is the Measure of per Capita GDP So Important?

Because one purpose of using GDP as a crude welfare measure is to relate output to human desires, we need to adjust for population change. If we do not take population growth into account, we can be misled by changes in real GDP values. For example, in some less-developed countries in some periods, real GDP has risen perhaps 2 percent a year, but the population has grown just as fast. In these cases, the real output of goods and services per person has remained virtually unchanged, but this would not be apparent in an examination of real GDP trends alone.

SECTION CHECK

1. It is difficult to compare real GDP over time because of the changing value of money over time.
2. Per capita real GDP is real output of goods and services per person. In some cases, real GDP may increase; but per capita real GDP may actually drop as a result of population growth.

---

1. If we overestimated inflation over time, would our calculations of real GDP growth be over- or underestimated?
2. Why would the growth in real GDP overstate the growth of output per person in a country with a growing population?

Section 21.5 Problems with GDP as a Measure of Economic Welfare

- What are some of the deficiencies of GDP as a measure of economic welfare?
- What are nonmarket transactions?
- What is the underground economy?

As we noted throughout this chapter, real GDP is often used as a measure of the economic welfare of a nation. The accuracy of this measure for that purpose is questionable, however, because several important factors are excluded from its calculation. These factors include nonmarket transactions, the underground economy, leisure, externalities, and the quality of the goods purchased.

Nonmarket Transactions

Nonmarket transactions include the provision of goods and services outside traditional markets for which no money is exchanged. We simply do not have reliable enough information on this output to include it in the GDP. The most important single nonmarket transaction omitted from the GDP is the services of housewives (or househusbands). These services are not sold in any market, so they are not entered into the GDP; but they are nonetheless performed. For example, if a single woman hires a tax accountant, those payments enter into the calculation of GDP. Suppose, though, that the woman marries her tax accountant. Now the woman no longer pays her husband for his accounting services. Reported GDP falls after the marriage, although output does not change.

In less-developed countries, where a significant amount of food and clothing output is produced in the home, the failure to include nonmarket economic activity in GDP is a serious deficiency. Even in the United States, homemade meals, housework, and the vegetables and flowers produced in home gardens are excluded, even though they clearly represent an output of goods and services.

The Underground Economy

It is impossible to know for sure the magnitude of the underground economy, which includes unreported income from both legal and illegal sources. For example, illegal gambling and prostitution are not included in the GDP, leading to underreporting of an unknown magnitude. The reason these activities are excluded, however, has nothing to do with the morality of the services performed; rather, the cause of the exclusion is that most payments made for these services are neither reported to government authorities nor go through normal credit channels. Likewise, cash payments made to employees "under the table" slip through the GDP net. Estimates of the size of the underground economy vary from less than 4 percent to more than 20 percent of GDP. It also appears that a significant portion of this unreported income comes from legal sources, such as self-employment.

Measuring the Value of Leisure

The value that individuals place on leisure is omitted in calculating GDP. Most of us could probably get a part-time job if we wanted to, earning some additional money by working in the evening or on weekends. Yet we choose not to do so. Why? The opportunity cost is too high—we would have to forgo some leisure. If you work on Saturday nights, you cannot see your friends, go to parties, attend concerts, watch television, or go to the movies. The opportunity cost of leisure is the income forgone by not working. For example, if people start taking more three-day weekends, GDP will surely fall, but can we necessarily say that the standard of living will fall? GDP will fall, but economic well-being may rise.

Leisure, then, has a positive value that does not show up in the GDP accounts. To put leisure in the proper perspective, ask yourself whether you would rather live in Country A, which has a per capita GDP of $25,000 a year and a 30-hour work week, or Country B, with a $25,000 per capita GDP and a 50-hour work week. Most people would choose Country A. The problem that this omission in GDP poses can be fairly significant in international comparisons or observations of one nation over time.

GDP and Externalities

As we have discussed in earlier chapters, positive and negative externalities may result from the production of some goods and services. As a result of these externalities, the equilibrium prices of these goods and services—the figures used in GDP calculations—do not reflect their true values to society (unless, of course, the externalities have been internalized). For example, if a

global WATCH: GROWING UNDERGROUND

Underground economies are large and growing rapidly in most countries. High taxes and labor market regulations are the reasons why 17 percent of economic activity goes unreported in OECD [Organization for Economic Co-operation and Development] countries, while corruption explains the large black market in some developing ones.

By definition, national income statistics capture economic activity reported by individuals and corporations. A large and growing portion of economic activity, however, goes unrecorded in most countries. This "underground" economy consists of legal activities that are concealed, mainly for reasons of tax evasion. Underground activity grew during the 1970s, when government became pervasive in national economies. As tax rates were raised to finance public spending programs, an increasing number of individuals risked dodging taxes. It is only since the 1980s that economists have attempted to estimate the size of underground economies. This task is inherently difficult.

Nevertheless, it is important to estimate the size and growth of all economic activity, not only the reported kind. For one thing, cross-country comparisons of per capita income depend on it. By one account, Italy would be one of the richest European countries if its large black market were included alongside reported income. More importantly, GDP growth figures and unemployment rates may be severely distorted if a sudden increase in taxes pushes more people underground. Accurate statistics about overall economic activity and true unemployment are essential for effective economic policy decisions.

An article in the *Journal of Economic Literature* takes a closer look at the size, causes, and consequences of underground economies. Its authors, Friedrich Schneider of the University of Linz and Dominick Enste of the University of Cologne, claim that no cross-country comparison of underground economies has yet been undertaken. In their research, the authors compare the relative size of underground economies for 76 countries, and track their growth over time. They point out that even though estimates of underground economies are naturally inexact, economists generally agree that they are growing in most countries. Moreover, underground economies vary significantly in size, from a small fraction of "official" GDP (Switzerland), to nearly three-quarters of economic output (Nigeria, Egypt, and Thailand).

But first, what drives people underground? The authors argue that underground activity grows when tax rates rise. This is most noticeable in Scandinavian countries where governments have created some of the most generous public programs over the past few decades, and have consequently witnessed a substantial rise in their underground economies. This unsurprising claim is substantiated by the data. Norway, for example, has seen its underground economy grow from a negligible 1.5 percent of GNP in 1960 to a staggering 18 percent in 1995 (based on the currency demand approach). The high fiscal burden in other Scandinavian countries has led to a similar growth in their underground economies. In contrast, countries with relatively small public sectors—such as Switzerland and the United States—have developed much smaller underground markets.

The study shows that underground economies have grown in all OECD countries over the past few decades, representing an alarming 17 percent of reported GDP by 1997. In countries such as Spain, Portugal, Italy, Belgium, and Greece, the estimated size of unreported economic activity stood at 22 to 30 percent. "In the European Union at least 20 million workers and in OECD countries about 35 million work in the unofficial economy. Moreover, the amount doubled within 20 years."

The authors find evidence that fewer regulations (that are properly enforced), lower tax rates, and a better rule of law lead to smaller underground economies, and consequently generate higher tax revenues. These factors are absent in many countries of Latin America, where underground economies amount to one-quarter to one-third of official GNP, and in the former Soviet Union, where underground economies stand at more than one-third of reported income.

SOURCE: Author's discussion of Friedrich Schneider and Dominick H. Enste, "Shadow Economies: Size, Causes and Consequences," *Journal of Economic Literature* (March 2000), and *Economic Intuition* (Summer 2000).

in the news | Time Well Spent

As America exits the twentieth century, we'd be hard-pressed to find a five and dime store. Penny candy now goes for a nickel or more. Five cents no longer buys a good cigar. Dime novels can't be found. Even a 3¢ stamp costs 44¢. Over the century, prices have gone up. The buying power of a dollar is down. We know this from statistical measures of inflation. We know it also from Grandpa's stories about paying 15¢ for a ticket to Gone with the Wind or 19¢ for a gallon of gasoline. Even a casual observer of the U.S. economy can see that the prices of milk, bread, houses, clothes, cars, and many other goods and services rise from year to year.

The cost of living is indeed going up—in money terms. What really matters, though, isn't what something costs in money; it's what it costs in time. Making money takes time, so when we shop, we're really spending time. The real cost of living isn't measured in dollars and cents but in the hours and minutes we must work to live. American essayist Henry David Thoreau (1817–62) noted this in his famous book, *Walden*: "The cost of a thing is the amount of . . . life which is required to be exchanged for it, immediately or in the long run."

The shortcoming of money prices is that they mean little apart from money wages. A pair of stockings cost just 25¢ a century ago. This sounds wonderful until we learn that a worker of the era earned only 14.8¢ an hour. So paying for the stockings took 1 hour 41 minutes of work. Today a better pair requires only about 18 minutes of work. Put another way, stockings cost an 1897 worker today's equivalent of $22, whereas now a worker pays only about $4. If modern Americans had to work as hard as their forebears did for everyday products, they'd be in a continual state of sticker shock—$67 scissors, $913 baby carriages, $2,222 bicycles, $1,202 telephones.

The best way to measure the cost of goods and services is in terms of a standard that doesn't change—time at work, or real prices. There's a regular pattern to real prices in our dynamic economy.

Americans come in all shapes and sizes. We differ in height and weight, gender, race, and age. We vary in talents, skills, education, experience, determination, and luck. Quite naturally, our paychecks differ, too. Some of us scrape by at minimum wage, while movie stars, corporate chieftains, and athletes sometimes make millions of dollars a year.

Calculations of the work time needed to buy goods and services use the average hourly wage for production and nonsupervisory workers in manufacturing. A century ago this figure was less than 15¢ an hour. By 1997 it had hit a record $13.18, a livable wage, but nothing worthy of *Lifestyles of the Rich and Famous*. What's most important about this wage is that it roughly represents what's earned by the great bulk of American society.

In calculating our cost of living, a good place to start is with the basics—food, shelter, and clothing. In terms of time on the job, the cost of a half-gallon of milk fell from 39 minutes in 1919 to 16 minutes in 1950, 10 minutes in 1975 and 7 minutes in 1997. A pound of ground beef steadily declined from 30 minutes in 1919 to 23 minutes in 1950, 11 minutes in 1975 and 6 minutes in 1997. Paying for a dozen oranges required 1 hour 8 minutes of work in 1919. Now it takes less than 10 minutes, half what it did in 1950. The money price of a 3-pound fryer chicken rose from $1.23 in 1919 to $3.15 in 1997, but its cost in work time fell from 2 hours 37 minutes to just 14 minutes. A sample of a dozen food staples—a market basket broad enough to provide three squares a day—shows that what required 9.5 hours to buy in 1919 and 3.5 hours in 1950 now takes only 1.6 hours.

SOURCE: W. Michael Cox and Richard Alm, *1997 Annual Report: Time Well Spent*, Federal Reserve Bank of Dallas. Reprinted with permission.

consider this:

According to Michael Cox and Richard Alm, the real cost of living, as measured in the hours and minutes we must work to live, is surely falling. That is, the cost to buy a particular good or service in terms of time on the job has decreased. Many goods such as microwaves, cellular phones, and camcorders have fallen in money price. This, coupled with higher wages and better-quality products, has been a real boon to the consumer.

steel mill produces 100,000 more tons of steel, GDP increases; GDP does not, however, decrease to reflect damages from the air pollution that results from the production of that additional steel. Likewise, additional production of a vaccine would be reflected in the GDP, but the positive benefit to members of society—other than the purchaser—would not be included in the calculation. In other words, while GDP measures the goods and services produced, it does not adequately measure the "goods" and "bads" that result from the production processes.

Quality of Goods

GDP can also miss important changes in the improvements in the *quality* of goods and services. For example, the quality of a computer bought today differs significantly from one that was bought 10 years ago, but it will not lead to an increase in measured GDP. The same is true of many other goods, from cellular phones to automobiles to medical care.

Other Measures of Economic Well-Being

Even if we included some of these statistics that are difficult to measure, such as nonmarket transactions, the underground economy, leisure, externalities, and the quality of products, GDP would still not be a precise measure of economic well-being. Many other indices of well-being should be considered: life expectancies, infant mortality rates, education and environmental quality, levels of discrimination and fairness, health care, low crime rates, and minimum traffic congestion, just to name a few. GDP is a measure of economic production, *not* a measure of economic well-being. However, greater levels of GDP can lead to improvements in economic well-being, because society will now be able to afford better education and health care and a cleaner, safer environment.

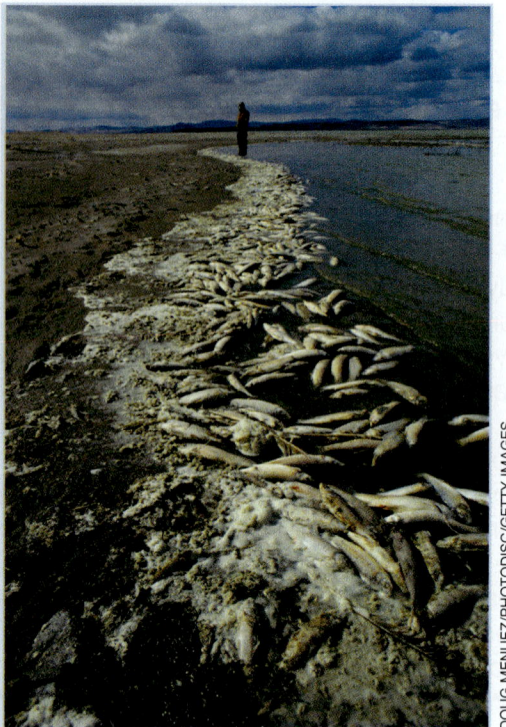

GDP doesn't measure everything that contributes to or detracts from our well-being; it is difficult to measure the value of those effects. Environmentalists believe that national income accounts should adjust for changes in the environment. But this leads to many conceptual problems, such as how to measure the marginal values of goods and services not sold in markets and how to adjust for geographical differences in environmental damage. The critical issue is whether important trends in "uncounted" goods and services result in questionable conclusions about whether we are becoming better or worse off.

SECTION CHECK

1. Several factors make it difficult to use GDP as a welfare indicator, including nonmarket transactions, the underground economy, leisure, externalities, and the quality of goods.
2. Nonmarket transactions are the exchanges of goods and services that do not occur in traditional markets and for which no money is exchanged.
3. The underground economy is the unreported production and income that come from legal and illegal activities.
4. The presence of positive and negative externalities makes it difficult to measure GDP accurately.

---

1. Why do GDP measures omit nonmarket transactions?
2. How would the existence of a high level of nonmarket activities in one country impact real GDP comparisons between it and other countries?

3. If we choose to decrease our hours worked because we value the additional leisure time more, will the resulting change in real GDP accurately reflect the change in our well-being? Why or why not?
4. How do pollution and crime affect GDP? How do pollution- and crime-control expenditures impact GDP?

Interactive Chapter Summary

Fill in the blanks:

1. _____ accounting was created to provide a reliable, uniform method of measuring economic performance.

2. _____ is defined as the value of all final goods and services produced in a country in a period of time, almost always one year.

3. A(n) _____ good or service is one that is ready for its designated ultimate use, in contrast to _____ goods or services, which are used in the production of other goods.

4. The two primary ways of calculating economic output are the _____ approach and the _____ approach.

5. With the _____ approach, GDP is calculated by adding up the expenditures of market participants on final goods and services over a period of time.

6. For analytical purposes, economists usually categorize expenditures into four categories: _____, _____, _____, and _____.

7. Consumption spending is usually broken down into three subcategories: _____ goods, _____ consumer goods, and _____.

8. Consumption refers to the purchase of consumer goods and services by _____.

9. The most important single category of consumer durable goods is consumer _____.

10. Sales of nondurable consumer goods tend to be _____ stable over time than sales of durable goods.

11. Investment, as used by economists, refers to the creation of _____ goods, whose purpose is to _____.

12. The two categories of investment purchases measured in the expenditures approach are _____ investment and _____ investment.

13. When the economy is booming, investment purchases tend to _____ dramatically.

14. _____ payments are not included in government purchases because that spending does not go to purchase newly produced goods or services.

15. Imports must be _____ from GDP in order to obtain an accurate measure of domestic production.

16. The _____ approach to measuring GDP involves summing the incomes received by producers of goods and services.

17. Output creates _____ of equal value.

18. Factor payments include _____ for the use of labor services, _____ for land, _____ payments for the use of capital goods, and _____ for entrepreneurs, who put labor, land, and capital together.

19. The incomes received by persons providing goods and services are actually payments to the owners of _____ resources and are sometimes called _____ payments.

20. _____ must be subtracted from gross domestic product to get net national product (NNP).

21. _____ income is the personal income available to individuals after taxes.

22. The formula for converting any year's nominal GDP into real GDP (in base year dollars) is real GDP equals _____ divided by the _____, times 100.

23. To calculate real per capita GDP, we divide _____ GDP by the _____ to get the value of real output of final goods and services per person.

24. We do not have _____ enough information on the output of nonmarket transactions to include it in the GDP.

25. The most important nonmarket transactions omitted from GDP are services provided directly _____.

26. The value that individuals place on leisure is _____ in calculating GDP.

Answers: 1. National income 2. GDP 3. final; intermediate 4. expenditure; income 5. expenditure 6. consumption; investment; government purchases; net exports 7. nondurable; durable; services 8. households 9. vehicles 10. more 11. capital; produce other goods 12. fixed; inventory 13. increase 14. Transfer 15. excluded 16. income 17. wages; rent; interest; profits 19. productive; factor 20. Depreciation 21. Disposable personal 22. nominal GDP; price-level index 23. real; total population 24. reliable 25. in the home 26. omitted

Key Terms and Concepts

national income accounting 607
gross domestic product (GDP) 608
double counting 608
expenditure approach 610
consumption 610
nondurable goods 610
durable goods 610
services 611
investment 611
fixed investment 611
producer goods 611
inventory investment 611
factor payments 613
gross national product (GNP) 613
depreciation 613
net national product (NNP) 613
indirect business taxes 613
national income (NI) 613
personal income (PI) 613
disposable personal income 613
real gross domestic product
    per capita 615

Section Check Answers

21.1 National Income Accounting: A Standardized Way to Measure Economic Performance

1. **Why does GDP measure only final goods and services produced, rather than all goods and services produced?**
   If the market value of every good and service sold were included in GDP, the same output would be counted more than once in many circumstances (as when the sales price of, say, bread includes the value of the flour that was used in making the bread, and the flour, in turn, includes the value of the wheat that was used to make the flour). Only final goods and services are included in GDP to avoid such double counting.

2. **Why aren't all of the expenditures on used goods in an economy included in current GDP?**
   Current GDP does not include expenditures on used goods because GDP is intended to measure the value of currently produced goods and services in the economy. Used goods are not currently produced and have already been counted for the year they were newly produced.

3. **Why do GDP statistics include real estate agents' commissions from selling existing homes and used car dealers' profits from selling used cars, but not the value of existing homes or used cars when they are sold?**
   Existing homes and used cars were both produced in the past and therefore aren't counted as part of current GDP. However, the services provided this year by real estate agents and used car dealers are currently produced, so the market value of those services, measured by real estate agent commissions and the profits earned by used car dealers, are included in GDP.

4. **Why are sales of previously existing inventories of hula hoops not included in the current year's GDP?**
   Previously existing inventories of any product are not newly produced and are therefore not included in current year GDP. They were already produced and counted in an earlier period.

21.2 Measuring Total Production

1. **What would happen to GDP if consumption purchases (*C*) and net exports (*X* − *M*) both rose, holding other things equal?**
   Since GDP is the sum of consumption purchases (*C*), investment purchases (*I*), government purchases (*G*), and net exports (*X* − *M*), an increase of any of these components of GDP will increase GDP, other things being equal. Since either an increase in consumption (*C*) or an increase in net exports (*X* − *M*) increases GDP, both changing in the same time period will also increase GDP, other things being equal.

2. **Why do you think economic forecasters focus so much on consumption purchases and their determinants?**
   Economic forecasters focus so much on consumption purchases and their determinants because consumption purchases are by far the largest component (roughly two-thirds) of GDP; what happens to consumption purchases is therefore crucial to what happens to GDP.

3. **Why are durable goods purchases more unstable than nondurable goods purchases?**
   Durable goods purchases are more unstable than nondurable goods purchases because nondurable goods are used up in a relatively short period of time; hence, their purchase is hard to shift from one time period to another. Durable goods, on the other hand, provide service for long periods of time, so consumer durable purchases can be significantly delayed to "make do" during economic hard times and significantly accelerated during good times.

4. **Why does the investment component of GDP include purchases of new capital goods but not purchases of company stock?**
   New capital goods are newly produced goods, by definition, so they are included in GDP. However, sales

of company stock do not involve a newly produced good or service (although the services of the broker, measured by the transaction fee, are included as a newly produced service). When someone buys shares of stock from someone else, no goods are being newly produced. Instead, already existing ownership claims on the future income of the company are simply being transferred from one person to another.

5. **If Mary received a welfare check this year, would that transfer payment be included in this year's GDP? Why or why not?**
   GDP includes only currently produced goods and services. But since transfer payments are not payments in exchange for newly produced goods and services, they are not included in GDP.

6. **Can inventory investment or net exports ever be negative?**
   Yes. If end-of-the-year inventories are smaller than beginning-of-the-year inventories, inventory investment is negative, and if the value of exports is smaller than the value of imports, net exports are negative.

21.3 Other Measures of Total Production and Total Income

1. **How is personal income different from national income?**
   Personal income, the amount of income available to spend by consumers, is not the same as national income, because owners of productive resources do not receive all of the income that they earn and they receive "unearned" transfer payments. Undistributed corporate profits and social insurance taxes, which are not received by the factors of production, must be subtracted from, and transfer payments must be added to, national income to get personal income.

2. **What is the difference between GDP and national income?**
   To find national income, we must subtract from GDP: (1) indirect business taxes, such as sales taxes; (2) depreciation—payments set aside for the replacement of worn-out capital; and (3) net income of foreigners in the United States.

21.4 Problems in Calculating an Accurate GDP

1. **If we overestimated inflation over time, would our calculations of real GDP growth be over- or underestimated?**
   Nominal GDP is deflated by the measure of inflation being used to calculate real GDP and real GDP growth. Therefore, for a given nominal GDP growth rate, overestimating inflation over time would result in underestimating real GDP growth over time.

2. **Why would the growth in real GDP overstate the growth of output per person in a country with a growing population?**
   Real GDP growth measures what happens to output for the economy as a whole. But if the population is growing, real GDP is being split among an increasing number of people, and thus real GDP growth exceeds per capita real GDP growth.

21.5 Problems with GDP as a Measure of Economic Welfare

1. **Why do GDP measures omit nonmarket transactions?**
   GDP measures omit nonmarket transactions because there is no accurate way to measure the values of those transactions, unlike for normal market transactions, where market prices can be used to measure the values involved.

2. **How would the existence of a high level of nonmarket activities in one country impact real GDP comparisons between it and other countries?**
   Since nonmarket activities are not included in GDP, GDP would understate the true value of total output more for a country with a relatively high level of nonmarket activities than for a country with a smaller proportion of nonmarket activities, making countries with smaller shares of nonmarket activities look more productive relative to countries with larger shares of nonmarket activities.

3. **If we choose to decrease our hours worked because we value the additional leisure time more, will the resulting change in real GDP accurately reflect the change in our well-being? Why or why not?**
   Decreasing hours worked will reduce real GDP, other things being equal. But if we choose to do so voluntarily, that would mean we place a higher value on the leisure time (which is not counted in GDP) than on the market output (which is counted in GDP) forgone by reducing hours worked, so the change in real GDP would not accurately reflect the change in our well-being.

4. **How do pollution and crime affect GDP? How do pollution- and crime-control expenditures impact GDP?**
   Neither pollution nor crime are included (as "bads" to be subtracted) in GDP calculations. However, market expenditures for pollution and crime control are included in GDP, as currently produced goods and services.

CHAPTER 21 STUDY GUIDE

True or False:

1. Not all goods and services exchanged in the current period are included in this year's GDP.
2. Measuring the performance of our economy is important to private businesses and to macroeconomic policymakers in setting goals and developing policy recommendations.
3. Following the expenditure method, GDP = C + I + G + (X − M).
4. The value of a good or service is determined by the market prices at which goods and services sell.
5. If we counted the value of intermediate goods as well as the full value of the final products in GDP, we would be double counting.
6. The distinction between whether a good is durable or nondurable is not clear and easy to apply.
7. In boom periods, expenditures on consumer durables increase less than expenditures on nondurables.
8. As incomes have risen, expenditures on services have been growing more rapidly than expenditures on goods.
9. The share of total consumption spent on goods rather than services exceeds 50 percent.
10. Purchases of stock are not included as part of investment in the national income accounts.
11. Fixed investments include all spending on capital goods except for residential construction.
12. Consumer spending is the most volatile category of GDP.
13. Government expenditures on goods and services as a proportion of GDP have grown over the last 30 years.
14. Even though exports are consumed in other countries, they are included in measures of domestic GDP.
15. Net exports are a small but positive category of GDP for the United States.
16. The net income of foreigners must be added to GDP to get GNP.
17. When someone makes an expenditure for a good or service, that spending creates income for someone else.
18. National income is a measure of the income earned by owners of resources.
19. The primary problem in calculating accurate U.S. GDP statistics over time is that the "yardstick" used in adding together the values of different products, the U.S. dollar, changes in value over time.
20. Real GDP equals nominal GDP divided by the price-level index, times 100.
21. In periods of inflation, real GDP growth will tend to be less than nominal GDP growth.
22. The measure of economic welfare most often cited is nominal per capita gross domestic product.
23. In a country with a growing population, real GDP per capita will rise whenever real GDP rises.
24. Nonmarket transactions, the underground economy, and the value of government purchase of military goods are all omitted from official measures of GDP.
25. Real GDP is a highly accurate measure of the economic welfare of a nation.
26. Marrying one's housekeeper, so that you stop paying her for her services, would decrease reported GDP.
27. In less-developed countries, the failure to include nonmarket economic activity in GDP measures is a less serious measurement problem than in more developed countries.
28. Severe shortcomings are involved when using real GDP as a welfare measure. Nonetheless, at the present time, no alternative measure is generally accepted as better.
29. GDP is not decreased to reflect pollution resulting from production.
30. Some of the underground economy represents income from illegal sources, such as drug dealing.

Multiple Choice:

1. GDP measures
   a. the value of all intermediate goods produced domestically within a given period.
   b. the value of all final goods and services produced domestically within a given period.
   c. the value of all final goods and services sold in an economy within a given period.
   d. the government's domestic product.

2. GDP is calculated including
   a. final products but not intermediate products.
   b. manufactured goods but not services.
   c. intermediate products but not final products.
   d. only goods purchased by consumers in a given year.

3. The expenditure measure of GDP accounting adds together
   a. consumption, interest, government purchases, and net exports.
   b. consumption, government purchases, wages and salaries, and net exports.
   c. wages and salaries, rent, investment, and profits.
   d. wages and salaries, rent, interest, and profits.
   e. consumption, investment, government purchases, and net exports.

4. GDP is defined as the
   a. value of all final services produced in a country in a period of time.
   b. value of all final goods produced in a country in a period of time.
   c. value of all goods and services produced in a country in a period of time.
   d. value of all final goods and services produced in a country in a period of time.

5. Which of the following is not included in the calculated gross domestic product?
   a. A new Ford Expedition sport-utility vehicle.
   b. A construction firm's purchase of lumber to build a four-bedroom home.
   c. A dinner at Burger King.
   d. The purchase of a newly constructed home.

6. Which of the following is not an example of an intermediate product?
   a. The purchase of tires by Ford Motor Company to put on its Ford Explorers.
   b. The purchase of wood by a home construction firm.
   c. The purchase of leather by a shoe manufacturer.
   d. The purchase of a window to be installed by a homeowner in his house.
   e. All of the above are examples of intermediate products.

7. Investment includes
   a. fixed investment plus subtractions from business inventories.
   b. fixed investment plus government investment plus additions to business inventories.
   c. fixed investment.
   d. fixed investment plus government investment.
   e. fixed investment plus additions to business inventories.

8. Which category of consumption spending tends to be the most unstable over the business cycle?
   a. Durable consumer goods.
   b. Services.
   c. Nondurable consumer goods.
   d. All of these categories of consumer spending are highly unstable over the business cycle.

9. Which of the following are most likely to be classified by economists as consumer durable goods?
   a. Automobiles, furniture, CD players.
   b. Stocks, bonds, EE savings bonds, CDs (certificates of deposit).
   c. Drugs, toys, magazines, books.
   d. Food, clothing, shelter.

10. Included in the investment category under the expenditure approach to GDP accounting is (are)
    a. additions to inventory.
    b. machines and tools.
    c. newly constructed residential housing.
    d. all of the above.

11. Which of the following is not included in government purchases?
    a. Government purchases of investment goods.
    b. Government spending on services.
    c. Transfer payments.
    d. None of the above is included in government purchases.
    e. Neither b. nor c. is included in government purchases.

12. We can be certain that net exports fall if
    a. both exports and imports rise.
    b. both exports and imports fall.
    c. exports fall and imports rise.
    d. exports rise and imports fall.
    e. either b or d occurs.

13. A negative amount of net exports in the GDP expenditures accounting means
    a. net exports have declined from the previous period.
    b. imports are less than exports.
    c. the sum of this period's exports and imports has declined from the previous period.
    d. exports are less than imports.
    e. none of the above.

14. If the United States imported $2.9 billion worth of goods and services and sold $1.5 billion worth of goods and services outside its borders, net exports would equal
    a. −$4.4 billion.
    b. $4.4 billion.
    c. $1.4 billion.
    d. −$1.4 billion.
    e. none of the above.

15. French perfume that is purchased in the United States is accounted for in which expenditure category of U.S. GDP?
    a. consumption
    b. investment
    c. government purchases
    d. net exports.

16. Which of the following will be counted as part of this year's U.S. GDP?
    a. Goods produced this year but not sold until next year
    b. Goods produced this year by an American working in Paris
    c. Purchases of Cisco Systems stock (not issued this year) that take place this March
    d. Sales of used lawn mowers that take place this year
    e. None of the above

17. The largest category of GDP is _____ and the most unstable category of GDP is _____ .
    a. consumption; investment.
    b. investment; consumption.
    c. consumption; consumption.
    d. government; investment.
    e. consumption; government purchases.

18. Which of the following is *not* considered a factor payment?
    a. Wages.
    b. Interest.
    c. Investment spending.
    d. Profit.
    e. Rent.

19. In the income approach to measuring GDP, factor payments do *not* include
    a. wages and salaries for the use of labor services.
    b. rent for land.
    c. interest payments for the use of capital goods.
    d. transfer payments.
    e. profits for entrepreneurs.

20. What is *not* subtracted from GDP to get national income?
    a. The net income of foreigners
    b. Depreciation
    c. Indirect business taxes
    d. All of the above are subtracted from GDP to get national income.

21. Disposable income is
    a. a measure of the market value of total output.
    b. a measure of the income households have to spend after paying taxes.
    c. a measure of household income from investment income, such as dividends and capital gains.
    d. a measure of the income households have to spend before paying taxes.

22. Disposable personal income will decrease when
    a. taxes rise and transfer payments rise.
    b. taxes rise and transfer payments fall.
    c. taxes fall and transfer payments rise.
    d. taxes fall and transfer payments fall.

23. Nominal GDP is
    a. the base year market value of all final goods and services produced domestically during a given period.
    b. the current year market value of all final goods and services produced domestically during a given period.
    c. usually greater than real GDP.
    d. the current year market value of domestic production of intermediate goods.
    e. Both b. and c. are correct.

24. Nominal GDP differs from real GDP in that
    a. real GDP excludes taxes paid to the government, while nominal GDP does not.
    b. nominal GDP tends to increase when total production of output in the economy increases, while real GDP does not.
    c. nominal GDP is measured in base year prices, while real GDP is measured in current year prices.
    d. nominal GDP is measured in current year prices, while real GDP is measured in base year prices.

25. The consumer price index
    a. does not take government purchases into account, unlike the GDP deflator.
    b. takes business investment purchases into account, unlike the GDP deflator.
    c. equals 100 in the base year, unlike the GDP deflator.
    d. is generally used to adjust nominal GDP to calculate real GDP.
    e. None of the above is true.

26. Real GDP in base year dollars equals
    a. nominal GDP times the price index.
    b. nominal GDP divided by the price index, times 100.
    c. nominal GDP divided by the price index.
    d. nominal GDP times the price index, divided by 100.
    e. none of the above.

27. Suppose that real GDP in 2010 equals $8,000 trillion and that in 2011 real GDP equals $8,500 trillion. It can be concluded that
    a. total output decreased from 2010 to 2011.
    b. total output increased from 2010 to 2011.
    c. the economy experienced inflation from 2010 to 2011.
    d. the economy experienced deflation from 2010 to 2011.
    e. Both b. and c. are true.

28. If real GDP per capita increases and population increases, then real GDP
    a. will rise.
    b. will fall.
    c. will remain unchanged.
    d. could either rise, fall, or remain unchanged.

29. If nominal GDP rises from $250 billion to $300 billion, when the GDP deflator goes from 100 to 125, real GDP
    a. rises.
    b. falls.
    c. stays the same.
    d. could either be rising or falling.

30. Which of the following is measured in per capita GDP?
    a. leisure.
    b. underground economic transactions.
    c. the services of homemakers.
    d. external benefits and costs.
    e. none of the above.

31. Important factors that are excluded from GDP measurements include
    a. leisure.
    b. the underground economy.
    c. nonmarket transactions.
    d. the value of changes in the environment.
    e. all of the above.

32. If country A has a bigger underground economy than country B, and country A's citizens work fewer hours per week than the citizens of country B, other things being equal, then
    a. GDP comparisons between the countries would understate the economic welfare of country A compared to B.
    b. GDP comparisons between the countries would overstate the economic welfare of country A compared to B.
    c. it is impossible to know which direction GDP comparisons between the countries would be biased as measures of the economic welfare of the two countries.
    d. it would not introduce any bias in using GDP to compare economic welfare between the countries.
    e. none of the above would be true.

Problems:

1. Which of the following are included in GDP calculations?
    a. Air pollution that diminishes the quality of the air you breathe.
    b. Toxic-waste cleanup performed by a local company.
    c. Car parts manufactured in the United States for a car assembled in Mexico.
    d. A purchase of 1,000 shares of IBM stock.
    e. Monthly Social Security payment received by a retiree.
    f. Cleaning services performed by Molly Maid Corporation.
    g. Lawn-mowing services performed by a neighborhood child.
    h. Drugs sold illegally on a local street corner.
    i. Prescription drugs manufactured in the United States and sold at a local pharmacy.
    j. A rug woven by hand in Turkey.

2. Answer the following questions about GDP:
   a. Why does GDP measure only the value of goods and services produced within a country?
   b. What is the definition of GDP?
   c. Why does GDP measure only the final value of goods and services?
   d. How does GDP treat the sales of used goods?
   e. How does GDP treat sales of corporate stock from one stockholder to another?

3. The expenditures on tires by the Ford Motor Company are not included directly in GDP statistics while consumer expenditures on replacement tires are included. Why?

4. To which category of U.S. GDP expenditure does each of the following correspond?
   a. F-22 fighter jets built by a U.S. aerospace corporation and contracted for by the government.
   b. A new steel mill.
   c. Department of Motor Vehicles services.
   d. Automobiles exported to Europe.
   e. A refrigerator.
   f. A newly constructed four-bedroom house.
   g. A restaurant meal.
   h. Additions to inventory at a furniture store.

5. Fill in the missing data for the following table (in billions):
   Consumption: _____
   Consumption of durable goods: $1,200
   Consumption of nondurable goods: $1,800
   Consumption of services: $2,400
   Investment: _____
   Fixed investment: $800
   Inventory investment: $600
   Government expenditures on goods and services: $1,600
   Government transfer payments: $500
   Exports: $500
   Imports: $650
   Net exports: _____
   GDP: _____

6. Using any relevant information below, calculate GDP using the expenditure approach.

Inventory investment	$50 billion
Fixed investment	$120 billion
Consumer durables	$420 billion
Consumer nondurables	$275 billion
Interest	$140 billion
Indirect business taxes	$45 billion
Government wages and salaries	$300 billion
Government purchases of goods and services	$110 billion
Imports	$80 billion
Exports	$40 billion
Profits	$320 billion
Services	$600 billion

7. Nominal GDP in Nowhereland in 2011 was $4 trillion and its Nominal GDP in 2012 was $4.8 trillion. Can you say that the production of goods and services in Nowhereland has increased between 2011 and 2012? Why or why not?

8. Fill in the missing data for the following table:

Year	GDP Deflator	Nominal GDP (in billions)	Real GDP (in billions)
2007	90.9	$7,000	_____
2008	100	_____	$8,000
2009	_____	$10,000	$8,000
2010	140	$14,000	_____
2011	150	_____	$12,000

9. Answer the following questions:
   a. How are consumer durable goods like investments?
   b. Can either fixed or inventory investment be negative in a given year?
   c. Why isn't all of government spending part of GDP?
   d. Do consumer durable goods or nondurable goods tend to change more over the course of the business cycle?

10. How does GDP compare to GNP when:
    a. earnings of foreigners and foreign firms in the U.S. exceed earnings of American citizens and firms overseas?
    b. earnings of foreigners and foreign firms in the U.S. are less than earnings of American citizens and firms overseas?
    c. earnings of foreigners and foreign firms in the U.S. equal earnings of American citizens and firms overseas?

11. Answer the following questions:
    a. Could real GDP grow at the same time that real GDP per capita falls?
    b. Could people's real consumption possibilities expand at the same time that real GDP per capita falls?
    c. Could next year's real GDP exceed next year's nominal GDP?
    d. How does changing amounts of leisure complicate comparisons of real well-being over time?

12. List, from the largest magnitude to the smallest, the following categories: disposable personal income, gross national product, national income, net national product, personal income.

Economic Growth in the Global Economy

22

22.1 Economic Growth
22.2 Determinants of Economic Growth
22.3 Public Policy and Economic Growth
22.4 Population and Economic Growth

John Maynard Keynes, one of the most influential economic thinkers of all time, once said that "in the long run, we are all dead."

He made this statement because he was primarily concerned with explaining and reducing short-term fluctuations in the level of business activity. He wanted to smooth out the business cycle, largely because of the implications that cyclical fluctuations had for buyers and sellers in terms of unemployment and price instability. No one would deny that Keynes's concerns were important and legitimate.

At the same time, however, Keynes's flippant remark about the long run discounts the fact that human welfare is greatly influenced by long-term changes in a nation's capacity to produce goods and services. Emphasis on short-run economic fluctuations ignores the longer-term dynamic changes that affect output, leisure, real income, and lifestyle.

What are the determinants of long-run economic change in our ability to produce goods and services? What are some of the consequences of rapid economic change? Why are some nations rich while others are poor? Does growth in output improve our economic welfare? We will explore these questions in this chapter.

SECTION 22.1 Economic Growth

* What is economic growth?
* What is the Rule of 70?
* What is productivity?

Defining Economic Growth

Economic growth is usually measured by the annual percentage change in real output of goods and services per capita (real GDP per capita), reflecting the expansion of the economy over time. We focus on per capita because we want to isolate the effect of increased population on economic growth. That is, an increase in population, *ceteris paribus,* will lower the standard of living because more people will be sharing a fixed real GDP. It is also important to note that our economic growth rate does not say anything about the distribution of output and income. For example, a country could have extraordinary growth in per capita output and yet the poor might make little or no improvement in their standard of living. That is, it is possible that income group made little or no gain.

In Chapter 3, we introduced the production possibilities curve. Along the production possibilities curve, the economy is producing at its potential output. How much the economy will produce at its potential output, sometimes called its *natural rate of output,* depends on the quantity and quality of its resources, including labor, capital (factories, machinery, tools, productive skills, etc.), and natural resources (land, coal, timber, oil, iron, etc.). In addition, technology can increase the economy's production capabilities. As shown in Exhibit 1, improvements in and greater stocks of land, labor, capital, and entrepreneurial activity will shift the production possibilities curve outward. Another way of saying that economic growth has shifted the production possibilities curve outward is to say that it has increased potential output.

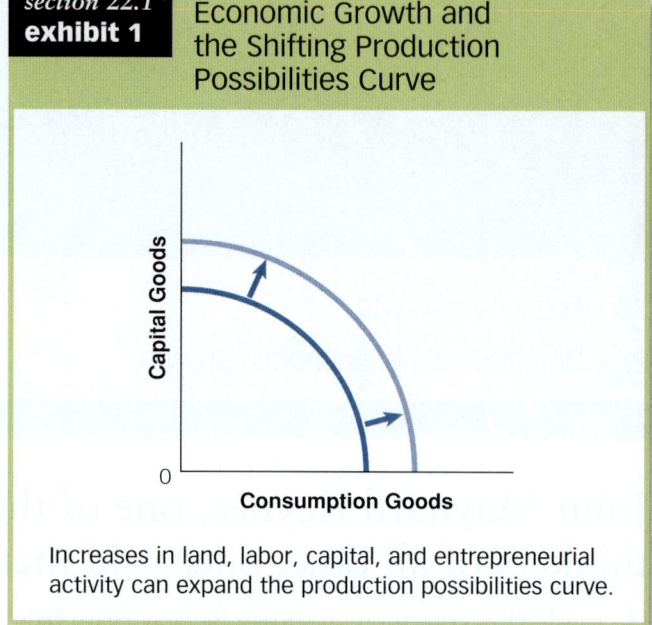

section 22.1 exhibit 1 Economic Growth and the Shifting Production Possibilities Curve

Increases in land, labor, capital, and entrepreneurial activity can expand the production possibilities curve.

economic growth an upward trend in the real per capita output of goods and services

The Rule of 70

If Nation A and Nation B start off with the same population and the same level of real GDP, will a slight difference in their growth rates over a long period of time make much of a difference? Yes. In the first year or two, the difference will be small; but even over a decade the difference will be large, and after 50 to 100 years it will be huge. The final effect will be a much higher standard of living in the nation with the greater economic growth, *ceteris paribus.*

A simple formula, called the Rule of 70, shows how long it will take a nation to double its output at various growth rates. If you take a nation's growth rate and divide it into 70, you will have the approximate time it will take to double the income level. For example, if a nation grows at 3.5 percent per year, then the economy will double every 20 years (70/3.5). However, if an economy only grows at 2 percent per year, the economy will double every 35 years (70/2); and at a 1 percent annual growth rate, it will take 70 years to double income (70/1). So even a small change in the growth rate of a nation will have a large impact over a lengthy period.

In Exhibit 2 we see the growth rates in real GDP for the United States since 1790. The exhibit shows U.S. Real GDP per capita (measured in 2000 dollars) grew from $917 in 1790 to $38,265 in 2008. Since the depth of the Great Depression in 1932 Americans today, on average, can purchase almost 9 times the amount of goods and services.

In Exhibit 3, we see a comparison of selected industrial countries. Because of differences in

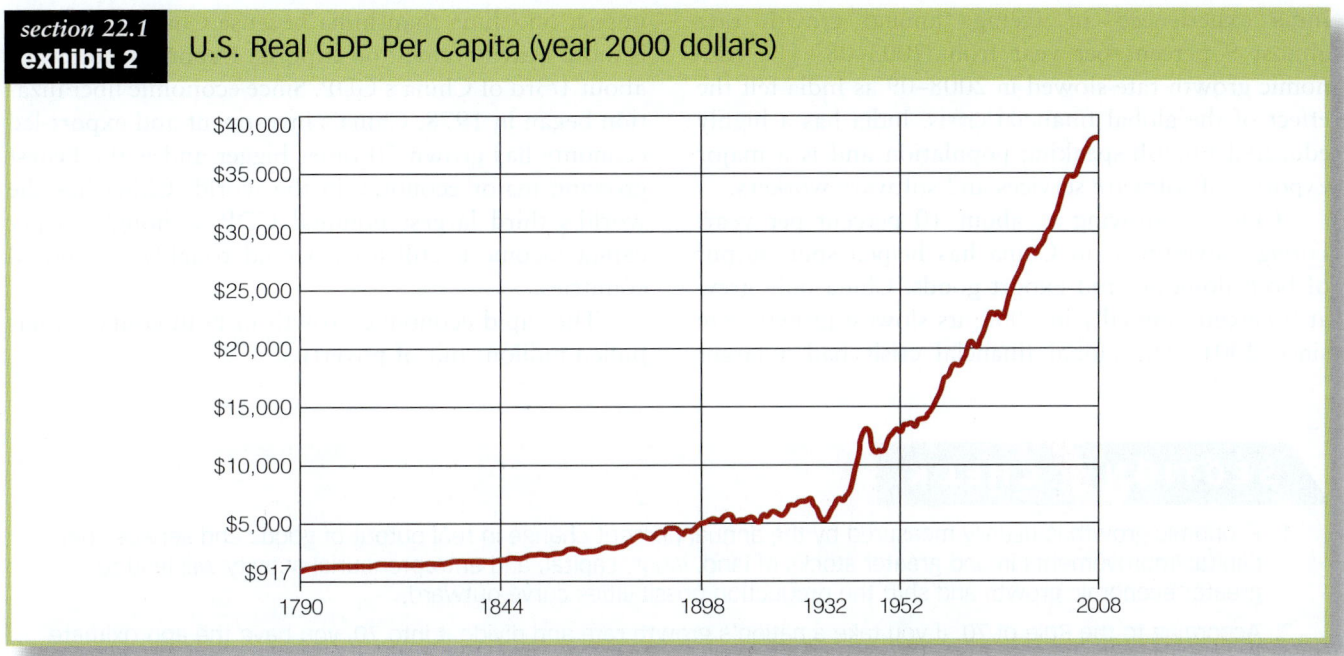

section 22.1 exhibit 2 U.S. Real GDP Per Capita (year 2000 dollars)

SOURCE: http://www.measuringgrowth.org

growth rates, some countries will become richer than others over time. With relatively slower economic growth, today's richest countries will not be the richest for very long. On the other hand, with even slight improvements in economic growth, today's poorest countries will not remain poor for long. China and India have both experienced spectacular economic growth over the past 20 years. Because of this economic growth, much of the world is now poorer than these two heavily populated countries. Other countries, such as Ireland, once one of the poorest countries in Western Europe, is now one of the richest. Disappointing growth rates over the past 30 years have left Argentina's economy and standard of living unchanged for a quarter of a century.

Because of past economic growth, the "richest" or "most-developed" countries today have many times the market output of the "poorest" or "least-developed" countries. Put differently, the most-developed countries produce and market more output in a day than the least-developed countries do in a year. The international differences in income, output, and wealth are indeed striking and have caused a great deal of friction between developed and less-developed countries. The United States and the nations of the European Union experienced sizable increases in real output over the past two centuries; but even in 1800 most of these nations were better off in terms of market output than many impoverished present-day countries such as Ethiopia, India, and Nepal. See the U.S. real GDP per capita growth from 1790–1860 in Exhibit 2.

section 22.1 exhibit 3 Growth in Real GDP per Capita in Selected Industrial Countries

	1979–2007
United States	1.8%
Japan	2.0
Germany	1.6
France	1.5
Italy	1.6
United Kingdom	2.1
Canada	1.6

SOURCE: International Monetary Fund, http://imf.org, December 2007.

China and India

Both China and India have per capita real GDP levels that are far less than the United States. The power of compound interest could well change this ranking in the future. As Nobel laureate Robert Lucas once said, "Once one starts to think about differences in growth rates among countries, it is hard to think about anything else." But the current rate of economic growth in these two countries will change things in the future.

India experienced an average annual growth rate almost 9 percent per year from 2003–08. The economic growth rate slowed in 2008–09 as India felt the effect of the global financial crisis. India has a highly educated English-speaking population and is a major exporter of software services and software workers.

China is growing at about 10 percent per year. Foreign investment in China has helped spur output of both domestic and export goods. China only grew at 9 percent annually in 2008; its slowest growth rate since 2001. The global financial crisis had a larger impact on China than India because China's economy is more heavily reliant on exports. Exports account for about 1/3rd of China's GDP. Since economic liberalization began in 1978, China's investment and export-led economy has grown 70 times bigger and is the fastest growing major economy in the world. China has the world's third largest nominal GDP, although its per capita income is still low, behind roughly a hundred countries.

The rapid economic growth in both countries has pulled millions out of poverty.

SECTION CHECK

1. Economic growth is usually measured by the annual percent change in real output of goods and services per capita. Improvements in and greater stocks of land, labor, capital, and entrepreneurial activity will lead to greater economic growth and shift the production possibilities curve outward.
2. According to the Rule of 70, if you take a nation's growth rate and divide it into 70, you have the approximate time it will take to double the income level.
3. Rising productivity plays a key role in determining standard of living and long-run economic growth.

---

1. Why does the production possibilities curve shift outward with economic growth?
2. Even if "in the long run, we are all dead," are you glad earlier generations of Americans worked and invested for economic growth?
3. If long-run consequences were not important, would many students go to college or participate in internship programs without pay?
4. When the Dutch "created" new land with their system of dikes, what did it do to their production possibilities curve? Why?

SECTION 22.2 Determinants of Economic Growth

* What factors contribute to economic growth?
* What is human capital?

Factors That Contribute to Economic Growth

any explanations of the process of economic growth have been proposed. Which is correct? No single description can give a complete picture of economic growth. However, each may be part of a more complicated reality. Economic growth is a complex process involving many important factors, no one of which completely dominates. We can, at a minimum, identify four factors that nearly everyone would agree have contributed to economic growth in some or all countries:

1. The quantity and quality of labor resources (labor and human capital)
2. Increase in the use of inputs provided by the land (natural resources)
3. Physical capital inputs (machines, tools, buildings, inventories)
4. Technological knowledge (new ways of combining given quantities of labor, natural resources, and capital inputs), allowing greater output than previously possible

Indeed, today's workers produce so much more than in years past because they have more physical capital (machinery and offices) to work with and they have more human capital (schooling and on-the-job training). Producing more output per worker is what economists call increased labor productivity.

Labor

We know that labor is needed in all forms of productive activity. But other things being equal, an increase in the quantity of labor inputs does not necessarily increase output per capita. For example, if the increase in the quantity of labor inputs is due to an increase in population, per capita growth might not occur, because the increase in output could be offset by the increase in population. However, if a greater proportion of the population works (i.e., the labor force participation rate rises) or if workers put in longer hours, output per capita will increase—assuming that the additional work activity adds something to output.

When workers acquire qualitative improvements (learning new skills, for example), output increases. Workers with a large stock of human capital are more productive than those with small stocks of human capital. Indeed, it has become popular to view labor skills as *human capital* that can be augmented or improved by education and on-the-job training. Like physical capital, human capital must be produced, usually by means of teachers, schoolrooms, libraries, computer labs, and time devoted to studying. Human capital may be more important than physical capital as a determinant of economic growth. It certainly can increase labor productivity. Human capital also includes improvements in health. Better health conditions allow workers to be more productive. In fact, University of Chicago economist and Nobel laureate Robert Fogel has shown that improved health from better nutrition has a significant impact on long-run economic growth.

Natural Resources

An abundance of natural resources, such as fertile soil, and other raw materials, such as timber and oil, can enhance output. Many scholars cite the abundance of natural resources in the United States as one reason for its historical success. Canada and Australia are endowed with a large natural resource base and high per capita incomes. Resources are, however, not the whole story; for example, Japan and Hong Kong have had tremendous economic success despite having relatively few natural resources. On the other hand, Brazil has a large and varied natural resource base, yet its income per capita is relatively low compared with many developed countries. It appears that a natural resource base can affect the initial development process, but sustained growth is influenced by other factors. However, most economists would agree that a limited resource base does pose an important obstacle to economic growth.

Physical Capital

Recall that physical capital (or just capital) includes goods like tools, machinery, and factories that have already been produced and are now producing other goods and services. Combining workers with more capital makes workers more productive. Thus, capital investment can lead to increases in labor productivity.

Even in primitive economies, workers usually have some rudimentary tools to further their productive activity. Consider the farmer who needs to dig a ditch to improve drainage in his fields. If he used just his bare hands, it might take a lifetime to complete the job. If he used a shovel, he could dig the ditch in hours or days. But with a big earth-moving machine, he could do it in minutes. Most economists agree that capital formation has played a significant role in the economic development of nations. Physical capital, like human capital, increases labor productivity.

Per-Worker Production Function

In chapter 3, we found that by increasing the rate of saving, we can produce a greater amount of new capital goods and increase the stock of productive capital for the future. Because resources are scarce, in order to invest in new capital, society must sacrifice some current consumption. To save more now, we need to consume less now. Ultimately, this will allow society to consume more in the future.

In Exhibit 1, we see how the amount of capital per worker influences the amount of output per worker. This positively sloped curve is called the per-worker production function. Holding the other determinants of output constant (human capital, natural resources and technology) we see that moving up along the production function, when the quantity of capital per worker rises, so does the amount of output per worker, but at a diminishing rate—the curve eventually becomes flatter as more capital per worker is added. That is, capital is subject to diminishing marginal returns. If the economy has a very low level of capital, an extra unit of capital leads to a relatively large increase in output—a movement from point A to point B in Exhibit 2. If the economy already has a great deal of capital, an extra unit of capital leads to a relatively smaller increase in output—a movement from point C to point D in Exhibit 2. Imagine that you owned a small store and you had 10 employees and one computer. As you added more computers, output per worker rose,

section 22.2 exhibit 1: Per-Worker Production Function

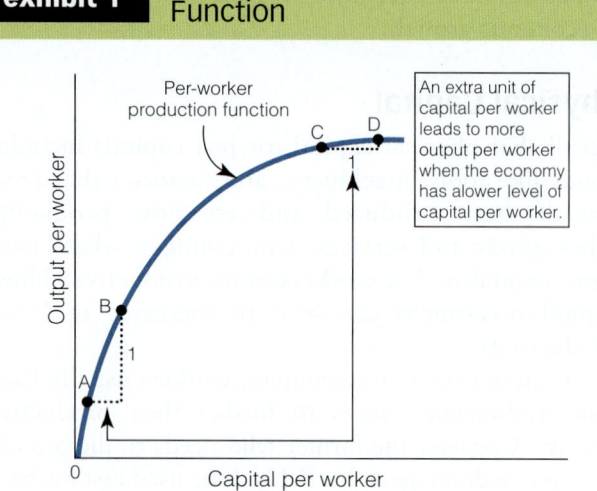

An extra unit of capital leads to a large increase in output per worker when the economy initially has a low level of capital per worker—a movement from point A to point B. However, when the economy has a high level of capital per worker, an extra unit of capital leads to a small increase in output—a movement from point C to point D. This occurs because of diminishing marginal returns to capital.

but only up to a point. What if you added 20 computers to you work force of 10? Adding more computers (capital) still adds to output but by smaller and smaller additional amounts. This is what is called diminishing marginal returns to capital. Thus, in the long run, other things equal, the benefits of a higher saving rate and additional capital stock become smaller and the rate of growth slows.

Some economists believe diminishing marginal returns to capital can help explain the variation in growth rates between rich and poor countries. In poor countries, where there is little capital, small increases in capital investment can lead to relatively large increases in productivity. In rich countries, where workers already have large amounts of capital, increases in capital investment may have a very small additional effect on productivity. Economists call this the catch up effect.

innovation
applications of new knowledge that create new products or improve existing products

Technological Advances

Most economists believe that it is the progress in technology that drives productivity. It is technology that allows workers to produce more. Technological change can lead to better machinery and equipment, increases in capital, and better organization and production methods. Technological advances stem from human ingenuity and creativity in developing new ways of combining the factors of production to enhance the amount of output from a given quantity of resources. The process of technological advance involves invention and innovation. **Innovation** is the adoption of the product or process. For example, in the United States, the invention and innovation of the cotton gin, the Bessemer steel-making process, and the railroad were important stimuli to economic growth. New technology, however, must be introduced into productive use by managers or entrepreneurs who weigh the perceived estimates of benefits of the new technology against estimates of costs. Thus, the entrepreneur is also an important economic factor in the growth process.

Technological advances permit us to economize on one or more inputs used in the production process. They can permit savings of labor. For example, when a new machine does the work of many workers, technology is said to be embodied in capital and to be labor saving. Technology, however, can also be land (natural resource) saving or even capital saving. For example, nuclear fission has permitted us to build power plants that economize on the use of coal, a natural resource. The reduction in transportation time that accompanied the invention and innovation of the railroad allowed businesses to reduce the capital they needed in the form of inventories. Because goods could be obtained more quickly, businesses could reduce the stock kept on their shelves.

And inventions can come in all sizes. Obviously, the semiconductor chip made a huge impact on productivity and growth, but so did the Post-it note that was introduced in the early 1980s, the laptop computer, or barcode scanners that were first introduced in Wal-Mart stores. We have also seen huge advances in communication (the Internet) and medicines.

In short, better methods of organization and production can lead to increases in labor productivity. When fewer workers are needed in a grocery store or a department store due to better methods of organization, or new machinery and equipment, labor productivity rises.

In Exhibit 2, we see that technological change can shift the per-worker production curve upward, producing more output per worker with the same amount of capital per worker.

Technological change allows the economy to escape the full impact of diminishing marginal returns to capital. Thus, in the long run, other things equal, an economy must experience technological advance in order to

section 22.2 exhibit 2 — Technological Change and the Per-Worker Production Function

Technological change causes the per-worker production function to shift upward from PF_1 to PF_2 allowing for the production of more output per worker with the same amount of capital per worker.

improve its standard of living and overcome the diminishing marginal returns to capital.

New Growth Theory

In Chapter 2, we discussed that most of economics reduces to stories about incentives. This is true for technology, too. The greater the reward for new technology, the more research and technology will occur. According to Paul Romer, a new growth economist, economic growth can continue unimpeded, as long as we keep coming up with new ideas. And there is a role for government, too—encouraging the creation of new ideas. While the market is a great engine for economic growth, it can be "turbocharged" with strong institutional support for education and science. Romer believes that it is ideas that drive economic growth. To Romer, economic growth comes from increases in value—rearranging fixed amounts of matter and making new combinations that are more valuable. "There are zillions of combinations that we can use to make new goods and services we value."

SECTION CHECK

1. The factors that contribute to economic growth are increased quantity and quality of labor, natural resources, physical capital, and technological advances.
2. Labor can be improved through investment in human capital—that is, education, on-the-job training, and experience can improve the quality of labor.

---

1. Why is no single factor capable of completely explaining economic growth patterns?
2. Why might countries with relatively scarce labor be leaders in labor-saving innovations? In what area would countries with relatively scarce land likely be innovative leaders?
3. Why could an increase in the price of oil increase real GDP growth in oil-exporting countries such as Saudi Arabia and Mexico, while decreasing growth in oil-importing countries such as the United States and Japan?
4. How is Hong Kong a dramatic example of why abundant natural resources are not necessary for rapid economic growth?

Section 22.3: Public Policy and Economic Growth

- Why is the saving rate so important for increasing economic growth?
- Why is research and development so important for economic growth?
- Why are property rights so important for increasing economic growth?
- What impact will free trade have on economic growth?
- Why is education so important for economic growth?

The Impact of Economic Growth

Economic growth means more than an increase in the real income (output) of the population. A number of other important changes accompany changes in output. Claims that economic growth stimulates political freedom or democracy have even been made, but evidence for that correlation is far from conclusive. Even though some democratic societies are rich and some authoritarian ones are poor, the opposite also holds. That is, some features of democracy, such as majority voting and special interest groups, may actually be growth retarding. For example, if the majority decides to vote for large land reforms and wealth transfers, the consequences will be higher taxes and market distortions that will reduce incentives for work, investment, and ultimately economic growth. However, a nation can pursue a number of policies that will increase economic growth.

Saving Rates, Investment, Capital Stock, and Economic Growth

One of the most important determinants of economic growth is the saving rate. To consume more in the future, we must save more now. Generally, higher levels of saving will lead to higher rates of investment and capital formation and, therefore, greater economic growth. Individuals can either consume or save their income. If individuals choose to consume all their income, they will have nothing left for saving, which businesses could use for investment purposes to build new plants or replace worn-out or obsolete equipment. With little investment in capital stock, there will be little economic growth. Capital can also increase as a result of injections of capital from abroad (foreign direct investments), but the role of national saving rates in economic growth is of particular importance.

Exhibit 1 clearly shows that sustained rapid economic growth is associated with high rates of saving and investment around the world. However, investment alone does not guarantee economic growth. Economic growth hinges on the quality and type of investment as well as on investments in human capital and improvements in technology.

Infrastructure

Infrastructure (e.g., highways, ports, bridges, power lines, airports, and information technology) is critical to economic coordination and activity. Some infrastructure is private and some is public. In the past several decades, the amount of government investment in U.S. infrastructure has fallen. Some economists argue that improvements in infrastructure could lead to higher productivity. Others argue the causality runs in the other direction; that higher productivity leads to greater infrastructure. In addition, a special interest problem concerns favored districts with political clout that end up as the recipients of improved infrastructure—which may not be an efficient solution. Most would agree, however, that poor infrastructure is a major deterrent to economic growth.

Research and Development

Some scholars believe that the importance of **research and development (R&D)** is understated. Research and development consists of the activities undertaken to create new products and processes that will lead to technological progress. The concept of R&D is broad indeed—it can include new products, management improvements, production innovations, or simply learning by doing. However, it is clear that investing in R&D and rewarding innovators with patents have paid big dividends in the past 50 to 60 years. Some would argue that even larger rewards for research and development would spur even more rapid economic growth. Some types of scientific research may have far-reaching

> **research and development (R&D)** activities undertaken to create new products and processes that will lead to technological progress

section 22.3 exhibit 1 — Saving Rates and GDP Growth During High-Growth Periods in Selected Economies

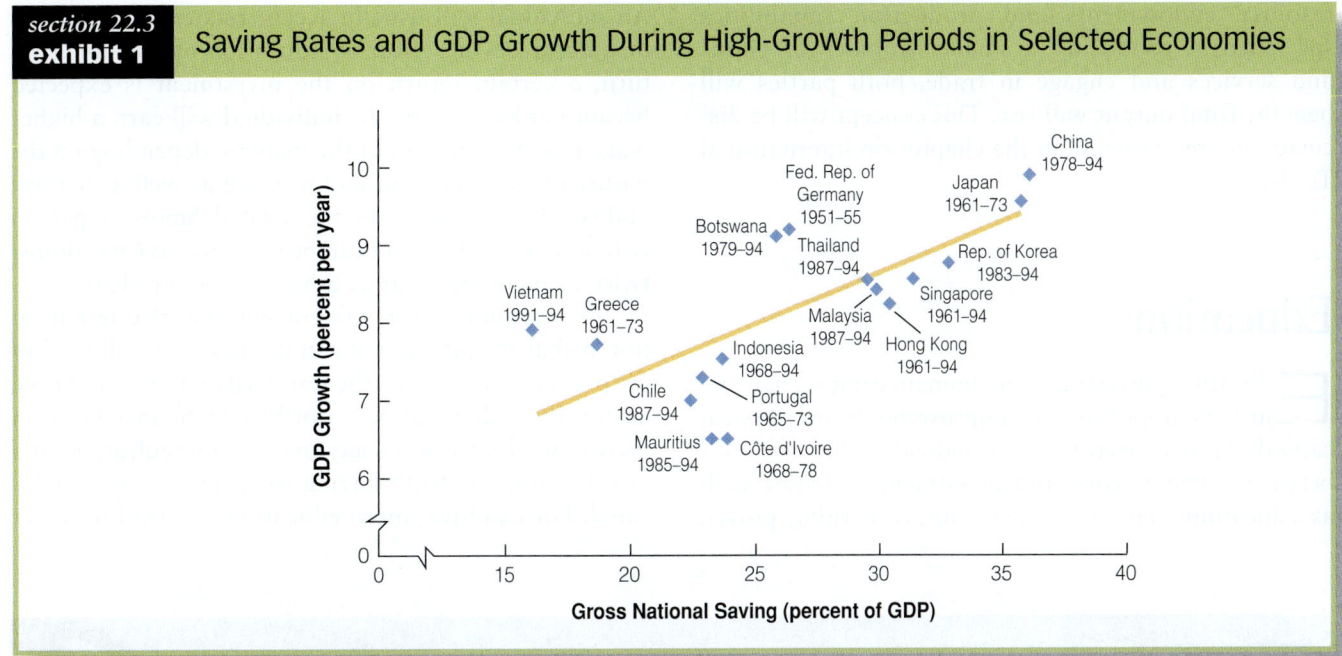

NOTE: Data are annual averages for the periods indicated.
SOURCE: World Bank, World Development Report, 1996, Oxford University Press, 1996. Republished with permission of the World Bank, from World Bank Development Report 1996; permission conveyed through Copyright Clearance Center, Inc.

benefits that cannot be captured by a private firm. Such a case presents a compelling argument for government support of basic research. GPS satellite systems in cars, for example, were originally designed for military purposes. In addition, an important link exists between R&D and capital investment. As already noted, when capital depreciates over time, it is replaced with new equipment that embodies the latest technology. Consequently, R&D may work hand in hand with investment to improve growth and productivity. Lastly, R&D may benefit foreigners as they import goods from technologically advanced countries to make their firms more efficient.

The Protection of Property Rights Impacts Economic Growth

Economic growth rates tend to be higher in countries where the government enforces property rights. Property rights give owners the legal right to keep or sell their properties—land, labor, or capital. Without property rights, life would be a huge "free-for-all," where people could take whatever they wanted. Economists call the government's ability to protect private property rights and enforce contracts the *rule of law*.

In most developed countries, property rights are effectively protected by the government. However, in developing countries, such protection is not usually the case. If the government does not enforce property rights, the private sector must respond in costly ways that stifle economic growth. For example, an unreliable judiciary system means that entrepreneurs must often rely on informal agreements that are difficult to enforce. As a result, they may have to pay bribes to get things done, and even then, they may not get the promised services. Individuals may have to buy private security or pay "organized crime" for protection against crime and corruption. In addition, landowners and business owners may be fearful of coups or takeovers from a new government, which might confiscate their property altogether. In short, if government is not adequately protecting property rights, the incentive to invest will be hindered, and political instability, corruption, and lower rates of economic growth will be likely. However, it may well be a two-way street. In the words of former U.N. Secretary-General Kofi Annan, "There will be no development without security and no security without development."

Free Trade and Economic Growth

Allowing free trade can also lead to greater output because of the principle of comparative advantage. Essentially, the principle of comparative advantage suggests that if two nations or individuals with different resource endowments and production capabilities specialize in producing a smaller number of goods and services and engage in trade, both parties will benefit. Total output will rise. This concept will be discussed in greater detail in the chapter on International Trade.

Education

Education, investment in human capital, may be just as important as improvements in physical capital. At any given time, an individual has a choice between current work and investment activities such as education that can increase future earning power. An individual will usually accept reduction in current income to devote effort to education and training. In turn, a certain return on the investment is expected because in later years, the individual will earn a higher wage rate (the amount of the increase depending on the nature of the education and training as well as natural ability). For example, in the United States, a person with a college education can be expected to earn almost twice as much per year as a high school graduate.

One argument for government subsidizing education is that the investment can increase the skill level of the population and raise the standard of living. However, even if the individual does not benefit financially from increased education, society may benefit culturally and in other respects from having its members highly educated. For example, more education can lead to lower

POLICY application: INSTITUTIONAL ECONOMICS

Douglass C. North, an economic historian, was the recipient of the Nobel Prize in Economics in 1993. One of North's contributions is his analysis of the linkage between institutional changes and economic growth. According to North, "the sources of sustained economic growth and the determinants of income distribution are to be found in the institutional structure of a society. Economic historians can no longer write good economic history without explicitly taking into account the institutional structure of the system, both economic and political. We can't avoid the political aspect because decisions made outside the marketplace have had, and will continue to have, a fundamental influence upon growth and welfare."

Institutions matter because they affect the choices open to people, shape incentives, and are an important determinant of human action. The institutional structure of a society (or the "rules of the game," as Mr. North calls it) includes formal rules (such as constitutions, property rights, laws of contract), informal constraints (conventions, customs, codes of conduct), and the means of enforcing both formal and informal standards of behavior (courts, social ostracism, personal beliefs). As in sports, the way the game is played and its outcome depend on the nature of the rules, the character of the players, and the fairness (impartiality) of the referee. Moreover, the choice of the rules and the enforcement mechanisms will be affected by prevailing ideology and culture.

According to North, rules must be credible if they are to be effective. That is, they must be enforced. Private enforcement is possible, but as economic life becomes more complex, political institutions become the major instrument for defining and enforcing property rights. The history of economic performance cannot be separated from the history of political performance. The New Institutional Economics studies both.

North has shown that those countries that (1) adopt a rule of law, one which limits the power of government over economic life and protects the rights of persons and property and (2) maintain open markets and freedom of contract are more likely to achieve long-run economic prosperity than those who do not.

According to North, economic change is "path dependent": The future depends on the past and present choices. History is not predetermined or based on some grand design; it is the sum of human actions. How we act will depend on the rules we inherit and formulate, as well as on our cultural and moral heritage. But ultimately, it is individuals who must choose.

SOURCES: See Douglass C. North, *Growth and Welfare in the American Past*, 2nd ed. (Englewood Cliffs, NJ: Prentice Hall, 1974); and James Dorn, "North Wins Nobel for New Institutional Economics," *The Margin* (Spring 1994), 56.

crime rates, new ideas that may benefit society, and more informed voters.

With economic growth, illiteracy rates fall and formal education grows. The correlation between per capita output and the proportion of the population that is able to read or write is striking. Improvements in literacy stimulate economic growth by reducing barriers to the flow of information; when information costs are high, out of ignorance, many resources flow to or remain in uses that are unproductive. Moreover, education imparts skills that are directly useful in raising labor productivity, whether it is mathematics taught to a sales clerk, engineering techniques taught to a college graduate, or just good ideas that facilitate production and design.

Many economists believe that the tremendous growth in East Asia (South Korea, Taiwan, Hong Kong, and Singapore) in the last half of the twentieth century was a result of good basic education for many of their citizens. This reason was one of many factors that contributed to growth, including high rates of saving and a large increase in labor force participation.

Improving education is a relatively inexpensive way to enrich the lives of people living in poorer countries. Education allows these countries to produce more advanced goods and services and enjoy the wealth created from trading in the global economy. Taiwan, India, and South Korea are now part of the high-tech global economy, but most of Africa, with the lowest levels of education, has been left behind.

global WATCH: EDUCATION REFORM IN ASIA AND LATIN AMERICA

The message of the Asian experience is clear: Good universal basic education makes most people more productive and satisfied with their own lives, more adaptable to changing circumstances, and better qualified to contribute to their own and national development, according to William Ratliff.

Reforming Asian countries have already taken long strides toward participating effectively in the modern world, he says, while most Latin American countries are hopping in that direction when they are not stumbling and falling back. Latin America's growth has been intermittent at best, in large part because most of that region's leaders have not promoted serious and systematic reforms that would allow the people to break out of the prison of traditional ways.

Latin America's implementation of substantive reforms, or failure to do so, is of direct interest to the United States:

* The failure of these countries to provide universal basic education will make it difficult for them to develop stable and productive economies.
* Without strong internal markets and economies, the countries themselves will not prosper, and the already enormous and potentially greater U.S. trade and investment in the hemisphere will be threatened.
* The failure to develop substantially will mean a continuation of the cycles of frustration among Latin Americans and make inevitable excessive migration to the United States.

What is more, failing economies create incentives for Latin Americans, from peasants to businesspeople to politicians, to become involved in the production and peddling of narcotics and the violence that follows.

Finally, Americans wish to see their southern neighbors able to participate actively in the unfolding of their own futures, in large part through higher standards of health and education. Thus, the United States should promote education reform among Latin Americans, bilaterally and multilaterally, and support serious efforts when they are made.

consider this:

In Brazil and other Latin American countries parents are receiving cash payments to keep their children in school. Human capital is a key component of economic growth and development.

SOURCE: *Doing It Wrong and Doing It Right: Education in Latin America and Asia*, by William Ratliff, Hoover Institution Press.

However, in poorer developing countries, the higher opportunity costs of education present an obstacle. Children in developing countries are an important part of the labor force starting at a young age. If they attend school, children cannot help in the fields—planting, harvesting, fence building, and many other tasks—which many households depend on in the rural areas of developing countries. A child's labor contribution to the family is far less important in a developed country. Thus, the higher opportunity cost of education in developing countries is one of the reasons that school enrollments are lower.

Education may also be a consequence of economic growth, because as incomes rise, people's tendency to consume education increases. People increasingly look to education for more than the acquisition of immediately applicable skills. Education becomes a consumption good as well as a means of investing in human capital. There are also a number of factors that can lead to slower economic growth. Countries that fail to enforce the rule of law, experience wars and revolutions, have poor education and health systems and low rates of saving and investment are not likely to grow very rapidly.

SECTION CHECK

1. Generally speaking, higher levels of saving will lead to higher rates of investment and capital formation and, therefore, to greater economic growth.
2. Larger rewards for research and development would spur even more rapid economic growth.
3. Economic growth rates tend to be higher in countries where the government enforces property rights more vigorously.
4. Allowing free trade can also lead to greater output because of the principle of comparative advantage.
5. Education, investment in human capital, is important to improving standards of living and economic growth.

---

1. Why does knowing what factors are correlated with economic growth not tell us what causes economic growth?
2. How does increasing the capital stock lead to economic growth?
3. How do higher saving rates affect long-run economic growth?
4. Why would you expect an inverse relationship between self-sufficiency and real GDP per capita?
5. If a couple was concerned about their retirement, why could that lead them to have more children if they lived in an agricultural society, but fewer children if they were in an urban society?
6. Why is the effective use of land, labor, capital, and entrepreneurial activities dependent on the protection of property rights and the rule of law?

SECTION 22.4 Population and Economic Growth

* When is population growth beneficial to per capita economic growth?
* When is population growth detrimental to per capita economic growth?
* Why are rising expectations detrimental to the desirability of economic growth?
* How do environmental concerns affect the desirability of economic growth?

Population Growth and Economic Growth

At the beginning of the English Industrial Revolution (c. 1750), the world's population was perhaps 700 million. It took 150 years (to 1900) for that population to slightly more than double to 1.6 billion. Just 64 years later (in 1964), it had doubled again to 3.2 billion.

After another 41 years (in 2005), the population doubled yet again to more than 6.4 billion. Economic development occurred amidst all this growth in population, but what role does population play in economic growth?

The effect of population growth on per capita economic growth is far from obvious. If population were to expand faster than output, per capita output would fall; population growth would inhibit growth with a larger population. With a larger population, however, comes a larger labor force. Also, economies of large-scale production may exist in some forms of production, so larger markets associated with greater populations lead to more efficient-sized production units. Certainly, rapid population growth—more than 3 percent a year—did not seem to impede U.S. economic growth in the mid-nineteenth century. U.S. economic growth until at least World War I was accompanied by population growth that was among the highest in the world for the time.

The general feeling, however, is that in many of the developing countries today, rapid population growth threatens the possibility of attaining sustained economic growth. These countries are predominantly agricultural with modest natural resources, especially land. The land-labor ratio is low. Why is population growth a threat in these countries? One answer was provided nearly two centuries ago by an English economist, the Reverend Thomas Malthus.

The Malthusian Prediction

Malthus formulated a theoretical model that predicted that per capita economic growth would eventually become negative and that wages would ultimately reach equilibrium at a subsistence level, or just large enough to provide enough income to stay alive. To create this model, Malthus made three assumptions: (1) the economy was agricultural, with goods produced by two inputs, land and labor; (2) the supply of land was fixed; and (3) human sexual desires worked to increase population.

The Law of Diminishing Marginal Returns

As population increases, the number of workers increases, and with greater labor inputs available, output also goes up. At some point, however, output will increase by diminishing amounts because of the law of diminishing returns, which states that if you add variable amounts of one input (in this case, labor) to fixed quantities of another input (in this case, land), output will rise but by diminishing amounts (because as the land-labor ratio falls, less land is available per worker). For example, a rapid growth in the labor force might make it more difficult to equip each worker with sufficient capital, and lower amounts of capital per worker lead to lower productivity and a lower real GDP per capita. In short, the increase in the one factor of production, labor, might cause the other factors of production to be spread too thinly.

Avoiding Malthus's Prediction

Fortunately, Malthus's theory proved spectacularly wrong for much of the world. Although the law of diminishing returns is a valid concept, Malthus's other assumptions were unrealistic. The quantity or quality of tillable land is not completely fixed. Irrigation, fertilizer, and conservation techniques effectively increase arable land. More important, Malthus implicitly neglected the potential for technological advances and ignored the real possibility that improved technology, often embodied in capital, could overcome the impact of the law of diminishing returns. Further, the Malthusian assumption that sexual desire would necessarily lead to population increase is not accurate. True, sexual desire will always be with us, but the number of births can be reduced by birth control techniques.

As we discussed earlier, some economists believe that population growth can lead to greater economic growth. In some countries, a larger population may lead to more entrepreneurs, engineers, and scientists who will contribute to even greater economic growth through technological progress. These factors turn Malthus's theory on its head; instead of population being the villain, it could actually turn out to be the hero.

Do Some Developing Countries Still Fit Malthus's Prediction Today?

Unfortunately, the Malthusian assumptions don't vary widely from reality for several developing countries today. Some developing nations of the world are having substantial population increases, with a virtually fixed supply of land, slow capital growth, and few technological advances. For example, in some African nations, the population growth rate is 3 percent per year, while food output is growing at only 2 percent per year. In these cases, population growth causes a negative effect on per capita output because the added output derived from having more workers on the land is small.

Some economists worry about population growth and the capital stock. The greater the production growth rate, the lower the capital stock per worker. This could lead to lower labor productivity, a reduction in one's standard of living, and slower economic growth.

In fact, some developing countries have tried to reduce the rate of population growth to achieve greater economic growth per capita and higher standards of living. For example, China tried to reduce its population growth rate through laws regulating the number of children a family may have. It is true that in many poor countries, the population growth rate is much higher, nearly 3 percent per year, than in richer countries, about 1 percent per year. High population growth rates may be one explanation for lower standards of living, but many non-Malthusian explanations help explain the recurring poverty that exists in developing countries today, such as political instability, the lack of defined and enforceable property rights, and inadequate investment in human capital.

SECTION CHECK

1. Population growth may increase per capita output in resource-rich countries such as the United States, Australia, and Saudi Arabia, because they have more resources for each laborer to produce with. They are more likely to be able to exploit economies of large-scale production, and they are more likely to have rapidly expanding technology.
2. In some countries, the Malthusian dilemma posed by population growth and diminishing returns is a problem, and they may suffer as a result of population growth.

---

1. What happens to per capita real output if population grows faster than output? If population grows more slowly than output?
2. How can economies of large-scale production allow per capita output to rise as population rises?
3. How did Malthus's prediction on population growth follow from the law of diminishing returns?
4. Why is population control a particularly important issue in countries with very low levels of per capita income?

Interactive Chapter Summary

Fill in the blanks:

1. John Maynard Keynes was primarily concerned with explaining and reducing _____ fluctuations in the level of business activity.
2. Many would argue that in the long run, economic growth is a(n) _____ determinant of people's well-being.
3. Economic growth is usually measured by the annual percent change in _____.
4. How much the economy will produce at its potential output depends on the _____ and _____ of an economy's resources.
5. _____ in technology can increase the economy's production capabilities.
6. A nation with _____ economic growth will end up with a much higher standard of living, *ceteris paribus*.
7. The Rule of 70 says that the number of years necessary for a nation to double its output is approximately equal to the nation's _____ rate divided into 70.
8. Several factors have contributed to economic growth in some or all countries: (1) growth in the quantity and quality of _____ resources used (human capital); (2) increase in the use of inputs provided by the _____ (natural resources); (3) growth in physical _____ inputs (machines, tools, buildings, inventories); and (4) _____ advances (new ways of combining given quantities of labor, natural resources, and capital inputs) allowing greater output than previously possible.
9. If the labor force participation rate in a country _____ or if workers put in _____ hours, output per capita will tend to increase.
10. It has become popular to view labor as _____ capital that can be augmented or improved by education and on-the-job training.
11. _____ formation has played a significant role in the economic development of nations.
12. _____ is the adoption of a new product or process.
13. Technological advance permits us to economize on _____, _____, or even _____.
14. Generally speaking, higher levels of saving will lead to _____ levels of investment and capital formation and, therefore, to _____ economic growth.
15. Investment alone does not guarantee economic growth, which hinges on the _____ and the _____ of investment as well.

16. Research and development can result in _____ products, management _____, production _____, or learning by _____.

17. Economic growth rates tend to be higher in countries where the government enforces _____.

18. If a country's government is not enforcing property rights, the private sector must respond in _____ ways that _____ economic growth.

19. _____ can lead to greater output because of the principle of comparative advantage.

20. Accepting a(n) _____ in current income to acquire education and training can _____ future earning ability, which can raise the standard of living.

21. With economic growth, illiteracy rates _____ and formal education _____.

22. Improvements in literacy stimulate economic growth by _____ barriers to the flow of information and _____ labor productivity.

23. One problem in providing enough education in poorer countries is that children in developing countries are an important part of the labor force at a young age; therefore, a(n) _____ opportunity cost of education is involved in terms of forgone contributions to family income.

Answers: 1. short-term 2. crucial 3. real GDP per capita 4. quantity, quality 5. Increases 6. greater 7. growth 8. labor; land; capital; technological 9. rises; longer 10. human 11. Capital 12. Innovation 13. labor (natural resources); capital 14. higher; greater 15. quality type 16. new; improvements; innovations; doing 17. property rights 18. costly; stifle 19. Free trade 20. reduction; increase 21. fall; grows 22. reducing; raising 23. higher

Key Terms and Concepts

economic growth 632   innovation 636   research and development (R&D) 638

Section Check Answers

22.1 Economic Growth

1. **Why does the production possibilities curve shift outward with economic growth?**
   Economic growth means that an economy is able to produce more goods and services than before. An outward shift in a country's production possibilities curve simply illustrates this fact graphically.

2. **Even if "in the long run, we are all dead," are you glad earlier generations of Americans worked and invested for economic growth?**
   The fact that earlier generations of Americans worked and invested for economic growth means that there is currently a greater stock of capital in the United States than there would have been otherwise. With more tools to work with, you are more productive, resulting in a higher income and greater consumption possibilities.

3. **If long-run consequences were not important, would many students go to college or participate in internship programs without pay?**
   No. These are two of many examples where people sacrifice in the short run in order to benefit in the long run. Saving and research and development are other obvious examples.

4. **When the Dutch "created" new land with their system of dikes, what did it do to their production possibilities curve? Why?**
   Building dikes in Holland increased the quantity of usable land the Dutch had to work with; an increase in the amount of usable natural resources shifts a country's production possibilities curve outward.

22.2 Determinants of Economic Growth

1. **Why is no single factor capable of completely explaining economic growth patterns?**
   No single factor is capable of completely explaining economic growth patterns because economic growth is a complex process involving many important factors, no one of which completely dominates.

2. **Why might countries with relatively scarce labor be leaders in labor-saving innovations? In what area would countries with relatively scarce land likely be innovative leaders?**
   Those in countries with relatively scarce and therefore more costly labor would benefit more from labor-saving innovations and so would be likely to be leaders in such innovations. Similarly, those in countries with

relatively scarce and therefore more costly land would likely be leaders in innovative ways to conserve land.

3. **Why could an increase in the price of oil increase real GDP growth in oil-exporting countries such as Saudi Arabia and Mexico, while decreasing growth in oil-importing countries such as the United States and Japan?**
Since GDP measures the market value of goods and services produced, an increase in prices for what a country exports adds to its GDP. However, an increase in the price of imported oil will raise costs and reduce output in that country, other things being equal.

4. **How is Hong Kong a dramatic example of why abundant natural resources are not necessary for rapid economic growth?**
Hong Kong has virtually no natural resources, yet has long been among the fastest-growing economies in the world, proving that abundant natural resources are not necessary for rapid economic growth.

5. **If a couple was concerned about their retirement, why could that lead them to have more children if they lived in an agricultural society, but fewer children if they were in an urban society?**
In an agricultural society, children can typically "earn their own keep," making them financially "profitable" investments, as well as helping to provide for parents' retirement. In an urban society, however, children are a substantial financial liability to their parents.

6. **Why is the effective use of land, labor, capital, and entrepreneurial activities dependent on the protection of property rights and the rule of law?**
Without protected property rights and the rule of law, both production and exchange become far more difficult, costly, and uncertain, undermining the ability of market incentives to induce the effective use of the factors of production. Similarly, the rewards to investors and those who seek new and better ways of doing things are also more uncertain, reducing the incentives to make such investments and innovations.

22.3 Public Policy and Economic Growth

1. **Why does knowing what factors are correlated with economic growth not tell us what causes economic growth?**
Knowing what factors are correlated with economic growth does not tell us what causes economic growth because correlation does not prove causation. A factor may cause changes in economic growth, or economic growth could cause changes in it, or changes in both the factor and economic growth may be caused by yet another variable.

2. **How does increasing the capital stock lead to economic growth?**
Increasing the capital stock adds to the tools workers have to work with, increasing their productivity over time, which in turn increases output over time.

3. **How do higher saving rates affect long-run economic growth?**
Higher savings rates provide more funds for capital investment, and greater capital investment (which often also embodies advances in technology) increases productivity and output growth.

4. **Why would you expect an inverse relationship between self-sufficiency and real GDP per capita?**
Because of different endowments and abilities, both people and countries have different opportunity costs of production for large numbers of goods and services (different comparative advantages). Specialization and large-scale production, combined with domestic and international trade, allow an expansion of productive and consumption possibilities by taking advantage of lower cost production, while self-sufficiency sacrifices those potential gains.

22.4 Population and Economic Growth

1. **What happens to per capita real output if population grows faster than output? If population grows more slowly than output?**
If population grows faster than real output, per capita real output falls, while if population grows more slowly than real output, per capita real output rises.

2. **How can economies of large-scale production allow per capita output to rise as population rises?**
Economies of large-scale production mean that output can expand more than proportionately to an increase in inputs. So that the increasing labor force that accompanies a larger population may increase output enough, through more efficient-sized production units, that per capita real output rises as population rises.

3. **How did Malthus's prediction on population growth follow from the law of diminishing returns?**
Malthus's prediction that population growth results in a subsistence level of wages was based on the assumption of an agricultural society with land and labor as the only factors of production. Assuming that the amount of land was fixed, population and the labor force would grow to where production exhibited the law of diminishing returns, with output growing more slowly than increases in the variable input, labor, which would reduce per capita incomes, eventually to the point of subsistence.

4. **Why is population control a particularly important issue in countries with very low levels of per capita income?**
In countries with a fixed supply of land and little if any technological advance, Malthus's assumptions are not far from the reality. Population control is one way to hold down the rate of population increase, to prevent the Malthusian subsistence wage result.

CHAPTER 22 STUDY GUIDE

True or False:

1. Human welfare is greatly influenced by long-term changes in a nation's capacity to produce goods and services.
2. Emphasis on the short run of the business cycle can ignore the longer-term dynamic changes that affect output and real incomes.
3. Economic growth is usually measured by the annual percent change in the nominal output of goods and services per capita.
4. Along the production possibilities curve, the economy is producing at its potential output, sometimes called its natural level of output.
5. Another way of saying that economic growth shifted the production possibilities curve outward is that it increased potential output.
6. Greater stocks of land, labor, or capital can shift the production possibilities curve outward.
7. The Rule of 70 says that the number of years necessary for a nation to double its output is approximately equal to the nation's growth rate divided by 70.
8. The "richest" or "most-developed" countries today have many times the per capita output of the "poorest" or "least-developed" countries.
9. Economic growth is a complex process involving many important factors, no one of which completely dominates.
10. If the quantity of physical capital in a country increases at the same time that the quantity or quality of labor resources used falls, that country would experience economic growth as a result.
11. Technological advances, even without any change in the quantity or quality of the labor resources used, tend to lead to economic growth.
12. An increase in labor input does not necessarily increase output per capita.
13. A limited resource base is no obstacle to economic growth.
14. Both the initial development process and the sustained growth of an economy are dependent on a large natural resource base.
15. Technological advances involve both invention and innovation.
16. Because new technology must be introduced into productive use by someone who weighs estimates of the benefits of the new technology against estimates of the costs, that person—the entrepreneur—is an important economic factor in the growth process.
17. Technological advance permits us to economize on labor, land, or even capital.
18. One of the most important determinants of economic growth is the saving rate.
19. Investment alone does not guarantee economic growth.
20. An important link between research and development and capital investment means that when capital depreciates over time, it is replaced with new equipment that embodies the latest technology.
21. In most developed countries, property rights are effectively protected by the government; but in developing countries, such protection is not normally the case.
22. Free-trade policies will tend to increase the value of total output in an economy.
23. Trade can make economies more productive, even if individual enterprises don't become more efficient.
24. The correlation between per capita output and the proportion of the population that is unable to read and write is small.
25. Education is both a consequence of economic growth and a cause of economic growth.

Multiple Choice:

1. John Maynard Keynes, who once said that "in the long run, we are all dead," was primarily concerned with
   a. long-run economic growth.
   b. long-run price stability.
   c. redirecting short-run fluctuations in the business cycle.
   d. all of these issues equally.

2. Economists typically measure economic growth by tracking
   a. the employment rate.
   b. the unemployment rate.
   c. the expansion index.
   d. real GDP per capita.
   e. nominal GDP.

3. Economic growth refers to a(n) _____ in the output of goods and services in an economy. The greater the economic growth, the _____ goods citizens and their descendants will have to consume.
   a. decrease; less
   b. decrease; more
   c. increase; more
   d. increase; less

4. Economic growth is usually measured by the annual percent change in
   a. nominal GDP.
   b. nominal GDP per capita.
   c. real GDP.
   d. real GDP per capita.

5. How much the economy can produce at its natural rate of output depends on
   a. technology.
   b. the quantity of available natural resources.
   c. the productivity of labor.
   d. the stock of available capital.
   e. all of the above.

6. The natural level of real output in a country will tend to fall if
   a. technology advances.
   b. an increasing fraction of the population retires.
   c. increased investment adds to the capital stock.
   d. existing supplies of natural resources are depleted.
   e. either b or d occurs.

7. The standard of living will decline if
   a. nominal GDP grows at a faster rate than real GDP.
   b. nominal GDP grows at a slower rate than real GDP.
   c. the rate of population growth exceeds the rate of growth of real GDP.
   d. the rate of population growth is less than the rate of growth of real GDP.

8. An economy's production possibilities curve will shift outward over time if
   a. technological progress occurs.
   b. the stock of available capital decreases.
   c. emigration results in a decrease in the supply of available labor.
   d. the productivity of labor increases.
   e. either a or d occurs.

9. Which of the following would *not* result in increasing the natural rate of output in a country?
   a. increasing current consumption by reducing current saving
   b. draining swampland to allow cultivation
   c. improving the transportation system
   d. raising the fraction of resources that the country devotes to education
   e. All of the above would tend to increase the natural rate of output in a country.

10. Which one of the following will cause the production possibilities curve to shift outward?
    a. improved public education
    b. improved health care systems
    c. larger budgets for research, development, and exploration
    d. all of the above

11. According to the Rule of 70, if a nation grows at a rate of 5 percent per year, it will take roughly _____ for national income to double.
    a. 10 years
    b. 7 years
    c. 70 years
    d. 14 years
    e. none of the above

12. A country will roughly double its GDP in 10 years if its annual growth rate is
    a. 5 percent.
    b. 7 percent.
    c. 10 percent.
    d. 12 percent.
    e. 20 percent.

13. According to the Rule of 70,
    a. if a country is growing at 7 percent per year, its output will double in approximately 10 years.
    b. if a country is growing at 3.5 percent per year, its output will double in approximately 20 years.
    c. if a country is growing at 1 percent per year, its output will double in approximately 70 years.
    d. all of the above are true.
    e. none of the above is true.

14. According to the Rule of 70, if a country's growth rate doubled, the amount of time before its output doubled would be
    a. quartered.
    b. halved.
    c. doubled.
    d. quadrupled.

15. In the long run, the most important determinant of a nation's standard of living is
    a. its rate of productivity growth.
    b. its ability to export cheap labor.
    c. its ability to control the nation's money supply.
    d. its endowment of natural resources.

16. Per capita real output would tend to rise, other things being equal,
    a. if the labor force participation rate in the country rose.
    b. if the population rose.
    c. if the population fell and the labor force participation rate in the country fell.
    d. in all of the above cases.
    e. in none of the above cases.

17. If both the capital stock and the technology in a country increased, other things being equal, the country's potential output would
    a. rise.
    b. fall.
    c. remain unchanged.
    d. change in an indeterminate direction.
18. If a country reduced its spending on education and used the resources to build capital goods, economic growth in that country
    a. would tend to rise.
    b. would tend to fall.
    c. would tend to remain the same.
    d. could rise, fall, or remain the same.
19. Technological advances can be
    a. labor saving.
    b. capital saving.
    c. land (natural resource) saving.
    d. any of the above.
20. If Goodland's population grows faster than Badland's population, but Badland's labor force participation rate is growing faster than Goodland's, other things being equal,
    a. real GDP will be growing faster in Badland.
    b. real GDP per capita will be growing faster in Badland.
    c. real GDP will be growing faster in Goodland.
    d. real GDP per capita will be growing faster in Goodland.
    e. both b and d will be true.
21. If a country increased its saving rate,
    a. its current consumption would have to fall.
    b. its current consumption would have to rise.
    c. its future consumption possibilities will fall.
    d. its future consumption possibilities will rise.
    e. both a and d will occur.
22. Which of the following statements is incorrect?
    a. One of the most important determinants of economic growth is a nation's saving rate.
    b. Injections of foreign capital from abroad may contribute to a nation's economic growth.
    c. Economic growth depends on the quality and type of investments made.
    d. Economic growth rates tend to be lower in countries where property rights are better enforced by government.
23. High rates of saving and investment in a country
    a. guarantee rapid economic growth.
    b. tend to increase economic growth but do not guarantee it.
    c. will result in greater economic growth if they are accompanied by advances in technology than if they are not.
    d. will result in greater economic growth if they are accompanied by more investment in human capital than if they are not.
    e. will result in all of the above except a.
24. Which of the following is considered a factor that contributes to economic growth?
    a. government protection of property rights
    b. increased specialization of labor
    c. research and development
    d. improved efficiencies through economies of scale
    e. all of the above

25. Economic growth tends to be greater in countries where
    a. the government effectively protects property rights.
    b. more resources are devoted to research and development.
    c. there is greater freedom to trade freely.
    d. any of the above is true.

26. During the Klondike gold rush, the first prospectors in the region arrived before any government authority was established. They followed a long goldfield tradition and created "miners' laws," which described how gold claims could be staked and how these claims would be enforced. The creation of "miners' laws" showed that these prospectors recognized the importance of which of the following factors that affect economic growth?
    a. increasing physical capital
    b. economies of scale
    c. well-defined and enforced property rights
    d. technological advance

27. In a country that has an unstable government or judiciary, would you expect to see more entrepreneurial activity, or less?
    a. less, because an unstable economy has fewer entrepreneurs
    b. less, because of an unreliable infrastructure for protecting property rights
    c. more, because of fewer governmental restrictions
    d. more, because of less taxation of commercial and research activities

28. Investment in human capital
    a. is of minor importance to economic growth.
    b. can be acquired through on-the-job training.
    c. is an important source of economic growth.
    d. does not affect economic growth; only physical capital does.
    e. is characterized by both b and c.

29. Other things being equal, the higher the rate of savings across countries,
    a. the higher the rate of change of real GDP per capita.
    b. the lower the rate of change of real GDP per capita.
    c. the lower the productivity of labor.
    d. the lower the rate of investment.

30. Reduced levels of illiteracy
    a. are, in part, a cause of economic growth.
    b. are, in part, caused by economic growth.
    c. are, in part, both a cause of economic growth and caused by economic growth.
    d. are largely unrelated to economic growth.

Problems

1. a. According to the Rule of 70, how many years will it take a country to double its output at each of the following annual growth rates?

Rate	Years
0.5 percent:	____ years
1 percent:	____ years
1.4 percent:	____ years
2 percent:	____ years
2.8 percent:	____ years
3.5 percent:	____ years
7 percent:	____ years

b. If a country has $100 billion of real GDP today, what will its real GDP be in 50 years if it grows at an annual growth rate of

   1.4 percent? _____
   2.8 percent? _____
   7 percent? _____

2. Answer these questions about GDP:
   a. How could real GDP grow, while, over the same period, real GDP per capita falls?
   b. If Country A has a 4 percent annual growth rate of real GDP and a 2 percent annual rate of population growth, while Country B has a 6 percent annual growth rate of real GDP and a 5 percent annual rate of population growth, which country will have a higher growth rate of real GDP per capita?

3. In which direction would the following changes alter GDP growth and per capita GDP growth in a country (increase, decrease, or indeterminate), other things being equal?

	Real GDP Growth	Real GDP Growth per Capita
An increase in population	_____	_____
An increase in labor force participation	_____	_____
An increase in population and labor force participation	_____	_____
An increase in current consumption	_____	_____
An increase in technology	_____	_____
An increase in illiteracy	_____	_____
An increase in tax rates	_____	_____
An increase in productivity	_____	_____
An increase in tariffs on imported goods	_____	_____
An earlier retirement age in the country	_____	_____
An increase in technology and a decrease in labor force participation	_____	_____
An earlier retirement age and an increase in the capital stock	_____	_____

4. Answer the following questions about real GDP per capita:
   a. If Country A had 4 times the initial level of real GDP per capita of Country B and it was growing at 1.4 percent a year, while real GDP was growing at 2.3 percent in Country B, how long would it take before the two countries had the same level of real GDP per capita?
   b. If two countries had the same initial level of real GDP per capita, and Country A grows at 2.8 percent, while Country B grows at 3.5 percent, how will their real per capita GDP levels compare at the end of a century?

5. Suppose that two poor countries experience different growth rates over time. Country A's real GDP per capita grows at a rate of 7 percent per year on average, and Country B's real GDP per capita grows at an average annual rate of only 3 percent. Predict how the standard of living will vary between these two countries over time as a result of divergent growth rates.

6. Could a country experience a fall in population and a rise in real GDP at the same time? Could an increase in labor force participation allow that?

7. What is the difference between labor and human capital? How can human capital be increased?

8. Would a shift from investment in capital goods to investment in education increase or decrease the growth rate of real GDP per capita?

9. Which of the following are likely to improve the productivity of labor and thereby lead to economic growth? Why?
   a. on-the-job experience
   b. vocational school
   c. a decrease in the amount of capital per worker
   d. improvements in management of resources

10. What is the implication about economic growth for an economic system with weak enforcement of patent and copyright laws? Why does weak property rights enforcement create an incentive problem?

11. How could permanently lower marginal tax rates increase the capital stock, the level of education, the level of technology, and the amount of developed natural resources over time?

Financial Markets, Saving, and Investment

23

23.1 Financial Institutions and Intermediaries
23.2 Saving, Investment, and the Financial System
23.3 The Financial Crisis of 2008
APPENDIX: Calculating Present Value

In this chapter we discuss how the financial system works. We begin with an introduction to financial institutions and financial intermediaries.

The two most important financial institutions are the stock market and the bond market. We also discuss financial intermediaries, including banks, savings and loans, mutual funds, and insurance companies. We then develop equations to connect the financial system to our macroeconomic model. In the rest of this section we present the supply and demand for loanable funds. Using this framework, we can examine a number of potential policy prescriptions that could alter real interest rates and, as a result, the amount of saving, investment, and capital formation—the foundation of growth in the economy. In the last section, we examine the causes of the financial crisis that officially started in December of 2007. ∎

Section 23.1 Financial Institutions and Intermediaries

- What are financial institutions?
- What are bonds?
- What are stocks?
- What are retained earnings?
- How do expected business conditions affect the price of a stock?
- What are financial intermediaries?

As we saw in the previous chapter, potential real GDP and economic growth depend on productive resources and the growth of these resources. In order for an economy to grow, there must be investment; firms invest in new capital (machines and factories) and new production techniques, often incorporating new technology. This makes labor more productive, leading to increases in real incomes and living standards.

Some people in the economy are seeking to save some of their income for the future, whereas others are seeking to borrow in order to finance investments that would grow their businesses. How do we get these two groups together?

Financial institutions exist to facilitate the channeling of saving into investment. The financial system is composed of both financial markets and financial intermediaries. Firms can obtain resources to invest in capital by using retained earnings; (the profits that are reinvested in the firm rather than distributed as dividends to shareholders). But there are several other methods they can use as well, including selling stocks or bonds in the financial markets or borrowing from financial intermediaries such as banks.

The loanable funds market is where households make their saving available to those who desire to borrow additional funds. Note that we said saving rather than savings. Saving without an s at the end refers to a flow concept—your rate of saving (how much you save per day, per week, per month, or per year). Savings with an s at the end, however, refers to how much you have accumulated at a particular moment in time—your stock of savings. When you save, you can put the funds in a bank, buy stocks or bonds, or invest in a variety of other financial assets, such as treasury bills or mutual funds. We begin by discussing two of the most important financial institutions—the bond market and the stock market.

Corporations obtain financial capital (dollars used to buy capital goods) by borrowing money in exchange for bonds, by selling stock or by reinvesting profits that are earned in the business.

Bonds

Although corporate borrowing takes different forms, corporations primarily borrow by issuing **bonds.** The holder of a bond is not a part owner of a corporation. Rather, a bondholder is a creditor to whom the corporation has a debt obligation. The obligation to bondholders is of higher legal priority than that of stockholders. Before any dividends can be paid, even to owners of preferred stock, the interest obligations to bondholders must be met. If a company is liquidated, bondholders must be paid the full face value of their bond holding before any disbursements can be made to stockholders. Bondholders have greater financial security than stockholders, but receive a fixed annual interest payment, with no possibility to receive increased payments as the company prospers. The possibility of the value of a bond increasing greatly—a capital gain—is limited compared to that of stocks.

However, there are some risks involved with holding bonds, such as from corporate bankruptcy or higher market interest rates. For example, suppose you buy a bond that pays 5 percent interest and the market interest rate rises, so that newly issued bonds are now paying, say, 7 percent. The value of your bond has now declined.

bonds
an obligation issued by the corporation that promises the holder to receive fixed annual interest payments and payment of the principal upon maturity

stockholders
entities that hold shares of stock in a corporation

Stocks

The owners of corporations own shares of stock in the company and are called **stockholders.** Each stockholder's ownership of the corporation and voting rights in the selection of corporate management are proportionate to the number of shares owned. Suppose a corporation has 1,000 shares of stock outstanding. If you own 10 shares, you own a 1 percent interest in the corporation (10 is 1 percent of 1,000). Another stockholder may only own one share and have but one-tenth the interest you do. Therefore, she earns one-tenth the dividend income from the stock that you do and has one-tenth the number of votes that you do in annual shareowner meetings to select members of the board of directors. (The board provides overall supervision of the business and hires the management.) Individuals and institutions buy shares of stock in the stock market, usually on one of the organized stock exchanges. The price that shares sell for will fluctuate (often many times a day) with changes in demand or supply. Corporations sometimes use proceeds from new sales of stock to finance expansion of their activities.

The two primary types of stock are preferred stock and common stock. Owners of **preferred stock** receive a regular, fixed dividend payment; the payment remains the same regardless of the profits of the corporation. No dividends can generally be paid to holders of common stock until the preferred stockholders receive a specified fixed amount per share of stock, assuming that funds are available after the debts of the corporation are paid.

Owners of **common stock** are the residual claimants on the resources of the corporation. They share in all profits remaining *after* expenses are paid, including interest payments to owners of debt obligations of the corporation and dividend payments to owners of preferred stock. Dividends in common stock frequently vary with profits, often going up in years of prosperity and down in less prosperous years. If the corporation is sold or liquidated, the common stockholders receive all the corporate assets after all debts are paid and preferred stockholders are paid a fixed amount per share. Owners of common stock assume greater risks than preferred stockholders, because the potential rewards are greater if the company is in fact successful.

Who Owns Stock in U.S. Corporations?

Individuals as well as institutions such as insurance companies, pension funds, mutual funds, trust departments of banks, and university and foundation endowment funds, all hold corporate stocks. To provide a perspective on the ease with which one can share in the ownership of a company, General Motors, IBM, and Microsoft have millions of individual stockholders. Indirectly, millions more are involved in stocks through their mutual funds, ownership of life insurance, vested rights in private pension funds, and so on.

preferred stock
a stock that pays fixed, regular dividend payments despite the profits of the corporation

common stock
residual claimants of corporate resources who receive a proportion of profits based upon the ratio of shares held

retained earnings
the practice of using corporate profits for capital investment rather than dividend payouts

securities
stocks and bonds

Retained Earnings

A third way a company can get money is through **retained earnings.** Instead of using its profits to pay out dividends, a firm might take some of its profits and plow them back into the company for new capital equipment. A company may decide, for example, to take its $10 million of after-tax profit and pay $3 million in dividends and plow back the $7 million into the firm. Reinvestment is by far the most important source of funding, accounting for almost 65 percent of a firm's finances. One reason firms find reinvestment an attractive source of funds is that issuing new stocks and bonds can be an expensive and lengthy process.

The Value of Securities

The two most important financial markets where savers can provide funds to borrowers are the stock market and the bond market. The values of **securities** (stocks and bonds) sold in financial markets change with expectations of benefits and costs. For example, if people expect corporate earnings to rise, prospective stockholders increase what they would be willing to pay for the fixed amount of securities, while existing stockholders become more reluctant to sell, leading to increased prices. If present business conditions or expectations about future profits worsen, stock prices will fall. A variety of other concerns, such as the economic policies of the government, business conditions in foreign countries, and concern over inflation, also influence the price of stocks (and, to a lesser extent, bonds). During periods of rising securities markets, optimism is generally great, and businesses are more likely to invest in new capital equipment, perhaps financing it by selling new shares of stock at current high prices.

in the news | Experts, Darts, Readers Take a Drubbing

A brutal six months led to the worst showing for investment professionals in the 10-year history of the column's stock picking contest—an average loss of 53 percent. The best of the four pro picks dropped 22 percent between July 11 and December 29, 2000. The worst plunged an eye-popping 90 percent.

Wall Street Journal readers didn't do much better. The four readers, whose picks were selected at random from among e-mail submissions to WSJ.com, posted an average 43 percent drop. However, a portfolio of stocks chosen by flinging darts at the stock tables did the best, it fell only 11 percent.

SOURCE: Adapted from Georgette Jasen, "Experts, Darts, Readers Take a Drubbing," *Wall Street Journal*, 11 January 2001, C1.

During periods of pessimism, stock prices fall, and businesses reduce expenditures on new capital equipment, partly because financing such equipment by stock sales is more costly. More shares have to be sold to get a given amount of cash, seriously diluting the ownership interest of existing stockholders.

Can You Consistently Pick Stock Winners?

Economists have a theory about the stock market. They call it a *random walk*. That is, it is difficult, without illegal inside information or a lot of luck, to consistently pick winners in the stock market. Not too long ago, a chimpanzee in Sweden beat that country's top analyst by throwing darts at a newspaper that included all the listings on the Swedish Stock Exchange. The fact remains that hot tips are only hot if you are one of only a few to know whether a company's stock is going to rise. Once that news hits the street, it will cease to be a source of profit. In sum, if markets are operating efficiently, the current stock prices will reflect all available information, and consistent, extraordinary profit opportunities will not exist. Many financial analysts think that the best stock market strategy is to diversify, buying several different stocks, and holding them for long periods. At least that way you don't have to continue to pay commissions on additional trades. Besides, over the long run the stock market has historically outperformed other financial assets.

Reading Stock Tables

Most newspapers (and many Web sites) provide a financial section that covers the prices of stocks so investors can have some of the information they need to make their decisions to buy and sell stocks. Some investors (day traders) watch these data by the second as they trade in and out of stocks a number of times during the day. At the other extreme, some investors pick a good company and hold the stock for a long time hoping that it will give them a better return than other assets—such as saving accounts. Exhibit 1 is a

section 23.1 exhibit 1 Reading a Stock Table

52-WEEK HI	52-WEEK LO	STOCK (DIV)	YLD %	PE	VOL 100s	CLOSE	NET CHG
29.08	7.99	HarleyDav .40	1.5	25	20,825	26.25	−0.59

reproduction of the *Wall Street Journal* on November 12, 2009. Let's look at the key indicators for one stock—Harley-Davidson—a company that makes motorcycles and accessories.

The first two columns show the stock's performance over the last 52 weeks—the highest price in the first column and the lowest price in the second column. We see that Harley-Davidson has been as high as $29.08 per share and as low as $7.99.

In column three we see the name of the stock—Harley-Davidson; the symbol for this stock is HOG. Also in column three is the **dividend**—this number indicates the annual amount the company has paid over the preceding year on each share of stock. Harley-Davidson paid $0.40 per share. If we divide the dividend by the price of the stock, we get the figure in the fourth column called the yield—1.5 percent.

The fifth column has the **price-earnings ratio (PE),** found by taking the price of the stock and dividing it by the amount the company earned per share over the past year. The price-earnings ratio is a measure of how highly a stock is valued. A typical price-earnings ratio is about 15; Harley-Davidson's PE is 25. If the PE ratio is higher, it means that the stock is relatively expensive in terms of its recent earnings; the stock might be overvalued or investors are expecting share prices to rise in the future. A lower PE ratio means that the stock is either undervalued or that investors may expect future earnings to fall.

The last three columns measure the performance of the stock on the last trading day—the stock's volume for the day, closing price, and net change from the closing price of the previous day.

> **dividend**
> the annual per share payment to shareholders based upon realized profits
>
> **price-earnings ratio (PE)**
> a measure of stock value that is determined by dividing the price of the stock by the amount of annual corporate earnings per share

Financial Intermediaries

Financial intermediaries are financial institutions that accept funds from households and make them available to firms. They are the intermediary between savers and borrowers. The most important financial intermediaries are banks, mutual funds, savings and loans, and insurance companies.

A bank is a financial intermediary that takes in deposits from customers who want to save and makes loans available to those who want to borrow. Banks make a profit by charging borrowers a higher interest rate than what they pay their depositors.

Banks also provide a medium of exchange—that is, it facilitates transactions. For example, by allowing people to write checks against their deposits, banks are lowering transaction costs. Imagine the difficulty of trying to trade a share of stock for groceries. Banks have also introduced debit cards, prepaid cards, smart cards and credit cards all to facilitate transactions and smooth consumption spending.

Another important financial intermediary is mutual funds. Mutual fund companies sell portfolio of stocks and bonds. The advantage of a mutual fund it is allows an individual with even a small amount of income to spread risk across hundreds of different companies. That is, adhere to the sage advice "do not put all your eggs in one basket." A far riskier strategy would be to invest in one stock. There is also the services of an "expert" money manager that watches your portfolio. If a stock is underperforming it can be sold. If a stock looks promising it can be purchased. Perhaps, this is expertise a small individual investor could not afford. However, it is not clear that the expert will do any better than someone picking stocks randomly. In fact, index funds are a type of fund that includes all the stocks in a given market like the Dow Jones Industrial average or the S&P 500. These index funds tend to outperform those managed by money managers. It costs less to run an index fund because there are no highly paid stock pickers or analysts.

Another financial intermediary is savings and loans. They accept deposits in savings accounts and pay interest for these funds. The most important purpose of these institutions is to make mortgage loans on residential property.

Another financial intermediary, insurance companies, will invest your premiums in financial markets. They can make a profit if their investment income is greater than their losses on insurance claims.

SECTION CHECK

1. The two most important financial institutions are stocks and bonds.
2. Corporate ownership and voting rights are dispersed among stockholders and are based on the proportion of shares owned.
3. Bonds are a financial instrument used by corporations to raise money by promising to repay the amount borrowed and pay the holder fixed annual interest payments.
4. Two different types of stocks can be issued: preferred stock and common stock.
5. Stockholders can consist of millions of individuals and institutions that hold an ownership stake in a corporation.
6. Companies can use retained earnings to finance growth by reinvesting their profits into the firm for new capital equipment.
7. Stock shares are bought and sold in an organized exchange—a stock market—with fluctuations in prices based on supply and demand.
8. The expectation of future profits, as well as government economic policies, foreign market conditions, and inflation concerns, influence the price of securities.
9. Investors obtain information about stocks from published stock tables that help them make purchasing and selling decisions.
10. Price tracking, dividends, and price-earnings ratio figures provide investors with indicators of the value of a stock.
11. Financial intermediaries include banks, savings and loans, mutual funds, and insurance companies.

---

1. If you believed a company's profitability was about to jump sharply, would you rather own bonds, preferred stock, or common stock in that company?
2. If almost all investors expected the profits of a company to jump sharply, would that make purchasing the stock today unusually profitable?
3. Why are issues of new stocks to finance business investments more common in periods of high and rising stock prices?
4. What are some of the reasons that stock prices rise and fall?
5. What is the random walk?
6. What is a dividend?
7. How do you calculate a price-earnings ratio?

SECTION 23.2
Saving, Investment, and the Financial System

- What is the demand for loanable funds curve?
- What is the supply of loanable funds curve?
- How is the real interest rate determined?
- How are shortages and surpluses eliminated in the loanable funds market?
- What is private saving? Public saving?

As we have discussed, saving and investment are critical components of long-run economic growth and living standards. We will now begin discussing how we can use national income accounting to understand the relationship between total saving and total investment.

The Macroeconomics of Saving and Investment

The key point that we will develop in this section is that for the entire economy, the total value of saving must equal the total value of investment, $S = I$. Recall from our discussion of national income accounts that GDP (or Y) = $C + I + G + (X - M)$. That is, aggregate expenditures (Y) must equal the sum of its four components, $C + I + G + (X - M)$. For simplicity, we begin by working in a closed economy, without the complications introduced by the international, or net export $(X - M)$, component. In a closed economy, net exports are zero, because there is no international trade—that is, exports are zero and imports are zero. So we can now write:

(1) $$Y = C + I + G$$

That is, GDP (Y) is the sum of consumption plus investment plus government purchases. If we subtract C and G from both sides of the equation, we have

(2) $$I = Y - C - G$$

The right hand side $(Y - C - G)$ is what is left over from total income (Y) when you subtract consumption and government purchases. Thus, in a closed economy, investment spending (I) is equal to total income (Y) minus consumption spending (C) minus government purchases (G).

We can also derive an expression for national (total) saving. There are two types of saving—private saving and public saving. Private saving is the amount of income households have left over after consumption and taxes, plus any transfer payments (social security and unemployment insurance payments) the household may receive. So private saving can be written then as:

(3) $$S_{private} = Y - C - T + TR$$

Public saving is the amount of income the government has left over after paying for its spending. So public saving (S_{public}) is equal to the amount of tax revenues (T) government has left over after paying for government purchases (G) and transfer payments (TR):

(4) $$S_{public} = T - G - TR$$

National (total) saving in an economy is the sum of private saving and public saving:

(5) $$S = S_{private} + S_{public}$$

or:

(6) $$S = (Y - C - T + TR) + (T - G - TR)$$

or; simplifying:

(7) $$S = Y - C - G$$

Since, from equation (2), we know that $I = Y - C - G$, we can then conclude that:

(8) $$S = I$$

That is, national (total) saving equals total investment.

Most people are familiar with the idea that households and firms can save, but are less familiar with the idea that the government can also save. If the government collects the same amount in taxes as it spends, we say there is a balanced budget. If the government collects more in taxes than it spends $(T > G + TR)$, it runs a budget surplus and public saving is positive. If the government spends more than it collects in taxes $(T < G + TR)$, it runs a deficit and public saving is negative. That is, the government has to borrow the money to fund the difference between taxes and spending.

In sum, for the economy as a whole, total saving must equal total investment. However, this equation need not hold for any individual household or firm. In the next section, we develop the market for loanable funds that brings saving and investment together.

The Market for Loanable Funds

As we have seen, potential GDP and economic growth depend on the extent of productive resources and the rate at which they increase. In order for an economy to grow, there must be investment. Firms invest in new capital (machines and factories) and new production techniques, often incorporating new technology. These investments make labor more productive, leading to increases in real incomes and living standards.

For simplicity, let us assume the loanable funds market is a single big financial market. All savers deposit their saving there and all borrowers go there to take out loans. Savers are spending less than they are earning and borrowers are spending more than they are earning. If there is one big market, there is just one interest rate, which represents both the cost to borrow and the return to saving. In the market for loanable funds, the market interest rate and the quantity of loanable funds is determined by the interaction of borrowers and lenders.

The Demand for Loanable Funds

The demand for loanable funds comes from households and firms.

Households and firms borrow in the loanable funds market. Households often take out loans to invest in new houses or cars. Firms borrow to invest in new capital equipment, such as factories. Thus, both firms and households borrow in the loanable funds market to make investments. The demand for loanable funds curve is negatively sloped. That is, a higher interest rate makes it more expensive to borrow, so the quantity of loanable funds demanded falls; a lower interest rate makes it less expensive to borrow, so the quantity of loanable funds demanded rises. For example, firm must compare the return they expect to make with the real interest rate they must pay to borrow. At a high real interest rate, firm will only pursue those investment activities that have an even higher expected rate of return. As the real interest rate falls, additional projects with lower expected rates of returns become profitable for firms and the quantity of loanable funds demanded rises. The idea that lower real interest rates stimulate investment is the reason that government often tries to combat recessions by lowering the interest rate.

The Supply of Loanable Funds

The loanable funds market is where households make their saving available to those who need to borrow funds. Households supply loanable funds because they earn interest in exchange. The higher the interest rate, the greater the reward for saving. With their saving, a household may buy stocks or bonds from firms, or save in banks that will use the new funds to make loans. Thus, saving provides the supply of loanable funds. The interest rate can be understood as the price of a loan. It is the price that borrowers pay for a loan and it is the price lenders receive for their saving.

The supply of loanable funds curve is positively sloped. The supply of loanable funds is determined by the willingness of households to save and the amount of government saving or dissaving (which we will discuss later). Households can either save or consume. The amount households consume or save depends to some extent on the interest rate. A higher interest rate makes saving more attractive, so that the quantity of loanable funds supplied rises; a lower interest rate makes saving less attractive, so that the quantity of loanable funds supplied falls.

The Equilibrium Adjusts to Balance the Demand and Supply of Loanable Funds

The interest rate adjusts to generate equilibrium in the loanable funds market. In equilibrium, the quantity of loanable funds demanded is equal to the quantity of loanable funds supplied at the equilibrium real interest

section 23.2 exhibit 1 The Market for Loanable Funds

The interest rate in the loanable funds market adjusts to balance the quantity of loans demanded with the quantity of loans supplied. The supply of national saving is the sum of private saving and public saving. The demand for loanable funds comes from firms and households that want to borrow for investment purposes. At the equilibrium interest rate, the quantity of loanable funds demanded equals the quantity of loanable funds supplied.

rate, r^*, as seen in Exhibit 1. At a real interest rate that is higher than equilibrium, the quantity of loanable funds supplied is greater than the quantity of loanable funds demanded—a surplus of loanable funds at the current real interest rate. As lenders (savers) compete against each other to attract borrowers (investors), the real interest rate falls. Alternatively, if the real interest rate, is below the equilibrium real interest rate, the quantity of loanable funds demanded is greater than the quantity of loanable funds supplied—a shortage of loanable funds at the current real interest rate. As a result of the shortage, lenders will raise their interest rates. A higher interest rate would encourage saving (increase the quantity of loanable funds supplied) and discourage borrowing (decrease the quantity of loanable funds demanded), eliminating the shortage when the interest rate hits the equilibrium level at r^*.

Recall that there is a difference between the nominal interest rate and the real interest rate. The stated interest rate on a loan is the nominal interest rate. However, we can calculate the real interest rate by subtracting the inflation rate from the nominal interest rate. The real interest rate is important because it shows how much borrowers pay and lenders receive in terms of purchasing power. Since inflation tends to erode the value of money over time, the real interest rate is a more accurate gauge of the return to savers and the cost to borrowers. Remember that the interest rate determined in the loanable funds market is the real interest rate, not the nominal interest rate.

Analyzing the Market for Loanable Funds

In this section we use the tools of supply and demand to examine how certain changes will impact real interest rates and the equilibrium quantity of loanable funds exchanged.

Saving Incentives

As we have discussed, saving is an important long-run determinant of real economic growth and the standard of living. Therefore, policymakers might want to encourage saving by changing the tax code—perhaps making Individual Retirement Accounts (IRAs) more attractive. This would encourage people to save more of their income, because it would not be taxed. How would this new tax law affect the market for saving and investment? It would shift the loanable funds supply curve to the right, from S_1 to S_2, leading to a lower equilibrium real interest rate and a higher equilibrium quantity of loanable funds exchanged—as seen in Exhibit 2. The increased supply of saving causes the interest rate to fall, which stimulates investment. Thus, the change in the tax law would increase saving and investment.

Consumption Tax

In Chapter 9, we discussed a consumption tax that could replace an income tax. That is, the government taxes what is spent, rather than what is earned. If consumers are now taxed only on what they buy, they will buy less—and buying less means saving more. Consequently, the supply of loanable funds curve will shift to the right from S_1 to S_2 in Exhibit 2, which lowers the interest rate from r_1 to r_2 and leads to a great equilibrium quantity of loanable funds—more saving and investment. Greater investment leads to a greater capital stock, greater output and productivity, higher real wages, and an improved standard of living. The problem, as we saw in Chapter 9, is transitioning from an income tax to a consumption tax.

An Investment Tax Credit

The passage of a new investment tax credit would give a tax advantage to any firm that invested in new

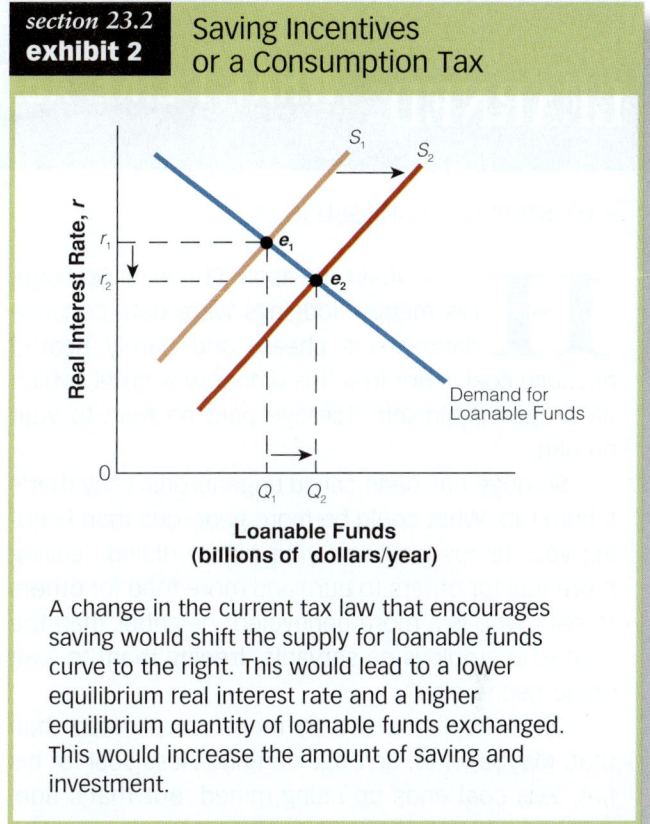

section 23.2 exhibit 2 Saving Incentives or a Consumption Tax

A change in the current tax law that encourages saving would shift the supply for loanable funds curve to the right. This would lead to a lower equilibrium real interest rate and a higher equilibrium quantity of loanable funds exchanged. This would increase the amount of saving and investment.

equipment or plant. Because firms would want to invest more, it would shift out (increase) the demand curve for loanable funds from D_1 to D_2, in Exhibit 3 leading to a higher real interest rate and a greater equilibrium quantity of loanable funds exchanged—greater levels of both saving and investment. That is, an investment tax credit would encourage investment and lead to a higher interest rate and greater saving. Of course, eliminating or reducing the investment tax credit would have the opposite effect: shifting the demand for loanable funds to the left, leading to a higher real interest rate and a lower equilibrium quantity of saving and investment.

Technological Change

Suppose a technological change causes an increase in demand for loanable funds, as firms see a new profitable opportunity for investment. The increase in the demand for loanable funds from D_1 to D_2 raises the real interest rate from r_1 to r_2 and leads to an increase in the equilibrium quantity of loanable funds from Q_1 to Q_2, as seen in Exhibit 3. At Q_2, there is greater levels of both saving and investment. This will ultimately lead to an increase in capital formation, more capital per worker, higher productivity, higher wages, and enhanced economic growth.

Use what you've LEARNED: WHAT I LIKE ABOUT SCROOGE

—BY STEVEN E. LANDSBURG

Here's what I like about Ebenezer Scrooge: His meager lodgings were dark because darkness is cheap, and barely heated because coal is not free. His dinner was gruel, which he prepared himself. Scrooge paid no man to wait on him.

Scrooge has been called ungenerous. I say that's a bum rap. What could be more generous than keeping your lamps unlit and your plate unfilled, leaving more fuel for others to burn and more food for others to eat? Who is a more benevolent neighbor than the man who employs no servants, freeing them to wait on someone else?

Oh, it might be slightly more complicated than that. Maybe when Scrooge demands less coal for his fire, less coal ends up being mined. But that's fine, too. Instead of digging coal for Scrooge, some would-be miner is now free to perform some other service for himself or someone else.

Dickens tells us that the Lord Mayor, in the stronghold of the mighty Mansion House, gave orders to his 50 cooks and butlers to keep Christmas as a Lord Mayor's household should—presumably for a houseful of guests who lavishly praised his generosity. The bricks, mortar, and labor that built the Mansion House might otherwise have built housing for hundreds; Scrooge, by living in three sparse rooms, deprived no man of a home. By employing no cooks or butlers, he ensured that cooks and butlers were available to some other household where guests reveled in ignorance of their debt to Ebenezer Scrooge.

In this whole world, there is nobody more generous than the miser—the man who could deplete the world's resources but chooses not to. The only difference between miserliness and philanthropy is that the philanthropist serves a favored few while the miser spreads his largess far and wide.

If you build a house and refuse to buy a house, the rest of the world is one house richer. If you earn a dollar and refuse to spend a dollar, the rest of the world is one dollar richer—because you produced a dollar's worth of goods and didn't consume them.

Who exactly gets those goods? That depends on how you save. Put a dollar in the bank and you'll bid down the interest rate by just enough so someone somewhere can afford an extra dollar's worth of vacation or home improvement. Put a dollar in your mattress and (by effectively reducing the money supply) you'll drive down prices by just enough so someone somewhere can have an extra dollar's worth of coffee with his dinner. Scrooge, no doubt a canny investor, lent his money at interest. His less conventional namesake Scrooge McDuck filled a vault with dollar bills to roll around in. No matter. Ebenezer Scrooge lowered interest rates. Scrooge McDuck lowered prices. Each Scrooge enriched his neighbors as much as any Lord Mayor who invited the town in for a Christmas meal.

Saving is philanthropy, and—because this is both the Christmas season and the season of tax reform—it's worth mentioning that the tax system should recognize as much. If there's a tax deduction for charitable giving, there should be a tax deduction for saving. What you earn and don't spend is your contribution to the world, and it's equally a contribution whether you give it away or squirrel it away.

Of course, there's always the threat that some meddling ghosts will come along and convince you to deplete your savings, at which point it makes sense (insofar as the taxation of income ever makes sense) to start taxing you. Which is exactly what individual retirement accounts are all about: They shield your earnings from taxation for as long as you save (that is, for as long as you let others enjoy the fruits of your labor), but no longer.

Great artists are sometimes unaware of the deepest meanings in their own creations. Though Dickens might not have recognized it, the primary moral of *A Christmas Carol* is that there should be no limit on IRA contributions. This is quite independent of all the other reasons why the tax system should encourage saving (e.g., the salutary effects on economic growth).

SOURCE: Copyright 2008 Washingtonpost.Newsweek Interactive Co. LLC

section 23.2 exhibit 3 — An Investment Tax Credit or a Technological Change

An investment tax credit, or other investment incentive would encourage businesses to invest more and increase the demand for loanable funds. Likewise, a technological change may increase the profitability of a new investment, increasing the firms' demand for loanable funds. An increase in the demand for loanable funds increases the real interest rate from r_1 to r_2, and the equilibrium quantity of loanable funds exchanged rises from Q_1 to Q_2. Consequently the amount of saving and investment increases.

section 23.2 exhibit 4 — Effects of a Government Budget Deficit

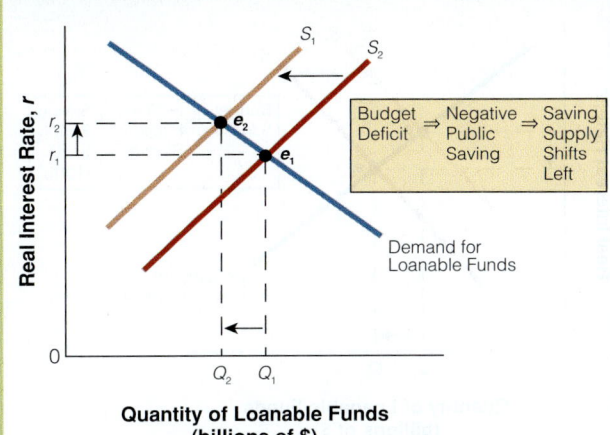

When the government runs a budget deficit, public saving is negative, lowering the supply of national saving and shifting the loanable funds supply curve leftward from S_1 to S_2. At the new equilibrium, the result is a higher real interest rate and a lower equilibrium quantity of loanable funds that is, less saving and investment. When the real interest rate rises as a result of the government budget deficit, it causes a decrease in private investment, known as the crowding-out effect.

Budget Deficits and Surpluses

When the government spends more than it receives in tax revenues, it experiences a budget deficit. Not including the effects of foreign saving, a budget deficit will lower national saving in the economy, causing a decrease in the supply of loanable funds from S_1 to S_2 in Exhibit 4. That is, the government is actually dissaving (borrowing), decreasing national saving. At the new equilibrium, there is a higher real interest rate and lower equilibrium quantity of loanable funds exchanged—less saving and investment. When the real interest rate rises as a result of the government budget deficit, it causes a decrease in private investment—households buy fewer homes and firms invest in fewer new factories. Economists call this the **crowding-out effect,** a topic we will return to in the chapter on fiscal policy. That is, the budget deficit reduces investment spending and long-term economic growth.

crowding-out effect
theory that government borrowing drives up the interest rate, lowering consumption by households and investment spending by firms

Now consider how a budget surplus (or a reduction in the budget deficit) will impact the real interest rate and the amount of saving and investment. In Exhibit 5, suppose that when the government has a balanced budget, the supply of loanable funds curve is S_1, the demand for loanable funds curve is D_1, the equilibrium real interest rate is r_1, and the equilibrium quantity of loanable funds exchanged is Q_1. If the government begins running a budget surplus—receiving more in tax revenues than it spends—there is an increase in public saving. Because national saving is the sum of private saving and public saving, national saving has now increased, shifting the supply of loanable funds curve right from S_1 to S_2. What impact does this budget surplus (government saving) have on the real interest rate, saving, and investment? The increase in the supply of loanable funds from S_1 to S_2 leads to a decrease in the real interest rate to r_2 and an increase in equilibrium of loanable funds exchanged from Q_1 to Q_2. The budget surplus has increased the supply of loanable funds, lowered the

section 23.2 exhibit 5 — Effects of a Government Budget Surplus

When the government runs a budget surplus, public saving is positive, increasing national saving and causing the saving supply curve to shift rightward from S_1 to S_2. This shift leads to a decrease in the real interest rate to r_2 and an increase in equilibrium saving and investment from Q_1 to Q_2. The budget surplus results in an increase in the supply of loanable funds, a lower real interest rate, and larger amounts of saving and investment. These factors cause increases in the capital formation and economic growth.

real interest rate, and increased the equilibrium quantity of loanable funds exchanged—that is, more saving and investment. This will ultimately lead to increases in capital formation and economic growth.

Tax Laws, Government Programs and the Saving Rate When the saving rate increases there are more resources available for investment. Investment in capital (plant and equipment) raises labor productivity, wages and national income. So, should we reform the tax laws to encourage a higher rate of saving? Currently, saving is taxed at a relatively high rate. Investors who save some of their wealth in stock are taxed twice—the corporation (shareholders) is taxed and then dividends are taxed again. Inheritance taxes can also discourage saving because it taxes a percentage of the wealth that many have saved to pass on to their children. Taxes on interest, dividends, capital gains, and estates raise the cost of saving versus consumption and drain capital from the economy.

Government programs, especially Social Security, discourage saving. Individuals use to save more for their retirement and health care but now rely more heavily on Medicare and other government health programs. Also means-tested government programs and colleges and universities have benefits and scholarships that are linked to wealth—which may discourage some from saving.

A consumption tax would encourage saving because saving would only be taxed when it was used to buy goods and services. In addition, there are currently some tax advantages for specific retirement programs like Individual Retirement Accounts (IRA's).

However, there are the equity effects of tax reform. High income families tend to save more—so the rich may benefit more from a tax policy aimed to encourage saving. There are also other ways to encourage saving like reducing the deficit—that is, increasing public saving. In fact, policymakers must be careful when they pass tax reform to encourage private saving because it may lead to less government revenue and higher deficits—a decrease in public saving. Policymakers face difficult choices.

POLICY application: BOOST PRIVATE INVESTMENT TO BOOST THE ECONOMY

—BY HAL VARIAN

These days it seems like it is our patriotic duty to consume more. And if we don't choose to spend more money ourselves, the government will do it for us.

But wait a minute. Isn't it excessive spending that got us into this mess in the first place? Spending more now seems like drinking Scotch to cure a hangover.

Despite this apparent paradox, there is some logic to providing a dose of economic stimulus. But it should be more like Alka-Seltzer than Scotch. To understand what sort of stimulus makes sense, consider the economic forces at work:

In the modern economy, there are four sources of demand (consumption, investment, government and exports) and two sources of supply (domestic

POLICY application: BOOST PRIVATE INVESTMENT TO BOOST THE ECONOMY (cont.)

production and imports). When a component of demand declines, supply will ultimately have to decline as well.

In the case of the U.S. economy now, the double-whammy of wealth shocks from the real-estate bubble and the stock-market crash has made consumers understandably cautious. Quite sensibly they want to consume less and save more.

In an ideal world, an increase in savings would automatically lead to an increase in investment. When consumers put more of their money in their savings accounts, the funds would be lent out to finance the production of factories, machines, computers and other forms of physical capital. These capital investments make more consumption possible in the future which is, after all, why people choose to save.

It is not just investment in physical capital that matters. Savings can also be recycled as student loans, which allow for the accumulation of human capital by increasing the supply of doctors, engineers and skilled workers of all kinds.

Unfortunately, savings are currently not getting translated into investment for three reasons. First, one of the largest categories of physical capital is real estate, and we have already overinvested in that area. Second, businesses are reluctant to invest in new plant and equipment due to the weakening economy. Third, the sorry condition of bank balance sheets has made them reluctant to lend. The net result is that money is piling up in ultrasafe assets like Treasury bills, without being invested in ways that would build a more productive economy.

Federal Reserve Chairman Ben Bernanke and Treasury Secretary Hank Paulson have rightly concentrated on getting the financial sector functioning again, since lending is a critical ingredient for private-sector investment. The Obama administration now wants to shift from monetary policy to fiscal policy and provide direct stimulus of demand. But which component: consumption, investment, government expenditures or exports?

Increasing exports would be great, but it's not going to happen. The rest of the world is having its own problems, so we are unlikely to see a big boost in demand for American goods.

Direct stimulus of consumption is tricky. In this economic climate, most of the money returned to consumers from tax cuts would probably be saved, and rightly so, since it is the prudent thing to do. Rather than relying entirely on direct stimulus of consumption, it is better to put a floor under consumption by making sure that unemployment benefits and food stamps are adequately funded.

That brings us to government expenditure, which is getting most of the press. The danger with this form of stimulus is twofold: First, it takes too long for the government spending to kick in, and second, spending may easily focus on pork-barrel projects that have little inherent value.

There *are* worthwhile public infrastructure projects; the trick is to find them and fund them promptly. One possible plan is to set up an independent commission to prioritize public investment projects, and then subject the plan to a single up-or-down vote in Congress.

One further warning about government stimulus: It makes little sense for the federal government to spend more if the states are forced to spend less. A significant part of the increase in federal government spending should be transfers to the states in order to keep basic government services available at the state and local level.

That brings us to private investment, which hasn't been getting nearly as much attention as it deserves. This is unfortunate, since private investment is what makes possible future increases in production and consumption. Investment tax credits or other subsidies for private-sector investment are not as politically appealing as tax cuts for consumers or increases in government expenditure. But if private investment doesn't increase, where will the extra consumption come from in the future?

Ultimately, we want to end up with a significantly higher savings rate in the U.S. than we have seen recently. That means some other component of demand must increase to compensate for the reduced consumption. And the most attractive candidate by far is private investment.

SOURCE: From Hal Varian, "Boost Private Investment to Boost the Economy, 'The Wall Street Journal', January 7, 2009, p. A13. Reprinted by permission of The Wall Street Journal, copyright © 2009 Dow Jones & Company, Inc. All Rights Reserved Worldwide.

Interest Rates and the Inflow and Outflow of Capital

In an open economy, individuals, firms, and governments are able to borrow from and lend to foreigners. When foreigners supply more funds than they demand, the result is a capital inflow. When foreigners demand more funds than they supply, the result is a capital outflow.

In Exhibit 6, we see that capital inflows from foreign countries add to the supply of domestic saving, increasing the funds available for domestic capital investment and causing the supply of loanable funds curve to be positioned to the right of the domestic saving curve. Capital outflows to foreign countries reduce the saving supply, reducing the funds available for domestic capital investment and causing the supply of loanable funds curve to be positioned to the left of the domestic saving curve, as shown in Exhibit 6. That is, capital inflows encourage capital formation and economic growth, and capital outflows hinder capital formation and reduce the rate of economic growth.

Notice in Exhibit 6 that when the real domestic interest rate is low and the demand for loanable funds is weak, capital will flow out to foreign markets where the real interest rate is higher (that is, a higher rate of return on investment). When the demand for loanable funds is strong, the real domestic interest rate is high, causing an inflow of capital because foreigners will look for a higher rate of return on their investments. Global financial markets tend to move toward equilibrium, at r^* and Q^* where the quantity of loanable funds demanded equals the quantity of loanable funds supplied including the net inflow and outflow of capital.

section 23.2 exhibit 6 — Net Inflow and Outflow of Capital in the Loanable Funds Market

When the demand for loanable funds is strong, the domestic real interest rate is high and capital inflows from foreign countries increase the supply of loanable funds, increasing the funds available for capital investment. When the demand for loanable funds is weak, the domestic real interest rate is low and capital flows out to foreign countries, lowering the supply of loanable funds and reducing the funds available for investment. That is, capital inflows encourage capital formation and economic growth, and capital outflows hinder capital formation and reduce the rate of economic growth.

SECTION CHECK

1. The loanable funds demand curve is downward sloping, reflecting the fact that the quantity of loanable funds demanded varies inversely with the real interest rate.
2. The supply of loanable funds is composed of both private saving and public saving.
3. The supply curve of loanable funds is upward sloping. At a higher real interest rate, the quantity of loanable funds supplied increases. At a lower real interest rate, the quantity of loanable funds supplied decreases.
4. In equilibrium, the demand for loanable funds equals the supply of loanable funds. If the real interest rate is above the equilibrium real interest rate, the quantity of loanable funds supplied is greater than the

quantity of loanable funds demanded at that interest rate; lenders will compete against each other to attract borrowers and the real interest rate falls. If the real interest rate is below the equilibrium real interest rate, the quantity of loanable funds demanded is greater than the quantity of loanable funds supplied at that interest rate; borrowers compete with each other for the available funds and drive the real interest rate up.

5. Private saving is the amount of income households have left over after consumption and net taxes.
6. Public saving is the amount of income the government has left over after paying for its spending.
7. National saving is the sum of private and public saving.
8. Government saving (a budget surplus) increases the saving supply leading to a lower real interest rate and an increase in equilibrium saving and investment.
9. Government dissaving (a budget deficit) reduces the saving supply leading to a higher real interest rate and a decrease in the equilibrium saving and investment.

1. Why does $Y - C - G = S$ in a simple, closed economy?
2. If net taxes rise, what happens to private saving? To public saving?
3. Why does the demand for loanable funds curve slope downward?
4. Why does the supply of loanable funds curve slope upward?
5. How is the real interest rate determined?
6. How are shortages and surpluses eliminated in the loanable funds market?
7. What factors can shift the demand for loanable funds curve?
8. What factors can shift the supply of loanable funds curve?
9. What would happen to the equilibrium interest rate and quantity of loanable funds exchanged if both the loanable funds demand and supply curves shifted right? What if the loanable funds demand curve shifted right and the loanable funds supply curve shifted left?
10. Other things equal, which direction will an increasing budget surplus change the equilibrium interest rate, the loanable funds supply curve, the level of investment in the economy, and the likely rate of economic growth?
11. Could the crowding-out effect sometimes be called the crowding-in effect?

SECTION 23.3 The Financial Crisis of 2008

* What role did the housing market play in the financial crisis?
* What impact did low short-term interest rates have on the housing market?
* What role did relaxed standards for mortgage loans have on the housing market?
* What impact did the higher interest rate of 2005 have on the housing market?

The best word to sum up the financial crisis of 2008 is DEBT. In technical terms, it is called excessive leverage. In short, too many homeowners and financial firms had assumed too much debt and taken on too much risk. Why did this happen? There is plenty of blame to go around—poorly informed borrowers, predatory mortgage lenders, incompetent rating agencies, lax regulators, misguided government policies, and outright fraud.

Many economists believe the crisis started in the housing market, with declining housing prices caused by overbuilding, excessive appreciation, and aggressive (i.e., risky) mortgages—a formula that only works when housing prices are rising.

Housing prices were rising at an extraordinary rate from 2000–2006. Housing prices peaked in 2006 and fell sharply in 2007; with the worst of the housing decline concentrated in California, Florida, Arizona, and Nevada.

section 23.3 exhibit 1 — Effective Federal Funds Rate (FEDFUNDS)

SOURCE: Board of Governors of the Federal Reserve System.

Low Interest Rates (2002–2004) Led to Aggressive Borrowing

After the 2001 recession, the Fed pursued an expansionary monetary policy that pushed interest rates down to historically low levels. The federal funds rate was maintained at 2 percent or lower for almost three years. Economists disagree on whether this was the correct government policy. Some argue that the Fed pursued the appropriate policy to stimulate economic growth and employment after the 2001 recession and terrorist attacks, in order to head off potential deflation. Once deflation sets in, it is very difficult to successfully use expansionary monetary policy. In addition, worldwide interest rates were very low at this time due to the large amount of savings in emerging markets. Because the US financial markets appeared relatively safe many of these global funds flowed into the United States lowering the interest rate and eventually helping to fuel the housing bubble.

Critics of the Fed argue that it lowered interest rates too much, for too long, in a growing economy, as shown in Exhibit 1. Most would agree that monetary policy was "too loose for too long" in the United States and around the world.

But whatever the reason for the low interest rates, there is common agreement that the low interest rates increased aggressive borrowing that encouraged less qualified buyers to purchase houses. The low interest rates set off a housing boom, especially in California, Florida, and the Northeast.

Deregulation in the Housing Market and Subprime Mortgages

In the last several decades the federal government encouraged the mortgage industry, especially Fannie Mae and Freddy Mac, to lower lending standards for low-income families in an effort to increase home ownership. Fannie Mae and Freddy Mac are the government-sponsored enterprises that fund or guarantee the majority of mortgage loans in the United States.

Specifically, lenders devised innovative adjustable rate mortgages with extremely low "teaser" rates, making it possible for many new higher risk buyers to purchase houses, often with little or no money as a down payment and, in some cases, no documentation of income. Most of these loans ended up in the hands of high-risk borrowers. These loans were called subprime loans because the borrower had less than a prime credit rating and many would not have qualified for a conventional loan.

In 2006, almost 70 percent of the subprime loans were in the form of a new innovative product called a

section 23.3 exhibit 2 — The Subprime Share of Home Mortgages Grows Rapidly Before the Big Decline (1995–Q2 2008)

SOURCES: Inside Mortgage Finance, Federal Reserve, Milken Institute.

hybrid. These loans started at a very low fixed rate for the initial period, say three to seven years, and then reset to a much higher rate for the remainder of the loan. Many subprime borrowers just expected to refinance later—thinking their property would continue to appreciate and interest rates would remain low. In retrospect, borrowers and lenders focused too much on the borrower's ability to cover the low initial payment and not enough on risk.

Speculators flipped (quickly bought and sold) properties with inflated appraisals and outright lying on loan applications. In addition, excessive credit provided to subprime borrowers (individuals who may not have qualified for conventional loans) fueled the housing bubble. Mortgage originators were not worried about making risky loans because they could pass on the risk to others (particularly Fannie Mae and Freddy Mac, who were aggressively buying such loans). Because origination fees on loans were due up front, and others would buy the loans, lenders were less concerned if the loan was ever repaid. It is safe to say that if mortgage companies had given loans only to safe investors, the United States would not have had a financial crisis.

Subprime mortgages jumped from 8 percent of the total in 2001 to 13.5 percent in 2005, as shown in Exhibit 2. These new buyers pushed housing prices higher. The increase in the lending to "subprime" borrowers helped inflate the housing bubble. The rising housing prices then led to overly optimistic expectations, with both borrowers and lenders thinking that with housing prices increasing, the risks were minimal. (After all, housing prices jumped almost 10 percent a year nationally from 2000–2006, as shown in Exhibit 3.)

Lenders were eager to make loans to anyone because they thought the prices for housing would continue to rise and, if borrowers defaulted, lenders would be left with an asset worth more than they were owed.

In short, the relaxed lending standards, backed by the government, put many low-income families into homes they could not afford. Unscrupulous mortgage brokers even falsified loan application forms, so clients could qualify for larger loans. Many borrowers also did not completely understand the terms of their loan.

Who Bought These Risky Subprime Mortgages?

Many of these risky subprime mortgages were sold to investors such as Bear Stearns and Merrill Lynch. They pooled them with other securities into packages and sold them all over the world. Part of the impetus for them was the great demand for mortgage-backed securities in the global market. A mortgage-backed security (MBS) is a package of mortgages bundled together and then sold to an investor, like a bond. Foreign investors were hungry to invest in these securities, because the U.S. housing market traditionally has been strong and stable. These mortgage-backed securities were also thought to have minimal risk because

section 23.3 exhibit 3 The Recent Run-Up of Nominal Home Prices was Extraordinary (1890–Q2 2008)

NOTE: The annualized growth rate is the geometric mean.
SOURCES: Shiller (2002), Milken Institute.

of the diversity of mortgages in each portfolio and because they had high security ratings. Security rating agencies gave their highest ratings to these securities—AAA (Standard's and Poor) and Aaa (Moody's). High ratings encouraged investors to buy securities backed by subprime mortgages, helping finance the housing boom. The rating agencies clearly underestimated the risk of these securities. The risk was spread among many different investment institutions, but no one knew exactly where the bad loans had ended up.

Consumers Borrowing Against Their Equity

To complicate matters further, consumers borrowed hundreds of billions of dollars against the equity from the appreciation in their homes, fueling consumption spending, and an increase in household debt, combined with a fall in personal saving. The low interest rates subsidized massive borrowing, and credit market debt soared as well.

The Fed Raises Interest Rates and the Housing Bust

The low interest rates of the 2002–2004 period and other factors led to the Fed becoming concerned about rising prices. In 2005–2006, therefore, the Fed reversed course and pushed short-term interest rates up, as shown in Exhibit 1. For those holding new adjustable rate mortgages (ARMs), it meant their monthly payments rose. Higher interest rates and falling housing prices were a recipe for disaster. Consequently, many homes went into default and foreclosure—both subprime borrowers and prime borrowers lost their homes. (The default rate was much lower on those holding fixed mortgage rates.)

When housing prices crashed, not only did too many homeowners find themselves over their heads, but there was also a huge excess inventory of new homes. From 2006–2008, housing construction fell by a whopping $350 billion—a huge hit on the economy. And by December of 2007, the United States was officially in a recession.

As housing prices fell and interest rates rose, foreclosures jumped. Once home prices fell below loan values, borrowers could not qualify to refinance and many were forced into foreclosure. When houses turn "upside down"—people owe more on their loan than the house is worth—many walk away from their houses. If a homeowner had put 20 percent down and had an appreciable amount of equity, she would have a greater incentive to make it work. Zero-down mortgages meant more defaults, especially when given to someone with a poor credit rating and little documentation of income. There was a major mispricing of risk in the mortgage markets.

in the news

That Freshman Course Won't Be Quite the Same

—BY N. GREGORY MANKIW

My day job is teaching introductory economics to about 700 Harvard undergraduates a year. Lately, when people hear that, they often ask how the economic crisis is changing what's offered in a freshman course.

They're usually disappointed with my first answer: not as much as you might think. Events have been changing so quickly that we teachers are having trouble keeping up. Syllabuses are often planned months in advance, and textbooks are revised only every few years.

But there is another, more fundamental reason: Despite the enormity of recent events, the principles of economics are largely unchanged. Students still need to learn about the gains from trade, supply and demand, the efficiency properties of market outcomes, and so on. These topics will remain the bread-and-butter of introductory courses.

Nonetheless, the teaching of basic economics will need to change in some subtle ways in response to recent events. Here are four:

The Role of Financial Institutions

Students have always learned that the purpose of the financial system is to direct the resources of savers, who have extra funds they are willing to lend, to investors, who have projects that need financing.

The economy's financial institutions—banks and insurance companies, for example—are mentioned as part of that system. But after a brief introduction in the classroom, they quickly fade into the background and are examined in detail only in more advanced courses.

The current crisis, however, has found these financial institutions at the center of the action. They will need to become more prominent in the classroom as well.

Financial institutions are like the stagehands who work behind the scenes at the theater. If they are there doing their jobs well, the audience can easily forget their presence. But if they fail to show up for work one day, their absence is very apparent, because the show can't go on. The process of financial intermediation is similarly most noteworthy when it fails.

The Effects of Leverage

Not long ago, I was explaining to a freshman that the economic crisis arose because some financial institutions had, in effect, invested in housing by holding mortgage-backed securities. When housing prices fell by about 20 percent nationwide, these institutions found themselves nearly insolvent.

But the student then asked an important question: "If housing prices have fallen only 20 percent, why did the banks lose almost 100 percent of their money?"

The answer was leverage, the use of borrowed money to amplify gains and, in this case, losses. Economists have yet to figure out what combination of mass delusion and perverse incentives led banks to undertake so much leverage. But there is no doubt that its effects have played a central role in the crisis and will need a more prominent place in the economics curriculum.

The Limits of Monetary Policy

The textbook answer to recessions is simple: When the economy suffers from high unemployment and reduced capacity utilization, the central bank can cut interest rates and stimulate the demand for goods and services. When businesses see higher demand, they hire more workers to meet it.

Only rarely in the past did students ask what would happen if the central bank cut interest rates all the way to zero and it still wasn't enough to get the economy going again. That is no surprise; after all, interest rates near zero weren't something that they, or even their parents, had ever experienced. But now, with the *Federal Reserve*'s target interest rate at zero to 0.25 percent, that question is much more pressing.

The Fed is acting with the conviction that it has other tools to put the economy back on track. These include buying a much broader range of financial

(continued)

in the news: That Freshman Course Won't Be Quite the Same (cont.)

assets than it typically includes in its portfolio. Students will need to know about these other tools of monetary policy—and will also need to know that economists are far from certain how well these tools work.

The Challenge of Forecasting

It is fair to say that this crisis caught most economists flat-footed. In the eyes of some people, this forecasting failure is an indictment of the profession.

But that is the wrong interpretation. In one way, the current downturn is typical: Most economic slumps take us by surprise. Fluctuations in economic activity are largely unpredictable.

Yet this is no reason for embarrassment. Medical experts cannot forecast the emergence of diseases like *swine flu* and they can't even be certain what paths the diseases will then take. Some things are just hard to predict.

Likewise, students should understand that a good course in economics will not equip them with a crystal ball. Instead, it will allow them to assess the risks and to be ready for surprises.

SOURCE: From N. Gregory Mankiw, "That Freshman Course Won't Be Quite the Same", 'New York Times', May 24, 2009. Copyright © 2009 The New York Times. All rights reserved. Used by permission and protected by the Copyright Laws of the United States. The printing, copying, redistribution, or retransmission of the Material without express writtten permission is prohibited.

When housing prices fell and mortgage delinquencies soared, the securities-backed subprime mortgages lost most of their value. When subprime borrowers defaulted, the investors that took the hit started demanding their money back by surrendering these securities to the banks. The result was a large decline in the capital of many banks and financial institutions, tightening credit around the world. Three investment banks either went bankrupt (Lehman Brothers) or were sold at fire-sale prices to other banks (Bear Stearns and Merrill Lynch) during September, 2008. The failures of three of the five largest investment banks augmented the instability in the global financial system. The remaining two investment banks, Morgan Stanley and Goldman Sachs, opted to become commercial banks, thereby subjecting themselves to more stringent regulation.

Banks ended up receiving a double hit. Their securities investors started demanding money and their borrowers were failing to pay their loans. And troubled banks were not able to raise more money, because other banks and investors sensed that they were in trouble and refused to lend to them.

It is also easy to see why the government-sponsored financial intermediaries, Freddy Mac and Fannie Mae, collapsed. Many economists believe it had to do with moral hazard, when individuals take additional risks because they are insured. Investors knew that the government supported Freddy and Fannie mortgage-backed securities, so they considered them very low risk. With the government behind them, Freddy and Fannie had an incentive to issue risky securities and buy risky mortgages from banks. Banks knew that Freddy and Fanny would buy almost any mortgage they created. However, when people stopped paying their mortgages, the two giant intermediaries lost billions of dollars. Their stocks became worthless and the government had to take control of both Fannie Mae and Freddy Mac.

Financial markets depend on lenders making funds available to borrowers. However, when lenders become reluctant to make loans, it becomes difficult to assess credit risk. This happened in 2008, which led the Federal Reserve and other central banks around the world to pour hundreds of billions of dollars (euros, pounds, etc.) into credit markets to ease the pain of the financial crisis. In addition, the government has enacted large fiscal stimulus packages of close to $1 trillion. The borrowing and spending is intended to offset the reduction in private sector demand caused by the crisis. We will return to this topic in the chapter on Fiscal Policy.

SECTION CHECK

1. There were several contributing factors to the financial crisis of 2008.
2. Maintaining very low real interest rates for a substantial period of time contributed to the housing price run-up.
3. The standards for low-income families to qualify for home loans were reduced, increasing the number of high-risk borrowers.
4. The rapid increase in housing prices during the housing bubble made both borrowers and lenders expect that the risks of subprime lending were not great.
5. After several years of maintaining low real interest rates, the Fed began pushing short-term interest rates up in 2005. The higher interest rates and falling housing prices pushed many homeowners into default and foreclosure.
6. The default rate on home loans was much lower on those holding fixed interest rate mortgage loans.

1. Why would history and the role of Fannie Mae and Freddy Mac have made investors consider mortgage-backed securities to be safe?
2. Why were those who took out hybrid loans at far greater risk of foreclosure when the Fed began raising interest rates?

Interactive Chapter Summary

Fill in the Blanks:

1. Investment cannot occur unless someone in the economy is _____.
2. The _____ market is where households make their saving available to those who desire to borrow additional funds.
3. Saving refers to a _____ concept, while savings refers to a _____ concept.
4. The two most important financial institutions are the _____ market and the _____ market.
5. An economy that invests a _____ fraction of its GDP tends to grow faster.
6. Owners of preferred stock receive a _____ dividend payment, whereas owners of _____ stock do not.
7. A _____ is an owner of a corporation, whereas a _____ is a creditor of a corporation.
8. The obligation to _____ is of higher legal priority than that to _____.
9. _____ is the most important source of funding for firms.
10. Better business conditions would tend to make the value of stocks _____.
11. The reason it is difficult, without inside information, to consistently pick winners in the stock market is because the value of a stock is a _____ _____.
12. Many financial analysts think that the best stock market strategy is to _____ and to hold stocks for _____ periods of time.
13. The _____ interest rate is determined by investment demand and national savings.
14. The loanable funds _____ curve for the economy is downward sloping.
15. As the real interest rate falls, _____ investment projects become profitable, _____ the dollar amount of investment.
16. The supply of national saving comprises both _____ saving and _____ saving.
17. At a _____ real interest rate, a greater quantity of loanable funds will be supplied.
18. Desired loanable funds demanded equals desired _____ at the equilibrium real interest rate.
19. If the real interest rate was above equilibrium, the quantity of loanable funds _____ would exceed the quantity of loanable funds _____.
20. At a real interest rate below equilibrium, a _____ for loanable funds would occur.

21. In a _____ economy, GDP is the sum of consumption plus investment plus government purchases.

22. Public saving is positive as the government _____ more in taxes than it _____.

23. Starting from a balanced budget, a government's move to a budget _____ would increase public saving and increase national saving, other things equal.

24. If the government moved into a budget _____, it would result in negative public saving, reduced national saving, a higher real interest rate, and reduced levels of investment.

25. If the government runs a budget _____, other things equal, it will tend to increase national saving, decrease the real interest rate, increase the amount of investment, and increase economic growth.

26. When foreigners supply more funds than they demand, a capital _____ occurs.

27. Capital inflows from foreign countries _____ to the supply of loanable funds.

28. When the domestic real interest rate is _____, capital will tend to flow out to foreign countries.

29. Too much _____, or excessive _____, was a major cause of the financial crisis of 2008.

30. Many economists think the financial crisis of 2008 began in the _____ market.

31. The worst of the housing market decline after 2006 was in _____, _____, _____, and _____.

32. After the 2001 recession, the Fed funds rate was maintained at _____ or lower for over three years.

33. In order to maintain investment yields as market interest rates decline requires an investor to take more _____.

34. In 2006, a majority of subprime loans were _____ loans, with a _____ fixed rate for the first few years, which then reset to a _____ rate for the rest of the term.

35. After several years of maintaining _____ real interest rates, the Fed reversed course and pushed short-term interest rates _____.

36. The default rate on home loans was much lower on those holding _____ interest rate mortgage loans.

Answers: 1. saving 2. loanable funds 3. flow 4. stock 5. bond 6. greater 6. fixed; stockholder; bondholder 8. bondholders, stockholders 9. Reinvestment 10. rise 11. random walk 12. diversify 13. substantial 14. real 15. demand 16. more; increasing 17. higher 18. loanable funds supplied 19. supplied; demanded 20. shortage 21. closed 22. collects; spends 23. surplus 24. deficit 25. surplus 26. inflow 27. add 28. low 29. debt; leverage 30. housing 31. California, Florida, Arizona, Nevada 32. 2 percent 33. risk 34. hybrid; low; higher 35. low; up 36. fixed

Key Terms and Concepts

bonds 654
stockholders 654
preferred stock 655

common stock 655
retained earnings 655
securities 655

dividend 657
price-earnings ratio 657
crowding-out effect 663

Section Check Answers

23.1 Financial Institutions and Intermediaries

1. **If you believed a company's profitability was about to jump sharply, would you rather own bonds, preferred stock, or common stock in that company?**
   You would rather own common stock because owners of common stock are the residual claimants on the resources of the corporation. If profits were about to jump sharply, common stock owners would benefit because that residual will get substantially larger. Preferred stocks, which pay regular, fixed dividends, and bonds, which pay fixed interest payments, would not benefit nearly as much from increased future profitability.

2. **If almost all investors expected the profits of a company to jump sharply, would that make purchasing the stock today unusually profitable?**
   No. Generally shared expectations of higher future profits will result in higher current prices that capitalize those expected profits. Once those expected profits are reflected in current stock prices, buyers of that stock will not earn unusually high profits as a result.

3. **Why are issues of new stocks to finance business investments more common in periods of high and rising stock prices?**
   In periods of high and rising stock prices, a firm can raise more money for a given number of new ownership shares issued.

4. **What are some of the reasons that stock prices rise and fall?**
   Stock prices rise and fall with expectations of corporate earnings, business conditions, economic policies of the government, business conditions in foreign countries, concern over inflation, and more. Anything that changes expectations of benefits or costs from holding securities will change stock prices.

5. **What is the random walk?**
   The random walk idea is that if markets are operating efficiently, the current stock prices will reflect all available information, so that consistent, extraordinary profit opportunities will not exist. That is, without illegal inside information or consistent good luck, one should not expect to be able to consistently pick winners in the stock market.

6. **What is a dividend?**
   The dividend reported on financial pages is the annual amount the company in question has paid over the preceding year on each share of stock.

7. **How do you calculate a price-earnings ratio?**
   The price-earnings ratio reported on financial pages is found by taking the price of the stock and dividing it by the amount the company earned per share over the past year.

23.2 Saving, Investment, and the Financial System

1. **Why does $Y - C - G = S$ in a simple, closed economy?**
   $Y - C - G$ is what is left over from income after spending on consumption and government purchases, which is what is available for investment. But in equilibrium, investment must equal saving.

2. **If net taxes rise, what happens to private saving? To public saving?**
   Increased net taxes reduce disposable income, which, in turn reduces private saving. However, increased net taxes move the government budget toward surplus, increasing public saving.

3. **Why does the demand for loanable funds curve slope downward?**
   As the real interest rate falls, additional investment projects with lower expected rates of return become profitable for firms, and the quantity of loanable funds demanded rises.

4. **Why does the supply of loanable funds curve slope upward?**
   At a higher real interest rate, the reward for saving and supplying funds to financial markets is greater, leading to an increased quantity of loanable funds supplied.

5. **How is the real interest rate determined?**
   The real interest rate is determined by the intersection of the loanable funds demand curve and the supply curve.

6. **How are shortages and surpluses eliminated in the loanable funds market?**
   If the real interest rate was above the equilibrium real interest rate, the quantity of loanable funds supplied would be greater than the quantity of loanable funds demanded—there would be a surplus of loanable funds. As lenders compete against each other to attract borrowers, the real interest rate will fall toward the equilibrium level. If the real interest rate was below the equilibrium real interest rate, the quantity of loanable funds supplied would be less than the quantity of loanable funds demanded—there would be a shortage of loanable funds. As borrowers compete against each other to attract lenders, the real interest rate will rise toward the equilibrium level.

7. **What factors can shift the demand for loanable funds curve?**
   The investment demand curve would increase (shift to the right) if firms expect higher rates of return on their investments; if profitable new products are developed; or if business taxes are lowered. The loanable funds demand curve would decrease (shift to the left) in the opposite situations.

8. **What factors can shift the supply of loanable funds curve?**
   The saving supply curve would increase (shift to the right) if disposable (after-tax) income rose (say, because taxes were reduced). The saving supply curve would decrease (shift to the left) if disposable (after-tax) income fell.

9. **What would happen to the equilibrium interest rate and quantity of loanable funds exchanged if both the loanable funds demand and supply curves shifted right? What if the loanable funds demand curve shifted right and the loanable funds supply curve shifted left?**
   Whenever both the supply and demand curves shift in any market, we add up the separate effects on price (interest rate) and quantity (of loanable funds) exchanged. When both the loanable funds demand and supply curves shift right, each would increase the quantity of loanable funds exchanged, but would have opposing effects on the interest rate, making that change indeterminate without knowing about the relative magnitudes of the changes.

When the loanable funds demand curve shifted right and the loanable funds supply curve shifted left, both effects would tend to increase the interest rate, but have opposing effects on the quantity of loanable funds exchanged, making that change indeterminate without knowing about the relative magnitudes of the changes.

10. **Other things equal, which direction will an increasing budget surplus change the equilibrium interest rate, the loanable funds supply curve, the level of investment in the economy, and the likely rate of economic growth?**

    An increasing budget surplus would increase the saving supply curve, which would decrease the equilibrium interest rate and increase the equilibrium level of investment in the economy, which would tend to increase economy growth.

11. **Could the crowding-out effect sometimes be called the crowding-in effect?**

    Just as larger government budget deficits crowd out investments by raising interest rates, smaller budget deficits or larger government surpluses would tend to reduce interest rates, increasing or crowding-in investment.

23.3 The Financial Crisis of 2008

1. **Why would history and the role of Fannie Mae and Freddy Mac have made investors consider mortgage-backed securities to be safe?**

   Historically, home loans in the United States had been very safe investments. In addition, both Fannie Mae and Freddy Mac were willing to buy large amounts of mortgage-backed securities and to guarantee others. Both made investors think mortgage-backed securities were not unduly risky.

2. **Why were those who took out hybrid loans at far greater risk of foreclosure when the Fed began raising interest rates?**

   Hybrid loans began, with a low fixed rate for the first few years, which then reset to a higher rate for the rest of the term. Hybrid loan borrowers also had far smaller down payments than traditional home borrowers. As a result, the combination of falling home prices and increasing interest rates hit those homeowners and their lenders particularly hard.

CHAPTER 23 STUDY GUIDE

True or False:

1. The only way for a firm to obtain resources to invest in capital is via borrowing in financial markets.
2. There is no difference in meaning between the terms *saving* and *savings*.
3. The amount of saving and investment are the foundation of economic growth.
4. New capital and new technology are completely separate factors of production.
5. In terms of economic growth, increases in the capital stock come at the expense of workers.
6. Owners of preferred stock are the residual claimants of the resources of a corporation.
7. Both bondholders and stockholders receive increased payments as a company prospers.
8. Preferred stockholders have a higher priority than bondholders and common stockholders when debts of the firm are settled.
9. Corporations can acquire additional financial resources by issuing new shares of stock or reinvesting profits.
10. Firms are more likely to issue new shares of stock and increase expenditures on new capital equipment in periods of optimism.
11. The values of securities change with the expectations of benefits and costs.
12. For a firm to raise additional capital through selling new shares of stock is more common when stock prices are high than when they are low.
13. If you and a large group of others have all received a "hot" stock tip, it is unlikely to be a source of unusually high profits.
14. Historically, the U.S. stock market has outperformed other financial assets.
15. A firm's price-earnings ratio is its stock price divided by its annual dividend.
16. The demand for loanable funds varies inversely with the real interest rate, other things equal.
17. If businesses expect higher rates of return on their investments, it would shift the loanable funds demand curve to the right.
18. An increase in business taxes would shift the loanable funds demand curve to the left.
19. The supply of national savings is the sum of all private savings.
20. Increases in current disposable income from a tax deduction will increase the loanable funds supply curve.
21. If the real interest rate is below equilibrium, the quantity of loanable funds demanded would be less than the quantity of loanable funds supplied.
22. At a real interest rate above equilibrium, a surplus of loanable funds would occur.
23. If the government spends more money than it collects in taxes, national saving is negative.
24. If the government goes from a balanced budget to a deficit, public saving would become negative and national saving would decrease, other things equal.
25. A move toward a government budget surplus would increase national saving, reduce real interest rates, and increase investment, other things equal.
26. A move toward a government budget deficit would tend to reduce private investment and reduce economic growth, other things equal.
27. A move toward a government budget surplus would tend to decrease the real interest rate, other things equal.
28. When foreigners supply fewer funds than they demand, a capital outflow from the United States occurs.
29. When the domestic real interest rate is high, capital will tend to flow out to foreign countries.
30. An increase in disposable income would shift the supply of loanable funds curve to the right.
31. Lower real interest rates will shift the loanable funds demand curve right.
32. Higher real interest rates will increase the quantity of loanable funds supplied, but not change the loanable funds supply curve.

33. If the loanable funds demand curve shifted right, we would expect higher real interest rates and an increased quantity of loanable funds demanded to result.
34. If the loanable funds supply curve shifted left, we would expect higher real interest rates and an increased quantity of loanable funds demanded to result.
35. If the loanable funds supply curve shifted right, it would cause a temporary surplus of loanable funds, which would result in a lower real interest rate.
36. There were only one or two major contributing factors to the financial crisis of 2008.
37. The housing market decline after 2006 was roughly similar throughout the United States.
38. Worldwide interest rates were low early in the twenty-first century in part because of a large amount of savings in emerging markets.
39. Maintaining very low real interest rates for a substantial period of time contributed to the housing price run-up.
40. Fannie Mae and Freddy Mac encouraged the lowering of standards for low-income families in an effort to increase homeownership.
41. Allowing mortgage borrowers to borrow with little or no money down increased the number of high-risk borrowers.
42. In 2006, a substantial minority of subprime loans were hybrid loans.
43. Excessive lending to subprime borrowers did not appreciably affect other homeowners.
44. The rapid increase in housing prices during the housing bubble made both borrowers and lenders expect that the risks of subprime lending was minimal.
45. The traditional safety of home loans in the United States helped make investors eager to buy mortgage-backed securities.
46. There was no one in the world who knew exactly where all the mortgage-backed securities were being held when they began to experience trouble.
47. After the Fed began pushing short-term interest rates up in 2005, the higher interest rates and falling housing prices pushed many homeowners into default and foreclosure.
48. When house prices began falling and many went into default and foreclosure, the housing industry continued to produce new housing at a rapid rate.
49. The fact that Fannie Mae and Freddy Mac were buying large amounts of risky mortgages meant that other buyers perceived the risks of such investments as lower than they really were.
50. The federal government had to take over both Fannie Mae and Freddy Mac as a result of the financial crisis.

Multiple Choice:

1. A firm can acquire financial resources through
   a. retained earnings.
   b. selling stocks.
   c. issuing bonds.
   d. all of the above.

2. You could invest your savings in
   a. treasury bills
   b. mutual funds.
   c. bank deposits.
   d. stocks and bonds.
   e. any of the above.

3. Which of the following entities do not hold corporate stocks?
   a. university and non-profit foundation endowment funds
   b. insurance companies
   c. other corporations
   d. pension funds
   e. All of the above entities hold corporate stocks.

4. Owners of stock in U.S. corporations include
   a. pension funds.
   b. insurance companies.
   c. mutual funds.
   d. all of the above.

5. Preferred stockholders
   a. assume greater risks than do common stockholders.
   b. receive payment before common stockholders in the event of liquidation.
   c. receive payment before bondholders in the event of liquidation.
   d. are characterized by all of the above.

6. Ownership of a share of stock in a corporation is different from ownership of a corporate bond in that
   a. the owner of a share of stock receives payment before a bondholder in the event of a corporation's liquidation.
   b. a bondholder receives a fixed interest payment plus a lump sum payment at maturity, whereas a stockholder may receive income in the form of dividends and capital gains.
   c. a bondholder has voting rights, a shareholder does not.
   d. a bondholder bears greater business risk than does a shareholder.

7. Corporations can finance their growth
   a. by issuing bonds.
   b. by issuing new shares of stock.
   c. through plowbacks.
   d. by all of the above.
   e. by either a or b.

8. Stock prices are influenced by
   a. concern over inflation.
   b. the economic policies of the government.
   c. business conditions in foreign economies.
   d. expectations about corporate earnings.
   e. all of the above.

9. The random walk theory suggests
   a. that stock prices fluctuate in highly predictable ways.
   b. that it is extremely difficult without inside information to consistently pick winners in the stock market.
   c. that if stock price fluctuations are scrutinized carefully, one can consistently pick winners in the stock market.
   d. that information filters sufficiently slowly that one can consistently profit by trading on newly released information.

10. A relatively high P/E ratio
    a. may indicate that investors expect future earnings to rise.
    b. may indicate that investors expect future earnings to fall.
    c. indicates that a stock is undervalued.
    d. indicates that the stock is trading at a price that is low relative to earnings.

11. A stock's P/E ratio
    a. is calculated by dividing the 52-week high price by the earnings per share of the firm over the past year.
    b. is calculated by dividing the 52-week low price by the earnings per share over the past year.
    c. indicates that the stock is overvalued if the P/E ratio is relatively low.
    d. indicates that investors may expect future earnings to fall if the P/E ratio is relatively low.

Use the following stock table to answer the next three questions (12–14).

52-week							Previous Day			
High	Low	Company	Symbol	Div.	Yield	P/E	High	Low	Close	Change
60.50	36.42	General Elec.	GE	.64	1.5	33	44.10	43.20	43.50	−.10
63.22	23.45	Hewlett-Pack.	HWP	.32	1.3	19	25.25	24.20	24.66	+.45

12. If a typical P/E ratio for companies that supply services and products comparable to General Electric is 20, then
    a. purchasing General Electric stock at this time cannot possibly be a wise decision.
    b. GE's P/E ratio suggests that its stock may be overvalued at this time.
    c. GE's P/E ratio suggests that its stock may be undervalued at this time.
    d. GE's P/E ratio suggests that investors may expect the stock price to rise in the near future.
    e. either b or d could be indicated by the information in the table.

13. If a typical P/E ratio for companies that supply services and products comparable to Hewlett-Packard is 40, then
    a. purchasing Hewlett-Packard stock at this time cannot possibly be a wise decision.
    b. Hewlett-Packard's P/E ratio suggests that its stock may be overvalued at this time.
    c. Hewlett-Packard's P/E ratio suggests that its stock may be undervalued at this time.
    d. Hewlett-Packard's P/E ratio suggests that investors may expect the stock price to rise in the near future.
    e. either c or d is indicated by the information in the table.

14. Based on the information in the preceding table, which of the following is true?
    a. Both General Electric and Hewlett-Packard stocks increased in price compared to the previous day's close.
    b. Both General Electric and Hewlett-Packard stocks decreased in price compared to the previous day's close.
    c. General Electric stock decreased in price from the previous day's close, while Hewlett-Packard's stock increased in price from the previous day's close.
    d. Both General Electric and Hewlett-Packard stocks are trading near their 52-week highs.

15. When the government runs a budget deficit, which of the following would have to be negative?
    a. public saving
    b. private saving
    c. national saving
    d. investment

16. Other things equal, if the government runs a budget surplus, it will tend to
    a. increase national saving.
    b. decrease the real interest rate.
    c. increase the amount of investment.
    d. increase economic growth.
    e. do all of the above.

17. Capital outflows to foreign countries tend to
    a. make domestic real interest rates higher than they would otherwise have been.
    b. reduce the funds available for domestic capital investment.
    c. cause the saving supply curve to be to the left of the national saving supply curve.
    d. do all of the above.

18. A lower real interest rate will
    a. increase the loanable funds demand curve.
    b. decrease the loanable funds demand curve.
    c. increase the dollar amount of loanable funds exchanged but not change the loanable funds demand curve.
    d. decrease the dollar amount of loanable funds exchanged but not change the loanable funds demand curve.

19. The discovery of profitable new technological investment opportunities
    a. would increase the loanable funds demand curve.
    b. would decrease the loanable funds demand curve.
    c. would leave the loanable funds demand curve unchanged.
    d. could either increase or decrease the loanable funds demand curve.

20. A combination of higher business taxes and a reduction in the level of new profitable technological investment opportunities
    a. would increase the loanable funds demand curve.
    b. would decrease the loanable funds demand curve.
    c. would leave the loanable funds demand curve unchanged.
    d. could either increase or decrease the loanable funds demand curve.

21. A higher real interest rate will
    a. increase the supply of loanable funds.
    b. decrease the supply of loanable funds.
    c. increase the dollar amount of loanable funds exchanged, but not shift the supply of loanable funds curve to the right.
    d. decrease the dollar amount of loanable funds exchanged, but not shift the supply of loanable funds curve to the left.

22. If at a given interest rate, the quantity of loanable funds supplied is less than the quantity of loanable funds demanded,
    a. there is a surplus of loanable funds and real interest rates will rise.
    b. there is a surplus of loanable funds and real interest rates will fall.
    c. there is a shortage of loanable funds and real interest rates will rise.
    d. there is a shortage of loanable funds and real interest rates will fall.

23. An increase in the loanable funds demand curve would
    a. increase real interest rates.
    b. decrease real interest rates.
    c. increase the dollar amount of loanable funds exchanged.
    d. decrease the dollar amount of loanable funds exchanged.
    e. do both a and c.

24. An increase in the supply of loanable funds would
    a. increase real interest rates.
    b. decrease real interest rates.
    c. increase the dollar amount of loanable funds exchanged.
    d. do both a and c.
    e. do both b and c.

25. At a higher than equilibrium real interest rate, the quantity of loanable funds supplied would be _____ than the quantity of loanable funds demanded—there would be a _____ of loanable funds at this real interest rate.
    a. greater; shortage
    b. greater; surplus
    c. less than; shortage
    d. less than; surplus

26. A budget deficit
    a. adds to national savings.
    b. lowers the interest rate.
    c. increases private investment.
    d. does none of the above, other things equal.

27. An increase in the real interest rate
    a. shifts the supply of loanable funds curve to the right.
    b. shifts the supply of loanable funds curve to the left.
    c. shifts the loanable funds demand curve to the right.
    d. shifts the loanable funds demand curve to the left.
    e. does none of the above.

28. An increase in expectations about the profitability of investment will tend to
    a. increase both the interest rate and the level of investment.
    b. decrease both the interest rate and the level of investment.
    c. increase the interest rate and decrease the level of investment.
    d. decrease the interest rate and increase the level of investment.

29. Suppose investors become pessimistic about the economy, lowering their expected returns on investment projects. The results would include
    a. a leftward shift in the supply of loanable funds.
    b. a rightward shift in demand for loanable funds.
    c. a smaller quantity of funds changing hands in the loanable funds market.
    d. the interest rate falling.
    e. both c and d.

30. If the equilibrium interest rate increases and quantity of funds traded in the loanable fund market decreases, it could have been caused by
    a. investors becoming more optimistic about profit prospects.
    b. investors becoming more pessimistic about profit prospects.
    c. households deciding to save less.
    d. households deciding to save more.

31. Which of the following was not a factor in the financial crisis of 2008?
    a. poorly informed borrowers
    b. credit rating agencies
    c. fraud
    d. misguided government policies
    e. All of the above were factors in the financial crisis of 2008

Problems:

1. Why are firms less likely to issue new shares of stock when consumers or businesses are pessimistic about economic conditions?

2. In the event of a corporate bankruptcy, would you rather be a bondholder, a preferred stockholder, or a stockholder in the ailing corporation? Explain.

3. Why might governments sometimes try to combat recessions by lowering interest rates?

4. What would happen to the loanable funds demand curve if new potentially profitable technologies arise and business taxes are raised at the same time?

5. What would happen to the loanable funds supply curve if there was both an increase in current disposable income and a decrease in new technologies creating investment opportunities?

6. Starting from equilibrium in the loanable funds market, what changes in loanable funds supply or demand would tend to cause a surplus of funds at the current interest rate? What changes in loanable funds supply or demand would tend to cause a shortage of funds at the current interest rate?

7. What happens to net taxes when transfer payments increase? When both taxes and transfer payments increase?

8. Other things equal, which direction will an increasing budget deficit change the equilibrium interest rate, the loanable funds supply curve, the level of loanable funds in the economy, and the likely rate of economic growth, other things equal?

9. Why will a given government budget deficit have a smaller effect on investment in an open economy than a closed economy?

10.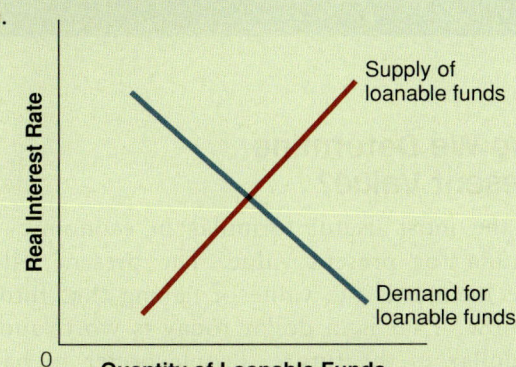
    a. What happens to the loanable funds supply and demand curves if business expectations and disposable income both increase?
    b. What happens to the loanable funds supply and demand curves if profitable new technologies are invented and disposable income decreases?
    c. What happens to the loanable funds supply and demand curves if taxes on investment increase and taxes on savings decrease?
    d. What happens to the loanable funds supply and demand curves if increasingly costly business regulations are imposed, along with increased taxes on current earnings?
11. In retrospect, what should have been the Federal Reserve's monetary policy during the 2008 financial crisis?
12. If housing prices had continued to rise during the 2008 financial crisis, would we still have had the same problem with subprime borrowers? Or would it have just been delayed?
13. Why was home building such an important factor in this crisis?
14. If the government had not encouraged a goal of homeownership with easy credit, would we have the current housing market problem?

APPENDIX
Calculating Present Value

Future Evaluation

One of the most important decisions a firm makes is investment in new capital. A lot of money will be invested in factory equipment and machines expected to last for many years. The firm making the investment decision must consider the price that it must pay *now* for the new capital compared with the additional revenue the capital should generate *over time*. That is, the firm must compare current costs with future benefits. To figure out how much those future benefits are worth today, economists use a concept called **present value**.

present value
the value in today's dollars of home future benefit

How Do We Determine the Present Value?

One of the most useful formulas in economics is the formula for present value. The present value of future income is the value of having that future income now. That is, a dollar today is worth more than a dollar in the future. People prefer to have money now rather than later, which is why they are willing to pay interest to borrow it. The present value of receiving $1,000 a year from now can be calculated by using the present value equation:

$$PV = \$X/(1 + r)^t$$

section 23.1 exhibit 1 Present Value Table

Year	3%	6%	8%	10%	15%
1	0.9709	0.9434	0.9259	0.9091	0.8696
2	1.9135	1.8334	1.7833	1.7355	1.6257
3	2.8286	2.6730	2.5771	2.4869	2.2832
4	3.7171	3.4651	3.3121	3.1699	2.8550
5	4.5797	4.2124	3.9927	3.7908	3.3522
6	5.4172	4.9173	4.6229	4.3553	3.7845
7	6.2303	5.5824	5.2064	4.8684	4.1604
8	7.0197	6.2098	5.7466	5.3349	4.4873
9	7.7861	6.8017	6.2469	5.7590	4.7716
10	8.5302	7.3601	6.7101	6.1446	5.0188
11	9.2526	7.8869	7.1390	6.4951	5.2337
12	9.9540	8.3838	7.5361	6.8137	5.4206
13	10.6350	8.8527	7.9038	7.1034	5.5831
14	11.2961	9.2950	8.2442	7.3667	5.7245
15	11.9379	9.7122	8.5595	7.6061	5.8474
16	12.5611	10.1059	8.8514	7.8237	5.9542
17	13.1661	10.4773	9.1216	8.0216	6.0472
18	13.7535	10.8276	9.3719	8.2014	6.1280
19	14.3238	11.1581	9.6036	8.3649	6.1982
20	14.8775	11.4699	9.8181	8.5136	6.2593
30	19.6004	13.7648	11.2578	9.4269	6.5660

where $X = \$1,000$; r = current market interest rate; and t = years from now. So the present value of $1,000 one year from now at the current market interest rate of 5 percent is

$$\$1,000/(1.05)^1 = \$952.38$$

The present value of $1,000 two years from now at a current market interest rate of 5 percent is

$$\$1,000/(1.05)^2 = \$907.03$$

To illustrate, suppose a company is contemplating the purchase of a new factory that they think will produce additional annual earnings of $100,000 a year for 10 years, at which time it will be obsolete (worthless). In this case, let us assume that we can get 10 percent annually on the use of our funds in some comparable alternative investment; a good proxy for this "comparable investment" is the market rate of interest. We can now calculate the present value of earnings to be received in each year (first, second, third, and so on) and sum them. Because these multiyear computations can be tedious, Exhibit 1 provides a present value table. For example, $100,000 per year over 10 years at 10 percent interest yields a present value of $614,460 ($100,000 × 6.1446). If the price of the factory were only $500,000, we would invest; if the price were $700,000, however, the marginal cost of $700,000 would exceed the present value, $614,460, so we would not invest in the new factory.

However, if interest rates were to fall to 6 percent, the present value of the flow of future earnings would grow to $736,010 ($1,000,000 × 7.3601), and we probably would make the investment even if the factory cost $700,000. Thus, falling interest rates lead to greater investment. In short, we see that an investor will buy capital (factory) if the expected discounted present value of the capital exceeds the current price.

Thus, the company's decision whether or not to invest in a new factory depends on the interest rate.

We can see from the example how the quantity of loanable funds demanded and investment is related to the interest rate. At a higher interest rate, the quantity of loanable funds demanded (and investments) falls and at a lower interest rate the quantity of loanable funds demanded (and investments) rises.

Key Terms and Concepts

present value 684

Problems:

1. Why is money worth more now than at some future date?

    Answer

    You can use the money that you have right now. You could save it and get interest on it or you can buy goods and services with that money. If you are receiving money a year from now—you can't use that money right now to save or consume. There is also a risk associated with lending the money. If you lend the money to a friend, he or she may not be able to pay it back in a year like you had expected.

2. How does the interest rate affect the present value payments?

    Answer

    The interest rate connects the present value with the future. The interest rate reflects *how much more* a person values a dollar today versus a dollar in the future.

3. If you won $10 million in the lottery and were given a choice of a lump sum payment or payment over a 20-year period, which would you choose?

    Answer

    Suppose you did win $10 million in the state lottery and your state will pay you this money over a 20-year period—$500,000 a year—or you can get a lump sum payment up front. What is the actual present value of this $10 million lottery prize? Using a 10 percent interest rate, the present value over a 20-year period is $4,256,800. That is, using the present value tables, we multiply $500,000 × 8.5136 = $4,256,800. If you want it up front, it is certainly less than $10 million. Oh yes, there are taxes, too.

PART 7
THE MACROECONOMIC MODELS

Chapter 24 Aggregate Demand and Aggregate Supply *688*

Chapter 25 The Aggregate Expenditure Model *731*

24 Aggregate Demand and Aggregate Supply

24.1 The Determinants of Aggregate Demand
24.2 The Aggregate Demand Curve
24.3 Shifts in the Aggregate Demand Curve
24.4 The Aggregate Supply Curve
24.5 Shifts in the Aggregate Supply Curve
24.6 Macroeconomic Equilibrium
24.7 The Classical and the Keynesian Macroeconomic Model

In this chapter, we develop the aggregate demand and aggregate supply model. The AD/AS model is a variable price model; that is, it allows us to see changes in the price level and changes in real GDP simultaneously.

We explain changes in the price level and real GDP in both the short run and long run. This model will help us understand such key macroeconomic variables as inflation, unemployment, and economic growth. In the following chapters, we will also use this model to help us understand how stabilization policies can help with problems that result from recession and inflationary expansion. ■

SECTION 24.1 The Determinants of Aggregate Demand

- What is aggregate demand?
- What is consumption?
- What is investment?
- What are government purchases?
- What are net exports?

What Is Aggregate Demand?

Aggregate demand (*AD*) is the sum of the demand for all final goods and services in the economy. It can also be seen as the quantity of real gross domestic product demanded at different price levels. The four major components of aggregate demand are consumption (*C*), investment (*I*), government purchases (*G*), and net exports (*X* − *M*). Aggregate demand, then, is equal to $C + I + G + (X - M)$.

Consumption (C)

Consumption is by far the largest component in aggregate demand. Expenditures for consumer goods and services typically absorb almost 70 percent of total economic activity, as measured by GDP. Understanding the determinants of consumption, then, is critical to an understanding of the forces leading to changes in aggregate demand, which, in turn, changes total output and income.

Investment (I)

Because investment spending (purchases of investment goods) is an important component of aggregate demand, which in turn is a determinant of the level of GDP, changes in investment spending are often responsible for changes in the level of economic activity. If consumption is determined largely by the level of disposable income, what determines the level of investment expenditure? As you may recall, investment expenditure is the most unstable category of GDP; it is sensitive to changes in economic, social, and political variables. In 2004, investment was roughly 16 percent of GDP.

Many factors are important in determining the level of investment. Good business conditions "induce" firms to invest because a healthy growth in demand for products in the future seems likely, based on current experience. We will consider the key variables that influence investment spending in the next section.

Government Purchases (G)

Government purchases, another component of aggregate demand, include spending by federal, state, and local governments for the purchase of new goods and services produced. Most of the purchases at the federal level are for the military. In 2004, the federal government accounted for roughly 19 percent of total spending. Government purchases at the state and local levels include education, highways, and police protection. Although volatile shifts in government purchases are less frequent than volatile shifts in investment spending, they do occasionally occur, often at the beginning or end of wars.

Net Exports (X − M)

The interaction of the U.S. economy with the rest of the world is becoming increasingly important. Up to this point, for simplicity, we have not included the foreign sector. However, international trade must be incorporated into the framework. Models that include the effects of international trade are called **open economy** models.

Remember, exports are goods and services that we sell to foreign customers, such as movies, wheat, and Ford Mustangs; imports are goods and services that we buy from foreign companies, such as BMWs, French wine, and Sony TVs. Exports and imports can alter aggregate demand. Exports minus imports is what we call **net exports**. If exports are greater than imports ($X > M$), we have positive net exports. If imports are greater than exports ($X < M$), net exports are negative.

> **aggregate demand (*AD*)**
> the total demand for all the final goods and services in the economy
>
> **open economy**
> a type of model that includes international trade effects
>
> **net exports**
> the difference between the value of exports and the value of imports

The impact of net exports (X − M) on aggregate demand is similar to the impact of government purchases on aggregate demand. Suppose that the United States has no trade surplus and no trade deficit—zero net exports. What would happen if foreign consumers started buying more U.S. goods and services, while U.S. consumers continued to buy imports at roughly the same rate? The result would be *positive net exports* (X > M) and greater demand for U.S. goods and services—a higher level of aggregate demand. What if a country has a trade deficit? Assuming, again, that the economy initially has zero net exports, a trade deficit, or *negative net exports* (X < M), would lower U.S. aggregate demand, *ceteris paribus*.

SECTION CHECK

1. Aggregate demand is the sum of the demand for all final goods and services in the economy. It can also be seen as the quantity of real GDP demanded at different price levels.
2. The four major components of aggregate demand are consumption (C), investment (I), government purchases (G), and net exports (X − M). Aggregate demand, then, is equal to C + I + G + (X − M).
3. Changes in investment spending are often responsible for changes in the level of economic activity.
4. Government purchases are made up of federal, state, and local purchases of goods and services.
5. Trade deficits lower aggregate demand, other things being equal; trade surpluses increase aggregate demand, other things being equal.

---

1. What are the major components of aggregate demand?
2. How would an increase in personal taxes or a decrease in transfer payments affect consumption?
3. What would an increase in exports do to aggregate demand, other things being equal? An increase in imports? An increase in both imports and exports, where the change in exports was greater in magnitude?

SECTION 24.2 The Aggregate Demand Curve

★ How is the aggregate demand curve different from the demand curve for a particular good?

★ Why is the aggregate demand curve downward sloping?

The **aggregate demand curve** reflects the total amount of real goods and services that all groups together want to purchase in a given period. In other words, it indicates the quantities of real gross domestic product demanded at different price levels. Note that this is different from the demand curve for a particular good presented in Chapter 4, which looked at the relationship between the relative price of a good and the quantity demanded.

aggregate demand curve
graph that shows the inverse relationship between the price level and RGDP demanded

How Is the Quantity of Real GDP Demanded Affected by the Price Level?

The aggregate demand curve slopes downward, which means an inverse (or opposite) relationship exists between the price level and real gross domestic product (RGDP) demanded. Exhibit 1

section 24.2 exhibit 1 — The Aggregate Demand Curve

The aggregate demand curve slopes downward, reflecting an inverse relationship between the overall price level and the quantity of real GDP demanded. When the price level increases, the quantity of RGDP demanded decreases; when the price level decreases, the quantity of RGDP demanded increases.

illustrates this relationship, where the quantity of RGDP demanded is measured on the horizontal axis and the overall price level is measured on the vertical axis. As we move from point A to point B on the aggregate demand curve, we see that an increase in the price level causes RGDP demanded to fall. Conversely, if a reduction in the price level occurs—a movement from B to A—RGDP demanded increases. Why do purchasers in the economy demand less real output when the price level rises and more real output when the price level falls?

Why Is the Aggregate Demand Curve Negatively Sloped?

Three complementary explanations exist for the negative slope of the aggregate demand curve: the real wealth effect, the interest rate effect, and the open economy effect.

The Real Wealth Effect

If you had $1,000 in cash stashed under your bed while the economy suffered a serious bout of inflation, the purchasing power of your cash would be eroded by the extent of the inflation. That is, an increase in the price level reduces real wealth and would consequently decrease your planned purchases of goods and services, lowering the quantity of RGDP demanded.

In the event that the price level falls, the reverse would hold true. A falling price level would increase the real value of your cash assets, increasing your purchasing power and increasing RGDP demanded. The connection can be summarized as follows:

↑Price level ⇒ ↓Real wealth ⇒ ↓Purchasing power ⇒ ↓RGDP demanded

and

↓Price level ⇒ ↑Real wealth ⇒ ↑Purchasing power ⇒ ↑RGDP demanded

The Interest Rate Effect

If the price level falls, households and firms will need to hold less money to conduct their day-to-day activities. Firms will need to hold less money for such inputs as wages and taxes; households will need to hold less money for such purchases as food, rent, and clothing. At a lower price level, households and firms will shift their "excess" money into interest-earning assets such as bonds or savings accounts. This will increase the supply of funds to the loanable funds market, leading to lower interest rates. As interest rates fall, households and firms will borrow more and buy more goods and services—thus, the quantity of RGDP demanded will increase. In sum:

↓Price level ⇒ Households and firms reduce their holdings of money and save more ⇒ Supply of loanable funds increases ⇒ Interest rates fall ⇒ Households and firms are encouraged to borrow and spend ⇒ RDP demanded increases

If the price level rises, households and firms will need to hold more money to buy goods and services and conduct their daily activities. Households and firms will need to borrow money, and this increased demand for loanable funds will result in higher interest rates. At higher interest rates, consumers may give up plans to buy new cars or houses, and firms may delay investments in plant and equipment. In sum:

↑Price level ⇒ Households and firms increase their holdings of money ⇒ Demand for loanable funds increases ⇒ Interest rates rise ⇒ Households and firms are discouraged from borrowing and spending ⇒ RDP demanded decreases

The Open Economy Effect

Many goods and services are bought and sold in global markets. If the price level in the United States rises relative to the price level in other countries, U.S. exports will become relatively more expensive and foreign imports will become relatively less expensive. Some U.S. consumers will shift from buying domestic goods to buying foreign goods (imports). Some foreign consumers will stop buying U.S. goods. U.S. exports will fall and U.S. imports will rise. Thus, net exports will fall, thereby reducing the amount of RGDP purchased in the United States. A lower price level makes U.S. exports less expensive and foreign imports more expensive. So U.S. consumers will buy more domestic goods, and foreign consumers will buy more U.S. goods. This will increase net exports, thereby increasing the amount of RGDP purchased in the United States.

SECTION CHECK

1. An aggregate demand curve shows the inverse relationship between the amounts of real goods and services (RGDP) that are demanded at each possible price level.
2. The aggregate demand curve is downward sloping because of the real wealth effect, the interest rate effect, and the open economy effect.

---

1. Why is the aggregate demand curve downward sloping?
2. How does an increased price level reduce the quantities of investment goods and consumer durables demanded?
3. What is the real wealth effect, and how does it imply a downward-sloping aggregate demand curve?
4. What is the interest rate effect, and how does it imply a downward-sloping aggregate demand curve?
5. What is the open economy effect, and how does it imply a downward-sloping aggregate demand curve?

SECTION 24.3 Shifts in the Aggregate Demand Curve

* What is the difference between a movement along and a shift in the aggregate demand curve?
* What variables shift the aggregate demand curve to the right?
* What variables shift the aggregate demand curve to the left?

Shifts Versus Movements Along the Aggregate Demand Curve

Like the supply and demand curves described in Chapter 4, the aggregate demand curve may experience both shifts and movements. In the previous section, we discussed three factors—the real wealth effect, the interest rate effect, and the open economy effect—that result in the downward slope of the aggregate demand curve. Each of these factors, then, generates a movement *along* the aggregate demand curve, in reaction to changes in the general price level. In this section, we will discuss some of the many factors that can cause the aggregate demand curve to shift to the right or left.

The whole aggregate demand curve can shift to the right or left, as shown in Exhibit 1. Put simply, if some nonprice level determinant causes total spending to increase, the aggregate demand curve will shift to the right. If a non-price level determinant causes the level of total spending to decline, the aggregate demand curve will shift to the left. Let's look at some specific factors that could cause the aggregate demand curve to shift.

Aggregate Demand Curve Shifters

Anything that changes the amount of total spending in the economy (holding price levels constant) will affect the aggregate demand curve. An increase in any component of GDP (C, I, G, or $X - M$) will cause the aggregate demand curve to shift rightward. Conversely,

section 24.3 exhibit 1 — Shifts in the Aggregate Demand Curve

An increase in aggregate demand shifts the curve to the right (from AD_1 to AD_2). A decrease in aggregate demand shifts the curve to the left (from AD_1 to AD_3).

decreases in C, I, G, or X − M will shift aggregate demand leftward.

Changing Consumption (C)

A whole host of changes could alter consumption patterns. For example, an increase in consumer confidence, an increase in wealth, or a tax cut can increase consumption and shift the aggregate demand curve to the right. An increase in population will also increase the aggregate demand because more consumers will be spending more money on goods and services.

Of course, the aggregate demand curve could shift to the left as a result of decreases in consumption demand. For example, if consumers sense that the economy is headed for a recession or if the government imposes a tax increase, the result will be a leftward shift of the aggregate demand curve. Because consuming less is saving more, an increase in saving, *ceteris paribus*, will shift aggregate demand to the left. Consumer debt may also cause some consumers to put off additional

Use what you've LEARNED — CHANGES IN AGGREGATE DEMAND

Q Any aggregate demand category that has the ability to change total purchases in the economy will shift the aggregate demand curve. That is, changes in consumption purchases, investment purchases, government purchases, or net export purchases shift the aggregate demand curve. For each component of aggregate demand (C, I, G, and X − M), list some changes that can increase aggregate demand. Then list some changes that can decrease aggregate demand.

A The following are some aggregate demand curve shifters.

INCREASES IN AGGREGATE DEMAND (RIGHTWARD SHIFT)	DECREASES IN AGGREGATE DEMAND (LEFTWARD SHIFT)
Consumption (C)	Consumption (C)
— lower personal taxes	— higher personal taxes
— a rise in consumer confidence	— a fall in consumer confidence
— greater stock market wealth	— reduced stock market wealth
— an increase in transfer payments	— a reduction in transfer payments
Investment (I)	Investment (I)
— lower real interest rates	— higher real interest rates
— optimistic business forecasts	— pessimistic business forecasts
— lower business taxes	— higher business taxes
Government purchases (G)	Government purchases (G)
— an increase in government purchases	— a reduction in government purchases
Net exports (X − M)	Net exports (X − M)
— income increases abroad, which will likely increase the sale of domestic goods (exports)	— income falls abroad, which leads to a reduction in the sale of domestic goods (exports)

spending. In fact, some economists believe that part of the 1990–1992 recession was due to consumer debt that had built up during the 1980s. In addition to maxing out their credit cards, some individuals lost equity in their homes and, consequently, experienced reductions in their wealth and purchasing power—again shifting aggregate demand to the left.

Changing Investment (I)

Investment is also an important determinant of aggregate demand. Increases in the demand for investment goods occur for a variety of reasons. For example, if business confidence increases or real interest rates fall, business investment will increase and aggregate demand will shift to the right. A reduction in business taxes would also shift the aggregate demand curve to the right, because businesses would now retain more of their profits to invest. However, if interest rates or business taxes rise, we would expect to see a leftward shift in aggregate demand.

Changing Government Purchases (G)

Government purchases are another part of total spending and therefore must have an impact on aggregate demand. An increase in government purchases, other things being equal, shifts the aggregate demand curve to the right, while a reduction shifts aggregate demand to the left.

Changing Net Exports (X − M)

Global markets are also important in a domestic economy. For example, when major trading partners experience economic slowdowns (as did the Asian market in the late 1990s), they will demand fewer U.S. imports. This causes U.S. net exports (X − M) to fall, shifting aggregate demand to the left. Alternatively, an economic boom in the economies of major trading partners may lead to an increase in our exports to them, causing net exports (X − M) to rise and aggregate demand to increase.

SECTION CHECK

1. A change in the price level causes a movement along the aggregate demand curve, not a shift in the aggregate demand curve.
2. Aggregate demand is made up of total spending, C + I + G + (X − M). Any change in these factors will cause the aggregate demand curve to shift.

---

1. How is the distinction between a change in demand and a change in quantity demanded the same for aggregate demand as for the demand for a particular good?
2. What happens to aggregate demand if the demand for consumption goods increases, *ceteris paribus*?
3. What happens to aggregate demand if the demand for investment goods falls, *ceteris paribus*?
4. Why would an increase in the money supply tend to increase expenditures on consumption and investment, *ceteris paribus*?

SECTION 24.4 The Aggregate Supply Curve

* What does the aggregate supply curve represent?
* Why do producers supply more as the price level increases in the short run?
* Why is the long-run aggregate supply curve vertical at the natural rate of output?

What Is the Aggregate Supply Curve?

The **aggregate supply (AS) curve** is the relationship between the total quantity of final goods and services that suppliers are *willing* and *able* to produce and the overall price level. The aggregate supply curve represents how much RGDP suppliers are willing to produce at different price levels. In fact, the two aggregate supply curves are a **short-run aggregate supply (SRAS) curve** and a **long-run aggregate** supply (*LRAS*) curve. The short-run relationship refers to a period when output can change in response to supply and demand, but input prices have not yet been able to adjust. For example, nominal wages are assumed to adjust slowly in the short run. The long-run relationship refers to a period long enough for the prices of outputs and all inputs to fully adjust to changes in the economy.

Why Is the Short-Run Aggregate Supply Curve Positively Sloped?

In the short run, the aggregate supply curve is upward sloping, as shown in Exhibit 1. At a higher price level, then, producers are willing to supply more real output, and at lower price levels, they are willing to supply less real output. Why would producers be willing to supply more output just because the price level increases? Two possible explanations are the profit effect and the misperception effect.

The Profit Effect

For many firms, input costs—wages and rents, for example—are relatively constant in the short run.

> **aggregate supply (*AS*) curve**
> the total quantity of final goods and services suppliers are willing and able to supply at a given price level
>
> **short-run aggregate supply (*SRAS*) curve**
> the graphical relationship between RGDP and the price level when output prices can change but input prices are unable to adjust
>
> **long-run aggregate supply (*LRAS*) curve**
> the graphical relationship between RGDP and the price level when output prices and input prices can fully adjust to economic changes

Workers and other material input suppliers often enter into long-term contracts with firms at prearranged prices. Thus, the slow adjustments of input prices are due to contracts that do not adjust quickly to output price level changes. So when the price level rises, output prices rise relative to input prices (costs), raising producers' short-run profit margins. With this short-run profit effect, the increased profit margins make it in producers' self-interest to expand production and sales at higher price levels.

If the price level falls, output prices fall and producers' profits tend to fall. Again, this is because many input costs, such as wages and other contracted costs, are relatively constant in the short run. When output price levels fall, producers find it more difficult to cover their input costs and, consequently, reduce their levels of output.

The Misperception Effect

The second explanation for the upward-sloping short-run aggregate supply curve is that producers can be fooled by price changes in the short run. For example, suppose a cotton farmer sees the price of his cotton rising. Thinking that the *relative price* of his cotton is rising (i.e., that cotton is becoming more valuable in real terms), he supplies more. Suppose, however, that cotton was not the only thing for which prices were rising. What if the prices of many other goods and services were rising at the same time as a result of an increase in the price level? The relative price of cotton, then, was not actually rising, although it appeared so in the short run. In this case, the farmer was fooled into supplying more based on his *short-run misperception* of relative prices. In other words, producers can be fooled into thinking that the relative prices of the items they are producing are rising and mistakenly increase production.

Why Is the Long-Run Aggregate Supply Curve Vertical?

Along the short-run aggregate supply curve, we assume that wages and other input prices are constant. This assumption is not the case in the long run, which is a period long enough for the price of all inputs to fully adjust to changes in the economy. When we move along the long-run supply curve, we are looking at the relationship between RGDP produced and the

section 24.4 exhibit 1 The Short-Run Aggregate Supply Curve

The short-run aggregate supply (*SRAS*) curve is upward sloping. Suppliers are willing to supply more RGDP at higher price levels and less at lower price levels, other things being equal.

price level, once input prices have been able to respond to changes in output prices. Along the long-run aggregate supply (LRAS) curve, two sets of prices are changing: the price of outputs and the price of inputs. That is, along the LRAS curve, a 10 percent increase in the price of goods and services is matched by a 10 percent increase in the price of inputs. The long-run aggregate supply curve is thus insensitive to the price level. As we can see in Exhibit 2, the LRAS curve is drawn as perfectly vertical, reflecting the fact that the level of RGDP producers are willing to supply is not affected by changes in the price level. Note that the vertical long-run aggregate supply curve will always be positioned at the natural rate of output, where all resources are fully employed ($RGDP_{NR}$). That is, in the long run, firms will always produce at the maximum level allowed by their capital, labor, and technological inputs, regardless of the price level.

The long-run equilibrium level is where the economy will settle when undisturbed and when all resources are fully employed. Remember that the economy will always be at the intersection of aggregate supply and aggregate demand; but that point will not always be at the natural rate of output, $RGDP_{NR}$. Long-run equilibrium will only occur where the aggregate supply and aggregate demand curves intersect along the long-run aggregate supply curve at the natural, or potential, rate of output.

section 24.4 exhibit 2 The Long-Run Aggregate Supply Curve

A change in the price level does not change the amount of RGDP supplied in the long run

Along the long-run aggregate supply curve, the level of RGDP does not change with a change in the price level. The position of the LRAS curve is determined by the natural rate of output, $RGDP_{NR}$, which reflects the levels of capital, land, labor, and technology in the economy.

SECTION CHECK

1. The short-run aggregate supply curve measures how much RGDP suppliers are willing to produce at different price levels.
2. In the short run, producers supply more as the price level increases because wages and other input prices tend to change more slowly than output prices. For this reason, producers can make a profit by expanding production when the price level rises. Producers also may be fooled into thinking that the relative price of the item they are producing is rising, and increase production as a result.
3. In the long run, the aggregate supply curve is vertical. In the long run, input prices change proportionally with output prices. The position of the LRAS curve is determined by the level of capital, land, labor, and technology at the natural rate of output, $RGDP_{NR}$.

1. What relationship does the short-run aggregate supply curve represent?
2. What relationship does the long-run aggregate supply curve represent?
3. Why is focusing on producers' profit margins helpful in understanding the logic of the short-run aggregate supply curve?
4. Why is the short-run aggregate supply curve upward sloping, while the long-run aggregate supply curve is vertical at the natural rate of output?
5. What would the short-run aggregate supply curve look like if input prices always changed instantaneously as soon as output prices changed? Why?
6. If the price of cotton increased 10 percent when cotton producers thought other prices were rising 5 percent over the same period, what would happen to the quantity of RGDP supplied in the cotton industry? What if cotton producers thought other prices were rising 20 percent over the same period?

SECTION 24.5 Shifts in the Aggregate Supply Curve

* Which factors of production affect the short-run and long-run aggregate supply curves?
* What factors shift the short-run aggregate supply curve exclusively?

Shifting Short-Run and Long-Run Supply Curves

We will now examine the determinants that can shift the short-run and long-run aggregate supply curves, as shown in Exhibit 1. Any change in the quantity of any factor of production available—capital, land, labor, or technology—can cause a shift in both the long-run and short-run aggregate supply curves. We will now see how these factors can change the positions of both types of aggregate supply curves.

How Capital Affects Aggregate Supply

Changes in the stock of capital will alter the amount of goods and services the economy can produce. Investing in capital improves the quantity and quality of the capital stock, which lowers the cost of production in the short run. This change in turn shifts the short-run aggregate supply curve rightward and firms will supply more output at every price level. It also allows output to be permanently greater than before, shifting the long-run aggregate supply curve rightward, *ceteris paribus*.

Changes in human capital can also alter the aggregate supply curve. Investments in human capital include educational or vocational programs and on-the-job training. All these investments in human capital cause productivity to rise. As a result, the short-run aggregate supply curve shifts to the right, because a more skilled workforce lowers the cost of production. The *LRAS* curve also shifts to the right, because greater output is achievable on a permanent, or sustainable, basis, *ceteris paribus*.

Technology and Entrepreneurship

Bill Gates of Microsoft, Steve Jobs of Apple Computer, and Larry Ellison of Oracle are just a few examples of entrepreneurs who, through inventive activity, developed innovative technology. Computers and specialized software led to many cost savings—ATMs, bar-code scanners, biotechnology, and increased productivity across the board. These activities shifted both the short-run and long-run aggregate supply curves rightward by lowering costs and expanding real output possibilities.

Land (Natural Resources)

Remember that, in economics, *land* has an all-encompassing definition that includes all natural resources. An increase in natural resources, such as successful oil exploration, would presumably lower the costs of production and expand the economy's sustainable rate of output, shifting both the short-run and long-run aggregate supply curves to the right. Likewise, a decrease in available natural resources would result in a leftward shift of both the short-run and long-run aggregate supply curves. For example, in the 1970s and early 1980s, when the OPEC cartel was strong and effective at raising world oil prices, both short-run and long-run aggregate supply curves shifted to the left, as the members of the cartel deliberately reduced the production of oil.

section 24.5 exhibit 1 — Shifts in Both Short-Run and Long-Run Aggregate Supply

Increases in any of the factors of production—capital, land, labor, or technology—can shift both the *LRAS* and *SRAS* curves to the right. Of course, changes that result in decreases in *SRAS* or *LRAS* will shift the respective curves to the left.

The Labor Force

The addition of workers to the labor force, *ceteris paribus,* can increase aggregate supply. For example, during the 1960s, women and baby boomers entered the labor force in large numbers. This increase tended to depress wages and increase short-run aggregate supply, *ceteris paribus*. The expanded labor force also increased the economy's potential output, increasing long-run aggregate supply. Japan's aging population is causing a decrease in the labor force in recent years—a leftward shift in the long-run aggregate supply curve, *ceteris paribus*.

Government Regulations

Increases in government regulations can make it more costly for producers. This increase in production costs results in a leftward shift of the short-run aggregate supply curve, and a reduction in society's potential output shifts the long-run aggregate supply curve to the left as well. Likewise, a reduction in government regulations on businesses would lower the costs of production and expand potential real output, causing both the *SRAS* and *LRAS* curves to shift to the right.

section 24.5 exhibit 2 — Shifts in Short-Run Aggregate Supply But Not Long-Run Aggregate Supply

A change in input prices that does not reflect a permanent change in the supply of those inputs will shift the *SRAS* curve but not the *LRAS* curve. Likewise, adverse supply shocks, such as those caused by natural disasters, may cause a temporary change that will only impact short-run aggregate supply.

What Factors Shift Short-Run Aggregate Supply Only?

Some factors shift the short-run aggregate supply curve but do not change the long-run aggregate supply curve. The most important of these factors are wages and other input prices, productivity, and unexpected supply shocks. Exhibit 2 illustrates the effect of these factors on short-run aggregate supply.

Wages and Other Input Prices

The price of factors, or inputs, that go into producing outputs will affect only the short-run aggregate supply curve if they do not reflect permanent changes in the supplies of some factors of production. For example, if wages increase without a corresponding increase in labor productivity, it will become more costly for suppliers to produce goods and services at every price level, causing the *SRAS* curve to shift to the left. As Exhibit 3 shows, long-run aggregate supply will not shift because, with the same supply of labor as before, potential output does not change. For example, a decrease in an input price (such as oil) will shift the *SRAS* curve to the right. If the price of steel or oil rises, automobile producers will find it more expensive to do business because their production costs will rise, again resulting in a leftward shift in the short-run aggregate supply curve. The *LRAS* curve will not shift, however, as long as the capacity to make steel has not been reduced.

Temporary Supply Shocks

Supply shocks are unexpected temporary events that can either increase or decrease the short-run aggregate supply. For example, major widespread flooding, earthquakes, droughts, and other natural disasters can increase the costs of production, causing the short-run aggregate supply curve to shift to the left, *ceteris paribus*. However, once the temporary effects of these disasters have been felt, no appreciable change in the economy's productive capacity has occurred, so the long-run aggregate supply doesn't shift as a result. Other temporary supply shocks, such as disruptions in trade due to war or labor strikes, will have similar effects on short-run aggregate supply. However, favorable weather conditions or temporary price reductions of imported resources like oil can shift the short-run aggregate supply curve rightward.

Exhibit 4 presents a table that summarizes the factors that can shift the short-run aggregate supply curve, the long-run aggregate supply curve, or both, depending on whether the effects are temporary or permanent.

supply shocks unexpected temporary events that can either increase or decrease aggregate supply

Use what you've LEARNED
SHIFTS IN THE SHORT-RUN AGGREGATE SUPPLY CURVE

Q Why do wage increases (and other input prices) affect the short-run aggregate supply but not the long-run aggregate supply?

A Remember, in the short run, wages and other input prices are assumed to be constant along the SRAS curve. If the firm has to pay more for its workers or any other input, its costs will rise. That is, the SRAS curve will shift to the left. This shift from $SRAS_1$ to $SRAS_2$ is shown in Exhibit 3. The reason the LRAS curve will not shift is that unless these input prices reflect permanent changes in input supply, those changes will only be temporary, and output will not be permanently or sustainedly different as a result. Other things being equal, if an input price is to be permanently higher, relative to other goods, its supply must have decreased; but that would mean that potential real output, and hence long-run aggregate supply, would also shift left.

section 24.5 exhibit 3 Supply Shifts

Along LRAS, price level and input prices rise by the same percentage.

An increase in input prices shifts the SRAS.

Along SRAS, price level changes but input prices do not.

section 24.5 exhibit 4 Factors That May Shift the Aggregate Supply

An Increase in Aggregate Supply (Rightward Shift)

Lower costs
- lower wages
- other input prices fall

Government policy
- tax cuts
- deregulation
- lower trade barriers

Economic growth
- improvements in human and physical capital
- technological advances
- an increase in labor

Favorable weather

A Decrease in Aggregate Supply (Leftward Shift)

Higher costs
- higher wages
- other input prices rise

Government policy
- overregulation
- waste and inefficiency
- higher trade barriers
- stagnation
- a decline in labor productivity
- capital deterioration

Unfavorable weather
Natural disasters and war

These factors can shift the short-run aggregate supply curve, the long-run aggregate supply curve, or both, depending on whether the effects are temporary or permanent.

SECTION CHECK

1. Any increase in the quantity of any of the factors of production—capital, land, labor, or technology—that is available will cause both the long-run and short-run aggregate supply curves to shift to the right. A decrease in any of these factors will shift both of the aggregate supply curves to the left.
2. Changes in the input price and temporary supply shocks will shift the short-run aggregate supply curve but will not affect the long-run aggregate supply curve.

1. Which of the aggregate supply curves will shift in response to a change in the expected price level? Why?
2. Why do lower input costs increase the level of RGDP supplied at any given price level?
3. What would discovering huge new supplies of oil and natural gas do to the short-run and long-run aggregate supply curves?
4. What would happen to short-run and long-run aggregate supply curves if the government required every firm to file explanatory paperwork each time a decision was made?
5. What would happen to the short-run and long-run aggregate supply curves if the capital stock grew and available supplies of natural resources expanded over the same period of time?
6. How can a change in input prices change the short-run aggregate supply curve but not the long-run aggregate supply curve? How could it change both long-run and short-run aggregate supply?
7. What would happen to short- and long-run aggregate supply if unusually good weather led to bumper crops of most agricultural produce?
8. If OPEC temporarily restricted the world output of oil, what would happen to short- and long-run aggregate supply? What would happen if the output restriction was permanent?

SECTION 24.6 Macroeconomic Equilibrium

* What is short-run macroeconomic equilibrium?
* What is the long-run macroeconomic equilibrium?
* What are recessionary and inflationary gaps?
* What is demand-pull inflation?
* What is cost-push inflation?
* How does the economy self-correct?
* What is wage and price inflexibility?

Determining Macroeconomic Equilibrium

The short-run equilibrium level of real output and the price level are given by the intersection of the aggregate demand curve and the short-run aggregate supply curve. When this equilibrium occurs at the potential output level, the economy is operating at full employment on the long-run aggregate supply curve, as shown in Exhibit 1. Only a short-run equilibrium that is at potential output is also a long-run equilibrium. Short-run equilibrium can change when the aggregate demand curve or the short-run aggregate supply curve shifts rightward or leftward; but the long-run equilibrium level of RGDP only changes when the *LRAS* curve shifts. Sometimes, these supply or demand changes are anticipated; at other times, however, the shifts occur unexpectedly. Economists call these unexpected shifts *shocks*.

Recessionary and Inflationary Gaps

As we have just seen, equilibrium will not always occur at full employment. In fact, equilibrium can occur at less than the potential output of the economy,

section 24.6 exhibit 1 — Long-Run Macroeconomic Equilibrium

Long-run macroeconomic equilibrium occurs at the level where short-run aggregate supply and aggregate demand intersect at a point on the long-run aggregate supply curve. At this level, real GDP will equal potential GDP at full employment ($RGDP_{NR}$).

Exhibit 3 shows that an increase in aggregate demand causes an increase in the price level and an increase in real output. The movement is along the SRAS curve from point E_1 to point E_2 and causes an inflationary gap. Recall that an increase in output occurs as a result of the increase in the price level in the short run, because firms have an incentive to increase real output when the prices of the goods they are selling are rising faster than the costs of the inputs they use in production.

Note that E_2 in Exhibit 3 is positioned beyond $RGDP_{NR}$—an inflationary gap. It seems strange that the economy can operate beyond its potential, but it is possible—temporarily—as firms encourage workers to work overtime, extend the hours of part-time workers, hire recently retired employees, reduce frictional unemployment through more extensive searches for employees, and so on. However, this level of output and employment *cannot* be sustained in the long run.

$RGDP_{NR}$ (a **recessionary gap**), temporarily beyond $RGDP_{NR}$ (an **inflationary gap**), or at potential GDP. Exhibit 2 shows these three possibilities. In (a), we have a recessionary gap at the short-run equilibrium, E_{SR}, at $RGDP_1$. When RGDP is less than $RGDP_{NR}$, the result is a recessionary gap—aggregate demand is insufficient to fully employ all of society's resources, so unemployment will be above the normal rate. In (c), we have an inflationary gap at the short-run equilibrium, E_{SR}, at $RGDP_3$, where aggregate demand is so high that the economy is temporarily operating beyond full capacity ($RGDP_{NR}$); this gap will lead to inflationary pressure, and unemployment will be below the normal rate. In (b), the economy is just right where AD_2 and SRAS intersect at $RGDP_{NR}$—the long-run equilibrium position.

Demand-Pull Inflation

Demand-pull inflation occurs when the price level rises as a result of an increase in aggregate demand. Consider the case in which an increase in consumer optimism results in a corresponding increase in aggregate demand.

recessionary gap
the output gap that occurs when the actual output is less than the potential output

inflationary gap
the output gap that occurs when the actual output is greater than the potential output

demand-pull inflation
a price-level increase due to an increase in aggregate demand

stagflation
a situation in which lower growth and higher prices occur together

cost-push inflation
a price-level increase due to a negative supply shock or increases in input prices

Cost-Push Inflation

The 1970s and early 1980s witnessed a phenomenon known as **stagflation**, where lower growth and higher prices occurred together. Some economists believe that this situation was caused by a leftward shift in the short-run aggregate supply curve, as shown in Exhibit 4. If the aggregate demand curve did not increase significantly but the price level did, then the inflation was caused by supply-side forces, which is called **cost-push inflation**.

The increase in oil prices was the primary culprit responsible for the leftward shift in the aggregate supply curve. As we discussed in the last section, an increase in input prices can cause the short-run aggregate supply curve to shift to the left; and this spelled big trouble for the U.S. economy—higher price levels, lower output, and higher rates of unemployment. The impact of cost-push inflation is illustrated in Exhibit 4.

In Exhibit 4, we see that the economy is initially at full-employment equilibrium at point E_1. A sudden increase in input prices, such as an increase in the price of oil, shifts the SRAS curve to the left—from $SRAS_1$ to $SRAS_2$. As a result of the shift in short-run aggregate supply, the price level rises to PL_2, and real

section 24.6 exhibit 2: Recessionary and Inflationary Gaps

a. Recessionary Gap

b. Long-Run Equilibrium

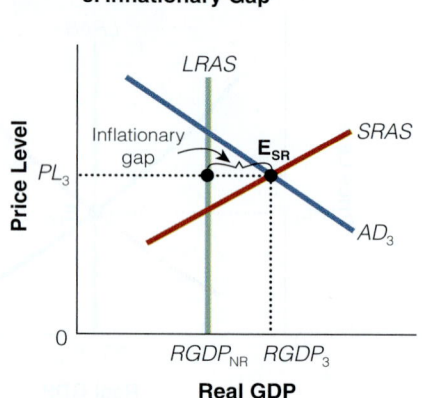

c. Inflationary Gap

In (a), the economy is currently in short-run equilibrium at E_{SR}. At this point, $RGDP_1$ is less than $RGDP_{NR}$. That is, the economy is producing less than its potential output and is in a recessionary gap. In (c), the economy is currently in short-run equilibrium at E_{SR}. At this point, $RGDP_3$ is greater than $RGDP_{NR}$. The economy is temporarily producing more than its potential output, and we have an inflationary gap. In (b), the economy is producing its potential output at $RGDP_{NR}$. At this point, the economy is in long-run equilibrium and is not experiencing an inflationary or a recessionary gap.

section 24.6 exhibit 3: Demand-Pull Inflation

Demand-pull inflation occurs when the aggregate demand curve shifts to the right along the short-run aggregate supply curve.

output falls from $RGDP_{NR}$ to $RGDP_2$ (point E_2). Firms demand fewer workers as a result of higher input costs that cannot be passed on to consumers. This lower demand, in turn, leads to higher prices, lower real output, and more unemployment—and a recessionary gap. In the United States these negative supply shocks occurred in 1974, 1979, 1990, 2005, and 2007–08. These supply shocks can change real GDP significantly, but temporarily, away from potential aggregate output at $RGDP_{NR}$. In 2007, the price of many raw materials shot up globally—a global negative supply shock. Many countries around the world felt the effects of the negative supply shock.

However, recessions are not all bad—they can at least slow the rate of inflation. Two periods of serious inflation, 1974–1975 and 1979–1981, were followed by recessions and a slower rate of inflation.

gate demand falls, shown in Exhibit 5 as the shift from AD_1 to AD_2, leaving the economy in a new short-run equilibrium at point E_2. Households, firms, and governments buy fewer goods and services at every price level. In response to this drop in demand, output falls from $RGDP_{NR}$ to $RGDP_2$, and the price level falls from PL_1 to PL_2. Therefore, in the short run, this fall in aggregate demand causes higher unemployment and a reduction in output—and it, too, can lead to a recessionary gap.

The recession of 2001 and the slow recovery that followed can be attributed to three shocks that affected aggregate demand: the end of the stock market boom, the terrorist attacks of September 11 (this event had an impact on both stock market wealth and consumer confidence), and a series of corporate scandals that rocked the stock market. Corrective stabilizing measures were taken following these events to prevent even further damage. For example, the Federal Reserve continued to lower interest rates. Lower interest rates stimulate the economy by encouraging investment and consumption spending. Other stabilizing measures included a tax cut passed by Congress in 2001 and increased government spending to help rebuild New York City and provide

section 24.6 exhibit 4 **Cost-Push Inflation**

Cost-push inflation is caused by a leftward shift in the short-run aggregate supply curve, from $SRAS_1$ to $SRAS_2$.

What Helped the United States Recover in the 1980s?

As far as energy prices are concerned, oil prices fell during the 1980s when OPEC lost some of its clout because of internal problems. In addition, many non-OPEC oil producers increased production. The net result in the short run was a rightward shift in the aggregate supply curve. Holding aggregate demand constant, this rightward shift in the aggregate supply curve leads to a lower price level, greater output, and lower rates of unemployment—moving the economy back toward E_1 in Exhibit 4.

A Decrease in Aggregate Demand and Recessions

Just as cost-push inflation may cause a recessionary gap, so may a decrease in aggregate demand. For example, consider the case in which consumer confidence plunges and the stock market "tanks." As a result, aggre-

section 24.5 exhibit 5 **Short-Run Decrease in Aggregate Demand**

A fall in aggregate demand due to a drop in consumer confidence can cause a short-run change in the economy. The decrease in aggregate demand (shown in the movement from E_1 to E_2) causes lower output and higher unemployment in the short run.

financial assistance to the ailing airline industry. Both the 2001 tax cut and the war on terrorism led to an increase in government spending. Both of these policies shifted the aggregate demand curve to the right, reducing the magnitude of the 2001 recession. The recovery did not pick up steam until 2003.

Most of the post war recessions have been caused by negative demand shocks. Negative supply shocks have been relatively few, but quite severe, in terms of unemployment rates. The 2007–08 recession appears to be the product of both negative demand and supply shocks. In the chapters on Fiscal and Monetary Policy, we will provide more details on the government's role in offsetting shocks to the economy.

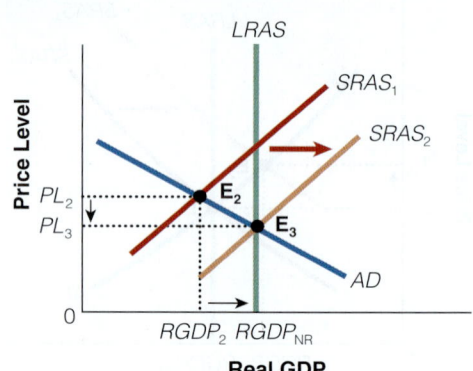

section 24.6 exhibit 6 Adjusting to a Recessionary Gap

At point E_2, the economy is in a recessionary gap. However, the economy may self-correct because laborers and other input suppliers are willing to accept lower wages and prices for the use of their resources, resulting in a reduction in production costs that shifts the short-run supply curve from $SRAS_1$ to $SRAS_2$. Eventually, the economy returns to a long-run equilibrium at point E_3, the intersection of $RGDP_{NR}$ and a lower price level, PL_3. However, if wages and other input prices are sticky, the economy's adjustment mechanism might take many months to totally self-correct.

Adjusting to a Recessionary Gap

Many recoveries from a recessionary gap occur because of increases in aggregate demand—perhaps consumer and business confidence picks up, or the government lowers taxes and/or lowers interest rates to stimulate the economy. That is, an eventual rightward shift in the aggregate demand curve takes the economy back to potential output—$RGDP_{NR}$.

However, it is possible for the economy to *self-correct* through declining wages and prices. In Exhibit 6, at point E_2, the intersection of PL_2 and $RGDP_2$, the economy is in a recessionary gap—that is, the economy is producing less than its potential output. At this lower level of output, firms lay off workers to avoid inventory accumulation. In addition, firms may cut prices to increase demand for their products. Unemployed workers and other input suppliers may also bid down wages and prices. That is, laborers and other input suppliers are now willing to accept lower wages and prices for the use of their resources, and the resulting reduction in production costs shifts the short-run supply curve from $SRAS_1$ to $SRAS_2$. Eventually, the economy returns to a long-run equilibrium at point E_3, the intersection of $RGDP_{NR}$ and a lower price level, PL_3.

wage and price inflexibility the tendency for prices and wages to only adjust slowly downward to changes in the economy

For example, in Exhibit 6 we see that the economy is in a recession at E_2 and $RGDP_2$. The economy will eventually self-correct to $RGDP_{NR}$ at E_3, as workers and other input owners accept lower wages and prices for their inputs, shifting the SRAS curve to the right from $SRAS_1$ to $SRAS_2$. However, if wages and other input prices are sticky, the economy's adjustment mechanism might take many months to totally self-correct.

Japan witnessed several recessionary gaps in the 1990s and even experienced deflation as the self-adjustment mechanism predicts. However, the adjustment out of the recessionary gap was slow and painful.

Slow Adjustments to a Recessionary Gap

Many economists believe that wages and prices may be slow to adjust, especially downward. This downward **wage and price inflexibility** may prolong the duration of a recessionary gap.

What Causes Wages and Prices to Be Sticky Downward?

Empirical evidence supports several explanations for the downward stickiness of wages and prices. Firms may not be able to legally cut wages because of long-term labor contracts (particularly with union workers) or a legal minimum wage. Efficiency wages may also limit a firm's ability to lower wage rates. Menu costs may cause price inflexibility as well.

Efficiency Wages

In economics, it is generally assumed that as productivity rises, wages will rise, and that workers can raise their productivity through investments in human capital such as education and on-the-job training. However, some economists believe that in some cases, *higher wages will lead to greater productivity*.

In the efficiency wage model, employers pay their employees more than the equilibrium wage as a means to increase efficiency. Proponents of this theory suggest that higher-than-equilibrium wages might attract the most productive workers, lower job turnover and training costs, and improve morale. Because the efficiency wage rate is greater than the equilibrium wage rate, the quantity of labor that would be willingly supplied is greater than the quantity of labor demanded, resulting in greater amounts of unemployment.

However, aside from creating some additional unemployment, the efficiency wage could also cause wages to be inflexible downward. For example, if aggregate demand decreases, firms that pay efficiency wages may be reluctant to cut wages, fearing that cuts could lead to lower morale, greater absenteeism, and general productivity losses. In short, if firms are paying efficiency wages, they may be reluctant to lower wages in a recession, leading to downward wage inflexibility.

Menu Costs

Some costs are associated with changing prices in an inflationary environment. Thus, the higher price level in an inflationary environment is often reflected slowly, as restaurants, mail-order houses, and department stores change their prices gradually so as to incur fewer *menu costs* (the costs of changing posted prices) in printing new catalogs, new mailers, new advertisements, and so on. Because businesses are not likely to change all their prices immediately, we can say that some prices are sticky, or slow to change. For example, many outputs, such as steel, are inputs in the production of other products, such as automobiles. As a result, these prices are slow to change.

Suppose aggregate demand unexpectedly decreases. This change could lower the price level. Some firms may adjust to the change quickly. Others, however, may move more slowly because of menu costs, causing their prices to become too high (above equilibrium). Ultimately, the sales and outputs will fall, potentially causing a recession. Firms not responding quickly to changes in demand fail to do so for a reason; and to some economists, menu costs are at least part of that reason.

Adjusting to an Inflationary Gap

In Exhibit 7, the economy is in an inflationary gap at E_2, where $RGDP_2$ is greater than $RGDP_{NR}$. Because the price level, PL_2, is higher than the one workers anticipated, PL_1, workers become disgruntled with wages that have not adjusted to the new price level (if prices have risen but wages have not risen as much, real wages have fallen). Recall that along the SRAS curve, wages and other input prices are assumed to be constant. Therefore, workers' and input suppliers' purchasing power falls as output prices rise. Real (adjusted for inflation) wages have fallen. Consequently, workers and other suppliers demand higher prices if they are to be willing to supply their inputs. As input prices respond to the higher level of output prices, the short-run aggregate

section 24.6 exhibit 7 Adjusting to an Inflationary Gap

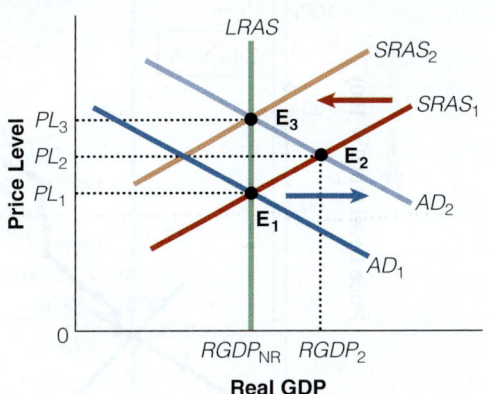

The economy is in an inflationary gap at E_2, where $RGDP_2$ is greater than $RGDP_{NR}$. Because the price level is higher than workers anticipated (that is, it is PL_2 rather than PL_1), workers become disgruntled with wages that have not adjusted to the new price level. Consequently, workers and other suppliers demand higher prices to be willing to supply their inputs. As input prices respond to the higher level of output prices, the short-run aggregate supply curve shifts to the left, from $SRAS_1$ to $SRAS_2$. Suppliers will continually seek higher prices for their inputs until they reach long-run equilibrium, at point E_3. At that point, input suppliers' purchasing power is restored to the natural rate, $RGDP_{NR}$, at a new higher price level, PL_3.

supply curve shifts to the left, from $SRAS_1$ to $SRAS_2$. Suppliers will continue to seek higher prices for their inputs until they reach the long-run equilibrium, at point E_3 in Exhibit 7. At point E_3, input suppliers' purchasing power is restored at the long-run equilibrium, at $RGDP_{NR}$ and a new higher price level, PL_3.

Price Level and RGDP Over Time

In Exhibit 8, we traced out the pattern of RGDP versus the price level. According to the Bureau of Economic Analysis, both the price level and RGDP have been rising over the last 36 years. So what is responsible for the changes? The answer is: both aggregate demand and aggregate supply. Aggregate demand has risen because of growing population (which impacts consumption and investment spending), rising income, increases in government purchases, and increases in the money supply. Aggregate supply has been generally increasing as well, including increases in the labor force and improvements in labor productivity and technology.

section 24.6
exhibit 8 — U.S. Price Level and RGDP

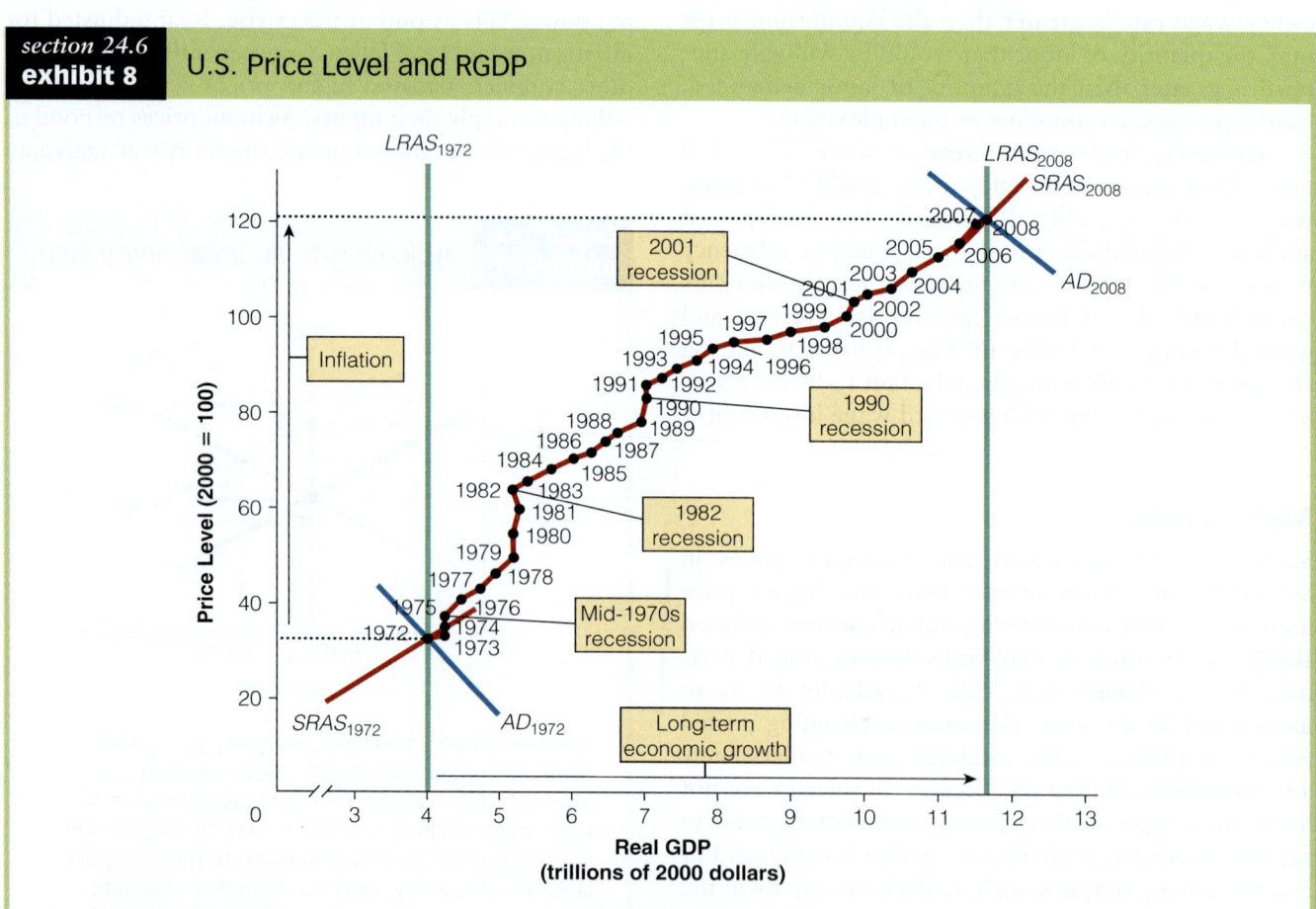

The price level and real GDP rose over the last 35 years. Inflation was rapid during the 1970s with little economic growth. However, the economy grew rapidly in the decades of the 1980s and 1990s with relatively little inflation—notice the red line that connects the dots is relatively flat during these periods but the economy is growing quite rapidly.

SOURCE: U.S. Department of Commerce, Bureau of Economic Analysis.

SECTION CHECK

1. Short-run macroeconomic equilibrium occurs at the intersection of the aggregate demand curve and the short-run aggregate supply curve. A short-run equilibrium is also a long-run equilibrium only if it is at potential output on the long-run aggregate supply curve.
2. If short-run equilibrium occurs at less than the potential output of the economy, $RGDP_{NR}$, the result is a recessionary gap. If the short-run equilibrium temporarily occurs beyond $RGDP_{NR}$, the result is an inflationary gap.
3. Demand-pull inflation occurs when the price level rises as a result of an increase in aggregate demand.
4. Cost-push inflation is caused by a leftward shift in the short-run aggregate supply curve.
5. It is possible for the economy to self-correct through declining wages and prices. For example, during a recession, laborers and other input suppliers are willing to accept lower wages and prices for the use of their resources, and the resulting reduction in production costs increases the short-run supply curve. Eventually, the economy returns to the long-run equilibrium, at $RGDP_{NR}$, and a lower price level.
6. Wages and other input prices may be slow to adjust, especially downward. This downward wage and price inflexibility may lead to prolonged periods of recession.
7. Firms might not be willing to lower nominal wages in the short run for several reasons, leading to downward wage and price inflexibility, or sticky prices. Firms may not be able to legally cut wages because of long-term labor contracts (particularly with union workers) or because of a legal minimum wage. In addition, efficiency wage and menu costs may lead to sticky wages and prices.

---

1. What is a recessionary gap?
2. What is an inflationary gap?
3. What is demand-pull inflation?
4. What is cost-push inflation?
5. Starting from long-run equilibrium on the long-run aggregate supply curve, what happens to the price level, real output, and unemployment as a result of cost-push inflation?
6. How would a drop in consumer confidence impact the short-run macroeconomy?
7. What would happen to the price level, real output, and unemployment in the short run if world oil prices fell sharply?
8. What are *sticky prices* and *wages*?
9. How does the economy self-correct?

SECTION 24.7 The Classical and the Keynesian Macroeconomic Model

* What is the classical school?
* What is Say's law?
* What was Keynes's criticism of the classical school?
* What is the full-employment classical school model?
* What is the Keynesian short-run supply curve?
* What is the modern Keynesian short-run supply curve?

The Classical School and Say's Law

Historically, the two primary approaches to macroeconomics have been the classical school and the Keynesian school. Let's begin with the classical school. The classical school of thought believed that wages and prices adjust quickly to changes in supply and demand.

Writing at the beginning of the nineteenth century, the French economist Jean Baptiste Say formulated a notion since dubbed Say's law, which in its simplest form states that "supply creates its own demand."

More precisely, the production of goods and services creates income for owners of inputs (land, labor, capital, and entrepreneurship) used in production, which in turn creates a demand for goods. According to Say's law, we need not worry about output not being utilized; production creates income, which creates demand for goods, which leads to still more production. That is, Say's law establishes that full employment can be maintained because total spending will be great enough for firms to sell all the output a fully employed economy can produce. Say's ideas were incorporated into the teaching of economists of the late nineteenth century who were considered classical economists.

Before the 1930s, the problem of unemployment was considered one that could be analyzed using microeconomic analysis; indeed, macroeconomics as we know it today did not exist. The theory that evolved to analyze unemployment suggested that joblessness could be eliminated by market forces, in the same way that shortages and surpluses of goods and services are eliminated by movement in the relative prices of those goods, as we discussed in Chapter 5.

The Full-Employment Classical School Model

The macroeconomic models presented in this text draw from both schools of thought and emphasize the commonality between the two schools. The classical school focuses on the economy at full employment, because both schools agree that in the long run both wages and prices adjust freely to changes in demand and supply and the economy moves back naturally to its potential, full-employment output level. That is, eventually (in the long run) all markets adjust to their equilibrium values. Recall that full employment does not mean zero unemployment; rather, it refers to zero cyclical unemployment. Some structural and frictional unemployment occurs naturally in a dynamic and vibrant economy.

The actual output that the economy produces need not be the same as potential output—what the economy can produce without leading to inflation. If the economy is producing at less than its potential output, unemployment is greater than the natural rate; if the economy is producing at greater than its potential output, unemployment is less than the natural rate, causing inflationary pressures. That is, it is possible on the peak of a business cycle that actual real GDP can exceed potential real GDP, but only for a short period of time. The problem is that the causal observer often confuses potential and actual output. When the economy is accelerating at a fast clip, some observers believe we are on a new growth trajectory. And when the economy slows, some observers confuse this change with doom and gloom.

Earlier in this chapter we discussed monetary and fiscal policy, using the AS/AD model to examine business cycles and short-run policy prescriptions that involve government intervention to help the economy get back to its long-run growth trajectory.

Changes in Aggregate Demand in the Classical Model

In Exhibit 1, we see the impact of either an increase or a decrease in aggregate demand in the classical model. According to Say's law, prolonged unemployment is impossible in the long-run classical model. Prices, wages, and interest rates all adjust quickly, which keeps workers and resources fully employed at the natural rate of real output, $RGDP_{NR}$. The classical school made very little distinction between the short run and the long run, so the only aggregate supply curve is the vertical long-run aggregate supply curve, *LRAS* in Exhibit 1. That is, there is no separate short-run aggregate supply curve in the classical model. Prices and wages adjust so quickly that the economy seldom remains far from $RGDP_{NR}$.

In Exhibit 1(a), if prices, wages, and interest rates were not completely and quickly flexible, an increase in aggregate demand from AD_1 to AD_2 might cause the economy to move toward point A beyond $RGDP_{AD}$. However, when the price level rises, input suppliers bid up input prices and the economy quickly adjusts to the new price level at PL_2, moving along the *LRAS*.

In Exhibit 1(b), there is a decrease in aggregate demand that could cause the economy to move toward point A, where resources (labor, factories, and other inputs) would be unemployed. However, because input suppliers will compete against each other, it will drive input prices down. If this occurs quickly, as predicted in the classical model, the economy will not experience prolonged unemployment and will adjust to the new price level, PL_2, along the *LRAS*.

Keynes's Criticism of the Classical School

In 1936, John Maynard Keynes's book, *The General Theory of Employment, Interest and Money*, was published. Along with Adam Smith's *The Wealth of Nations* in the eighteenth century, *The General Theory of Employment, Interest and Money* was one of the most influential books in economics. In his book, Keynes attacked the classical economic theory. He pointed out the naiveté of Say's law: Not all income generated from output need be used to buy goods and services; it can also be saved, hoarded, or taxed away. Supply does not automatically create an adequate

section 24.7 exhibit 1 — Changes in Aggregate Demand in the Classical Model

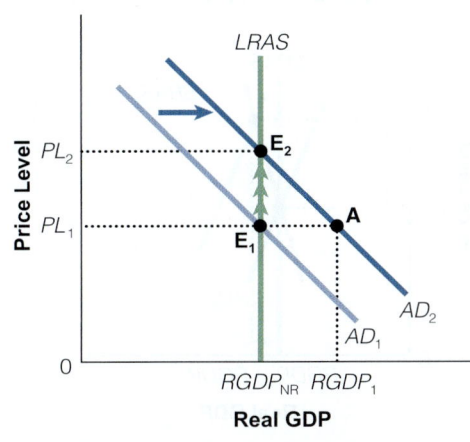

a. An Increase in Aggregate Demand

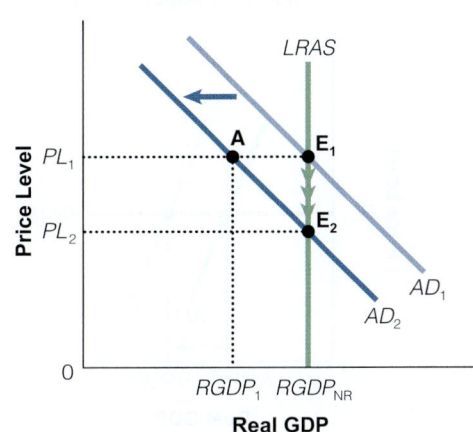

b. A Decrease in Aggregate Demand

In the classical model, wages, prices and interest rates are completely and quickly flexible so the economy will quickly adjust to an increase in AD moving from E_1 to E_2 as seen in 1(a) and quickly adjust to a decrease in AD moving from E_1 to E_2 as seen in 1(b). If wages and prices were not completely flexible the economy could move toward point A from E_1.

demand. Keynes's severest attacks were against classical ideas about unemployment. With unemployment rates at that time in the double digits, where did the classicists go wrong?

To begin with, when a recession begins, wages rarely fall quickly to a new equilibrium level consistent with full employment. Long-term labor contracts with unions, minimum wage laws, and other factors often prevent wages from falling as quickly as the classical model suggests. Thus, wage inflexibility prevents the market solution from working rapidly enough to avert a prolonged recession.

The Keynesian Short-Run Aggregate Supply Curve—Sticky Prices and Wages

Keynes and his followers argued that wages and price are inflexible downward. As we just discussed, wage stickiness can arise as a result of long-term labor and raw material contracts, unions, and minimum wage laws. If wages and prices are sticky and the economy has sufficient excess capacity, then the short-run aggregate supply curve is flat, because full employment of all resources is not reached until $RGDP_{NR}$. That is, with so many resources idle, producers will not have to compete with each other for machinery or labor and input prices will tend to stay flat.

In Exhibit 2(a), we see that in the flat portion of the SRAS curve an increase in AD from AD_1 to AD_2 has little impact on the price level but considerable impact on real GDP and employment. When AD_1 increases to AD_2, we see an increase in real gross domestic product from $RGDP_1$ to $RGDP_2$—a new equilibrium where resources are more fully utilized. Similarly, a reduction in AD in this region will also leave the price level unchanged. Specifically, it means that the price level does not rise or fall in this situation, but RGDP does. This price and wage inflexibility when AD is falling played a significant part in the Keynesian theory. With stickiness of wages and other input costs, a reduction in aggregate demand will not lead to a lower price level if the economy has sufficient excess capacity—say at $RGDP_1$. Historically, the mid- to late 1930s seems to fit the Keynesian model quite well—increases in RGDP without simultaneous increases in the price level. It was a period of high unemployment of resources and double-digit unemployment—that is, sufficient level of excess capacity and little competition to bid up input prices.

Most macroeconomists now believe that price and wages are not completely inflexible downward. However, wages and prices do tend to be less flexible when excess capacity is available—the slope of the SRAS is flatter the further it is below full employment. However, when the economy is temporarily operating beyond $RGDP_{NR}$, the SRAS is steep because higher output prices are necessary if firms are expanding output in this unsustainable region beyond full employment. This is seen in Exhibit 2(b). That is, the firm can increase output by working labor and capital more intensively. When resources are idle, output will be more responsive

section 24.7 exhibit 2 — The Keynesian Aggregate Supply Curve

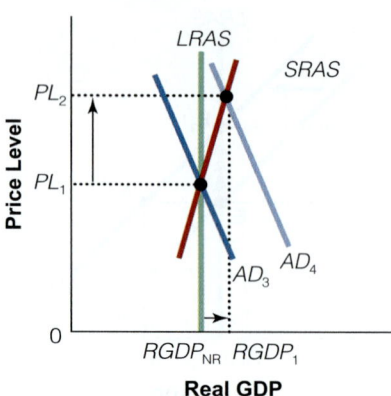

a. Keynesian Short-Run Aggregate Supply Curve

b. Modern Keynesian Short-Run Aggregate Supply Curve

In the flat portion of the SRAS curve, an increase in AD, from AD_1 to AD_2, has little impact on the price level but considerable impact on real GDP and employment. Similarly, a reduction in AD in this region will also leave the price level relatively unchanged—the price level does not rise or fall much in this situation, but RGDP does. In Exhibit (b), when resources are at (or temporarily beyond) the natural rate, output is not highly responsive to changes in AD but the price level is responsive—as shown in the move from AD_3 to AD_4.

to changes in AD, and the price level will not be as responsive—the SRAS is flatter—as it moves from AD_1 to AD_2. And when resources are at full capacity, output is less responsive to changes in AD and the price level is highly responsive—the SRAS is steeper—as it moves from AD_3 to AD_4.

However, economists continue to debate about the actual shape of the aggregate supply curve.

SECTION CHECK

1. Say's law stated that "supply creates its own demand."
2. Say's law argued that full employment could be maintained in the economy.
3. Keynes rejected Say's law because, in addition to spending income from production on goods and services, it can go toward saving, hoarding, or taxes.
4. Potential real output is the level of real output the economy can produce without leading to inflation.
5. If the economy is producing less than potential output, unemployment is greater than its natural rate.
6. If the economy is temporarily producing more than potential output, unemployment is less than its natural rate.
7. When prices are sticky, the SRAS curve is flat, meaning that changes in aggregate demand result in little change in the price level, but significant changes in RGDP.
8. Price stickiness is likely when the economy has excess capacity, but is less likely when the economy is operating at full capacity.

1. What are the two primary approaches to macroeconomics?
2. Which school of thought emphasized that markets can rapidly adjust to changes?
3. Why was the double-digit unemployment of the Great Depression when Keynes wrote *The General Theory of Employment, Interest and Money* helpful in leading to its general acceptance?
4. What would keep wages from falling quickly in a recession?
5. If wages are sticky downward, why will a decrease in aggregate demand primarily reduce real output?

Interactive Chapter Summary

Fill in the blanks:

1. Aggregate demand (AD) refers to the quantity of _____ at different price levels.
2. _____ is by far the largest component of AD.
3. Government purchases tend to be a(n) _____ volatile category of aggregate demand than investment.
4. Models that include international trade effects are called _____ models.
5. Exports minus imports equals _____.
6. The AD curve slopes _____, which means a(n) _____ relationship between the price level and real gross domestic product (RGDP) demanded.
7. Three complementary explanations exist for the negative slope of the aggregate demand curve: the _____ effect, the _____ effect, and the _____ effect.
8. As the price level decreases, the real value of people's cash balances _____ so that their planned purchases of goods and services _____.
9. The real wealth effect can be summarized as follows: A higher price level → _____ real wealth → _____ purchasing power → _____ RGDP demanded.
10. At higher interest rates, the opportunity cost of borrowing _____; and _____ interest-sensitive investments will be profitable, which will result in a(n) _____ quantity of RGDP demanded.
11. The interest rate effect process can be summarized as follows: A higher price level → _____ the demand for loanable funds → _____ the interest rate → _____ investments → _____ RGDP demanded.
12. If the prices of goods and services in the domestic market rise relative to those in global markets as a result of a higher domestic price level, consumers and businesses will buy _____ from foreign producers and _____ from domestic producers.
13. If the price level in the United States rises, U.S. exports will become _____ expensive, imports will become _____ expensive, and net exports will _____.
14. The real wealth effect, the interest rate effect, and the open economy effect all contribute to the _____ slope of the AD curve.
15. An increase in any component of GDP (C, I, G, or X − M) can cause the AD curve to shift _____.
16. If consumers sensed that the economy was headed for a recession or the government imposed a tax increase, this would result in a(n) _____ shift of the AD curve.
17. Because consuming less is saving more, an increase in savings, *ceteris paribus*, would shift AD to the _____.
18. A reduction in business taxes would shift AD to the _____, while an increase in real interest rates or business taxes would shift AD to the _____.
19. An increase in government purchases, other things being equal, shifts AD to the _____.
20. If major trading partners are experiencing economic slowdowns, then they will demand _____ imports from the United States, shifting AD to the _____.
21. The _____ curve is the relationship between the total quantity of final goods and services that suppliers are willing and able to produce and the overall price level.
22. The two aggregate supply curves are a(n) _____ aggregate supply curve and a(n) _____ aggregate supply curve.
23. The short-run relationship refers to a period when _____ can change in response to supply and demand, but _____ prices have not yet been able to adjust.
24. In the short run, the aggregate supply curve is _____ sloping.
25. In the short run, at a higher price level, producers are willing to supply _____ real output, and at lower price levels, they are willing to supply _____ real output.
26. The two explanations for why producers would be willing to supply more output when the price level increases are the _____ effect and the _____ effect.
27. When the price level rises in the short run, output prices _____ relative to input prices (costs), _____ producers' short-run profit margins.
28. If the price level falls, output prices _____, producers' profits will _____, and producers will _____ their level of output.
29. If the overall price level is rising, producers can be fooled into thinking that the _____ price of their output is rising and as a result supply _____ in the short run.

30. The long run is a period long enough for the price of _____ to fully adjust to changes in the economy.

31. Along the LRAS curve, two sets of prices are changing: the prices of _____ and the prices of _____.

32. The level of RGDP producers are willing to supply in the long run is _____ by changes in the price level.

33. The vertical LRAS curve will always be positioned at the _____ of output.

34. The long-run equilibrium level is where the economy will settle when undisturbed and all resources are _____ employed.

35. Long-run equilibrium will only occur where AS and AD intersect along the _____.

36. The underlying determinant of shifts in short-run aggregate supply is _____.

37. _____ production costs will motivate producers to produce less at any given price level, shifting the short-run aggregate supply curve _____.

38. A permanent increase in the available amount of capital, entrepreneurship, land, or labor can shift the LRAS and SRAS curves to the _____.

39. A decrease in the stock of capital will _____ real output in the short run and _____ real output in the long run, ceteris paribus.

40. Investments in human capital would cause productivity to _____.

41. A(n) _____ in the amount of natural resources available would result in a leftward shift of both SRAS and LRAS.

42. An increase in the number of workers in the labor force, ceteris paribus, tends to _____ wages and _____ short-run aggregate supply.

43. _____ output per worker causes production costs to rise and potential real output to fall, resulting in a(n) _____ shift in both SRAS and LRAS.

44. A(n) _____ in government regulations on businesses would lower the costs of production and expand potential real output, causing both SRAS and LRAS to shift to the right.

45. The most important of the factors that shift SRAS but do not impact LRAS are a change in _____ prices and _____.

46. If the price of steel rises, it will shift SRAS _____, while the LRAS will _____ as long as the capacity to make steel has not been reduced.

47. A fall in input prices, which shifts SRAS right, shifts LRAS right only if _____ has risen, and this situation only occurs if the _____ of those inputs is increased.

48. _____ supply shocks, such as natural disasters, can increase the costs of production.

49. Only a short-run equilibrium that is at _____ output is also a long-run equilibrium.

50. The short-run equilibrium level of real output and the price level are determined by the intersection of the _____ curve and the _____ curve.

51. The long-run equilibrium level of RGDP changes only when the _____ curve shifts.

52. Economists call unexpected shifts in supply or demand _____.

53. When short-run equilibrium occurs at less than the potential output of the economy, it results in a(n) _____ gap.

54. _____ inflation occurs when the price level rises as a result of an increase in aggregate demand.

55. Demand-pull inflation causes a(n) _____ in the price level and a(n) _____ in real output in the short run, illustrated by a movement up along the SRAS curve.

56. Demand-pull inflation causes a(n) _____ gap.

57. When AD increases, real (adjusted for inflation) wages _____ in the short run.

58. In response to an inflationary gap in the short run, real wages and other real input prices will tend to _____, which is illustrated by a(n) _____ shift in the SRAS curve.

59. _____ is the situation in which lower economic growth and higher prices occur together.

60. An increase in input prices can cause the SRAS curve to shift to the _____, resulting in _____ price levels, _____ real output, and _____ rates of unemployment in the short run.

61. With the economy initially at full-employment equilibrium, a sudden increase in oil prices would result in _____ unemployment and in real output _____ than potential output in the short run.

62. Falling oil prices would result in a(n) _____ shift in the SRAS curve.

63. Holding AD constant, falling oil prices would lead to _____ prices, _____ output, and _____ rates of unemployment in the short run.

64. An economy can self-correct from a recessionary gap through _____ wages and prices.

65. The long-run result of a fall in aggregate demand is an equilibrium _____ potential output and a(n) _____ price level.

Chapter 24 Aggregate Demand and Aggregate Supply

66. Wages and prices may be sticky downward because of _____ labor contracts, a legal _____ wage, employers paying _____ wages, and _____ costs.

67. If the economy is currently in an inflationary gap, with output greater than potential output, the price level is _____ than workers anticipated.

68. The _____ of the *AD* and *AS* curves makes the *AD/AS* analysis less than completely satisfactory.

69. Say's law could be stated as "_____ creates its own _____."

70. When real output is below potential real output, unemployment is _____ than its natural rate.

71. Unlike our modern understanding, the classical model has no separate _____ _____ curve.

72. The economy will not experience unemployment in the _____ model.

73. When resources are idle, output will be _____ responsive to changes in aggregate demand and the price level will be _____ responsive to changes in aggregate demand.

Answers: 1. real GDP demanded 2. Consumption 3. less 4. open economy 5. net exports 6. downward; inverse 7. real wealth; interest rate; open economy 8. rises; increase 9. reduced; reduced; reduced 10. rises; fewer; lower 11. increases; increases; reduces; reduces 12. more; less 13. more; less fall 14. downward 15. rightward 16. leftward 17. left 18. right; left 19. right 20. fewer; left 21. aggregate supply 22. short-run; long-run 23. output; input 24. upward 25. more; less 26. profit; misperception 27. rises; raising 28. fall; fall; reduce 29. relatively more 30. all inputs 31. outputs; inputs 32. not affected 33. natural rate 34. fully 35. long-run aggregate supply curve 36. production costs 37. Higher; leftward 38. right 39. reduces; reduce 40. rise 41. decrease 42. depress; increase 43. Lower; leftward 44. reduction 45. input 46. left; not shift 47. Adverse 48. supply 49. potential output 50. aggregate demand; short-run aggregate supply 51. LRAS 52. shocks 53. recessionary 54. Demand-pull 55. increase 56. inflationary 57. fall 58. rises 59. Stagflation 60. left; higher; lower; higher 61. higher; less 62. rightward 63. lower; greater; lower 64. declining 65. at; lower 66. long-term; minimum; efficiency; menu 67. higher 68. interdependence 69. supply; demand 70. greater 71. short-run aggregate supply 72. classical 73. more; less

Key Terms and Concepts

aggregate demand (*AD*) 689
open economy 689
net exports 689
aggregate demand curve 690
aggregate supply (*AS*) curve 695

short-run aggregate supply (*SRAS*) curve 695
long-run aggregate supply (*LRAS*) curve 695
supply shocks 698
recessionary gap 701

inflationary gap 701
demand-pull inflation 701
stagflation 701
cost-push inflation 701
wage and price inflexibility 704

Section Check Answers

24.1 The Determinants of Aggregate Demand

1. **What are the major components of aggregate demand?**

   The major components of aggregate demand are consumption, planned investment, government purchases, and net exports.

2. **How would an increase in personal taxes or a decrease in transfer payments affect consumption?**

   An increase in taxes or a decrease in transfer payments would decrease the disposable income of households, hence reducing their demand for consumption goods.

3. **What would an increase in exports do to aggregate demand, other things being equal? An increase in imports? An increase in both imports and exports, where the change in exports was greater in magnitude?**

   An increase in exports would increase aggregate demand, other things being equal, since net exports are part of aggregate demand. An increase in imports would decrease aggregate demand, other things being equal, by reducing net exports (demand shifts from domestic producers to foreign producers). An increase in both imports and exports would increase aggregate demand if the increase in exports exceeded the increase in imports, other things being equal, because the combination would increase net exports.

24.2 The Aggregate Demand Curve

1. **Why is the aggregate demand curve downward sloping?**
   Aggregate demand shows what happens to the total quantity of all real goods and services demanded in the economy as a whole (that is, the quantity of real GDP demanded) at different price levels. Aggregate demand is downward sloping because of the real wealth effect, the interest rate effect, and the open economy effect as the price level changes.

2. **How does an increased price level reduce the quantities of investment goods and consumer durables demanded?**
   An increased price level increases the demand for money, which, in turn, increases interest rates. Higher interest rates increase the opportunity cost of financing both investment goods and consumer durables, reducing the quantities of investment goods and consumer durables demanded.

3. **What is the real wealth effect, and how does it imply a downward-sloping aggregate demand curve?**
   A reduced price level increases the real value of people's currency holdings; as their real wealth increases, so does the quantity of real goods and services demanded, particularly consumption goods. Therefore, the aggregate demand curve, which represents the relationship between the price level and the quantity of real goods and services demanded, slopes downward as a result.

4. **What is the interest rate effect, and how does it imply a downward-sloping aggregate demand curve?**
   A reduced price level reduces the demand for money, which lowers interest rates, thereby increasing the quantity of investment goods and consumer durable goods people are willing to purchase. Therefore, the aggregate demand curve, which represents the relationship between the price level and the quantity of real goods and services demanded, slopes downward as a result.

5. **What is the open economy effect, and how does it imply a downward-sloping aggregate demand curve?**
   The open economy effect occurs when a higher domestic price level raises the prices of domestically produced goods relative to the prices of imported goods. This reduces the quantity of domestically produced goods demanded (by both citizens and foreigners) as relatively cheaper foreign-made goods are substituted for them. The result is a downward-sloping aggregate demand curve, as a higher price level results in a lower quantity of domestic real GDP demanded.

24.3 Shifts in the Aggregate Demand Curve

1. **How is the distinction between a change in demand and a change in quantity demanded the same for aggregate demand as for the demand for a particular good?**
   Just as a change in the price of a particular good changes its quantity demanded but not its demand, a change in the price level changes the quantity of real GDP demanded but not aggregate demand. Just as a change in any of the demand-curve shifters (factors other than the price of the good itself) changes the demand for a particular good, a change in any of the $C + I + G + (X - M)$ components of aggregate demand not caused by a change in the price level changes aggregate demand.

2. **What happens to aggregate demand if the demand for consumption goods increases, *ceteris paribus*?**
   Since consumption purchases are part of aggregate demand, an increase in the demand for consumption goods increases aggregate demand, *ceteris paribus*.

3. **What happens to aggregate demand if the demand for investment goods falls, *ceteris paribus*?**
   Since planned investment purchases are part of aggregate demand, a falling demand for investment goods makes aggregate demand fall, *ceteris paribus*.

4. **Why would an increase in the money supply tend to increase expenditures on consumption and investment, *ceteris paribus*?**
   An increase in the money supply would increase how many now relatively more plentiful dollars people would be willing to pay for goods in general. This would increase expenditures on consumption and investment, increasing aggregate demand, *ceteris paribus*.

24.4 The Aggregate Supply Curve

1. **What relationship does the short-run aggregate supply curve represent?**
   The short-run aggregate supply curve represents the relationship between the total quantity of final goods and services that suppliers are willing and able to produce (the quantity of real GDP supplied) and the overall price level, before all input prices have had time to completely adjust to the price level.

2. **What relationship does the long-run aggregate supply curve represent?**
   The long-run aggregate supply curve represents the relationship between the total quantity of final goods and services that suppliers are willing and able to produce (the quantity of real GDP supplied) and the

overall price level, once all input prices have had time to completely adjust to the price level. (Actually, it shows there is no relationship between these two variables, once input prices have had sufficient time to completely adjust to the price level.)

3. **Why is focusing on producers' profit margins helpful in understanding the logic of the short-run aggregate supply curve?**

   Profit incentives are the key to understanding what happens to real output as the price level changes in the short run (before input prices completely adjust to the price level). When the prices of outputs rise relative to the prices of inputs (costs), as when aggregate demand increases in the short run, profit margins increase, which increases the incentives to produce, which leads to increased real output. When the prices of outputs fall relative to the prices of inputs (costs), as when aggregate demand decreases in the short run, profit margins decrease, which decreases the incentives to produce, which leads to decreased real output.

4. **Why is the short-run aggregate supply curve upward sloping, while the long-run aggregate supply curve is vertical at the natural rate of output?**

   The short-run aggregate supply curve is upward sloping because in the short run, before input prices have completely adjusted to the price level, an increase in the price level increases profit margins by increasing output prices relative to input prices, leading producers to increase real output. The long-run aggregate supply curve is vertical because in the long run, when input prices have completely adjusted to changes in the price level, input prices as well as output prices have adjusted to the price level; hence, profit margins in real terms do not change as the price level changes, and therefore there is no relationship between the price level and real output in the long run. The long-run aggregate supply curve is vertical at the natural rate of real output because that is the maximum output level allowed by capital, labor, and technological inputs at full employment (that is, given the determinants of the economy's production possibilities curve), which is therefore sustainable over time.

5. **What would the short-run aggregate supply curve look like if input prices always changed instantaneously as soon as output prices changed? Why?**

   If input prices always changed instantaneously as soon as output prices changed, the short-run aggregate supply curve would look the same as the long-run aggregate supply curve—vertical at the natural rate of real output. This is because both input and output prices would then change proportionately, so that real profit margins (the incentives facing producers), and therefore real output, would not change as the price level changes.

6. **If the price of cotton increased 10 percent when cotton producers thought other prices were rising 5 percent over the same period, what would happen to the quantity of RGDP supplied in the cotton industry? What if cotton producers thought other prices were rising 20 percent over the same period?**

   If the price of cotton increased 10 percent when cotton producers thought other prices were rising 5 percent over the same period, the quantity of RGDP supplied in the cotton industry would increase, because with other prices (including input prices) falling relative to cotton prices, the profitability of growing cotton would be rising. If the price of cotton increased 10 percent when cotton producers thought other prices were rising 20 percent over the same period, the quantity of RGDP supplied in the cotton industry would decrease, because with other prices (including input prices) rising relative to cotton prices, the profitability of growing cotton would be falling.

24.5 Shifts in the Aggregate Supply Curve

1. **Which of the aggregate supply curves will shift in response to a change in the expected price level? Why?**

   The short-run aggregate supply curve shifts in response to a change in the expected price level by changing the expected production costs and therefore the expected profitability of producing output at any given output price level. Remember that the long-run aggregate supply curve assumes that people have had enough time to completely adjust to a changing price level, so a change in the expected price level does not change expected profit margins along the long-run aggregate supply curve.

2. **Why do lower input costs increase the level of RGDP supplied at any given price level?**

   Lower input costs increase the level of RGDP supplied at any given (output) price level by increasing the profit margin for any given level of output prices.

3. **What would discovering huge new supplies of oil and natural gas do to the short-run and long-run aggregate supply curves?**

   Discovering huge new supplies of oil and natural gas would increase both the short-run and long-run aggregate supply curves, because those additional resources would allow more to be produced in the short run, at any given output price level, as well as on a sustainable, long-run basis (since such a discovery would shift the economy's production possibilities curve outward).

4. **What would happen to short-run and long-run aggregate supply curves if the government required every firm to file explanatory paperwork each time a decision was made?**

   This would shift both the short-run and long-run aggregate supply curves to the left. It would permanently raise producers' costs of producing any level of output, which would reduce how much producers would produce in the short run at any given price level, as well as on a sustainable, long-run basis (since such a requirement would shift the economy's production possibilities curve inward).

5. **What would happen to the short-run and long-run aggregate supply curves if the capital stock grew and available supplies of natural resources expanded over the same period of time?**

   An increase in the capital stock together with increased available supplies of natural resources would shift both the short-run and long-run aggregate supply curves to the right (shifting the economy's production possibilities curve outward), increasing the short-run and sustainable levels of real output.

6. **How can a change in input prices change the short-run aggregate supply curve but not the long-run aggregate supply curve? How could it change both long-run and short-run aggregate supply?**

   A temporary change in input prices can change the short-run aggregate supply curve by changing profit margins in the short run. However, when input prices return to their previous levels (reflecting a return to their previous relative scarcity) in the long run, the sustainable level of real output will be no different from before. If, on the other hand, input price changes reflect a permanently changed supply of inputs (lower input prices reflecting an increased supply), a change in input prices would increase both the long-run and short-run aggregate supply curves by increasing the real output producible both currently and on an ongoing basis (permanently shifting the economy's production possibilities curve outward).

7. **What would happen to short- and long-run aggregate supply if unusually good weather led to bumper crops of most agricultural produce?**

   Since this would mean only a temporary change in output, it would increase the short-run aggregate supply curve but not the long-run aggregate supply curve.

8. **If OPEC temporarily restricted the world output of oil, what would happen to short- and long-run aggregate supply? What would happen if the output restriction was permanent?**

   A temporary oil output restriction would temporarily increase oil (energy input) prices, reducing the short-run aggregate supply curve (shifting it left) but not the long-run aggregate supply curve. If the oil output restriction was permanent, the oil price increase would also reduce the level of real output producible on a sustainable basis, and so would shift both short-run aggregate supply and long-run aggregate supply to the left.

24.6 Macroeconomic Equilibrium

1. **What is a recessionary gap?**

   A recessionary gap exists when the macroeconomy is in equilibrium at less than the potential output of the economy because aggregate demand is insufficient to fully employ all of society's resources.

2. **What is an inflationary gap?**

   An inflationary gap exists when the macroeconomy is in equilibrium at more than the potential output of the economy because aggregate demand is so high that the economy is operating temporarily beyond its long-run capacity.

3. **What is demand-pull inflation?**

   Demand-pull inflation reflects an increased price level caused by an increase in aggregate demand.

4. **What is cost-push inflation?**

   Cost-push inflation is output price inflation caused by an increase in input prices (that is, by supply-side forces rather than demand-side forces). It is illustrated by a leftward or upward shift of the short-run aggregate supply curve for given long-run aggregate supply and demand curves.

5. **Starting from long-run equilibrium on the long-run aggregate supply curve, what happens to the price level, real output, and unemployment as a result of cost-push inflation?**

   Starting from long-run equilibrium on the long-run aggregate supply curve, cost-push inflation causes the price level to rise, real output to fall, and unemployment to rise in the short run.

6. **How would a drop in consumer confidence impact the short-run macroeconomy?**

   A drop in consumer confidence would decrease the demand for consumer goods, other things being equal, which would reduce (shift left) the aggregate demand curve, resulting in a lower price level, lower real output, and increased unemployment in the short run for a given short-run aggregate supply curve.

7. **What would happen to the price level, real output, and unemployment in the short run if world oil prices fell sharply?**

   If world oil prices fell sharply, it would increase (shift right) the short-run aggregate supply curve, resulting in a lower price level, greater real output, and reduced unemployment in the short run for a given aggregate demand curve.

8. **What are *sticky prices* and *wages*?**

   Sticky prices and *wages* are terms for input prices and wages that may be very slow to adjust in the downward direction, causing the economy's adjustment mechanism to take a substantial amount of time to self-correct from a recession.

9. **How does the economy self-correct?**

   The economy self-corrects for a short-run recession through declining wages and prices, brought on by reduced demand for labor and other inputs; the economy self-corrects for a short-run boom through increasing wages and prices, brought on by increased demand for labor and other inputs.

24.7 The Classical and the Keynesian Macroeconomic Model

1. **What are the two primary approaches to macroeconomics?**

   The classical school and the Keynesian school are the two primary approaches to macroeconomics.

2. **Which school of thought emphasized that markets can rapidly adjust to changes?**

   The classical school emphasized that markets can rapidly adjust to change.

3. **Why was the double-digit unemployment of the Great Depression when Keynes wrote *The General Theory of Employment, Interest and Money* helpful in leading to its general acceptance?**

   The classical school held that persistent high unemployment would not occur in a market economy, so the high unemployment in the Great Depression—a central aspect of it—appeared to be something the classical approach could not explain.

4. **What would keep wages from falling quickly in a recession?**

   The two reasons cited most often that prevent wages from falling quickly in a recession are long-term union contracts and minimum wage laws.

5. **If wages are sticky downward, why will a decrease in aggregate demand primarily reduce real output?**

   For a decrease in *AD*, if wages are sticky downward, the short-run aggregate supply curve will be nearly horizontal over the relevant range, and the fall in real output would be nearly as great as the fall in *AD*.

CHAPTER 24 STUDY GUIDE

True or False:

1. Aggregate demand (AD) = Consumption (C) + Investment (I) + Government purchases (G) − Net exports (X − M).
2. Because consumption is such a large part of GDP, analyzing its determinants is important for an understanding of the forces leading to changes in aggregate demand.
3. In good business conditions, the level of investment by firms tends to decrease.
4. A $1 million increase in exports has the same direct effect on aggregate demand as a $1 million increase in government purchases.
5. Either a decrease in exports or an increase in imports would increase net exports.
6. *Ceteris paribus,* negative net exports would increase aggregate demand.
7. The aggregate demand (AD) curve indicates the quantities of real GDP demanded at different price levels.
8. The AD curve is downward sloping for different reasons than why the demand curve for a particular product is downward sloping.
9. An increase in the price level causes the quantity of RGDP demanded to rise.
10. The real wealth effect reflects the fact that the real (adjusted for inflation) value of any asset of fixed dollar value, such as cash, rises as the price level increases.
11. A lower price level, other things being equal, will lead to increased real wealth and an increase aggregate demand.
12. At a higher price level, interest rates will rise, other things being equal.
13. If the price level rose, interest rates would fall, which would trigger greater investment and consumer durable spending.
14. A lower price level, other things being equal, would decrease both the interest rate and the quantity of RGDP demanded.
15. If domestic prices of goods and services rise relative to foreign prices, more domestic products will be bought, increasing RGDP demanded.
16. A decreased price level will tend to increase the quantity of RGDP demanded.
17. The AD curve is not shifted by the real wealth effect, the interest rate effect, or the open economy effect.
18. A change in the price level will change aggregate demand.
19. A decrease in C, I, G, or X − M because of changes in the price level will shift AD leftward.
20. An increase in consumer confidence, an increase in wealth or a tax increase would shift AD to the right.
21. An increase in consumer debt, other things being equal, would tend to shift AD to the right.
22. If either business confidence increases or real interest rates fall, business investment will increase and AD will shift to the right.
23. A reduction in government purchases shifts AD to the right.
24. An economic recession in the economies of major trading partners may lead to an increase in U.S. exports to them, causing net exports to rise and AD to increase.
25. The aggregate supply curve represents how much RGDP suppliers will be willing to produce at different price levels.
26. Nominal wages do not adjust quickly in the short run.
27. The long-run relationship refers to a period long enough for the prices of outputs and all inputs to fully adjust to changes in the economy.
28. In the long run, the aggregate supply curve is vertical.
29. In the short run, the slow adjustments of input prices are due to the longer-term input contracts that do not adjust quickly to price-level changes.
30. When price level rises in the short run, it will decrease producers' profit margins and make it in the producers' self-interest to reduce their production.

31. If the output price level falls, ceteris paribus, producers' profits and real output will fall in the short run.
32. When the price level rises, producers can be fooled into supplying more as a result of a short-run misperception of relative prices.
33. Along the short-run aggregate supply curve, we assume that wages and other input prices do not have time to fully adjust.
34. Along the long-run aggregate supply curve, we are looking at the relationship between RGDP produced and the price level, before input prices have been able to respond to changes in output prices.
35. In the long run, the economy will produce at the maximum sustainable level allowed by its capital, labor, and technological inputs, regardless of the price level.
36. Along the *LRAS* curve, a 10 percent increase in the price of goods and services is matched by a 10 percent increase in the price of inputs.
37. Along the *LRAS* curve, the economy is assumed to be at full employment.
38. Short-run equilibrium occurs wherever *SRAS* and *AD* intersect.
39. The economy cannot be in short-run equilibrium without being in long-run equilibrium.
40. *Ceteris paribus,* lower production costs will motivate producers to produce more at any given price level, shifting *AS* rightward.
41. Any permanent change in the quantity of any factor of production available—capital, entrepreneurship, land, or labor—can cause a shift in the long-run aggregate supply curve as well as the short-run aggregate supply curve.
42. Less and lower-quality capital will shift the short-run aggregate supply curve, but not the long-run aggregate supply curve, to the left.
43. Added investments in human capital will shift both the short-run aggregate supply curve and the long-run aggregate supply curve to the right.
44. If entrepreneurs can find ways to lower the costs of production, then the short-run and long-run aggregate supply curves both shift to the right.
45. The discovery of an oil field that will last for a century would increase *LRAS*.
46. An expanded labor force increases the economy's potential output, increasing *LRAS*.
47. Increases in government regulations that make it more costly for producers shift both SRAS and *LRAS* left.
48. The price of factors, or inputs, that go into producing outputs will affect only *LRAS* if they don't reflect permanent changes in the supplies of some factors of production.
49. If wages increase without a corresponding increase in labor productivity, *SRAS* will shift to the left; but *LRAS* will not shift, because with the same supply of labor as before, potential output does not change.
50. Changes in input prices only affect *LRAS* if they reflect permanent changes in the supplies of those inputs.
51. Adverse supply shocks can increase the costs of production, shifting *SRAS* to the left; but once the temporary effects of these disasters have been felt, no appreciable change in the economy's productive capacity occurs, so *LRAS* doesn't shift as a result.
52. In long-run equilibrium, the economy operates at full employment, regardless of the level of the aggregate demand curve.
53. Short-run equilibrium will change when the short-run aggregate supply curve shifts.
54. A change in aggregate demand will change RGDP in the short-run equilibrium and the long-run equilibrium.
55. When short-run equilibrium occurs beyond the economy's level of potential output, it results in a recessionary gap.
56. Demand-pull inflation causes an inflationary gap.
57. Demand-pull inflation causes the prices of the inputs they use in production to rise faster than prices the goods producers sell.
58. If *AD* is increasing at the same rate as the *LRAS* curve, the economy will tend toward both economic growth and stable prices.

59. The economy cannot operate beyond its potential output for a sustained period of time.
60. Short-run real output beyond potential output (and employment beyond full employment) cannot be sustained in the long run.
61. In response to a recessionary gap in the short run, real wages and other real input prices will tend to rise.
62. When an increase in *AD* causes an inflationary gap in the short run, the long-run levels of real output and the price level will be higher.
63. A leftward shift in the aggregate supply curve can cause cost-push inflation.
64. The primary culprits responsible for the leftward shift in *SRAS* in the 1970s were oil price increases.
65. Starting with the economy initially at full-employment equilibrium, a sudden increase in oil prices would result in an inflationary gap.
66. Holding *AD* constant, falling oil prices would lead to a lower price level, higher rate of real output and lower rates of unemployment.
67. A fall in *AD* would reduce real output, the price level and and unemployment in the short run.
68. If the economy is currently in a recessionary gap, with output less than potential output, the price level is lower than workers anticipated.
69. When aggregate demand increases, workers' wages and input suppliers' purchasing power rises in the short run but not in the long run.
70. In a recession, unemployed workers and other input suppliers will bid down wages and prices, and the resulting reduction in production costs shifts the short-run aggregate supply curve to the right.
71. Downward wage stickiness may lead to prolonged periods of recession in response to decreases in aggregate demand by making the economy's adjustment mechanism slower.
72. The *AD/AS* model is not precise tool for analyzing the economy.
73. In the simple Keynesian model, the price level decreases as real output falls in the short run.
74. On the steeper part of a short-run aggregate supply curve, a decrease in aggregate demand will decrease real output, but not decrease the price level very much.
75. Historically, the first two primary approaches to macroeconomics were the classical school and the Monetarist school.
76. It is not possible for actual real GDP to remain above potential real GDP for a sustained period of time.
77. Since real output can exceed potential real output only for a short period of time, unemployment can exceed the natural rate of unemployment only for a short period of time.
78. The extended high unemployment rate in the Great Depression was is inconsistent with the conclusions of classical economists.
79. The degree of wage and price flexibility decreases with the extent of excess capacity in the Keynesian model.

Multiple Choice:

1. The largest component of aggregate demand is
   a. consumption.
   b. net exports.
   c. government purchases.
   d. investment.

2. Empirical evidence suggests that consumption _____ with any _____.
   a. decreases, increase in income.
   b. decreases, tax cut.
   c. increases, increase in income.
   d. increases, decrease in consumer confidence.
   e. Both a. and b. are true.

3. A reduction in personal income taxes, other things being equal, will
   a. leave consumers with less disposable income.
   b. decrease aggregate demand.
   c. leave consumers with more disposable income.
   d. increase aggregate demand.
   e. do both c and d.

4. Aggregate demand is the sum of _____.
   a. $C + I + G$.
   b. $C + I + G + X$.
   c. $C + I + G + (X + M)$.
   d. $C + I + G + (X - M)$.

5. If private consumption in the United States were 67 percent of GDP, investment were 16 percent, government purchases were 13 percent, exports were 12 percent, and imports were 8 percent, net exports would be equal to _____ percent of GDP.
   a. 20.
   b. -20.
   c. 4.
   d. -4.
   e. None of the above.

6. Investment includes
   a. the amount spent on stocks and bonds.
   b. the amount spent on new factories and machinery.
   c. the amount spent on consumer goods that last more than one year.
   d. the amount spent on purchases of art.
   e. all of the above.

7. If our exports of final goods and services increase less than our imports, other things being equal, aggregate demand will
   a. increase.
   b. be negative.
   c. decrease.
   d. stay the same.
   e. do none of the above.

8. As the price level increases, other things being equal,
   a. the quantity of real gross domestic product demanded decreases.
   b. aggregate demand decreases.
   c. the quantity of real gross domestic product demanded increases.
   d. aggregate demand increases.
   e. both a. and b. occur.

9. The aggregate demand curve
   a. is negatively sloped.
   b. demonstrates an inverse relationship between the price level and real gross domestic product demanded.
   c. shows how real gross domestic product demanded changes with the changes in the price level.
   d. All of the above are correct.

10. As the price level increases, interest rates _____, investments _____, and the quantity of RGDP demanded _____.
    a. decrease; increase; decreases.
    b. increase; increase; decreases.
    c. increase; decrease; decreases.
    d. decrease; decrease; increases.
    e. decrease; increase; increases.

11. According to the real wealth effect, if you are living in a period of falling price levels on a fixed income (that is not indexed), the cost of the goods and services you buy _____ and your real income _____.
    a. decreases; increases
    b. decreases; decreases
    c. increases; increases
    d. decreases; remains the same

12. As the price level decreases, real wealth _____, purchasing power _____, and the quantity of RGDP demanded _____.
    a. decreases; decreases; decreases.
    b. decreases; decreases; increases.
    c. increases; decreases; decreases.
    d. increases; decreases; increases.
    e. increases; increases; increases.

13. Which of the following helps explain the downward slope of the aggregate demand curve?
    a. The real wealth effect.
    b. the interest effect.
    c. The open economy effect.
    d. All of the above.
    e. None of the above.

14. Which of the following describes the open economy effect?
    a. If prices of the goods and services in the domestic market rise relative to those in global markets as a result of a higher domestic price level, consumers and businesses will buy less from foreign producers and more from domestic producers.
    b. If prices of the goods and services in the domestic market rise relative to those in global markets as a result of a higher domestic price level, consumers and businesses will buy more from foreign producers and less from domestic producers, other things being equal.
    c. People are allowed to trade with anyone, anywhere, anytime.
    d. It is the ability of firms to enter or leave the marketplace—easy entry and exit with low entry barriers.

15. Which of the following will increase when the price level falls, other things equal?
    a. The real level of investment.
    b. Money demand.
    c. The real interest rate.
    d. Both a. and b.
    e. Both b. and c.

16. Which of the following will result as part of the interest rate effect when the price level rises?
    a. Money demand will increase.
    b. Interest rates will increase.
    c. The dollar amount of investment will decrease.
    d. A lower quantity of real GDP will be demanded.
    e. All of the above will result.

17. An economic bust or severe downturn in the Japanese economy will likely result in a(n)
    a. decrease in U.S. imports and U.S. aggregate demand.
    b. increase in U.S. exports and U.S. aggregate demand.
    c. decrease in U.S. exports and U.S. aggregate demand.
    d. increase in U.S. imports and U.S. aggregate demand.

18. A decrease in the U.S. price level will
    a. increase U.S. imports.
    b. increase U.S. exports.
    c. increase RGDP demanded in the United States.
    d. do both a. and c.
    e. do both b. and c.

19. Which of the following will cause consumption and, as a result, aggregate demand to increase?
    a. A tax decrease.
    b. A fall in consumer confidence.
    c. Reduced stock market wealth.
    d. Rising levels of consumer debt.
    e. All of the above.

20. A massive increase in interstate highway construction will affect aggregate demand through which sector? Will this change increase or decrease aggregate demand?
    a. Investment; increase.
    b. Consumption; decrease.
    c. Government purchases; increase.
    d. Government purchases; decrease.

21. An increase in government purchases, combined with an increase in investment, would have what effect on aggregate demand?
    a. *AD* would increase.
    b. *AD* would decrease.
    c. *AD* would stay the same.
    d. *AD* could either increase or decrease, depending on which change was of greater magnitude.

22. An increase in consumption, combined with a decrease in exports, would have what effect on aggregate demand?
    a. *AD* would increase.
    b. *AD* would decrease.
    c. *AD* would stay the same.
    d. *AD* could either increase or decrease, depending on which change was of greater magnitude.

23. What would happen to aggregate demand if the federal government increased military purchases and state and local governments increased their road-building budgets at the same time?
    a. *AD* would increase.
    b. *AD* would decrease.
    c. *AD* would increase if the change in federal purchases were greater than the change in state and local purchases.
    d. *AD* would decrease if the change in federal purchases were greater than the change in state and local purchases.

24. If exports and imports both decrease, but exports decrease less than imports,
    a. *AD* would decrease.
    b. *AD* would increase.
    c. *AD* would be unaffected.
    d. *AD* could either increase or decrease.

25. If exports decreased and imports increased,
    a. *AD* would decrease.
    b. *AD* would increase.
    c. *AD* would be unaffected.
    d. *AD* could either increase or decrease.

26. The short-run aggregate supply curve slopes
    a. downward because firms can sell more, and hence, will produce more when prices are lower.
    b. downward because firms find it costs less to purchase labor and other inputs when prices are lower, and hence they produce more.
    c. upward because firms find that it costs more to purchase labor and other inputs when prices are higher, and hence they must produce and sell more in order to make a profit.
    d. upward because when the price level rises, output prices rise relative to input prices (costs), raising profit margins and increasing production and sales.

27. If the price level rises, what will happen to the quantity of RGDP produced along the long-run aggregate supply curve?
    a. It will increase.
    b. It will usually increase, but not always.
    c. It will usually decrease, but not always.
    d. It will decrease.
    e. Nothing will happen to it.

28. If the price level falls, what happens to the level of real GDP supplied?
    a. It will increase in both the short run and long run.
    b. It will increase in the short run but not in the long run.
    c. It will decrease in both the short run and long run.
    d. It will decrease in the short run but not in the long run.
    e. It will usually decrease, but not always.

29. What is the typical response of firms to a decrease in the price of what they sell, for given input prices?
    a. An increase in output.
    b. An increase in hiring factors of production.
    c. An increase in the profit level of firms.
    d. A decrease in employment in the industry.
    e. None of the above.

30. The short run is
    a. a time period in which the prices of output cannot change but in which the prices of inputs have time to adjust.
    b. a time period in which neither the prices of output nor the prices of inputs are able to change.
    c. a time period in which output prices can change in response to supply and demand but in which all input prices have not yet been able to completely adjust.
    d. any time period of less than a year.

31. With respect to the profit effect,
    a. When the price level rises, output prices rise relative to input prices (costs), raising producers' short-run profit margins.
    b. When the price level decreases, output prices rise relative to input prices (costs), raising producers' short-run profit margins.
    c. At equilibrium, when costs rise, profit margins are able to float with them and be passed along.
    d. The profit effect is only a long-run phenomenon.

32. The text's explanation of the misperception effect for an upward-sloping short-run aggregate supply curve is based on
    a. falling profit margins as the price level rises.
    b. the fact that producers may be fooled into thinking that the relative price of the item they are producing is rising and as a result increase production.
    c. fixed-wage labor contracts.
    d. rising costs of production as the price level rises.

33. In the short run, an increase in the price level
    a. increases output prices relative to input prices.
    b. increases the profit margins of many producers.
    c. decreases RGDP supplied.
    d. decreases unemployment rates.
    e. does all of the above except c.

34. The short-run aggregate supply curve will shift to the left, other things being equal, if
    a. a short-term increase in input prices occurs.
    b. technology and productivity increase in the nation.
    c. energy prices fall.
    d. the capital stock of the nation increases.

35. Which of the following would shift the long-run aggregate supply curve if it changed?
    a. The level of capital in the economy
    b. The amount of usable land in the economy
    c. The amount of labor in the economy
    d. The technology in the economy
    e. Any of the above would shift the long-run aggregate supply curve if it changed.

36. A decrease in input prices causes
    a. the short-run aggregate supply curve to shift rightward, which means the quantity supplied at any price level declines.
    b. the short-run aggregate supply curve to shift leftward, which means the quantity supplied at any price level declines.
    c. the short-run aggregate supply curve to shift leftward, which means the quantity supplied at any price level increases.
    d. the short-run aggregate supply curve to shift rightward, which means the quantity supplied at any price level increases.

37. How will a decrease in money wages affect the short-run aggregate supply curve?
    a. It will shift left (a decrease in short-run aggregate supply).
    b. It will shift left (an increase in short-run aggregate supply).
    c. It will shift right (a decrease in short-run aggregate supply).
    d. It will shift right (an increase in short-run aggregate supply).

38. An unusual series of rainstorms washes out the grain crop in the upper plains states, severely curtailing the supply of corn and wheat, as well as soybeans. What effect would this situation have on aggregate supply?
    a. It would shift both the *SRAS* and the *LRAS* left.
    b. It would shift the *SRAS* left, but not the *LRAS*.
    c. It would shift the *SRAS* right, but not the *LRAS*.
    d. It would shift both the *SRAS* and the *LRAS* right.

39. Any permanent decrease in the quantity of any of the factors of production—capital, land, labor, or technology—available, will cause
    a. the *SRAS* to shift to the left and *LRAS* to remain constant.
    b. the *SRAS* to shift to the right and *LRAS* to remain constant.
    c. both *SRAS* and *LRAS* to shift to the right.
    d. both *SRAS* and *LRAS* to shift to the left.

40. A temporary negative supply shock will shift _____; a permanent negative supply shock will shift _____.
    a. *SRAS* but not *LRAS* left; *SRAS* and *LRAS* left.
    b. *SRAS* and *LRAS* left; *SRAS* and *LRAS* left.
    c. *SRAS* and *LRAS* left; *SRAS* but not *LRAS* left.
    d. *SRAS* but not *LRAS* left; *SRAS* but not *LRAS* left.

41. Which of the following could be expected to shift the short-run aggregate supply curve upward?
    a. A rise in the price of oil.
    b. A natural disaster.
    c. Wage increases without increases in labor productivity.
    d. All of the above.

42. A year of unusually bad weather for agriculture would
    a. increase *SRAS* but not *LRAS*.
    b. increase *SRAS* and *LRAS*.
    c. decrease *SRAS* but not *LRAS*.
    d. decrease *SRAS* and *LRAS*.

43. When the price of oil experiences a temporary sharp decrease, which curve(s) will shift left?
    a. *SRAS*.
    b. *LRAS*.
    c. Neither *SRAS* nor *LRAS*.
    d. Both *SRAS* and *LRAS*.

44. Assuming a constant level of aggregate demand, the short-run effects of a positive supply shock include
    a. an increase in the price level and a decrease in real output.
    b. a decrease in the price level and an increase in real output.
    c. an increase in the price level and an increase in real output.
    d. a decrease in the price level and a decrease in real output.

45. Cost-push inflation occurs when
    a. the aggregate demand curve shifts left and aggregate supply is fixed.
    b. the short-run aggregate supply curve shifts right.
    c. the aggregate demand curve shifts right at a faster rate than short-run aggregate supply.
    d. the short-run aggregate supply curve shifts left, while aggregate demand is fixed.

46. Inflation that occurs as a result of a decrease in aggregate supply is called
    a. cost-push.
    b. demand-pull.
    c. inflationary push.
    d. none of the above.

47. A recession could result from
    a. an increase in short-run aggregate supply.
    b. an increase in long-run aggregate supply.
    c. an increase in aggregate demand.
    d. a decrease in aggregate demand.
    e. none of the above.

48. Where *SRAS* and *AD* currently intersect at a real output level less than the natural level of real output,
    a. it is a short-run equilibrium, and real output will tend to fall from its current level as it adjusts to long-run equilibrium.
    b. it is a short-run equilibrium, and real output will tend to rise from its current level as it adjusts to long-run equilibrium.
    c. it is a short-run disequilibrium, and real output will tend to fall from its current level as it adjusts to long-run equilibrium.
    d. it is a short-run disequilibrium, and real output will tend to rise from its current level as it adjusts to long-run equilibrium.

49. When *SRAS* and *AD* intersect at the natural level of real output, it is
    a. a short-run equilibrium but not necessarily a long-run equilibrium.
    b. a short-run equilibrium and a long-run equilibrium.
    c. just a short-run equilibrium.
    d. not necessarily either a short-run equilibrium or a long-run equilibrium.

50. Starting from long-run equilibrium, a decrease in aggregate demand will cause
    a. an inflationary gap in the short run.
    b. a recessionary gap in the short run.
    c. an inflationary gap in the short run and long run.
    d. a recessionary gap in the short run and long run.
    e. neither an inflationary nor a recessionary gap in the short run or the long run.

51. When an inflationary gap occurs,
    a. real output exceeds the natural level of output, and unemployment exceeds its natural rate.
    b. real output exceeds the natural level of output, and unemployment is less than its natural rate.
    c. real output is less than the natural level of output, and unemployment exceeds its natural rate.
    d. real output is less than the natural level of output, and unemployment is less than its natural rate.

52. Which of the following could begin an episode of demand-pull inflation?
    a. An increase in consumer optimism.
    b. A faster rate of economic growth for a major trading partner country.
    c. Expectations of higher rates of return in investment.
    d. Any of the above.
    e. None of the above.

53. If real output is currently less than the natural level of real output, a decrease in aggregate demand will
    a. make the current recessionary gap larger.
    b. make the current recessionary gap smaller.
    c. make the current inflationary gap larger.
    d. make the current inflationary gap smaller.

54. In the short run, demand-pull inflation
    a. increases both unemployment and the price level.
    b. increases unemployment but not the price level.
    c. decreases unemployment and increases the price level.
    d. increases the price level but not unemployment.

55. In a stagflation situation,
    a. unemployment increases and the price level decreases.
    b. unemployment increases and the price level increases.
    c. unemployment decreases and the price level increases.
    d. unemployment decreases and the price level decreases.

56. A sharp rise in oil prices will cause a(n) ____; a sudden decrease in the wages demanded by workers will cause a(n) ____.
    a. recessionary gap; inflationary gap.
    b. recessionary gap; recessionary gap.
    c. inflationary gap; inflationary gap.
    d. inflationary gap; recessionary gap.

57. Starting from long-run equilibrium, a decrease in aggregate demand
    a. causes an inflationary gap.
    b. results in a lower price level.
    c. increases unemployment.
    d. does all of the above.
    e. does b. and c., but not a.

58. During the self-correction process after an increase in aggregate demand,
    a. the price level increases and real output increases.
    b. the price level increases and real output decreases.
    c. the price level decreases and real output increases.
    d. the price level decreases and real output decreases.

59. An unexpected decrease in aggregate demand will
    a. increase real wages in the short run but not the long run.
    b. increase real wages in the short run and long run.
    c. decrease real wages in the short run but not the long run.
    d. decrease real wages in the short run and long run.

60. Which of the following can contribute to slowing the adjustment to a recessionary gap?
    a. Efficiency wages.
    b. The minimum wage.
    c. Menu costs.
    d. All of the above.
    e. B. or c., but not a.

61. If the economy was operating on a completely flat segment of the short-run aggregate supply curve, a decrease in aggregate demand would
    a. increase real output and increase the price level.
    b. increase real output and decrease the price level.
    c. decrease real output and increase the price level.
    d. decrease real output and decrease the price level.
    e. do none of the above.

62. Which of the following statements is true?
    a. The classical short-run aggregate supply curve gets steeper as real output increases.
    b. The Keynesian short-run aggregate supply curve gets steeper as real output increases.
    c. The classical long-run aggregate supply curve gets steeper as real output increases.
    d. The Keynesian long-run aggregate supply curve gets steeper as real output increases.

63. "In the long run, both wages and prices adjust freely to changes in demand and supply, and the economy will be at its full employment level of real output."
    a. Classical economists, but not Keynesian economists, would accept that statement.
    b. Keynesian economists, but not classical economists, would accept that statement.
    c. Both classical economists and Keynesian economists would accept that statement.
    d. Neither classical economists nor Keynesian economists would accept that statement.

Problems:

1. Fill in the blanks in the following explanations:
   a. The real wealth effect is described by the following: A decrease in the price level leads to a(n) _____ in real wealth, which leads to a(n) _____ in purchasing power, which leads to a(n) _____ in RGDP demanded.
   b. The interest rate effect is described by the following: An increase in the price level leads to a(n) _____ in the interest rate, which leads to a(n) _____ in investments, which leads to a(n) _____ in RGDP demanded.
   c. The open economy effect is described by the following: A decrease in the price level leads to a(n) _____ in the demand for domestic goods, which leads to a(n) _____ in RGDP demanded.

2. Describe what the effect on aggregate demand would be, other things being equal, if
   a. exports decrease.
   b. both imports and exports decrease.
   c. the price level increases.
   d. the price level decreases.
   e. consumption increases.
   f. investment decreases.
   g. investment decreases and government purchases increase.

3. Use the accompanying diagram to answer questions a. and b.

a. On the exhibit provided, illustrate the short-run effects of an increase in aggregate demand. What happens to the price level, real output, employment, and unemployment?
b. On the exhibit provided, illustrate the long-run effects of an increase in aggregate demand. What happens to the price level, real output, employment, and unemployment?

4. How will each of the following changes alter aggregate supply?

	Short-Run Aggregate Supply	Long-Run Aggregate Supply
A temporary adverse supply shock		
An increase in aggregate demand	_____	_____
An increase in the stock of capital	_____	_____
A reduction in the labor force's size	_____	_____
A decrease in input prices (that reflects Permanent changes in their supplies)	_____	_____
An increase in input prices (not reflecting permanent changes in their supplies)	_____	_____
A decrease in aggregate demand	_____	_____
An increase in usable natural resources	_____	_____
Increased costs of regulations		

5. Use the accompanying diagram to answer questions a and b.

a. Illustrate a recessionary gap on the diagram provided.
b. Using the results in a, illustrate and explain the eventual long-run equilibrium in this case.

6. Use the accompanying diagram to answer questions a. and b.

a. Illustrate an inflationary gap on the diagram provided.
b. Using the results in a, illustrate and explain the eventual long-run equilibrium in this case.

7. Use the diagram below to answer questions a and b.

   a. On the exhibit provided, illustrate the short-run effects of a decrease in aggregate demand. What happens to the price level, real output, employment, and unemployment?
   b. On the exhibit provided, illustrate the long-run effects of a decrease in aggregate demand. What happens to the price level, real output, employment, and unemployment?
8. How does a higher price level in the U.S. economy affect purchases of imported goods? Explain.
9. Explain how a recession in Latin America may affect aggregate demand in the U.S.
10. If retailers such as Wal-Mart and Target find that inventories are rapidly being depleted, would it have been caused by a rightward or leftward change in the aggregate demand curve? What are the likely consequences for output and investment?
11. You operate a business in which you manufacture furniture. You are able to increase your furniture prices by 5 percent this quarter. You assume that the demand for your furniture has increased and begin increasing furniture production. Only later do you realize that prices in the macroeconomy are rising generally at a rate of 5 percent per quarter. This is an example of what effect? What does it imply about the slope of the short-run aggregate supply curve?
12. Evaluate the following statement: "A higher price level decreases the purchasing power of the dollar and reduces RGDP."
13. Is it ever possible for an economy to operate above the full-employment level in the short term? Explain.
14. Distinguish cost-push from demand-pull inflation. Provide an example of an event or shock to the economy that would cause each.
15. How does the slope of the Keynesian short-run aggregate supply curve depend on the degree of excess capacity in the economy?
16. Why does the effect of a given increase in aggregate demand have a larger effect on real output in the short run, the more excess capacity exists in the economy?
17. Why do classical economists and Keynesian economists agree on the long-run effects of a fall in aggregate demand, but not agree on the short run effects?
18. Evaluate the following statement: The Keynesian assumption of wage and price rigidity best corresponds to the steepest portion of the aggregate supply curve, where factories are operating at or beyond normal capacity.

The Aggregate Expenditure Model

25

- 25.1 Simple Aggregate Expenditure Model
- 25.2 Finding Equilibrium in the Aggregate Expenditure Model
- 25.3 Adding Investment, Government Purchases, and Net Exports
- 25.4 Shifts in Aggregate Expenditure and the Multiplier
- 25.5 From Aggregate Expenditures to Aggregate Demand

The Keynesian expenditure model is based on the condition that the components of aggregate demand (consumption, investment, government purchases, and net exports) must equal total output.

Keynes believed that total spending was the critical determinant of the overall level of economic activity. When total spending increases, firms increase their output and hire more workers. Even though Keynes ignored an important component—aggregate supply—his model still provides a great deal of information about aggregate demand. ∎

SECTION 25.1 Simple Aggregate Expenditure Model

- Why do we assume a fixed price level?
- What economic variables influence aggregate demand?
- What are the autonomous factors that influence consumption spending?

In this chapter, we go into a more detailed description of the causes of short-run business cycles. We assume that we are in the Keynesian region of the aggregate supply curve, where the aggregate supply curve is horizontal and RGDP is completely determined by aggregate demand. Recall that Keynes believed that in the short run wages and prices were inflexible, so inflation is not a concern; real values and nominal values are equal in the aggregate expenditure model. Keynes focused on how unanticipated changes in expenditure, particularly investment expenditures, had an impact on real GDP. Keynes's model enlightens our understanding of the short-run business cycle. The model is called the aggregate expenditure model (sometimes the Keynesian cross model), because its focus is aggregate expenditures (aggregate demand), which has historically been especially important to the economy in the short run.

The key to the aggregate expenditure model is that the amount of goods and services (real GDP) depends on aggregate expenditures (total spending). When aggregate expenditures fall, it causes a decrease in output and employment. When aggregate expenditures rise, it causes an increase in output and employment. Thus, in the short run, the level of RGDP is determined by the level of aggregate expenditure.

Recall that Keynes pointed out the naiveté of Say's law. Not all income generated from output is used to buy goods and services; some is saved, hoarded, or taxed away. Supply does not automatically create an adequate demand. In other words, income is not always spent in the period that it is produced. Keynes recognized the volatility of investment spending. A decline in investment would lead to insufficient total spending—inventories would accumulate, and firms will cut production and lay off workers. To fully understand investment fluctuations, Keynes believed you had to study people's income and consumption spending patterns.

Why Do We Assume the Price Level Is Fixed?

Because Keynes believed wages and prices were inflexible in the short run, in this chapter we will assume that the price level is fixed or constant. If the price level is fixed, then changes in nominal income will be equivalent to changes in real income. That is, when we assume the price level is fixed, we do not have to distinguish real variable changes from nominal variable changes. Keynes believed that prices and wages were rigid or fixed until we reached full employment. But let us begin by looking at the most important aggregate demand determinant—consumption.

The Simplest Aggregate Expenditure Model: Autonomous Consumption Only

It is useful to begin by considering consumption spending by households. Household spending on goods and services is the largest single component of the demand for final goods, accounting for more than 65 percent of GDP.

Numerous economic variables influence aggregate demand for consumer goods and services, and thus, aggregate consumption expenditures. Using you or your family as an example, you know that such things as family disposable income (after-tax income), credit conditions, the level of debt outstanding, the amount of financial assets, and expectations are important determinants of consumption purchases. Most economists believe that disposable income is one of the dominant factors.

Let's begin by simplifying things quite a bit. Imagine an economy in which only consumption spending exists (no investment, government purchases, or net exports; later, we'll add in these other sectors). To begin with the simplest situation possible, let's suppose that each household has the same level of disposable income. This kind of analysis that relies on averages is called a representative household analysis. On a graph of consumption spending (vertical axis) for our representative household and the household's representative disposable income (horizontal axis), we could represent average consumption of disposable income at point A in Exhibit 1. From point A, a horizontal dotted line to

section 25.1 exhibit 1 Autonomous Changes in Consumption Spending

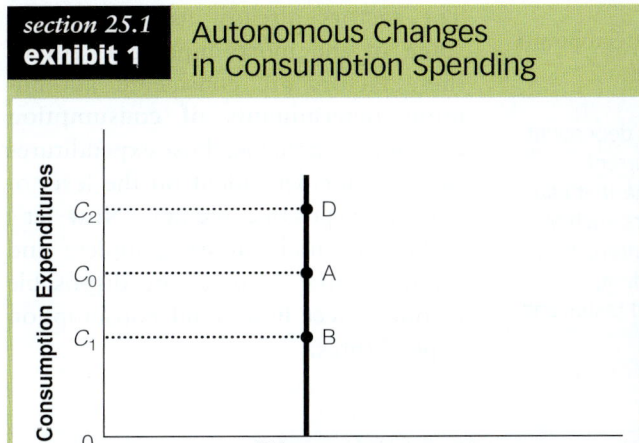

An increase in real wealth would raise consumption spending to C_2, at point D. A decrease in real wealth would tend to lower the level of consumption spending to C_1, at point B. A higher interest rate tends to cause a decrease in consumption spending from point A to point B. As household debt increases, other things equal, consumption spending would fall from point A to point B. In general, an increase in consumer confidence would act to increase household spending (a movement from point A to point D) and a decrease in consumer confidence would act to decrease household spending (a movement from point A to point B).

the vertical axis permits us to read the value of average consumption spending, C_0.

What Are the Autonomous Factors That Influence Spending?

Even though income is given for the representative household, other economic factors that influence consumption spending are not. When consumption (or any of the other components of spending, such as investment) does not depend on income, we call it *autonomous* (or independent). Let's look at some of these other autonomous factors and see how they would change consumption spending.

Real Wealth

The larger the value of a household's real wealth (the money value of wealth divided by the price level, which indicates the amount of consumption goods that the wealth could buy), the larger the amount of consumption spending, other things equal. Thus, in Exhibit 1, an increase in real wealth would raise consumption to C_2, at point D, for a given level of current income. Similarly, something that would lower the value of real wealth, such as a decline in property values or a stock market decline, would tend to lower the level of consumption to C_1, at point B in Exhibit 1.

The Interest Rate

A higher interest rate tends to make the consumption items that we buy on credit more expensive, which reduces expenditures on those items. An increase in the interest rate increases the monthly payments made to buy such things as automobiles, furniture, and major appliances and reduces our ability to spend out of a given income. This shift is shown as a decrease in consumption from point A to point B in Exhibit 1. Moreover, an increase in the interest rate provides a higher future return from reducing current spending, which motivates increasing savings. Thus, a higher interest rate in the current period would likely motivate an increase in savings today, which would permit households to consume more goods and services at some future date.

Household Debt

Remember when that friend of yours ran up his credit card obligations so high that he stopped buying goods except the basic necessities? Well, our average household might find itself in the same situation if its outstanding debt exceeds some reasonable level relative to its income. So, as debt increases, other things equal, consumption expenditure would fall from point A to point B in Exhibit 1.

Expectations

Just as in microeconomics, decisions to spend may be influenced by a person's expectations of future disposable income, employment, or certain world events. Based on monthly surveys conducted that attempt to measure consumer confidence, an increase in consumer confidence generally acts to increase household spending (a movement from point A to point D in Exhibit 1) and a decrease in consumer confidence would act to decrease spending (a movement from A to B in Exhibit 1). For example, a decline in the consumer confidence index after the financial crisis that begun in December of 2007 and a subsequent fall in household spending are considered factors in the recession in the United States.

Tastes and Preferences

Of course, each household is different. Some are young and beginning a working career; some are without children; others have families; still others are older and perhaps retired from the workforce. Some households like to save, putting dollars away for later spending, while others spend all their income, or even borrow to spend more than their current disposable income. These saving and spending decisions often vary over a household's life cycle.

As you can see, many economic factors affect consumption expenditures.

autonomous determinants of consumption expenditures
expenditures not dependent on the level of current disposable income that can result from factors such as real wealth, the interest rate, household debt, expectations, and tastes and preferences

The factors already listed represent some of the most important. All of these factors are considered **autonomous determinants of consumption expenditures;** that is, those expenditures that are not dependent on the level of current disposable income. Now let's make our model more complete and evaluate how changes in disposable income affect household consumption expenditures.

SECTION CHECK

1. The aggregate expenditure model is based on the idea that the components of aggregate demand must equal total output, implying that changes in aggregate demand cause fluctuations in real GDP.
2. In the simplest aggregate expenditure model, the price level is fixed to allow for easy evaluation of changes in demand due to real income.
3. In the simplest aggregate expenditure model, consumption spending is the primary determinant of aggregate demand.
4. Representative household analysis allows the determination of the value of average consumption spending.
5. Autonomous consumption is not dependent on income, but does depend on real wealth, the interest rate, household debt, future expectations, and tastes and preferences.

---

1. How does the assumption of a fixed price level in the Keynesian expenditure model solve the problem of distinguishing between changes in the real value of a variable (such as GDP) and changes in its nominal value?
2. Would it be possible for some consumption expenditures to be autonomous and other parts of consumption expenditures not to be autonomous?
3. In what two ways does a higher interest rate tend to reduce current consumption?
4. What would happen to autonomous consumption expenditures if the value of a consumer's stock market investments rose and his household debt rose at the same time?
5. What would happen to your autonomous consumption if you expected to get a job paying 10 times your current salary next week?
6. Why do households headed by a 50-year-old tend to save a larger fraction of their incomes than those headed by either a 30-year-old or a 70-year-old?

SECTION 25.2
Finding Equilibrium in the Aggregate Expenditure Model

* What factors determine consumer spending?
* How do we find equilibrium in the aggregate expenditure model?
* Why does income equal output?
* Why does expenditure equal output?

In our first model, we looked at the economic variables that affected consumption expenditures when disposable income was fixed. This assumption is clearly unrealistic, but it allows us to develop some of the basic building blocks of the aggregate expenditure model. Now we'll look at a slightly more complicated model in which consumption also depends on disposable income.

If you think about what determines your own current consumption spending, you know that it depends on many factors previously discussed, such as your age, family size, interest rates, expected future disposable income, wealth, and, most importantly, your current disposable income. Recall from earlier chapters, disposable income is your after-tax income. Your personal consumption spending depends primarily on your current disposable income. In fact, empirical studies confirm that most people's consumption spending is closely tied to their disposable income.

Revisiting Marginal Propensity to Consume and Save

What happens to current consumption spending when a person earns some additional disposable income? Most people will spend some of their extra income and save some of it. The percentage of your extra disposable income that you decide to spend on consumption is what economists call your **marginal propensity to consume (MPC)**. That is, MPC is equal to the *change* in consumption spending (ΔC) divided by the *change* in disposable income (ΔDY).

$$MPC = \Delta C / \Delta DY$$

For example, suppose you won a lottery prize of $1,000. You might decide to spend $750 of your winnings today and save $250. In this example, your marginal propensity to consume is 0.75 (or 75%) because out of the extra $1,000, you decided to spend 75 percent of it (0.75 × $1,000 = $750).

The term *marginal propensity to consume* has two parts: (1) *marginal* refers to the fact that you received an extra amount of disposable income—in addition to your income, not your total income; and (2) *propensity to consume* refers to how much you tend to spend on consumer goods and services out of your additional income.

Marginal Propensity to Save

The flip side of the marginal propensity to consume is the **marginal propensity to save (MPS),** which is the proportion of an addition to your income that you would save or not spend on goods and services today.

marginal propensity to consume (MPC)
the additional consumption that results from an additional dollar of income

marginal propensity to save (MPS)
the additional saving that results from an additional dollar of income

That is, MPS is equal to the *change* in savings (ΔS) divided by the change in disposable income (ΔDY).

$$MPS = \Delta S / \Delta DY$$

In the earlier lottery example, your marginal propensity to save is 0.25, or 25 percent, because you decided to save 25 percent of your additional disposable income (0.25 × $1,000 = $250). Because your additional disposable income must be either consumed or saved, the marginal propensity to consume plus the marginal propensity to save must add up to 1, or 100 percent.

Let's illustrate the marginal propensity to consume in Exhibit 1. Suppose you estimated that you had to spend $16,000 a year, even if you earned no income for the year, for "necessities" such as food, clothing, and shelter. And suppose for every $1,000 of added disposable income you earn, you spend 75 percent of it and save 25 percent of it. So if your disposable income is $0, you spend $16,000 (that means you have to borrow or reduce your existing savings just to survive). If your disposable income is $40,000, you'll spend $16,000 plus 75 percent of $40,000 (which equals $30,000), for total spending of $46,000. If your disposable income is $80,000, you'll spend $16,000 plus 75 percent of $80,000 (which equals $60,000), for total spending of $76,000.

What's your marginal propensity to consume? In this case, if you spend 75 percent of every additional $1,000 you earn, your marginal propensity to consume is 0.75 or 75 percent. And if you save 25 percent of every additional $1,000 you earn, your marginal propensity to save is 0.25.

In Exhibit 1, the slope of the line represents the marginal propensity to consume. To better understand this concept, look at what happens when your disposable income rises from $36,000 to $40,000. At a disposable income of $36,000, you spend $16,000 plus 75 percent of $36,000 (which is $27,000), for total spending of $43,000. If your disposable income rises to $40,000, you spend $16,000 plus 75 percent of $40,000 (which is $30,000), for total spending of $46,000. So when your disposable income rises by $4,000 (from $36,000 to $40,000), your spending goes up by $3,000 (from $43,000 to $46,000). Your marginal propensity to consume is $3,000 (the increase in spending) divided by $4,000 (the increase in disposable income), which equals 0.75, or 75 percent. But notice that this calculation is also the calculation of the slope of the line from point A to point B in the exhibit. Recall that the slope of the line

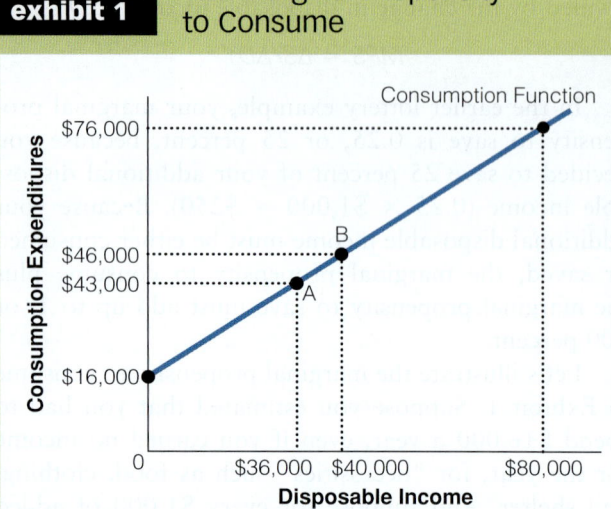

section 25.2 exhibit 1 — The Marginal Propensity to Consume

The slope of the line represents the marginal propensity to consume. At a disposable income of $36,000, you spend $16,000 plus 75 percent of $36,000 (which is $27,000), for total spending of $43,000. If your disposable income rises to $40,000, you spend $16,000 plus 75 percent of $40,000 (which is $30,000), for total spending of $46,000. So when your disposable income rises by $4,000 (from $36,000 to $40,000), your spending goes up by $3,000 (from $43,000 to $46,000). Your marginal propensity to consume is $3,000 (the increase in spending) divided by $4,000 (the increase in disposable income), which equals 0.75, or 75 percent. But notice that this MPC calculation is also the calculation of the slope of the line from point A to point B.

is the rise (the change on the vertical axis) over the run (the change on the horizontal axis). In this case, that's $3,000 divided by $4,000, which makes 0.75 the marginal propensity to consume. So the marginal propensity to consume is the same as the slope of the line in our graph of consumption and disposable income.

Now, let's take this same logic and apply it to the economy as a whole. If we add up, or aggregate, everyone's consumption and everyone's income, we'll get a line that looks like the one in Exhibit 1, but that applies to the entire economy. This line or functional relationship is called a *consumption function*. Let's suppose consumption spending in the economy is $1 trillion plus 75 percent of income.

Now, with consumption equal to $1 trillion plus 75 percent of income, consumption is partly autonomous (the $1 trillion part, which people would spend no matter what their income, which depends on the cur-

rent interest rate, real wealth, debt, and expectations), and partly *induced*, which means it depends on income. The induced consumption is the portion that's equal to 75 percent of income.

What is the total amount of expenditure in this economy? Because we've assumed that investment, government purchases, and net exports are zero, aggregate expenditure is just equal to the amount of consumption spending represented by our consumption function.

Equilibrium in the Aggregate Expenditure Model

The next part of the aggregate expenditure model is to examine what conditions are needed for the economy to be in equilibrium. In order to determine equilibrium, we need to show (1) that income equals output in the economy, and (2) that in equilibrium, aggregate expenditure (or consumption in this example) equals output. First, income equals output because people earn income by producing goods and services. For example, workers earn wages because they produce some product that is then sold on the market, and owners of firms earn profits because the products they sell provide more income than the cost of producing them. So any income that is earned by anyone in the economy arises from the production of output in the economy. From now on, we'll use this idea and say that income equals output; we'll use the terms *income* and *output* interchangeably. Another way to remember this concept is to recall the circular flow diagram; the top half (output) is always equal to the bottom half (income—the sum of wages, rents, interest payments, and profits).

The second condition needed for equilibrium (aggregate expenditure in the economy equals output) is the distinctive feature of the aggregate expenditure model. Just as income must equal output (because income comes from selling goods and services), aggregate expenditure equals output because people can't earn income until the products they produce are sold to someone. Every good or service that is produced in the economy must be purchased by someone or added to inventories. Exhibit 2 plots aggregate expenditure against output. As you can see, it's a 45-degree line (slope = 1). The 45-degree line shows that the number on the horizontal axis, representing the amount of output in the economy, real GDP (Y), is equal to the number on the vertical axis, representing the amount

section 25.2 exhibit 2 — In Equilibrium, Aggregate Expenditure Equals Output

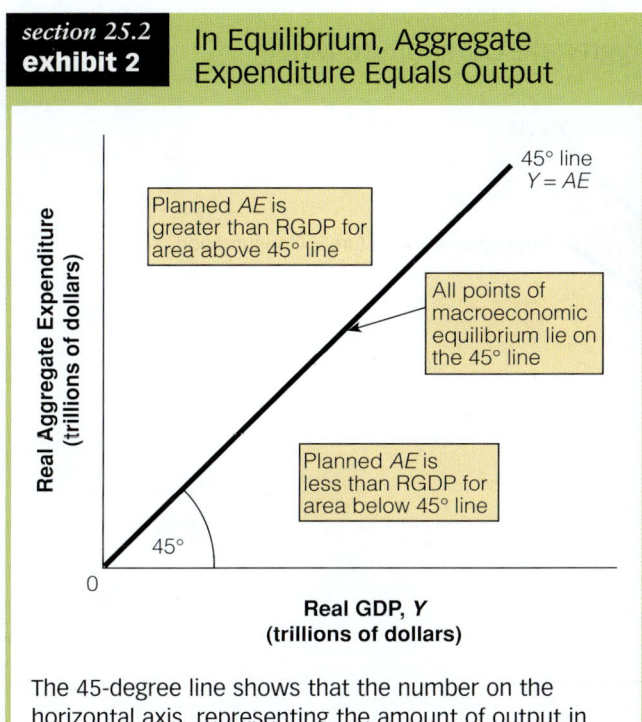

The 45-degree line shows that the number on the horizontal axis, representing the amount of output in the economy, is equal to the number on the vertical axis, representing the amount of aggregate expenditure in the economy. If output is $14 trillion, then in equilibrium, aggregate expenditure must equal $14 trillion.

of real aggregate expenditure (AE) in the economy. If output is $14 trillion, then in equilibrium, aggregate expenditure must equal $14 trillion. All points of macroeconomic equilibrium lie on the 45-degree line.

Disequilibrium in the Aggregate Expenditure Model

What would happen if, for some reason, output were lower than its equilibrium level, as would be the case if output were Y_1 in Exhibit 3? Looking at the vertical dotted line, we see that when output is Y_1, aggregate expenditure (shown by the consumption function) is greater than output (shown by the 45-degree line). This amount is labeled the distance AB on the graph. So people would be trying to buy more goods and services (A) than were being produced (B), which would cause producers to increase the amount of production, which would increase output in the economy. This process would continue until output reached its equilibrium level, where the two lines intersect. Another way to think about this disequilibrium is that consumers would be buying more than is currently produced, causing a decrease in inventories on shelves and in warehouses from their desired levels. Clearly, profit-seeking businesspeople would increase production to bring their inventory stocks back up to the desired levels. In doing so, they would move production to the equilibrium level.

Similarly, if output were above its equilibrium level, as would occur if output were Y_2 in Exhibit 3, economic forces would act to reduce output. At this point, as you can see by looking at the graph, at point Y_2 on the horizontal axis aggregate expenditure (D) is less than output (C). People wouldn't want to buy all the output that is being produced, so producers would want to reduce their production. They would keep reducing their output until reaching the equilibrium level. Using the inventory adjustment process, inventories would be bulging from shelves and warehouses and firms would reduce output and production until inventory stocks returned to the desired level. For example, automobile companies might close plants to reduce inventories.

This basic model—in which we've assumed that consumption spending is the only component of aggregate expenditure (that is, we've ignored investment, government spending, and net exports) and that some consumption spending is autonomous—is quite simple, yet it is the essence of the aggregate expenditure model. Equilibrium in this model, and in more complicated versions of the model, always occurs where one line representing aggregate expenditure crosses another line that represents the equilibrium condition where aggregate expenditure equals output (the 45-degree line).

Now let's put Exhibits 1 and 2 together to find the equilibrium in the economy, shown in Exhibit 3. As you might guess, the point where the two lines cross is the equilibrium point. Why? Because it is only at this point that aggregate expenditure is equal to output. Aggregate expenditure is shown by the flatter line (Aggregate expenditure = Consumption). The equilibrium condition is shown by the 45-degree line (Y = AE). The only point for which consumption spending equals aggregate expenditure equals output is the point where those two lines intersect, labeled "Equilibrium." Because these points are on the 45-degree line, equilibrium output Y^*, equals equilibrium aggregate expenditure AE^*.

section 25.2 exhibit 3 — Disequilibrium and Equilibrium in the Aggregate Expenditure Model

When RGDP is Y_1, aggregate expenditure is greater than output—distance AB on the graph. Consumers are trying to buy more goods and services (A) than are being produced (B), which causes producers to increase the amount of production, increasing output in the economy. This process continues until output reaches its equilibrium level, Y^*, where the two lines intersect. If RGDP is at Y_2, aggregate expenditure (D) is less than output (C). Consumers wouldn't want to buy all the output that is being produced, so producers would want to reduce their production. They would keep reducing their output until the equilibrium level of output was reached. The only point for which consumption spending equals real aggregate planned expenditure equals output is the point where those two lines intersect. Because these points are on the 45-degree line, equilibrium output, Y^* equals equilibrium aggregate expenditure AE^*.

SECTION CHECK

1. The magnitude of change in consumption spending due to a change in income is the marginal propensity to consume (MPC); change in consumption divided by change in disposable income.
2. The counterpart of the marginal propensity to consume is the marginal propensity to save (MPS); the additional savings realized as a result of a change in income. MPS equals the change in saving divided by the change in disposable income.
3. When the aggregate expenditure model is in equilibrium, income equals output and aggregate expenditure equals output.
4. Income equals output because individuals earn income through production.
5. Aggregate expenditure equals output because income is earned when goods and services are sold.

---

1. If consumption purchases rise with disposable income, how would an increase in taxes affect consumption purchases?
2. If your marginal propensity to consume was 0.75, what is your marginal propensity to save? If your marginal propensity to consume rose to 0.80, what would happen to your marginal propensity to save?
3. Could a student have a positive marginal propensity to save, and yet have negative savings (increased borrowing) at the same time?
4. What would happen to the slope of the consumption function if the marginal propensity to save fell?
5. Why would an increase in disposable income increase induced consumption but not autonomous consumption?

6. What tends to happen to inventories if aggregate expenditures exceed output? What tends to happen to output?

7. What tends to happen to inventories if output exceeds aggregate expenditures? What tends to happen to output?

SECTION 25.3 Adding Investment, Government Purchases, and Net Exports

* What is the impact of adding investment, government purchases, and net exports to aggregate expenditures?
* What is planned investment?
* What is unplanned investment?
* How does the aggregate expenditure model help explain the process of the business cycle?

Now we can complicate our model in another important way by adding in the other three major components of expenditure in the economy: investment, government purchases, and net exports. As a first step, we'll add these components to the model but assume that they are autonomous, that is, they don't depend on the level of income or output in the economy. Later, we'll relax that assumption.

Suppose that consumption depends on the level of income or output in the economy, but investment, government purchases, and net exports don't; instead, they depend on other things in the economy, such as interest rates, political considerations, or the condition of foreign economies (we'll discuss these things in more detail later). Now, aggregate expenditure (AE) consists of consumption (C) plus investment (I) plus government purchases (G) plus net exports (NX):

$$AE \equiv C + I + G + NX$$

This equation is nothing more than a definition (indicated by the ≡ rather than =): Aggregate expenditure equals the sum of its components.

When we add up all the components of aggregate expenditure, we'll get an upward-sloping line, as we did in the previous section, because consumption increases as income increases. But because we're now allowing for investment, government purchases, and net exports, the autonomous portion of aggregate expenditure is larger. Thus, the intercept of the aggregate expenditure line is higher, as shown in Exhibit 1.

What is the new equilibrium? As before, the equilibrium occurs where the two lines cross, that is, where the aggregate expenditure line intersects the equilibrium line, which is the 45-degree line.

Now that we've added in the other components of spending, especially investment spending, we can begin to discuss some of the more realistic factors related to the business cycle. This discussion of what happens to the economy during business cycles is a major element of Keynesian theory, which was designed to explain what happens in recessions.

If you look at historical economic data, you'll see that investment spending fluctuates much more than overall output in the economy. In recessions, output declines, and a major portion of the decline occurs because investment falls sharply. In expansions, investment is the major contributor to economic growth. The two major explanations for the volatile movement of investment over the business cycle involve planned investment and unplanned investment.

The first explanation for investment's strong business cycle movement is that *planned* investment responds dramatically to perceptions of future changes in economic activity. If business firms think that the economy will be good in the future, they'll build new factories, buy more computers, and hire more workers today, in anticipation of being able to sell more goods in the future. On the other hand, if firms think the economy will be weak in the future, they'll cut back on both investment and hiring. Economists find that planned investment is extremely sensitive to firms' perceptions about the future. And if firms desire to invest more today, it generates ripple effects that make the economy grow even faster.

The second explanation for investment's movement over the business cycle is that businesses encounter *unplanned* changes in investment as well. The idea here is that recessions, to some extent, occur as

section 25.3 exhibit 1 — Adding Investment, Government Purchases, and Net Exports to Aggregate Expenditures

Adding $I + G + NX$ leads to a larger intercept of the aggregate expenditure line. Because consumption is the only component of aggregate expenditure that depends on income, the slope of the line is the same as the slope of the line in Exhibit 3 of Section 25.2.

the economy is making a transition, before it reaches equilibrium. We'll use Exhibit 2 to illustrate this idea. In the exhibit, equilibrium occurs at output of Y^*. Now, consider what would happen if, for some reason, firms produced too many goods, bringing the economy to output level Y_2. At output level Y_2, aggregate expenditure is less than output because the aggregate expenditure line is below the 45-degree line at that point. When people aren't buying all the products that firms are producing, unsold goods begin piling up. In the national income accounts, unsold goods in firms' inventories are counted in a subcategory of investment—inventory investment. The firms didn't plan for this to happen, so the piling up of inventories reflects **unplanned inventory investment**. Of course, once firms realize that inventories are rising because they've produced too much, they cut back on production, reducing output below Y_2. This process continues until firms' inventories are restored to normal levels and output returns to Y^*.

Now let's look at what would happen if firms produced too few goods, as occurs when output is

unplanned inventory investment collection of inventory that results when people do not buy the products firms are producing

section 25.3 exhibit 2 — Unplanned Inventory Investment

At Y_2, AE is less than output and unsold goods pile up. As unplanned inventory investment builds up, firms cut back on production until equilibrium output is restored at Y^*. At Y_1, AE is greater than output: Consumers want to buy more than firms are producing. Inventories become depleted and firms increase production until inventories are restored and output returns to equilibrium at Y^*.

at Y_1. At output level Y_1, aggregate expenditure is greater than output because the aggregate expenditure line is above the 45-degree line at that point. People want to buy more goods than firms are producing, so firms' inventories begin to decline or become depleted. Again, this change in inventories shows up in the national income accounts, this time as a decline in firms' inventories and thus a decline in investment. Again, the firms didn't plan for this situation, so once they realize that inventories are declining because they haven't produced enough, they'll increase production beyond Y_1. Equilibrium is reached when firms' inventories are restored to normal levels and output returns to Y^*.

So, our Keynesian expenditure model helps to explain the process of the business cycle, working through investment. Next, let's see how other economic events can act to affect the equilibrium level of output in the economy. We'll begin by looking at how changes in autonomous spending (consumption, investment, government purchases, and net exports) can influence output.

SECTION CHECK

1. Aggregate expenditure consists of consumption (C), investment (I), government expenditures (G), and net exports (NX). Hence, in the aggregate expenditure model, output is the result of these components.
2. Changes in planned or unplanned investment contribute to the fluctuations evident in the business cycle.

---

1. When all the nonconsumption components of aggregate expenditures are autonomous, why does the aggregate expenditures line have the same slope as the consumption function?
2. If net exports are negative, what happens to the aggregate expenditures line, other things equal? What will happen to equilibrium income?
3. As the economy turns toward a recession, what happens to unplanned inventory investment? Why? What happens to planned investment? Why?
4. How does unplanned inventory investment signal which way real GDP will tend to change in the economy?

SECTION 25.4 Shifts in Aggregate Expenditure and the Multiplier

* How do changes in the components of aggregate expenditure affect the aggregate expenditure curve?
* How does the multiplier affect aggregate expenditures?

What happens if one of the components of aggregate expenditure increases for reasons other than an increase in income? Remember that we called these components or parts *autonomous*. Households' expectations might become more optimistic, or households may find credit conditions easier as interest rates decline, or their real wealth might increase as the stock market rises. All these factors increase autonomous consumption, and thus total consumption at every level of income increases. Firms might increase their investment (especially if their productivity rises or the interest rate declines), government might increase its spending, or net exports could rise as foreign economies improve their economic health. Any of these things would increase aggregate expenditure for any given level of income, shifting the aggregate expenditure curve up, as shown in Exhibit 1.

Suppose that firms optimistic about their future profitability increase their planned investment spending on plants, factories and machines by $100 billion. In Exhibit 1, we see that the increase in planned investment spending shifts the aggregate expenditure curve upward and results in a $400 billion gain in equilibrium real GDP; the difference between the equilibrium

section 25.4
exhibit 1

Increases in the Autonomous Components of Aggregate Expenditure

If one of the "autonomous" components of aggregate expenditure increases for reasons other than an increase in income like: optimistic consumer or business expectations, a decrease in the interest rate, or real wealth increases, government might increase its spending, or net exports could rise as foreign economies improve their economic health. Any of these things would increase aggregate expenditure for any given level of income, shifting the aggregate expenditure curve up, as shown in Exhibit 1.

profits, so they spend more. The higher level of economic activity encourages even more spending, until a new equilibrium with higher output is reached, Y_2 rather than Y_1. In this example, the increase in output is four times as big as the initial increase in investment spending that started the cycle. Let's see how this process works in more detail.

Exhibit 2 shows what happens along the way. We begin at point A, with output of $14 trillion. The increase in investment spending of $100 billion directly increases aggregate expenditure by that amount, represented by point B. Firms observe the increase in aggregate expenditure (perhaps because they see their inventories declining), so over the next few months they produce more output, moving the economy to point C, with output of $14.1 trillion. But now consumers have an extra $100 billion in income and they wish to spend three-fourths of it (because the marginal propensity to consume is 0.75). Three-fourths of $100 billion is $75 billion, so consumers now spend an additional $75 billion, increasing aggregate expenditure to $14.075 trillion at point D. Again, firms observe the increase in expenditure, so over the next few months they increase output, bringing the economy to point E. This process continues until the economy eventually reaches point Z, at which output is $14.4 trillion.

You can see on the graph how the economy reaches its new equilibrium at point Z. We can also calculate it numerically by adding up an infinite series of numbers in the following way. The first increase in output was $100 billion, which comes directly from the increase in investment spending. Then consumers, with higher incomes of $100 billion, want to spend three-fourths of it, so they increase spending: $100 billion × 3/4 = $75 billion. Now, with incomes higher by $75 billion, consumers want to spend an additional three-fourths of it: $75 billion × 3/4 = $56 billion. Again, incomes are higher, so consumers will spend more, this time in the amount $56 billion × 3/4 = $42 billion. The process continues indefinitely. To find the total increase in output (or income), we simply need to add up all these amounts. It turns out that an infinite sum with this pattern is exactly $100 billion/(1 − 3/4) = $400 billion. So output increases by $400 billion from $14 trillion to $14.4 trillion.

This calculation of the sum of all the increases to output can be written in a convenient way. As you saw in this example, the multiplier depends on how much consumers spend out of any additions to their income. So in this model in which consumption spending is the

real GDP at point A and the equilibrium real GDP at point B. How did the $100 billion increase in autonomous investment raise real GDP demanded by $400 billion? This result might seem amazing—that an increase in planned investment spending of a $100 billion can result in a $400 billion increase in real GDP—but it merely reflects a well-understood process, known as the **expenditure multiplier**.

expenditure multiplier the multiplier that only considers the impact of consumption changes on aggregate expenditures

A caution here: Do not assume that the multiplier applies only to changes in planned investment spending. Multipliers apply to any increase in autonomous expenditure. As an example, if the stock market went up to increase the amount of autonomous household spending by $100 billion, the level of output would go up the same $400 billion as found in the preceding example.

The idea of the multiplier is that permanent increases in spending in one part of the economy lead to increased spending by others in the economy as well. When firms increase investment spending private resource owners earn more wages, interest, rents, and

section 25.4 exhibit 2 — Aggregate Expenditures and the Multiplier Process

At point A, output is $14 trillion and the increase in government purchases of $500 billion directly increases aggregate expenditure by that amount, represented by point B. Firms observe the increase in aggregate expenditure and produce more output, moving the economy to point C, with output of $14.075 trillion. But now consumers have an extra $100 billion in income and they wish to spend three-fourths of it (the MPC is 0.75). Three-fourths of $100 billion is $75 billion, so consumers now spend an additional $75 billion, increasing aggregate expenditure to $14.075 trillion at point D. Again, firms observe the increase in expenditure and increase output, bringing the economy to point E. This process continues until the economy eventually reaches point Z, at which output is $14.4 trillion.

only component of aggregate expenditure that depends on income, the multiplier is equal to $1/(1 - MPC)$, where MPC is the marginal propensity to consume. In the previous example, MPC = 3/4, so the multiplier is $1/(1 - 3/4) = 4$. The same multiplier holds whether the increase in aggregate expenditures arises from an increase in investment spending, as in the example, or from an increase in other autonomous elements of spending, such as government purchases, net exports, or the autonomous portion of consumption spending. The larger (smaller) the MPC the larger (smaller) the multiplier. For example, if the MPC is .8 (1/1 - .8 or 1/.2 = 5) than the multiplier would be 5. If the MPC is .5 (1/1 - .5 or 1/.5 = 2). The true multiplier is usually smaller because of complications that we will discuss in the chapter on Fiscal Policy.

The multiplier can operate in both directions. During the Great Depression, both consumption spending and planned investment fell causing a decease in aggregate expenditure. As sales fell, workers were laid off and falling levels of production and income led to further declines in consumption spending as the economy fell into a downward spiral. The downturn can also start in a certain sector and than spread via the multiplier to other sectors of the economy. Recall, the information technology recession of 2001. The initial impact of the decline in investment spending was felt in the computer and telecommunications industries but eventually the declines in production, income and spending spread into other industries; like automobiles, furniture, appliances, airlines and restaurants.

SECTION CHECK

1. Autonomous changes in the components of aggregate expenditure change the total level of aggregate expenditure, and thus output.
2. The effect of spending in one part of the economy is magnified by the multiplier and can affect the other components; the change in output may be greater than the change in spending.
3. Where consumption spending is the only variable of aggregate expenditure dependent on income, the multiplier is 1/(1 − MPC).

---

1. If autonomous expenditure rises and the marginal propensity to consume rises, what would happen to equilibrium income?
2. If autonomous expenditure rises and the marginal propensity to consume falls, what would happen to equilibrium income?
3. If the marginal propensity to consume was 0.75, what would happen to equilibrium income if government purchases increased by $500 billion and investment fell by $500 billion at the same time? What if government purchases increased by $500 billion and investment fell by $400 billion at the same time?
4. Why does a larger marginal propensity to consume lead to a larger multiplier?
5. If autonomous consumption was $300 billion, investment was $200 billion, government purchases were $400 billion, and net exports were a negative $100 billion, what would autonomous consumption be? What would equilibrium income be?
6. What would happen to equilibrium income if, other things equal, imports increased by $100 billion and the marginal propensity to consume was 0.9?

SECTION 25.5 From Aggregate Expenditures to Aggregate Demand

- Why do aggregate expenditures depend on the price level?
- How do we move from aggregate expenditures to aggregate demand?

To go from the Keynesian-cross aggregate expenditure model to aggregate demand, all we need to add is how the price level affects the components of aggregate demand.

The effect of different price levels can be seen in Exhibit 1. Let's consider three different price levels, $P = 90$, $P = 100$, and $P = 110$, where P is a price index like the GDP deflator. Suppose the price level is 100, and suppose at that level of prices, the aggregate expenditure curve is given as the curve labeled $AE (P = 100)$, shown in the top diagram. The equilibrium in the Keynesian aggregate expenditure model occurs at point A. Now we plot point A in the bottom diagram, corresponding to a price level of 100 and output of $8 trillion.

What happens if the price level falls from 100 to 90? Recall from the previous chapter, that a lower price level will cause an increase in RGDP demanded through the real wealth, interest rate and open economy effects. The lower price level will (1) increase the real value of household's money holdings (part of their wealth) causing purchasing power to rise leading to greater consumption expenditures (2) firms and households reduce their holdings of money and save more causing interest rates to fall increasing investment and consumption expenditures and (3) it leads to an increase in imports and a decrease in exports. As a consequence of the increase in RGDP demanded associated with the lower price level there is a higher level of planned expenditures, so the aggregate expenditure curve shifts up to $(AE, P = 90)$ and the new equilibrium is at point B. So we plot B in the bottom diagram, corresponding to the price level 90 and output $15 trillion, as seen in Exhibit 1.

Finally, what happens if the price level rises to 110? The higher price level will (1) decrease the value of household's money holdings (part of their wealth) causing purchasing power to fall leading to reduced consumption expenditures (2) firms and households increase their holdings of money and increase the demand for loanable funds causing interest rates to rise decreasing consumption and investment expenditures and (3) it leads to an increase in exports and a decrease in imports. As a consequence of the decrease in RGDP demanded associated with the higher price level there is a lower level of planned expenditures (AE, $P = 110$) and a lower level of output, $13 trillion, as seen in Exhibit 1. The higher price level means lower aggregate expenditure, so the aggregate expenditure curve shifts down to $AE(P = 110)$, and the equilibrium in the Keynesian-cross diagram is at point C. We plot point C in the bottom diagram, corresponding to a price level of 110 and output of $13 trillion.

Notice that the higher the price level, the lower is aggregate demand. Imagine carrying out this same experiment for every possible price level. Then the points like A, B, and C in the lower diagram would trace out the entire aggregate demand curve.

Shifts in Aggregate Demand

In the previous section, we used the relationship between aggregate expenditure and the price level to derive the aggregate demand curve. Now we'll show that changes in any of the components of aggregate expenditure that occur for any reason other than a change in the price level or output lead to a shift of the aggregate demand curve. We'll start with Exhibit 1 (but to keep things readable we'll only draw in one of the aggregate expenditure lines in the top half of the exhibit), then consider what happens when the autonomous parts of consumption, investment, government purchases, or net exports change. Such a change would shift the aggregate expenditure curve upwards, as shown in Exhibit 2, where we denote the original aggregate expenditure curve AE_1 and the new aggregate expenditure curve AE_2.

Originally, we had equilibrium at point A with output of $14 trillion when the price level was 100. After the increase in government spending, the aggregate expenditure curve shifts up, and we get equilibrium at point D with output of $14.5 trillion when the price level is 100. Similarly, for any other given price level, equilibrium output would be higher. So, the new aggregate demand curve on the lower diagram has shifted to the right. In sum, changes in the price level create the real wealth, interest rate, and open economy effects which shift the aggregate expenditure curve changing RGDP demanded and these price quantity combinations generate the aggregate demand curve. But at a given price level, changes in spending plans, C, I, G or (X-M), shift the aggregate demand curve.

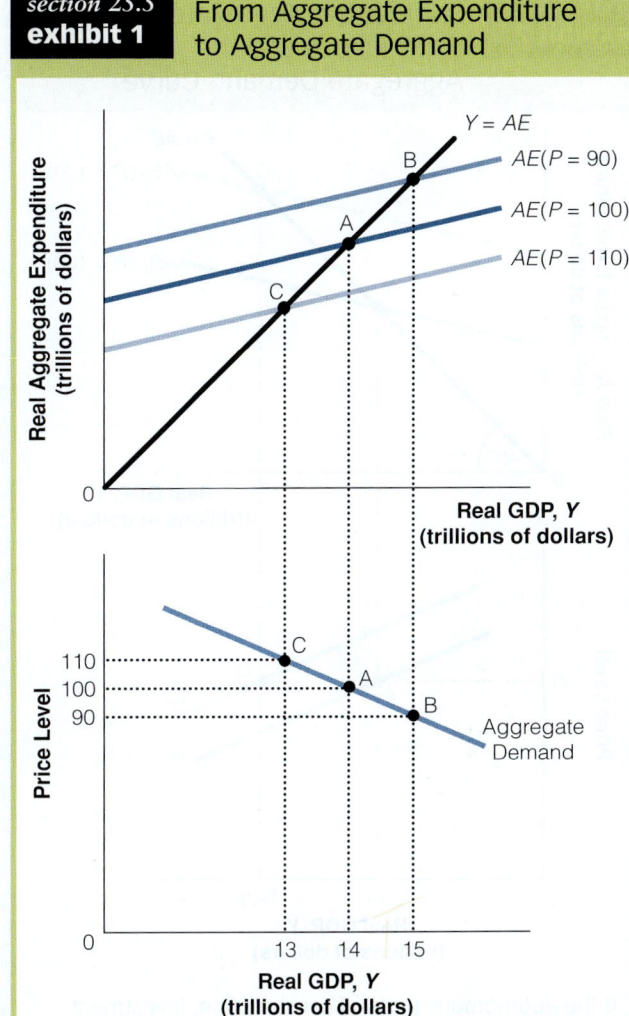

section 25.5 exhibit 1 — From Aggregate Expenditure to Aggregate Demand

Suppose the price level is 100, and suppose at that level of prices, the aggregate expenditure curve is given as the curve labeled $AE(P = 100)$, shown in the top diagram. The equilibrium in the aggregate expenditure model occurs at point A. Now we plot point A in the bottom diagram, corresponding to a price level of 100 and output of $14 trillion. If the price level falls from 100 to 90, the aggregate expenditure curve shifts up to $AE(P = 90)$, and the equilibrium in the Aggregate-cross diagram is at point B. So we plot point B in the bottom diagram, corresponding to price level 90 and output $15 trillion. If the price level rises to 110 the aggregate expenditure curve shifts down to $AE(P = 110)$, and the equilibrium is at point C. We plot point C in the bottom diagram, corresponding to a price level of 110 and output of $13 trillion.

The aggregate demand curve can now be combined with a model of aggregate supply in the economy. As an example, suppose the aggregate supply curve is vertical, as it must be in the long run, because the price level has no long-lasting effect on output. Now, consider our example of an increase

section 25.5 exhibit 2 — Shifting the Aggregate Expenditure and the Aggregate Demand Curve

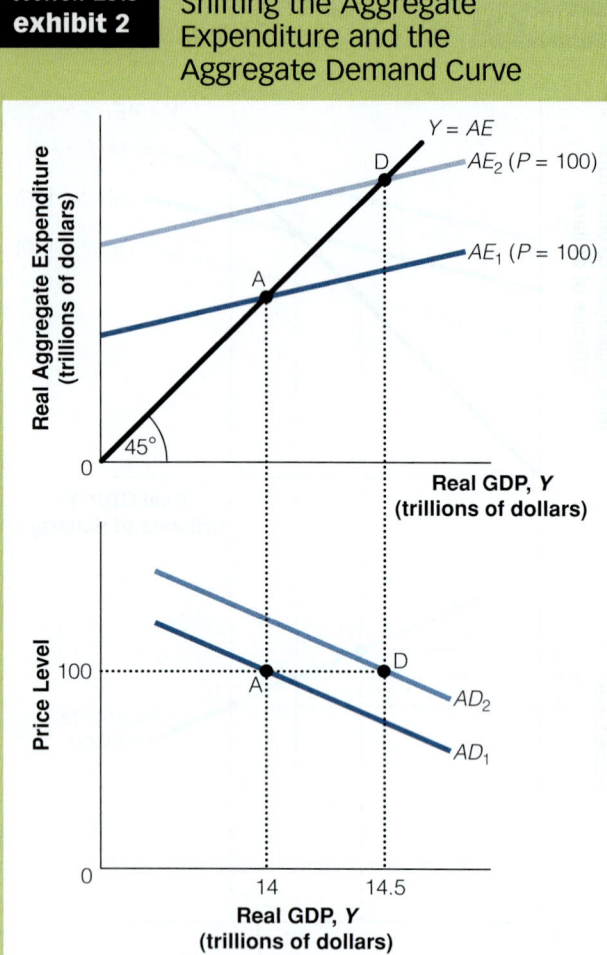

If the autonomous parts of consumption, investment, government purchases, or net exports change, it shifts the aggregate expenditure curve upwards from AE_1 to AE_2. Originally, we had equilibrium at point A with output of $14 trillion when the price level was 100. Now suppose the government increased spending, the aggregate expenditure curve shifts up, and we get equilibrium at point D with output of $14.5 trillion when the price level is 100. Similarly, for any other given price level, equilibrium output would be higher. So, the new aggregate demand curve on the lower diagram has shifted to the right.

section 25.5 exhibit 3 — Aggregate Demand and Aggregate Supply

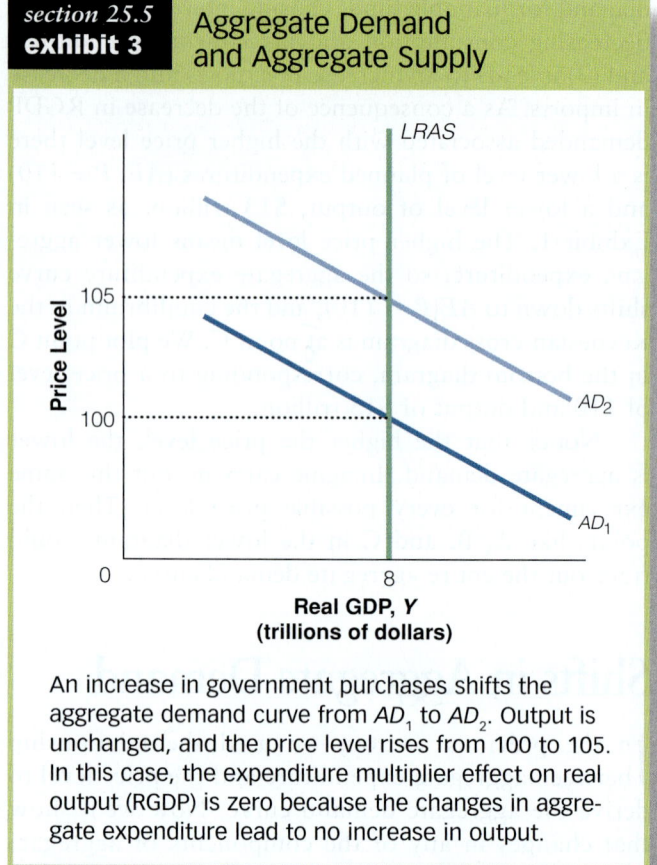

An increase in government purchases shifts the aggregate demand curve from AD_1 to AD_2. Output is unchanged, and the price level rises from 100 to 105. In this case, the expenditure multiplier effect on real output (RGDP) is zero because the changes in aggregate expenditure lead to no increase in output.

in government purchases (or any other autonomous change). As shown in Exhibit 3, the original aggregate demand curve is AD_1 and the increase in government purchases shifts the aggregate demand curve to AD_2. What happens to output? It is unchanged from its original level. A rise in the price level from 100 to 105 is the only effect of the higher level of government expenditures.

Recall in the short run the aggregate supply curve slopes upward, so an increase in aggregate demand will lead to some increase in output in the short run. In that case, the effect on real output in the short run will be greater than zero.

Therefore, the important point is that supply considerations are important in constraining the impact of a change in aggregate expenditure on output.

Limitations of the Aggregate Expenditure Model

The aggregate expenditure model is helpful in explaining how short-run business cycles occur. However, the model fails to show price level changes so there is no way to measure inflation. The model also fails to explain the stagflation of the 1970s—unemployment and inflation together—that is, it does not incorporate possible shifts in the aggregate supply curve. In other words, it cannot explain cost-push inflation. It also does not take into consideration the expectations of consumers and firms as they react to changes in policies designed to stabilize the economy. It does not take into account that an economy can *temporarily* produce beyond the natural rate of real output, $RGDP_{NR}$. It does not allow for the economy to self-correct.

GREAT ECONOMIC THINKERS: JOHN MAYNARD KEYNES (1883–1946)

John Maynard Keynes was born in Cambridge, England, in 1883. Keynes's father was a political economist and logician, his mother a justice of the peace who eventually became the mayor of Cambridge, England.

Many would argue that Keynes was one of the most brilliant minds of the twentieth century. He was educated at Eton and Cambridge, where he studied mathematics and philosophy. Keynes had a brief tutelage under Alfred Marshall who tried to convince Keynes to pursue economics. Keynes began his career in the India Office of the British government. He soon became bored and returned to King's College, Cambridge, to lecture in economics, a post he held until his death in 1946.

Keynes had many interests outside of economics, including mathematics, art, and theater. Keynes married a Russian ballerina and, for a time, he associated with a group of intellectuals known as Bloomsbury Group (which included such notables as E. M. Forster and Virginia Wolff).

Keynes's contributions to the field of economics have influenced public policy since 1930. He is the father of discretionary fiscal policy—deliberating using government spending and taxes to stabilize the economy.

Keynes believed that the economy could stay in a period of unemployment for a long time and not self-correct. Specifically, Keynes emphasized the idea that wages and prices do not always adjust rapidly to bring about full employment in an economy. Keynes believed that government spending could stimulate the economy back to full employment.

Keynes was also a successful investor in the commodity and stock markets. His own net worth increased from a miniscule level in 1920 to over $2 million by the time of his death.

SECTION CHECK

1. The aggregate demand curve is derived by the relationship of the price level and output, plotted by the Keynesian-cross equilibrium at varying price levels.
2. Changes in aggregate expenditures for reasons other than price level or output will shift the aggregate demand curve.
3. When prices are sticky, the *SRAS* curve is flat, meaning that changes in aggregate demand result in little change in the price level, but significant changes in RGDP.
4. Price stickiness is likely when the economy has excess capacity, but is less likely when resources are at full capacity.

---

1. In the aggregate expenditure model, does a lower price level lead to an increase in the real quantity of goods and services demanded or an increase in demand?
2. If autonomous expenditures increased by $20 billion, what is the change in aggregate demand at a given price level if the marginal propensity to consume is 0.75?
3. If autonomous expenditures decreased by $50 billion, what is the change in aggregate demand at a given price level if the marginal propensity to consume is 0.8?
4. Along a vertical long-run aggregate supply curve, what effect will a $10 billion increase in government expenditures have on real output?
5. If the short-run aggregate supply curve is upward sloping, why will the change in real output due to an increase in autonomous expenditures in the short run be less than that indicated by the change in aggregate demand?
6. If wages are sticky downward, why will a decrease in autonomous expenditures reduce real output much like the Keynesian expenditure model indicates?

Interactive Chapter Summary

Fill in the blanks:

1. Keynes believed that _____ was the critical determinant of the overall level of economic activity.
2. In the simple Keynesian model, we assume that the price level is _____ as output changes.
3. _____ spending is the largest component of the demand for final goods and services.
4. The _____ factors affecting consumption are those that do not depend on income.
5. A(n) _____ in real wealth would decrease autonomous consumption.
6. A higher interest rate today tends to make items purchased on credit _____ expensive and _____ expenditures on those items.
7. Either lower interest rates or lower household debt would tend to _____ autonomous consumption.
8. An increase in consumer confidence would tend to _____ consumption spending.
9. Personal consumption spending depends most importantly on your current _____.
10. Your marginal propensity to consume is equal to the change in _____ divided by the change in _____.
11. The more you spend out of any given increase in income, the _____ your marginal propensity to consume.
12. Your marginal propensity to save is equal to the change in _____ divided by the change in _____.
13. The MPC and MPS must add up to _____.
14. The MPC is equal to the _____ of the consumption function.
15. Consumption spending is partly _____, or independent of income, and partly _____, or dependent on income.
16. Income and _____ are always the same in the economy.
17. Aggregate _____ equal _____ when the economy is in equilibrium.
18. In the Keynesian model, if output were lower than its equilibrium level, inventories would _____ desired levels and producers would _____ output.
19. When inventories rise above desired levels, output will _____.
20. When aggregate expenditures exceed output, output will _____.
21. In addition to consumption, the major components of aggregate expenditures are _____, _____, and _____.
22. Only in equilibrium do aggregate expenditures _____ output.
23. One reason that investment contributes to the business cycle is that _____ investment responds dramatically to perceptions about future changes in business activity.
24. When unplanned inventory investment is _____, output will tend to fall.
25. In equilibrium, unplanned business investment _____ zero.
26. An increase in autonomous government purchases by $2 billion will increase output by _____ $2 billion in the simple Keynesian model.
27. The expenditure multiplier is equal to 1 divided by _____, when consumption is the only component of aggregate expenditures.
28. When autonomous investment increases, the level of consumption will _____ as a result.
29. The _____ is MPC, the smaller is the expenditure multiplier.
30. To go from the aggregate expenditure model to aggregate demand, we need to add how the _____ affects each of the aggregate expenditure components.
31. Consumption, investment, and net exports all increase as a result of a _____ in the price level.
32. In terms of the aggregate expenditure model, a fall in the price level shifts the aggregate expenditures curve _____.
33. Changes in any of the components of aggregate expenditures for any reason other than a change in the _____ or _____ will also shift the aggregate demand curve.
34. When the aggregate expenditure curve shifts up for reasons other than changes in the price level, the aggregate demand curve shifts _____.
35. The aggregate supply curve must be _____ in the long run.

36. If the short-run aggregate supply curve slopes upward, an increase in aggregate demand will increase real output _____ than aggregate expenditures in the short run.

37. The aggregate expenditure model could not explain the _____ of the 1970s.

Answers: 1. total spending 2. constant 3. Consumption 4. autonomous 5. decrease 6. more; reduces 7. increase 8. increase 9. disposable income 10. consumption spending; disposable income 11. greater 12. savings; disposable income 13. 1 14. slope 15. autonomous; induced 16. output 17. expenditures; output 18. fall below; increase 19. fall 20. rise 21. investment; government purchases; net exports 22. equal 23. planned 24. positive 25. equals 26. more than 27. $(1 - MPC)$ 28. increase 29. smaller 30. price level 31. fall 32. up 33. price level; income 34. right 35. vertical 36. less 37. stagflation

Key Terms and Concepts

autonomous determinants of consumption expenditures 734

marginal propensity to consume (MPC) 735

marginal propensity to save (MPS) 735

unplanned inventory investment 740

expenditure multiplier 742

Section Check Answers

25.1 Simple Aggregate Expenditure Model

1. **How does the assumption of a fixed price level in the Keynesian expenditure model solve the problem of distinguishing between changes in the real value of a variable (such as GDP) and changes in its nominal value?**
   If the price level is fixed, a change in nominal income is equivalent to a change in real income.

2. **Would it be possible for some consumption expenditures to be autonomous and other parts of consumption expenditure not to be autonomous?**
   Yes. Some consumption depends on income, but other consumption is autonomous (not changing with income), depending on variables such as real wealth, interest rates, and so on.

3. **In what two ways does a higher interest rate tend to reduce current consumption?**
   A higher interest rate reduces current consumption by (1) increasing the cost of consumption items bought on credit and (2) increasing the return to current saving, which increases savings, which in turn reduces consumption.

4. **What would happen to autonomous consumption expenditures if the value of a consumer's stock market investments rose and his household debt rose at the same time?**
   If the value of a consumer's stock market investments rose, it would increase autonomous consumption, but if household debt rose, it would reduce autonomous consumption. Since these effects are in opposite directions, the net effect would be indeterminate, without more information.

5. **What would happen to your autonomous consumption if you expected to get a job paying 10 times your current salary next week?**
   Since your expected future income will rise substantially, just like an increase in real wealth, it will increase your current consumption.

6. **Why do households headed by a 50-year-old tend to save a larger fraction of their incomes than those headed by either a 30-year-old or a 70-year-old?**
   A 50-year-old is in his peak earning years and is also trying to save for retirement, both of which increase saving. A 70-year-old is in retirement and drawing down previous savings. A 30-year-old has a relatively low income and is often faced with the expenses of raising a family.

25.2 Finding Equilibrium in the Aggregate Expenditure Model

1. **If consumption purchases rise with disposable income, how would an increase in taxes affect consumption purchases?**
   An increase in taxes reduces disposable income, which in turn reduces consumption purchases.

2. **If your marginal propensity to consume was 0.75, what is your marginal propensity to save? If your marginal propensity to consume rose to 0.80, what would happen to your marginal propensity to save?**

   Since the marginal propensity to consume plus the marginal propensity to save must equal 1, if MPC = 0.75, MPS = 0.25. If MPC = 0.8, MPS = 0.2.

3. **Could a student have a positive marginal propensity to save, and yet have negative savings (increased borrowing) at the same time?**

   Yes. A student could be increasing his saving (decreasing his dissaving) with each dollar of income earned, yet still have an income low enough (less than autonomous consumption divided by MPS) that he must borrow.

4. **What would happen to the slope of the consumption function if the marginal propensity to save fell?**

   Since the slope of the consumption function equals MPC, a fall in MPS implies an increase in MPC and a steeper consumption function.

5. **Why would an increase in disposable income increase induced consumption but not autonomous consumption?**

   Autonomous consumption is defined as consumption spending that does not depend on income, while induced consumption spending is induced by increases in disposable income.

6. **What tends to happen to inventories if aggregate expenditures exceed output? What tends to happen to output?**

   If aggregate expenditures exceed output, inventories will fall, which will give producers incentives to increase output.

7. **What tends to happen to inventories if output exceeds aggregate expenditures? What tends to happen to output?**

   If output exceeds aggregate expenditures, inventories will rise, giving producers incentives to decrease output.

25.3 Adding Investment, Government Purchases, and Net Exports

1. **When all the nonconsumption components of aggregate expenditures are autonomous, why does the aggregate expenditures line have the same slope as the consumption function?**

   The slope of the aggregate expenditures line equals the change in aggregate expenditures divided by the change in income, but where only consumption depends on income, the change in aggregate expenditures equals the change in consumption, and the aggregate expenditures line has the same slope as the consumption function.

2. **If net exports are negative, what happens to the aggregate expenditures line, other things equal? What will happen to equilibrium income?**

   Autonomous expenditures equals the sum of autonomous consumption plus investment plus government purchases plus net exports. If net exports are negative, autonomous expenditures are lower and the aggregate expenditure line shifts down, resulting in lower equilibrium income.

3. **As the economy turns toward a recession, what happens to unplanned inventory investment? Why? What happens to planned investment? Why?**

   As the economy turns toward a recession, unplanned inventory investment is positive because sales are less than producers' planned. Planned inventory falls because it is very sensitive to perceptions of future changes in business conditions.

4. **How does unplanned inventory investment signal which way real GDP will tend to change in the economy?**

   Unplanned inventory increases signal that demand was weaker than expected, which will tend to result in a decrease in real output and income. Unplanned inventory decreases signal that demand was stronger than expected, which will tend to result in an increase in real output and income.

25.4 Shifts in Aggregate Expenditure and the Multiplier

1. **If autonomous expenditure rises and the marginal propensity to consume rises, what would happen to equilibrium income?**

   Either of these changes moves the AE intersection with the 45° line to the right, increasing equilibrium income.

2. **If autonomous expenditure rises and the marginal propensity to consume falls, what would happen to equilibrium income?**

   Since the first change moved the AE intersection with the 45° line to the right, the second moved it left. Since the two changes would change equilibrium income in opposite directions, we do not know the net effect without more information.

3. **If the marginal propensity to consume was 0.75, what would happen to equilibrium income if government purchases increased by $500 billion and investment fell by $500 billion at the same time? What if government purchases increased by $500 billion and investment fell by $400 billion at the same time?**

   If government purchases increased by $500 billion and investment fell by $500 billion at the same time, there would be no change in autonomous expenditures and therefore no change in equilibrium income. If government purchases increased by $500 billion and investment fell by $400 billion at the same time, autonomous expenditures would increase by $100 billion. It would increase equilibrium income by $100 billion times one over one minus 0.75, or $400 billion.

4. **Why does a larger marginal propensity to consume lead to a larger multiplier?**

   A larger marginal propensity to consume makes the denominator of the multiplier smaller, which makes the multiplier larger.

5. **If autonomous consumption was $300 billion, investment was $200 billion, government purchases were $400 billion, and net exports were a negative $100 billion, what would autonomous consumption be? What would equilibrium income be?**

   Autonomous expenditures are the autonomous components of consumption, investment, and government purchases plus net exports. Here that would be $300 billion plus $200 billion plus $400 billion minus $100 billion, or $800 billion. Equilibrium income would be $800 billion times one over one minus MPC. We cannot calculate that number without knowing MPC.

6. **What would happen to equilibrium income if, other things equal, imports increased by $100 billion and the marginal propensity to consume was 0.9?**

   Net exports would decrease by $100 billion, which would decrease autonomous expenditures by $100 billion. Income would fall by $100 billion times one over one minus 0.9, or $1 trillion.

25.5 From Aggregate Expenditures to Aggregate Demand

1. **In the aggregate expenditure model, does a lower price level lead to an increase in the real quantity of goods and services demanded or on increase in demand?**

   A lower price level increases the real quantity of goods and services demanded. However, because it was caused by a changing price level rather than a change in autonomous expenditures, it does not cause a change in aggregate demand.

2. **If autonomous expenditures increased by $20 billion, what is the change in aggregate demand at a given price level if the marginal propensity to consume is 0.75?**

   AD would increase by the increase in autonomous expenditures times one over one minus MPC, or $20 billion × 4 = $80 billion.

3. **If autonomous expenditures decreased by $50 billion, what is the change in aggregate demand at a given price level if the marginal propensity to consume is 0.8?**

   AD would decrease by the decrease in autonomous expenditures times one over one minus MPC, or $50 billion × 5 = $250 billion.

4. **Along a vertical long-run aggregate supply curve, what effect will a $10 billion increase in government expenditures have on real output?**

   A change in aggregate expenditures, increasing aggregate demand, will have no effect on real output along a vertical long-run aggregate supply curve, regardless of MPC.

5. **If the short-run aggregate supply curve is upward sloping, why will the change in real output due to an increase in autonomous expenditures in the short run be less than that indicated by the change in aggregate demand?**

   If the short-run aggregate supply curve is upward sloping, real output will increase less than the change in aggregate demand.

6. **If wages are sticky downward, why will a decrease in autonomous expenditures reduce real output much like the Keynesian expenditure model indicates?**

   A decrease in autonomous expenditures will reduce AD by the amount indicated by the multiplier formula. If wages are sticky downward, the short-run aggregate supply curve will be nearly horizontal over the relevant range, and the fall in real output would be nearly as great as the fall in AD.

CHAPTER 25 STUDY GUIDE

True or False:

1. In the aggregate expenditure model, when total spending increases, firms increase their output and hire more workers.
2. When we assume the price level is constant, we do not have to distinguish real variable changes from nominal variable changes.
3. The aggregate expenditure approach assumes that prices and wages are constant until we reach full employment.
4. Disposable income is one of the dominant factors in determining the demand for consumer goods.
5. An increase in property values or a stock market boom would tend to reduce autonomous consumption.
6. If either interest rates fell or the level of household debt rose, autonomous consumption would tend to fall.
7. A decrease in consumer confidence would tend to reduce consumption spending.
8. Consumption spending depends most importantly on people's expected future disposable income.
9. If your disposable income increased by $10,000 and as a result, your consumption spending increased by $8,000, you would have a marginal propensity to consume of 0.8.
10. The higher is MPC, the lower is MPS.
11. If your MPC was equal to 0.5, your MPS would also be 0.5.
12. The greater is the MPS, the steeper is the slope of the consumption function.
13. When your disposable income rises, both your total consumption and your total saving rise.
14. Aggregate expenditures always equal consumption expenditures.
15. Income equals output in the economy only in equilibrium.
16. When output is greater than the equilibrium level, inventories would build up above desired levels and producers would reduce output.
17. In the aggregate expenditure model, when inventories fall below desired levels, output will rise.
18. When output is less than aggregate expenditures, output will fall.
19. The greater is savings, for a given level of income, the greater is aggregate expenditures.
20. If investment, government purchases, and net exports are autonomous, the aggregate expenditures curve will have the same slope as the consumption function.
21. Planned investment is sensitive to firms' perceptions about the future.
22. If businesspeople are confident that the economy will be good in the future, output tends to increase.
23. When unplanned inventory investment is negative, output will tend to fall.
24. Increasing planned investment would tend to increase output, but positive unplanned inventory investment would tend to decrease output.
25. The expenditure multiplier applies to any increase in autonomous expenditures.
26. An increase of $10 million in autonomous consumption has the same effect on output as a $10 million increase in autonomous investment.
27. The multiplier process takes place almost instantaneously.
28. Whenever a component of autonomous expenditures increases, consumption will tend to increase as a result.
29. The greater is MPC, the greater is the expenditure multiplier.
30. If MPC equals 0.75, the expenditure multiplier equals 4.
31. Investment as well as consumption spending can depend on current income.
32. An autonomous increase in saving would also be a decrease in autonomous consumption, resulting in decreased output, in the aggregate expenditure model.

33. The aggregate expenditure model is best seen as a model of aggregate demand, and not a complete model of the economy.
34. The components of aggregate demand depend on the price level.
35. An increase in the price level would increase investment but decrease net exports.
36. An increase in the price level shifts up the aggregate expenditure function.
37. A change in the price level would shift the aggregate expenditure function but not aggregate demand.
38. When the aggregate expenditures function shifts up because of an increase in autonomous expenditures due to increased optimism, aggregate demand will shift right.
39. The price level has no effect on real output in the long run.
40. In the long run, an increase in government purchases will increase aggregate demand but not real output.
41. On the flat part of a short-run aggregate supply curve, a decrease in aggregate demand will primarily decrease real output and not change the price level.

Multiple Choice:

1. Demand for consumer goods will be affected by which of the following?
   a. disposable income
   b. credit conditions
   c. the level of debt outstanding
   d. expectations about the future
   e. all of the above

2. Autonomous consumption will increase when
   a. real wealth increases.
   b. the interest rate increases.
   c. household debt increases.
   d. any of the above occur.

3. If autonomous consumption fell, it could have been caused by
   a. falling interest rates.
   b. falling household debt.
   c. more optimistic expectations about future disposable income.
   d. increasing real wealth.
   e. none of the above.

4. If an economy's marginal propensity to consume was 0.75, which of the following is not true?
   a. The consumption function would have a slope of 0.75.
   b. The marginal propensity to save would be 0.25.
   c. Increases in disposable income would increase consumption spending by three times as much as it would increase saving.
   d. Consumption will always equal 75 percent of disposable income.
   e. All of the above would be true.

5. If an economy's MPC was 0.8, which of the following is true?
   a. The MPS would be 1 divided by 0.8, or 0.125.
   b. Consumption would always be four-fifths of income.
   c. The slope of the consumption function would also be 0.8.
   d. An increase in income would not result in four times as large an increase in consumption than the increase in savings.

6. If the MPS is 0.25, which of the following is true?
   a. The slope of the consumption function would be 0.75.
   b. The MPC is 0.75.
   c. Consumption would not always be 75 percent of income.
   d. All of the above are true.

7. Which of the following need not be equal at equilibrium in the aggregate expenditure model?
   a. income and output
   b. aggregate expenditures and output
   c. consumption and income
   d. All of the above must be equal at equilibrium in the aggregate expenditure model.

8. If output was less than the equilibrium level in the aggregate expenditure model, people would be trying to buy _____ goods and services than are being produced, so producers would _____ the amount of production.
   a. more; increase
   b. more; decrease
   c. less; increase
   d. less; decrease

9. If output was greater than the equilibrium level in the aggregate expenditure model, unplanned inventory investment would be _____, leading real output to _____.
   a. positive; increase
   b. positive; decrease
   c. negative; increase
   d. negative; decrease

10. If output was lower than its equilibrium level,
    a. inventories will exceed their desired level.
    b. output will rise.
    c. total expenditures will fall.
    d. the marginal propensity to consume will rise.

11. Output equals income
    a. always.
    b. only in equilibrium.
    c. only when MPC equals MPS.
    d. unless inventories are changing.

12. In addition to consumption, the major components of aggregate expenditures do not include
    a. investment.
    b. saving.
    c. government purchases.
    d. net exports.
    e. All of the above are included in aggregate expenditures.

13. When the autonomous level of investment increases,
    a. at first, inventories will fall below desired levels.
    b. output will rise.
    c. consumption spending will rise.
    d. all of the above will occur.

14. Equilibrium output will tend to increase when
    a. planned investment increases.
    b. unplanned investment is positive.
    c. either planned investment increases or unplanned investment is positive.
    d. either planned investment decreases or unplanned investment is negative.

15. Which of the following would increase aggregate expenditures?
    a. Households become more optimistic about the future.
    b. Interest rates fall.
    c. Foreign economies improve.
    d. Government purchases increase.
    e. Any of the above would increase aggregate expenditures.

16. Real GDP would tend to decrease when planned investment _____ or unplanned inventory investment _____.
    a. increases; increases
    b. increases; decreases
    c. decreases; increases
    d. decreases; decreases
17. Which of the following is true?
    a. A lower price level shifts the aggregate expenditure function upward, moving the economy down along the aggregate demand curve.
    b. A lower price level shifts the aggregate expenditure function upward, shifting the aggregate demand curve to the right.
    c. A lower price level shifts the aggregate expenditure function downward, moving the economy up along the aggregate demand curve.
    d. A lower price level shifts the aggregate expenditure function downward, shifting the aggregate demand curve to the right.
18. Equilibrium output would tend to rise when
    a. autonomous expenditures increase.
    b. the MPC increases.
    c. either autonomous expenditures increase or the MPC increases.
    d. neither autonomous expenditures increase nor the MPC increases.
19. If the MPC equals 0.5,
    a. the expenditure multiplier will equal 2.
    b. a $5 billion increase in investment would tend to increase output by $10 billion.
    c. the expenditure multiplier is less than if the MPC = 0.8.
    d. all of the above are true.
20. Investment can depend on
    a. expectations.
    b. taxes.
    c. interest rates.
    d. current income.
    e. all of the above.
21. When the price level falls,
    a. consumption increases because real wealth increases.
    b. investment rises because interest rates decline.
    c. net exports rise because exchange rates decline.
    d. all of the above are true.
22. Which of the following would shift both the aggregate expenditure function and aggregate demand?
    a. an increase in consumption because disposable income rose
    b. an increase in consumption because the price level fell
    c. an increase in consumption because of increased consumer optimism
    d. All of the above would shift both the aggregate expenditure function and aggregate demand.
23. If the economy was operating on a completely flat segment of the short-run aggregate supply curve, an increase in aggregate demand would
    a. increase output and increase the price level.
    b. increase output and decrease the price level.
    c. decrease output and increase the price level.
    d. decrease output and decrease the price level.
    e. do none of the above.

Problems:

1. Which of the following are likely to cause a reduction in consumption?
   a. an increase in interest rates
   b. an increase in the value of stock market portfolios
   c. a decrease in disposable income
   d. an increase in income taxes
   e. deflation
2. Identify the most volatile component of aggregate expenditure. Identify its largest component.
3. Which of the following will cause the aggregate expenditure schedule to increase?
   a. an increase in consumer optimism
   b. an increase in the purchase of imports
   c. an increase in the sale of exports
   d. pessimism by business owners about the outlook of the economy
   e. an increase in government spending due to the outbreak of war
4. What would happen to autonomous consumption if household debt fell and the interest rate rose over the same time period?
5. What would happen to autonomous consumption if real wealth increased and expectations of the future became more optimistic?
6. Consumption equals $32,000 when disposable income equals $40,000. Consumption increases to $38,000 when disposable income increases to $50,000. What is the marginal propensity to consume? The marginal propensity to save?
7. If the marginal propensity to save increases, what happens to the consumption function?
8. If MPC was equal to 0.5, would doubling your income double your consumption spending?
9. Why can't an economy with an MPC greater than one reach a stable equilibrium in the aggregate expenditure model?
10. Why are unplanned inventory changes the key to predicting future changes in real GDP in the aggregate expenditure model?
11. Why would an increase in planned investment increase real GDP, but an unplanned increase in inventory investment decrease real GDP, in the aggregate expenditure model?
12. If the economy is a net importer, what will that do to the aggregate expenditure function and equilibrium level of real GDP?
13. Why are planned and unplanned investment unlikely to both increase over the same period of time?
14. Why do the aggregate expenditure function and the aggregate demand curve both shift upward at the same time?
15. Evaluate the following statement: The Keynesian assumption of wage and price rigidity best corresponds to the steepest portion of the aggregate supply curve where factories are operating below capacity.
16. Visit the Economy at a Glance page at the Bureau of Economic Analysis, http://www.bea.gov/bea/glance.htm. Locate information about recent changes in inventory levels as well as the ratio of inventory to sales. Can you detect a trend upward or downward in inventory levels? What does the trend bode for national output according to the aggregate expenditure model?

PART 8
MACROECONOMIC POLICY

Chapter 26 Fiscal Policy *758*

Chapter 27 Monetary Institutions *801*

Chapter 28 The Federal Reserve System and Monetary Policy *832*

Chapter 29 Issues in Macroeconomic Theory and Policy *877*

26 Fiscal Policy

26.1 Fiscal Policy
26.2 Fiscal Policy and the *AD/AS* Model
26.3 The Multiplier Effect
26.4 Supply-Side Effects of Tax Cuts

26.5 Possible Obstacles to Effective Fiscal Policy
26.6 Automatic Stabilizers
26.7 The National Debt

In earlier chapters, we discussed how an economy can face a recessionary gap when aggregate demand is deficient or an inflationary gap when there is excessive aggregate demand.

In this chapter, we will see how the government can employ fiscal policy—the use of government purchases, transfers, and/or taxes—to combat recessions or curb inflationary pressures. We will also see that a number of problems are associated with successfully enacting and applying fiscal policy to stabilize an economy. Finally, we will examine the supply-side effects of taxes. ■

SECTION 26.1 Fiscal Policy

- What is fiscal policy?
- How does expansionary fiscal policy affect the government's budget?
- How does contractionary fiscal policy affect the government's budget?

Fiscal Policy

Fiscal policy is the use of government purchases, taxes, and transfer payments to alter RGDP and the price level. Sometimes it is necessary for the government to use fiscal policy to stimulate the economy during a contraction (or recession) or to try to curb an expansion in order to bring inflation under control. In the early 1980s, large tax cuts helped the U.S. economy out of a recession. In the 1990s, Japan used large government spending programs to try to spend itself out of a recessionary slump. In 2001, a large tax cut was implemented to combat an economic slowdown and to promote long-term economic growth in the United States. And the fiscal stimulus package that the Obama administration enacted in 2009 to combat the recession was the largest fiscal stimulus since World War II. But that was small compared to the $2.5 trillion spent on the financial system. When should the government use such policies and how well do they work are just a couple of the questions we will answer in this chapter.

Fiscal Stimulus Affects the Budget

Government spending (for purchases of goods and services and transfer payments) that exceeds tax revenues causes a **budget deficit.** When tax revenues are greater than government spending, a **budget surplus** exists. A balanced budget, where government expenditures equal tax revenues, seldom occurs unless efforts are made to deliberately balance the budget as a matter of public policy.

When the government wishes to stimulate the economy by increasing aggregate demand, it will increase government purchases of goods and services, increase transfer payments, lower taxes, or use some combination of these approaches. Any of those options will increase a budget deficit (or reduce a budget surplus). Thus, **expansionary fiscal policy** is associated with increased government budget deficits. Likewise, if the government wishes to dampen a boom in the economy by reducing aggregate demand, it will reduce its purchases of goods and services, increase taxes, reduce transfer payments, or use some combination of these approaches. Thus, **contractionary fiscal policy** will tend to create or expand a budget surplus, or reduce a budget deficit, if one exists.

> **fiscal policy**
> use of government purchases, taxes, and transfer payments to alter equilibrium output and prices
>
> **budget deficit**
> occurs when government spending exceeds tax revenues for a given fiscal year
>
> **budget surplus**
> occurs when tax revenues are greater than government expenditures for a given fiscal year
>
> **expansionary fiscal policy**
> use of fiscal policy tools to foster increased output by increasing government purchases, lowering taxes, and/or increasing transfer payments
>
> **contractionary fiscal policy**
> use of fiscal policy tools to reduce output by decreasing government purchases, increasing taxes, and/or reducing transfer payments

The Government and Total Spending

In a previous chapter, we learned that the aggregate demand is equal to consumer spending, investment spending, government purchases, and net exports $(X - M)$: $AD = C + I + G + (X - M)$. The government directly controls government purchases, but government can also indirectly affect aggregate demand through taxes and transfer programs. For example, an increase in taxes and/or a reduction in transfer payments can reduce disposable income and decrease consumer spending. Similarly, a decrease in taxes and/or an increase in transfer payment can increase disposable income and lead to an increase in consumer spending. The government can also influence investment spending through business taxes. For example, a tax cut for firms may increase investment spending and shift the aggregate demand curve to the right. Thus, the government can change aggregate demand in a number of ways.

section 26.1 exhibit 1: Summary of Fiscal Policy Tools

Macroeconomic Problem	Fiscal Policy Prescription	Fiscal Policy Tools
Unemployment (Slow or negative RGDP growth rate—below $RGDP_{NR}$)	Expansionary fiscal policy to increase aggregate demand	Cut taxes Increase government purchases Increase government transfer payments
Inflation (Rapid RGDP growth rate—beyond RGDP)	Contractionary fiscal policy to decrease aggregate demand	Raise taxes Decrease government purchases Decrease government transfer payments

global WATCH: JAPAN'S FISCAL POLICY EXPERIMENT

Prior to the 1990s, Japan experienced several decades of rapid economic growth with only a mild recession in 1974. However, the 1990s were a different story—the exuberant bubble burst, as the stock market made a major correction and land values plunged. Consequently, consumption and investment spending—two major components of aggregate demand—fell.

In the decade of the 1990s, Japan grew at an unusually slow rate—1.2 percent per year—almost 3 percentage points below the average growth rate of the previous decade. In order to combat the recession, the Japanese launched a fiscal policy stimulus package of unprecedented tax cuts and spending increases. Government expenditures rose from slightly over 30 percent of GDP to almost 40 percent of GDP. The Japanese government spent well over a trillion dollars during the decade to heal their ailing economy. Because of the tax cuts, government tax revenues fell from 34 percent to 31 percent of GDP. And the continued fiscal efforts, financed with lower taxes and higher government spending, led to a growing debt problem. (The debt-to-GDP ratio almost doubled in the decade of the 1990s—from 0.58 in 1991 to 1.1 in 2000.)

The results of the fiscal policy are mixed. The fiscal policy clearly did not bring about a full recovery. However, some economists argue that without the spending and tax cuts, the Japanese would have suffered a depression rather than a sustained period of slow economic growth. Other economists argue that the wasteful nature of government spending was the reason that fiscal policy was not more successful. The Japanese built bridges, railroad lines, tunnels, and highways to sparsely populated areas. It is safe to say that none of these projects would have been undertaken by the private sector. Thus, a better-designed fiscal policy might have been more effective.

SECTION CHECK

1. Fiscal policy is the use of government purchases of goods and services, taxes, and/or transfer payments to affect aggregate demand and to alter RGDP and the price level.
2. Expansionary fiscal policies will increase the budget deficit (or reduce a budget surplus) through greater government spending, lower taxes, or both.
3. Contractionary fiscal policies will create a budget surplus (or reduce a budget deficit) through reduced government spending, higher taxes, or both.

---

1. If, as part of its fiscal policy, the federal government increases its purchases of goods and services, is that an expansionary or contractionary tactic?
2. If the federal government decreases its purchases of goods and services, does the budget deficit increase or decrease?
3. If the federal government increases taxes and/or decreases transfer payments, is that an expansionary or contractionary fiscal policy?
4. If the federal government increases taxes or decreases transfer payments, does the budget deficit increase or decrease?
5. If the federal government increases government purchases and lowers taxes at the same time, does the budget deficit increase or decrease?

SECTION 26.2 Fiscal Policy and the *AD/AS* Model

* How can government stimulus of aggregate demand reduce unemployment?
* How can government reduction of aggregate demand reduce inflation?

Fiscal Policy and the *AD/AS* Model

The primary tools of fiscal policy, government purchases, taxes, and transfer payments, can be presented in the context of the aggregate supply and demand model. In Exhibit 1, we have used the *AD/AS* model to show how the government can use fiscal policy as either an expansionary or contractionary tool to help close a recessionary or an inflationary gap.

As we discussed earlier, when the government purchases more, taxes less, and/or increases transfer payments, the size of the government's budget deficit will grow. Although budget deficits are often thought to be bad, a case can be made for using budget deficits to stimulate the economy when it is operating at less than full capacity. Such expansionary fiscal policy may have the potential to move an economy out of a contraction (or a recession) and closer to full employment.

Expansionary Fiscal Policy to Close a Recessionary Gap

If the government decides to purchase more, cut taxes, and/or increase transfer payments, other things constant, total purchases will rise. That is, increased government purchases, tax cuts, or transfer payment increases can increase consumption, investment, and government purchases, shifting the aggregate demand curve to the right. The effect of this increase in aggregate demand depends on the position of the macroeconomic equilibrium before the government stimulus. For example, in Exhibit 1, the initial equilibrium is at E_1, a recession scenario, with real output below potential RGDP. Starting at this point and moving along the short-run aggregate supply curve, an increase in government purchases, a tax cut, and/or an increase in transfer payments would increase the size of the budget deficit and lead to an increase in aggregate demand, ideally from AD_1 to AD_2. The result of such a change would be an increase in the price level, from

section 26.2 exhibit 1: Expansionary Fiscal Policy to Close a Recessionary Gap

The increase in government purchases, a tax cut, and/or an increase in transfer payments leads to a rightward shift in aggregate demand. This shift results in a change in equilibrium from E_1 to E_2, reflecting a higher price level and a higher RGDP. Thus, the expansionary fiscal policy can close the recessionary gap and move the economy from $RGDP_1$ to $RGDP_{NR}$. Because this result is on the LRAS curve, it is a long-run, sustainable equilibrium.

section 26.2 exhibit 2

Contractionary Fiscal Policy to Close an Inflationary Gap
The reduction in government purchases, a tax increase, or transfer payment decrease leads to a leftward shift in aggregate demand and a change in the short-run equilibrium from E_1 to E_2, reflecting a lower price level and a return to full-employment RGDP ($RGDP_{NR}$). The final long-run effect is a new lower price level and real output that has returned to $RGDP_{NR}$, and the inflationary gap is closed.

PL_1 to PL_2, and an increase in RGDP, from $RGDP_1$ to $RGDP_{NR}$. If the policy change is of the right magnitude and timed appropriately, the expansionary fiscal policy might stimulate the economy, pull it out of the contraction and/or recession, and result in full employment at $RGDP_{NR}$. The recessionary gap is then closed.

Contractionary Fiscal Policy to Close an Inflationary Gap

Suppose that the price level is at PL_1 and that short-run equilibrium is at E_1, as shown in Exhibit 2. Say that the government decides to reduce its purchases, increase taxes, or reduce transfer payments. A government purchase change may directly affect aggregate demand.

A tax increase on consumers or a decrease in transfer payments will reduce households' disposable incomes, reducing purchases of consumption goods and services, and higher business taxes will reduce investment purchases. The reductions in consumption, investment, and/or government purchases will shift the aggregate demand curve leftward, ideally from AD_1 to AD_2. This lowers the price level from PL_1 to PL_2 and brings RGDP back to the full-employment level at $RGDP_{NR}$, resulting in a new short- and long-run equilibrium at E_2, and the inflationary gap is closed.

Global Watch

GLOBAL TAX COMPARISONS: TAX REVENUES AS A PERCENTAGE OF GDP

This chart takes into account the total taxes, including "stealth" taxes (green and carbon taxes, for example) imposed by a country at all levels, national and local, as a share of GDP. It includes as well overall government spending, which will only get worse in reaction to the economic meltdown and contracting economies around the world. Some countries, such as Norway, are running large surpluses because of North Sea oil taxes. Others, such as France, are spending more than they're taking in. The resulting deficits are covered by public debt repaid through future taxes and stealth taxes.

[1] OECD 2007 report.

SOURCE: OECD, 2006 report.

POLICY application: THE NEW DEAL AND EXPANSIONARY FISCAL POLICY?

Roosevelt's sweep into office allowed him to push through Congress a massive amount of legislation in the first 100 days of his administration. Roosevelt did not enter the presidency with the idea that government deficit spending was a necessary stimulus to economic recovery. In fact, it was only later in his administration that he appears to have believed deficit spending would help the economy in its gravely depressed state.

Despite all of the fanfare about the first 100 days of Roosevelt's campaign for programs against the Depression, it is not really clear that they had much effect on aggregate demand. After all, besides considering what programs were instituted, we also have to look at how they were paid for and at what other programs were dropped.

In Roosevelt's campaign, he criticized Hoover for large budget deficits that had been marked up after the Crash of 1929. In fact, Hoover's administration had the largest federal deficit in the history of the United States prior to Roosevelt's election. Once elected, Roosevelt told Congress that he did not want the country to be "wrecked on the rocks of loose fiscal policy." Deficits during the Depression years were indeed small. In fact, in 1937 the total government budget, including federal, state, and local levels, had a surplus of $0.3 billion. During this time, taxes were repeatedly raised.

Fiscal policies, then, were in fact extremely weak, and even perverse. At the same time that the federal government was increasing expenditures, local and state governments were decreasing them. If we measure the total of state, federal, and local fiscal policies, we find that they were truly expansive only in 1931 and 1936 as compared to what the government was doing prior to the Depression. These two years were expansive only because of large veterans' payments, passed by Congress in both years—by the way, over the vigorous opposition of both Hoover and Roosevelt. In both 1933 and 1937, and, to a lesser degree, in 1938, fiscal policy was quite a bit less expansionary than in 1939.

Continued tepid use of increased government spending and a slow increase in private investment led to a slow improvement, and finally by 1939 output exceeded 1929 in real terms. Because of productivity advances and a growth in the labor force, however, the return to 1929 output levels did not mean an end to unemployment. The 1939 unemployment rate of 17.2 percent was much lower than the 1933 rate, but still well above a typical unemployment rate of 5 percent.

Preparations for war in 1941 led to a 77 percent increase in government spending over the previous year. This $11 billion increase in government purchases of goods and services, followed by still greater increases in subsequent years as the United States entered World War II, led to aggregate demand increases of a magnitude to wipe out unemployment and end the Depression, which was by far the worst in U.S. history.

SOURCE: From *Issues in American Economic History 1st edition* by MILLER/SEXTON. 2005. Reprinted with permission of South-Western, a division of Thomson Learning: http://www.thomsonrights.com. Fax 800 730-2215.

SECTION CHECK

1. If the government decided to purchase more, cut taxes, and/or increase transfer payments, that would increase total purchases and shift the aggregate demand curve to the right.
2. If the correct magnitude of expansionary fiscal policy is used in a recession, it could potentially bring the economy to full employment at a higher price level.
3. Contractionary fiscal policy has the potential to offset an overheated inflationary boom.

---

1. If the economy is in recession, what sort of fiscal policy changes would tend to bring it out of recession?
2. If the economy is at a short-run equilibrium at greater than full employment, what sort of fiscal policy changes would tend to bring the economy back to a full-employment equilibrium?
3. What effects would an expansionary fiscal policy have on the price level and real GDP, starting from a full-employment equilibrium?
4. What effects would a contractionary fiscal policy have on the price level and real GDP, starting from a full-employment equilibrium?

SECTION 26.3 The Multiplier Effect

* What is the multiplier effect?
* How does the marginal propensity to consume affect the multiplier effect?
* How does investment interact with the multiplier effect?

Government Purchases, Taxes, and Aggregate Demand

Recall from our earlier discussion that any one of the major spending components of aggregate demand (C, I, G, or $X - M$) can initiate changes in aggregate demand, thereby producing a new short-run equilibrium. If policymakers are unhappy with the present short-run equilibrium GDP, perhaps they consider unemployment too high because of a current aggregate demand shortfall. If government were to increase its purchases of jet fighters, highways, and schools, this increased spending would lead to an increase in aggregate demand. That is, they can deliberately manipulate the level of government purchases to obtain a new short-run equilibrium value. But how much new additional government purchasing is necessary?

The Multiplier Effect

Usually, when an increase in purchases of goods or services occurs, the ultimate increase in total purchases tends to be greater than the initial increase, which is known as the **multiplier effect**. But how does this effect work? Suppose the government increases its defense budget by $10 billion to buy aircraft carriers. When the government purchases the aircraft carriers, not only does it add to the total demand for goods and services directly, but it also provides $10 billion in added income to the companies that actually construct the aircraft carriers. These companies will then hire more workers and buy more capital equipment and other inputs to produce the new output. The owners of these inputs therefore receive more income because of the increase in government purchases. What will they do with this additional income? Although behavior will vary somewhat among individuals, collectively they will probably spend a substantial part of the additional income on additional consumption purchases, pay some additional taxes incurred because of the income, and save a bit of it as well. The **marginal propensity to consume (MPC)** is the fraction of additional disposable (after-tax) income that a household consumes rather than saves. That is, MPC is equal to the *change* in consumption

multiplier effect
a chain reaction of additional income and purchases that results in total purchases that are greater than the initial increase in purchases

marginal propensity to consume (MPC)
the additional consumption resulting from an additional dollar of disposable income

spending (ΔC) divided by the *change* in disposable income (ΔDY).

$$MPC = \Delta C/\Delta DY$$

For example, suppose you won a lottery prize of $1,000. You might decide to spend $750 of your winnings today and save $250. In this example, your marginal propensity to consume is 0.75 (or 75 percent), because out of the extra $1,000, you decided to spend 75 percent of it (0.75 × $1,000 = $750). The term *marginal propensity to consume* has two parts: (1) *marginal* refers to the fact that you received an *extra* amount of disposable income—an addition to your income, not your total income; and (2) *propensity to consume* refers to how much you tend to spend on consumer goods and services out of your additional income.

The flip side of the marginal propensity to consume is the **marginal propensity to save (MPS),** which is the proportion of an addition to your income that you would save, or not spend on goods and services today. That is, MPS is equal to the change in savings (ΔS) divided by the change in disposable income (ΔDY).

$$MPS = \Delta S/\Delta DY$$

In the lottery example, your marginal propensity to save is 0.25, or 25 percent, because you decided to save 25 percent of your additional disposable income (0.25 × $1,000 = $250). Because your additional disposable income must be either consumed or saved, the marginal propensity to consume plus the marginal propensity to save must add up to 1, or 100 percent.

marginal propensity to save (MPS)
the change in savings divided by the change in disposable income

purchases, individuals collectively spend two-thirds, or 67 cents, on consumption purchases. In other words, the MPC is 2/3. The initial $10 billion increase in government purchases causes both a $10 billion increase in aggregate demand and an income increase of $10 billion to suppliers of the inputs used to produce aircraft carriers; the owners of those inputs, in turn, will spend an additional $6.67 billion (2/3 of $10 billion) on additional consumption purchases. A chain reaction has been started. The added $6.67 billion in consumption purchases by those deriving income from the initial investment brings a $6.67 billion increase in aggregate demand and in new income to suppliers of the inputs that produced the goods and services. These persons, in turn, will spend some two-thirds of their additional $6.67 billion in income, or $4.44 billion, on consumption purchases. This $4.44 billion becomes aggregate demand and income to still another group of people, who will then proceed to spend two-thirds of that amount, or $2.96 billion, on consumption purchases.

The chain reaction continues, with each new round of purchases providing income to a new group of people who in turn increase their purchases. As successive changes in consumption purchases occur, the feedback becomes smaller and smaller. The added income generated and the number of resulting consumer purchases get smaller because some of the increase in income goes to savings and tax payments that do not immediately flow into greater investment or government spending. As indicated in Exhibit 1, the fifth change in consumption is indeed much smaller than the first change in consumption.

What is the total impact of the initial increase in government purchases on additional consumption and

The Multiplier Effect at Work

Suppose that out of every dollar in *added* disposable income generated by increased investment

section 26.3 exhibit 1 — The Multiplier Process

Change in government purchases	$10.00 billion—direct effect on *AD*	
First change in consumption purchases	6.67 billion (2/3 of 10)	
Second change in consumption purchases	4.44 billion (2/3 of 6.67)	The sum of the indirect effect on *AD*, through induced additional consumption purchases, is equal to $20 billion
Third change in consumption purchases	2.96 billion (2/3 of 4.44)	
Fourth change in consumption purchases	1.98 billion (2/3 of 2.96)	
Fifth change in consumption purchases	1.32 billion (2/3 of 1.98)	
⋮	⋮	

$30 billion = Total change in aggregate demand

income? We can find the answer by using the multiplier formula, calculated as follows:

$$Multiplier = 1/(1 - MPC)$$

In this case,

$$Multiplier = 1/(1 - 2/3) = 1/(1/3) = 3$$

An initial increase in government purchases of $10 billion will increase total purchases by $30 billion ($10 billion $\times$ 3), as the initial $10 billion in government purchases also generates an additional $20 billion in consumption.

Changes in the MPC Affect the Multiplier Process

Note that the larger the marginal propensity to consume, the larger the multiplier effect, because relatively more additional consumption purchases out of any given income increase generates relatively larger secondary and tertiary income effects in successive rounds of the process. For example, if the MPC is 3/4, the multiplier is 4:

$$Multiplier = 1/(1 - 3/4) = 1/(1/4) = 4$$

If the MPC is only 1/2, however, the multiplier is 2:

$$Multiplier = 1/(1 - 1/2) = 1/(1/2) = 2$$

The Multiplier and the Aggregate Demand Curve

As we discussed earlier, when the federal Department of Defense decides to buy additional aircraft carriers, it affects aggregate demand. It increases the incomes of owners of inputs used to make the aircraft carriers, including profits that go to the owners of the firms involved. That is the initial effect. The secondary effect—the greater income that results—will lead to increased consumer purchases. In addition, the higher profits for the firms involved in carrier construction may lead them to increase their investment purchases. So the initial effect of the government's purchases will tend to have a multiplied effect on the economy. In Exhibit 2, we can see that the initial impact of a $10 billion additional purchase by the government directly shifts the aggregate demand curve from AD_1 to AD_2. The multiplier effect then causes the aggregate demand to shift out $20 billion further, to AD_3. If MPC is 2/3, the total effect on aggregate demand of a $10 billion increase in government purchases is therefore $30 billion.

section 26.3 exhibit 2 The Multiplier Aggregate Demand

In this hypothetical example, an increase in government purchases of $10 billion for new aircraft carriers will shift the aggregate demand curve to the right by more than the $10 billion initial purchase, other things being equal. It will shift aggregate demand by a total of $30 billion, to AD_3. (The shifts are shown larger than they would really be for visual ease; $30 billion is a small shift in a $10,000 billion economy.)

Tax Cuts and the Multiplier

If the government finds that it needs to use fiscal stimulus to move the economy to the natural rate, increased government spending is only one alternative. The government can also stimulate business and consumer spending through tax cuts. Both Japan (1999) and the United States (2001 and 2003) have recently employed tax cuts to stimulate their economies.

How much of an AD shift do we get from a change in taxes? As in the case of government spending, it depends on the marginal propensity to consume. However, the tax multiplier is smaller than the government spending multiplier because government spending has a direct impact on aggregate demand, while a tax cut has only an indirect impact on aggregate demand. Why? Because consumers will save some of their income from the tax cut. So if the MPC is 3/4, then when their disposable income rises by $1,000, households will increase their consumption by $750 while saving $250 of the added income.

To compare the multiplier effect of a tax cut with an increase in government purchases, suppose there were a $10 billion tax cut and that the MPC is 2/3. The initial increase in consumption spending from the tax cut would be 2/3 $\times$ $10 billion (MPC $\times$ tax cut) = $6.67 billion. Because in this case people would save one-third of their tax cut income, the effect on aggregate demand of the change in taxes would be smaller than that of a change of equal size in government purchases. The cumulative change in spending (the increase in AD) due to the $10 billion tax cut is found by plugging the initial effect of the changed consumption spending into our earlier formula: $1/(1 - \text{MPC}) \times \$6.67$ billion, which is $3 \times \$6.67 = \$20$ billion. So the initial tax cut of $10 billion leads to a stimulus of $20 billion in consumer spending. Although this amount is less than the $30 billion from government purchases, it is easy to see why tax cuts and government purchases are both attractive policy prescriptions for a slow economy.

Taxes and Investment Spending

Taxes can also stimulate investment spending. For example, if a cut in corporate-profit taxes leads to expectations of greater after-tax profits, it could fuel additional investment spending. That is, tax cuts designed for consumers and investors can stimulate both the C and I components of aggregate demand. A number of administrations have used this strategy to stimulate aggregate spending and shift the aggregate demand curve to the right: Kennedy (1963), Reagan (1981), and Bush (2001 and 2003).

A Reduction in Government Purchases and Tax Increases

A reduction in government purchases and tax increases are magnified by the multiplier effect, too. Suppose the government made cutbacks in the space program. Not only would it decrease government purchases directly, but aerospace workers would be laid off and unemployed workers would cut back on their consumption spending; this initial cutback would have a multiplying effect through the economy, leading to an even greater reduction in aggregate demand. Similarly, tax hikes would leave

---

Use what you've LEARNED: THE BROKEN WINDOW FALLACY

Whenever a government program is justified not on its merits but by the jobs it will create, remember the broken window: Some teenagers toss a brick through a bakery window. A crowd gathers and laments, "What a shame." But before you know it, someone suggests a silver lining to the situation: Now the baker will have to spend money to have the window repaired. This will add to the income of the repairman, who will spend his additional income, which will add to another seller's income, and so on. You know the drill. The chain of spending will multiply and generate higher income and employment. If the broken window is large enough, it might produce an economic boom! . . .

Most voters fall for the broken window fallacy, but not students of economic principles. They will say, "Hey, wait a minute!" If the baker hadn't spent his money on window repair, he would have spent it on the new suit he was saving to buy. Then the tailor would have the new income to spend, and so on. The broken window didn't create net new spending; it just diverted spending from somewhere else. The broken window does not create new activity, just different activity. People see the activity that takes place. They don't see the activity that *would* have taken place.

The broken window fallacy is perpetrated in many forms. Whenever job creation or retention is the primary objective, I call it the job-counting fallacy. Students of economics principles understand the nonintuitive reality that real progress comes from job destruction. It once took 90 percent of our population to grow our food. Now it takes 3 percent. Pardon me, but are we worse off because of the job losses in agriculture? The would-have-been farmers are now college profs and computer gurus or singing the country blues on Sixth Street.

If you want jobs for jobs' sake, trade in bulldozers for shovels. If that doesn't create enough jobs, replace shovels with spoons. But there will always be more work to do than people to work. So instead of counting jobs, we should make every job count.

SOURCE: Robert D. McTeer Jr., "The Dismal Science? Hardly," *The Wall Street Journal*, June 4, 2003. Copyright © 1998 by Robert D. McTeer Jr.

consumers with less disposable income, so they would cut back on their consumption, which would lower aggregate demand and set off the multiplier process, leading to an even larger cumulative effect on aggregate demand.

Time Lags, Saving, and Imports Reduce the Size of the Multiplier

The multiplier process is not instantaneous. If you get an additional $100 in income today, you may spend two-thirds of that on consumption purchases eventually, but you may wait six months or even longer to do it. Such time lags mean that the ultimate increase in purchases resulting from an initial increase in purchases may not be achieved for a year or more. The extent of the multiplier effect visible within a short time will be less than the total effect indicated by the multiplier formula. In addition, saving and money spent on import goods (which are not part of aggregate demand for domestically produced goods and services) will reduce the size of the multiplier, because each of them reduces the fraction of a given increase in income that will go to additional purchases of domestically produced consumption goods.

It is also important to note that the multiplier effect is not restricted to changes in government purchases and taxes. The multiplier effect can apply to changes that alter spending in any of the components of aggregate demand: consumption, investment, government purchases, or net exports.

Some have argued that the multiplier effect of a new sports stadium, for example, will lead to additional local spending that will be three or four times the amount of the initial investment. However, this outcome is unlikely. It is important to remember that money spent on the stadium (taxpayer dollars) could also have been spent on food, clothing, entertainment, recreation, and many other goods and services. So the expenditures on the stadium come at the expense of other consumer expenditures. In addition, the multiplier is most effective when it brings idle resources into production. If all resources are fully employed, the expansion in demand and the multiplier effect will lead to a higher price level, not increases in employment and RGDP.

The 2008-09 Recession

The 2008-09 recession will probably end up being the worst recession since the Great Depression. It has lead to the largest peacetime fiscal expansion in history. Many countries around the world have been increasing the size of their budget deficits by cutting taxes and increased government spending. There is debate among economists on the effectiveness of fiscal policy to stimulate the economy and much of that debate depends on the size of the multiplier. A multiplier of 1 means that an increase in government purchases of $1 billion would increase aggregate demand and lead to an increase in $1 billion of RGDP. The economy could now have new highways, bridges, fighter jets and aircraft carriers without sacrificing other components of aggregate demand like private consumption and investment. How is this possible? The answer is that these are idle resources that are now being put to use. If the multiplier is greater than 1 it is even more magical; RGDP rises by more than than the increase in government purchases.

The Obama economists believe the multiplier for government purchases is close to 1.6 (a $1 billion increase in government spending will increase a country's GDP by $1.6 billion) and the multiplier for taxes is closer to 1. Other economists believe that the multiplier is much smaller and will boost the economy by about 20 percent of what the Obama team expects.

However, economists do agree that the multiplier is very small—close to zero—when the economy is at or near full employment and that the effectiveness of fiscal policy depends on the type of action that is taken. For example, the short-run effect of government spending on infrastructure like highways and bridges tends to be greater than, say, that of a tax cut where individuals will save a large portion of their tax windfall. Tax cuts for poorer people may be more effective than those for richer, because the poor tend to spend a larger proportion of their additional (marginal) income. Economists also agree that tax multipliers are much higher when taxes are permanent than when they are temporary and that fiscal multipliers will be lower in heavily indebted economies than in prudent ones.

In the words of macroeconomist Robert Barro, "Do not use the cover of fiscal policy to undertake massive public works programs that do not pass muster from the perspective of cost-benefit analysis . . . it is wrong now to think that added government spending is free."

SECTION CHECK

1. The multiplier effect is a chain reaction of additional income and purchases that results in a final increase in total purchases that is greater than the initial increase in purchases.
2. An increase in the marginal propensity to consume leads to an increase in the multiplier effect.
3. Because of a time lag, the full impact of the multiplier effect on GDP may not be felt until a year or more after the initial investment.
4. An increase in government purchases will also cause an increase in aggregate income and stimulate additional consumer purchases, which will result in a magnified (or multiplying) effect on aggregate demand.

---

1. How does the multiplier effect work?
2. What is the marginal propensity to consume?
3. Why is the marginal propensity to consume always less than one?
4. Why does the multiplier effect get larger as the marginal propensity to consume gets larger?
5. If an increase in government purchases leads to a reduction in private-sector purchases, why will the effect on the economy be smaller than that indicated by the multiplier?

SECTION 26.4 Supply-Side Effects of Tax Cuts

* What is supply-side?
* How do supply-side policies affect long-run aggregate supply?
* What do its critics say about supply-side ideas?

What Is Supply-Side?

The debate over short-run stabilization policies has been going on for some time, with no sign that it is close to being settled. When policymakers discuss methods of stabilizing the economy, the focus since the 1930s has been on managing the economy through demand-side policies. But a group of economists believes that we should be focusing on the supply side of the economy as well, especially in the long run, rather than just on the demand side. In particular, they believe that individuals will save less, work less, and provide less capital when taxes, government transfer payments (such as welfare), and regulations are too burdensome on productive activities. In other words, they believe that fiscal policy can work on the supply side of the economy as well as the demand side.

Impact of Supply-Side Policies

Supply-siders would encourage government to reduce individual and business taxes, deregulate, and increase spending on research and development. Supply-siders believe that these types of government policies could generate greater long-term economic growth by stimulating personal income, savings, and capital formation.

Research and Development and the Supply Side of the Economy

Some economists believe that investment in research and development will have long-run benefits for the economy. In particular, greater research and development will lead to new technology and knowledge, which will permanently shift the short- and long-run aggregate supply curves to the right. The government could encourage investments in research and development by giving tax breaks or subsidies to firms. The challenge, of course, is to produce *productive* research and development.

How Do Supply-Side Policies Affect Long-Run Aggregate Supply?

We see in Exhibit 1 that rather than being primarily concerned with short-run economic stabilization, supply-side policies are aimed at increasing both the short-run and long-run aggregate supply curves. If these policies are successful and maintained, output and employment will increase in the long run, as reflected in the shift from $RGDP_{NR}$ to $RGDP'_{NR}$. Both short- and long-run aggregate supply will increase over time, as the effects of deregulation and major structural changes in plant and equipment work their way through the economy. It takes workers some time to fully respond to improved work incentives.

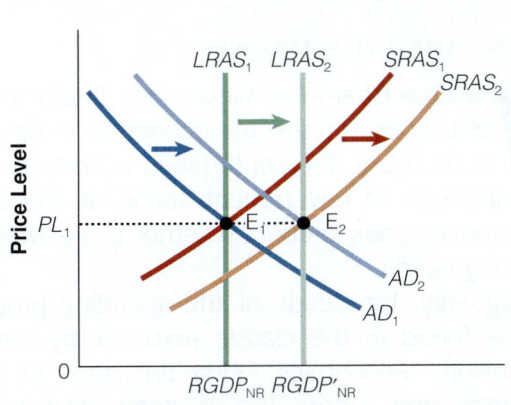

section 26.4 exhibit 1 The Impact of Supply-Side Policies on Short-Run and Long-Run Aggregate Supply

The impact of a permanent reduction in tax rates and regulations together with investments in research and development could create long-term effects on income, saving, and capital formation, shifting both the SRAS curve and the LRAS curve rightward. As income rises and is spent, the aggregate demand curve shifts to the right.

Critics of Supply-Side Economics

Of course, those who believe in supply-side economics have their critics. These critics are skeptical about the magnitude of the impact of lower taxes on work effort and the impact of deregulation on productivity. Critics claim that the tax cuts of the 1980s led to moderate real output growth but only through a reduction in real tax revenues, inflation, and large budget deficits.

Although real economic growth followed the tax cuts, supply-side critics say that it came as a result of a large budget deficit. The critics raise several questions: What will happen to the distribution of income if most supply-side policies focus on benefits to those with capital? Will people save and invest much more if capital gains taxes are reduced (capital gains are increases in the value of an asset)? It may be more likely that saving and investment is driven by changes in income and expectations of profitability. How much more work effort will we see if marginal tax rates are lowered? The increase in the quantity of labor supplied following a tax cut is likely to be limited since most workers are already working 40 hour weeks and do not have opportunities to work more hours. Will the new production that occurs from deregulation be enough to offset the benefits thought by many to come from regulation?

The Supply-Side and Demand-Side Effects of a Tax Cut

A tax cut can lead to greater incentives to work and save—an increase in aggregate supply (short-run and long-run)—and to demand-side stimulus from the increased disposable income (income after taxes) and an increase in aggregate demand. But how much will the tax rate affect aggregate demand and aggregate supply? We do not know for sure, but let's look at two possible outcomes of the supply-side effects of a tax cut. We will focus on the aggregate demand curve and the SRAS curve. Suppose the tax cut leads to a large increase in AD but only a small increase in SRAS. What happens to the price level and RGDP? The more traditional view of a fiscal policy tax cut is shown in Exhibit 2(a). We can see that RGDP increases from $RGDP_1$ to $RGDP_2$ and price level increases from PL_1 to PL_2. The good news

in the news

Is Government Spending Too Easy an Answer?

—BY N. GREGORY MANKIW

When the Obama administration finally unveils its proposal to get the economy on the road to recovery, the centerpiece is likely to be a huge increase in government spending. But there are ample reasons to doubt whether this is what the economy needs.

Arguably, the seeds of the spending proposal can be found in the classic textbook by Paul A. Samuelson, "Economics." First published in 1948, the book and others like it dominated college courses in introductory economics for the next half-century. It is a fair bet that much of the Obama team started learning how the economy works through Mr. Samuelson's eyes. Most notably, Lawrence H. Summers, the new head of the National Economic Council, is Mr. Samuelson's nephew.

Written in the shadow of the Great Depression and World War II, Mr. Samuelson's text brought the insights of John Maynard Keynes to the masses. A main focus was how to avoid, or at least mitigate, the recurring slumps in economic activity.

"When, and if, the next great depression comes along," Mr. Samuelson wrote on the first page of the first edition, "any one of us may be completely unemployed—without income or prospects." He added, "It is not too much to say that the widespread creation of dictatorships and the resulting World War II stemmed in no small measure from the world's failure to meet this basic economic problem adequately."

Economic downturns, Mr. Keynes and Mr. Samuelson taught us, occur when the aggregate demand for goods and services is insufficient. The solution, they said, was for the government to provide demand when the private sector would not. Recent calls for increased infrastructure spending fit well with this textbook theory.

But there is much to economics beyond what is taught in Econ 101. In several ways, these Keynesian prescriptions make avoiding depressions seem too easy. When debating increased spending to stimulate the economy, here are a few of the hard questions Congress should consider:

How Much Bang for Each Buck?

Economics textbooks, including Mr. Samuelson's and my own more recent contribution, teach that each dollar of government spending can increase the nation's gross domestic product by more than a dollar. When higher government spending increases G.D.P., consumers respond to the extra income they earn by spending more themselves. Higher consumer spending expands aggregate demand further, raising the G.D.P. yet again. And so on. This positive feedback loop is called the multiplier effect.

In practice, however, the multiplier for government spending is not very large. The best evidence comes from a recent study by Valerie A. Ramey, an economist at the University of California, San Diego. Based on the United States' historical record, Professor Ramey estimates that each dollar of government spending increases the G.D.P. by only 1.4 dollars. So, by doing the math, we find that when the G.D.P. expands, less than a third of the increase takes the form of private consumption and investment. Most is for what the government has ordered, which raises the next question.

Will the Extra Spending Be on Things We Need?

If you hire your neighbor for $100 to dig a hole in your backyard and then fill it up, and he hires you to do the same in his yard, the government statisticians

in the news

report that things are improving. The economy has created two jobs, and the G.D.P. rises by $200. But it is unlikely that, having wasted all that time digging and filling, either of you is better off.

People don't usually spend their money buying things they don't want or need, so for private transactions, this kind of inefficient spending is not much of a problem. But the same cannot always be said of the government. If the stimulus package takes the form of bridges to nowhere, a result could be economic expansion as measured by standard statistics but little increase in economic well-being.

The way to avoid this problem is a rigorous cost-benefit analysis of each government project. Such analysis is hard to do quickly, however, especially when vast sums are at stake. But if it is not done quickly, the economic downturn may be over before the stimulus arrives.

How Will It All End?

Over the last century, the largest increase in the size of the government occurred during the Great Depression and World War II. Even after these crises were over, they left a legacy of higher spending and taxes. To this day, we have yet to come to grips with how to pay for all that the government created during that era—a problem that will become acute as more baby boomers retire and start collecting the benefits promised.

Rahm Emanuel, the incoming White House chief of staff, has said, "You don't ever want to let a crisis go to waste: it's an opportunity to do important things that you would otherwise avoid."

What he has in mind is not entirely clear. One possibility is that he wants to use a temporary crisis as a pretense for engineering a permanent increase in the size and scope of the government. Believers in limited government have reason to be wary.

Might Tax Cuts Be More Potent?

Textbook Keynesian theory says that tax cuts are less potent than spending increases for stimulating an economy. When the government spends a dollar, the dollar is spent. When the government gives a household a dollar back in taxes, the dollar might be saved, which does not add to aggregate demand.

The evidence, however, is hard to square with the theory. A recent study by Christina D. Romer and David H. Romer, then economists at the University of California, Berkeley, finds that a dollar of tax cuts raises the G.D.P. by about $3. According to the Romers, the multiplier for tax cuts is more than twice what Professor Ramey finds for spending increases.

Why this is so remains a puzzle. One can easily conjecture about what the textbook theory leaves out, but it will take more research to sort things out. And whether these results based on historical data apply to our current extraordinary circumstances is open to debate. . . .

N. Gregory Mankiw is a professor of economics at Harvard. He was an adviser to President Bush.

SOURCE: From N. Gregory Mankiw, "Is Government Spending Too Easy an Answer?", 'New York Times', January 11, 2009. Copyright © 2009 The New York Times. All rights reserved. Used by permission and protected by the Copyright Laws of the United States. The printing, copying, redistribution, or retransmission of the Material without express written permission is prohibited.

---

is that the price level rises less than it would if there were no supply-side effect to the tax cut. Without the supply-side effect from the tax cut, the price level would rise to PL_3. But what if the supply-side effect were much larger, as shown in Exhibit 2(b)? It could completely offset the higher price-level effect of an expansionary fiscal policy, as RGDP rises from $RGDP_1$ to $RGDP_2$ and the price level stays constant at PL_1.

Both the Kennedy tax cut (1964) and the Reagan tax cut of the early 1980s, which lowered marginal tax rates and helped the economy recover from the 1980–1981 recession, likely raised the growth rate of potential GDP—shifting the $LRAS$ rightward.

Fiscal policy was used infrequently in the United States and Europe from the 1980s to the late 1990s because of concerns over large budget deficits. However,

section 26.4 exhibit 2 — Two Possible Supply-Side Effects of a Tax Cut

If the supply-side tax cut has a small effect on the *SRAS* but a large effect on *AD*, then RGDP increases from $RGDP_1$ to $RGDP_2$, while the price level rises from PL_1 to PL_2, as shown in (a). However, if the supply-side tax cut has a large effect on *SRAS* and a large effect on *AD*, then RGDP increases from $RGDP_1$ to $RGDP_2$, and the price level is constant at PL_1, as shown in (b).

the budget surplus that emerged in the latter half of the 1990s opened the gate for increased government spending and the Bush tax cut in 2001. Most economists agree that taxes alter incentives and distort market outcomes, as we learned in Chapter 6. Taxes clearly change people's behavior; and the tax cuts that lead to the strongest incentives to work, save, and invest will lead to the greatest economic growth and will be the least inflationary.

SECTION CHECK

1. Supply-side fiscal policy advocates believe that people will save less, work less, and provide less capital when taxes, government transfers, and regulations are too burdensome.
2. Supply-side policies are designed to increase output and employment in the long run, causing the long-run and short-run aggregate supply curves to shift to the right.
3. Critics of supply-side economics question the magnitude of the impact of lower taxes on work effort, saving, and investment, as well as the impact of deregulation on productivity.

1. Is supply-side economics more concerned with short-run economic stabilization or long-run economic growth?
2. Why could you say that supply-side economics is really more about after-tax wages and after-tax returns on investment than it is about tax rates?
3. Why do government regulations have the same sort of effects on businesses as taxes?
4. Why are the full effects of supply-side policies not immediately apparent?
5. If taxes increase, what would you expect to happen to employment in the underground economy? Why?

SECTION 26.5 Possible Obstacles to Effective Fiscal Policy

* How does the crowding-out effect limit the economic impact of increased government purchases or reduced taxes?
* How do time lags in policy implementation affect policy effectiveness?

The Crowding-Out Effect

The multiplier effect of an increase in government purchases implies that the increase in aggregate demand will tend to be greater than the initial fiscal stimulus, other things being equal. However, because all other things will not tend to stay equal in this case, the multiplier effect may not hold true. For example, when an increase in government purchases stimulates aggregate demand, it also drives up the interest rate. In particular, when the government borrows money to finance the deficit, it increases the overall demand for money in the money market. The increase in the demand for money increases the price paid for borrowing money—the interest rate. As a result of the higher interest rate, consumers may decide against buying a car, a home, or other interest-sensitive goods, and businesses may cancel or scale back plans to expand or buy new capital equipment. In short, the higher interest rate will choke off private spending on goods and services; and, as a result, the impact of the increase in government purchases may be smaller than first assumed. Economists call this the **crowding-out effect.**

In Exhibit 1, suppose government purchases initially increased by $10 billion. This change by itself would shift aggregate demand to the right by $10 billion times the multiplier, from AD_1 to AD_2. However, when the government borrows in the money market to pay for increases in government purchases, the interest rate increases. The higher interest rate crowds out investment spending, causing the aggregate demand curve to shift left, from AD_2 to AD_3. Because both these processes are taking place at the same time, the net effect is an increase in aggregate demand from AD_1 to AD_3 rather than to AD_2.

Critics of the Crowding-Out Effect

Critics of the crowding-out effect argue that the increase in government spending, particularly if the economy is in a severe recession, may actually improve consumer and business expectations and encourage private investment spending. It is also possible for the monetary authorities to increase the money supply in order to offset the higher interest rate, resulting from the crowding-out effect.

crowding-out effect
theory that government borrowing drives up the interest rate, lowering consumption by households and investment spending by firms

The Crowding-Out Effect in the Open Economy

Another form of crowding out can take place in international markets. For example, say the government increases spending, which leads to an increase in the demand for money to pay for the spending and drives up the interest rate (assuming the money supply is unchanged). The higher U.S. interest rate will attract funds from abroad. To invest in the

section 26.5 exhibit 1 The Crowding-Out Effect

Government borrowing to finance a deficit leads to a higher interest rate and lower levels of private investment spending. The lower levels of private spending can crowd out the fiscal policy effect, shifting aggregate demand to the left from AD_2 to AD_3. The net effect of the fiscal policy is a small increase in aggregate demand, AD_1 to AD_3, not the larger increase from AD_1 to AD_2.

U.S. economy, foreigners will first have to convert their currencies into dollars. The increase in the demand for dollars relative to other currencies will cause the dollar to appreciate in value, making foreign imports relatively cheaper in the United States and U.S. exports relatively more expensive in other countries. This change will cause net exports $(X - M)$ to fall, for two reasons. One, because of the higher relative price of the dollar, foreign imports will become cheaper for those in the United States, and imports will increase. Two, because of the higher relative price of the dollar, U.S.-made goods will become more expensive to foreigners, and exports will decrease. The increase in imports and the decrease in exports will cause a reduction in net exports and a fall in aggregate demand. The net effect will be that fiscal policy will have a smaller effect on aggregate demand than it would otherwise.

Time Lags in Fiscal Policy Implementation

It is important to recognize that in a democratic country, fiscal policy is implemented through the political process, and that process takes time. Often, the lag between the time that a fiscal response is desired and the time an appropriate policy is implemented and its effects felt is considerable. Sometimes a fiscal policy designed to deal with a contracting economy may actually take effect during a period of economic expansion, or vice versa, resulting in a stabilization policy that actually destabilizes the economy.

The Recognition Lag

Government tax or spending changes require both congressional and presidential approval. Suppose the economy is beginning a downturn. It may take two or three months before enough data are gathered to indicate the actual presence of a downturn. This time span is called the *recognition lag*. Sometimes a future downturn can be forecast through econometric models or by looking at the index of leading indicators, but usually decision makers are hesitant to plan policy on the basis of forecasts that are not always accurate.

The Implementation Lag

At some point, however, policymakers may decide that some policy change is necessary. At this point, experts are consulted, and congressional committees hold hearings and listen to testimony on possible policy approaches. During the consultation phase, many decisions have to be made. If, for example, a tax cut is recommended, what form should the cut take, and how large should it be? Across-the-board income tax reductions? Reductions in corporate taxes? More generous exemptions and deductions from the income tax (e.g., for child care, casualty losses, education of children)? In other words, who should get the benefits of lower taxes? Likewise, if the decision is made to increase government expenditures, which programs should be expanded or initiated, and by how much? Because these questions have profound political consequences, reaching decisions is seldom easy and usually involves substantial compromise and a great deal of time.

Finally, once the House and Senate have completed their separate deliberations and have arrived at a final version of the fiscal policy bill, it is presented to Congress for approval. After congressional approval is secured, the bill then goes to the president for approval or veto. These steps are all part of what is called the *implementation lag*.

During the period 1990–1991, the actual output of the economy was less than the potential output of the economy—a recessionary gap. Because automatic stabilizers resulted in lower taxes and larger transfer payments, consumption did not fall as far as it might have.

However, before President Clinton began his term in 1993, he believed that more was needed, so he put together a stimulus package of additional government spending and tax cuts. But by the time the bill reached the floor of Congress, the recession was over, illustrating how difficult it is to time fiscal stimulus. When the economy went into recession in March of 2001, but it was not until a year later that the stimulus package was signed into law. Another example is when President John F. Kennedy thought the economy was operating below its potential in 1962; Congress finally passed a tax cut in 1964.

The Impact Lag

Even after legislation is signed into law, it takes time to bring about the actual fiscal stimulus desired. If the legislation provides for a reduction in withholding taxes, for example, it might take a few months before the changes show up in workers' paychecks. With respect to changes in government purchases, the delay is usually much longer. If the government increases spending for public works projects such as sewer systems, new highways, or urban renewal, it takes time to draw up plans and get permissions, to advertise for bids from

in the news: Fiscal Policy and the Financial Crisis

This [financial] crisis is rubbing salt in old wounds. It is reopening debates about one of the most contentious questions in macro, namely, the ability of government deficit spending (i.e., fiscal policy) to stimulate demand and get people back to work.

In January the fight over fiscal policy broke out in public after then-President-elect Barack Obama made what probably seemed to him a safe claim, saying: "There is no disagreement that we need action by our government, a recovery plan that will help to jump-start the economy." Not long after, some 250 conservative economists, in an open letter published in major newspapers, wrote: "With all due respect Mr. President, that is not true."

. . . Believing in the power of the Fed, economists mostly stopped researching the use of fiscal policy to fight recessions or depressions. What's more, recessions had become rarer and milder—the so-called Great Moderation. So who needed stimulus? Says New York University economist Xavier Gabaix: "Up until a year ago, you would look very old-fashioned if you were talking about optimal fiscal policy."

Mainstream economists' adherence to orthodoxy was also apparent in their casual dismissal of worries about bubbles in housing and stocks. Former Fed Chairman Alan Greenspan denied that a national housing bubble was even possible, since housing was not a single national market. He also brushed off the dangers of Wall Street concoctions such as derivatives. Only last year did he concede he was wrong. In Senate testimony, he said he was shocked to have found a "flaw" in his ideology, adding: "I have been going for 40 years or more with very considerable evidence that it was working exceptionally well."

Politics compounded the trouble. As a rough first cut, you can divide macroeconomists based on how concerned they are about economic instability. One group, in the tradition of Keynes, worries about self-perpetuating economic declines that leave the economy in a deep trough it can't escape. Members of this group say government needs to break downward spirals with the kinds of aggressive policies the U.S. is following now—cutting interest rates and raising government spending. The group includes Paul R. Krugman, the Princeton University economist and Nobel laureate; NYU's Nouriel Roubini, who was early in predicting a severe recession; and Yale University's Robert J. Shiller, who predicted the housing bust and the tech-stock bust.

Other economists have more confidence that the economy is self-equilibrating. They believe low interest rates and heavy deficit spending will be ineffective while leaving the U.S. with a mountain of debt. Count Harvard's Robert Barro in this

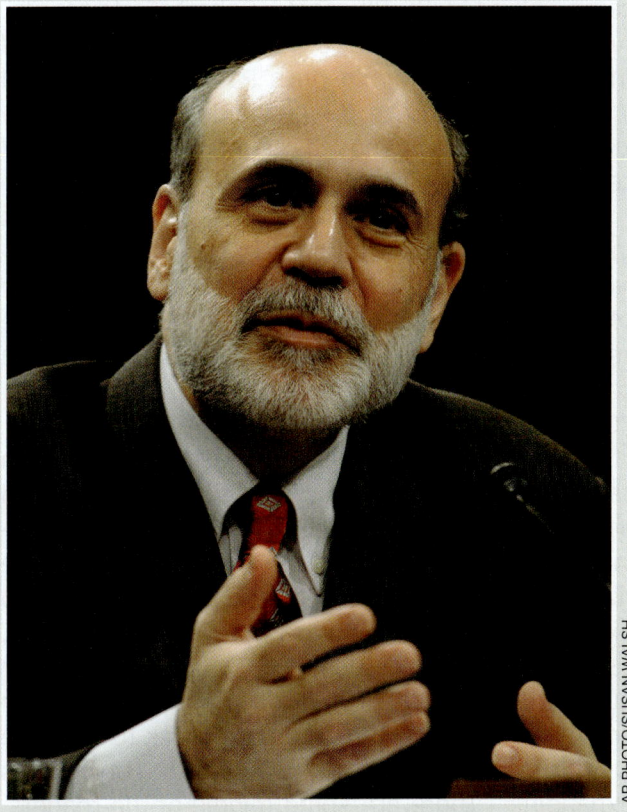

"You're right, we did it. We're very sorry. But thanks to you, we won't do it again" Ben Bernanke, In a Speech on Milton Friedman's 90th Birthday Acknowledging the Fed's Role in Deepening the Great Depression, Nov. 8, 2002

(continued)

in the news (cont.)

camp, along with Chicago's Robert E. Lucas Jr., Arizona State University's Edward C. Prescott, and the University of Minnesota's Patrick J. Kehoe and V. V. Chari. No surprise, the equilibrium school mainly leans Republican, and the interventionist school seems to be crawling with Democrats.

Before this crisis, it seemed that economists might resolve their differences. The oft-combative Krugman, in the first edition of his textbook *Macroeconomics* in 2006, wrote that "the clean little secret of modern macroeconomics is how much consensus economists have reached over the past 70 years."

The mood now is uglier. On the left, Krugman says: "This is really fairly shameful, that we should be wasting precious months as a profession retracing debates that were settled 70 years ago." On the right, John H. Cochrane of the University of Chicago dismisses those who advocate Keynesian stimulus, saying: "Professional economists, the guys I hang out with, are not reverting to ancient Keynesianism any more than physicists are going back to Aristotle when they can't understand how fast the universe is expanding." There are some middle-of-the-roaders, such as Columbia University's Michael Woodford, who argue that macroeconomists are converging on a methodology for asking questions. But even Woodford agrees that "recent debates don't particularly make the field look unified."

The easiest criticism of macroeconomists is that nearly all failed to foresee the recession despite plenty of warning signs. In early September 2008, the median growth forecast for the fourth quarter was 0.2%, according to a survey by *Blue Chip Economic Indicators*. The actual outcome was a 6.3% annualized decline. The Fed didn't do any better. In July 2008, Fed officials projected unemployment in the fourth quarter of 2008 would end up between 5.5% and 5.8%. The actual number was 6.9%. Their projection for the fourth quarter of 2009, done at the same time, was for a range of 5.2% to 6.1%. Today, with unemployment at 8.5%, most forecasters expect the rate to be nearing double digits by the end of 2009.

Now that fiscal policy is back on the table, economists are fighting over the size of the ripple effect—or "multiplier"—of increased government spending. Interventionist economists think multipliers are large when the economy is operating below capacity—and it certainly is now. According to a Fed report on Apr. 15, one-third of manufacturing's productive capacity is going unused, the biggest share on record back to 1948.

Obama Administration officials believe that their fiscal policy is on the right track. The stimulus program "is putting a little more energy into the consumer," National Economic Council Director Summers told Maria Bartiromo (page 12). "Two months ago you couldn't find anything positive." Christina D. Romer, Obama's chief economic adviser and a historian of the Depression, said in March that "at some point, recovery will take on a life of its own." Until then, she said, government should watch closely "to make sure the private sector is back in the saddle" before easing off.

Other economists say increased government spending may actually depress private employment. At a Council on Foreign Relations event on Mar. 30, Chicago's Lucas called the Administration's multiplier math "kind of schlock economics."

The truth is, even backers of stimulus can't be sure it will work. As World War II ended, many economists worried that growth would lapse as military spending fell. Sewell Avery, the CEO of Montgomery Ward, was so anxious about a postwar depression that he refused to open new stores. Economists still aren't sure why he was wrong, so they can't say reliably whether fiscal stimulus will end this recession or just interrupt it. "Is it possible to engineer a durable recovery with fiscal expansion, or are you just buying time?" asks Krugman, who favors coupling stimulus with drastic action to fix the banks.

What, then, is the way forward? Once this crisis is past, the next agenda for macroeconomists will be to help make the economy far more robust—enough to survive the blunders of politicians, bankers, and economists of the future.

contractors, to get contracts, and then to begin work. Further delays might occur because of government regulations. For example, an environmental impact statement must be completed before most public works projects can begin, a process that often takes many months or even years, called the *impact lag*.

> ### SECTION CHECK
>
> 1. The crowding-out effect states that as the government borrows to pay for the deficit, it drives up the interest rate and crowds out private investment spending.
> 2. If crowding out causes a higher U.S. interest rate, it will attract foreign funds. In order to invest in the U.S. economy, foreigners will have to first convert their currencies into dollars. The increase in the demand for dollars relative to other currencies will cause the dollar to appreciate in value, making foreign imports relatively cheaper in the United States and U.S. exports relatively more expensive in other countries. This change will cause net exports (X − M) to fall and is called the crowding-out effect in the open economy.
> 3. The lag time between when a fiscal policy may be needed and when it is actually implemented is considerable.
>
> 1. Why does a larger government budget deficit increase the magnitude of the crowding-out effect?
> 2. Why does fiscal policy have a smaller effect on aggregate demand the greater the crowding-out effect is?
> 3. How do time lags affect the effectiveness of fiscal policy?

SECTION 26.6 Automatic Stabilizers

* What are automatic stabilizers?
* Which automatic stabilizers are the most important?

Automatic Stabilizers

Some changes in government transfer payments and taxes take place automatically as business cycle conditions change, without deliberations in Congress or the executive branch of the government. Changes in government transfer payments or tax collections that automatically tend to counter business cycle fluctuations are called **automatic stabilizers**.

automatic stabilizers changes in government transfer payments or tax collections that automatically help counter business cycle fluctuations

How Do the Tax System and Transfer Payments Stabilize the Economy?

The most important automatic stabilizer is the tax system. Personal income taxes vary directly in amount with income and, in fact, rise or fall by greater percentages than income itself. Big increases and big decreases in GDP are both lessened by automatic changes in income tax receipts. Because incomes, earnings, and profits all fall during a recession, the government collects less in taxes. When you work less, you are paid less and therefore pay less in taxes. It's like an automatic tax cut that acts to reduce the severity of a recession. This is also true for payroll taxes, which depend on a worker's earnings, and corporate income taxes, which depend on a firm's profits. When earnings and profits fall during a recession, so do government revenues. So, like the personal income tax, the corporate income tax and payroll taxes are automatic stabilizers, too. This reduced tax burden partially offsets the magnitude of the recession. Beyond this factor, the unemployment compensation program is another source of automatic stabilization. During recessions, unemployment is usually high and unemployment

Automatic stabilizers work without legislative action. The stabilizers serve as shock absorbers for the economy. But the key is that they do it quickly.

compensation payments increase, providing income that will be consumed by recipients. During boom periods, such payments will fall as the number of unemployed decreases. The system of public assistance (such as food stamps, Temporary Assistance for Needy Families, and Medicaid) payments tends to be another important automatic stabilizer because the number of low-income persons eligible for some form of assistance grows during recessions (stimulating aggregate demand) and declines during booms (reducing aggregate demand). Perhaps the Great Depression would not have been so "great" if automatic stabilizers had been in place. Many had to dig into their savings and cut back on their spending, which made matters worse.

Automatic stabilizers are not strong enough to completely offset a serious recession. However, they certainly reduce the severity of a recession, without the problems associated with lags that were discussed in the last section.

SECTION CHECK

1. Automatic stabilizers are changes in government transfer payments or tax collections that happen automatically and with effects that vary inversely with business cycles.
2. The tax system is the most important automatic stabilizer; it has the greatest ability to smooth out swings in GDP during business cycles. Other automatic stabilizers are unemployment compensation and welfare payments.

1. How does the tax system act as an automatic stabilizer?
2. Are automatic stabilizers affected by a time lag? Why or why not?
3. Why are transfer payments such as unemployment compensation effective automatic stabilizers?

SECTION 26.7 The National Debt

* What are budget deficit and budget surplus?
* How is the national debt financed?
* What has happened to the federal budget balance?
* What impact does a budget deficit have on the interest rate?
* What impact does a budget surplus have on the interest rate?

Fiscal Stimulus Affects the Budget

As discussed earlier in the chapter, when government spending exceeds tax revenues, a budget deficit results. When tax revenues are greater than government spending, a budget surplus exists. A balanced budget occurs through deliberate efforts that are a matter of public policy.

Budget Deficit:

Government Spending > Tax Revenues

Budget Surplus:

Tax Revenues > Government Spending

How Government Finances the Debt

For many years, the U.S. government ran budget deficits and built up a large federal debt. How did it pay for those budget deficits? After all, it has to have some means of paying out the funds necessary to support government expenditures that are in excess of the funds derived from tax payments. One thing the government can do is simply print money—dollar bills. This approach was used to finance much of the Civil War budget deficit, both in the North and in the Confederate states. However, printing money to finance activities is highly inflationary and also undermines confidence in the government. Typically, the budget deficit is financed by issuing debt. The federal government in effect borrows an amount necessary to cover the deficit by issuing bonds, or IOUs, payable typically at some maturity date. The total of the values of all bonds outstanding constitutes the federal debt. Exhibit 1 shows the improvement in the federal budget balance since the early 1990s as a result of economic growth and the efforts of the president and Congress to control the growth of government spending.

Why Run a Budget Deficit?

From 1960 through 1997, the federal budget was in deficit every year except one—in 1969, the government ran a small budget surplus. Budget deficits can be important because they provide the federal government with the flexibility to respond appropriately to changing economic circumstances. For example, the government may run deficits during special emergencies such as military involvements, earthquakes, fires, or floods. The government may also use a budget deficit to avert an economic downturn.

Historically, the largest budget deficits and a growing government debt occur during war years, when defense spending escalates and taxes typically do not rise as rapidly as spending. The federal government will also typically run budget deficits during recessions, as taxes are cut and government spending increases. However, in the 1980s, deficits and debt soared in a relatively peaceful and prosperous time. In 1980, President Reagan ran a platform of lowering taxes and reducing the size of government. Although the tax cuts occurred, the reduction in the growth of government spending did not. The result was huge peacetime budget deficits and a growing national debt that continued through the early 1990s, as shown in Exhibit 1.

However, when President Clinton took office in 1993, he set a goal to reduce the budget deficit. This goal was a high priority for both Democrats and Republicans. And after nearly a decade of uninterrupted economic growth, the deficit eventually turned into a budget surplus. In 2001 the budget surplus slipped into a deficit for three primary

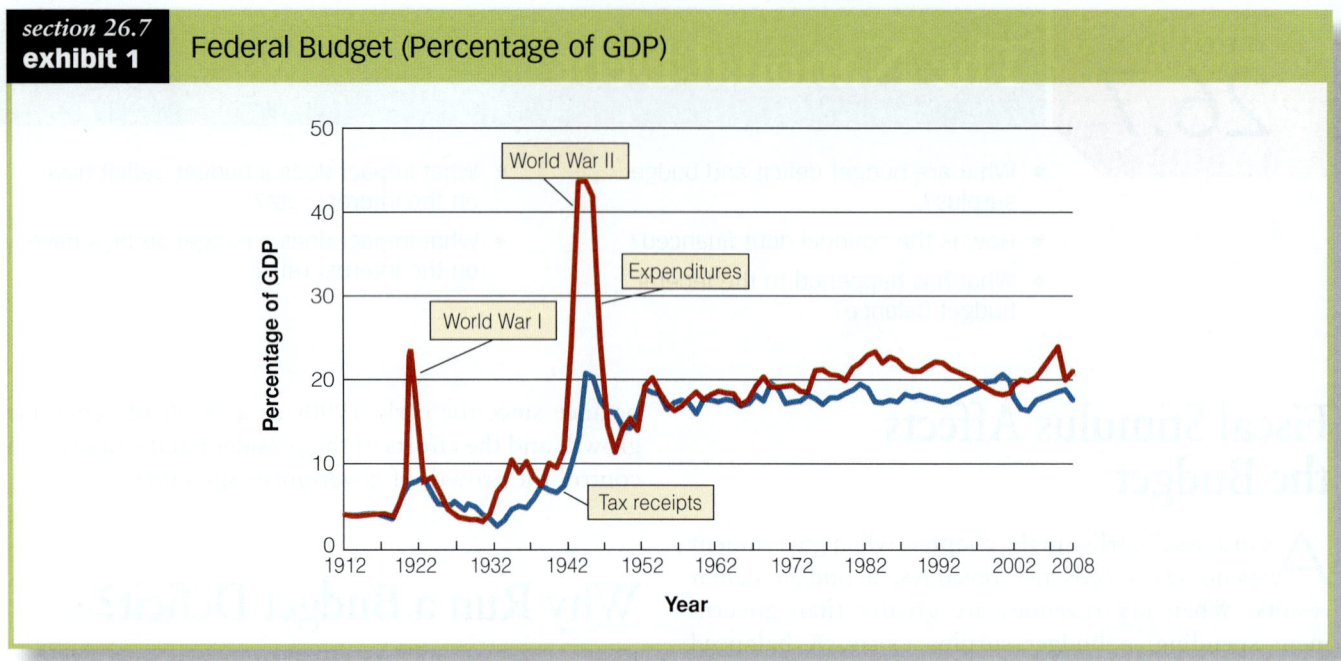

section 26.7 exhibit 1 Federal Budget (Percentage of GDP)

SOURCE: Office of Management and Budget, Historical Tables, Budget of the United States Government, Fiscal Year 2009.

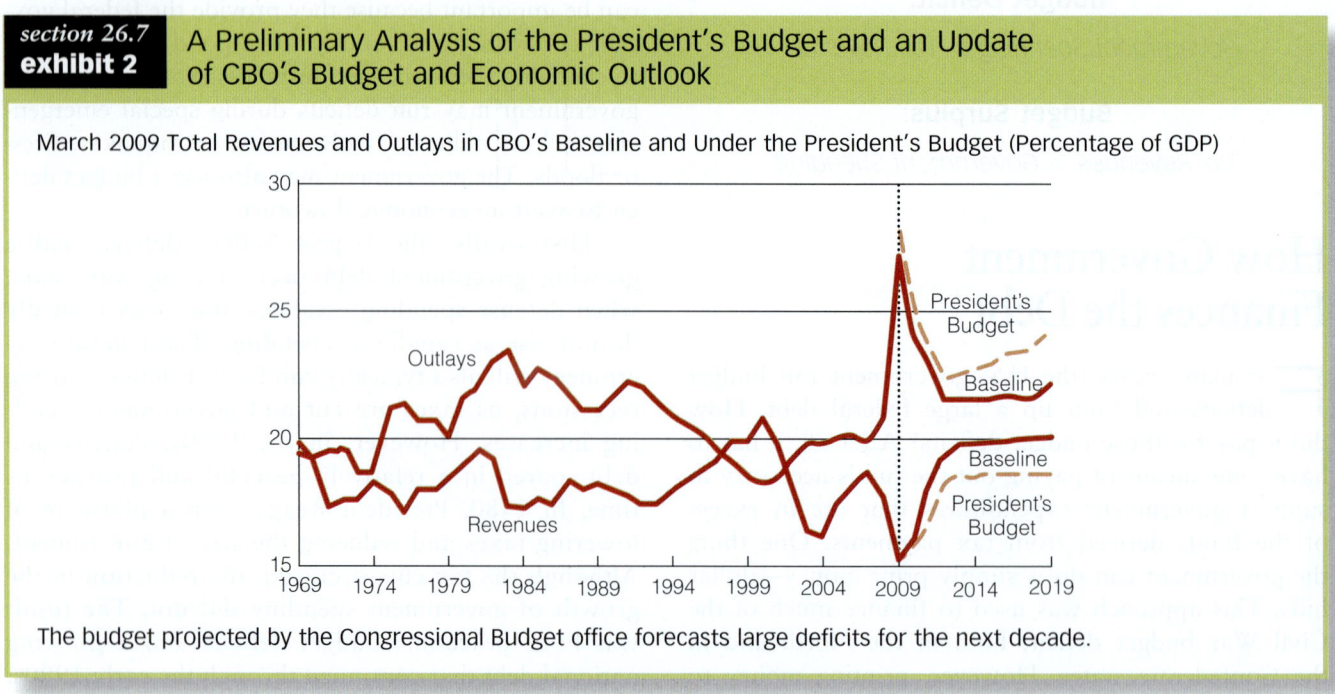

section 26.7 exhibit 2 A Preliminary Analysis of the President's Budget and an Update of CBO's Budget and Economic Outlook

March 2009 Total Revenues and Outlays in CBO's Baseline and Under the President's Budget (Percentage of GDP)

The budget projected by the Congressional Budget office forecasts large deficits for the next decade.

reasons: (1) the 2001 tax cut that President Bush promised in his presidential campaign; (2) the war on terrorism and wars in Iraq and Afghanistan; and (3) the 2001 recession that led to less tax revenue and greater government spending. However, in looking at the future projections in Exhibit 2, it appears the United States will face large deficits for the next decade.

An Increase in the Budget Deficit: Short-Run and Long-Run Effects

Recall that when the government borrows to finance a budget deficit, it causes the interest rate to rise. The higher interest rate will crowd out private

section 26.7 exhibit 3 Reducing a Budget Deficit—The Short-Run Effects

In the short run, a reduction in the budget deficit (higher taxes and/or a reduction in government purchases) will lead to a reduction in aggregate demand. The leftward shift of aggregate demand from AD_1 to AD_2 leads to a lower price level and a lower level of RGDP.

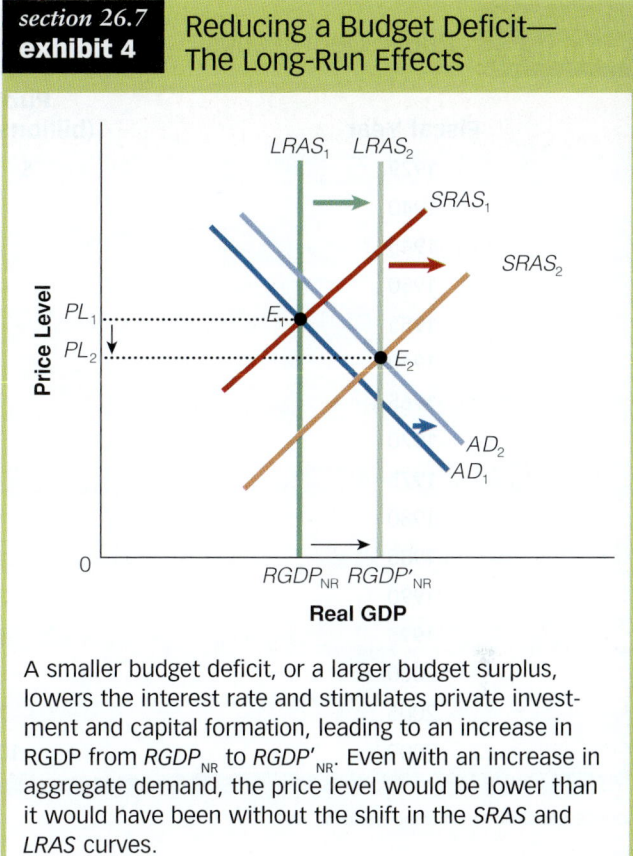

section 26.7 exhibit 4 Reducing a Budget Deficit—The Long-Run Effects

A smaller budget deficit, or a larger budget surplus, lowers the interest rate and stimulates private investment and capital formation, leading to an increase in RGDP from $RGDP_{NR}$ to $RGDP'_{NR}$. Even with an increase in aggregate demand, the price level would be lower than it would have been without the shift in the SRAS and LRAS curves.

investment by households and firms. Higher private investment and increases in capital formation are critical in a growing economy. However, what if the government runs a budget deficit reduction (or surplus)?

In the short run, deficit reduction is the same as running contractionary fiscal policy; either tax increases and/or a reduction in government purchases will shift the aggregate demand curve to the left, from AD_1 to AD_2, as seen in Exhibit 3. Unless this shift is offset by expansionary monetary policy (a topic we discuss in The Federal Reserve System and Monetary Policy when we cover monetary policy), a lower price level and lower RGDP will result. That is, in the short run, an aggressive program of deficit reduction can lead to a recession.

In the long run, however, the story is different. Lowering the budget deficit, or running a larger budget surplus, leads to a lower real interest rate, which increases private investment and stimulates higher growth in capital formation and economic growth. In fact, this situation happened in the 1990s as the budget deficit was reduced and finally turned into a budget surplus. The reduction in the deficit increased the potential rate of output, shifting the SRAS and LRAS curves rightward in Exhibit 4. The final effect was a higher RGDP and a lower price level than would have otherwise prevailed. Both investment and RGDP grew as the budget deficit shrank. The long-run effects of a deficit reduction are greater economic growth and a lower price level, *ceteris paribus*. The short-run recessionary effects of a budget deficit reduction can be avoided through the appropriate monetary policy, as we will explore in The Federal Reserve System and Monetary Policy chapter.

The Burden of Public Debt

The "burden" of the debt is a topic that has long interested economists, particularly whether it falls on present or future generations. Exhibit 5 shows the burden as a percentage of GDP from 1929 to 2009. Arguments can be made that the generation of taxpayers living at the time that the debt is issued shoulders the true cost of the debt, because the debt permits the government to take command of resources that might be available for other, private uses. In a sense, the resources it takes to purchase government bonds might take away from private activities, such as private investment financed

section 26.7 exhibit 5 — Public Debt Trends

Fiscal Year	Public Debt (billions of dollars)	Public Debt as a Percentage of GDP
1929	$ 16.9	18.0%
1940	43.0	45.0
1945	260.2	120.0
1950	256.8	94.0
1955	274.4	69.0
1960	290.5	56.0
1965	322.3	47.0
1970	380.9	38.0
1975	541.9	35.0
1980	909.1	33.0
1985	1,817.5	44.0
1990	3,206.6	56.0
1995	4,921.0	67.2
2000	5,629.0	57.9
2005	7,905.3	64.6
2009	10,438.4	70.4

SOURCE: Economic Report of the President, 2009.

by private debt. No economist can deny, however, that the issuance of debt does involve some intergenerational transfer of incomes. Long after federal debt is issued, a new generation of taxpayers is making interest payments to people of the generation that bought the bonds issued to finance that debt.

If public debt is created intelligently, however, the "burden" of the debt should be less than the benefits derived from the resources acquired as a result, particularly when the debt allows for an expansion in real economic activity or for the development of vital infrastructure for the future. The opportunity cost of expanded public activity may be small in terms of private activity that must be forgone to finance the public activity if unemployed resources are put to work. The real issue of importance is whether the government's activities have benefits that are greater than their costs; whether it is done through raising taxes, printing money, or running deficits, it is, for the most part, a "financing issue." It is also possible that parents can offset some of the intergenerational debt by leaving larger bequests.

POLICY application: WOULD A BALANCED BUDGET AMENDMENT WORK?

What are the arguments for and against balancing the budget? If we had a balanced budget, how could we allow the government to run deficits during emergencies?

From 1960 to 1998, the federal budget was in deficit every year except one, when the government ran a small balanced surplus in 1969. In 1998, the federal government ran a surplus and continued to run surpluses for the next three years. However, a series of events—the recession of 2001, the terrorist attacks, financing the wars in Iraq and Afghanistan, and a financial crisis—brought deficits back in the picture.

Some individuals believe that we must control the deficits through responsible fiscal restraint—a belief that has prompted a drive to add a balanced budget amendment to the U.S. Constitution.

But the possibility that the spending activities of the federal government may be constitutionally restricted is terrifying to some. Opponents' arguments can be summarized as follows:

First, at best, a balanced budget amendment would be ineffective because it is impossible to guarantee that revenues and expenditures will always match up on an annual basis. Second, at worst, a balanced budget amendment would reduce the fiscal flexibility of the federal government, thereby making it more difficult to respond appropriately to changing economic circumstances. Furthermore, if the public really wants the government to balance its budget, our elected representatives already have the power to respond to this desire.

It is certainly true that no amendment to the Constitution can ensure that the budget will ever be perfectly balanced. No one can exactly predict either revenues or expenditures over a specified interval. And in some circumstances, budget flexibility can be justified. Finally, it is true that Congress has the control over taxing and spending needed to eliminate the chronic deficits if it chooses to do so. Given all these factors, why should we clutter up the Constitution with a balanced budget amendment?

Proponents of a balanced budget amendment argue that, in the absence of fiscal restraints, excessive government spending will occur because the private advantages that each of us realizes from spending on our government programs are paid for almost entirely by other taxpayers. Of course, each of us suffers from having to pay for the programs of others, and most of us would be willing to reduce our special interest demands if others would do the same. But we all recognize that as long as we continue to pay for the programs of others, we enjoy no advantage from reducing our individual demands on the government treasury. In this uncontrolled setting, we are in a spending free-for-all, with penalties for the fiscally responsible and rewards for the fiscally irresponsible.

Of course, a balanced budget amendment could be written that would allow the government to run deficits in time of special emergencies such as military involvement, earthquakes, financial crises, fires, or floods. In addition, the voters might adopt a plan that would allow for a two-thirds vote to increase the deficit or that would opt for a running average balanced budget instead of balancing the budget every year. Any of these proposals could work toward controlling runaway federal spending to some degree. A balanced budget would mean greater national saving, investment and economic growth. A smaller debt would also lead to less of a burden on future generations of taxpayers. Inheriting this debt will lower future standards of living, other things equal. However, what if the deficit is reduced by cutting back on spending in education? With less education, future generations could be less productive with lower incomes. If the deficit became so large that financing the debt (sometimes called monetizing the debt) became problematic than there might be a temptation to turn to inflation to finance the debt. In addition, parents and grandparents could offset some of this problem to the extent that they save more now and bequeath larger inheritances to their children.

The most important issue of all might be at what *level* the budget should be balanced. Many would prefer deficits in a small budget to a much larger, but balanced, budget. However, the real issue, as always, is: Are we getting government goods and services with benefits that are greater than costs?

SECTION CHECK

1. The budget deficit is financed by issuing debt.
2. Improvement in the federal budget balance since the early 1990s resulted from economic growth and the efforts of the president and Congress to control the growth of government spending. From 1960 through 1997, the federal budget had been in deficit every year except one, when the government ran a small balance surplus in 1969. However, with the recession in 2001 and the war on terrorism, the budget surplus slipped into a budget deficit.
3. When the government borrows to finance a budget deficit, it causes the interest rate to rise.
4. When the government runs a budget surplus, it adds to national saving, lowers the interest rate, and stimulates private investment and capital formation.

---

1. What will happen to the interest rate when a budget deficit occurs?
2. What will happen to the interest rate when a budget surplus occurs?
3. What are the intergenerational effects of a national debt?
4. What must be true for Americans to be better off as a result of an increase in the national debt?

Interactive Chapter Summary

Fill in the blanks:

1. _____ is the use of government spending and/or taxes to alter real GDP and price levels.

2. When government spending (for purchases of goods and services and transfer payments) exceeds tax revenues, the result is a budget _____.

3. When the government wishes to stimulate the economy by increasing aggregate demand, it will _____ government purchases of goods and services, _____ taxes, or use some combination of these approaches.

4. Expansionary fiscal policy is associated with _____ government budget deficits.

5. If the government wishes to dampen a boom in the economy, it will _____ its purchases of goods and services, _____ taxes, or use some combination of these approaches.

6. By changing tax rates, the government can alter the amount of _____ income of households and thereby bring about changes in _____ purchases.

7. Increased budget _____ will stimulate the economy when it is operating at less than full capacity.

8. The result of an expansionary fiscal policy in the short run would be a(n) _____ in the price level and a(n) _____ in RGDP.

9. If the government wants to use fiscal policy to help "cool off" the economy when it has overheated and inflation has become a serious problem, it will tend to _____ government purchases and/or _____ taxes.

10. A tax _____ on consumers will reduce households' disposable incomes and thus their purchases of _____ goods and services, while higher business taxes will reduce _____ purchases.

11. Contractionary fiscal policy will result in a(n) _____ price level and _____ employment in the short run.

12. The _____ effect explains why, when an initial increase in purchases of goods or services occurs, the ultimate increase in total purchases will tend to be greater than the initial increase.

13. When the government purchases additional goods and services, not only does it add to the total demand for goods and services directly, but the purchases also add to people's _____.

14. When people's incomes rise because of increased government purchases of goods and services, collectively people will spend a substantial part of the additional income on additional _____ purchases.

15. The additional consumption purchases made as a portion of one's additional income is measured by the _____.

16. With each additional round of the multiplier process, the added income generated and the resulting consumer purchases get _____ because some of each round's increase in income goes to _____ and _____ payments.
17. _____ is equal to 1/(1 − MPC).
18. The larger the marginal propensity to consume, the _____ the multiplier effect.
19. If the marginal propensity to consume were smaller, a given increase in government purchases would have a(n) _____ effect on consumption purchases.
20. The extent of the multiplier effect visible within a short time period will be _____ than the total effect indicated by the multiplier formula.
21. The multiplier effect triggered by an increase in spending arises because of the additional _____ spending that it leads to.
22. If your MPC were equal to 0.7, your MPS would equal _____.
23. Savings and money spent on imported goods will each _____ the size of the multiplier.
24. The multiplier effect of an increase in government purchases implies that the increase in aggregate demand will tend to be _____ than the initial fiscal stimulus, other things being equal.
25. Supply-side economists believe that individuals will save _____, work _____, and provide _____ capital when taxes, government transfer payments (such as welfare), and regulations are too burdensome on productive activities.
26. The _____ curve shows that high tax rates could conceivably reduce work incentives to the point that government revenues are lower at high marginal tax rates than they would be at somewhat lower rates.
27. If the demand-side stimulus from reduced tax rates is _____ than the supply-side effects, the result will be a higher price level and a greater level of real output.
28. Changes in government transfer payments or tax collections that automatically tend to counter business cycle fluctuations are called _____.
29. The most important automatic stabilizer is the _____ system.
30. Big increases and big decreases in GDP are both _____ by automatic changes in income tax receipts.
31. Because incomes, earnings, and profits all fall during a recession, the government collects _____ in taxes. This reduced tax burden partially _____ any contractionary fall in aggregate demand.
32. When the government borrows money to finance a deficit, it _____ the overall demand for money in the money market, driving interest rates _____.
33. The _____ effect refers to the theory that when the government borrows money to finance a deficit, it drives interest rates up, choking off some private spending on goods and services.
34. The monetary authorities could _____ the money supply to offset the _____ interest rates due to the crowding-out effect of expansionary fiscal policy.
35. Expansionary fiscal policy will tend to _____ the demand for dollars relative to other currencies.
36. Expansionary fiscal policy will tend to cause net exports to _____.
37. The larger the crowding-out effect, the _____ the actual effect of a given change in fiscal policy.
38. Because of the _____ in implementing fiscal policy, a fiscal policy designed to deal with a contracting economy may actually take effect during a period of economic expansion.
39. Timed correctly, contractionary fiscal policy could correct a(n) _____; timed incorrectly, it could cause a(n) _____.
40. If the federal government is running a(n) _____, the federal debt would be getting smaller.
41. Historically, the largest budget deficits have tended to be in _____ years.
42. Deficit reduction is a(n) _____ fiscal policy in the short run.
43. _____ a federal budget deficit could be an appropriate fiscal policy if the economy were in a recession.
44. If unemployed resources are put to work by government spending, the opportunity cost of expanded public activity would be _____ than otherwise.
45. Starting at a full-employment equilibrium, the only long-term effect of an increase in aggregate demand will be an increase in the _____ level.

46. Starting at a full-employment equilibrium, once the economy has returned to its long-run equilibrium after an increase in government purchases, employment will be _____ full employment.

Answers: 1. Fiscal policy 2. deficit 3. increase; increased 4. increased 5. reduce; increase 6. disposable; consumption 7. deficits 8. increase; increase 9. reduce; increase 10. increase; consumption; investment 11. lower; lower 12. multiplier 13. incomes 14. consumption 15. marginal propensity to consume 16. smaller; savings; tax 17. The expenditure multiplier 18. larger 19. smaller 20. less 21. consumption 22. 0.3 23. reduce 24. greater 25. less; less 26. Laffer 27. greater 28. automatic stabilizers 29. tax 30. lessened 31. less offsets 32. increases; up 33. crowding-out 34. increase 35. higher; increase 36. fall 37. smaller 38. time lags 39. inflationary boom; recession 40. surplus 41. war 42. contractionary 43. Increasing 44. lower 45. price 46. equal to

Key Terms and Concepts

fiscal policy 759
budget deficit 759
budget surplus 759
expansionary fiscal policy 759
contractionary fiscal policy 759
multiplier effect 765
marginal propensity to consume (MPC) 765
marginal propensity to save (MPS) 766
crowding-out effect 775
automatic stabilizers 779

Section Check Answers

26.1 Fiscal Policy

1. **If, as part of its fiscal policy, the federal government increases its purchases of goods and services, is that an expansionary or contractionary tactic?**

   An increase in government purchases of goods and services would be an expansionary tactic, increasing aggregate demand, other things equal.

2. **If the federal government decreases its purchases of goods and services, does the budget deficit increase or decrease?**

   If the federal government decreased its purchases of goods and services, for a given level of tax revenue, the budget deficit (the difference between government spending and government revenues) would decrease.

3. **If the federal government increases taxes and/or decreases transfer payments, is that an expansionary or contractionary fiscal policy?**

   Either an increase in taxes or a decrease in transfer payment would be a contractionary tactic, decreasing aggregate demand by decreasing people's disposable incomes and therefore reducing the demand for consumption goods.

4. **If the federal government increases taxes or decreases transfer payments, does the budget deficit increase or decrease?**

   If the federal government increased taxes or decreased transfer payments, for a given level of government purchases, a budget deficit (the difference between government spending and government revenues) would decrease.

5. **If the federal government increases government purchases and lowers taxes at the same time, does the budget deficit increase or decrease?**

   Increased government purchases would increase a budget deficit, other things equal. Lowered taxes would also increase a budget deficit, other things equal. Therefore, both changes together would increase a budget deficit.

26.2 Fiscal Policy and the AD/AS Model

1. **If the economy is in recession, what sort of fiscal policy changes would tend to bring it out of recession?**

   If the economy is in recession, aggregate demand intersects short-run aggregate supply to the left of the long-run aggregate supply curve. Expansionary fiscal policy—increased government purchases, decreased taxes, and/or increased transfer payments—addresses a recession by shifting aggregate demand to the right.

2. **If the economy is at a short-run equilibrium at greater than full employment, what sort of fiscal policy changes would tend to bring the economy back to a full-employment equilibrium?**

   If the economy is at a short-run equilibrium at greater than full employment, aggregate demand intersects short-run aggregate supply to the right of the long-run aggregate supply curve. Contractionary fiscal policy—decreased government purchases, increased taxes, and/or decreased transfer payments—addresses a short-run equilibrium at greater than full employment by shifting aggregate demand to the left.

3. **What effects would an expansionary fiscal policy have on the price level and real GDP, starting from a full-employment equilibrium?**

   Starting from a full-employment equilibrium, an expansionary fiscal policy would increase aggregate demand, increasing the price level and real GDP in the short run. However, in the long run, real GDP will return to its full-employment long-run equilibrium level as input prices adjust (the short-run aggregate supply curve shifts up or left), and only the price level will end up higher.

4. **What effects would a contractionary fiscal policy have on the price level and real GDP, starting from a full-employment equilibrium?**

   Starting from a full-employment equilibrium, a contractionary fiscal policy would decrease aggregate demand, decreasing the price level and real GDP in the short run. However, in the long run, real GDP will return to its full-employment long-run equilibrium level as input prices adjust (the short-run aggregate supply curve shifts down or right), and the price level will end up lower.

26.3 The Multiplier Effect

1. **How does the multiplier effect work?**

   The multiplier effect occurs because the increased purchases during each "round" of the multiplier process generate increased incomes for the owners of the resources used to produce the goods purchased, which leads them to increase consumption purchases in the next "round" of the process. The result is a final increase in total purchases, including the induced consumption purchases, that is greater than the initial increase in purchases.

2. **What is the marginal propensity to consume?**

   The marginal propensity to consume is the proportion of an additional dollar of income that would be spent on additional consumption purchases.

3. **Why is the marginal propensity to consume always less than one?**

   This is true because all expenditures ultimately have to be financed out of income, so each dollar of added income cannot lead to more than a dollar of added purchases. In addition, taxes and savings also have to be financed out of income.

4. **Why does the multiplier effect get larger as the marginal propensity to consume gets larger?**

   The larger the marginal propensity to consume, the larger the fraction of increased income in each "round" of the multiplier process that will go to additional consumption purchases. Since each round of the multiplier process will therefore be larger the greater the marginal propensity to consume, the multiplier will also be larger.

5. **If an increase in government purchases leads to a reduction in private-sector purchases, why will the effect on the economy be smaller than that indicated by the multiplier?**

   At the same time that the increased government purchases are leading to a multiple expansion of income and purchases for one set of citizens, the "crowded-out" private-sector purchases are causing a multiple contraction of income and purchases for other citizens. The net effect on the economy will therefore be smaller than the increase in government purchases times the multiplier.

26.4 Supply-Side Effects of Tax Cuts

1. **Is supply-side economics more concerned with short-run economic stabilization or long-run economic growth?**

   Supply-side economics is more concerned with long-run economic growth than short-run economic stabilization. It is focused primarily on adopting policies that will increase the long-run aggregate supply curve (society's production possibilities curve) over time, by increasing incentives to work, save, and invest.

2. **Why could you say that supply-side economics is really more about after-tax wages and after-tax returns on investment than it is about tax rates?**

   Changes in after-tax wages and after-tax returns on investment are the incentives that change people's behavior, not changes in the tax rates themselves.

3. **Why do government regulations have the same sort of effects on businesses as taxes?**
   To the extent that government regulations impose added costs on businesses, the effects of these added costs are the same—a decrease (leftward or upward shift) in supply—as if a tax of that amount were imposed on the business.

4. **Why are the full effects of supply-side policies not immediately apparent?**
   It often takes a substantial period of time before improved productivity incentives have their complete effects. For instance, an increase in the after-tax return on investment will increase investment, but it will take many years before the capital stock has completed its adjustment. The same is true for human capital investments in education, research and development, and so forth—if a student or researcher learns more today, the full effect won't be observed immediately.

5. **If taxes increase, what would you expect to happen to employment in the underground economy? Why?**
   The primary benefit of employment in the underground economy is the savings due to not having to pay taxes (or bear some of the costs of regulations imposed on legitimate employment). The cost includes the risk of being caught, the difficulty of dealing on a cash-only or barter basis, and so on. As tax rates increase, the benefits of working in the underground economy increase relative to the costs, and employment in the underground economy will tend to increase, other things being equal.

26.5 Possible Obstacles to Effective Fiscal Policy

1. **Why does a larger government budget deficit increase the magnitude of the crowding-out effect?**
   A larger government budget deficit increases the demand for loanable funds, thereby increasing the magnitude of the increase in interest rates and crowding out more private-sector investment as a result.

2. **Why does fiscal policy have a smaller effect on aggregate demand the greater the crowding-out effect is?**
   The greater the crowding-out effect, the smaller the net effect (the increase in government purchases minus the private-sector purchases crowded out) fiscal policy has on aggregate demand. For example, if each dollar of added government purchases crowds out 50 cents worth of private-sector purchases, fiscal policy will have only half the effect on aggregate demand that it would if there were no crowding-out effect.

3. **How do time lags affect the effectiveness of fiscal policy?**
   The time lag between when a policy change is desirable and when it is adopted and implemented (for data gathering, decision making, etc.), as well as the time lag between when a policy is implemented and when it has its effects, makes it difficult for fiscal policy to have the desired effect at the desired time, particularly given the difficulty in forecasting the future course of the economy.

26.6 Automatic Stabilizers

1. **How does the tax system act as an automatic stabilizer?**
   Some taxes, such as progressive income taxes and corporate profits taxes, automatically increase as the economy grows, and this increase in taxes restrains disposable income and the growth of aggregate demand below what it would have been otherwise. Similarly, they automatically decrease in recessions, and this decrease in taxes increases disposable income and acts as a partial offset to the fall in aggregate demand. The result is reduced business cycle instability.

2. **Are automatic stabilizers affected by a time lag? Why or why not?**
   Since automatic stabilizers respond to business cycle changes without the need for legislative or executive action, there is no appreciable lag between when business cycle conditions justify a change in them and when they do change. However, there is still a lag between when those stabilizers change and when their full effects are felt.

3. **Why are transfer payments such as unemployment compensation effective automatic stabilizers?**

   Some transfer payment programs, such as unemployment compensation, act as automatic stabilizers because when business cycle conditions worsen, people can start receiving increased transfer payments as soon as they become eligible (lose their jobs, in the case of unemployment compensation). The same is true of some other welfare-type programs, such as food stamps.

26.7 The National Debt

1. **What will happen to the interest rate when a budget deficit occurs?**

   When the government borrows to finance a budget deficit, it causes the interest rate to rise, other things equal.

2. **What will happen to the interest rate when a budget surplus occurs?**

   When there is a budget surplus, it adds to national saving and lowers the interest rate, other things equal.

3. **What are the intergenerational effects of a national debt?**

   Arguments can be made that the generation of the taxpayers living at the time that the debt is issued shoulders the true cost of the debt, because the debt permits the government to take command of resources that would be available for other, private uses. However, the issuance of debt does involve some intergenerational transfer of incomes. Long after federal debt is issued, a new generation of taxpayers is making interest payments to persons of the generation that bought the bonds issued to finance that debt. If public debt is created intelligently, however, the "burden" of the debt should be less than the benefits derived from the resources acquired as a result; this is particularly true when the debt allows for an expansion in real economic activity or for the development of vital infrastructure for the future.

4. **What must be true for Americans to be better off as a result of an increase in the national debt?**

   For Americans to be better off as a result of an increase in the federal debt, the value of the investments and other spending financed by the debt must be greater than the cost of financing it.

CHAPTER 26 STUDY GUIDE

True or False:

1. The government can use fiscal policy to stimulate the economy out of a recession or to try to bring inflation under control.
2. When tax revenues are greater than government spending, a budget surplus exists.
3. A budget surplus is the most common result of government fiscal policy.
4. An increase in government purchases of goods and services will stimulate the economy by increasing aggregate demand.
5. An increase in taxes will increase aggregate demand.
6. Contractionary fiscal policy will tend to reduce a federal budget surplus or increase a federal budget deficit.
7. Real GDP will tend to change anytime the amount of consumption, investment, government purchases, or net exports changes.
8. If policymakers are unhappy about the present short-run equilibrium GDP, they can deliberately manipulate the level of government purchases in order to obtain a new short-run equilibrium value.
9. Expansionary fiscal policy has the potential to move an economy out of recession.
10. The effect of an increase in aggregate demand depends on the position of the macroeconomic equilibrium prior to the government stimulus.
11. Starting from an initial recession equilibrium, expansionary fiscal policy could potentially increase employment to $RGDP_{NR}$.
12. Starting from an initial recession equilibrium, a government tax increase would tend to reduce the severity of the recession.
13. An increase in government spending and/or a tax cut will tend to move the economy up along its short-run aggregate supply curve.
14. Contractionary fiscal policy has the potential to offset an overheated, inflationary boom.
15. Contractionary fiscal policy will tend to increase a current government budget deficit.
16. When an initial increase in government purchases of goods and services occurs, the ultimate increase in total purchases will tend to be greater than the initial increase.
17. If the marginal propensity to consume is two-thirds, a $6 million increase in disposable income to certain households will lead them to increase their consumption spending by $18 million.
18. The multiplier is equal to 1 divided by the marginal propensity to consume.
19. The multiplier would be smaller if the marginal propensity to consume were smaller.
20. If the MPC were equal to two-thirds, the multiplier would be equal to 3.
21. The multiplier may be written as $1/(1 - MPC)$ or as $1/MPS$.
22. A person's MPC and MPS can be equal only if MPC = 0.5.
23. The multiplier effect of a reduction in taxes is larger than the multiplier effect of an equal increase in government spending on goods and services.
24. If MPC = 0.67, the effects of a change in taxes on *AD* would be two-thirds the magnitude of the effects of an equal change in government spending.

25. The effect of a $5 billion change in government spending on *AD* would be greater than that of an equal change in taxes, regardless of the MPC.
26. The multiplier process is virtually instantaneous.
27. Savings and money spent on imported goods will each reduce the size of the multiplier because each reduces the fraction of a given increase in income that will go to additional purchases of domestically produced consumption goods.
28. Supply-siders would encourage government to reduce individual and business taxes, deregulate, and increase spending on research and development.
29. Supply-siders' primary focus is on stabilizing aggregate demand in the short run.
30. A lower marginal tax rate will raise after-tax earnings, improving productive incentives.
31. Higher marginal tax rates will lead investors to spend more scarce resources looking for tax shelters, which harms the economy as high-return but highly taxed investments give way to lower-return tax shelters.
32. If greater research and development leads to new technology and knowledge, it will shift the short- and long-run aggregate supply curves to the right.
33. If tax rates are reduced, it will affect aggregate supply but not aggregate demand.
34. One of the advantages of automatic stabilizers is that they take place without the necessity for deliberations in Congress or the executive branch of the government.
35. Unemployment compensation and public assistance payments act as automatic stabilizers, stimulating aggregate demand during recessions and reducing aggregate demand during booms.
36. Starting at a full-employment equilibrium, the gains in employment that result from expansionary fiscal policy will not be sustainable in the long run.
37. Starting at full employment, contractionary fiscal policy could cause a recession in the short run.
38. Starting at full employment, the long-run result of contractionary fiscal policy includes a lower price level and reduced real output.
39. The crowding-out effect will tend to reduce the magnitude of the effects of increases in government purchases.
40. The crowding-out effect implies that expansionary fiscal policy will tend to reduce private purchases of interest-sensitive goods.
41. The crowding-out effect does not occur with a tax change.
42. Critics of the crowding-out effect argue that an increase in government purchases (or a tax cut), particularly if the economy is in a severe recession, could improve consumer and business expectations and actually encourage private investment spending.
43. Expansionary U.S. fiscal policy will tend to move funds out of the United States.
44. Expansionary fiscal policy will tend to be partly crowded out by a reduction in net exports.
45. Sometimes fiscal policy designed to stabilize the economy may actually destabilize the economy.
46. Time lags in the legislative process are a serious problem in the implementation of fiscal policy.
47. After expansionary fiscal policy legislation is signed into law, it takes time to bring about the actual fiscal stimulus desired.
48. The sum total of the values of all bonds outstanding constitutes the federal debt.
49. Printing money to finance government activities is inflationary.

50. If public debt is created intelligently, the "burden" of the debt should be less than the benefits derived from the resources acquired as a result.
51. If the U.S. government has a large current federal debt, it must be running a current year deficit.
52. One way the federal government can finance deficits is to print money.
53. When the federal government spends more, other things being equal, it tends to increase both that year's deficit and the federal debt.
54. Sometimes special emergencies, such as military involvements and natural disasters, may lead governments to run deficits.
55. The U.S. federal government has never run a surplus in the last decade.
56. If the economy were in an unsustainable boom, appropriate countercyclical policy would be to increase the budget deficit.
57. If the economy were in recession, a fiscal policy that decreased the budget deficit would make the recession worse.
58. If the federal debt rises as a result of increasing government spending, the burden of the debt will necessarily be greater than the benefit.

Multiple Choice:

1. Traditionally, government has used _____ to influence _____.
   a. taxing and spending; the demand side of the economy
   b. spending; the supply side of the economy
   c. supply management; the demand side of the economy
   d. demand management; the supply side of the economy

2. Contractionary fiscal policy consists of
   a. increased government spending and increased taxes.
   b. decreased government spending and decreased taxes.
   c. decreased government spending and increased taxes.
   d. increased government spending and decreased taxes.

3. Budget deficits are created when
   a. government spending exceeds its tax revenues.
   b. government tax revenues exceed its spending.
   c. government spending equals its tax revenues.
   d. none of the above.

4. If the government wanted to move the economy out of a current recession, which of the following might be an appropriate policy action?
   a. decrease taxes
   b. increase government purchases of goods and services
   c. increase transfer payments
   d. any of the above

Using the accompanying graph, answer question 5.

5. In order for the economy pictured here to return to $RGDP_{NR}$, this economy could use
   a. decreased taxes and increased government purchases.
   b. increased taxes and increased government purchases.
   c. decreased taxes and decreased government purchases.
   d. decreased taxes and increased government purchases.

6. If government policymakers were worried about the inflationary potential of the economy, which of the following would not be a correct fiscal policy change?
   a. increase consumption taxes
   b. increase government purchases
   c. reduce government purchases
   d. decrease government purchases of goods and services

7. In the short run, expansionary fiscal policy can cause a rise in real GDP
   a. in combination with a rise in the price level.
   b. in combination with no rise in the price level.
   c. in combination with a reduction in the price level.
   d. in combination with a rise or reduction in the price level, depending on the economy.

8. If the government wanted to offset the effect of a boom in consumer and investor confidence on AD, it might
   a. decrease government purchases.
   b. decrease taxes.
   c. increase taxes.
   d. do either a or c.

9. An increase in taxes combined with a decrease in government purchases would
   a. increase AD.
   b. decrease AD.
   c. leave AD unchanged.
   d. have an indeterminate effect on AD.

10. A combination of an increase in government purchases and a decrease in taxes would
    a. increase AD.
    b. decrease AD.
    c. leave AD unchanged.
    d. have an indeterminate effect on AD.

11. *AD* will shift to the right, other things being equal, when
    a. the government budget deficit increases because government purchases rose.
    b. the government budget deficit increases because taxes fell.
    c. the government budget deficit increases because transfer payments rose.
    d. any of the above circumstances exist.

12. If the marginal propensity to consume is two-thirds, the multiplier is
    a. 30.
    b. 66.
    c. 1.5.
    d. 3.

13. The multiplier effect is based on the fact that _____ by one person is (are) _____ to another.
    a. income; income
    b. expenditures; expenditures
    c. expenditures; income
    d. income; expenditures

14. The expenditure multiplier is
    a. 1/MPC.
    b. 1/(1 − MPC).
    c. (1 − MPC)/1.
    d. 1/change in MPC.

15. The federal government buys $20 million worth of computers from Dell. If the MPC is 0.60, what will be the impact on aggregate demand, other things being equal?
    a. Aggregate demand will increase $12 million.
    b. Aggregate demand will increase $13.33 million.
    c. Aggregate demand will increase $20 million.
    d. Aggregate demand will increase $50 million.
    e. Aggregate demand will not change.

16. When taxes are increased, disposable income _____, and hence consumption _____.
    a. increases; increases
    b. increases; decreases
    c. decreases; increases
    d. decreases; decreases
    e. stays the same; stays the same

17. If the MPC is 0.5, a $1 million change in taxes will have _____ effect as a $1 million change in government spending.
    a. the same
    b. half the
    c. double the
    d. none of the above

18. Lower marginal tax rates stimulate people to work, save, and invest, resulting in more output and a larger tax base. This statement most closely reflects which of the following views?
    a. the Keynesian
    b. the crowding-out theory of budget deficits
    c. the aggregate demand theory
    d. the supply-side view

19. Other things being constant, an increase in marginal tax rates will
    a. decrease the supply of labor and reduce its productive efficiency.
    b. decrease the supply of capital and decrease its productive efficiency.
    c. encourage individuals to buy goods that are tax deductible instead of those that are more desired but nondeductible.
    d. do all of the above.

20. According to the Laffer curve,
    a. decreasing tax rates on income will always increase tax revenues.
    b. decreasing tax rates on income will always decrease tax revenues.
    c. decreasing tax rates are more likely to increase tax revenues the higher tax rates are to start with.
    d. decreasing tax rates are more likely to increase tax revenues the lower tax rates are to start with.

21. One of the real-world complexities of countercyclical fiscal policy is that
    a. fiscal policy is based on forecasts, which are not foolproof.
    b. a lag occurs between a change in fiscal policy and its effect.
    c. how much of the multiplier effect will take place in a given amount of time is uncertain.
    d. All of the above are correct.

22. According to the crowding-out effect, if the federal government borrows to finance deficit spending,
    a. the demand for loanable funds will decrease, driving interest rates down.
    b. the demand for loanable funds will increase, driving interest rates up.
    c. the supply for loanable funds will increase, driving interest rates up.
    d. the supply for loanable funds will decrease, driving interest rates down.

23. Automatic stabilizers
    a. reduce the problems caused by lags, using fiscal policy as a stabilization tool.
    b. are changes in fiscal policy that act to stimulate *AD* automatically when the economy goes into recession.
    c. are changes in fiscal policy that act to restrain *AD* automatically when the economy is growing too fast.
    d. All of the above are correct.

24. During a recession, government transfer payments automatically _____ and tax revenue automatically _____.
    a. fall; falls
    b. increase; falls
    c. increase; increases
    d. fall; increases

25. If U.S. budget deficits (which require the borrowing of funds) raise interest rates and attract investment funds from abroad,
    a. the foreign exchange value of the dollar will appreciate, and U.S. net exports will decrease.
    b. the foreign exchange value of the dollar will depreciate, and U.S. net exports will decrease.
    c. the foreign exchange value of the dollar will depreciate, and U.S. net exports will increase.
    d. the foreign exchange value of the dollar will appreciate, and U.S. net exports ($X - M$) will increase.

26. When the crowding-out effect of an increase in government purchases is included in the analysis,
    a. *AD* shifts left.
    b. *AD* doesn't change.
    c. *AD* shifts right, but by more than the simple multiplier analysis would imply.
    d. *AD* shifts right, but by less than the simple multiplier analysis would imply.

27. How does the government finance budget deficits?
    a. The Federal Reserve creates new money.
    b. It issues debt to government agencies, private institutions, and private investors.
    c. It is primarily financed by foreign investors.
    d. It does nothing to finance budget deficits.

28. When government debt is financed internally, future generations will
    a. inherit a lower tax liability.
    b. inherit neither higher taxes nor interest payment liability.
    c. inherit higher taxes.
    d. do none of the above.

29. After briefly running federal surpluses, in 2001 the budget returned to deficits because of
    a. a recession.
    b. the war on terrorism.
    c. a tax cut.
    d. all of the above.

30. Higher budget deficits would tend to
    a. raise interest rates.
    b. reduce investment.
    c. reduce the growth rate of the capital stock.
    d. do all of the above.

31. If the government budget deficit became a budget surplus because of cuts in federal government spending, other things being equal, which of the following would fall in the short run?
    a. interest rates
    b. investment
    c. unemployment
    d. the money supply
    e. None of the above would fall in the short run.

32. Deficit reduction will tend to
    a. decrease real output in both the short run and long run.
    b. decrease real output in the short run, but increase real output in the long run.
    c. increase real output in both the short run and long run.
    d. increase real output in the short run, but decrease real output in the long run.

33. A policy which increased the federal government deficit would tend to increase which of the following in the short run, other things being equal?
    a. aggregate demand
    b. real output
    c. the price level
    d. employment
    e. all of the above

34. Starting at full employment, if MPC = 2/3, an increase in government purchases of $10 billion would lead AD to _____ and _____ real output in the long run.
    a. increase $30 billion; increase
    b. increase $30 billion; not change
    c. decrease $30 billion; decrease
    d. decrease $30 billion; not change
    e. none of the above

35. A decrease in government purchases will do which of the following in the long run?
    a. increase unemployment
    b. decrease real output
    c. decrease the price level
    d. all of the above

Problems:

1. Why are federal government actions that increase deficits considered expansionary fiscal policy and those that decrease deficits considered contractionary fiscal policy?

2. Are increases in both government purchases and net taxes at the same time expansionary or contractionary? Would both changes together increase or decrease the federal government deficit?

3. Answer the following questions:
   a. If the current budget shows a surplus, what would an increase in government purchases do to it?
   b. What would that increase in government purchases do to aggregate demand?
   c. When would an increase in government purchases be an appropriate countercyclical fiscal policy?

4. Answer the following questions:
   a. If the current budget shows a deficit, what would an increase in taxes do to it?
   b. What would that increase in taxes do to aggregate demand?
   c. When would an increase in taxes be an appropriate contractionary fiscal policy?

5. Use the accompanying diagram to answer questions a–f.

   a. At what short-run equilibrium point might expansionary fiscal policy make sense to help stabilize the economy?
   b. What would be the result of appropriate fiscal policy in that case?
   c. What would be the long-run result if no fiscal policy action were taken in that case?
   d. At what short-run equilibrium point might contractionary fiscal policy make sense to help stabilize the economy?
   e. What would be the result of appropriate fiscal policy in that case?
   f. What would be the long-run result if no fiscal policy action were taken in that case?

6. What is a recessionary gap? What would be the appropriate fiscal policy to combat or offset one? What is an inflationary gap? What would be the appropriate fiscal policy to combat or offset one?

7. What would the multiplier be if the marginal propensity to consume was
   a. 1/3?
   b. 1/2?
   c. 3/4?

8. If government purchases increased by $20 billion, other things being equal, what would be the resulting change in aggregate demand, and how much of that change would be a change in consumption, if the MPC were
   a. 1/3?
   b. 1/2?
   c. 2/3?
   d. 3/4?
   e. 4/5?

9. Could the multiplier be written as 1 divided by the marginal propensity to save (MPS)?

10. Why does it take a larger reduction in taxes to create the same increase in *AD* as a given increase in government purchases?

11. Explain why an equal dollar increase in both government purchases and net taxes would increase aggregate demand.

12. Use the accompanying diagram to answer questions a and b.

   a. Starting from the initial equilibrium in the diagram, illustrate the case of a supply-side fiscal policy that left the price level unchanged.
   b. Compared to your answer in a, when would a supply-side fiscal policy result in an increase in the price level?

13. Why can a decrease in tax rates increase *AS* as well as *AD*, whereas an increase in government purchases will increase *AD* but not *AS*?

14. How do automatic stabilizers affect budget deficits and surpluses? How would automatic stabilizers be affected by an annually balanced budget rule?

15. Why do automatic stabilizers minimize the lag problem with fiscal policy?

16. Answer the following questions:
   a. Describe the crowding-out effect of an increase in government purchases.
   b. Why does the magnitude of the crowding-out effect depend on how responsive interest rates are to increased government borrowing and how responsive investment is to changes in interest rates?
   c. How would the size of the crowding-out effect affect the size of the change in aggregate demand that would result from a given increase in government purchases?

17. Illustrate diagrammatically the short-run and long-run effects of a government budget deficit. Describe the mechanism that makes these effects different.

Monetary Institutions

27

27.1 What Is Money?
27.2 Measuring Money
27.3 How Banks Create Money

27.4 The Money Multiplier
27.5 The Collapse of America's Banking System, 1920–1933

Money is very important to the economy. Recall the circular flow model in which households trade money for the goods and services they buy in product markets, and firms exchange money for inputs they buy to produce the goods and services they sell in factor markets. In this chapter, we will discuss the different forms of money, the different functions of money, and how banks create money. We will learn how the Federal Reserve works to keep banks safe. At the end of the chapter, we will examine some periods of bank failure in the twentieth century.

SECTION 27.1 What Is Money?

* What is money?
* Is using money better than barter?
* How does money lower the costs of making transactions?
* How does money serve as a store of value?

Money is anything that is generally accepted in exchange for goods and services. In colonial times, commodities such as tobacco and wampum (Native American trinkets, such as shells) were sometimes used as money. At some times and in some places, even cigarettes and whiskey have been used as money. Using commodities as money has several disadvantages, however, the most important of which is that many commodities deteriorate easily after a few trades. Precious metal coins have been used for money for millennia, partly because of their durability.

The Functions of Money

Money has four important functions in the economy: as a medium of exchange, a unit of account, a store of value, and a means of deferred payment. Let's examine the four important functions of money and see how they are different than other assets in the economy like stocks, bonds, art, real estate, and a comic book collection.

The primary function of money is to serve as a **medium of exchange,** to facilitate transactions, and to lower transaction costs. That is, sellers will accept it as payment in a transaction. However, money is not the only medium of exchange; rather, it is the only medium that is generally accepted for most transactions. How would people trade with one another in the absence of money? They would **barter** for goods and services that they desire.

The Barter System Is Inefficient

Under a barter system, individuals pay for goods or services by offering other goods and services in exchange. Suppose you are a farmer who needs some salt.

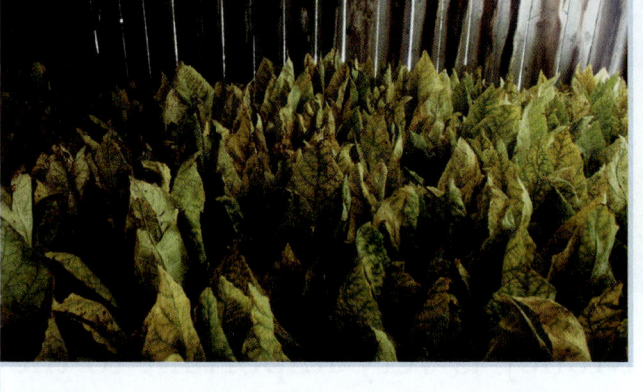

Tobacco was once used as money in colonial America—in particular, in Virginia and Maryland. Tobacco was used rather than other commodities because it was resistant to spoilage. In the seventeenth century, colonists used wampum (polished shells) as lawful money. The ancient Chinese used chisels for money, while other societies have used fish and cattle and, of course, gold coins as money.

money anything generally accepted in exchange for goods or services

medium of exchange the primary function of money, which is to facilitate transactions and lower transaction costs

barter direct exchange of goods and services without the use of money

You go to the merchant selling salt and offer her 30 pounds of wheat for 2 pounds of salt. The wheat that you use to buy the salt is not money, because the salt merchant may not want wheat and therefore may not accept it as payment. This issue is one of the major disadvantages of barter: The buyer may not have appropriate items of value to the seller. The salt merchant may reluctantly take the wheat that she does not want, later bartering it away to another customer for something that she does want. In any case, barter is inefficient because several trades may be necessary to receive the desired goods. That is, the problem with barter is that it requires a double coincidence of wants—both traders must be willing to trade their products with each other. Money solves

in the news

Mackerel Economics in Prison Leads to Appreciation for Oily Fillets

—JUSTIN SCHECK

When Larry Levine helped prepare divorce papers for a client a few years ago, he got paid in mackerel. Once the case ended, he says, "I had a stack of macks."

Mr. Levine and his client were prisoners in California's Lompoc Federal Correctional Complex. Like other federal inmates around the country, they found a can of mackerel—the "mack" in prison lingo—was the standard currency.

"It's the coin of the realm," says Mark Bailey, who paid Mr. Levine in fish. Mr. Bailey was serving a two-year tax-fraud sentence in connection with a chain of strip clubs he owned. Mr. Levine was serving a nine-year term for drug dealing. Mr. Levine says he used his macks to get his beard trimmed, his clothes pressed and his shoes shined by other prisoners. "A haircut is two macks," he says, as an expected tip for inmates who work in the prison barber shop.

There's been a mackerel economy in federal prisons since about 2004, former inmates and some prison consultants say. That's when federal prisons prohibited smoking and, by default, the cigarette pack, which was the earlier gold standard.

Prisoners need a proxy for the dollar because they're not allowed to possess cash. Money they get from prison jobs (which pay a maximum of 40 cents an hour, according to the Federal Bureau of Prisons) or family members goes into commissary accounts that let them buy things such as food and toiletries. After the smokes disappeared, inmates turned to other items on the commissary menu to use as currency.

Books of stamps were one easy alternative. "It was like half a book for a piece of fruit," says Tony Serra, a well-known San Francisco criminal-defense attorney who last year finished nine months in Lompoc on tax charges. Elsewhere in the West, prisoners use PowerBars or cans of tuna, says Ed Bales, a consultant who advises people who are headed to prison. But in much of the federal prison system, he says, mackerel has become the currency of choice.

Mackerel supplier Global Source Marketing Inc. says demand from prisons has grown since 2004. In recent years, demand has switched from cans—which wardens don't like because inmates can turn them into makeshift knives—to plastic-and-foil pouches of mackerel fillets, says Jon Linder, a vice president at supplier Power Commissary Inc., in Bohemia, N.Y.

Mackerel is hot in prisons in the U.S., but not so much anywhere else, says Mark Muntz, president of Global Source, which imports fillets of the oily, dark-fleshed fish from Asian canneries. Mr. Muntz says he's tried marketing mackerel to discount retailers. "We've even tried 99-cent stores," he says. "It never has done very well at all, regardless of the retailer, but it's very popular in the prisons."

Mr. Muntz says he sold more than $1 million of mackerel for federal prison commissaries last year. It accounted for about half his commissary sales, he says, outstripping the canned tuna, crab, chicken and oysters he offers.

Unlike those more expensive delicacies, former prisoners say, the mack is a good stand-in for the greenback because each can (or pouch) costs about $1 and few—other than weight-lifters craving protein—want to eat it.

So inmates stash macks in lockers provided by the prison and use them to buy goods, including illicit ones such as stolen food and home-brewed "prison hooch," as well as services, such as shoe-shines and cell cleaning.

The Bureau of Prisons views any bartering among prisoners as fishy. "We are aware that

(continued)

in the news

Mackerel Economics in Prison Leads to Appreciation for Oily Fillets (cont.)

inmates attempt to trade amongst themselves items that are purchased from the commissary," says bureau spokeswoman Felicia Ponce in an email. She says guards respond by limiting the amount of goods prisoners can stockpile. Those who are caught bartering can end up in the "Special Housing Unit"—an isolation area also known as the "hole"—and could lose credit they get for good behavior.

For that reason—and since communications between inmates and nonprisoners are monitored by prison officials—current inmates can't discuss mackerel transactions without risking discipline, say several lawyers and consultants who represent incarcerated clients.

. . . "I paid gambling debts" with mackerel, he says. "One time I bought cigarettes for a friend who was in the hole."

Mr. Roberts and other ex-inmates say some prisoners make specially prepared food with items from the prison kitchen and sell it for mackerel.

"I knew a guy who would buy ingredients and use the microwaves to cook meals. Then people used mack to buy it from him," says Jonson Miller, an adjunct history professor at Drexel University in Philadelphia who spent two months in federal prison after being arrested at a protest on federal property.

Mr. Miller was released in 2003, when prisoners were getting ready for cigarettes to be phased out, and says inmates then were already moving to mackerel.

. . . There are other threats to the mackerel economy, says Mr. Linder, of Power Commissary. "There are shortages world-wide, in terms of the catch," he says. Combined with the weak dollar, that's led to a surging mack. Now, he says, a pouch of mackerel sells for more than $1 in most commissaries.

Another problem with mackerel is that once a prisoner's sentence is up, there's little to do with it—the fish can't be redeemed for cash, and has little value on the outside. As a result, says Mr. Levine, prisoners approaching their release must either barter or give away their stockpiles.

That's what Mr. Levine did when he got out of prison last year. Since then, he's set up a consulting business offering advice to inmates and soon-to-be prisoners. He consults on various matters, such as how to request facility transfers and how to file grievances against wardens.

It's similar to the work he provided fellow inmates when he was in prison. But now, he says, "I get paid in American dollars."

SOURCE: Wall Street Journal, p. A1, October 2, 2008, Justin Scheck, Mackerel Economics in Prison Leads to Appreciation for Oily Fillets Packs of Fish Catch On as Currency, Former Inmates Say; Officials Carp.

---

the problem of double coincidence of wants because people will accept money for the items they sell.

Moreover, barter is extremely expensive over long distances. What would it cost me, living in California, to send wheat to Maine in return for an item in the L.L. Bean catalog? It is much cheaper to mail a check. Finally, barter is time-consuming because of difficulties in determining the value of the product that is being offered for barter. For example, the person selling the salt may wish to inspect the wheat first to make sure that it is pure and not contaminated with dirt or insects. Barter, in short, is expensive and inefficient, and it generally prevails only where limited trade is carried out over short distances, which generally means in relatively primitive economies. The more complex the economy (e.g., the higher the real GDP per capita), the greater the economic interactions between people, and consequently, the greater the need for one or more universally accepted assets serving as money. Only in a Robinson Crusoe economy, where people live in isolated settlements and are generally self-sufficient, is the use of money unnecessary.

Money as a Unit of Account

Besides serving as a medium of exchange, money is also a unit of account. With a barter system, one does not know precisely what 30 pounds of wheat are worth relative to 2 pounds of salt. With money, a common "yardstick" exists, so people can precisely compare the values of diverse goods and services. Thus, if wheat costs 50 cents a pound and salt costs $1 a pound, we can say that a pound of salt is valued precisely two times as much as a pound of wheat ($1/$0.50 = 2). By providing a universally understood unit of account, money serves to lower the information costs involved in making transactions. Without money, a person might not know what a good price for salt is, because so many different commodities can be bartered for it. With money, only one price for salt is necessary, and that price is readily available as information to the potential consumer. We use money as a unit of account when we measure and record economic value.

Money as a Store of Value

Money also serves as a store of value. It can provide a means of saving or "storing" things of value in an efficient manner. A farmer in a barter society who wants to save for retirement might accumulate enormous inventories of wheat, which he would then gradually trade away for other goods in his old age. This approach is a terribly inefficient way to save. The farmer would have to construct storage buildings to hold all his wheat; and the interest payments he would earn on the wheat would actually be negative, because it is quite likely that rats would eat part of it or it would otherwise deteriorate. Most important, physical goods of value would be tied up in unproductive use for many years. With money, the farmer saves pieces of paper that can be used to purchase goods and services in his old age. It is both cheaper and safer to store paper rather than wheat.

means of deferred payment
the attribute of money that makes it easier to borrow and to repay loans

Money as a Means of Deferred Payment

Finally, money is a **means of deferred payment.** Money makes it much easier to borrow and to repay loans. With barter, lending is cumbersome and subject to an added problem. What if a wheat farmer borrows some wheat and agrees to pay it back in wheat next year, but the value of wheat soars because of a poor crop resulting from drought? The debt will be paid back in wheat that is far more valuable than that borrowed, creating a problem for the borrower. Of course, fluctuations in the value of money can also occur; indeed, inflation has been a major problem in our recent past and continues to be a problem in many countries. But the value of money fluctuates far less than the value of many individual commodities, so lending in money imposes fewer risks on buyers and sellers than lending in commodities.

SECTION CHECK

1. Money is anything that is generally accepted in exchange for goods and services.
2. Barter is inefficient compared to money because a person may have to make several trades before receiving something that is truly wanted.
3. By providing a universally understood unit of account, money serves to lower the information costs involved in making transactions.
4. Money is both cheaper and easier to store than other goods.
5. Because the value of money fluctuates less than specific commodities, it imposes fewer risks on borrowers and lenders.

---

1. Why does the advantage of monetary exchange over barter increase as an economy becomes more complex?
2. How can uncertain and rapid rates of inflation erode money's ability to perform its functions efficiently?
3. In a world of barter, would useful financial statements such as balance sheets be possible? Would stock markets be possible? Would it be possible to build cars?
4. Why do virtually all societies create something to function as money?

SECTION 27.2 Measuring Money

* What is currency?
* What is liquidity?
* What is included in the money supply?
* What backs our money?

Currency

Currency consists of coins and/or paper that some institution or government has created to be used in the trading of goods and services and the payment of debts. Currency in the form of metal coins is still used as money throughout the world today. But metal currency has a disadvantage: It is bulky. Also, certain types of metals traditionally used in coins, such as gold and silver, are not available in sufficient quantities to meet our demands for a monetary instrument. For these reasons, metal coins have for centuries been supplemented by paper currency, often in the form of bank notes. In the United States, the Federal Reserve System (the Fed) issues Federal Reserve notes in various denominations, and this paper currency, along with coins, provides the basis for most transactions of relatively modest size in the United States today. (The Federal Reserve system will be discussed at length in the next chapter.)

What makes this paper and metal valuable? Paper and metal are valuable if they are acceptable to people who want to sell goods and services. Sellers must be confident that the money they accept is also acceptable where they want to buy goods and services. Imagine if money in California were not accepted as money in Texas or New York. It would certainly make it more difficult to carry out transactions.

Currency as Legal Tender

In the United States and most other nations of the world, metallic coins and paper currency are the only forms of **legal tender**. In other words, coins and paper money have been officially declared to be money—to be acceptable for the settlement of debts incurred in financial transactions. In effect, the government says, "We declare these instruments to be money, and citizens are expected to accept them as a medium of exchange." Legal tender is **fiat money**—a means of exchange that has been established not by custom and tradition or because of the value of the metal in a coin but by government fiat, or declaration.

currency
coins and/or paper created to facilitate the trade of goods and services and the payment of debts

legal tender
coins and paper officially declared to be acceptable for the settlement of financial debts

fiat money
a means of exchange established by government declaration

demand deposits
balances in bank accounts that depositors can access on demand

Demand Deposits and Other Checkable Deposits

Most of the money that we use for day-to-day transactions, however, is not official legal tender. Rather, it is a monetary instrument that has become "generally accepted" in exchange over the years and has now, by custom and tradition, become money. What is this instrument? It is balances in checking accounts in banks, more formally called **demand deposits**.

Demand deposits are defined as balances in bank accounts that depositors can access on demand by simply writing checks. Some other forms of accounts in financial institutions also have virtually all the attributes of demand deposits. For example, other checkable deposits earn interest but have some restrictions, such as higher monthly fees or minimum balance requirements. These interest-earning checking accounts effectively permit the depositors to write "orders" similar to checks and assign the rights to the deposit to other persons, just as we write checks to other parties. Practically speaking, funds in these accounts are the equivalent of demand deposits and have become an important component in the supply of money. Both these types of accounts are forms of **transaction deposits** because they can be easily converted into currency or used to buy goods and services directly. **Traveler's checks,** like currency and demand deposits, are also easily converted into currency or used directly as a means of payment.

transaction deposits deposits that can be easily converted to currency or used to buy goods and services directly

traveler's checks transaction instruments easily convertible into currency

goods and services because he has to be able to identify himself as a representative of the telephone company. If someone steals your checkbook, the thief can use your checks as money only if he can successfully forge your signature and provide some identification. Hence, transacting business by check is much less risky than using legal tender; an element of insurance or safety exists in the use of transaction deposits instead of currency.

Lower Transaction Costs

Suppose you decide that you want to buy a sweater that costs $81.28 from the current Urban Outfitters mail-order catalog. It is much cheaper, easier, and safer for you to send a check for $81.28 rather than four $20 bills, a $1 bill, a quarter, and three pennies. Transaction deposits are popular precisely because they lower transaction costs compared with the use of metal or paper currency. In small transactions, the gains in safety and convenience of checks are outweighed by the time and cost required to write and process them; in these cases, transaction costs are lower with paper and metallic currency. Therefore, it is unlikely that the use of paper or metallic currency will disappear entirely.

Transaction Records

Another useful feature of transaction deposits is that they provide a record of financial transactions. Each month, the bank sends the depositor canceled checks and/or a statement recording the deposit and withdrawal of funds. In an age when detailed records are often necessary for tax purposes, this feature is useful. Of course, it can work the other way, too. Paper currency transactions are also popular in business activities in which participants prefer no records for tax collectors to review.

The Popularity of Demand Deposits and Other Checkable Deposits

Demand deposits and other checkable deposits have replaced paper and metallic currency as the major source of money used for larger transactions in the United States and in most other relatively well-developed nations for several reasons, including the ease and safety of transactions, lower transaction costs, and transaction records.

Ease and Safety of Transactions

Paying for goods and services with checks is easier (meaning cheaper) and less risky than paying with paper money. Paper money is readily transferable: If someone takes a $20 bill from you, it is gone, and the thief can use it to buy goods with no difficulty. If, however, someone steals a check that you have written to the telephone company to pay a monthly bill, that person will probably have great difficulty using it to buy

Credit Cards

A credit card is "generally acceptable in exchange for goods and services." At the same time, however, a credit card payment is actually a guaranteed loan available on demand to the cardholder, which merely defers the cardholder's payment for a transaction using a demand deposit. Ultimately, an item purchased with a credit card must be paid for with a check; monthly payments on credit card accounts are required to continue using the card. A credit card, then, is not money but rather a convenient tool for carrying out transactions that minimizes the physical transfer of checks or currency. In this sense, it is a substitute for the use of money in exchange and allows the cardholder to use any given amount of money in future exchanges.

Savings Accounts

Economists are not completely in agreement on what constitutes money for all purposes. They agree, nearly universally, that coins, paper currency, demand and other checkable deposits, and traveler's checks are certainly forms of money, because all are accepted as direct means of payment for goods and services. Some economists, however, argue that for some purposes *money* should be more broadly defined to include **nontransaction deposits.** Nontransaction deposits are fund accounts against which the depositor *cannot* directly write checks—hence the name. If these funds cannot be used directly as a means of payment but must first be converted into money, why do people hold such accounts? People use these accounts primarily because they generally pay higher interest rates than transaction deposits.

Two primary types of nontransaction deposits exist—savings accounts and time deposits (sometimes referred to as certificates of deposit, or CDs). Most purists would argue that nontransaction deposits are **near money** assets but not money itself. Why? Savings accounts and time deposits cannot be used directly to purchase a good or service. They are not a direct medium of exchange. For example, you cannot go into a supermarket, pick out groceries, and give the clerk the passbook to your savings account. You must convert funds from your savings account into currency or demand deposits before you can buy goods and services. Thus, strictly speaking, nontransaction deposits do not satisfy the formal definition of money. At the same time, however, savings accounts are assets that can be quickly converted into money at the face value of the account. In the jargon of finance, savings accounts are highly liquid assets. True, under federal law commercial banks legally can require depositors to request withdrawal of funds in writing and then defer making payment for several weeks. But in practice no bank prohibits immediate withdrawal, although early withdrawal from some time deposits, especially certificates of deposit, may require the depositor to forgo some interest income as a penalty.

Money Market Mutual Funds

Money market mutual funds are interest-earning accounts provided by brokers who pool funds into investments such as Treasury bills. These funds are invested in short-term securities, and depositors are allowed to write checks against their accounts subject to certain limitations. This type of fund experienced tremendous growth over the last 20 years. Money market mutual funds are highly liquid assets. They are considered to be near money because they are relatively easy to convert into money for the purchases of goods and services.

Stocks and Bonds

Virtually everyone agrees that many other forms of financial assets, such as stocks and bonds, are not money. Suppose you buy 1000 shares of common stock in Microsoft at $30 per share, for a total of $30,000. The stock is traded daily on the New York Stock Exchange and elsewhere; you can readily sell the stock and get paid in legal tender or a demand deposit. Why, then, is this stock not considered money? First, it will take a few days for you to receive payment for the sale of stock; you cannot turn the asset into cash as quickly as you can a savings deposit in a financial institution. Second, and more importantly, the value

---

nontransaction deposits funds that cannot be used for payment directly but must be converted into currency for general use

near money nontransaction deposits that are not money but can be quickly converted into money

money market mutual funds interest-earning accounts provided by brokers that pool funds into such investments as Treasury bills of the stock fluctuates over time, and as the owner of the asset, you have no guarantee that you will be able to obtain its original nominal value at any time. Thus, stocks and bonds are not generally considered to be money.

Liquidity

Money is an asset that we generally use to buy goods or services. In fact, it is so easy to convert money into goods and services that we say it is the most liquid of assets. When we speak of **liquidity,** we are referring to the ease with which one asset can be converted into another asset or goods and services. For example, to convert a stock into goods and services would prove to be somewhat more difficult—contacting your broker or going online, determining at what price to sell your stock, paying the commission for the service, and waiting for the completion of the transaction. Clearly, stocks are not as liquid an asset as money. But other assets are even less liquid—for example, converting your painting collection or your baseball cards or Barbie dolls into other goods and services.

The Money Supply

Because a good case can be made either for including or for excluding savings accounts, certificates of deposit (CDs), and money market mutual funds from an operational definition of the money supply depending on its intended purpose, we will compromise and do both. Economists call the narrow definition of money—currency, checkable deposits, and traveler's checks—**M1.** The broader definition of money, encompassing M1 plus savings deposits, time deposits (except for some large-denomination certificates of deposit), and noninstitutional money market mutual fund shares, is called **M2.**

The difference between M1 and M2 is striking, as evidenced by the different sizes of the total stock of money depending on which definition is used. As Exhibit 1 shows, M2 is more than four times the magnitude of M1. In other words, people strongly prefer to keep the bulk of their liquid assets in the form of savings accounts of various kinds.

How Was Money "Backed"?

Until fairly recently, coins in most nations were largely made from precious metals, usually gold or silver. These metals had a considerable intrinsic worth: If the coins were melted down, the metal would be valuable for use in jewelry, industrial applications, dentistry, and so forth. Until 1933, the United States was on an internal **gold standard,** meaning that the dollar was defined as equivalent in value to a certain amount of gold, and paper currency or demand deposits could be

liquidity
the ease with which one asset can be converted into another asset or into goods and services

M1
the narrowest definition of money; includes currency, checkable deposits, and traveler's checks

M2
a broader definition of money that includes M1 plus savings deposits, time deposits, and noninstitutional money market mutual fund shares.

gold standard
defining the dollar as equivalent to a set value of a quantity of gold, allowing direct convertibility from currency to gold

---

section 27.2 exhibit 1 Two Definitions of the Money Supply: M1 and M2

Currency = $863 billion
M1: Currency + Checkable deposits + Traveler's checks = $1633 billion
M2: M1 + Savings deposits + Small-denomination time deposits + Noninstitutional money market mutual fund shares + Money market deposit accounts = $8310 billion

SOURCE: Federal Reserve, October 2009.

freely converted to gold coin. The United States abandoned the gold standard, however, eventually phasing out gold currency. Some silver coins and paper money convertible into silver remained; but by the end of the 1960s, even this tie between the monetary system and precious metals was gone—in part because the price of silver soared so high that the metal in coins had an intrinsic worth greater than its face value, leading people to hoard coins or even melt them down. When two forms of money are available, people prefer to spend the form of money that is less valuable. This tendency is a manifestation of **Gresham's Law:** "Cheap money drives out dear money."

> **Gresham's Law**
> the principle that "cheap money drives out dear money"; given an alternative, people prefer to spend less valuable money

What Really Backs Our Money Now?

Consequently, today no meaningful precious metal "backing" gives our money value. Why, then, do people accept dollar bills in exchange for goods? After all, a dollar bill is a piece of generally wrinkled paper about 6 inches by 2.5 inches in size, with virtually no inherent utility or worth. Do we accept these bills because it states on the front of the bills, "This note is legal tender for all debts, public and private"? Perhaps, but we accept some forms of currency and money in the form of demand deposits without that statement.

The true backing behind money in the United States is faith that people will take it in exchange for goods and services. People accept with great eagerness these small pieces of green paper with pictures of long-deceased people with funny-looking hair simply because we believe that they will be exchangeable for goods and services with an intrinsic value. If you were to drop two pieces of paper of equal size on the floor in front of 100 students, one a blank piece of paper and the other a $100 bill, and then leave the room, most of the group would probably start scrambling for the $100 bill, while the blank piece of paper would be ignored. Such is our faith in the green paper's practical value that some will even fight over it. As long as people have confidence in something's convertibility into goods and services, "money" will exist and no further backing is necessary.

Because governments represent the collective will of the people, they are the institutional force that traditionally defines money in the legal sense. People are willing to accept pieces of paper as money only because of their faith in the government. When people lose faith in the exchangeability of pieces of paper that the government decrees as money, even legal tender loses its status as meaningful money. Something is money only if people will generally accept it. Governments play a key role in defining money, but much of its value is actually created by private businesses in the pursuit of profit. A majority of U.S. money, whether M1 or M2, is in the form of deposits at privately owned financial institutions.

People who hold money, then, must have faith not only in their government but also in banks and other financial institutions. If you accept a check drawn on a regional bank, you believe that bank or, for that matter, any bank will be willing to convert that check into legal tender (currency), enabling you to buy goods or services that you want to have. Thus, you have faith in the bank as well. In short, our money is money because of the confidence we have in private financial institutions and our government.

Use what you've LEARNED
PAWN SHOPS AND LIQUIDITY

Q What do pawn shops sell?

A The typical response is that they sell used goods. In fact, they sell few used goods. However, they do sell something that is even more important to their clientele. They sell liquidity. When individuals hock their wares at pawn shops they are usually desperate—and are willing to pledge their watches, rings, or whatever as collateral. The pawn shop will allow you to buy your pawned item back in some specified time period for a higher price (that is, an interest charge). In this sense, pawn shops are like banks and will lend you money for a specified period of time if you are willing to pay the interest. But even if individuals don't buy their pawned item back, this behavior of selling and taking a lower price than could be obtained through the classifieds in order to get the money now, demonstrates that buyers are willing to pay for liquidity.

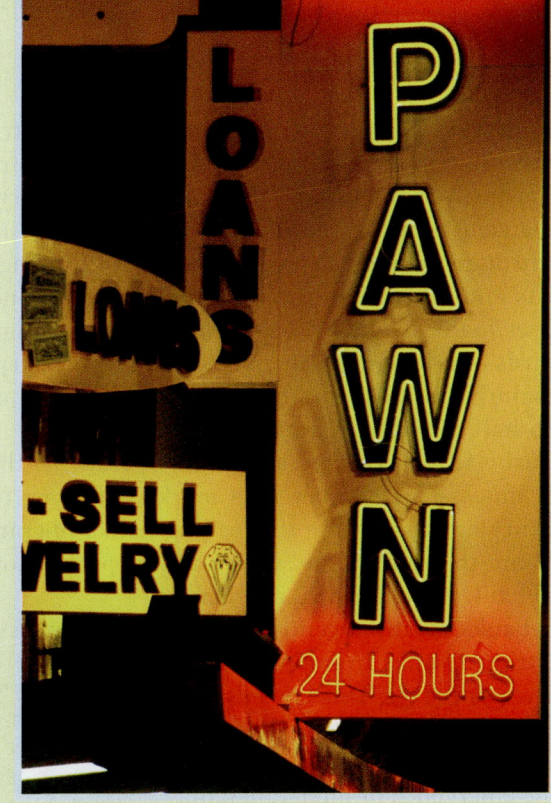

SECTION CHECK

1. Coins, paper currency, demand and other checkable deposits, and traveler's checks are all forms of money.
2. The ease with which one asset can be converted into another asset or goods and services is called liquidity.
3. M1 is made up of currency, checkable deposits, and traveler's checks. M2 is made up of M1, plus savings accounts, time deposits, and money market mutual funds.
4. Money is no longer backed by gold. The true backing is our faith that others will accept it from us in exchange for goods and services.

---

1. If everyone in an economy accepted poker chips as payment in exchange for goods and services, would poker chips be money?
2. If you were buying a pack of gum, would using currency or a demand deposit have lower transaction costs? What if you were buying a house?
3. What is the main advantage of transaction deposits for tax purposes? What is their main disadvantage for tax purposes?
4. Are credit cards money?
5. What are M1 and M2?
6. How have interest-earning checking accounts and overdraft protection led to the relative decline in demand deposits?

SECTION 27.3 How Banks Create Money

- How is money created?
- What is a reserve requirement?
- How do reserve requirements affect how much money can be created?

Financial Institutions

The biggest players in the banking industry are **commercial banks**. Commercial banks are financial institutions organized to handle the everyday financial transactions of businesses and households through demand deposit accounts and savings accounts and by making short-term commercial and consumer loans. These banks account for more than two-thirds of all the deposits in the banking industry; they maintain almost all the demand deposits and close to half the savings accounts.

Nearly 1,000 commercial banks operate in the United States. This number is in marked contrast to most other nations, where the leading banks operate throughout the country and where a large proportion of total bank assets are held in a handful of banks. Until recently, federal law restricted banks from operating in more than one state. This law has now changed, and the structure of banking as we know it will inevitably change with the emergence of interstate banking, mergers, and "hostile" takeovers.

Aside from commercial banks, the banking system includes two other important financial institutions: **savings and loan associations** and **credit unions**. Savings and loan associations provide many of the same services as commercial banks, including checkable deposits, a variety of time deposits, and money market deposit accounts. The almost 2,000 members of savings and loan associations have typically invested most of their savings deposits in home mortgages. Credit unions are cooperatives, made up of depositors with some common affiliation, for example, the same employer or union.

commercial banks financial institutions organized to handle everyday financial transactions of businesses and households through demand deposit accounts and savings accounts and by making short-term commercial and consumer loans

savings and loan associations financial institutions organized as cooperative associations that hold demand deposits and savings of members in the form of dividend-bearing shares and make loans, especially home mortgage loans

credit unions financial cooperatives made up of depositors with a common affiliation

The Functions of Financial Institutions

Financial institutions offer a large number of financial functions. For example, they often will pay an individual's monthly bills by automatic withdrawals, administer estates, and rent safe-deposit boxes, among other things. Most important, though, they are depositories for savings and liquid assets that are used by individuals and firms for transaction purposes. They can create money by making loans. In making loans, financial institutions act as intermediaries (the middle persons) between savers, who supply funds, and borrowers seeking funds to invest.

How Do Banks Create Money?

As we have already learned, most money, narrowly defined, is in the form of transaction deposits—assets that can be directly used to buy goods and services. But how did the balance in, say, a checking account get there in the first place? Perhaps it was through a loan made by a commercial bank. When a bank lends to a person, it does not typically give the borrower cash (paper and metallic currency). Rather, it gives the borrower the funds by issuing a check or by adding funds to an existing checking account. If you go into a bank and borrow $1,000, the bank probably will add $1,000 to your checking account at the bank, creating a new checkable deposit—money.

How Do Banks Make Profits?

Banks make loans and create checkable deposits to make profits. How do they make their profits? By collecting higher interest payments on the loans they make than they pay their depositors for those funds. If you borrow $1,000 from Bank One, the interest payment you make, less the expenses the bank incurs in making the loan, including their costs of acquiring the funds, represents profit to the bank.

Reserve Requirements

Because the way to make more profit is to make more loans, banks want to make a large volume of loans. Stockholders of banks want the largest profits possible; so what keeps banks from making nearly infinite quantities of loans? Primarily, government regulatory authorities limit the loan issuance of banks by imposing **reserve requirements.** Banks are required to keep on hand a quantity of cash or reserve accounts with the Federal Reserve equal to a prescribed proportion of their checkable deposits.

Fractional Reserve System

Even in the absence of regulations restricting the creation of checkable deposits, a prudent bank would put some limit on their loan (and therefore deposit) volume. Why? For people to accept checkable deposits as money, the checks written must be generally accepted in exchange for goods and services. People will accept checks only if they know that they are quickly convertible at par (face value) into legal tender. For this reason, banks must have adequate cash reserves on hand (including reserves at the Fed that can be almost immediately converted to currency, if necessary) to meet the needs of customers who wish to convert their checkable deposits into currency or spend them on goods or services.

It's a Wonderful Life has a scene showing a run on a savings and loan that demonstrates the power of the fractional reserve banking system—"You're thinking of this place all wrong; as if I had the money in a safe. Your money is not here. Your money is in Joe's house and in the Kennedy's house and hundreds of others."

reserve requirements
holdings of assets at the bank or at the Federal Reserve Bank as mandated by the Fed

fractional reserve system
a system that requires banks to hold reserves equal to some fraction of their checkable deposits

Our banking system is sometimes called a **fractional reserve system,** because banks, by law as well as by choice, find it necessary to keep cash on hand and reserves at the Federal Reserve equal to some fraction of their checkable deposits. If a bank were to create $100 in demand deposits for every $1 in cash reserves that it had, the bank might well find itself in difficulty before too long. Why? Consider a bank with $10,000,000 in demand and time deposits and $100,000 in cash reserves. Suppose a couple of large companies with big accounts decide to withdraw $120,000 in cash on the same day. The bank would be unable to convert into legal tender all the funds requested. The word would then spread that the bank's checks are not convertible into lawful money, possibly causing a "run on the bank." The bank would have to quickly convert some of its other assets into currency, or it would be unable to meet its obligations to convert its deposits into currency and it would have to close.

Therefore, even in the absence of reserve regulations, few banks would risk maintaining fewer reserves on hand than they thought prudent for their amount of deposits (particularly demand deposits). Reserve requirements exist primarily to control the amount of demand and time deposits and thus the size of the money supply; they do not exist simply to prevent bank failures.

While banks must meet their reserve requirements, they do not want to keep any more of their funds as additional reserves than necessary for safety, because cash assets do not earn any interest. To protect themselves but also earn some interest income, banks usually keep some of their assets in highly liquid investments, such as U.S. government bonds. These types of highly liquid, interest-paying assets are often called **secondary reserves**.

> **secondary reserves**
> highly liquid, interest-paying assets held by the bank
>
> **balance sheet**
> a financial record that indicates the balance between a bank's assets and its liabilities plus capital

bonds, and its buildings), including contractual obligations of individuals and firms to pay funds to the bank (loans). The largest asset item for most banks is loans. Banks maintain most of their assets in the form of loans because interest payments on loans are the primary means by which they earn revenue. Some assets are kept in the form of non-interest-bearing cash and reserve accounts at the Federal Reserve to meet legal reserve requirements (and to meet the cash demands of customers). Typically, relatively little of a bank's reserves, or cash assets, is physically kept in the form of paper currency in the bank's vault or at tellers' windows. Most banks keep the majority of their reserves as reserve accounts at the Federal Reserve. As previously indicated, banks usually also keep some assets in the form of bonds that are quickly convertible into cash if necessary (secondary reserves).

A Balance Sheet

Earlier in this chapter, we learned that money is created when banks make loans. We will now look more closely at the process of bank lending and its impact on the stock of money. In doing so, we will examine the structure and behavior of our hypothetical bank, Bank One. To get a good picture of the size of the bank, what it owns, and what it owes, we look at its **balance sheet**, which is like a financial "photograph" of the bank at a single moment. Exhibit 1 presents a balance sheet for Bank One.

Assets

The assets of a bank are the items of value that the bank owns (e.g., cash, reserves at the Federal Reserve,

Liabilities

All banks have substantial liabilities, which are financial obligations that the bank has to other people. The predominant liability of virtually all banks is deposits. If you have money in a demand deposit account, you have the right to demand cash for that deposit at any time. Basically, the bank owes you the amount in your checking account. Time deposits similarly constitute a liability of banks.

Capital Stock

For a bank to be healthy and solvent, its assets, or what it owns, must exceed its liabilities, or what it owes others. In other words, if the bank were liquidated and all the assets converted into cash and all

section 27.3 exhibit 1 Balance Sheet, Bank One

Assets		Liabilities and Capital	
Cash (reserves)	$ 2,000,000	Transaction deposits (checking deposits)	$ 5,000,000
Loans	6,100,000	Savings and time deposits	4,000,000
Bonds (U.S. government and municipal)	1,500,000	Total Liabilities	$ 9,000,000
Bank building, equipment, fixtures	400,000	Capital	1,000,000
Total Assets	**$10,000,000**	**Total Liabilities and Capital**	**$10,000,000**

the obligations to others (liabilities) paid off, some cash would still be left to distribute to the owners of the bank, that is, its stockholders. This difference between a bank's assets and its liabilities constitutes the bank's capital. Note that this definition of capital differs from the earlier definition, which described capital as goods used to further production of other goods (machines, structures, tools, etc.). In this case, the capital stock is the equity owned by shareholders both in and out of the community. As you can see in Exhibit 1, capital is included on the right side of the balance sheet, so that both sides (assets and liabilities plus capital) are equal in amount. Any time the aggregate amount of bank assets changes, the aggregate amount of liabilities and capital must also change by the same amount, by definition.

required reserve ratio the percentage of deposits that a bank must hold at the Federal Reserve Bank or in bank vaults

excess reserves reserve levels held above that required by the Fed

The Required Reserve Ratio

Suppose for simplicity that Bank One faces a reserve requirement of 10 percent on all deposits. This percentage is often called the **required reserve ratio.** But what does a required reserve ratio of 10 percent mean? It means that the bank *must* keep cash on hand or at the Federal Reserve Bank equal to one-tenth (10 percent) of its deposits. For example, if the required reserve ratio is 10 percent, banks are required to hold $100,000 in required reserves for every $1 million in deposits. The remaining 90 percent of cash is called **excess reserves.**

Reserves in the form of cash and reserves at the Federal Reserve earn no revenue for the bank; no profit is made from holding cash. Whenever excess reserves appear, banks will invest the excess reserves in interest-earning assets—sometimes bonds, but usually loans.

Loaning Excess Reserves

Let's see what happens when someone deposits $100,000 at Bank One. We will continue to assume that the required reserve ratio is 10 percent. That is, the bank is required to hold $10,000 in required reserves for this new deposit of $100,000. The remaining 90 percent, or $90,000, becomes excess reserves, most of which will likely become available for loans for individuals and businesses.

However, the story doesn't end here. Let's say that the bank loans all its new excess reserves of $90,000 to an individual who is remodeling her home. At the time the bank makes the loan, its money supply increases by $90,000. Specifically, no one has less money—the original depositor still has $100,000, and the bank adds $90,000 to the borrower's checking account (demand deposit). A new demand deposit, or checking account, of $90,000 has been created. *Because demand deposits are money, the issuers of the new loan have created money.*

Furthermore, borrowers are not likely to keep borrowed money in their checking accounts for long, because they usually take out loans to make purchases. If a loan is used for remodeling, the borrower pays the construction company; the owner of the construction company, in turn, will likely deposit the money into his account at another bank to add even more funds for additional money expansion. This whole process is summarized in Exhibit 2.

Now suppose that Bank One faces a reserve requirement of 20 percent. The bank must keep cash on hand or at the Federal Reserve Bank equal to one-fifth (20%) of its deposits. If the bank's deposits (demand and time) sum to $9,000,000, required reserves are calculated as follows:

Deposits × *Reserve ratio* = $9,000,000 × 0.20
= $1,800,000

The bank then, is required to maintain $1,800,000 in cash. Bank One, however, actually has $2 million in cash, meaning that it has excess reserves, or $200,000. (Excess reserves = Actual reserves − Required reserves, or $2,000,000 − $1,800,000.)

Excess reserves = *Actual reserves*
− *Required reserves*
= $2,000,000 − $1,800,000
= $200,000

Suppose Bank One decided to make loans with its $200,000 in excess reserves. For simplicity's sake, let us suppose it makes one loan of $200,000 to a manufacturer for an addition to its chocolate factory. What will be the bank's balance sheet after it makes the loan? As Exhibit 3 indicates, both assets and liabilities rise by $200,000. The bank simply gives the borrower a checking account with $200,000 in it, a new deposit liability of the bank. In return, the borrower gives the bank an

section 27.3 exhibit 2 — Fractional Reserve Banking System

When a new deposit enters the banking system, much of that money will be used for loans. Banks create money when they increase demand deposits through the process of creating loans.

section 27.3 exhibit 3 — Balance Sheet for Bank One After Loan

Assets		Liabilities and Capital	
Cash (reserves)	$ 2,000,000	Demand deposits	$ 5,200,000
Loans	6,300,000	Time deposits	4,000,000
Bonds (U.S. government and municipal)	1,500,000	Total Liabilities	$ 9,200,000
Bank building, equipment, fixtures	400,000	Capital	1,000,000
Total Assets	$10,200,000	Total Liabilities and Capital	$10,200,000

IOU agreeing to pay back the $200,000 plus interest at some future date. Thus, loans rise by $200,000 over the level on the initial balance sheet.

Note that in making the loan, Bank One did not have to reduce its cash reserves. It did not give the borrower cash; it simply created new money by giving the borrower $200,000 in a checking account. Therefore, even after making a loan equal to its initial excess reserves of $200,000, the bank still has some excess reserves. The bank's deposits rose to $9,200,000; 20 percent of that is $1,840,000. Yet the bank has $2,000,000 in actual reserves. Excess reserves are still $160,000 ($2,000,000 − $1,840,000 = $160,000).

If it still has some excess reserves, should the bank make still more loans? No. Why? Because when the

section 27.3 exhibit 4: Balance Sheet for Bank One After Loan Funds Are Spent

Assets		Liabilities and Capital	
Cash (reserves)	$ 1,800,000	Demand deposits	$ 5,000,000
Loans	6,300,000	Time deposits	4,000,000
Bonds (U.S. government and municipal)	1,500,000	Total Liabilities	$ 9,000,000
Bank building, equipment, fixtures	400,000	Capital	1,000,000
Total Assets	$10,000,000	Total Liabilities and Capital	$10,000,000

chocolate manufacturer borrowed $200,000, it did so in order to expand the factory. Few people borrow money and simply let the money sit in a checking account while they pay interest on the loan. It is reasonable to assume that the chocolate maker will shortly take all or part of the $200,000 out of the checking account, probably in the form of a check to a construction company for $200,000. What will the construction company do with the check? Put it in its bank. With many different banks in the United States, it is likely that the construction company has its checking account in another bank. Suppose its account is in Bank Two. Bank Two credits the account of the construction company with $200,000 in demand deposits, then takes the check and uses the facilities of the Federal Reserve System or a bank clearinghouse to present the check to Bank One for payment. Bank One will then have to pay Bank Two $200,000 in cash.

Therefore, Bank One will eventually (depending on how long it takes the chocolate manufacturer to spend the $200,000 it borrowed) face losing cash reserves equal to the loan. After Bank Two presents the check that was written by the chocolate manufacturer to Bank One for payment, Bank One's balance sheet changes again, as indicated in Exhibit 4.

As the chocolate maker spends the $200,000, demand deposits fall by that amount, so that the bank's liabilities also decline by $200,000. The bank transfers $200,000 in cash to Bank Two. Incidentally, rarely is cash actually physically moved, given the expense and risk. Typically, the local Federal Reserve Bank simply reduces the cash reserves of Bank One by $200,000 and increases Bank Two's by $200,000.

When the smoke clears, the chocolate manufacturer has its factory addition, and Bank One has an interest-paying IOU equal to $200,000. Bank One's cash reserves have fallen, however, to an amount ($1,800,000) exactly equal to its required reserves. Had the bank initially loaned out more than its $200,000 in excess reserves, the bank would have found its reserves below the required level as soon as the borrower spent the loan, assuming that the receiver of the funds had his or her bank account in another bank. Therefore, one important rule of thumb in banking is that a single bank in a banking system of many banks can safely make loans only equal to the amount of its excess reserves.

Is More Money More Wealth?

When banks create more money by putting their excess reserves to work, they make the economy more liquid—more of a medium of exchange. Clearly, more money is in the economy after the loan, but is the borrower any wealthier? The answer is no. Even though borrowers have more money to buy goods and services, they are not any richer, because the new liability, the loan, has to be repaid.

In short, banks create money when they increase demand deposits through the process of creating loans. However, the process does not stop here. In the next section, we will see how the process of loans and deposits has a multiplying effect throughout the banking industry.

SECTION CHECK

1. Money is created when banks make loans. Borrowers receive newly created demand deposits.
2. Required reserves are the amount of cash or reserves—equal to a prescribed proportion of their deposits—that banks are required to keep on hand or in reserve accounts with the Federal Reserve.
3. A balance sheet is a financial record that indicates the balance between a bank's assets and its liabilities plus capital.

1. What is happening to the number of banks now that interstate banking is allowed?
2. In what way is it true that "banks make money by making money"?
3. How do legal reserve deposit regulations lower bank profits?
4. Is a demand deposit an asset or a liability?
5. If the Bonnie and Clyde National Bank's only deposits were demand deposits of $20 million and it faced a 10 percent reserve requirement, how much money would it be required to hold in reserves?
6. Suppose you found $10,000 while digging in your backyard and you deposited it in the bank. How would your new demand deposit account create a situation of excess reserves at your bank?

SECTION 27.4 The Money Multiplier

* How does the process of multiple expansions of the money supply work?
* What is the money multiplier?

The Multiple Expansion Effect

We just learned that banks can create money (demand deposits) by making loans and that the monetary expansion of an individual bank is limited to its excess reserves. However, this point ignores the further effects of a new loan and the accompanying expansion in the money supply. New loans create new money directly, but they also create excess reserves in other banks, which leads to still further increases in both loans and the money supply. With this multiple expansion effect, a given volume of bank reserves creates a multiplied amount of money.

New Loans and Multiple Expansions

To see how the process of multiple expansion works, consider what happens when Bank One receives a new cash deposit of $100,000. For convenience, say the bank is only required to keep new cash reserves equal to one-tenth (10 percent) of new deposits. Thus, Bank One is only required to hold $10,000 of the $100,000 deposit for required reserves. The bank therefore has $90,000 in excess reserves as a consequence of the new cash deposit.

Bank One will probably put its newly acquired excess reserves to work in some fashion earning income in the form of interest. Most likely, it will make one or more new loans totaling $90,000.

When the borrowers from Bank One get their loans, the borrowed money will almost certainly be spent on something—new machinery, a new house, a new car, or greater store inventories. The new money will lead to new spending.

The $90,000 spent by people borrowing from Bank One will likely end up in bank accounts in still other banks, such as Bank Two in Exhibit 1. Bank Two now has a new deposit of $90,000 with which to make more loans and create still more money. So Bank Two's T-account now looks like this:

Bank Two

Assets		Liabilities	
Reserves	$ 9,000	Checking	
Loans	81,000	deposits	$90,000

After the deposits, Bank Two has liabilities of $90,000. Thus, Bank Two creates $81,000 of money. Now if the money deposited in Bank Two is made available for a loan and is then deposited in Bank Three, the T-account for Bank Three will be:

Bank Three

Assets		Liabilities	
Reserves	$ 8,100	Checking	
Loans	72,900	deposits	$81,000

This process continues with Bank Three, Bank Four, Bank Five, and others. The initial cash deposit made by Bank One thus has a chain-reaction effect that ultimately involves many banks and a total monetary impact that is far greater than would be suggested by the size of the original deposit of $100,000. That is, every new loan gives rise to excess reserves, which lead to still further lending and deposit creation. Of course, each round of lending is smaller than the preceding one, because some (we are assuming 10 percent) of the new money created must be kept as required reserves.

The Money Multiplier

The **money multiplier** measures the potential amount of money that the banking system generates with each dollar of reserves. The following formula can be used to measure the total maximum potential impact on the supply of money:

> *Potential money creation = Initial deposit × Money multiplier*

money multiplier measures the potential amount of money that the banking system generates with each dollar of reserves

To find the size of the money multiplier, we simply divide 1 by the reserve requirement (1/R). The larger the reserve requirement, the smaller the money multiplier. Thus, a reserve requirement of 25 percent, or one-fourth, means a money multiplier of 4. Likewise, a reserve requirement of 10 percent, or one-tenth, means a money multiplier of 10.

In the example given in Exhibit 1, where Bank One (facing a 10% reserve requirement) receives a new $100,000 cash deposit, the initial deposit equals $100,000. Potential money creation, then, equals $100,000 (initial deposit) multiplied by 10 (the money multiplier), or $1,000,000. Using the money multiplier, we can calculate that the total potential impact of the initial $100,000 deposit is some $1,000,000 in money being created. In other words, the final monetary impact is 10 times as great as the initial deposit. Most of this increase, $900,000, has been created by the increase in demand deposits generated when banks make loans; the remaining $100,000 is from the initial deposit.

Why Is It Only "Potential" Money Creation?

Note that the expression "potential money creation" was used in describing the impact of creating loans and deposits out of excess reserves. Why "potential"? Some banks could choose not to lend all their excess reserves. Some banks might be extremely conservative and keep some extra newly acquired cash assets in that form. When they do, the chain reaction effect is reduced by the amount of excess reserves not loaned out.

Moreover, some borrowers may not spend all their newly acquired bank deposits, or they may wait a considerable period before doing so. Others may put their borrowed funds into time deposits rather than checkable deposits, which would reduce the M1 expansion process but not the M2 money expansion process. Still others may choose to keep some of their loans as currency in their pockets. Such leakages and time lags in the bank money expansion process usually mean that the actual monetary impact of an initial deposit created out of excess reserves within a short time is less than that indicated by the money multiplier. Still, the multiplier principle does work, and a multiple expansion of deposits will generally occur in a banking system that is characterized by fractional reserve requirements.

section 27.4 exhibit 1 — The Multiple Expansion Process

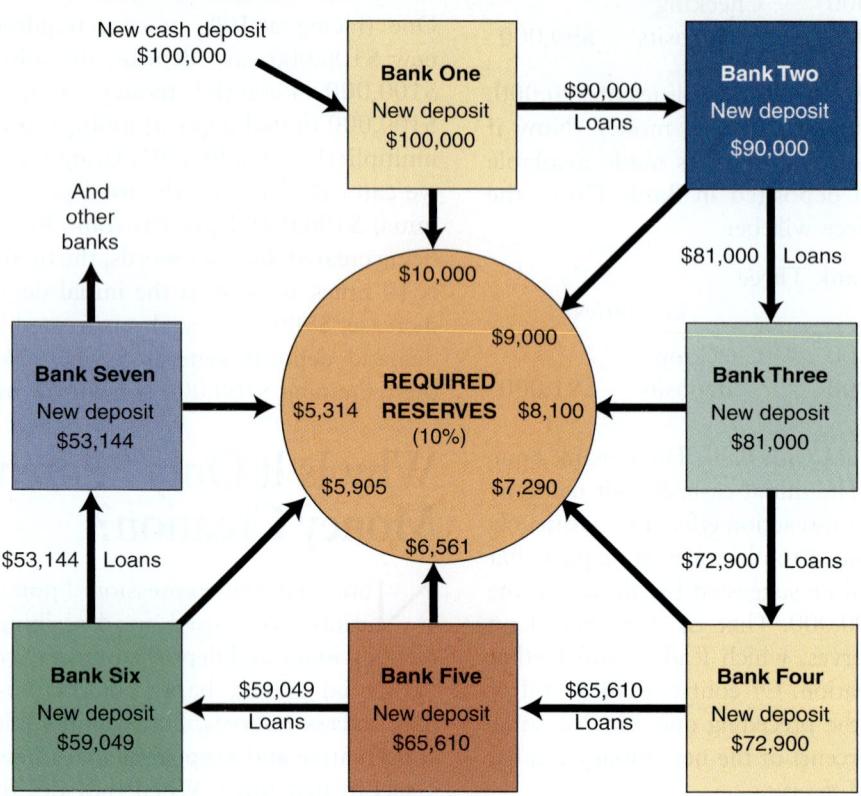

A $100,000 new cash deposit at Bank One has the potential to create $1,000,000 in a chain reaction that involves many banks. The process repeats itself, as the money lent by one bank becomes a new deposit in another bank.

SECTION CHECK

1. New loans mean new money (demand deposits), which can increase spending as well as the money supply.
2. The banking system as a whole can potentially create money equal to several times the amount of total reserves or new money equal to several times the amount of excess reserves; the exact amount may be determined by the money multiplier, which is equal to one divided by the reserve requirement.

1. Why do the supply of money and the volume of bank loans both increase or decrease at the same time?
2. Why would each bank involved in the process of multiple expansions of the money supply lend out a larger fraction of any new deposit it receives the lower the reserve requirement?
3. If a particular bank with a reserve requirement of 10 percent has $30,000 in new cash deposits, how much money could it create through making new loans?
4. Why do banks choosing to hold excess reserves or borrowers choosing to hold some of their loans in the form of currency reduce the actual impact of the money multiplier below that indicated by the multiplier formula?

SECTION 27.5 The Collapse of America's Banking System, 1920–1933

* What caused the collapse of the banking system between 1920 and 1933?
* How are bank failures avoided today?

Perhaps the most famous utterance from Franklin D. Roosevelt, the president of the United States from 1933 to 1945, was made on the day he assumed office, when he declared, "The only thing we have to fear is fear itself." These 10 words succinctly summarize the problems that led the world's leading economic power to a near total collapse in its system of commercial banking and, with that, to an abrupt and unprecedented decline in the money supply. The decline in the money supply, in turn, contributed to an economic downturn that had dire consequences for many, especially for the one-fourth of the labor force unemployed at the time of Roosevelt's first inaugural address.

What Happened to the Banking Industry?

In 1920, 30,000 banks were operating in the United States; by 1933, the number declined to about 15,000. What happened? In some cases, bank failure reflected imprudent management or even criminal activity on the part of bank officers (stealing from the bank). More often, though, banks in rural areas closed as a consequence of having large sums of assets tied up in loans to farmers who, because of low farm prices, were not in a position to pay off the loans when they came due. Rumors spread that a bank was in trouble, and those rumors, even if false, became self-fulfilling prophecies. Bank "runs" developed, and even conservatively managed banks with cash equal to 15 percent or 20 percent of their deposit liabilities found themselves with insufficient cash reserves to meet the withdrawal requests of panicky depositors.

The bank failures of the 1920s, while numerous, were generally scattered around small towns in the country. In general, confidence in banks actually increased during that decade; and by the fall of 1929, there were $11 in bank deposits for every $1 in currency in circulation.

The first year following the stock market crash of 1929 saw little dramatic change in the banking system; but in late 1930, a bank with the unfortunately awesome-sounding name of the Bank of the United States failed—the largest bank failure in the country up to that time. This failure had a ripple effect. More runs on banks occurred as depositors became jittery. Banks, fearing runs, stopped lending their excess reserves, thereby aggravating a fall in the money supply and reducing business investment.

As depositors converted their deposits to currency, bank reserves fell, as did the ability of banks to support deposits. The situation improved a bit in 1932, when a newly created government agency, the Reconstruction Finance Corporation (RFC), made loans to distressed banks. By early 1933, however, the decline in depositor confidence had reached the point that the entire banking system was in jeopardy. On March 4, newly inaugurated President Roosevelt declared a national bank holiday, closing every bank in the country for nearly two weeks. Then, only the "good" banks were allowed to reopen, an action that increased confidence. By this time the deposit-currency ratio had fallen from 11 to 1 (in 1929) to 4 to 1. Passage of federal deposit insurance in mid-1933 greatly strengthened depositor confidence and led to money reentering the banks. The recovery process began.

What Caused the Collapse?

The collapse occurred for several reasons. First, the nation had thousands of relatively small banks. Customers believed that depositor withdrawals could force a bank to close, and the mere fear of bank runs made them a reality. Canada, with relatively few banks, most of them large with many branches, had no bank runs. Second, governmental attempts to stem the growing distress were weak and too late. Financial aid to banks was nonexistent; the Federal Reserve System and other governmental efforts began only in 1932—well into the decline. Third, deposit insurance, which would have bolstered customer confidence, did not exist. The financial consequences of bank failures were correctly perceived by the public to be dire. Fourth, growing depositor fear was enhanced by the fact that the economy was in a continuous downward spiral, eroding the basis for any optimism that bank loans would be safely repaid.

Bank Failures Today

The combination of the Federal Deposit Insurance Corporation (FDIC) and the government's greater willingness to assist distressed banks has reduced the number of bank failures in recent times. Now, when a bank runs into financial difficulty, the FDIC may assist another bank in taking over the assets and liabilities of the troubled bank so that no depositor loses a cent. We do not see depositors run on banks because the FDIC will make good on deposits. There are costs and benefits of insuring deposits. On the cost side is that bankers whose deposits are insured may take greater risks. On the benefit side deposit insurance means that, changes in the money supply due to a loss of deposits from failed banks are no longer a big problem. Better bank stability means a greater stability in the money supply, which means, as will be more explicitly demonstrated in the next chapter, a greater level of economic stability.

However, in the 1980s, a savings and loan crisis occurred, one of the worst financial crises since the Great Depression. The inflation of the 1970s had created a problem for many savings and loans. They had made a large number of real estate loans in the early 1970s, when the inflation rate was relatively low at about 5 percent. Then, during most of the rest of that decade, inflation rates rose rapidly and nominal interest rates soared. The savings and loans were in a squeeze—they had to pay high interest rates to attract depositors but were earning low interest rates on their real estate loans from the early 1970s. This disastrous combination for the savings and loans caused many of them to go belly up.

Unfortunately, interest rates were not the only problem. The government eased regulations to make it easier for savings and loans to compete for deposits with other financial institutions in the national market. Deregulation, coupled with deposit insurance, put savings and loans in a gambling mood. Many savings and loans poured money into high-risk real estate projects and other risky ventures. Depositors had little incentive to monitor their banks because they knew they would be protected up to $100,000 on their accounts by the government. Eventually, more than a thousand thrift institutions went bankrupt. Depositors were saved, but taxpayers were not. Taxpayers ended up paying the bill for much of the savings and loan debacle—the bailout for the financial losses has been estimated to be more than $150 billion. The Thrift Bailout Bill of 1989 provided funds for the bailout and new, stricter provisions for banks.

Financial crisis are a little like earthquakes. We know that they will happen but we don't know exactly when and the magnitude. For example, not many economists forecasted the financial crisis of 2008.

SECTION CHECK

1. The banking collapse of 1920–1933 occurred because of customers' fears and the weakness of the government's attempts to correct the problem.
2. The creation of the Federal Deposit Insurance Corporation has largely eliminated bank runs in recent times.

---

1. How did the combination of increased holding of excess reserves by banks and currency by the public lead to bank failures in the 1930s?
2. What are the four reasons cited in the text for the collapse of the U.S. banking system in this period?
3. What is the FDIC, and how did its establishment increase bank stability and reassure depositors?

Interactive Chapter Summary

Fill in the blanks:

1. The most important disadvantage of using commodities as money is that they _____ easily after a few trades.

2. _____ consists of coins and/or paper that some institution or government has created to be used in the trading of goods and services and the payment of debts.

3. Legal tender is _____ money.

4. Assets in checking accounts in banks are more formally called _____ deposits.

5. Demand deposits are deposits in banks that can be _____ on demand by simply writing a check.

6. _____ deposits are assets that can be easily converted into currency or used to buy goods and services directly.

7. _____ deposits and _____ deposits have replaced paper and metallic currency as the primary source of money used for transactions in the United States.

8. Transaction deposits are a popular monetary instrument precisely because they lower _____ costs compared with the use of metal or paper currency.

9. Credit card payments are actually guaranteed _____, which merely defer customer payment.

10. Credit cards are not money; they are _____ for the use of money in exchange.

11. _____ deposits are fund accounts against which the depositor cannot directly write checks.

12. Two primary types of nontransaction deposits exist: _____ accounts and _____ deposits.

13. Assets that can be quickly converted into money are considered highly _____ assets.

14. Money market mutual funds are considered _____ money because they are relatively easy to convert into money for the purchase of goods and services.

15. _____ includes M1, plus saving accounts, time deposits (except for some large-denomination certificates of deposit), and money market mutual funds.

16. _____ Law states that "cheap money drives out dear money."

17. Something is money only if people will generally _____ it.

18. Our money is money because of confidence that we have in _____ institutions as well as in our _____.

19. The primary function of money is to serve as a(n) _____.

20. The more complex the economy, the _____ the need for one or more universally accepted assets serving as money.

21. Money is both a(n) _____ of value and a(n) _____ of value.

22. With money, a common _____ exists, so that the values of diverse goods and services can be precisely compared.

23. The value of money fluctuates far _____ than the value of many individual commodities.

24. The biggest players in the banking industry are _____.

25. Aside from commercial banks, the banking system includes two other important financial institutions: _____ and _____.

26. Most important, financial institutions are _____ for savings and liquid assets that are used by individuals and firms for transaction purposes.

27. In making loans, financial institutions act as intermediaries between _____, who supply funds, and _____ seeking funds to invest.

28. If you go into a bank and borrow $1,000, the bank probably will simply _____ to your checking account at the bank.

29. Banks make their profit by collecting _____ interest payments on the loans they make than they pay their depositors for those funds.

30. _____ require banks to keep on hand a quantity of cash or reserve accounts with the Federal Reserve equal to a prescribed proportion of their checkable deposits.

31. Our banking system is sometimes called a(n) _____ system because banks find it necessary to keep cash on hand and reserves at the Federal Reserve equal to some fraction of their checkable deposits.

32. Money is created when banks _____.

33. The largest asset item for most banks is _____.

34. Most banks keep a majority of their reserves as _____.

35. Checking account deposits and time deposits constitute _____ of banks.

36. Any time the aggregate amount of bank _____ changes, the aggregate amount of liabilities and capital must also change by the same amount, by definition.

37. Required reserves equal _____ times _____.

38. Whenever excess reserves appear, banks will convert the _____ reserves into other _____ assets.

39. The monetary expansion of an individual bank is limited to its _____ reserves.

40. Potential money creation from a cash deposit equals that initial deposit times _____.

41. The actual monetary impact of an initial deposit created out of excess reserves within a short time period is _____ indicated by the money multiplier.

42. When a person pays a loan back to a bank, demand deposits _____ and the money supply _____.

Answers: 1. deteriorate 2. Currency 3. fiat 4. demand 5. withdrawn 6. Transaction 7. Demand; other checkable 8. transaction 9. loans 10. substitutes 11. Nontransaction 12. savings; time 13. liquid 14. near 15. M2 16. Gresham's 17. accept 18. private financial; government 19. medium of exchange 20. greater 21. standard; store 22. yardstick 23. less 24. commercial banks 25. savings and loan associations; credit unions 26. depositories 27. savers; borrowers 28. add $1,000 29. higher 30. Reserve requirements 31. fractional reserve 32. make loans 33. loans 34. reserve accounts at the Federal Reserve 35. liabilities 36. assets 37. deposits; the required reserve ratio 38. non-interest-earning; interest-earning 39. excess 40. the money multiplier 41. less than that 42. declines; declines

Key Terms and Concepts

money 802
medium of exchange 802
barter 802
means of deferred payment 805
currency 806
legal tender 806
fiat money 806
demand deposits 806
transaction deposits 807
traveler's checks 807

nontransaction deposits 808
near money 808
money market mutual funds 808
liquidity 809
M1 809
M2 809
gold standard 809
Gresham's Law 810
commercial banks 812
savings and loan associations 812

credit unions 812
reserve requirements 813
fractional reserve system 813
secondary reserves 814
balance sheet 814
required reserve ratio 815
excess reserves 815
money multiplier 819

Section Check Answers

27.1 What Is Money?

1. **Why does the advantage of monetary exchange over barter increase as an economy becomes more complex?**

   As the economy becomes more complex, the number of exchanges between people in the economy grows very rapidly. This means that the transaction cost advantages of using money over barter for those exchanges also grows very rapidly as the economy becomes more complex.

2. **How can uncertain and rapid rates of inflation erode money's ability to perform its functions efficiently?**

   Uncertain and rapid rates of inflation erode money's ability to perform its functions efficiently because money lowers transaction costs most effectively when its value is stable and therefore more predictable. Uncertain and rapid rates of inflation reduce the stability and predictability of the value of money, reducing its usefulness as a universally understood store of value. It therefore reduces money's ability to reduce transaction costs.

3. **In a world of barter, would useful financial statements such as balance sheets be possible? Would stock markets be possible? Would it be possible to build cars?**

   In a world of barter, there is no common standard of value to allow comparisons of all the "apples and oranges" that must be summarized in financial statements, making such statements virtually impossible. Without money to act as a common standard of value, stock and other financial markets, as well as very complex (many transactions) production processes, would also be virtually impossible.

4. **Why do virtually all societies create something to function as money?**

   Having some good function as money lowers transaction costs, allowing increasing specialization and exchange to create increasing wealth for a society. That increase in wealth made possible by using money is why virtually all societies create something to function as money.

27.2 Measuring Money

1. **If everyone in an economy accepted poker chips as payment in exchange for goods and services, would poker chips be money?**
   Since money is anything that is generally accepted in exchange for goods or services (a medium of exchange), if everyone in an economy accepted poker chips as payment in exchange for goods and services, poker chips would be money.

2. **If you were buying a pack of gum, would using currency or a demand deposit have lower transaction costs? What if you were buying a house?**
   If you were buying a pack of gum, or making any other such small purchase, using currency would generally have lower transaction costs than a demand deposit (checking account). However, if you were buying a house, or any other very large purchase, using a demand deposit would generally have lower transaction costs than paying with currency (it would be cheaper, easier, and safer, and it would generate a more reliable financial record).

3. **What is the main advantage of transaction deposits for tax purposes? What is their main disadvantage for tax purposes?**
   The main advantage of transaction deposits for tax purposes is that they provide more reliable financial records for complying with record-keeping requirements for tax purposes. The financial records that transaction deposits generate, on the other hand, are their main disadvantage for those who wish to hide their financial activities from tax authorities.

4. **Are credit cards money?**
   Credit cards are not money. They are actually guaranteed loans available on demand to users, which can be activated by consumers. Credit cards are convenient substitutes for making transactions directly with money; that is, they are substitutes for the use of money in exchange.

5. **What are M1 and M2?**
   M1 is a narrow definition of money that focuses on money's use as a means of payment (for transaction purposes). M1 includes currency in circulation, checkable deposits, and traveler's checks. M2 is a broader definition of money, which focuses on money's use as a highly liquid store of purchasing power or savings. M2 equals M1 plus other "near moneys," including savings accounts, small-denomination time deposits, and money market mutual funds.

6. **How have interest-earning checking accounts and overdraft protection led to the relative decline in demand deposits?**
   Interest-earning checking accounts provide the same ability to make transactions as non-interest-earning demand deposit accounts but are more attractive to many consumers because they earn interest. Overdraft protection means that consumers do not have to keep as much money in demand deposit accounts "just in case" in order to protect against overdrawing their accounts.

27.3 How Banks Create Money

1. **What is happening to the number of banks now that interstate banking is allowed?**
   Laws against interstate banking prevented the formation of large, interstate banking organizations, resulting in a large number of American banks. However, now that interstate banking is allowed, mergers are resulting in fewer, larger, interstate banks.

2. **In what way is it true that "banks make money by making money"?**
   Banks make money (profits) by loaning out their deposits at a higher interest rate than they pay their depositors. However, it is the extension of new loans in search of profits that creates new demand deposits, thereby increasing the stock of money.

3. **How do legal reserve deposit regulations lower bank profits?**
   Unlike other bank assets, legal reserves do not earn interest. Therefore, requiring a larger portion of bank assets to be held in such non-interest-earning accounts than prudent banking practice would dictate reduces bank earnings and profits.

4. **Is a demand deposit an asset or a liability?**
   A demand deposit is an asset for its owner but a liability for the bank at which the account is kept.

5. **If the Bonnie and Clyde National Bank's only deposits were demand deposits of $20 million and it faced a 10 percent reserve requirement, how much money would it be required to hold in reserves?**
   The Bonnie and Clyde National Bank would have to hold 10 percent of its $20 million in demand deposits, or $2 million, as reserves.

6. **Suppose you found $10,000 while digging in your backyard and you deposited it in the bank. How would your new demand deposit account create a situation of excess reserves at your bank?**
   A new $10,000 deposit adds that amount both to your demand deposit account and to the reserves of your bank. But only a fraction of the added reserves

are required by the addition to your demand deposit account. The rest are excess reserves, which the bank will look to convert to interest-earning loans or other assets.

27.4 The Money Multiplier

1. **Why do the supply of money and the volume of bank loans both increase or decrease at the same time?**

   The supply of money and the volume of bank loans both increase or decrease at the same time because issuing new bank loans adds to the money supply, while calling in existing bank loans reduces the money supply.

2. **Why would each bank involved in the process of multiple expansions of the money supply lend out a larger fraction of any new deposit it receives the lower the reserve requirement?**

   Each bank involved in the process of multiple expansions of the money supply can lend up to the amount of its excess reserves. But the excess reserves created by each dollar deposited in a bank equals 1 minus the required reserve ratio. The lower this reserve requirement, the greater the excess reserves created by each new deposit, and therefore the greater the fraction of any new deposit that will be loaned out in this process.

3. **If a particular bank with a reserve requirement of 10 percent has $30,000 in new cash deposits, how much money could it create through making new loans?**

   A bank can loan up to the amount of its excess reserves. If it faces a reserve requirement of 10 percent, a new $30,000 cash deposit would add $3,000 (10 percent of $30,000) to its required reserves but $30,000 to its total reserves. This deposit would therefore create $27,000 in excess reserves that the bank could lend out, and that $27,000 in increased loans would increase the money stock by an equal amount.

4. **Why do banks choosing to hold excess reserves or borrowers choosing to hold some of their loans in the form of currency reduce the actual impact of the money multiplier below that indicated by the multiplier formula?**

   If banks choose to hold excess reserves, each bank involved in the process of multiple expansions of the money supply will lend out less, and therefore create less new money, than if it loaned out all its excess reserves. The result will be a smaller money supply than that indicated by the multiplier formula because the formula assumes that banks lend out all their excess reserves. If borrowers hold some of their loans as currency, this will reduce the amount of vault cash, which counts as a reserve, at banks. This then will reduce the amount that can be loaned at each stage of the money-supply creation process and will therefore reduce the actual money multiplier below the level indicated by the multiplier formula.

27.5 The Collapse of America's Banking System, 1920–1933

1. **How did the combination of increased holding of excess reserves by banks and currency by the public lead to bank failures in the 1930s?**

   The desire by the public for increased currency holdings, caused largely by the fear of bank failures, also forced banks to sharply increase excess reserves and reduce lending, together resulting in a sharp fall in the money stock. Despite substantial excess reserves, however, bank runs led to the failure of even many conservatively run banks.

2. **What are the four reasons cited in the text for the collapse of the U.S. banking system in this period?**

   The cited reasons include: (1) the large number of small banks, which were more at risk from bank runs; (2) governmental attempts to stem the distress in the banking industry that were both weak and too late; (3) the absence of deposit insurance, which would have bolstered consumer confidence; and (4) fear that the economy was in a continuous downward cycle, so that there was little basis for optimism that bank loans would be safely repaid.

3. **What is the FDIC, and how did its establishment increase bank stability and reassure depositors?**

   The Federal Deposit Insurance Corporation insures bank deposits. This guarantee of deposits eliminated the risk to depositors if their bank failed, thus eliminating the bank runs that resulted from the fear of bank insolvency. Without having to face the risk of bank runs, banks became more stable.

CHAPTER 27 STUDY GUIDE

True or False:

1. Money is anything that is generally accepted in exchange for goods or services.
2. Metallic coins, paper currency and checks are the only forms of legal tender.
3. In the United States, the Treasury issues paper currency.
4. Checks provide the basis for most transactions of small size in the United States today.
5. Most of the money that we use for day-to-day transactions is not official legal tender.
6. Economists are in complete agreement on what constitutes money for all purposes.
7. Credit cards are not included in any measures of the money supply.
8. The use of transaction deposits instead of currency provides an element of insurance or safety.
9. Other checkable deposits that earn interest but have some restrictions have become an important component in the supply of money.
10. Liquidity refers to the ease with which one asset can be converted into another asset or goods and services.
11. People use transaction accounts primarily because they generally pay higher interest rates than non-transaction deposits.
12. Most purists would argue that nontransaction deposits are near money assets but not money itself, because they are not a direct medium of exchange.
13. Money market mutual funds are highly liquid assets that have experienced tremendous growth over the last 20 years.
14. M2 is substantially larger than M1.
15. M2 includes currency, checkable deposits, and traveler's checks, but not savings accounts.
16. People prefer to keep the bulk of their liquid assets in the form of savings accounts of various kinds rather than in currency or transaction accounts.
17. When the United States was on an internal gold standard, the dollar was defined as equivalent in value to a certain amount of gold.
18. When two forms of money are available, people prefer to spend the form of money that is less valuable.
19. Even if people lose faith in the exchangeability of pieces of paper that the government decrees as money, legal tender never loses its status as meaningful money.
20. As long as people have confidence in something's convertibility into goods and services, no further backing is necessary for it to serve as money.
21. Money is the only medium of exchange that is generally accepted for most transactions.
22. A majority of U.S. money, whether M1 or M2, is in the form of deposits at privately owned financial institutions.
23. Unlike in other nations, many separate commercial banks operate in the United States.
24. Lending in money imposes more risks on buyers and sellers than lending in commodities.
25. Financial institutions can create money by making loans.
26. If you go into a bank and borrow $5,000, the bank probably will simply add $5,000 to a checking account balance in your name at the bank, which will create new money in the process.
27. In the absence of legal reserve requirements, a prudent bank would not need to limit its loan volume.
28. Reserve requirements exist primarily to eliminate bank runs.
29. Even though banks must meet their reserve requirements, they generally want to keep far more of their funds as excess reserves.
30. The predominant liability of virtually all banks is deposits.
31. Excess reserves equal actual reserves minus required reserves.

32. The difference between a bank's assets and its liabilities constitutes the bank's capital, or net worth.
33. Banks have historically earned no interest on reserves, whether kept as cash on hand or in accounts with the Federal Reserve.
34. If a bank lends out its excess reserves of $75,000, the money supply will not increase.
35. New loans create new money directly, but they also create excess reserves in other banks, which leads to still further increases in both loans and the stock of money.
36. When banks create more money, they also directly create wealth.
37. Assume that Bank One receives a new cash deposit of $100,000. With a 20 percent required reserve ratio, this creates $20,000 of required reserves and $100,000 of excess reserves.
38. The money multiplier is 1 divided by one minus the required reserve ratio.
39. The higher the required reserve ratio, the smaller the money multiplier.
40. If some banks choose not to lend all of their excess reserves, the total amount of money created by the banking system in response to an initial cash deposit will be larger.
41. When a person pays a loan back to a bank, demand deposits decline, but the money supply is not affected.

Added T/F?

42. In the Depression, the country experienced an abrupt and unprecedented decline in the supply of money.
43. In the Depression, banks tried to lend out their excess reserves, increasing the money supply.
44. In the Depression, banks, runs could leave even conservatively managed banks with insufficient cash reserves to meet the withdrawal requests of panicky depositors.
45. The combination of the Federal Deposit Insurance Corporation (FDIC) and the government's greater willingness to assist distressed banks has largely eliminated bank runs and failures in recent times.
46. In the Depression, governmental attempts to stem the growing distress in the banking system were rapid but too weak.

Multiple Choice:

1. Barter is inefficient compared to using money for trading because
   a. it is more expensive over long distances.
   b. potential buyers may not have appropriate items of value to sellers with which to barter.
   c. it is more time consuming, since it is more difficult to evaluate the products that are being offered for barter than to evaluate money.
   d. of all of the above.
   e. of none of the above.

2. Money's principal role is to serve as
   a. a standard for credit transactions.
   b. a standard for making bank loans.
   c. a medium of exchange.
   d. a standard for the real bills doctrine.

3. Currency is a poor store of value when
   a. the unemployment rate is high.
   b. the rate of inflation is very high.
   c. banks are failing at an abnormally high rate.
   d. gold can be purchased at bargain prices.
   e. All of the above are correct.

4. Credit cards
   a. are not included in any definition of the money supply.
   b. are included in the M1 definition of the money supply.
   c. are included in the M2 definition of the money supply.
   d. are included in the M3 definition of the money supply.
   e. are included only in the broadest definition of the money supply.

5. The money supply that includes only currency, checkable deposits, and traveler's checks is known as
   a. M1.   b. M2.
   c. M3.   d. L.

6. The distinction between M1 and M2 is based on
   a. portability—the ease with which an asset can be moved to make a payment on the spot.
   b. storability—the ease with which an asset can be stored.
   c. divisibility—the ease with which an asset can be used to make specific payments.
   d. liquidity—the ease with which an asset can be converted into cash.
   e. all of the above.

7. Money is
   a. a highly illiquid asset.
   b. an object to be consumed.
   c. whatever is generally accepted in exchange for goods and services.
   d. widely used in a barter economy.

8. Without money to serve as a medium of exchange,
   a. gains from trade would be severely limited.
   b. our standard of living would probably be reduced.
   c. the transactions costs of exchange would increase.
   d. All of the above are true.

9. Money makes it easier to borrow and repay loans. This function of money is referred to as
   a. a means of deferred payment.
   b. a unit of account.
   c. a standard of value.
   d. a store of value.
   e. none of the above.

10. Liquidity is defined as
    a. the cash value of fiat money.
    b. the ease with which an asset can be converted into cash.
    c. the speed at which money is spent.
    d. the ease with which money can be divided to make payments.
    e. the value of fiat money when used to buy a good or service.

11. An increase in demand deposits combined with an equal decrease in currency in circulation would
    a. directly increase both M1 and M2.
    b. directly increase M1 and decrease M2.
    c. directly decrease M1 and increase M2.
    d. have no direct effect on M1 or M2.

12. Under fractional reserve banking, when a bank lends to a customer,
    a. borrowers receive a newly created demand deposit; that is, money is created.
    b. reserves drain away from the system.
    c. the bank is protected from a run.
    d. bank credit decreases.
    e. bank profitability is decreased.

13. Required reserves of a bank are a specific percentage of their
    a. loans.   b. cash on hand.
    c. deposits.   d. total assets.

14. Which of the following will lead to an increase in the money supply?
    a. You pay back a $10,000 loan that you owe to your bank.
    b. You pay $10,000 in cash for a new motorcycle.
    c. Your bank gives you a $10,000 loan by adding $10,000 to your checking account.
    d. You bury $10,000 in cash in your backyard.

15. If a banking transaction created new excess reserves in the banking system, the result would tend to be
    a. a decrease in the amount of loans made by banks and an increase in the supply of money.
    b. a decrease in the amount of loans made by banks and a decrease in the supply of money.
    c. an increase in the amount of loans made by banks and an increase in the supply of money.
    d. an increase in the amount of loans made by banks and a decrease in the supply of money.

16. If many people were to suddenly withdraw large sums of currency from their checking accounts, and no offsetting actions were taken by the Fed, the result would be
    a. a reduction in the U.S. money supply.
    b. a decrease in M1 but an increase M2.
    c. an increase in interest rates.
    d. an increase in reserves of banks and therefore an increase in the money supply.
    e. both a. and c.

17. A reserve requirement of 25 percent means a money multiplier of
    a. 25.   b. 4.
    c. 1.33.   d. 1.

18. If the required reserve ratio were decreased, then
    a. the money supply would tend to decrease, but the outstanding loans of banks would tend to increase.
    b. both the money supply and the outstanding loans of banks would tend to decrease.
    c. the money supply would tend to increase, but the outstanding loans of banks would tend to decrease.
    d. both the money supply and the outstanding loans of banks would tend to increase.

Problems:

1. Why do people who live in countries experiencing rapid inflation often prefer to hold American dollars rather than their own country's currency? Explain.

2. Explain the difficulties that an economics professor might face in purchasing a new car under a barter system.

3. Which one of each of the following pairs of assets is most liquid?
    a. A savings account or 10 acres of real estate.
    b. A 30-year bond or a six-month Treasury bill.
    c. Microsoft stock or a traveler's check.
    d. A certificate of deposit or a demand deposit.

4. Indicate whether each of the following belongs on the asset or liability side of a bank's balance sheet:
    a. Demand deposits.   b. Vault cash.
    c. Certificates of deposit.   d. Loans.
    e. Holdings of government securities.   f. Deposits at the Fed.
    g. Bank buildings.

5. What would each of the following changes do to M1 and M2?

Change	M1	M2
a. An increase in currency in circulation	___	___
b. An increase in credit card balances	___	___
c. A decrease in demand deposits	___	___
d. An increase in savings deposits	___	___
e. A conversion of savings account balances into checking account balances	___	___
f. A conversion of savings account balances into time account balances	___	___
g. A conversion of checking account balances into money market mutual funds	___	___

6. What would the money multiplier be if the required reserve ratio were
   4 percent? _____   20 percent? _____
   5 percent? _____   25 percent? _____
   12.5 percent? _____

7. Assume there was a new $500,000 deposit into a checking account at a bank.
   a. What would be the resulting excess reserves created by that deposit if banks faced a reserve requirement of

   50 percent? _____   10 percent? _____
   25 percent? _____   5 percent? _____
   20 percent? _____

   b. How many additional dollars could that bank lend out as a result of that deposit if banks faced a reserve requirement of

   15 percent? _____   10 percent? _____
   25 percent? _____   5 percent? _____
   20 percent? _____

   c. How many additional dollars of money could the banking system as a whole create in response to such a new deposit if banks faced a reserve requirement of

   50 percent? _____   10 percent? _____
   25 percent? _____   5 percent? _____
   20 percent? _____

8. If the required reserve ratio is 10 percent, calculate the potential change in demand deposits under the following circumstances:
   a. You write a check for $2,500 drawn on your bank (Wells Fargo) to an auto mechanic who deposits the funds in his bank (Bank of America).
   b. You take $5,000 from under your mattress and deposit it in your bank.
   c. You withdraw $50 from the bank and leave it in your wallet for emergencies.

9. Calculate the magnitude of the money multiplier if banks were to hold 100 percent of deposits in reserve. Would banks be able to create money in such a case? Explain.

10. a. If a bank had reserves of $90,000 and demand deposits of $600,000 (and no other deposits), how much could it lend out if it faced a required reserve ratio of

   10 percent? _____
   15 percent? _____
   20 percent? _____

   b. If the bank then received a new $40,000 deposit in a customer's demand deposit account, how much could it now lend out if it faced a required reserve ratio of

   10 percent? _____
   15 percent? _____
   20 percent? _____

11. An alternative version of Gresham's Law is that "Bad money drives out good money." Why is it true that, in choosing between different currencies to transact in, good money drives out bad money?

12. Why do you think asking whether money is an asset or a liability is a trick question in economics?

13. Why would the increasing liquidity of savings accounts make some monetary economists track the size of M1 plus savings account balances (called MZM) over time?

14. Given that the Fed currently imposes reserve requirements on checking deposits, but not on savings deposits, why would banks prefer to hold deposits as saving accounts rather than checking accounts, other things equal?

15. If the Fed paid interest on bank reserves at the Fed, would banks still want to avoid holding excess reserves?

16. Why have ATMs and online banking made savings accounts more liquid than they used to be?

28 The Federal Reserve System and Monetary Policy

28.1 The Federal Reserve System

28.2 How Does the Federal Reserve Change the Money Supply?

28.3 Money, Interest Rates, and Aggregate Demand

28.4 Expansionary and Contractionary Monetary Policy

28.5 Money and Inflation

28.6 Problems in Implementing Monetary and Fiscal Policy

The chairperson of the Federal Reserve System is one of the most important policymakers in the country. The importance of the Federal Reserve System and monetary policy cannot be overestimated. In this chapter, we will see how deliberate changes in the money supply can affect aggregate demand and lead to short-run changes in the output of goods and services as well as the price level. That is, monetary policy can be an effective tool for helping to achieve and maintain price stability, full employment, and economic growth. We will also see that monetary-policy tools, just like fiscal-policy tools, have problems of implementation.

SECTION 28.1 The Federal Reserve System

* What are the functions of a central bank?
* Who controls the Federal Reserve System?
* How is the Fed tied to Congress and the executive branch?

The Functions of a Central Bank

In most countries of the world, the job of manipulating the supply of money belongs to the "central bank." A central bank performs many functions. First, the central bank is a "banker's bank." It is the bank where commercial banks maintain their own cash deposits—their reserves. Second, the central bank performs a number of service functions for commercial banks, such as transferring funds and checks between various commercial banks in the banking system. Third, the central bank typically serves as the primary bank for the central government, handling, for example, its payroll accounts. Fourth, the central bank buys and sells foreign currencies and generally assists in the completion of financial transactions with other countries. Fifth, it serves as the "lender of last resort," helping banking institutions in financial distress. Sixth, the central bank is concerned with the stability of the banking system and the money supply, which, as we have already seen, results from the loan decisions of banks. The central bank can and does impose regulations on private commercial banks; it thereby regulates the size of the money supply and influences the level of economic activity. The central bank also implements monetary policy, which, along with fiscal policy, forms the basis of efforts to direct the economy to perform in accordance with macroeconomic goals.

Commercial banks keep reserves with the central bank. Roughly 4,000 U.S. banks are members of the Federal Reserve System. While this is less than half the number of total banks, the member banks hold roughly 75 percent of U.S. bank deposits. Furthermore, all banks must meet the Fed's requirements, whether they are members or not.

Location of the Federal Reserve System

In most countries, the central bank is a single bank; for example, the central bank of Great Britain, the Bank of England, is a single institution located in London. In the United States, however, the central bank is 12 institutions, closely tied together and collectively called the Federal Reserve System. The Federal Reserve System, or Fed, as it is nicknamed, comprises separate banks in Boston, New York, Philadelphia, Richmond, Atlanta, Dallas, Cleveland, Chicago, St. Louis, Minneapolis–St. Paul, Kansas City, and San Francisco. As Exhibit 1 shows, these banks and their branches are spread all over the country, but they are most heavily concentrated in the eastern states.

Each of the 12 banks has branches in key cities in its district. For example, the Federal Reserve Bank of Cleveland serves the fourth Federal Reserve district and has branches in Pittsburgh, Cincinnati, and Columbus. Each Federal Reserve Bank has its own board of directors and, to a limited extent, can set its own policies. Effectively, however, the 12 banks act in unison on major policy issues, with control of major policy decisions resting with the Board of Governors and the Federal Open Market Committee, headquartered in Washington, D.C. The Chairman of the Federal Reserve Board of Governors (currently Ben Bernanke) is generally regarded as one of the most important and powerful economic policymakers in the country.

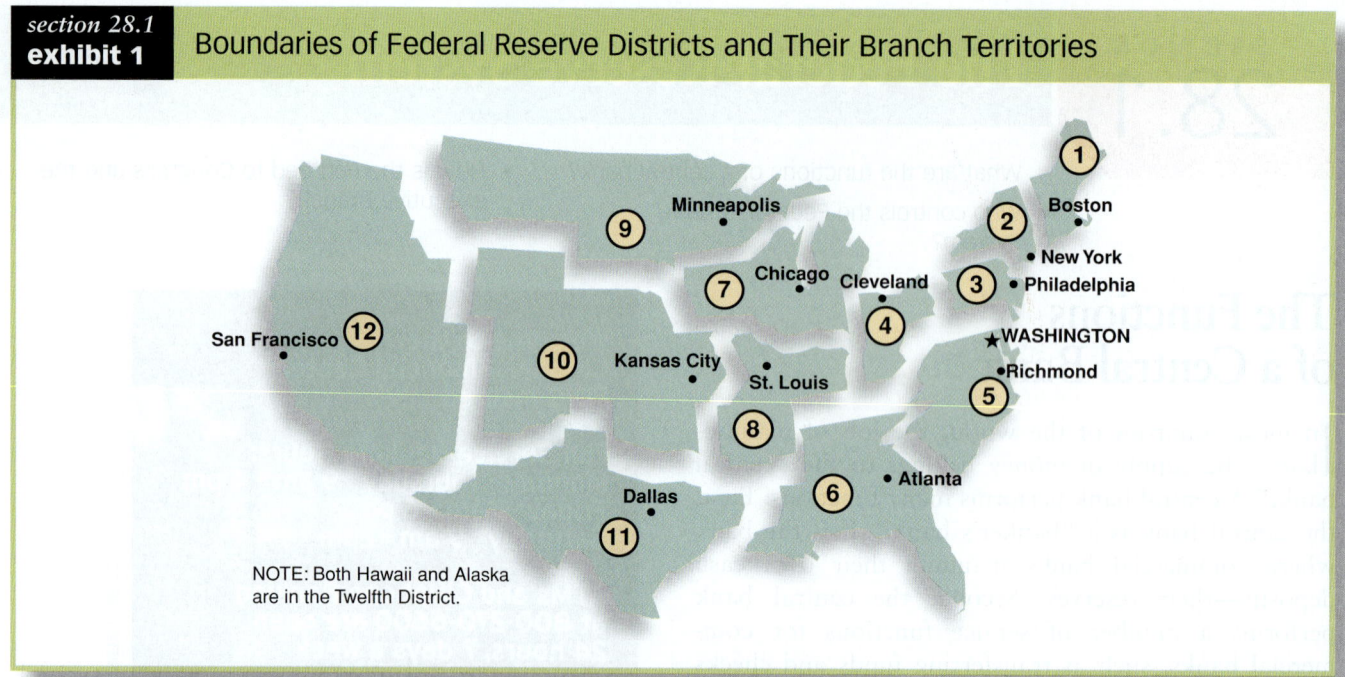

section 28.1 exhibit 1 Boundaries of Federal Reserve Districts and Their Branch Territories

NOTE: Both Hawaii and Alaska are in the Twelfth District.

The Fed's Relationship to the Federal Government

The Federal Reserve System was created in 1913 because the U.S. banking system had so little stability and no central direction. Technically, the Fed is privately owned by the banks that "belong" to it. Banks are not required to belong to the Fed; however, since the passage of new legislation in 1980, virtually no difference exists between the requirements for member and nonmember banks.

The private ownership of the Fed is essentially meaningless, because the Federal Reserve Board of Governors, which controls major policy decisions, is appointed by the president of the United States, not by the stockholders. The owners of the Fed have relatively little control over its operations and receive only small fixed dividends on their modest financial stake in the system. Again, the feature of private ownership but public control was a compromise made to appease commercial banks opposed to direct public (government) regulation.

The Fed's Ties to the Executive Branch

An important aspect of the Fed's operation is that, historically, it has enjoyed a considerable amount of independence from both the executive and legislative

section 28.1 exhibit 2 Central Bank Independence and Inflation, 1960–1992

There is often a strong negative correlation between a country's average annual inflation rate and the degree of independence of its central bank.

SOURCE: "Monetary Metamorphosis," *The Economist*, September 23, 1999.
© The Economist Newspaper Limited, London 1999. Reprinted with permission.

branches of government. In fact, central banks with greater degrees of independence appear to have a lower annual inflation rate, see Exhibit 2. True, the president appoints the seven members of the Board of Governors, subject to Senate approval; but the term of appointment is 14 years. No member of the Federal Reserve

The chair of the Fed is truly the chief executive officer of the system. The Fed chair is required by law to testify to Congress twice a year. In addition to the chair, all seven members are appointed by the president and confirmed by the Senate to sit on the Board of Governors. Governors are appointed for 14-year terms, staggered every two years, in an attempt to insulate them from political pressure.

the terms of board members are staggered, so a new appointment is made only every two years. It is practically impossible for a single president to appoint a majority of the members of the board; and even were it possible, members have little fear of losing their jobs as a result of presidential wrath. The chair of the Federal Reserve Board is a member of the Board of Governors and serves a four-year term. The chair is truly the chief executive officer of the system and effectively runs it, with considerable help from the presidents of the 12 regional banks.

Fed Operations

Many of the key policy decisions of the Federal Reserve are actually made by its Federal Open Market Committee (FOMC), which consists of the seven members of the Board of Governors; the president of the New York Federal Reserve Bank; and four other presidents of Federal Reserve Banks, who serve on the committee on a rotating basis. The FOMC makes most of the key decisions influencing the direction and size of changes in the money supply; and their regular, closed meetings are accordingly considered important by the business community, news media, and government.

Board will face reappointment from the president who initially made the appointment, because presidential tenure is limited to two four-year terms. Moreover,

SECTION CHECK

1. Of the six major functions of a central bank, the most important is its role in regulating the money supply.
2. The Federal Reserve System consists of 12 Federal Reserve banks. Although these banks are independent institutions, they act largely in unison on major policy decisions.
3. The Federal Reserve Board of Governors and the Federal Open Market Committee are the prime decision makers for U.S. monetary policy.
4. The president of the United States appoints members of the Federal Reserve Board of Governors to a 14-year term, with only one appointment made every two years. The president also selects the Chair of the Federal Reserve Board, who serves a four-year term. The only other government intervention in the Fed can come from legislation passed in Congress.

1. What are the six primary functions of a central bank?
2. What is the FOMC, and what does it do?
3. How is the Fed tied to the executive branch? How is it insulated from executive branch pressure to influence monetary policy?

SECTION 28.2 How Does the Federal Reserve Change the Money Supply?

* What are the three major tools of the Fed?
* What is the purpose of the Fed's tools?
* What other powers does the Fed have?
* How are bank failures avoided today?

As noted previously, the Federal Reserve Board of Governors and the FOMC are the prime decision makers for U.S. monetary policy. They decide whether to expand the money supply and, it is hoped, the real level of economic activity, or to contract the money supply, hoping to cool inflationary pressures. How does the Fed control the money supply, particularly when it is the privately owned commercial banks that actually create and destroy money by making loans, as we discussed earlier?

The Fed has three major methods by which to control the supply of money: It can engage in open market operations, change reserve requirements, or change its discount rate. Of these three, by far the most important is open market operations.

Open Market Operations

Open market operations involve the purchase and sale of government bonds by the Federal Reserve System. At its regular meetings, the FOMC decides to buy or sell government bonds. Open market operations are the most important method the Fed uses to influence the money supply for several reasons. First, it is a device that can be implemented quickly and cheaply—the Fed merely calls an agent who buys or sells bonds. Second, it can be done quietly, without a lot of political debate or a public announcement. Third, it is a rather powerful tool, as any given purchase or sale of bonds has an ultimate impact several times the amount of the initial transaction. Fourth, the Fed can use this tool to change the money supply by a small or large amount on any given day.

When the Fed buys bonds, it pays the seller of the bonds by a check written on one of the 12 Federal Reserve banks. The person receiving the check will likely deposit it in his or her bank account, increasing the money supply in the form of added transaction deposits. More important, the commercial bank, in return for crediting the account of the bond seller with a new deposit, gets cash reserves or a higher balance in its reserve account at the Federal Reserve Bank in its district.

open market operations purchase and sale of government securities by the Federal Reserve System

For example, suppose our example bank, Bank One, has no excess reserves and that one of its customers sells a bond for $10,000 through a broker to the Federal Reserve System. The customer deposits the check from the Fed for $10,000 in his or her account, and the Fed credits Bank One with $10,000 in reserves. Suppose the reserve requirement is 10 percent. Bank One, then, needs new reserves of only $1,000 ($10,000 × 0.10) to support its $10,000, meaning that it has acquired $9,000 in new excess reserves ($10,000 new actual reserves minus $1,000 in new required reserves). Bank One can, and probably will, lend out its excess reserves of $9,000, creating $9,000 in new deposits in the process. The recipients of the loans, in turn, will likely spend the money, leading to still more new deposits and excess reserves in other banks.

In other words, the Fed's purchase of the bond directly creates $10,000 in money in the form of bank deposits and indirectly permits up to $90,000 in additional money to be created through the multiple expansion in bank deposits. (The money multiplier is 1/.10, or 10; 10 × $9,000 = $90,000.) Thus, if the reserve requirement is 10 percent, a potential total of up to $100,000 in new money is created by the purchase of one $10,000 bond by the Fed.

The process works in reverse when the Fed sells a bond. The individual purchasing the bond will pay the Fed by check, lowering demand deposits in the banking system. Reserves of the bank where the bond purchaser has a bank account will likewise fall. If the bank had zero excess reserves at the beginning of the process, it now has a reserve deficiency. The bank must sell secondary reserves or reduce loan volume, either of which leads to further destruction of deposits. Thus, a multiple contraction of deposits begins.

In short, if the Fed believes the economy needs to be stimulated, it will buy bonds from the private sector with open market purchases. If the Fed wishes to slow the economy down, it will sell bonds to the private sector with open market sales.

Use what you've LEARNED: OPEN MARKET OPERATIONS

Q How does the money supply increase and decrease as the result of open market operations?

To increase the money supply, the Fed instructs its bond traders at the Fed bank in New York to buy government bonds in the bond market.

A For people to want to put more money in banks and less in government bonds, the Fed must offer bondholders an attractive price. If the Fed's price is high enough, it will tempt some investors to sell their government bonds to the Fed. When these individuals place the proceeds from the sale in the bank, new deposits are created, increasing reserves in the banking system. The excess reserves can then be loaned by the banks, creating more new deposits and increasing the excess reserves in still other banks.

To reduce the money supply, the Fed does the opposite. It sells government bonds in the bond market. The buyer pays for bonds from a checking account and bank reserves fall. When banks have fewer reserves, it reduces their ability to lend. That is, when the Fed sells bonds, it is taking the money exchanged for these bonds out of the hands of the public.

The Reserve Requirement

Even though open market operations are the most important and widely utilized tool for achieving monetary objectives that the Fed has at its disposal, they are not its potentially most powerful tool. The Fed possesses the power to change the reserve requirements of member banks by altering the reserve ratio. It can have an immediate and significant impact on the ability of member banks to create money. Suppose the banking system as a whole has $500 billion in deposits and $60 billion in reserves, with a reserve ratio of 12 percent. Because $60 billion is 12 percent of $500 billion, the system has no excess reserves. Suppose now that the Fed lowers reserve requirements by changing the reserve ratio to 10 percent. Banks then are required to keep only $50 billion in reserves ($500 billion × 0.10), but they still have $60 billion. Thus, the lowering of the reserve requirement gives banks $10 billion in excess reserves. The banking system as a whole can expand deposits and the money stock by a multiple of this amount, in this case 10 (10% equals 1/10; the banking multiplier is the reciprocal of this, or 10). The lowering of the reserve requirement in this case, then, would permit an expansion in deposits of $100 billion, which represents a 20 percent increase in the stock of money, from $500 to $600 billion.

When Does the Fed Use This Tool?

Relatively small reserve requirement changes can thus have a big impact on the potential supply of money. This tool is so potent, in fact, that it is seldom used. In other words, the power of the reserve requirement is not only its advantage but also its disadvantage, because a small reduction in the reserve requirement can make a huge change in the number of dollars that are in excess reserves in banks all over the country. Such huge changes in required reserves and excess reserves have the potential to disrupt the economy.

Frequent changes in the reserve requirement would make it difficult for banks to plan. For example, a banker might worry that if she makes loans now and then the Fed raises the reserve requirement, she would not have enough reserves to meet the new reserve requirements. If she does not make loans and the Fed leaves the reserve requirement alone, she loses the opportunity to earn income on those loans.

Carpenters don't use sledgehammers to hammer small nails or tacks; the tool is too big and powerful to use effectively. For the same reason, the Fed changes reserve requirements rather infrequently, and when it does make changes, it is by small amounts. For example, between 1970 and 1980, the Fed changed the reserve requirement only twice, and less than 1 percent on each occasion. Furthermore, changes in the reserve requirement, because they are so powerful, are a sign that monetary policy has swung strongly in a new direction.

The Discount Rate

Banks having trouble meeting their reserve requirement can borrow funds directly from the Fed at its discount window. The interest rate the Fed charges on these borrowed reserves is called the **discount rate.** The Fed can control the money supply by altering the discount rate. If the Fed raises the discount rate, it discourages banks from borrowing reserves from the Fed. This reduces the quantity of reserves in the banking system, which leads to a reduction in the money supply. That is, if the Fed wants to contract the money supply, it will raise the discount rate, making it more costly for banks to borrow reserves.

If the Fed is promoting an expansion of money and credit, it will lower the discount rate, making it cheaper for banks to borrow reserves. Thus, a lower discount rate will encourage banks to borrow from the Fed, increasing the quantity of reserves and the money supply.

The discount rate sometimes changes fairly frequently, often several times a year. Sometimes the rate will be moved several times in the same direction within a single year, which has a substantial cumulative effect.

> **discount rate**
> interest rate that the Fed charges commercial banks for the loans it extends to them
>
> **federal funds market**
> market in which banks provide short-term loans to other banks that need cash to meet reserve requirements

The Significance of the Discount Rate

The discount rate is a relatively unimportant tool, mainly because member banks do not rely heavily on the Fed for borrowed funds and often the Fed would not lend them all they want to borrow. It is something most of them believe should be reserved for real emergencies. In October of 1987, when the stock market crashed, Fed chair Alan Greenspan used discount lending to help financial institutions that were in trouble. Many Wall Street brokerage firms needed temporary funds to finance the high volume of stock trades. The Fed was there to help. Also, in the financial crisis of 2008, the collapse of the housing market coupled with mortgage defaults meant that many financial institutions were in trouble. The Fed provided loans to many of these financial institutions that were in trouble.

When banks have short-term needs for cash to meet reserve requirements, they are more likely to take a short-term (often overnight) loan from another bank in the **federal funds market.** For that reason, many people pay a lot of attention to the interest rate on federal funds.

In recent years, the Federal Reserve has increased its focus on the federal funds rate as the primary indicator of its stance on monetary policy. The Fed announces a federal funds rate target at each FOMC meeting. This rate is watched closely, because it affects all the interest rates throughout the economy—auto loans, mortgages, and so on.

Since January 2003, the discount rate has been set between 0.5 and 1.0 percentage points above the federal funds rate target. Setting the discount rate above the fund rate is designed to keep banks from turning to this source. Thus, most of discount lending is small.

The Fed could use the discount rate by altering the discount rate relative to the federal funds rate. However, the discount rate's main significance is that changes in the rate are commonly viewed as a signal of the Fed's intentions with respect to monetary policy. Discount rate changes are widely publicized, unlike open market operations, which are carried out in private and announced several weeks later in the minutes of the FOMC.

How the Fed Reduces the Money Supply

The Fed can do three things to reduce the money supply or reduce the rate of growth in the money supply: (1) sell bonds, (2) raise reserve requirements, or (3) raise the discount rate. Of course, the Fed could also opt to use some combination of these three tools in its approach.

These moves tend to decrease aggregate demand, reducing nominal GDP—ideally, through a decrease in P rather than Q. These actions are the monetary policy equivalent of a fiscal policy of raising taxes, lowering transfer payments, and/or reducing government purchases.

How the Fed Increases the Money Supply

If the Fed is concerned about underutilizing resources (e.g., unemployment), it can engage in precisely the opposite policies: (1) buy bonds, (2) lower reserve requirements, or (3) lower the discount rate. The Fed can also use some combination of these three approaches.

These moves tend to increase aggregate demand, increasing nominal GDP—ideally, through an increase in Q (in the context of the equation of exchange) rather than P. Equivalent expansionary fiscal policy actions include reducing taxes, increasing transfer payments, and/or increasing government purchases.

Difficulties in Controlling the Money Supply

In a fractional reserve banking system, the Fed cannot precisely control the money supply because of two problems: people and banks.

The Fed cannot precisely control the amount of money that people want to hold as currency in circulation versus as deposits in their financial institutions. The more cash people put in the bank, the more excess reserves the bank has for lending purposes and the more money created. Alternatively, if people are concerned about the health of the financial system and choose to take money out of the bank in order to hold more currency, it would reduce banks' excess reserves, reducing lending and the stock of money. Either change can alter the money supply without any action from the Fed.

Banks can also choose to not lend out all of their excess reserves. When banks keep more excess reserves, the Fed has less control over the money supply because banks rather than Fed policy dictates how much will be lent out. If banks make money by making loans, why would they keep excess reserves? Banks may choose to become more cautious because of the current economic climate; to avoid risk they may choose to hold on to more excess reserves. Consequently, the banking system would create less money with a given level of reserves than it normally would and the money supply would fall.

This may not be a huge problem because the Fed keeps massive amounts of data on the behavior of banks and their depositors. As a result, changes in currency circulation or excess reserve holdings by banks can be remedied with offsetting policies the Fed can control.

SECTION CHECK

1. The three major tools of the Fed are open market operations, changing reserve requirements, and changing the discount rate.
2. If the Fed wants to stimulate the economy (increase aggregate demand), it will increase the money supply by buying government bonds, lowering the reserve ratio, and/or lowering the discount rate.
3. If the Fed wants to restrain the economy (decrease aggregate demand), it will lower the money supply by selling government bonds, increasing the reserve ratio, and/or raising the discount rate.

---

1. What three main tactics could the Fed use in pursuing a contractionary monetary policy?
2. What three main tactics could the Fed use in pursuing an expansionary monetary policy?
3. Would the money supply rise or fall if the Fed made an open market purchase of government bonds, *ceteris paribus*?
4. If the Fed raised the discount rate from 12 to 15 percent, what effect would this have on the money supply?

SECTION 28.3 Money, Interest Rates, and Aggregate Demand

* What causes the demand for money to change?
* How do changes in income change the money market equilibrium?
* How does the Fed's buying and selling bonds affect RGDP in the short run?
* What is the relationship between bond prices and the interest rate?
* Why does the Fed target the interest rate rather than the money supply?
* How are the real and nominal interest rates connected in the short run?

The Money Market

The Federal Reserve's policies with respect to the money supply have a direct effect on short-run nominal interest rates and, accordingly, on the components of aggregate demand. The **money market** is the market where money demand and money supply determine the equilibrium *nominal* interest rate. When the Fed acts to change the money supply by changing one of its policy variables, it alters the money market equilibrium.

Money has several functions, but why would people hold money instead of other financial assets? That is, what is responsible for the demand for money? Transaction purposes, precautionary reasons, and asset purposes are at least some of the determinants of the demand for money.

Transactions Demand for Money

First, the primary reason that money is demanded is for transaction purposes—to facilitate exchange. Workers are generally paid by the week or month. However, most people want to hold on to money so they can buy goods and services on a continual basis, not just on payday. They want to keep money for everyday predictable expenses. For example, nobody would want to buy pizza with stocks and bonds. How costly would it be to convert less liquid assets like stocks or bonds into goods and services? Those costs would include the loss of interest and possible withdrawal penalties. In addition, the higher a person's income, the more transactions that person is likely to make (because consumption is income related); the greater will be GDP; and the greater will be the demand for money from transaction purposes, other things being equal.

money market
market in which money demand and money supply determine the equilibrium interest rate

Precautionary Demand for Money

Second, people like to have money on hand for precautionary reasons—so called "mattress money." If unexpected medical or other expenses require an unusual outlay of cash, people want to be prepared. The extent to which an individual holds cash for precautionary reasons depends partly on that person's income and partly on the opportunity cost of holding money, which is determined by market rates of interest. The higher the market interest rates, the higher the opportunity cost of holding money; and so people will hold less of their financial wealth as money.

Asset Demand for Money

Third, money has a trait—liquidity—that makes it a desirable asset. Other things being equal, people prefer assets that are more liquid to those that are less liquid. That is, people want to be able to easily convert some of their money into goods and services. For this reason, most people wish to have some of their portfolio in the form of money. At higher interest rates on other assets, the amount of money desired for this purpose will be smaller, because the opportunity cost of holding money will have risen.

The Demand for Money and the Nominal Interest Rate

The quantity of money demanded varies inversely with the nominal interest rate. When interest rates are higher, the opportunity cost—in terms of the interest income on alternative assets—of holding monetary assets is higher, and persons will want to hold less money. At the same time, the demand for money, particularly for transaction purposes, is highly dependent on income levels, because the transaction volume varies directly with income. Finally, the demand for money depends on the price level. If the price level increases, buyers will need more money to purchase their goods and services. If the price level falls, buyers will need less money to purchase their goods and services.

The demand curve for money is presented in Exhibit 1. At lower interest rates, the quantity of money demanded is greater, illustrated by a movement from A to B. That is, the lower the interest rate the lower the opportunity cost of holding money. An increase in income will lead to an increase in the demand for money, depicted by a rightward shift in the money demand (MD) curve, a movement from A to C.

section 28.3 exhibit 1 Money Demand, Interest Rates, and Income

An increase in the level of income will increase the amount of money that people want to hold for transaction purposes for any given interest rate; the demand for money therefore shifts to the right, from MD_1 to MD_2. The money demand curve is downward sloping, because at the lower nominal interest rate, the opportunity cost of holding money is lower.

Why Is the Supply of Money Relatively Inelastic?

The supply of money is largely governed by the regulatory policies of the central bank. Whether interest rates are 4 percent or 14 percent, banks seeking to maximize profits will increase lending as long as they have reserves above their desired level. Even a 4 percent return on loans provides more profit than maintaining those assets in non-interest-bearing cash or reserve accounts at the Fed, which currently earn very low interest rate from the Fed. Given this fact, the money supply is effectively almost perfectly inelastic with respect to interest rates over their plausible range. Therefore, we draw the money supply (MS) curve as vertical, other things being equal, in Exhibit 2, with changes in Federal Reserve policies acting to shift the money supply curve.

The Money Market

Equilibrium in the money market is found by combining the money demand and money supply curves in Exhibit 2. Money market equilibrium occurs at that *nominal* interest rate where the quantity of money demanded equals the quantity of money supplied. Initially, the money market is in equilibrium at i^* in Exhibit 2.

Money Market Equilibrium

In Exhibit 2, we see that equilibrium occurs at point E, where the quantity of money demanded by the public is equal to the quantity of the money supplied by the banking system, given the policies adopted by the Fed. At i_2, below the equilibrium interest rate, the quantity of money that people want to hold is greater than the quantity that is available from the banking system—there is a shortage at i_2. Consequently, people will try to increase their holdings of money by reducing their holdings of bonds or other interest-bearing assets. Because many people are trying to rid themselves of bonds, bond sellers realize they must increase interest on bonds to attract buyers. Thus, the interest rate rises to the equilibrium level, i^*.

At i_1, the interest rate is above the equilibrium level, the quantity of money people want to hold is less than the quantity that is available from the banking system; there is a surplus of money at i_1. Those that are holding the surplus of money (cash and checkable deposits) will try to exchange money for other assets such as bonds.

section 28.3 exhibit 2 **Money Market Equilibrium**

At equilibrium E, the quantity of money demanded is equal to the quantity of money supplied by the banking system. The equilibrium interest rate is i^* and the equilibrium quantity of money is Q^*. At i_1, there is a surplus. At i_2 there is a shortage.

As the demand for bonds rises, bond sellers can pay less interest but still attract enough buyers. As the interest rate falls, people become more willing to hold money, until the interest rate reaches equilibrium at i^*, where people are content holding the money the banking system has supplied.

The Money Market and the Aggregate Demand Curve

Recall the interest rate effect that moved us along the aggregate demand curve when the price level changed. We now look at that relationship in more detail. Specifically, when the price level rises from PL_1 to PL_2 in Exhibit 3, people demand more money and the money demand curve shifts from MD_1 to MD_2. That is, at the new higher price level, PL_2, many goods and services will have higher prices, so people will want to hold more money, MD_2 rather than MD_1.

How does an increase in the demand for money affect the money market? The increase in the demand for money, coupled with a fixed money supply (controlled by the Fed), will cause the interest rate to

section 28.3 exhibit 3 — The Money Market and the Aggregate Demand Curve

When the price level increases from PL_1 to PL_2, people desire to hold more money—an increase in the demand for money from MD_1 to MD_2. The increase in the demand for money causes the interest rate to rise from i_1 to i_2. The increase in interest leads to a reduction in RGDP demanded from $RGDP_1$ to $RGDP_2$.

increase from i_1 to i_2. At the higher interest rate, the cost of borrowing and the return to saving are higher. In short, fewer households will be borrowing for houses and cars, and fewer firms will be investing in new factories and equipment. Thus, the quantity at RGDP demanded falls from $RGDP_1$ to $RGDP_2$.

Of course, the reverse is true as well. A lower price level leads to a decrease in the demand for money because, on average, goods and services have lower price tags. The reduction in the demand for money causes a reduction in the interest rate, which encourages consumption and investment that reduces RGDP demanded. Hence, this leads to the downward sloping aggregate demand curve—a higher price level leads to reduction in RGDP demanded.

How Do Income Changes Affect the Equilibrium Position?

Rising national income increases the demand for money, shifting the money demand curve to the right from MD_1 to MD_2, and leading to a new higher equilibrium interest rate.

How Would an Increase in the Money Supply Affect Equilibrium Interest Rates and Aggregate Demand?

A Federal Reserve policy change that increased the money supply would be depicted by a shift in the money supply curve to the right. As a result of this shift, the equilibrium quantity of money demanded increases as equilibrium interest rates fall. The immediate impact of expansionary monetary policy is to decrease the interest rate. Because the money demand curve has not changed, the interest rate falls to the new equilibrium at E_2. The interest rate falls to induce people to hold the additional money supplied by the banking system, MS_2. The lower interest rate, or the fall in the cost of borrowing money, then leads to an increase in aggregate demand for goods and services at the current price level. The lower interest rate will increase home sales, car sales, business investments, and so on. That is, an increase in the money supply will lead to lower interest rates and an increase in aggregate demand, as seen in Exhibit 4. Thus, when the Fed changes policy

section 28.3 exhibit 4 — The Impact of an Increase in the Supply of Money

The increase in the money supply causes the interest rate to fall in the short run, as seen in Exhibit 4(a). At lower interest rates, households and businesses invest more and buy more goods and services, shifting the aggregate demand curve to the right, as shown in Exhibit 4(b).

to increase the money supply, the interest rate falls. This increases RGDP demanded at each and every price level. If the Fed changes policy to reduce the money supply, the interest rate would rise, which would lower RGDP demanded at each and every price level.

Does the Fed Target the Money Supply or Interest Rates?

Some economists believe that the Fed should try to control the money supply. Other economists believe that the Fed should try to control interest rates. Unfortunately, the Fed cannot do both—it must pick one or the other.

The economy is initially at point A in Exhibit 5, where the interest rate is i_1 and the quantity of money is at Q_1. Now, suppose the demand for money were to increase because of an increase in national income, an increase in the price level, or because people desire to hold more money. As a result, the demand curve for money shifts to the right, from MD_1 to MD_2. If the Fed decides it does not want the money supply to increase, it can pursue a policy of no monetary growth, which leads to an increase in the interest rate to i_2 at point C. The Fed could also try to keep the interest rate stable at i_1, but it can only do so by increasing the growth in the money supply through expansionary monetary policy.

section 28.3 exhibit 5 — Fed Targeting Money Supply Versus the Interest Rate

When the demand curve for money shifts outward, the Fed must settle for either a higher interest rate, a greater money supply, or some combination of both. The Fed cannot completely control both the growth in the money supply and the interest rate. If it attempts to keep the interest rate steady, it must increase the growth in the money supply. If it tries to keep the growth of the money supply in check, the interest rate will rise.

The Fed cannot simultaneously pursue policies of no monetary growth and monetary expansion; it must choose—a higher interest rate, a greater money supply, or some combination of both. The Fed cannot completely control both the growth in the money supply and the interest rate. If it attempts to keep the interest rate steady in the face of increased money demand, it must increase the growth in the money supply. If it tries to keep the growth of the money supply in check in the face of increased money demand, the interest rate will rise.

In short, monetary policy can be applied in terms of the money supply or the interest rate (the federal funds rate). When FOMC sets a federal funds rate target, the Fed's bond traders are told to do whatever is necessary to get the equilibrium interest rate to the target level. To lower the federal funds rate, Fed bond traders buy government bonds. This increases the money supply and lowers the interest rate. If FOMC raises the target for the federal funds rate, its bond traders sell government bonds. This decreases the money supply and raises the interest rate.

The Problem

The problem with targeting the money supply is that the demand for money fluctuates considerably in the short run. Focusing on the growth in the money supply when the demand for money is changing unpredictably leads to large fluctuations in interest rates, as occurred in the U.S. economy during the late 1970s and early 1980s. These erratic changes in interest rates could seriously disrupt the investment climate.

Keeping interest rates in check also creates problems. For example, when the economy grows, the demand for money also grows, so the Fed has to increase the money supply to keep interest rates from rising. If the economy is in a recession, the demand for money falls, and the Fed has to contract the money supply to keep interest rates from falling. This approach leads to the wrong policy prescription—expanding the money supply during a boom eventually leads to inflation, and contracting the money supply during a recession makes the recession even worse.

Which Interest Rate Does the Fed Target?

The Fed targets the federal funds rate. Remember the federal funds rate is the interest rate that banks charge each other for short-term loans. A bank that may be short of reserves might borrow from another bank that has excess reserves. The Fed has been targeting the federal funds rate since about 1965. At the close of the meetings of the FOMC, the Fed usually announces whether the federal funds rate target will be increased, decreased, or left alone as shown in Exhibit 6.

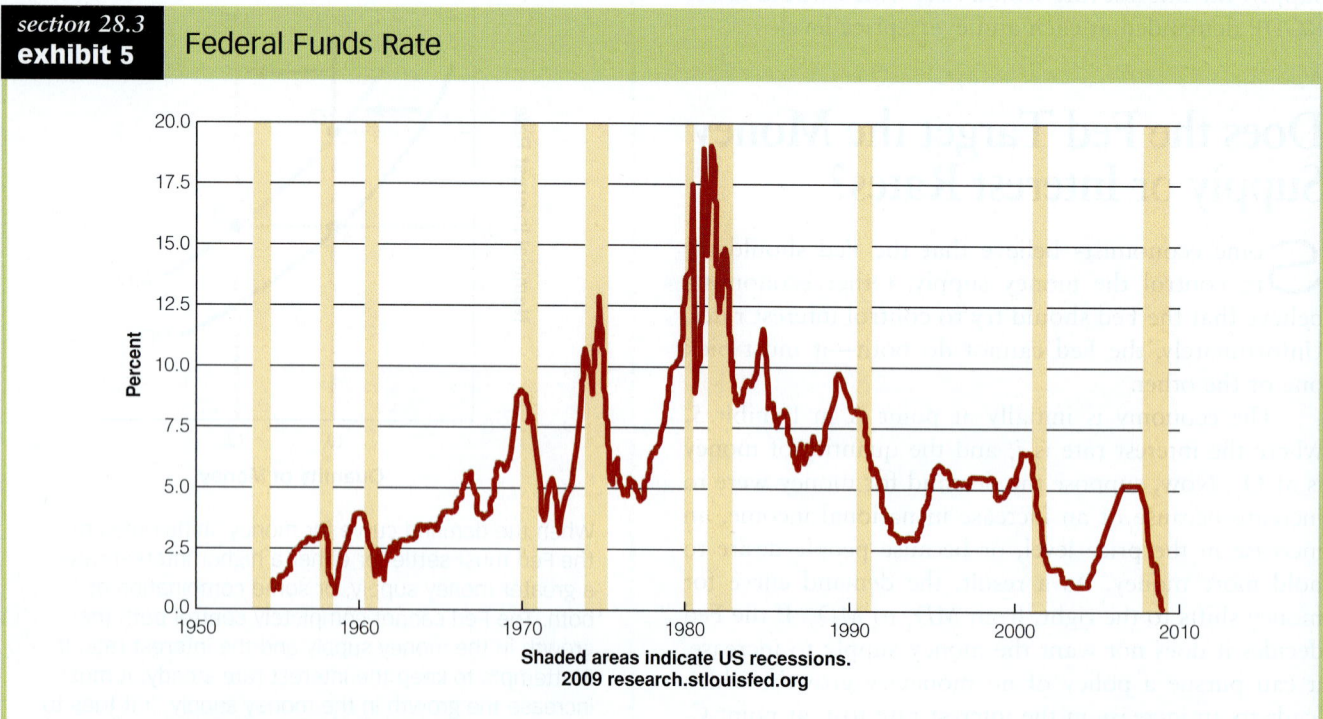

section 28.3 exhibit 5 Federal Funds Rate

Shaded areas indicate US recessions.
2009 research.stlouisfed.org

The Federal Reserve sets its policies according to the federal funds rate. Notice in the shaded areas (recession) that the federal funds rate has fallen considerably.

SOURCE: Board of Governors of the Federal Reserve System.

section 28.3 exhibit 6: Summary of Fed Tools for Monetary Policy

Macroeconomic Problem	Monetary Policy Prescription	Fed Policy Tools
Unemployment (Slow or negative RGDP growth rate—below $RGDP_{NR}$)	Expansionary monetary policy to increase aggregate demand	Buy bonds Lower discount rate Lower reserve requirement
Inflation (Rapid RGDP growth rate—beyond $RGDP_{NR}$)	Contractionary monetary policy to decrease aggregate demand	Sell bonds Raise discount rate Raise reserve requirement

Monetary policy decisions may be enacted either through the money supply or through the interest rate. That is, if the Fed wants to pursue a contractionary monetary policy (a reduction in aggregate demand), this policy can take the form of a reduction in the money supply or a higher interest rate. If the Fed wants to pursue an expansionary monetary policy (an increase in aggregate demand), this policy can take the form of an increase in the money supply or a lower interest rate. So why is the interest rate used? First, many economists believe that the primary effects of monetary policy are felt through the interest rate. Second, the money supply is difficult to measure accurately. Third, as we mentioned earlier, changes in the demand for money may complicate money supply targets. Last, people are more familiar with changes in the interest rate than with changes in the money supply.

Does the Fed Influence the Real Interest Rate in the Short Run?

Most economists believe that in the short run the Fed can control the nominal interest rate and the real interest rate. Recall that the real interest rate is equal to the nominal interest rate minus the expected inflation rate. Therefore, a change in the nominal interest rate tends to change the real interest rate by the same amount, because the expected inflation rate is slow to change in the short run. That is, if the expected inflation rate does not change, the relationship between the nominal and real interest rates is a direct relationship: A 1 percent reduction in the nominal interest rate will generally lead to a 1 percent reduction in the real interest rate in the short run. However, for the long run—several years after the inflation rate has adjusted—the equilibrium real interest rate will be given by the intersection of the demand and supply of loanable funds curves.

Exhibit 7 summarizes the preceding discussion of the tools available to the Fed for enacting monetary policy.

POLICY application: BERNANKE IS THE BEST STIMULUS RIGHT NOW

—BY ROBERT E. LUCAS JR.

The Federal Reserve's lowering of interest rates last Tuesday was welcome, but it was also received with skepticism. Once the federal-funds rate is reduced to zero, or near zero, doesn't this mean that monetary policy has gone as far as it can go? This widely held view was appealed to in the 1930s to rationalize the Fed's passive role as the U.S. economy slid into deep depression.

It was used again by the Bank of Japan to rationalize its unwillingness to counteract the deflation and recession of the 1990s. In both cases, constructive monetary policies were in fact available but remained unused. Fed Chairman Ben Bernanke's statement last Tuesday made it clear that he does not share this view and intends to continue to take actions to stimulate spending.

There should be no mystery about what he has in mind. Over the past four months the Fed has put

(continued)

POLICY application: BERNANKE IS THE BEST STIMULUS RIGHT NOW (cont.)

more than $600 billion of new reserves into the private sector, using them to discount—lend against—a wide variety of securities held by a variety of financial institutions. (The addition is to be weighed against September 2007's total outstanding level of reserves of about $50 billion.)

This action has been the boldest exercise of the Fed's lender-of-last-resort function in the history of the Federal Reserve System. Mr. Bernanke said that he is prepared to continue or expand this discounting activity as long as the situation dictates.

Why do I describe this as an action to stimulate spending? Financial markets are in the grip of a "flight to quality" that is very much analogous to the "flight to currency" that crippled the economy in the 1930s. Everyone wants to get into government-issued and government-insured assets, for reasons of both liquidity and safety. Individuals have tried to do this by selling other securities, but without an increase in the supply of "quality" securities these attempts do nothing but drive down the prices of other assets. The only other action people can take as individuals is to build up their stock of cash and government-issued claims to cash by reducing spending. This reduction is a main factor in inducing or worsening the recession. Adding directly to reserves—the ultimate liquid, safe asset—adds to supply of "quality" and relieves the perceived need to reduce spending.

When the Fed wants to stimulate spending in normal times, it uses reserves to buy Treasury bills in the federal-funds market, reducing the funds' rate. But as the rate nears zero, Treasury bills become equivalent to cash, and such open-market operations have no more effect than trading a $20 bill for two $10s. There is no effect on the total supply of "quality" assets.

A dead end? Not at all. The Fed can satisfy the demand for quality by using reserves—or "printing money"—to buy securities other than Treasury bills. This is the way the $600 billion got out into the private sector.

This expansion of Fed lending has not violated the constraint that "the" interest rate cannot be less than zero, nor will it do so in the future. There are thousands of different interest rates out there and the yield differences among them have grown dramatically in recent months. The yield on short-term governments is now about the same as the yield on cash: zero. But the spreads between governments and privately-issued bonds are large at all maturities. The flight to quality means exactly that many are eager to trade private paper for non-interest bearing (or low-interest bearing) reserves and with the Fed's help they are doing so every day.

Could the $600 billion in new reserves be called a bailout? In a sense, yes: The Fed is lending on terms that private banks are not willing to offer. They are not searching for underpriced "bargains" on behalf of the public, nor is it their mission to do so. Their mission is to provide liquidity to the system by acting as lender-of-last-resort. We don't care about the quality of the assets the Fed acquires in doing this. We care about the quantity of its liabilities.

There are many ways to stimulate spending, and many of these methods are now under serious consideration. How could it be otherwise? But monetary policy as Mr. Bernanke implements it has been the most helpful counter-recession action taken to date, in my opinion, and it will continue to have many advantages in future months. It is fast and flexible. There is no other way that so much cash could have been put into the system as fast as this $600 billion was, and if necessary it can be taken out just as quickly. The cash comes in the form of loans. It entails no new government enterprises, no government equity positions in private enterprises, no price fixing or other controls on the operation of individual businesses, and no government role in the allocation of capital across different activities. These seem to me important virtues.

Mr. Lucas, a professor of economics at the University of Chicago, received the Nobel Prize in Economic Sciences in 1995.

From Robert E. Lucas, Jr., "Bernanke is the Best Stimulus Right Now", 'The Wall Street Journal', December 12, 2008, p. A13. Reprinted by permission of The Wall Street Journal, copyright © 2008 Dow Jones & Company, Inc. All Rights Reserved Worldwide.

SECTION CHECK

1. The money market is the market where money demand and money supply determine the equilibrium interest rate.
2. The three primary reasons for the demand for money are transaction purposes, precautionary reasons, and asset purposes.
3. The quantity of money demanded varies inversely with interest rates (a movement along the money demand curve) and directly with income (a shift of the money demand curve). Monetary policies that increase the supply of money will lower interest rates in the short run, other things being equal.
4. Rising incomes increase the demand for money and lead to a new, higher equilibrium interest rate, other things being equal.
5. The supply of money is effectively almost perfectly inelastic with respect to interest rates over their plausible range, as controlled by Federal Reserve policies.
6. Money market equilibrium occurs at the intersection of the money demand and money supply curves. At the equilibrium nominal interest rate, the quantity of money demanded equals the quantity of money supplied.
7. When the Fed sells bonds to the private sector, bond purchasers take the money out of their checking accounts to pay for the bonds, and those banks' reserves are reduced by the size of the check. This reduction in bank reserves leads to a reduction in the money supply, which in turn leads to a higher interest rate and a reduction in aggregate demand, at least in the short run.
8. When the Fed buys bonds, bond sellers will likely deposit their check from the Fed in their banks and the money supply will increase. The increase in the money supply will lead to lower interest rates and an increase in aggregate demand.
9. An inverse relationship between the interest rate and the price of bonds means that when the price of bonds rises (falls), the interest rate falls (rises).
10. A change in the nominal interest rate tends to change the real interest rate by the same amount in the short run.
11. The Fed signals its intended monetary policy through the federal funds rate target it sets.

---

1. What are the determinants of the demand for money?
2. If the earnings available on other financial assets rose, would you want to hold more or less money? Why?
3. For the economy as a whole, why would individuals want to hold more money as GDP rises?
4. Why might people who expect a major market "correction" (a fall in the value of stock holdings) wish to increase their holdings of money?
5. How is the money market equilibrium established?
6. Who controls the supply of money in the money market?
7. How does an increase in income or a decrease in the interest rate affect the demand for money?
8. What Federal Reserve policies would shift the money supply curve to the left?
9. Will an increase in the money supply increase or decrease the short-run equilibrium real interest rate, other things being equal?
10. Will an increase in national income increase or decrease the short-run equilibrium real interest rate, other things being equal?
11. What is the relationship between interest rates and aggregate demand in monetary policy?
12. When the Fed sells bonds, what happens to the price of bonds and the interest rate?
13. When the Fed buys bonds, what happens to the price of bonds and the interest rate?
14. Why is the relationship between bond prices and interest rates an inverse one?

SECTION 28.4
Expansionary and Contractionary Monetary Policy

- What is expansionary monetary policy?
- What is contractionary monetary policy?
- How does monetary policy work in the open economy?
- How does monetary policy impact real GDP and the price level?

Expansionary Monetary Policy in a Recessionary Gap

If the Fed engages in expansionary monetary policy to combat a recessionary gap, the increase in the money supply will lower the interest rate. The lower interest rate reduces the cost of borrowing and the return to saving. Therefore, firms invest in new plant and equipment, while households increase their investment in housing at the lower interest rate. In short, when the Fed increases the money supply, interest rates fall and the quantity demanded of goods and services increases at each and every price level. The aggregate demand curve shifts from AD_1 to AD_2, as seen in Exhibit 1. The result is greater RGDP growth at a higher price level at E_2. In this case, the Fed has eliminated the recession, and RGDP is equal to the potential level of output at $RGDP_{NR}$. During the recession of 2001, the Fed aggressively lowered the federal funds rate to stimulate aggregate demand when it was faced with a recessionary gap.

For example, in the first half of 2001, the Fed slashed interest rates to their lowest levels since August 1994. Between January 2001 and August 2001, the Fed cut the federal funds rate target by 3 percentage points, clearly demonstrating that it was concerned that the economy was dangerously close to falling into a recession. Then came the events of September 11 and the corporate scandals. By the end of the year, the federal funds rate, which began at 6.5 percent, was at 1.75 percent, the lowest rate since 1961. With the slow recovery, the Fed pushed the rate down further, to 1.25 percent in November 2002. The Fed's actions were aimed at increasing consumer confidence, restoring stock market wealth, and stimulating investment. That is, the Fed's move was designed to increase aggregate demand in an effort to increase output and employment to long-run equilibrium at E_2.

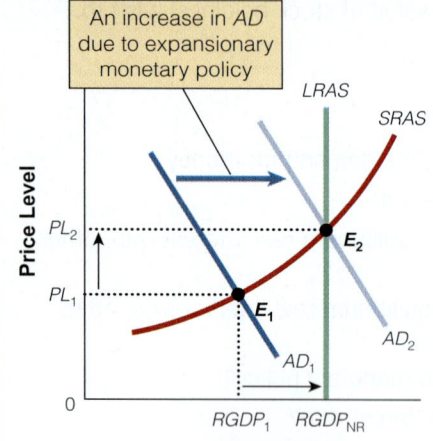

section 28.4 exhibit 1 Expansionary Monetary Policy in a Recessionary Gap

If the Fed is combatting a recessionary gap, it can increase the money supply, which leads to a change in aggregate demand from AD_1 to AD_2. The result is greater RGDP of a higher price level. The expansionary monetary policy has moved the economy to the natural rate (where RGDP = potential GDP).

Contractionary Monetary Policy in an Inflationary Gap

The Fed may engage in contractionary monetary policy if the economy faces an inflationary gap. Suppose the economy is at initial short-run equilibrium, E_1, in Exhibit 2. In order to combat inflation, suppose the Fed engages in an open market sale of bonds. This would lead to a decrease in the money supply, causing the interest rate to rise. The higher interest rate means that borrowing is more expensive and the return to saving is higher. Consequently, firms find it more costly to invest in plant and equipment and households find it more costly to finance new homes. In short, when the Fed increases the money

in the news — The U.S. Economy in the Wake of September 11

The devastating events of September 11 further set back an already fragile economy. Heightened uncertainty and badly shaken confidence caused a widespread pullback from economic activity and from risk taking in financial markets, where equity prices fell sharply for several weeks and credit risk spreads widened appreciably. The most pressing concern of the Federal Reserve in the first few days following the attacks was to help shore up the infrastructure of financial markets and to provide massive quantities of liquidity to limit potential disruptions to the functioning of those markets. The economic fallout of the events of September 11 led the Federal Open Market Committee (FOMC) to cut the target federal funds rate after a conference call early the following week and again at each meeting through the end of the year.

Displaying the same swift response to economic developments that appears to have characterized much business behavior in the current cyclical episode, firms moved quickly to reduce payrolls and cut production after mid-September. Although these adjustments occurred across a broad swath of the economy, manufacturing and industries related to travel, hospitality, and entertainment bore the brunt of the downturn. Measures of consumer confidence fell sharply in the first few weeks after the attacks, but the deterioration was not especially large by cyclical standards, and improvement in some of these indexes was evident in October. Similarly, equity prices started to rebound in late September, and risk spreads began to narrow somewhat by early November, when it became apparent that the economic effects of the attacks were proving less severe than many had feared.

Consumer spending remained surprisingly solid over the final three months of the year in the face of enormous economic uncertainty, widespread job losses, and further deterioration of household balance sheets from the sharp drop in equity prices immediately following September 11. Several factors were at work in support of household spending during this period. Low and declining interest rates provided a lift to outlays for durable goods and to activity in housing markets. Nowhere was the boost from low interest rates more apparent than in the sales of new motor vehicles, which soared in response to the financing incentives offered by manufacturers. Low mortgage interest rates not only sustained high levels of new home construction but also allowed households to refinance mortgages and extract equity from homes to pay down other debts or to increase spending. Fiscal policy provided additional support to consumer spending. The cuts in taxes enacted [in 2001], including the rebates paid out over the summer, cushioned the loss of income from the deterioration in labor markets. And the purchasing power of household income was further enhanced by the sharp drop in energy prices during the autumn. With businesses having positioned themselves to absorb a falloff of demand, the surprising strength in household spending late in the year resulted in a dramatic liquidation of inventories. In the end, real gross domestic product posted a much better performance than had been anticipated in the immediate aftermath of the attacks.

SOURCE: Federal Reserve Board of Governors, "Monetary Policy and the Economic Outlook," *88th Annual Report*, 2001, pp. 3–5.

section 28.4 exhibit 2 — Contractionary Monetary Policy in an Inflationary Gap

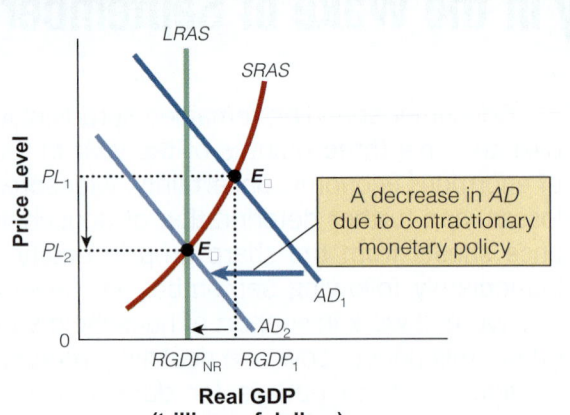

If the Fed is combatting an inflationary gap at E_1, it can decrease the money supply, which would lead to a change from AD_1 to AD_2. The result is a lower RGDP and a lower price level at E_2, and the economy moves to the natural rate (where RGDP = potential GDP).

supply it lowers the interest rate and increases the quantity of goods and services demanded at every price level. That is, the aggregate demand curve shifts leftward from AD_1 to AD_2 in Exhibit 2. The result is a lower RGDP and a lower price level, at E_2. The economy is now at $RGDP_{NR}$ where RGDP equals the potential level of output.

Monetary Policy in the Open Economy

For simplicity, we have assumed that the global economy does not affect domestic monetary policy. This assumption is incorrect. Suppose the Fed decides to pursue an expansionary policy by buying bonds on the open market. As we have seen, when the Fed buys bonds on the open market, the immediate effect is that the money supply increases and interest rates fall. With lower domestic interest rates, some domestic investors will invest funds in foreign markets, exchanging dollars for foreign currency, which leads to a depreciation

Use what you've LEARNED: MONEY AND THE AD/AS MODEL

Q During the Great Depression in the United States, the price level fell, the money wage rate fell, real GDP fell, and unemployment reached 25 percent. Investment fell, and as banks failed, the money supply fell dramatically. Can you show the effect of these changes from a vibrant 1929 economy to a battered 1932 economy using the AD/AS model?

A The 1929 economy was at PL_{1929} and $RGDP_{NR}$ in Exhibit 3. The lack of consumer confidence coupled with the large reduction in the money supply, wealth lost in the stock market crash, and falling investment sent the aggregate demand curve reeling. As a result, the aggregate demand curve fell from AD_{1929} to AD_{1932}, real GDP fell to $RGDP_{1932}$, and the price level fell to PL_{1932}.

section 28.4 exhibit 3 — The Great Depression

in the news: The Science (and Art) of Monetary Policy

Are there rules for designing and implementing good monetary policy that all economists agree on? Or is policymaking inherently a subjective task, one that depends critically on combining both good economics and insightful judgment?

Is Monetary Policy a Science?
Currently, many economists are in agreement with three basic principles that form the core of the "scientific" approach to monetary policy. Each of these principles is designed to guide central bankers.

Principle 1: Focus on the output gap. A huge literature in the 1980s and 1990s showed how excessive inflation can result if a central bank aims for output objectives that are too ambitious. If, for example, the central bank engages in expansionary policies in an attempt to keep output above potential, the net result will only be a higher average rate of inflation.

Many solutions to this problem have been suggested. The simplest is to have the central bank adopt a realistic output objective. Specifically, the central bank should strive to stabilize output around potential output, sometimes also called full-employment or natural rate output.

Principle 2: Follow the Taylor Principle. The second principle in the "scientific" approach to monetary policy is to follow the Taylor Principle. This principle states that the central bank's policy interest rate should be increased more than one for one with increases in the inflation rate. Named after Stanford University economist John Taylor, the Taylor Principle ensures that an increase in the inflation rate produces a policy reaction that increases the real rate of interest—the interest rate corrected for inflation. The rise in the real interest rate reduces private spending, slows the economy down, and brings inflation back to the central bank's inflation target. Conversely, if inflation falls below the central bank's target, the Taylor Principle calls for a more than one for one cut in the central bank's policy interest rate. This reduces the real rate of interest, stimulates private spending, and pushes inflation back to its target level....

One way to implement the Taylor Principle is to follow a Taylor rule, also named after John Taylor, which specifies exactly how much to change the federal funds rate in response to changes in inflation and the output gap.

Principle 3: Be forward looking. Monetary policy actions affect the economy with a lag. An interest rate cut may not have its maximum impact on real output for 12 or even 18 months, and the effects on inflation may take longer still. Central banks cannot wait to act until inflation has increased or the economy has gone into a recession. These lags mean that central banks must be forward looking. For example, when the Fed raised interest rates in 2000, inflation was still quite low, once the volatile food and energy components were removed. The Fed acted because it was concerned that inflation would otherwise begin to rise.

One policy framework that satisfies these three principles is *inflation* forecast targeting. Under an inflation forecast targeting procedure, the central bank is concerned with stabilizing inflation at low levels and with stabilizing the output gap. Because of the lags in policy, the emphasis is on responding to the central bank's forecast of future inflation. If the forecast says inflation will rise, the central bank should act to slow the economy down—it doesn't wait until inflation actually has increased. Because inflation forecast targeting is based on the three policy principles, it has gained many adherents among academic and central bank economists.

Is there more to achieving good monetary policies than simply following the economist's scientific principles?

(continued)

in the news: The Science (and Art) of Monetary Policy (cont.)

Is Monetary Policy an Art?
Perhaps the public believes that Alan Greenspan's [former chair of the Fed] leadership matters because it perceives monetary policy to be, in part, an art. It requires the fine touch of a master policymaker, one whose feel for the correct moment to change interest rates cannot be reduced to a few scientific principles. But if making policy isn't a science, what exactly is nonscientific about it? The best way to understand the "art" of policymaking is to revisit our three policy principles.

How can we focus on the output gap when we don't know what it is? It's all very well to tell central banks to focus on the output gap, but how are they supposed to know what the gap is? When major shifts in productivity growth occur—as happened in the 1970s with the productivity slowdown and again in the 1990s with the productivity speedup—measuring the output gap can be difficult. The output gap is the difference between something we can measure (real GDP) and something we can't (the economy's potential output level).

Implementing the Taylor Principle. The Taylor Principle calls for adjusting the policy interest rate more than one for one with changes in inflation. But how much more? If inflation rises by 1 percentage point, should the federal funds rate be increased by 1.5 percentage points? 2 percentage points? Or 1.01 percentage points? The Taylor Principle alone does not offer guidance.

The art of forecasting. Implementing inflation forecast targeting means the central bank has to be able to forecast future economic conditions. This is not an easy task. Last summer, economic forecasts did not foresee the growth slowdown that began during the third quarter. The Fed had to respond quickly in early 2001 as signs of an economic slowdown developed.

Good forecasts are based on good data, good economic models, and good judgment. Mechanical forecasts based on a few key indicators inevitably ignore information that might be relevant. While statistical models provide a baseline for developing economic forecasts, good forecasters always supplement the models' predictions with judgmental adjustment.

SOURCE: Reprinted from Carl E. Walsh, "The Science (and Art) of Monetary Policy," Federal Reserve Bank of San Francisco. *Economic Letter* 2001–13 (May 4, 2001). The opinions expressed in this article do not necessarily reflect the views of the management of the Federal Reserve Bank of San Francisco, or of the Board of Governors of the Federal Reserve System.

GREAT ECONOMIC THINKERS
MILTON FRIEDMAN (1912–2006)

Milton Friedman was born in New York City in 1912. He was an undergraduate at Rutgers and a graduate student at Columbia University. Prior to his death in November 2006, he was a senior research fellow at the Hoover Institute at Stanford University. He was also Paul Snowden Russell Distinguished Service Professor Emeritus of Economics at the University of Chicago, where he taught from 1946 to 1976, and was a member of the research staff of the National Bureau of Economic Research from 1937 to 1981.

He is probably best known as the leader of the Chicago School of Monetary Economics, which stressed the importance of the quantity of money as an instrument of government policy and as a determinant of business cycles and inflation.

During the 1950s and 1960s, researching the relationship between the money supply and the economy was considered a waste of time. But in the 1970s Friedman convinced many of his colleagues, even his most ardent critics, that money matters in the economy. Friedman knew that money mattered, but he also knew that it is not easy to successfully manipulate monetary policy to stabilize the economy when the lags between implementation and impact can be long and unpredictable. Friedman thought that continued aggregate demand stimulation would not increase output, but would cause inflation. He believed that most recessions were caused by monetary misuse. Friedman also developed the permanent income hypothesis: People's spending decisions depend on expectations of future income not just current income.

In addition to his work on monetary economics, Friedman wrote extensively on public policy, always with a primary emphasis on the preservation and extension of individual freedom. In fact, many of Friedman's economic ideas have been tested: flexible exchange rates, educational vouchers, an all-volunteer army, and the privatization and deregulation of many industries.

of the dollar (a decrease in the value of the dollar). The depreciation of the dollar makes the U.S. market more attractive to foreign buyers and foreign markets relatively less attractive to domestic buyers. That is, this shift means an increase in net exports—fewer imports and greater exports—and an increase in RGDP in the short run.

Similarly, the Fed may pursue a contractionary monetary policy by selling bonds on the open market. When the Fed sells bonds on the open market, the immediate effect is it reduces the money supply and causes interest rates to rise; foreign investors will convert their currencies to dollars to take advantage of the relatively higher interest rates. These purchases will lead to an appreciation of the dollar (an increase in the value of a currency), which will make U.S. goods and services relatively more expensive—foreigners will import less and domestic consumers will buy more exports. The result is a decrease in net exports and a reduction in RGDP in the short run.

SECTION CHECK

1. An expansionary monetary policy at less than full employment can cause an increase in real GDP and price level.
2. An expansionary monetary policy at full employment can temporarily increase real GDP, but in the long run, only the price level will rise.

---

1. How will an expansionary monetary policy affect RGDP and the price level at less than full employment?
2. How will a contractionary monetary policy affect RGDP and the price level at a point beyond full employment?

SECTION 28.5 Money and Inflation

* What is the equation of exchange?
* What is the velocity of money?
* What is the quantity theory of money and prices?

For many centuries, scholars have known that there is a positive relationship between the money supply, the price level, the growth in the money supply, and the inflation rate. In the 1500s, there was a huge influx of gold and silver that flowed into Europe following the Spanish conquest in the New World. The influx of precious metals almost tripled the money supply of Europe. Too many coins were chasing what goods were available and prices rose steadily in the sixteenth century.

The Inflation Rate and the Growth in the Money Supply

One of the major reasons that the control of the money supply is so important is that, in the long run, the amount of money in circulation and the overall price level are closely linked. It is virtually impossible for a country to have sustained inflation without a rapid growth in the money supply. The inflation rate tends to be greater in periods of rapid monetary expansion than in periods of slower growth in the money supply. In Exhibit 1, we see that international data supports the relationship between higher money growth and a higher inflation rate.

The Equation of Exchange

In the early twentieth century, Yale economist Irving Fisher formalized the relationship between money and the price level with the equation of exchange. The equation of exchange (or quantity equation) can be written as:

$$M \times V = P \times Q$$

where M is the money supply, however defined (usually M_1 or M_2), V is the velocity of money, P is the price level, and Q is real output (RGDP).

The **velocity of money** refers to its "turnover" rate, or the intensity with which money is used. Specifically, V represents the average number of times that each dollar is used in purchasing final goods or services in a one-year period. For example, a $20 bill may travel from you to the delicatessen owner, who passes it on to a doctor for the co-payment on medical services, who passes it on to a car dealership as part of a down payment for a new car. The faster money circulates, the higher the velocity. Velocity is defined as the nominal or current dollar value of output divided by the money supply, or:

$$V = \text{Nominal GDP}/M$$

velocity of money
a measure of how frequently money is turned over

section 28.5 exhibit 1 Money Supply Growth and Inflation Rates in Selected Countries, 1980–2002

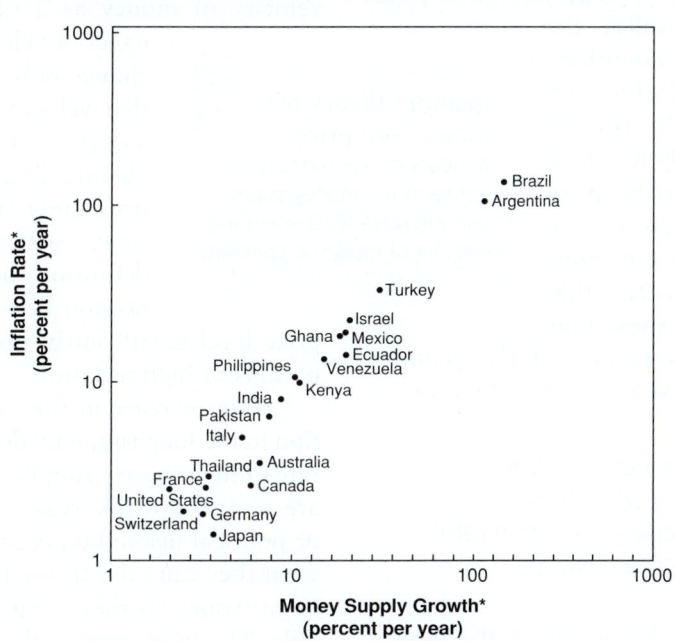

*Logarithmic Scale

We often see a strong positive correlation between a country's average annual inflation rate and its annual growth in money supply.

SOURCE: World Bank, *World Development Indicators*, 2004.

Suppose we have a simple economy that only produces frozen yogurt. The economy produces 200 quarts of frozen yogurt per year. The frozen yogurt sells for $5 a quart and the quantity of money in the economy is $100. Plugging the numbers into our equation, we get:

$$V = \text{Nominal GDP}/M$$
$$= P \times Q/M$$
$$= (\$5 \times 200)/\$100 = 10$$

That is, the people in the economy spend $1,000 per year on frozen yogurt. If there is only $100 of money in the economy, each dollar must change hands on average 10 times per year. Thus, the velocity is 10.

The Quantity Theory of Money and Prices

If we make certain assumptions about the variables in the equation of exchange we can clearly see the relationship between the money supply and the price level. This relationship is called the **quantity theory of money and prices.** If velocity (V) and real GDP (Q) both remain constant, then a 10 percent increase in the money supply will lead to a 10 percent increase in the price level—that is, the money supply and the price level change by the same proportion. We can then extend this equation to link the growth rates of these four variables. Using the *growth version of the quantity equation*, we can transform $M \times V = P \times Q$ into:

Growth rate of the money supply
+ Growth rate of velocity =
Growth rate of the price level (inflation rate)
+ Growth rate of real output

quantity theory of money and prices a theory of the connection between the money supply and the price level when the velocity of money is constant

This makes it easier to see the effects of the money supply on the inflation rate. Suppose money growth is 5 percent per year, the growth of real output is 3 percent per year, and velocity has not changed at all—its growth rate is 0 percent. What is the inflation rate? The growth rate of M (5 percent) + the growth rate of V (0 percent) = the growth rate of prices ___ + the growth rate of Q (3 percent). In this situation, the growth rate of prices (the inflation rate) is equal to 2 percent. We can also extend the analysis to predict the inflation rate when real GDP and velocity also vary. For example, if velocity grew at 1 percent annually rather than zero in our example, the inflation rate would be 3 percent rather than 2 percent.

If velocity remains constant, then the growth rate of velocity (the percentage change from one year to the next) will be zero. Then we can simplify our equation once more:

Inflation rate = Growth rate of the money supply
− Growth rate of real GDP

If this is the case, there are three possible scenarios:

1. If money supply grows at a faster rate than real GDP, then there will be inflation.
2. If money supply grows at a slower rate than real GDP, then there will be deflation.
3. If money supply grows at the same rate as real GDP, the price level will be stable.

Economists once expected they could treat the velocity of money as a given, because the determinants of velocity they focused on would change only very slowly. We now know that velocity is not constant, but often moves in a fairly predictable pattern. Historically, the velocity of money has been quite stable over a long period of time, particularly when using the M_2 definition of money. Thus, the connection between money supply and the price level is still fairly predictable, especially during periods of high inflation.

If an increase in the money supply leads to inflation in the long run, why do countries allow the growth rate of their money supply to increase so rapidly? There are several possible reasons. For instance, due to war or political instability, countries' spending may exceed what they can raise through borrowing from the public or taxation, so they create more money to pay their bills. The more money they create, the larger amount of inflation they will experience.

Hyperinflation

The relationship between the growth rate of the money supply and the inflation rate is particularly strong when there is very rapid inflation, called hyperinflation.

One of the most famous cases of hyperinflation was in Germany in the 1920s—inflation rose to roughly 300 percent *per month* for over a year. The German government had incurred large amounts of debt as a result of World War I and could not raise enough money to pay its expenses, so it printed huge amounts of money. The inflation rate became so rapid that store owners would change their prices in the middle of the day, firms had to pay workers several times a week, and many resorted to barter. Recently, Zimbabwe, Brazil, Argentina, and Russia have all experienced hyperinflation. The cause of hyperinflation is simply excessive money growth.

SECTION CHECK

1. The equation of exchange is expressed as $M \times V = P \times Q$, where M is the money supply, V is the velocity of money, P is the average level of prices of final goods and services, and Q is real GDP in a given year.
2. The velocity of money (V) represents the average number of times that a dollar is used in purchasing final goods or services in a one-year period.
3. The equation of exchange is a particularly useful tool when analyzing the effects of a change in the money supply on the price level or inflation rate in the aggregate economy.

---

1. If M_1 is $10 billion and velocity is 4, what is the product of the price level and real output (nominal GDP)? If the price level is 2, what does the dollar value of output (nominal GDP) equal?
2. If nominal GDP is $200 billion and the money supply is $50 billion, what must velocity be?
3. If the money supply increases and velocity does not change, what will happen to nominal GDP?
4. If velocity is unstable, does stabilizing the money supply help stabilize the economy? Why or why not?

SECTION 28.6 Problems in Implementing Monetary and Fiscal Policy

* What problems exist in implementing monetary policy?
* What problems exist in coordinating monetary and fiscal policies?

Problems in Conducting Monetary Policy

The lag problem inherent in adopting fiscal policy changes is less acute for monetary policy, largely because the decisions are not slowed by the same budgetary process. That is, the implementation lag is longer for fiscal policy. The FOMC of the Federal Reserve, for example, can act quickly (in emergencies almost instantly, by conference call) and even secretly to buy or sell government bonds, the key day-to-day operating tool of monetary policy. However, the length and variability of the lag before its effects on output and employment are felt are still significant, and the time before the full price-level effects are felt is even longer and more variable. According to the Federal Reserve Bank of San Francisco, the major effects of a change in policy on growth in the overall production of goods and services usually are felt within three months to two years; the effects on inflation tend to involve even longer lags, one to three years or more.

How Do Commercial Banks Implement the Fed's Monetary Policies?

One limitation of monetary policy is that it ultimately must be carried out through the commercial banking system. The central bank (the Federal Reserve System in the United States) can change the environment in which banks act, but the banks themselves must take the steps necessary to increase or decrease the money supply. Usually, when the Fed is trying to constrain monetary expansion, it has no difficulty in getting banks to make appropriate responses. Banks must meet their reserve requirements; and if the Fed raises bank reserve requirements, sells bonds, and/or raises the discount rate, banks must obtain the necessary cash or reserve deposits at the Fed to meet their reserve requirements. In response, banks will call in loans that are due for collection, sell secondary reserves, and so on in order to obtain the necessary reserves. In the process of collecting loans, the banks decrease the money supply.

When the Federal Reserve wants to induce monetary expansion, however, it can provide banks with excess reserves (e.g., by lowering reserve requirements or buying government bonds), but it cannot force the banks to make loans, thereby creating new money. Ordinarily, of course, banks want to convert their excess reserves to interest-earning income by making loans. But in a deep recession or depression, banks might be hesitant to make enough loans to put all those reserves to work, fearing that they will not be repaid. Their pessimism might lead them to perceive that the risks of making loans to many normally creditworthy borrowers outweigh any potential interest earnings (particularly at the low real interest rates that are characteristic of depressed times). Some have argued that banks maintaining excess reserves rather than loaning them out was, in fact, one of the monetary policy problems that arose in the Great Depression.

Banks That Are Not Part of the Federal Reserve System and Policy Implementation

A second problem with monetary policy relates to the fact that the Fed can control deposit expansion at member banks, but it has no control over global and nonbank institutions that also issue credit (loan money) but are not subject to reserve requirement limitations; examples are pension funds and insurance companies. Therefore, while the Fed may be able to predict the impact of its monetary policies on loans issued by member banks, global and nonbanking institutions can alter the impact of monetary policies adopted by the Fed. Hence, the real question is how precisely the Fed can control the short-run real interest rates and the money supply through its monetary policy instruments.

Fiscal and Monetary Coordination Problems

Another problem that may arise out of existing institutional policymaking arrangements is the coordination of fiscal and monetary policy. Congress and the president make fiscal policy decisions, while monetary policymaking is in the hands of the Federal Reserve System. A macroeconomic problem arises if the federal government's fiscal decision makers differ with the Fed's monetary decision makers on policy objectives or targets. For example, the Fed may be more concerned about keeping inflation low, while fiscal policymakers may be more concerned about keeping unemployment low.

Alleviating Coordination Problems

In recognition of potential macroeconomic policy coordination problems, the chairman of the Federal Reserve Board has participated for several years in meetings with top economic advisers of the president. An attempt is made in these meetings to reach a consensus on the appropriate policy responses, both monetary and fiscal. Still, they sometimes disagree, and the Fed occasionally works to partly offset or even neutralize the effects of fiscal policies that it views as inappropriate. Some people believe that monetary policy should be more directly controlled by the president and Congress, so that all macroeconomic policy will be determined more directly by the political process. Also, it is argued that such a move would enhance coordination considerably. Others, however, argue that it is dangerous to turn over control of the nation's money supply to politicians, rather than allowing decisions to be made by technically competent administrators who are more focused on price stability and more insulated from political pressures applied by the public and special interest groups.

section 28.6 exhibit 1 — Timing Expansionary Policy

Initially, the macroeconomy is at equilibrium at point E_1. With high unemployment (at $RGDP_1$), the government decides to increase government purchases and cut taxes to stimulate the economy, or the Fed could have increased the money supply. Aggregate demand shifts from AD_1 to AD_2 over time, perhaps 12 to 16 months. In the meantime, if consumer confidence increases, the aggregate demand curve might shift to AD_3, leading to much higher prices (PL_4) in the long run, rather than at the target level, point E_2, at price level PL_2.

Timing Is Critical

The timing of fiscal policy and monetary policy is crucial. Because of the significant lags before the fiscal and monetary policy has its impact, the increase in aggregate demand may occur at the wrong time. For example, imagine that we are initially at AD_1 in Exhibit 1. The economy is currently suffering from low levels of output and high rates of unemployment. In response, policymakers decide to increase government purchases and implement a tax cut, or alternatively they could have increased the money supply. But from the time when the policymakers recognize the problem to the time when the policies have a chance to work themselves through the economy, business and consumer confidence both increase, shifting the aggregate demand curve rightward from AD_1 to AD_2—increasing RGDP and employment. When the fiscal policy takes hold, the policies will have the undesired effect of causing inflation, with little permanent effect on output and employment. This effect may be seen in Exhibit 1, as the aggregate demand curve shifts from AD_2 to AD_3. At E_3, input owners will require higher input prices, shifting the SRAS leftward from $SRAS_1$ to $SRAS_2$ and to the new long-run equilibrium at E_4.

Imperfect Information

In addition, the problem of imperfect information enters the picture. For example, in order to know how much to stimulate the economy, policymakers must know the size of the multiplier and by how much RGDP should increase. But some economists disagree on the natural rate of real output ($RGDP_{NR}$), and it may be difficult to know where RGDP is at any given moment in time; government estimates are approximations and are often corrected at a later period. The government must also know the exact MPC. If the estimate is too low, the multiplier will be less than expected and the stimulus will be too small. If the estimate of MPC is too high, the multiplier will be more than expected and the stimulus will be too large.

Overall Problems with Monetary and Fiscal Policy

Much of macroeconomic policy in this country is driven by the idea that the federal government can counteract economic fluctuations: stimulating the economy (with increased government spending, tax

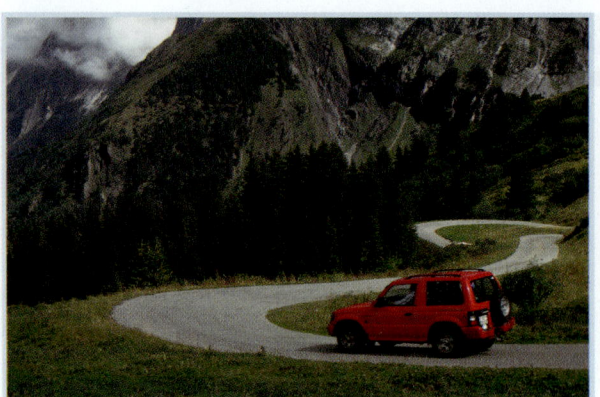

Some economists believe that fine-tuning the economy is like driving a car with an unpredictable steering lag on a winding road, or driving while looking only through the rearview mirror.

cuts, and easy money) when it is weak and restraining it when it is overheating. However, policymakers must adopt the right policies in the right amounts at the right time for such "stabilization" to do more good than harm; and to do this, government policymakers need far more accurate and timely information than experts can give them.

First, economists must know not only which way the economy is heading but also how rapidly it is changing. Even the most current data on key variables such as employment, growth, productivity, and so on, reflect conditions in the past, not the present. The unvarnished truth is that in our incredibly complicated world, no one knows exactly what the economy will do, no matter how sophisticated the econometric models used; our models are only approximations. It has often been said, and not completely in jest, that the purpose of economic forecasting is to make astrology look respectable.

But let's assume that economists can outperform astrologers at forecasting. Indeed, let's be completely unrealistic and assume that economists can provide completely accurate economic forecasts of what will happen if macroeconomic policies are unchanged. Even then, they cannot be certain of how best to promote stable economic growth.

If economists knew, for example, that the economy was going to dip into another recession in six months, they would then need to know exactly how much each possible policy would spur activity to keep the economy stable. But such precision is unattainable, given the complexity of economic forecasting. Furthermore, despite assurances to the contrary, economists aren't always certain what effect a policy will have on the economy. Will an increase in government purchases quicken economic growth? It is widely assumed so; but how much? Moreover, increasing government purchases increases the budget deficit, which could send a frightening signal to the bond markets. The result might be to drive up interest rates and choke off economic activity. Thus, even when policymakers know in which direction to nudge the economy, they cannot be sure which policy levers to pull, or how hard to pull them, in order to fine-tune the economy to stable economic growth.

But let's further assume that policymakers know when the economy will need a boost and which policy will provide the right boost. A third crucial consideration is how long it will take a policy before it has its effect on the economy. The trouble is that, even when increased government purchases or an expansionary monetary policy does give the economy a boost, no one knows precisely how long it will take to do so. The boost may come quickly or it may come many months (even years) in the future, when it may add inflationary pressures to an economy already overheating rather than help the economy to recover from a recession.

Macroeconomic policymaking is rather like driving down a twisting road in a car with an unpredictable lag and degree of response in the steering mechanism. If you turn the wheel to the right; the car will eventually veer to the right, but you don't know exactly when or how much. In short, severe practical difficulties are inherent in trying to fine-tune the economy. Even the best forecasting models and methods are far from perfect. Economists are not exactly sure where the economy is or where or how fast it is going, making it difficult to prescribe an effective policy. Even if we do know where the economy is headed, we cannot be sure how large a policy's effect will be or when it will take effect.

SECTION CHECK

1. Monetary policy faces somewhat different implementation problems from those faced by fiscal policy. Both face difficult forecasting and lag problems; however, the Fed can take action much more quickly. But its effectiveness depends largely on the reaction of the private banking system to its policy changes, and its intended effects can be offset by global and nonbank financial institutions, over which the Fed lacks jurisdiction.
2. In the United States, monetary and fiscal policy are carried out by different decision makers, thus requiring cooperation and coordination for effective policy implementation.
3. An aggregate demand shift in the flat portion of the *SRAS* curve will result in a large change in RGDP and a small change in the price level.
4. An aggregate demand shift in the steep portion of the *SRAS* curve will result in a small change in RGDP and a large change in the price level.

---

1. Why is the lag time for adopting policy changes shorter for monetary policy than for fiscal policy?
2. Why would a banking system that wanted to keep some excess reserves rather than lending out all of them hinder the Fed's ability to increase the money supply?
3. How can the activities of global and nonbank institutions weaken the Fed's influence on the money market?
4. If fiscal policy was expansionary, but the Fed wanted to counteract the fiscal policy effect on aggregate demand, what could it do?
5. What are the arguments for and against having monetary policy more directly controlled by the political process?
6. How is fine-tuning the economy like driving a car with an unpredictable steering lag on a winding road?

Interactive Chapter Summary

Fill in the blanks:

1. In most countries, the job of manipulating the supply of money belongs to the _____.
2. Effective control of major monetary policy decisions rests with the _____ and the _____ of the Federal Reserve System.
3. The Federal Reserve was created in 1913 because the U.S. banking system had little _____ and no _____ direction.
4. The _____ consists of the seven members of the Board of Governors, the president of the New York Federal Reserve Bank, and four other presidents of Federal Reserve banks, who serve on the committee on a rotating basis.
5. Perhaps the most important function of the Federal Reserve is its ability to regulate the _____.
6. The Fed has three major methods that it can use to control the supply of money: It can engage in _____ operations, change _____ requirements, or change its _____ rate.
7. _____ are by far the most important device used by the Fed to influence the money supply.
8. Open market operations involve the purchase or sale of _____ by _____.
9. When the Fed buys government bonds in an open market operation, it _____ the money supply.
10. The most a bank can lend out at a given time is equal to its _____.
11. If the reserve requirement is 10 percent, a total of up to _____ in new money is potentially created by the purchase of $100,000 of government bonds by the Fed.

12. When the Fed sells a bond, the reserves of the bank where the bond buyer keeps his bank account will _____.

13. If the Fed _____ reserve requirements, other things being equal, it will create excess reserves in the banking system.

14. An increase in the required reserve ratio would result in a _____ in the money supply.

15. Small reserve requirement changes have a _____ impact on the potential supply of money.

16. Banks having trouble meeting their reserve requirement can borrow reserves directly from the Fed at an interest rate called the _____ rate.

17. If the Fed raises the discount rate, it makes it _____ costly for banks to borrow funds from it to meet their reserve requirements, which will result in _____ new loans being made and _____ money created.

18. If the Fed wants to expand the money supply, it will _____ the discount rate.

19. When banks have short-term needs for cash to meet reserve requirements, they are more likely to take a short-term (often overnight) loan from other banks in the _____ market than to borrow reserves directly from the Fed.

20. The current extent of discount lending is _____.

21. In recent years, the Federal Reserve has _____ its focus on the federal funds rate as the primary indicator of its stance on monetary policy.

22. The Fed can do three things if it wants to reduce the money supply: _____ government bonds, _____ reserve requirements, or _____ the discount rate.

23. An increase in the money supply would tend to _____ nominal GDP.

24. People have three basic motives for holding money instead of other assets: for _____ purposes, _____ reasons, and _____ purposes.

25. The quantity of money demanded varies _____ with the rate of interest.

26. If the price level falls, buyers will need _____ money to purchase their goods and services.

27. We draw the money supply curve as _____, other things being equal, with changes in _____ policies acting to shift the money supply curve.

28. Money market equilibrium occurs at that _____ interest rate where the quantity of money demanded equals the quantity of money supplied.

29. Rising national income will shift the demand for money to the _____, leading to a new _____ equilibrium nominal interest rate.

30. An increase in the money supply will lead to _____ interest rates and a(n) _____ in aggregate demand.

31. When the Fed sells bonds, it _____ the price of bonds, _____ interest rates, and _____ aggregate demand in the short run.

32. If the demand for money increases, but the Fed doesn't allow the money supply to increase, interest rates will _____, and aggregate demand will _____.

33. When the economy grows, the Fed would have to _____ the money supply to keep interest rates from rising.

34. The _____ is the interest rate the Fed targets.

35. A contractionary policy can be thought of as a(n) _____ in the money supply or a(n) _____ in the interest rate.

36. The real interest rate is equal to _____ minus _____.

37. Countercyclical monetary policy would _____ the supply of money to combat a potential inflationary boom.

38. The Fed selling bonds will lead to a(n) _____ in the money supply, a(n) _____ in interest rates, a(n) _____ of the dollar, a(n) _____ in net exports, and a(n) _____ in RGDP in the short run.

39. The quantity equation of money can be presented as: _____ = _____.

40. _____ represents the average number of times that a dollar is used in purchasing final goods or services in a one-year period.

41. If M increases and V remains constant, then P must _____, Q must _____, or P and Q must each _____.

42. Expanding the money supply, other things being equal, will have a similar impact on aggregate demand as _____ government spending or _____ taxes.

43. Some economists, often called _____, believe that monetary policy is the most powerful determinant of macroeconomic results.

44. Velocity is _____ stable when measured using the M_1 definition and over shorter periods of time.

45. An increase in the interest rates will cause people to hold _____ money, which, in turn, means that the velocity of money _____.

46. Higher rates of anticipated inflation would tend to _____ velocity.

47. The inflation rate tends to rise _____ in periods of rapid monetary expansion.

48. The lag problem inherent in adopting fiscal policy changes is much _____ acute for monetary policy.

49. According to the Federal Reserve Bank of San Francisco, the major effects of a change in policy on growth in the overall production of goods and services usually are felt within _____ months to _____ years, and the effects on inflation tend to involve even longer lags, perhaps _____ to _____ years or more.

50. In the process of calling in loans to obtain necessary banking reserves, banks _____ the supply of money.

51. Ordinarily, banks want to convert excess reserves into interest-earning _____, but in a deep recession or a depression, banks might be hesitant to make enough loans to put all those reserves to work.

52. The Fed can control deposit expansion at _____ banks, but it has no control over global and nonbank institutions that also _____.

53. Decision making with respect to fiscal policy is made by _____ and _____, while monetary-policy decision making is in the hands of _____.

54. Some people believe that monetary policy should be more directly controlled by the president and Congress, so that all macroeconomic policy will be determined _____ directly by the political process, which will _____ policy coordination.

55. Policymakers must adopt the _____ policies in the _____ amounts at the _____ time for such "stabilization" to do more good than harm.

56. When increased government purchases or expansionary monetary policy does give the economy a boost, _____ knows precisely how long it will take to do so.

Answers: 1. central bank 2. Board of Governors; Federal Open Market Committee 3. stability; central 4. Federal Open Market Committee 5. money supply 6. open market; reserve; discount 7. Open market operations 8. government securities; the Federal Reserve System 9. increases 10. excess reserves 11. $1,000,000 12. fall 13. lowers 14. decrease 15. big 16. discount 17. more; fewer; less 18. lower 19. federal funds 20. small 21. increased 22. sell; raise; raise 23. raise 24. transaction; precautionary; asset 25. inversely 26. less 27. vertical; Federal Reserve 28. nominal 29. right; holder 30. lower; increase 31. lowers; raises; reduces 32. rise; fall 33. increase 34. federal funds rate 35. decrease; increase 36. the nominal interest rate; the expected inflation rate 37. reduce 38. decrease; increase; appreciation; decrease; decrease 39. $M \times V$; $P \times Q$ 40. Velocity 41. rise; rise 42. increasing; reducing 43. monetarists 44. less 45. less; increases 46. increase 47. more 48. less 49. three; two; one; three 50. reduce 51. loans 52. member; issue credit 53. Congress; the president; the Federal Reserve System 54. more; improve 55. right; right; right 56. no one

Key Terms and Concepts

open market operations 836
discount rate 838
federal funds market 838

money market 840
velocity of money 855

quantity theory of money and prices 856

Section Check Answers

28.1 The Federal Reserve System

1. **What are the six primary functions of a central bank?**
   A central bank (1) is a "banker's bank," where commercial banks maintain their own deposits; (2) provides services, such as transferring funds and checks, for commercial banks; (3) serves as the primary bank for the federal government; (4) buys and sells foreign currencies and assists in transactions with other countries; (5) serves as a "lender of last resort" for banking institutions in financial distress; and (6) regulates the size of the money supply.

2. **What is the FOMC, and what does it do?**
   The Federal Open Market Committee is a committee of the Federal Reserve System, made up of the seven members of the Board of Governors, the president of the New York Federal Reserve Bank and four other presidents of Federal Reserve banks. It makes most of the key decisions influencing the direction and size of changes in the money stock.

3. **How is the Fed tied to the executive branch? How is it insulated from executive branch pressure to influence monetary policy?**
   The president selects the seven members of the Board of Governors, subject to Senate approval, one every two years, for 14-year terms. He also selects the chair of the Board of Governors for a four-year term. However, since the president can only select one member every two years, he cannot appoint a majority of the Board of Governors during his term in office. Also, the president cannot use reappointment of his nominees or threats of firing members to pressure the Fed on monetary policy.

28.2 How Does the Federal Reserve Change the Money Supply?

1. **What three main tactics could the Fed use in pursuing a contractionary monetary policy?**
   The Fed could conduct an open market sale of government securities (bonds), mandate an increase in reserve requirements, and/or mandate an increase in the discount rate if it wanted to pursue a contractionary monetary policy.

2. **What three main tactics could the Fed use in pursuing an expansionary monetary policy?**
   The Fed could conduct an open market purchase of government securities (bonds), mandate a decrease in reserve requirements, and/or mandate a decrease in the discount rate if it wanted to pursue an expansionary monetary policy.

3. **Would the money supply rise or fall if the Fed made an open market purchase of government bonds, *ceteris paribus*?**
   An open market purchase of government bonds by the Fed would increase banking reserves, thereby increasing the money stock, *ceteris paribus*.

4. **If the Fed raised the discount rate from 12 to 15 percent, what effect would this have on the money supply?**
   Raising the discount rate makes it more costly for banks to borrow reserves directly from the Fed. To the extent that banks borrow fewer reserves directly from the Fed, this reduces total banking reserves, thereby decreasing the money stock, *ceteris paribus*.

28.3 Money, Interest Rates, and Aggregate Demand

1. **What are the determinants of the demand for money?**
   There are three motives for the demand for money: transaction purposes (to facilitate exchange), precautionary purposes (just in case), and asset purposes (to keep some assets in the liquid form of money). The demand for money increases (shifts to the right) if either real incomes or the price level is higher, because that will increase the nominal amount of transactions. A decrease in the interest rate will decrease the opportunity cost of holding money, increasing the quantity of money people wish to hold (moving down along the demand for money curve), but not increasing the demand for money (shifting the demand for money curve).

2. **If the earnings available on other financial assets rose, would you want to hold more or less money? Why?**
   Since holding wealth in the form of other financial assets is the alternative to holding it in the form of

money, nonmoney financial assets are substitutes for holding money. When the earnings (interest) available on alternative financial assets rise, the opportunity cost of holding money instead also rises; so you would want to hold less money, other things being equal.

3. **For the economy as a whole, why would individuals want to hold more money as GDP rises?**

   Individuals conduct a larger volume of transactions as GDP rises. Therefore, they would want to hold more money as GDP rises in order to keep the costs of those increasing transactions down.

4. **Why might people who expect a major market "correction" (a fall in the value of stock holdings) wish to increase their holdings of money?**

   When the value of alternative financial assets is expected to fall, holding money, which will not similarly fall in value, becomes more attractive. Therefore, in the case of an expected fall in the value of stocks, bonds, or other financial assets, people would want to increase their holdings of money as a precaution.

5. **How is the money market equilibrium established?**

   In the money market, money demand and money supply determine the equilibrium nominal interest rate.

6. **Who controls the supply of money in the money market?**

   The banking system, through the loan expansion process, directly determines the supply of money in the money market. However, the Fed, through the policy variables it controls (primarily open market operations, reserve requirements, and the discount rate), indirectly controls the supply of money by controlling the level of reserves and the money multiplier.

7. **How does an increase in income or a decrease in the interest rate affect the demand for money?**

   An increase in income increases (shifts right) the demand for money, as people want to hold down the transactions costs on the increasing volume of transactions taking place. A decrease in interest rates, on the other hand, increases the quantity of money demanded (moving down along the money demand curve) but does not change the demand for money.

8. **What Federal Reserve policies would shift the money supply curve to the left?**

   An open market sale of government securities (bonds), an increase in reserve requirements, and/or an increase in the discount rate would shift the money supply curve to the left.

9. **Will an increase in the money supply increase or decrease the short-run equilibrium real interest rate, other things being equal?**

   An increase in the money supply would decrease the short-run equilibrium real interest rate, other things being equal, as the rightward shift of the money supply curve pushes the money market equilibrium down along the money demand curve.

10. **Will an increase in national income increase or decrease the short-run equilibrium real interest rate, other things being equal?**

    An increase in national income will shift the money demand curve to the right, which would increase the short-run equilibrium real interest rate, other things being equal.

11. **What is the relationship between interest rates and aggregate demand in monetary policy?**

    Lower interest rates will tend to stimulate aggregate demand for goods and services, other things being equal.

12. **When the Fed sells bonds, what happens to the price of bonds and the interest rate?**

    When the Fed sells bonds, it increases the supply of bonds, decreasing bond prices. The process results in reserves being removed from the banking system when the buyer's payment to the Fed is subtracted from his or her bank's reserve account, leading to a decrease in the money supply and an increase in the interest rate.

13. **When the Fed buys bonds, what happens to the price of bonds and the interest rate?**

    When the Fed buys bonds, it increases the demand for bonds, increasing bond prices. The process results in reserves being added to the banking system when the Fed's payment is deposited back into the banking system, leading to an increase in the money supply and a decrease in the interest rate.

14. **Why is the relationship between bond prices and interest rates an inverse one?**

    There is an inverse relationship between bond prices and interest rates because the process that creates more money, lowering interest rates, is triggered by the

Fed's buying bonds, bidding up bond prices. Similarly, the process that reduces the money supply, lowering interest rates, is triggered by the Fed's selling bonds, bidding down bond prices.

28.4 Expansionary and Contractionary Monetary Policy

1. **How will an expansionary monetary policy affect RGDP and the price level at less than full employment?**

   An expansionary monetary policy shifts aggregate demand to the right. Starting from less than full employment, the result will be an increase in the price level, an increase in real output, and a decrease in unemployment as the economy moves up along the short-run aggregate supply curve. This increased output will be sustainable if it does not exceed the natural level of real output.

2. **How will a contractionary monetary policy affect RGDP and the price level at a point beyond full employment?**

   A contractionary monetary policy, starting from a point beyond full employment, will reduce aggregate demand and will move the economy from the short-run equilibrium position beyond full employment toward the new long-run equilibrium position at full employment, preventing an inflationary boom. There is, then, a reduction in both RGDP and the price level.

28.5 Money and Inflation

1. **If M_1 is $10 billion and velocity is 4, what is the product of the price level and real output (nominal GDP)? If the price level is 2, what does the dollar value of output (nominal GDP) equal?**

   If the money supply is $10 billion and velocity is 4 (so that $M \times V$ = $40 billion), the product of the price level and real output ($P \times Q$, or nominal output), must also be $40 billion. If the price level is 2, real output would equal the $40 billion nominal output divided by the price level of 2, or $20 billion.

2. **If nominal GDP is $200 billion and the money supply is $50 billion, what must velocity be?**

   Since $M \times V = P \times Q$, $V = P \times Q/M$. V = $200 billion/$50 billion, or 4, in this case.

3. **If the money supply increases and velocity does not change, what will happen to nominal GDP?**

   If M increases and V does not change, $M \times V$ must increase. Since $M \times V = P \times Q$, and $P \times Q$ equals nominal GDP, nominal GDP must also increase as a result.

4. **If velocity is unstable, does stabilizing the money supply help stabilize the economy? Why or why not?**

   If V is unstable, stabilizing M does not stabilize $M \times V$. Since $M \times V$ will not be stabilized, $P \times Q$, or nominal GDP, will not be stabilized either.

28.6 Problems in Implementing Monetary and Fiscal Policy

1. **Why is the lag time for adopting policy changes shorter for monetary policy than for fiscal policy?**

   The lag time for adopting monetary policy changes is shorter than for fiscal policy changes because decisions regarding monetary policy are not slowed by the budgetary process that fiscal tax and expenditure policy changes must go through.

2. **Why would a banking system that wanted to keep some excess reserves rather than lending out all of them hinder the Fed's ability to increase the money supply?**

   A desire on the part of the banking system to keep some excess reserves would reduce the money supply, other things being equal. Such a change would thus at least partly offset the effects of the Fed's expansionary policy changes, which would hinder the Fed's ability to successfully use expansionary monetary policy to increase the money supply.

3. **How can the activities of global and nonbank institutions weaken the Fed's influence on the money market?**

   The Fed has no control over global and nonbank institutions that issue credit (loan money), as do U.S. commercial banks, but are not subject to reserve requirement limitations. The Fed cannot control their behavior and the resulting effects on economic activity through its policy variables, as it can with U.S. commercial banks.

4. **If fiscal policy was expansionary, but the Fed wanted to counteract the fiscal policy effect on aggregate demand, what could it do?**

   Expansionary fiscal policy would increase aggregate demand. To counteract that fiscal policy effect on aggregate demand, the Fed would want to adopt contractionary monetary policy (through an open market sale of government securities, an increase in reserve requirements, and/or an increase in the discount rate), which would tend to reduce aggregate demand, other things being equal.

5. **What are the arguments for and against having monetary policy more directly controlled by the political process?**

   The argument for having monetary policy more directly controlled by the political process is basically that since fiscal policy is already determined by the political process, and since monetary policy (which is not determined by the same political process) can offset or even neutralize the macroeconomic effects of fiscal policy, it would be better for all macroeconomic policy to be directly controlled by the political process. The argument against having monetary policy more directly controlled by the political process is that it would be dangerous to turn over control of the nation's money supply to politicians rather than having monetary policy decisions be made by technically competent administrators who are focused more on price stability and are more insulated from political pressures coming from the public and special interest groups.

6. **How is fine-tuning the economy like driving a car with an unpredictable steering lag on a winding road?**

   Fine-tuning the economy is like driving a car with an unpredictable steering lag on a winding road because to steer the economy successfully requires that policymakers have an accurate map of both which way and how rapidly the economy is headed; that they know exactly how much each possible policy would affect the economy, so that they "turn the policy wheels" just the right amount; and that they know how long it will take each possible policy to "turn" the economy.

CHAPTER 28 STUDY GUIDE

True or False:

1. A central bank has only one function—controlling the supply of money in a country.
2. The central bank typically serves as the major bank for the central government.
3. The central bank implements monetary and fiscal policy for the government.
4. The 12 member banks of the Federal Reserve System act largely in unison on major monetary policy issues.
5. Banks are not all required to belong to the Fed; but there is currently virtually no difference in the requirements for member and nonmember banks.
6. Historically, the Fed has had limited independence from the executive and legislative branches of government.
7. No member of the Federal Reserve Board will face reappointment by the president who initially made the appointment.
8. The Federal Open Market Committee makes most of the key decisions influencing the direction and size of changes in the money supply.
9. The Fed controls the supply of money, even though privately owned commercial banks actually create and destroy money by making loans.
10. Open market purchases or sales of bonds by the Fed have an ultimate impact on the money supply that is several times the amount of the purchase or sale.
11. If the Fed buys bonds in an open market operation, and the seller deposits the payment in her bank account, the money supply will increase and lead to an increase in the bank's reserves.
12. With a 10 percent required reserve ratio, a $10,000 cash deposit in a bank would result in an increase in the bank's excess reserves of $1,000.
13. With a 10 percent required reserve ratio, a $1,000 bond purchase by the Fed directly creates $1,000 in money in the form of bank deposits, and indirectly permits up to $9,000 in additional money to be created through the multiple expansion in bank deposits.
14. The Fed selling government bonds will tend to cause a multiple expansion of bank deposits.
15. Generally, in a growing economy, where the real value of goods and services is increasing over time, an increase in the supply of money is needed to maintain stable prices.
16. Changes in required reserve ratios are such a potent monetary policy tool that they are frequently used.
17. If the Fed raises the discount rate, the money supply will tend to increase.
18. The discount rate is a relatively unimportant monetary policy tool, mainly because member banks do not rely heavily on the Fed for borrowed funds.
19. The discount rate's main significance is that changes in the rate signal the Fed's intentions with respect to monetary policy.
20. Currently, the Fed sets the discount rate below the federal funds target.
21. The Fed funds rate target tends to affect interest rates throughout the economy.
22. Setting the discount rate above the Fed funds target tends to discourage borrowing from the Fed's discount window.
23. If the Fed wanted to increase the money supply, it would buy bonds, lower reserve requirements, or lower the discount rate.
24. When interest rates are lower, the opportunity cost of holding monetary assets is higher.

25. The demand for money, particularly for transactions purposes, is highly dependent on income levels because the transaction volume varies directly with income.
26. At lower interest rates, the quantity of money demanded, but not the demand for money, is greater.
27. An increase in the money supply raises the equilibrium nominal interest rate.
28. The Fed buying bonds on the open market is an example of an expansionary monetary policy.
29. When the price of bonds rises, the interest rate rises.
30. The Fed cannot control both the money supply and the interest rate at the same time.
31. If the demand for money increases, and the Fed wants to keep the interest rate stable, it will have to increase the money supply.
32. Focusing on growth in the money supply when the demand for money is changing unpredictably will lead to large fluctuations in the interest rate.
33. An expansionary policy can be thought of as an increase in the money supply or an increase in the interest rate.
34. A change in the nominal interest rate tends to change the real interest rate by the same amount in the short run because the expected inflation rate is slow to change in the short run.
35. An increase in AD brought about through monetary policy can lead to only a temporary, short-run increase in real GDP if the economy is initially operating at or above full employment, with no long-run effect on output or employment.
36. If the Fed pursues a contractionary monetary policy when the economy is at full employment, the Fed could cause a recession.
37. The Fed buying bonds on the open market will lead to an appreciation of the dollar, an increase in net exports, and an increase in RGDP in the short run.
38. The money supply times velocity equals the price level times real GDP.
39. If individuals are writing lots of checks on their checking accounts and spending currency as fast as they receive it, velocity will tend to be low.
40. Velocity equals nominal GDP divided by the money supply.
41. The magnitude of velocity does not depend on the definition of money that is used.
42. If the money supply increases and the velocity of money does not change, the result will be higher prices (inflation), greater real output of goods and services, or a combination of both.
43. Expanding the money supply, unless counteracted by increased hoarding of currency (leading to a decline in V), will have the same type of impact on aggregate demand as an expansionary fiscal policy.
44. Reducing the money supply, other things being equal, will have a contractionary impact on aggregate demand.
45. The velocity of money is a constant.
46. If velocity changes but moves in a fairly predictable pattern, the connection between money supply and GDP is still fairly predictable.
47. The cause of hyperinflation is excessive money growth.
48. The FOMC of the Federal Reserve is unable to act quickly in emergencies.
49. The length and variability of the impact lag before the effects of monetary policy on output and employment are felt longer and are more variable than for fiscal policy.

50. The Fed can change the environment in which banks act, but the banks themselves must take the steps necessary to increase or decrease the supply of money.
51. If the Fed raises bank reserve requirements, sells bonds, and/or raises the discount rate, banks will call in loans that are due for collection, sell secondary reserves, and so on, to obtain the necessary reserves; and in the process of contracting loans, they decrease the supply of money.
52. When the Fed is trying to constrain monetary expansion, it often has difficulty in getting banks to make appropriate responses.
53. When the Federal Reserve wants to induce monetary expansion, it can provide banks with excess reserves; but it cannot force the banks to make loans, thereby creating new money.
54. Banks maintaining excess reserves hinder attempts by the Fed to induce monetary expansion.
55. The Fed may be able to predict the impact of its monetary policies on loans by member banks, but the actions of global and nonbanking institutions can serve to offset, at least in part, the impact of monetary policies adopted by the Fed on the money and loanable funds markets.
56. The Fed can precisely control the short-run real interest rates through its monetary policy instruments.
57. A macroeconomic problem arises if the federal government's fiscal decision makers differ with the Fed's monetary decision makers on policy objectives or targets.
58. The Fed occasionally works to partly offset or even neutralize the effects of fiscal policies that it views as inappropriate.
59. For government policymakers to be sure of doing more good than harm, they need far more accurate and timely information than experts can give them.
60. Economic advisers, using sophisticated econometric models, can forecast what the economy will do in the future with reasonable accuracy.
61. Even if economists could provide completely accurate economic forecasts of what will happen if macroeconomic policies are unchanged, they could not be certain of how to best promote stable economic growth.
62. Given the difficulties of timing stabilization policy, an expansionary monetary policy intended to reduce the severity of a recession may instead add inflationary pressures to an economy that is already overheating.
63. Most of the effects of a given monetary policy will be on prices rather than RGDP in the short run, if the *SRAS* is relatively steep over the relevant range.
64. If the "new" economy increases productivity, the Fed, in trying to allow for greater economic growth without creating inflationary pressures, must estimate how much faster productivity is increasing and whether those increases are temporary or permanent.

Multiple Choice:

1. The most important role of the Federal Reserve System is
   a. raising or lowering taxes.
   b. regulating the supply of money.
   c. increasing or reducing government spending.
   d. none of the above.
2. Which of the following is not a function of the Federal Reserve System?
   a. being a lender of last resort
   b. being concerned with the stability of the banking system
   c. serving as a major bank for the central government
   d. setting currency exchange rates

3. The Fed is institutionally independent. A major advantage of this is that
    a. monetary policy is subject to regular ratification by congressional votes.
    b. monetary policy is not subject to control by politicians.
    c. monetary policy cannot be changed once it has been determined.
    d. monetary policy will always be coordinated with fiscal policy.
    e. monetary policy will always offset fiscal policy.

4. In order to increase the rate of growth of the money supply, the Fed can
    a. raise the discount rate.
    b. raise the reserve requirement.
    c. buy government bonds on the open market.
    d. sell government bonds on the open market.

5. The monetary policies generated by the Federal Reserve System
    a. must be consistent with fiscal policies that are formatted in Congress.
    b. are sometimes inconsistent with fiscal policies.
    c. must be ratified by Congress.
    d. must be approved by the president.

6. If the Fed buys a bond from an individual instead of a bank, what is the effect on the money supply?
    a. There will be no effect at all.
    b. The money supply will shrink.
    c. The money supply will grow by smaller amounts than if the Fed bought from a bank.
    d. The money supply will grow by larger amounts than if the Fed bought from a bank.
    e. The effect will be the same as if the Fed had bought the bond from a bank.

7. When the Fed purchases government bonds from a commercial bank, the bank
    a. automatically becomes poorer.
    b. loses equity in the Fed.
    c. receives reserves that can be used to make additional loans.
    d. loses its ability to make loans.

8. If the Fed wishes to expand the money supply, it
    a. buys stocks.
    b. sells stocks.
    c. buys government bonds.
    d. sells government bonds.

9. If the Fed sells a U.S. government bond from a member of the public,
    a. the banking system has more reserves, and the money supply tends to grow.
    b. the banking system has fewer reserves, and the money supply tends to grow.
    c. the banking system has more reserves, and the money supply tends to fall.
    d. the banking system has fewer reserves, and the money supply tends to fall.

10. An open market purchase of government bonds by the Fed would tend to cause
    a. the money supply to fall and bond prices to go up.
    b. the money supply to rise and bond prices to go up.
    c. the money supply to rise and bond prices to go down.
    d. the money supply to fall and bond prices to go down.

11. If the Fed lowers the discount rate, what will be the effect on the money supply?
    a. The money supply will tend to increase.
    b. The money supply will tend to decrease.
    c. The money supply will not change nor influence an expansion or contraction process.
    d. Not enough data are given to answer.

12. When the Fed sells a U.S. government bond,
    a. the volume of loans issued by the banking system increases, and investment will tend to increase.
    b. the volume of loans issued by the banking system increases, and investment will tend to decrease.
    c. the volume of loans issued by the banking system decreases, and investment will tend to increase.
    d. the volume of loans issued by the banking system decreases, and investment will tend to decrease.

13. Reducing reserve requirements, other things being equal, would tend to
    a. increase the dollar volume of loans made by the banking system.
    b. increase the money supply.
    c. increase aggregate demand.
    d. do all of the above.
    e. do a and b, but not c.

14. The combination of a decrease in the required reserve ratio and a decrease in the discount rate would
    a. increase the money supply.
    b. decrease the money supply.
    c. leave the money supply unchanged.
    d. have an indeterminate effect on the money supply.

15. When the money supply increases, other things being equal,
    a. real interest rates fall, and investment spending rises.
    b. real interest rates fall, and investment spending falls.
    c. real interest rates rise, and investment spending falls.
    d. real interest rates rise, and investment spending rises.

16. The money demand curve shows
    a. the various amounts of money that individuals will hold at different price levels.
    b. the various amounts of money that individuals will spend at different levels of GDP.
    c. the various amounts of money that individuals will hold at different interest rates.
    d. the quantity of bonds that the Fed will buy at different price levels.

17. What will happen to the demand for money if real GDP rises?
    a. It will decrease.
    b. It will be unchanged.
    c. It will increase.
    d. It depends on what happens to interest rates.

18. Contractionary monetary policy will tend to have what effect?
    a. increase the money supply and lower interest rates
    b. increase the money supply and increase interest rates
    c. decrease the money supply and lower interest rates
    d. decrease the money supply and increase interest rates

19. The combination of an increase in the discount rate and an open market sale of government bonds by the Fed will tend to result in
    a. a higher loan volume issued by the commercial banking system.
    b. higher bond prices.
    c. a lower price level.
    d. a decrease in unemployment rates.

20. When money demand increases, the Fed can choose between
    a. increasing interest rates or increasing the supply of money.
    b. increasing interest rates or decreasing the supply of money.
    c. decreasing interest rates or increasing the supply of money.
    d. decreasing interest rates or decreasing the supply of money.

21. When the economy is initially at full employment,
    a. expansionary monetary policy can potentially result in increased real output, but only in the short run.
    b. expansionary monetary policy can potentially result in increased real output in both the short run and long run.
    c. contractionary monetary policy can potentially result in increased real output, but only in the short run.
    d. contractionary monetary policy can potentially result in increased real output in both the short run and long run.

22. If a reduction in the money supply were desired in order to slow inflation, the Federal Reserve might
    a. decrease reserve requirements.
    b. buy U.S. bonds on the open market.
    c. raise the discount rate.
    d. do either b or c.

23. Suppose the Fed purchases $100 million of U.S. bonds from the public. If the reserve requirement is 20 percent and all banks keep zero excess reserves, the total impact of this action on the money supply will be a
    a. $100 million decrease in the money supply.
    b. $100 million increase in the money supply.
    c. $200 million increase in the money supply.
    d. $500 million increase in the money supply.

24. Which of the following Federal Reserve actions would most likely help counteract an oncoming recession?
    a. an increase in reserve requirements and an increase in the discount rate
    b. the sale of government bonds and an increase in the discount rate
    c. the sale of foreign currencies and an increase in reserve requirements
    d. the purchase of government bonds and a reduction in the discount rate

25. In a recession, appropriate monetary policy would tend to be for the Fed to _____ bonds to _____ AD.
    a. buy; increase
    b. buy; decrease
    c. sell; increase
    d. sell; decrease

26. To offset an inflationary boom, appropriate Fed policy could be to _____ reserve requirements to _____ AD.
    a. increase; increase
    b. increase; decrease
    c. decrease; increase
    d. decrease; decrease

27. The quantity of money that households and businesses will demand
    a. increases if income rises but decreases if interest rates rise.
    b. increases if income rises and increases if interest rates rise.
    c. decreases if income rises but increases if interest rates rise.
    d. decreases if income rises and decreases if interest rates rise.
    e. None of the above is true.

28. Starting from an initial long-run equilibrium, an unanticipated shift to more expansionary monetary policy would tend to increase
    a. prices and unemployment in the long run.
    b. real output in the short run, but not in the long run.
    c. real output in the long run, but not the short run.
    d. real output in both the long run and short run.

29. The Fed unexpectedly increasing the money supply will cause an increase in aggregate demand because
    a. real interest rates will fall, stimulating business investment and consumer purchases.
    b. the dollar will depreciate on the foreign exchange market, leading to an increase in net exports.
    c. lower interest rates will tend to increase asset prices, which increases wealth and thereby stimulates current consumption.
    d. of all the above reasons.

30. Which one of the following would be the most appropriate stabilization policy if the economy is operating beyond its long-run potential capacity?
    a. an increase in the discount rate
    b. an increase in government purchases, holding taxes constant
    c. a reduction in reserve requirements
    d. a reduction in taxes, holding government purchases constant

31. In the long run, a sustained increase in growth of the money supply relative to the growth rate of potential real output will most likely
    a. cause the nominal interest rate to fall.
    b. cause the real interest rate to fall.
    c. reduce the natural rate of unemployment.
    d. increase real output growth.
    e. do none of the above.

32. Which of the following is true?
    a. An unanticipated shift to a more expansionary monetary policy will temporarily stimulate real output and employment.
    b. Once decision makers come to anticipate the inflationary side effects, expansionary monetary policy will fail to stimulate either real output or employment.
    c. The primary long-run effect of persistent growth of the money supply at a rapid rate will be inflation.
    d. All of the above are true.

33. Which of the following would cause the U.S. money supply to expand?
    a. a commercial bank calling in a loan to build up more excess reserves
    b. a commercial bank purchasing U.S. bonds from the Fed as an investment
    c. a decrease in reserve requirements
    d. an increase in the discount rate

34. Which of the following would tend to reduce the price level?
    a. a commercial bank using excess reserves to extend a loan to a customer
    b. a commercial bank purchasing U.S. bonds from an individual as an investment
    c. an increase in reserve requirements
    d. an increase in the discount rate
    e. a purchase of U.S. government bonds by the Fed

35. The P in the equation of exchange represents the
    a. profit earned in the economy.
    b. average level of prices of final goods and services in the economy.
    c. marginal level of prices.
    d. marginal propensity to spend.

36. The equation of exchange can be written as
    a. $M \times P = V \times Q$.
    b. $M \times V = P \times Q$.
    c. $M \times Q = P \times V$.
    d. $Q \times M = P \times V$.

37. If an economist divides the level of nominal GDP by the number of dollars in the money supply, she has computed
    a. the velocity of money.
    b. the price level.
    c. the level of real GDP.
    d. the economic growth rate.

38. If nominal GDP is $3,200 billion and M_1 is $800 billion, then velocity is
    a. 0.5.
    b. 2.
    c. 4.
    d. 8.
    e. 400.

39. According to the simple quantity theory of money, a change in the money supply of 6.5 percent would, holding velocity constant, lead to
    a. a 6.5 percent change in real GDP.
    b. a 6.5 percent change in nominal GDP.
    c. a 6.5 percent change in velocity.
    d. a 6.5 percent change in aggregate supply.

40. If people expect increasing inflation, what would be the expected reaction of velocity in the equation of exchange?
    a. Velocity would be expected to remain the same.
    b. Velocity would be expected to decrease.
    c. Velocity would be expected to increase.
    d. none of the above

41. If M increases and V increases,
    a. nominal GDP increases.
    b. nominal GDP decreases.
    c. nominal GDP stays the same.
    d. the effect on nominal GDP is indeterminate.

42. If the velocity of money (V) and real output (Q) were increasing at approximately the same rate, then
    a. it would be impossible for monetary authorities to control inflation.
    b. monetary acceleration would not lead to inflation.
    c. inflation would be closely related to the long-run rate of monetary expansion.
    d. both a and b would be true.

43. Compared to fiscal policy, which of the following is an advantage of using monetary policy to attain macroeconomic goals?
    a. It takes a long time for fiscal policy to have an effect on the economy, but the effects of monetary policy are immediate.
    b. The effects of monetary policy are certain and predictable, while the effects of fiscal policy are not.
    c. The implementation of monetary policy is not slowed down by the same budgetary process as fiscal policy.
    d. The economists who help conduct monetary policy are smarter than those who help with fiscal policy.

44. An important limitation of monetary policy is that
    a. it is conducted by people in Congress who are under pressure to get reelected every two years.
    b. when the Fed tries to buy bonds, it is often unable to find a seller.
    c. when the Fed tries to sell bonds, it is often unable to find a buyer.
    d. it must be conducted through the commercial banking system, and the Fed cannot always make banks do what it wants them to do.

Problems:

1. Why is the private ownership of the Federal Reserve System essentially meaningless?
2. How is central bank independence related to average inflation rates across countries? How is the Fed insulated from executive branch pressures?
3. Why does the fact that the Fed finances its operations out of interest earned on its portfolio, with the excess returned to the U.S. Treasury, make it more independent of congressional pressure?
4. How does an open market purchase by the Fed increase bank reserves? How does it increase the money supply?
5. Why would the Fed seldom do an open market purchase of government securities at the same time that it raises the discount rate or the required reserve ratio?
6. Why is a reduction in the required reserve ratio such a powerful monetary policy tool? Why is it so seldom used?
7. Why would a reduction in the required reserve ratio not be a powerful tool when banks choose to hold substantial quantities of excess reserves?
8. In which direction would the money supply change if
   a. the Fed raised the reserve requirement?
   b. the Fed conducted an open market sale of government bonds?
   c. the Fed raised the discount rate?
   d. the Fed conducted an open market sale of government bonds and raised the discount rate?
   e. the Fed conducted an open market purchase of government bonds and raised reserve requirements?
9. Why would the transactions motive and the precautionary motive for holding money both tend to vary directly with the price level? Why would the quantity of money people desire to hold for both motives tend to vary inversely with interest rates?
10. In the move from a below equilibrium interest rate to the equilibrium interest rate, what happens in the bond market and the loan market? In the move from an above equilibrium interest rate to the equilibrium interest rate, what happens in the bond market and the loan market?
11. How does a higher price level affect the money market? How does it affect aggregate demand?
12. Why can't the Fed target both the money supply and the interest rate at the same time?
13. Answer questions a–e.
    a. What is the equation of exchange?
    b. In the equation of exchange, if V doubled, what would happen to nominal GDP as a result?
    c. In the equation of exchange, if V doubled and Q remained unchanged, what would happen to the price level as a result?
    d. In the equation of exchange, if M doubled and V remained unchanged, what would happen to nominal GDP as a result?
    e. In the equation of exchange, if M doubled and V fell by half, what would happen to nominal GDP as a result?
14. Why have ATMs and online banking made savings accounts more liquid than they used to be?
15. Given that the Fed currently imposes reserve requirements on checking deposits, but not on savings deposits, why would banks prefer to hold deposits as savings accounts rather than checking accounts, other things equal?

Issues in Macroeconomic Theory and Policy

29

29.1 The Phillips Curve

29.2 The Phillips Curve over Time

29.3 Rational Expectations and Real Business Cycles

29.4 Controversies in Macroeconomic Policy

We begin this chapter by asking whether policymakers face a trade-off between inflation and unemployment. If a trade-off is inevitable, does it exist in the short run and the long run?

If the economy is faced with a recessionary or an inflationary gap, how quickly will it recover to its long-run equilibrium position? And what is the best way to stabilize the economy? Should policymakers use expansionary and contractionary monetary and fiscal policies? Or should policymakers allow the economy to self-correct? Macroeconomists do not completely agree on this question, a topic we will discuss throughout this chapter.

After 10 years of unprecedented economic growth, the economy started to slip into a recession in early 2001, although it was one of the mildest recessions on record. This recession was set off by a serious drop in investment spending. The technology sector led to higher productivity during the 1990s, but the bursting of the dot-com bubble resulted in considerable loss in stock market wealth. The slowdown in the tech sector started to affect other segments of the economy. This situation, coupled with the 9/11 terrorist attacks, created a negative shock that rippled through the economy, especially in the travel sector. Hotels and airlines were hit particularly hard. The corporate accounting scandals of Enron and WorldCom also influenced investment attitudes. Uncertainty and fading optimism reduced both investment and consumption spending and reduced aggregate demand. To combat, or weaken, the recession, the government stimulated aggregate demand with increases in government expenditures for security and defense, the tax cut of 2001, and aggressive reductions in the federal funds rate by the Federal Reserve. The Fed started to cut its federal funds rate by 0.5 percentage point (it usually only changes the rate by 0.25 percent) in January of 2001. In the week following the attacks on the World Trade Center (September 2001), it temporarily set the federal funds rate as low as 1.25 percent. By November 2001, the recession was officially over but the federal funds rate had fallen from 6.5 percent to 2 percent—4.5 percent lower than the previous year. The Fed looked like it had done its job.

However, the Fed may have set the Federal Funds rate too low for too long. This Fed policy may have been at least partially responsible for causing a housing bubble that was reminiscent of the stock market bubble of the 1990s. The 2007–08 period also witnessed risky lending that was similar to the lending practices that occurred during the saving and loans crisis of the 1980s. There were also bank runs as a crisis of confidence in our financial institutions ensued, not unlike the Great Depression (but certainly smaller in scope).

Was it the best way to stabilize an economy?

SECTION 29.1 The Phillips Curve

* What is the Phillips curve?
* How does the Phillips curve relate to the aggregate supply and demand model?

Unemployment and Inflation

Despite legislation committing the federal government to the goal of full employment and the development of macroeconomic theory arguing that full employment can be achieved by manipulating aggregate demand, periods of high unemployment still occur.

We usually think of inflation as an evil—higher prices mean lower real incomes for people on fixed incomes, while those with the power to raise the prices charged for goods or services they provide may actually benefit. Nevertheless, some economists believe that inflation could actually help eliminate unemployment. For example, if output prices rise but money wages do not go up as quickly or as much, real wages fall. At the lower real wage, unemployment is less because the lower wage makes it profitable to hire more, now cheaper, employees than before. The result is real wages that are closer to the full-employment equilibrium wage that clears the labor market. Hence, with increased inflation, one might expect lower unemployment in the short run.

The Phillips Curve

In fact, an inverse relationship between the rate of unemployment and the changing level of prices has been observed in many periods and places in history. Credit for identifying this relationship generally goes to British economist A. H. Phillips, who in the late 1950s published a paper setting forth what has since been called the *Phillips curve*. Phillips and many others since suggested that at higher rates of inflation, the rate of unemployment is lower, while during periods of relatively stable or falling prices, unemployment is substantial. In short, the cost of lower unemployment appears to be greater inflation, and the cost of greater price stability appears to be higher unemployment.

Exhibit 1 shows the actual inflation-unemployment relationship for the United States for the 1960s. The points in this graph represent the combination of the inflation rate and the rate of unemployment in each of the 10 years of the decade. The curved line—the Phillips curve—is the smooth line that best "fits" the data points.

The Slope of the Phillips Curve

In examining Exhibit 1, it is evident that the slope of the Phillips curve is not the same throughout its length. The curve is steeper at higher rates of inflation and lower levels of unemployment. This relationship suggests that once the economy has relatively low unemployment rates, further reductions in the unemployment rate can occur only if the economy can accept larger increases in the inflation rate. Once the unemployment rate is low, it takes larger and larger doses of inflation to eliminate a given quantity of unemployment. Presumably, at lower unemployment rates, an increased part of the economy is already operating at or near full capacity. Further fiscal or monetary stimulus primarily triggers inflationary pressures in sectors already at capacity, while eliminating decreasing amounts of unemployment in those sectors where some excess capacity and unemployment still exist.

section 29.1 exhibit 1: The Phillips Curve Relationship, United States, 1960s

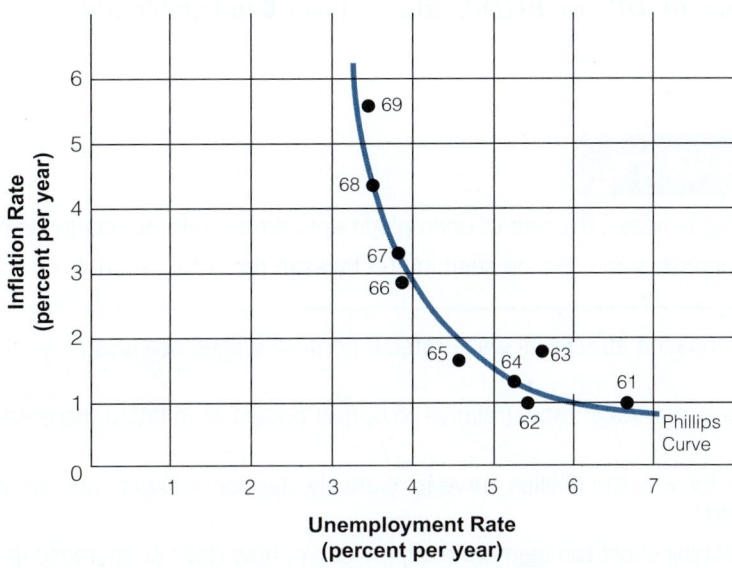

The Phillips curve illustrates an inverse relationship between the rate of unemployment and the rate of inflation. The slope of the Phillips curve becomes more steep as the unemployment rate drops, indicating that at low unemployment rates, further decreases in unemployment can occur only if the economy can accept much larger increases in inflation rates.

The Phillips Curve and Aggregate Supply and Demand

In Exhibit 2, we see the relationship between aggregate supply and demand analysis and the Phillips curve. Suppose the economy moved from a 2 percent annual inflation rate to a 4 percent inflation rate, and the unemployment rate simultaneously fell from 5 percent to 4 percent. In the Phillips curve, we see this shift as a move up the curve from point A to point B in Exhibit 2(a). We can see a similar relationship in the

section 29.1 exhibit 2: The Phillips Curve and the AD/AS Curves

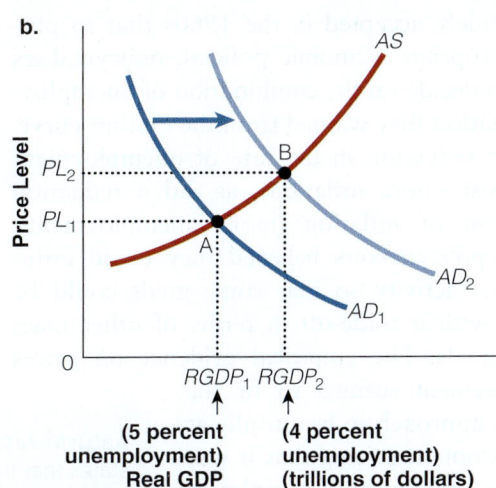

As shown in (b), if the aggregate supply curve is positively sloped, an increase in aggregate demand will cause higher prices and higher output (lower unemployment); a decrease in aggregate demand will cause lower prices and lower output (higher unemployment). This same trade-off is illustrated in the Phillips curve in (a), in the shift from point A to point B.

AD/AS model in Exhibit 2(b). Imagine that an increase in aggregate demand occurs. Consequently, the price level increases from PL_1 to PL_2 (the inflation rate rises) and output increases from $RGDP_1$ to $RGDP_2$ (the unemployment rate falls). To increase output, firms employ more workers, so employment increases and unemployment falls—the movement from point A to point B in Exhibit 2(b).

SECTION CHECK

1. The inverse relationship between the rate of unemployment and the rate of inflation is called the Phillips curve.
2. The Phillips curve relationship can also be seen indirectly from the AD/AS model.

---

1. How does the rate of inflation affect real wage rates if nominal wages rise less or more slowly than output prices?
2. How does the change in real wage rates (relative to output prices) as inflation increases affect the unemployment rate?
3. What is the argument for why the Phillips curve is relatively steeper at lower rates of unemployment and higher rates of inflation?
4. For a given upward-sloping short-run aggregate supply curve, how does an increase in aggregate demand correspond to a movement up and to the left along a Phillips curve?

SECTION 29.2 The Phillips Curve over Time

* How reliable is the Phillips curve?
* Is the Phillips curve stable over time?
* What is the difference between the long-run and short-run Phillips curves?

The Phillips Curve—The 1960s

It became widely accepted in the 1960s that to pursue the appropriate economic policies, policymakers merely had to decide on the combination of unemployment and inflation they wanted from the Phillips curve. To be sure, a reduction in the rate of unemployment came at a cost (more inflation), as did a reduction in the amount of inflation (more unemployment). Nonetheless, policymakers believed they could influence economic activity so that some goals could be met, though with a trade-off in terms of other macroeconomic goals. The empirical evidence on prices and unemployment seemed to fit the Phillips curve approach so beautifully at first that it is not surprising that it was embraced so rapidly and completely. Economists such as Milton Friedman and Edmund Phelps, who questioned the long-term validity of the Phillips curve, were largely ignored in the 1960s. These economists believed there might be a short-term trade-off between unemployment and inflation but not a permanent trade-off. That is, a trade-off happens in the short run but not in the long run. According to Friedman, the short-run trade-off comes from *unanticipated* inflation.

The Short-Run Phillips Curve Versus the Long-Run Phillips Curve

The **natural rate hypothesis** states that the economy will self-correct to the natural rate of unemployment. Let us examine the reason behind the natural rate hypothesis. Suppose the

natural rate hypothesis states that the economy will self-correct to the natural rate of employment

section 29.2 exhibit 1 — The Short-Run and Long-Run Phillips Curve

The economy initially moves along the short-run Phillips curve (SRPC) as actual inflation deviates from expected inflation. When expected inflation rates then adapt to actual inflation rates, the SRPC shifts to intersect the long-run Phillips curve (LRPC) at the new inflation rate—point C in (a) and point F in (b). If the actual inflation rate remains at the new level, then output returns to the natural level of real output, and unemployment returns to the natural rate of unemployment at that inflation rate on the LRPC.

economy is at point A in Exhibit 1(a). At that point, the inflation rate is 3 percent and the unemployment rate is at the natural rate, 5 percent. Now suppose the growth rate of the money supply increases. The increase in the growth rate of the money supply stimulates aggregate demand. In the short run, the increase in aggregate demand increases output and decreases unemployment. As the economy moves up along the short-run Phillips curve, from point A to point B, the actual inflation rate increases from 3 percent to 6 percent, and the unemployment rate falls below the natural rate to 3 percent.

Because the increase in inflation was unanticipated, real wages fall. Firms are now receiving higher prices relative to their input costs, so they expand output. Consequently, unemployment rates fall, seen in Exhibit 1(a) as a movement along the short-run Phillips curve from A to B. Eventually, workers (and other input owners) realize that their real wages have fallen because of the increase in the inflation rate that was not initially anticipated—in short, they were fooled in the short run. Workers now vigorously negotiate for higher wages. These demands increase costs to producers, and as a result, they reduce output and unemployment rises—causing a rightward shift in the short-run Phillips curve in Exhibit 1(a).

In short, the higher-than-expected inflation rate shifts the short-run Phillips curve to the right. If the 6 percent inflation rate continues, the adjustment of expectations will move the economy from point B to point C, where the expected and actual inflation rates are equal at the natural level of output and the natural rate of unemployment.

In the long run, the economy moves from A to C as inflation increases from 3 percent to 6 percent. This graph reveals that no trade-off occurs between the inflation rate and the unemployment rate in the long run. The policy implication is that the use of fiscal or monetary policy to alter real output from the natural level of real output or unemployment from the natural rate of unemployment is ineffective in the long run.

Alternatively, suppose the rate of growth in the money supply decreases as a result of the Federal Reserve System's inflationary concerns. The decrease in the rate of growth in the money supply reduces aggregate demand. In the short run, the decrease in aggregate demand moves the economy down along the short-run Phillips curve from point D to point E, where the actual inflation rate has decreased from 6 percent to 3 percent and the unemployment rate has risen above the natural rate to 7 percent. The decrease in aggregate demand leads to lower production and a higher unemployment rate.

Initially, the reduction in the inflation rate is unanticipated, and real wages rise; firms are now receiving lower prices relative to their input costs, so they reduce their output. This leads to a higher unemployment rate, as seen in the movement from point D to point E in Exhibit 1(b). If this new inflation rate remains steady at 3 percent, the actual and expected inflation rates will eventually become the same. The growth in wages will slow, lowering the cost of production, increasing output, and lowering the unemployment rate as the short-run Phillips curve shifts leftward in Exhibit 1(b).

If the 3 percent inflation rate continues, the adjustment of expectations will move the economy from point E to point F in Exhibit 1(b), where the expected and actual inflation rates are equal at the natural level of output and the natural rate of unemployment. In this scenario, a lower inflation rate comes at the expense of higher unemployment in the short run, until people adapt their expectations to the new lower inflation rate in the long run.

adaptive expectations an individual's belief that the best indicator of the future is recent information on inflation and unemployment

These expectations are called **adaptive expectations**—individuals believe that the best indicator of the future is recent information on inflation and unemployment.

In Exhibit 2 (a), we see that the negative relationship between the inflation rate and the unemployment rate breaks down in the early 1970s. Notice that the inflation rate was in the 5–6% range in the early 1970s; and consumers and firms, expected it to remain high. However, the unemployment rate rose back to the rates of the early 1960s. The movement from point A to point B in Exhibit 2 (a) resembles the movement along the short run Phillips Curve and the movement from point B to point C resembles the curve shifting back towards the natural rate of unemployment.

In Exhibit 2(b), we see inflation and unemployment data for the period 1979 to 1985. The late 1970s and early 1980s was a period of very high inflation and the the Chair of the Federal Reserve, Paul Volker decided to reduce the growth rate of the money supply to slow the rate of inflation. The contractionary monetary policy moved the economy down along the short run Phillips curve from point D to point E. When workers and firms lowered their inflationary expectations, the short run Phillips curve shifted inward from point E to point F.

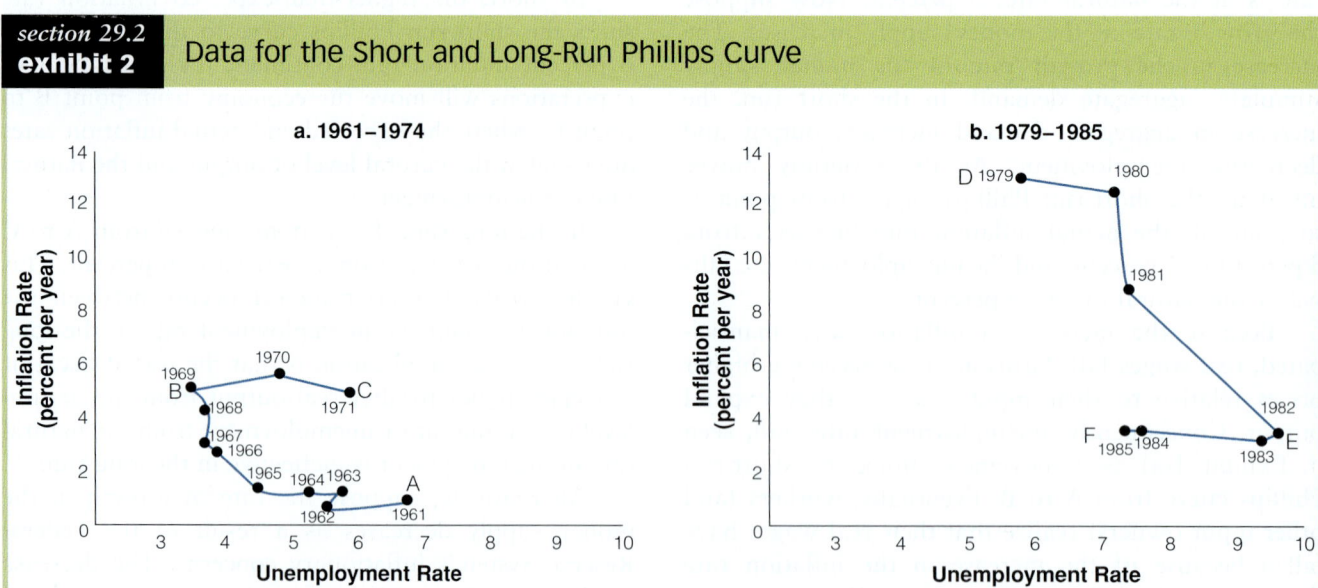

section 29.2 **exhibit 2** Data for the Short and Long-Run Phillips Curve

In Exhibit 2 is annual data for 1961-74 and 1979-85. Notice that this data in Exhibit 2(a) and (b) closely correspond to point label a, b, c, d, e, and f in Exhibit 1(a) and (b).

Supply Shocks

Earlier in this chapter, we assumed that the inverse relationship in the short-run Phillips curve was created by changes in aggregate demand. Further, as we have just seen, a change in the expected inflation rate can cause a shift in the short-run Phillips curve. However, another explanation applies to a change in the short-run Phillips curve—supply shocks.

Many economists believe that the higher energy prices in the early and late 1970s created an adverse supply shock. Higher oil prices had important implications for the macroeconomy because they meant higher production costs for many goods and services. Higher production costs caused a leftward shift in the SRAS curve from $SRAS_1$ to $SRAS_2$, as seen in Exhibit 3(a). Because the leftward shift in SRAS was greater than the rightward shift in AD, the price level increased from PL_1 to PL_2 and RGDP fell from $RGDP_1$ to $RGDP_2$ in Exhibit 3(a). The adverse supply shock led to a higher price level and less output—stagflation. A stagnant economy means fewer jobs and a higher unemployment rate. A higher price level leads to a higher inflation rate (the percentage change in the price level from the previous year) and a higher rate of unemployment. The short-run Phillips curve shifts to the right from $SRPC_1$ to $SRPC_2$, in Exhibit 3(b). Point B indicates a higher rate of inflation and a higher rate of unemployment than at point A.

A favorable supply shock (large technological improvements, bountiful harvest, or lower energy prices) lowers the inflation rate and lowers the rate of unemployment. Specifically, a favorable supply shock lowers the costs of production and causes a rightward shift in the SRAS curve from $SRAS_1$ to $SRAS_2$, as seen in Exhibit 4(a). Because the rightward shift in SRAS is greater than the rightward shift in AD, the price level falls from PL_1 to PL_2, and RGDP rises from $RGDP_1$ to $RGDP_2$ in Exhibit 4(a). The favorable supply-side shock leads to a lower price level and greater output. A growing economy means more jobs and a lower unemployment rate. With a lower price level, a lower inflation rate and a lower rate of unemployment occur; the short-run Phillips curve shifts to the left, from $SRPC_1$ to $SRPC_2$ in Exhibit 4(b). That is, at point B, both the rate of inflation and the rate of unemployment are lower than at point A. For example, in the late 1990s, a number of economists believed we witnessed

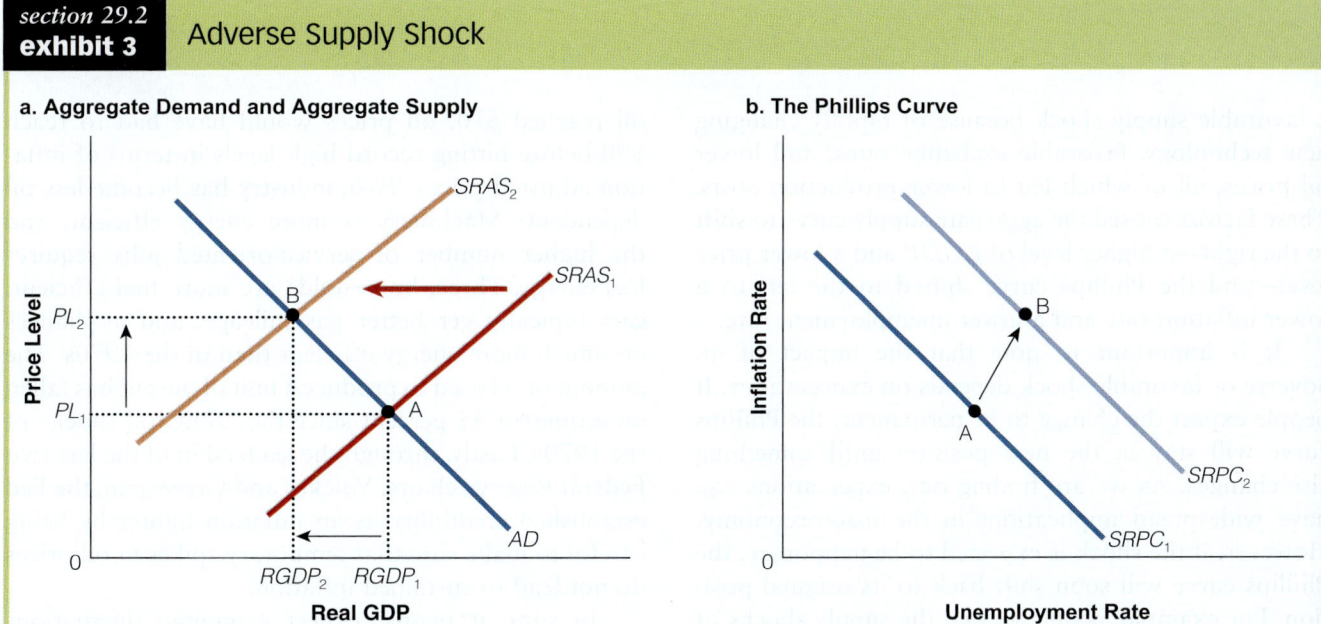

section 29.2 exhibit 3 — Adverse Supply Shock

The higher energy prices in the early and late 1970s created an adverse supply shock. In (a), the higher production costs causes a leftward shift in the SRAS curve from $SRAS_1$ to $SRAS_2$, an increase in the price level from PL_1 to PL_2, and a decrease in RGDP from $RGDP_1$ to $RGDP_2$. With a higher price level comes a higher inflation rate, and with less output comes a higher rate of unemployment. The short-run Phillips curve shifts to the right from $SRPC_1$ to $SRPC_2$ in (b). At point B, both the inflation rate and the unemployment rate are higher than at point A.

section 29.2 exhibit 4 — Favorable Supply Shock

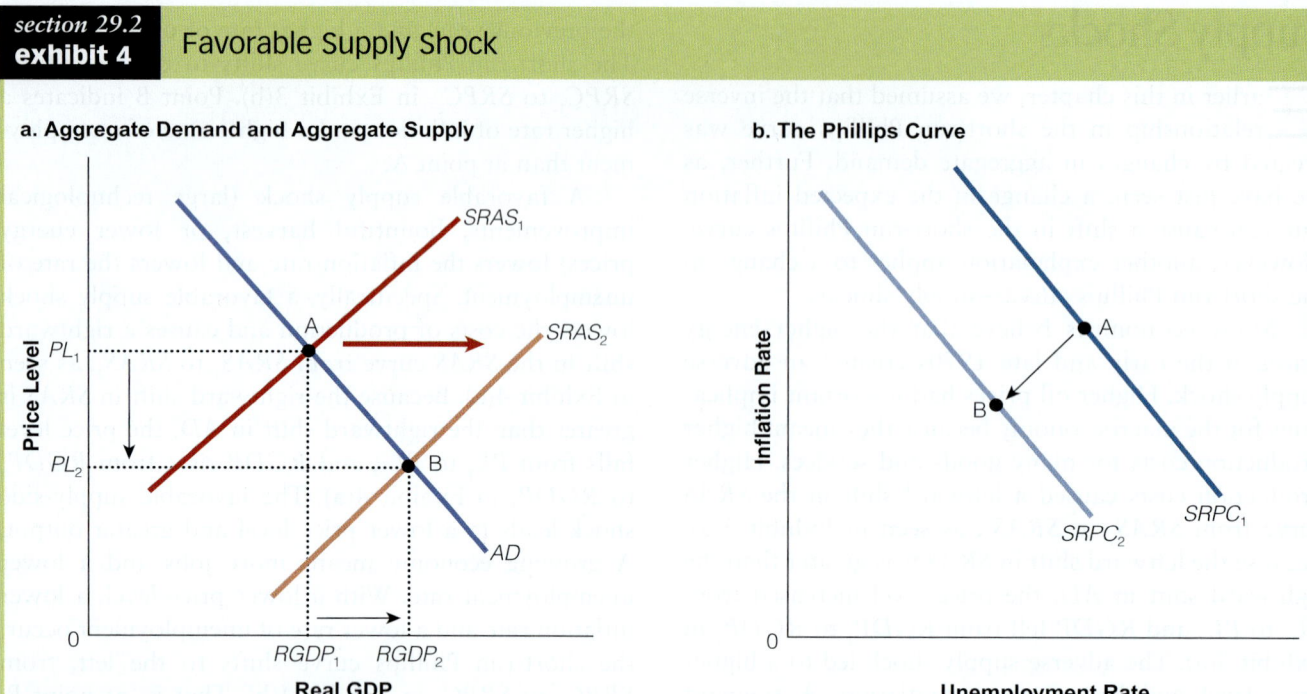

In (a), lower costs of production caused by the favorable supply shock cause a rightward shift in the SRAS curve from SRAS$_1$ to SRAS$_2$, the price level falls from PL$_1$ to PL$_2$, and RGDP rises from RGDP$_1$ to RGDP$_2$. The favorable supply-side shock leads to a lower price level and greater output. With a lower price level comes a lower inflation rate and a lower rate of unemployment. The short-run Phillips curve shifts to the left, from SRPC$_1$ to SRPC$_2$ in (b). At point B, both the inflation rate and the unemployment rate are lower than at point A.

a favorable supply shock because of rapidly changing new technology, favorable exchange rates, and lower oil prices, all of which led to lower production costs. These factors caused the aggregate supply curve to shift to the right—a higher level of *RGDP* and a lower price level—and the Phillips curve shifted to the left to a lower inflation rate and a lower unemployment rate.

It is important to note that the impact of an adverse or favorable shock depends on expectations. If people expect the change to be permanent, the Phillips curve will stay in the new position until something else changes. As we are finding out, expectations can have widespread implications in the macroeconomy. However, if the shock is expected to be temporary, the Phillips curve will soon shift back to its original position. For example, people viewed the supply shocks of the 1970s as permanent and the Phillips curve shifted to the right—a new position with a higher rate of inflation and a higher rate of unemployment.

Why did the United States not experience a negative supply shock in 2005 when oil prices jumped to more than $70 a barrel? The answer is based on several possible reasons. One, although the nominal price of oil reached $70, oil prices would have had to reach $90 before hitting record high levels in terms of inflation adjusted prices. Two, industry has become less oil dependent: Machinery is more energy efficient, and the higher number of service-oriented jobs requires less energy. Three, households are more fuel efficient: cars typically get better gas mileage, and appliances are much more energy efficient than in the 1970s. The amount of oil used to produce a unit of output has fallen an estimated 35 percent since the OPEC oil shocks of the 1970s. Lastly, through the leadership of the last two Federal Reserve chairs, Volcker and Greenspan, the Fed established credibility as an inflation fighter by being careful to make sure that temporary spikes in oil prices do not lead to sustained inflation.

In sum, if people expect economic fluctuations to be permanent and caused primarily by supply-side shifts, then the result is likely to be a positive relationship between the inflation rate and the unemployment rate—a shifting Phillips curve. Higher rates of inflation will be coupled with higher rates of unemployment, and lower rates of inflation will be coupled with lower rates of unemployment.

SECTION CHECK

1. The Phillips curve depicting the period of high inflation and unemployment in the 1970s no longer suggests the strong inverse relationship between the two variables that was evident in the 1960s.
2. The short-run Phillips curve relationship is seen as unstable and not a permanent relationship between unemployment and inflation rates.
3. The long-run Phillips curve shows the relationship between the inflation rate and the unemployment rate when the actual and expected inflation rates are the same.
4. Along the long-run Phillips curve, the natural rate of unemployment can occur at any rate of inflation.
5. If economic fluctuations are expected to be permanent and caused primarily by supply-side shifts, then a positive relationship may occur between the inflation rate and the unemployment rate—a shifting short-run Phillips curve. Higher rates of inflation will be coupled with higher rates of unemployment and lower rates of inflation will be coupled with lower rates of unemployment.

---

1. Is the Phillips curve stable over time?
2. Why would you expect no relationship between inflation and unemployment in the long run?
3. Why is the economy being on the long-run Phillips curve equivalent to its being on the long-run aggregate supply curve?
4. Why would inflation have to accelerate over time to keep unemployment below its natural rate (and real output above its natural level) for a sustained period?
5. What does the long-run Phillips curve say about the relationship between macroeconomic policy stimulus and unemployment in the long run?

SECTION 29.3 Rational Expectations and Real Business Cycles

* What is the rational expectations theory?
* What do critics say about the rational expectations theory?
* What is the real business cycle theory?
* What do the critics say about the real business cycle theory?

Can Human Behavior Counteract Government Policy?

Is it possible that people can anticipate the plans of policymakers and alter their behavior quickly to neutralize the intended impact of government action? For example, if workers see that the government is allowing the money supply to expand rapidly, they may quickly demand higher money wages to offset the anticipated inflation. In the extreme form, if people could instantly recognize and respond to government policy changes, it might be impossible to alter real output or unemployment levels through policy actions, because government policymakers could no longer surprise households and firms. An increasing number of economists believe that there is at least some truth to this point of view. At a minimum, most economists accept the notion that real output and the unemployment rate cannot be altered with the ease that was earlier believed; some believe that the unemployment rate can seldom be influenced by fiscal and monetary policies.

The Rational Expectations Theory

The relatively new extension of economic theory that leads to this rather pessimistic conclusion regarding macroeconomic policy's ability to achieve our economic goals is called the **theory of rational expectations.** The notion that expectations or anticipations of future events are relevant to economic theory is not new; for decades, economists have incorporated expectations into models analyzing many forms of economic behavior. Only in the recent past, however, has a theory evolved that tries to incorporate expectations as a central factor in the analysis of the entire economy.

> **theory of rational expectations**
> belief that workers and consumers incorporate the likely consequences of government policy changes into their expectations by quickly adjusting wages and prices

The interest in rational expectations has grown rapidly in the last decade. Acknowledged pioneers in the development of the theory include Professor Robert Lucas of the University of Chicago and Professor Thomas Sargent of the University of Minnesota. In 1995, Professor Lucas won the Nobel Prize for his work in rational expectations.

Rational expectations economists believe that wages and prices are flexible and that households and firms incorporate the likely consequences of government policy changes quickly into their expectations. In addition, rational expectations economists believe that the economy is inherently stable after macroeconomic shocks and that tinkering with fiscal and monetary policy cannot have the desired effect unless households and firms are caught "off guard" (and catching them off guard gets harder the more you try to do it).

Rational Expectations and the Consequences of Government Macroeconomic Policies

Rational expectations theory, then, suggests that government economic policies designed to alter aggregate demand to meet macroeconomic goals are of limited effectiveness. When policy targets become public, it is argued, people will alter their own behavior from what it would otherwise have been to maximize their own utility, and in so doing, they largely negate the intended impact of policy changes. If government policy seems tilted toward permitting more inflation to try to reduce unemployment, people start spending their money faster than before, become more adamant in their demands for wages and other input prices, and so on. In the process of quickly altering their behavior to reflect the likely consequences of policy changes, they make it more difficult (costly) for government authorities to meet their macroeconomic objectives. Rather than fooling people into changing real wages, and therefore unemployment, with inflation "surprises," changes in inflation are quickly reflected into expectations with little or no effect on unemployment or real output even in the short run. As a consequence, policies intended to reduce unemployment through stimulating aggregate demand will often fail to have the intended effect. Fiscal and monetary policy, according to this view, will work only if the people are caught off guard or are fooled by policies and thus do not modify their behavior in a way that reduces policy effectiveness.

Anticipation of an Expansionary Monetary Policy

Consider the case in which an increase in aggregate demand is a result of an expansionary monetary policy. This increase is reflected in Exhibit 1 in the shift from AD_1 to AD_2. Because of the predictable inflationary consequences of that expansionary policy, prices immediately adjust to a new level at PL_2. Consumers, producers, workers, and lenders who *anticipated* the

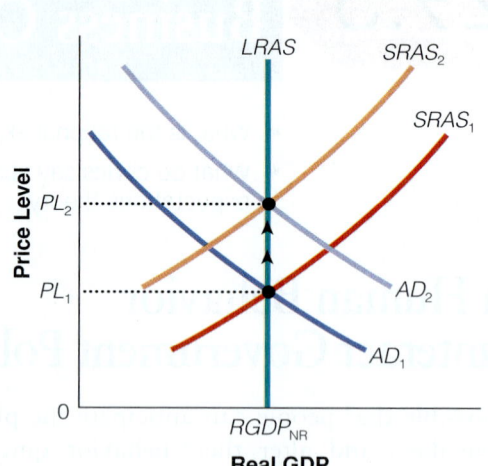

section 29.3 exhibit 1 Rational Expectations and the *AD/AS* Model

Expansionary monetary policy (or fiscal policy) will not affect RGDP if wages and prices are completely flexible, as in the rational expectations model. This means that the SRAS curve will shift leftward from $SRAS_1$ to $SRAS_2$ at the same time as the AD curve. Therefore, an expansionary policy, an increase in aggregate demand from AD_1 to AD_2, will lead to a higher price level but no change in RGDP or unemployment.

effects of the expansionary policy simply build the higher inflation rates into their product prices, wages, and interest rates. That is, households and firms realize that expansionary monetary policy can cause inflation if the economy is working close to capacity. Consequently, in an effort to protect themselves from the higher anticipated inflation, workers ask for higher wages, suppliers increase input prices, and producers raise their product prices. Because wages, prices, and interest rates are assumed to be flexible, the adjustments take place immediately. This increase in input costs for wages, interest, and raw materials causes the aggregate supply curve to shift up or leftward, shown as the movement from $SRAS_1$ to $SRAS_2$ in Exhibit 1. So the desired policy effect of greater real output and reduced unemployment from a shift in the aggregate demand curve is offset by an upward or leftward shift in the aggregate supply curve caused by an increase in input costs.

Unanticipated Expansionary Policy

Again, consider the case of an increase in aggregate demand that results from an expansionary monetary policy. However, this time it is *unanticipated*. The increase in the money supply is reflected in Exhibit 2 in the shift from AD_1 to AD_2. This unanticipated change in monetary policy stimulates output and employment in the short run, as the equilibrium moves from point A to point B. At the new short-run equilibrium, the output is at $RGDP_2$ and the price level is at PL_2. This output is beyond $RGDP_{NR}$, so it is not sustainable in the long run. Because it is unanticipated, workers and other input owners are expecting the price level to remain at PL_1, rather than PL_2. However, when input owners eventually realize that the actual price level has changed, they will require higher input prices, shifting the SRAS from $SRAS_1$ to $SRAS_2$. At point C, we see that output has returned to $RGDP_{NR}$ but at a higher price level, PL_3.

Therefore, when the expansionary policy is unanticipated, it leads to a short-run expansion in output and employment. But in the long run, the only impact of the change in monetary policy is a higher price level—inflation. In short, when the change is correctly anticipated, expansionary monetary (or fiscal) policy does not result in a change in real output. However, if the expansionary monetary (fiscal) policy is unanticipated, the result is a short-run increase in RGDP and employment, but in the long run, it just means a higher price level.

section 29.3 exhibit 2 An Expansionary Policy That Is Unanticipated

An unanticipated change in monetary policy stimulates output and employment in the short run, as the equilibrium moves from point A to point B. At the new short-run equilibrium, the output is at $RGDP_2$ and the price level is at PL_2. Because the expansionary policy is unanticipated, workers and other input owners are expecting the price level to remain at PL_1, rather than PL_2. When input owners eventually realize that the actual price level has changed, they will require higher input prices, shifting the SRAS curve from $SRAS_1$ to $SRAS_2$. At point C, we see that output has returned to $RGDP_{NR}$ but at a higher price level, PL_3. If the expansionary policy is unanticipated, it leads to a short-run expansion in output and employment. In the long run, however, the impact of the change in the expansionary policy is a higher price level.

In fact, the only way that monetary or fiscal policy can change output in the rational expectations model is with a surprise—an unanticipated change. For example, on April 18, 2001, between regularly scheduled meetings of the Federal Open Market Committee, the Fed surprised financial markets with an aggressive half-point cut in the interest rate. The Fed was trying to boost consumer confidence and impact falling stock market wealth. The surprise reduction in the interest rate sent the stock market soaring as the Dow posted one of its largest single-day point gains, and the NASDAQ had its fourth largest percentage gain. Former Fed Chairman Greenspan hoped that this move would shift the AD curve rightward, leading to higher levels of output.

When an Anticipated Expansionary Policy Change Is Less Than the Actual Policy Change

In the context of the rational expectations model (wages and prices are flexible), suppose people are expecting a large increase in the money supply as a result of expansionary monetary policy. Then, the *anticipated* price level increases from PL_1 to PL_3 when the anticipated aggregate demand increases from AD_1 to AD_3, as seen in Exhibit 3. If people anticipate the new price level PL_3, wages and other input prices adjust quickly, and the SRAS shifts leftward from $SRAS_1$ to $SRAS_2$. But what if the increase in the money supply ends up being less than people anticipated? Say the *actual* increase in the money supply only shifts AD from AD_1 to AD_2? The economy moves from point A to point B rather than to point C as many had expected, which leads to a higher price level but a lower level of RGDP—a recession.

That is, a policy designed to increase output may actually reduce output if prices and wages are flexible and the expansionary effect is less than people anticipated.

Critics of Rational Expectations Theory

Of course, rational expectations theory does have its critics. Critics want to know whether households and firms are completely informed about the impact that, say, an increase in money supply will have on the economy. In general, all citizens will not be completely informed, but key players such as corporations, financial institutions, and labor organizations may well be informed about the impact of these policy changes. But other problems arise. For example, are wages and other input prices really that flexible? That is, even if decision makers could anticipate the eventual effect of policy changes on prices, those prices may still be slow to adapt (e.g., what if you had just signed a three-year labor or supply contract when the new policy was implemented?).

section 29.3 exhibit 3 An Actual Expansionary Policy That Is Less Than the Anticipated Policy

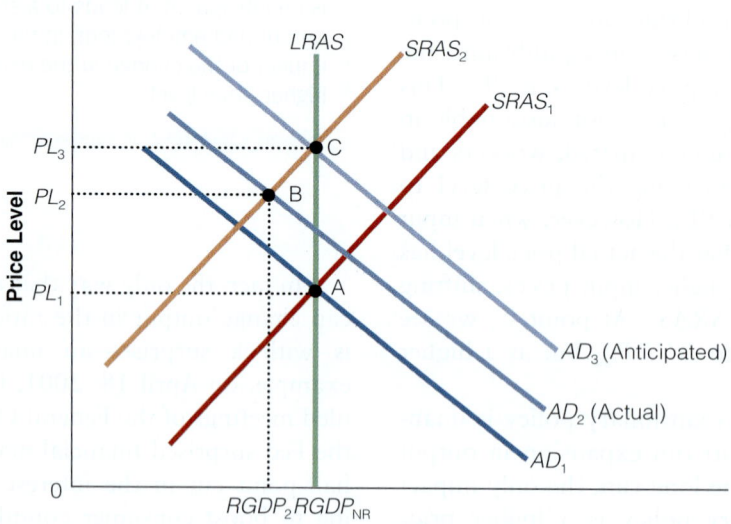

If people are expecting a large increase in the money supply as a result of expansionary monetary policy, the anticipated price level increases from PL_1 to PL_3 and the anticipated AD shifts from AD_1 to AD_3. Because wages and prices are completely flexible, the SRAS shifts leftward from $SRAS_1$ to $SRAS_2$ at the same time the AD curve shifts to the right. But if the actual increase in the money supply only shifts AD from AD_1 to AD_2, the economy moves from point A to point B rather than to point C, and the result is a higher price level but a lower level of RGDP—a recession, not the intended policy prescription.

Most economists reject the extreme rational expectations model of complete wage and price flexibility. In fact, most economists still believe a short-run trade-off between inflation and unemployment results because some input prices are slow to adjust to changes in the price level. However, in the long run, the expected inflation rate adjusts to changes in the actual inflation rate at the natural rate of unemployment, $RGDP_{NR}$.

New Keynesians and Rational Expectations

Recall that in the Keynesian model, wages and prices are assumed to be inflexible. For example, workers who work under contracts that fix their wages for several years may be aware of price increases, but cannot renegotiate their labor contracts. The same may be true for other input suppliers. That is, firms may have negotiated fixed-price contracts with their suppliers for substantial periods of time.

Suppose that many people anticipate an increase in aggregate demand from AD_1 to AD_2 in Exhibit 4. In the rational expectations model, where wages and prices are completely flexible, that means that SRAS will quickly move from $SRAS_1$ to $SRAS_3$ when AD_1 moves to AD_2, so RGDP does not change.

However, if some wages and other input supply prices are fixed, when aggregate demand shifts from AD_1 to AD_2, then the SRAS curve does not shift from $SRAS_1$ to $SRAS_3$. It may shift from $SRAS_1$ to $SRAS_2$ instead, leading to an increase in real aggregate output to $RGDP_2$ in the short run.

What Is the Real Business Cycle Theory?

The **real business cycle theory** shares some of the same assumptions as the rational expectations theory: Households and firms form their expectations rationally, and wages and prices adjust quickly. However, instead of unexpected changes in the money supply causing fluctuations in real GDP, the real business cycle theorists believe that technological changes lead to changes in the growth rate of productivity. In short, they believe that positive and negative productivity shocks are the cause of the business cycle. That is, these economists believe real shocks such as new technology (new products or production methods), resource prices (like oil), changes in government regulation, unusually good or bad weather, international disturbances, or any other factor that can change productivity can cause fluctuations in the economy. In short, negative shocks cause recessions, and positive shocks cause expansion.

real business cycle theory the belief that economic fluctuations are the result of external negative and positive productivity shocks to the economy

For example, real business cycle theorists believe that significant changes in technology can lead to stronger productivity growth and therefore greater economic expansion. For example, productivity (output per worker) could fall as a result of large increases in oil prices, similar to what occurred in the 1970s.

With a negative productivity shock, the marginal productivity of labor falls leading to a fall in real wages and a subsequent reduction in the quantity of labor supplied as people choose to work less. Lower profit expectations cause firms to cut back on new capital purchases (new or remodeled plants and equipment) and lay off workers. In short, several quarters of below-average productivity output lead to declines in investment and average hours worked as well as an economy that finds itself in a recession. This event may have been the case in the 2001 recession.

section 29.3 exhibit 4 New Keynesians and Rational Expectations

When an increase in aggregate demand from AD_1 to AD_2 is anticipated the SRAS curve shifts from $SRAS_1$ to $SRAS_3$. However, because some wages and input prices are inflexible in the short run, in the Keynesian model SRAS may only shift from $SRAS_1$ to $SRAS_2$, or from point A to point B.

Of course, the reverse could happen after large, and perhaps unexpected, productivity improvements. This scenario characterized the second half of the 1990s and resulted in an increase in the marginal productivity of labor, higher real wages, and people choosing to work more. In addition, firms with expectations of higher profits will invest in new capital and equipment. Together, these factors will lead to an increase in output consumption and investment—an economic expansion.

In the real business cycle theory, it is the potential output that fluctuates (the *LRAS*); not the output deviating from potential output—as is the case with recessionary or inflationary gaps. According to real business cycle theorists, prices and wages are sufficiently flexible that they adjust quickly. Because the economy is always operating close to full employment, the Fed just needs to keep an eye on inflation and intervention should be unnecessary.

The empirical evidence shows a strong correlation between declining productivity and the business cycle. However, some economists argue that the causality could go in the opposite direction—the recession causes the declining productivity. Other critics argue that the model assumes that wages and prices are completely flexible, a claim that is at odds with the facts. And others believe that technology shocks are incapable of explaining *all* of the swings in productivity; they claim that some of the changes must come from aggregate demand. However, the real business cycle theorists do force economists to think more about the supply side.

SECTION CHECK

1. Rational expectations economists believe that wages and prices are flexible and thus should be left alone. They also believe that households and firms form rational expectations that essentially negate the desired effect of a policy change.
2. Critics of rational expectations theory believe that most people are not truly informed about the effects of a policy change and therefore do not adjust their behavior. Additionally, they question whether prices and wages are really that flexible.
3. Real business cycle theorists believe that technological change leads to changes in the growth of productivity. They believe that positive and negative productivity shocks are the cause of the business cycle.
4. Empirical evidence shows a strong correlation between declining productivity and the business cycle. However, some economists argue that the causality could go in the opposite direction—the recession causes the declining productivity. The real business cycle theory also assumes, like the rational expectations model, that wages and prices are completely flexible, a claim that is at odds with the facts. Still others believe that technology shocks are incapable of explaining *all* of the swings in productivity.

---

1. What is the rational expectations theory?
2. Why could an unexpected change in inflation change real wages and unemployment, while an expected change in inflation could not?
3. Why can the results of rational expectations be described as generating the long-run results of a policy change in the short run?
4. In a world of rational expectations, why is it harder to reduce unemployment below its natural rate but potentially easier to reduce inflation rates?
5. Even if individuals could quickly anticipate the consequences of government policy changes, how could long-term contracts (e.g., three-year labor agreements and 30-year fixed rate mortgages) and the costs of changing price lists and catalogs result in unemployment still being affected by those policy changes?
6. Why do expected rainstorms have different effects on people than unexpected rainstorms?
7. What is the real business cycle theory?
8. Give an example of a positive productivity shock.
9. According to real business cycle theorists, what happens when a negative productivity shock occurs?
10. What does it mean when we say that real business cycle theorists have made us think more about the supply side?

SECTION 29.4 Controversies in Macroeconomic Policy

* Are fiscal and monetary policies effective?
* Should monetary policy use a rule or discretion?
* Should central banks target inflation?
* Could indexing reduce the costs of inflation?

Are Fiscal and Monetary Policies Effective?

Economies tend to fluctuate. Consumer or business pessimism leads to a reduction in aggregate demand. As aggregate demand falls, so does output and employment. The rising unemployment and the fall in income cause additional damage to the economy. The economy is now operating to the left of the *LRAS* (or inside its production possibilities curve); resources are not being used efficiently when actual output is less than potential output. Many economists believe that in the short run, policymakers have the ability to alter aggregate demand. If the aggregate demand is insufficient, policymakers can stimulate aggregate demand by increasing government spending, cutting taxes, and increasing the growth rate of the money supply. If aggregate demand is excessive, policymakers can reduce aggregate demand by decreasing government spending, increasing taxes, and reducing the growth rate of the money supply.

These macroeconomists are called *activists*, and they believe that in the short run, discretionary monetary and fiscal policy can stimulate the economy that is in a recessionary gap or dampen the economy that is in an inflationary boom with aggregate demand management. However, other economists believe that aggregate demand stimulus cannot *keep* the rate of unemployment below the natural rate. Most economists accept the basic notion of the natural rate hypothesis that suggests the unemployment rate will be close to the natural rate in the long run. Other economists, *rational expectations theorists*, believe that government economic policies designed to alter aggregate demand are not all that effective because households and firms form expectations to economic policy causing prices and wages to adjust quickly, leaving the output roughly the same but at a higher price level. To these economists, monetary and fiscal policy will only work if it comes as a surprise to the public.

The *real business cycle theorists* believe that economic fluctuations are the result of external shocks to the economy. The shocks change productivity, which shifts the *LRAS*. The real business cycle theorist, like the new classical school (rational expectations), believes that prices and wages are flexible and that the market adjusts quickly and restores full employment at the new level of output. That is, fiscal or monetary policies are not needed except to keep inflation in check.

However, most economists do not accept the notion that households and firms have rational expectations and that wages and prices adjust quickly because of wage and other input contracts. Even if households and firms formed rational expectations, if prices and wages adjusted slowly, expansionary monetary policy could lead to a lower unemployment level.

Most macroeconomists believe both that monetary and fiscal policy can shift the aggregate demand and that the intervention can be counterproductive. Recall our discussion in the previous chapter about the lags associated with both fiscal and monetary policies. The long and uncertain lags may lead to policies that are counterproductive. In other words, the policies aimed at closing a recessionary gap may cause an inflationary gap if the stimulus occurs at the wrong time. Or policies aimed at closing an inflationary gap may overshoot the goal and cause a recessionary gap. The problem is that we do not operate with a clear crystal ball. For policymakers, timing and the exact size of the stimulus are essential for effective stabilization policies.

Other economists believe that the potency of expansionary fiscal policy will be diminished by the crowding-out effect. That is, expansionary fiscal policy increases the real interest rate when it borrows money to finance its deficit, which crowds out private investment. It is also possible that the economy is stimulated with fiscal or monetary policy in the short run for political gains that will only be inflationary in the long run. Recall that expansionary monetary policy lowers the real interest rate and stimulates private investment.

Other questions the policymakers will have to answer are: What are the output effects of the fiscal or monetary policy? What is the marginal propensity to consume (MPC) of the tax cut? How much will the central bank have to change the real interest rate to get the desired change in residential and commercial spending?

For most economists, monetary policy is the preferred tool for stabilization because the inside lags (the time from when a policy is needed to the time it is implemented) are much shorter. Recall that the federal open market committee (FOMC) meets eight times a year. Fiscal policy requires Congress to convene and debate the tax cuts or expenditure increases. However, fiscal policy may be used in special circumstances when monetary policy alone cannot do the job. Automatic stabilizers (e.g., taxes that impact disposable income and unemployment compensation) are an important part of fiscal policy and have a much smaller lag because they are implemented automatically.

Policy Difficulties with Supply Shocks

Recall that a negative supply shock, like those the United States experienced in the 1970s and 2007–08, leads to an increase in the price level and a reduction in real aggregate output ($RGDP$), as seen in Exhibit 1.

After a negative demand shock (not shown but a leftward shift in the AD curve from say point A), policy makers can employ expansionary fiscal and/or monetary policy which can help shift the economy back to its original position. However, this is not the case with a negative supply shock. For example, suppose policy makers choose to use expansionary fiscal and/or monetary policy as a response to the recession caused by the supply shock; this increase in aggregate demand causes an increase in aggregate output ($RGDP$) but leads to even greater inflation, as seen in Exhibit 2(a). Or if policy makers choose to use contractionary fiscal and/or monetary policy to control inflation this decrease in aggregate demand leads to a lower price level but causes an even lower level of aggregate output with higher rates of unemployment, as seen in Exhibit 2(b). In short, stagflation caused by a supply shock makes economic policy making very difficult.

What Should the Central Bank Do?

Most economists believe that monetary policy should take the lead in stabilization policy and that the central bank should be independent and insulated from political pressure to avoid political business cycles. Political business cycles may occur if central banks ally themselves with an incumbent party and pursue expansionary monetary policy prior to an election. Even though the short-run impact may be increased output, employment, and a victory for the

section 29.4 exhibit 1 A Negative Supply Shock

A negative supply shock (e.g., an increase in global oil prices) cause production costs to rise and lowers the amount producers are willing to supply at any given aggregate price level. The result is a lower aggregate output at $RGDP_1$ and a higher price level at PL_2

incumbent party in the election, the long-run impact will be inflation. So, faced with these potential problems, how should the central bank set its monetary policy?

Some macroeconomists believe that the central bank should adopt rules, such as a constant growth rate in the money supply. According to the rule advocates, if the money supply were only allowed to increase by say 3–5 percent per year (enough to accommodate new economic growth), the result would be less uncertainty and greater economic stability. In other words, if the fixed rule is followed and the growth rate is 3 percent per year and the monetary growth rate is 3 percent per year, the average rate of inflation is zero. This situation seldom occurs, but the point here is that it would add credibility to the Federal Reserve as being tough on inflation. It would make it clear that what the Fed says it's going to do is consistent with what it actually does.

Inflation Targeting

Some macroeconomists believe that we can do better than targeting the growth rate of monetary aggregates. These economists believe we should target the inflation rate. Targeting the inflation rate would

section 29.4 exhibit 2 — Policy Response to a Supply Shock

a. Expansionary Monetary and/or Fiscal Policy

If policy makers increase aggregate demand at $E_{SR'}$, aggregate output increase to $RGDP_{NR}$ and employment increases but the price level rise to PL_3. The increase in AD helps aggregate output but causes even more inflation.

b. Contractionary Monetary and/or Fiscal Policy

If policy makers decrease aggregate demand at E_{SR} aggregate output falls further to $RGDP_2$ but the price level returns to PL_1. The decrease in AD curbs inflation but causes a reduction in aggregate output and a rise in unemployment.

---

require the central bank to attempt to stay in a certain band of inflation for a specified period of time—say 2–3 percent. The key to targeting is that it enhances credibility and could help to "anchor" inflationary expectations and lead to greater price stability. After all, successful monetary policy hinges critically on the ability to manage expectations. Several countries have inflation targets in place: The Bank of England is at 2 percent; the Bank of Canada is at 2 percent; Brazil is at 4.5 percent; and Chile is at the range between 2 percent and 4 percent. Empirical studies show a tendency for inflation rates to fall in countries that use inflation targeting.

Critics of inflation targeting will argue that central banks need flexibility. Good leaders, like Volker and Greenspan, proved that they can handle the job without set rules or targets. In other words, the United States has kept inflation low without rules or targeting, so those opposed to targets say, "If it ain't broke, don't fix it." Others argue that it may cause banks to focus too much attention on inflation at the expense of other goals such as output and employment. For example, a recessionary gap will normally cause the central bank to lower the interest rate to stimulate spending, output, and employment rather than just focus on inflation. Some might ask: If the Fed is going to put a target band on inflation, why not put one on unemployment and long-term interest rates too?

Targeting Inflation at Zero

So, if central banks are targeting low inflation rates of 2 percent, why not target inflation rates at 0 percent? After all, we have seen the costs to inflation: shoe leather costs, menu costs, changes in tax liabilities, changes in the distribution of income—and it leads to a distortion of the price system. However, these costs are probably small if inflation rates are low and expected to stay low. The other problem associated with a zero inflation rate is that it would be difficult to precisely hit the target all the time, and it could lead to deflation (the average price level of goods and services are falling) as it did in Japan in the 1990s. Also, some macroeconomists worry that if the inflation rate is targeted at zero the interest rate may fall to zero in a recession and render expansionary macroeconomic policy powerless. Other problems are unanticipated shocks and unanticipated financial crises. Monetary authorities need the flexibility to respond to these shocks by temporarily going outside the target range. In recent times, the Federal Reserve was there to respond to the stock market crash of October 19, 1987—when stock prices

POLICY application
WHY PERMANENT TAX CUTS ARE THE BEST STIMULUS

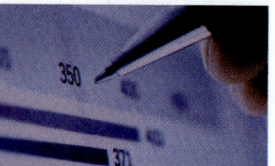

—BY JOHN B. TAYLOR

The incoming Obama administration and congressional Democrats are now considering a second fiscal stimulus package, estimated at more than $500 billion, to follow the Economic Stimulus Act of 2008. As they do, much can be learned by examining the first.

The major part of the first stimulus package was the $115 billion temporary rebate payment program targeted to individuals and families that phased out as incomes rose. Most of the rebate checks were mailed or directly deposited during May, June, and July.

The argument in favor of these temporary rebate payments was that they would increase consumption, stimulate aggregate demand, and thereby get the economy growing again. What were the results? The chart nearby reveals the answer.

The upper line shows disposable personal income through September. Disposable personal income is what households have left after paying taxes and receiving transfers from the government. The big blip is due to the rebate payments in May through July.

The lower line shows personal consumption expenditures by households. Observe that consumption shows no noticeable increase at the time of the rebate. Hence, by this simple measure, the rebate did little or nothing to stimulate consumption, overall aggregate demand, or the economy.

These results may seem surprising, but they are not. They correspond very closely to what basic economic theory tells us. According to the permanent-income theory of Milton Friedman, or the life-cycle theory of Franco Modigliani, temporary increases in income will *not* lead to significant increases in consumption. However, if increases are longer-term, as in the case of a permanent tax cut, then consumption is increased, and by a significant amount.

After years of study and debate, theories based on the permanent-income model led many economists to conclude that discretionary fiscal policy actions, such as temporary rebates, are not a good policy tool. Rather, fiscal policy should focus on the "automatic stabilizers" (the tendency for tax revenues to decline in a recession and transfer payments such as unemployment compensation to increase in a recession), which are built into the tax-and-transfer system, and on more permanent fiscal changes that will positively affect the long-term growth of the economy.

Why did that consensus seem to break down during the public debates about the fiscal stimulus early this year? One reason may have been the apparent success of the rebate payments in 2001. However, those rebate payments were the first installment of more permanent, multiyear tax cuts passed that same year. Hence, they were not temporary.

What are the implications for a second stimulus early next year? The mantra often heard during debates about the first stimulus was that it should be temporary, targeted and timely. Clearly, that mantra must be replaced. In testimony before the Senate Budget Committee on Nov. 19, I recommended

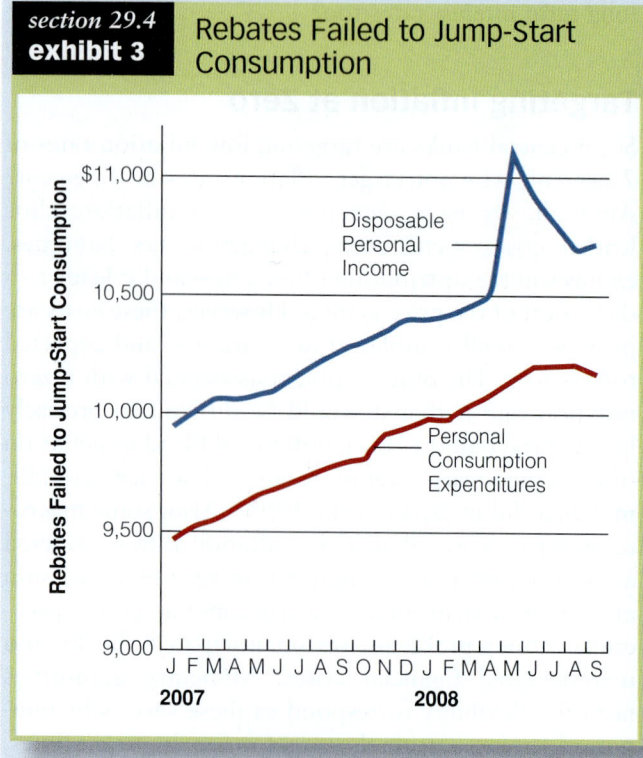

section 29.4 exhibit 3 — Rebates Failed to Jump-Start Consumption

SOURCE: Bureau of Economic Analysis.

POLICY application: WHY PERMANENT TAX CUTS ARE THE BEST STIMULUS (cont.)

alternative principles: permanent, pervasive and predictable.

Permanent. The most obvious lesson learned from the first stimulus is that temporary is not a principle to follow if you want to get the economy moving again. Rather than one- or two-year packages, we should be looking for permanent fiscal changes that turn the economy around in a lasting way.

Pervasive. One argument in favor of "targeting" the first stimulus package was that, by focusing on people who might consume more, the impact would be larger. But the stimulus was ineffective with such targeting. Moreover, targeting implied that increased tax rates, as currently scheduled, will not be a drag on the economy as long as increased payments to the targeted groups are larger than the higher taxes paid by others. But increasing tax rates on businesses or on investments in the current weak economy would increase unemployment and further weaken the economy. Better to seek an across-the-board approach where both employers and employees benefit.

Predictable. While timeliness is an admirable attribute, it is only one property of good fiscal policy. More important is that policy should be clear and understandable—that is, predictable—so that individuals and firms know what to expect.

Many complain that government interventions in the current crisis have been too erratic. Economic policy—from monetary policy to regulatory policy, international policy and fiscal policy—works best if it is as predictable as possible.

Many good fiscal packages are consistent with these principles. But what can Congress and the incoming Obama administration do to give the economy a real boost on Jan. 20? Here are a few fairly bipartisan measures worth considering:

First, make a commitment, passed into law, to keep all income-tax rates where they are now, effectively making current tax rates permanent. This would be a significant stimulus to the economy, because tax-rate increases are now expected on a majority of small business income, capital gains income, and dividend income.

Second, enact a worker's tax credit equal to 6.2% of wages up to $8,000 as Mr. Obama proposed during the campaign—but make it permanent rather than a one-time check.

Third, recognize explicitly that the "automatic stabilizers" are likely to be as large as 2.5% of GDP this fiscal year, that they will help stabilize the economy, and that they should be viewed as part of the overall fiscal package even if they do not require legislation.

Fourth, construct a government spending plan that meets long-term objectives, puts the economy on a path to budget balance, and is expedited to the degree possible without causing waste and inefficiency.

Some who promoted the first stimulus package have reacted to its failure by saying that we must now switch to large increases in government spending to stimulate demand. But government spending does not address the causes of the weak economy, which has been pulled down by a housing slump, a financial crisis and a bout of high energy prices, and where expectations of future income and employment growth are low.

The theory that a short-run government spending stimulus will jump-start the economy is based on old-fashioned, largely static Keynesian theories. These approaches do not adequately account for the complex dynamics of a modern international economy, or for expectations of the future that are now built into decisions in virtually every market.

SOURCE: Wall Street Journal NOVEMBER 25, 2008, p. A-15, John Taylor, Why Permanent Tax Cuts Are the Best Stimulus.

fell by more than 20 percent in a single day (the biggest ever one-day decline)—and to the shock created by the terrorist attacks on September 11, 2001, when the Federal Reserve made massive discount loans to banks to avoid a financial crisis.

Critics of targeting a zero inflation rate believe that achieving zero inflation is almost impossible and the costs are too high. The costs of disinflation (lowering the rate of inflation) can be high. Reducing the inflation rate by 1 percent may reduce output by as much as 5 percent. Disinflation is not painless.

The Taylor Rule

A variant of monetary rules and inflation targeting is the Taylor rule. It is a hybrid—part rule, part discretion. Taylor's formula uses a rule to decide when to use discretionary decisions. According to John Taylor, "The federal funds rate is increased or decreased according to what is happening to both real GDP and inflation. In particular, if real GDP rises 1 percent above potential GDP the federal funds rate should be raised, relative to the current inflation rate, by .5 percent. And if inflation rises by 1 percent above its target of 2 percent, then the federal funds rate should be raised by .5 percent relative to the inflation rate. When real GDP is equal to potential GDP and inflation is equal to its target of 2 percent, then the federal funds rate should remain at about 4 percent, which would imply a real interest rate of 2 percent on average. The policy rule was purposely chosen to be simple. Clearly, the equal weights on inflation and the GDP gap are an approximation reflecting the finding that neither variable should be given a negligible weight." If the central bank used this rule, market participants could easily predict central bank behavior, creating greater stability and certainty.

indexing
use of payment contracts that automatically adjust for changes in inflation

Asset Price Inflation

Some economists believe that the Fed should be concerned about asset pricing—especially housing and stock market prices. The period 1999–2004 saw inflation at a low rate of about 2.5 percent per year, yet housing prices were rising 25 percent and higher in some markets. In some countries, Australia and Great Britain, the central banks are paying closer attention to the growth in asset prices even when consumer price inflation is low. Others believe that the central bank should not concern itself with the value that consumers place on stocks and housing. If the bubble bursts, the Fed can lower interest rates to bolster the economy.

Of course, as we found out during the financial crisis of 2007–2008, there are several questions that must be answered. One of the most important is: Can you identify housing or stock bubbles when they are appearing? The extent of monetary policy intervention may depend on the bubble. In the recession of 2007–2008, the housing bubble spread throughout the economy quickly and violently, before interest rate policy could be used to offset the damaging effects.

Indexing and Reducing the Costs of Inflation

Another approach to some of the problems posed by inflation is **indexing**. As you recall, inflation poses substantial equity and distributional problems only when it is unanticipated or unexpected. One means of protecting parties against unanticipated price increases is to write contracts that automatically change the prices of goods or services whenever the overall price level changes, effectively rewriting agreements in terms of dollars of constant purchasing power. Wages, loans, and mortgage payments—everything possible—would be changed every month or so by an amount equal to the percentage change in some broad-based price index. Thus, if prices rose by 1.2 percent this month and your last month's wage was $1,000, your wage this month would be $1,012 ($1,000 × 1.012). By making as many contracts as possible payable in dollars of constant purchasing power, those involved could protect themselves against unanticipated changes in inflation.

Why Isn't Indexing More Extensively Used?

Indexing seems to eliminate most of the wealth transfers associated with unexpected inflation. Why then is it not more commonly used? One main argument against indexing is that it can worsen inflation. As prices go up, wages and certain other contractual obligations (e.g., rents) also automatically increase. This immediate and comprehensive reaction to price increases leads to greater inflationary pressures. One price increase leads to a second, which in turn leads to a third, and so on.

Other Problems Associated with Indexing

We might ask, so what? If prices rise rapidly, but wages, rents, and so forth, move up with prices, real wages and rents remain constant. However, if inflation gets bad enough, it could become almost impossible administratively to maintain the indexing scheme. The index, to be effective, might have to be changed every few days, but the information to make such frequent changes is not currently available. To get the necessary information quickly, then, might be quite expensive, involving a small army of price-checking bureaucrats and a massive electronic communications system. Other inefficiencies occur as well. During the German hyperinflation of the early 1920s, prices at one point rose so rapidly that workers demanded to be paid twice a day, at noon and at the end of the workday. During their lunch hour, workers would rush money to their wives, who would then run out and buy real goods before prices increased further.

Other big problems include the fact that indexing reduces the ability for relative price changes to allocate resources where they are more valuable. Not everything can be indexed, so indexing would cause wealth redistribution. In addition, costs would necessarily be incurred as a result of renegotiating cost-of-living (COLA) clauses.

Excessive inflation, then, leads to great inefficiency, as well as to a loss of confidence in the issuer of money—namely, the government. Furthermore, inflation influences world trade patterns. Limited indexing, in fact, has already been adopted, as some wage and pension payments are changed with changes in the cost-of-living index. Whether on balance those escalator clauses are "good" or "bad" is a debatable topic—a normative judgment that we will leave to the reader to make.

SECTION CHECK

1. Proponents of active monetary and fiscal policy view the economy as inherently unstable and believe that expansionary and contractionary fiscal and monetary policy can stabilize the economy. Critics believe that lags and uncertainty make it virtually impossible to stabilize the economy, and the stabilization policies are more likely to be counterproductive.

2. Proponents of the monetary rule believe that a constant growth rate in the money supply will lead to less uncertainty and greater credibility. Other macroeconomists believe it is better to target inflation than an aggregate monetary growth rate. Critics of rules and targeting argue that the central bank needs flexibility. They believe that competent, independent central bank leaders can be effective in controlling inflation. Other critics believe that the central bank should not just focus on inflation—they should be concerned about employment and growth, too.

3. Inflation targeting requires the central bank to stay in a certain band of inflation for a specified period of time. Targeting could enhance credibility and "anchor" inflationary expectations. Critics argue that the central banks need flexibility and competent leaders can do the job without rules or targeting.

4. Advocates of zero inflation believe that no inflation is better than some inflation and that it "anchors" expectations. It is a sign that the central bank is completely committed to eliminating inflation even if the short-run costs include reduced employment and output. Critics believe that achieving zero inflation is almost impossible and its costs too high. The costs of disinflation (lowering the rate of inflation) can be as high a ratio as 5:1. That is, to reduce the inflation rate by 1 percent may reduce output by as much as 5 percent. Disinflation is not painless.

5. Indexing is a process of adjusting payment contracts to automatically reflect changes in inflation. Indexing reduces the impact of inflation on the distribution of income but may also intensify the inflationary effects of expansionary monetary policy by increasing inflationary pressures.

---

1. What impact do lags have on discretionary fiscal and monetary policy?
2. What is a political business cycle? What are the possibilities for conflict of interest to arise?
3. How does credibility impact inflation?
4. What are the arguments for and against inflation targeting?
5. What are the problems associated with targeting a zero rate on inflation?
6. If each possible good were indexed to changes in the general price level, would it be easy for relative price changes to signal changing relative scarcities? Why or why not?

Interactive Chapter Summary

Fill in the blanks:

1. The recession in early 2001 was set off by a serious drop in _____.

2. The Phillips curve describes a short-run trade-off between _____ and _____.

3. If output prices rise but money wages do not go up as quickly, real wages will _____, tending to _____ unemployment.

4. The Phillips curve suggests that at lower rates of inflation, the rate of unemployment will be _____.

5. The Phillips curve is _____ at higher rates of inflation and lower rates of unemployment.

6. An increase in aggregate demand would cause the economy to move _____ along a Phillips curve, causing the inflation rate to _____ and the rate of unemployment to _____.

7. When moving up along a Phillips curve, employment rates tend to _____.

8. Economists who questioned the long-term validity of the Phillips curve were largely _____ in the 1960s.

9. According to Milton Friedman, a trade-off occurs between inflation and unemployment in the _____ run but not in the _____ run; the trade-off comes from _____ inflation.

10. The data from the 1970s indicated that the Phillips curve _____ remain in place.

11. In the long run when the expected inflation rate falls, the short-run Phillips curve shifts _____.

12. The _____ hypothesis states that the economy will self-correct to the natural rate of unemployment.

13. An increase in the growth rate of the money supply _____ aggregate demand, _____ output, _____ inflation, and _____ unemployment.

14. An unanticipated increase in inflation will _____ real wages, resulting in a _____ unemployment rate.

15. In the long run, when expected inflation rises, workers adjust to the higher rate of inflation by shifting the short-run Phillips curve _____.

16. When actual inflation equals expected inflation, real output equals its _____ level and unemployment equals the _____.

17. In the long run, when inflation increases, there is _____ in unemployment.

18. A decrease in inflation will _____ real wages at first, _____ real output and _____ unemployment.

19. If inflation is steady, actual inflation _____ expected inflation.

20. When people adapt their inflationary expectations after actual inflation changes, it is called _____ expectations.

21. Higher production costs due to adverse supply shocks shift the short-run Phillips curve _____.

22. An adverse supply shock _____ cause inflation to increase and unemployment to increase at the same time.

23. A favorable supply shock can result in both unemployment and inflation _____ at the same time.

24. If people expect supply shocks to be permanent, the result would be inflation and unemployment both _____ for adverse supply shocks and both _____ for favorable supply shocks.

25. An increase in oil prices is considered a(n) _____ supply shock.

26. If people could _____ to policy changes, it might not be possible to increase real output or employment through policy actions.

27. The theory of rational expectations leads to a(n) _____ conclusion about macroeconomic policy's ability to achieve our economic goals.

28. Rational expectations economists believe that wages and prices are _____ and workers _____ incorporate the likely consequences of government policy changes into their expectations.

29. Rational expectations economists think the economy tends to be inherently _____ and that government policy has the desired effects only when consumers and workers are caught _____.

30. According to rational expectations, when policy targets become public, people will alter their behavior to largely _____ the intended effects.

31. If changes in the inflation rate are quickly reflected in expectations, unemployment or real output from macroeconomic policy would experience _____ effect.

32. An increase in aggregate demand that is correctly anticipated and responded to will _____ the price level, _____ real output and _____ the unemployment rate.

33. When expansionary macroeconomic policy is unanticipated, the short-run aggregate supply curve _____ in the short run, but when it is correctly anticipated, the short-run aggregate supply curve _____.

34. Whether a macroeconomic policy change is anticipated or unanticipated it will not change real output or unemployment in the _____ run.

35. In the short run, an increase in aggregate demand will _____ the price level, whether it is anticipated or not, but it will increase real output only if it is _____.

36. If people expect a larger increase in aggregate demand than the actual increase in aggregate demand that occurs, the price level would _____ and real output would _____ in the short run.

37. If input prices adjust _____, the rational expectations view that changes in government policy would have no effect on real output in the short run would be incorrect.

38. Real business cycle theorists believe that _____ shocks due to _____ changes are the cause of business cycles.

39. In real business cycle analysis, negative shocks cause _____ and positive shocks cause _____.

40. A productivity boom would tend to _____ the marginal productivity of labor, _____ real wages, _____ average hours worked, _____ investment, leading to an economic _____.

41. In real business cycle analysis, several quarters of below-average productivity would cause real output, investment, and average hours worked to _____, and the economy would tend toward _____.

42. In real business cycle analysis, the key is that the long-run aggregate supply curve _____, rather than short-run _____ deviating from the long-run aggregate supply curve.

43. If aggregate demand is insufficient, policymakers can stimulate aggregate demand by _____ government spending, _____ taxes, or _____ the growth rate of the money supply.

44. Activist macroeconomists believe that in the short run, discretionary macroeconomic policy can _____ economic fluctuations.

45. Most economists accept the notion that unemployment will be close to the natural rate of unemployment in the _____ run.

46. The rational expectations school, the form that assumes instant adjustment, believes that government _____ impact real output in the short run.

47. With _____ expectations, but not _____ expectations, inflation could potentially be lowered by macroeconomic policy without causing a recession.

48. Real business cycle theorists as well as rational expectations economists believe that wages and prices are _____ and that markets adjust _____.

49. If the timing or the magnitude of a macroeconomic policy change is not what is intended, it could make the economy _____ stable.

50. Monetary policy is often the preferred stabilization tool due to its _____ inside lags.

51. Monetary policy rules and inflation targeting are intended to add _____ to the Federal Reserve's determination to hold inflation down.

52. Inflation targeting is intended to help _____ inflation expectations and lead to _____ price stability.

53. Shoe leather costs and menu costs are probably small if inflation is _____ and expected to _____.

54. One worry about inflation targeting is that it would reduce monetary authorities' _____ to respond to _____ shocks and crises.

55. To reduce the inflation rate by one percentage point may require reducing real output by _____ 1 percent.

56. The Taylor approach uses a _____ to decide when to use _____ actions.

57. The Taylor rule suggests changes in the _____ rate when real output or inflation rates deviate from their targets.

58. Under a Taylor rule, when real GDP falls below potential GDP, the federal funds rate should _____, and when inflation falls above the target the federal funds rate should _____.

59. Under a Taylor rule, for each one percentage point deviation from potential GDP or from the target inflation rate, the federal funds rate should change by _____ point.

60. _____ is a way of protecting parties against unanticipated changes in inflation by using contracts that automatically adjust to changes in purchasing power.

61. One main argument against indexing is that it can _____ inflation, by making one price increase lead to others.

62. If _____ becomes rapid, it could be almost impossible to administer an indexing scheme.

63. Another problem with indexing is that it reduces the ability for _____ changes to efficiently allocate resources.

Answers: 1. investment 2. inflation; unemployment 3. fall; reduce 4. higher 5. steeper 6. up; rise; fall 7. rise 8. ignored 9. short; long; unanticipated 10. did not 11. leftward 12. natural rate 13. increases; increasing; decreasing 14. decreases; lower 15. rightward 16. natural; natural rate of unemployment 17. no change 18. increase; lowering; raising 19. equals 20. adaptive 21. rightward 22. can 23. falling 24. increasing; decreasing 25. negative or adverse 26. instantly recognize and respond 27. pessimistic 28. flexible; quickly 29. stable; off-guard 30. negate 31. little or no 32. increase; leave unchanged 33. does not change; shifts upward 34. long 35. increase; unanticipated 36. increase; decrease 37. slowly 38. productivity; technological 39. recessions; expansions 40. increase; increase; expansion 41. fall; recession 42. shifts; real output 43. increasing; decreasing; increasing 44. reduce 45. long 46. cannot 47. rational; adaptive 48. flexible; quickly 49. less 50. shorter 51. credibility 52. anchor; greater 53. low; stay low 54. flexibility; unanticipated 55. more than 56. rule; discretionary 57. federal funds 58. fall; rise 59. 0.5 60. Indexing 61. worsen 62. inflation 63. relative price

Key Terms and Concepts

natural rate hypothesis 880
adaptive expectations 882
theory of rational expectations 886
real business cycle theory 889
indexing 896

Section Check Answers

29.1 The Phillips Curve

1. How does the rate of inflation affect real wage rates if nominal wages rise less or more slowly than output prices?

When nominal wages rise less or more slowly than output prices, real (adjusted for inflation) wages fall.

2. How does the change in real wage rates (relative to output prices) as inflation increases affect the unemployment rate?

The fall in real wage rates (relative to output prices) as inflation increases reduces the unemployment rate, because the lower real wage rates make it profitable to hire more, now relatively cheaper, employees than before.

3. What is the argument for why the Phillips curve is relatively steeper at lower rates of unemployment and higher rates of inflation?

The argument is that once capacity utilization is high and unemployment is low, an increased part of the economy is already operating at or near full capacity, and further fiscal or monetary policy stimulus primarily triggers inflationary pressures in sectors already at capacity, while eliminating decreasing amounts of unemployment in those fewer sectors where excess capacity and high unemployment still exist.

4. For a given upward-sloping short-run aggregate supply curve, how does an increase in aggregate demand correspond to a movement up and to the left along a Phillips curve?

For a given upward-sloping short-run aggregate supply curve, an increase in aggregate demand moves the economy up along the short-run aggregate supply curve to an increased price level and increased real GDP. The increase in the price level is an increase in inflation and the increase in real GDP is accompanied by a decrease in unemployment, so the same effect is shown by a move up (higher inflation) and to the left (lower unemployment) along a Phillips curve.

29.2 The Phillips Curve over Time

1. Is the Phillips curve stable over time?

No. While the short-run Phillips curve was once considered to be stable, economists now recognize that it is unstable and does not represent a permanent relationship between unemployment and inflation rates.

2. Why would you expect no relationship between inflation and unemployment in the long run?

This is the natural rate hypothesis. You would expect there to be no relationship between inflation and unemployment in the long run because the long run represents what happens once people have completely adjusted to changed conditions. Therefore, in the long run, actual and expected rates of inflation are the same, and changes in rates of inflation do not change people's "real" behavior (reflected in unemployment and real GDP) because those changes are not unexpected.

3. Why is the economy being on the long-run Phillips curve equivalent to its being on the long-run aggregate supply curve?

Unemployment equals its natural rate along the long-run Phillips curve. Real GDP is equal to its natural level along the long-run aggregate supply curve. But the natural level of real GDP is the output level consistent with unemployment equal to its natural rate, so points on both curves illustrate the same results.

4. **Why would inflation have to accelerate over time to keep unemployment below its natural rate (and real output above its natural level) for a sustained period of time?**

Inflation would have to accelerate over time to keep unemployment below its natural rate (and real output above its natural level) for a sustained period of time because over time, people would adapt to any given level of inflation. Therefore, at a given rate of inflation, unemployment would return to its natural rate over time. To keep people "fooled" into unemployment below its natural rate requires more inflation than people expected, and to maintain this requires accelerating inflation over time.

5. **What does the long-run Phillips curve say about the relationship between macroeconomic policy stimulus and unemployment in the long run?**

The vertical long-run Phillips curve indicates that there is no relationship between macroeconomic policy stimulus and unemployment in the long run, once people have had time to completely adapt to it. Unemployment will equal its natural rate in the long run, and macroeconomic policy will therefore only change the inflation rate in the long run.

29.3 Rational Expectations and Real Business Cycles

1. **What is the rational expectations theory?**

The rational expectations theory incorporates expectations as a central factor in the analysis of the entire economy. It is essentially the idea that people will rationally anticipate the predictable future consequences of present decisions, and change their behavior today to reflect those future consequences. For example, this would mean that people can anticipate the inflationary long-run consequences of macroeconomic policies adopted today, and that anticipation leads them to change their current behavior in a way that can quickly neutralize the intended impact of a government action.

2. **Why could an unexpected change in inflation change real wages and unemployment, while an expected change in inflation could not?**

An unexpected change in inflation could change real wages and unemployment precisely because it was unexpected, and people were "fooled" into changing their behavior (in the short run). An expected change in inflation would not change real wages and unemployment because no one is fooled, so people don't change their real behavior as a result.

3. **Why can the results of rational expectations be described as generating the long-run results of a policy change in the short run?**

The long run refers to the situation once people have had time to completely adjust their behavior to current circumstances. But under rational expectations, the long-run consequences will be anticipated and responded to today, so that people have completely adjusted their behavior to new policies in the short run. Therefore, the results of rational expectations can be described as generating the long-run results of a policy change in the short run.

4. **In a world of rational expectations, why is it harder to reduce unemployment below its natural rate but potentially easier to reduce inflation rates?**

Reducing unemployment below its natural rate requires that inflation is greater than expected. But under rational expectations, people are not fooled by inflationary policies (unless they are surprised), so this is very hard to do. It is potentially easier to reduce inflation rates under rational expectations, though, because people will be more quickly convinced that inflation will fall when credible government policies are put in place, and it will not take an extended period of high unemployment before they adapt to the lower inflation rate that results.

5. **Even if individuals could quickly anticipate the consequences of government policy changes, how could long-term contracts (e.g., three-year labor agreements and 30-year fixed rate mortgages) and the costs of changing price lists and catalogs result in unemployment still being affected by those policy changes?**

Even if individuals could quickly anticipate the consequences of government policy changes, long-term contracts can't be instantly adjusted, so the real prices and wages subject to such contracts will be at least temporarily changed by inflation "surprises," at least until such contracts can be rewritten. Similarly, price lists and catalogs will not be changed instantly when new policies are adopted, because of the cost of doing so, and those prices will not instantly adapt to new inflationary expectations. Since these prices will be "wrong" for a period after new policies are adopted, real wages and prices, and therefore unemployment, can still be affected for a period of time by policy changes.

6. **Why do expected rainstorms have different effects on people than unexpected rainstorms?**

Expected rainstorms don't catch you by surprise, so you prepare for them in a way that minimizes their effects (umbrellas, jackets, etc.). Unexpected rainstorms catch you by surprise, and have much greater effects, because they haven't been prepared for.

7. **What is the real business cycle theory?**
   In short, real business cycle theory points to positive and negative supply shocks as the cause of the business cycle. Real shocks can include changes in technology, resource prices, government regulation, good or bad weather, and international disturbances. Negative shocks cause recessions and positive shocks cause expansion.

8. **Give an example of a positive productivity shock.**
   A technological advance, which leads to unexpected productivity improvements, would be a positive productivity shock. It would increase the marginal productivity of labor, increase real wages, and increase the quantity of labor supplied. In addition, expectations of higher profits would increase investment in new capital and equipment. Together, these lead to an increase in output, consumption, and investment—an economic expansion.

9. **According to real business cycle theorists, what happens when a negative productivity shock occurs?**
   A negative supply shock is the opposite of a positive supply shock. It would decrease the marginal productivity of labor, decrease real wages, and decrease the quantity of labor supplied. In addition, expectations of lower profits would decrease investment in new capital and equipment. Together, these lead to a decrease in output, consumption, and investment—an economic recession.

10. **What does it mean when we say that real business cycle theorists have made us think more about the supply side?**
    In real business cycle theory, potential output (the *LRAS*) fluctuates, so changes on the supply side drive business cycles, rather than booms and recessions being caused by output deviating from potential output.

29.4 Controversies in Macroeconomic Policy

1. **What impact do lags have on discretionary fiscal and monetary policy?**
   Since for stabilization policy to be effective it requires that the policy be appropriate in direction, magnitude, and timing, lag problems can cause policy to be ineffective or even worsen problems. This means that policies aimed at closing a recessionary gap may cause an inflationary gap, or that policies aimed at closing an inflationary gap may cause a recessionary gap, if the policies have their effects at the wrong time. Further, this leads many economists to believe that monetary authorities should take the lead in stabilization policy, because of the much shorter inside lags for monetary policy. Shorter lags are also an advantage for automatic stabilizers over discretionary fiscal policy.

2. **What is a political business cycle? What are the possibilities for conflict of interest to arise?**
   Political business cycles can occur when economic policies are timed for political effect, as when a central bank pursues expansionary monetary policy prior to an election. The conflict of interest arises because while the short-run impact may be electoral success because of the increased output and employment, the long-run effect will be inflation and the costs entailed in dealing with it or overcoming it.

3. **How does credibility impact inflation?**
   Credibility is particularly important to make it clear that government authorities, such as the Federal Reserve, will actually do what they say they will do (e.g., when they say they will be tough on inflation, they actually will be). This dramatically reduces the risk that such government policy will fool you in substantial ways, so that you need not worry so much about protecting yourself against policy-induced mistakes, and social coordination is improved as a result.

4. **What are the arguments for and against inflation targeting?**
   The argument for inflation targeting is that rules are important in creating policy credibility and that inflation targeting works more effectively than other rules, such as targeting the growth of monetary aggregates. Targeting inflation is said to enhance credibility and to help "anchor" inflationary expectations and lead to greater price stability. Critics argue that inflation targeting removes the flexibility that central banks need to respond to changing situations and may focus too much attention on inflation and not enough on employment and output.

5. **What are the problems associated with targeting a zero rate on inflation?**
   While there are costs of low rates of inflation (e.g., shoe leather and menu costs), those costs are small when inflation is low and expected to remain low. A zero inflation rate, however, would be difficult to precisely hit, and could even lead to deflation, which also causes economic problems. Some economists also worry that targeting zero inflation could sometimes result in a zero interest rate, which would render expansionary monetary policy powerless to stimulate the economy. Further, when there are unanticipated shocks and crises, it would eliminate the flexibility that central banks need to respond.

6. **If each possible good were indexed to changes in the general price level, would it be easy for relative price changes to signal changing relative scarcities? Why or why not?**
   When all prices tend to change together (e.g., when one price goes up, the price level goes up, and so other indexed prices also go up as a result), it is harder for relative prices to change to reflect changing relative scarcity.

CHAPTER 29 STUDY GUIDE

True or False:

1. The inverse relationship between the rate of unemployment and the rate of inflation is called the Phillips curve.
2. If output prices rise faster than money wages, real wages will fall, as will the unemployment rate.
3. According to the short-run Phillips curve, the cost of lower unemployment appears to be greater inflation, and the cost of lower inflation appears to be higher unemployment.
4. Along any particular Phillips curve, the slope and therefore the trade-off between unemployment and inflation is constant.
5. The Phillips curve concept was developed by looking at the relationship between inflation and wage rates.
6. A single short-run Phillips curve can accurately describe the behavior of the economy since 1969.
7. If aggregate demand stimulus occurs in a fully employed economy, the result will mostly be higher prices in the economy, even in the short run, if the Phillips curve is steep over the relevant range.
8. The Phillips curve shows the relationship between the rate of inflation and the rate of growth in real GDP.
9. The natural rate of unemployment is the level that will occur after the economy completely self-corrects from a change in aggregate demand.
10. If the government tried to maintain unemployment below its natural rate for a sustained period of time, it would accelerate inflation.
11. Rational expectations economists tend to believe that people anticipate the results of government policy moves.
12. If people's expectations instantly and accurately reflected the likely result of government policy changes, the *SRAS* and *LRAS* curves would be the same.
13. Rational expectations models assert that in an effort to protect themselves from a higher anticipated inflation rate, workers ask for higher wages, suppliers increase input prices, and producers raise their product prices.
14. Rational expectations economists believe that wages and prices are relatively rigid.
15. Rational expectations theory suggests that government economic policies have limited effectiveness. As a result, monetary and fiscal policy will affect output and employment only if people are fooled by policy moves.
16. Real business cycle theorists believe the business cycle is primarily caused by aggregate demand shocks.
17. According to real business cycle theorists, rapid productivity growth causes economic expansions and productivity slowdowns cause recessions.
18. Unexpected productivity improvements would tend to increase both real wages and average hours worked.
19. The occurrence of productivity shocks tends to change the marginal productivity of labor, real wages, average hours worked, and the level of investment all in the same direction.
20. In real business cycle theory, shocks change the long-run aggregate supply curve rather than leading real output to deviate from the long-run aggregate supply curve.
21. Activist economists believe that discretionary macroeconomic policy can make the economy less unstable.
22. Most economists think that unemployment will remain close to the natural rate of unemployment in the short run.
23. Real business cycle theorists agree with rational expectations economists that wages and prices are flexible and that markets adjust quickly to economic shocks.
24. For many economists, monetary policy's shorter outside lag is an advantage in using monetary policy for stabilization efforts.
25. If monetary authorities respond to political pressures during a recession, the result could be a decrease in interest rates and a decrease in unemployment in the short run, but higher inflation in the long run.
26. One of the advantages of monetary policy rules is to increase the Federal Reserve System's credibility in its fight against inflation.
27. Monetary policy rules have the advantage of giving the Fed discretion to deal with sudden shocks and crises.

28. An example of indexing is an escalator clause, linking wage rates to a cost-of-living measure.
29. Some economists oppose widespread indexing on the grounds that it could worsen inflation.
30. As a practical matter, indexing can only be used with wage contracts.

Multiple Choice:

1. If output prices rise faster than money wages, the likely result will be that
   a. real wages will fall, as will the unemployment rate.
   b. real wages will fall, and the unemployment rate will rise.
   c. real wages will rise, as will the unemployment rate.
   d. real wages will rise, and the unemployment rate will fall.

2. Society faces a
   a. long-run trade-off between price inflation and unemployment.
   b. short-run trade-off between inflation and unemployment.
   c. short-run trade-off between the actual unemployment rate and the natural rate of unemployment.
   d. long-run trade-off between inflation and real output.
   e. Both b and d are correct.

3. If policymakers expand aggregate demand, they can lower unemployment _____, but only by _____.
   a. temporarily; decreasing inflation
   b. temporarily; increasing inflation
   c. permanently; decreasing inflation
   d. permanently; increasing inflation

4. If the Phillips curve is steeper at higher rates of inflation, it suggests that
   a. once the economy has relatively low unemployment rates, further reductions in the unemployment rate can occur only by accepting larger increases in the inflation rate.
   b. once the economy has relatively low unemployment rates, further reductions in the unemployment rate can occur only by reducing the rate of inflation.
   c. only reducing the rate of inflation can reduce the high unemployment rate.
   d. When the economy is experiencing low inflation rates, the unemployment rate can be reduced only by accepting lower rates of inflation.

5. If decision makers underestimate inflation, the real wage will
   a. rise, increasing unemployment.
   b. rise, reducing unemployment.
   c. fall, increasing unemployment.
   d. fall, reducing unemployment.

6. At the natural rate of unemployment, the long-run Phillips curve is
   a. horizontal.
   b. upward sloping.
   c. downward sloping.
   d. vertical.

7. An increase in aggregate demand will cause a larger increase in the price level when the economy
   a. is operating at or near full employment.
   b. is operating with substantial excess capacity.
   c. is operating with high unemployment.
   d. is in a depression.

8. Which of the following is consistent with a movement along a short-run Phillips curve?
   a. a decrease in the inflation rate with no change in unemployment
   b. a decrease in unemployment with no change in the inflation rate
   c. a decrease in inflation with an increase in unemployment
   d. a decrease in unemployment and a decrease in inflation

9. Most economists today believe that the Phillips curve is
    a. downward sloping in the short run but vertical in the long run.
    b. vertical in the short run but downward sloping in the long run.
    c. upward sloping in the short run but vertical in the long run.
    d. vertical in the short run but upward sloping in the long run.

10. The short-run Phillips curve trade-off implies
    a. that if the curve shifts over time, society must accept decreases in unemployment for decreases in inflation.
    b. that if the curve is stable, society must accept increases in inflation for increases in unemployment.
    c. that if the curve shifts over time, society must accept increases in inflation for decreases in unemployment.
    d. that if the curve is stable, society must accept increases in unemployment for decreases in inflation.

11. Which of the following would shift the Phillips curve to the left?
    a. an adverse supply shock
    b. an increase in inflationary expectations
    c. a favorable supply shock
    d. all of the above

12. If the inflation rate is increasing while unemployment is increasing,
    a. the short-run Phillips curve must have shifted right.
    b. the short-run Phillips curve must have shifted left.
    c. it involved a movement along the short-run Phillips curve.
    d. it would be inconsistent with any possible Phillips curve scenario.

13. Which of the following is true?
    a. Inflation and unemployment rates can both increase in the short run in response to adverse supply shocks.
    b. Inflation and unemployment rates can both decrease in the short run in response to reduced aggregate demand.
    c. Inflation and unemployment rates can both decrease in the short run in response to adverse supply shocks.
    d. The short-run Phillips curve relationship appears to be relatively stable over time.
    e. None of the above is true.

14. The short-run Phillips curve could shift to the right as a result of either _____ or _____.
    a. rising oil prices; increasing inflation expectations
    b. rising wages; falling prices
    c. declining oil prices; falling inflation expectations
    d. falling wages; rising prices
    e. none of the above

15. If people expect a higher inflation rate, the
    a. short-run Phillips curve will shift to the right.
    b. long-run Phillips curve will shift to the right.
    c. short-run and long-run Phillips curves will both shift to the right.
    d. short-run Phillips curve will shift to the left.

16. A current short-run Phillips curve can remain stable over time
    a. only if there is no inflation.
    b. if inflation remains steady at its current rate.
    c. if inflation is accelerating.
    d. if inflation is decelerating.

17. As the economy moves up and to the right along a short-run aggregate supply curve, it
    a. moves up and to the right along the short-run Phillips curve.
    b. moves up and to the left along the short-run Phillips curve.
    c. moves down and to the right along the short-run Phillips curve.
    d. moves down and to the left along the short-run Phillips curve.

18. If the actual unemployment rate exceeds the natural rate of unemployment, there will be a tendency toward
    a. increased inflation and a leftward shift of the short-run Phillips curve.
    b. decreased inflation and a rightward shift of the short-run Phillips curve.
    c. increased inflation and a rightward shift of the short-run Phillips curve.
    d. decreased inflation and a leftward shift of the short-run Phillips curve.

19. An increase in the expected level of inflation will cause short-run aggregate supply to _____ and the short-run Phillips curve to _____.
    a. shift left; shift right
    b. shift left; shift left
    c. shift right; shift right
    d. shift right; shift left
    e. none of the above

20. A decrease in inflation expectations causes producers to push for _____ input prices, which results in a(n) _____ shift in the short-run Phillips curve.
    a. lower; rightward
    b. lower; leftward
    c. higher; rightward
    d. higher; leftward

21. Whenever the actual rate of inflation is less than the expected rate of inflation,
    a. the unemployment rate will fall.
    b. the unemployment rate will exceed the natural rate of unemployment.
    c. the unemployment rate will rise.
    d. the unemployment rate will be below the natural rate of unemployment.
    e. both c and d will occur.

22. In the long run, an increase in the actual annual rate of inflation from 8 percent to 10 percent will
    a. not affect the natural rate of unemployment.
    b. not affect the actual rate of unemployment.
    c. increase the natural rate of unemployment.
    d. increase the actual rate of unemployment.
    e. not affect either the natural rate of unemployment or the actual rate of unemployment.

23. According to rational expectations, if workers and firms forecast inflation accurately,
    a. the real wage will not decline as the price level rises.
    b. workers will not lose from inflation, and firms will not gain.
    c. the aggregate supply curve will be vertical.
    d. all of the above are correct.

24. If increased inflation exceeds forecast inflation in the short run but not in the long run, what are the shapes of the aggregate supply curves?
    a. *AS* is vertical in the short run and long run.
    b. *AS* is vertical in the short run, and upward sloping in the long run.
    c. *AS* is upward sloping in the short run, and vertical in the long run.
    d. *AS* is upward sloping in the short run, and horizontal in the long run.
    e. *AS* is horizontal in the short run and the long run.

25. If expectations are rational,
    a. a predictable change in inflation can make the expected inflation rate deviate from the actual inflation rate.
    b. unemployment can exceed the full-employment rate even in the long run.
    c. the inflation rate cannot be reduced without a sustained period of high unemployment, because the short-run Phillips curve is downward sloping.
    d. an increase in aggregate demand due to government policy will not necessarily increase real output.

26. According to the rational expectations view, the government can change real output
    a. with appropriate, well-publicized fiscal and monetary policies.
    b. with appropriate, well-publicized fiscal and monetary policies in the short run, but not in the long run.
    c. only by making unexpected changes in aggregate demand.
    d. without ever affecting the price level.

27. The theory of rational expectations says that
    a. workers make excellent choices of places to work.
    b. economists expect workers to always correctly forecast the inflation rate.
    c. economists, but not workers, are expected to always correctly forecast the inflation rate.
    d. workers and consumers incorporate the likely consequences of government policy into their expectations rapidly.

28. If expectations are rational, can fiscal and monetary policy control real output?
    a. Yes, provided policies are announced in advance.
    b. Yes, both policies are effective in altering real output in the desired way.
    c. No, because policymakers can't accurately predict how people's expectations will be affected by the policies they adopt.
    d. No, only fiscal policy can alter unemployment in the short run.
    e. No, only monetary policy can alter unemployment in the short run.

29. If expectations are rational, is it possible to reduce inflation without causing increased unemployment?
    a. Yes, simply by using monetary policy to reduce aggregate demand instead of fiscal policy.
    b. No, no economic theory assumes that this is possible under any conditions.
    c. Yes, simply by making a quick move to reduce aggregate demand with no announcement.
    d. No, rational expectations theory assumes that any decrease in inflation always triggers mass unemployment.
    e. Yes, simply by reducing the growth aggregate demand to a lower level and announcing this in a credible way.

30. Employment will be affected by inflation only if
    a. the inflation rate gets above a certain level.
    b. the inflation is expected.
    c. the inflation rate is different from what was expected.
    d. unemployment is above the natural rate.

31. Rational expectations theory implies that accurately anticipating aggregate demand
    a. will increase RGDP in the short run.
    b. will affect RGDP and inflation only in the long run.
    c. may affect RGDP but not nominal GDP in the short run.
    d. will do none of the above.

32. Whether people quickly anticipate the effects of government policy changes or not, an increase in the growth rate of aggregate demand will tend to increase nominal GDP
    a. in both the short run and the long run.
    b. in the short run but not the long run.
    c. in the long run but not the short run.
    d. in neither the short run nor the long run.

33. If an increase in the growth rate of *AD* leads to an increase in real GDP in the short run,
    a. the increase in *AD* could have been correctly anticipated.
    b. the increase in *AD* could have been greater than anticipated.
    c. the increase in *AD* could have been less than anticipated.
    d. the increase in *AD* could have been any of the above.

34. With rational expectations, a policy that would increase *AD* would lead to
    a. higher inflation and lower unemployment in the short run.
    b. higher inflation and higher unemployment in the short run.
    c. higher inflation and no change in unemployment in the short run.
    d. higher inflation and an indeterminate effect on unemployment in the short run, unless people's expectations were correct.

35. With rational expectations, a policy that would increase *AD* would lead to
    a. higher inflation and lower unemployment in the short run if people underestimated the effect of the policy on inflation.
    b. higher inflation and higher unemployment in the short run if people underestimated the effect of the policy on inflation.
    c. higher inflation and no change in unemployment in the short run, if people's expectations were correct.
    d. higher inflation and an indeterminate effect on unemployment in the short run, if people's expectations were correct.
    e. both a and c.

36. If the rational expectations theory is accurate, equilibrium real GDP will change in the short run
    a. whenever the aggregate demand curve shifts.
    b. only if discretionary fiscal policy is used.
    c. only if there is a shift in aggregate demand that could not have been predicted from the information available to the public.
    d. only if discretionary monetary policy is used.
    e. none of the above

37. A conclusion of the theory of rational expectations is that, in the short run, the impact of a correctly anticipated fiscal policy designed to increase *AD* will
    a. result in no net change in *AD* once people's expectations of adjustments have been accounted for.
    b. shift *AD* in the opposite direction intended once people's expectations of adjustments have been accounted for.
    c. result in no change in the price level.
    d. increase the price level.
    e. be characterized by both a and d.

38. Critics of rational expectations theory believe
    a. that most people are truly not well informed about the effects of a policy change.
    b. that most people do not adjust their behavior rapidly to changes in government policies, in part because they are not informed about the effects of policy changes.
    c. that wages and prices are not as flexible as the rational expectations theory assumes.
    d. all of the above.

39. Which of the following is false?
    a. If people can anticipate the plans of policymakers and alter their behavior quickly, their behavior could neutralize the intended impact of government action on real GDP.
    b. The theory of rational expectations leads to optimistic conclusions regarding macroeconomic policy's ability to achieve its intended economic goals.
    c. Rational expectations economists believe that wages and prices are flexible, and that workers and consumers incorporate the likely consequences of government policy changes quickly into their expectations.
    d. Catching consumers and businesspeople off-guard with macroeconomic policy changes gets harder the more you try to do it.
    e. None of the above is false; all are true.

40. Which of the following is true?
    a. A correctly anticipated increase in *AD* from expansionary monetary or fiscal policy will not change real output, employment, or unemployment in the short run.
    b. In the rational expectations model, when people expect a larger increase in *AD* than actually results from a policy change, it leads to a lower price level and a higher level of RGDP in the short run.
    c. If some input prices are slow to adjust to changes in the price level, the rational expectations model of complete wage and price flexibility will be correct.
    d. In the long run and the short run, the expected inflation rate equals the actual inflation rate.

41. Under rational expectations, a fully anticipated decrease in the inflation rate from 6 percent to 2 percent will
    a. lower unemployment at first, but then unemployment will return to its natural rate.
    b. lower unemployment permanently.
    c. not change unemployment in either the short run or the long run.
    d. raise unemployment at first, but then unemployment will return to its natural rate.
    e. raise unemployment permanently.

42. Which of the following is not a factor emphasized by real business cycle theorists as a cause of business cycles?
    a. the growth rate of productivity
    b. technological advances
    c. slow adjustments of markets to changes in inflation
    d. all of the above are emphasized by real business cycle theorists as causes of business cycles.

43. According to real business cycle theorists, as a result of a negative productivity shock,
    a. the marginal productivity of labor will fall.
    b. the real wage rate will fall.
    c. the average hours of work will fall.
    d. investment will fall.
    e. All of the above will occur.

44. Which of the following would move in a different direction from the others in the case of a positive productivity shock?
    a. investment
    b. the average amount of vacation time taken by workers
    c. real wages
    d. real output
    e. the marginal productivity of labor

45. Under the Taylor rule, the federal funds rate would be increased by half a point when
    a. real GDP exceeds target real GDP by 1 percentage point.
    b. target GDP exceeds real GDP by 1 percentage point.
    c. inflation exceeds the inflation target by 1 percentage point.
    d. either a or c occurs.

46. The primary purpose of indexing is to
    a. lower the inflation rate.
    b. reduce the social costs of inflation.
    c. help the government maintain wage and price controls.
    d. All of the above are primary purposes of indexing.

47. Indexing is a method of fighting inflation by
    a. tying monetary payments to changes in price indexes.
    b. lowering the level of the consumer price index.
    c. keeping prices from rising above government set ceilings.
    d. all of the above.

48. An escalator clause generally allows wage increases
    a. without annual negotiations.
    b. only when prices increase by more than 5 percent.
    c. when unemployment threatens a major industry.
    d. to protect workers from increases in the prices of a few selected products.

49. Indexing
    a. is a process of adjusting payment contracts to automatically adjust for changes in the price level.
    b. can reduce the impact of inflation on the distribution of income.
    c. may intensify the inflationary effects of expansionary monetary policy by increasing inflationary pressures.
    d. is characterized by all of the above.

Problems:

1. Use the following diagrams and
    a. show what would happen in both diagrams if government purchases increase in the short run.
    b. show what would happen in both diagrams if the growth rate of the money supply was reduced in the short run.
    c. show what would happen in both diagrams if people came to expect a higher rate of inflation.
    d. show what would happen in both diagrams if a favorable supply shock occurred.

2. Use the diagram to answer the following questions:
   a. At which point might expansionary government policy help stabilize the economy?
   b. At which point might contractionary government policy help stabilize the economy?

3. Use the diagram from problem 2 and
   a. indicate which movement would correspond to an unanticipated expansionary government policy in the short run.
   b. indicate which movement would correspond to an unanticipated contractionary government policy in the short run.
   c. indicate which movement would correspond to a completely anticipated expansionary government policy, under rational expectations.
   d. indicate which movement would correspond to a completely anticipated contractionary government policy in the short run.
   e. indicate what would happen if an expansionary government policy occurred, but its inflationary effects were smaller than they were expected to be.

4. Abraham Lincoln once said "You can fool all of the people some of the time, and some of the people all of the time, but you cannot fool all of the people all of the time." How can a central bank that conducts monetary policy "fool people" and thereby affect the level of unemployment in the economy? What happens if people begin to anticipate future monetary policy correctly based upon past experience?

5. Predict the impact an unexpected decrease in the money supply would have on the following variables in the short run and in the long run.
   a. the inflation rate
   b. the unemployment rate
   c. real output
   d. real wages

6. Predict whether unemployment will increase or decrease as a result of each of the following monetary policies. If it is unanticipated? What if it is anticipated?
   a. a reduction in the discount rate from 6 percent to 5.5 percent
   b. an open market sale by the Federal Reserve Bank
   c. an increase in the required reserve ratio from 10 percent to 12 percent
7. If money wages are rising faster than output prices,
   a. what is happening to real wages?
   b. what would happen to unemployment as a result?
   c. what would happen to SRAS as a result?
8. Is there any way that, starting from a long-run stable price equilibrium, an increase in aggregate demand could result in an increase in unemployment and a decrease in RGDP?
9. Answer the following questions.
   a. Why does an upward shift in the Phillips curve correspond to an upward shift in the short-run aggregate supply curve?
   b. Why does a movement up and to the left along a Phillips curve correspond to a movement up and to the right along a short-run aggregate supply curve?
10. Why is the credibility of the monetary authorities so crucial to quickly overcoming expected inflation?
11. Suppose the following data represent points along a short-run Phillips curve. Are the data consistent with what you would expect? Why or why not?

	Inflation Rate	Unemployment Rate
A	0%	5%
B	1%	4.5%
C	2%	3.75%
D	3%	2.75%
E	4%	1.5%

12. How are the long-run Phillips curve and the long-run aggregate supply curve related?
13. How would each of the following likely affect long-run and/or short-run aggregate supply and employment in the macro-economy?
    a. an increase in the productivity of the labor force due to increased education
    b. the coldest year in a century leads to frequent ice and snow storms
    c. major advances in computer and Internet technologies
14. Why do economists who believe people form rational expectations have little faith that announced changes in monetary policy will have substantial effects on real output?
15. Does stagflation contradict the theory of the Phillips curve?

PART 9 THE GLOBAL ECONOMY

Chapter 30 International Trade 914

Chapter 31 International Finance 949

30 International Trade

30.1 The Growth in World Trade
30.2 Comparative Advantage and Gains from Trade
30.3 Supply and Demand in International Trade
30.4 Tariffs, Import Quotas, and Subsidies

Economics is largely about exchange. But up to this point we have focused on trade between individuals within the domestic economy. In this chapter, we extend our coverage to international trade.

Why do countries trade? Hong Kong has no oil—how are they going to get it? What is comparative advantage? Bananas could be grown in the most tropical parts of the United States or in expensive greenhouses, but wouldn't it be easier to import bananas from Honduras?

Stop for a moment and imagine a world without international trade. Chocolate is derived from cocoa beans that are imported from South America and Africa. There are imported cars from Germany and Japan, shoes and sweaters from Italy, shirts from India, and watches and clocks from Switzerland. Consumers love trade because it provides us with more choices. It is good for producers, too; and the speed of transportation and communication has opened up world markets. In addition, lower costs are sometimes the result of economies of scale. Free trade gives firms access to large world markets. It also fosters more competition, which helps to keep prices down.

In this chapter, we will study the theoretical reasons for the importance of trade. We will also look at the arguments for and against trade protection. ∎

SECTION 30.1 The Growth in World Trade

- What has happened to the volume of international trade over time?
- Who trades with the United States?
- What does the United States export? Import?

Importance of International Trade

In a typical year, about 15 percent of the world's output is traded in international markets. Of course, the importance of the international sector varies enormously from place to place across the world. Some nations are virtually closed economies (no interaction with other economies), with foreign trade equaling only a small proportion (perhaps 5 percent) of total output, while in other countries, trade is much more important. In the last three decades, the sum of U.S. imports and exports has increased from 11 percent of GDP to roughly 30 percent. In addition, incoming and outgoing investments (capital flows) have risen from less than 1 percent to roughly 3 percent of GDP. In Germany, roughly 30 percent of all output produced is exported, while Ireland and Belgium each export more than 70 percent of GDP.

U.S. exports include capital goods, automobiles, industrial supplies, raw materials, consumer goods, and agricultural products. U.S. imports include crude oil and refined petroleum products, machinery, automobiles, consumer goods, industrial raw materials, food, and beverages.

Trading Partners

In the early history of the United States, international trade largely took place with Europe and with Great Britain in particular. Now the United States trades with a number of countries, the most important of which are Canada, China, Japan, Mexico, Germany, and the United Kingdom as seen in Exhibit 1.

section 30.1 exhibit 1 — Major U.S. Trading Partners

Top Trading Partners—Exports of Goods in 2007			Top Trading Partners—Imports of Goods in 2007		
Rank	Country	Percent of Total	Rank	Country	Percent of Total
1	Canada	21.4%	1	China	16.9%
2	Mexico	11.7	2	Canada	15.7
3	China	5.6	3	Mexico	10.6
4	Japan	5.4	4	Japan	7.4
5	United Kingdom	4.3	5	Germany	4.8
6	Germany	4.3			

SOURCE: CIA, *The World Factbook* 2009.

global WATCH: INTERNATIONAL TRADE MAY REDUCE INEQUALITY IN THE UNITED STATES

Conventional wisdom says globalization has increased US income inequality. This column says that is dead wrong, as China and Wal-Mart have increased the purchasing power of the poor more than the rich....

How rich you are depends on two things: how much money you have and how much the goods you buy cost. If your income doubles but the prices of the goods you consume also double, then you are no better off. Unfortunately, the conventional wisdom on US inequality is based on official measures that only look at the first half, the income differential. National statistics ignore the fact that inflation affects people in different income groups unevenly because the rich and poor consume different baskets of goods.

Inflation differentials between the rich and poor dramatically change our view of the evolution of inequality in America. Inflation of the richest 10 percent of American households has been 6 percentage points higher than that of the poorest 10 percent over the period 1994–2005. This means that real inequality in America, if you measure it correctly, has been roughly unchanged. And the reason is just as dramatic as the result. Why has inflation for the poor been lower than that for the rich? In large part it is because of China and Wal-Mart!

Poor families in America spend a larger share of their income on goods whose prices are directly affected by trade—like clothing and food—relative to wealthier families. By contrast, the higher your income, the more you spend on services, which are less subject to competition from abroad. Since 1994 the price of goods in the U.S. has risen much less than the price of services—and, yes, this includes the recent surge in food prices. Paradoxically, focusing only in the last few quarters of high relative food prices misses the fact that the main trend we have observed for decades is exactly the opposite.

This trend can partly be explained by China. In U.S. stores, prices of consumer goods have fallen the most in sectors where Chinese presence has increased the most. Take canned seafood or cotton shirts, for instance. Exports of China to the rest of the world in these categories have increased

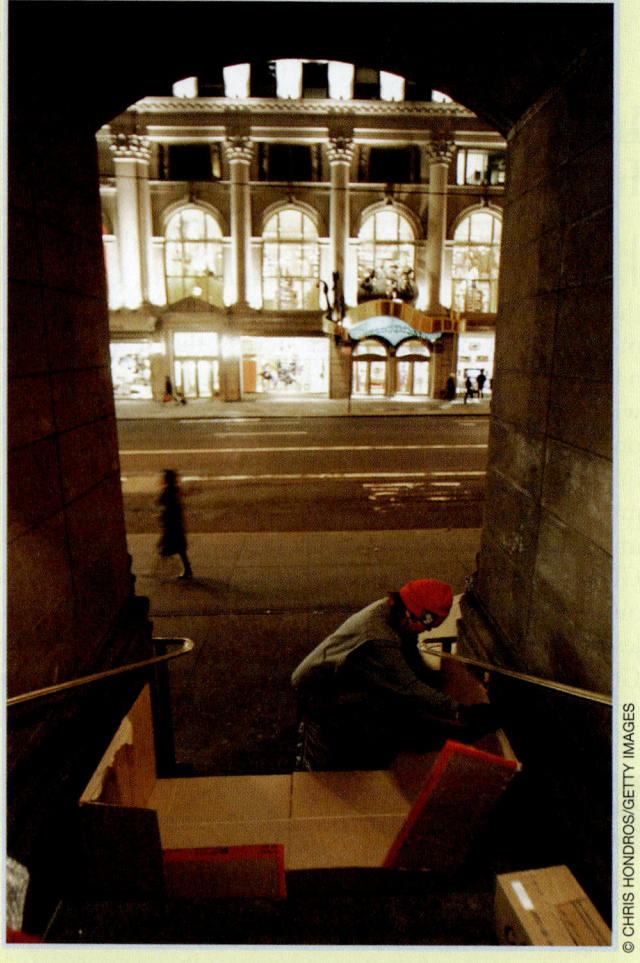

dramatically over this decade. Inflation in these sectors has been negative over the last decade, while in other sectors with no Chinese presence inflation has been over 20 percent. Moreover, as China produces goods of relatively low quality, sectors with strong Chinese presence are disproportionately consumed by the poor.

The expansion of superstores—like Wal-Mart and Target—has also played an important role in accounting for the inflation differentials between rich and poor. Superstores sell the same products as traditional shops at much lower prices. Today the poor do roughly twice as much of their buying of non-durable goods in these stores than the rich. So poor consumers have been the biggest beneficiaries of Wal-Mart coming to town.

global WATCH: INTERNATIONAL TRADE MAY REDUCE INEQUALITY IN THE UNITED STATES (cont.)

What is really worrying is that, *despite* these facts, we have had a backlash against China and Wal-Mart in America.

We need to remind politicians and the public that the gains from trade are broadly shared. Every time the discussion over trade is diverted towards the problems facing specific producers, be they farmers in France or textile workers in the U.S., we miss the central point. Trading allows everyone, and *especially* the poor, to buy things that they could not otherwise afford. Without better public understanding of these facts, governments will not only keep supporting policies aimed against China and Wal-Mart but may receive the uninformed support of many consumers who are benefitting from trade.

SOURCE: Vox, July 3, 2008 http://www.voxeu.org.

SECTION CHECK

1. The volume of international trade has increased substantially in the United States over the last 30 years. During that time, exports and imports have grown from 11 percent to 30 percent of GDP.
2. Our single most important trading partner, Canada, accounts for roughly one-fourth of our exports and almost one-fifth of our imports. Trade with Japan, Mexico, China, Germany, the United Kingdom, France, and Taiwan is also particularly important to the United States.
3. U.S. exports include capital goods, automobiles, industrial supplies, raw materials, consumer goods, and agricultural products. U.S. imports include crude oil and refined petroleum products, machinery, automobiles, consumer goods, industrial raw materials, food, and beverages.

---

1. Why is it important to understand the effects of international trade?
2. Why would U.S. producers and consumers be more concerned about Canadian trade restrictions than Swedish trade restrictions?

SECTION 30.2 Comparative Advantage and Gains from Trade

- Does voluntary trade lead to an improvement in economic welfare?
- What is the principle of comparative advantage?
- What benefits are derived from specialization?

Economic Growth and Trade

sing simple logic, we conclude that the very existence of trade suggests that trade is economically beneficial. Our conclusion is true if we assume that people are utility maximizers and are rational, are intelligent, and engage in trade on a voluntary basis. Because almost all trade is voluntary, it would seem that trade occurs because the participants feel that they are better off because of the trade. Both participants in an exchange of goods and services anticipate an improvement in their economic welfare. Sometimes, of course, anticipations are not realized (because the world is uncertain); but the motive behind trade remains an expectation of some enhancement in utility or satisfaction by both parties.

Granted, "trade must be good because people do it" is a rather simplistic explanation. The classical economist David Ricardo is usually given most of the credit for developing the economic theory that more precisely explains how trade can be mutually beneficial to both parties, raising output and income levels in the entire trading area.

comparative advantage occurs when a person or country can produce a good or service at a lower opportunity cost than others

The Principle of Comparative Advantage

Ricardo's theory of international trade centers on the concept of comparative advantage. Persons, regions, or countries can gain by specializing in the production of the good in which they have a comparative advantage. That is, if they can produce a good or service at a lower opportunity cost than others, we say that they have a 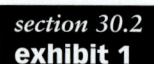 in the production of that good or service. In other words, a country or a region should specialize in producing and selling those items that it can produce at a lower opportunity cost than other regions or countries.

Comparative advantage analysis does not mean that nations or areas that export goods will necessarily be able to produce those goods or services more cheaply than other nations in an absolute sense. What is important is *comparative* advantage, not *absolute* advantage. For example, the United States may be able to produce more cotton cloth per worker than India can, but this capability does not mean that the United States should necessarily sell cotton cloth to India. For a highly productive nation to produce goods in which it is only marginally more productive than other nations, the nation must take resources from the production of other goods in which its productive abilities are markedly superior. As a result, the opportunity costs in India of making cotton cloth may be less than in the United States. With that, both can gain from trade, despite potential absolute advantages for every good in the United States.

Comparative Advantage, Specialization, and the Production Possibilities Curves

Wendy and Calvin live on opposite ends of a small town. Wendy can produce either food or cloth. On a daily basis, she can produce 10 pounds of food, 5 yards of cloth, or any linear combination between the two goods along her production possibilities curve in Exhibit 1 (to simplify the calculations we have drawn linear production possibilities curves). If Wendy spends the whole day producing food, she can produce 10 pounds. If she spends the whole day producing cloth, she can produce 5 yards. Recall that the production possibilities curve represents the maximum possible combinations of food and cloth she can produce, given her fixed set of resources and technology.

The negatively sloped production possibilities curve means that when she produces one good, with her fixed resources, she gives up the opportunity to produce another good.

What is Wendy's opportunity cost of producing cloth? It is what Wendy gives up in food production for each unit of cloth production, which is 2 pounds of food per yard of cloth. Therefore, her opportunity cost of producing a yard of cloth is 2 pounds of food. What is the opportunity cost of Wendy producing food? If is what she gives up in cloth production for each unit increase

section 30.2 exhibit 1 Wendy's Production Possibilities Curve

$$OC_{CLOTH} = \frac{\text{loss in food}}{\text{gain in cloth}} = \frac{10}{5} = \frac{2 \text{ pounds of food}}{1 \text{ yard of cloth}}$$

$$OC_{FOOD} = \frac{\text{loss in cloth}}{\text{gain in food}} = \frac{5}{10} = \frac{1 \text{ yard in cloth}}{2 \text{ pounds of food}}$$

or

1 yard of cloth costs 2 pounds of food
1 pound of food costs ½ yard of cloth

Wendy can produce either food or cloth along her production possibilities curve. For Wendy, the opportunity cost of producing a yard of cloth is 2 pounds of food; and the opportunity cost of producing a pound of food is ½ yard of cloth.

GREAT ECONOMIC THINKERS
DAVID RICARDO (1772–1823)

David Ricardo was born in London to a wealthy, Jewish immigrant stockbroker, the third of 17 children. His father trained him in the stock brokerage business, which he entered at age 14. At 21, he married a young Quaker woman, leaving the Jewish faith to become a Unitarian. This upset his father, who disowned David. The young Ricardo joined a bank and entered the stock market on his own. He was very successful in this enterprise, making millions of pounds and quickly surpassing the wealth accumulated by his father, with whom he later reconciled. Ricardo retired from the stock exchange business at age 43 and died of an ear infection at 51, leaving behind a large fortune.

Ricardo could accredit much of his success in the stock market to his brilliant ability to predict human nature and public reaction. As a member of the House of Commons, he was also an undaunted advocate of government reform, religious and political freedom, and free trade. A man of firm convictions, he often lobbied for class-leveling policies that conflicted with his personal interests as a landowner and a man of wealth.

In his late 20s, while vacationing in Bath, England, Ricardo picked up a copy of Adam Smith's *The Wealth of Nations* and became interested in economics. It was a few years later that Ricardo, who had no formal education past age 14, improved upon Smith's principle of absolute advantage. Ricardo's ideas, though difficult for many of his fellow politicians to understand, were ingenious.

Smith argued that two countries should engage in trade if one was better at producing one good than the other—absolute advantage. For example, if one country is better at producing hats and the other at producing shoes, the two countries can produce more total output by producing those goods that they can produce best. However, Ricardo demonstrated that even if one country was absolutely more productive than another in making all goods and services, it would still be mutually beneficial for the two countries to engage in trade, as each had a comparative advantage in one of the goods.

Ricardo argued this point at a time in British history when the wealthy landowners, who had a clutch on parliament, had a virtual monopoly on grain in England in the form of the Corn Laws, passed in 1815. These acts prevented the importation of grain from France, although, as Ricardo argued, France could afford to feed the British for less than it would cost them to feed themselves. Despite Ricardo's argument and the fact that English laborers were spending one-fourth of their income on bread, the Corn Laws persisted until 1846. Ricardo did, however, leave behind a remarkable concept that convinced future economists that free trade is almost always in the best interest of an economy as a whole.

Use what you've LEARNED
COMPARATIVE ADVANTAGE AND ABSOLUTE ADVANTAGE

Q Renee Saunts is a successful artist, who can complete one painting in each 40-hour workweek. Each painting sells for $4,000. As a result of her enormous success, however, Renee is swamped in paperwork. To solve the problem, Renee hires Drake to handle all the bookkeeping and typing associated with buying supplies, answering inquiries from prospective buyers and dealers, writing art galleries, and so forth. Renee pays Drake $300 per week for his work. After a couple of weeks in this arrangement, Renee realizes that she can handle Drake's chores more quickly than Drake does. In fact, she estimates that she is twice as fast as Drake, completing in 20 hours what it takes Drake 40 hours to complete. Should Renee fire Drake?

A Clearly, Renee has an absolute advantage over Drake in both painting and paperwork, because she can do twice as much paperwork in 40 hours as Drake can and Drake can't paint well at all. Still, it would be foolish for Renee to do both jobs. If Renee did her own paperwork, it would take her 20 hours per week, leaving her only 20 hours to paint. Because each watercolor takes 40 hours to paint, Renee's output would fall from one painting per week to one painting per two weeks.

When Drake works for her, Renee's net income is $3,700 per week ($4,000 per painting minus $300 in Drake's wages); when Drake does not work for her, it is only $2,000 per week (one painting every two weeks). Even though Renee is both a better painter and better at Drake's chores than Drake, it pays for her to specialize in painting, in which she has a comparative advantage, and allow Drake to do the paperwork. The opportunity cost to Renee of paperwork is high. For Drake, who lacks skills as a painter, the opportunity costs of doing the paperwork are much less.

---

in food production = 1 yard of cloth per 2 pounds of food. That is, for each pound of food Wendy produces, she gives up producing ½ yard of cloth.

Calvin, who lives on the other side of town, can also produce food or cloth. On a daily basis, he could produce 3 pounds of food, 4 yards of cloth, or any linear combination between the two along his production possibilities curve in Exhibit 2. When he spends the day producing cloth, he can produce 4 yards. When he spends the day producing food, he can produce 3 pounds. To produce cloth, Calvin must decrease his production of food. What is Calvin's opportunity cost of producing cloth? It is what he gives up in producing food for each unit of cloth production, which is 3 pounds of food per 4 pounds of cloth. Therefore, his opportunity cost of producing cloth is ¾ pound of food. What is Calvin's opportunity cost of producing food? It is what he gives up in cloth production for each unit of food production which is 4 yards of cloth per 3 pounds of food. Therefore, the opportunity cost of producing a pound of food is 4/3 yards of cloth per day.

Absolute and Comparative Advantage

Now let's compare Wendy's production possibilities curve to Calvin's production possibilities curve to see who has an absolute advantage in producing cloth and who has an absolute advantage in producing food. An absolute advantage occurs when one producer can do a task using fewer inputs than the other producer. In Exhibit 3, we see that Wendy is more productive than Calvin at producing food. Along the vertical axis, we can see that if Wendy uses all of her resources to produce food, she can produce 10 pounds of food per day. If Calvin devotes all of his resources to producing food, he can only produce 3 pounds of food per day. We say that Wendy has an absolute advantage over Calvin in the production of food.

Along the horizontal axis in Exhibit 3, we can see that Wendy is also more productive than Calvin at producing cloth. If Wendy devotes all of her resources to producing cloth, she can produce 5 yards of cloth per day. If Calvin devotes all of his resources to producing cloth, he can only produce 4 yards of cloth per day. We say that Wendy also has an absolute advantage over Calvin in the production of cloth. She has an absolute advantage in producing both food and cloth. Therefore, should Wendy produce both food and cloth and Calvin produce nothing? No!

Recall from Chapter 2 that a comparative advantage exists when one person can produce a good at a lower opportunity cost than another person. So who

section 30.2 exhibit 2 — Calvin's Production Possibilities Curve

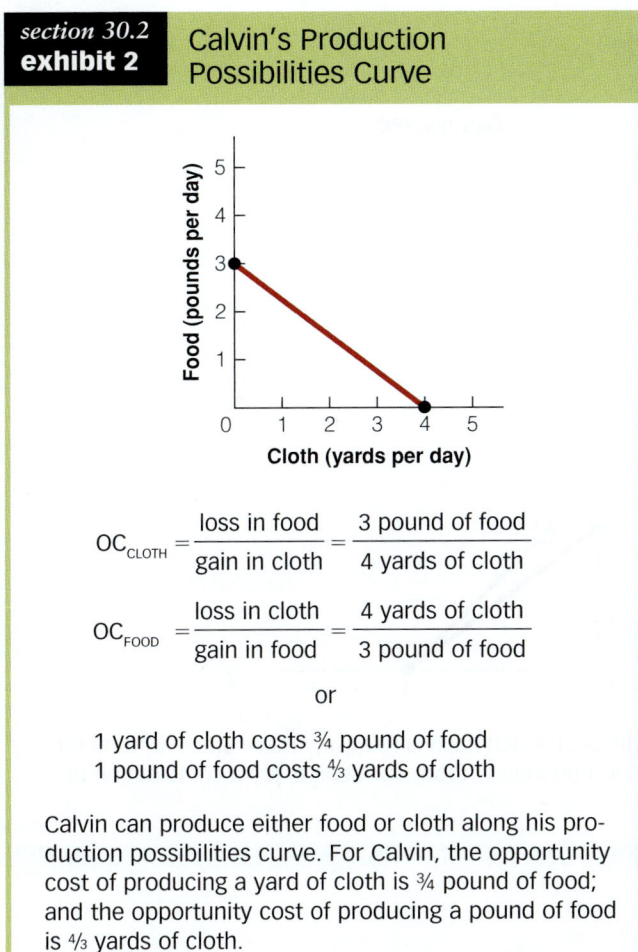

$$OC_{CLOTH} = \frac{\text{loss in food}}{\text{gain in cloth}} = \frac{3 \text{ pound of food}}{4 \text{ yards of cloth}}$$

$$OC_{FOOD} = \frac{\text{loss in cloth}}{\text{gain in food}} = \frac{4 \text{ yards of cloth}}{3 \text{ pound of food}}$$

or

1 yard of cloth costs ¾ pound of food
1 pound of food costs 4/3 yards of cloth

Calvin can produce either food or cloth along his production possibilities curve. For Calvin, the opportunity cost of producing a yard of cloth is ¾ pound of food; and the opportunity cost of producing a pound of food is 4/3 yards of cloth.

section 30.2 exhibit 3 — Absolute and Comparative Advantage

	Cloth (yds/day)	Food (lbs/day)	OC of Cloth	OC of Food
Wendy	5	10	2 lb of food	½ yd of cloth
Calvin	4	3	¾ lbs of food	4/3 yds of cloth

In this case, Wendy has an absolute advantage producing food and cloth. It is easy to see the absolute advantage, because if she devotes all her resources to producing cloth she can produce 10 yards per day, while Calvin could only produce 5 yards. But she also has a comparative advantages because she has a lower opportunity cost of producing cloth, ½ lb of food versus Calvin's ¾ lbs of food.

In addition, if she devotes all her resources to producing food she could produce 5 pounds of food and Calvin could only produce 4 pounds of food.

---

has the comparative advantage (lowest opportunity cost) in producing food? In this case, Wendy's opportunity cost of producing food is less than Calvin's. Wendy's opportunity cost of producing a pound of food is ½ yard of cloth, whereas Calvin's opportunity cost of producing 1 pound of food is 4/3 yards of cloth. Therefore, Wendy is the more efficient producer of food—she gives up less in cloth when she produces food, compared to Calvin. Remember, comparative advantage is always a relative concept.

Who has the comparative advantage in producing cloth? That is, who can produce cloth at the lowest opportunity cost? That would be Calvin, because he gives up only ¾ pound of food to produce 1 yard of cloth. If Wendy were to produce a yard of cloth, she would have to give up 2 pounds of food. The lowest opportunity cost producer of cloth is Calvin. In other words, to produce one more yard of cloth, Calvin gives up fewer pounds of food than Wendy. Therefore, Calvin is the more efficient producer of cloth—he gives up less in food when he produces cloth, compared to Wendy. Calvin has a comparative advantage in producing cloth.

Gains from Specialization and Exchange

Suppose Wendy and Calvin meet and decide to specialize in those activities in which they have a comparative advantage. Wendy would specialize in the production of food and Calvin would specialize in the production of

section 30.2 exhibit 4 — The Gains from Specialization and Trade

After meeting, Wendy and Calvin decided to specialize in the activity in which each is relatively more efficient; food for Wendy and cloth for Calvin. When they trade 3 pounds of cloth for 3 pounds of food, each can enjoy a combination of food and cloth they could not have produced on their own.

cloth. By specializing, Wendy can produce 10 pounds of food per day (point B' in Exhibit 4) and Calvin can produce 4 yards of cloth per day (point B in Exhibit 4). However, *to achieve any of the gains from comparative advantage and specialization, there must be trade.*

After specializing in the good in which they have a comparative advantage, suppose Wendy and Calvin agree to trade at the exchange "price" of 1 pound of food for 1 yard of cloth. If Wendy trades 3 pounds of cloth for 3 pounds of food, she can obtain a position along the new production possibilities curve which is beyond her original production possibilities curve, point C in Exhibit 4. Wendy can now have 7 pounds of food and 3 yards of cloth—a combination she could not have obtained without specialization and trade.

Calvin also benefits from specialization and trade. In the trade, he receives 3 pounds of food for 3 yards of cloth and now can enjoy 3 pounds of food and 1 yard of cloth a combination, at point C, he could not have obtained without specialization and trade. In sum, the exchange has allowed both Wendy and Calvin to produce and consume a combination of the two goods beyond what would have been attainable if it were not for specialization and exchange.

Individuals and Nations Gain from Specialization and Trade

Just as Calvin and Wendy benefit from specialization and trade, so do the people of different nations. Because of specialization, according to comparative advantage, both nations can be better off, even if one nation has an absolute advantage in both goods over the other. Furthermore, the greater the difference in opportunity cost between the two trading partners, the greater the benefits from specialization and exchange.

Note that when we say nations trade with nations, we really mean that the people of a nation trade with people of other nations. When China trades clothes to the United States for Boeing 787 jetliners, they both benefit from the exchange, because they are able to obtain them at a lower cost than if they produced those goods themselves. Free trade does not guarantee that each individual will be better off or that everyone will receive the same benefits, but it does mean that collectively, the population of each nation will benefit from the trade. Indeed, unskilled workers in high wage countries may temporarily lose jobs. Recall that when NAFTA was passed, its critics argued that low skilled workers would lose jobs because of U.S. trade with Mexico. However, that does not appear to have happened to any large extent. Instead, consumers have been enjoying lower priced goods because of the trade.

Regional Comparative Advantage

Using a production possibilities curve, we saw how Wendy and Calvin could benefit from specialization and trade. The principle of comparative advantage can be applied to regional markets as well. In fact, trade has evolved in large part because different geographic areas have different resources and therefore different production possibilities. The impact of trade between two areas with differing resources is shown in Exhibit 5. To keep the analysis simple, suppose two trading areas can produce only two commodities, grain and computers. A "trading area" may be a locality, a region, or even a nation, but for our example suppose we think in terms of two hypothetical regions, Grainsville and Techland.

Grainsville and Techland have various potential combinations of grain and computers that they can produce. For each region, the cost of producing more grain is the output of computers that must be forgone, and vice versa. We see in Exhibit 5 that Techland can

section 30.2 exhibit 5 Production Possibilities, Techland and Grainsville

Region	Grain (bushels per day)	Computers (units per day)
Techland	0	100
	10	75
	20	50
	30	25
	40	0
Grainsville	0	30
	6	24
	12	18
	18	12
	24	6
	30	0
Before Specialization		
Techland	10	75
Grainsville	18	12
Total	28	87
After Specialization		
Techland	0	100
Grainsville	30	0
Total	30	100

Use what you've LEARNED
THE SECRET TO WEALTH

Do what you do relatively best. Trade for the rest. In other words, specialize and then trade.

The farmer grows wheat, the baker makes bread, the weaver produces cloth, the tailor sews clothing, the lumberjack harvests wood, the carpenter builds houses. By exchanging the fruits of their labor in the marketplace, they all can enjoy more food, clothing, and shelter than they could if each tried to meet his needs in isolation. . . .

It's a matter of working smarter, not harder.

Societies reaped the benefits of specialization and trade for thousands of years before English economist David Ricardo (1772–1823) finally demonstrated why it works. His theory of comparative advantage helps explain why the United States exports soybeans to China and imports shoes in return.

Suppose an average American worker can produce 100 bushels of soybeans or five pairs of shoes and a typical Chinese worker can turn out 8 bushels of soybeans or four pairs of shoes. [See Exhibit 6.]

The United States is more productive than China in both industries, but consumers in both countries can still gain from specialization and trade. Shifting a U.S. worker from shoe factory to soybean farm produces a gain of 100 bushels of soybeans at the cost of five pairs of shoes. Shifting two Chinese workers from farm to factory raises shoe output by eight pairs

(continued)

Use what you've LEARNED
THE SECRET TO WEALTH (cont.)

but cuts soybean production by 16 bushels. The net effect is an increase of 84 bushels of soybeans and three pairs of shoes.

Total output of both products reaches a maximum when the United States specializes in soybeans and China in shoes. Through trade, the two countries can divide the added production between themselves, leaving both better off than they were on their own.

In the real world, trade isn't a two-party swap meet. The United States does business with more than 225 other nations—from Albania to Zimbabwe. The dizzying number of potential transactions increases the opportunities to gain from trade.

This potent international division of labor enables America to take advantage of its expertise in such industries as jet-aircraft manufacturing and financial services while other countries exploit their edge in oil production or hand assembly.

Specialization and trade arise out of the profit motive. Except when transaction costs are too high or governments impose barriers, buyers and sellers will find each other. We're not meant to go it alone.

SOURCE: W. Michael Cox and Richard Alm "The Secret to Wealth," 2002 *Annual Report: The Fruits of Free Trade*, Federal Reserve Bank of Dallas.

section 30.2 exhibit 6 — The Alchemy of Exchange

	Autarky		Free Trade	
	China	U.S.	China	U.S.
Labor Force	500	100	500	100
Output per worker				
Shoes	4	5	4	5
Soybeans	8	100	8	100
Employment				
Shoes	125	60	500	0
Soybeans	375	40	0	100
Production				
Shoes	500	300	2,000	0
Soybeans	3,000	4,000	0	10,000
Consumption				
Shoes	500	300	1,500	500
Soybeans	3,000	4,000	5,000	5,000
Consumption per person				
Shoes	1	3	3	5
Soybeans	6	40	10	50

Five hundred Chinese workers can each produce four pairs of shoes or 8 bushels of soybeans. One hundred U.S. workers can each produce five pairs or 100 bushels—more productive in both jobs but comparatively more so in farming. Under an autarkic regime—isolated from foreign trade—Chinese workers can afford one pair of shoes each and 6 bushels of soybeans; Americans, three and 40. Trading freely, China will specialize in shoes and America in soybeans, raising world production of shoes from 800 to 2,000 pairs and soybeans from 7,000 to 10,000 bushels. Chinese workers can then afford three pairs of shoes and 10 bushels of soybeans; American workers, five and 50. In this case, the United States trades 10 bushels of soybeans to China for each pair of shoes.

produce more grain (40 bushels) and more computers (100 units) than Grainsville can (30 bushels and 30 units, respectively), perhaps reflecting superior resources (more or better labor, more land, and so on). These numbers mean that Techland has an absolute advantage in both products.

Suppose that, before specialization, Techland chooses to produce 75 computers and 10 bushels of grain per day. Similarly, suppose Grainsville decides to produce 12 computers and 18 bushels of grain. Collectively, then, the two areas are producing 87 computers (75 + 12) and 28 bushels of grain (10 + 18) per day before specialization.

Now, suppose the two nations specialize. Techland decides to specialize in computers and devotes all its resources to making that product. As a result, computer output in Techland rises to 100 units per day, some of which is sold to Grainsville. Grainsville, in turn, devotes all its resources to grain, producing 30 bushels of grain per day and selling some of it to Techland. Together, the two areas are producing more of both grain and computers than before—100 instead of 87 computers and 30 instead of 28 bushels of grain. Both areas could, as a result, have more of both products than before they began specializing and trading.

How can this happen? In Techland, the opportunity cost of producing grain is high—25 computers must be forgone to get 10 more bushels of grain. The cost of one bushel of grain, then, is 2.5 computers (25 divided by 10). In Grainsville, by contrast, the opportunity cost of producing six more units of grain is six units of computers that must be forgone; so the cost of one unit of grain is one unit of computers. In Techland, a unit of grain costs 2.5 computers, while in Grainsville the same amount of grain costs only one computer. Grain is more costly in Techland in terms of the computers forgone than in Grainsville, so Grainsville has the comparative advantage in the production of grain, even though Techland has an absolute advantage in grain.

With respect to computers, an increase in output by 25 units, say from 25 to 50 units, costs 10 bushels of grain forgone in Techland. The cost of one more computer is 0.4 bushel of grain (10 divided by 25). In Grainsville, an increase in computer output of six units, say from 12 to 18, is accompanied by a decrease in grain production by 6 bushels, as resources are converted from grain to computer manufacturing. The cost of one computer is 1 bushel of grain. Computers are more costly (in terms of opportunity cost) in Grainsville and cheaper in Techland, so Techland should specialize in the production of computers.

Thus, by specializing in products in which it has a comparative advantage, an area has the potential of having more goods and services, assuming it trades the additional output for other desirable goods and services that others can produce at a lower opportunity cost. In the scenario presented here, the people in Techland would specialize in computers, and the people in Grainsville would specialize in farming (grain). We can see from this example that specialization increases both the division of labor and the interdependence among groups of people.

SECTION CHECK

1. Voluntary trade occurs because the participants feel that they are better off as a result of the trade.
2. A nation, geographic area, or even a person can gain from trade if the good or service is produced relatively cheaper than anyone else can produce it. That is, an area should specialize in producing and selling those items that it can produce at a lower opportunity cost than others.
3. Through trade and specialization in products in which it has a comparative advantage, a country can enjoy a greater array of goods and services at a lower cost.

---

1. Why do people voluntarily choose to specialize and trade?
2. How could a country have an absolute advantage in producing one good or service without also having a comparative advantage in its production?
3. Why do you think the introduction of the railroad reduced self-sufficiency in the United States?
4. If you can wash the dishes in two-thirds the time it takes your younger sister to wash them, do you have a comparative advantage in washing the dishes with respect to her?

SECTION 30.3
Supply and Demand in International Trade

* What is consumer surplus?
* What is producer surplus?
* Who benefits and who loses when a country becomes an exporter?
* Who benefits and who loses when a country becomes an importer?

The Importance of Trade: Producer and Consumer Surplus

Recall from Chapter 7 that the difference between the most a consumer would be willing to pay for a quantity of a good and what a consumer actually has to pay is called **consumer surplus**. The difference between the lowest price for which a supplier would be willing to supply a quantity of a good or service and the revenues a supplier actually receives for selling it is called **producer surplus**. With the tools of consumer and producer surplus, we can better analyze the impact of trade. Who gains? Who loses? What happens to net welfare?

The demand curve represents the maximum prices that consumers are willing and able to pay for different quantities of a good or service; the supply curve represents the minimum prices suppliers require to be willing to supply different quantities of that good or service. For example, in Exhibit 1, the consumer is willing to pay up to $7 for the first unit of output and the producer would demand at least $1 for producing that unit. However, the equilibrium price is $4, as indicated by the intersection of the supply and demand curves. It is clear that the two would gain from getting together and trading that unit, because the consumer would receive $3 of consumer surplus ($7 − $4), and the producer would receive $3 of producer surplus ($4 − $1). Both would also benefit from trading the second and third units of output—in fact, from every unit up to the equilibrium output. Once the equilibrium output is reached at the equilibrium price, all the mutually beneficial opportunities from trade between suppliers and demanders will have taken place; the sum of consumer surplus and producer surplus is maximized.

It is important to recognize that the total gain to the economy from trade is the sum of the consumer and the producer surpluses. That is, consumers benefit from additional amounts of consumer surplus, and producers benefit from additional amounts of producer surplus.

consumer surplus
the difference between the price a consumer is willing and able to pay for an additional unit of a good and the price the consumer actually pays; for the whole market, it is the sum of all the individual consumer surpluses—the area below the market demand curve and above the market price

producer surplus
the difference between what a producer is paid for a good and the cost of producing that unit of the good; for the market, it is the sum of all the individual sellers' producer surpluses—the area above the market supply curve and below the market price

section 30.3 exhibit 1 — Consumer and Product Surplus

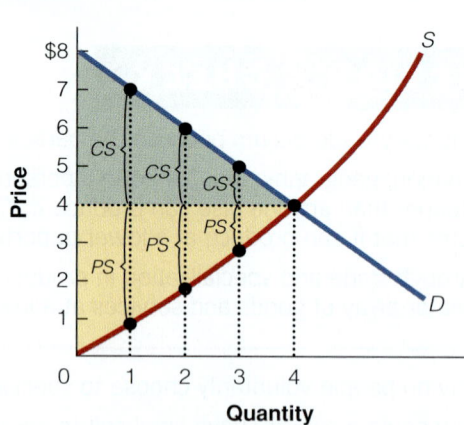

Consumer surplus is the difference between what a consumer has to pay ($4) and what the consumer is willing to pay. For unit 1, consumer surplus is $3 ($7 − $4). Producer surplus is the difference between what a seller receives for selling a good or service ($4) and the price at which the seller is willing to supply that good or service. For unit 1, producer surplus is $3 ($4 − $1).

Free Trade and Exports—Domestic Producers Gain More Than Domestic Consumers Lose

Using the concepts of consumer and producer surplus, we can graphically show the net benefits of free trade. Imagine an economy with no trade, where the equilibrium price, P_{BT}, and equilibrium quantity, Q_{BT}, of wheat are determined exclusively in the domestic economy, as shown in Exhibit 2. Suppose that this imaginary economy decides to engage in free trade. You can see that the world price (established in the world market for wheat), P_{AT}, is higher than the domestic price before trade, P_{BT}. In other words, the domestic economy has a comparative advantage in wheat, because it can produce wheat at a lower relative price than the rest of the world. So this wheat-producing country sells some wheat to the domestic market and some wheat to the world market, all at the going world price.

The price after trade (P_{AT}) is higher than the price before trade (P_{BT}). Because the world market is huge, the demand from the rest of the world at the world price (P_{AT}) is assumed to be perfectly elastic. That is, domestic wheat farmers can sell all the wheat they want at the world price. If you were a wheat farmer in Nebraska, would you rather sell all your bushels of wheat at the higher world price or the lower domestic price? As a wheat farmer, you would surely prefer the higher world price. But this preference is not good news for domestic cereal and bread eaters, who now have to pay more for products made with wheat because P_{AT} is greater than P_{BT}.

Graphically, we can see how free trade and exports affect both domestic consumers and domestic producers. At the higher world price, P_{AT}, domestic wheat producers are receiving larger amounts of producer surplus. Before trade, they received a surplus equal to area e + f; after trade, they received surplus b + c + d + e + f, for a net gain of area b + c + d. However, part of the domestic producers' gain comes at domestic consumers' expense. Specifically, consumers had a consumer surplus equal to area a + b + c before the trade (at P_{BT}), but they now have only area a (at P_{AT})—a loss of area b + c.

Area b reflects a redistribution of income, because producers are gaining exactly what consumers are losing. Is that good or bad? We can't say objectively whether

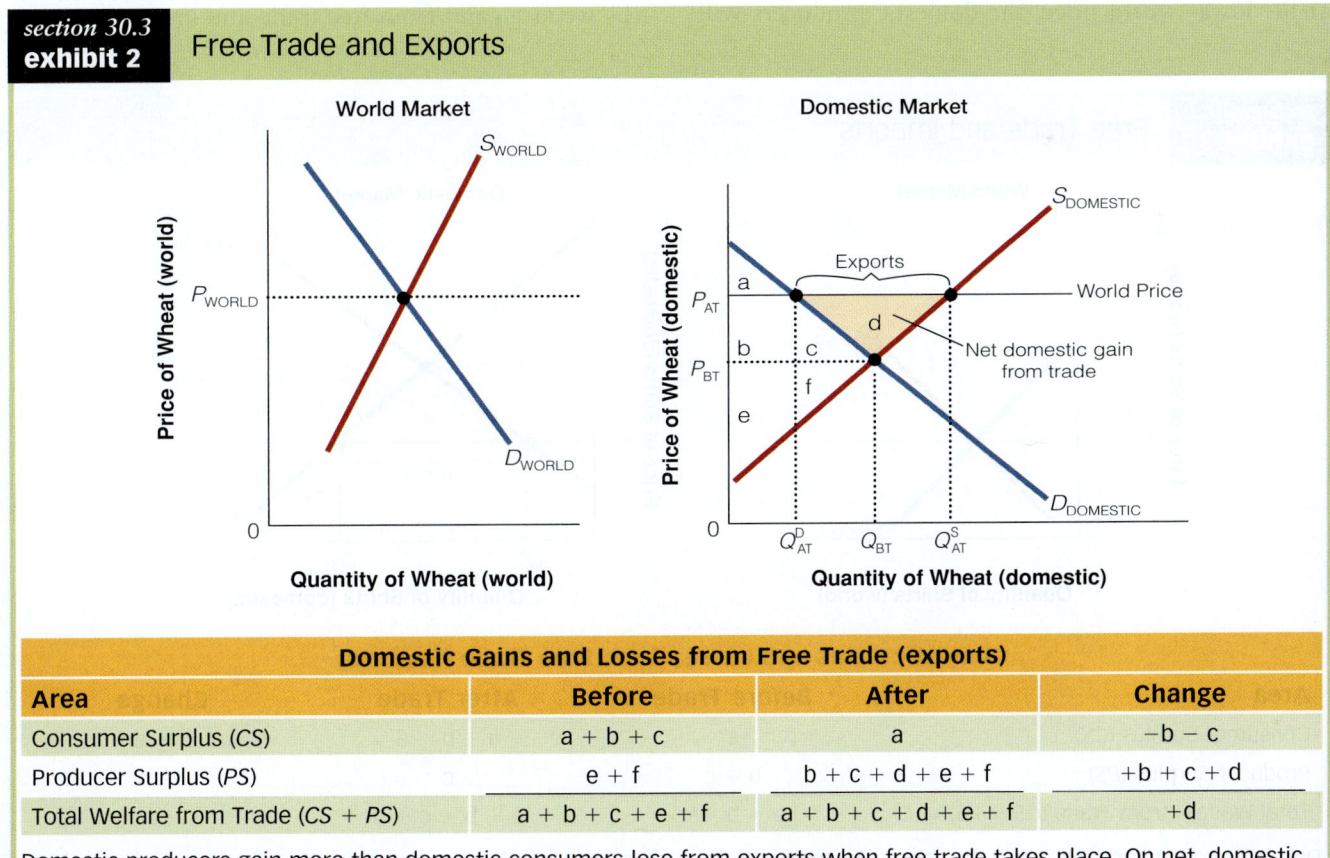

section 30.3 exhibit 2 Free Trade and Exports

Domestic Gains and Losses from Free Trade (exports)

Area	Before	After	Change
Consumer Surplus (CS)	a + b + c	a	− b − c
Producer Surplus (PS)	e + f	b + c + d + e + f	+ b + c + d
Total Welfare from Trade (CS + PS)	a + b + c + e + f	a + b + c + d + e + f	+ d

Domestic producers gain more than domestic consumers lose from exports when free trade takes place. On net, domestic wealth rises by area d.

consumers or producers are more deserving. However, the net benefits from allowing free trade and exports are clearly visible in area d. Without free trade, no one gets area d. That is, on net, members of the domestic society gain when domestic wheat producers are able to sell their wheat at the higher world price. Although domestic wheat consumers lose from the free trade, those negative effects are more than offset by the positive gains captured by producers. Area d is the net increase in domestic wealth (the welfare gain) from free trade and exports.

Free Trade and Imports—Domestic Consumers Gain More Than Domestic Producers Lose

Now suppose that our economy does not produce shirts as well as other countries of the world. In other words, other countries have a comparative advantage in producing shirts, and the domestic price for shirts is above the world price. This scenario is illustrated in Exhibit 3. At the new, lower world price, the domestic producer will supply quantity Q^S_{AT}. However, at the lower world price, the domestic producers will not produce the entire amount demanded by domestic consumers, Q^D_{AT}. At the world price, reflecting the world supply and demand for shirts, the difference between what is domestically supplied and what is domestically demanded is supplied by imports.

At the world price (established in the world market for shirts), we assume that the world supply to the domestic market curve is perfectly elastic—that the producers of the world can supply all that domestic consumers are willing to buy at the going price. At the world price, Q^S_{AT} is supplied by domestic producers, and the difference between Q^D_{AT} and Q^S_{AT} is imported from other countries.

Who wins and who loses from free trade and imports? Domestic consumers benefit from paying a lower price for shirts. In Exhibit 3, before trade, consumers only received area a in consumer surplus. After trade, the price fell and quantity purchased increased, causing the area of consumer surplus to increase from area a to area a + b + d, a gain of b + d. Domestic producers lose because they are now selling their shirts at the lower world price, P_{AT}. The producer surplus before trade was b + c. After trade, the producer surplus falls to area c, reducing producer surplus by area b. Area b, then, represents a redistribution from producers to consumers; but area d is the net increase in domestic wealth (the welfare gain) from free trade and imports.

section 30.3 exhibit 3 Free Trade and Imports

Domestic Gains and Losses from Free Trade (imports)

Area	Before Trade	After Trade	Change
Consumer Surplus (CS)	a	a + b + d	b + d
Producer Surplus (PS)	b + c	c	−b
Total Welfare from Trade (CS + PS)	a + b + c	a + b + c + d	+d

Domestic consumers gain more than domestic producers lose from imports when free trade is allowed. On net, domestic wealth rises by area d.

SECTION CHECK

1. The difference between what a consumer is willing and able to pay and what a consumer actually has to pay is called consumer surplus.
2. The difference between what a supplier is willing and able to supply and the price a supplier actually receives for selling a good or service is called producer surplus.
3. With free trade and exports, domestic producers gain more than domestic consumers lose.
4. With free trade and imports, domestic consumers gain more than domestic producers lose.

---

1. How does voluntary trade generate both consumer and producer surplus?
2. If the world price of a good is greater than the domestic price prior to trade, why does it imply that the domestic economy has a comparative advantage in producing that good?
3. If the world price of a good is less than the domestic price prior to trade, why does it imply that the domestic economy has a comparative disadvantage in producing that good?
4. When a country has a comparative advantage in the production of a good, why do domestic producers gain more than domestic consumers lose from free international trade?
5. When a country has a comparative disadvantage in a good, why do domestic consumers gain more than domestic producers lose from free international trade?
6. Why do U.S. exporters, such as farmers, favor free trade more than U.S. producers of domestic products who face competition from foreign imports, such as the automobile industry?

SECTION 30.4 Tariffs, Import Quotas, and Subsidies

* What is a tariff?
* What are the effects of a tariff?
* What are the effects of an import quota?
* What is the economic impact of subsidies?

Tariffs

A **tariff** is a tax on imported goods. Tariffs are usually relatively small revenue producers that retard the expansion of trade. They bring about higher prices and revenues for domestic producers, and lower sales and revenues for foreign producers. Moreover, tariffs lead to higher prices for domestic consumers. In fact, the gains to producers are more than offset by the losses to consumers. With the aid of a graph we will see how the gains and losses from tariffs work.

tariff
a tax on imports

The Domestic Economic Impact of Tariffs

The domestic economic impact of tariffs is presented in Exhibit 1, which illustrates the supply and demand curves for domestic consumers and producers of shoes. In a typical international supply and demand illustration, the intersection of the world supply and demand curves would determine the domestic market price. However, with import tariffs, the

section 30.4 exhibit 1 — Free Trade and Tariffs

Area	Before Tariffs	After Tariffs	Change
Consumer Surplus (CS)	a + b + c + d + e + f	a + b	−c − d − e − f
Producer Surplus (PS)	g	c + g	+c
Government Revenues (Tariff)	0	e	+e
Total Welfare from Tariff (CS + PS + Tariff Revenues)	a + b + c + d + e + f + g	a + b + c + e + g	−d − f

In the case of a tariff, we see that consumers lose more than producers and government gain. On net, the deadweight loss associated with the new tariff is represented by area d + f.

domestic price of shoes is greater than the world price, as in Exhibit 1. We consider the world supply curve (S_W) for domestic consumers to be perfectly elastic; that is, we can buy all we want at the world price (P_W). At the world price, domestic producers are only willing to provide quantity Q_S, but domestic consumers are willing to buy quantity Q_D—more than domestic producers are willing to supply. Imports make up the difference.

As you can see in Exhibit 1, the imposition of the tariff shifts the perfectly elastic supply curve from foreigners to domestic consumers upward from S_{WORLD} to $S_{WORLD+TARIFF}$, but it does not alter the domestic supply or demand curve. At the resulting higher domestic price (P_{W+T}), domestic suppliers are willing to supply more, Q'_S, but domestic consumers are willing to buy less, Q'_D. At the new equilibrium, the domestic price (P_{W+T}) is higher and the quantity of shoes demanded (Q'_D) is lower. But at the new price, the domestic quantity demanded is lower and the quantity supplied domestically is higher, reducing the quantity of imported shoes. Overall, then, tariffs lead to (1) a smaller total quantity sold, (2) a higher price for shoes for domestic consumers, (3) greater sales of shoes at higher prices for domestic producers, and (4) lower sales of foreign shoes.

Although domestic producers do gain more sales and higher earnings, consumers lose much more. The increase in price from the tariff results in a loss in consumer surplus, as shown in Exhibit 1. After the tariff, shoe prices rise to P_{W+T}, and, consequently, consumer surplus falls by area c + d + e + f, representing the welfare loss to consumers from the tariff. Area c in Exhibit 1 shows the gain to domestic producers as a result of the tariff. That is, at the higher price, domestic producers are willing to supply more shoes, representing a welfare gain to producers resulting from the tariff. As a result of the tariff revenues, government gains area e. This is the import tariff—the revenue government collects from foreign countries on imports. However, we see from Exhibit 1 that consumers lose more than producers and government gain from the tariff. That is, on net, the deadweight loss associated with the tariff is represented by area d + f.

Arguments for Tariffs

Despite the preceding arguments against trade restrictions, they continue to be levied. Some rationale for their existence is necessary. Three common arguments for the use of trade restrictions deserve our critical examination.

Temporary Trade Restrictions Help Infant Industries Grow

A country might argue that a protective tariff will allow a new industry to more quickly reach a scale of operation at which economies of scale and production efficiencies can be realized. That is, temporarily shielding the young industry from competition from foreign firms will allow the infant industry a chance to grow. With early protection, these firms will eventually be able to compete effectively in the global market. It is presumed that without this protection, the industry could never get on its feet. At first hearing, the argument sounds valid, but it involves many problems. How do you identify "infant industries" that genuinely have potential economies of scale and will quickly become efficient with protection? We do not know the long-run average total cost curves of industries, a necessary piece of information. Moreover, if firms and governments are truly convinced of the advantages of allowing an industry to reach a large scale, would it not be wise to make massive loans to the industry, allowing it to begin large-scale production all at once rather than slowly and at the expense of consumers? In other words, the goal of allowing the industry to reach its efficient size can be reached without protection. Finally, the history of infant industry tariffs suggests that the tariffs often linger long after the industry is mature and no longer in need of protection.

Tariffs Can Reduce Domestic Unemployment

Exhibit 1 shows how tariffs increase output by domestic producers, thus leading to increased employment and reduced unemployment in industries where tariffs have been imposed. Yet the overall employment effects of a tariff imposition are not likely to be positive; the argument is incorrect. Why? First, the imposition of a tariff by the United States on, say, foreign steel is going to be noticed in the countries adversely affected by the tariff. If a new tariff on steel lowers Japanese steel sales to the United States, the Japanese will likely retaliate by imposing tariffs on U.S. exports to Japan, say, on machinery exports. The retaliatory tariff will lower U.S. sales of machinery and thus employment in the U.S. machinery industries. As a result, the gain in employment in the steel industry will be offset by a loss of employment elsewhere.

Even if other countries did not retaliate, U.S. employment would likely suffer outside the industry gaining tariff protection. The way that other countries pay for U.S. goods is by getting dollars from sales to the United States—imports to us. If new tariffs lead to restrictions on imports, fewer dollars will be flowing overseas in payment for imports, which means that foreigners will have fewer dollars available to buy our exports. Other things being equal, this situation will tend to reduce our exports, thus creating unemployment in the export industries.

Tariffs Are Necessary for Reasons of National Security

Sometimes it is argued that tariffs are a means of preventing a nation from becoming too dependent on foreign suppliers of goods vital to national security. That is, by making foreign goods more expensive, we can protect domestic suppliers. For example, if oil is vital to operating planes and tanks, a cutoff of foreign supplies of oil during wartime could cripple a nation's defenses.

The national security argument is usually not valid. If a nation's own resources are depletable, tariff-imposed reliance on domestic supplies will hasten depletion of domestic reserves, making the country even *more* dependent on imports in the future. If we impose a high tariff on foreign oil to protect domestic producers, we will increase domestic output of oil in the short run; but in the process, we will deplete the stockpile of available reserves. Thus, the defense argument is of questionable validity. From a defense standpoint, it makes more sense to use foreign oil in peacetime and perhaps stockpile "insurance" supplies so that larger domestic supplies would be available during wars.

Are Tariffs Necessary to Protect Against Dumping?

Dumping occurs when a foreign country sells its products at prices below their costs or below the prices for which they are sold on the domestic market. For example, the Japanese government has been accused for years of subsidizing Japanese steel producers as they attempt to gain a greater share of the world steel market and greater market power. That is, the short-term losses from selling below cost may be offset by the long-term economic profits from employing this strategy. Some have argued that tariffs are needed to protect domestic producers against low-cost dumpers because they will raise the cost to foreign producers and offset their cost advantage.

The United States has antidumping laws; if a foreign country is found guilty of dumping, the United States can impose antidumping tariffs on that country's products, thereby raising the price of the foreign goods that are being dumped. In practice, however, it is often difficult to prove dumping; foreign countries may simply have lower steel production costs. So what may seem like dumping may in fact be comparative advantage.

Import Quotas

Like tariffs, **import quotas** directly restrict imports, leading to reductions in trade and thus preventing nations from fully realizing their comparative advantage. The case for quotas is probably even weaker than the case for tariffs. Unlike what occurs with a tariff, the U.S. government does not collect any revenue as a result of the import quota. Despite the higher prices, the loss in consumer surplus, and the loss in government revenue, quotas come about because people often view them as being less protectionist than tariffs—the traditional, most-maligned form of protection.

Besides the rather blunt means of curtailing imports by using tariffs and quotas, nations have devised still other, more subtle means of restricting international trade. For example, nations sometimes impose product standards, ostensibly to protect consumers against inferior merchandise. Effectively, however, those standards may be simply a means of restricting foreign competition. For example, France might keep certain kinds of wine out of the country on the grounds that they are made with allegedly inferior grapes or have an inappropriate alcoholic content. Likewise, the United States might prohibit automobile imports that do not meet certain standards in terms of pollutants, safety, and gasoline mileage. Even if these standards are not intended to restrict foreign competition, the regulations may nonetheless have that impact, restricting consumer choice in the process.

The Domestic Economic Impact of an Import Quota

The domestic economic impact of an import quota on autos is presented in Exhibit 2. The introduction of an import quota increases the price from the world price, P_W (established in the world market for autos) to P_{W+Q}. The quota causes the price to rise above the world price. The domestic quantity demanded falls and the domestic quantity supplied rises. Consequently, the number of imports is much smaller than it would be without the import quota. Compared with free trade, domestic producers are better off but domestic consumers are worse off. Specifically, the import quota results in a gain in producer surplus of area c and a loss in consumer surplus of area c + d + e + f. However, unlike the tariff case, where the government gains area e in revenues, the government does not gain any revenues with a quota. Consequently, the deadweight loss is even greater with quotas than with tariffs. That is, on net, the deadweight loss associated with the quota is represented by area d + e + f. Recall that the deadweight loss was only d + f for tariffs.

import quota
a legal limit on the imported quantity of a good that is produced abroad and can be sold in domestic markets

rent seeking
efforts by producers to gain profits from government protections such as tariffs and import quotas

If tariffs and import quotas hurt importing countries, why do they exist? The reason they exist is that producers can make large profits or "rents" from tariffs and import quotas. Economists call these efforts to gain profits from government protection **rent seeking**. Because this money, time, and effort spent on lobbying could have been spent producing something else, the deadweight loss from tariffs and quotas will likely understate the true deadweight loss to society.

The Economic Impact of Subsidies

Working in the opposite direction, governments sometimes try to encourage exports by subsidizing producers. With a subsidy, revenue is given to producers for each exported unit of output, which stimulates exports. Although not a barrier to trade like tariffs and quotas, subsidies can distort trade patterns and lead to inefficiencies. How do these distortions happen? With subsidies, producers will export goods not because their costs are lower than those of a foreign competitor but because their costs have been artificially reduced by government action, transferring income from taxpayers to the exporter. The subsidy does not reduce the amounts of actual labor, raw material, and capital costs of production—society has the same opportunity costs as before. The nation's taxpayers end up subsidizing the output of producers who, relative to producers in other countries, are inefficient. The nation, then, is exporting products in which it does

section 30.4 exhibit 2 — Free Trade and Import Quotas

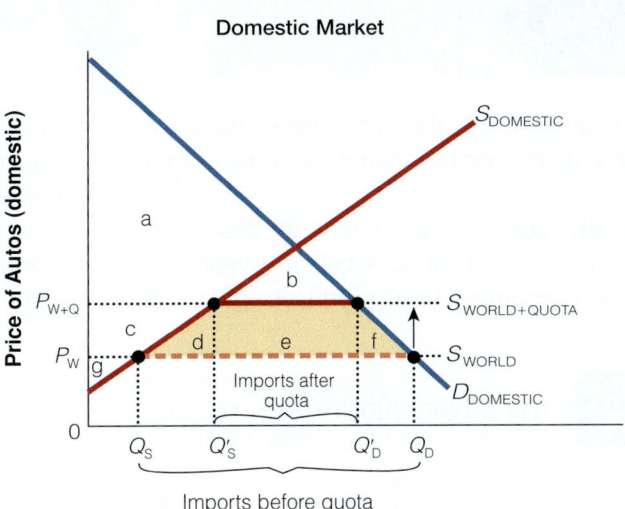

Gains and Losses from Import Quotas			
Area	Before Quota	After Quota	Change
Consumer Surplus (CS)	a + b + c + d + e + f	a + b	−c − d − e − f
Producer Surplus (PS)	g	c + g	+c
Total Welfare (CS + PS) from Quota	a + b + c + d + e + f + g	a + b + c + g	−d − e − f

With an import quota, the price rises from P_W to P_{W+Q}. Compared with free trade, consumers lose area c + d + e + f, while producers gain area b. The deadweight loss from the quota is area d + e + f. Under quotas, consumers lose and producers gain. The difference in deadweight loss between quotas and tariffs is area d, which the government is not able to pick up with import quotas.

Policy application: THE SUGAR QUOTA

The world price of sugar is much lower than the U.S. price. For example, in recent years, the U.S. price of sugar has been as high as 25 cents per pound while the world price was less than a nickel per pound. Why? The reason is that a sugar import quota protects the domestic sugar industry, by controlling how much foreign sugar can enter the country. This policy raised the price of U.S. sugar and helps both domestic producers and those foreign producers who have lobbied successfully for quota allotment. In 2006, five of the largest producing Caribbean nations received increases in their quota because of the devastation done to the sugar plantations in Louisiana by Hurricane Katrina.

The sugar quota impacts the price of everything from beverages to birthday cakes. As we can see graphically in Exhibit 3, this policy may be good for domestic sugar producers but it is clearly bad for consumers (and those producers who use sugar as an input to further production such as candy makers, several of whom have moved out of the United States). Even though the numbers are hypothetical

(continued)

POLICY application: THE SUGAR QUOTA (cont.)

for ease of quantifying, they are close enough to reality that you can see the monetary impact of the quota.

Notice the cost to consumers of this policy is area a + b + c + d, or $2.1 billion a year. But, part of what consumers lose, producers gain. U.S. producers gain area a, or $850 million, and foreign producers with quota allotments for the U.S. market received $600 million (remember they would have had to sell their sugar for $0.10, instead of $0.20, on the world market). Areas b and d represent the deadweight loss from this policy—$650 million.

section 30.4 exhibit 3 — The Sugar Quota

Gains and Losses Associated with Sugar Quota	
Loss of Consumer Surplus	Area a + b + c + d = $2.1 billion
Gain to U.S. Producers of Sugar	Area a = $850 million
Gain to Foreign Sugar Producers with Quota Allotments	Area c = $600 million
Deadweight Loss	Area b + d = $650 million
Area a = $850 million ($0.10 × 11 billion × 0.5) + ($0.10 × 3 billion)	Area c = $600 million ($0.10 × 6 billion)
Area b = $550 million ($0.10 × 11 billion × 0.5)	Area d = $100 million ($0.10 × 2 billion × 0.5)

in the news

True or False: Outsourcing Is a Crisis

—BY EDUARDO PORTER

If you read only the headlines, the future of globalization may seem scary, indeed.

American jobs have already been heading abroad. And as telecommunications and more powerful computers enable companies to take even more jobs overseas, the service sector, which accounts for about 85 percent of the United States work force, will be increasingly vulnerable to competition from the cheap labor pools of the developing world.

So the question looms: Is America on the verge of losing oodles of white-collar jobs?

Probably not. The threat of global outsourcing is easily overstated.

The debate over the global competition for jobs is awash in dire projections. All those legal assistants in New York and Washington, for example, could be replaced with smart young graduates from Hyderabad. Office support occupations—jobs like data entry assistant, file clerk and the entire payroll department - could also be carried out in remote locations. "We are really at the beginning stages of this, and it is accelerating rapidly," said Ron Hira, assistant professor of public policy at the Rochester Institute of Technology.

In a study published this year, two economists at the Organization for Economic Cooperation and Development in Brussels estimated that 20 percent of the developed world's employment could be "potentially affected" by global outsourcing. That could include all American librarians, statisticians, chemical engineers and air traffic controllers, the study said.

What does "potentially affected" mean? Even if offshoring didn't drain away all these jobs, global competition for employment—including workers in developing countries who earn so little by

chart 1 — A Variety of Jobs Being Outsourced

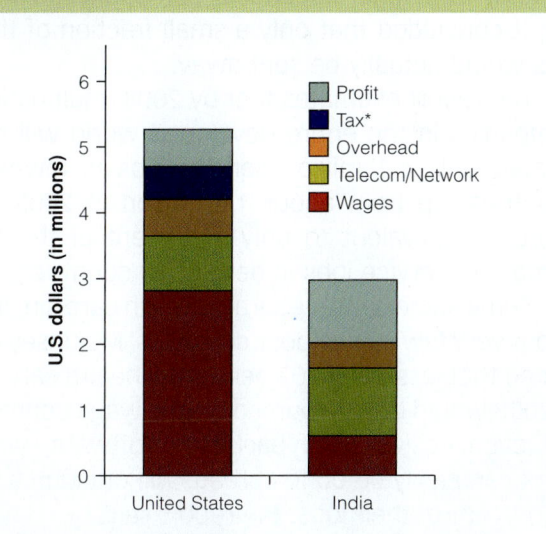

- Office 53%
- Computer 26%
- Business 11%
- Sales 4%
- Architecture 3%
- Legal 2%
- Art, design 1%

NOTE: Percentages computed on estimates for 2000.

SOURCE: John C. McCarthy (2002), "3.3 Million U.S. Services Jobs to Go Offshore," TechStrategy Research Brief, Forrester Research Inc., November 11.

chart 2 — Outsourcing to India Can Net Large Savings

(U.S. dollars in millions; United States ≈ 5.3, India ≈ 3.0)
Categories: Profit, Tax*, Overhead, Telecom/Network, Wages

*India exempts taxes for exports, including call centers for foreign businesses.
NOTE: This comparison is based on annual costs for a 100-seat call center.

SOURCE: Antonio Riera, Janmejaya Sinha, and Alpesh Shah (2002), "Passage to India: The Rewards of Remote Business Processing," The Boston Consulting Group.

continued

in the news

True or False: Outsourcing Is a Crisis (cont.)

comparison—could severely dent the livelihoods of American workers. "It isn't going to hurt in terms of jobs," said William J. Baumol, an economics professor at New York University who has studied the costs of globalization. "It is going to hurt in terms of wages."

But even if millions of tasks can be done by cheaper labor on the other side of the planet, businesses won't rush to move every job they can to wherever the cost is lowest. The labor market isn't quite that global, and it's unlikely to be anytime soon.

In a new set of reports, the McKinsey Global Institute, a research group known for its unabashedly favorable view of globalization, argued that 160 million service jobs—about 10 percent of total worldwide employment—could be moved to remote sites because these job functions don't require customer contact, local knowledge or complex interactions with the rest of a business.

Yet after surveying dozens of companies in eight sectors, from pharmaceutical companies to insurers, it concluded that only a small fraction of these jobs would actually be sent away.

The report estimates that by 2008, multinational companies in the entire developed world will have located only 4.1 million service jobs in low-wage countries, up from about 1.5 million in 2003. The figure is equivalent to only 1 percent of the total number of service jobs in developed countries.

Some sectors, like retail and health care, are likely to put very few jobs in poor countries. McKinsey estimated that less than 0.07 percent of health care jobs in 2008 would be outsourced to low-wage countries. But even designers of packaged software, whose work can easily be done abroad, will outsource only 18 percent of their jobs, the report said.

Moving tasks to faraway sites isn't simple. According to McKinsey's study, many business processes are difficult to separate into discrete chunks that can be sent away. Many insurance companies use information technology systems that have been cobbled together over time and would be difficult to manage remotely. Managers can be unwilling or unprepared to work overseas. And sometimes the tasks that can be sent offshore are too small to make the move worthwhile.

To top it off, there aren't that many suitable cheap workers available. Human-resources managers interviewed for the McKinsey study said that for reasons ranging from poor language skills to second-rate education systems, only about 13 percent of the young, college-educated professionals in the big developing countries are suitable to work for multinationals. And competition from local companies reduces this pool.

Sure, there are a billion Indians, but only a tiny percentage of the Indian work force have the appropriate qualifications. "Only a fraction have English as a medium of instruction, and only a fraction of those speak English that you or I can understand," said Jagdish N. Bhagwati, a professor of economics at Columbia University.

Of course, many of these obstacles can be overcome with time. The pool of adequate workers in poorer countries will grow, and companies will eventually iron out many of the logistical complications.

But that is likely to take a while."

From The New York Times, © June 19, 2005 The New York Times All rights reserved. Used by permission and protected by the Copyright Laws of the United States. The printing, copying, redistribution, or retransmission of the Material without express written permission is prohibited. www.nytimes.com.

not have a comparative advantage. Gains from trade in terms of world output are eliminated or reduced by such subsidies. Thus, subsidies, usually defended as a means of increasing exports and improving a nation's international financial position, are usually of dubious worth to the world economy and even to the economy doing the subsidizing.

According to the World Bank and the International Monetary Fund (IMF), world trade has benefited enormously from greater openness in trade since 1950. Tariffs on goods have fallen from a worldwide average of 26 percent to less than 9 percent today. On average, trade has grown more than twice as fast as world output.

Buy American. The Job You Save May Be Your Own. A common myth is that it's better for Americans to spend their money at home than abroad. The best way to expose the fallacy in this argument is to take it to its logical extreme. If it's better for me to spend my money here than abroad, then it's even better to buy in Texas than in New York, better yet to buy in Dallas than in Houston . . . in my own neighborhood . . . within my own family . . . to consume only what I can produce. Alone and poor.

SECTION CHECK

1. A tariff is a tax on imported goods.
2. Tariffs bring about higher prices and revenues to domestic producers and lower sales and revenues to foreign producers. Tariffs lead to higher prices and reduce consumer surplus for domestic consumers. Tariffs result in a net loss in welfare because the loss in consumer surplus is greater than the gain to producers and the government.
3. Arguments for the use of tariffs include: tariffs help infant industries grow; tariffs can reduce domestic unemployment; new tariffs can help finance our international trade; and tariffs are necessary for national security reasons.
4. Like tariffs, import quotas restrict imports, lowering consumer surplus and preventing countries from fully realizing their comparative advantage. The net loss in welfare from a quota is proportionately larger than for a tariff because it does not result in government revenues.
5. Sometimes government tries to encourage production of a certain good by subsidizing its production with taxpayer dollars. Because subsidies stimulate exports, they are not a barrier to trade like tariffs and import quotas. However, they do distort trade patterns and cause overall inefficiencies.

1. Why do tariffs increase domestic producer surplus but decrease domestic consumer surplus?
2. How do import tariffs increase employment in "protected" industries but at the expense of a likely decrease in employment overall?
3. Why is the national security argument for tariffs questionable?
4. Why is the domestic argument for import quotas weaker than the case for tariffs?
5. Why would foreign producers prefer import quotas to tariffs, even if they resulted in the same reduced level of imports?
6. Why does subsidizing exports by industries without a comparative advantage tend to harm the domestic economy, on net?

Interactive Chapter Summary

Fill in the blanks:

1. In a typical year, about _____ percent of the world's output is traded in international markets.

2. In the global economy, one country's exports are another country's _____.

3. _____ trade implies that both participants in an exchange of goods and services anticipate an improvement in their economic welfare.

4. The theory that explains how trade can be beneficial to both parties centers on the concept of _____.

5. A person, a region, or a country has a comparative advantage over another person, region, or country in producing a particular good or service if it produces a good or service at a lower _____ than others do.

6. What is important for mutually beneficial specialization and trade is _____ advantage, not _____ advantage.

7. Trade has evolved in large part because different geographic areas have _____ resources and therefore _____ production possibilities.

8. If Techland can produce more of both grain and computers than Grainsville, Techland has a(n) _____ advantage in both products.

9. The difference between the most a consumer would be willing to pay for a quantity of a good and what a consumer actually has to pay is called _____ surplus.

10. We can better analyze the impact of trade with the tools of _____ and _____ surplus.

11. Once the equilibrium output is reached at the equilibrium price, the sum of _____ and _____ is maximized.

12. When the domestic economy has a comparative advantage in a good because it can produce it at a lower relative price than the rest of the world can, international trade _____ the domestic market price to the world price, benefiting domestic _____ but harming domestic _____.

13. When the domestic economy has a comparative advantage in a good, allowing international trade redistributes income from domestic _____ to domestic _____, but _____ surplus increases more than _____ surplus decreases.

14. When a country does not produce a good relatively as well as other countries do, international trade will _____ the domestic price to the world price, with the difference between what is domestically supplied and what is domestically demanded supplied by _____.

15. When a country does not produce a good relatively as well as other countries do, international trade redistributes income from domestic _____ to domestic _____ and causes a net _____ in domestic wealth.

16. A(n) _____ is a tax on imported goods.

17. Tariffs bring about _____ prices and revenues to domestic producers, _____ sales and revenues to foreign producers, and _____ prices to domestic consumers.

18. With import tariffs, the domestic price of goods is _____ than the world price.

19. If import tariffs are imposed, at the new price the domestic quantity demanded is _____, and the quantity supplied domestically is _____, _____ the quantity of imported goods.

20. Import tariffs benefit domestic _____ and _____ but harm domestic _____.

21. One argument for tariffs is that tariff protection is necessary _____ to allow a new industry to more quickly reach a scale of operation at which economies of scale and production efficiencies can be realized.

22. Tariffs lead to _____ output and employment and reduced unemployment in domestic industries where tariffs are imposed.

23. If new tariffs lead to restrictions on imports, _____ dollars will be flowing overseas in payment for imports, which means that foreigners will have _____ dollars available to buy U.S. exports.

24. If a nation's own resources are depletable, tariff-imposed reliance on domestic supplies will _____ depletion of domestic reserves.

25. An import _____ gives producers from another country a maximum number of units of the good in question that can be imported within any given time span.

26. The case for import quotas is _____ than the case for import tariffs.

27. Tariffs and import quotas are rather suspect and exist because of producers' lobbying efforts to gain profits from government protection, which is called _____.

28. Dumping occurs when a foreign country sells its products at prices _____ their costs or _____ the prices they are sold at in the domestic market.

29. If a foreign country is found guilty of dumping, the United States can impose _____ tariffs.

30. Governments sometimes try to encourage exports by _____ producers.

31. With subsidies, a nation's taxpayers end up subsidizing the output of producers who, relative to producers in other countries, are _____.

32. Gains from trade in terms of world output are _____ by export subsidies.

Answers: 1. 15 2. imports 3. Voluntary 4. comparative advantage 5. comparative 6. opportunity cost 7. different; different 8. absolute 9. consumer; producer 10. consumer; producer 11. consumer surplus; producer surplus 12. raises; producers; consumers 13. consumers; producers; producer; consumer 14. lower; imports 15. producers; consumers; increase 16. tariff 17. higher; lower; higher 18. greater 19. lower; greater; reducing 20. producers; the government; consumers 21. temporarily 22. increased 23. fewer; fewer 24. hasten 25. quota 26. weaker 27. rent seeking 28. below; below 29. antidumping 30. subsidizing 31. inefficient 32. reduced

Key Terms and Concepts

comparative advantage 918
consumer surplus 926
producer surplus 926
tariff 929
import quota 932
rent seeking 932

Section Check Answers

30.1 The Growth in World Trade

1. **Why is it important to understand the effects of international trade?**
   All countries are importantly affected by international trade, although the magnitude of the international trade sector varies substantially by country. International connections mean that any of a large number of disturbances that originate elsewhere may have important consequences for the domestic economy.

2. **Why would U.S. producers and consumers be more concerned about Canadian trade restrictions than Swedish trade restrictions?**
   The United States and Canada are the two largest trading partners in the world. This means that the effects of trade restrictions imposed by Canada would have a far larger effect on the United States than similar restrictions imposed by Sweden. (For certain items, however, the magnitude of our trade with Sweden is greater than it is with Canada, so for these items Swedish restrictions would be of more concern.)

30.2 Comparative Advantage and Gains from Trade

1. **Why do people voluntarily choose to specialize and trade?**
   Voluntary specialization and trade among self-interested parties only takes place because all the parties involved expect that their benefits from this specialization (according to comparative advantage) and exchange will exceed their costs.

2. **How could a country have an absolute advantage in producing one good or service without also having a comparative advantage in its production?**
   If one country was absolutely more productive at everything than another country but wasn't equally more productive at everything, there would still be some things in which it had a comparative disadvantage. For instance, if country A was three times as productive in making X and two times as productive in making Y as country B, it would have a comparative advantage in making X (it gives up less Y for each X produced) and a comparative disadvantage in making Y (it gives up more X for each Y produced), relative to country B.

3. **Why do you think the introduction of the railroad reduced self-sufficiency in the United States?**
   Prior to the introduction of the railroad, the high cost of transportation overwhelmed the gains from specializing according to comparative advantage in much of the United States (production cost differences were smaller than the costs of transportation). The railroads reduced transportation costs enough that specialization and exchange became beneficial for more goods and services, and self-sufficiency due to high transportation costs declined.

4. **If you can wash the dishes in two-thirds the time it takes your younger sister to wash them, do you have a comparative advantage in washing the dishes with respect to her?**
   We can't know the answer to this question without more information. It is not the time taken to wash the dishes that matters in determining comparative advantage but the opportunity cost of the time in terms of

forgone value elsewhere. If your younger sister is less than two-thirds as good at other chores than you, she is relatively better at washing the dishes and so would have a comparative advantage in washing the dishes. If she is more than two-thirds as good at other chores, she is relatively better at these chores and so would have a comparative disadvantage in washing the dishes.

30.3 Supply and Demand in International Trade

1. **How does voluntary trade generate both consumer and producer surplus?**

   Voluntary trade generates consumer surplus because a rational consumer would not purchase if he did not value the benefits of purchase at greater than its cost, and consumer surplus is the difference between that value and the cost he is forced to pay. Voluntary trade generates producer surplus because a rational producer would not sell additional units unless the price he received was greater than his marginal cost, and producer surplus is the difference between the revenues received and the costs producers must bear to produce the goods that generate those revenues.

2. **If the world price of a good is greater than the domestic price prior to trade, why does it imply that the domestic economy has a comparative advantage in producing that good?**

   If the world price of a good is greater than the domestic price prior to trade, this implies that the domestic marginal opportunity cost of production is less than the world marginal opportunity cost of production. But this means that the domestic economy has a comparative advantage in that good.

3. **If the world price of a good is less than the domestic price prior to trade, why does it imply that the domestic economy has a comparative disadvantage in producing that good?**

   If the world price of a good is less than the domestic price prior to trade, this implies that the domestic marginal opportunity cost of production is greater than the world marginal opportunity cost of production. But this means that the domestic economy has a comparative disadvantage in that good.

4. **When a country has a comparative advantage in the production of a good, why do domestic producers gain more than domestic consumers lose from free international trade?**

   When a country has a comparative advantage in producing a good, the marginal benefit from exporting is the world price, which is greater than the forgone value domestically (along the domestic demand curve) for those units of domestic consumption "crowded out" and greater than the marginal cost of the expanded output. Therefore, there are net domestic gains to international trade (the gains to domestic producers exceed the losses to domestic consumers).

5. **When a country has a comparative disadvantage in a good, why do domestic consumers gain more than domestic producers lose from free international trade?**

   When a country has a comparative disadvantage in producing a good, the marginal cost of importing is the world price, which is less than the additional value (along the domestic demand curve) for those units of expanded domestic consumption and less than the marginal cost of the domestic production "crowded out." Therefore, there are net domestic gains to international trade (the gains to domestic consumers exceed the losses to domestic producers).

6. **Why do U.S. exporters, such as farmers, favor free trade more than U.S. producers of domestic products who face competition from foreign imports, such as the automobile industry?**

   Exporters favor free trade over restrictions on what they sell in other countries because it increases the demand and therefore the price for their products, which raises their profits. Those who must compete with importers want those imports restricted rather than freely traded because it increases the demand and therefore the price for their domestically produced products, which raises their profits.

30.4 Tariffs, Import Quotas, and Subsidies

1. **Why do tariffs increase domestic producer surplus but decrease domestic consumer surplus?**

   Tariffs raise the price of imported goods to domestic consumers, resulting in higher prices received by domestic producers as well. Thus, the higher price reduces domestic consumer surplus but increases domestic producer surplus.

2. **How do import tariffs increase employment in "protected" industries but at the expense of a likely decrease in employment overall?**

   Import tariffs increase employment in "protected" industries because the barriers to lower-price imports increase the demand faced by domestic producers, increasing their demand for workers. However, imports are the means by which foreigners get the dollars to buy our exports, so restricted imports will mean restricted exports (even more so if other countries retaliate with import restrictions of their own). In addition, by raising the prices domestic consumers pay for the protected products (remember that domestic consumers lose more than domestic producers gain from protectionism), consumers are made poorer in real terms, which will reduce demand for goods, and therefore the labor to make them, throughout the economy.

3. **Why is the national security argument for tariffs questionable?**

   The national security argument for tariffs is questionable because tariffs increase current reliance on domestic supplies, which depletes the future stockpile of available reserves. With fewer domestic reserves, the country will be even more dependent on foreign supplies in the future. Buying foreign supplies and stockpiling them makes more sense as a way of reducing reliance on foreign supplies in wartime.

4. **Why is the domestic argument for import quotas weaker than the case for tariffs?**

   Tariffs at least use the price system as the basis of trade. Tariff revenues end up in a country's treasury, where they can be used to produce benefits for the country's citizens or to reduce the domestic tax burden. Import quotas, however, transfer most of those benefits to foreign producers as the higher prices they receive.

5. **Why would foreign producers prefer import quotas to tariffs, even if they resulted in the same reduced level of imports?**

   Restricting imports reduces supply, which increases the price that foreign producers receive on the units they sell, thus benefiting them. Tariffs, on the other hand, reduce the after-tariff price that foreign producers receive. If both reduce foreign sales by the same amount, foreign producers would clearly prefer import restrictions over tariffs.

6. **Why does subsidizing exports by industries without a comparative advantage tend to harm the domestic economy, on net?**

   Subsidizing industries in which a country has a comparative disadvantage (higher costs) must, by definition, require shifting resources from where it has a comparative advantage (lower costs) to where it has a comparative disadvantage. The value of the output produced from those resources (indirectly in the case of specialization and exchange) is lower as a result.

CHAPTER 30 STUDY GUIDE

True or False:

1. Although the importance of the international sector varies enormously from place to place, the volume of international trade increased substantially.
2. U.S. imports are considered a credit item in the balance of payment because the dollars sold to buy the necessary foreign currency add to foreign claims against U.S. buyers.
3. Our imports provide the means by which foreigners can buy our exports.
4. Nations' imports and exports of services are the largest component of the balance of payments.
5. When the United States runs a trade deficit in goods and services with the rest of the world, the rest of the world must be running a trade surplus in goods and services with the United States.
6. When the United States runs a trade deficit in goods, it must run a trade surplus in services.
7. In the global economy, imports equal exports because one country's exports are another country's imports.
8. In voluntary trade, both participants in an exchange anticipate an improvement in their economic welfare.
9. An area should specialize in producing and selling those items in which it has an absolute advantage.
10. Differences in opportunity costs provide an incentive to gain from specialization and trade.
11. The principle of comparative advantage can be applied to regional markets.
12. A trading area may be a locality, a region, or a nation.
13. If two nations with different opportunity costs of production specialize, total output of both products may be higher as a result.
14. By specializing in products in which it has a comparative advantage, an area can have more goods and services if it trades the added output for other goods and services that others can produce at a lower opportunity cost.
15. By specialization according to comparative advantage and trade, two parties can each achieve consumption possibilities that would be impossible for them without trade.
16. The difference between the least amount for which a supplier is willing to supply a quantity of a good or service and the revenues a supplier actually receives for selling it is called consumer surplus.
17. Trading at the market equilibrium price generates both consumer surplus and producer surplus.
18. Once the equilibrium output is reached at the equilibrium price, all of the mutually beneficial opportunities from trade between suppliers and demanders will have taken place.
19. The total gain to the economy from trade is the sum of consumer and producer surpluses.
20. When the domestic economy has a comparative advantage in a good, allowing international trade benefits domestic consumers but harms domestic producers.
21. When the domestic economy has a comparative advantage in a good, exporting that good increases domestic wealth because, while domestic consumers lose from the free trade, these negative effects are more than offset by the positive gains captured by producers.
22. When a country does not produce a good relatively as well as other countries do, international trade benefits domestic consumers but harms domestic producers.
23. When a country does not produce a good relatively as well as other countries do, allowing international trade will increase consumer surplus less than producer surplus decreases.
24. Tariffs are usually relatively large revenue producers for governments.
25. Tariffs result in gains to domestic producers that are more than offset by losses to domestic consumers.
26. The history of infant-industry tariffs suggests that the tariffs often linger long after the industry is mature and no longer in need of protection.
27. When foreign countries are dumping, they are trying to gain a greater share of the world market for their products.

28. What may seem like dumping may in fact be comparative advantage.
29. The overall domestic employment effects of a tariff imposition are likely to be positive.
30. If the imposition of a tariff leads to retaliatory tariffs by other countries, domestic employment outside the industry gaining the tariff protection will likely suffer.
31. Exporters in a country would generally be supportive of their country's imposing import tariffs.
32. From a national defense standpoint, rather than imposing import tariffs, it makes more sense to use foreign supplies in peacetime and perhaps stockpile "insurance" supplies so that large domestic supplies would be available during wars.
33. Like tariffs, quotas directly restrict imports; but the U.S. government does not collect any revenue as the result of an import quota, as it does with tariffs.
34. Nations have sometimes used product standards ostensibly designed to protect consumers against inferior, unsafe, dangerous, or polluting merchandise as a means of restricting foreign competition.
35. Because resources being spent on lobbying efforts could have produced something instead, the measured deadweight loss from tariffs and quotas will likely understate the true deadweight loss to society.
36. Unlike import tariffs and quotas, export subsidies tend to increase efficiency.
37. With subsidies, producers export goods not because their costs are lower than those of a foreign competitor but because their costs have been artificially reduced by government action transferring income from taxpayers to the exporter.
38. Export subsidies lead nations to export products in which they do not have a comparative advantage.

Multiple Choice:

1. Assume that the opportunity cost of producing a pair of pants in the United States is 2 pounds of rice, while in China, it is 5 pounds of rice. As a result,
   a. the United States has a comparative advantage over China in the production of pants.
   b. China has a comparative advantage over the United States in the production of rice.
   c. mutual gains from trade can be realized by both countries if the United States exports rice to China in exchange for shoes.
   d. mutual gains from trade can be realized by both countries if the United States exports pants to China in exchange for rice.
   e. all of the above except c are true.
2. In Samoa the opportunity cost of producing one coconut is four pineapples, while in Guam the opportunity cost of producing one coconut is five pineapples. In this situation,
   a. if trade occurs, both countries will be able to consume beyond the frontiers of their original production possibilities.
   b. Guam will be better off if it exports coconuts and imports pineapples.
   c. both Samoa and Guam will be better off if Samoa produces both coconuts and pineapples.
   d. mutually beneficial trade cannot occur.
3. Mutually beneficial trade will occur whenever the exchange rate between the goods involved is set at a level where
   a. each country can export a good at a price above the opportunity cost of producing the good in the domestic market.
   b. each country can import a good at a price above the opportunity cost of producing the good in the domestic market.
   c. the exchange ratio is exactly equal to the opportunity cost of producing the good in each country.
   d. each country will specialize in the production of those goods in which it has an absolute advantage.
   e. either b or d is true.

Questions 4–6 refer to the following data: Alpha can produce either 18 tons of oranges or 9 tons of apples in a year, while Omega can produce either 16 tons of oranges or 4 tons of apples in a year.

4. The opportunity costs of producing 1 ton of apples for Alpha and Omega, respectively, are
   a. 0.25 ton of oranges and 0.5 ton of oranges.
   b. 9 tons of oranges and 4 tons of oranges.
   c. 2 tons of oranges and 4 tons of oranges.
   d. 4 tons of oranges and 2 tons of oranges.
   e. 0.5 ton of oranges and 0.25 ton of oranges.

5. Which of the following statements is true?
    a. Alpha should export to Omega, but Omega should not export to Alpha.
    b. Because Alpha has an absolute advantage in both goods, no mutual gains from trade are possible.
    c. If Alpha specializes in growing apples and Omega specializes in growing oranges, they could both gain by specialization and trade.
    d. If Alpha specializes in growing oranges and Omega specializes in growing apples, they could both gain by specialization and trade.
    e. Because Alpha has a comparative advantage in producing both goods, no mutual gains from trade are possible.

6. Which of the following exchange rates between apples and oranges would allow both Alpha and Omega to gain by specialization and exchange?
    a. 1 ton of apples for 3 tons of oranges
    b. 3 tons of apples for 3 tons of oranges
    c. 2 tons of apples for 3 tons of oranges
    d. 1 ton of oranges for 0.2 ton of apples
    e. 1 ton of oranges for 0.8 ton of apples

7. After the United States introduces a tariff in the market for steel, the price of steel in the United States will
    a. decrease.
    b. increase.
    c. remain the same.
    d. change in an indeterminate manner.

8. If Japan does not have a comparative advantage in producing rice, the consequences of adopting a policy of reducing or eliminating imports of rice into Japan would include the following:
    a. Japan will be able to consume a combination of rice and other goods beyond their domestic production possibilities curve.
    b. The real incomes of Japanese rice producers would rise, but the real incomes of Japanese rice consumers would fall.
    c. The real incomes of Japanese rice consumers would rise, but the real incomes of Japanese rice producers would fall.
    d. The price of rice in Japan would fall.

9. The infant-industry argument for protectionism claims that an industry must be protected in the early stages of its development so that
    a. firms will be protected from subsidized foreign competition.
    b. domestic producers can attain the economies of scale to allow them to compete in world markets.
    c. adequate supplies of crucial resources will be available if needed for national defense.
    d. None of the above reflect the infant-industry argument.

10. Protectionist legislation is often passed because
    a. employers in the affected industry lobby more effectively than the workers in that industry.
    b. both employers and workers in the affected industry lobby for protectionist policies.
    c. trade restrictions often benefit domestic consumers in the long run, even though they must pay more in the short run.
    d. none of the above

11. Introducing a tariff on vitamin E would
    a. reduce imports of vitamin E.
    b. increase U.S. consumption of domestically produced vitamin E.
    c. decrease total U.S. consumption of vitamin E.
    d. do all of the above.
    e. do none of the above.

12. A new U.S. import quota on imported steel would be likely to
    a. raise the cost of production for steel-using American firms.
    b. generate tax revenue to the government.
    c. decrease U.S. production of steel.
    d. increase the production of steel-using American firms.
    e. do all of the above.

13. An import quota does which of the following?
    a. decreases the price of the imported goods to consumers
    b. increases the price of the domestic goods to consumers
    c. redistributes income away from domestic producers of those products toward domestic producers of exports
    d. a and c
    e. b and c

14. A crucial difference between the impacts of import quotas and of tariffs is that
    a. import quotas generate revenue to the domestic government, but tariffs do not.
    b. import quotas generate no revenue to the domestic government, but tariffs do.
    c. tariffs increase the prices paid by domestic consumers, but quotas do not.
    d. a and c
    e. b and c

15. If the United States could produce 0.5 ton of potatoes or 1 ton of wheat per worker per year, while Ireland could produce 3 tons of potatoes or 2 tons of wheat per worker per year, the country with the comparative advantage in producing wheat is _____ and the country with the absolute advantage in producing potatoes is _____.
    a. the United States; the United States
    b. the United States; Ireland
    c. Ireland; the United States
    d. Ireland; Ireland

16. According to international trade theory, a country should
    a. import goods in which it has an absolute advantage.
    b. export goods in which it has an absolute advantage.
    c. import goods in which it has a comparative disadvantage.
    d. import goods in which it has an absolute disadvantage.
    e. import goods when it has either a comparative or absolute disadvantage in producing them.

17. Relative to a no-international-trade initial situation, if the United States imported wine, the U.S. domestic price of wine
    a. would rise, but domestic output would fall.
    b. would fall, but domestic output would rise.
    c. would rise, and domestic output would rise.
    d. would fall, and domestic output would fall.

18. Relative to a no-international-trade initial situation, if the United States exported wine, the U.S. domestic price of wine
    a. would rise, but domestic output would fall.
    b. would fall, but domestic output would rise.
    c. would rise, and domestic output would rise.
    d. would fall, and domestic output would fall.

Problems:

1. Bud and Larry have been shipwrecked on a deserted island. Their economic activity consists of either gathering berries or fishing. We know that Bud can catch four fish in one hour or harvest two buckets of berries. In the same time Larry can catch two fish or harvest two buckets of berries.
    a. Fill in the following table assuming that they *each* spend four hours a day fishing and four hours a day harvesting berries.

	Fish per Day	Buckets of Berries per Day
Bud	_____	_____
Larry	_____	_____
Total	_____	_____

    b. If Bud and Larry don't trade with each other, who is better off? Why?

c. Assume that Larry and Bud operate on straight-line production possibilities curves. Fill in the following table:

	Opportunity Cost of a Bucket of Berries	Opportunity Cost of a Fish
Bud	_____	_____
Larry	_____	_____

d. If they traded, who has the comparative advantage in fish? In berries?
e. If Larry and Bud specialize in and trade the good in which they have a comparative advantage, how much of each good will be produced in an eight-hour day? What are the gains from trade?

2. The following table represents the production possibilities in two countries:

Country A		Country B	
Good X	Good Y	Good X	Good Y
0	32	0	24
4	24	4	18
8	16	8	12
12	8	12	6
16	0	16	0

Which country has a comparative advantage at producing Good X? How can you tell?
Which country has a comparative advantage at producing Good Y?

3. Suppose the United States can produce cars at an opportunity cost of two computers for each car it produces. Suppose Mexico can produce cars at an opportunity cost of eight computers for each car it produces. Indicate how both countries can gain from free trade.

4. Evaluate the following statement: "Small developing economies must first become self-sufficient before benefiting from international trade."

5. Evaluate the following statement: "The United States has an absolute advantage in growing wheat. Therefore, it must have a comparative advantage in growing wheat."

6. NAFTA (North American Free Trade Agreement) is an agreement among the United States, Canada, and Mexico to reduce trade barriers and promote the free flow of goods and services across borders. Many U.S. labor groups were opposed to NAFTA.
    Can you explain why? Can you predict how NAFTA might alter the goods and services produced in the participating countries?

7. If country A is the lowest opportunity cost producer of X and country B is the lowest opportunity cost producer of Y, what happens to their absolute and comparative advantages if country A suddenly becomes three times more productive at producing both X and Y than it was before?

8. Assume that Freeland could produce 8 units of X and no Y, 16 units of Y and no X, or any linear combination in between, and Braveburg could produce 32 units of X and no Y, 48 units of Y and no X, or any linear combination in between.
    a. What is the opportunity cost of producing X in Freeland? In Braveburg?
    b. If Freeland and Braveburg specialize according to comparative advantage, which directions will goods flow in trade?
    c. If trade occurs, what will the terms of trade between X and Y be?
    d. How large would transactions costs, transportation costs, or tariffs have to be to eliminate trade between Freeland and Braveburg?

9. To protect its domestic apple industry, Botswana has for many years prevented international trade in apples. The following graph represents the Botswana domestic market for apples. P_{BT} is the current price, and P_{AT} is the world price.

a. If the government allows world trade in apples, what will happen to the price of apples in Botswana? Why?
b. Indicate the amount of apples domestic producers produce after there is trade in apples as Q_{DT}. How many apples are imported?
c. Trade in imports causes producer surplus to be reduced by the amount b. Show b on the graph.
d. The gains from trade equal the amount increased consumer surplus exceeds the loss in producer surplus. Show this gain, g, on the graph.
e. Explain why consumers in Botswana would still be better off if they were required to compensate producers for their lost producer surplus.

10. Use the accompanying graphs to illustrate the effects of imposing a tariff on imports on the domestic price, the domestic quantity purchased, the domestic quantity produced, the level of imports, consumer surplus, producer surplus, the tariff revenue generated, and the total welfare effect from the tariff.

11. Using the accompanying graphs, illustrate the effects of opening up the domestic market to international trade on the domestic price, the domestic quantity purchased, the domestic quantity produced, imports or exports, consumer surplus, producer surplus, and the total welfare gain from trade.

12. Explain why imposing a tariff causes a net welfare loss to the domestic economy.

13. If imposing tariffs and quotas harms consumers, why don't consumers vigorously oppose the implementation of these protectionist policies?

14. Why does rent seeking imply that the traditional measure of deadweight loss from tariffs and quotas will likely understate the true deadweight loss to society?

15. Would you be in favor of freer trade or against it in the following circumstances?
    a. The move to freer trade is in another country and you are an exporter to that country.
    b. The move to freer trade is in your country and you compete with imports from other countries.
    c. The move to freer trade is in your country and you import parts for products you sell domestically.

16. Go through your local newspaper and locate four news items regarding the global economy. Identify the significance of each of these news items to the U.S. economy and whether they are likely to affect international trade.

International Finance

31

- 31.1 The Balance of Payments
- 31.2 Exchange Rates
- 31.3 Equilibrium Changes in the Foreign Exchange Market
- 31.4 Flexible Exchange Rates

When people travel to foreign countries, they pay for their goods and services in foreign currencies. For example, if we were in Italy and were buying Italian shoes, we would have to pay in euros—and we might want to know how much that will cost us in U.S. currency. In this chapter, we will learn how nations pay each other in world trade and how we measure how much buying and selling is going on. We will also learn about exchange rates.

SECTION 31.1 The Balance of Payments

* What is the balance of payments?
* What are the three main components of the balance of payments?
* What is the balance of trade?

Balance of Payments

The record of all of the international financial transactions of a nation over a year is called the balance of payments. The **balance of payments** is a statement that records all the exchanges requiring an outflow of funds to foreign nations or an inflow of funds from other nations. Just as an examination of gross domestic product accounts gives us some idea of the economic health and vitality of a nation, the balance of payments provides information about a nation's world trade position. The balance of payments is divided into three main sections: the current account, the capital account, and an "error term" called the statistical discrepancy. These are highlighted in Exhibit 1. Let's look at each of these components, beginning with the current account, which is made up of imports and exports of goods and services.

balance of payments
the record of international transactions in which a nation has engaged over a year

current account
a record of a country's imports and exports of goods and services, net investment income, and net transfers

The Current Account

Export Goods and the Current Account

A **current account** is a record of a country's imports and exports of goods and services, net investment income, and net transfers. Any time a foreign buyer purchases a good from a U.S. producer, the foreign buyer must pay the U.S. producer for the good. Usually, the foreign buyer must pay for the good in U.S. dollars, because the producer wants to pay his workers' wages and other input costs with dollars. Making this payment requires the foreign buyer to exchange units of her currency at a foreign exchange dealer for U.S. dollars. Because the United States gains claims for foreign goods by obtaining foreign currency in exchange for the dollars needed to buy exports, all exports of U.S. goods abroad are considered a credit, or plus (+), item in the U.S. balance of payments. Those foreign currencies are

section 31.1 exhibit 1 — U.S. Balance of Payments, 2008 (billions of dollars)

Type of Transaction				
Current Account			**Capital Account**	
1. Exports of goods	$ 1,291		10. U.S.-owned assets abroad	$ −54
2. Imports of goods	−2,112		11. Foreign-owned assets in the United States	599
3. Balance of trade (lines 1 + 2)		−821	12. Capital account balance (lines 10 + 11)	545
4. Service exports	544		13. Statistical discrepancy	128
5. Service imports	−405		14. Net Balance (lines 9 − 12 + 13)	$0
6. Balance on goods and services (lines 3 + 4 + 5)		−682		
7. Unilateral transfers (net)	−120			
8. Investment income (net)	129			
9. Current account balance (lines 6 + 7 + 8)		−673		

SOURCE: Bureau of Economic Analysis, Table 1.

later exchangeable for goods and services made in the country that purchased the U.S. exports.

Import Goods and the Current Account

When a U.S. consumer buys an imported good, however, the reverse is true: The U.S. importer must pay the foreign producer, usually in that nation's currency. Typically, the U.S. buyer will go to a foreign exchange dealer and exchange dollars for units of that foreign currency. Imports are thus a debit (−) item in the balance of payments, because the dollars sold to buy the foreign currency add to foreign claims for foreign goods, which are later exchangeable for U.S. goods and services. U.S. imports, then, provide the means by which foreigners can buy U.S. exports.

Nations import and export services like tourism.

Services and the Current Account

Even though imports and exports of goods are the largest components of the balance of payments, they are not the only ones. Nations import and export services as well. A particularly important service is tourism. When U.S. tourists go abroad, they are buying foreign-produced services in addition to those purchased by citizens there. Those services include the use of hotels, sightseeing tours, restaurants, and so forth. In the current account, these services are included in imports. On the other hand, foreign tourism in the United States provides us with foreign currencies and claims against foreigners, so they are included in exports. Airline and shipping services also affect the balance of payments. When someone from Italy flies American Airlines, that person is making a payment to a U.S. company. Because the flow of international financial claims is the same, this payment is treated just like a U.S. export in the balance of payments. If an American flies on Alitalia, however, Italians acquire claims against the United States; and so it is included as a debit (import) item in the U.S. balance-of-payments accounts.

Net Transfer Payments and Net Investment Income

Other items that affect the current account are private and government grants and gifts to and from other countries. When the U.S. gives foreign aid to another country, a debit occurs in the U.S. balance of payments because the aid gives foreigners added claims against the United States in the form of dollars. Private gifts, such as individuals sending money to relatives or friends in foreign countries, show up in the current account as debit items as well. Because the United States usually sends more humanitarian and military aid to foreigners than it receives, net transfers are usually in deficit.

Net investment income is also included in the current account (line 8)—U.S. investors hold foreign assets and foreign investors hold U.S. assets. Payments received by U.S. residents are added to the current account and payments made by U.S. residents are subtracted from the current account. In 2008, a net flow of $2 billion came into the United States.

The Current Account Balance

The balance on the current account is the net amount of credits or debits after adding up all transactions of goods (merchandise imports and exports), services, and transfer payments (e.g., foreign aid and gifts). If the sum of credits exceeds the sum of debits, the nation is said to run a balance-of-payments surplus on the current account. If debits exceed credits, however, the nation is running a balance-of-payments deficit on the current account.

The Balance of Trade and the Balance of the Current Account

The balance of payments of the United States for 2008 is presented in Exhibit 1. Notice that exports and imports of goods and services are by far the largest credits and debits. Notice also that U.S. exports of goods were $821 billion less than imports of goods. The import/export goods relationship is often called the **balance of trade.** The United States, therefore, experienced a balance-of-trade deficit that year of $821 billion.

balance of trade
the net surplus or deficit resulting from the level of exportation and importation of merchandise

However, some of the $821 billion trade deficit is offset by credits from a $139 billion surplus in services. This difference leads to a $682 billion deficit in the balance of goods and services. When $120 billion of net unilateral transfers (gifts and grants between the United States and foreigners) and $129 billion of investment income (net) from the United States are added (the foreigners gave more to the United States than the United States gave to the foreigners), the total deficit on the current account is $673 billion. Exhibit 2 shows the balance on the current account since 1975.

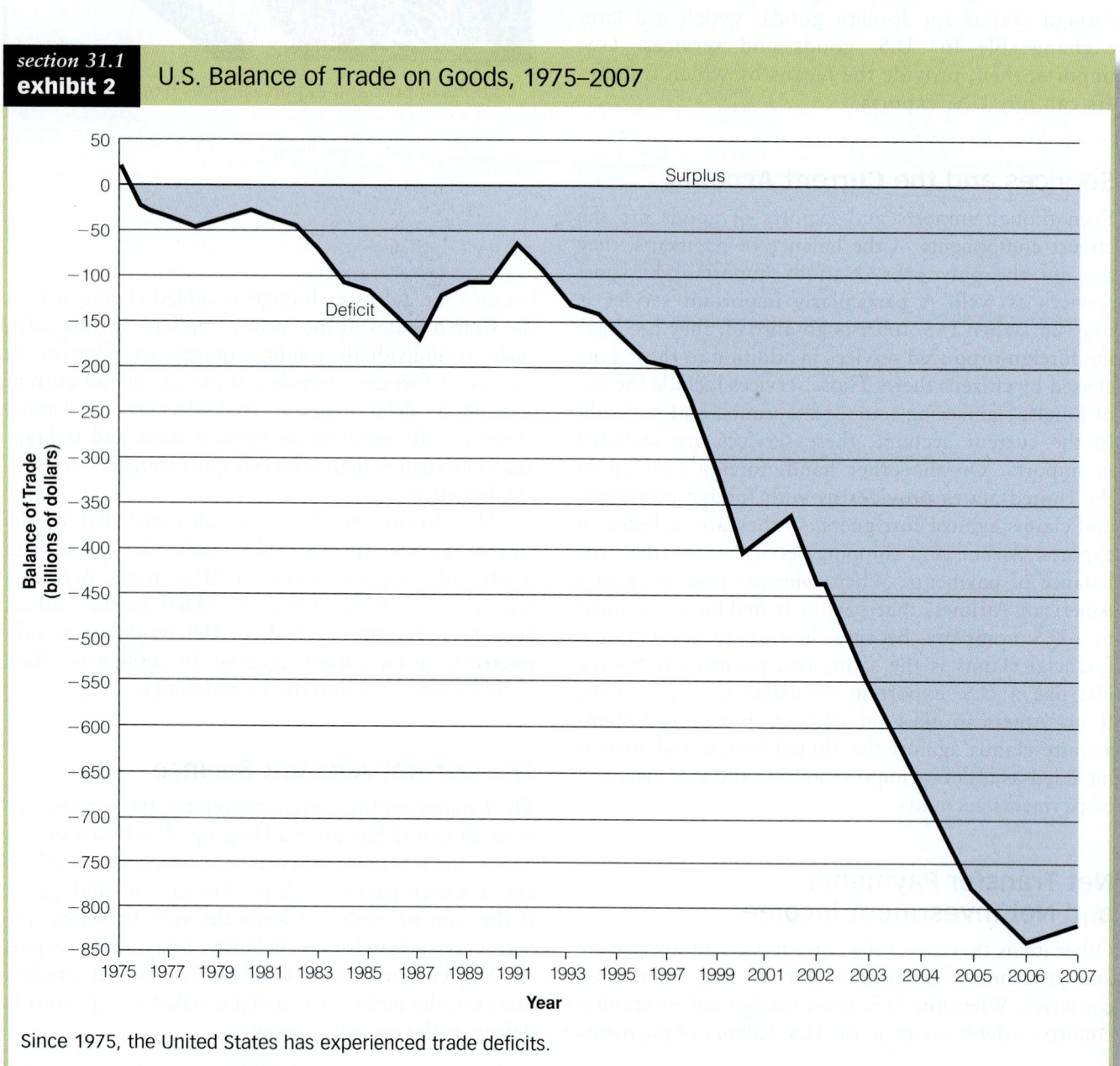

section 31.1
exhibit 2 U.S. Balance of Trade on Goods, 1975–2007

Since 1975, the United States has experienced trade deficits.

SOURCE: Bureau of Economic Analysis, 2009.

The Capital Account

How was this deficit on the current account financed? Remember that U.S. credits give us the financial means to buy foreign goods and that our credits were $545 billion less than our debits from imports and net unilateral transfers to foreign countries. This deficit on the current account balance is settled by movements of financial, or capital, assets. These transactions are recorded in the *capital account*, so that a current account deficit is financed by a capital account surplus. In short, the **capital account** records the foreign purchases or assets in the United States (a monetary inflow) and U.S. purchases of assets abroad (a monetary outflow).

capital account records the foreign purchases or assets in the domestic economy (a monetary inflow) and domestic purchases of assets abroad (a monetary outflow)

What Does the Capital Account Record?

Capital account transactions include such items as international bank loans, purchases of corporate securities, government bond purchases, and direct investments in foreign subsidiary companies. In 2008, the United States purchased foreign assets of $54 billion, which was a further debit because it provided foreigners with U.S. dollars. On the other hand, foreign investments in U.S. bonds, stocks, and other items totaled more than $599 billion. In addition, the United States and other governments buy and sell dollars. On net in 2008, foreign-owned assets in the United States made about $545 billion more than did U.S. assets abroad. On balance, then, a surplus (positive credit) in the capital account from capital movements amounted to $545 billion, offsetting the $673 billion deficit on current account.

The Statistical Discrepancy

In the final analysis, it is true that the balance-of-payments account (current account minus capital account) must balance so that credits and debits are equal. Why? Due to the reciprocal aspect of trade, every credit eventually creates a debit of equal magnitude. These errors are sometimes large and are entered into the balance of payments as the *statistical discrepancy*. Including the errors and omissions recorded as the statistical discrepancy, the balance of payments does balance. That is, the number of U.S. dollars demanded equals the number of U.S. dollars supplied when the balance of payments is zero.

Balance of Payments: A Useful Analogy

In concept, the international balance of payments is similar to the personal financial transactions of an individual. Each individual has a personal "balance of payments," reflecting that person's trading with other economic units: other individuals, corporations, and governments. People earn income or credits by "exporting" their labor service to other economic units or by receiving investment income (a return on capital services). Against that, they "import" goods from other economic units; we call these imports consumption. This debit item is sometimes augmented by payments made to outsiders (e.g., banks) on loans and so forth. Fund transfers, such as gifts to children or charities, are other debit items (or credit items for recipients of the assistance).

As individuals, if our spending on consumption exceeds our income from exporting our labor and capital services, we have a "deficit" that must be financed by borrowing or selling assets. If we "export" more than we "import," however, we can make new investments and/or increase our "reserves" (savings and investment holdings). Like nations, an individual who runs a deficit in daily transactions must make up for it through accommodating transactions (e.g., borrowing or reducing personal savings or investment holdings) to bring about an ultimate balance of credits and debits in his or her personal account.

SECTION CHECK

1. The balance of payments is the record of all the international financial transactions of a nation for any given year.
2. The balance of payments is made up of the current account and the capital account, as well as an "error term" called the statistical discrepancy.
3. The balance of trade refers strictly to the import and export of goods (merchandise) from/to other nations. If our imports of foreign goods are greater than our exports, we are said to have a balance-of-trade deficit.

(continued)

1. What is the balance of payments?
2. Why must British purchasers of U.S. goods and services first exchange pounds for dollars?
3. How is it that our imports provide foreigners with the means to buy U.S. exports?
4. What would have to be true for the United States to have a balance-of-trade deficit and a balance-of-payments surplus?
5. What would have to be true for the United States to have a balance-of-trade surplus and a current account deficit?
6. With no errors or omissions in the recorded balance-of-payments accounts, what should the statistical discrepancy equal?
7. A Nigerian family visiting Chicago enjoys a Chicago Cubs baseball game at Wrigley Field. How would this expense be recorded in the balance-of-payments accounts? Why?

SECTION 31.2 Exchange Rates

* What are exchange rates?
* How are exchange rates determined?
* How do exchange rates affect the demand for foreign goods?

The Need for Foreign Currencies

When a U.S. consumer buys goods from a seller in another country—who naturally wants to be paid in her own domestic currency—the U.S. consumer must first exchange U.S. dollars for the seller's currency in order to pay for those goods. American importers must, therefore, constantly buy yen, euros, pesos, and other currencies in order to finance their purchases. Similarly, someone in another country buying U.S. goods must sell his domestic currency to obtain U.S. dollars to pay for those goods.

The Exchange Rate

The price of a unit of one foreign currency in terms of another is called the **exchange rate**. If a U.S. importer has agreed to pay euros (the currency of the European Union) to buy a cuckoo clock made in the Black Forest in Germany, she would then have to exchange U.S. dollars for euros. If it takes $1 to buy 1 euro, then the exchange rate is $1 per euro. From the German perspective, the exchange rate is 1 euro per U.S. dollar.

exchange rate
the price of one unit of a country's currency in terms of another country's currency

derived demand
the demand for an input derived from consumers' demand for the good or service produced with that input

Changes in Exchange Rates Affect the Domestic Demand for Foreign Goods

Prices of goods in their currencies combine with exchange rates to determine the domestic price of foreign goods. Suppose the cuckoo clock sells for 100 euros in Germany. What is the price to U.S. consumers? Let's assume that tariffs and other transaction costs are zero. If the exchange rate is $1 = 1 euro, then the equivalent U.S. dollar price of the cuckoo clock is 100 euros times $1 per euro, or $100. If the exchange rate were to change to $2 = 1 euro, fewer clocks would be demanded in the United States, because the effective U.S. dollar price of the clocks would rise to $200 (100 euros × $2 per euro). The higher relative value of a euro compared to the dollar (or, equivalently, the lower relative value of a dollar compared to the euro) would lead to a reduction in U.S. demand for German-made clocks.

The Demand for a Foreign Currency

The demand for foreign currencies is known as a **derived demand**, because the demand for a foreign

Use what you've LEARNED
EXCHANGE RATES

Q Why is a strong dollar (i.e., exchange rate for foreign currencies is low) a mixed blessing?

A A strong dollar will lower the price of imports and make trips to foreign countries less expensive. Lower prices on foreign goods also help keep inflation in check and make investments in foreign financial markets (foreign stocks and bonds) relatively cheaper. However, it makes U.S. exports more expensive. Consequently, foreigners will buy fewer U.S. goods and services. The net effect is a fall in exports and a rise in imports—net exports fall. Note that some Americans are helped (vacationers going to foreign countries and those preferring foreign goods), while others are harmed (producers of U.S. exports, operators of hotels dependent on foreign visitors in the United States). A stronger dollar also makes it more difficult for foreign investors to invest in the United States.

---

currency derives directly from the demand for foreign goods and services or for foreign investment. The more that goods from a foreign country are demanded, the more of that country's currency is needed to pay for those goods. This increased demand for the currency will push up the exchange value of that currency relative to other currencies.

The Supply of a Foreign Currency

Similarly, the supply of foreign currency is provided by foreigners who want to buy the exports of a particular nation. For example, the more that foreigners demand U.S. products, the more of their currencies they will supply in exchange for U.S. dollars, which they use to buy our products.

Determining Exchange Rates

We know that the demand for foreign currencies is derived from the demand for foreign goods, but how does that affect the exchange rate? Just as in the product market, the answer lies with the forces of supply and demand. In this case, it is the supply of and demand for a foreign currency that determine the equilibrium price (exchange rate) of that currency.

The Demand Curve for a Foreign Currency

As Exhibit 1 shows, the demand curve for a foreign currency—the euro, for example—is downward sloping, just as it is in product markets. In this case,

section 31.2 exhibit 1 Equilibrium in the Foreign Exchange Market

Suppose the foreign exchange market is in equilibrium at 1 euro = $1.50. At any price higher than $1.50, a surplus of euros will result. At any price lower than $1.50, a shortage of euros will result.

however, the demand curve has a negative slope because as the price of the euro falls relative to the dollar, European products become relatively more inexpensive to U.S. consumers, who therefore buy more European goods. To do so, the quantity of euros demanded by U.S. consumers will increase to buy more European goods as the price of the euro falls. For this reason, the demand for foreign currencies is considered to be a derived demand.

The Supply Curve for Foreign Currency

The supply curve for a foreign currency is upward sloping, just as it is in product markets. In this case, as the price, or value, of the euro increases relative to the dollar, U.S. products will become relatively less expensive to European buyers, who will thus increase the quantity of dollars they demand. Europeans will, therefore, increase the quantity of euros supplied to the United States by buying more U.S. products.

Hence, the supply curve is upward sloping.

Equilibrium in the Foreign Exchange Market

Equilibrium is reached where the demand and supply curves for a given currency intersect. In Exhibit 1, the equilibrium price of a euro is $1.50. As in the product market, if the dollar price of euros is higher than the equilibrium price, an excess quantity of euros will be supplied at that price; that is, a surplus of euros will exist. Competition among euro sellers will push the price of euros down toward equilibrium.

Likewise, if the dollar price of euros is lower than the equilibrium price, an excess quantity of euros will be demanded at that price; that is, a shortage of euros will occur. Competition among euro buyers will push the price of euros up toward equilibrium.

On January 1, 1999, the euro became the currency in 11 countries: Belgium, Germany, Spain, France, Ireland, Italy, Luxembourg, the Netherlands, Austria, Portugal, and Finland. If the euro becomes relatively less expensive in terms of dollars (it now costs less to buy a euro), what will happen to the U.S. demand for European goods? If the price of the euro falls relative to the dollar, European products become relatively less expensive to U.S. consumers, who will tend to buy more European goods.

SECTION CHECK

1. The price of a unit of one foreign currency in terms of another is called the exchange rate.
2. The exchange rate for a currency is determined by the supply of and demand for that currency in the foreign exchange market.
3. If the dollar appreciates in value relative to foreign currencies, foreign goods become more inexpensive to U.S. consumers, increasing U.S. demand for foreign goods.

---

1. What is an exchange rate?
2. When a U.S. dollar buys relatively more British pounds, why does the cost of imports from England fall in the United States?
3. When a U.S. dollar buys relatively fewer yen, why does the cost of U.S. exports fall in Japan?
4. How does an increase in domestic demand for foreign goods and services increase the demand for those foreign currencies?
5. As euros get cheaper relative to U.S. dollars, why does the quantity of euros demanded by Americans increase? Why doesn't the demand for euros increase as a result?
6. Who brings exchange rates down when they are above their equilibrium value? Who brings exchange rates up when they are below their equilibrium value?

SECTION 31.3
Equilibrium Changes in the Foreign Exchange Market

* What factors cause the demand curve for a currency to shift?
* What factors cause the supply curve for a currency to shift?

Determinants in the Foreign Exchange Market

The equilibrium exchange rate of a currency changes many times daily. Sometimes, these changes can be quite significant. Any force that shifts either the demand for or supply of a currency will shift the equilibrium in the foreign exchange market, leading to a new exchange rate. Among such factors are changes in consumer tastes for goods, income levels, relative real interest rates, and relative inflation rates, as well as speculation.

Increased Tastes for Foreign Goods

Because the demand for foreign currencies is derived from the demand for foreign goods, any change in the U.S. demand for foreign goods will shift the demand schedule for foreign currency in the same direction. For example, if a cuckoo clock revolution sweeps through the United States, German producers will have reason to celebrate, knowing that many U.S. buyers will turn to Germany for their cuckoo clocks. However, because Germans will only accept payment in the form of euros, U.S. consumers and retailers must convert their dollars into euros before they can purchase their clocks. The increased taste for European goods in the United States will, therefore, lead to an increased demand for euros. As shown in Exhibit 1, this increased demand for euros shifts the demand curve to the right, resulting in a new, higher equilibrium dollar price of euros.

Relative Income Increases or Reductions in U.S. Tariffs

Any change in the average income of U.S. consumers will also change the equilibrium exchange rate, *ceteris paribus*. If on the whole incomes were to increase

section 31.3 exhibit 1 — Impact on the Foreign Exchange Market of a U.S. Change in Taste, Income Increase, or Tariff Decrease

An increase in the taste for European goods, an increase in U.S. incomes, or a decrease in U.S. tariffs can cause an increase in the demand for euros, shifting the demand for euros to the right from D_1 to D_2 and leading to a higher equilibrium exchange rate.

What impact will an increase in travel to Paris by U.S. consumers have on the dollar price of euros? For a consumer to buy souvenirs at the Eiffel Tower, she will need to exchange dollars for euros. It will increase the demand for euros and result in a new, higher dollar price of euros.

in the United States, Americans would buy more goods, including imported goods, hence more European goods would be bought. This increased demand for European goods would lead to an increased demand for euros, resulting in a higher exchange rate for the euro. A decrease in U.S. tariffs on European goods would tend to have the same effect as an increase in incomes, by making European goods more affordable. Exhibit 1 shows that it would again lead to an increased demand for European goods and a higher short-run equilibrium exchange rate for the euro.

European Incomes Increase, Reductions in European Tariffs, or Changes in European Tastes

If European incomes rose, European tariffs on U.S. goods fell, or European tastes for American goods increased, the supply of euros in the euro foreign exchange market would increase. Any of these changes would cause Europeans to demand more U.S. goods and therefore more U.S. dollars to purchase those goods. To obtain these added dollars, Europeans would have to exchange more of their euros, increasing the supply of euros on the euro foreign exchange market. As Exhibit 2 demonstrates, the result would be a rightward shift in the euro supply curve, leading to a new equilibrium at a lower exchange rate for the euro.

section 31.3 exhibit 2 — Impact on the Foreign Exchange Market of a European Change in Taste, Income Increase, or Tariff Decrease

If European incomes increase, European tariffs on U.S. goods fall, or European tastes for American goods increase, the supply of euros increases. The increase in demand for dollars causes an increase in the supply of euros, shifting it to the right, from S_1 to S_2.

How Do Changes in Relative Real Interest Rates Affect Exchange Rates?

If interest rates in the United States were to increase relative to, say, European interest rates, other things being equal, the rate of return on U.S. investments would increase relative to that on European investments. European investors would then increase their demand for U.S. investments and therefore offer euros for sale in order to buy dollars to buy U.S. investments, shifting the supply curve for euros to the right, from S_1 to S_2 in Exhibit 3.

In this scenario, U.S. investors would also shift their investments away from Europe by decreasing their demand for euros relative to their demand for dollars, from D_1 to D_2 in Exhibit 3. A subsequent, lower equilibrium price ($1.50) would result for the euro as a result of the increase in U.S. interest rates. That is, the euro would depreciate, because euros could now buy fewer units of dollars than before. In short, the higher U.S. interest rates would attract more investment to the United States, leading to a relative appreciation of the dollar and a relative depreciation of the euro.

Changes in the Relative Inflation Rate

If Europe experienced an inflation rate greater than that experienced in the United States, other things being equal, what would happen to the exchange rate? In this case, European products would become more expensive to U.S. consumers. Americans would then decrease the quantity of European goods demanded and thus decrease their demand for euros. The result would be a leftward shift of the demand curve for euros.

On the other side of the Atlantic, U.S. goods would become relatively cheaper to Europeans, leading Europeans to increase the quantity of U.S. goods demanded and thus to demand more U.S. dollars. This increased demand for dollars would translate into an increased supply of euros, shifting the supply curve for euros outward. Exhibit 4 shows the shifts of the supply and demand curves and the new lower equilibrium price for the euro resulting from the higher European rate.

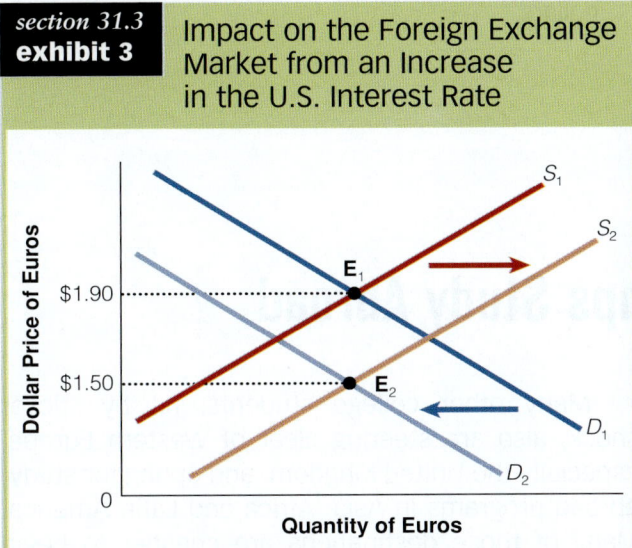

section 31.3 exhibit 3 Impact on the Foreign Exchange Market from an Increase in the U.S. Interest Rate

When U.S. interest rates increase, European investors increase their supply of euros to buy dollars—the supply curve of euros increases from S_1 to S_2. In addition, U.S. investors shift their investments away from Europe, decreasing their demand for euros and shifting the demand curve from D_1 to D_2. This shift leads to a depreciation of the euro; that is, euros can now buy fewer units of dollars.

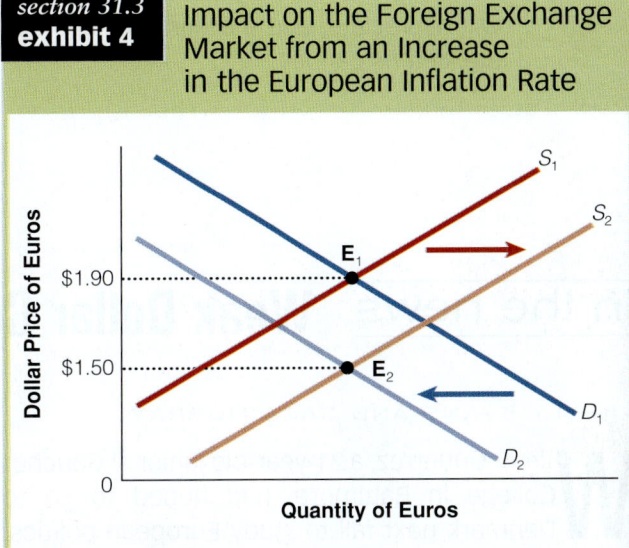

section 31.3 exhibit 4 Impact on the Foreign Exchange Market from an Increase in the European Inflation Rate

If Europe experiences a higher inflation rate than does the United States, European products become more expensive to U.S. consumers. As a result, those consumers demand fewer euros, shifting the demand for euros to the left, from D_1 to D_2. At the same time, U.S. goods become relatively cheaper to Europeans, who then buy more dollars by supplying euros, shifting the euro supply curve to the right, from S_1 to S_2. The result: a new, lower equilibrium price for the euro.

Expectations and Speculation

Every trading day, roughly a trillion dollars in currency trades hands in the foreign exchange markets. Suppose currency traders believe that in the future, the United States will experience more rapid inflation than will Japan. If currency speculators believe that the value of the dollar will soon be falling because of the anticipated rise in the U.S. inflation rate, those who are holding dollars will convert them to yen. This move will lead to an increase in the demand for yen—the yen appreciates and the dollar depreciates relative to the yen, *ceteris paribus*. In short, if speculators believe that the price of a country's currency is going to rise, they will buy more of that currency, pushing up the price and causing the country's currency to appreciate.

Use what you've LEARNED: DETERMINANTS OF EXCHANGE RATES

Q How will each of the following events affect the foreign exchange market?
a. American travel to Europe increases.
b. Japanese investors purchase U.S. stock.
c. U.S. real interest rates abruptly increase relative to world interest rates.
d. Other countries become less politically and economically stable relative to the United States.

A
a. The demand for euros increases (demand shifts right in the euro market), the dollar will depreciate, and the euro will appreciate, *ceteris paribus*.
b. The demand for dollars increases (demand shifts right in the dollar market), the dollar will appreciate, and the yen will depreciate, *ceteris paribus*. Alternatively, you could think of it as an increase in supply in the yen market.
c. International investors will increase their demand for dollars in the dollar market to take advantage of the higher interest rates. The dollar will appreciate relative to other foreign currencies, *ceteris paribus*.
d. More foreign investors will want to buy U.S. assets, resulting in an increase in demand for dollars.

---

in the news: Weak Dollar Crimps Study Abroad

—KELLY EVANS AND SARA MURRAY

Wilmer Gutierrez, a 21-year-old junior at Goucher College in Baltimore, had hoped to go to Denmark next fall to study European politics. But the weak dollar has prompted a change of plan: Now, he will head to Argentina to study the Latin American political system.

With the greenback down 20% against the Danish krone and up 4% against the Argentine peso in the past two years, Mr. Gutierrez says he has little choice but to head south. "It's very frustrating," he says.

Many other college students, hit by sticker shock, also are steering clear of Western Europe, especially the United Kingdom, and opting for study-abroad programs in Asia, Africa and Latin America. Many of those destinations are cheaper to begin with and have currencies that haven't been as rough on the dollar.

Over the past two years, the dollar, while up a bit from recent lows, has lost more than 20% of its value against the euro and about 6% against the pound. The result: While programs in places like Rome, Paris, Barcelona and London are still at the

in the news: Weak Dollar Crimps Study Abroad (cont.)

top of students' lists, enrollment there is slowing. And interest in alternative destinations is surging.

Nearly a quarter of a million students from the U.S. studied abroad for academic credit during the 2005–06 school year, according to the most recent data from the Institute of International Education, a New York–based nonprofit organization that administers study-abroad programs. Each college handles study-abroad programs differently—some directly host programs in other countries so students pay the same tuition as they would for a semester at home in the U.S. Others allow students to enroll in programs offered by other colleges or by third-party study-abroad providers that enroll them directly in foreign institutions.

Language students often choose their location to become fluent speakers and learn about the culture of a chosen region; others, such as business students, may choose a program that enhances their resume (like China, India, or the Middle East).

Geoffrey Bannister, president and chief academic officer of Cultural Experiences Abroad, a company based in Tempe, Ariz., that runs study-abroad programs, says enrollment in the company's Western Europe programs grew just 8% for next fall, much less than the usual increase of 20% to 25%. Buenos Aires, meanwhile, is getting a lot of interest, he says.

Nathan Bullock, a University of Richmond sophomore who is majoring in history and international studies, considered expenses carefully when deciding between Hong Kong and France for the current semester.

The university was going to charge him the same tuition regardless of where he went, so his decision came down to room and board—and he knew his dollars would go further in Hong Kong, where the currency is pegged to the dollar.

"Just getting an apartment or living with a family would be so expensive in France," he says. In Hong Kong, his room and board costs about HK$3,000, or about US$385 a semester. In addition, it's an easy jumping-off point for other parts of Asia, where traveling can be a bargain.

Even in Shanghai, the most expensive place he has visited, Mr. Bullock spent only 55 yuan a night—less than $8—for a room in a hostel. By comparison, in Paris, the cheapest hostels run 12 to 16 euros, or about $18 to $24.

American students in Europe understand the need to scale back. "Just to lead a normal student life here is so expensive," says Sarah Ott, a junior at Ohio's Kenyon College who is studying in Paris.

To save money, Ms. Ott says, she and other students avoid cozy cafes, which can easily charge $7 or $8 for a glass of soda. Instead, they get takeout sandwiches and carry around six-packs of Coca-Cola. They patronize bars offering cheap beer rather than nightclubs. And they pinch pennies during sightseeing jaunts to nearby cities.

"I went into it thinking traveling would be a cheap little weekend away," Ms. Ott says. "Not so much."

Daeya Malboeuf, a spokeswoman for Syracuse University's study-abroad programs, says the school urges students in its London program to save money by staying in the city on weekends. And it serves free coffee, so students "don't have to go to Starbucks," where a medium-size latte runs about 2.40 pounds, or about $4.75.

"We used to be able to say the cost of a semester abroad was the same as a semester here," Ms. Malboeuf says, because a strong dollar made traveling overseas relatively cheap. "We don't say that anymore."

While London, Florence and Madrid continue to be top destinations for Syracuse students, she says, Hong Kong, Beijing and Santiago are growing quickly in popularity.

consider this:

In March of 2009 it would cost you $125 to get 100 euros; a year earlier it would have cost you a $160. That is, the price of travel to nations using the euro is now less expensive. However since March the dollar has weakened against the Euro and in October of 2009 it cost $1.50 to get 100 Euros.

SOURCE: From 'The Wall Street Journal' May 14, 2008. Reprinted by permission of 'The Wall Street Journal', Copyright © 2008 Dow Jones & Company, Inc. All Rights Reserved Worldwide.

SECTION CHECK

1. Any force that shifts either the demand or the supply curves for a foreign currency will shift the equilibrium in the foreign exchange market and lead to a new exchange rate.
2. Any changes in tastes, income levels, relative real interest rates, or relative inflation rates will cause the demand for and supply of a currency to shift.

---

1. Why will the exchange rates of foreign currencies relative to U.S. dollars decline when U.S. domestic tastes change, reducing the demand for foreign-produced goods?
2. Why does the demand for foreign currencies shift in the same direction as domestic income? What happens to the exchange value of those foreign currencies in terms of U.S. dollars?
3. How would increased U.S. tariffs on imported European goods affect the exchange value of euros in terms of dollars?
4. Why do changes in U.S. tastes, income levels, or tariffs change the demand for euros, while similar changes in Europe change the supply of euros?
5. What would happen to the exchange value of euros in terms of U.S. dollars if incomes rose in both Europe and the United States?
6. Why does an increase in interest rates in Germany relative to U.S. interest rates increase the demand for euros but decrease their supply?
7. What would an increase in U.S. inflation relative to Europe do to the supply and demand for euros and to the equilibrium exchange value (price) of euros in terms of U.S. dollars?

SECTION 31.4 Flexible Exchange Rates

* How are exchange rates determined today?
* How are exchange rate changes different under a flexible-rate system than in a fixed system?
* What major problems exist in a fixed-rate system?
* What are the major arguments against flexible rates?

The Flexible Exchange Rate System

Since 1973, the world has essentially operated on a system of flexible exchange rates. Flexible exchange rates mean that currency prices are allowed to fluctuate with changes in supply and demand, without governments stepping in to prevent those changes. Before that, governments operated under what was called the *Bretton Woods fixed exchange rate system*, in which they would maintain a stable exchange rate by buying or selling currencies or reserves to bring demand and supply for their currencies together at the fixed exchange rate. The present system evolved out of the Bretton Woods fixed-rate system and occurred by accident, not design. Governments were unable to agree on an alternative fixed-rate approach when the Bretton Woods system collapsed, so nations simply let market forces determine currency values.

Are Exchange Rates Managed at All?

To be sure, governments sensitive to sharp changes in the exchange value of their currencies do still intervene from time to time to prop up their currency's exchange rate if it is considered to be too low or falling too rapidly, or to depress its exchange rate if it is considered to be too high or rising too rapidly. Such was the case when the U.S. dollar declined in value in the late 1970s, but the U.S. government intervention appeared to have little if any effect in preventing the dollar's decline. However, present-day fluctuations in exchange rates are not determined solely by market forces. Economists sometimes say that the current exchange rate system is a **dirty float system,** meaning that fluctuations in currency values are partly determined by market forces and partly influenced by government intervention. Over the years, however, such governmental support attempts have been insufficient to dramatically alter exchange rates for long, and currency exchange rates have changed dramatically.

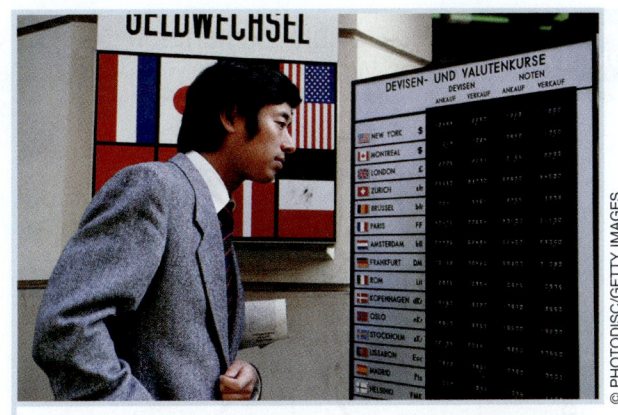

The exchange rate is the rate at which one country's currency can be traded for another country's currency. Under a flexible-rate system, the government allows the forces of supply and demand to determine the exchange rate. Changes in exchange rates occur daily or even hourly.

When Exchange Rates Change

When exchange rates change, they affect not only the currency market but the product markets as well. For example, if U.S. consumers were to receive fewer and fewer British pounds and Japanese yen per U.S. dollar, the effect would be an increasing price for foreign imports, *ceteris paribus.* It would now take a greater number of dollars to buy a given number of yen or pounds, which U.S. consumers use to purchase those foreign products. It would, however, lower the cost of U.S. exports to foreigners. If, however, the dollar increased in value relative to other currencies, then the relative price of foreign goods would decrease, *ceteris paribus.* But foreigners would find that U.S. goods were more expensive in terms of their own currency prices, and, as a result, would import fewer U.S. products.

dirty float system
a description of the exchange rate system that means that fluctuations in currency values are partly determined by government intervention

rampages and major currency revaluations under the fixed Bretton Woods system have significantly diminished. Under the fixed-rate system, price changes in currencies came infrequently, but when they came, they were of a large magnitude: 20 percent or 30 percent changes overnight were fairly common. Today, price changes occur daily or even hourly, but each change is much smaller in magnitude, with major changes in exchange rates typically occurring only over periods of months or years.

The Advantages of Flexible Rates

As mentioned earlier, the present system of flexible exchange rates was not planned. Indeed, most central bankers thought that a system where rates were not fixed would lead to chaos. What in fact has happened? Since the advent of flexible exchange rates, world trade has not only continued but expanded. Over a one-year period, the world economy adjusted to the shock of a four-fold increase in the price of its most important internationally traded commodity, oil. Although the OPEC oil cartel's price increase certainly had adverse economic effects, it did so without paralyzing the economy of any one nation.

The most important advantage of the flexible-rate system is that the recurrent crises that led to speculative

Fixed Exchange Rates Can Result in Currency Shortages

Perhaps the most significant problem with the fixed-rate system is that it can result in currency shortages, just as domestic price and wage controls lead to shortages. Suppose we had a fixed-rate system with the price of one euro set at $1.00, as shown in Exhibit 1. In this example, the original quantity of euros demanded and supplied is indicated by curves D_1 and S, so $1.00 is the equilibrium price. That is, at a price of $1.00, the quantity of euros demanded (by U.S. importers of European products and others wanting euros) equals the quantity supplied (by European importers of U.S. products and others).

Suppose that some event happens to increase U.S. demand for Dutch goods. For this example, let us

section 31.4 exhibit 1 — How Flexible Exchange Rates Work

An increase in demand for euros shifts the demand curve to the right, from D_1 to D_2. Under a fixed-rate system, this increase in demand results in a shortage of euros at the equilibrium price of $1, because the quantity demanded at this price, Q_2, is greater than the quantity supplied, Q_1. If the exchange rate is flexible, however, no shortage develops. Instead, the increase in demand forces the exchange rate higher, to $1.50. At this higher exchange rate, the quantity of euros demanded doesn't increase as much, and the quantity of euros supplied increases as a result of the now relatively lower cost of imports from the United States.

assume that Royal Dutch Shell discovers new oil reserves in the North Sea and thus has a new product to export. As U.S. consumers begin to demand Royal Dutch Shell oil, the demand for euros increases. That is, at any given dollar price of euros, U.S. consumers want more euros, shifting the demand curve to the right, to D_2. Under a fixed exchange rate system, the dollar price of euros must remain at $1, where the quantity of euros demanded (Q_2) now exceeds the quantity supplied, Q_1. The result is a shortage of euros—a shortage that must be corrected in some way. As a solution to the shortage, the United States may borrow euros from the Netherlands, or perhaps ship the Netherlands some of its reserves of gold. The ability to continually make up the shortage (deficit) in this manner, however, is limited, particularly if the deficit persists for a substantial time.

Flexible Rates Solve the Currency Shortage Problem

Under flexible exchange rates, a change in the supply or demand for euros does not pose a problem. Because rates are allowed to change, the rising U.S. demand for European goods (and thus for euros) would lead to a new equilibrium price for euros, say at $1.50. At this higher price, European goods are more costly to U.S. buyers. Some of the increase in demand for European imports, then, is offset by a decrease in quantity demanded resulting from higher import prices. Similarly, the change in the exchange rate will make U.S. goods cheaper to Europeans, thus increasing U.S. exports and, with that, the quantity of euros supplied. For example, a $40 software program that cost Europeans 40 euros when the exchange rate was $1 per euro costs less than 27 euros when the exchange rate increases to $1.50 per euro ($40 divided by $1.50).

Flexible Rates Affect Macroeconomic Policies

With flexible exchange rates, the imbalance between debits and credits arising from shifts in currency demand and/or supply is accommodated by changes in currency prices, rather than through the special financial borrowings or reserve movements necessary with fixed rates. In a pure flexible exchange rate system, deficits and surpluses in the balance of payments tend to disappear automatically. The market mechanism itself is able to address world trade imbalances, dispensing with the need for bureaucrats attempting to achieve some administratively determined price. Moreover, the need to use restrictive monetary and/or fiscal policy to end such an imbalance while maintaining a fixed exchange rate is alleviated. Nations are thus able to feel less constraint in carrying out internal macroeconomic policies under flexible exchange rates. For these reasons, many economists welcomed the collapse of the Bretton Woods system and the failure to arrive at a new system of fixed or quasi-fixed exchange rates.

The Disadvantages of Flexible Rates

Despite the fact that world trade has grown and dealing with balance-of-payments problems has become less difficult, flexible exchange rates have not been universally endorsed by everyone. Several disadvantages of this system have been cited.

Flexible Rates and World Trade

Traditionally, the major objection to flexible rates was that they introduce considerable uncertainty into international trade. For example, if you order some perfume

Use what you've LEARNED: BIG MAC INDEX

The **Big Mac Index** is published by *The Economist* as an informal way of measuring the purchasing power parity (PPP) between two currencies and provides a test of the extent to which market exchange rates result in goods costing the same in different countries. It "seeks to make exchange-rate theory a bit more digestible."

The index takes its name from the Big Mac, a hamburger sold at McDonald's restaurants.

McDonald's Big Mac Purchased in Australia

The Big Mac Index was introduced in *The Economist* in September 1986 by Pam Woodall as a semi-humorous illustration and has been published by that paper annually since then. The index also gave rise to the word *burgernomics*.

UBS Wealth Management Research has expanded the idea of the Big Mac Index to include the amount of time that an average worker in a given country must work to earn enough to buy a Big Mac. The working-time based Big Mac Index might give a more realistic view of the purchasing power of the average worker, as it takes into account more factors, such as local wages.

One suggested method of predicting exchange rate movements is that the rate between two currencies should naturally adjust so that a sample basket of goods and services should cost the same in both currencies (PPP). In the Big Mac Index, the "basket" in question is considered to be a single Big Mac burger as sold by the McDonald's fast food restaurant chain. The Big Mac was chosen because it is available to a common specification in many countries around the world, with local McDonald's franchisees having significant responsibility for negotiating input prices. For these reasons, the index enables a comparison between many countries' currencies.

The Big Mac PPP exchange rate between two countries is obtained by dividing the price of a Big Mac in one country (in its currency) by the price of a Big Mac in another country (in its currency). This value is then compared with the actual exchange rate; if it is lower, then the first currency is under-valued (according to PPP theory) compared with the second, and conversely, if it is higher, then the first currency is over-valued.

For example, using figures in July 2008:

* the price of a Big Mac was $3.57 in the United States
* the price of a Big Mac was £2.09 in the United Kingdom (Britain) (Varies by region)
* the implied purchasing power parity was $1.56 to £1, that is $3.57/£2.29 = 1.56
* this compares with an actual exchange rate of $2.00 to £1 at the time
* the pound was thus overvalued against the dollar by 28%
  * i.e. the actual exchange rate divided by implied purchasing parity → 2 divided by 1.56 = 1.28

The Euro-zone is mixed, as prices differ widely in the EU area. As of April 2009, the Big Mac is trading in

(continued)

Use what you've LEARNED

BIG MAC INDEX (cont.)

Germany at 2,99EUR, which translates into 3,96 US$, which would imply that the Euro is slightly trading above the PPP, with the difference being 10.9%.

The Economist sometimes produces variants on the theme. For example in January 2004, it showed a *Tall Latte index* with the Big Mac replaced by a cup of Starbucks coffee. In a similar vein, in 1997, the newspaper drew up a "Coca-Cola map" that showed inverse proportionality between the amount of Cola consumed per capita in a country and that country's health.

In 2007, an Australian bank, Commonwealth Securities, adapted the idea behind the Big Mac Index to create an "iPod index." The bank's theory is that since the iPod is manufactured at a single place, the value of iPods should be more consistent globally. However, this theory can be criticized for ignoring shipping costs, which will vary depending on how far the product is delivered from its "single place" of manufacture.

The burger methodology has limitations in its estimates of the PPP. In many countries, eating at international fast-food chain restaurants such as McDonald's is relatively expensive in comparison to eating at a local restaurant, and the demand for Big Macs is not as large in countries like India as in the United States. Social status of eating at fast food restaurants like McDonald's, local taxes, levels of competition, and import duties on selected items may not be representative of the country's economy as a whole. In addition, there is no theoretical reason why non-tradable goods and services such as property costs should be equal in different countries: this is the theoretical reason for PPPs being different from market exchange rates over time. Nevertheless, economists widely cite the Big Mac Index as a real world measurement of purchasing power parity. McDonald's is also using different commercial[s] which can result in huge differences for a product, whereas there is a smaller price difference between both countries. For example, a Hamburger sandwich costs only 1 € in France, and 1,50 € in Belgium, but overall, McDonald's restaurants are cheaper in Belgium. In Estonia, the price difference between a Big Mac burger and the whole meal is sometimes as small as 3 EEK (0,20 USD), or 5% of the price of the burger alone.

---

from France with a commitment to pay 1,000 euros in three months, you are not certain what the dollar price of euros, and therefore of the perfume, will be three months from now, because the exchange rate is constantly fluctuating. Because people prefer certainty to uncertainty and are generally risk averse, this uncertainty raises the costs of international transactions. As a result, flexible exchange rates can reduce the volume of trade, thus reducing the potential gains from international specialization.

Proponents of flexible rates have three answers to this argument. First, the empirical evidence shows that international trade has, in fact, grown in volume faster since the introduction of flexible rates. The exchange rate risk of trade has not had any major adverse effect. Second, it is possible to, in effect, buy insurance against the proposed adverse effect of currency fluctuations. Rather than buying currencies for immediate use in what is called the "spot" market for foreign currencies, one can contract today to buy foreign currencies in the future at a set exchange rate in the "forward" or "futures" market. By using this market, a perfume importer can buy euros now for delivery to her in three months; in doing so, she can be certain of the dollar price she is paying for the perfume. Since floating exchange rates began, booming futures markets in foreign currencies have opened in Chicago, New York, and in foreign financial centers. The third argument is that the alleged certainty of currency prices under the old Bretton Woods system was fictitious, because the possibility existed that nations might, at their whim, drastically revalue their currencies to deal with their own fundamental balance-of-payments problems. Proponents of flexible rates, then, argue that they are therefore no less disruptive to trade than fixed rates.

Flexible Rates and Inflation

A second, more valid criticism of flexible exchange rates is that they can contribute to inflationary pressures. Under fixed rates, domestic monetary and fiscal authorities have an incentive to constrain their domestic prices, because lower domestic prices increase the attractiveness of exported goods. This discipline is not present to the same extent with flexible rates. The consequence of a sharp monetary or fiscal expansion under flexible rates would be a decline in the value of one's currency relative to those of other countries. Yet even that may not seem to be as serious a political consequence as the Bretton Woods solution of an abrupt devaluation of the currency in the face of a severe balance-of-payments problem.

Advocates of flexible rates would argue that inflation need not occur under flexible rates. Flexible rates do not cause inflation; rather, it is caused by the expansionary macroeconomic policies of governments and central banks. Actually, flexible rates give government decision makers greater freedom of action than fixed rates; whether they act responsibly is determined not by exchange rates but by domestic policies.

global WATCH: CHINA'S CURRENCY

From 1994 until July 2005, China maintained a policy of pegging its currency, the renminbi or yuan, to the U.S. dollar at an exchange rate of roughly 8.28 yuan to the dollar. The Chinese central bank maintained this peg by buying (or selling) as many dollar-denominated assets in exchange for newly printed yuan as needed to eliminate excess demand (supply) for the yuan. As a result, the exchange rate between the yuan and the dollar basically stayed the same, despite changing economic factors which could have otherwise caused the yuan to either appreciate or depreciate relative to the dollar. Under a floating exchange rate system, the relative demand for the two countries' goods and assets would determine the exchange rate of the yuan to the dollar. Many economists contend that for the first several years of the peg, the fixed value was likely close to the market value. But in the past few years, economic conditions have changed such that the yuan would likely have appreciated if it had been floating. The sharp increase in China's foreign exchange reserves (which grew from $403 billion in 2003 to $1.95 trillion as of March 2009) and China's large trade surplus with the world ($297 billion in 2008) are often viewed by critics of China's currency policy as proof that the yuan is significantly undervalued.

The Chinese government modified its currency policy on July 21, 2005. It announced that the yuan's exchange rate would become "adjustable, based on market supply and demand with reference to exchange rate movements of currencies in a basket" (it was later announced that the composition of the basket includes the dollar, the yen, the euro, and a few other currencies) and that the exchange rate of the U.S. dollar against the yuan was adjusted from 8.28 to 8.11, an appreciation of 2.1%. Unlike a true floating exchange rate, the yuan would be allowed to fluctuate by up to 0.3% (later changed to 0.5%) on a daily basis against the basket.

Since July 2005, China has allowed the yuan to appreciate steadily, but very slowly. It has continued to accumulate foreign reserves at a rapid pace, which suggests that if the yuan were allowed to freely float it would appreciate much more rapidly. The current situation might be best described as a "managed float"—market forces are determining the general direction of the yuan's movement, but the government is retarding its rate of appreciation through market intervention. From July 21, 2005 to April 13, 2009, the dollar-yuan exchange rate went from 8.11 to 6.83, an appreciation of 18.7%. The effects of the yuan's appreciation are unclear. The price index for U.S. imports from China in 2008, rose by 3.0% (compared to a 0.9% rise in import prices for total U.S. imports of non-petroleum products). In 2008, U.S. imports from China rose by 5.1% over the previous year, compared to import growth of 11.7% in 2007; however, U.S. exports over this period were up 9.5% compared with an 18.1% rise in 2007.

Many Members of Congress charge that China's policy of accumulating foreign reserves (especially U.S. dollars) to influence the value of its currency constitutes a form of currency manipulation intended to make its exports cheaper and imports into China more expensive than they would be under free market conditions. They further contend that this policy has caused a surge in the U.S. trade deficit

(continued)

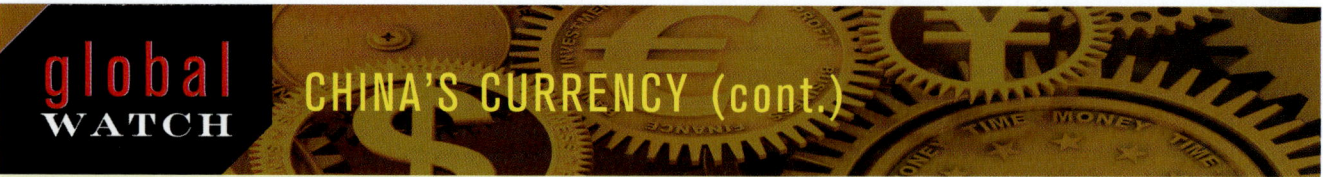

Global Watch: CHINA'S CURRENCY (cont.)

with China and has been a major factor in the loss of U.S. manufacturing jobs. Although China made modest reforms to its currency policy in 2005, resulting in a gradual appreciation of its currency (about 19% through mid-April 2009), many Members contend the reforms have not gone far enough and have warned of potential punitive legislative action.

Although an undervalued Chinese currency has likely hurt some sectors of the U.S. economy, it has also benefited others. For example, consumers have gained from the supply of low-cost Chinese goods (which helps to control inflation), as well as U.S. firms using Chinese-made parts and materials (which helps such firms become more globally competitive). In addition, China has used its abundant foreign exchange reserves to buy U.S. securities, including U.S. Treasury securities, which are used to fund the Federal budget deficit. Such purchases help keep U.S. interest rates relatively low.

The current global economic crisis has further complicated the currency issue for both the United States and China. Although China is under pressure from the United States to appreciate its currency, it is reluctant to do so because it could cause further damage to export sector and lead to more layoffs. China has halted its gradual appreciation of its currency, the renminbi (RMB) or yuan to the dollar in 2009; keeping it at about 6.83 yuan per dollar (from January 1 through April 13, 2009). The federal budget deficit has increased rapidly since FY2008, causing a sharp increase in the amount of Treasury securities that must be sold. The Obama Administration has encouraged China to continue purchasing U.S. debt. However, if China were induced to further appreciate its currency against the dollar, it could slow China's accumulation of foreign exchange reserves, thus reducing the need to invest in dollar assets, such as Treasury securities.

China's currency policy appears to have created a policy dilemma for the Chinese government. A strong and stable U.S. economy is in China's national interest since the United States is China's largest export market. Thus, some analysts contend that China will feel compelled to keep funding the growing U.S. debt. However, Chinese officials have expressed concern that the growing U.S. debt will eventually spark inflation in the United States and a depreciation of the dollar, which would negatively impact the value of China's holdings of U.S. securities. But if China stopped buying U.S. debt or tried to sell off a large portion of those holdings, it could also cause the dollar to depreciate and thus reduce the value of its remaining holdings, and such a move could further destabilize the U.S. economy. Chinese concerns over its large dollar holdings appear to have been reflected in a paper issued by the governor of the People's Bank of China, Zhou Xiaochuan on March 24, 2009, which called for the replacing the U.S. dollar as the international reserve currency with a new global system controlled by the International Monetary Fund. China has also signed currency swap agreements with six of its trading partners, which would allow those partners to settle accounts with China using the yuan rather than the dollar.

CRS Report RL32165, *China's Currency: Economic Issues and Options for U.S. Trade Policy*, by Wayne M. Morrison and Marc Labonte.

SOURCE: *Congressional Research Service*, April 2009.

SECTION CHECK

1. Today, rates are free to fluctuate based on market transactions, but governments occasionally intervene to increase or depress the price of their currencies.
2. Changes in exchange rates occur more often under a flexible-rate system, but the changes are much smaller than the drastic, overnight revaluations of currencies that occurred under the fixed-rate system.
3. Under a fixed-rate system, the supply and demand for currencies shift, but currency prices are not allowed to shift to the new equilibrium, leading to surpluses and shortages of currencies.

4. The main arguments presented against flexible exchange rates are that international trade levels will be diminished due to uncertainty of future currency prices and that the flexible rates would lead to inflation. Proponents of flexible exchange rates have strong counter-arguments to those views.

1. What are the arguments for and against flexible exchange rates?
2. When the U.S. dollar starts to exchange for fewer Japanese yen, other things equal, what happens to U.S. and Japanese imports and exports as a result?
3. Why is the system of flexible exchange rates sometimes called a dirty float system?
4. Were exchange rates under the Bretton Woods system really stable? How could you argue that exchange rates were more uncertain under the fixed-rate system than with floating exchange rates?
5. What is the uncertainty argument against flexible exchange rates? What evidence do proponents of flexible exchange rates cite in response?
6. Do flexible exchange rates cause higher rates of inflation? Why or why not?

Interactive Chapter Summary

Fill in the blanks:

1. A current account is a record of a country's current _____ and _____ of goods and services.
2. Because the United States gains claims over foreign buyers by obtaining foreign currency in exchange for the dollars needed to buy U.S. exports, all exports of U.S. goods abroad are considered a(n) _____ or _____ item in the U.S. balance of payments.
3. Nations import and export _____, such as tourism, as well as _____ (goods).
4. The merchandise import/export relationship is often called the balance of _____.
5. Foreigners buying U.S. goods must _____ their currencies to obtain _____ in order to pay for exported goods.
6. The price of a unit of one foreign currency in terms of another is called the _____.
7. A change in the euro-dollar exchange rate from $1 per euro to $2 per euro would _____ the U.S. price of German goods, thereby _____ the number of German goods that would be demanded in the United States.
8. The demand for foreign currencies is a derived demand because it derives directly from the demand for foreign _____ or for foreign _____.
9. The more foreigners demand U.S. products, the _____ of their currencies they will supply in exchange for U.S. dollars.
10. The supply of and demand for a foreign currency determine the equilibrium _____ of that currency.
11. The quantity of euros demanded by U.S. consumers will increase to buy more European goods as the price of the euro _____.
12. As the price, or value, of the euro increases relative to the dollar, American products become relatively _____ expensive to European buyers, which will _____ the quantity of dollars they will demand.
13. The supply curve of a foreign currency is _____ sloping.
14. If the dollar price of euros is higher than the equilibrium price, an excess quantity of euros will be _____ at that price, and competition among euro _____ will push the price of euros _____ toward equilibrium.
15. An increased demand for euros will result in a(n) _____ equilibrium price (exchange value) for euros, while a decreased demand for euros will result in a(n) _____ equilibrium price (exchange value) for euros.
16. Changes in a currency's exchange rate can be caused by changes in _____ for goods, changes in _____, changes in relative _____ rates, changes in relative _____ rates, and _____.
17. An increase in tastes for European goods in the United States would _____ the demand for euros, thereby _____ the equilibrium price (exchange value) of euros.
18. A decrease in incomes in the United States would _____ the amount of European imports purchased by Americans, which would _____ the demand for euros, resulting in a(n) _____ exchange rate for euros.

19. If European incomes _____, European tariffs on U.S. goods _____, or European tastes for U.S. goods _____, Europeans would demand more U.S. goods, leading them to increase their supply of euros to obtain the added dollars necessary to make those purchases.

20. If interest rates in the United States were to increase relative to European interest rates, other things being equal, the rate of return on U.S. investments would _____ relative to that on European investments, thereby _____ Europeans' demand for U.S. investments.

21. If Europe experienced a higher inflation rate than the United States, European products would become _____ expensive to U.S. consumers, thereby _____ the quantity of European goods demanded by Americans, and thus _____ the demand for euros.

Answers: 1. imports; exports 2. credit; plus 3. services; merchandise 4. trade 5. sell; U.S. dollars 6. exchange rate 7. increase; reducing 8. goods and services; capital 9. more 10. exchange rate 11. falls 12. less; increase 13. upward 14. supplied; sellers; down 15. higher; lower 16. tastes; income; real interest; inflation; speculation 17. increase; decrease; lower 19. rose; increased; increased 20. increase; increasing 21. more; decreasing; decreasing

Key Terms and Concepts

balance of payments 950
current account 950
balance of trade 952

capital account 953
exchange rate 954

derived demand 954
dirty float system 963

Section Check Answers

31.1 The Balance of Payments

1. **What is the balance of payments?**
   The balance of payments is the record of all the international financial transactions of a nation—both those involving inflows of funds and those involving outflows of funds—over a year.

2. **Why must British purchasers of U.S. goods and services first exchange pounds for dollars?**
   Since U.S. goods and services are priced in dollars, a British consumer who wants to buy U.S. goods must first buy dollars in exchange for British pounds before he can buy the U.S. goods and services with dollars.

3. **How is it that our imports provide foreigners with the means to buy U.S. exports?**
   The domestic currency Americans supply in exchange for the foreign currencies to buy imports also supplies the dollars with which foreigners can buy American exports.

4. **What would have to be true for the United States to have a balance-of-trade deficit and a balance-of-payments surplus?**
   A balance-of-trade deficit means that we imported more merchandise (goods) than we exported. A balance-of-payments surplus means that the sum of our goods and services exports exceeded the sum of our goods and services imports, plus funds transfers from the United States. For both to be true would require a larger surplus of services (including net investment income) and/or net fund transfer inflows than our trade deficit in merchandise (goods).

5. **What would have to be true for the United States to have a balance-of-trade surplus and a current account deficit?**
   A balance-of-trade surplus means that we exported more merchandise (goods) than we imported. A current account deficit means that our exports of goods and services (including net investment income) were less than the sum of our imports of goods and services, plus net fund transfers. For both to happen would require that the sum of our deficit in services plus net transfers must be greater than our surplus in merchandise (goods) trading.

6. **With no errors or omissions in the recorded balance-of-payments accounts, what should the statistical discrepancy equal?**
   If there were no errors or omissions in the recorded balance-of-payments accounts, the statistical discrepancy should equal zero, since when properly recorded, credits and debits must be equal because every credit creates a debit of equal value.

7. **A Nigerian family visiting Chicago enjoys a Chicago Cubs baseball game at Wrigley Field. How would this expense be recorded in the balance-of-payments accounts? Why?**
   This would be counted as an export of services, because it would provide Americans with foreign currency (a claim against Nigeria) in exchange for those services.

31.2 Exchange Rates

1. **What is an exchange rate?**
   An exchange rate is the price in one country's currency of one unit of another country's currency.

2. **When a U.S. dollar buys relatively more British pounds, why does the cost of imports from England fall in the United States?**
   When a U.S. dollar buys relatively more British pounds, the cost of imports from England falls in the United States because it takes fewer U.S. dollars to buy a given number of British pounds in order to pay English producers. In other words, the price in U.S. dollars of English goods and services has fallen.

3. **When a U.S. dollar buys relatively fewer yen, why does the cost of U.S. exports fall in Japan?**
   When a U.S. dollar buys relatively fewer yen, the cost of U.S. exports falls in Japan because it takes fewer yen to buy a given number of U.S. dollars in order to pay American producers. In other words, the price in yen of U.S. goods and services has fallen.

4. **How does an increase in domestic demand for foreign goods and services increase the demand for those foreign currencies?**
   An increase in domestic demand for foreign goods and services increases the demand for those foreign currencies because the demand for foreign currencies is derived from the demand for foreign goods and services and foreign capital. The more foreign goods and services are demanded, the more of that foreign currency that will be needed to pay for those goods and services.

5. **As euros get cheaper relative to U.S. dollars, why does the quantity of euros demanded by Americans increase? Why doesn't the demand for euros increase as a result?**
   As euros get cheaper relative to U.S. dollars, European products become relatively more inexpensive to Americans, who therefore buy more European goods and services. To do so, the quantity of euros demanded by U.S. consumers will rise to buy them, as the price (exchange rate) for euros falls. The demand (as opposed to quantity demanded) of euros doesn't increase because this represents a movement along the demand curve for euros caused by a change in exchange rates, rather than a change in demand for euros caused by some other factor.

6. **Who brings exchange rates down when they are above their equilibrium value? Who brings exchange rates up when they are below their equilibrium value?**
   When exchange rates are greater than their equilibrium value, there will be a surplus of the currency, and frustrated sellers of that currency will bring its price (exchange rate) down. When exchange rates are less than their equilibrium value, there will be a shortage of the currency, and frustrated buyers of that currency will bring its price (exchange rate) up.

31.3 Equilibrium Changes in the Foreign Exchange Market

1. **Why will the exchange rates of foreign currencies relative to U.S. dollars decline when U.S. domestic tastes change, reducing the demand for foreign-produced goods?**
   When U.S. domestic tastes change, reducing the demand for foreign-produced goods, the reduced demand for foreign-produced goods will also reduce the demand for the foreign currencies to buy them. This reduced demand for those foreign currencies will reduce their exchange rates relative to U.S. dollars.

2. **Why does the demand for foreign currencies shift in the same direction as domestic income? What happens to the exchange value of those foreign currencies in terms of U.S. dollars?**
   An increase in domestic income increases the demand for goods and services, including imported goods and services. This increases the demand for foreign currencies with which to buy those additional imports, which increases their exchange rates (the exchange value of those currencies) relative to U.S. dollars.

3. **How would increased U.S. tariffs on imported European goods affect the exchange value of euros in terms of dollars?**
   Increased U.S. tariffs on imported European goods would make them less affordable in the United States. This would lead to a reduced demand for European goods in the United States, and therefore a reduced demand for euros. And this would reduce the exchange value of euros in terms of dollars.

4. **Why do changes in U.S. tastes, income levels, or tariffs change the demand for euros, while similar changes in Europe change the supply of euros?**
   Changes in U.S. tastes, income levels, or tariffs change the demand for euros because they change the American demand for European goods and services, thereby changing the demand for euros with which to buy them. Similar changes in Europe change the supply of euros because they change the European demand for U.S. goods and services, thus changing their demand for dollars with which to buy those goods and services. This requires them to change their supply of euros in order to get those dollars.

5. **What would happen to the exchange value of euros in terms of U.S. dollars if incomes rose in both Europe and the United States?**
   These changes would increase both the demand (higher incomes in the United States) and supply

(higher incomes in Europe) of euros. The effect on the exchange value of euros would be determined by whether the supply or demand for euros shifted more (rising if demand shifted relatively more and falling if supply shifted relatively more).

6. **Why does an increase in interest rates in Germany relative to U.S. interest rates increase the demand for euros but decrease their supply?**
An increase in interest rates in Germany relative to U.S. interest rates increases the rates of return on German investments relative to U.S. investments. U.S. investors therefore increase their demand for German investments, increasing the demand for euros with which to make these investments. This would also reduce the demand by German investors for U.S. investments, decreasing the supply of euros with which to buy the dollars to make the investments.

7. **What would an increase in U.S. inflation relative to Europe do to the supply and demand for euros and to the equilibrium exchange value (price) of euros in terms of U.S. dollars?**
An increase in U.S. inflation relative to Europe would make U.S. products relatively more expensive to European customers, decreasing the amount of U.S. goods and services demanded by European customers and thus decreasing the supply of euros with which to buy the dollars necessary for those purchases. It would also make European products relatively cheaper to American customers, increasing the amount of European goods and services demanded by Americans and thus increasing the demand for euros needed for those purchases. The decreased supply of and increased demand for euros results in an increasing exchange value of euros in terms of U.S. dollars.

31.4 Flexible Exchange Rates

1. **What are the arguments for and against flexible exchange rates?**
The arguments for flexible exchange rates include: the large expansion of world trade under flexible exchange rates; the fact that they allowed the economy to adjust to a quadrupling in the price of the world's most important internationally traded commodity—oil; and especially that it diminished the recurring crises that caused speculative rampages and currency revaluations, allowing the market mechanism to address currency shortages and world trade imbalances. The arguments against flexible exchange rates are that it increases exchange rate uncertainty in international trade, and can contribute to inflationary pressures, due to the lack of the fixed-rate system's incentives to constrain domestic policies which would erode net exports.

2. **When the U.S. dollar starts to exchange for fewer Japanese yen, other things equal, what happens to U.S. and Japanese imports and exports as a result?**
When the U.S. dollar starts to exchange for fewer Japanese yen, other things equal, the U.S. cost of Japanese imports rises, decreasing the value of Japanese exports to the United States. It also decreases the cost to the Japanese of buying U.S. goods, increasing the value of U.S. exports to Japan.

3. **Why is the system of flexible exchange rates sometimes called a dirty float system?**
The system of flexible exchange rates is sometimes called a dirty float system because governments do intervene at times in foreign currency markets to alter their currencies' exchange rates, so that exchange rates are partly determined by market forces and partly by government intervention.

4. **Were exchange rates under the Bretton Woods system really stable? How could you argue that exchange rates were more uncertain under the fixed-rate system than with floating exchange rates?**
Exchange rates under the Bretton Woods system were not really stable. While exchange rate changes were infrequent, they were large, with large effects. It could be argued that the cost of the uncertainty about the less frequent but larger exchange rate changes that resulted was actually greater as a result than for the more frequent but smaller exchange rate changes under the fixed-rate system.

5. **What is the uncertainty argument against flexible exchange rates? What evidence do proponents of flexible exchange rates cite in response?**
The uncertainty argument against flexible exchange rates is that flexible exchange rates add another source of uncertainty to world trade, which would increase the cost of international transactions, reducing the magnitude of international trade. Proponents of flexible exchange rates cite the faster growth of international trade since the introduction of flexible exchange rates, the fact that markets exist on which to hedge exchange rate risks (through forward, or futures, markets), and that the alleged exchange rate certainty was fictitious, since large changes could take place at a nations' whim, in response.

6. **Do flexible exchange rates cause higher rates of inflation? Why or why not?**
Flexible exchange rates do not cause higher rates of inflation. However, they do reduce the incentives to constrain domestic inflation for fear of reducing net exports under the fixed exchange rate system. Inflation, though, is ultimately caused by expansionary macroeconomic policies adopted by governments and their central banks.

CHAPTER 31 STUDY GUIDE

True or False:

1. U.S. consumers must first exchange U.S. dollars for a foreign seller's currency in order to pay for imported goods.
2. The exchange rate can be expressed either as the number of units of currency A per unit of currency B or as its reciprocal, the number of units of currency B per unit of currency A.
3. The more foreign goods that are demanded, the more of that foreign currency will be needed to pay for those goods, which will tend to push down the exchange value of that currency relative to other currencies.
4. The supply of foreign currency is provided by foreigners who want to buy the exports of a particular nation.
5. As the price of the euro falls relative to the dollar, European products become relatively more inexpensive to U.S. consumers, who therefore buy more European goods.
6. As the value of the euro increases relative to the dollar, American products become relatively more inexpensive to European buyers and increase the quantity of dollars they will demand. Europeans will, therefore, increase the quantity of euros supplied to the United States by buying more U.S. products.
7. If the dollar price of euros is lower than the equilibrium price, a surplus of euros will result, and competition among euro sellers will push the price of euros down toward equilibrium.
8. Any force that shifts either the demand for or supply of a currency will shift the equilibrium in the foreign exchange market, leading to a new exchange rate.
9. Any change in the demand for foreign goods will shift the demand curve for foreign currency in the opposite direction.
10. A decrease in tastes for European goods in the United States would decrease the demand for euros, hence decreasing the equilibrium price (exchange value) of euros.
11. An increase in incomes in the United States would increase the amount of European imports purchased by Americans, which would increase the demand for euros, resulting in a higher exchange rate for euros.
12. If European incomes rose, European tariffs on U.S. goods increased, or European tastes for U.S. goods increased, the exchange rate for euros would tend to increase.
13. A decrease in U.S. tariffs on European goods would tend to have the same effect on the exchange rate for euros as an increase in U.S. incomes.
14. If interest rates in the United States were to increase relative to European interest rates, the result would be a new, lower exchange rate for euros, other things being equal.
15. If Europe experienced a higher inflation rate than the United States, the supply of euros would tend to increase and the demand for euros would tend to decrease, leading to a new, lower exchange rate for euros.
16. If currency speculators believe that the United States is going to experience more rapid inflation than Japan in the future, they believe that the value of the dollar will soon be falling, which will increase the demand for the yen, and so the yen will appreciate relative to the dollar.

Multiple Choice:

1. Which of the following would be recorded as a credit in the U.S. balance-of-payments accounts?
    a. the purchase of a German business by a U.S. investor
    b. the import of Honda trucks by a U.S. automobile distributor
    c. European travel expenditures of an American college student
    d. the purchase of a U.S. Treasury bond by a French investment company
2. What is the difference between the balance of merchandise trade and the balance of payments?
    a. Only the value of goods imported and exported is included in the balance of merchandise trade, while the balance of payments includes the value of all payments to and from foreigners.
    b. The value of goods imported and exported is included in the balance of merchandise trade, while the balance of payments includes only capital account transactions.
    c. The value of all goods, services, and unilateral transfers is included in the balance of merchandise trade, while the balance of payments includes both current account and capital account transactions.
    d. Balance of merchandise trade and balance of payments both describe the same international exchange transactions.

3. If consumers in Europe and Asia develop strong preferences for U.S. goods, the U.S. current account will
   a. not be affected, because purchases of U.S. goods by foreigners are recorded in the capital account.
   b. not be affected, because purchases of U.S. goods based on mere preferences are recorded under statistical discrepancy.
   c. move toward surplus, because purchases of U.S. goods are recorded as credits on our current account.
   d. move toward deficit, because purchases of U.S. goods by foreigners are counted as debits in our current account.

4. Which of the following would supply dollars to the foreign exchange market?
   a. the sale of a U.S. automobile to a Mexican consumer
   b. spending by British tourists in the United States
   c. the purchase of Canadian oil by a U.S. consumer
   d. the sale of a U.S. corporation to a Saudi Arabian investor

5. Which of the following will enter as a credit in the U.S. balance-of-payments capital account?
   a. the purchase of a Japanese automobile by a U.S. consumer
   b. the sale of Japanese electronics to an American
   c. the sale of an American baseball team to a Japanese industrialist
   d. the purchase of a Japanese electronic plant by an American industrialist

6. If the value of a nation's merchandise exports exceeds merchandise imports, then the nation is running a
   a. balance-of-payments deficit.
   b. balance-of-payments surplus.
   c. merchandise trade deficit.
   d. merchandise trade surplus.

7. When goods or services cross international borders,
   a. money must generally move in the opposite direction.
   b. payment must be made in another good, using barter.
   c. a future shipment must be made to offset the current sale/purchase.
   d. countries must ship gold to make payment.

8. The balance-of-payments accounts for and records information about
   a. purchases of U.S. financial assets by foreigners.
   b. purchases of foreign financial assets by Americans.
   c. the levels of imports and exports of goods and services for a country.
   d. all of the above.

9. Suppose the United States imposed a high tariff on a major imported item. Under a system of flexible rates of exchange, this tariff would tend to
   a. cause the dollar to appreciate in value.
   b. cause the dollar to depreciate in value.
   c. increase the U.S. balance-of-trade deficit.
   d. increase the U.S. balance-of-payments deficit.
   e. do b, c, and d.

10. Under a system of flexible exchange rates, a deficit in a country's balance of payments will be corrected by
    a. depreciation in the nation's currency.
    b. appreciation in the nation's currency.
    c. a decline in the nation's domestic price level.
    d. an increase in the nation's inflation rate.

11. If high-yield investment opportunities attract capital from abroad and lead to a capital account surplus, then the
    a. nation's currency must appreciate.
    b. nation's currency must depreciate.
    c. nation must run a current account deficit under a flexible exchange rate system.
    d. nation must run a current account surplus under a flexible exchange rate system.
    e. Both a and c are true.

12. If the dollar *depreciates,* it can be said that
    a. foreign countries no longer respect the United States.
    b. other currencies appreciate.
    c. it falls in value just as it does during inflation.
    d. it takes fewer dollars to buy units of other currencies.
    e. all of the above are correct.

13. On May 16, 1999, it cost $0.667 to buy one Canadian dollar. How many Canadian dollars would $1 U.S. buy?
    a. $1.50
    b. $1.30
    c. $1.00
    d. $0.67

14. If the exchange rate between the dollar and the euro changes from $1 = 1 euro to $2 = 1 euro, then
    a. European goods will become less expensive for Americans, and imports of European goods to the United States will rise.
    b. European goods will become less expensive for Americans, and imports of European goods to the United States will fall.
    c. European goods will become more expensive for Americans, and imports of European goods to the United States will rise.
    d. European goods will become more expensive for Americans, and imports of European goods to the United States will fall.

15. If the price in dollars of Mexican pesos changes from $0.10 per peso to $0.14 per peso, the peso has
    a. appreciated.
    b. depreciated.
    c. devalued.
    d. stayed at the same exchange rate.

16. Which of the following is most likely to favor the appreciation of the American dollar?
    a. a German professor on vacation in Iowa
    b. an American professor on extended vacation in Paris
    c. an American farmer who relies on exports
    d. Disney World

17. If the dollar appreciates relative to other currencies, which of the following is true?
    a. It takes more of the other currency to buy a dollar.
    b. It takes less of the other currency to buy a dollar.
    c. No change occurs in the currency needed to buy a dollar.
    d. Not enough information is available to make a determination.

18. If the United States experiences a sharp increase in exports, what will happen to demand for the U.S. dollar?
    a. It will decrease.
    b. It will increase.
    c. It will be unchanged.
    d. It will change at the same rate as the supply of dollars will change.
    e. There is not enough information to make a determination.

19. If fewer British tourists visit the Grand Canyon, what is the effect in the exchange market?
    a. It will increase the supply of British pounds.
    b. It will decrease the supply of British pounds.
    c. It will increase the demand for British pounds.
    d. It will decrease the demand for British pounds.

20. Suppose that the dollar rises from 100 to 125 yen. As a result,
    a. exports to Japan will likely increase.
    b. Japanese tourists will be more likely to visit the United States.
    c. U.S. businesses will be less likely to use Japanese shipping lines to transport their products.
    d. U.S. consumers will be more likely to buy Japanese-made automobiles.

21. Other things being constant, which of the following will most likely cause the dollar to appreciate on the exchange rate market?
    a. higher domestic interest rates
    b. higher interest rates abroad
    c. expansionary domestic monetary policy
    d. reduced inflation abroad

22. A depreciation in the U.S. dollar would
    a. discourage foreigners from making investments in the United States.
    b. discourage foreign consumers from buying U.S. goods.
    c. reduce the number of dollars it would take to buy a Swiss franc.
    d. encourage foreigners to buy more U.S. goods.

23. If the exchange rate between euros and dollars were 2 euros per dollar, when an American purchased a good valued at 80 euros, its cost in dollars would be
    a. $160.
    b. $80.
    c. $40.
    d. none of the above.

24. Suppose that the exchange rate between Mexican pesos and dollars is 8 pesos per dollar. If the exchange rate goes to 10 pesos per dollar, it would tend to
    a. increase U.S. exports to Mexico.
    b. decrease U.S. exports to Mexico.
    c. increase Mexican exports to the United States.
    d. decrease Mexican exports to the United States.
    e. do both b and c.

25. If a dollar is cheaper in terms of a foreign currency than the equilibrium exchange rate, a _____ exists at the current exchange rate that will put _____ pressure on the exchange value of a dollar.
    a. surplus of dollars; downward
    b. surplus of dollars; upward
    c. shortage of dollars; downward
    d. shortage of dollars; upward

26. In foreign exchange markets, the supply of dollars is determined
    a. by the level of U.S. imports and the demand for foreign assets by U.S. citizens and the U.S. government.
    b. solely by the level of U.S. merchandise exports.
    c. solely by the level of U.S. merchandise imports.
    d. solely by the levels of U.S. merchandise exports and merchandise imports.
    e. by the level of U.S. exports and the demand for U.S. assets by foreigners.

27. In foreign exchange markets, the effect of an increase in the demand for dollars on the value of the dollar is the same as that of
    a. an increase in the supply of foreign currencies.
    b. a decrease in the supply of foreign currencies.
    c. a decrease in the demand for dollars.
    d. none of the above.

28. If the demand by foreigners for U.S. government securities increased, other things being equal, it would tend to
    a. increase the exchange value of the dollar and increase U.S. merchandise exports.
    b. increase the exchange value of the dollar and decrease U.S. merchandise exports.
    c. decrease the exchange value of the dollar and increase U.S. merchandise exports.
    d. decrease the exchange value of the dollar and decrease U.S. merchandise exports.

29. If the rate of inflation in the United States falls relative to the rate of inflation in foreign nations, U.S. net exports will tend to _____, causing the exchange value of the U.S. dollar to _____.
    a. rise; rise
    b. rise; fall
    c. fall; rise
    d. fall; fall

30. If real incomes in foreign nations were growing more rapidly than U.S. real incomes, one would expect that, as a result,
    a. the exchange value of the dollar would decline relative to other currencies.
    b. the exchange value of the dollar would increase relative to other currencies.
    c. the exchange value of the dollar relative to other currencies would not change.
    d. the effect on the exchange value of the dollar relative to other currencies would be undeterminable.

31. If real interest rates in the United States fell relative to real interest rates in other countries, other things being equal,
    a. the exchange value of the dollar would decline relative to other currencies.
    b. the exchange value of the dollar would increase relative to other currencies.
    c. the exchange value of the dollar relative to other currencies would not change.
    d. the effect on the exchange value of the dollar relative to other currencies would be undeterminable.

32. Sweden's currency will tend to appreciate if
    a. the demand for Sweden's exports increases.
    b. the demand for imports by Swedes increases.
    c. real interest rates in Sweden decrease relative to those of the rest of the world.
    d. Sweden's inflation rate rises relative to inflation in the rest of the world.

33. A country will tend to experience currency depreciation relative to that of other countries if
    a. the profitability of investments in other countries increases relative to the profitability in that country.
    b. people in the foreign currency markets expect the value of the currency to fall in the near future.
    c. the foreign demand for its exports decreases.
    d. any of the above occur.
    e. any of the above except c occur.

34. If the dollar depreciates relative to the yen, we would expect
    a. that the Japanese trade surplus with the United States would increase.
    b. that Japanese imports from the United States would decrease.
    c. that Japanese exports to the United States would decrease.
    d. that a and b would occur.

35. As the number of British pounds that exchange for a dollar falls on foreign currency markets,
    a. the British will have an incentive to import fewer U.S. goods.
    b. the British will find it easier to export goods to the United States.
    c. the British will find U.S. goods to be more expensive in their stores.
    d. all of the above will be true.
    e. none of the above will be true.

36. If real interest rates in the United States rose and real interest rates in England fell, we would expect people to
    a. increase their demand for British pounds.
    b. borrow more from U.S. sources.
    c. buy relatively more U.S. assets.
    d. buy relatively more British assets.
    e. do both b and c.

37. If the Federal Reserve were to sell U.S. dollars on the foreign exchange market, a likely result would be
    a. a rightward shift in the dollar supply curve.
    b. at least a temporary decline in the exchange value of the U.S. dollar.
    c. at least a temporary increase in the exchange value of the U.S. dollar.
    d. a and b.
    e. a and c.

Problems:

1. Indicate whether each of the following represents a credit or debit on the U.S. current account.
   a. an American imports a BMW from Germany
   b. a Japanese company purchases software from an American company
   c. the United States gives $100 million in financial aid to Israel
   d. a U.S. company in Florida sells oranges to Great Britain

2. Indicate whether each of the following represents a credit or debit on the U.S. capital account.
   a. a French bank purchases $100,000 worth of U.S. Treasury notes
   b. the central bank in the United States purchases 1 million euros in the currency market
   c. a U.S. resident buys stock on the Japanese stock market
   d. a Japanese company purchases a movie studio in California

3. How are each of the following events likely to affect the U.S. trade balance?
   a. the European price level increases relative to the U.S. price level
   b. the dollar appreciates in value relative to the currencies of its trading partners
   c. the U.S. government offers subsidies to firms that export goods
   d. the U.S. government imposes tariffs on imported goods
   e. Europe experiences a severe recession

4. How are each of the following events likely to affect the value of the dollar relative to the euro?
   a. interest rates in the European Union increase relative to the United States
   b. the European Union price level rises relative to the U.S. price level
   c. the European central bank intervenes by selling dollars on currency markets
   d. the price level in the United States falls relative to the price level in Europe

5. If the demand for a domestic currency decreases in a country using a fixed exchange rate system, what must the central bank do to keep the currency value steady?

6. What happens to the supply curve for dollars in the currency market under the following conditions?
   a. Americans wish to buy more Japanese consumer electronics
   b. the United States wishes to prop up the value of the yen

7. Evaluate the following statement: "The balance of payments equals −$200 million and the statistical discrepancy equals zero."

8. Assume that a product sells for $100 in the United States.
   a. If the exchange rate between British pounds and U.S. dollars is $2 per pound, what would the price of the product be in the United Kingdom?
   b. If the exchange rate between Mexican pesos and U.S. dollars is 125 pesos per dollar, what would the price of the product be in Mexico?
   c. In which direction would the price of the $100 U.S. product change in a foreign country if Americans' tastes for foreign products increased?
   d. In which direction would the price of the $100 U.S. product change in a foreign country if incomes in the foreign country fell?
   e. In which direction would the price of the $100 U.S. product change in a foreign country if interest rates in the United States fell relative to interest rates in other countries?

9. How would each of the following affect the supply of euros, the demand for euros, and the dollar price of euros?

Change	Supply of Euros	Demand for Euros	Dollar Price of Euros
Reduced U.S. tastes for European goods			
Increased incomes in the United States			
Increased U.S. interest rates			
Decreased inflation in Europe			
Reduced U.S. tariffs on imports			
Increased European tastes for U.S. goods			

10. How are each of the following classified, as debits or credits, in the U.S. balance-of-payments accounts?

	Credit	Debit
a. Americans buy autos from Japan.		
b. American tourists travel to Japan.		
c. Japanese consumers buy rice grown in the United States.		
d. United States gives foreign aid to Rwanda.		
e. General Motors, a U.S. company, earns profits in France.		
f. Royal Dutch Shell earns profits from its U.S. operations.		
g. General Motors builds a new plant in Vietnam.		
h. Japanese investors purchase U.S. government bonds.		

11. What will happen to the supply of dollars, the demand for dollars, and the equilibrium exchange rate of the dollar in each of the following cases?

	Supply of Dollars	Demand for Dollars	Equilibrium Exchange Rates
a. Americans buy more European goods.			
b. Europeans invest in U.S. stock market.			
c. European tourists flock to the United States.			
d. Europeans buy U.S. government bonds.			
e. American tourists flock to Europe.			

Glossary

ability to pay principle belief that those with the greatest ability to pay taxes should pay more than those with less ability to pay

accounting profits total revenues minus total explicit costs

adaptive expectations an individual's belief that the best indicator of the future is recent information on inflation and unemployment

adverse selection a situation where an informed party benefits in an exchange by taking advantage of knowing more than the other party

aggregate the total amount—such as the *aggregate level of output*

aggregate demand (AD) the total demand for all the final goods and services in the economy

aggregate demand curve graph that shows the inverse relationship between the price level and RGDP demanded

aggregate supply (AS) curve the total quantity of final goods and services suppliers are willing and able to supply at a given price level

allocative efficiency where $P = MC$ and production will be allocated to reflect consumer preferences

asymmetric information occurs when the available information is initially distributed in favor of one party relative to another in an exchange

automatic stabilizers changes in government transfer payments or tax collections that automatically help counter business cycle fluctuations

autonomous determinants of consumption expenditures expenditures not dependent on the level of current disposable income that can result from factors such as real wealth, the interest rate, household debt, expectations, and tastes and preferences

average cost pricing setting price equal to average total cost

average fixed cost (AFC) a per-unit measure of fixed costs; fixed costs divided by output

average revenue (AR) total revenue divided by the number of units sold

average total cost (ATC) a per-unit cost of operation; total cost divided by output

average variable cost (AVC) a per-unit measure of variable costs; variable costs divided by output

backward-bending labor supply curve above a certain wage rate, a worker may prefer to enjoy more leisure and less work to meet his or her own personal preferences (the income effect dominates the substitution effect)

bads items that we do not desire or want, where less is preferred to more, like terrorism, smog, or poison oak.

balance of payments the record of international transactions in which a nation has engaged over a year

balance of trade the net surplus or deficit resulting from the level of exportation and importation of merchandise

balance sheet a financial record that indicates the balance between a bank's assets and its liabilities plus capital

bandwagon effect a positive network externality in which a consumer's demand for a product increases because other consumers own it

bar graph visual display showing the comparison of quantities

barter direct exchange of goods and services without the use of money

bonds an obligation issued by the corporation that promises the holder to receive fixed annual interest payments and payment of the principal upon maturity

boom period of prolonged economic expansion

budget deficit occurs when government spending exceeds tax revenues for a given fiscal year

budget surplus occurs when tax revenues are greater than government expenditures for a given fiscal year

business cycles short-term fluctuations in the economy relative to the long-term trend in output

capital the equipment and structures used to produce goods and services

capital account records the foreign purchases or assets in the domestic economy (a monetary inflow) and domestic purchases of assets abroad (a monetary outflow)

capital intensive production that uses a large amount of capital

cartel a collection of firms that agree on sales, pricing, and other decisions

cash transfers direct cash payments like welfare, Social Security, and unemployment compensation

causation when one event brings about another event

ceteris paribus holding all other things constant

change in demand the prices of related goods, income, number of buyers, tastes, and expectations can change the demand for a good; that is, a change in one of these factors shifts the entire demand curve

change in quantity demanded a change in a good's own price leads to a change in quantity demanded, a move along a given demand curve

Coase theorem states that where property rights are defined in a clear-cut fashion, externalities are internalized

collective bargaining negotiations between representatives of employers and unions

collude when firms act together to restrict competition

command economy economy in which the government uses central planning to coordinate most economic activities

commercial banks financial institutions organized to handle everyday financial transactions of businesses and households through demand deposit accounts and savings accounts and by making short-term commercial and consumer loans

common resource a rival good that is nonexcludable

common stock residual claimants of corporate resources who receive a proportion of profits based upon the ratio of shares held

comparative advantage occurs when a person or country can produce a good or service at a lower opportunity cost than others

competitive market a market where the many buyers and sellers have little market power—each buyer's or seller's effect on market price is negligible

complements an increase (decrease) in the price of one good shifts the demand curve for another good to the left (right)

constant-cost industry an industry where input prices (and cost curves) do not change as industry output changes

constant returns to scale occur in an output range where LRATC does not change as output varies

consumer equilibrium allocation of consumer income that balances the ratio of marginal utility to the price of goods purchased

consumer price index (CPI) a measure of the cost of a market basket that represents the consumption of a typical household

consumer sovereignty consumers vote with their dollars in a market economy; this accounts for what is produced

consumer surplus the difference between the price a consumer is willing and able to pay for an additional unit of a good and the price the consumer actually pays; for the whole market, it is the sum of all the individual consumer surpluses

consumption purchases of final goods and services

consumption tax tax collected based on a taxpayer's spending

contraction when the economy is slowing down—measured from the peak to the trough

contractionary fiscal policy use of fiscal policy tools to reduce output by decreasing government purchases, increasing taxes, and/or reducing transfer payments

cooperative game collusion by two firms in order to improve their profit maximizations

correlation when two events occur together

cost-push inflation a price-level increase due to a negative supply shock or increases in input prices

credit unions financial cooperatives made up of depositors with a common affiliation

cross-price elasticity of demand the measure of the impact that a price change of one good will have on the demand of another good

crowding-out effect theory that government borrowing drives up the interest rate, lowering consumption by households and investment spending by firms

currency coins and/or paper created to facilitate the trade of goods and services and the payment of debts

current account a record of a country's imports and exports of goods and services, net investment income, and net transfers

cyclical unemployment unemployment due to short-term cyclical fluctuations in the economy

deadweight loss net loss of total surplus that results from an action that alters a market equilibrium

deflation a decrease in the overall price level, which increases the purchasing power of money

demand deposits balances in bank accounts that depositors can access on demand

demand-pull inflation a price-level increase due to an increase in aggregate demand

depreciation annual allowance set aside to replace worn-out capital

depression severe recession or contraction in output

derived demand the demand for an input derived from consumers' demand for the good or service produced with that input

diminishing marginal product as a variable input increases, with other inputs fixed, a point will be reached where the additions to output will eventually decline

diminishing marginal utility a good's ability to provide less satisfaction with each successive unit consumed; the concept that states that as an individual consumes more and more of a good, each successive unit generates less and less utility (or satisfaction)

dirty float system a description of the exchange rate system that means that fluctuations in currency values are partly determined by government intervention

discount rate interest rate that the Fed charges commercial banks for the loans it extends to them

discouraged worker an individual who has left the labor force because he or she could not find a job

diseconomies of scale occur in an output range where LRATC rises as output expands

disposable personal income the personal income available after personal taxes

dividend the annual per share payment to shareholders based upon realized profits

dominant strategy strategy that will be optimal regardless of opponents' actions

double counting adding the value of a good or service twice by mistakenly counting the intermediate goods and services in GDP

durable goods longer-lived consumer goods, such as automobiles

Earned Income Tax Credit (EITC) a welfare program that allows the working poor to receive income refunds that can be greater than the taxes they paid during the last year

economic goods scarce goods created from scarce resources—goods that are desirable but limited in supply

economic growth an upward trend in the real per capita output of goods and services

the economic problem scarcity forces us to choose, and choices are costly because we must give up other opportunities that we value

economic profits total revenues minus explicit and implicit costs

economic rent the payment for the use of any resource above its opportunity cost

economics the study of choices we make among our many wants and desires given our limited resources

economies of scale occur in an output range where *LRATC* falls as output increases

efficiency when an economy gets the most out of its scarce resources

efficiency wage model theory stating that higher wages lead to greater productivity

elastic when the quantity demanded is greater than the percentage change in price ($E_D > 1$)

empirical analysis the use of data to test a hypothesis

Employment Act of 1946 a commitment by the federal government to hold itself accountable for short-run economic fluctuations

entrepreneurship the process of combining labor, land, and capital to produce goods and services

equilibrium price the price at the intersection of the market supply and demand curves; at this price, the quantity demanded equals the quantity supplied

equilibrium quantity the quantity at the intersection of the market supply and demand curves; at the equilibrium quantity, the quantity demanded equals the quantity supplied

excess capacity occurs when the firm produces below the level where average total cost is minimized

excess reserves reserve levels held above that required by the Fed

exchange rate the price of one unit of a country's currency in terms of another country's currency

excise tax a sales tax on individual products such as alcohol, tobacco, and gasoline

expansion when output (real GDP) is rising significantly—the period between the trough of a recession and the next peak

expansionary fiscal policy use of fiscal policy tools to foster increased output by increasing government purchases, lowering taxes, and/or increasing transfer payments

expansion path shows the least-cost input solutions for providing a given output

expenditure approach calculation of GDP by adding the expenditures by market participants on final goods and services over a given period

expenditure multiplier the multiplier that only considers the impact of consumption changes on aggregate expenditures

explicit costs the opportunity costs of production that require a monetary payment

externality a benefit or cost from consumption or production that spills over onto those who are not consuming or producing the good

factor (or input) markets markets where households sell the use of their inputs (capital, land, labor, and entrepreneurship) to firms

factor payments wages (salaries), rent, interest payments, and profits paid to the owners of productive resources

fallacy of composition the incorrect view that what is true for the individual is always true for the group

featherbedding practice of hiring workers who may not be necessary

federal funds market market in which banks provide short-term loans to other banks that need cash to meet reserve requirements

fiat money a means of exchange established by government declaration

fiscal policy use of government purchases, taxes, and transfer payments to alter equilibrium output and prices

fixed costs costs that do not vary with the level of output

fixed investment all new spending on capital goods by producers

fixed-proportions production function when it is impossible to substitute one input for another so inputs must be used in fixed proportions

flat tax a tax that charges all income earners the same percentage of their income

fractional reserve system a system that requires banks to hold reserves equal to some fraction of their checkable deposits

free rider deriving benefits from something not paid for

frictional unemployment the unemployment that results from workers searching for suitable jobs and firms looking for suitable workers

game theory firms attempt to maximize profits by acting in ways that minimize damage from competitors

GDP deflator a price index that helps measure the average price level of all final consumer goods and services produced

gold standard defining the dollar as equivalent to a set value of a quantity of gold, allowing direct convertibility from currency to gold

goods items we value or desire

Gresham's Law the principle that "cheap money drives out dear money"; given an alternative, people prefer to spend less valuable money

gross domestic product (GDP) the measure of economic performance based on the value of all final goods and services produced within a country during a given period

gross national product (GNP) the difference between net income of foreigners and GDP

health maintenance organization (HMO) an organization that contracts with physicians, medical facilities, employers, and individuals to provide medical care to a group of individuals. Health care services are usually provided at a fixed price per patient. The cost of providing care is contained through the rationing of health care resources.

human capital the productive knowledge and skill people receive from education, on-the-job training, health, and other factors that increase productivity

hyperinflation extremely high rates of inflation for sustained periods of time

hypothesis a testable proposition

implicit costs the opportunity costs of production that do not require a monetary payment

import quota a legal limit on the imported quantity of a good that is produced abroad and can be sold in domestic markets

income effect reduction in quantity demanded of a good when its price increases because of a consumer's decreased purchasing power

income elasticity of demand the percentage change in demand divided by the percentage change in consumer's income

increasing-cost industry an industry where input prices rise (and cost curves rise) as industry output rises

increasing opportunity cost the opportunity cost of producing additional units of a good rises as society produces more of that good

indemnity coverage compensation toward the cost of medical services in the event of illness or injury

indexing use of payment contracts that automatically adjust for changes in inflation

indirect business taxes taxes, such as sales tax, levied on goods and services sold

individual demand curve a graphical representation that shows the inverse relationship between price and quantity demanded

individual demand schedule a schedule that shows the relationship between price and quantity demanded

individual supply curve a graphical representation that shows the positive relationship between the price and quantity supplied

inelastic when the quantity demanded is less than the percentage change in price ($E_D < 1$)

inferior good if income increases, the demand for a good decreases; if income decreases, the demand for a good increases

inflation a rise in the overall price level, which decreases the purchasing power of money

inflationary gap the output gap that occurs when the actual output is greater than the potential output

in-kind transfers in-kind transfers are transfers in the form of goods and services instead of money. In-kind transfers include food stamps, school lunch programs, housing subsidies, and Medicaid, among others.

innovation applications of new knowledge that create new products or improve existing products

intangible goods goods that we cannot reach out and touch, such as friendship and knowledge

interest the cost of borrowed funds

internalized externalities when an industry is forced to compensate those enduring some negative externality caused by its production

inventory investment purchases that add to the stocks of goods kept by the firm to meet consumer demand

investment the creation of capital goods to augment future production

isocost (equal cost) lines graphical display of the various possible quantities of the two factors that can be purchased with a given outlay of money

isoquant curve showing the various factor combinations that can produce a given level of output

job-entry discrimination a worker is denied employment on the basis of some biological feature, such as sex or race, without any regard to productivity

job leaver a person who quits his or her job

job loser an individual who has been temporarily laid off or fired

joint profit maximization determination of price based on the marginal revenue derived from the market demand schedule and marginal cost schedule of the firms in the industry

kinked demand curve indicates the price rigidity in oligopoly when competitors show a greater tendency to follow price reductions than price increases

labor the physical and human effort used in the production of goods and services

labor force the number of people aged 16 and over who are available for employment

labor force participation rate the percentage of the working age population in the labor force

labor intensive production that uses a large amount of labor

land the natural resources used in the production of goods and services

law of demand the quantity of a good or service demanded varies inversely (negatively) with its price, *ceteris paribus*

law of supply the higher (lower) the price of the good, the greater (smaller) the quantity supplied

leading economic indicators factors that economists at the Commerce Department have found typically change before changes in economic activity

legal tender coins and paper officially declared to be acceptable for the settlement of financial debts

liquidity the ease with which one asset can be converted into another asset or into goods and services

long run a period over which all production inputs are variable

long-run aggregate supply (LRAS) curve the graphical relationship between RGDP and the price level when output prices and input prices can fully adjust to economic changes

M1 the narrowest definition of money; includes currency, checkable deposits, and traveler's checks

M2 a broader definition of money that includes M1 plus savings deposits, time deposits, and noninstitutional money market mutual fund shares.

macroeconomics the study of the whole economy, including the topics of inflation, unemployment, and economic growth

marginal cost (MC) the change in total costs resulting from a one-unit change in output

marginal product (MP) the change in total output of a good that results from a one-unit change in input

marginal productivity theory of income distribution income is distributed according to marginal revenue product of the factors of production individuals own

marginal propensity to consume (MPC) the additional consumption resulting from an additional dollar of disposable income

marginal propensity to save (MPS) the additional saving that results from an additional dollar of income

marginal rate of technical substitution of labor for capital (MRTS) the quantity of capital that can be given up by using one additional unit of labor while producing the same level of output

marginal resource cost (MRC) the amount that an extra input adds to the firm's total cost

marginal revenue (MR) the increase in total revenue resulting from a one-unit increase in sales

marginal revenue product (MRP) marginal product times the price of the product

marginal thinking focusing on the additional, or marginal, choices; marginal choices involve the effects of adding or subtracting, from the current situation, the small (or large) incremental changes to a plan of action

marginal utility extra satisfaction generated by consumption of an additional good or service during a specific time period

market the process of buyers and sellers exchanging goods and services

market demand curve the horizontal summation of individual demand curves

market economy an economy that allocates goods and services through the private decisions of consumers, input suppliers, and firms

market equilibrium the point at which the market supply and market demand curves intersect

market failure when the economy fails to allocate resources efficiently on its own

market supply curve a graphical representation of the amount of goods and services that suppliers are willing and able to supply at various prices

means of deferred payment the attribute of money that makes it easier to borrow and to repay loans

means-tested income transfer program program in which eligibility is dependent on low income; food stamps, Medicaid, and housing subsidies are examples of means-tested income transfer programs

median voter model a model that predicts candidates will choose a position in the middle of the distribution

medium of exchange the primary function of money, which is to facilitate transactions and lower transaction costs

menu costs the costs imposed on a firm from changing listed prices

microeconomics the study of household and firm behavior and how they interact in the marketplace

minimum efficient scale the output level where economies of scale are exhausted and constant returns to scale begin

minimum wage rate an hourly wage floor set above the equilibrium wage

mixed economy an economy where government and the private sector determine the allocation of resources

money anything generally accepted in exchange for goods or services

money market market in which money demand and money supply determine the equilibrium interest rate

money market mutual funds interest-earning accounts provided by brokers that pool funds into such investments as Treasury bills

money multiplier measures the potential amount of money that the banking system generates with each dollar of reserves

monopolistic competition a market structure with many firms selling differentiated products

monopoly the single supplier of a product that has no close substitute

monopsony a market with a single buyer

moral hazard taking additional risks because you are insured

multiplier effect a chain reaction of additional income and purchases that results in total purchases that are greater than the initial increase in purchases

mutual interdependence when a firm shapes its policy with an eye to the policies of competing firms

national income (NI) a measure of income earned by owners of the factors of production

national income accounting a uniform means of measuring economic performance

natural monopoly a firm that can produce at a lower cost than a number of smaller firms can

natural rate hypothesis states that the economy will self-correct to the natural rate of employment

natural rate of unemployment the median, or "typical," unemployment rate, equal to the sum of frictional and structural unemployment when they are at a maximum

near money nontransaction deposits that are not money but can be quickly converted into money

negative externality occurs when costs spill over to an outside party who is not involved in producing or consuming the good

negative incentive an incentive that either increases costs or reduces benefits, resulting in a decrease in the activity or behavior

negative network externality increase in a consumer's demand for a good because fewer consumers are purchasing the same good

negative relationship when two variables change in opposite directions

net benefit the difference between the expected marginal benefits and the expected marginal costs

net exports the difference between the value of exports and the value of imports

net national product (NNP) GNP minus depreciation

network externality when the number of other people purchasing the good influences quantity demanded

new entrant an individual who has not held a job before but is now seeking employment

nominal interest rate the reported interest rate that is not adjusted for inflation

noncooperative game each firm sets its own price without consulting other firms

nondurable goods tangible items consumed in a short period of time, such as food

nontransaction deposits funds that cannot be used for payment directly but must be converted into currency for general use

normal good if income increases, the demand for a good increases; if income decreases, the demand for a good decreases

normative statements a subjective, contestable statement that attempts to describe what should be done

open economy a type of model that includes international trade effects

open market operations purchase and sale of government securities by the Federal Reserve System

opportunity cost the value of the best forgone alternative that was not chosen

optimum factor combination a point of tangency between the given isoquant and the lowest possible isocost line

payoff matrix a summary of the possible outcomes of various strategies

peak the point in time when expansion comes to an end, that is, when output is at the highest point in the cycle

peak load pricing when producers charge different prices during different periods because the demand and the cost of producing a product vary over time

permanent income hypothesis the hypothesis that consumption is more closely related to permanent income than current income

personal income (PI) the amount of income received by households before personal taxes

pie chart visual display showing the relative size of various quantities that add up to 100 percent

pollution tax tax levied by government on a firm for environmental pollution

positive externality occurs when benefits spill over to an outside party who is not involved in producing or consuming the good

positive incentive an incentive that either reduces costs or increases benefits, resulting in an increase in an activity or behavior

positive network externality increase in a consumer's quantity demanded for a good because a greater number of other consumers are purchasing the good

positive relationship when two variables change in the same direction

positive statement an objective, testable statement that describes what happens and why it happens

potential output the amount of real output the economy would produce if its labor and other resources were fully employed, that is, at the natural rate of unemployment

poverty line a set of money income thresholds, established by the federal government, that vary by family size and are used to detect who is poor; if a family's total income is less than the established family threshold, then that family, and every individual in it, is considered poor

poverty rate the percentage of the population who fall below the poverty line

predatory pricing setting a price deliberately low in order to drive out competitors

preferred provider organization (PPO) a network of doctors who agree to provide services to a health plan's enrollees at discounted fees

preferred stock a stock that pays fixed, regular dividend payments despite the profits of the corporation

present value the value in today's dollars of home future benefit

price ceiling a legally established maximum price

price controls government-mandated minimum or maximum prices

price discrimination the practice of charging different consumers different prices for the same good or service

price-earnings ratio (PE) a measure of stock value that is determined by dividing the price of the stock by the amount of annual corporate earnings per share

price elasticity of demand the measure of the responsiveness of quantity demanded to a change in price

price elasticity of supply the measure of the sensitivity of the quantity supplied to changes in price of a good

price floor a legally established minimum price

price follower a competitor in an oligopoly that goes along with the pricing decision of the price leader

price index a measure of the trend in prices paid for a certain bundle of goods and services over a given period

price leader a large firm in an oligopoly that unilaterally makes changes in its product prices that competitors tend to follow

price leadership when a dominant firm that produces a large portion of the industry's output sets a price that maximizes its profits, and other firms follow

price level the average level of prices in the economy

price takers a perfectly competitive firm that takes the price it is given by the intersection of the market demand and market supply curves

prisoners' dilemma the basic problem facing noncolluding oligopolists in maximizing their own profit

private good a good with rivalrous consumption and excludability

private property rights consumers' right to use their property as they see fit

producer goods capital goods that increase future production capabilities

producer price index a measure of the cost of goods and services bought by firms

producer surplus the difference between what a producer is paid for a good and the cost of producing that unit of the good; for the market, it is the sum of all the individual sellers' producer surpluses—the area above the market supply curve and below the market price

product differentiation goods or services that are slightly different, or perceived to be different, from one another

product markets markets where households are buyers and firms are sellers of goods and services

production function the relationship between the quantity of inputs and the quantity of outputs

production possibilities curve the potential total output combinations of any two goods for an economy

productive efficiency where a good or service is produced at the lowest possible cost

profit-maximizing level of output a firm should always produce at the output where $MR = MC$

profits the difference between total revenues and total costs

progressive tax tax designed so that those with higher incomes pay a greater proportion of their income in taxes

progressive tax system tax system that imposes higher marginal tax rates on higher incomes; the federal income tax is designed to be a progressive tax system

public good a good that is nonrivalrous in consumption and nonexcludable

quantity of money and prices a theory of the connection between the money supply and the price level when the velocity of money is constant

rational behavior people do the best they can, based on their values and information, under current and anticipated future circumstances

rational ignorance lack of incentive to be informed

real business cycle theory the belief that economic fluctuations are the result of external negative and positive productivity shocks to the economy

real gross domestic product per capita real output of goods and services per person

real gross domestic product (RGDP) the total value of all final goods and services produced in a given period, such as a year or a quarter, adjusted for inflation

real interest rate the nominal interest rate minus the inflation rate; also called the inflation-adjusted interest rate

recession a period of significant decline in output and employment

recessionary gap the output gap that occurs when the actual output is less than the potential output

reentrant an individual who worked before and is now reentering the labor force

regressive tax as a person's income rises, the amount his or her tax as a proportion of income falls

relative price the price of a specific good compared to the price of other goods

rent seeking efforts by producers to gain profits from government protections such as tariffs and import quotas

required reserve ratio the percentage of deposits that a bank must hold at the Federal Reserve Bank or in bank vaults

research and development (R&D) activities undertaken to create new products and processes that will lead to technological progress

reservation price the maximum amount a customer would be willing to pay for a unit of output

reserve requirements holdings of assets at the bank or at the Federal Reserve Bank as mandated by the Fed

resources inputs used to produce goods and services

retained earnings the practice of using corporate profits for capital investment rather than dividend payouts

rule of rational choice individuals will pursue an activity if the expected marginal benefits are greater than the expected marginal costs

savings and loan associations financial institutions organized as cooperative associations that hold demand deposits and savings of members in the form of dividend-bearing shares and make loans, especially home mortgage loans

scarcity exists when human wants (material and nonmaterial) exceed available resources

scatter diagram a graph showing the relationship of one variable to another

secondary reserves highly liquid, interest-paying assets held by the bank

securities stocks and bonds

services intangible items of value provided to consumers, such as education

shoe-leather cost the cost incurred when individuals reduce their money holdings because of inflation

shortage a situation where quantity demanded exceeds quantity supplied

short run a period too brief for some production inputs to be varied

short-run aggregate supply (SRAS) curve the graphical relationship between RGDP and the price level when output prices can change but input prices are unable to adjust

short-run market supply curve the horizontal summation of the individual firms' supply curves in the market

short-run supply curve the portion of the MC curve above the AVC curve

simple circular flow model an illustration of the continuous flow of goods, services, inputs, and payments between firms and households

slope the ratio of rise (change in the Y variable) over run (change in the X variable)

special interest groups groups with an intense interest in particular voting issues that may be different from that of the general public

specializing concentrating in the production of one, or a few, goods

stagflation a situation in which lower growth and higher prices occur together

stockholders entities that hold shares of stock in a corporation

structural unemployment the unemployment that results from workers not having the skills to obtain long-term employment

substitutes an increase (decrease) in the price of one good causes the demand curve for another good to shift to the right (left)

substitution effect a consumer's switch to another similar good when the price of the preferred good increases

sunk costs costs that have been incurred and cannot be recovered

Supplemental Security Income (SSI) a welfare program designed for the most needy, elderly, disabled, and blind

supply shocks unexpected temporary events that can either increase or decrease aggregate supply

surplus a situation where quantity supplied exceeds quantity demanded

switching costs the costs involved in changing from one product to another brand or in changing suppliers

Taft-Hartley Act legislation enacted in 1947 to somewhat restrict the power of unions granted by the Wagner Act

tangible goods items we value or desire that we can reach out and touch

tariff a tax on imports

Temporary Assistance for Needy Families (TANF) a welfare program designed to help families that have few financial resources

theory statement or proposition used to explain and predict behavior in the real world

theory of rational expectations belief that workers and consumers incorporate the likely consequences of government policy changes into their expectations by quickly adjusting wages and prices

time-series graph visual tool to show changes in a variable's value over time

tit-for-tat strategy strategy used in repeated games where one player follows the othe player's move in the previous round; leads to greater cooperation

total cost (TC) the sum of the firm's total fixed costs and total variable costs

total fixed cost (TFC) the sum of the firm's fixed costs

total product (TP) the total output of a good produced by the firm

total revenue (TR) the amount sellers receive for a good or service, calculated as the product price times the quantity sold

total utility total amount of satisfaction derived from the consumption of a certain number of goods or services

total variable cost (TVC) the sum of the firm's variable costs

total welfare gains the sum of consumer and producer surpluses

transaction deposits deposits that can be easily converted to currency or used to buy goods and services directly

transferable pollution rights a right given to a firm to discharge a specified amount of pollution; its transferable nature creates incentive to lower pollution levels

traveler's checks transaction instruments easily convertible into currency

trough the point in time when output stops declining, that is, when business activity is at its lowest point in the cycle

underemployment a situation in which a worker's skill level is higher than necessary for a job

unemployment rate the percentage of the population aged 16 and older who are willing and able to work but are unable to obtain a job

unintended consequences the secondary effects of an action that may occur after the initial effects

unit elastic demand demand with a price elasticity of 1; the percentage change in quantity demanded is equal to the percentage change in price

unplanned inventory investment collection of inventory that results when people do not buy the products firms are producing

util one unit of satisfaction

utility a measure of the relative levels of satisfaction consumers get from consumption of goods and services

variable something that is measured by a number, such as your height

variable costs costs that vary with the level of output

velocity of money a measure of how frequently money is turned over

vertical equity different treatment based on level of income and the ability to pay principle

wage and price controls legislation used to combat inflation by limiting changes in wages and prices

wage and price inflexibility the tendency for prices and wages to only adjust slowly downward to changes in the economy

wage discrimination when a worker is given employment at a wage lower than that of other workers, based on something other than productivity

Wagner Act legislation enacted in 1935 that protected workers' rights to organize and bargain collectively

welfare effects the gains and losses associated with government intervention in markets

winner's curse a situation that arises in certain auctions where the winner is worse off than the loser because of an overly optimistic value placed on the good

X-axis the horizontal axis on a graph

Y-axis the vertical axis on a graph

Index

ability to pay principle, 243–244
Abreu, Sabrina De, 19
absolute advantage, 918, 920–921
abstraction, economic theory and, 10–11
accounting profits, 291–292
activists, 891
adaptive expectations, 882
AD/AS model, 761–762, 879–880
adjustable rate mortgages (ARMs), 670
adverse selection, 220, 222, 223, 544
advertising, 411–413, 436, 438, 546
age, 487, 566
aggregate, 13
aggregate demand (AD), 689–690, 703–704, 708, 744–746
aggregate demand curve, 690–694, 767, 841–842
aggregate expenditure model, 732–738
aggregate supply curve, 694–699
allocative efficiency, 347, 348, 376, 409
Alm, Richard, 488
amenities, 463
American Economic Association, 20
anchoring, 269
Angulo, Roberto, 18–19
Annan, Kofi, 639
antitrust policies and laws, 374–375, 430, 432
arms race, 436, 438
assets, of banks, 814
assumptions, 11
asymmetric information, 219–223
Auerbach, Alan, 244
automatic stabilizers, 779–780
autonomous consumption, 732–734
autonomous determinants of consumption expenditures, 734
availability heuristic, 269
average cost pricing, 376–378
average fixed cost (AFC), 296, 298–299
average revenue (AR), 333, 364, 404
average total cost (ATC), 296, 297, 298–299, 301–303
average variable cost (AVC), 296, 298–299, 302–303
Avery, Sewell, 778

backward-bending labor supply curve, 460
bads, 38
Bailey, McKinley, 215
balanced budget amendment, 785
balance of payments, 950–953
balance of trade, 952
balance sheets, 814–815
bandwagon effect, 440
banking system, collapse of, 821–822
banks, 657, 812–817, 858
bar graph, 28, 29
barriers to entry, 362–363, 423, 546
Barro, Robert, 769, 777–778
barter, 802, 804
Becker, Gary, 271

behavioral economics, 269–272
Belichick, Bill, 44
benefit-cost analysis, 217–218
benefits received principle, 244
Bentham, Jeremy, 260, 261
Bernanke, Ben, 665, 845–846
Bhagwati, Jagdish N., 936
Big Mac index, 965–966
black market, 194–195
bonds, 654, 808–809
boom, 588
Boskin, Michael, 581
Bretton Woods fixed exchange rate system, 962
Brooks, David, 499–500
budget deficit, 663–664, 759, 781–783
budget line, consumer choice and, 281–282, 283–284
budget surplus, 759
Bureau of Economic Analysis (BEA), 613
Bureau of Labor Statistics (BLS), 566, 569, 578, 581–582
business cycle, 587–590
Business Cycle Dating Committee, 588–589
buyers, 94, 101, 329

cap and trade, 522–523
capital, 37, 468, 635, 666, 697
capital account, 953
capital gains taxes, 585
capital goods, vs. consumption goods, 78–79
capital intensive production, 68
capital stock, of banks, 814–815
Caplan, Bryan, 271
Carlyle, Thomas, 92
cartel, 424–427
cash transfers, 498
catch up effect, 636
causation, correlation vs., 14
Cellar-Kefauver Act (1950), 374
central bank, 833, 892
ceteris paribus, 12, 94
Chandra, Anita, 16
change in demand, 98, 102–104
change in quantity demanded, 97–98, 102–104
change in quantity supplied, 106, 109, 110
change in supply, 106–110
Chari, V. V., 778
chart, pie, 28, 29
Chinamasa, Patrick, 136
choice, scarcity and, 40–42
circular flow model, 608, 609
classical macroeconomic model, 707–708
Clayton Act (1914), 374
Clean Air Act (1970), 519
climate change, 522–523
Clinton, Bill, 776, 781
Coase, Ronald, 525, 526
Coase theorem, 525–527
Cochrane, John H., 778
cognitive dissonance, 269
collective bargaining, 466

collude, 424
collusion, 424, 546
command economy, 68
commercial banks, 812
common resources, 218–219
common stock, 655
comparative advantage, 49, 50, 51, 918, 920–925
compartmentalize, 269
competition, imperfect, 545–546
competitive market, 94
complements, 99, 100, 280, 281
complements in production, 107, 108
concentration ratios, 422–423
conceptual order, of facts, 12
conglomerate merger, 430
Congressional Budget Office, 549
constant-cost industry, 344, 345
constant returns to scale, 306
consumer behavior, 259–263
consumer choice, 266–267
consumer equilibrium, 266–267
consumer optimization, 282–283
consumer preferences, 101
consumer price index (CPI), 542, 578, 579, 581–582
consumer sovereignty, 67
consumer surplus, 183–188, 190–192, 194–196, 197, 926
consumption, 213–214, 610, 689, 693–694
consumption function, 736
consumption goods, vs. capital goods, 78–79
consumption tax, 244, 662
contraction, 587–588
contractionary fiscal policy, 759, 762
contractionary monetary policy, 848, 850
cooperative game, 433–434
Corcoran, Terence, 526
corporate income taxes, 243
correlation, causation vs., 14
cost curves, 304–306
cost of living allowance (COLA), 585
cost-push inflation, 701–702, 703
costs, 40–41, 296–299, 377
Council of Economic Advisers, 242, 550
Cox, Michael, 488
credit cards, 807–808
credit unions (CU), 812
cross-price elasticity of demand, 163
crowding-out effect, 663, 775–776
currency, 806
current account, 950–952
curves, movement vs. shift, 31, 32
cyclical unemployment, 570–571

deadweight loss, 187–188, 191–192, 193, 194, 196
decreasing-cost industry, 346–347
deficiency payment program, 198, 199
deflation, 577
degree-of-equity arguments, 54

demand, 94–97, 102–104, 127–134, 363–367, 456–460, 468–469, 659–660
demand curve, 30–31, 97–104, 127, 152–153, 162, 183, 184, 190, 330–332, 366–367, 403–404, 405, 457–458, 955
demand deposits, 806–807
demand-pull inflation, 701, 702
demographics, 101, 544
Department of Commerce, 578, 589
Department of Labor, 564, 578
depreciation, 613
depression, 588
deregulation, 668–669
derived demand, 455–545, 954–955
determinants of demand, 98
diamond-water paradox, 264
diminishing marginal product, 294–295
diminishing marginal utility, 259, 261, 267, 491
direct relationship, 30
dirty float system, 963
discount rate, 837–838
discouraged workers, 566
discrimination, 493–495
diseconomies of scale, 306
disposable personal income, 613
dissaving, 486
distribution, 68–69
dividend, 657
dominant strategy, 434
double counting, 608
drugs, 169–170
Duggan, Mark, 550
dumping, 931–932
durable goods, 610–611
Dzirutwe, MacDonald, 136

Earned Income Tax Credit (EITC), 498
econometric models, 589
economic behavior, 7, 10
economic efficiency, 347–348
economic fluctuations, 587–590
economic goods, 38
economic growth, 78–80, 587, 632–644
economic losses, 337–338, 340, 341–343, 369–370
the economic problem, 3
economic profits, 290–292
economic rent, 468
economics, 3, 4–6
Economic Stimulus Act (2008), 894
economic theories, 10–13, 17
economic welfare, 617
economies of scale, 306, 362–363, 423, 546
education, 487, 566, 640–642
efficiency, 52, 76
efficiency wage model, 574
efficiency wages, 705
elastic, 152
elasticity, 192, 193
elasticity of demand, 367
elastic supply curve, 166
Elster, Jon, 271
emotions, 269
empirical analysis, 11
Employment Act (1946), 563
Enste, Dominick, 618
entrepreneurship, 37, 697
environment, 513–527

Environmental Protection Agency (EPA), 519, 521
equality, 54, 491
equation of exchange, 855–857
equilibrium, 368–370, 461–464, 660, 662, 734–738, 956
equilibrium output, 338
equilibrium price, 122, 127–134, 423
equilibrium quantity, 122
equity-premium puzzle, 271
Estonia, 48
Evans, Kelly, 960–961
excess capacity, 408–409
excess reserves, 815–817
exchange rates, 954–956, 962–967
exchanges, 921–922
excise tax, 239
executive branch, 834–835
expansion, 587
expansionary fiscal policy, 759, 761–762, 764
expansionary monetary policy, 848, 886–888
expansion path, 323–325
expectations, 101, 107, 733, 960
expenditure approach, 610
expenditure multiplier, 742
explicit costs, 290, 291
exports, 612, 927–928
external diseconomies of scale, 346, 347
externalities, 210–216, 515–516, 617, 620

factor markets, 71
factor payments, 613
fallacy of composition, 15–16
Fannie Mae, 668, 672
Farber, Henry, 272
farm prices, 169
featherbedding, 466
Federal Deposit Insurance Corporation (FDIC), 822
federal funds market, 838
Federal Open Market Committee (FOMC), 835, 849, 887
Federal Reserve System (the Fed), 833–854
Federal Trade Commission (FTC), 374, 430
Feldstein, Martin S., 522
fiat money, 806
final goods and services, 608
financial crisis of 2008, 667–672, 769
financial institutions, 671, 812
financial intermediaries, 657
fiscal policy, 759–764, 857–860
fixed costs, 296
fixed investment, 611
fixed-proportions production function, 322
flat tax, 240, 243
flexible exchange rates, 962–967
Flexible Savings Account, 550, 551
Fogel, Robert, 635
Ford, Henry, 574
forecasting, 672, 851, 852
foreign currency, 955
foreign exchange market, 957–960
fractional reserve system, 813–814, 816
Freakonomics (Levitt), 18
Freddy Mac, 668, 672
Freeman, Richard, 467
free rider, 217
free trade, 639–640, 927–928, 930
frictional unemployment, 569–570

Friedman, Milton, 853, 894
Fuchs, Victor, 548–549
Full Employment and Balanced Growth Act (1978), 563
full-employment classical school model, 708
Fuller, Ida May, 241

Gabaix, Xavier, 777
game theory, 433, 437
GDP deflator, 578, 579
gender, unemployment and, 566
The General Theory of Employment, Interest and Money (Keynes), 708
Gertler, Mark, 18
Gini coefficient, 484–485
global warming, 522–523
gold standard, 809–810
goods, 38, 67–70
Goolsbee, Austan, 550–551
government
    benefit-cost analysis and, 217–218
    failure of, 54
    functions of, 234, 236
    pollution taxes, 211, 213
    purchases, 689, 694, 739–741, 768
    regulation, 211, 213, 214, 375–377, 519, 698
    spending and taxation, 237–244, 759, 772–773
    subsidies, 109, 193, 194, 214, 236, 499
    supply and, 108–109
Grabowski, David, 550
graphs/graphing, 28–33
Greenspan, Alan, 244, 777, 852, 887, 893
Gresham's Law, 810
gross domestic product (GDP), 608, 612, 614–616, 617–620
gross national product (GNP), 613
group behavior, 12, 13
growth version of the quantity equation, 856
Gruber, Jonathan, 549, 550

health care, 540–551
health maintenance organization (HMO), 545
health saving account (HSA), 547–549
Heckman, James, 501–502
Herfindahl-Hirshman Index (HHI), 430
hindsight bias, 269
homogenous products, 329
horizontal merger, 430
household debt, 733
housing market, 667–668
human behavior, 12, 13
human capital, 37, 487, 489, 635
human organs, 547
Humphrey-Hawkins Act (1978), 563
Hurricane Katrina, 125–126
hyperinflation, 583, 856–857
hypothesis, 11

ice cream vendor model, 439
identical products, 329
immigration, labor market and, 463
impact lag, 776, 780
imperfect competition, 545–546
implementation lag, 776
implicit costs, 290, 291
import quotas, 932, 933
imports, 928
incentives, positive and negative, 47, 48

income, 99–100, 156, 542–543, 608
income distribution, 470, 483–489
income effect, 259, 285, 460
income elasticity of demand, 163–165
income inequality, 483
income redistribution, 234, 236, 490–492, 498–499
increasing-cost industry, 344, 346
increasing opportunity cost, 76–77
indemnity coverage, 545
indeterminate, 129
indexing, 896–897
indifference curves, 279–280, 285, 286
indirect business taxes, 613
individual behavior, 13
individual consumption-payment link, 246
individual demand curve, 95
individual demand schedule, 95
Individual Retirement Account (IRA), 662
individual supply curve, 105
industry concentration, measuring, 422–423
inefficiency, 76, 371
inelastic, 152
inelastic supply curve, 166
inferior goods, 100–101, 102
inflation, 576–586, 854–857, 878, 892–893, 896–897, 966–967
inflationary gap, 700–701, 702, 705–706, 762, 848, 850
inflation rate, 959
infrastructure, 638
in-kind transfers, 485
innovation, 373, 636
input markets, 71, 455–545, 469
input prices, 107
institutional economics, 640
insufficient competition, 234
insurance, 543–544, 545
insurance companies, as financial intermediary, 657
intangible goods, 38
interest, 469
interest rate effect, 691
interest rates, 584, 666, 668, 670, 672, 733, 843–845
internalized externalities, 515
international finance, 949–968
international trade, 914–937
inventory investment, 611
inverse relationship, 30
investment, 611, 659, 689, 694, 739–741
investment tax credit, 662
isocost (equal cost) lines, 322
isoquants, 320–325
Iyengar, Radha, 302

job-entry discrimination, 493
job leaver, 566, 567
job loser, 566, 567
job market signaling, 221
job preferences, 489
job search, 574
joint profit maximization, 424–427
Jotwani, Pooja, 18
Journal of Economic Education, 18
Journal of Petroleum Technology, 224
Justice Department, 430

Kahneman, Daniel, 270
Kehoe, Patrick J., 778

Kennedy, John F., 776
Keynes, John Maynard, 6, 189, 526, 631, 708–709, 731, 732, 747, 772
Keynesian cross model, 732
Keynesian macroeconomic model, 708–710
kinked demand curve, 427–428
Krugman, Paul R., 777, 778

labor, 37, 635
labor demand curve, 461–463
labor force, 564, 698
labor force participation rate, 568
labor intensive production, 68
labor market, 456–460, 565–566
labor productivity, 461
labor supply curve, 463
labor unions, 465–467, 574
land, 37, 468, 697
Landrum-Griffen Act (1959), 466
Landsburg, Steven E., 661
law of demand, 94–97, 267
law of diminishing marginal returns, 643
law of increasing opportunity cost, 76–77
law of supply, 104–105
leading economic indicators, 589
legal tender, 806
leisure, 617
Leslie, Phillip, 382
leverage, 671
Levitt, Steven, 18
liabilities, of banks, 814
life-cycle model, 894
Lindbeck, Assar, 140
linear curve, slope of, 31–32
linear demand curve, 162
liquidity, 809
Lo, Andrew, 272
loanable funds, 659–666
long run, 293
long-run aggregate supply, 771
long-run aggregate supply (LRAS) curve, 694–698
long-run cost curves, 304–306
long-run equilibrium, 341–343, 406–407
long-run supply, 344–348
Lorenz curve, 484–485
Lucas, Robert, 633, 886
Lucas, Robert E., 778
Lucas, Robert E. Jr., 845–846
luxury tax, 168

M1, 809
M2, 809
macroeconomic equilibrium, 700–706
macroeconomic goals, 563
macroeconomics, 13
magical thinking, 269
majority rule, 246–247
majors, salaries and, 5
Malthusian prediction, 643–644
Mankiw, N. Gregory, 242, 522–523, 526, 551, 671–672, 772–773
marginal benefits, 183
marginal cost (MC), 185, 297–298, 299, 302–303
marginal productivity theory of income distribution, 470, 492
marginal product (MP), 294, 300, 457
marginal propensity to consume (MPC), 735, 765–766, 767

marginal propensity to save (MPS), 735–736, 766
marginal rate of technical substitution of labor for capital (MRTS), 321–322
marginal resource cost (MRC), 456–460
marginal revenue curve, 403–404, 405
marginal revenue (MR), 333–335, 363–367
marginal revenue product (MRP), 456–460
marginal thinking, 42–43, 45–46
marginal utility, 261–263, 268
marginal willingness, 183, 184
market, 52, 93–94
market demand curve, 95–97
market economy, 53, 68, 134
market efficiency, 185–188
market entry, 429–430
market equilibrium, 122
market failure, 53–54
market labor supply curve, 459–460
market prices, 52–53, 331, 332
market segregation, 379
market supply curve, 105, 106
Marshall, Alfred, 121, 189
Masterov, Dimitriy, 501–502
McFadden, Daniel, 218
means of deferred payment, 805
means-tested income transfer program, 498
median voter model, 246, 247
Medicare, 498
medium of exchange, 802
Medoff, James, 467
Melville, Kate, 164
menu costs, 583, 705
mergers, 430
Metcalf, Gilbert, 522
microeconomics, 13
midpoint method, 154–155
minimum efficient scale, 306
minimum wage, 137–138
minimum wage rate, 573
misperception effect, 695
mixed economy, 68
Modigliani, Franco, 894
monetary policy, 671–672, 857–860
money, 802–817, 854–857
money market, 839–840, 841–842
money market mutual funds (MMMF), 808
money multiplier, 818–820
money prices, 40–41
money supply, 809, 836–839
monopolistic competition, 401–411, 441
monopoly, 54, 362–379, 441
monopsony, 464
moral hazard, 222–223, 543–544, 550–551
mortgage-backed security (MBS), 669
Morton, Fiona Scott, 550
multiple expansion effect, 818–819
multiplier effect, 765–769
Murray, Sara, 960–961
mutual funds, as financial intermediary, 657
mutual interdependence, 422, 432

Nash, John, 435
Nash equilibrium, 435–436, 437, 439
National Association of Colleges and Employers, 18
National Bureau of Economic Research (NBER), 588–589
National Conference of State Legislatures, 215